ON TH

MANNERS AND CUSTOMS

OF

THE ANCIENT IRISH.

A SERIES OF LECTURES

DELIVERED BY THE LATE

EUGENE O'CURRY, M.R.I.A.,

PROFESSOR OF IRISH HISTORY AND ARCHAEOLOGY IN THE CATHOLIC UNIVERSITY OF IRELAND;
CORRESPONDING MEMBER OF THE SOCIETY OF ANTIQUARIES OF SCOTLAND, ETC.

EDITED, WITH

AN INTRODUCTION, APPENDIXES, ETC.,

BY

W. K. SULLIVAN, PH.D.,

SECRETARY OF THE ROYAL IRISH ACADEMY, AND PROFESSOR OF CHEMISTRY TO THE
CATHOLIC UNIVERSITY OF IRELAND, AND TO THE ROYAL COLLEGE OF SCIENCE.

VOL. III.

LECTURES, VOL. II.

WILLIAMS AND NORGATE,
14 HENRIETTA STREET, COVENT GARDEN, LONDON,
AND 20 SOUTH FREDERICK STREET, EDINBURGH.
W. B. KELLY, 8 GRAFTON STREET, DUBLIN.
SCRIBNER, WELFORD, & CO., NEW YORK.
1873.

CONTENTS.

LECTURE XIX. Of Buildings, Furniture, etc., in Ancient Erinn . . . . 1—22

(VII.) Of Buildings, Furniture, etc. (continued). Of the number and succession of the colonists of ancient Erinn. Tradition ascribes no buildings to *Parthalon* or his people; their sepulchral mounds at Tallaght near Dublin. Definitions of the *Rath*, the *Dun*, the *Lis*, the *Caiseal*, and the *Cathair;* the latter two were of stone; many modern townland-names derived from these terms; remains of many of these structures still exist. *Rath na Righ* or "Rath of the Kings", at Tara; the *Teach Mór Milibh Amus*, or "Great House of the Thousands of Soldiers". Several houses were often included within the same *Rath, Dun, Lis*, or *Caiseal.* Extent of the demesne lands of Tara. The *Rath* or *Cathair* of *Aileach;* account of its building; the houses within the *Rath* as well as the latter were of stone; why called *Aileach Frigrind?* *Aileach* mentioned by Ptolemy. Account of the *Rath* of *Cruachan* in the *Táin Bó Fraich.* The "House of the Royal Branch". Description of a *Dun* in Fairy Land. The terms *Rath, Dun,* and *Lis* applied to the same kind of enclosure. The *Foradh* at Tara. Description of the house of *Credé.* Two classes of builders,—the *Rath*-builder, and the *Caiseal*-builder; list of the professors of both arts from the Book of Leinster. *Dubhaltach Mac Firbissigh's* copy of the same list (note); his observations in answer to those who deny the existence of stone-building in ancient Erinn. The story of *Bricriu's* Feast; plan of his house; his *Grianan* or "sun house"; his invitation to *Conchobar* and the Ultonians; he sows dissensions among the women; the *Briathar Ban Uladh;*—his house was made of wicker-work.

LECTURE XX. Of Buildings, Furniture, etc., in Ancient Erinn . . . . 23—38

(VII.) Buildings, Furniture, etc.; (continued). The description of buildings in our ancient MSS., even when poetical in form, and not strictly accurate as to date, are still valuable for the object of these lectures. Veracity of the evidence respecting the "Great

Banqueting Hall" of Tara in the time of *Cormac Mac Airt*, as given by Dr. Petrie; no record of the changes which took place at Tara subsequent to that time. Residences of the monarchs of Erinn after the desertion of Tara. Desertion of other celebrated royal residences: —*Emania*, *Cruachan*, etc. Division of the people into classes; this division did not impose perpetuity of caste; increase of wealth enabled a man to pass from one rank to another; crime alone barred this advancement; the qualifications as to furniture and houses of the several classes of *Aires* or landholders; fines for injury to the house of the *Aire Reiré Breithé*; of the *Aire Desa*; of the *Aire-Ard*; of the *Aire Forgaill*; of the king of a territory. Law against damage or disfigurement of buildings and furniture; of the house of a *Bó-Aire*; of the house of an *Aire-Desa*; of the house of an *Aire-Tuise*; of the house of an *Aire-Ard*. Law directing the provision to be made for aged men. Shape of houses in ancient Erinn; construction of the round house; reference to the building of such a house in an Irish life of St. *Colman Ela*; a similar story told of St. *Cumin Fada*. No instance recorded of an ecclesiastical edifice built of wicker work; two instances of the building of oratories of wood;—story of the oratory of St. *Moling*; quatrain of *Rumand Mac Colmain* on the oratory of *Rathan Ua Suanaigh*; account of *Rumand* writing a poem for the *Galls* of Dublin; he carries his wealth to *Cill Belaigh*; statement of seven streets of *Galls* or foreigners at that place; importance of the account of *Rumand*.

LECTURE XXI. OF BUILDINGS, FURNITURE, ETC. IN ANCIENT ERINN . . . . . . 39—63

(VII.) OF BUILDINGS, FURNITURE; (continued). Of the *Gobban Saer*; mistakes concerning him; explanation of his name; he was a real personage. Old Irish writers fond of assigning a mythological origin to men of great skill or learning. The legend of *Tuirbhi*, the father of *Gobban Saer*; observations of Dr. Petrie on this legend; error of Dr. Petrie. Story of *Lug Mac Eithlenn*, the *Sabh Ildenach* or "trunk of all arts". *Tuirbhi* a descendant of *Oilioll Oluim*. References to *Gobban Saer* in ancient Gaedhelic MSS.;—one in the Irish life of St. *Abban*; the name of the place where *Gobban* built the church for St. *Abban* not mentioned; another in the life of St. *Moling*. The name of *Gobban* mentioned in a poem in an ancient Gaedhelic MSS. of the eighth century;—original and translation of this poem (note); original and translation of a poem of St. *Moling* from the same MS. which is also found in a MS. in Ireland—great importance of this poem (note). Oratories generally built of wood, but sometimes of stone. Ancient law regulating the price to be paid for ecclesiastical buildings;—as to the oratory; as to the *Damh-liag* or stone church; explanation of the rule as to the latter (note); as to the *Cloicteach* or belfry. Explanation of the preceding rule quoted from Dr. Petrie; reasons for reëxamining these rules. Dr. Petrie's opinion about the Round Towers unassailable. Law regulating the proportionate stipends of *Ollamhs*; stipends of the *Ollamh*-builder;

Dr. Petrie's observation on the passage regarding the stipend of the *Ollamh*-builder; dwelling houses omitted from the list of buildings; mistake made by Dr. Petrie about the passage concerning the *Ollamh*-builder; author's correction of this mistake: meaning of the word *Coictighis*,—new interpretation by the author. Artistic works of the *Ollamh*-builder; the *Iubroracht* or working in yew-wood; carving in yew-wood at *Emania* and *Cruachan*, and in Armagh cathedral. Romantic origin of work in yew-wood—legend of *Fintann*, son of *Bochra;* no trace of the doctrine of metempsychosis among the Gaedhil; legend of *Fintann*, continued. List of articles of household furniture mentioned in the laws regarding lending or pledging. Law regarding the house of a doctor.

LECTURE XXII. OF BUILDINGS, FURNITURE, ETC., IN ANCIENT ERINN . . . . 64—86

(VII.) OF BUILDINGS, FURNITURE, ETC.; (continued). Stone buildings; *Cathairs* and *Clochans;* O'Flaherty's notice of the *Clochans* of the Arann Islands; *Clochans* still existing in those islands; *Clochans* on other islands of the western coast. Mr. Du Noyer's account of ancient stone buildings in Kerry; his ethnological comparisons; summary of his views; apart his speculations, his paper is important. Different members of the same family had distinct houses in ancient Erinn. Mr. Du Noyer's claim to priority in the discovery of the stone buildings of Kerry inadmissible; Mr. R. Hitchcock had already noticed them; ancient burial grounds also noticed by the latter in the same district. The two names of "Cahers" given by Mr. Du Noyer, not ancient; his opinion of the use of *Dunbeg* fort not correct; this and the other forts did not form a line of fortifications. Instance of a bee-hive house or *Clochan* having been built within the *Rath* of *Aileach*. Limited use of the term *Cathair;* the same term not always applied to the same kind of building. Tale of the dispute about the "champion's share"; Smith's notice of *Sliabh Mis* and *Cathair Conroi;* story of the dispute about the "champion's share" (continued). The "guard room" or "watching seat". The position of *Cathair Conroi* not exactly ascertained. Story of "the slaughter of *Cathair Conroi*". Reference to *Cathair Conroi* in the tale of "the Battle of Ventry Harbour". Modern hypothesis of the inferiority of the Milesians. Stone-building in ancient Erinn not exclusively pre-Milesian. The *Aitheach Tuatha* or *Atticotti*. The Firbolgs still powerful in the sixth century. Townland names derived from *Cathairs*. No evidence that the Milesians were a ruder race than their predecessors in Erinn.

LECTURE XXIII. OF DRESS AND ORNAMENTS . . . 87—107

(VIII.) Early sumptuary law regulating the colours of dress, attributed to the monarchs *Tighernmas* and *Eochaidh* and *Edgudach*. Native gold first smelted by *Iuchadan*, and golden ornaments made in Ireland in the reign of *Tighernmas*. The uses of colours to distinguish the several classes of society, also attributed to the same *Eochaidh;* the nature of those colours not specified. Household utensils, ornaments, and variously coloured dresses of *Ailill* and *Medhbh* mentioned in the tale of the *Táin Bó Chuailgne*; the material or fashion of the dress not specified. *Medhbh's* preparation for the war of the first *Táin*; description of the parties summoned. Description of the Ultonian clanns at the hill of *Slemain*, forming the army in pursuit of *Ailill* and *Medhbh*, by the herald of the latter, *Mac Roth*, from the tale of the *Táin Bó Chuailgne*; his description of *Conchobar Mac Nessa*; of *Causcraid Mend*; of *Sencha*; of *Eogan Mac Durthachta*; of *Laegaire Buadach*; of *Munremur*; of *Connud*; of *Reochaid*; of *Amargin*; of *Feradach Find Fechtnach*; of *Fiachaig* and *Fiachna*; of *Celtchair Mac Uthair* and his clann; of *Eirrge Echbel*; of *Mend*, son of *Salcholgan*; of *Fergna*; of *Ercc*, son of *Carpri Nia Fer* and his clann; of *Cuchulaind's* clans. Note: *Cuchulaind* is removed to *Muirtheimne* after his fight with *Ferdiadh*, to get the benefit of the healing properties of its stream or river; enumeration of them; while there, *Cethern*, who had gone to his assistance, arrives covered with wounds, and is visited by physicians from the enemy's camp, whom he drives away; *Cuchulaind* then sends for *Fingin Fathliagh*, who examines each of his wounds, and *Cethern* describes the persons who gave them—his description of *Illand*, son of *Fergus*; of queen *Medhbh*; of *Oll* and *Othine*; of *Bun* and *Mecconn*; of *Broen* and *Brudni*, sons of *Teora Soillsi*, king of *Caille*; of *Cormac* [*Mac*] *Colomarig* and *Cormac* the son of *Maelefoga*; of *Mane Mathremail* and *Mane Athremail*, sons of *Ailill* and *Medhbh*; of the champions from *Iruade* [Norway]; of *Ailill* and his son *Mane*; of the marrow bath by which *Cethern* was healed, whence the name of *Smirammair*, now Smarmore, in the county Louth. *Medhbh* enumerates her dowry to *Ailill*; gifts promised by her to *Long Mac Emonis*; gifts promised by her to *Ferdiadh*; one of those gifts, her celebrated brooch, weighed more than four pounds. Story of *Mac Conglinde*; his extravagant dream; his description of a curious dress of a doorkeeper; analysis of the dress—the *Cochall*, the *Ionar*, the *Ochrath*; analysis of *Mac Conglinde's* own dress; his *Leinidh*. Distinction between the *Léine* and the *Leinidh*—the latter was a kilt. Description of the dress of the champion *Edchu Rond* in the tale of the Exile of the Sons of *Duildermait*; he wore a kilt. Ancient law regulating the wearing of the *Leinidh* or kilt, and the *Ochrath* or pantaloon.

LECTURE XXIV. Of Dress and Ornaments in Ancient Erinn . . . . 108—134

(VIII.) Dress and Ornaments (continued). Constant references to fringes of gold thread; mention of this ornament in the account of *Medbh's* visit to her chief Druid in the commencement of the *Táin Bó Chuailgne*,—description of *Fedelm* the prophetess weaving a fringe; the fringe sword or lath mentioned in a poem of *Dallan Forgaill* (circa A.D. 560). Ancient laws relating to the pledging of ornaments, etc.; law relating to the pledging of a needle; the pledging of a queen's work bag; the work bag of an *Aireck Feibhe*. The legal contents of a workbag formed only a small part of a lady's personal ornaments. References to dyeing, weaving, embroidering, etc., in the ancient laws regulating Distress; objects connected with those arts for the recovery of which proceedings might have been taken under those laws. Coloured thread and wool paid as rent or tribute, The dye-stuffs used were of home growth. Legend of St. *Ciaran* and the blue dye stuff called *Glaisin*. Summary of the processes in the textile arts mentioned in the extracts quoted in the lecture. Reference to embroidery in the tale of the *Tochmarc nEimire*, and in the *Dinnseanchas*. *Coca* the embroideress of St. *Columcille*. The knowledge of the Gaedhils about colours shown by the illuminations to the Book of Kells. Reference in the Book of Ballymote to the colours worn by different classes. Cloth of various colours formed part of the tributes or taxes paid as late as the ninth and tenth centuries. Tributes to the king of *Caiseal* according to the Book of Rights from: *Ara*; *Boirinn*; Leinster; *Uaithne*; *Duibhneach* and *Drung*; *Corcumruadh*; the *Deise*; *Orbraidhe*. Stipends paid by the king of *Caiseal* to the kings of Kerry; *Raithlenn*; *Ara*. Tributes to the king of Connacht from *Umhall*; the *Greagraidhe*; the *Conmaicne*; the *Ciarraidhe*; the *Luighne*; the *Dealbhna*; *Ui Maine*. Stipends paid by the king of Connacht to the kings of: *Dealbhna*; *Ui Maine*. Tributes to the king of *Aileach* from: the *Cuileantraidhe*; the *Ui Mic Caerthainn*; *Ui Tuirtre*. Stipends paid by the king of *Aileach* to the kings of: *Cinel Boghaine*; *Cinel Enanna*; *Craebh*; *Ui Mic Caerthainn*; *Tulach Og*. Stipends paid by the king of Oriel to the kings of: *Ui Breasail*; *Ui Eachach*; *Ui Meith*; *Ui Dortain*; *Ui Briuin Archoill*; *Ui Tuirtre*; *Feara Manach*; *Mughdhorn* and *Ros*. Stipends paid by the king of *Uladh* to the kings of: *Cuailgne*; *Araidhe*; *Cobhais*; *Muirtheimne*. Tributes to the king of *Uladh* from: *Semhne*; *Crothraidhe*; *Cathal*. Gifts to the king of Tara. Stipends paid by the king of Tara to the kings of: *Magh Lacha*; *Cuircne*; *Ui Beccon*. Tributes to the king of Tara from: the *Luighne*; the *Feara Arda*; the *Saithne*; *Gailenga*; the *Ui Beccon*. Stipends paid by the king of Leinster to the: *Ui Fealain*; the chief of *Cualann*; *Ui Feilmeadha*; king of *Raeilinn*; *Ui Criomhthannan*. Tributes to the king of Leinster from the: Galls; *Forthuatha*; *Fotharta*; men of South Leinster. Gifts from the monarch of Erinn to the king of *Emain Macha*. Stipends of the king of *Emain Macha* to the kings of: *Rathmor*; *Ui Briuin*; *Conmaicne*. Gifts bestowed on the king of Leinster by the monarch of Erinn whenever he visited Tara. Gift of the king of Leinster on his return from Tara to the king of *Ui Fealain*. Gifts of the monarch of Erinn to the king of *Caiseal* when at *Teamhair Luachra*. Stipends given by the king of *Caiseal* at the visitation of the monarch of Erinn to the: *Deise*; *Ui Chonaill*. Stipends paid by the king of Connacht to the kings of: *Ui Maine*; *Luighne*. Colours of winds, according to the preface to the *Seanchas Mór*.

LECTURE XXV. Of Dress and Ornaments in ancient Erinn 135—154

(VIII.) Dress and Ornaments (continued). Of *Conaire Mór*, monarch of Erinn (circa B.C. 100 to B.C. 50) and the outlawed sons of *Dond Dess*, according to the ancient tale of the *Bruighean Daderga*; the sons of *Dond Dess* associate with the British outlaw *Ingcel* to plunder the coasts of Britain and Erinn; the monarch, in returning from *Corca Bhaiscinn* in the Co. Clare, being unable to reach Tara, goes to the court of *Daderg*; *Ingcel* visits the court to ascertain the feasibility of plundering it; he gives descriptions on his return to his companions of those he saw there, and *Ferrogain* identifies them; *Ingcel's* description of the Ultonian warrior *Cormac Conloinges* and his companions; of the *Cruithentuath* or Picts; of the nine pipe players; of *Tuidle* the house steward; of *Oball*, *Oblini*, and *Coirpre Findmor*, sons of *Conaire Mór*; of the champions *Mal Mac Telbaind*, *Muinremor*, and *Birderg*; of the great Ultonian champion *Conall Cearnach*; of the monarch himself, *Conaire Mór*; of the six cup bearers; of *Tulchinne*, the royal Druid and juggler; of the three swine-herds; of *Causcrach Mend*; of the Saxon princes and their companions; of the king's outriders; of the king's three judges; of the king's nine harpers; of the king's three jugglers; of the three chief cooks; of the king's three poets; of the king's two warders; of the king's nine guardsmen; of the king's two table attendants; of the champions *Sencha*, *Dubthach Dael Uladh*, and *Goibniu*; of *Daderg* himself; of the king's three door keepers; of the British exiles at the court of the monarch; of the three jesters or clowns; of the three drink bearers. Summary of the classes of persons described. The exaggerations of such descriptions scarcely affect their value for the present purpose; very little exaggeration on the whole in the tales of the *Bruighean Daderga* and *Táin Bó Chuailgne*. Antiquity and long continued use of the colour of certain garments shown by the tale of the *Amhra Chonrai*, by *Mac Liag's* elegy on *Tadgh* O'Kelly, and also by a poem of *Gillabrighde Mac Conmidhe*.

LECTURE XXVI. Of Dress and Ornaments in ancient Erinn 155—170

(VIII.) Dress and Ornaments (continued). Very early mention of ornaments of gold, etc., *e. g.* in the description of *Eladha* the Fomorian king, in the second battle of *Magh Tuireadh*. Champions sometimes wore a finger ring for each king killed. Allusion to bracelets in an ancient poetical name of the river Boyne. Ornaments mentioned in a description of a cavalcade given in an ancient preface to the *Táin Bó Chuailgne*, and in the description of another cavalcade in the same tract. Some of the richest descriptions of gold and silver ornaments are to be found in the romantic tale of the "Wanderings of *Maelduin's* Canoe" (circa A.D. 700). Bronze *Buidne* for the hair in Dr. Petrie's collection. Ornaments described in the tale of the *Tochmarc Bec Fola*. Story of *Aithirne Ailgisach*, king *Fergus*

Fairge, and the gold brooch found at *Ard Brestine;* the finding of ornaments unconnected with human remains explained by this tale. Mention of a large sized brooch in the legendary history of Queen *Edain*. Ancient law respecting the mode of wearing large brooches. Large brooches mentioned in the tale of the "Wanderings of *Maelduin's* Canoe". Thistle headed or Scottish brooches; reference to Scottish brooches in the story of *Cano* son of *Gartnan*. Carved brooches mentioned in the tale of the *Bruighean Daderga*. Reference to a carved brooch in the Book of Munster. Another reference to a carved brooch in a poem ascribed to *Oisin*. Brooches of bronze and *Findruine*. Chased gold pins used down to the beginning of the thirteenth century. Of the different kinds of rings. The *Fainne* used to confine the hair. Hair rings used in the seventeenth century. *Fails* were worn up the whole arm for the purpose of bestowing them upon poets, etc.; example of this from the Book of Lismore. Of the bracelet called a *Budne, Buidne*, or *Buinne*.

LECTURE XXVII. Of Dress and Ornaments in Ancient Erinn 171—184

(VIII.) Dress and Ornaments (continued). Anonymous notice of Irish Torques; description of two found at Tara; accounts of Torques found in England; no account of Torques in the works of older Irish antiquaries; those found at Tara bought in 1813 by Alderman West of Dublin; the author does not agree with the anonymous as to the mode of production of the Tara Torques. Uses of the Tara Torques; reference to such a ring of gold for the waist in an ancient preface to the *Táin Bó Chuailgne;* another reference to such a ring in an account of a dispute about the manner of death of *Fothadh Airgteach* between king *Mongan* and the poet *Dallan Forgaill* from the *Leabhar na h-Uidhre; Cailte's* account of his mode of burial; a hoop or waist-torque among the ornaments placed on *Fothadh's* stone coffin. Story of *Cormac Mac Airt* and *Lugaidh Laga*, showing one of the uses of rings worn on the hands. Ornaments for the neck; the *Muinche;* first used in the time of *Muineamhon* (circa B.C. 1300); mentioned in a poem of *Ferceirtne* on *Curoi Mac Daire;* also in account of the Battle of *Magh Leana*. The *Niamh Land* or flat crescent of gold worn on the head, as well as on the neck. The Neck-Torque of *Cormac Mac Airt*. Descriptions of the dress and ornaments of *Bec Fola*. The *Muinche* mentioned in the tale of the "Wanderings of *Maelduin's* Canoe", and in the story of *Cano*. *Muinche* and *Land* used also for the neck ornaments of animals and spears. Use of the term *Muintorcs*. Of the *Mael-Land* mentioned in the *Táin Bó Fruich*. The ferrule of a spear called a *Muinche* in the account of the Battle of *Magh Leana;* discovery of such a ring in Kerry; the term also used for the collars of grayhounds, chiefly in Fenian tales. Mention of the *Torc* in its simple form in the Book of Leinster. Of the *Land* or lunette; it formed part of the legal contents of a lady's workbag, and of the inheritance of daughters. The *Land* was worn on the head as well as on the neck, as shown by the descriptions of *Conaire Mór's* head charioteer and apprentice charioteers; and also of his poets.

LECTURE XXVIII. Of Dress and Ornaments in Ancient Erinn 185—1

(VIII.) Dress and Ornaments (continued). Of Ear-rings: the *An-Nasc* mentioned in *Cormac's* Glossary, and in the accounts of *Tulchinne* the druid and juggler, and the harpers in the tale of the *Bruighean Daderga.* Of the *Gibne*: it was a badge of office, especially of charioteers; it is mentioned in the description of *Rian Gabhra*, *Cuchulaind's* charioteer; and also in a legend about him in *Leabhar na h-Uidhre*; the word *Gibne* is explained in an ancient glossary in a vellum MS.; the story of *Edain* and *Midir* shows that the *Gibne* was not worn exclusively by charioteers. The spiral ring for the hair mentioned in the "Wanderings of *Maelduin's* Canoe". Men as well as women divided the hair. Hollow golden balls fastened to the tresses of the hair; mention of such ornaments in the tale of the *Bruighean Daderga*; curious poem from the tale of *Eochaidh Fedhleach* and *Edain* (foot note); golden balls for the hair also mentioned in the "Sick Bed of *Cuchulaind*"; two such balls mentioned in the tales of *Bec Fola* and *Bruighean Daderga*, and only one in that of the "Sick Bed". The *Mind oir* or crown not a *Land* or crescent; it is mentioned in the Brehon Laws, and in a tale in the *Leabhar na h-Uidhre*; the second name used in the tale in question proves that the *Mind* covered the head. The *Mind* of *Medb* at the *Táin Bó Chuailgne.* The *Mind* was also worn in Scotland, as is shown by the story of prince *Cano.* Men also wore a golden *Mind*, as appears from the *Táin Bó Chuailgne*; this ornament called in other parts of the tale an *Imscind.* The curious *Mind* worn by *Cormac Mac Airt* at the meeting of the States at *Uisnech.*

LECTURE XXIX. Of Dress and Ornaments in Ancient Erinn 199—21

(VIII.) Dress and Ornaments (continued). Story of a *Mind* called the *Barr Bruinn* in the tale of the *Táin Bó Aingen.* Another legend about the same *Mind* from the Book of Lismore; another celebrated *Mind* mentioned in the latter legend; origin of the ancient name of the Lakes of Killarney from that of *Lén Linfhiaclach*, the maker of this second *Mind.* The ancient goldsmiths appear to have worked at or near a gold mine. *Lén* the goldsmith appears to have flourished circa B.C. 300. The names of ancient artists are generally derived from those of their arts, but that of *Len* is derived from a peculiarity of his teeth; this circumstance shows that he was not the legendary representative of his art, but a real artist. Gold ornaments found in a bog near Cullen in the county of Tipperary; circumstances under which they were found, and enumeration of the articles found—note. *Cerdraighe* or ancient territory of the goldsmiths near the present Cullen. Pedigree of the *Cerdraighe* of *Tulach Gossa*; this family of goldsmiths are brought down by this pedigree to circa A.D. 500; the eldest branch became extinct in St. *Mo-*

themnioc, circa A.D. 550; but other branches existed at a much later period. The mineral districts of Silvermines and Meanus are not far from Cullen. The *At* and the *Cleitme*. The *Barr*, *Cennbarr*, *Æobarr*, and *Righbarr*. The goldsmith in ancient times was only an artizan; other artizans of the same class. *Creidne* the first *Cerd* or goldsmith; his death mentioned in a poem of *Flann* of Monasterboice; this poem shows that foreign gold was at one time imported into Ireland. The first recorded smelter of gold in Ireland was a native of Wicklow. References to the making of specific articles not likely to be found in our chronicles; there is, however, abundant evidence of a belief that the metallic ornaments used in Ireland were of native manufacture.

LECTURE XXX. OF MUSIC AND MUSICAL INSTRUMENTS IN ANCIENT ERINN . . . . 212—233

(IX.) OF MUSIC AND MUSICAL INSTRUMENTS. Antiquity of the harp in Erinn. The first musical instrument mentioned in Gaedhelic writings is the *Cruit*, or harp, of the *Daghda*, a chief and druid of the *Tuatha Dé Danann*; his curious invocation to his harp; the three musical feats played upon it; examination of the names of this harp; the word *Coir*, forming part of the name of the *Daghda's* harp, came down to modern times, as is shown by a poem of Keating on *Tadgh* O'Coffey, his harper. The *Daghda's* invocation to his harp further examined; the three musical modes compared to the three seasons of the year in ancient Egypt; myth of the discovery of the lyre; Dr. Burney on the three musical modes of the Greeks; the three Greek modes represented by the Irish three feats; conjectural completion of the text of the *Daghda's* invocation; what were the bellies and pipes of the *Daghda's* harp; ancient painting of a lyre at Portici, with a pipe or flute for cross-bar, mentioned by Dr. Burney. Legend of the origin of the three feats, or modes of harp playing, from the *Táin Bó Fraich*; meaning of the name *Uaithne* in this legend. No mention of strings in the account of the *Daghda's* harp, but they are mentioned in the tale of the *Táin Bó Fraich*. Legend of *Find Mac Cumhaill*; *Scathach* and her magical harp; *Scathach's* harp had three strings; no mention of music having been played at either of the battles of the northern or southern *Magh Tuireadh*; this proves the antiquity of those accounts. The *Daghda's* harp was quadrangular; a Greek harp of the same form represented in the hand of a Grecian Apollo at Rome; example of an Irish quadrangular harp on the *Theca* of an ancient missal. Dr. Ferguson on the antiquity and origin of music in Erinn; musical canon of the Welsh regulated by Irish harpers about A.D. 1100; his account of the *Theca* above mentioned, and of figures of the harp from ancient Irish monumental crosses which resembled the old Egyptian one; he thinks this resemblance supports the Irish traditions; Irish MSS. little studied twenty years ago, but since they have been; from this examination the author thinks the *Firbolgs* and *Tuatha Dé Danann* had nothing to do with Egypt, but that the Milesians had. Migration of the *Tuatha Dé*

Danann from Greece; the author does not believe they went into Scandinavia; he believes their cities of *Falias*, *Gorias*, etc., were in Germany; they spoke German, according to the Book of *Lecan*. The similarity of the harps on the monument of Orpheus at Petau in Styria and on the *Theca* of the Stowe MS. may point to Murrhart as the *Murias* of the *Tuatha Dé Danann*.

LECTURE XXXI. OF MUSIC AND MUSICAL INSTRUMENTS IN ANCIENT ERINN 234–

(IX.) OF MUSIC AND MUSICAL INSTRUMENTS (continued). Legendary origin of the Harp according to the tale of *Imtheacht na Trom Dhaimhe*, or the "Adventures of the Great Bardic Company"; *Seanchan's* visit to *Guaire*; interview of *Marbhan*, *Guaire's* brother, with *Seanchan*; *Marbhan's* legend of *Cuil* and *Canoclach Mhór* and the invention of the Harp; his legend of the invention of verse; his legend concerning the *Timpan*; the strand of *Camas* not identified. Signification of the word *Cruit*. The Irish *Timpan* was a stringed instrument. Another etymology for *Cruit*; Isidore not the authority for this explanation. Reference to the *Cruit* in the early history of the Milesians. *Eimher* and *Ereamhon* cast lots for a poet and harper. Skill in music one of the gifts of the *Eberian* or southern race of Erinn. Mention of the *Cruit* in the historical tale of *Orgain Dindrighe* or the "destruction of *Dindrigh*". First occurrence of the word *Ceis* in this tale; it occurs again in connection with the assembly of *Drom Ceat*, A.D. 573; *Aidbsi* or *Corus Crondin* mentioned in connection with poems in praise of St. *Colum Cille*, sung at this assembly; meaning of the word *Aidbsi*; the author heard the *Cronán* or throat accompaniment to dirges; origin of the word "crone"; the Irish *Aidbsi* known in Scotland as *Cepóg*; the word *Cepóg* known in Ireland also, as shown by a poem on the death of *Athairne*. The assembly of *Drom Ceat* continued; *Dallan Forgaill's* elegy on St. *Colum Cille*; the word *Ceis* occurs in this poem also; *Ceis* here represents a part of the harp, as shown by a scholium in *Leabhar na h-Uidhre*; antiquity of the tale of the "Destruction of *Dindrigh*" proved by this scholium; the word *Ceis* glossed in all ancient copies of the elegy on St. *Colum Cille*; scholium on the same poem in the MS. H. 2. 16. T.C.D.; gloss on the poem in Liber Hymnorum; parts of the harp surmised to have been the *Ceis*,—the *Cobluighe* or "sisters", and the *Leithrind*; *Leithrind* or half harmony, and *Rind* or full harmony; difficulty of determining what *Ceis* was; it was not a part of the harp; summary of the views of the commentators as to the meaning of *Ceis*. Fourth reference to the word *Ceis* in an ancient tale in *Leabhar na h-Uidhre*. Fifth reference to *Ceis* in another ancient poem. *Coir*, another term for harmony, synonymous with *Ceis*; the author concludes that *Ceis* meant either harmony, or the mode of playing with a bass. The word *Gles* mentioned in the scholium in H. 2. 16. is still a living word; the *Crann Gleasta* mentioned in a poem of the eighteenth century; this poem contains the names of the principal parts of the harp; the names of the different classes of strings are only to be found in the scholium in the *Leabhar na h-Uidhre* to the elegy on St. *Colum Cille*.

LECTURE XXXII. OF MUSIC AND MUSICAL INSTRUMENTS IN ANCIENT ERINN . . . . 258—278

(IX.) MUSIC AND MUSICAL INSTRUMENTS (continued). Reference to the different parts of a harp in a poem of the seventeenth century. The number of strings not mentioned in references to harps, except in two instances; the first is in the tale of the *Iubar Mic Aingis* or the "Yew Tree of *Mac Aingis*"; the instrument mentioned in this tale was not a *Cruit*, but a three stringed *Timpan;* the second reference is to be found in the Book of *Lecan;* and the instrument is eight stringed. The instrument called "Brian Boru's Harp" has thirty strings. Reference to a many stringed harp in the seventeenth century. Attention paid to the harp in the twelfth and thirteenth centuries. Reference to the *Timpan* as late as the seventeenth century, proving it to have been a stringed instrument. The *Timpan* was distinguished from the *Cruit* or full harp. No very ancient harp preserved. The harp in Trinity College, Dublin; Dr. Petrie's account of it; summary of Dr. Petrie's conclusions. Dr. Petrie's serious charge against the Chevalier O'Gorman. Some curious references to harps belonging to O'Briens which the author has met with: *Mac Conmidhe's* poem on *Donnchadh Cairbreach* O'Brien; *Mac Conmidhe's* poem on the harp of the same O'Brien; the poem does not explain how the harp went to Scotland. What became of this harp? Was it the harp presented by Henry the Eighth to the Earl of Clanrickard? Perhaps it suggested the harp-coinage, which was in circulation in Henry the Eighth's time. The Chevalier O'Gorman only mistook one Donogh O'Brien for another. There can be no doubt that this harp did once belong to the Earl of Clanrickard. If the harp was an O'Neill harp, how could its story have been invented and published in the lifetime of those concerned? Arthur O'Neill may have played upon the harp. But it could not have been his; this harp is not an O'Neill, but an O'Brien one; Dr. Petrie's antiquarian difficulties: author's answer; as to the monogram I. H. S.; as to the arms on the escutcheon. The assertion of Dr. Petrie, that the sept of O'Neill is more illustrious than that of O'Brien, is incorrect.

LECTURE XXXIII. OF MUSIC AND MUSICAL INSTRUMENTS IN ANCIENT ERINN . . . . 279—303

(IX.) MUSIC AND MUSICAL INSTRUMENTS (continued). *Donnchadh Cairbreach* O'Brien sent some prized jewel to Scotland some time before *Mac Conmidhe's* mission for *Donnchadh's* harp. The Four Masters' account of the pursuit of *Muireadhach* O'Daly by O'Donnell; O'Daly sues for peace in three poems, and is forgiven; no copies of these poems existing in Ireland; two of them are at Oxford. The Four Masters' account of O'Daly's banishment not accurate; his poems to Clanrickard and O'Brien give some particulars of his flight. Poem of O'Daly to Morogh O'Brien, giving some account of the poet after his flight to Scotland. The poet Brian O'Higgins and David Roche of Fermoy. O'Higgins writes a poem to him which is in the Book of Fermoy; this poem gives a somewhat different account of O'Daly's return from that of the Four Masters. O'Daly was perhaps not allowed to leave Scotland without ransom; what was the jewel paid as this ransom? The author believes that it was the harp of O'Brien. This harp did not come back to Ireland directly, and may have passed into the hands of Edward the First, and have been given by Henry the Eighth to Clanrickard. The armorial bearings and monogram not of the same age as the harp. Objects of the author in the previous discussion. Poem on another straying harp of an O'Brien, written in 1570; the O'Brien was Conor Earl of Thomond; the Four Masters' account of his submission to Queen Elizabeth; it was during his short absence that his harp passed into strange hands; the harp in T.C.D. not this harp. Mr. Lanigan's harp. Owners of rare antiquities should place them for a time in the museum of the R.I.A. Some notes on Irish harps by Dr. Petrie.—"He regrets the absence of any ancient harp"; "present indifference to Irish harps and music"; "some ecclesiastical relics preserved"; Dr. Petrie would have preferred the harp of St. Patrick or St. Kevin; "our bogs may yet give us an ancient harp"; Mr. Joy's account of such a harp found in the county Limerick; according to Dr. Petrie, this harp was at least 1,000 years old. What has become of the harps of 1782 and 1792? A harp of 1509. "*Brian Boru's*" harp is the oldest of those known; the Dalway harp is next in age; the inscriptions on this harp imperfectly translated in Mr. Joy's essay. Professor O'Curry's translation of them; Mr. Joy's description of this harp. The harp of the Marquis of Kildare. Harps of the eighteenth century: the one in the possession of Sir Hervey Bruce; the Castle Otway harp; a harp formerly belonging to Mr. Hehir of Limerick; a Magennis harp seen by Dr. Petrie in 1832; the harp in the possession of Sir G. Hodson; the harp in the museum of the R.I.A. purchased from Major Sirr; the so-called harp of Carolan in the museum of the R.I.A. The harps of the present century all made by Egan; one of them in Dr. Petrie's possession. Dr. Petrie's opinion of the exertions of the Harp Society of Belfast. "The Irish harp is dead for ever, but the music won't die". The harp in Scotland known as that of Mary Queen of Scots. Rev. Mr. Mac Lauchlan's "Book of the Dean of Lismore"; it contains three poems ascribed to O'Daly or *Muireadhach Albanach*; Mr. Mac Lauchlan's note on this poet; his description of one of the poems incorrect as regards O'Daly; Mr. Mac Lauchlan not aware that *Muireadhach Albanach* was an Irishman. The author has collected all that he believes authentic on the *Cruit*. The statements about ancient Irish music and musical instruments of Walker and Bunting of no value; these writers did not know the Irish language; the author regrets to have to speak thus of the work of one who has rescued so much of our music.

LECTURE XXXIV. Of Music and Musical Instruments 304—326

(IX.) Of Music and Musical Instruments (continued). Names of musical instruments found in our MSS.—The *Benn-Buabhaill;* the *Corn-Buabhaill* a drinking horn The *Benn-Chroit.* The *Buinne.* The *Coir-Ceathairchuir.* The *Corn;* the *Cornaire* or horn-player mentioned in the *Táin Bó Fraich*, in the "Courtship of *Ferb*", and in a legendary version of the Book of Genesis; no reference to trumpets in the *Táin Bó Chuailgne*, but the playing of harps in the encampments is mentioned; instance of musicians in the trains of kings and chiefs on military expeditions:—the Battle of *Almhain* and the legend of *Dondbo.* Musical instruments mentioned in the Tale of the Battle of *Almhain*, and in the poem on the Fair of *Carman.* The *Cornaire*, or horn-blower, also mentioned in the poem on the Banqueting-House of Tara. The *Craebh-Ciúil*, or Musical Branch, mentioned in the Tale of *Fled Bricrind* or "*Bricriu*'s Feast"; the musical branch a symbol of poets and used for commanding silence, as shown by the Tales of "*Bricriu*'s Feast", and the "Courtship of *Emer*"; the Musical Branch mentioned in the Tale of the "Dialogue of the Two Sages"; and also in the Tale of the "Finding of *Cormac's* Branch"; and lastly in a poem of about the year A.D. 1500; the Musical Branch symbolical of repose and peace; it was analogous to the Turkish silver crescent and bells; some bronze bells in the museum of the R.I.A. belonged perhaps to such an instrument. The bells called "Crotals" described in the *Penny Journal;* Dr. Petrie's observations thereon; "Crotals" not used by Christian priests; explanation of the term; the Irish words *crothaidh*, *crothla*, and *clothra;* they are the only words at all like *crotalum*, except *crotal*, the husks of fruit, *i.e.* castanets; bells put on the necks of cows, and on horses; the *Crotal* not known in Ireland. The *Crann-Ciúil*, or Musical Tree; it was a generic term for any kind of musical instrument, *e.g.* a *Cruit*, a *Cuisle*, or tube, or a *Timpan.* The *Cuiseach;* mentioned in the poem on the Fair of *Carman*, and in the Tale of the Battle of *Almhain.* The *Cuisle Ciúil* another name for *Crann Ciúil; Cuisle* a living word meaning a vein, or a kind of cock: mentioned in the Book of Invasions; *Cuisle* explained in H. 3. 18. T.C.D., as a Musical Tree.

LECTURE XXXV. Of Music and Musical Instruments 327—350

(IX.) Of Music and Musical Instruments (continued). The *Fedán;* mentioned in the Book of Lismore; *Fedán* players mentioned in the Brehon Laws. The *Fidil* or Fiddle; mentioned in the poem on the fair of *Carman*, and in a poem written in 1680. The *Guth-Buinde;* mentioned in an Irish life of Alexander the Great; the *Ceólán* also mentioned in this tract; incorrect meaning given to this word in Macleod's and Dewar's Dictionary; *Ceólán* not a diminutive of *ceol*, but the name of a tinkling bell; the *Ceólán* mentioned in the Irish life of St. *Mac Creiche.* The *Guthbuine* also mentioned in an Irish tract on the Siege of Troy. The *Ocht Tedach.* The *Oircin;* mentioned in the Irish Triads; one of the bards of *Seanchan Tor-*

peist's "Great Bardic Company" called *Oircne;* no explanation of *Oircne* known, except that it was the name of the first lap-dog. Of the *Pip* or Pipe, and in the plural *Pipai* or Pipes; mentioned in the poem on the Fair of *Carman;* the only ancient reference to the *Pipaireadha*, or *Piobaire*, or Piper, known to author is in a fragment of Brehon Law. Of the *Stoc;* mentioned in a paraphrase of the Book of Genesis in the *Leabhar Breac*, and in the version of the "Fall of Jericho" in the same book; and again in describing the coming of Antichrist; and in the plural form *Stuic* in the poem on the Fair of *Carman*, and in the *Táin Bó Flidais.* Another instrument, the *Sturgan*, mentioned in this tract; and also in a poem on Randal lord of Arran. The *Sturganuidhe* or *Sturgan* player mentioned in Keating's "Three Shafts of Death". Specimens of the *Corn, Stoc*, and *Sturgan* are probably to be found in the Museum of the R.I.A. The *Corn* was the Roman Cornua. The *Stoc* represents the Roman Buccina. The *Sturgan* corresponds to the Roman Lituus. Mr. R. Ousley's description of the *Stuic* and the *Sturgana* in the Museum of the R.I.A. Ancient Irish wind instruments of graduated scale and compass; the trumpets mentioned in Walker's Irish Bards first described and figured in Smith's History of Cork; Walker's observations on them; they are figured in Vetusta Monumenta; a similar trumpet found in England; the author agrees with Walker that there must have been another joint in the trumpets; discrepancy between the figures of Smith and the Vetusta Monumenta; Smith's opinion that they were Danish, erroneous; Smith's error that the Cork trumpets formed but one instrument, reproduced by Mr. R. MacAdam; Sir W. Wilde's novel idea of the use of the straight tubes; his idea that they were part of a "Commander's Staff", borrowed from Wagner; Sir William Wilde's illustration of the use of the straight part of a trumpet as a "Commander's Staff", unsatisfactory; his separation of the straight tube from the curved parts in the Museum of the R.I.A. a mistake which ought to be corrected. *Sturgana, Stuic*, and *Corna* in the Museums of the Royal Irish Academy, and Trinity College, Dublin.

LECTURE XXXVI. OF MUSIC AND MUSICAL INSTRUMENTS 351—363

(IX.) MUSIC AND MUSICAL INSTRUMENTS (continued). The word *Teillin*, the name of a harp in Welsh, is not applied in Gaedhelic to a musical instrument; meaning of *Telyn* according to Owen's Welsh Dictionary; *Telyn* originally perhaps a derisive name; *Caradoc*'s account of the introduction of harp music from Ireland into Wales; author unable to find what Welsh word *Caradoc* used for harp; the *Telyn* and *Cruth* were the *Cruit* and *Timpan* of Ireland; Owen's definition of a Welsh *Cruit.* The Irish *Cruit* was a lyre, and not a cithara. The Welsh *Crud* or Crowd could not represent the Irish *Cruit.* The Welsh word *Telyn* apparently the same as the Irish *Teillin*, applied to the humming bee and humble bee; *Teillin* occurs in the *Dinnseanchas;* also in a poem about *Marbhan* and *Guaire;* and in one by O'Donnelly written about 1680. The word *Teillin* applied to the humming of bees; it has become obsolete in Ireland, but not in Scotland; occurs in the Highland Society's dictionary as *Seillean*. *Telyn* could not be a modification of the Greek Chelys. Some think the fiddle represents the ancient *Cruit;* the poem on the Fair of *Carman* proves this to be erroneous. Of the *Timpan: Cormac's* derivation of this word gives us the materials of which the instrument was made; the *Timpan* mentioned in an ancient paraphrase of the Book of Exodus; also in the Tale of the Battle of *Magh Lena;* and in that of the Exile of the Sons of *Duil Dermaid;* another reference in the Dialogue of the Ancient Men; the passage in the latter the only one which explains *Lethrind;* in this passage *Lethrind* signifies the treble part; another description of the *Timpan* given in the Siege of *Dromdamhghaire*. The *Timpan* was a stringed instrument played with a bow; this is fully confirmed by a passage from a vellum MS. compiled by Edmund *O'Deórain* in 1509. The same person may have played the harp and *Timpan*, but they were two distinct professions. The *Timpan* came down to the seventeenth century. Important passage from the Brehon Law respecting the Timpanist; it would appear from this that, in addition to the bow, the deeper strings were struck with the nail. Harpers and Timpanists are separately mentioned in the *Tochmarc Emere*. The harper alone always considered of the rank of a *Bó Aire;* the timpanist, only when chief Timpanist of a king. Relative powers of the harp and *Timpan* illustrated by a legend from the Book of Lismore. Professional names of musical performers; the *Buinnire;* the *Cnaimh-Fhear;* the *Cornair;* the *Cruitire;* the *Cuisleannach;* the *Fedánach;* the *Fer Cengail;* the *Graice;* the *Pipaire;* the *Stocaire;* the *Sturganaidhe;* the *Timpanach*.

LECTURE XXXVII. OF MUSIC AND MUSICAL INSTRUMENTS 370—389

(IX.) OF MUSIC AND MUSICAL INSTRUMENTS (continued). The particular kinds of music mentioned in ancient manuscripts; the *Aidbsi;* the *Cepóc*. *Cepóc* only another name for *Aidbsi*; the word *Cepóc* used in Ireland also, as shown by the Tale of "*Mac Datho's* Pig", and in an elegy on *Aithirne* the poet. *Aidbsi* or *Cepóc* a kind of *Cronán* or guttural murmur. The *Certan* referred to particularly in the *Cain Adamhnain*. The *Cronán*, mentioned in the account of the assembly of *Drom Ceat;* and also in the Adventures of the "Great Bardic Company". The *Crann-Dord;* it consisted of an accompaniment produced by the clashing of spear handles, as shown by a passage in the *Táin Bó Chuailgne;* and in a legend from the Book of Lismore in which the term occurs. Other musical terms used in this tale: the *Dordán;* the *Fodord;* the *Abran;* the *Fead;* the *Dord Fiansa;* the *Dord;* the *Fiansa;* the *Andord;* the latter word occurs in the Tale of the "Sons of *Uisnech*"; this passage shows that the pagan Gaedhil sang and played in chorus and in concert; though *Dord* and its derivatives imply music, the word *Dordán* was applied to the notes of thrushes. Character of the *Crann-Dord* shown by a passage from the "Dialogue of the Ancient Men"; and by another passage from the same Dialogue in a MS. in the Royal Irish Academy; the *Dord-Fiansa* was therefore a kind of wooden gong accompaniment. The *Duchand*, explained as *Luinneog* or music; *Luinneog* obsolete in Ireland, but used in Scotland for a ditty or chorus; *Duchand* was probably a dirge; *Duan*, a laudation; *Duchand* occurs in *Cormac's* Glossary explaining *Esnad;* the latter a moaning air or tune in chorus. The *Esnad*. The Three Musical Modes. The *Géim Druadh* or "Druid's Shout", mentioned in the Tale of the Battle of *Almhain*. The *Golghaire Bansidhe*, or wail of the *Bansidhe*, mentioned in the *Táin Bó Fraich;* it probably came down to a late period. The *Gúbha*. The *Logairecht* or funeral wail, occurs in *Cormac's* Glossary at the word *Amrath;* meaning of the latter term. The *Luinneog*. The *Samhghúba*, or sea nymph's song as it is explained in an old glossary. The *Sian* or *Sianan*, applied in the Tale of the Battle of the second *Magh Tuireadh* to the whizzing of a spear; applied to a song in the Tale of the Sons of *Uisnech;* and also in the wanderings of the priests *Snedgus* and *Mac Riaghla;* it designated soft plaintive music. *Sirectach* applied to low music; synonymous with *Adbond;* the latter word occurs in the Festology of *Aengus Ceilé Dé; Adband Trirech*, or triple *Adbond*, explained in Michael O'Clery's glossary as the Three Musical Modes; *Trirech* occurs in Zeuss' *Grammatica Celtica; Trirech* was applied to a species of lyric poetry; the term *Trirech* not exclusively applied to the music or quantity of verse, but also to a particular kind of laudatory poem; the stanza in question sings to the air of "For Ireland I would not tell who she is".

LECTURE XXXVIII. Of Music and Musical Instruments 390—40

(IX.) Of Music and Musical Instruments (continued). The ancient lyric verse adapted to an ancient air referred to in last lecture; the existence of old lyric compositions having a peculiar structure of rhythm adapted to old airs still existing, unknown in the musical history of any other country; many such known; there exists in the Book of Ballymote a special tract on versification containing specimen verses; the specimens are usually four-lined verses, but they sing to certain simple solemn airs; these are chiefly the poems called Ossianic; the author has heard his father sing the Ossianic poems; and has heard of a very good singer of them named O'Brien; the author only heard one other poem sung to the air of the Ossianic poems; many other old poems would, however, sing to it. The tract on versification contains specimens which must read to music at first sight; three examples selected. The first called *Ocht-Foclach Corranach Beg*, or, "the little eight-line curved verse"; this class of poems written to a melody constructed like that known as the "Black Slender Boy"; description of this kind of verse. The second is the *Ocht Foclach Mór* or "great eight line verse"; this stanza was written to the musical metre of an air of which the first half of "John O'Dwyer of the Glen" is an example; description of this kind of verse. The third is the *Ocht Foclach Mór*

Corranach, or "great curving eight line verse"; measure, accents, cadences, and rhyme are the same as in the second. Another specimen of verse from a long poem in the Book of *Lecan*; the kind called *Ocht Foclach hi-Eimhin*, or the "eight line verse of *O' h-Eimhin*"; the *Ui* or *O* prefixed to the name of the author of the poem does not necessarily imply his having lived after the permanent assumption of surnames; description of this kind of poem; this poem written to a different kind of air from the other stanzas quoted; will sing to any one of three well known airs. The author does not say that these verses were written for the airs mentioned, but only that they sing naturally to them. That these stanzas were not written by the writers on Irish prosody to support a theory, is shown by poems in the Tale of the *Táin Bó Chuailgne*; e.g. the poem containing the dialogue between *Medb* and *Ferdiad*; musical analysis of this poem; there are five poems of the same kind in this tale. The author does not want to establish a theory, but only to direct attension to the subject. Antiquity of the present version of the *Táin Bó Chuailgne*: the copy in the *Leabhar na h-Uidhri*; the copy in the Book of Leinster. At least one specimen of the same kind of ancient verse in the *Dinnseanchas*, e.g. in the legend of *Ath Fadad*, or Ahade: the *Dinnseanchas*, was written about 590 by *Amergin*, chief poet to *Diarmait*, son of *Fergus Ceirbheoil*; these various compositions are at least 900 years old, and prove that the most enchanting form of Irish music is indigenous. The author is conscious of his unfitness to deal with the subject of music technically; complaint on the neglect of Irish music; appeal to Irishmen in favour of it.

No clear allusion in the very old Irish MSS. to dancing. The modern generic name for dancing is *Rinnceadh*; it is sometimes called *Damhsa*; meaning of those terms. *Fonn* and *Port* the modern names for singing and dancing music; Michael O'Clery applies the term *Port* to lyric music in general. *Cor*, in the plural *Cuir*, an old Irish word for music, perhaps connected with *Chorea*; the author suggests that *Port* was anciently, what it is now, a "jig", and *Cor*, a "reel"; "jig" borrowed from the French or Italian. *Rinnceadh fada*, "long dance", not an ancient term; applied to a country dance. Conclusion.

APPENDIX.

I. The Fight of Ferdiad and Cuchulaind, from the *Táin Bó Chuailgne* 412–463

II. Two Old Law Tracts:

1. The *Crith Gablach* 465–512

2. A Law Tract without a title, on the classes of society 513–522

III. The Ancient Fair of *Carman* 523–547

Glossarial Index of Irish Words 549-604

Index Nominum 605-634

Index Locorum 635–653

General Index 654

CORRIGENDA.

The following errors have been noticed in preparing the I

		FOR	READ
Page 4, note	1,	with water,	with water between
„ 10, line	3,	*Ubtaire,*	*Fubtaire.*
„ 18 „	32,	way,	day.
„ 20 „	12,	ridges,	*Fothairbes.*
„ 25 „	2,	*Cradbh dearg,*	*Crobh derg.*
„ „ „	11,	their,	his.
„ 26 „	44,	four times seven,	twice seven.
„ 27 „	19,	and perfect.	and a perfect.
„ 30 „	2,	[of the posts.]	the front posts.
„ 31 „	6,	with salt; and a vessel of sour milk,	with condiments, an sel of skimmed m
„ 40 „	13,	the mouth,	a mouth.
„ 42 „	6,	*Lamhfhada,*	*Lamhfada.*
„ 52 „	36,	on *Ollamh,*	an *Ollamh.*
„ 79 „	9,	*Midir,*	*Mind.*
„ 90 „	39,	sons,	sons of.
„ 92 „	2,	three times three thousand men,	three *Triucha Ced*
„ „ „	31,	black-green,	black-gray.
„ 93 „	16,	deep-gray,	light-gray.
„ „ „	23,	a man of hound-like, hateful face,	and he fierce and te
„ „ „	25,	close napped cloak,	cloak with little ca
„ 94 „	4,	a dark gray long wooled cloak,	a loose fitting da cloak.
„ „ „	12,	squinting,	round.
„ 98 „	11,	*after* me there, *add*	with a glossy curled hair upon him.
		FOR	READ
„ 99 „	4,	*Othme,*	*Othine.*
„ „ „	32,	two woodrings,	two kings of *Caill.*
„ „ „	48,	of the household youths of,	sons of.
„ 101, note 59, col. 1, line 13		óɼ,	óp.
„ 104 line	45,	with *Bille,*	with seven *Bille.*

FOR — READ

Page 106 „ 19, a *Mac*, — *Mac*.
„ 110, note 71, col. 2, line 11, fnrri, — furri.
„ 111, line 6, fastening, — fastenings.
„ 131 „ 25, m n. *Fortharta*, — *Fotharta*.
„ 136 „ 9, fifty, — seventy.
„ 149 „ 8, white shirt and collar, — white collared shirt.
„ „ „ 29, sons renowned for valour, — sons of *Ersand* (jamb) and *Comlad* (door).
„ 157 „ 15, *after* silver and, *add* flesh-mangling spears with veins of gold and silver, and *Creduma* (bronze).

FOR — READ.

„ 157, note 234, col. 2, line 4, at im cech fer, — at di ór im cech fer.
„ 165, line 3, yellow silk, — yellow silk with silver upon them.
„ 166, side note line 2, reference of carved in Book of Munster, — reference to carved brooches in Book of Munster.
„ 186, line 40, side note, dress of *Riangabhra*, — dress of *Laegh*, son of *Riangabhra*.
„ 192 „ 4, Fair haired woman, — fair woman.
„ 196 „ 2, places, — pieces.
„ „ „ 9, *Lacair*, — *lán ecair*.
„ 197 „ 11, In a former lecture an account, — In a former lecture I gave an account.
„ 215, note 297, ile ich, — ileich.
„ 202, line 16, "Lady *Nar* of *Badbh Dearg's* mansion". The lady *Nar* mentioned in this tale, was daughter of *Loch*, son of *Doire Leith*, of the *Cruitentuaith* or Irish Picts, and wife of *Crimthan Nia Nar*, and not *Nar Tuathcaech* of *Badbh Derg's* mansion, who was swineherd to *Badbh Derg*, and a great warrior. See *Lindsenchas*, *MS. Book of Lecan*.

FOR — READ

„ 219 „ 20, rings, — coils.
„ 220 „ 23, hills, — *Sidhe*.
„ 245 „ 40, *after last line add:* "and it was together they made that music".

FOR — READ

„ 249 „ 6, the *Ceis*, — the musical *Ceis*.
„ 251, note 328, col. 2, line 1, leiges "cure", — is scaradh, parting in *Leb. na h-Uidhri*, p. 9.
„ 254, line 5, counter part strings of that part in their proper places, — *Lethrind* with its strings in it.
„ 265 „ 2, *Laoighseal*, — *Laoighseach*.
„ 266 „ 36, in position, — in a position.
„ 301 „ 7, *Croibhdhearg*, — *Crobhdearg*.
„ 305, line 12, *Cruiseach* — *Cuiseach*.

	FOR	READ
Page 308, note 352, col. 1, line 8,	bá táp,	bátáp.
„ 312, note 359, col. 1, line 15,	cupla,	cuala.
„ 313 „ 360, col. 2,	vol. ii,	vol. i.
„ 328 „ 377, col. 2 line, 3,	do eann,	do ceann.
„ 339, line 26, side note,	also a poem,	also in a poe
„ 342 „ 15, side note,	*Stuic* or *Sturgana*,	*Stuic* and *St*
„ 344 „ 4,	may seem,	may be seen
„ 357 „ 17,	Dusky *Tellins*,	buzzing *Cia*
„ 364 „ 17-18, side note,	there were,	they were.
„ „ „ 5,	*Inis Cathargh*,	*Inis Cathagh.*
„ 373 „ 20, et seq.,	lady *Luain*,	lady *Luan.*
„ 375, note 429, col. 2, line 4,	linnpa,	limpa.
„ 379, line 36,	*Dord Fiansa*,	*Crann Dord.*
„ „ { „ 37, }	*Crann Dord*,	*Dordfiansa.*
„ 380 { „ „ }	This mistake is repeated, pp. 379-3 Introduction, p. cclix.	
„ 417 „ 38,	will kill,	wilt kill.
„ 418 „ 39,	ocap,	ocap.
„ 467 „ 2 (marg. note),	352,	252.
„ „ „ 24,	*Airè Desa, Airè Tuisi,*	*Airé Desa,* *Ard, Air*
„ 497 „ 37,	a cow,	a new calve
„ 500 „ 39,	bond,	bond *Ceiles.*
„ 501 „ 38,	ten not,	ten on.

LECTURE XIX.

[Delivered 6th July, 1859.]

(VII.) OF BUILDINGS, FURNITURE, ETC., in ancient Erinn. Of the number and succession of the colonists of ancient Erinn. Tradition ascribes no buildings to *Parthalon* or his people; their sepulchral mounds at Tallaght near Dublin. Definitions of the *Rath*, the *Dun*, the *Lis*, the *Caiseal*, and the *Cathair;* the latter two were of stone; many modern townland-names derived from these terms; remains of many of these structures still exist. *Rath na Righ* or "Rath of the Kings", at Tara; the *Teach Mór Milibh Amus*, or "Great House of the Thousands of Soldiers". Several houses were often included within the same *Rath*, *Dun*, *Lis*, or *Caiseal*. Extent of the demesne lands of Tara. The *Rath* or *Cathair* of *Aileach;* account of its building; the houses within the *Rath* as well as the latter were of stone; why called *Aileach Frigrind?* *Aileach* mentioned by Ptolemy. Account of the *Rath* of *Cruachan* in the *Táin Bo Fraich*. The "House of the Royal Branch". Description of a *Dun* in Fairy Land. The terms *Rath*, *Dun*, and *Lis* applied to the same kind of enclosure. The *Foradh* at *Tara*. Description of the house of *Credé*. Two classes of builders,—the *Rath*-builder, and the *Caiseal*-builder; list of the professors of both arts from the Book of Leinster. *Dubhaltach Mac Firbissigh*'s copy of the same list (note); his observations in answer to those who deny the existence of stone-building in ancient Erinn. The story of *Bricrind*'s Feast; plan of his house; his *grianan* or "sun house"; his invitation to *Conchobar* and the Ultonians; he sows dissensions among the women; the *Briathar Ban Uladh;*—his house was made of wicker-work.

IN the last Lecture I concluded what I had to say concerning the Arms, the Military System, and the modes of Warfare, of the ancient Gaedhil. I now proceed to the consideration of their Domestic Life; and, as the erection of dwellings, and with these the adoption of means of defence against external aggression, must have been the first care of every people where society began to be formed, we may naturally commence with the arrangement of their houses and the appliances of comfortable life within them.

In dealing with this subject I shall naturally go back first to the very earliest colonists of ancient Erinn; and in doing so, I must premise by repeating the caution I have already intimated, —that here again I adopt the number and succession of these colonists, as I have hitherto done, simply in the order in which I find them in the ancient "Book of Invasions"; because the time has not yet come for entering on the consideration of the grounds upon which those ancient accounts have been, or to what extent they ought to have been, so implicitly relied on by the Gaedhelic writers of the last eighteen hundred years. Without at all then entering at present into any investigation of the

ECT. XIX. long discussed question of the veracity of our ancient records and traditions, which declare that this island was occupied in succession by the Parthalonians, the Nemedians, the Firbolgs, the *Tuatha Dé Danann*, and, finally, the Milesians or Scoti; or from what countries or by what routes they came hither; it must strike every unprejudiced reader as a very remarkable fact, that the Scoti, who were the last colony, and consequently the historians of the country, should actually have recorded, by name and local position, several distinct monuments, still existing, of three out of the four peoples or races who are said to have occupied the country before themselves. And although much has been incautiously written of the tendency of our old Scotic writers to the wild and romantic in their historical compositions, I cannot discover any sufficient reason why they should concede to their predecessors the credit of being the founders of Tara, the seat of the monarchy, as well as of some others of the most remarkable and historic monuments of the whole country, unless they had been so.

re Scoti ention the onuments their edecessors.

Etymological speculations and fanciful collations of the ancient Gaedhelic with the Semitic languages, were taken up by a few very incompetent persons in this country within our own memory, and carried to such an extent of absurdity, that both subject and the authors became a bye-word among the truly learned historians and philologists of Europe. Still, etymology and philology must have an important bearing on the ethnological history of Europe. It forms, however, no part of my present plan to enter upon any arguments based on these studies; though I may of course have occasion now and again to refer to proofs or illustrations ascertained by their means.

o buildings cribed to rthalon.

It is a remarkable fact, and one not to be despised among the evidences of the extreme antiquity of the tradition, that no account that has come down to us ascribes to the Parthalonian colony the erection of any sort of building, either for residence or defence. *Parthalon* and his people came into the island A.M. 2520, B.C. 2674 (according to the chronology adopted in the Annals of the Four Masters); and although the descendants of this colony are said to have continued in Erinn for over three hundred years, still no memorial of them has been preserved save what we may find in a few topographical names derived from those of their chiefs, excepting only the ancient sepulchral mounds still remaining on the hill of *Tamhlacht* (or Tallaght, in the county of Dublin), where the last remnant of this colony are recorded to have been interred, after having been, as it is said, swept off by a plague. The word *tamh* in the Gaedhelic signifies a sudden or unnatural death; and *leacht* a monumental mound or heap of stones; and hence those ancient monumental mounds have from a period beyond the reach of history preserved the name of *Tamhleachta Muintiré Phartolain*, that is, the Mortality Mounds of the people of *Parthalon*.

The forts of *Nemhidh*.

Thirty years after the destruction of the people of *Parthalon*, according to the Four Masters, *Nemhidh* came into Erinn at the head of a large colony; and although this colony also remained in the country for three hundred years, we have no record of any sort of buildings having been erected by them, any more than by their predecessors, excepting two only, both of which are said to have been erected by *Nemhidh* himself; namely, *Rath-Cinn-Eich*, in *Ui Niallain* (now the barony of Oneilland in the county of Armagh); and *Rath Cimbaoith*, in *Seimhné* (which was the ancient name of that part of the seaboard of the present county of Antrim, opposite to which lies Island Magee).

That these *Raths*, or Forts, of *Nemhidh* could not have been of any great extent or importance according to our present notions, is evident, since we find it stated in the "Book of Invasions", that *Rath-Cinn-Eich*, (lit. the Horse-Head-Fort), was built in one day, by four Fomorian brothers, who it would appear were condemned by *Nemhidh*, as prisoners or slaves, to perform the work, but who were put to death the next day lest they should demolish their work again. No trace of these ancient edifices now remains, at least under their ancient names.

It may be as well to state here what is exactly meant by the different words *Rath*, *Dun*, *Lis*, *Caiseal*, and *Cathair*; the prevailing names for fortified places of residence, as well as for the fortifications themselves, among the Gaedhil.

The *Rath*.

The *Rath* was a simple circular wall or enclosure of raised earth, enclosing a space of more or less extent, in which stood the residence of the chief and sometimes the dwellings of one or more of the officers or chief men of the tribe or court. Sometimes also the *Rath* consisted of two or three concentric walls or circumvallations; but it does not appear that the erection so called was ever intended to be surrounded with water.

The *Dun*.

The *Dun* was of the same form as the *Rath*, but consisting of at least two concentric circular mounds or walls, with a deep trench full of water between them. These were often encircled by a third, or even by a greater number of walls, at increasing distances; but this circumstance made no alteration in the form or in the signification of the name. *Dun* is defined strictly in so authoritative a MS. as the ancient Gaedhelic Law tract preserved in the vellum MS. H. 3., 18. T. C. D., thus: "*Dun*, i.e.

two walls with water".[1] The same name, according to this derivation, would apply to any boundary or mearing formed of a wet trench between two raised banks or walls of earth.

The *Lis*.

The *Lis*, as far as I have been able to discover, was precisely the same as the *Rath;* the name, however, was applied generally to some sort of fortification, but more particularly those formed of earth. That this was so, we have a curious confirmation, in the life of Saint *Mochuda*, or *Carthach*, (the founder of the once famous ecclesiastical establishment of *Lis-Mór*, now Lismore in the county of Waterford). The life states, that when Saint *Mochuda*, on being driven out of *Rathin* (his great foundation, near the present town of Tullamore, King's County), came to the place on which *Lis-Mór* now stands, with the consent of the king of the *Deisé* he commenced forthwith to raise what is described as a circular enclosure of earth. A religious woman who occupied a small cell in the neighbourhood, perceiving the crowd of monks at work, came up and asked what they were doing. "We are building a small *Lis* here", said saint *Mochuda*. "A small *Lis! [Lis Beg]*", said the woman: "this is not a small *Lis*, [*Lis Beg*], but a great *Lis* [*Lis Mór*]", said she; and so we are told, that church ever since continued to be called by that name. It matters little to the present purpose whether this legend is strictly true or not; but it is quite sufficient to show what the ancient Gaedhils understood the word *Lis* to mean.

Origin of name *Lis-Mór* or Lismore.

So much for the *Rath*, the *Dun*, and the *Lis*, all of which were generally built of earth. The *Caiseal* and the *Cathair* are to be distinguished from these especially, because they were generally, if not invariably, built of stone.

The *Caiseal* and *Cathair*

The *Caiseal* was nothing more than a Stone *Rath* or enclosure within which the dwelling-house, and in after times churches, stood; and the *Cathair*, in like manner, was nothing more than a Stone *Dun*, (with loftier and stronger walls), with this exception, that the *Cathair* was not necessarily surrounded with water, as far as I know.

were of stone.

No reliable analysis of the term *Caiseal* is to be found among the writings of the Gaedhils; but our experience of existing monuments enables us to decide that the *Caiseal* and *Cathair* were both of stone; and that the words are cognate with the British "Caer", the Latin "Castrum", and the English "Castle". There can be no doubt, however, but that our ancient writers often used the terms *Dun*, *Rath*, *Lis*, and *Cathair*, indifferently, to designate a stronghold or well-fortified place; and these terms afterwards came to give names to the towns and cities which in

[1] original:—dún .i. dá ċlad im uisce.

time sprang up at or around the various forts so designated, or in which those fortified residences were situated, which naturally became the centres of increasing population. Thus we have *Rath-Gaela*, (now the town of Rathkeale, in the county of Limerick); *Rath-Naoi* (now the town of Rathnew, in the county of Wicklow); *Dun-Duibh-linné*, (now the city of Dublin); *Dun-Dealca*, (now the town of Dundalk, in the county of Louth); *Dun-Chealtchair*, which was afterwards called *Dun-da-Leath-Ghlas*, (now the town of Downpatrick, in the county of Down); *Lis-Mór*, (now the town of Lismore, in the county of Waterford); *Lis Tuathail*, (now the town of Listowel, in the connty of Kerry); *Cathair-Dun-Iascaigh*, (now the town of Cahir, in the county of Tipperary); *Cathair-Chinn-Lis*, (now the town of Caherconlish, in the county of Limerick); etc., etc.

Names of modern towns derived from *Rath*, *Dun*, etc.

Remains of many of the residences and forts known as *Rath*, *Dun*, *Lis*, and *Cathair*, still exist throughout Ireland, some of which belong to the most remote antiquity. The *Cathair* or Stone Fort is seldom or never met with but where stone is in great abundance; such as in the counties of Kerry and Limerick; in Burren, in the county of Clare; and in the Arann Islands, on the coast of Clare, in which there are fine examples of these stone edifices, though singularly enough, still bearing the names of *Duns*, such as *Dun-Ænghuis*, *Dun-Ochaill*, *Dun-Eoghanacht*, and *Dubh Chathair*, (or the Black Fortress), on the great or western island; and *Dun-Chonchraidh*, on the middle island; these remarkable fortresses on the Arann islands, are referred to the *Clann Umoir*, (a *Firbolg* tribe, who occupied the seaboard of Clare and Galway, shortly before the Christian era), excepting one, *Dun-Eoghanacht*. This fort must have been erected after the close of the third century, when the *Eoghanachts*, (that is, the descendants of *Eoghan Mór*, son of *Oilioll Oluim*, king of Munster), took their tribe-title from that chivalrous prince, in whose time, and for centuries afterwards, those islands belonged to Munster.

Remains of *Raths*, *Duns*, etc. still existing.

In any attempt to treat of the early or primitive buildings or habitations of Erinn, we must of course give the first place to Tara, which, according to all our old accounts, had been first founded by the Firbolgs, the third in the series of the early colonists of the island. In the ancient account of the battle of the first or Southern *Magh Tuireadh*, we are told that the Firbolgs, who had been dispersed into three parties on their approach to the Irish coast by a storm, had, on their landing, repaired by one consent to *Rath na Righ*, (i.e. the Rath or Palace of the Kings), at Tara. And again, when *Breas* goes out from the camp of the *Tuatha Dé Danann* to meet *Sreng*, the Fir-

Rath na Righ at Tara.

LECT. XIX. bolg warrior whom they saw coming towards them, *Breas* asks *Sreng* where he had slept the night before; and *Sreng* answers, that it was at "the *Rath* of the Kings at Tara".

It is stated in an ancient poem on Tara, the author of which is not known, that the "*Rath* of the Kings" was first founded by *Slaingé*, one of the *Firbolg* chiefs; and it is rather singular that, in the time of *Cuan O'Lothchain*, who died in the year 1024, this same *Rath-na-Righ* was the most conspicuous and by far the most extensive enclosure upon or around the Hill of Tara; and that it was within its ample circuit that, in an earlier era, the palace of the monarch *Cormac Mac Airt*, as well as other edifices, once stood. This will be very plainly seen from the map of ancient Tara, prepared by the officers of the Ordnance Survey, from *Cuan O'Lothchain*'s poem (described in a former lecture)[2] for the illustration of Dr. Petrie's History of the Antiquities of Tara Hill, published in the year 1839.[3]

There were two remarkable buildings at Tara in ancient times, namely, the *Teach Mór Milibh Amus*, i.e. the "Great House of the Thousands of Soldiers"; and the *Teach Midhchuarta*, i.e. the "Mead-circling House", in other words, the great Banqueting House or Hall of Tara.

The "Great House of the Thousands of Soldiers".

The "great House of the Thousands of Soldiers" was the particular palace of the monarch; it stood within the *Rath-na-Righ*, or Rath of the Kings, and was called also *Tigh-Temrach*, or the House of Tara. Of its extent and magnificence in the time of King *Cormac Mac Airt*, in the middle of the third century, we may form some notion from an ancient poem preserved in the Book of Leinster, and ascribed to *Cormac Filé*, or the poet. The precise time of this writer I have not been able to ascertain, but he must have flourished in or before the middle of the tenth century; since we find *Cineadh O'Hartagan*, who flourished at that period, set down in the Yellow Book of *Lecan*, the Book of Ballymote, and others, as the author of the same poem. Dr. Petrie has published this poem in his essay on the "History and Antiquities of Tara Hill".[4]

The following short account of the extent and arrangement of the Great House of the Thousands of Soldiers, is translated from the Book of Leinster (folio 15).

"As regards the arrangement of the Palace of Tara by *Cormac*, it was larger than any house. The *Rath* was nine hundred feet in *Cormac*'s time. His own house was seven hundred feet;—[and there were] seven bronze candelabras in the middle of it. [There were] nine mounds around the house. There were three times fifty compartments (*imdadh*) in the house;

[2] See Lect. vii., *ante*, vol. i. p. 140. [3] P. 143. [4] P. 199.

The "Great House of the Thousands of Soldiers".

and three times fifty men in each compartment; and three times fifty continuations of compartments (*airel*); and fifty [men] in each of these continuations.

"Three thousand persons, each day, is what *Cormac* used to maintain in pay; besides poets and satirists; and all the strangers who sought the king: Galls; and Romans; and Franks; and Frisians; and Longbards; and Albanians, [i.e., Caledonians]; and Saxons; and *Cruithneans*, [i.e., Picts]; for all these used to seek him, and [it was] with gold and with silver, with steeds and with chariots, [that] he paid them off. They used all come to *Cormac*, because there was not in his time, nor before him, any one more celebrated in honour, and in dignity, and in wisdom, except only Solomon, the son of David".

It is not easy to conceive how this "Great House" of Tara could have received into its compartments, and sub-compartments, the "thirty thousand men", which, on the authority both of the prose and the verse account in the Book of Leinster, it is stated to have accommodated; but although no plan of the Great House has been preserved to our time, the plan of the *Teach Midhchuarta*, or Banqueting Hall of Tara, as preserved in the Book of Leinster and in the Yellow Book of *Lecan*, enables us to form some idea of the arrangement. I must, however, add, that even the whole compass of the *Rath-na-Righ*, or Rath of the Kings, within which the "Great House" stood, could not possibly accommodate anything like the number of persons just mentioned. The enclosure of this Rath of the Kings, when measured in 1839 by the officers of the Ordnance Survey,[5] was found to measure across, from south-east to north-west, within the ring, only 775 feet.

The *Dun*, *Rath*, etc. often contained several houses.

It may be noted here, that the *Rath*, *Dun*, *Lis*, or *Caiseal*, which formed the fortification of ancient residences, often contained within them more than one house; and thus the whole ancient city of Tara was composed of seven *Duns*, or enclosures, each containing within it a certain number of houses. We learn this fact from an ancient poem of thirty-seven stanzas, of which there is an old paper copy in the Library of Trinity College, Dublin, (MS. H. 1, 15). This poem begins:

"The plain of Temair was the residence of the kings".[6]

The following are the twenty-eighth, twenty-ninth, and thirtieth stanzas of this valuable poem:

"The demesne of *Temur* they ploughed not;
It was seven full *bailés* [townlands], seven full *lisses* [houses],

(5) See Petrie's *History and Antiquities of Tara Hill*, page 128

(6) original:—baile na ríg ros temrach.

Seven ploughs to each full *lis;*
Of the best class land was fair-skinned *Temur.*
"The demesne of *Temur* was a pleasant abode;
A mound surrounded it all around;
I know besides the name of every house
Which was in the wealthy *Temur.*
"Seven *duns* in the *Dun* of *Temur,*—
Is it not I that well remember;
Seven score houses in each *dun,*
Seven hundred warriors in each brave *dun*".

[Ex]tent of [th]e demesne [la]nds of [Ta]ra.

We find from this poem that the demesne-lands of Tara, which were never distributed or cultivated, consisted of seven *bailés*, that is, "ballys", or townlands, as they would be now called; and from an ancient poem which I took occasion to print some years ago in connection with the Historic Tale of the "Battle of *Magh Leana*",[7] it will be found that a *bailé* contained grazing for three hundred cows, and as much of tillage land as seven ploughs could turn over in the year. This was the quantity of land that by law appertained to the *dun* or *lis.* And as the demesne of *Temair* contained seven such *bailés*, the quantity was equal to the feeding of two thousand one hundred cows, and the ploughing of forty-nine ploughs, for a year.

[T]he *Rath* or [C]*athair* of [A]*ileach.*

The next great building, in point of antiquity and historical reminiscence, is the great *Rath*, or rather *Cathair*, of *Aileach* (in the county of Derry), so well described by Dr. Petrie, in the Ordnance Memoir of the parish of Templemore. This great *Cathair* is said to have been originally built by the *Daghda*, the celebrated king of the *Tuatha Dé Danann*, who planned and fought the battle of the second or northern *Magh Tuireadh*, against the Fomorians. The fort was erected around the grave of his son *Aedh*, (or Hugh), who had been killed through jealousy by *Corrgenn*, a Connacht chieftain.

The history of the death of *Aedh*, and the building of *Aileach*, (or "the Stone Building"), is given at length in a poem preserved in the Book of *Lecan*;[8] which poem has been printed, with an English translation, (but with two lines left out at verse 38), by Dr. Petrie, in the above Memoir. The following extract from this curious and important poem, beginning at verse 32, will suffice for my present purpose:

"Then were brought the two good men
In art expert,

[7] *Cath Mhuighé Leana*, etc., pub. by the Celtic Society; Dublin, 1855; pp. 106–7, note (t).
[8] See also Lect. vii., *ante*, vol. i. p. 151.

The *Rath* or *Cathair* of *Aileach*.

Garbhan and *Imcheall*, to *Eochaid* [*Daghda*],
The fair-haired, vindictive;
And he ordered these a *rath* to build,
Around the gentle youth:
That it should be a *rath* of splendid sections—
The finest in Erinn.
Neid, son of *Indai*, said to them,
[He] of the severe mind,
That the best hosts in the world could not erect
A building like *Aileach*.
Garbhan the active proceeded to dress
And to cut [the stones];
Imcheall proceeded to set them
All around in the house.
The building of *Aileach*'s fastness came to an end,
Though it was a laborious process;
The top of the house of the groaning hostages
One stone closed".

In a subsequent verse of this poem, (verse 54), the author says that *Aileach* is the senior, or father of the buildings of Erinn:

"It is the senior of the buildings of Erinn,—
Aileach Frigrind:
Greater praise than it deserves,
For it I indite not".

This *Rath* and its houses were of stone.

It appears clearly from this very ancient poem that not only was the outer *Rath*, or protective circle of *Aileach*, built of stone by the regular masons *Imcheall* and *Garbhan;* but that the palace and other houses within the enclosure were built also of stone, (nay, even of chipped and cut stone). All these buildings, probably, were circular, as the house or Prison of the Hostages certainly must have been, when, as the poem says, it was "closed at the top with one stone". This, however, is a matter concerning which I shall have something to say in a future Lecture.

The time to which the first building of *Aileach* may be referred, according to the chronology of the Annals of the Four Masters, would be about seventeen hundred years before the Christian era. But another and much later erection within the same *Rath* of *Aileach* is also spoken of in ancient story, and as having conferred a name upon this clebrated palace.

Why called *Aileach Frigrind*.

It is stated further in this poem, that *Aileach* in after ages obtained the name of *Aileach Frigrind*, as it is in fact called in the stanza quoted last. According to another poem[9] (written by *Flann* of Monasterboice), and preserved in the Book of Lein-

[9] See Lect. vii., *ante*, vol. i., p. 153.

LECT. XIX. ster, this *Frigrind* was a famous builder, or architect, as he would be called in our day. Having travelled in Scotland he was well received at the court of *Ubtaire*, the king of that country, where having gained the affections of the king's daughter, the beautiful *Ailech*, she eloped with him, and he returned to his own country with her. Fearing pursuit, however, he claimed the protection of the then monarch of Erinn, *Fiacha-Sraibhthinè*, (the same who was slain in the battle of *Dubh-Chomar*, in Meath, A.D. 322); and the monarch accorded it at once, and gave them the ancient fort of *Aileach* for their dwelling-place for greater security. Here *Frigrind* built a splendid house of wood for his wife. The material of this house, we are told, was red yew, carved, and emblazoned with gold and bronze; and so thickset with shining gems, that "day and night were equally bright within it". I may observe that *Aileach* is one of the few spots in Erinn marked in its proper place by the geographer Ptolemy of Alexandria, who flourished in the second century, or nearly two hundred years before the time of *Frigrind*. By Ptolemy it is distinguished as a royal residence.

Aileach mentioned by Ptolemy.

To proceed to the next in order of importance of the great royal residences of Erinn, we find in an ancient tale, called *Táin Bo Fraich*, or the carrying off the cows of *Fraech Mac Fidhaidh*, (a tale which in fact forms part of the *Táin Bo Chuailgnè*), a curious instance of the existence of more than one house within the great *Rath* of *Cruachan*, the residence of the kings of Connacht.

Fraech Mac Fidhaidh was a famous warrior and chieftain: his mother, *Bé-binn*, was one of the mysterious race of the *Tuatha Dé Danann*, and by her supernatural powers, according to this tale, her son was enabled to enjoy many advantages both of person and of fortune over other young princes of this time. After some time, accordingly, he was encouraged by his mother to seek an alliance with the celebrated *Ailill* and *Medbh*, the king and queen of Connacht, by proposing for the hand of their beautiful daughter, the celebrated *Finnabhair*, ["the fair-browed"]. So his mother supplied him with a gorgeous outfit; and *Fraech* set out for the palace of *Cruachan*, with a train of fifty young princes in his company, as well as attended by all the usual retinue which accompanied friendly progresses of this kind, such as musicians, players, huntsmen, hounds, etc. Arrived at *Cruachan*, they alight, and take their seats at the door of the royal *Rath;* a steward then comes from king *Ailill* to inquire who they were and whence they came; and he was told (the tale goes on to say) that it was *Fraech Mac Fidhaidh;* and the steward returned and informed the king and queen: "The man is welcome", said *Ailill* and *Medbh;* "and let them all come into the lis", said *Ailill*.

Description of *Rath Cruachain*.

"A quarter of the *Dun*", proceeds the story, "was then assigned to them. The manner of that house was this: There were seven companies in it; seven compartments from the fire to the wall, all round the house. Every compartment had a front of bronze. The whole were composed of beautifully carved red yew. Three strips of bronze were in the front of each compartment. Seven strips of bronze from the foundation of the house to the ridge. The house from this out was built of pine, [*gius*]. A covering of oak shingles was what was upon it on the outside. Sixteen windows was the number that were in it, for the purpose of looking out of it and for admitting light into it. A shutter of bronze to each window. A bar of bronze across each shutter; four times seven *ungas* of bronze was what each bar contained. *Ailill* and *Mebdh*'s compartment was made altogether of bronze; and it was situated in the middle of the house, with a front of silver and gold around it. There was a silver wand at one side of it, which rose to the ridge of the house, and reached all round it from the one door to the other.

"The arms of the guests were hung up above the arms of all other persons in that house; and they sat themselves down, and were bade welcome".

Such is the description of one of the four "royal houses" which, in the heroic age of our history, that of *Ailill* and *Medbh*, (the century preceding the Christian era), are said to have stood within the ancient *Rath* of *Cruachan*.

The House of the Royal Branch.

The description of the *Craebh-Ruadh*, or house of the "Royal Branch", at Emania, the capital city of ancient Ulster, (as described in the Ancient Historic Tale of *Tochmarc nEimiré*, or "the Courtship of the Lady *Emer* by *Cuchulainn*"), agrees very nearly with this description of the house at *Cruachan;* and we know that there were three great Houses at least within the circle of the great *Rath* of *Emania*, raised by queen *Macha*, more than three hundred years before the Christian era.

Description of a *Dun* in Fairy Land.

Again, we find the same general features of a royal fort alluded to in a short description of another *Dun*, or enclosure, (preserved in the Book of Ballymote and in the Yellow Book of *Lecan*), in a romantic account of the adventures of king *Cormac Mac Airt* in the Land of Promise, or Fairy-land, of the Gaedhils. According to this wild story, as *Cormac* was traversing this unknown land in search of his wife, "he saw another very large, kingly *Dun*, and another palisade of bronze around it; four houses in the *Dun*. He went into the *Dun;* and he saw

LECT. XIX. a very large house, with its rafters of bronze, and its wattling of silver, and its thatch of the wings of white birds; and he saw, too, a sparkling well within the *Lis*, and five streams issuing from it, and the hosts around, drinking the waters of these streams".

The same kind of enclosure called a *dun*, *rath*, or *lis*.

From these various descriptions of Tara, *Aileach*, *Cruachan*, the *Craebh Ruadh*, and the *Dun* in the Land of Promise, it will be seen that our old writers applied the terms *Rath*, *Dun*, and *Lis*, indiscriminately, to the earthen enclosure or fort within which the houses of the ancient Gaedhils stood. We have seen also that these enclosures frequently contained more than one "house"; and we know, from actual existing monuments, that the "*Rath* of the Kings" at Tara contained, besides the "Great House of the Thousands of Soldiers", at least two other remarkable edifices; though, whether they were houses or mere mounds, it remains yet to be shown with certainty. The first of these was the *Mur Tea*, or Mound of *Tea*, the wife of *Eremon*, one of the Milesian brothers who took Erinn from the *Tuatha Dé Danann*. It was because *Tea* was, in accordance with her own request, buried in the rampart of this primitive "house", that the name of *Tea-Mur* (that is, *Tea*'s *Mur*, or rampart, now Tara), was first given to the hill by the Milesians. A small mound remained still, at the time of *Cuan O'Lothchain*, about the year 1000, as the remains of this once famous mound; but all vestiges of it have now disappeared, though its situation is still pointed out as a little hill which lies to the south, between the *Foradh* and *Cormac*'s House.

The *Foradh* at Tara.

There was a second and more important building within the Rath of the Kings, besides *Cormac*'s Great House. This was the edifice called the *Foradh*, large remains of which still exist, adjoining the Great House of *Cormac*. This does not appear to have been a house at all, but rather, what its name implies, the mound upon which the royal residents of Tara used to sit, to enjoy the sports which were celebrated on the slopes to the west and south of it.

The house of *Credé*.

I introduced into a former Lecture[10] a poetical description, from one of the ancient Fenian Poems, of the mansion-house of a young princess of Kerry, in the time of *Finn Mac Cumhaill*; but the subject is so appropriate to the purpose of the present Lecture, that I feel I cannot with propriety omit to notice it again here. I allude to the story of the Courtship of *Credé* and *Cael*, preserved in the Book of Lismore in the Royal Irish Academy, which contains the curious poem descriptive of the

[10] *Lect. on the MS. Materials of Ancient Irish History*; p. 309; and App. No. XCIV.; p. 594.

The house of *Credé*.

construction of the lady's mansion, as well as of the rich furniture contained within it. The following verses are those to which I especially allude:

"Delightful the house in which she is,
Between men, and children, and women,
Between druids and musical performers,
Between cup-bearers and door-keepers.
"Between horse-boys who are not shy,
And table servants who distribute;
The command of each and all of these
Hath *Credé* the fair, the yellow-haired.
"It would be happy for me to be in her *dun*,
Among her soft and downy couches.
Should *Credé* deign to hear [my suit],
Happy for me would be my journey.
"A bowl she has whence berry-juice flows,
By which she colours her eye-brows black;
[She has] clear vessels of fermenting ale;
Cups she has, and beautiful goblets.
"The colour [of her *dun*] is like the colour of lime,
Within it are couches and green rushes;
Within it are silks and blue mantles;
Within it are red gold and crystal cups.
"Of its *grianan* [sunny chamber] the corner stones
Are all of silver and of yellow gold;
Its thatch in stripes of faultless order,
Of [birds'] wings of brown and crimson-red.
"Two door-posts of green I see;
Nor is its door devoid of beauty;
Of carved silver, long has it been renowned,
Is the lintel that is over its door.
"*Credé's* chair is on your right hand,
The pleasantest of the pleasant it is;
All over a blaze of Alpine gold,
At the foot of the beautiful couch.
"A gorgeous couch in full array,
Stands directly above the chair,
It was made by [or at?] *Túllé*, in the east,
Of yellow gold and precious stones.
"There is another couch on your right hand,
Of gold and silver, without defect;
With curtains, with soft [pillows];
And with graceful rods of golden bronze.
"The household which are in her house,
To the happiest of conditions have been destined;

LECT. XIX.

The house of *Credé.*

Gray and glossy are their garments,
Twisted and fair is their flowing hair.
"Wounded men would sink in sleep,
Tho' ever so heavily teeming with blood,
With the warbling of the fairy birds
From the eaves of her sunny *grianan.*

* * * * * *

"One hundred feet are in *Credé*'s house,
From the one gable to the other;
And twenty feet in measure,
There are in the breadth of its noble door.
"Its portico with its thatch
Of the wings of birds, blue and yellow;
Its lawn in front, and its well
[Formed] of crystal and of *carmogal* [carbuncles?]
"Four posts to every bed,
Of gold and of silver gracefully carved;
A crystal gem between every two posts;
They are no cause of unpleasantness.
"There is a vat there of kingly bronze,
From which flows the pleasant juice of malt;
There is an apple-tree over the vat,
In the abundance of its heavy fruit".

* * * * * *

This poem is of especial value, inasmuch as it describes with such minuteness not only the form, size, and materials of what a poet in the earliest period of our literature would have regarded as a beautiful house, but also the nature, position, and materials of the principal articles of furniture in a mansion of those primitive times.

To return now to more general considerations:

The *Rath*-builder and the *Caiseal*-builder.

It appears from our ancient authorities, that the pagan Gaedhil had two classes of professional builders: the *Rath-bhuidhé*, or *Rath*-builder, who built the *Rath*, *Dun*, and *Lis*, which were formed of earth; and the *Caisleoir*, or *Caiseal*-builder, who built the *Caiseal*, the *Cathair*, and the *Dun* when it was constructed of stone. These authorities go as far as even to preserve the names of some of the most ancient professors of both arts, not only in Erinn, but even in the far east. Thus, the Book of Leinster (fol. 27, b) presents us with the following list, headed: "*Hi sunt nomina virorum componentium lapides*": which I believe is bad Latin for, "These are the names of the men who built in stone".—"*Cabar* was the *Caiseal* [i.e. stone-work] builder of Tara; *Ilian* was Solomon's *Caiseal* builder. *Caior* was Nimrod's *Caiseal* builder. *Barnib* was the *Caiseal* builder

LECT. XIX.

The Rath-builder and the Caiseal-builder.

of Jericho. *Cir* was the *Caiseal* builder of Rome. *Arann* was the *Caiseal* builder of Jerusalem. *Alen* was the *Caiseal* builder of Constantinople. *Buchur* was the *Rath* [i.e. earthwork] builder of Nimrod. *Cingdorn* was *Curoi-Mac-Dairé's* stone (*Caiseal*) builder", [who built for him *Cathair Conroi*, the ruins of which may still exist, somewhere to the west of Tralee, in the county of Kerry]. *Goll-Clochair*, the son of *Bran*, it was that built *Caiseal* [Cashel], the place so-called, for *Ængus Mac Nadfraich*. *Rigrinn* [elsewhere *Frigrinn*] was the stone (*caiseal*) builder of *Aileach*, assisted by *Gablan* the son of *U-Gairbh*. *Traighlethan* was the *Rath*-builder of Tara. *Blocc*, son of *Blar*, was the *Rath*-builder of *Cruachan*. *Blancé*, son of *Dalran*, was the *Rath*-builder of *Emania*. *Balar*, the son of *Buarainech*, was the *Rath*-builder of *Breas* [the king of the *Tuatha Dé Danann*], and who built for him *Rath-Breisi*, in Connacht. *Crichel*, the son of *Dubhchluithé*, was the Rath-builder of *Alinn*" (in Leinster). *Dubhaltach Mac Firbissigh*, commonly called Dudley Mac Firbis, the last great antiquary of that celebrated Connacht family, has preserved a copy of this list of builders, in prose and verse, with some slight differences, in the preface to his great genealogical work, compiled in the year 1650.[31]

[31] "Here", he says, "are the names of some of the masons (or builders) who are called the masons (or builders) of the chief stone buildings.—

"*Alan* was Solomon's *Caiseal*-builder. *Cabur* was the *Caiseal*-builder of *Temair*. *Barnb* was the *Caiseal*-builder of Jericho. *Bocus* was the *Rath*-builder of Nimrod. *Cingdorn* was *Curoi Mac Daire's Caiseal*-builder. *Cir* was the *Caiseal*-builder of Rome. *Arann* was the *Caiseal*-builder of Jerusalem. *Oilen* was the *Caiseal*-builder of Constantinople. *Bolc*, the son of *Blar*, was the *Rath*-builder of *Cruachan*. *Goll* of *Clochar* [now Manister, in the county of Limerick] was the *Caiseal*-builder of *Nadfraech* [who founded the first stone building at the place still called Cashel]. *Casruba* was the *Caiseal*-builder of *Ailinn*. *Ringin*, or *Rigrin*, and *Gabhlan* the son of *U-Gairbh*, or *Garbhan* the son of *U-Gairbh*, were the two *Caiseal*-builders of *Aileach* [near Derry]. *Troighlethan* was the *Rath*-builder of *Temair*. *Bainché* or *Bailchné*, the son of *Dobhru*, was the *Rath*-builder of *Emania*. *Balur*, the son of *Buan-lamhach*, was the *Rath*-builder of *Rath-Breisi* [in Connacht]. *Crichel*, the son of *Dubh-chruit*, was the *Rath*-builder of the *Rath* of *Ailinn*" [in Leinster].

"And these", he continues, "were the chief stone-builders, as the poet says:—

"*Ailinn* with Solomon of the hosts,
A beautiful, noble *Caiseal*-builder;
With Nimrod, as graceful builder,
Caur it was that built a *Caiseal*.

"*Barnab* in his own good time,
Was the *Caiseal*-builder of Jericho's land;
Rome took *Cir*,—graceful was his chisel;
Arann was the mason of Jerusalem.

"In Constantinople, with activity,
Cleothor was powerful in his art;
With Nimrod, without fear of weakness,
Bacus the noble was *Rath*-builder.

"*Curoi's Caiseal*-builder was gifted *Cingdorn*;
With the son of *Natfraech* was *Goll* of *Clochar*;
Casruba was the priceless *Caiseal*-builder,

LECT. XIX.

Mac Firbis on stone building in ancient Erinn.

Mac Firbis, in answer to those who would deny the existence of stone-building in ancient Erinn, offers some fair remarks, from which I quote the following passages:

"It is only because lime-cast walls are not seen standing in the place in which they were erected a thousand and a half, or two thousand, or three thousand and more years since, what it is no wonder should not be; for, shorter than that is the time in which the ground grows over buildings when they are once ruined, or when they fall down of themselves with age. In proof of this, I have myself seen within (the last) sixteen years, many lofty lime-cast castles, built of limestone; and at this day, (having fallen) there remains of them but a mound of earth; and hardly could a person ignorant of their former existence, know that there had been buildings there at all. Let this, and the works that were raised hundreds and thousands of years ago, be put together [compared], and it will be no wonder, were it not for the firmness of the old work over the work of these times, if a stone or an elevation of earth can be recognized in their place. But such is not the case, for such is the durability of the ancient work, that there are great royal *raths* and *lisses* in abundance throughout Erinn; in which there are many hewn, smooth stones, and cellars or apartments, under ground, within their enclosures, such as *Rath Mailcatha*, at Castle Connor, Bally-O'Dowda in *Tir Fhiachrach*, on the brink of the [river] *Muaidhe* [Moy]. There are nine smooth stone cellars under the mound of this rath; and I have been within in it, and I think it is one of the oldest raths in Erinn; and the height of its walls would be a good height for a cow-keep".

I make this quotation from Mac Firbis only for what it is worth; for he does not absolutely assert that the masonry con-

Who used to have great stone-
hewing hatchets.
"The two *Caiseal*-builders of armed
Aileach,
Rigru and *Garbhan* son of *U-
Gairbh*;
Troiglethan, an hereditary beauti-
ful builder,
Was the *Rath*-builder of the strong
king of *Temair*.
"*Bolc* the son of *Blar*, from sweet
Ath-Blair,
Was the *Rath*-builder of the circu-
lar *Cruachan*;
Bainché the gifted, from *Bearbha*,
Was the *Rath*-builder of the noble
king of *Emania*.
"*Balur*, of whom it was worthy,
It was that formed the strong
Rath-Breisé;
Cricel the son of *Dubhraith*, with-
out reproach,
Was the acute builder of *Aillinn*.
"May the high and happy heavens
Be given to *Domhnall*, the son of
Flanncan,
Who has composed a poem, no in-
direct numbers,
From *Ailian* down to *Aillinn*.
[*Ailian*".

I have not been able to obtain any other reference to *Domhnall*, the son of *Flanncan*, the author of this poem; but I am satisfied the poem as it stands is as old as the tenth century.

tained lime and mortar; and there can be no denial of the existence of stone forts in this country from the earliest times, as evidenced not only by our oldest historical records and traditions, but by the very great number of them of the remotest antiquity, which still remain in wonderful preservation.

The following extract from a large fragment of a curious and very ancient tale, preserved in the *Leabhar na h-Uidhre* (R.I.A.), will tend to explain more closely the actual mode of building, and the materials of those ancient houses of which I have been speaking. The story is referred to a remote period in Irish History; and the substance of it may be told in a few words.

Story of the Feast of Bricriud:

In the time of *Conchobar Mac Nessa*, the celebrated king of Ulster, who was contemporary of our Saviour, there lived in Ulster a famous satirist, called *Bricrind Nemh-thenga*, or "*Bricrind* of the Poisoned Tongue", (from whom *Loch-Bricrend*, now called Loch-Brickland, in the county of Down, derives its name). *Bricrind* was a constant guest at the court of King *Conchobar*, at *Emania;* where it may well be supposed the purchase of silence from his bitter tongue brought him many a gift from a people always, even to this day, peculiarly sensitive to the shafts of satire. This *Bricrind* once proposed to himself to prepare a great feast for the king, the knights of the Royal Branch, and the other nobles of Ulster, and their wives; not, however, out of gratitude or hospitality, but simply to gratify his mere love of mischief, and to work up a serious quarrel, if possible, by exciting such a spirit of envy and jealousy among the ladies, as would draw their husbands into war with one another. In the very commencement of the tale, in which these scenes are related, occurs a passage which I may translate directly from the original, because it bears at once on our present subject.

"*Bricrind* of the Poisoned Tongue had a great feast for *Conchobar Mac Nessa*, and for all the Ultonians. A full year was he preparing for the feast. There was built by him, in the meantime, a magnificent house in which to serve up the feast. This house was built by *Bricrind* at *Dun-Rudhraidhe*, [probably the exact place now called Dundrum, in the county of Down], in likeness to [the house of] the Royal Branch at *Emain-Macha*, (or *Emania*), except alone that his house excelled in material and art, in beauty and gracefulness, in pillars and facings, in emblazonments and brilliancy, in extent and variety, in porticoes and in doors, all the houses of its time.

plan of his house;

"The plan upon which this house was built was on the plan of the *Teach-Midhchuarta*, [i.e. the great Banqueting House of

SCT. XIX. Tara]. [There were] nine couches in it from the fire to the wall: Thirty feet was the height of every gold-gilt bronze front of them all. There was a kingly couch built for *Conchobar* [the king] in the front part of that kingly house, above all the other couches of the house; [and it was] inlaid with carbuncles, and other brilliants besides, and emblazoned with gold, and silver, and carbuncles, and the finest colours of all countries; so that day and night were the same in it. The twelve couches of the twelve heroes of Ulster were built around it. The style of the work, and the material, were equally ponderous. Six horses were [employed] to draw home [from the wood] every post; and [it required] seven of the strong men of Ulster to entwine (or set) every rod; and thirty builders of the chief builders of Erinn were [engaged], in the building and the ordering of it.

his *grianan* or sun-house; "There was a *grianan* (or sun-house) built by *Bricrind* for himself, on a range with the couches of *Conchobar* and the heroes of Ulster. That *grianan* was built with carvings and ornaments of admirable variety; and windows of glass were set in it on all sides. There was one of these windows set over his own couch; so that he could see the state of the entire of the great house before him from his couch; [he built this] because he well knew that the [great chiefs of the] Ultonians would not admit him [to feast] into the [same] house [with them].

"Now, when *Bricrind* had finished his great house, and his *grianan*, and furnished both with coverlets and beds and pillows, as well as with a full supply of ale and of food, and when he saw that there was nothing whatever in which it was deficient, of the furniture and the materials of the feast, then he went forth until he arrived at *Emain-Macha*, to invite *Conchobar*, and the nobles of the men of Ulster along with him.

his invitation to *Conchobar* and the Ultonians; "This was the way, now, on which the Ultonians held a fair at *Emain-Macha*. He receives welcome there, and he sat at *Conchobar*'s shoulder; and then he addressed *Conchobar* and the Ultonians: 'Come with me', said he, 'to accept a banquet with me'. 'I am well pleased', said *Conchobar*, 'if the Ultonians are pleased'. But *Fergus Mac Róigh*, and the nobles of Ulster answered, and said: 'We shall not go', said they, 'because our dead would be more numerous than our living, after we should be set at variance by *Bricrind*, if we were to go to partake of his banquet'. 'That will be worse for ye, then, indeed', said he, 'which I shall do to ye if ye do not come with me'. 'What is it thou wilt do then?' said *Conchobar*, 'if they do not go with thee?'" [They then argue for some time; and at last:] 'It is better for us to go', said *Fergus Mac*

Rôigh; 'what he has said he will verify', said he. But as a precaution against his subtle tongue, *Sencha* the son of *Ailill*, the chief poet of Ulster, advised them: 'Since', said he, 'there is an objection to going with *Bricrind*, exact securities from him; and place eight swordsmen around him for the purpose of conveying him out of the house when he has shown them the feast'. So *Fus baidé Ferbeann*, the son of [king] *Conchobar*, went with this message, and told *Bricrind*. 'I am well pleased', said *Bricrind*, 'to act accordingly'. So the Ultonians went forth from *Emain-Macha;* each division with his king; each battalion with its chief; and each company with its leader".

he sows dissension among the women;

The story goes on to describe how, on the way, *Bricrind* contrived to sow jealousies among all the principal champions, by flattering each separately at the expense of the others; so that, when they took their places in the banqueting house, he could see from his *grianan* that they were soon almost at daggers drawn. It then proceeds.

"It happened just to his desire, that, at this very time, *Fedelm Noi-chridhé*, [i.e. "the Ever-blooming *Fedelm*"] the wife of *Laeghairé Buadhach*, was leaving the house with fifty of her attendant women, to take the cool air outside for a while; and *Bricrind* accosted her, and said.—'Well done this night, thou wife of *Laeghairé Buadhach;* it is no nickname to call thee *Fedelm* the ever-blooming, because of the excellence of thy shape, and because of thy intelligence, and because of thy family. *Conchobar*, the king of the chief province of Erinn, is thy father, and *Laeghairé Buadhach* thy husband. Now I would not think it too much for thee that none of the women of Ulster should come before thee into the banqueting house; but that it should be after thy heels that the whole band of the women of Ulster should come, [and I say to thee that] if it be thou that shalt be the first to enter the house this night, thou shalt be queen over all the other women of Ulster'. *Fedelm* went forth then as far as three ridges out from the house.

"Immediately after, came out *Lendabair*, the daughter of *Eoghan Mac Duirtheacht* [king of Farney], and wife of *Conall Cearnach* [the great champion]; and *Bricrind* addressed her, and said.—'Well done, *Lendabair*', said he; 'it is no nickname to call thee *Lendabair*, [i.e. the Favourite], because thou art the beloved and desired of the men of the whole world, for the splendour and lustre [of thy beauty]. As far as thy husband excels the warriors of the world in beauty and valour, thou excellest the women of Ulster'. And so, though much of flattering praise he had bestowed upon *Fedelm*, he lavished twice as much upon *Lendabair*.

LECT. XIX.

he sows dissension among the women;

" *Emer*, *Cuchulainn*'s wife, came out next.—' A safe journey to thee, O *Emer*, daughter of *Forgall Manach*', said *Bricrind*: 'thou wife of the best man in Erinn: *Emer* of the beautiful hair. The kings and the princes of Erinn are at enmity about thee. As far as the sun excels the stars of heaven, so far dost thou excel the women of the whole world, in face, and in shape, and in family, in youth and in lustre, in fame and in dignity, and in eloquence'. So, though great the flattering praise he bestowed on the other women, he lavished twice as much upon *Emer*.

" The three women moved on then till they reached the same place, that is, three ridges from the house; and none of them knew that the other had been spoken to by *Bricrind*. They returned to the house then. They passed over the first ridge with a quiet, graceful, dignified carriage; hardly did any one of them put one foot beyond another. In the second ridge their steps were closer and quicker. The ridge nearest to the house [in getting over it] each woman sought to forcibly take the lead of her companions; and they even took up their dresses to the calves of their legs, vying with each other who should enter the house first; because what *Bricrind* said to each, unknown to the others, was, that she who should first enter the house should be queen of the whole province. And such was the noise they made in their contest to enter the kingly house, that it was like the rush of fifty chariots arriving there; so that they shook the whole kingly house, and the champions started up for their arms, each striking his face against the other throughout the house.

" ' Stop', said *Sencha*, [the judge], ' they are not foes that have come there; but it is *Bricrind* that has raised a contest between the women since they have gone out. I swear by the oaths of my territory', said he, ' that if the house is not closed against them, their dead will be more numerous than their living'. So the door-keepers shut the door immediately. But *Emer*, the daughter of *Forgall Manach* and wife of *Cuchulainn*, advanced in speed before the other women, and put her back to the door, and hurled the door-keepers from it before the other women came up. Then their husbands stood up in the house, each of them anxious to open the door before his wife, that his own wife should so be the first to enter the house. ' This will be an evil night', said *Conchobar* the king. Then he struck his silver pin against the bronze post of his couch; and all immediately took their seats. ' Be quiet', said *Sencha* [the judge]; ' it is not a battle with arms that shall prevail here, but a battle of words'. Each woman then put herself under the protection of her husband outside: and it was then they delivered those speeches which are called by the poets the *Briatharchath Ban Uladh*, the 'battle-speeches of the women of Ulster'". the *Briath-archath Ban Uladh*;

We must for the present pass over these long-celebrated speeches, remarkable though they are in point of mere language, as examples of the copiousness and delicacy of the ancient Gaedhelic tongue in terms of laudation, such as these three princesses of Ulster lavished on their husbands on this occasion.

At the conclusion of the harangues, the champions *Laeghairé Buadhach* and *Conall Cearnach* rushed suddenly at the wooden wall of the house, and, knocking a plank out of it, brought in their wives. Not so *Cuchulainn;* "he raised up", the story tells us, "that part of the house which was opposite his couch, so that the stars of heaven were visible from beneath the wall; and it was through this opening that his wife came in to him". And the tale goes on to say that, "*Cuchulainn* then let the house fall down suddenly again, so that he shook the whole fabric, and laid *Bricrind's grianan* prostrate on the ground, so that *Bricrind* himself and his wife were cast into the mire, among the dogs. Then *Bricrind* harangued the Ultonians, and conjured them to restore his house to its original position, as it still remained inclined to one side. And all the champions of the Ultonians united their strength and exerted themselves to restore the balance of the house, but without effect". They then begged of *Cuchulainn* to try his own strength on it, which he did, and alone restored the house to its perpendicular.

This is an extravagant tale in form; and a great part of it may at first sight appear somewhat irrelevant to the purpose of this Lecture. It was proper, however, to give so much at least of the story as to explain the occasion of the singular performance attributed, in the exaggerated language of the poet, to the hero *Cuchulainn*, who fills completely the part of Hercules in our ancient tales. And it happens that none of the other great houses already mentioned have been described, in some respects, with the same minuteness as to form, material, preparation for building, furniture, and internal arrangement, as this celebrated house and *grianan* of *Bricrind*. For instance: we are told that there were six horses to carry home every post or plank of the walls; that it took seven of the stoutest men in Ulster to weave or interlace between the upright posts, each of the stout rods which, like basket-work, filled up the space between these posts; and there were thirty builders or carpenters besides. The rods thus used were, I believe, uniformly of hazle, perhaps because that was the smoothest of all the forest *Bricrind's* house was made of wicker-work.

LECT. XIX. trees. Again, we are told, that this house was supplied with glass windows; and that it was supplied, as well as *Bricrind's* own *grianan*, with coverlets, beds, and pillows. And we learn that the panels and posts of these beds or couches, (for they answered both purposes,) were gorgeously adorned and emblazoned. So that, making due allowance for the poetry of the description, this house of *Bricrind* must have been an elegant, as well as a commodious building; and though we must not take the description as representing more than the poet's ideal of what he would have regarded as a splendid house in his own time, still there can be no doubt but that such edifices as that described, were in their main characteristics the prevailing form of house in ancient times in this country; and in fact the use of the wooden basket-work building, with its decorations, came down, as we shall soon see, to a comparatively late period of our history.[(10)]

[(10) See INTRODUCTION on the similar houses of the Gauls and the illustrations from the Colonne Antonine in the Louvre, Figs. 54, 55.]

LECTURE XX.

[Delivered 12th July, 1859.]

(VII.) OF BUILDINGS, FURNITURE, ETC.; (continued). The descriptions of buildings in our ancient MSS., even when poetical in form, and not strictly accurate as to date, are still valuable for the object of these lectures. Veracity of the evidence respecting the "Great Banqueting Hall" of Tara in the time of *Cormac Mac Airt*, as given by Dr. Petrie; no record of the changes which took place at Tara subsequent to that time. Residences of the monarchs of Erinn after the desertion of Tara. Desertion of other celebrated royal residences,—*Emania*, *Cruachan*, etc. Division of the people into classes; this division did not impose perpetuity of caste; increase of wealth enabled a man to pass from one rank to another; crime alone barred this advancement; the qualifications as to furniture and houses of the several classes of *Airés* or landholders; fines for injury to the house of the *Airé Reiré Breithe*; of the *Airé Desa*; of the *Airé-Ard*; of the *Airé Forgaill*; of the king of a territory. Law against damage or disfigurement of buildings and furniture: of the house of a *Bo-Airé*; of the house of an *Airé-Desa*; of the house of an *Airé-Tuisa*; of the house of an *Airé-Ard*. Law directing the provision to be made for aged men. Shape of houses in ancient Erinn; construction of the round house; reference to the building of such a house in an Irish life of St. *Colman Ela*; a similar story told of St. *Cumin Fada*. No instance recorded of an ecclesiastical edifice built of wicker work; two instances of the building of oratories of wood;—story of the oratory of St. *Moling*; quatrain of *Rumand Mac Colman* on the oratory of *Rethan Ua Suanaigh*; account of *Rumand* writing a poem for the *Galls* of Dublin; he carries his wealth to *Cill Belaigh*; statement of seven streets of *Galls* or foreigners at that place; importance of the account of *Rumand*.

It is of very little moment to the history of the country whether the descriptions, preserved in our ancient manuscripts, of the "Great Houses" of the Royal Branch, of Emania, in Ulster; of the "Great House" into which *Fraech*, the son of *Fidhadh*, was ushered with his followers, at *Cruachan*, in Connacht; or of the "Great House" which *Bricrind* built at *Rath Rudhraidhé*, in Ulster (all these accounts referring to the period of the Incarnation), be strictly correct in all their dates, or tinged with somewhat of the story-teller's exaggeration. The imagination of writers say of the fourth, fifth, and sixth centuries must have been grounded, at least, on what they were accustomed to see about them; and they must have described (be it indeed with some colouring as to accessories) merely that state of things which still continued in vivid recollection, if not in actual existence, in their time. In this way even the most poetic accounts are important to history; just as those of Homer are so with reference to similar matters, although mixed up with so much of the fabulous and the impossible in action.

LECT. XX.

As to the character of the "Great House of the Thousands of Soldiers", and the Great Banqueting House at Tara, in the time of *Cormac Mac Airt* (that is, in the middle of the third century), and in the reign of *Laeghairé Mac Neill* (that is, at the time of the coming of Saint Patrick in the fifth century), no candid reader will for a moment refuse credence to the evidences of them published by Dr. Petrie in his admirable Essay on the History and Antiquities of Tara Hill, at least to the extent to which their probable veracity is measured by that thoughtful and most cautious writer.

Of the changes or improvements, if any, in the mansions of Tara, between the death of *Laeghairé Mac Neill* and its total desertion as a royal residence and seat of the central government of the kingdom (about the middle of the sixth century), no record has come down to us, as far as I know. Neither have we any account, that I have seen, of the style or particular character of the dwellings of the monarchs, or of the provincial kings of Erinn, who succeeded *Diarmait*, the son of *Fergus Cerrbhéoil*, the last occupier of the Great House of Tara, down to the final overthrow of the monarchy in the twelfth century.

Residences of the monarchs of Erinn after the desertion of Tara.

For, after the desertion of the ancient seat of the supreme royalty, each of the succeeding monarchs fixed his residence in some part of his own provincial territories; so, the *Clann Colmain*, or Southern *Ui-Neill*, who were the hereditary princes of Tara and Meath, and who subsequently took the name of *O'Maeilsheachlainn*, had their chief seat at *Dun-na-Sciath*, on the bank of *Loch Aininn* (now called Loch Ennel, near Mullingar, in Westmeath); whilst the northern *Ui-Neill*, subsequently represented by the O'Neills, whenever they succeeded to the monarchy, held their court and residence at the ancient provincial palace of *Aileach*, near Derry, of which mention was made in the last Lecture; and when *Brian Borumha* came to the supreme throne in the year 1002, he continued to reside at the celebrated *Ceann-Coradh* (a name which signifies literally, the "Head of the Weir", at the place now called Killaloe, in the county of Clare), a place about a mile south by east from *Grianan-Lachtna*, near *Craig-Liath*, the once noble residence of his great-grandfather *Lachtna*, some traces of which even still remain.

So also, when *Torloch Mór O'Conor*, and his son *Rudhraidhe* after him, became monarchs, in the first part of the twelfth century, they had their residence on the bank of *Loch En* (a place now represented, I believe, by the castle of Roscommon). This is sufficiently shown in the Annals of the Four Masters, at the year 1225. For, it appears that, in that year, Hugh O'Conor having succeeded his father, *Cathal Cradbh-dearg* (i.e. "of the Red Hand"), in the kingship, dispossessed an important chief, named *Donn-óg Mac Erachtaigh*, of his lands; that *Mac Erachtaigh* invited O'Neill to his assistance against his own king; and that the latter proceeded to Athlone, in the neighbourhood of which he remained two nights, and totally plundered *Loch En*, from whence, we are informed, he carried off O'Conor's jewels. It seems, however, that this place was abandoned afterwards by the O'Conors; as I find, from two contemporaneous poems in my own possession, that *Aedh*, the son of *Eoghan* O'Conor, removed their residence from *Loch En* to *Cluain Fraich* (a place near Strokestown, in the same county), where he built a residence, in the year 1309. It is in description and praise of this new palace of *Cluain Fraich* that the two poems to which I allude (and to which I shall have occasion to refer again) were written.

Emania, Cruachan, etc., also deserted. It appears from an ancient poem, also in my possession, that *Emania* ceased to be the royal residence of the kings of Ulster after the death of *Ferghus Fogha*, in the year 331; *Cruachan*, to be the residence of the kings of Connacht, after the death of *Raghallach* in 645; *Caiseal* (Cashel), to be the residence of the kings of Munster, after the death of *Cormac Mac Cuilenndin* in 903; *Nás* [now Naas], the residence of the kings of Leinster, after the death of *Cearbhall*, son of *Muiregan*, in 904; and *Aileach*, to be the residence of the kings of Ulster of the *Ui-Neill* line, after the death of *Muircheartach*, the son of *Niall Glun-dubh*, who was killed in a battle with the Danes, at *Ath Firdiadh* (now Ardee), in the year 941. The poem in which these facts are preserved, was written about A.D. 1620, by *Eochaidh O'h-Eoghusa*, for the revived castle of Mac-Dermot's Rock, of *Loch Cé*.

Having disposed, so far, of our reference to special buildings and residences of the higher classes, in the more ancient time, we proceed now to the consideration of the dwellings of the less exalted classes, the arrangements of which were, in some respects, regulated by law according to the rank of the owner.

Division of the people into classes; The people in ancient Erinn were divided, as I explained on a former occasion,[1] into several classes; those who had no land nor dwellings; those who had land at rent not amounting to the value of that number of cows which was required to support the rank of a cow-chief, or rich grazier; those who had the required quantity of land to entitle them to that rank; and the degrees of that rank itself, in accordance with the increased number of cows or their grazing; and lastly, those who inherited

[1] See Lect. ii., *ante*, vol. i. p. 33 *et seq.* [See also Appendix for the entire of the fragment of the *Crith Gabhlach* referred to in Lect. ii.

LECT. XX.

or otherwise obtained any quantity of land for an absolute estate; and of whom, again, there were three ranks.

The general name for a man of any one of these classes was *Airé*, or *Flaith*, that is, something like our landlord; a term which may be applied at the present day to a man who lets ten acres of land, as well as to the man who lets ten thousand.

this division did not impose perpetuity of caste.

The law did not impose perpetuity of caste upon any of those ranks, but left it open for them to ascend still higher in the scale of social dignity, should the prudence or industry of any man, or any of the chances of life, enable him to acquire more land and cattle; provided only that his moral status in society was not impeachable, this being always deemed essential by the social law of the country. Thus, no perjurer, no thief, no receiver of stolen property, no absconder from his lawful debts, no murderer, no homicide, no unlawful or unnecessary wounder of another, could ever legally rise in the scale of society, until he had made full and ample satisfaction, according to law, for his misdeeds. All the professors of the mechanical arts were eligible to rise in rank in the same manner, under the same conditions.

Of the furniture and houses of the several classes of *Airés*:—

I have alreadyin a former Lecture explained from the ancient laws the nature of the different ranks of the *Airés*, or landholders, and the qualification of each rank in point of wealth.[12] I shall only here repeat so much of the laws respecting the different classes of society, as regards the size, the furniture, and the appointments of the houses allowed to or required to be kept by each of them, according to his rank; because these laws contain much important information as to our immediate subject.

of the *Og Airé*;

1st, The *Og Airé*, or Young *Airé*. He was required to have a fourth part in a ploughing apparatus, namely, an ox, a sock (or plough-share), a goad, and head-gear for the control of the ox. He had a share in a kiln; a share in a mill; a share in a barn; and an exclusive cooking-caldron. His house was ordained to be nineteen feet long, and his kitchen, or store room, thirteen feet.

of the *Bo Airé*;

2nd, The *Aitheach ar Athrebha*, or *Bo-Airé*, who succeeded his father. He counted his stock by tens: he had ten cows, ten pigs, ten sheep, and a fourth part of a ploughing machine, namely, an ox, a sock, and a goad, and head-gear for control. He had a house twenty feet long, and a store room of fourteen feet.

of the *Bo Airé Febhsa*;

3rd, The *Bo-Airé Febhsa*, or Best Cow-keeper. He had the land of four times seven *Cumhals:* his dwelling house measured

(12) *Ubi supra*, p. 35.

twenty-seven feet, and his store room fifteen feet; he had also a share in a mill, in which his family and his refection-companies ground their corn; he had a kiln, a barn, a sheep-house, a cow-house, a calf-house, and a pig-sty; and he had within the enclosure of his dwelling-house six ridges of onions, and one or more of leeks [etc.].

of the Bo Airé Gen.

4th, The *Bo-Airé Gensa*, or Chaste Cow-keeper. The furniture of his house (the dimensions of which are not given) included a large caldron, with its hooks and its bars; a vat for brewing ale; and an ordinary working boiler, with minor vessels; as well as spits, and flesh-forks; kneading-troughs, and skins (to sift meal and flour on); a washing-trough, and a "head-bathing basin"; tubs; candlesticks; knives (or hooks), for cutting or reaping rushes; a rope; an adze; an auger; a saw; shears; a forest-axe, for cutting every quarter's fire-wood; —every item of these without borrowing; and a grinding-stone; a billet-hook; a dagger for slaughtering cattle; perpetual fire, and a candle in a candlestick, without fail [i.e. he was bound to keep a fire always kindled, and lights in the evening]; and perfect ploughing apparatus, with all its necessary works.

of the Air Reiré Breithé;

5th, The *Airé Reiré Breithé*, or the Judgment-distributing Cow-keeper. He had seven houses; namely, a kiln, a barn, a mill (that is a share in it) for his grinding purposes; a dwelling-house of twenty-seven feet in length, with a store room of twelve feet; a pig-sty; a calf-house; and a sheep-house.

fines for injury to house or furniture of the fifth class of Airé;

The fines appointed by law for injury to the house or furniture of a man of this class, may also be quoted as recording some further particulars, thus.—He was entitled to five *seds*, [the *sed* was sometimes a calf, and sometimes a heifer, or a cow], for a person climbing over the *lis* (or rampart of his house), without his leave; but it was lawful to open its gate from without. Five *seds* for opening the door of his house without consent; a cow for spying into it; a calf for taking a handful of its thatch off; a year-old calf for two (handfuls); a two-year-old heifer, for an armful; a three-year-old heifer (not bulled), for half a bundle; a cow for a whole bundle, as well as restitution of the straw; five *seds* for entering his house or his cow-house by breaking the doors; a calf for breaking the withe (of the door) below; a yearling for breaking the withe above; a heifer for breaking a wattle below; an older heifer for breaking a wattle above [that is, should the cow-house door be fastened by a wattle or bar, and not by a twig or gad, below and above]; a yearling for disfiguring the door-posts of the front of his house; a calf for the door-posts of the back of his house. The seventh part of the price of honour of every rank is paid for stealing anything out of his lawn (or green); a calf for disfiguring the lintel of his back door; a yearling for the lintel of his front door; for stripping his couch, if it be a lock (of hair) from its pillow, two pillows are to be paid for it; if it be a lock from the part on which he sits, two skins are to be paid; if it be a lock from the foot, a pair of shoes are to be paid.

From these extracts we may form some idea of the style of the establishment of what, in old times, was looked upon as a farmer or landholder of the middle rank; but there is very much more connected with his position, privileges, and liabilities, too minute to be introduced into a lecture of this kind, and too technical to be understood without explanatory notes, which would lead us too far from our immediate object. All this information, however, will appear in the forthcoming publications of the Brehon Law Commissioners.

of the *Airé-Désa*;

6th, The next *Airé*, or landlord, was the *Airé-Désa*; that is, an *Airé* who possessed *Dés*, or free land derived from his father and grandfather. Of this class of *Airés* there were four ranks, of which the simple *Airé-Désa* was the lowest. The dwelling house of the *Airé-Désa* was twenty-seven feet long, with a proper store house; it was to have eight beds, with their furniture in it, as well as vats and caldrons, and the other vessels becoming the house of an *Airé*, together with keeves.

of the *Airé-Ard*;

7th, The *Airé-Ard*, or High *Airé*, was so called because he was higher than the simple *Airé-Désa*, and took precedence of him. His dwelling house was to be twenty-nine feet in length; his store house nineteen feet. Eight beds were to be in the dwelling house, with their full furniture, befitting the house of an *Airé-Tuisé*, with six *brothrachs* (or couches), with their proper furniture of pillows, and (stuffed) skins for sitting upon: he was also to have proper stands (or racks) in the house, furnished with vessels of yew of various sizes, and iron ones for different kinds of work; and bronze vessels, with a (bronze) boiler, in which would fit a cow, and a pig in bacon, etc.

of the *Airé-Forgaill*;

8th, The *Airé-Forgaill*, the third of this rank of *Airés*, so called because his evidence is good against all those before enumerated, wherever he undertakes to deny a charge; because his qualifications are higher than those of his fellows, as thirty feet was to be the length of his dwelling house, and twenty that of his store house. The furniture of his house was of the highest order.

of the king of a territory.

9th, From those intermediate ranks of society we pass to the king of a territory or province. And the proper establishment for a king who is constantly resident at the head of his people (or territory) was as follows. Seven score feet of properly measured feet is the measure of his *dun* (or circular fort) each way; seven feet is the thickness of its mound at top; twelve feet at its base. He is a king only when his *dun* is surrounded with *drechta giallna*, that is, with a trench made by his own tenants. Twelve feet is the breadth of its mouth and its depth; and it is as long as the *dun*. Thirty feet is its length at the outside. Clerics are to bless his house; and every one who damages it is to pay a cart load of wattles, and a cart load of rushes by way of fine.

Such were, shortly, as indicated by the laws, the different classes of private houses in ancient Erinn, as distinguished from those great edifices of which I spoke in the last Lecture. But the Laws contain many passages in which still more minute details concerning the arrangement of personal residences are happily preserved to us.

Law against damage of houses and furniture:—

There is one chapter, or version, in particular, of the special law against damage or disfigurement of buildings and furniture, preserved in another part of the ancient code, which is so curious and precise, that I think it will not be deemed an unnecessary repetition of some part of what has been already said on the subject. This law was specially intended to punish disfigurement by scratching or cutting the door-posts, the columns, and the fronts and heads of beds and couches. It runs as follows.—

of a Bo-Aire;

"The house of a *Bo-Airé* (or Cow-chief). To disfigure its south door-post, a sheep is paid for it; a lamb for its north door-post: why is the south side more noble? Answer. Because it is it that is in the view of the good man [of the house], who always sits in the north end (or part) of the house: because that is the part in which the good man always sits. Its lintel: a sheep for disfiguring its front; a lamb for the back (or inside). The incasement of his bed (or his couch): a *dairt* [i.e. yearling calf] for it in front; a sheep for the back.

of an Airé-Dèsa;

"The house of an *Airé-Dèsa.* For cutting its south door-post, there is a *dairt* (or yearling,) paid; a sheep for the northern post. The door of this house receives the finish of a Gaulish axe (*Gaill biail*), and carving (*aurscartadh*). To disfigure (or cut) its south door-post, so as to render it useless, there is a cow paid for it; and a heifer for the other post (at the back of the house); and restitution, [that is, posts in place of them]. It is the same that is paid for its lintel, and the fronts of his beds, (and couches) receive the finish of a channel-plane (*rungcin*): should they be disfigured in front, there is a cow paid; and an heifer for the back. If they be disfigured so as to be rendered

LECT. XX. useless, there are five *seds*, that is, a cow and a heifer, paid for the front, and restitution [of the posts]; a cow only for the back.

of an Airé-Tuisé; "The house of an *Airé-Tuisé*. Both its doors receive the finish of a channel plane (*rungcin*) and carving (*aurscartadh*). For disfiguring its south door-post there is a cow paid; and a heifer for the northern. The same is paid for its lintel. For disfiguring the front of his bed (or couch), five *seds*, or a cow and an heifer, are paid; and a cow for the backs. For disfiguring it till it is rendered useless, there is half a *cumhal*, or a cow and an half, paid for the front; and five *seds*, or a cow and an heifer, paid for the back.

of an Airé Ard. "The house of an *Airé-Ard*. Its door-posts and the sides of its beds receive the finish of a diversifying plane (*rungcin*); and the carvings on his bed must be of the best kind that can be found in any house. For its disfigurement in its southern door-posts, five *seds*, or a cow and a heifer, are paid; a cow for the northern posts. It is the same for its lintel. For disfigurement of the sides of its beds from the front, there is half a *cumhal*, or a cow and a-half, paid; five *seds*, or a cow and a heifer, for the back; for its disfigurement till it is rendered useless, there is a *cumhal*, or three cows, paid for the front, and half a *cumhal* for the back", [etc.].

These regulations contain abundant evidences of the amount of ornament and workmanship bestowed upon our domestic architecture and furniture in the earliest times.

And here, before we pass from the special subject of the houses ordered by law to be kept by particular classes of men, and for particular purposes, let me make one more extract. It is one not merely useful in connection with my immediate subject (as affording yet some further information as to the nature of the construction and furniture of ancient dwelling-houses), but interesting as a very curious instance of the care for the welfare of the people which so very strongly marks the code of our ancestors. It proves that even two thousand years ago, the legislators of ancient Erinn did not forget to make provision for those of the population who through age or infirmity were no longer able to take care of themselves, by working for their subsistence upon their share of the tribe-land. The article of law in question is that which prescribes directions for the houses in which "superannuated men" were to be provided with the means of comfortable existence, and is as follows:

Law directing provision for the aged. "The special law of a superannuated man's rent, that is, a man who has fallen into old age. He has a foster-child to whom he says: 'Go from me to my family, and tell them that they shall maintain me'. They come to him; and they say unto him: 'What rent [or maintenance] shall we give thee? How many items of maintenance are allowed by the law?' Answer. Three: maintenance in food, maintenance in attendance, maintenance of milk. The maintenance in food is, half a *bairghin* (or cake) of wheaten meal, with salt; and a vessel of sour milk. The maintenance of attendance is, to wash his body every twentieth night, and to wash his head every Saturday. The maintenance of milk is, one milch-cow every month throughout the year. His house of maintenance is to be seventeen feet long; it is to be woven [as basket-work] till it reaches the lintel of the door; there is to be a wing [or weather-board] between every two weavings from that up to the ridge; there are to be two doorways in it: a door to one, a hurdle to the other. A chest to be at one side of the house, a bed at the other side; it is to have a kitchen [or store-house] to it. In the fort [or enclosure] of maintenance [that is, the little garden within which the house stood], there can fit but four ridges; that is, two ridges at each side of the house: twelve feet is to be the length of each ridge; and eight its breadth. The bundle of firewood of maintenance is to consist of seventeen sticks, each tree of which should be of such size that, if split into four parts, each part would be sufficient for the handle of a forest-axe or hatchet. [As to] the can (*ploit*) of maintenance, seven hands is to be its circumference at the base; six hands in the middle; and four hands at top".

Shape of houses in ancient Erinn.

From the measurement of the buildings described in the foregoing extracts, the houses in ancient Erinn would appear to have been in some instances of a rectangular or oblong form. There is, however, absolute proof of the existence of round or circular houses, made chiefly, or wholly, of wicker-work; and it is even probable that this was the more general form. The plan of this description of house was very simple, and may be seen still preserved in the wicker or wattle sheep-cots in many of those parts of Ireland where timber is abundant enough to render its use more economical in raising these simple temporary structures, than either stone or earth.

Construction of the round house.

The plan of the round house was precisely that of the ordinary tent or pavilion, with one exception in detail, however. While the usual canvas tent rises tapering, from a certain extent of circumference, to the top of a central upright pole, the round wicker-house was built by setting up perpendicularly a number of poles or posts, of more or less solidity, ranged in a circle of the necessary diameter, and at equal distances from each other. The interstices between these poles or posts were then filled up with stout hazle and other rods, in the form of

LECT. XX. wicker or basket-work, until it reached the required height of the wall. In the meantime there was firmly set up in the centre within, a stout post, called a *tuireadh*, of length commensurate with the required height of the roof; into which were inserted by mortices, or otherwise attached, a certain number of rafters, which descended slantingly all round to the tops of the upright posts of the wall, into which they were received by tenon and mortice, or otherwise attached, in the same way as at the roof-tree. The number of these main rafters, as we shall call them, need not, and could not, have been great; because, according as their distance asunder increased as they radiated from the centre, cross-beams or pieces were inserted between them, as often as was needed, until at last a regular shield-roof, with a sharp pitch, was formed above; across the rafters and ribs, thus inserted were then laid bands or laths, or narrow slips of wood, which were fastened with pegs, or with gads, that is, twisted withes, forming a regular network from the top of the roof-tree to the walls. On these, again, were laid or fastened, at short distances, what may be called a sheeting of rods and thin branches of trees, stretching from the roof-tree to the wall. And now, the shell of the house being finished, it was thatched with straw, rushes, or sedge, and neatly fastened down with what are now Anglicised "scollops" (from the Gaedhelic word *scolb*, literally, a thin twig pointed at both ends), an ancient art of which the use, as we all know, is not yet forgotten among us. I cannot say how they staunched the walls of the round wicker-house, whether with clay, moss, or skins; but it appears, from what we have seen in the last Lecture, that some houses at least were covered with the wings and skins of birds, though probably only by way of ornament.[13]

There is a curious reference to the building of a round wicker-house preserved in the ancient Gaedhelic Life of Saint *Colman Ela*, of *Lann Ela* (now called Lynally, in the King's County). The story is this—

Account of the building of a round house in a life of St. *Colman Ela*.

The celebrated Saint *Baoithin*, the nephew of Saint *Colum Cillé*, was placed by the latter under the tuition of Saint *Colman Ela*. *Baoithin*'s understanding was clear and acute enough, but his memory failed him, and all his master's instructions availed him nothing. It happened that one day, Saint *Colman* was so irritated at the dulness of his pupil that he struck him; whereupon the latter fled from the church into the neighbouring wood, to hide himself, to avoid his lessons. Here, however, he discovered a man, alone, building a house; and the

(13) [See INTRODUCTION on the similar Gaulish houses figured on the Colonne Antonine in the Louvre.]

process is described, for the story says, that according as he came to the end of setting or weaving one rod into the wall, he would immediately introduce the head of another; and so worked on, from rod to rod, setting one only at a time. Slow as this process appeared to the young student, still he saw the house rising apace; and he said to himself: "Had I pursued my learning with this assiduity, it is probable that I might have become a scholar". A heavy shower of rain fell at the same time, and *Baoithin* took shelter from it under an oak-tree. Here he perceived a drop of the rain dripping from one leaf of the tree upon a particular spot. The youth pressed his heel upon this spot, forming a little hollow, which was soon filled up by the dripping of the single drop. *Baoithin* said then: "Ah! if I had pursued my learning even by such slow degrees, I would doubtless have become a scholar"; and then he spoke this lay:—

"Of drops a pond is filled;
Of rods a round-house is built;
The house which is favoured of God,
More and more numerous will be its family.
"Had I attended to my own lessons
At all times and in all places,
Tho' small my progress at a time,
Still I would acquire sufficient learning
"[It is a] single rod which the man cuts,
And which he weaves upon his house:
The house rises pleasantly,
Tho' singly he sets the rod.
"The hollow which my heel hath made,
Be thanks to God and Saint Colman,
Is filled in every shower by the single drop;
The single drop becomes a pool.
"I make a vow, that while I live,
I will not henceforth my lessons abandon;
Whatever the difficulty may be to me,
It is cultivating learning I shall always be".

Similar story told of St. *Cumin Fada.*

A similar story is told of the celebrated Saint *Cumin Fada*, Bishop of Clonfert (who died A.D. 661), as to his having taken a lesson in perseverance from seeing a little pool formed by the dripping of a single drop, and seeing a house rising to completion by the weaving in of a single rod at a time.

It does not appear that, even so late as this period (the seventh century), stone dwellings were in much repute or use, excepting ecclesiastical edifices; and that these too were frequently if not generally built of wood down to the seventh and eighth centuries, we have the clearest proofs. It appears, how-

LECT. XX. ever, from another passage in the Life of Saint *Colman Ela*, quoted above, that stone buildings must have been occasionally used at the same time as wood. Thus says the Life:

"One of the days that *Colman* was building the causeway which is situated at the rock on the western side [of the Church] [it happened that] there was no one engaged in setting the stones in the walls of the church, nor in the *Caiseal* [*i.e.* the encircling wall], nor in the *Tochar* [*i.e.* the causeway], on that day, who did not receive attendance from *Duinechadh*, who was the "second son of the king of that country, but who thus showed his humility and the fervour of his faith".

In dealing with the subject of the dwelling houses and other buildings here in the early ages after the introduction of Christianity, it would be impossible to separate the ecclesiastical and the laical buildings; because the builders and architects of both were the same. The same architect planned the great stone church and the belfry, as well as the oratory, which was sometimes built of stone, but more generally of timber, in the first three centuries of our national Church.

It does not appear in any ancient writing with which I am acquainted, that any kind of ecclesiastical edifice was built of basket or wicker work, like the houses of the laity just described. There are, however, at least two instances on record of the actual building of oratories, or small churches for private prayer, of wood, and instances of such interest that I cannot but cite them here. Both are connected with the life of the celebrated builder, *Gobban Saer*, of whom I shall have something to say by and by.

Story of the building of the oratory of St. *Moling*.

The first of these instances is that of the oratory of Saint *Moling* of *Tech Moling* (now Saint Mullin's, in the county of Carlow), and is recorded in the ancient Gaedhelic life of that saint. The story is so singularly told, wild as it is in part, that I cannot but give it in full. But it is, of course, only valuable in our present inquiry as preserving a statement of the materials of which the oratory was built. It is as follows:

"It was at this time the great ancient yew tree called the *Eo Rossa* [*i.e.* the Yew of *Ross*] was blown down. This famous tree became the property of Saint *Molaisé* of *Leithglinn*, who had it cut up and distributed among the saints of Erinn. Saint *Moling* went to him and asked him for a share of the Yew of *Ross;* and Saint *Molisé* presented him with as much of it as would make shingles for his oratory. Saint *Moling* then brought *Gobban Saer* to build his oratory. His company consisted of eight carpenters and their eight wives, and eight boys. They continued with the saint for a whole year

Story of the building of the oratory of St. *Moling*.

without commencing the work, and during this time their entertainment was never the worse. *Gobban* used every morning to press them to go to the wood; and what he said every day was: 'Let us go in the name of the Heavenly Father to-day'. Then at the end of the year he said: 'Let us go in the name of the Father, and of the Son, and of the Holy Ghost'.

"They went then at the end of the year to the wood, Saint *Moling* and *Gobban*, and having found a suitable tree, they began to cut it down. The first chip that flew from the tree struck Saint *Moling* on the eye and broke it; he drew his cowl over it; and, without informing them of what had happened, he bade them work well, while he should return home to read his office: this he did, and had his eye miraculously healed. *Gobban* and his assistants soon returned from the wood; and the oratory was built forthwith.

"In the meantime *Gobban*'s wife, *Ruadsech Derg*, had received a milch cow as a present from the saint. This cow was soon after stolen by a notorious thief named *Drac*, who infested the neighbourhood. The woman went to Saint *Moling* to complain of this. The saint sent a party of his people in search of the thief; and they found him roasting the cow at a large fire on the brink of the Barrow. When he saw them he quickly climbed a high tree which stood near; but one of the men wounded him with a spear, and he fell down into the river and was drowned. The party took up the carcase of the cow, one side of which had been put to the fire; and they rolled it up in the hide, and carried it back to the saint, who by his prayers called it to life again, in the same condition that it had been before, except that the side which had been to the fire remained of a dark gray colour ever after. *Gobban*'s wife having heard that the cow had been recovered, came again to the saint requesting that it should be restored to her. To this request, however, Saint *Moling* did not accede; and the woman returned in high anger to her husband.

"*Gobban* had just finished the building of the oratory at this time; and his wife addressed him, and said that she would not henceforth live with him, unless he should demand from the saint as the price of his work what she should name. 'It shall be done so', said *Gobban*. 'Well then', said she, 'the oratory is finished, and accept not any other payment for it but its full of rye'. 'It shall be so done', said *Gobban*. *Gobban* went then to Saint *Moling;* and the latter said to him, 'Make thy own demand now, because it was thy own demand that was promised to thee'. 'I shall', said *Gobban;* 'and it is, that its (the oratory's) full of rye be paid to me'. 'Invert it', said Saint *Moling*, 'and

LECT. XX.

Story of the building of the oratory of St. *Moling.*

turn its mouth up, and it shall be filled for thee'. So *Gobban* applied machinery and force to the oratory, so that he turned it upside down, and not a plank of it went out of its place, and not a joint of a plank gave the smallest way beyond another.

"Saint *Moling*, on hearing his exorbitant demand, sent immediately to his paternal relatives, the *Ui-Deagha*, on all sides, for assistance to meet it; and he spoke the following poem:

"Grief has seized upon me,
Between the two mountains,
Ui-Deagha by me upon the east,
Ui-Deagha by me on the west.

"There has been demanded from me
The full of a brown oratory
(A demand that is difficult to me)
Of bare rye grain.

"If you should pay this to him,
He shall not be much a gainer;
It shall not be malt, of a truth,
It shall not be seed, nor dried.

"The *Ui-Deagha*, to serve me,
Will relieve me from grief;
Because I must desire
To remain here in sorrow.

"On receiving this message the *Ui-Deagha* assembled, from the east and from the west, to him, until the hill was covered with them. He then explained to them the demand which had been made upon him. 'If we had the means', said they, 'you should have what you want; but in fact we have not among all *Ui-Deagha* more than the full of this oratory of all kinds of corn'. 'That is true', said he; 'and go ye all to your houses for this night, and come back at rising time on to-morrow, and reserve nothing in the way of corn, and nuts, and apples, and green rushes, until this oratory be filled'. They came on the morrow, and they filled the oratory, and God on this occasion worked a miracle for Saint *Moling*, so that nothing was found in the oratory but bare rye grain. So *Gobban* took away his corn then; and what he discovered it to be, on the next day, was a heap of maggots".

The second of the two instances on record of the building of a wooden *Duirtheach*, or oratory, though not in connection with the name of any architect, and although the passage describing it has already been published in Dr. Petrie's Essay on the Round Towers (page 348), is, however, so valuable in relation to my subject, that I cannot omit to give it here.

"It is found", [says Dr. Petrie] "in an account of the circumstances which occasioned the writing of a poem for the Galls, or foreigners of Dublin, by the celebrated Irish poet Rumann, who has been called by the Irish writers the Virgil of Ireland, and whose death is thus entered in the Annals of Tighernach at the year 747: '*Ruman Mac Colmain, Poeta optimus quievit*'. It refers to the building of the *duirtheach mór*, or great oratory of *Rathain Ua Suanaigh*, now Rahen, [near Tullamore] in the King's County; and the original, which is preserved in an ancient vellum MS. in the Bodleian Library at Oxford, is said to have been copied from the Book of Rathain Ua Suanaigh: 'Rumann, son of Colman, i.e. the son of the king of Laegairé, [in Meath], of the race of Niall, royal poet of Ireland, was he that composed this poem, and Laidh Luascach is the name of the measure in which he composed it. He came on a pilgrimage to Rathan in a time of great dearth. It was displeasing to the people of the town that he should come thither, and they said to the architect who was making the great *duirtheach* [or oratory], to refuse admittance to the man of poetry. Upon which the builder said to one of his people: Go meet Rumann, and tell him that he shall not enter the town until he makes a quatrain in which there shall be an enumeration of what boards there are here for the building of the *duirtheach*. And then it was that he composed this quatrain:

Quatrain of *Rumand* on the oratory of *Rathan Ua Suanaigh*.

"'O my Lord! what shall I do
About these great materials?
When shall be [seen] in a fair jointed edifice
These ten hundred boards?'

"This was the number of boards there, i e. one thousand boards; and then he could not be refused [*admittance*], since God had revealed to him, through his poetic inspiration, the number of boards which the builder had.

Poem of *Rumand* for the *Galls* of Dublin.

"He composed a great poem for the Galls of Ath-Cliath [that is, the Foreigners of Dublin] immediately after, but the Galls said that they would not pay him the price of his poem; upon which he composed the celebrated distich in which he said:

"'To refuse me, if any one choose, he may';

upon which his own award was given him. And the award which he made was a *pinginn* [or penny] from every mean Gall, and two *pinginns* from every noble Gall so that there was not found among them a Gall who did not give him two *pinginns*, because no Gall of them deemed it worth while to be esteemed a mean Gall. And the Galls then told him to praise the sea, that they might know whether his was original poetry. Whereupon he praised the sea while he was drunk, when he spoke [as follows]:

"'A great tempest on the Plain of *Lear*'" [*i.e.*, the sea].

"And he then carried his wealth with him to Cell Belaigh in Magh Constantine [or Constantine's Plain, near *Rathan*], for this was one of the churches of Ua-Suanaigh, and the whole of Magh Constantine belonged to him. For every plain and land which Constantine had cleared belonged to [Saint] Mochuda; so that the plain was named after Constantine. At this time Cell Belaigh had seven streets of Galls [or foreigners] in it; and Rumann gave the third [part] of his wealth to it because of its extent; and a third part to schools; and he took a third part with himself to Rathain, where [in course of time] he died, and was buried in the same bed [or tomb] with Ua-Suanaigh, for his great honour with God and [with] man".

Mention of seven streets of foreigners at *Cill Belaigh*.

This extract contains for us an undeniably curious piece of history. First, it gives us a clear idea of the materials of which the great oratory at *Rathan* was built, and of the size of it, which could not have been inconsiderable, since there were no less than one thousand planks prepared for its use.

It also supports the old account, which states that Constantine, the king of the Britons (perhaps of *Ailcluaidé* in Scotland) retired from the care of his government, and entered the monastery of *Rathan*, under Saint *Mochuda*, who preceded *Ua-Suanaigh*. All our old martyrologies give this fact, and assign the 11th of March as the festival day of this royal penitent.

A second curious fact established, to my mind at least, by this story, is that of the existence of "seven streets" exclusively inhabited by foreign pilgrims or students at *Cill Belaigh*, in the middle of the eighth century. And a third remarkable fact is that of the residence in Dublin of a large population of foreigners so early in this century; for it is only towards the close of that and in the beginning of the succeeding century that our annals begin to notice the descent on our coasts of the hostile foreigners whom we call Danes. There is no doubt, however, but that there were foreigners settled in Dublin, and in other parts of the east and south-east of the island, in the peaceful pursuits of trade and commerce, long before the fierce invaders of the ninth century.

LECTURE XXI.

[Delivered July 14th, 1859.]

(VII.) OF BUILDINGS, FURNITURE; (continued). Of the *Gobban Saer;* mistakes concerning him; explanation of his name; he was a real personage. Old Irish writers fond of assigning a mythological origin to men of great skill or learning. The legend of *Tuirbhi*, the father of *Gobban Saer;* observations of Dr. Petrie on this legend; error of Dr. Petrie. Story of *Lug Mac Eithlenn*, the *Sabh Ildenach* or "trunk of all arts". *Tuirbhi* a descendant of *Oilioll Oluim*. References to *Gobban Saer* in ancient Gaedhelic MSS.;—one in the Irish life of St. *Abban;* the name of the place where *Gobban* built the church for St. *Abban* not mentioned; another in the life of St. *Moling*. The name of *Gobban* mentioned in a poem in an ancient Gaedhelic MSS. of the eighth century;—original and translation of this poem (note); original and translation of a poem of St. *Moling* from the same MS. which is also found in a MS. in Ireland—great importance of this poem (note). Oratories generally built of wood, but sometimes of stone. Ancient law regulating the price to be paid for ecclesiastical buildings;—as to the oratory; as to the *Damh-liag* or stone church; explanation of the rule as to the latter (note); as to the *Cloicteach* or belfry. Explanation of the preceding rule quoted from Dr. Petrie; reasons for reëxamining these rules. Dr. Petrie's opinion about the Round Towers unassailable. Law regulating the proportionate stipends of *ollamhs;*—stipends of the *ollamh*-builder; Dr. Petrie's observation on the passage regarding the stipend of the *ollamh*-builder; dwelling houses omitted from the list of buildings; mistake made by Dr. Petrie about the passage concerning the *ollamh*-builder; author's correction of this mistake: meaning of the word *Coictighis*,—new interpretation by the author. Artistic works of the *ollamh*-builder, the *Iubroracht* or working in yew-wood; carving in yew-wood at *Emania* and *Cruachan*, and in Armagh cathedral. Romantic origin of work in yew wood—legend of *Fintann*, son of *Bochra;* no trace of the doctrine of metempsychosis among the Gaedhil; legend of *Fintann*, continued. List of articles of household furniture mentioned in the laws regarding lending or pledging. Law regarding the house of a doctor.

It would have interrupted too much the thread of the last lecture, as well as unreasonably prolonged its length, if I had introduced what I have to say concerning *Gobban Saer*, when I alluded to his works in connection with the wooden oratory of Saint *Moling*. I shall, therefore, begin the present lecture with some observations concerning this remarkable man. This is the more necessary because his name has been associated so long with modern legendary lore, that, I believe, many persons are content to doubt his existence altogether, and to look upon him as an impersonation of building or architecture in our national mythology. Some writers, again, whose want of acquaintance with the ancient language, and whose ignorance of the genuine history and archaeology of the Gaedhils, betray them into so many fanciful speculations, nay, even into the assump-

Of *Gobban Saer.*

Mistakes about him;

 tion of theoretic facts, if I may so call such inventions, accept the *Gobban Saer* indeed as a personage who had a real existence, but, in order to assist in supporting a whole series of false theories concerning the history and the life of our remote ancestors, refer back his era, together with that of the Round Towers, to pre-historic times. It is, therefore, very necessary to show that the celebrated builder in question, as well as his works (some of the Round Towers included), belonged to a time not only quite within the historic period, but more than a century after the time of the mission of Saint Patrick.

explanation of his name;

And, first, as to the name,—*Gobban Saer*. The man's *Christian* name was *Gobban*,—a word which means literally one with the mouth like the bill of a bird; and the word *saer* signifies, in the old as well as in the modern Gaedhelic, both a carpenter and a mason, and generally a builder; so that *Gobban Saer* signifies, simply, *Gobban* "the Builder". That *Gobban* is not a fanciful or merely mythological name is well shown by the fact that *Cill-Gobbain*, now Kilgobbin, near Dundrum, in the county of Dublin, is named after a saint of this name. Very little is known of the real history of this remarkable man, and it was only lately that the precise period at which he lived has been with certainty ascertained. Dr. Petrie, in his unanswerable Essay on the Round Towers and other ecclesiastical buildings of Ireland, published in 1845, gives all that could then be found concerning him, among our ancient writings at home and the popular traditions of the country. Some small additional information has, however, been since discovered, which I shall give hereafter.

a real personage.

It is not necessary for my present purpose that I should quote from Dr. Petrie, anything more than his belief in the real existence of *Gobban Saer*, and his high character as an architect,—because the original passages from native Gaedhelic authorities, printed in his beautiful book, I shall give also from the original sources, and with my own independent translation, though these can, indeed, differ but little from the translation given by him, in which I had some small share myself.

A mythological origin assigned to men of great skill or learning.

Our old Irish writers were very fond of tracing to some romantic and mysterious origin, men who at any time had exhibited artistic or scientific skill, or philosophical knowledge of an uncommon and extraordinary order, and particularly those who were, or who were supposed to be, of *Tuatha Dé Danann* descent. Such were, for instance, *Manannan Mac Lir*, the great mariner; *Diancecht*, the great physician; *Goibniu*, the great smith; *Lug Mac Eithlenn*, the great polytechnic trunk or block; and so on. And so in accordance with this tendency of our ancestors, we find that, in order, it would appear, to give our *Gobban Saer* a claim to an hereditary and mysterious excellence in his art, they give him a father of equally mysterious origin and talents. The legend of *Gobban's* father is given in the well-known ancient topographical tract called the *Dinnseanchas*, where it professes to trace the origin of the name of *Traigh Tuirbhi*, now the strand of Turvey on the coast of the county of Dublin. This curious legend, taken from the Books of Lecan and Ballymote, and which is also given by Dr. Petrie, is as follows:—

The legend of *Tuirbhi* the father of *Gobban Saer*.

"The strand of *Tuirbhi*, whence was it named? Answer: It is not unpleasant to tell. *Tuirbhi Traghmhar*, that is, *Tuirbhi* 'of the Strand', the father of *Gobban Saer*, it was he that owned it [the strand] and the land. He it was that used to throw a cast of his hatchet from *Tuladh-an-Bhiail*, [that is, Hill of the Hatchet], in the face of the flowing tide, and it used to stop the [flowing of the] sea, and it [the sea] used not come in past it. His true pedigree is not known, unless he was one of the disgraced men who fled from Tara before [that is, from] the *Sabh Ildanach* (or Polytechnic Block), and who remain in the *Diamhraibh* (or deserts) of *Bregia* [now Diamor, in Meath]. Hence the strand of *Tuirbhi dicitur*".

This legend is next thrown into verse as follows:

"The strand of *Tuirbhi* received its name,
According to authors I relate,
[From] *Tuirbhi* of the strands, [lord] over all strands,
The affectionate acute father of *Gobban*.

"His hatchet he would fling after ceasing [from work]
The rusty-faced, black, big fellow,
From the pleasant Hill of the Hatchet,
Which is washed by the great flood.

"The distance to which his hatchet he used to send,
The tide beyond [or within] it, flowed not;
Though *Tuirbhi* in his land in the south was strong,
It is not known of what stock was his race.

"Unless he was of the mystical black race,
Who went out of Tara from the heroic *Lug*,
It is not known for what benefit he avoided to meet him,
The man of the feats from the strand of *Tuirbhi*".

Dr. Petrie on the foregoing legend.

On this wild and unsatisfactory legend the thoughtful and accomplished Doctor Petrie makes the following remarks:

"It is not, of course, intended to offer the preceding extract as strictly historical: in such ancient documents we must be content to look for the substratum of truth beneath the covering of fable with which it is usually encumbered, and not reject the one on account of the improbability of the other; and, viewed in this way, the passage may be regarded as, in many respects, of interest and value, for it shows that the artist spoken of was not one of the Scotic or dominant race in Ireland, who are always referred to as light-haired; and further, from the supposition, grounded on the blackness of his hair and his skill in arts, that he might have been of the people that went with Lugaidh Lamhfadha from Tara,—that is, of the Tuatha Dé Danann race, who are always referred to as superior to the Scoti in knowledge of the arts. We learn that in the traditions of the Irish, the Tuatha De Danann were no less distinguished from their conquerors in their personal than in their mental characteristics. The probability, however, is, that Turvey was a foreigner, or descendant of one who brought a knowledge of art into the country, not then known, or at least prevalent".

Error in preceding observations. There is an error in the reading of the above legend, where it is conjectured that *Tuirbhi*, the reputed father of *Gobban Saer*, was descended from one of the party of artists who went forth from Tara along with *Lug Mac Eithlenn;* that *Lug*, who was the great stock or trunk of all the arts and sciences in Erinn, according to our ancient writers,—who was king of the *Tuatha Dé Danann*, and whose exploits at and before the battle of the second *Magh Tuireadh*, have been already mentioned at considerable length in a former lecture.

Story of *Lug Mac Eithlenn.* The story of *Lug* as a man skilled beyond all others in the arts and sciences, is as follows:—When he came first to Tara, he introduced himself as a young man possessed of all the arts and sciences then known, at home and abroad; and hence it was that he was afterwards called the *Sabh Ildanach*, that is, the "stock or trunk of all the arts". When first he came to the gate of Tara, the door-keeper refused to pass him in unless he was the master of some art or profession. *Lug* said that he was a *saer*, that is, a carpenter or mason, or both. The door-keeper answered that they were not in want of such an artist, as they had a very good one, whose name was *Luchta*, the son of *Luchad*. The young artist then said that he was an excellent smith: "We don't want such an artist", said the door-keeper, "as we have a good one already, namely *Colum Cuaellemeach*, professor of the three new designs" [*greisa*]. *Lug* then said that he was a champion: "We don't want a champion", said the door-keeper, "since we have a champion, namely, *Ogma*, the son of *Eithlenn*". "Well then", said *Lug*, "I am a harper". "We are not in want of a harper", said the door-keeper, "since we have a most excellent one, namely, *Abhcan*, the son of *Becelmas*". "Well then", said *Lug*, "I am a poet and an antiquarian". "We don't want a man of these professions", said the door-keeper, "because we have already an accomplished professor of these sciences, namely, *En*,

Story of *Lug Mac Eithlenn.*

; son of *Ethoman*". "Well then", said *Lug*, "I am a necro-ncer". "We are not in want of such a man", said the door-;per, "because our professors of the occult sciences and our uids are very numerous". "Well then, I am a physician", said *ıg*. "We are not in want of a professor of that art", said the or-keeper, "as we have an excellent one already, namely, *'ancecht*". "Well then, I am a good cup-bearer", said *Lug*. *We* don't want such an officer", said the door-keeper, "because ; are already well supplied with cup-bearers, namely, *Delt*, d *Drucht*, and *Daithe*, and *Taei*, and *Talom*, and *Trog*, and *lei*, and *Glan*, and *Glesi*". [These, I may observe, are all fe-ıle names.] "Well then", said *Lug*, "I am an excellent arti-ɛ (*cerd*)". "We are not in want of an artifex", said the door-eper, "as we have already a famous one, namely, *Creidne* the ificer". "Well then", said *Lug*, "go to the king, and ask him he has in his court any one man who embodies in himself these arts and professions; and if he has, I shall not remain iger, nor seek to enter Tara". It is needless to say that the ıg was overjoyed to lay hold of such a wonderful person as *ug*, and that he was immediately admitted into the palace, d placed in the chair of the *ollamh*, or chief professor of the s and sciences.

Lug, as we have already seen, rendered the *Tuatha Dé Da-nns* the most important services in the battle of the second or rthern *Magh Tuireadh*, which they fought against the Fomo-ıas, and in which he slew his own grandfather, *Balor* "of e evil eye". After this he became king of the *Tuatha Dé anann*, over whom he reigned forty years, until he was slain *Mac Cuill*, one of the three sons of *Cermat*, son of the *aghda Mor*, who were the joint kings of Erinn when the *'ilesians* arrived, and conquered them.

I have gone into this digression for the purpose of showing at this *Lug*, who was otherwise, or poetically, called the *Sabh danach*, never fled from or left Tara accompanied by any ımber of artists; but the great probability is, and indeed it is stated in the prose and verse accounts above quoted, that hen the artists of the court of Tara found themselves so far 'ershadowed by the superior abilities of the newcomer, they tired in disgrace to the solitudes of Bregia, or the eastern parts Meath, where the fruitful imagination of our romancists eserved them in concealment, even down to *Tuirbhi*, the ther of the celebrated *Gobban Saer*, who lived to the close of e seventh century. And notwithstanding the veil of mystery hich the poet throws over the lineage of the talented *Tuirbhi*, ere can be little doubt but that he was descended, if he ex-

Tuirbhi a descendant of *Oilioll Oluim.*

isted at all, from no other than *Teige*, the son of *Cian*, son of *Oilioll Oluim*, the celebrated king of Munster. This *Teige*, in the third century, settled in the territory which runs along the coast from the river Boyne [*Boind*] to the river Liffey, where his descendants continued to rule as chiefs until supplanted by the Danes in the ninth century; and their chief descendants were, in latter times, represented in the family of *Mac Cormac*.

References to *Gobban Saer* in ancient Gaedhelic MSS.;

To proceed, however, with the account of the *Gobban Saer*: I have never had the good fortune to meet with any old written reference to him but in two instances, although I have read a great many of the lives of our Irish saints, with whom, he is believed, on the authority at least of more than one tradition, to have maintained a close professional intercouse. But these two instances conclusively establish the date at which he flourished.

one in the life of St. *Abban*;

We read in the ancient Irish life of Saint *Abban*, a distinguished saint of Leinster, of which I possess a copy, that after he had travelled into Connacht and Munster, and founded many churches in those provinces, he returned to his native province, and decided on settling down there for the future. "There was", says the writer of this life, "a distinguished builder residing convenient to Saint *Abban*, and *Gobban* was his name; and it was his constant occupation to do the work of the saints in every place in which they were; until at length he had lost his sight because of the displeasure of the saints, on account of his dearness and the greatness of his charge. Saint *Abban* went to him to ask him to build a church for him. *Gobban* told him that it was not possible because of his being blind. Saint *Abban* said to him, you shall get your sight while you are doing the work, and it shall go from you again when you have finished the work. And so it was done, and the name of God, and of Saint *Abban*, were magnified by this".[16]

The name of the place where *Gobban* built the church not given.

It is to be lamented that the writer of the life does not give the name of the place where *Gobban* built this church for Saint *Abban*. The life states that his chief monastery was at *Camros*, but does not name the chieftaincy. The name *Camros*, however, remains still as that of a townland in the parish of Offerlane, barony of Upperwood, and Queen's County; but I am not aware of the existence of any ecclesiastical ruin remaining in it. There

[16] [original:—Baoi ar aile saor anórać agcoṁḟogus do Aban, acus Goban a ainm, acus ro buḋ e agnaṫuġaḋ, oibreacha na naoṁ do ḋenaṁ an gaċ áit ambiodis go ro dallaḋ é le hoirbire na naoṁ fair ar a ḋaoire forṫa, acus ar ṁéid alúiġ. teid Abban da iarraiġ do ḋenaṁ reigleise dó, adbert Goban nar bu héidir do ar ba dall. airbert Aban fris, do ġebair do rosġ an feḋ béir aig denaṁ na hoibre, acus adul uait iar nḋéanaṁ na hoibre, acus ro fioraḋ gaċ ní ḋiob sin, acus do máraḋ ainm de, acus Abain de sin.]

is another Camros near Barry's Cross in the county of Carlow. This parish of Offerlane is situated in the western side of the Queen's County, adjoining the King's County, where there is a church and parish still called Killabban, situated in the eastern part of the Queen's County, in the barony of Ballyadams, and on the boundary of Kildare. There is reason to think that this may be the real church of Saint *Abban*, and that the name *Camros* is a mistake of some old transcriber, for *Cnamh-ros*, which was certainly situated in the place now occupied by *Cil Abbain*, or in its immediate neighbourhood. Bishop *Ibar*, Saint *Abban's* maternal uncle, died in the year 500; so that *Abban* himself must have lived far into the sixth century.

The second reference to *Gobban Saer*

The second, and only other mention that I have found of *Gobban Saer*, is that in the life of Saint *Moling* (of *Tech Moling*, now Saint Mullin's, on the river Barrow, in the county of Carlow), which I gave in full in the last lecture. This Saint *Moling* fills a distinguished place in the civil as well as in the ecclesiastical history of ancient Erinn: his father was chief of the territory of *Ui-Deaghaidh*, in the south-eastern part of the present county of Kilkenny, and his mother was the daughter of a Munster chieftain, of the county of Kerry.

So far, we are able to follow with certainty the history of this celebrated architect of the Milesians. I have, however, the satisfaction of being able to refer, in corroboration of the authenticity of these references to *Gobban* in the lives of the Saints, to a Gaedhelic manuscript so old as the eighth century, now in the monastery of Saint Paul in Carinthia. From this ancient manuscript, through the kindness of my learned friend, Mr. Whitley Stokes, I am in possession of two or three stanzas of a poem, into which the name of *Gobban Saer* enters; but as yet I have not been able to ascertain whether these stanzas stand as mere fragments in the book, or whether they have not been transcribed as specimens by a distinguished scholar, Herr Mone of Carlsruhe. In any case they seem to form only a fragment of a longer poem. The language is very archaic and obscure, so that it is very difficult to make a satisfactory translation of it. I should not indeed have attempted to do so before collating my text with the original manuscript, were it within my reach. The *Suibne Geilt*, to whom the poem is attributed in the ancient codex, ended his life at *Tech Moling* as a much favoured member of the household of St. *Moling*, for whom *Gobban Saer* built the oratory just described. He was therefore coëval with St. *Moling* and with *Gobban Saer*, and his testimony may be regarded as that of an eye witness. This poem consequently affords a piece of very important evi-

Mention of *Gobban* in a MS. of the 8th century.

LECT. XXI. dence in favour of the Christian character of the round towers, if indeed any further evidence beyond what has been already given by Dr. Petrie were needed. The following is the best translation I can offer of it:

Mention of *Gobban* in a MS. of the 8th century.

Suibne, the mad, *Barr Edin.*

A *mairiu* I have heard in Tuaim Inbir,
  Nor is there a house more auspicious,
  With its stars last night,
  With its sun, with its moon.
Gobban made there
  A black *Conecestar* and a tower,
  My believing in the God of Heaven,
  That raised the choicest towers.
The house of the *Ire Fera Flechod*,
  The place [house] of the chief Virgin he built
  More conspicuous than the orchard's food,
  And it without an *Udnucht* upon it.[17]

The same MS. contains two other poems, one a speech of the devil to St. *Moling* after he had failed to seduce him into his own allegiance. It begins:

He is pure gold, he is a nimbus around the sun.

Suibne geilt barr edin.

[17] Mairiu* clun hi tuaim inbir
  ni lan techdais bes festu,
  cona retglannaib arein,
  cona grein cona escu.†
Gobban du rigni in sin
  conecestar‡ duib a's toir;
  mu chridecan dia du nim
  is hé tuga tóir rodtoig.
Tech h-ira fera flechod,§
  maigen na aigder,‖ rindi;
  soilsiu bidi lubgurt
  ose cen udnucht¶ n-imbi.

* *Mairiu* is perhaps an obsolete form of a verb derived from *mair*=*mór*, great, with the archaic verbal ending *-iu* instead of the more usual *-ughudh*. Cf. *mairiughudh*, *merughadh* to praise, to exalt, to magnify, Cf. also *Murughadh*, building, from *mur*, a stone wall, and *-ughudh*, the participial ending of a verb, and *muraighim*, I wall in or fortify, etc., so that *mairiu* might also be translated "a house-building".

† These lines indicate the antiquity of the custom of drawing auguries from the heavenly bodies, as to the auspiciousness of commencing a house.

‡ *Conecestar duib*, a black penitentiary or house of mortification, from *cestar*, is mortified or castigated. Cf. *Conae clu*, a house of good fame, a place where renown is fostered and preserved. MS. Egerton 88, Brit. Mus. 80, a. 3. *voce*, *alt.* The word may also be read as an obsolete form of *confecestar*, may be seen, the *f* being elided; and if the *u* in *duib* could be overlooked, and the *o* in *toir* (a tower) made *a*, the line might be read, "That it may be perceptible to you in history".

§ *Ire Fera Flechod*, the land or territory of the *Fera Flechod*.

‖ *Aigder*, chief Virgin, the Blessed Virgin, from *aig*, a chief, as in *aige fine*, a family chief, and *der*, a daughter, a virgin, as in *ainder*, a maid.

¶ *Udnucht* was the hurdle roof of a round house, upon which the thatch was laid. It also meant a palisade or hurdle fence which marked an inviolable sanctuary. The absence of an *Udnucht* implies that it was easily accessible to all, and as visible as the apples in an orchard.

Of this poem I have a copy from a vellum MS.[17a] of the twelfth century. The second poem is a panegyric on a king of Leinster named *Aedh*, of which the following is a translation: LECT. XXI.

Aedh great to promote happiness,
 Aedh ready to dispense hospitality,
 The thorny rod, the most beautiful
 Of the nobles of cleared *Roerin*.
The body which enshrines the wisdom of faith,—
 A great splendour under choicest thatches,—
 Who was exalted above all generations
 Of *Maisten* of smoothest meadows.
The son of *Dermot* dear to me,
 Whatever is desired is not difficult to him.
 To praise him, richest in treasures,
 Poems shall be sung by me.
Beloved the name,—the fame is not new,—
 Of *Aedh* who lowered not his dignity;
 The chaste form, the fame unconcealed,
 Whose patrimony is the smooth Liffey.
The descendant of *Muireadhach* without disgrace,
 A chosen cliff of loudly proclaimed dignity,
 A descendant whose like has not been found—
 Or kings of the clans of *Cualann*.
The chief, these are his inheritance,—
 All good be to him [from] God in the highest,—
 The scion of the reproachless race
 Of the renowned kings of *Marggae*.
He is the stem of a great illustrious noble tree,
 For battle he is a prop of valour;
 He is a silver sprig of exalted power,
 Of the race of a hundred kings, a hundred queens.
At ale-drinking emulatory poems are sung
 Between chivalrous people;
 Sweet-singing bards extol
 Through foamy ale the name of *Aedh*. *Aedh* great.[18]

When we remember that the book in Carinthia containing these poems is considered by so competent a judge as Herr

[17a] Is or glan, is nem grein.—MS. H. 2, 18, T.C.D., f. 204, b a.; Book of Ballymote, R.I.A., f. 140, b.a.; Book of Lismore, part ii. f. 25, a.a.; MS. Laud. 610, Bodleian Library, Oxford.

[18] Aed oll fri andud n-ane,
 Aed fonn fri fuilted fele,
 in deil delgnaidi, as chóemem
 di dindgnaib Roerenn rede.

In chli compar cond credail,—
 ollmar fu thocaid tugaib,—
 du farclu sech cach n-doine
 di moisten mine m[b]rugaib.

Mac diarmata dil damsa,
 cid iarfactha ni insa,
 a molad maissiu maénib,
 luaidfidir laéoib limmsa.

LECT. XXI.

Mention of *Gobban* in a MS. of the 8th century.

Mone to be of the eighth century, and that St. *Abban*, with whom *Gobban* was contemporary, lived perhaps to the middle of the sixth century, or little more than one hundred and fifty years before the presumed date of the codex, we have, I think, good evidence of the real existence of *Gobban Saer* as an architect; and also of the authenticity of our Gaedhelic records, and of the truth of the statements so frequently made in our manuscripts of later date, that they were compiled from more ancient books.

Oratories generally built of wood, but sometimes of stone.

I have dwelt too long, I fear, on the subject of these wooden oratories, to which, after all, we have so few historical references; the subject, however, is not an unimportant one, as it shows, as far as we can ascertain, that those edifices were often, probably generally, if not always, built of wood, where that material was most abundant; while it is certain that, in the stony and rocky countries on the south and west coasts, and on the islands, they were built of stone, that being the most abundant and ready material. And the same rule that applies to these sacred edifices will doubtless apply as well to the ordinary edifices for human habitation, whether round, oval, or quadrangular in shape.

Before passing from this subject I must mention another, indeed I may say the most important, reference to the special law which regulated the remuneration for building such edifices in the ancient times; a law which, it is very probable, arose from the circumstance of the exorbitant prices which such distinguished builders as the *Gobban Saer*, and other men of his class of abilities, had put upon their works, in the seventh and eighth centuries. This important regulation is found in a distinct article in a volume of the Brehon Laws,[19] and with a notice prefixed recommending special attention to it. The article, as will be seen, deals with the group which, of old, formed a regular ecclesiastical establishment, namely, a *Duirtheach*, or oratory, a *Damh-liag*, or stone-built principal church, and a *Cloicteach*, or belfry, or bell-house, as it is more appro-

Inmain na-ainm,—mit ut nuabla,—
aeda nad-airolig digna;
in cruth glan, clú nad cliche,
dian duchaig líphe ligda.

Aue Muiredaich cen chair,
all togu fri ordduin uallán,
aue ni frith nach ammail—
na rig dichlandaib cualan

Ind flaith, issed a orbbae,—
cach maith dó Dé no ardae,—
in gar fine cen dibail
di rígaib marraib margae.

Is bun cruinn máir miad roerda,
fri báig is bunad phindae;
is garne arggait ardd brig,
di chlaind chéit rig, ceit rignae.

Oc cormaim gaibtir dúana drenga
itir drerra daena;
arbertet bairgni bindi
tri laith linni ainm n-aeda.
Aed oll.

(19) Class H. 3, 17, in the Library of Trinity College, Dublin.

priately termed in the Gaedhelic, and with the proportionate price paid for the building of each. LECT. XXI.

"If it be an Oratory", [says this rule] "of fifteen feet, or less than that, that is, fifteen feet in its length and ten in its breadth, it is a *samaisc* [or three-year-old heifer] that is paid for every foot of it across, or for every foot and an half in length; this is when it is thatched with rushes; and if it be a covering of shingles, it is a cow for every foot of it across, or for every foot and an half in length. If it be greater than fifteen feet, there is a *samaisc* paid for every two-thirds of a foot across of it, or for every foot in length: this is with its covering of rushes; if it be a covering of shingles, there is a cow for every two-thirds of a foot across of it, or for a foot in length. as to the Oratory;

"That is the price of the oratories, according to law; and a third of it goes to art [that is, to the builder], and a third to material, and a third to food and to attendance and to smiths; and it is according as smiths may be wanted that this is assigned to them; and half the third goes to the smiths alone [if they be wanted at all], that is, a sixth part; the other sixth to be divided into two parts between food and attendance, one-twelfth to each of them; and if a division should remain, where smiths are not required, it is then to be divided into two parts between food and attendance. If it be a work for which land is required, [that is, the site of which must be purchased], and at which a smith is not, a third [goes] to art, and a third to land, and a third to material and to food and to attendance: half of that [last third] goes to material alone, that is, a sixth; the other sixth goes to food and attendance, that is, a twelfth part to each of them.

"The *Damhliag* [or stone church]. If it be a covering of shingles that is upon it, the price of it is the same as of an oratory which is equal in size to it. If it be a covering of rushes ['*rushes*' is clearly a mistake here; and we must read—if it be a roof of stone] that is upon it, the proportion which stone bears to wood, it is that proportion of full price that shall be upon it; and the proportion which wood bears to stone, it is that proportion of half price that shall be upon it; and the division which shall be made of these proportions is, the division which was made at the oratory.[30] as to the *Damhliag*;

[30] It has been found very difficult to understand clearly this very curious old mode of computation, nor has it, up to this day, been clearly explained by any one. I shall, however (with the condition of correcting the word rushes in the text to what it really must have been—*stone*), endeavour to explain the meaning of the writer's words, as that meaning appears, at least to my own satisfaction.

The writer says, that when the stone church was roofed with timber and

LECT. XXI.

as to the *Cloicteach.*

"The belfry [*Cloicteach*]. The base of this is measured with the base of the stone church, for determining its proportion; and the excess which is in the length and breadth of the stone church over that, that is, over the measure of the belfry, is the rule for the height of the belfry; and should there be an excess upon it, that is, upon the height of the belfry, as compared with the stone church which is of equal price with it, the proportionate price [of that excess] is to be paid for the belfry".

The necessity of making the translation as literal as possible, so as to express as nearly as could be done the peculiar idiom of the original, in the latter article, as well as in the two previous ones, renders a short explanation necessary. And yet, the rule laid down here for the height of the round tower or belfry, in proportion to the dimensions of the church, to which it was a mere appendage, is quite simple and intelligible; and as the whole article respecting the three edifices has been published by Doctor Petrie in his "Round Towers", I may as well quote for you, from that admirable work, the cautious but accurate reading of this rule by its learned author, and the decided proofs of its correct application which his extensive researches enabled him to put on record.

Dr. Petrie's explanation of the preceding rules.

"It is not, of course, necessary to my purpose to attempt an explanation of the rule for determining the height of the belfry; yet, as a matter of interest to the reader, I am tempted to hazard a conjecture as to the mode in which it should be understood. It appears then, to me, that by the measurement of the base of the tower, must be meant its external circumference, not its diameter; and, in like manner, the measurement of the base of the *Damhliag* must be its perimeter, or the external measurement of its four sides. If, then, we understand these terms in this manner, and apply the rule as directed, the result will very well agree with the measurements of the existing ancient churches and towers. For example, the cathedral church of Glendalough, as it appears to have been originally constructed, for the present chancel seems an addition of later time,—was fifty-

covered with shingles or boards, the price of building it was the same as the price of building an oratory of the same dimensions altogether of wood. But if the roof were stone [not rushes, which would be nonsense], then the full price which should be paid for it would be determined by the proportions which the price of a house built altogether of stone would bear to one built altogether of wood; and this is clearly explained immediately after, when the writer says of the proportion which wood bears to stone, that that was the half price which should be paid for it. In other words, when the church was stone, and stone-roofed, as was often the case, the price of building it was double that of the wooden oratory of the same dimensions; and the wooden oratory was but half the price of the stone-roofed church. This rule appears to have been modified in after times, as we shall see further on.

feet in length, giving a perimeter of one hundred and eighty-: feet. If from this we subtract the circumference of the er; at the base, or foundation, which is fifty-two feet, we shall e a remainder of one hundred and thirty-two feet, as the pre-bed height of this structure; for, to its present height of one dred and ten feet should be added from fifteen to eighteen for its conical roof, now wanting, and perhaps a few feet at its ;, which are concealed by the accumulation of earth around In cases of churches having a chancel as well as nave, the thus understood is equally applicable; for instance, the rch of Iniscaltra gives a perimeter of one hundred and sixty-feet, from which deducting forty-six feet, the circumference he tower, we have one hundred and sixteen feet as the pre-bed height of the latter, which cannot be far from the actual inal height of the tower; for, to its present height of eighty must be added ten or twelve feet for the upper story, which ow wanting, fifteen feet for its conical roof, and a few feet a portion concealed at its base".[(31)]

Reason for reëxamining these rules.

; may, as I have observed, appear to some persons that an :le which has been already published, which does not deal ı the dwellings of the people, but with ecclesiastical build-, need not be republished here. To such an objection I answer, that I was myself the first who had the good for-: to discover this most important little tract, in the year 7, at a time when the round-tower controversy had attracted gree of critical examination and public discussion which it er enjoyed before. And although the article was published Dr. Petrie's work, yet, considering the suddenness of its overy, and the extreme caution observed in its translation, vell as the entire abstinence of the editor from any attempt leal with the discrepancies and ambiguities of the text, I eve I may, with some advantage, at this distance of time, with a much more mature acquaintance with such writings r than then, take advantage of this opportunity of reëx-ning the meaning of this piece, and of leaving on record, e confirmed or refuted by future inquirers, of greater ability, reading which I am about to give, and which so little differs a the reading published fourteen years ago, that I am myself prised that it could have been so well understood then.

. shall also bring under the reader's notice, and chiefly for reasons just mentioned, another article connected with build-s in ancient Erinn. This second piece was also published Dr. Petrie; for, I may say, there was no reference whatever ich, at the time, could be discovered in our ancient manu-

[n] Petrie's *Round Towers*, p. 361.

LECT. XXI.

Dr. Petrie's opinion about the round towers unassailable.

scripts bearing in any way on the erection of ecclesiastical and other buildings, that was not pressed into the pages of Dr. Petrie's book; and it is satisfactory to that eminent scholar and artist, and to those who lent their more humble efforts to relieve him of some part of his laborious investigations, to say, that although all our ancient Gaedhelic manuscripts at home, and several in England and in foreign countries, have since that time undergone a much more thorough examination, nothing has been discovered—indeed nothing, I believe, ever can—to throw the smallest doubt upon the clear conclusions on the origin and uses of the round towers of Ireland, to which, after long thought and research, he had come.

Law regulating the stipend of *ollamhs*;

The following is the article to which I have just alluded; it is found in a Brehon Law tract preserved in the Book of Ballymote, in the Royal Irish Academy, and also in a fragment of another copy of the same tract preserved in a vellum manuscript of the same date, 1391, in the library of Trinity College, Dublin.[32] The tract is one which defines the rank and privileges of all the higher classes of ecclesiastical and civil society, the fines and penalties for injury, death, or dishonour, brought upon any of them, and the public stipends which the chiefs or *ollamhs*, and the other professors in the various departments of literature and the social arts, received from the chiefs, provincial kings, or the monarchs of Erinn, when attached to their respective courts. The stipend, however, advanced in proportion to the rank of the patron, as we may easily believe that any of the *ollamh* professors of the monarch received a much higher stipend than he would under a provincial king or a chief of one or more territories. These dignities and stipends were not arbitrarily and immediately conferred by king or chief. The man who aspires to an ollaveship in any profession or art, should submit his works for examination by one or more *ollamhs*, who pronounced judgment on it,[33] and if the judgment were favourable, the king, or chief, as the case might be, conferred on the candidate the rank and degree of an *ollamh* or master in all the departments of his profession;—such as, if he were an *ollamh* in building, he should be a master of all the varieties of the arts of a mason and a carpenter. And at the same time that these were necessary qualifications of the *ollamh*, there was a *sai* or chief professor of every one, or more, of these arts, who had also some privileges. It was the same with poets, lawyers, judges, doctors, etc.[34]

(32) Class H, 2, 16.

(33) See *Agallamh an da Shuadh*, or the *Dialogue of the Two Sages*.

(34) It is not to be supposed, however, that the *ollamh* in many arts, or the

These proportionate stipends are all set out in the present tract, and the section of it that I have to deal with at present, is that which regards the *ollamh*, or chief professor of the building art, and which is as follows: LECT. XXI

"If he be an *ollamh* builder he advances to twenty *seds* in his pay; that is, if he be a chief who professes the mastership of the building art, there are twenty-one *seds* assigned to him for his stipend. There are twenty-one cows to the chief master in the building art; and a month's refections, that is, a month is his full relief of food and attendance; for, although from remote times the chief builder was entitled to more than this in reward of the versatility of his genius, or his being master of many arts in various other departments, the author [of these laws, i.e., the legislator] felt a repugnance to allow him more than an equality with the chief poet, or with the chief professor in languages, or with the chief teacher. Wherefore, what the author [legislator] did was, to allow him to have two principal arts fundamentally, namely, stone-building and wood-building; and of these to have the two noblest exclusively, namely, the *damhliag* [or stone church], and the *duirtheach* [or oratory]. He had twelve cows for these, that is, six cows for each; and his superiority was recognized over the other arts from that out; and he was to take an equivalent to a sixth [of their price] out of each [work of] art of them, that is, his own sixth, six cows for *iubroracht*, [that is, vessels and furniture from the [wood of the] yew-tree]; and six cows for *coictighes;* and six cows for mill-building; take three cows from these [which] added to the twelve cows which he has exclusively, and they make fifteen cows. Four cows for ships, and four cows for *barcas*, and four cows for *curachs* [canoes]; take two cows from these, which added to the fifteen cows above, and they make seventeen cows. Four cows for wooden vessels, namely, vats and tubs, and keeves of oak, and small vessels besides; and two cows for ploughing machinery; one cow out of these added to the seventeen cows above makes eighteen cows. Two cows for causeways, and two cows for stone walls, and two cows for stepping stones [in swamps and rivers]; a cow out of these added to the eighteen cows above, and it makes nineteen cows. Two cows for carvings, and two cows for crosses, and two cows for chariots; a cow out of these added to the nineteen cows above, and it makes twenty cows.

Stipend of the *ollamh*-builder.

professor of one art or science, was debarred by his public stipend from following his profession at large and receiving its emoluments. This would be quite absurd, because, for instance, in the case of the *ollamh* builder, twenty-one cows would be but a poor reward for the exercise of his versatile genius: he ranked with the chief *ollamh* in poetry, who also received twenty-one cows for his stipend, and twenty-one cows for every poem which he wrote.

LECT. XXI. Two cows for rod [or wicker] houses, and two cows for shields, and two cows for casks; a cow out of these added to the twenty cows above, and it makes twenty-one cows for the chief builder, in that manner; provided he is master of all these arts".[35]

Dr. Petrie's observation on the preceding passage; It is but justice to Dr. Petrie to quote his observations on this article, as far as it regarded the object of his Essay. "It is to be regretted", he says, "that of the preceding curious passage, which throws so much light upon the state of society in Ireland anterior to the twelfth century, but two manuscript copies have been found, and of these one is probably a transcript from the other, for it seems in the highest degree probable that by the occasional omission or change of a letter, the sense of the original commentary has been vitiated. Thus, where it is stated that six cows was the payment for kitchen-building, which is the same as that for building a *damhliag*, or *duirtheach*, it would appear much more likely that the word originally used was *cloictighes*, or belfry-building, which we may assume was a much more important labour than the other, and which, if the word be truly *coicthiges* [rectè, *coicthigis*] is omitted altogether, though, as I shall show in the succeeding section from another commentary on the Brehon Laws, ranked amongst the Irish as one of the most distinguished works of the *saer*, or builder. But till some older or better copy of the passage be found, it must of course remain as of no authority in reference to the Round Towers; and I have only alluded to it with a view of directing attention to the manuscript copies of the Brehon Laws not immediately within my reach".

Such are Dr. Petrie's judicious observations, and it does appear rather strange, at first view, that the *cloicteach*, or round tower, should have found no place in this enumeration of buildings, unless, as he has conjectured, that it might be concealed by misspelling in the word *coictighis*, which only wants the letter *l* after the initial *c* to make it the round tower. Yet, however strange the absence of the *cloicteach* from the list may appear, it is not more so, nor even as much so, as the total absence of all allusion to dwelling-houses, except to the inferior kind which were built with wattles and wicker-work.

an apparent omission in the same passage;

There is another remarkable fact that cannot be passed over in the article, and it is this:—It sets out with stating that the *ollamh* or chief builder of a territory received from the chief an annual stipend of twenty-one cows in right of his office; and the writer then goes on to show how these twenty-one cows were calculated, counting one by one the various works of art of which

(35) See original and also a similar translation in Dr. Petrie's *Essay on the Round Towers*, p. 341. The original tract is in H. 2, 16, 930, T.C.D.

the *ollamh* was master, and upon the prices paid for which the calculation of that stipend was made. And there is a simple rule laid down for this calculation, namely, that for every building, or work of art, for which six cows were paid, there was a cow allowed to his stipend; not that it was taken from the actual price, and given to him, but calculated on the price. And where single works of art did not cost six cows, the writer groups them into twos and threes until they amount to six cows; and for the *ollamh*-mastery in these arts there is another cow put to his stipend; and so on to the end, where we find the sum total of twenty-one cows, premised in the rule, completely made up, and this without any shortcoming on account of the absence of the *cloicteach* or of the dwelling-house, either of which, most certainly, the word *coictighis* was intended to signify; for it will be clear to any one that a kitchen could not enter into the group of buildings in which it is found.

mistake made by Dr. Petrie about this passage;

The mistake—a very natural one in the state of antiquarian researches at the time—into which Dr. Petrie and those who endeavoured to assist him (of whom I was myself one), fell, was this: we thought that the twenty-one cows was the entire actual pay of the *ollamh*-builder; that he received six cows for building an oratory, six cows for building a church, and a cow out of every six cows paid for the other enumerated groups. I have shown, however, that this was not the case. And notwithstanding that we had seen, in a former article, that an oratory of fifteen feet in length and ten feet in breadth, when covered with shingles, and at the rate of a cow for every foot in breadth, cost ten cows, and that the church and the belfry were paid for at the same rate; still, when we found it stated in the present rule that the *ollamh*-builder, in more remote times, received a higher rate than this, we took it for granted, and it is no matter of surprise, that it was a higher price for the building of these several edifices that was meant by it, and that the *cloicteach*, which we thought ought to appear in this group, was, though of equal importance with its fellow-buildings, thrown by some mistake or accident into the next incongruous group, and written inaccurately by leaving the letter *l* out of it.

author's correction of this mistake;

This view of the case, however, appears to me to be a mistaken one; and I now believe the calculation of the *ollamh's* stipend did not imply the appropriation by him of any part of the price paid to any other builder for his work, nor even to himself; but that, on the contrary, if he were the builder of the oratory, the church, and the tower, himself, he was paid the full price set forth in the former rule, quite independently of his stipend of twenty-one cows a year which he received from his chief in right of his ollaveship. In this view of the case, which I am now confident is the correct one, it was not at all necessary to introduce the tower, because of its being clearly implied in the group. I have now to consider the real signification of the word *coictighis*, and endeavour to explain the apparent absence of the dwelling-house from the above list of works.

meaning of the word *coictighis*;

This word—*coictighis*, is compounded, according to the published translation,—of *coic*, a cook, and *tighis*, the plural of *tigh*, a house, that is, literally, "cook-houses". But from the fact, as before stated, of finding it grouped with works of so high an order of art as mills, and the manufactures from the yew-wood, we are, of necessity, driven to find another and more congenial signification for it. It is curious enough that, without altering a letter, such a signification, on a further examination of the Brehon Laws, has been found; a signification too, which, leaving the idea of a belfry out, fills up in the most satisfactory manner the other defect which appeared in our list of works, namely, the absence from it of the dwelling-house.

new interpretation by the author.

The word *coic-tighis*, in the sense in which I now propose to take it, will remain still composed of the same identical letters, and compounded exactly of *coic* and *tighis*, as before, the latter part retaining its former proper signification of houses, but the first part changed from "cook" to "five"; so that, in place of translating the compound word "kitchens", or "cook-houses", I propose now to translate it "five-houses", and for the following reasons:—First, it is quite unreasonable to suppose that such an important item as the building of the superior class of dwelling-houses should be omitted from the above list of works, whilst the building of the inferior class—those formed of wattles and wicker work—is introduced, and classed in price with the making of shields and casks, for each of which two cows was the pay of the artist. Secondly, we know now, from these very laws, that the regular establishment of a farmer of the first class, as well as of a chief, consisted of five houses; and that if he were deficient in any one of these houses, he was not entitled to the full privileges and dignity of his rank. Thus saith the law in this respect: that is, "the five privileges are—a great house, a cow-house, a pig-sty, a sheep-house, and a calves'-house".[26]

Even a slave, when he came to possess these *coic-tighis*, or five-houses, with the lawful stock that required them, became forthwith emancipated.

I need not, I think, pursue this argument any farther, as the object I have in view is, not to criticise any one, but to set

[26] original:—Itiat na cuic turba, tech mór, bo-teaċ, foil-muc, lias caerach, lias-laeg—H. 3, 18, p. 121½. T.C.D.

myself and others right as far as I can, in a matter that some years ago presented apparent contradictions which it was then found difficult to explain. But before passing from the immediate subject of these remarks, namely, the article from the Brehon Laws which enumerates the various artistic works of which the *ollamh*-builder was master, I must bring that enumeration or list of works more directly under the reader's notice again.

Artistic work of the *ollamh*-builder;

It may be remembered that the first item in the list is the ecclesiastical establishments, consisting of a wooden oratory, a stone church, and a stone round tower or belfry; and these, we have seen, were the works which required and received the highest exercise of the builder's art, both in stone and woodwork. For the building of these three edifices, according to certain proportions of one with another, the builder received thirty cows; but out of this he was to supply materials, tradesmen, labourers, and sometimes even the site of the edifices. It does not appear, however, that the other requisite buildings which must have formed part of the establishment, were included in the sum of thirty cows, such as a cook house, refectory, dormitory, the ordinary residence of the clergyman, and so forth.

The *Iubroracht*, or working in yew-wood.

The next exercise of the artist's skill was the *Iubroracht*, or working in *iubar*, or yew-wood. The working in this material must have embraced a wide range of objects, as it formed, with some exceptions, the material of all the most elegant articles of furniture in beds, bed-posts, buckets, cans, mugs, *medars*, [or square mead-drinking mugs], cups, and sometimes large vessels; as well as, we may fairly infer, various other articles of convenience and ornament for the houses of the higher classes of society. The stealing, breaking, or defacing of this class of articles came within the range of the criminal law, which injury to similar articles manufactured from any other native wood, did not. The yew was also largely used in cornices, wainscoting, or some such ornamentation of houses, from the very early times, as may be seen from the description of the palace of the Royal Branch at *Emania*, and of the house assigned to *Fraech*, the son of *Fidhadh*, at *Rath Cruachain*, mentioned in a previous lecture.[37] Where the palace of the Royal Branch is described it is said,[38] i.e. "ornamentation of the red yew in it". And where the house in *Rath Cruachain* is described, it is said,[39] i.e. "an ornamental carving of red yew upon the entire of it". We are told in this tract that the house itself was built of *giús*, what we now

Carved yew at *Emania* and *Cruachan*.

[37] Lect. xix., *ante*, vol. ii. p. 10.
[38] original:—erscor din dercc iubar and.
[39] original:—aurscartad do derg iubar fo brecht imchain uile.

LECT. XXI. call "deal"; and I am obliged to use the general term ornamentation, because there is nothing from which I could understand the precise character of the work in yew. I have, however, been so fortunate as to meet with one passage, which clearly defines the use to which the yew was put in the particular case to which it refers. This passage occurs in a poem of forty-seven stanzas, or one hundred and eighty-eight lines, written by *Giolla-Brighde Mac Conmidhe*, a distinguished Ulster poet who flourished between the years 1220 and 1250, in praise and description of the cathedral of Armagh founded by Saint Patrick. The only copy of this curious and important poem in Ireland, so far as I am aware, is a fine one in my own possession. The verses 6, 7, and 12, bear particularly on the subject I am at present discussing, and are as follows:

"The church of Armagh, of the polished walls,
Is not smaller than three churches;
The foundation of this conspicuous church,
Is one solid, indestructible rock.

"A capacious shrine of chiselled stone,
With ample oaken shingles covered;
Well hath its polished sides been warmed,
With lime as white as plume of swans.

* * * * * * *

Carving in yew-wood in Armagh cathedral.

"Upon the arches of this white-walled church,
Are festooned clusters of rosey grapes,
From ancient yew profusely carved;
This place where books are freely read".(30)

I have quoted these verses in order to show that down to the middle of the thirteenth century the cathedral of Armagh, though its walls were built with chiselled stone, was covered with oak shingles or boards in place of slates; and in the second place, that the arches at least of that venerable historical edifice were festooned with clusters of the ripe vine-berry, carved from ancient yew, and apparently coloured to imitate the natural grapes, proba-

(30) [original:—Teampall aird ṁaċa an ṁúir ċuirr
ní lughaḋ náid trí teampuill
grian an teampaill ḃric ḃadḃa
na lic ceanntruim ċatharrda.
Mionn luchṁar cloiche cuirre
slinnteach darach dioghuinne
do téideadh a taoḃ sleaṁain,
le heol n-gleigeal n-geisreaṁail.
* * * * *
Ar sduaigh an teampaill theoiḃghil,
caora de na ndeargaoiḃlibh
semioḃar do geḃtha glan
deighionadh leaghta leaḃar.
From the Book of *Fearan Connaill.*]

LECT. XI

bly some part of a more ancient roof of the church itself. From this curious fact, for, as a fact I am satisfied to receive it, we may easily imagine in what way the yew was applied to the adornment of the ancient palace of the Royal Branch at *Emania*, the Great House in *Rath Cruachain*, and many others which may be met with in our old writings.

Romantic origin of work in yew wood;—

The romantic origin ascribed by the poets to the manufacturing even of vessels for domestic use from the yew-tree, is preserved in our ancient writings. We are told that in the days of the monarch *Dermot Mac Fergusa Cerrbheoil*, who died at Tara in the year 558, there appeared an ancient sage who had outlived the general deluge. This man's name was *Finntann*, the son of *Bochra*, and he was one of the three men who came to Erinn along with the lady *Ceasair*, a short time before the deluge. But, as the legend is short, and as it may not be generally known, I shall tell it in a few words, as recorded in the Book of Leinster.

Legend of *Finntann* son of *Bochra*.

When Noah received the command of the Lord to build the ark, and the number of persons he should take into it, he had a fourth son whose name was *Bith*, or *Life*, who was not included in the number. *Bith*, accompanied by his daughter *Ceasair*, went to his father begging to be taken into the ark, but Noah refused, and desired them to take shipping and sail to the western borders of the earth, where, probably, the deluge would not reach them. This they did, in three ships, two of which were lost; but the third, containiug fifty women and three men, reached the coast of Kerry, and landed safely in that country. Among the women who arrived in safety was the lady *Ceasair*, and the three men were—her father, *Bith*, *Ladhra*, and *Finntan*, the son of *Bochra*, son of *Bith*, son of Noah. The whole party, however, are stated to have died before the flood came, except *Finntann*, who, when it commenced, was cast into a deep sleep which continued for twelve months, until the waters were dried up, when he found himself in *Dun-Tulcha*, his own former residence, a place situated somewhere near the head of Kenmare Bay, in Kerry. Here he continued to live, contemporaneously with the various succeeding series of colonists, and down, as I have already said, to the time of the monarch *Dermot*, in the middle of the sixth century, before whom he appeared at Tara, accompanied by eighteen companies of his own descendants; but it does not appear who his wife was. To show the antiquity of these tales, and that they are not isolated stories found only in some local compilation, I may mention that, in the very ancient account of the battle of the first or southern *Magh Tuireadh* (fought between the *Firbolgs*

LECT. XXI and the *Tuatha Dé Danann*), it is stated that the *Firbolgs* sent for *Finntann*, to take his advice on the course they should adopt towards their enemies; and also that thirteen of his sons took part in the battle.

No trace of the doctrine of metempsychosis among the Gaedhil.

While speaking of this *Finntann*, the son of *Bochra*, I wish to correct an error in which some persons have been indulging for many years; namely, that the ancient Gaedhils, Pagan and Christian, believed in the doctrine of the transmigration of souls —in other words, that when people died their earthly existence was not terminated, but that their souls were transferred to other corporeal forms, generally to animals. I would not think it necessary to notice the subject now, however important it would be in connection with the psychology of the Gaedhils, but that the opinion that the belief in metempsychosis did really exist among the people of ancient Erinn has been more than once lately put forward with all the pomp of supposed historical data, and on the authority of a gentleman whose mere word has, for many years, been deemed sufficient guarantee for the value of any assertion connected with Irish archæology and history. I have applied myself to test these opinions by the simple evidence of that history to which appeal has been made with so much confidence; and, in the course of an examination of the original of the celebrated legend of *Finntann*, I have found abundant proof of the entire absence of foundation for the reckless assertions which have been made on the authority of this tract. This subject, however, would evidently require so much space for its discussion as to lead me into an unwarrantable digression, if I were to go into it here in full; and I therefore content myself for the present with denying that there are any data in our existing Gaedhelic literature which could give the slightest support to the opinion that the doctrine of metempsychosis existed among the ancient Gaedhils, either Christian or Pagan.

To return then to the account of old *Finntann*, who is said, as I have above mentioned, to have survived the deluge, and whom I left on his arrival at the court of the monarch, *Dermot Mac Fergusa Cerrbheoil*, at Tara (about the middle of the sixth century), I shall now tell, in as few words as possible, how this strange event was supposed to have occurred.

Legend of *Finntann*, son of *Bochra*, continued.

In the time of the monarch *Dermot*, land, it would appear, began to become scarce, and the descendants of *Niall* of the Nine Hostages, who at this time were the owners of all East and West Meath, and who are commonly called by English writers the southern *Hy-Niall*, became dissatisfied with the waste of the great extent of the royal demesne of Tara, which was never allowed to be cultivated, or otherwise to contribute

Legend of *Finntann*, son of *Bochra*, continued.

to the support of the royal establishment. The monarch heard these complaints, and said that he was quite willing to contract the limits of the royal demesne in accordance with their reasonable wishes, provided any one could be found to show that it now exceeded what it had been in all times from the foundation of the monarchy. They then sent for the oldest and most intelligent men of the country. These were *Cennfaeladh*, the successor of Saint Patrick at Armagh; *Fiachra*, the son of *Nadruig; Cennfaeladh*, the son of *Ailill; Finnchadh* of Leinster; *Cualadh* from *Cruachan; Conaladh; Bran-Bairne* from Burren, in the county of Clare; *Duban*, the son of *Degha;* and *Tuan Mac-Carrill* (of whom I may have more to say hereafter). The latter five sages were commanded to appear forthwith at Tara; and when they arrived, and heard the point that was proposed to them to settle, they all declined to offer any opinion on it as long as their senior—by an immense distance—in age and in wisdom was still living, and accessible for consultation, namely, *Finntann*, the son of *Bochra*, who was the son of *Bith*, son of Noah, and which *Finntann* resided at *Dun Tulcha*, in the south-west of Kerry.

Bearran, *Cennfaeladh*'s servant, went then to request *Finntann*'s appearance at Tara. *Finntann* acceded to the request, and appeared at the palace, accompanied by eighteen companies or bands of men—nine before him, and nine after him—all his own descendants. He received a hearty welcome at Tara from king and people, and, after resting himself, he related to them his own wonderful history, and that of Tara from its very foundation:—"That is very good", said they, when he had finished, "and we should like to know from you an instance of the tenacity of your own memory". "You shall have it", said he: "I passed one day through a wood in West Munster: I brought home with me a red berry of the yew tree, which I planted in the vegetable-garden of my mansion, and it grew there until it was as tall as a man. I then took it out of the garden, and I planted it in the green lawn of my mansion; and it grew in the centre of that lawn until an hundred champions could fit under its foliage, and find shelter there from wind, and rain, and cold, and heat. I remained so, and my yew remained so, spending our time alike, until at last its leaves all fell off from decay. When afterwards I thought of turning it to some profit, I went to it and cut it from its stem, and I made from it seven vats, seven keeves, and seven *stans*, and seven churns, and seven pitchers, and seven *milans* [i.e. an *urna*], and seven *medars*, with hoops for all. I remained still with my yew-vessels, until their hoops all fell off from decay and old age. After this I re-made them, but could only get a keeve out of the vat, and a *stan* out of the keeve, and a mug out of the *stan*, and a *cilorn* [pitcher] out of the mug, and a *milán* [an *urna*] out of the *cilorn*, and a *medar* out of the *milán;* and I leave it to 'Almighty God'", said he, "that I do not know where their dust is now, after their dissolution with me from decay".

Such is the legendary account of the first manufacture of household vessels of yew, valuable at least for the list it contains of the different household utensils of the earlier ages.

List of articles of household furniture.

We find also in the laws concerning the lending or pledging of certain articles of house furniture, that, if they were not restored after one day's notice, a "smart" fine fell upon the persons who overheld them; and among these were the following articles: A flesh fork, and a boiler; a kneading-trough, and a sieve; a wide-mouthed pan, or vat; a narrow-mouthed barrel, or churn; a mirror, for men and women to view themselves in when preparing to attend a fair or assembly; play-things for children, to drive away decline from them, such as "kittens", "pups", balls, "hurlies", etc.; bridles with single and double reins; hatchets and forest-axes; the iron reaping-hook of a widow's house, which she had for reaping the straw and rushes of her house, and also to cut ivy and holly with; the chess-board of a gentleman's house; the salt of a farmer's house; griddles, and gridlets, or the small spatulas with which the cakes were turned on them; candlesticks of various kinds; bellows and flanges, with which to blow the fire in respectable houses; the *cilorn*, or pitcher with a handle at its side; or the *milan*, or *medar;* and any or all of the seven requisites of a gentleman's house, namely, a caldron; a keeve; a water-cask, or bucket; a pan; a plough; a horse-bridle, and a brooch; and all articles manufactured from the yew-tree; and besides these, all beautiful drinking vessels, such as goblets of glass and of silver, with cups, mugs, and flagons of bronze, brass, or copper. These fines extended to the over-holding or withholding of splendid clothes and trinkets, from men and women, at the approach of a fair or assembly, as well as to chariots and various other things.

It would be difficult to bring together and arrange in any readable order, all the various articles of household furniture, domestic economy, and personal ornament, to be met with in our ancient laws and historical and romantic tales and poems.

Law regarding the house of a doctor.

There is, however, a passage in the laws which shows with what jealous care the arrangements for domestic life were guarded by even formal legislation in the olden time. The passage in question has reference to the house of a doctor, and provides as follows: "He shall arrange his lawful house; a house of great work; it shall not be a dirty, slovenly house; it shall not be one of the three houses; [i.e. a cow-house, pig-house, or sheep-house.] There must be four doors upon it; so that the sick man may perceive it from all sides; and there must be a stream of water passing through its middle".

LECTURE XXII.

[Delivered July 19th, 1859.]

(VII.) Of Buildings, Furniture, etc.; (continued). Stone buildings; *Cathairs* and *Clochans*; O'Flaherty's notice of the *Clochans* of the Arann Islands; *Clochans* still existing in those Islands; *Clochans* on other islands of the western coast. Mr. Du Noyer's account of ancient stone buildings in Kerry; his ethnological comparisons; summary of his views; apart his speculations his paper is important. Different members of the same family had distinct houses in ancient Erinn. Mr. Du Noyer's claim to priority in the discovery of the stone buildings of Kerry inadmissible; Mr. R. Hitchcock had already noticed them; ancient burial grounds also noticed by the latter in the same district. The two names of "Cahers" given by Mr. Du Noyer, not ancient; his opinion of the use of *Dunbeg* fort not correct; this and the other forts did not form a line of fortifications. Instance of a bee-hive house or *Clochan* having been built within the *Rath* of *Aileach*. Limited use of the term *Cathair*; the same term not always applied to the same kind of building. Tale of the dispute about the "champion's share"; Smith's notice of *Sliabh Mis* and *Cathair Conroi*; story of the dispute about the "champion's share" (continued). The "guard room" or "watching seat". The position of *Cathair Conroi* not exactly ascertained. Story of "the slaughter of *Cathair Conroi*". Reference to *Cathair Conroi* in the tale of "the Battle of Ventry Harbour". Modern hypothesis of the inferiority of the Milesians. Stone-building in ancient Erinn not exclusively pre-Milesian. The *Aitheach Tuath* or *Atticotti*. The Firbolgs still powerful in the sixth century. Townland names derived from *cathairs*. No evidence that the Milesians were a ruder race than their predecessors in Erinn.

Stone buildings;

I shall conclude the present division of my subject—that of the buildings and domestic furniture of the people of ancient Erinn—by some observations upon the stone erections of the primitive periods of our history, and particularly upon those constructed for the purpose of the fortification of the settlement of a tribe, or the palace or court of a king, the remains of some of which fortunately still exist in a state which allows us, even at the present day, to form some conjectures as to the original design of their first builders.

Cathairs and *Clochans*

The subject of ancient cyclopean architecture—that is, that of buildings of stone constructed without mortar or application of the mason's hammer—has for a long time occupied the attention of Irish antiquaries, particularly those edifices which are known by the names of *cathairs* and *clochans*. The *cathair* was always a stone fort or wall of enclosure; while the *clochan*, as it is called, is a small hut, generally of one chamber, built of uncemented, undressed stones, usually circular, in the form of a bee-hive, but sometimes oval or lozenge-shaped, and in a few instances square within though circular without. Both *cathairs* and *clochans* are found chiefly, if not exclusively, on the south and west coasts of Ireland, and on the islands of these coasts, but particularly in the district lying to the west and north of the town of Ventry in Kerry.

The first antiquary who appears to have paid any attention to these *clochans* on the western coast, was Roderick O'Flaherty, the author of the *Ogygia*, in his Chorographical Description of West Connacht,—a work written in the year 1684, and which was edited by the late James Hardiman for the Irish Archæological Society in 1846. O'Flaherty, in describing the Arann Islands, on the coast of Clare, in the Bay of Galway, speaks as follows:—

"The soil is almost paved over with stones, soe as, in some places, nothing is to be seen but large stones with wide openings between them, where cattle break their legs. Scarce any other stones there but limestones, and marble fit for tomb-stones, chymney mantel-trees, and high crosses. Among those stones is very sweet pasture, so that beefe, veal, mutton, are better and earlier in season here than elsewhere; and late there is plenty of cheese and tillage-mucking, and corn is the same with the sea-side tract. In some places the plow goes. On the shore grows samphire in plenty, ringroot or sea-holy, and sea-cabbage. Here are Cornish choughs, with red legs and bills. Here are ayries of hawkes, and birds which never fly but over the sea; and, therefore, are used to be eaten on fasting-days; to catch which people goe down with ropes tyed about them into the caves of cliffs by night, and with a candle-light kill abundance of them. Here are severall wells and pooles, yet in extraordinary dry weather, people must turn their cattell out of the islands, and the corn failes. They have no fuell but cow-dung dryed with the sun, unless they bring turf in from the western continent. They have *cloghans*, a kind of building of stones laid one upon another, which are brought to a roof without any manner of mortar to cement them, some of which cabins will hold forty men on their floor; so ancient that no body knows how long agoe any of them was made. Scarcity of wood, and store of fit stones, without peradventure found out the first invention".[31]

O'Flaherty's notice of the *clochans* of Arann;

Of the *clochans* mentioned above by O'Flaherty, several remain still on the Great or Western Island of Arann; some of them in ruins, and others still in a state of good preservation. Of these latter, four or five are to be seen in the immediate vicinity of the beautiful little ruined church called *Tempall an*

clochans still existing on the islands of Arann;

(31) Page 68.

LECT. XXII. *Cheathrair Aluinn*, or the "Church of the Four Beautiful Persons". These "four beautiful persons", according to the bishop *Malachias O'Cadhla*, or Kiely (who so informed Father John Colgan, about the year 1645), were Saint *Fursa*, Saint *Brendan* of Birr, Saint *Conall*, and Saint *Bearchan*. One of these *clochans* is in almost perfect preservation; it is built of dry stones, and measures about twenty feet in length, about nine in breadth, and nine in height to the top of the arch. It stands north and south, and had three doors, one at each side, nearly in the middle, and one in the east end, and it has a square aperture in the top near the south end, made, probably, to answer the purpose of a chimney. There is a square apartment, now in ruins, projecting from the south jamb side of the door on the western side of this *clochan*, with an entrance immediately at the same jamb, on the outside of the main building; but there is no communication with this apartment from within. The work of the whole is of the rudest and simplest character; and most probably when it was inhabited it must have been covered with sods, or the interstices at least stuffed with moss or mud to keep out the wind. This edifice was occupied by a poor school-master within the memory of some people still living on the island; but it does not appear to have undergone any change whatever from its original condition, during this or any other occupancy. There are three or four other *clochans* a little to the west of this, but they are now reduced to heaps of ruin; still one or two of them appear to have been circular, and one of them has the remains of a little porch which stood against, and appears even to have entered into, the main wall, immediately adjoining the north jamb of the door in the east side. There may be many more in this immediate neighbourhood, but to one so much burdened with lameness as I am, it would have been a work of no ordinary trouble to move among the rugged rocks and constantly recurring dry stone walls with which the place is beset; and I did not venture to attempt this on the occasion of my late visit to the island.

There is another *clochan*, one at least, in more perfect preservation, situated between Murvey Strand and the Seven Churches of Saint *Brecan*, on the left hand side of the road; but I was not able to visit it. There is another also, in ruins, near *Tempall Benen*, in the eastern part of the island; and there are some two or three, in ruins, within the great stone fortress of *Dun Concraidh*, on the middle island.

Clochans on other islands of the W. coast.

Besides these *clochans* on the Arann Islands, there are four more such edifices of bee-hive form, in ruins, on the island of *Inis-Gluaire* on the Connacht coast, together with three small churches. There are others of them again on *Ard-Oilean*, or

High Island, where Saint *Fechin* founded a church in the sixth century. The island of *Inis-Erca* too, near *Inis-Bo-finne* (now Boffin, off the coast of Galway), contains the ruins of an ancient church, called Saint *Leo*'s church, and near it is a cross called *Leo*'s Flag. On the south shore of this island there is a cave called *Uaimh Leo*, where the saint is said to have passed much of his time in prayer and meditation. There is here also a ruin called *Clochan Leo*, in which he is said to have dwelt. Coming back again southward, we find a *clochan* of the bee-hive shape on the Bishop's Island, a little to the west of the mouth of the bay of Kilkee on the Clare coast. I know this island well from my earliest boyhood, and have seen the *clochan* from the mainland, from which the island is distant but a short space; but I have never been on the island, and can only speak of the precise form of the "bishop's house", as it is popularly called, on the authority of the fishermen, who are almost the only persons able to climb the steep precipitous cliffs which wall it in. I may here mention that the name *clochan* for this, or indeed for any other kind of habitation, is not known in any part of the county of Clare that I am aware of.

Mr. Du Noyer's account of ancient stone buildings in Kerry.

I have been induced to go thus minutely into an account of these curious old edifices, on account of some statements made by Mr. George V. Du Noyer in a paper read by him before the British Association for the Advancement of Science, at its meeting in Dublin in 1857.[38] The preface to Mr. Du Noyer's paper is so short that it will occupy less time and space to give it as it stands than if I were to make any analysis of it.

"The earliest vestiges", says Mr. Du Noyer, "which are still in existence, of any dwellings of the inhabitants of Ireland, consist generally of a simple circular mound of earth, surrounded by one or more fosses and earthen ramparts; but they are for the most part so defaced by time, that archaeologists have passed them by as undeserving of attention. When, however, we find stone buildings of an equally remote period occurring in groups, surrounded by a massive circular wall, as if intended for warlike defences, and in detached houses comprising one, two, or three apartments, more or less circular in plan, and all evincing considerable skill and ingenuity in their designs, the investigation of them is attended with no little interest; for it may throw some light on the social condition of a race who occupied Ireland at a period so remote, that scarcely a trace of their arts has been

(38) "*On the remains of ancient Stone-built Fortresses and Habitations occurring to the West of Dingle, county of Kerry*", and published in the fifty-seventh number of the *Journal of the Archaeological Institute.*

XII. preserved to us, and even their specific name as a people has not been rescued from oblivion.

"It was my good fortune", he continues, "in the summer of 1856, while engaged on the Geological Survey of Ireland in the Dingle promontory, to meet with an extensive group of such buildings. They are known as Cahers and Cloghauns,[39] and had till then escaped the notice both of tourists and antiquaries. These buildings, amounting probably to seventy or eighty in number, are in the parishes of Ventry, Ballinvogher, and Dunquin, and occupy, in groups as well as singly, the narrow and gently sloping plateau which extends along the southern base of Mount Eagle, from Dunbeg fort or Caher on the east to the village of Coumeenole on the west, a distance of three miles. An ancient bridle-path, still in use, winds along the slope of the hill near the northern limit, and was near the original road which led to them. They occur principally in the townland of Fahan: hence the collection of buildings which I am about to describe, may with propriety be called the ancient Irish city of Fahan. Proceeding west from the coast-guard station at Ventry, along the bridle-road just alluded to, at a short distance south-east of Fahan village, we arrive at a group of small Cloghauns, or bee-hive shaped huts, which appear to have served as an outpost, to guard the place on that side from any hostile surprise; and close to them, nearer to the sea, are two groups of standing stones called gallauns, which mark the eastern limit of the city.

"The Caher or fort of Dunbeg [little fort], which protected the city of Fahan on the east, is the first of these structures which requires a detailed description. By reference to the map it will be seen that it lies due south of the present village of Fahan on the sea coast. This remarkable fort has been formed by separating the extreme point of an angular headland from the main shore by a massive stone-wall, constructed without cement, from 15 to 25 feet in thickness, and extending 200 feet in length from cliff to cliff. This wall is pierced near its middle by a passage, which is flagged overhead, the doorway to which is at present 3 feet 6 inches high, 2 feet wide at top, and 3 feet at its present base, having a lintel of 7 feet in length; as the passage recedes from the doorway it widens to 8 feet, and becomes arched overhead; to the right hand, and constructed in the thickness of the wall, is a rectangular room—perhaps a guard-room—measuring about 10 feet by 6 feet, and communi-

[39] "*Caher* signifies a circular wall of dry masonry, as well as a fort or stone house of large size. *Cloghaun*, as here used means, a hut or house formed of dry masonry, with the room or rooms dome-shaped, having each stone over lapping the other, and terminating in a single stone".

cating with the passage by means of a low square opening, opposite to which, in the passage, is a broad bench-like seat; a second guard-room, similar to the one just described, has been constructed in the thickness of the wall on the left hand of the main entrance, but unconnected with it, the access to this being from the area of the fort through a low square opening".[34]

Mr. Du Noyer's ethnological comparisons;

Further on Mr. Du Noyer gives us a little of that kind of speculative ethnology which now too commonly passes for science, and which many writers, too superficial to follow out the true and only method by which archæology, like all other sciences, can progress, namely, patient research and careful induction from facts, usually indulge in to the great injury of true knowledge. As I shall have to notice these speculations of Mr. Du Noyer, I cannot avoid adding the following extract from his paper: "The smallness of the sleeping-chambers and of the entrances leading into them is very remarkable; indeed this addition to the Cloghaun is a singular feature in the habits of the people who used them. Taking both into account, we may suppose that the attainment of warmth by animal heat was the chief object they had in view in their construction; if so, it at once lowers them to the scale of the Esquimaux, whose circular Inglöe, or stone huts, closely resemble the smaller and more insignificant of our Cloghauns; indeed the resemblance may go even yet further, for it is likely that in many instances there were long covered stone passages, conducting to the door of the Cloghaun, similar in design to the long, low, and straight stone passages, covered with sods, which lead into the winter Inglöe. When we consider what an important addition to our comfort is a chamber set apart for sleeping in, no matter how small it may be, we are surprised to find that so few of the Cloghauns have this important addition to them; it is sufficient, however, to know that such was sometimes required, and we may regard this fact as evincing some degree of refinement in a people whose habits must have been rude and simple".

summary of his views.

These conclusions of Mr. Du Noyer's amount simply to this: that some of the ancient Irish people built beehive-shaped houses of stone, without cement, sometimes of small, and sometimes of comparatively large dimensions, for at this day sixty men might stand together on the floor of some of them; that some of these round houses were divided into two or three apartments; that some of the apartments were pretty large, and some small; and that in some of the buildings there was no second apartment at all. The additional apartments in the former class of buildings were believed by Mr. Du Noyer to be sleeping-rooms; and taking

(34) See INTRODUCTION, Figs. 56, 57, and 58.

LECT. XXII. the smallest of them for his rule, he delicately concludes that the sleeping parties were composed of savages of both sexes, huddled together promiscuously for the purposes of animal warmth; and then, arguing from this assumed fact, he at once leaps to the conclusion that such a people must have been lower even than the poor Esquimaux of North America in the scale of human civilization. Then again, this estimate of the people being taken for granted, he deems it conclusive as to the remote antiquity of these dwellings, and of the people who built them; and he unhesitatingly assures us accordingly, that neither the buildings nor the builders have any place in our oldest traditions or historical documents.

It is sufficient to summarize, as I have just done, the conclusions to which Mr. Du Noyer has arrived, to show how illogical and gratuitous they are. It would surely be a waste of time, and not very complimentary to the reader's intelligence, to disprove them. Indeed I would not have noticed them at all, only that the passage affords an admirable example of the modern ethnological theories put forward with such parade by popular writers. Apart from these absurd ethnological comparisons, Mr. Du Noyer's paper is a valuable and important contribution to Irish topographical archæology, illustrated as it is by admirable drawings.

In all the civilized countries in the world there have been, and must continue to be, two extremes of society, one high and one low; and to judge of the high by the low is what no man of intelligence would think of. And so, in the case of the edifices at Glennfahan, if we find the house of one apartment, we also find, alongside of it, perhaps, the strong *cathair* enclosing within it two, three, four, or more, small and large houses; but we are not to infer from this fact that these enclosed houses were inhabited by different families; for we have distinct statements in our ancient records that different members of the same family had distinct houses, and not apartments within the same *rath*, *dun*, *lis*, or *cathair;* that the lord or master had a sleeping-house, his wife a sleeping-house, his sons and daughters, if he had such, separate sleeping-houses, and so on, besides places of reception for strangers and visitors.

Different members of the same family had distinct houses.

I shall presently refer to the buildings described by Mr. Du Noyer, but before doing so I must correct a mistake which he has made regarding the first discovery of the stone buildings of the Dingle promontory. The mistake occurs in the following note which he has appended to his paper: "In reply to some remarks which have reached me relative to the bee-hive houses of the county of Kerry and other districts, especially in the west

Mr. Du Noyer's claim of priority

of Ireland, I feel called upon to state distinctly that, until I examined and sketched the Fahan buildings, in the summer of 1856, they had lain unknown to, or at least undescribed by, any tourist or antiquary; even that acute observer and recorder of so many of the pre-historic relics of the Dingle promontory, the late lamented Mr. Hitchcock, passed them by without examination".

not admissible.

Now, in justice to the late lamented Richard Hitchcock, it must be said that Mr. Du Noyer does not here deal quite fairly with him. It is true that Mr. Hitchcock did not write, or at least did not publish, any description of the *Clochans* at Ventry; but on the other hand it is certain that he did not pass them by without examination. Mr. Hitchcock's antiquarian researches were chiefly, if not wholly, confined to the discovery and sketching of stones with *ogham* inscriptions, and these he did discover, and preserve in sketches, with wonderful industry and accuracy. His too inadequate means, and the impossibility of his absenting himself long from his official duties in Dublin, could not, of course, permit him such opportunities and so much time for collateral examinations, as Mr. Du Noyer enjoyed in the fulfilment of his professional duties on the Geological Survey of Ireland; but that Mr. Hitchcock saw, and, I believe, examined them, is beyond dispute. For, in a manuscript book of "notes on *oghams*", in Mr. Hitchcock's handwriting, deposited with his other books after his death in the Royal Irish Academy, by his widow, we find at page 103, where he is describing the *ogham* on the *Dunmore* stone in the townland of Coumeenvole, the following words:—"The locality of this ogham inscription appears on sheet 52 of the Ordnance Survey of the county [of Kerry], where the stone is named 'monumental pillar'. *Cloghauns* are very numerous to the south-east, and there are also a few *caluragh* burial grounds. The townlands of Coumeenole, South Glanfahan and Fahan, at the sea-side, are actually filled with *cloghauns*".

Ancient burial ground noticed in the same district.

This note was written in the year 1850, and I think it shows clearly enough that Mr. Hitchcock not only discovered the "cloghauns" at Ventry, but discovered among, or about them, what appears to have escaped Mr. Du Noyer's notice, at least some few *cealluraehs*, that is, sites of ancient churches and burial grounds. And it is not at all improbable that all these beehive houses described by Mr. Du Noyer were in fact but the cells of Christian hermits, like all the other buildings of the same class known along the western coast of Ireland. It is quite clear, however, that the Glenfahan "city", so called, has not yet received a thorough antiquarian examination; and until it shall have been

The buildings described by Mr. Du Noyer are probably Christian.

LECT. XXII. properly investigated, I do not wish to be understood as expressing any positive opinion upon this conjecture.

The names of cahers given by Mr. Du N. not ancient.

Mr. Du Noyer has recovered but two names of "cahers" among the group at Ventry, and both these names, in the form in which he puts them, are grammatically inaccurate: one is *cahernamactirech*, which he translates "the stone fort of the wolves"; and the other, *caher-fada-an-dorais*, or the "long fort of the doors". These are certainly names either entirely modern, or else inaccurately taken down. I cannot, however, examine them further at present, and shall therefore return to the immediate subject of this lecture.

The fort of Dun-beg not peculiar.

In the first place, there is nothing extraordinary or peculiar, nor anything necessarily implying a very remote antiquity, in the "caher" or Fort of *Dun-beg* (a word which signifies the little *dun* or fort), on which Mr. Du Noyer expatiates so warmly, and which evidently received its name of *Dun-beg* to distinguish it from *Dun-mór* (or the great fort), also described by Mr. Du Noyer. The latter was constructed in a manner exactly like it, by drawing a thick wall or mound of earth, lined with stones on the inside, across the narrow neck of another point of land which projects into the Atlantic ocean about three miles or so due-west from the *Dun-beg*, a point which forms, I may observe, the most western point of land in Europe.

Mr. Du Noyer's view of the use of *Dun-beg* fort not correct;

Mr. Du Noyer believes that the *Dun-beg* fort in the east was intended as a protection to the supposed "city" of Fahan, which he thinks lay scattered over a distance of three miles west from it; but he gives no place in the protective idea to the *Dun-mór* fort which is at the other end of the line, although it is quite clear that the idea which suggested the erection of the one must have suggested the erection of the other; and if the idea of both was the protection of the presumed "city", there was a very lamentable defect in the design, for, whilst one or both ends of the "city" may have had the benefit of protection from one or both of the forts, the whole sea and land lines in front and rear of the "city" were left without any protection whatever. It cannot, of course, be supposed that a stronghold erected on a point of land projecting considerably into the sea beyond the front line, and at one end of the presumed "city", could have formed any possible protection to it, while its front and rear were quite exposed by water and land; and the same objection holds good as regards the Great Fort at the other end.

this and the other forts did not form part of a line of fortifications;

These forts in fact were not intended for the immediate protection of anything but what happened to be permanently (or at all events occasionally, in time of danger) kept or placed within their walls If the fort of *Dun-beg* had been multiplied into a line of forts or "cahers", or continued into such a wall as formed itself, but carried on northwards from it to the harbour of Smerwick, that is, across the entire neck of the head-land, then indeed would there have been a protection for the inhabitants of Fahan, as well as for all the others within this line. Again, there is not anything in the character of these particular *cathairs* and *clochans* to warrant the conclusion that they belong to an age of an antiquity beyond our historic period. And it can be shown from the most ancient historical authorities which we possess, that the two kinds of building to be found at *Glenn Fahan*, namely, the stone forts now called "cahers", and the bee-hive stone houses found within them, now called *clochans*, have their types in one of the most ancient buildings—indeed the most ancient now identified—in Ireland, namely that of *Aileach* in the county of Donegal, of which I have already spoken.

And are not prehistoric.

This ancient *Rath* of *Aileach*, as you may remember, was originally built by orders of the *Daghda Mór*—the great king of the *Tuatha Dé Dananns*—around the sepulchre of his son, fourteen hundred years it is supposed before the Christian era. We are told that the work was performed by his two *caisleors*, or stone-castle builders, namely *Garbhan* and *Imcheall*. *Garbhan* is recorded to have shaped and chipped the stones, while *Imcheall* set them all round the house, until the laborious work was finished, and until the top of the house called that of the "groaning hostages" was closed by a single stone. This house was one of those within the circle of the great *rath*, which contained, of course, all the various houses or buildings requisite for the establishment of the king even of a very comparatively small number of subjects; the whole ending with that very necessary appendage to a king's palace in those days, a house or prison for hostages and pledges. As this house is described as having been closed at the top with one stone, there can be no doubt of the shape of it,—a shape which was probably common to it with all the others.

A clochan built within the Rath of Aileach.

And here, as to the name of *cathair*: it is remarkable that in the old poem already quoted, as well as in several other pieces in prose and verse which refer to this ancient structure ("the senior or parent of all the edifices of Erinn", as the poem calls it)—this stone building never goes by the name of *cathair*. The old poem calls it alternately *rath*, and *dun*, and even *caislen*, or castle, but never *cathair*; nor do we find any other edifice of the early *Firbolgs*, *Tuatha Dé Danann*, or Milesians, called a *cathair*, except in one instance alone, where it is stated in an ancient poem that Tara was called *Cathair Crofin* in the time of the *Tuatha Dé Danann*. And this fact holds good even to a comparatively

Limited use of the term cathair.

 late period as regards the *Firbolgs*. On their return to Erinn —after an absence of several hundred years, after the battle of *Magh Tuireadh* (under the designation of the *Clann Umoir*), the people of this race received liberty from *Ailill* and *Medbh*, the king and queen of Connacht, to settle in the western half and on the sea-board of the present counties of Galway and Clare, as well as in the Arann Islands. And here, where they raised for themselves, as on the Arann Islands, those enormous fortresses of stone, some of which remain in wonderful preservation to this day, these fortresses were never called *cathairs;* and those on the Arann Islands are still, as well as in all ancient times, called *duns*, and named after their respective builders or owners, as *Dun-Ænghuis* and *Dun-Ochaill*, on the great island, and *Dun-Chonchraidh*, on the middle island. There is also, indeed, on the great island, another most ancient fortress, bearing the name of no particular person, but called simply *Dubh-Chathair*,[35] or the "Black *Cathair*". These are all built of stone, and I imagine simply because no other material could be procured on those rocky islands.

It is remarkable that there are no *clochans*, or bee-hive houses, remaining around any of these great forts, whilst they are found with the Christian churches; save that there are some traces of the ruins of such edifices within the area of *Dun-Conchraidh* on the middle island; though whether they were of the same date as the fortress cannot now be ascertained.

The same term not always applied to the same kind of building.

It may be remembered that the period to which the erection of these edifices is referred by all our old writings, is the century immediately preceding the Incarnation. And to show that in those ancient times this people were not wedded to any particular descriptive names for their residences,[36] we find from the same authorities, that others of the *Clann Umoir* gave other names to their residences, as in the case of *Daolach*, who, with *Endach*, his brother, settled on the river *Davil* (on the coast of Burren, in the county of Clare), whose dwelling was called *Teach Eandaich*, literally *Eandach*'s House; and this house was most undoubtedly built of stone, since other materials are as scarce in the district as in Arann; and as it was intended for a fortress as well as a residence, it must have been of large dimensions, and could not, therefore, have been of the bee-hive

[35] This *Dubh Chathair* would seem to be a common modern name, like Mr. Du Noyer's "Fort of the doors", etc. This fortress is not apparently coeval with the others on the islands: why has it no name? The name could not have been lost, any more than the others.

[36] Just as at the present day large mansions, some of them castellated, are called "halls", "houses", "courts", "manors", etc. *Cathair* is like the French *chateau* (a castle or grand residence).

shape. This house is not now known, as far as I am aware, though the locality still bears the ancient name of *Daolach*. LECT. XXII.

While, however, we have no account of stone-built cities, towns, or even villages, in ancient Erinn, it is yet certain that wherever the provincial king, or the chief and leader of a territory, as well as the head of a tribe, had his residence, it was surrounded by a town or village, as the case might be; and that the houses were built of such materials as were most convenient and compatible with the position and resources of the inhabitants. And we may, I think, also reasonably suppose, if we do not actually believe it, that wherever the requirements of position, or the peculiar taste of an individual chief or tribe, made stone the material of the "head-house" of the territory, there the houses of the next in importance at least, if not all the houses of the tribe which must have surrounded it, were built, if possible, of the same material.

As an instance of the character and condition of the *dun*, *rath*, or *cathair*, in very ancient times, I may be permitted to give you here a short extract from an ancient tract preserved in *Leabhar na h-Uidhre*, a manuscript of about the eleventh century, preserved in the Royal Irish Academy, and so often quoted in the course of these lectures. The story from which I am about to quote is one which grew out of that *Bricrind's Feast*, already described.

Tale of the dispute about the "champion's share".

Cuchulainn, *Conall Cearnach*, and *Laeghaire Buadhach* were the great leading champions of Ulster at the period of, as well as a short time previous to, the Incarnation. Between these three knights of the Royal Branch of Ulster there had been for a long time a dispute as to which of them was best entitled to what was called the *curadh-mir*, or "champion's share" at table at all the great feasts and solemnities of the province. After having submitted their case together with their respective claims, to several parties for arbitration, but without success, they were at last advised to repair to the *cathair*, or mansion of *Curoi Mac Dáire*, king of West Munster. And this *cathair* was situated on a shoulder of a high mountain which is said to be called even to this day *Cathair Conroi*, and which is a part of *Sliabh Mis*, situated on the peninsula which separates the bay of Tralee on the north from the bay of Dingle or Castlemaine on the south, in the county of Kerry.

Smith's notice of *Sliabh Mis*.

As to this mountain, Smith in his History of Kerry, published in the year 1756, and at page 156, says: "On the top of this mountain is a circle of massy stones, laid one on the other in the manner of a Danish intrenchment: several of them are from eigth to ten cubical feet, but they are all very rude.

"From the situation of the place, it resembles a beacon or place of guard to alarm the country; but from the prodigious size of the stones, it rather seems to be a monument of some great action performed near this place, or perhaps a sepulchral trophy raised over some eminent person.

"This piece of antiquity stands on the summit of a conical mountain, which is more than seven hundred yards above the level of the sea, and forms a kind of peninsula between two very fine bays. The country people, from the height and steepness of it, and the largeness of the stones, will have it to be the work and labour of a giant, and it seems indeed wonderful how human strength, unassisted by engines, could possibly raise stones of such a prodigious weight to the summit of so steep and high a mountain".

Dr. Smith adds two notes, one on the way in which stones of enormous size and weight were carried, in comparatively modern times, in other parts of the world, for purposes and to situations similar to the present; and in the other note he gives from Keting's History of Ireland, the popular but ancient story of the destruction of this formidable fortress.

Story of the dispute about the "champion's share", continued.

But to return to our story. The three contending champions of Ulster set out from *Emania*, and in due time arrived at *Cathair Conroi*. *Curoi*, the lord of the fortress, was not at home on their arrival, being absent on a foreign expedition, so that the visitors were received by his wife, the beautiful *Blathnaid*. When night came the lady told the three knights that when her husband was leaving home he acquainted her with this intended visit, and requested that they should keep watch over his palace during their sojourn,—each in turn to watch a night, according to seniority. This request was at once acceded to; and *Laeghaire Buadhach*, the eldest of the three, undertook the watch for the first night.

After this the story proceeds in an exaggerated strain of fable; but even in the midst of the greatest extravagance of incident, it contains so many details of the form and the various appurtenances of an ancient fortified mansion, that I believe I shall best make use of the piece by translating a portion of it with all its extravagance, just as it stands in the original:—

"*Laeghaire Buadhach* then went to the watching the first night, because he was the senior of the three of them. He was in the warder's seat after that until the end of the night, when he saw a champion away from him as far as his eye could reach, on the sea to the west, coming towards him. Huge, and ugly, and hateful appeared this champion to him, for it seemed to him that his head reached the sky in height, and he could plainly see the broad expanse of the ocean between his legs. The phantom

Story of the dispute about the "champion's share", continued.

came towards him, with only his two handsful of oak saplings, and each bare pole of them was sufficient to make the swingle-tree of a plough, and no pole of them required the repetition of the one stroke of the sword by which it was cut from its stem. He threw one of these branches at *Laeghaire*, but *Laeghaire* evaded it. He repeated this twice or thrice, but none of them reached *Laeghaire's* body or shield. *Laeghaire* cast at him a spear, but it did not reach him. He stretched his arm towards *Laeghaire* then, and the arm was so long that it reached over the three ridges that were between them at the casting, and he then grasped him in his hand. Though large and though portly a man was *Laeghaire*, he fitted in the one hand of the man whom he encountered, with as much ease as would a child of one year old; and he pressed him between his two palms, in the same way that a chessman is pressed in a groove. When at length he was half dead in that way, he threw a cast of him over the *cathair* from without, so that he fell upon the bench at the door of the royal house [within], and the *cathair* was not opened for that purpose at all. The other two champions and all the inhabitants of the *cathair* thought it was by a leap over the *cathair* that he came from without, in order to leave the watching to the other men. They spent that day together till the evening, when the watch hour came, when *Conall Cearnach* went out to the warder's seat, because he was older than *Cuchulainn;* but he met with exactly the same adventure which *Laeghaire* met with on the previous night. The third night came, and *Cuchulainn* took his place in the warder's seat. This was precisely the night upon which the three green men of *Seiscenn Uairbeoil*, and the three *Buagelltaigh* [or itinerant cow-keepers] of *Bregia*, and the three sons of the musical *Dornmar*, had appointed to come to the *cathair*. It was, too, the night which had been prophesied that the monster which inhabited the lake near the *cathair* would devour the occupants of the whole establishment, both man and beast. *Cuchulainn*, however, continued to watch throughout the night, and he experienced many mishaps. When midnight came, he heard a loud noise approach: 'Speak, speak!' said *Cuchulainn;* 'whoever are there, let them speak if friends, let them attack if foes'. Thereupon there was set up a fearful shout at him. *Cuchulainn* sprang upon them then, so that it was dead the nine men came to the ground. He then cut off their heads and placed them near him in the watching-seat. Suddenly nine more shouted at him; but, to make the story short, he killed the three times nine plunderers in the same manner, and he heaped up their heads and their arms in one heap in the same place. He kept his place after that till the end of the night, tired, weary, and

LECT. XXII.

Story of the dispute about the "champion's share", continued.

fatigued, when he heard the uprising of the lake, as if it were the noise of a great sea. His ardour induced him, notwithstanding his great fatigue, to go to see the cause of the great noise which he had heard, and he presently perceived the tumult which the monster had produced. It appeared to him that there were thirty cubits of it above the lake. It then raised itself up into the air, and sprang towards the *cathair;* and it so opened its jaws that the vat of a king's house might enter them. He [*Cuchulainn*] then executed his *form-ehleas*, and sprang up [in the air too], and with the velocity of a twisting-wheel flew around the monster. He closed his two hands around its neck then, and then directed one of them to its mouth and down its throat, and tore the heart out of it. He then cast it from him upon the ground, and he plied its sword upon it, cutting it to pieces, and carried its head to the watching-seat, where he placed it along with the other heads.

"*Cuchulainn* took some rest after these mighty exploits, until the dawn of the morning, when he saw the great phantom coming from off the western sea towards him". But, without repeating details, it is sufficient for our present purpose to state, that his good fortune and his stout heart and arm stood to him on this occasion as it did in his previous encounters, and that he overthrew the phantom giant, as he did the rest of the enemies of *Curoi*'s court.

Our hero then bethought him that his companions, who preceded him in the wardership the two previous nights, must have jumped over the wall of the *cathair*, as they had been seen to fall from the air within, when cast over by the giant, and he determined not to be outdone by them in this stupendous feat. The story then goes on in the same extravagant style of language which we meet in the tale of the battle of *Magh-Rath* (published by the Archæological Society), and in many other such pieces, as follows:—

"He attempted twice to leap over, but he failed. 'Alas!' said he, 'that I have taken so much trouble hitherto to secure the "Champion's share", and to lose it now by failing to take the leap which the other knights have accomplished'. What *Cuchulainn* did at these words was this: He would fly from where he stood, at one time, until his face would come plump against the *cathair*. At another time he would spring up into the air, so that he could see all that was within the *cathair*. At another time he would fall down and sink to his knees in the ground, from the pressure of his ardour and his strength. At another time he would not disturb the dew from the top of the grass, from the buoyancy of his spirit, and the velocity

LECT. XXII. Story of the dispute about the "champion's share", continued.

of his motion, and the vehemence of his action, such was the bounding fury into which he had been excited. At last, in one of these furious fits he flew over the *cathair* from without and alighted in the middle of the *cathair* within, at the door of the royal house; and the place [or print] of his two feet remains still in the flag which is in the middle of the *cathair*, where it stood at the door of the royal house. He entered the house then, and heaved a deep sigh: upon which *Blathnaid*, the daughter of *Midir* and wife of *Curoi*, said: 'That is not a sigh after treachery', said she; 'it is a sigh after victory and triumph'. The daughter of the king of *Firfalgia* indeed knew what difficulties had beset *Cuchulainn* on that night. They had not been long there after that when they saw *Curoi* entering the house, having with him the battle suits of the three nines *Cuchulainn* had slain, together with their heads and the head of the monster. He said then—after having put all the heads down on the floor of the house: 'The youth whose trophies of one night are all these', said he, 'is a youth most qualified to keep perpetual watch over a king's *dun*'. And *Curoi* then awarded *Cuchulainn* the 'Champion's share' at all the feasts of Ulster, and to his wife precedence of all the ladies of Ulster, at feasts, fairs, and assemblies, the queen of the province excepted".

I have not, as will be seen, been deterred by the wildness of this very ancient tale from quoting directly from the original, as much of it as bears directly on the condition and circumstances of this ancient *cathair*, of the existence and rational history of which there cannot be the least doubt.

It is of some importance in the discussion on ancient stone edifices, to find still in existence one not only of undoubted authenticity, but even preserving through ages down even to the present day the name of the man for whom it was built, as well as that of the man who built it; for in the list of builders in stone who were attached to certain great men, already quoted from the Book of Leinster, *Cingdorn* is set down as *Curoi Mac Dáiré's caisleoir*, or stone-builder.

The "guard room" or "watching seat".

The description of this *cathair* when occupied is important, in as far as it explains on authority the actual use and intention of those small internal and external chambers, the ruins of which are found among the "cahers" and "*cloghauns*" represented in Mr. Du Noyer's beautiful plates, and to some of which he properly gives the names of "guard rooms". One of these described in connection with *Cathair Conroi* is called a *suidhe-faire*, or "watching-seat", and was one of those situated outside the wall.

The royal mansion of *Curoi Mac Dáiré*, king of West Mun-

ECT. XXII. ster, which stood in the middle of this once great *cathair*, was, no doubt, one of considerable dimensions, and built of stone; but unfortunately, as no trace of it is known to remain now, and as no precise description of it is given in our story, we are left to guess that it was probably a building somewhat of the size and form of the house of the royal branch at *Emania*, or of the house in *Rath Cruachain* which I have already described. Even the exact situation of the historic *Cathair Conroi* has not been satisfactorily ascertained; although Dr. Charles Smith in his History of Kerry, already quoted, places it on the very summit of a conical mountain of that name, and describes by this title the highest of the *Sliabh Mis* range, a mountain 2,100 feet above the level of the sea. This, however, could scarcely be correct, as no human dwelling, much less the fortified palace of a king, would be placed in so inaccessible a position. And, therefore, the heaps of large stones which Dr. Smith mentions as existing on the top of this mountain, if they be ancient remains at all, must probably be those of a ruined sepulchral monument, and not those of *Curoi*'s *Cathair*.

osition of *athair onroi* not xactly ascrtained.

On the Ordnance Survey map *Cathair Conroi* is marked but at an elevation of one thousand feet above the level of the sea, and at or near the source of the little river *Finnghlais*, which runs down the side of the mountain and falls into the bay of Tralee near its western extremity. This would certainly be the proper position for *Cathair Conroi*, according to the old topographical tract called the *Dinnseanchas*, which professes to give the origin of the name of this stream. And as this story too has reference to *Cathair Conroi*, and as the substance of it, given in a few words, may enable some one who hears or reads them to identify with certainty the site of this famous *cathair*, I shall briefly narrate it here.

tory of the rigin of the ame of the iver *Finnhlais.*

We have seen before how graciously the lady *Blathnaid*, king *Curoi Mac Dáiré*'s wife, had received the three rival champions of Ulster at her court, and how warmly *Curoi* himself, on his return home, had eulogized *Cuchulainn*'s valour in guarding his court. Yet, notwithstanding these commendations from *Curoi*, there existed an old cause of dissension between him and *Cuchulainn*. *Curoi*'s wife, the beautiful *Blathnaid*, was the daughter of *Midir*, king of the island of *Firfalgia*, which some of our old writers say was a name for the present Isle of Mann. In a successful attack made on this island by the chief heroes of Ulster, headed by *Cuchulainn*, and assisted by *Curoi Mac Dáiré*, who joined them in disguise as a simple champion, the chief prize among the spoils obtained was the king's daughter, this lady *Blathnaid*. Accordingly, on the return of the party to Ulster,

Cuchulaind, on the division of the spoil, claimed the fair princess as his share. To this, however, *Curoi Mac Dáiré* objected, and said that, as the highest exploit connected with the assault on *Midir*'s court had been performed by him (*Curoi*), he thought it but fair that he should carry off the highest prize. A combat ensued, in which *Curoi*'s more mature strength, joined with equal military skill, prevailed over the more youthful *Cuchulaind*. The latter was left vanquished on the field, tied hand-and-foot, and his long hair cut off close to the back of his head by the sword of his proud conqueror. *Curoi* and his beautiful captive set out then, and arrived in due time at the famous *Cathair* on *Sliabh Mis*.

LECT. XXI

It does not appear that *Cuchulaind* had any subsequent knowledge of the fate of the fair captive until he saw her in the court of her husband; and it seems that it was then for the first time that he discovered who his victorious antagonist for her possession had been, as *Curoi* had gone on the expedition completely disguised. It would seem, however, that some understanding of a friendly nature sprang up between *Cuchulaind* and his fair hostess during his short sojourn at her court, from what we are told in the old story of *Orgain Cathrach Chonrai* (or "the Slaughter of *Cathair Chonrai*"), which was one of the Great Stories the *ollamh* was accustomed and bound to relate before the king. In this old story we are told that, in some time after the visit of the three Ulster knights to *Cathair Chonrai*, the lady *Blathnaid* sent a secret message to *Cuchulaind*, inviting him to come at an appointed time, and well attended, to the foot of the hill upon which her court was situated, and to stop at an appointed place on the brink of the river which flowed down by the *Cathair*, until he should see its waters changing colour, and then rapidly to ascend the mountain to the *Cathair*, where she would contrive to place her husband, unarmed, in his absolute power. All this was done accordingly; and *Cuchulaind* had not remained long watching the flowing water of the river, until he saw it suddenly change in colour from dark to white. This change of colour was produced by the spilling of several tubs of milk into the stream, where it passed by the *Cathair*, by orders of the lady *Blaithnaid;* and soon this silent message informed *Cuchulaind* that all was ready.

Story of "the Slaughter of *Cathair Chonrai*".

Cuchulaind immediately ascended to the *Cathair*, which he found, as was promised to him, open and unguarded. He found the royal mansion within in the same condition; and, on entering that, the lady *Blathnaid* sitting on a couch by the side of her husband, who lay asleep with his head in her lap, his sword and spears hanging on a rack over the couch. *Cuchulaind*'s first care was to secure the sword and spears; and then

LECT. XXII. giving the sleeping warrior a smart prick of his sword in the side, to awaken him—so that it should not be said he slew him while in his sleep—he cut off his head.

The court was next stripped of all its valuables; and *Cuchulaind* with the treacherous *Blathnaid*, taking with them a quantity of rich spoils gathered from all parts of the world, returned in safety to Ulster. If the stream which passed by *Cathair Chonrai* had received a name before this time, it thenceforth lost it, for it is ever since, even to this day, known as the *Finnghlais*, or "white-stream". And therefore any person taking this white-stream, still so well known in the locality, as his guide, and following it up the mountain, may perhaps discover the ancient *Cathair Chonrai*, some vestiges of which must still exist.

Reference to *Cathair Chonrai* in the tale of the "Battle of Ventry Harbour".

Cathair Chonrai appears to have been well known at the time of writing the old tale called *Cath Finntragha*, or Battle of Ventry Harbour. The name Ventry is a vulgar anglicised form of *Finntraigh;* a name which literally signifies "white-strand", and which is very applicable to the shore of that famous harbour, which is covered with beautiful white sand.

In this old story we are told that when *Find Mac Cumhaill* was marching from the eastern parts of Ireland to the great battle of Ventry, he passed over the river Maige, in the county of Limerick, into *Ciarruidhe Luachra*, or Kerry, and then passed over the long white strand (of the bay) of Tralee, with his left hand to *Cathair na-Claen Ratha*, which was called *Cathair Chonrai*, and to *Sliabh Mis*, and so from that to the mouth of the *Labhrand*, and so on to *Finntraigh* [Ventry].

I cannot take upon myself to say that the places mentioned in this march are all correctly set down; but the reference to *Cathair Chonrai* appears to be correct, as it was after *Find* had passed over the strand of Tralee, that he is said to have passed by it leaving it on his left; and this would exactly agree with the position on the map of the river *Finnghlais*, which falls into the western extremity of the bay of Tralee.

Another curious bit of additional information, if it be correct, is supplied by this tale, namely, that *Cathair Chonrai* was also called *Cathair na-Claen Ratha*, that is, the "*Cathair* of the sloping *Rath*"; and probably *Claen Rath*, or "sloping *Rath*" only. And this may lead farther to the identification of the old *Cathair*, since, perhaps, it may be still known under the name of *Cathair na-Claen Ratha*, or of *Claen Rath* only.

So much for the construction, position, and history of one of the most celebrated of the ancient stone buildings of the Milesians, of which we are fortunate in having an example preserved so well in the description of *Cathair Chonrai*.

Some writers, I know not why, have assumed that the more ancient colonists of Erinn, the *Firbolgs* and *Tuatha Dé Danann*, from a superiority of knowlege and taste, erected stone buildings in preference to earthen ones; whilst their successors, the Milesians, being of a lower order of intellect, and having reached only a lower scale of cultivation, were content with forts and houses built of earth, or of wood. Nothing could be more unfounded than this assertion. And I have already, I think, fully shown its fallacy by placing before the reader a list of the buildings ascribed during the first occupation of this island, to those two colonies, in which our oldest chronicles and traditions ascribe but the one single stone building of *Aileach*, to the *Firbolgs* and *Tuatha Dé Danann*. And if the *Firbolgs*, who, after centuries of absence, returned to Erinn a short time before the Incarnation of our Lord, erected for themselves some fortresses of stone on the western coast of Erinn, where no other building material could be found, yet, nothing remains in writing, in tradition, or in any existing monumental ruin, to show that those chiefs of that tribe who at the same time settled inland, in the territories of South Connacht and North Munster, where stone was scarce and other material abundant, built their fortresses and residences of the former and not of the latter. It may also be asked why did not the *Firbolgs* and the *Tuatha Dé Danann* erect some stone building at Tara during their successive occupations of it? Surely, if they preferred stone to wood, they would have been more likely to have indulged that taste at the seat of royalty than elsewhere.

Modern hypothesis of the inferiority of the Milesians.

All that can be said in favour of this modern theory of the superiority of the older colonists over the Milesians, is, that tradition ascribes necromantic power and a superiority of inventive genius to the *Tuatha Dé Danann;* but among the specimens of ancient personal decorative art which have come down in such abundance to our own times, nothing has been as yet found to equal in ingenuity, or in artistic taste and excellence, articles, such as brooches, girdles, and torques, in the precious metals, the fabrication of which can be clearly shown to be Milesian.

The most artistic works are Milesian.

Then, as regards those stone buildings about the southern and western coasts of Ireland, being all of *Firbolg* or *Tuatha Dé Danann*, or of pre-historic erection, whatever may be said in favour of the hypothesis as regards all places on the coast north of the Shannon, there can certainly be no reason for extending it to the coast south of that river.

Stone buildings not all pre-Milesian.

There is to be found in the Books of Ballymote and *Lecan*, and in *Dubhaltach Mac Firbhisigh*'s Book of Genealogies, a

The *Aitheach Tuatha* or *Attecotti*.

LECT. XXII. very curious list of the tribes who took part in the great *Aitheach Tuatha* revolution in the first century, and of the dispersion and enslavement—to some extent—of these tribes, in the same century, by the monarch *Tuathal Teachtmhar*, on recovering the throne of his father, who had been killed in that revolution.[37] Those revolutionary tribes are very generally believed to have been the oppressed and degraded descendants of the pre-Milesian colonists; but, although great numbers of them belonged to the earlier races, yet a great many of them belonged to the decayed Milesian race also, as well as to the Picts who had settled in the east of Ireland. These revolutionists have been called *Attacotti* by modern Irish writers; but, whether they really were the *Attacotti* of Romano-British history is a question that, I fear, will never be cleared up. It is, however, certain from the detailed list just alluded to, that they consisted not all of one race, but of a number of tribes belonging to the various races which then inhabited the country. There can be no doubt, however, that among those revolutionary tribes there was a large proportion of the *Firbolg* race, who, from a list of the battles in which they were defeated, appear to have been in valour and social position the most formidable opponents that *Tuathal* had to contend with. And it is not to be supposed that, when these various tribes were reduced to the condition of rent-payers to the state, they therefore disappeared, or even sunk into insignificance. It was not so: for, we find about the close of the sixth century that the whole country of *Ui-Maine*, in the present counties of Galway and Roscommon, was in the actual possession of the *Firbolgs* when, about that time, it was forcibly wrested from them by *Maine Mór* of the race of *Colla da Chrioch*, ancestor of the O'Kellys of that country. There is a curious and somewhat romantic account of this conquest in the Life of Saint *Greallan*, patron of the territory, preserved in the Royal Irish Academy, an extract from which is published in the "Tribes and Customs of Hy-Maine", printed in 1843 by the Irish Archæological Society.

The *Firbolgs* still powerful in the sixth century.

Now, the Firbolgs down to the historic times preserved territories and importance; and we have very fair evidence to show that, during a space of more than a thousand years, they held possession, one way or another, of the whole province of Connacht, often as sovereigns. It would be but reasonable, therefore, to expect—if "cahers" and stone-building were peculiar characteristics of their civilization—that vestiges of such building should even still remain, in connection with the townland

(37) See in Appendix the note on this subject.

and other topographical names, without any reference to the immediate presence or absence of stone in any particular district of their extensive territory. I have made out a list from the census of 1851 of all the townland names in Ireland, as taken from the Ordnance Survey, into the names of which the word *Cathair* enters, and, as the list is not long, I shall, without going into the local distribution of the names, give a summary of it here.

Townland names derived from *Cathairs*.

In the whole province of Ulster there is not one townland taking its name from a *Cathair*. In Leinster there are but two—one in the county of Longford, and one in the Queen's County. In Munster there are 151, distributed as follows among the counties: Clare, 58; Cork, 32; Kerry, 35; Limerick, 17; Tipperary, 5; and Waterford, 4. In Connacht there are 91, distributed as follows: Galway, 67; Mayo, 22, of which there are 15 in the inland barony of Castlemaine; and in Roscommon there are 2; thus showing, among the many thousands of townlands in Ireland, that there are but 244 which take their names from *Cathairs;* whilst the number of names compounded of *Dún*, *Lis*, and *Rath*, is very great, but particularly the latter, which is more than three times the number of all the others. Nor can this paucity of *Cathairs*, to be found at the present day in our topography, be ascribed, to any extent, to modern changes; since we find that they held exactly the same places and proportions in the inquisitions of Leinster and Ulster, taken in the reigns of Elizabeth, James the First, Charles the First, and Charles the Second, and published—so far as these two provinces about thirty years ago, under the direction of the Irish Record Commission.

It is also worth noticing that while the county of Galway preserves the names of sixty-seven *Cathairs*, of these only six are found in the eastern or Shannon-board baronies of the county, while in the neighbouring baronies of Athlone and Moycarne, in the county of Roscommon, there are none to be found. And yet we know that the eastern parts of Galway and Roscommon were the places longest and last held by the *Firbolgs* in Erinn.

No evidence that the Milesians were a ruder race than the previous colonists.

From all that I have said, then, it may be collected concerning the primitive colonists of Erinn, as we find them set down in our chronicles, as well as in our oral traditions, and—what is even more important—in our topographical names, that nothing now remains to show, with any certainty, that the periods of occupation of the various races were marked by any distinct characteristics of civilization or social refinement. And surely it is not to be supposed that the Milesians, who came in the last,

LECT. XXII. even if they were, as pretended—a ruder race—would conti[illegible] to adhere to their own less refined habits and tastes, after t[illegible] had become masters of the country, and that in presence of [illegible] superior civilization of their now fallen predecessors, who [illegible] remained in peace under their rule, and lived in import[illegible] numbers around them.

LECTURE XXIII.

[Delivered July 5th, 1860.]

(VIII.)—**Of Dress and Ornaments.** Early sumptuary law regulating the colours of dress, attributed to the monarchs *Tighernmas* and *Eochaidh Edgudach*. Native gold first smelted by *Iuchadan*, and golden ornaments made in Ireland in the reign of *Tighernmas*. The uses of colours to distinguish the several classes of society, also attributed to the same *Eochaidh*; the nature of those colours not specified. Household utensils, ornaments and variously coloured dresses of *Ailill* and *Medhbh* mentioned in the tale of the *Táin Bo Chuailgne*; the material or fashion of the dress not specified. *Medhbh*'s preparation for the war of the first *Táin*; description of the parties summoned. Description of the Ultonian clanns at the hill of *Slemain*, forming the army in pursuit of *Ailill* and *Medhbh*, by the herald of the latter, *Mac Roth*, from the tale of the *Táin Bo Chuailgne*; his description of *Conchobar Mac Nessa*; of *Causcraid Mend*; of *Sencha*; of *Eogan Mac Durthachta*; of *Loaegaire Buadach*; of *Munremur*; of *Connud*; of *Reochaid*; of *Amargin*: of *Feradach Find Fechtnach*; of *Fiachaig* and *Fiachna*; of *Celtchair Mac Uthair* and his clann; of *Eirrge Echbel*; of *Mend*, son of *Salcholgan*; of *Fergna*; of *Ercc*, son of *Carpri Nia Fer* and his clann; of *Cuchulaind*'s clann. Note: *Cuchulaind* is removed to *Muirtheimne* after his fight with *Ferdiadh*, to get the benefit of the healing properties of its stream or river; enumeration of them; while there, *Cethern*, who had gone to his assistance, arrives covered with wounds, and is visited by physicians from the enemy's camp, whom he drives away; *Cuchulaind* then sends for *Fingin Fathliagh*, who examines each of his wounds, and *Cethern* describes the persons who gave them—his description of *Illand*, son of *Fergus*; of queen *Medhbh*; of *Oll* and *Othine*; of *Bun* and *Meccon*; of *Broen* and *Brudni*, sons of *Teora Soillsi*, king of *Caille*; of *Cormac* [*Mac*] *Colomarig* and *Cormac* the son of *Maelefoga*; of *Mane Mathremail*, and *Mane Athremail*, sons of *Ailill* and *Medhbh*; of the champions from *Iruade* [Norway]; of *Ailill* and his son *Mane*; of the marrow bath by which *Cethern* was healed, whence the name of *Smirammair*, now Smarmore, in the county Louth. *Medhbh* enumerates her dowry to *Ailill*; gifts promised by her to *Long Mac Emonis*; gifts promised by her to *Ferdiadh*; one of those gifts, her celebrated brooch, weighed more than four pounds. Story of *Mac Conglinde*; his extravagant dream; his description of a curious dress of a door-keeper; analysis of the dress—the *Cochall*, the *Ionar*, the *Ochrath*; analysis of *Mac Conglinde*'s own dress; his *Leinidh*. Distinction between the *Léine* and the *Leinidh*—the latter was a kilt. Description of the dress of the champion *Edchu Rond* in the tale of the Exile of the Sons of *Duildermait*; he wore a kilt. Ancient law regulating the wearing of the *Leinidh* or kilt, and the *Ochrath* or pantaloon.

In the last four lectures I applied myself to the subject of the dwellings of the people of ancient Erinn, the forms in which their houses and their strong places were built, the materials used, and the manner of building adopted in those early ages. I proceed now to give some account of the personal dress and ornaments, and of the laws connected with dress, its materials and manufacture, as we find them described in our ancient

XXIII. writings, as well as the various sumptuary laws by which particular robes and ornaments were regulated in very early times.

One of the earliest entries in our ancient books connected with my present subject, and referring to a period usually considered so remote as fifteen hundred years before the Christian era, is a notice of a sumptuary law regulating the colours to be worn in dress. Such a law implies necessarily a considerable advance in the arts connected with weaving and dyeing. The introduction of diversity of colours in dress is attributed to the monarch *Tighernmas*, who is said to have reigned at the remote period just mentioned. To the monarch *Eochaidh Edgudach* or "*Eochaidh*, the cloth designer", is attributed the extension and complete establishment of this early sumptuary law. The Book of Leinster, which is the oldest authority that I am acquainted with on this subject, thus speaks of it: "*Tighernmas*, the son of *Ollaig*, then assumed the sovereignty, and he broke three times nine battles before the end of a year upon the descendants of *Eber*. It was by him that drinking horns (or cups) were first introduced into Erinn. It was by him that gold was first smelted [the word used means literally boiled] in Erinn, and that colours were first put into cloths (namely—brown, red, and crimson), and ornamental borders. It was by him that ornaments and brooches of gold and silver were first made. *Iuchadan* was the name of the artificer who smelted the gold in the forests on the east side of the river Liffey. And *Tighernmas* was seventy-seven years in the sovereignty, and he nearly extirpated the descendants of *Eber* during that time. And he died in *Magh Slecht*, in the great meeting of *Magh Slecht*, and three-fourths of the men of Erinn died along with him, whilst adoring *Crum Cruach*, the king-idol of Erinn; and there survived accordingly but one-fourth of the men of Erinn. . . . The one-fourth who survived of the men of Erinn gave the sovereignty to *Eochaidh Edgudach*, the son of *Dairé Domthig*, of the seed of *Lugaidh*, the son of *Ith*".[38] It

Sumptuary law regulating the colours of dress.

First smelting of gold;

and making of golden ornaments.

(38) [original:—Gabas Tigernmas mac Ollaig rige iar clanna Conn [? . . . .] tain acas bris tri noi caṫa re cind bliaḋna for Claind Eber. Is leis tuca cuirn atuis in Heren. Is les ro berbad or ar tus in Herinn, acas [tucaḋ*] daṫa for etaige acas corcara [.i. ruamna dearga, acas corcra] is leis denaḋ Ċumtaige acas bretnasa óir, acas argit in Herenn. Iuċadan ainm na cerda ro berbad inór hiroċraib qas [?] Lire. Acas bai lxxvii. m-bliaḋain irrigain Herenn, acas is bec nar doilgend Claind Eber as in re sin. Conerbailt in Maig Sleċt immóṙdáil Maig Sleċt acas teora cethramthana fer n-Erenn malle fris, ic adrad Ċroim Ċroiċ, rig idaill Herenn. Conaterna amlaitisin act cenċeċramtha fer nHerenn . . . Do rat in cethramthu Herenn dororaib (Erenn) rige do Eochaidh Edgudaċ mac Daire Domthig, do sil Lugdaċ mac Iṫa". H. 2. 18. f. 8. b. col. 2. mid.]

* Word effaced, but was probably that in brackets.

was by this *Eochaidh*, we are told by Keating, on the authority of a similar ancient record in existence in his time, but now lost, that cloth was first coloured crimson, blue, and green, in Erinn. It was by him that various colours were introduced into the wearing clothes of Erinn, namely, one colour in the clothes of servants; two colours in the clothes of rent-paying farmers; three colours in the clothes of officers; five colours in the clothes of chiefs; six colours in the clothes of *ollamhs* and poets; seven colours in the clothes of kings and queens. It is from this that (says the old book) the custom has grown this day, that all these colours are in the clothes of a bishop.

Variety of colours in dress first used to distinguish classes;

Although the number of colours, which are here mentioned as having distinguished each of the seven classes into which the people of Erinn at so early a period had been divided by the Milesian colonists, are given, yet we have no description specifying what these colours were exactly, which were then employed in dress, excepting brown, red, and crimson, which *Tighernmas* is stated to have previously established. It could scarcely be expected, indeed, that such a description would survive to our times in any other way than by accidental references in the course of history to the costume or wardrobes of particular individuals. And although we may not find any personal description identical with that of the higher classes in the above list, it happens that we have a very ancient reference to, and even an enumeration of, the various colours which were used in the select wardrobe of royalty, at a period which, though far within that of *Tighernmas*, is yet remote enough from us indeed. I allude here to the account of the display of their valuables of all kinds, made by the celebrated *Medbh*, queen of Connacht, and her consort, *Ailill*, as described in the opening of the ancient tale of the *Táin Bo Chuailgne*, so often quoted from in the course of these lectures.

exact nature of these colours not specified.

Ailill and *Medbh*, it may be remembered, flourished in the century immediately preceding the Christian era. The reader will, doubtless, remember the account of their conversation in the palace of *Cruachan*, said to have been the remote origin of the celebrated war of the *Táin Bo Chuailgne*. They had been boasting of their respective possessions, and comparing their wealth together, when, at last to settle their dispute, they proceeded to make a complete examination of their furniture and trinkets. They had brought unto them, says the tale, the most brilliant of their jewels and valuables, that they might know which of them had the most of jewels and wealth. There were brought before them also, it continues, their vessels of carved yew, and their two-handled keeves, and their iron vessels; their

Household utensils, ornaments, and dress of *Ailill* and *Medbh*;

XXIII. small wooden vessels; their cauldrons and their small keeves; their rings, and their bracelets, and their robes, and their thumb-rings, and also their clothes; and of these clothes the colours enumerated are these: crimson, and blue, and black, and green, and yellow, and speckled, and pale, and gray, and blay, and striped.[39] Now, if we consider the tale of the *Táin Bo Chuailgne*, from which the above enumeration is taken, to have been originally written even as late as the time set down for the recovery of a much older version in the seventh century, no one will deny that the list of primary colours which it contains, independently of combinations, is ample enough. But the existing tale bears internal evidence of being composed of fragments of a thoroughly pagan tale connected anew into a connected narrative.

material or fashion of the dress not specified.

It does not appear from the passage in question what the materials of the robes alluded to were, but we may presume that they were native wool and flax, and probably imported silk, or *Siriac*, as it is called in some of our ancient tracts. Neither does it appear of what shape or fashion were the robes, nor of what particular articles they consisted. Indeed almost all our personal descriptions are silent on the number of garments worn by either men or women, as it seldom happens that any distinguished persons, except warriors in or going to battle, are described, and in those cases the description is of a very general character. As instances, however, of the diversity of colours which distinguished various classes in ancient times, and the general character of their clothes, we shall have to draw again to a great extent on the same grand old tale of the *Táin Bo Chuailgne*.

I have in former lectures sufficiently described the origin of the war of the *Táin Bo Chuailgne*, and need not therefore say anything further on that subject here, and may consequently take up the story where the preparations for the war commence.

Medbh's preparation for war;

When queen *Medbh*, stung by the refusal of *Daire Mac Fiachna* to sell or lend his famous bull the *Donn Chuailgne*, had vowed vengeance against the whole province of Ulster, and had determined to get possession of the bull by force, she bethought her of the means of carrying her plans into execution. She accordingly summoned to her court the seven *Mainés* her sons, with all their followers, and their cousins, the seven sons

(39) [original:—Tucad dóib anba tárru da setaib co fesstair cia dib dambad lia séoit, acas móine, acas indmassa. Tucad chuca a n-ena, acas a n-dabcha, acas a n-iarnlestair, a milain, acas a lóthommair, acas a n-drolmacha. Tucait dana cucu, a fáinne, acas a failge, acas a fornasca, acas a n-órdúise, acas a n-etguda, etir chorcair, acas gorm, acas dub, acas uáine, buide, acas brecc acas láchtna, odor, alad, acas riabach.—H. 2. 18. f. 41. *b*. col. 1.]

Magach, with their followers, and *Cormac Conloingeas*, the son of *Conchobar*, king of Ulster, who had been in exile in her kingdom, with his exiled followers, numbering about fifteen hundred men.

These three parties immediately answered the queen's summons, and appeared before the palace of *Cruachan;* and they are separately described in the tale in the following order. The description, though short, will be found very important for the purpose I have at present in view. The first party came with black uncut hair; they wore green cloaks, with silver brooches; the shirts which they wore next their skin were interwoven with thread of gold. The second company had closely cut hair, light gray cloaks, and pure white shirts next their skin. The third and last party had broad cut, fair yellow, golden loose flowing hair upon them; they wore crimson embroidered cloaks, with stone set brooches over their breasts (in the cloaks) and fine long silken shirts, falling to the insteps of their feet.

description of the parties summoned by her.

But there is yet another passage containing references still more minute, and much more numerous, to the characteristic differences of costume, used by different leaders and their clanns (no doubt the far originals of the Scottish tartans), as well as to the details of personal clothing. It is where, after the retreat from Ulster, the army of Connacht under queen *Medbh* is overtaken by the Ulstermen under *Conchobar Mac Nessa* at *Slemain* (now well known as the townland of Sleamhain near Mullingar in the county of Westmeath). Here *Ailill* and *Medbh* held a council; and *Ailill* ordered his herald *Mac Roth*, to go forward to observe the approach of the enemy; and when he had carefully ascertained their military order, their dress, their weapons, and their numbers, to return to him with the information. *Mac Roth* went forth and took up a favourable position at *Slemain*, where he waited until the Ultonian chiefs with their respective clanns had arrived, and having viewed and well noted their appearance, he then returned to *Ailill* and *Medbh*, with whom was Fergus the exiled prince of Ulster, to inform them of what he had seen.

Description of costume of Irish Clanns from the *Táin Bo Chuailgne:*

I have already quoted the descriptions of the arms given by *Mac Roth*,[40] and shall therefore confine myself now to those of the costume of the warriors of Ulster, both as to colour and materials, only adding figure, face, hair, complexion, etc., which are almost as necessary to our present purpose of endeavouring to form an accurate idea of the appearance of the nobles and chieftains of those early days.

[40] Lect. XV., *ante*, vol. i., p. 315.

XXIII.

c Roth's scription Conchobar c Nessa at hill of main;

The first party described by *Mac Roth* consisted of three times three thousand men, according to the story; and after describing how they raised a mound for their chief to sit on, the poetic herald continues: "A tall graceful champion of noble, polished, and proud mien, stood at the head of the party. This most beautiful of the kings of the world, stood among his troops with all the signs of obedience, superiority, and command. He wore a mass of fair, yellow, curling drooping hair. He had a pleasing, ruddy countenance. He had a deep blue, sparkling, piercing, terrific eye in his head; and a two branching beard, yellow, and curling upon his chin. He wore a crimson, deep-bordered five folding *Fuan*, or tunic; a gold pin in the tunic over his bosom; [and also] a brilliant white shirt, interwoven with thread of red gold, next his white skin".[41] Such is the description of the renowned champion *Conchobar Mac Nessa* himself, the king of Ulster.

Causcraid nd;

The next company at the hill of *Slemain* was under twice three thousand, and, says *Mac Roth*, "this party too was led by a comely man. He had fair yellow hair upon him. He had a glossy curling beard. He wore a green cloak wrapping him about; and there was a bright silver brooch (*Cassan*) in that cloak at his breast. He had a brown-red shirt, interwoven with thread of red gold, next his skin and descending to his knees".[42] This was *Causcraid Mend Macha*, son of the king *Conchobar*.

Sencha;

The third company is described by *Mac Roth* as similar to the last in order, in number, and in dress. "There was", he said, "a comely broad headed champion at the head of that party, with long, flowing, brown yellow hair; he had a sharp black blue eye rolling restlessly in his head. He had a divided, curling, two-branching narrow (or confined) beard upon his chin. He wore a black-green, long-wooled cloak, wrapped around him; and a foliated brooch (*Delg Duillech*) of *Findruine* in that cloak at his breast. He had a white shirt, with a collar, next his skin. A bright shield with devices in silver hung at his shoulder.

(41) [original:—óclach seta fata n-airard n-aromin foruallach in airinuċ na buidni sin. Cáiniú di flaitib in domuin rita caemnacair, etir a sluagaib, etir urud, acas grain, acas báig, acas ċosud. Folt findbuide is sé cass deiss drumneċ tóbaċ faride [.i. fair]. Cuindsiu ċaem ċorcarglan leis. Rosc ro glass gorsarda, issé cicarda aduathmar ina ċind; ulċa degablach iss i buide urċass ḃa smech. Fuan corcra corrtharaċ caéic diabuil imbi; eó óir isin brutt ós abruinne; léine glégel ċulpataċ ḃa derg intliud do derg ór fria gellchness.—H. 2. 18. f. 65. col. 1.]

(42) [original:—Fer cáin and dna, in airinuċ na buidne sin caedessin. Folt findbuide fair. Ulċa eicsi imċass imma smeċ. Brat uanidei forcipul imme; cassán gel argit is in brut ósabruinni. Léinidh donderg mileta ḃa derg indliud do derg ór, fri gel ċness i caustul go glunib dó.—H, 2. 18. f. 65. col. 1.]

A silver-hilted sword in a flaming scabbard at his side. A spear like a column of a king's palace beside him". This champion sat upon a mound of sods in presence (or front) of the first champion (king *Conchobar*) who came to the hill, and his company sat around him.[43] "Sweeter to me", continues *Mac Roth*, "than the sound of triangular harps in the hands of professional performers on them, were the melodious sounds of the voice and the eloquence of that young hero, when addressing him who had first come to the hill, and advising him in all things".[44] This was *Sencha* the orator: he was king *Conchobar's* chief minister at the time.

"There came another company to the same hill of *Slemain* of *Midhe*", said *Mac Roth*. "A fair, tall, great, man was at the head of that party, of a florid, noble, countenance: with soft brown hair, falling upon him in thin, smooth locks upon his forehead. He had a deep gray cloak wrapped around him, and a silver brooch in the cloak at his breast. He wore a soft white shirt to his skin".[45] This was *Eogan Mac Durthachta*, chief of *Fernmaige*, now Farney in the county of Monaghan. *of Eogan Mac Durthachta;*

Another clann is described by *Mac Roth* as advancing fiercely and in greater disorder. All of them, he said, had their clothes thrown back. "A large-headed, warlike champion took the front of that party; a man of houndlike, hateful face. He had light grisly hair, and large yellow eyes in his head. He wore a yellow, close-napped cloak upon him; and a gold brooch (*Delg*) in that cloak at his breast. He had a yellow fringed shirt next his skin".[46] This was *Loegaire Buadach*, that is "*Loeghaire* the victorious", chief of *Immail* in Ulster. *of Loegaire Buadach;*

The next clann is described as having "a thicknecked, corpulent champion at their head; he wore black, short, bushy *of Muinreamhar;*

(43) [original:—Laeċ caem cendlethan in airinuch na buidni sin; folt dualaċ dondbuide fair; Rosc duilleċ dubgorm for foluamain ina chind. Ulċa éicsi imcass issí degablaċ imċáel imma smeċ. Brat dubglass ba loss isforcipul imme; delg duilleċ de findruine sin brutt ósa bruine. Léne gel ċulpataċ fri ċness. Gel sciaṫ co tuagmilaib argait inti fair. Maeldorn find argait in intiuċ badba faċomm. tuse rigthige fri a aiss.—H. 2. 18. f. 65. col. 2.]

(44) [original:—aċt ba binniṫir limsa fogor téṫ mendċrott illámaib suad ica sirṡenmm, bindḟogrugud a goṫa acas a irlabra in n-óclaig ac acallaim in óclaig thoesig thanic isin tulaig, acas ac tabairt caċa comairle dó.—H. 2. 18. f. 65. col. 2.]

(45) [original:—Fer findfata mór inairinuċ nabuidni sin, isé grísta gormaineċ; folt dond temin fair, isé slím tanaide bar a étun. Bratt forglass i filliud imme, delg argit isin brutt ós a bruinni. Lénni gel manaiseċ fri chness.—H. 2. 18. f. 65. col. 1.]

(46) [original:—Láeċ cendmar curata in airinuċ na buidnisin; isé ciċarda uathmar. Folt n-etrom n-grelliaċ fair, súle bude móra na ċind. Bratt buide cáiclamaċ imme; delg oirbuide sin brutt ós abruinne. Léne bude corrṫarach fri chness.—H. 2. 18. f. 65. col. 1.]

XXIII. hair, and he had a scarred crimson face, and gray sparkling eyes. A wounding shadowy spear over him. A black shield with a hard rim of white bronze hung at his shoulder. He wore a dark gray long-wooled cloak with a brooch of pale gold in that cloak at his breast. A shirt of striped silk lay next his skin. A sword with hilt of ivory, and an ornamentation of gold thread upon the outside of his dress".[47] This champion was *Munremur* the son of *Gercin*, chief of the territory of *Modurn* in Ulster.

of Connud; The next clann had "a broad-faced thickset champion at its head. And he was irritable, and had prominent, dull, and squinting eyes. He wore yellow, close curling hair. A streaked gray cloak hung upon him, with a bronze brooch at the breast. He wore a shirt with a collar, descending to the calves of his legs on him. An ivory-hilted sword hung at his left hip".[48] This was *Connud* the son of *Morna*, from *Callaind* in Ulster.

of Reochaid; The leader of the next clann described by *Mac Roth* appears to be a specimen of manly beauty according to the herald's ideas. No more comely champion had yet arrived, he says: and he describes him as having a head of bushy red yellow hair; a face broad above and narrow below [the true Celtic head of Ireland]; a deep gray, flashing, flaming, brilliant eye in his head, and pearly white teeth. He wore a white and red cloak or wrapper, and a brooch (*Eó*) of gold in that cloak at his breast. He had on a shirt of kingly silk, turned up with a red hem of gold, next his white skin".[49] This was *Reochaid* the son of *Fatheman* from *Rigdond* in Ulster.

of Amargin The next clann is distinguished by *Mac Roth* as steady and diversified. "A beautiful, active champion was at the head of

(47) [original:—laeċ munremur collaċ in airinuċ na buidni sin; folt dub tóbaċ fair, gnúis ċnedaċ ċorcarda sua, rosc ro glass lainnerda na ċinn. Gae súleċ go forcadaib uasu. Dubsciaċ co calad bualid findruini fair, bratt dodorda da ċuaslae imme. Bretnas bán óir is in brutt ósa bruinne. Léine ċrebraid side sria ċnes. Claideb co n-eltaib déd, acas co n-imdenam órsnáiċ ar a etaig immaig a neċtair.—H. 2. 18. f. 65. col. 1.]

(48) [original:—laeċ ceċeirleċan comremtir in airinuċ na buidni sin. Isé anisc dodorda. Ise derisc carbda, srunnrosc odarda n-adárd ina ċinn. Folt buide roċass fair. Srunnsciaċ derg co m-bil ċalad argait ina imċimchiull uasu; gae slindleċan, slegfota na láim. Bratt riabaċ imme, eo uma isin brutt ar a bruinni. Léni ċulpataċ i ċaustul ga forcnib dó. Colg dét iar na ċoss-barait ċlí.—H. 2. 18. f. 65. b. col. 1.]

(49) [original:—Ni tanic laeċ is ċaemiu ná in laeċ fail inairinuċ na buidni sin. Folt tóbaċ derg buide fair; aged roċáin forleċan lais; rosc roglass gorrsarda, isé caindelda gairéċtaċ na ċinn. Fer cóir cutrumma isé sara roċael foleċan, béoil derg tanaide leiss; déoit niamda nemanda; corp gel cnesta. Cassán gelderg i faen uasu; eó óir isin brutt ós a bruinni. Léne de ṡról ríg ina dergṡilliud de derg ór, fri gel ċness.—H. 2. 18. f. 65. b. col. 2.]

this company; he wore a blue, fine-bordered shirt next his skin, with carved and interlaced clasps of white bronze, with real buttons of burnished red gold in its openings and breast. He wore above it a cloak mottled with the splendour of all the most beautiful of colours".[50] This was *Amargin*, the son of *Ecelsalach* the smith, the good poet from the river *Buais* in Ulster. XXIII.

The next clann was that of *Feradach Fin Fechtnach* of *Slebe Fuaid* in Ulster, described as a champion entirely fair, hair, eyes, beard, eyebrows, and dress.[51] *of Feradach Fin Fechtnach;*

At the head of the next company the herald describes "two soft youths with two green cloaks wrapped around them, and two brooches (*Cassán*) of shining silver in these cloaks over their breasts; they wore two shirts of smooth yellow silk next their skins".[52] These were *Fiachaig* and *Fiachna*, the two younger sons of king *Conchobar* himself. *of Fiachaig and Fiachna;*

Another clann noted by *Mac Roth* in his poetical report is described as "overwhelming in magnitude; fiery-red in a heat; a battalion in numbers; a rock in strength; a destruction in battle; as thunder in impetuosity. The chieftain at its head was [one certainly of no very enviable style of beauty; for he is described as] "an angry, terrific, hideous man, long-nosed, large-eared, apple-eyed; with coarse, dark-gray hair. He wore a striped cloak, and instead of a brooch, he had a stake (*Cuaille*) of iron in that cloak over his breast, which reached from one shoulder to the other. He wore a coarse, streaked shirt next his skin".[53] This was the great *Celtchair Mac Uthair*, from *Dun-da-leth-glass*, now Downpatrick in Ulster. *of Celtchair Mac Uthair and his clann;*

The next in order among the clanns of Ulster is reported by *Mac Roth* as, firm and furious, hideous and terrible; "its leader a champion, one of whose eyes was black, and the other white; a wrynecked man with long hands; he had brown, thick, *of Eirrge Echbel;*

(50) [original:—Laech alaind escaid in airinuch na buidni sin; gorm anart cael corrtarach, go stuagaib srithi figthi féta findruini, go cnappib dilsi deligthi derggóir for bernadaib, acas brollaig do sri chness. Bratt bommanach co m-buaid cach data tharisss.—H. 2. 18. f. 65. *b*. col. 1.]

(51) [original:—Laech findbuide in airinuch na buidni sin. Find uile, in fer sain etir, ḟolt acas rosc acas ulcha acas abratchur acas decelt.—H. 2. 18. f. 66. *a*. col. 1.]

(52) [original:—Dias máeth óclách in airinuch na buidnisin. Da bratt uaine i forcipul impu, da chassán gel argait is na brattaib ás a m-brunnib; dá lene di ṡlemun ṡitu buide fria cnessaib.—H. 2. 18. f. 66. *a*. col. 1.]

(53) [original:—Is bádud ar méit; is tene ruad loss.; is cath arlin; is ald ar nirt; is brath; ar bláriud; is torandar tairpige. Fer fergach; uathmar, irggráin, in airinuch na buidni sin; isé srónmar, ómar, uball ruisc; folt n-garb n-greliach. Bratt ribáin imme; cuailli iairn isin brutt ós a bruinni, con geib on gualaind go a raile dó. Léne garb threbnaid fri chness.—H. 2. 18. f. 66. *a*. col. 1.]

XXIII. curling hair. He wore a black flowing cloak with a brooch of red bronze over his breast; and an embroidered shirt next his skin".[34] This was *Eirrge Echbel* from *Bri Ergi* in Ulster.

of Mend son of Salcholgan; We have next a clann with a large fine man at its head. He had foxy red hair, and foxy red large eyes in his head, and he wore a speckled cloak.[35] This was *Mend* the son of *Salcholgan*, from the headlands of the river *Boind*.

of Fergna; At the head of the next clann that came to the hill of *Slemain* was a chief described as a long-cheeked swarthy man with black hair upon him, and long-limbed. "He had a red longwooled cloak, with a clasp of white silver in it, over his breast, and a linen shirt next his skin".[36] This was *Fergna* the son of *Findconna* the king of *Burach* in Ulster.

of Erce son of Carpri Nia-Fer and his clann; Then we have a company described as steady, and different from the other companies: "some of them had red cloaks; others gray cloaks, others blue cloaks, and others cloaks of green, blay, white, and yellow; and these cloaks all floating splendidly and brightly upon them". "There is", said *Mac Roth*, "a red speckled little boy, with a crimson cloak, among them in the centre; he has a brooch (*Eó*) of gold in that cloak over his breast: and a shirt of kingly silk interwoven with red gold next his white skin".[37] This was *Erce* the son of *Carpri Nia-Fer*, monarch of Erinn, and of *Fedilm Nucruthach* (literally *Fedilm* the ever blooming), daughter of king *Conchobar*. This was the *Erce* mentioned in a former lecture, at whose death his sister *Acaill* died of grief, and was buried on the hill of *Acaill*, so called after her, and now known as the hill of Skreene, near ancient Tara.

of Cuchulaind's clann. Lastly a clann is described by *Mac Roth*, which counted, he said, no less than thirty hundred blood red, furious warriors,

(34) [original:—Is h-i bale bruċhmar, issi eitig uáċhmar; Láec [anarain?] bruasaċ belmar inairinuċ na buidnisin. Is hé leċgleóir, leich inċind, lamfada [in airinuch na buidni sin;] folt dond fo ċass fair. Bratt dubluascaċ imme; roċ creda sin brutt ás a bruinni. Léni derg scaigchi fri cness.—H. 2. 18. f. 66. a. col. 1.]

(35) [original:—Fer mór bresta in airinuċ na buidni sin. Folt ruad-derg fair. Súle ruadderga móra na chind. Sithithir ri Ċrummċir meóir miled ceċtarnai, dina rig rosc ruad ramóra failet lais. Bratt brecc imme.—H. 2. 18. f. 66. a. col. 2.]

(36) [original:—Laec lecconfota dodorda in airinuċ na buidni sin. Folt dub fair; sith ballrad .i. cassa fata. Bratt derg ra ċaslái imme; bretnas bán argait is in brut ós a bruinni. Léni lindi fri ċness.—H. 2. 18. f. 66. a col. 2.]

(37) [original:—Is hi forsud écsamail ris na buidnib aile, aill bruitt deirg; aill bruitt glass, aill bruitt guirm, aill bruitt uane, blae [blana], bána, buide; iciat alle etrocta uasu. Undsed mac m-bec m-brecderg co m-brutt corcra ecurru bar medón danessin. Eó óir isin brutt ós a bruinni, léne de sról ríg ba dergginluid de dergór fri gel ċness.—H. 2. 18. f. 66. a. col. 2.]

white, clean, dignified, crimson faced men. They had long fair yellow hair [upon them], splendid, bright countenances, and sparkling kingly eyes; and they wore glossy, long, flowing robes, with noble brooches (*Deilge*) of gold, pure shining gauntlets (*Iarndota*), and shirts of striped silk.[58] These were the men of *Muirtheimne*, the hereditary patrimony of *Cuchulaind*, the great hero of the tale. XXIII.

These descriptions are surely specific enough to afford us a very vivid glimpse of the dress and accoutrements, as well as the personal appearance of the Gaedhelic warriors of two thousand years ago. But the same remarkable tale contains much besides on the subject.[59]

(58) [original:—Nao uatti tricha-cét mói, fianna feochra for dergga, fir gil glain guirm chorcarda. Monga fata finbuidi, gnúri álle derochtai; ruisc reilli rígdaidi; etaige ligda lendmassa, deilge órda airegda, iarndótaib dendglana; lénti síti srebnaide.—H. 2. 18. f. 66. col. 1.]

(59) [All the clanns whose dress and personal ornaments are described in the text belong to the Ultonian party; there are, however, some descriptions, though not so full in other parts of the tale of the *Táin Bo Chuailgne*, of the champions of Connacht, and the allies of *Ailill* and *Medhbh*, a few of which may be given here, in order to show that, so far at least as that tale is concerned, there is no evidence of difference of costume and arms between the ruling class in the northern and western parts of ancient Erinn.

After the great combat between *Ferdiadh* and *Cuchulaind*, the latter was obliged to retire from before the enemy, and betake him to his bed of green rushes, in order to obtain relief from the fearful wounds which he had received from *Ferdiadh*. He had not remained long in this position, when some of his northern friends arrived to his assistance; finding him, however, in a very dangerous state, they took him away to his native *Muirtheimne*, to whose streams and rivers, and the plants which grew in them, the *Tuatha Dé Danann* had communicated healing properties. The names of these healing streams were:—*Sais*, *Buain*, *Bithlain*, *Findglais*, *Gleoir*, *Gleanamain*, *Bedg*, *Tadg*, *Telameit*, *Rind*, *Bir*, *Brenidé*, *Dicaem*, *Muach*, *Miliuc*, *Comung*, *Culend*, *Gaisemain*, *Drong*, *Delt*, *Dubglas*. While *Cuchulaind* was taking the benefit of these waters, the famous *Cethern*, who was described in Lecture xv. (vol. i., p. 313), as making such haste from the north to the assistance of *Cuchulaind*, that he could only arm himself with an iron spit, arrived. Making straight for the camp of the invaders, he attacked like a maniac every one he met with his spit, and received in return so many wounds, that he was at length obliged to withdraw to where *Cuchulaind* was undergoing medical treatment.

Having arrived there, *Cethern* asked *Cuchulaind* to procure him some medical attendance. The latter immediately complied with his request, by inviting a party of medical men from the enemy's camp to come out to him, as none of the Ultonian physicians were at the time available. The angry northern champion, rendered fretful by his many wounds, had no patience for the dilatory deliberations of the doctors, and he accordingly dismissed them with blows and wounds, some, as we are told, to a bed of sickness, and some to death. *Cuchulaind*, therefore, sent his charioteer *Laegh* for *Fingin Fathliagh* (or *Fingin* the prophetic leech or physician), king *Conchobar Mac Nessa*'s chief physician, to *Ferta Fingin* on the brow of *Slebe Fuaid*, in the present county of Armagh. The physician returned with the messenger, and the narrator of the tale avails himself of the dialogue between *Fingin* and his patient in the presence of *Cuchulaind*, to introduce to the reader by descriptions of their forms, dress, personal ornaments and arms, several of the champions of the

XXIII.

Medbh's gifts to Ailill.

At the opening of the pillow controversy already spoken of, between queen *Medbh* and her consort *Ailill*, the irritated

invading force. These descriptions it is, which it is proposed to add by way of supplement to those of *Mac Roth* in the text.

"The physician having arrived at *Cethern's* bed, the latter exhibits his wounds to him one by one, and asks his opinion of each.

Fegais Fingin in fuil sin: Singal ectrom indechrachtach andso, ale bar in liaig, ocas ni berad immucha. Is fir ám, ale bar Cethern, dom riachtsa oen fer and cuidmáile sair; bratt gorm i filliud imme, delg n-argit is in brutt ara bruinne; crommsciach go faebur chondualach; fair sleg cuicrind in na láim, fága faegablaige na farrad. Do bert in fuil sain. Rucsom fuil m-bic uaimse nó. Ra tá fetammar in fer sain, ale bar Cuchulaind,—Illand ilar chless mac Fergusa sain, ocas ni ba dúthracht leis do thuttimsiu da láim.—H. 2. 18. f. 61. col. 2.

"*Fingin* examined that blood: 'This is a light unwilling wound', said the physician, 'and it will not carry thee off very soon'. 'True', said *Cethern*, 'a single man approached me there; a blue cloak wrapped around him, a brooch of silver in that cloak at his breast; a curved shield with sharp carved edges upon his shoulder; a flesh-seeking *slegh* (or light spear) in his hand, and a *Faga Faegablaige* (or a small down-headed spear) near it. It was he that gave this wound; and he got a slight wound from me'. 'We know that man', said *Cuchulaind*, 'he is *Illand*, the accomplished warrior, son of *Fergus*, and he was not desirous that thou shouldst fall by his hand'.

Fega latt dam in fuil seo dna, a mo phopa Fhingin, bar Cethern. Fechais Fingin in fuil sin: ban gala banualach and so, ale bar in liaig. Is fir ám, ale bar Cethern, dompiachtsa oen ben and, ben chain bánainech, leccan fata mór, monng ór buide fursi; bratt corcra gendaichi impi, eó óir is in brutt ós a bruinni; sleg dirich drumnech ar derglassad na láim. Ra bert in fuil sin, Formsa; ruc si fuil m-bic uaimse nó. Rata fetammar in mnai sin, ale bar Cuchulaind,—Medb ingen Echaid Feidlig, ingen ardrig h-Erenn, ari da riacht san congrammumsin. Ba buaid ocas chosgor ocas commaidium le sia do faicherceru da lámaib.—H. 2. 18. fol. 61. b. a. col. 1.

"'Look at this blood [wound] for me, my good *Fingin*', said *Cethern*. *Fingin* examined this blood: 'This is the deed of a haughty woman', said the physician. 'It is true', said *Cethern*, 'there came to me one beautiful, pale, long-faced, woman, with long flowing golden yellow hair upon her; [she had] a crimson cloak, with a brooch of gold in that cloak over her breast; a straight-ridged *slegh* (or light spear) blazing red in her hand. She it was that gave me that wound; and she got a slight wound from me'. 'We know that woman well', said *Cuchulaind*, 'she is *Medbh*, the daughter of *Echaid Feidlig*, the daughter of the high king of Erinn [and queen of Connacht]; it is she that came thus unto me. She would have deemed it a great victory and a triumph that thou shouldst have fallen by her hands'.

Fecha latt dam in fuilse no a mo phopa Fhingin, bar Cethern. Fechais Fingin in fuilsein:—Galach da fenned and so, ale bar in liaig. Is fir ám, bar Cethern, dammiachtatarsa dias and, dá thoomaile foraib; dá bratt a gorma i filliud impu; delgi argait is na brattaib ós a m-bruinnib; munchobrach argit oengil im bragit cechtarnai dib. Rócta fetammar in dis sein, ale bar Cuchulaind,—Oll ocas Ochme sain,

"'Look at this blood [wound] for me, my good *Fingin*', said *Cethern*. *Fingin* examined that blood: 'This is the deed of two champions', said the physician. 'It is true indeed', said *Cethern*; 'two men came to me there with two glossy curled heads of hair; two blue cloaks wrapped around them; brooches of silver in the cloaks over their breasts; a chain of bright silver around the neck of each of them'. 'We know these two

queen does not hesitate to say to her husband, that she had paid him a high compliment, when she selected him as her XXIII.

do sain muintir Ailella ocus Medba.—H. 2. 18. f. 61. b. a. col. 1.

Fécha latt dam in fuilseo no a mo phopa Fingin, for Cethern. Fechais Fingin in fuilsain:—Domriachtatarsa dias óac fénne and, congrum n-anfebdaide forro; cumaing bir imniumsa cechtarnai dib, cumanngsa in m-birsa tri sin dara nai dibsium. Fechais Fingin in fuil sin. Dub ule, in fuilseo, ale bar in liaig. Tri cride do chrotair dait co n-derna chrois dib trit chride, ocus ni furchanaimsea icc andso; acht do gebainnse daitseo do lossaib icci ocus slánsen ni nachat bertais immucha. Nata fetammar in dis sain, alé bar Cuculaind,—Ban ocus Meccon sain, do sain, muintir Ailella ocus Medba. Ba duthracht leo sea do faethaistesu da lámaib.—H. 2. 18. f. 61. b. a. col. 1.

Fécha lat dam in fuilsea no a mo phopa Fingin, ar Cethern. Fechais Fingin in fuilsain:—Dergruathur da rig Caille andso, alebar in liaig. Is fir ám, bar Cethern, domriachtatarsa dá óclach aigfinna abratgorma móra and, go mindaib óir uasu; da bratt uane isorchipul impu; da chassán gel argit is na-brattaib ós a m-brunnib; da sleig cuicrinni ina lámaib. It immaicsi na fuili do bertatar forc, alebar in liaig: it chraes da chuatar dait, co comarnectatar renna na n-gae innut, ocus ni h-assu aicc andso. Na ta fetammar in dis sain, bar Cuculaind, Broen ocus Bruidni sain, meic Theora Soillsi, da mac rig Caille. Bá buaid, ocus choscur, ocus commaidib leo gia do fáethaistesu leo.—H. 2. 18. f. 61. b. a. col. 1.

Fécha latt dam in fuilsea no a mo phopa Fhingin, ar Cethern. Fechais Fingin in fuil sain: Comgas dambráthar andso, ale bar in liaig. Is fir ám, bar Cethern; domriachtatarsa dias cétrighlach and, fuilt

men well', said *Cuchulaind*, 'they are *Oll* and *Othine*, of the special household of *Ailill* and *Medhbh*'.

"'Look at this blood [wound], for me, my good *Fingin*', said *Cethern*. *Fingin*, looked at that blood, [and *Cethern* said]: 'There came to me two young warriors, who have not as yet come to full manhood; each of them thrust a spit into me, and I wounded each of them in return with this spit'. *Fingin* examined that blood [wound]. 'This blood is all black', said the physician. 'It was through thy heart they pierced thee, so that they formed a cross in thy heart, and I cannot pronounce a cure here; but I can procure for thee such plants of healing and saving properties as shall save thee from an early death'. 'We know these two men', said *Cuchulaind*, 'they are *Ban* and *Meccons*, of the special household troops of *Ailill* and *Medhbh*. It would be pleasing to them that thou shouldst receive thy death wounds from their hands'.

"'Look at this wound for me, my good *Fingin*', said *Cethern*. *Fingin* looked at this blood [wounds]: 'These are the red rush of two woodrings', said the leech. 'True', said *Cethern*, 'there came to me two fair-faced youths, with large blue eyes and with golden diadems on them; two green cloaks wrapped around them; two brooches of bright silver in these cloaks over their breasts; and two flesh-seeking spears in their hands'. 'The wounds they have given thee are invisible wounds: it is down thy throat thou hast received them, where the points of the spears met within thee, and a cure is not easy here'. 'We know these two well', said *Cuchulaind*, 'they are *Broen* and *Brudni*, of the household youths of *Teora Soillsi*, the two sons of the king of *Caille*. They would consider it a victory, and a triumph, and a cause of universal exultation, that thou shouldst receive thy death wounds from them'.

"'Look at this blood [wound] for me, my good *Fingin*', said *Cethern*. *Fingin* looked at that blood [wound]. 'This is the joint deed of two brothers', said the physician. 'True indeed', said *Cethern*, 'there came two kingly

XXIII. husband, while he was only a younger son of the king of Leinster; and she reminds him that she had presented him at

buide forro; bruitt dubglassa fá loss i forcipul impu; delgi duilleċa do finnruiniu is na brattaib ór a m-brunnib; mánaisi lethan glassa na lamaib. Rata fetammar in dis sain, ale bar Cuculaind, Cormac [mac] colomárig sain, acas Cormac mac Maelefoga, do sain muntir Aililla ocas Medba. Ba dutḟract leo gea do taeċaisteru da lémaib.—H. 2. 18. f. 61. b. a. col. 1.

Fecha latt dam in fuilsea no a ma ṗopa Fingin, ar Cethern. Fechais Fingin in fuilsain:—Attaċ da n-derbraṫar andso, ar in liaig. Is fír am, ale bar Cethern, domriaċtarsa dias maeth oclác ann, iciat comċosmaile diblinaib, folt cass bar in dara nai dib, folt casbuide bar araile; da bratt uaine i forcipul impu, da ċassan gel argit is na brattaib as a m-brunib; da leni di ṡlemain ṡíta buide sria cnessaib; claidbi gelduirn sar a cressaib; da gel sciaṫ co tuagmiliab argit finnoi foraib; da ṡleig cúicrind go ferranaib argit dengil ina lámaib. Ra ta fetammar in dis sain, ale bar Cuculaind,—Mane Maṫremail sain, ocas Mane Aṫremail, da mac Aililla ocas Medbá. Ocas ba buaid ocas coscur ocas commaidium leo gae ro taeċáisteru dá lámaib.—H. 2. 18. f. 61. b. a. col. 2.

Feċa lat dam in fuilsea a mo ṗopa Ḟhingin, bar Cethern. Domriaċtar dias oac féinne ann, conngnam n-ecside, ice erarda serdaide forro, etaige allmarda ingantacha impo. Cumaing bir inniumsa ceċtarnai dib, cumanngsa (bir) tri cheċtarnai dibrium. Feċais Fingin in fuil sain: Atamaing na fuili ra bertatar fort, ale ar in liaig, gonda rubdatar féiċe do ċride inniut, conda n-imbir do ċride it ċliab, immar abull i rabull, ná mar ċerctli i fásbulg, co naċ fail féiċ itir icá immulung, ocas ni dergenaimse ícc

champions to me, with yellow hair upon them; black gray cloaks with fringes wrapped around them; and foliated brooches of *Findruinin* in their cloaks at their breasts; broad green *Manaisé* (or spears) in their hands'. 'We know these two very well', said *Cuchulaind*, 'they are *Cormac*, [son of] *Colamarig*, and *Cormac*, the son of *Maelefogha*, of the special household of *Ailill* and *Medhbh*. It would be delightful to them that thou shouldst receive thy death wound at their hands'.

"'Look at this blood [wound] for me, my good *Fingin*', said *Cethern*. *Fingin* looked at that blood [wound]: 'This is the deed of two brothers', said the physician. 'True indeed', said *Cethern*, 'there came two young warriors to me resembling each other, one had curling [dark] hair, and the other curling yellow hair; two green cloaks wrapped around them, with two brooches of bright silver in their cloaks at their breasts; two soft smooth shirts of yellow silk to their skin; two bright hilted swords at their girdles; two bright shields with fastenings of bright silver upon them; and two flesh seeking *sleghs* (or light spears) with bright veinings of pure bright silver on their handles'. 'We know these two very well', said *Cuchulaind*, 'they are *Mane Mathremail*, and *Mane Athremail*, two sons of *Ailill* and *Medhbh*. And they would deem it a victory, and a triumph, and a cause of universal exultation, that thou shouldst fall by their hands'.

"'Look at this blood for me, my good *Fingin*', said *Cethern*. 'There came to me there two young champions with clear, noble, manly features, and with wonderful foreign clothes upon them. Each of them thrust a spit into me, and I sent this spit into each of them'. *Fingin* examined the wounds [blood]: 'They have inflicted dangerous wounds on thee', said the physician, 'for they have severed the strings of thy heart within thee, so that it plays in thy body like an apple in the air, or a ball of thread in an empty sack, so that there is not a string sustaining it, and I cannot perform any cure in this

the outset with twelve suits of robes, a chariot worth three times seven *cumals* (or sixty-three cows), the breadth of his face of red gold, and a bracelet of *Findruine* or carved white metal (silver bronze) to fit his left wrist.[60] The breadth of his face of red gold spoken of here, and of which we shall have occasion to speak again, was doubtless one of those deep crescents of red gold of which there are so many magnificent specimens preserved in our national museum in the Royal Irish Academy.

Gifts promised by *Medbh* to *Long Mac Emonis*.

Again, when queen *Medbh* is inducing one of her warriors, named *Long Mac Emonis*, to fight *Cuchulaind* in single combat, she "promises him great rewards, namely, twelve suits of robes, and a chariot worth four times seven *cumals* or eighty-four cows, and her daughter *Findabair* to wife".[61] And again, when queen *Medbh* summoned *Ferdiadh* to fight *Cuchu-*

asoro. Ra ta fetamar in dis sain, ale bar Cuculaind, dias sain de feinnedaib na h-Iruade forroeglass doen toisc o Ailill ocas o Meidb ar dáig do gonasu.

Feċa latt dam in fuilse no a mo phopa Fhingin, bar Cethern. Feċas Fingin in fuil sain no: Imrubad mic ocas atar andso, ale ar in liaig. Is fír am, bar Cethern, dommiaċtatarsa dá fer móra, gamdel derca and, go mindaib óir ós lassaig uasu, errud rigdaidi impu, claidbi órduirn intlassi bar a cressaib, go ferbolgaib airgit óen gil, go frithatartaib óir bricc friu a neċtair. Ra ta fetamar in dis sain, ale bar Cuculaind, Ailill acas a mac sain Mane, condergeib ule. Ba buaid ocas coscur acas commaidium leo gea ro fechaistesu dia lámaib.—H. 2. 18. f. 61. b. a. col. 2.

place [here'.] 'We know these two very well', said *Cuchulaind*, 'they are two choice champions of *Irruade* [Norway] who were sent specially by *Ailill* and *Medhbh* to kill thee'.

"'Look at this blood [wound] for me, my good *Fingin*', said *Cethern*. *Fingin* examined the blood [wounds] and said: 'This is the joint piercing of a father and son', said the physician. 'True', said *Cethern*, 'there came to me there two large men with flaming eyes, having diadems of lustrous gold on their heads, with kingly dress upon them, with long gold hilted swords at their girdles, in scabbards of bright shining silver, with frettings of mottled gold on their lower ends'. 'We know these two very well', said *Cuchulaind*, 'they are *Ailill* and his son *Mainé*, who have inflicted those wounds upon thee. They would think it a victory and a triumph, and a cause of universal exultation, that thou shouldst fall by their hands'".

Notwithstanding the unfavourable opinion pronounced by *Fingin* upon some of *Cethern's* wounds, he succeeded, we are told, in curing him, or at least in enabling him to share again in the conflict. This he is said to have done by means of a curious bath formed of the marrow of a great number of cows which *Cuchulaind* had killed for the purpose. The place where this bath was prepared received the name of *Smiramair* or the Marrow-bath, which is still preserved in that of Smarmore in the county of Louth.]

(60) [original:—Tucasa cor acas coibchi duit amail as dech téit do mnái, .i. timthaċ dá ferdéc d'étaċ, carpat tri secht cumal, comleṫet t-aigthi do derg ór, comṫrom do riged clí do findruini.—H. 2 18. f. 41. b. a. col. 1.]

(61) [original:—Gellas Medb morċoma do, .i. timṫeċt da fer deg do etgud, ocas carpat cethre secht cumal, ocas Findabair domnaoi".—Prof. O'Curry's copy. Fol. 53 of H. 2. 18, which must have contained this passage, is now apparently wanting.]

XXIII. *laind* in that great combat described in a former lecture,[62] which proved fatal to himself at *Ath Ferdiaidh* (now Ardee) we are told that when he came to the queen's pavilion, "he was honoured and supplied with the best of food, and plied with the choicest, most delicious, and most exhilarating of liquors, until he became intoxicated and hilarious. And he was promised great rewards for undertaking to fight and combat, namely, a chariot worth four times seven *cumals* or eighty-four cows; and suits of clothes for twelve men, of cloth of all colours; and the size of his own territory of the smoothest part of *Magh Ai* (in the present county of Roscommon) free of rent and tribute, and of attendance at court or upon expeditions; without any forcible exaction whatever; and to his son and his grandsons and great-grandsons to the breast of eternity, and end of the world; and the queen's daughter (*Findabair*) as his wife, and the brooch (*Eó*) of gold which was in (queen) *Medbh*'s mantle over all that", or, as she is made to say in the copy of the *Táin* preserved in the vellum MS. H. 2. 16. T.C.D.: "My spear brooch (*Duillend-Dealc*) of gold which weighs thirty *Ungas* (or ounces) and thirty half *Ungas* and thirty *Crossachs*, and thirty quarter [*Crossachs*]".[63]

Gifts promised by *Medhbh* to *Ferdiadh*; one of them, a gold brooch, weighed more than four pounds.

Persons often find it difficult to believe that some of the gold bracelets and silver brooches to be seen in the museum of the Royal Irish Academy could, from their massiveness, have ever been worn as personal ornaments; but after this great gold brooch of queen *Medbh*, which, according to our calculation, must have weighed more than four pounds Troy, we need wonder no longer at the weight of those that have come down to us from those remote ages. I have indeed so frequently had occasion to refer to the use of these large heavy pins in narrating more than one historical event or anecdote, that I need scarcely insist on the abundance of evidence we possess as to the use of brooches even larger and heavier than those in the museum of the Academy: and there is in fact a fragment of one such silver brooch in that museum, sufficient to show how easily queen *Macha Mongruadh* might have marked out the tracing of the great *Rath* of *Emania* with hers.

Story of *Mac Conglinde*;

There is another curious reference to the imaginary costume of an imaginary individual, preserved in the *Leabhar Mór Duna Doighre* (now called the *Leabhar Breac*) in the Royal Irish

(62) [See Lect. XIV., *ante*, vol. i., p. 302; and also Appendix, where the whole episode descriptive of this fight is given.]

(63) [See Appendix, where the original of this passage will be found as part of the text of the whole episode of the combat of *Cuchulaind* and *Ferdiadh*.]

XXIII. Story of Mac Conglinde;

Academy; but, although the dress is imaginary as regards its materials (indeed of the most ludicrous character), the description given of it is not the less true and valuable as regards the names and the destination of the different articles spoken of. The tract in which we find this reference, is of a very wild character. I have already briefly alluded to it in a former lecture,[64] but I shall have to refer here to some parts of it more specifically.

The story commences with informing us that about the time to which it refers (say about the year 740) there were at the great college of Armagh eight divinity students, who in after life became distinguished personages in their country. One of these students was *Anier Mac Conglinde*, a youth not more distinguished for his literary acquirements, than he was for his natural talent and his inclination for bitter sarcasm and satirical rhyming. *Mac Conglinde* after some time discovered that his vocation for the Church was doubtful, while his preference for poetry and history was every day becoming more and more apparent. At last he retired from Armagh and resorted to his former tutor at Roscommon, where he devoted himself for some time to the cultivation and study of his favourite pursuits. At length he bethought him of the best place in which to commence his practice in his new character; and having heard that *Cathal Mac Finghuine*, king of Munster (who died in 742), was suffering from a demoniac, voracious, unappeasable appetite, he decided upon paying him a visit and endeavour to cure him of his malady. "With this intention *Mac Conglinde*", the story says, "sold the few effects that he possessed for two wheaten cakes and a piece of cured beef; these he put into his book-wallet; after which he shaped for himself a pair of *Cuarans*, or shoes, of brown leather, seven times doubled. He arose early the next morning; tucked his *Leinidh* above his hips; he put on his white cloak of five doubles, firmly wrapped about him, and with an iron pin (*Milech*) in that cloak at his breast.[65] Thus accoutred *Mac Conglinde* went on to Cork, where he heard the king of Munster was making a visitation of his territories; and after some adventures he found himself in the royal presence. The young poet had then recourse to various devices to draw

(64) See Lect. IV., *ante*, vol. i., p. 81.

(65) [original:—Iar sin rechad in m-bec sprédi boi acca, .i. for da bairgin do cruithnecht acas for choicht sen-saille co tiert dar dos alar; rac sin ina ceig libair; acas cumais dicuaran corro co-dligo do dondlechar, .uii. fillte do in agaid sin. Atracht moch iarnabarach; acas gabaid a leinid in árdgabail os mellaib a larac; acas gabaid a lummain find forcotbalta i forcipal imme; milech iarnaige uasu ina brutt.—*Leabhar Breac*, f. 97. a.]

XXIII.

Story of Mac Conglinde;

forth the demon which it was believed had taken up his abode in the king's stomach and tormented him with an unappeasable appetite. One of the devices to which he had recourse was, to exhibit to the eyes of the king food of the most tempting character, but, Tantalus-like, in such a way as that although it came up to his lips, he had not the power to touch it. Another of his plans was to give a vivid and tormenting description of plenty of viands and sumptuous food which he had seen in his dreams or his imagination. Nothing can be more grotesque or extravagant than this description as preserved in the piece before us. But though it is impossible not to laugh at it, it contains however much detail of quite serious importance with reference to our present subject.

his extravagant dream;

The extravagance to which I allude may be judged by the commencement of *Mac Conglinde's* story to the king, in which he describes how he was carried in his dream to a lake of new milk, in which stood an island of wheaten bread, and a mansion built of butter, cheese, sweet curds, and various kinds of preparations of milk, as well as of many sorts of flesh and fleshy substances. Having reached the brink of the lake, he found there a little boat made of fat beef, and well graved with suet, with seats of sweet curds, with prow of lard, with stern of butter, with sculls (or paddles) of marrow, and with oars of bacon.

Having found himself rowed over in this singular equipage to this singular island, *Mac Conglinde* landed and walked up to the mansion, where he met the doorkeeper; and of him he speaks in these words, in which the most minute account is given of the several articles of dress worn by such a functionary, and in which the only absurd portion consists of the ludicrous character of the materials of which they were supposed to have been made.

his description of a curious dress of a doorkeeper;

"Comely was the face of that young man", said *Mac Conglinde;* "his name was *Maelsaille* (that is, a person dedicated to fat meat), and he was the son of *Mael-imme* (that is, of a person dedicated to rich butter), who was the son of rich lard. There he stood", continues *Mac Conglinde*, "with his smooth *Assai* or sandals of old hung beef upon his feet; with his *Ochrath* or trews of sweet curds upon his shins; with his *Inar* (tunic, or frock) of fresh fat cow-beef upon his body; with his *Oris* or girdle of salmon fish around him; with his *Cochall*, or cape, of *Tōsaidh*, or fat heifer beef, upon his shoulders; with his seven *Corniu* or garlands of butter around his head; with his seven rows of onions in each garland of them separately; with his seven epistles of sausages around his neck, with *Bille* or bosses of rendered lard upon the head of each epistle of them".(88) XXIII.

I shall not at present follow *Mac Conglinde*'s humorous description farther. Let us stop to analyze the doorkeeper's dress, so precisely and minutely noted, and, abstracting from it the absurdities of the fanciful materials mentioned, we can very easily call up the image of a man in the costume of the time. And in fact it happens, most singularly, with the exception of the sandals, the girdle, the garlands, and what is called the *Epistle* or necklace, there is still in existence in the Museum of the Royal Irish Academy an ancient and most faithful copy of the doorkeeper's dress: that is, as regards the principal articles of which it consisted, namely the trews, the frock, and the cape. analysis of this dress;

Of these last three articles of dress it is quite unnecessary to say any more here, as they come within the knowledge of every one. We all know that the *Cochall* is the ordinary cape or short cloak for the shoulder, such as is worn at this day. Secondly, the *Inar*, or tunic, is almost identical with the tight, military frock of modern times, but without a collar of any kind as far as we know. The third article of the dress, the *Ochrath*, or trews, was a very graceful fashion of tight-fitting pantaloons, reaching from the hips to the ankles. These three, it will be remembered, were the principal articles of *Mac Conglinde*'s doorkeeper's dress, and they are sufficiently explicit. Not so, however, with *Mac Conglinde*'s own dress, as described at the opening of the tale. There we are told that the night before his departure for Roscommon, our young poet made for himself a pair of *Cuarans*, or shoes, of brown leather of seven doubles. He arose in the morning, and of course dressed himself. The particulars of the dress are not given, but we are told that he tucked up his *Leinidh* over his hips, and wrapped his white cloak around his body. Here we have no account of the pantaloons, nor of the frock, because they were close fitting articles, that required no tucking up to facilitate the traveller's motion. The white cloak does not demand any particular attention; but the *Leinidh* which he tucked up above his hips, is an article that has not hitherto attracted the notice of any writer on Irish antiquities. the *Cochall*; the *Inar*; the *Ochrath*; analysis of *Mac Conglinde*'s own dress; his *Leinidh*.

(88) [original:—Ba cain delb inóclaig sin, acas ba hé a ċómáinm .i. Maelsaille mac Mailimme mic Blongi, cona assaib slemna sensaille ima bunnu; cona ochraib do bind scaibline imalurgib; cona h-mar bo-saille imme; cona cris do lechar sinérc taris; cona ċochall diċarcaid imme; cona vii. cornib imme ima chind; ocas batar .vii. n-imaire do sirċainnind incaċ coraind dibside fóleth; cona .vii. n-epislib do ċaelanu inbid fo bragait, Cona .vii. m-bille do blonaig bruti for cind caċa h-episli dibside.—*Leabhar Breac*, f. 100. b.]

XXIII.

Distinction between the Léine and the Léinidh,—the latter was a kilt.

The word *Leine*, though written in two different ways, and signifying two different things, is and must be invariably pronounced the same way. When it signifies a shirt, as it does at the present day, it is witten *Léine;* but when, as in the present case, it signifies a sort of petticoat or kilt, it is then written *Léinidh;* but I am not able to explain the reason of the difference in orthography. I am very well aware that these words have been often thoughtlessly and carelessly written, one for the other, even in very old manuscripts; whenever we find a person described with a *Léine* of some beautiful stuff placed upon his white skin, we may, however, be certain, whatever the orthography may be, that the article spoken of is a shirt. And again, when we find a person described with a *Léinidh* having a costly border or fringe, and descending to his knees, we may be equally certain that the article spoken of was a kilt or petticoat. I happen to have met two references to the word in its latter signification, that leave no doubt of its distinctive character and its assigned place on the human body.

Description of the dress of the champion Edchu Rond;

In the ancient tale called *Loinges nMac nDuildermaita*, or the Exile of the Sons of *Duildermait*, we are told that on a certain occasion as *Ailill* and *Medbh*, the king and queen of Connacht, were in their palace of *Cruachan*, the warder of the castle came out and informed the queen that he saw a body of men coming towards them from the south: and then the story says that, "as they were looking out then, they saw the cavalcade upon the plain; and they saw a champion leading them, having on a crimson four-folding cloak, with its four borders of gold upon it; a shield with eight joints of *Findruine* at his back; a *Leinidh* reaching from his knees to his hips; fair yellow hair upon his head, falling down both flanks of the steed he rode; a bunch of thread of gold depending from it of the weight of seven ounces; and it was hence he was called *Edchu Rond* [that is, *Edchu* of the gold thread or wire]. A gray black-spotted stallion under him, [having] a golden mouthpiece in his mouth; two spears with ribs of *Findruine* in his hand, and a gold-hilted sword upon his side".[87] This splendid champion was the king of *Ui Maine* in the present counties of Galway and Roscommon, and one of the *Firbolg* race.

he wore a kilt.

[87] [original:—amail robatar and iar sin, condacatar insluaig san mag; acas conacatar in loech remib, acas brat corcra cethardia bail imm, cona ceoceoraib oir [*recte* oraib] fair; sciath chonoct nairlib findruine fora muin; lene cona clar argait imm o aglun co-sodbrunn; mong findbuidi fair combid for dib slesaib inneich; rond oir eissice roibe coticrom .uii. nungi, ba de ro hainmniged Edchu Rond fair. Gabair brec glasa forsidiu, conabelltc oir sriae; dagai cona narnadaib findruine inalaim, cloidib orduirnn for a chriss.—H. 2. 16. col. 961, line 6.]

Here, I think, there can be no doubt of the precise character and use of the *Léinidh;* and the following passage from the ancient Gaedhelic Triads, gives us even the very law which regulated the wearing of the *Leinidh*, as well as of the *Ochrath*, or trews; and the length of the hair (or beard). Thus speaks this Triad:

"Three legal handsbreadths, that are, namely—a handsbreadth between his shoes and his *Ochrath*, or pantaloons; a handsbreadth between his ear and his beard (or hair); and a handsbreadth between the border of his *Leinidh* and his knee.[88]

Law regulating the wearing of the *Leinidh* or kilt, and the *Ochrath* or pantaloons.

I need not, I think, say another word to show what the *Ochrath* and the *Leinidh* were, but it would appear from the absence of the *Leinidh* in the description of the fat doorkeeper, that that article of dress was not worn by the inferior people, but that it appertained to the higher classes and to the professions. The identification of this article of dress is, I must confess, a late discovery, and time has not allowed me to pursue the subject farther at present; but I have no doubt but that I shall be able hereafter to add to these descriptions some more striking illustrations from some of the illuminations to be met with so often in our ancient books and from our sculptures.[89]

(88) [original:—Tri basa techta (.i. dligteacha). Bas eitir a ussa (.i. assam) acas na hailt agas a ochrat (.i. alt), bas eitir a u (.i. a cluas) agas a berrat (.i. mullach a chinn), bas eitir curtar aleine agas a ghlun (.i. cuirter le h-ór no le himioll an échtuig (.i. imioll lásaite)".—H. 1. 15. p. 955, line 7.]

(89) [*Vide postea*, Lecture xxv. vol. ii. p. 143, where a striking illustration of the nature of the *Leinidh* is given from the tale of the *Bruighean Da Derga*.]

LECTURE XXIV.

[Delivered July 10th, 1860.]

(VIII.) Dress and Ornaments (continued). Constant references to fringes of gold thread; mention of this ornament in the account of *Medbh's* visit to her chief Druid in the commencement of the *Táin Bo Chuailgne*,—description of *Fedelm* the prophetess weaving a fringe; the fringe sword or lath mentioned in a poem of *Dallan Forgaill* (circa A.D. 560). Ancient laws relating to the pledging of ornaments, etc.; law relating to the pledging of a needle; the pledging of a queen's work bag; the work bag of an *Aireach Feibhe*. The legal contents of a work bag formed only a small part of a lady's personal ornaments. References to dyeing, weaving, embroidering, etc., in the ancient laws regulating Distress; objects connected with those arts for the recovery of which proceedings might have been taken under those laws. Objects connected with the textile arts mentioned in other ancient laws. Coloured thread and wool paid as rent or tribute. The dye-stuffs used were of home growth. Legend of St. *Ciaran* and the blue dye stuff called *Glaissin*. Summary of the processes in the textile arts mentioned in the extracts quoted in the lecture. Reference to embroidery in the tale of the *Tochmarc nEimire*, and in the *Dinnseanchas*. *Coca* the embroideress of St. *Columcillé*. The knowledge of the Gaedhils about colours shown by the illuminations to the Book of Kells. Reference in the Book of Ballymote to the colours worn by different classes. Cloth of various colours formed part of the tributes or taxes paid as late as the ninth and tenth centuries. Tributes to the king of *Caiseal* according to the Book of Rights from: *Ara*; *Boirinn*; Leinster; *Uaithne*; *Duibhneach* and *Drung*; *Corcumruadh*; the *Deise*; *Orbraidhe*. Stipends paid by the king of *Caiseal* to the kings of Kerry; *Raithlenn*; *Ara*. Tributes to the king of Connacht from *Umhall*; the *Greagraidhe*; the *Conmaicne*; the *Ciarraidhe*; the *Luighne*; the *Dealbhna Ui Maine*. Stipends paid by the king of Connacht to the kings of: *Dealbhna*; *Ui Maine*. Tributes to the king of *Aileach* from: the *Cuileantraidhe*; the *Ui Mic Caerthainn*; *Ui Tuirtre*. Stipends paid by the king of *Aileach* to the kings of: *Cinel Boghaine*; *Cinel Eanna*; *Craebh*; *Ui Mic Caerthainn*; *Tulach Og*. Stipends paid by the king of Oriel to the kings of: *Ui Breasail*; *Ui Eachach*; *Ui Meith*; *Ui Dortain*; *Ui Briuin Archoill*; *Ui Tuirtre*; *Feara Manach*; *Mughdhorn* and *Ros*. Stipends paid by the king of *Uladh* to the kings of: *Cuailgne*; *Araidhe*; *Cobhais*; *Muirtheimne*. Tributes to the king of *Uladh* from: *Semhne*; *Crothraidhe*; *Cathal*. Gifts to the king of Tara. Stipends paid by the king of Tara to the kings of: *Magh Lacha*; *Cuircne*; *Ui Becon*. Tributes to the king of Tara from: the *Luighne*; the *Feara Arda*; the *Saithne*; *Gailenga*; the *Ui Beccon*. Stipends paid by the king of Leinster to the: *Ui Fealain*; the chief of *Cualann*; *Ui Feilmeadha*; king of *Raeilinn*; *Ui Criomhthannan*. Tributes to the king of Leinster from the: Galls; *Forthuatha*; *Fotharta*; men of South Leinster. Gifts from the monarch of Erinn to the king of *Emain Macha*. Stipends of the king of *Emain Macha* to the kings of: *Rathmor*; *Ui Briuin*; *Conmaicne*. Gifts bestowed on the king of Leinster by the monarch of Erinn whenever he visited Tara. Gift of the king of Leinster on his return from Tara to the king of *Ui Fealain*. Gifts of the monarch of Erinn to the king of *Caiseal* when at *Teamhair Luachra*. Stipends given by the king of *Caiseal* at the visitation of the monarch of Erinn to the: *Deise*; *Ui Chonaill*. Stipends paid by the king of Connacht to the kings of: *Ui Maine*; *Luighne*. Colours of winds, according to the preface to the *Seanchas Mor*.

In the last lecture, I brought together a considerable number of general descriptions of the costume of kings and warriors armed for battle, taken chiefly from the historic tale of the great war between Connacht and Ulster in the time of *Conchobar Mac Nessa*, about one thousand nine hundred years ago. I purpose in this lecture to give as detailed descriptions of the manufacture of ornamental dresses, as the accounts preserved in our old books will enable me to do. XXIV.

We have seen, and shall see hereafter, in the description of the clothes of men and women, constant reference to borders, or fringes of thread of gold and other materials and of various colours. And in fact we find a very circumstantial, and therefore most interesting, reference to the actual manufacture of this beautiful ornament at the beginning of the tale of the *Táin Bo Chuailgne*.

Medhbh's visit to her chief druid before the great *Táin*;

When the three great parties already spoken of, consisting of queen *Medbh*'s seven sons, their cousins, the seven sons of *Magach*, *Cormac Conloingeas*, the exiled Ulster prince, and their followers, had arrived at the palace of *Cruachan* and quartered themselves for the time on the surrounding territory, queen *Medbh* herself began to entertain serious thoughts on the probable results of the great war on which she was about to enter. To satisfy herself as far as possible, the queen ordered her chariot and drove to the residence of her chief Druid, and demanded knowledge and prediction of the future from him. "Numbers", said *Medbh*, "shall separate from their companions and from their friends this day, and from their country, and from their lands; from father, and from mother; and if they do not all return in safety, it is upon me their groans and their curses shall be poured out; however, there goes not forth and there remains not at home any one more precious to us than ourselves, and ascertain thou for us", said she, "shall we return or shall we not". And the Druid answered: "Whosoever returns not, you yourself shall return".(70)

The story then goes on as follows:

description of *Fedelm* the prophetess who appeared to her when returning;

"The charioteer then turned the chariot, and *Medbh* returned back. She saw what was a surprise to her, namely, a single woman sitting upon the shaft of the chariot beside her in her presence. What the woman was doing was, weaving a border with a sword [that is, a lath or rod] of *Findruini* (or white

(70) [original:—Soċaiḋe scaras fria ċoemu acas fria ċairdiu sund indiu, ar Meḋb, acas fria ċriċ, acas fria ferand; fria athair, acas fria mathair, acas meni ṫisec uli in imslan, is formsa co m-bensat an osnaid acas a mallachtain. Ar ai sin ni teit immaċ acas ni anand isus ar diliu lind oldammit fadessin, acas fintassu dún in tecam fo na tecam. Acas ra raid in drui: "Cipé no na tic ticfasu fessin".—H. 2. 18. f. 42. a. col. 2.]

XXIV. bronze) in her right hand, having seven ribs of red gold in its points (or ends). She had a green spot-speckled cloak upon her; and a round heavy headed brooch (*Bretnas*) in that cloak over her breast. Her countenance was crimson, rich-blooded; her eyes gray and sparkling; her lips red and thin; her teeth shining and pearly, so that you would think it was a shower of fair pearls that had been set in her head; like fresh *Partaing* [Coral] were her lips; as sweet as the strings of sweet harps played by the hands of long practised masters, were the sounds of her voice and her fine speech; whiter than the snow shed in one night were her skin and her body appearing through her dress; she had long, even, white feet; and her nails were crimson, well cut, circular, and sharp; she had long fair yellow hair; three wreaths of her hair were braided around her head; and another braid descending as low down as the calves of her legs".[71]

Queen *Medbh* questioned this strange visitor as to her name and the cause of her visit. The lady answered that she was a handmaid of her own, from the fairy mansion of *Cruachan;* that her name was *Fedelm* the prophetess; and that she had come to tell her royal mistress beforehand, the losses and misfortunes which would result from the intended expedition. The prophetess then in a poem of ten stanzas, describes minutely the person of *Cuchulaind*, who was to bring such losses and disasters upon the queen; and disappears.

the weaving of a border or fringe the most important part of this description.

The most remarkable matter in this short description is the fact of the speaker being engaged in weaving a fringe or border in the same way that such an operation is carried on at this day: for the poetical sword which she made use of for the purpose is represented by the less costly sword-like lath of our more matter of fact times. The fringe sword or lath is mentioned also in the ancient and obscure poem, believed to have been written by *Dallan Forgaill* for the shield of *Aedh* or Hugh, king of *Oirghialla* or Oriel about the year 560.

The fringe-sword mentioned in a poem of *Dallan Forgaill* (circa A.D. 560).

(71) [original:—Impáis in t-ara in carpat, acas do ċaét Medb for cúlu. Conaccai ni raringnad lé, .i. in n-aen mnái for fertais in ċarpait na farrad ina doċum. Is amlaid boi ind inden ic figi corr-ṫairi acas claideb findruini ina láim deiss, cona secc n-aslib do dergór ina dessaib. Bratt balla-brecc uani impi; bretnas corrach ċren-cend sin brutt os a bruinni. Gnúis ċorcra ċrumaineċ lé; rosc glass gaireċtaċ lé; beóil derga thanaide; deit ṁamda nemanda, anndaslec batar frossa find-nemand ertais ina cend; cosmail do nua partaing a beóil; binnidir teta mend-ċrot aca seinm allámaib sírṡuad, bind-ṡogur a goṫa acas a cáin urlabra; gilidir sneċta snigeo sri oen aidċi taidleċ a cniss acas a colla, seċ a timṫaċ seċtair; traigṫi seta sithgela; ingn. corcra, cori, cruind-gera, lé; folt sind-buidi fata forórda sairi; teora tuillri da fult imma cend; trilis aile combenad forcaid sri colpṫa.—H, 2. 18. f. 42. a col. 2.]

This singular composition consists of twenty-one stanzas, the fourteenth of which runs as follows: XXIV.

["It was not woven with a beam or heddles
Nor a wooden lath of the whitest
Nor [was it] the handiwork of a dexterous embroideress,
Nor did red fastening fasten it.][72]

This is said of the king of Oriel's shield *Dubhghilla*, and from the negative allusions to the absence of the weaver's beam, the weaving swords, or heddles, the hand of an expert woman, and the fastening pins in its manufacture, it is evident that the shield was one of those formed of wickerwork or woven laths.

It would be easy to multiply examples of the references to rich borders or laces in our old historic and romantic tales, but the following one or two instances will be sufficient to illustrate this article of our ancient luxury.

Ancient la relating to the pledgi of ornaments and articles belonging women;

The following curious enactments found in the ancient Institutes of Erinn commonly called the Brehon Laws, relate to the pledging of certain articles peculiarly appertaining to women, and is of great interest in connection with the present subject. These laws were enacted to provide against the loss or misappropriation of articles of domestic use, as well as of personal adornment and convenience, when these happened to have been pledged and not delivered up when demanded, and upon payment of the sum lent; in which case the overholders were liable to "smart" fines. And these fines varied according to the importance of the article to the owner, as for instance: if a man or woman pledged a ring, a bracelet, or a brooch, and wished to release it on the eve of a great fair or assembly, the disgrace of the owner for having to appear without his proper ornaments or not at all, was included in the calculation of the fine for overholding the article.[73] Thus says the law: "If there happens to be a day of solemnity, such as Easter or Christmas, or an assembly, such as a fair, or a convocation of the state, to entertain a question, by a king, or by a synod [of the clergy], if his pledged

(72) [original:—.i. nir figed aggarmain na aclaidmib.

Ni caill garman ga fige
Ni cloidbi croinn co n-gile
Ni lamach dag-mna druine
Ni derg airrge gairige.—H. 3. 18. p. 560]

(73) [original:—Ma tecmai lith laithe, no dáil, no thorcomracc tuaithe, mani toirc a gell dó, no séd berid fiú, dosli lan log aenech do cach, fo miad, la eraicc do neoch do ruirmesem di smachtaib ocus aithgenaib.—H. 2. 15. f. 30? The whole of the passages from the fragment of the *Seanchas Mór* in H. 2. 15. T.C.D. quoted in this lecture are contained, as well as I can recollect, on pp. 27 to 30 of that MS. It was not available to me for collation, and the references to the pages where given are consequently only approximations.]

XXIV. article is not restored to the pledger, that is his brooch, and everything which is composed of [gold or of] silver, or an article equal to it in value, there shall be a fine of dishonour, and other enumerated fines, together with restitution of the pledge [upon the overholder]".(74)

the pledging of a needle; The law then goes into more minute details as follows:—

"What has the law laid down as the fine of a pledged needle? Answer—it is a *dairt* [or yearling calf] that is paid as the fine for it. If it be a cloak needle, it is a heifer that is paid as its fine. And it is the same fine that is paid to any person [for needles], but women are the most proper to put them in pledge".(75)

This article is further explained as follows: "What does the law lay down as the fine of a pledged needle? Answer—A *dairt* [or yearling calf] worth four *screpalls* [of three pennies each] is what is paid as the fine of the needle, that is of the fine needle. That is to say: a yearling calf to every woman whatever as the fine for her needle, except the embroideress, for, as regards her, it is the value of an ounce of silver that shall be paid her as the fine for her needle; provided, however, that this may not be paid her except for the needle with which she works her ornamentation, that is, her embroidery".(76)

This article is further explained by another section, which says:—

"The lawful right of the pledged needle of an embroideress is laid down by the law. It is in ornamentation she is paid as far as the value of an ounce of silver; because every woman who is an embroideress is entitled to more profit (or value) than a queen".(77)

This is a remarkable instance of protection to skilled industry so many ages ago! The law proceeds:—

(74) [original:—Lith Laithe, .i. cairt no noclaig. dáil, .i. oenaig, chomracc tuaithe, .i. im caingin fri rig, no senad, a gelldo, .i. adealg, acas doneoch is aicde airgid, smachtaib, .i. dairtib, aithginaib, .i. na naigde.—H. 2. 15. f. 30?]

(75) [original;—Cid forso ro suidiged techta sullema gill snaċaite la feine? Ain.—Dairt direnar inna suillema side. Madbratsnaċat is colbtach ina suillemsido. Noch is comdire di cech recht, act ic mna aca corus dia tabairt ingell.—H. 2. 15. Vide ante, p. 111.]

(76) [original:—Cid forso .i. cia ara samaigea dliged suillem gill snaċaide da seir ino fenecais? Dairt, .i. dairte .iiii. screbull isead eirniċer ina suillemside .i. na snaċaite caile .i. dairt do caċ mnai uile a suillem a snataici cenmotá in druinig, uair mad iside is log uingi airgit bias di a suillem a snaċaiti; no dno, cona beit sin di act isin snaċsec da nugnead a himdenam, .i. a druinechus". [Noch is comdire .i. neoch seċim goneċ comór inni is dir du gaċ sicc duine ga mi si. Acht ic mna .i. aċtaigim conid iad na mna is cors dia tabairt ingill.—H. 2. 15. Vide ante, p. 111.]

(77) [original:—Techta sullema gill snatate, druinige la féine. Imdénmaib direnar corruicce log uinge argit; air iss mo do chorbu dosli cachben bes druinech lo daite rigna.—H. 2. 15. Vide ante, p. 111.]

XXIV.

"The lawful right of the pledged needle of an embroideress is laid down in the law. She is paid the value of an ounce of silver in ornamentation [which we may suppose means materials for ornamentation], for every needle which she has [pledged]". "Or it is half an ounce of silver she is paid for the needle with which she works her ornamentation; and the same to her, as to any other woman for every needle which she has from that out. The greater profit [which the embroideress was entitled to beyond the queen], consisted of *Breac-Glas* [green-spotted cloth] and *Srol* [i. e. satin or silk], and fringes (or borders); and that all these ornamentations were worth an ounce of silver".(77)

the pledging of a queen's work-bag;

In the following article the contents of a queen's workbag are minutely recorded.

"The lawful fine of the pledged workbag of the king's wife. If it contains but two of its lawful articles, there are two ounces of silver paid for it.(78)

"If it contains its legitimate property, namely, a veil of one colour, and a *Mind* or crown of gold, and a *Land*, or crescent of gold, and thread of silver. This then is the workbag of the wives of the kings, and when all these articles are in it, three cows (or six heifers) are its fine: and if they are not in it, it is double of every article which is in it [that is paid], until it reaches the three cows, and when it does so reach, it goes no further".(79)

And again the law says, "If it contains its legitimate property, namely, a veil of one colour, and thread of silver, and a *Land*, or crescent of gold, and a *Mind* or crown [of gold]—if all these are in it, it is three ounces [of silver that are paid]. If it is one of them that [it contains] it is one ounce that is paid. But if the four articles are in it, it is three cows that are paid for it; and if they are not [in it] it is double [the value] of every article that it contains [that is paid for it] until

(77) [original:—Techta fuillemagill, .i. dliged fuillema gill snataite na druinige. Imdenmaib, .i. esraincer log uingi airgid d'imdenam di in gaċ snaṫaid uili bis aici. No is leṫ uingi airgid di is an snaṫaid da nidenand a imdenam; acas cutruma di, acas da gaċ mnai eile in gaċ snaṫaid uile bis aice o hsroinimaċ. Do thorba, .i. do breaclas acas srol, acas corrtaraib; acas arbat siu uinge uile na imdenma. H. 2. 15. Vide ante, p. 111.]

(78) [original:—Techta fuillema gill iadaige mna rig, .i. dliged fuillema gill iadaigi mná in rig. Mad deide dib, it di uinge.—H. 2. 15. Vide ante, p. 111.]

(79) [original:—Iadaige, .i. tiag, ma beith cona thothguraib, .i. ma dia rab si go na toċaraib dligthea-ċaib, .i. caille aen daṫe, acas mind oir, acas land oir, acas rand airgid, .i. iadaċ ban na rig seo, acas o beid, na neiċi sin inti is trí ba ina fuillem, acas mana rabad, is diablad gaċa neiċ bis inti no go ria na tri ba, ácas ord sia naċo teid tairsib.—H. 2. 15. Vide ante, p. 111.]

XXIV. it reaches three cows, and when it reaches [the three cows] it goes no further".[80]

the work-bag of the wife of an Airech Feibhe.

The law then passes from the professional and from the amateur embroideress and from the king's wife, to the wife of an *Airech Feibhe*, or chief of dignity, of whom it says:

"The workbags of the wives of the noble [or lord] grades, that is, a workbag with its legitimate property of [silver] thread, with a veil, and with a diadem of gold, and a silk handkerchief, and if so, there are three heifers paid as its fine; and if these are not in it, it is the double of every article which is in it that is paid until it reaches three heifers".[81]

This text is further explained as follows:

"If it be a bag without its legitimate property, namely, a veil, and silver thread, and a crescent of silver, and a diadem of gold; or what contains a painted mask, that is, what contains a painted face, [or mask] for assemblies, namely, the banner or the handkerchief of silk, or the gold thread, that is when it does not contain those things; and if those things were contained in it, three heifers [would have been the lawful fine for it]; but when those [articles] are not in it, it is double the value of everything which is in it until it reaches the three heifers [that is paid for it, but when it so reaches] it goes no further".[82] This is a very curious entry regarding ladies' dress, and indicates, I think, a peculiar and advanced state of civilization.

The legal contents of a work bag only a small part of a lady's personal ornaments, etc.

So much then for the legal protection of an embroideress in ancient Erinn, and for the legal requisites of what is, I believe, in our times called a lady's workbag or work-box. We must remember, however, that the articles required by law to constitute the contents of a lady's treasure bag, formed only a small, though an important part of the articles intended to grace and decorate her person. Neither her ordinary nor her state garments are enumerated here; neither are her rings, bracelets, clasps, anklets, brooches, earrings, necklaces, or torques, nor the

(80) [original:—Techtaib, .i. caille aen sinna, acas rond, acas land oir, acas mind—ma beit inne uile it teora uinge. Mad én dib es én uinge. No matait na triur inti is tri ba ina fuillem; acas mana fuilet is diablad cach neich inntí co ria tri ba, acas ono ra noco téit tairrib.—H. 2. 15 f. 28.]

(81) [original:—Techta fuillema, .i. iadaċ ban na ngrad flaṫa, .i. iadaċ cona toċas techta rainde, gu caille, acas gu mind oir, acas breidsida, acas tri samaisce ina fuillem, acas mani uilet sed inti is diablad gaċ neiċ uil inti, no gu ria na tri samaisce.—H. 2. 15. f. 29. a.]

(82) [original:—Manis iadach, .i. manas tiag gan a toċos dligtaiġ, .i. caille, acas rond, acas land airgit, acas mind oir; ni conai sechal, .i. no ni coimedas ecos dála coin, .i. in meirgi, no in brat sida, no in rainde, uair noċo fuil and inni sin; acas da mbeċ rabat tri samaisci; uair naċ fuil is diablad gaċ neiċ uil inti no go ria na tri samaisci; acas noco téid tairsib.—H. 2. 15. f. 29. a.]

golden balls, rings, and pins of her hair, all of which articles, we know, were worn by the ladies of those times at the great fairs, assemblies, and state meetings of the country.

References to dyeing, weaving, embroidering, etc., in the Ancient Laws regulating Distress;

In a similar law to that just referred to, we find some details regarding the dyeing of cloth, weaving it, and preparing it for use, all which were employments of women. It is only from these allusions that we can discover clearly what they had to wear in those ancient times. The law I allude to is one regulating the recovery of debts by distress or seizure, and the time allowed for the distrained property to remain in the hands of the owner, in order to give him time to procure means to pay the debt. This law was general and complicated; and the time of stay, as it was called, varied according to circumstances, from the immediate carrying away of the distress, to a period of one, two, three, five, ten, and fifteen days, or more. Two days, however, was the stay of sale of all seizures made on the part of women only, either for their pay as manufacturers, or for articles connected with their manufactures, sold, lent, or taken away from them. The following are the items for the recovery of which women had recourse to the aid of the law, as far as this particular enactment is concerned.

objects connected with those arts for the recovery of which proceedings might have been taken under the laws.

1. The price (or wages) of hand produce [labour], that is, the price of what she produced with her hand, namely, teasing and colouring and weaving (wool), the price or pay being one-tenth part of each work [i.e. of the value of the woven piece].[83]

Also for napping [or also sleeking] the cloth, half the wages of the weaving woman, i.e. the wages given, i.e. the price of weaving.[84]

2. For materials, such as of gray flax and gray woollen yarn, when upon the spindles.[85]

3. For a flax-spinning spindle.[86]

4. For a spindle, i.e. a wool-spinning spindle, or a spindle of weft.[86]

5. For a foot-bag, that is, a bag [which contains the sorted wool], and which is placed under (or at) the woman's feet, out of which she combs (or cards) her materials, that is, the combing (or carding) bag.[87]

(83) [original:—athgabail aile, .i. ar ata anad naili. im log lamchoraid, .i. im log in toraid do ni si ó láim, .i. tocad, acas brecad, acas sige, .i. dechmad cacha dúla.—*Seanchus Mór*, Harleian MSS. 432. Brit. Mus. f. 10. a. a.]

(84) [original: im forbriche, .i. leth na ruba don mnái sigi, .i. ruba berr-tha[r], i. logh sige.—*Ibid.*]

(85) [original:—im cach naadbur, .i. glas lin. bis i fertsib, .i. snáth glas olla.—*Ibid.*]

(86) [original:—im fertais, .i. lin. im snimaire, .i. olla no in fertais loim, .i. innoich.—*Ibid.*]

(87) [original:—im ser bolg, .i. inin bolg bis fo péis fochaige, as a cirann a abras, .i. in cirbolc.—*Ib.*]

XXIV.

objects connected with those arts for the recovery of which proceedings might have been taken under the laws.

6. For a *Feith-Géir*, which puts a sharp [smooth] face upon her weaving.[88] [This, I believe, was the sleeking stick or bone which weavers still use to close and flatten linen cloth on the breast beam of the loom while in process of being woven.]

7. For all the weaving implements, i.e. for all the instruments used in weaving, including beams and heddles, that is, weaving rods.[89]

8. For the flax scutching-stick, i.e. by which the flax is scutched. For the distaff or flax rock [or for] the spindle for spinning wool.[90]

9. For a rolling beam, that is, the beam without the radiating head, without sharp points.[91] [This was, I believe, the front beam of the loom upon which the warp was rolled up to be woven.]

10. For a border (or fringe) sword, that is, [the sword or lath] upon which the border (or fringe) is woven.[92]

11. For materials, that is, for the finished material, the material which wants only to be woven; that is, the white balls, the white (bleached) thread.[93]

12. For the instrument of the manufacturing woman, namely, the winding bars, that is, the tree upon which she prepares the yarn, the winding reel.[94] [This was not the vertical reel upon which the skene of yarn was formed from off the spool or the spindle, but it was the horizontal reel upon which the skene of yarn, when taken off the vertical reel, was laid, and wound off into balls or bottoms, as they still call them in the rural districts.]

13. For a border fringe upon itself, [i.e. cloth having a bordered edge or fringe made of its own warp, and not sewed on].[95]

14. For the facilitater of her handiwork [namely], that which facilitates to her the work she produces from her hand; the pattern piece of leather, which is placed before her, in which is delineated the pattern of the work.[96]

(88) [original:—im feċ [no fiḋ] geir [.i. do beir feiṫ ger dar a figi.]—*Ibid.* and vol. i. p. 152 of *Senchus Mór* of Brehon Law Commis.]

(89) [original:—im aiceḋ fige uile .i. comobar na fige do garmnib ocus do claidmib .i. na slata fige. Harl. MSS. 432, fol. 10. a. a.]

(90) [original:—im slese lin, .i. da slesther in lin. im cuicil, .i. cuicil lin, .i. in fertais, .i. nolla.—*Ibid.*]

(91) [original:—im lugarmain, .i. luga garman, no lingua garman, .i. in garman cen buirr [cenbair], .i. cen faebar.—*Ibid.*]

(92) [original:—im cloidem corthaire, .i. ara figther in corrthair.—*Ibid.*]

(93) [original:—im abras, .i. adbar uais acht a figi, .i. na certle gela, .i. snath finn.—*Ibid.*]

(94) [original:—im comorair na-bairse [.i. ini ar a comoibrigenn in abairsech a h-abras], .i. crann cochartai [.i. in crann cocartha.] no cochrais [.i. cranda beca a cinn corthar]. nabairse, .i. gnim ar gnim.—*Ib.*]

(95) [original.—im corthair, .i. uissi féin.—*Ibid.*]

(96) [original:—im airce lamthoraid, .i. uraice le in torad do gni ó láim; in nuaċ leob ina fiadnaisi, .i. fuaċ in gresa innti.—*Ibid.*]

XXIV.

Objects connected with those arts for the recovery of which proceedings might have been taken under the laws.

This most curious fact, of a pattern, cut or painted, by an artist or designer in leather, was probably made available for figured weaving as well as embroidery and other needlework. Several bones of animals have been discovered, and are now in the museum of the Royal Irish Academy, containing patterns of illuminated letters for ancient books, and delicate interlacings for such letters, or for the embellishment of shrines, croziers, covers of books, etc.; and an ancient box or pouch of strong leather, with various interlacings and grotesque figures, embossed by pressure, and which was intended for, and used as, a *case* for the ancient Book of Armagh, is now preserved, as well as the book itself, in the Library of Trinity College, Dublin. There is good reason to believe that this case was made in the tenth century.

14. For a wallet with its contents, that is, a bag with what is put to keep in it. For the material, that is, the *Aiteog*, that is, the string that is about it, that is, about its mouth.[97]

15. For a *Crioll*, that is, a bag formed of strips of leather stitched together with a thong.[98]

[This *Crioll*-making was a trade in itself, but included the making of leather bottles. The maker was called a *Cliaraidhe*, from *Clera*, a word synonymous with *Crioll;* and he was also called a *Pataire*, from *Pait*, a bottle, when he practised that branch of the trade. The brogue-maker, or *Cuaranaigh*, sometimes made bag and bottle making part of his trade.]

16. For a leathern tube-bag, that is a bag (or case) with a wooden tube, that which encased the cosmetic or oil bottle.[99]

17. For a *Rinde* [that is, a round wooden bucket].[100]

18. For a *Cusal* [that is, a long wooden bin (or box).] These were small wooden repositaries of prepared materials, which the women kept in ancient times".[101]

19. For a needle [i.e. the thread passes through its eye].[102]

20. For ornamentation thread, that is, coloured thread.[103]

21. For a *Scaideirc*, that is, the reflector of the woman's image, that is, a mirror".[104]

(97) [original:—im iadag cona ecortaig, .i. in tiag cus ani ecarthar innti. In [im] tabrús, .i. aiteog, .i. in loman bis imbe, .i. im a beolu.—*Ibid.*]

(98) [original:—im criol, .i. im croiall, cro fuaigther d'i allaib, no cro assoiallaib.—*Ibid.*]

(99) [original:—im crandbolg, .i. lechair, .i. bolg ar ambid crann-belan anallud, .i. bis fon pait foilcti.—*Ibid.*]

(100) [original:—im rinde, .i. in fota.—*Ibid.*]

(101) [original:—im chusail, .i. gairit, .i. cruind rigind, .i. crandoga beca no biṫ aca anallót im an abras.—*Ibid.*]

(102) [original:—im snáthait, .i. sét int snaiṫ ina cró.—*Ibid.*]

(103) [original:—im snáithe liga, .i. snaṫ daṫa.—*Ibid.*]

(104) [original:—im scaideirc, .i. scat derc na mban, .i. scáṫán.—*Ibid.*]

XXIV.

For *Focoisle ben*, that is, anything which one woman borrows from another".[105]

Objects connected with the textile arts mentioned in other ancient laws.

To this curious list of articles, connected with the manufacture of domestic clothing, may be added the following few items, which are found in the Brehon Laws, which relate to a separation between husband and wife, when each of the parties took of the common property, as it stood at the time of separation, an amount proportioned to their respective stocks when first married, the property of the wife not resting in her husband under the Irish law. The following is an extract from the law alluded to:

"Four divisions there are upon wool [at the time of separation], of which the woman takes a seventh part, if it be only in the fleece, and a sixth part if it be in flakes, and a third part when almost ready [for the rock], half after oil was put into it, and also when in cloth".[106]

"Four divisions there are upon the *Glaissin* [that is, the dye-stuff]. A ninth part for plucking it, a sixth part for bruising it, and until it is applied to the colouring, that is, until the wool passes from the *Glaisin* into the first, or ground colour. A third part, if it has passed out of the first dying into the second She takes half if it is fully dyed.[107]

"Four divisions that are upon flax for her. She takes but a measure of the seed if it is only standing, that is, if the flax be still growing, or in bundles unbroken. She takes a sixth part if it is broken. She takes half if it has passed from the scutch".[108]

To these curious references to the materials of cloth, and linen, and their manufacture, to be found in our ancient laws, I shall here add another small item from an ancient tract called the Book of Rights, published by the Celtic Society in the year 1847. This curious book gives an account of the tributes and services paid by the various chiefs and territories of Erinn to the provincial and petty kings, and these again to the monarch, as well as the monarch's stipends and presents to these in return.

Coloured thread and wool paid as rent or tribute.

Among the tributes and services paid to the king of Leinster

(105) [original:—Focoisleben ar araile, .i. berir in ben ó céili.—Harleian MSS. 432. fol. 10. a. a.]

(106) [original:—Cetheora randa fuil for olland .i. u in [.un.?] mad ar lomrad, acas .ui. ed alloaib, acas trian a eircho adbalam, Lech o do cae beoil ind icir abrus acas etach.—H. 2. 15.]

(107) [original:—Cetheora bi for glaisin, .i. nomad ar na buain .ui. ed iar na minugad, co techt a cro [.i. arin nglaisin ina cet cro]. Trian iar na cet codad [.i. is in cru tanaisi]. Lech mad co taide.—H. 2. 15.]

(108) [original:—Cetheora randa di for lin. Hes Cra ruis di mad for a cois bech in lin, no mad as tuaraib cen chuagain. Seissed mad inas ta [main dartai]. Lech óod to oclar.—H. 2. 15.]

are the following few: "The burnishing, and renewing, and washing, and cleansing of his court was performed by the *Cocarts* of the lower order of the people; and the supply of his court with crimson [thread] and crimson dye, and red, and light blue thread, and white, and blay, and yellow, and 'bindean wool', from the better class of *Cocarts*".[199]

Here we see how the manufacture of cloth, and the supply of its materials, were distributed among the lower and middle classes of peasants in ancient times, so that it could never cease to be cultivated in a respectable degree, since even the king's wardrobe as well as his presents were supplied from the wool and yarn dyed and spun by them.

The dye stuffs used were of home growth.

Another curious fact connected with those manufactures was, that it appears that the various dye-stuffs were of home growth or produce.

The first part of the process of wool dyeing is called in Irish *Ruamadh*, or *Rimeing*, and this is effected by steeping and boiling the wool with the twigs or brushwood of the alder tree, to which they give the name of *Ruaim*, or "*Rime*". This process produces a good reddish brown colour, and forms the ground for black, blue, or red: green I have never seen produced at home, except by one woman, Catherine Collins, an intelligent mantua-maker in Clare, who kept her knowledge a profound secret all her life.

If the colour is to be a black, after the wool is "rimed" as described above, it is again put down with a black sediment, which is taken up from the bottom of certain pools, ponds, and holes, in the bogs and boggy borders of lakes, and which is called *Dubh-Poill* or black of the pond, a stuff which imparted a strong but rather dull black colour; the addition, however, of oak chips or twigs improves the undecided colour to a clear glossy jet black. Now, of course, logwood and copperas, whenever they can be readily got, are generally substituted for the bog stuff and oak chips. In order to dye the same "rimed" wool of a splendid crimson red, they cultivated a plant in

[199] [See original in *Leabhar na g-Ceart* or The Book of Rights, p. 218. The following is the poetical account of these tributes:

The unfree tribes,—a condition not oppressive
That are on his [the king's] own lands;
Servile rent by them, it is the truth,
Is to be supplied to the palaces of the chief king.
The tribute which is due of these
[Is] of fire-bote and wood;
[Also] the renewing of his cloaks, constant the practice
A tribute in washing and in cleansing.
There is due of the best party of these
Ruu and purple of fine strength
Red thread, white wool, I will not conceal it,
Yellow *blaan* and *bindean*.
Leabhar na g-Ceart, p. 223.]

XXIV. ancient Erinn which they called *Rudh* and *Roidh;* but as the plant is not now known in the country, I cannot designate it by any more intelligible name. In the ancient laws it classed with corn and onions; and they speak of a ridge of *Rudh* or *Roidh* as they would of a ridge of onions or corn.

The other ingredient already mentioned, which is called *Glaissin*, and with which they produced the various shades of blue, appears to have been the plant now called "woad", formerly much used by dyers.[116] The late Mr. Francis Mahony, of Limerick, made a handsome fortune by the cultivation in fields of this plant, and its application to the purposes of dyeing, which he carried on very extensively for many years.

Legend of St. *Ciaran*, and the blue dye-stuff called *Glaissin*.

There is a curious reference to the application of the *Glaissin*, in colouring wool, preserved in the ancient Gaedhelic life of St. *Ciaran* of Clonmacnoise, who died A.D. 548. The following is a literal translation:—

"On a certain day *Ciaran*'s mother was preparing *Glaissin*. And when she had it ready to put the cloth into it, then his mother said to him: 'Go out, *Ciaran*', said she, 'people do not deem it lucky to have men in the house with them when they are putting cloth down to be dyed'. 'May there be a dark gray stripe in it then', said *Ciaran*. And so of all the cloth that was put into the *Glaissin*, there was no piece of them without a dark gray stripe in it.

"The *Glaissin* was prepared again, and his mother said to him: 'Go thou out now this time, *Ciaran*, and let there be no dark gray stripe in the cloth this turn'".

It was then he said:

"Allelujah Domine.
May my mother's *Glaissin* be white!
Every time it comes back to thy hand
May it be as white as bone;
Every time it comes out of the boiling,
May it be whiter than curds".

And so every piece of cloth that was put into it after this was white.

"The *Glaissin* was prepared the third time. '*Ciaran*', said his mother, 'do not spoil the *Glaissin* upon me this turn, but let it be blessed by you', [this *Ciaran* did] and after it was blessed by *Ciaran*, there was not made before or after it a *Glaissin* as good as it, for though it were all the cloth of all the *Cinel*

(116) [The Isatis tinctoria (*Lin.*) *Glastum* or *Guadum*. The French call it *Pastel*; the Italians, *Guado* and *Glastro*; and the Spaniards, *Pastel* and *Glasto*. See on this subject *Introduction*.]

XXIV.

Legend of St. *Ciaran* and the blue dye-stuff called *Glaisin*.

Fiachrach [that is, the people of the south-eastern part of the present county of Galway] that had been put into its after-dye, [i.e. the mother-liquor of the dye vat], it would colour it blue; and it afterwards made blue the hounds and the cats and the trees which it touched".[111]

This curious legend supplies us with an interesting bit of ancient social history, and it is valuable, not only for the distinct manner in which we are told that manufactured cloth was dyed in the piece, but also for the antiquity of the superstition which deemed it unlucky to have men in the house at the time of putting the cloth into the dye. This superstition does not, to my knowledge, exist now, but there are certain days of the month and week upon which no housewife in Munster would put wool or cloth down to be dyed.

Summary of processes in the textile arts mentioned in foregoing extracts.

In these few extracts we have allusions to all the processes of the manufacture of cloth in ancient Erinn. In the extracts from the laws, as well as from the Book of Rights given above, we have the processes of dyeing, carding, spinning wool, and weaving it into cloth. We have also the progress of the preparation of flax—the pulling of it out of the ground, the tying of it in bundles, the retting or steeping of it in water, the taking of it up and drying, and tying of it into bundles again; the breaking of it with a mallet, and the scutching of it. [The cloving and hackling are omitted, unless we take the combing, as of the wool, to be the hackling of the flax.] We have it put on the rock or distaff; spun upon the spindle; formed into skenes from off the spindle upon the vertical reel; taken off the vertical reel in skenes; [boiled with home-made potash, and put out on the grass to bleach, which is omitted here, though the bleached thread is spoken of;] we next have the skene when bleached laid on the horizontal reel, and wound up into balls for warping, as well as for weft [warped then upon the wooden pins,

(111) [original:—"Ina raili la do ṁaṫair Chiarain, oc denum glaisne cero riaċt co tabuirt eduig innti. Is ann ro raiḋ a ṁaṫair fris. Amaċ dom a Chiarain ni hada leosum fir an aeintig fria daṫugaḋ eduig. Sruaḃ odur annsuiṁ on ol Ciaran. Do neoċ tra do eduċ tucaḋ isin nglaisin ni raiḃi naċ netuċ diḃ cen sruiḃ nuiḋir ann. Do gniṫir dorisi in glaisin condebairt a ṁaṫair frisium. Eiristi imaċ dan infeċtsa a Chiarain acas na biḋ sruaḃ odur ann a Chiarain nosa. Is ann sin do raiḋsium.

Alleluia domine
Rob geal glaisin mo ṁuim
Ceċ tanti am laiṁ
Rop gilither cnaim
Caċ ti a bruṫ,
Rop giliter gruṫ.

Ceċ eduċ din de raṫaḋ innti robaengeal iarsin. Do gniṫer an tresas feċt inglaisin. A Chiarain ol a ṁaṫair na mill umam innosa innglaisin aċt bennaċtar lat hi. Oros benaḋ umorro Chiarain. Ni dearnad roimpi na nadiaig glaisin buḋ commaiṫ riasan ciḋ edaċ cenitil Fiaċraċ uili do berṫi ina hiarċain nos gormfaḋ acas nogormaḋ sa deoig na conu acas na catu ina crunda fris acoṁraiced".—*Book of Lismore*, f. 78. b. col. 1.]

XXIV. either driven into the walls of a house, or on a frame specially made for the purpose], and then put into the loom and woven.

On the subject of embroidery and elegant needlework, it would be very easy indeed to extend this lecture much farther; but for the present I will content myself with a very few references of striking interest.

Reference to embroidery in the tale of the Tochmarc nEimire;

In the ancient tale called *Tochmarc nEimire*, that is, the courtship of the lady *Emer*, described in a former lecture, we are told that when *Cuchulaind*, the great champion of Ulster, came in his chariot from *Emania* to Lusk, in the present county of Dublin (where *Forghall Monach Emer*'s father kept his high court of universal hospitality), he found her sitting on the lawn of her father's court surrounded by fifty young ladies, the daughters of the surrounding gentlemen, whom she was instructing in needlework and embroidery.

and in the Dinseanchas.

Again, in the ancient topographical tract called the *Dinnseanchas*, and in that article of it which professes to give the derivation of the famous and well known hill and Rath of *Maistiu*, now called Mullaghmast in the county of Kildare, we find the following curious passage:

"*Maistiu* [from whom the hill is named] was the born daughter of *Aengus Mac Umor*, and embroideress to *Aengus Mac Inog*. She was the first person that formed the figure of a cross in Erinn, in the breast border of *Aengus*' tunic".[112] The *Aengus Mac Umor* mentioned here, as the father of the lady *Maistiu*, was that *Aengus* of the Firbolg race who, shortly before the Incarnation, built the great stone fort on the great island of Arann, so well known to this day as *Dun Aenghuis*, and of which I had much to say in a former lecture. The other *Aengus*, who, I dare say, was the first that was ever decorated with the order of the cross at the hands of a fair lady, was the celebrated *Tuatha Dé Danann* chief of *Brugh na Boinne*, or "the Palace of the Boyne", near Slane, of whom so many mythological legends are still preserved in Ireland.

But no sooner did Christianity raise its heavenly banner in our island, than the charming ingenuity of woman was put in requisition to adorn with befitting dignity and splendour the glorious and devoted soldiers of the Cross. St. Patrick kept three embroideresses constantly at work, with, we may be sure, a sufficient staff of assistants. These were *Lupait*, his own sister, and *Erc*, the daughter of king *Daire*, and *Cruimthoris* of *Cenngoba*.

Coca the embroideress of St. Columb Cillé.

St. *Columb Cillé* also had his special embroideress, whose name

(112) [original:—"Maistiu ingen genni Aengusa mac Umoir bandruinneach Aengusa mac Inog ar i rus comdealb chroiss rriuss an Erinn; a corrtair brollaich inair Aengusa'.—*Book of Lecan*, f. 233. a. b.]

was *Coca*, from whom *Cille Choca*, now Kilcock, in the county of Kildare, is named. This pious lady is mentioned in a note to the ***Feilire Aenghuis***, or Festology of *Aengus* the *Ceile Dé* or Culdee at her festival day, the 8th of January. This note is as follows: "*Ernat*, the virgin nun, was cook and robe maker to St. *Columb Cillé*, and her church is *Cille Choca* [or Kilcock] in *Cairbre ua Ciardha* [now Carbury, in the county of Kildare]. *Ernat* was her true name, which means an embroideress, because *Ercadh*, in the ancient Gaedhelic was the same as drawing and embroidering now; for it was that virgin who was the embroideress, cutter, and sewer of clothes to St. *Columb Cillé* and his disciples".

The knowledge of colours of the Gaedhils shown by the Book of Kells.

The intimate acquaintance of the ancient Gaedhils of Erinn with the cardinal colours in their highest degree of purity, and with a great variety of other shades and tints, can be clearly established by existing evidence of a very certain character. The Book of Kells, which is an ancient copy of the four Gospels, preserved in the library of Trinity College, Dublin, contains in its pictorial representations, as well as in its illuminations of the written text, a display of beautiful colouring, sufficient of itself to prove the taste and knowledge of the beautiful in colours possessed by our remote ancestors. The figures in the Book of Kells are no doubt ecclesiastical and scriptural; but this circumstance does not in the least invalidate our claim to originality in the production and combination of the colours used in the vestments there pourtrayed. On the contrary, the fact of finding them in illuminations such as these, still preserving all their brilliancy, in a book written, perhaps, about A.D. 590, only bears the stronger evidence to the truthfulness of the use of brilliant dyes in the colouring of costume to which attention has been directed in the course of these lectures. The purity and brilliancy of the green, the blue, the crimson, the scarlet, the yellow, and the purple of the book, like its penmanship, stand perhaps unrivalled, and can only be realized by an actual examination of this very beautiful manuscript itself.

This book, it has been always believed, was written by the hand of St. *Columb Cillé* himself, the original founder of the church of *Ceanannus*, now called Kells, in the county of Meath; and the following passage from the Annals of the Four Masters will show the esteem and veneration in which, from its antiquity and splendour, it was held even at the beginning of the eleventh century:

"The great gospels of [St.] *Columb Cillé* was sacrilegiously stolen at night out of the western sacristy of the great stone church at *Ceanannus* [or Kells]. It was the chief relic of the

XXIV.

western world, even as regarded its shrine of human workmanship; and it was found in twenty nights and two months, after all its [ornamentation of] gold had been stolen off it; with sods turned over it".[113]

Reference in B. of Ballymote to colours worn by different classes.

I have found in the Book of Ballymote a curious old stanza, headed with these Latin words:

"Ordo vestimentorum per colores"; that is, the order of the cloths according to their colours.

"The following is the stanza:

"Mottled to simpletons; blue to women;
Crimson to the kings of every host;
Green and black to noble laymen;
White to clerics of proper devotion".[114]

Clothes of various colours formed part of the tributes or taxes paid as late as the ninth and tenth centuries.

It is probable that this stanza is only a fragment of a longer poem, since we have undoubted authority that at the close of the ninth century (say about the year 900), clothes of various colours such as cloaks, tunics, mantles, and capes, continued to be paid by way of tribute or tax to and by the monarch, the provincial kings, and their subordinate kings. The following stanzas from the Book of Rights will show to what extent this reciprocity of stipends, or presents, and tributes existed between the supreme and petty rulers of the land in ancient times.

Tributes to the king of *Caiseal* from: *Ara*;

To the kings of Cashel were paid as follows:

"Two hundred wethers from the host were given;
An hundred hogs in statute tribute;
An hundred cows that enriched the farmer's dairy;
An hundred green mantles from the men of Ara.[115]

Boirinn;

"A thousand oxen, a thousand cows I exact;
To the palace in one day I ordain,
A thousand rams swelled out with wool,
[And] a thousand cloaks from *Boirinn*.[116]

Leinster;

"He himself, the king of noble Cashel, is entitled
To three hundred suits of cloths at *Samhain* [from Leinster];
To fifty steeds of a dark gray colour
In readiness for every battle.[117]

"This is what is due, and no falsehood:
Fifty oxen and fifty cows,
Fifty steeds with noble bridles,

(113) Annals of Four Masters. Dr. O'Donovan's Edition. Year A.D. 1006.

(114) Original:—Ordo uestimentorum percolores, .i. ordna nedaċ daċaib.
Brec do druċaib, gorm do mnaib
Corcair do rigaib gach sloig
Uaine is dub do laeċraid feil
Find do ċleircib crabaid cruaid
[no coir]!—folio 161. b.

(115) See for original *Leabhar na g-Ceart*, p. 44.

(116) Ibid., p. 48.

(117) Ibid., p. 54.

And an hundred cloaks of the cloaks of *Umall*.[118]
"Three hundred hogs from the men of *Uaithne*
To Cashel without failure;
Three hundred mantles of bright mixture, [i.e. varigated]
With an hundred strong milch cows.[119]

Uaithne;

"Thirty short cloaks well stitched,
Which with crimson are trimmed;
Thirty good cows from the men of *Duibhneach*,
Thirty oxen from *Drung*.[120]

Duibhneach and *Drung*;

"There are due from the county of *Corcumruadh*
An hundred sheep, an hundred sows;
A thousand oxen from brown *Boirinn*,
A thousand cloaks not white.[121]

Corcumruadh;

"Ten hundred oxen from the *Deise*,
A thousand fine sheep,
A thousand cloaks with white borders,
A thousand cows after calving.[122]

the *Deise*;

"An hundred from the men of *Orbhraidhe*
Of cows are given to him;
An hundred white cloaks to fair Cashel,
An hundred sows for the sty".[123]

Orbhraidhe.

Such were the tributes, including those in clothes, which the king of Cashel received from his tributaries; and from the scanty number of garments with which he presented them in return, it is evident that by far the greater part of his stock was bestowed on persons of inferior rank, in his own tribe perhaps, including his men-at-arms. Thus:—

"Seven mantles with wreaths of gold,
And seven cups for social drinking,
Seven steeds not accustomed to falter,
To the king of Kerry of the combats.[124]

Stipends paid by the king of *Caiseal* to the kings of: Kerry;

"The prosperous king of *Rathlenn* is entitled
To the stipend of a brave great man;
Ten swords, and ten drinking horns,
Ten red cloaks, ten blue cloaks.[125]

Rathlenn;

"The king of *Ara* of beauty is entitled
From the king of *Eire* of the comely face
To six swords, six praised shields,
And six mantles of deep crimson".[126]

Ara;

The tributes of the king of Connacht come next, of which our poet says:—

Tributes to the king of Connacht from: *Umall*;

"Five score cows long to be praised,

(118) Ibid., p. 56. (119) Ibid., p. 62. (120) Ibid., p. 64.
(121) Ibid., p. 64. (122) Ibid., p. 66. (123) Ibid., p. 66.
(124) Ibid., p. 74. (125) Ibid., p. 82. (126) Ibid., p. 86.

XXIV.

Five score hogs of broad sides,
Five score mantles of beautiful colour,
From *Umall* to the king of Connacht.[127]

the Greagraidhe;

"Three score hogs, great the tribute,
And three score kingly cloaks,
Three score milch cows hither come,
From the *Greagraidhe* of the fine trees.[128]

the Conmaicne;

"Twelve score of costly cloaks,
Two hundred cows without error in reckoning,
Eighty hogs of great report
Are due from the *Conmaicne*.[129]

the Ciarraidhe;

"Three score red cloaks, not black,
Three score hogs of long sides,
From the *Ciarraidhe*,—a hard sentence,—
And all to be brought hither together.[130]

the Luighne;

"Thrice fifty bull-like hogs,
And all to come hither at *Samhain;*
Thrice fifty superb cloaks
To the king of Connacht and *Cruachan*[131]
[From the *Luighne*].

the Dealbhna;

"Three times fifty crimson mantles it is known,
Without injustice, without transgression,
Of the *Dealbhna* are these due
To the king of Connacht at *Cruachan*.[132]

Ui Maine.

"The great tribute of *Ui Maine* of the plain
Is well known to every historian;
Eighty cloaks, it is no falsehood,
Eighty hogs, a weighty herd".[133]

Stipends paid by the king of Connacht to the kings of: *Dealbhna;*

Next come the disbursements of the king of Connacht, as our poet sings:—

"Entitled is the king of *Dealbhna* of *Druim Leith*
To six swords and six shields,
Six steeds, six tunics with gold [embroidery],
Six drinking horns for banquets.[134]

Ui Maine.

"Entitled is the king of *Ui Maine* the illustrious
To seven cloaks, seven horses over the valley,
Seven hounds to follow the chase,
And seven bright red tunics".[135]

Tributes to the king of *Aileach* from: the *Cuilenntraidhe;*

Next come the tributes paid to the king of *Aileach* or *Tir Eoghain* in Ulster:—

"An hundred sheep, and an hundred cloaks, and an hundred cows,

(127) Ibid., p. 98. (128) Ibid., p. 98. (129) Ibid., p. 100.
(130) Ibid., p. 102. (131) Ibid., p. 102. (132) Ibid., p. 104.
(133) Ibid., p. 106. (134) Ibid., p. 112. (135) Ibid., p. 114.

XXIV.

And an hundred hogs are given to him,
From the *Cuileantraidhe* of the wars,
To the king of *Aileach*, beside labour.[136]

"An hundred beeves from the *Ui Mic Caerthainn*,
And an hundred hogs—not very trifling,
Fifty cows in lawful payment,
Fifty cloaks with white borders.[137]

the *Ui Mic Caerthainn*;

"An hundred milch cows from the *Tuathas* of *Tort* [*Ui Tuirtre*].
Fifty hogs in bacon, fifty (live) hogs,
With fifty coloured cloaks to him are given
From *Dun na h-Uidhre* in one day".[138]

Ui Tuirtre.

When the king of *Aileach* was not himself the monarch of Erinn, he was entitled to three hundred suits of clothes from the monarch; and of the distribution of these three hundred suits among the king of *Aileach*'s subordinate kings or chiefs, the poet sings only of the following:—

Stipends paid by the king of *Aileach* to the kings of:

"The king of the *Cinel Boghaine* the firm
Is entitled to five steeds for cavalry,
Six shields, six swords, six drinking horns,
Six green cloaks, six blue cloaks.[139]

Cinel Boghaine;

"Entitled is the king of *Cinel Eanna*
To five beautiful powerful steeds,
Five shields, five swords for battle,
Five mantles, five coats of mail.[140]

Cinel Eanna;

"Entitled is the king of *Craebh* to a gift,
Three strong steeds as a stipend,
Three shields, three swords of battle,
Three green cloaks of uniform colour.[141]

Craebh;

"Entitled is the king of *Ui Mic Caerthainn*
To three tunics with golden borders,
Three beautiful statute mantles,
Three befitting bondwomen.[142]

Ui Mic Caerthainn;

"Entitled is the king of *Tulach Og*
To fifty serviceable foreign bondmen,
Fifty swords, fifty steeds,
Fifty white mantles, fifty coats of mail".[143]

Tulach Og.

Next comes the king of *Oirghialla* or *Oriel*'s distribution of rich garments among his subordinate kings, of which our poet sings:—

Stipends paid by the king of *Oriel* to the kings of:

"The stipend of the king of *Ui Breasail* is
Three crimson cloaks of lightning lustre,

Ui Breasail;

(136) Ibid., p. 120. (137) Ibid., p. 122. (138) Ibid., p. 124.
(139) Ibid., p. 130. (140) Ibid., p. 130. (141) Ibid., p. 132.
(142) Ibid., p. 132. (143) Ibid., p. 134.

XXIV.

Five shields, five swords of battle,
Five swift steeds of beautiful colour.[144]

Ui Eachach;

"Entitled is the king of *Ui Eachach* the noble
To five crimson square cloaks,
Five shields, five swords, five drinking horns,
Five gray dark-forked steeds.[145]

Ui Meith;

"Entitled is the king of *Ui Meith* the hero,
From the king of *Macha* [*Oirghialla*] of great assemblies,
To four swords, four drinking horns,
'Four cloaks, four iron-gray steeds.[146]

Ui Dortain;

"The stipend of the king of *Ui Dortain* is
Three crimson cloaks with borders,
Three shields, three swords of battle,[147]
Three white mantles, three coats of mail.

Ui Briuin Archoill;

"Entitled is the king of *Ui Briuin Archoill*
To three tunics with golden borders,
Six steeds, six heavy bondmen,
Six befitting bondwomen".[148]

Ui Tuirtre;

The king of *Ui Tuirtre* was further entitled to gifts from the king of *Oirghialla*, such as:—

"Eight bay steeds are due to him,
Eight crimson cloaks of beautiful texture,
Eight shields, eight swords, eight drinking horns,
Eight hardworking, dexterous-handed bondmen.[149]

Feara Manach;

"Entitled is the great king of *Feara Manach*
To five cloaks with golden borders,
Five shields, five swords of battle,
Five ships, five coats of mail.

Mughdhorn and *Ros.*

"Entitled is the king of *Mughdhorn* and *Ros*
To six bondmen of great vigour,
Six swords, six shields, six drinking horns,
Six crimson cloaks, six blue cloaks".[150]

Stipends paid by the king of *Uladh* to the king of: *Cuailgne;*

Next comes the distribution by the king of *Uladh*, or *Ulidia*, that is Down and Antrim, of his gifts among his chiefs, firstly to the king of *Cuailgne*, as our poet sings:

"Fifty swords, fifty shields,
Fifty cloaks, fifty gray steeds,
Fifty capes, fifty pack-saddles,
And fifty pleasing coats of mail.[151]

Araidhe;

"Twenty speckled cloaks,—no small present,
Twenty mantles of softest sheen,

(144) Ibid., p. 146. (145) Ibid., p. 148. (146) Ibid., p. 148.
(147) Ibid., p. 150. (148) Ibid, p. 150. (149) Ibid., p. 152.
(150) Ibid., p. 154. (151) Ibid., p. 158.

Twenty drinking-horns, twenty quern-women,
To the valorous king of *Araidhe*.[152]
"The stipend of the victorious king of *Cobhais*
Ten drinking horns, ten wounding swords,
Ten ships to which crews belong,
Ten cloaks with their borders of gold.[153]
"Entitled is the heroic king of *Muirtheimne*—the hero?
To six tall drinking horns full of ale,
Ten ships to the champion of *Ealga* [Erinn],
Ten steeds, ten scarlet tunics".[154]

Cobhais; *Muirtheimne*.

Next come the tributes paid to the king of *Uladh* by his subordinate chiefs and tribes, among which we find the following, as sung by our poet:

Tributes to the king of *Uladh* from:

"Three times fifty excellent cloaks from *Semhne*,
This from all,
Three times fifty excellent dairy cows,
All within two days.[155]
"There is due from *Crothraidhe* of the fleet,
Bear it in thy memory,—
An hundred wethers, an hundred cows not sickly,
And an hundred cloaks.[156]
"Three hogs from the lands of *Cathal*,
Not very severe,
Three hundred well coloured cloaks,
He is entitled to in the north".[157]

Semhne; *Crothraidhe*; *Cathal*.

Next comes the hereditary king of Tara and Meath, with his gifts from the monarch, when he was not himself the monarch of Erinn; and his own liabilities to the petty kings and chiefs of Meath, as our poet sings.

Gifts to king of Tara.

"An hundred swords, and an hundred shields,
The king of Tara of lords is entitled to,
An hundred suits of clothes, and an hundred steeds,
An hundred white cloaks, and an hundred suits of mail.[158]
"Entitled is the king of *Magh Lacha*
To five shields, five swords of battle,
Five short cloaks, and five steeds,
Five white hounds, in a fine leash.[159]
"Entitled is the king of *Cuircne* of the shore
To six shields and six horses,
Six cloaks and six shepherds,
Six drinking horns, full, ready for use.[160]

Stipends paid by king of Tara to the king of: *Magh Lacha*; *Cuircne*;

(152) Ibid., p. 158. (153) Ibid., p. 164. (154) Ibid., p. 166.
(155) Ibid., p. 170. (156) Ibid., p. 170. (157) Ibid., p. 172.
(158) Ibid., p. 178. (159) Ibid., p. 178. (160) Ibid., p. 180.

XXIV.

Ui Beccon;

"The stipend of the king of *Ui Beccon* is,
Five swift ready steeds,
Five speckled cloaks of permanent colour,
And five swords for battle".[161]

Tributes to the king of Tara from:

Next come the tributes paid to the king of Tara, or Meath, from his territories, and of which the poet sings:—

the *Luighne;*

"Thrice fifty white cloaks, from the *Luighne*,
Thrice fifty hogs, as were reckoned,
Thrice fifty beeves, without default,
To be brought to great *Teamair*.[162]

The *Feara Arda;*

"An hundred beeves from the *Feara Arda*,
An hundred white wethers besides,
An hundred hogs, heavy to be remembered,
An hundred cloaks the enumeration of the great *Luighne*.[163]

the *Saithne;*

"An hundred best cloaks from the *Saithne*,
An hundred sows, a stock of wealth,
An hundred beeves from the plains,
And an hundred wethers to be slaughtered.[164]

Gailenga;

"Three hundred hogs from the territory of *Gailenga*,
Three hundred wethers, three hundred white cloaks,
Three hundred oxen, great the relief
To the *Claen Raith* [at Tara] ye have heard.[165]

the *Ui Beccon.*

"Sixty cloaks from the *Ui Beccon*,
Sixty beeves, great the strength,
With sixty excellent sows,
And sixty tunics (?) to the great hill" [of *Teamair*].[166]

Stipends paid by the king of Leinster to the:

We come next to the king of Leinster, and his rights and liabilities when not himself monarch of Erinn. He was, among other presents from the monarch, entitled to fifty short cloaks and ten kingly mantles. Of the king of Leinster's liabilities to his tributaries, we take the following stanzas from the poet:—

Ui Fealain;

"Six drinking horns, six rings to the *Ui Fealain*,
Six white cloaks at the same time,
Six swift steeds, with their caparisons,
Though they boast of this it is not brotherhood.[167]

chief of *Cualand;*

"Eight ships from the champion to the chief of *Cualand*
With sails and with sailing masts,[168]
Eight drinking horns, eight keen-edged swords,

(161) Ibid., p. 182. (162) Ibid., p. 186 (163) Ibid., p. 186.
(164) Ibid., p. 186. (165) Ibid., p. 188. (166) Ibid., p. 190.
(167) Ibid., p. 204.
(168) [Ocht longa ó'n laech do ḟlaith Chualand,
Co seolaib co seol bratáib.
Dr. O'Donovan translates the second line:
"With sails [and] with satin flags (banners)".]

Eight tunics, eight gold worked mantles.
"Seven steeds to the fair *Ui Feilmeadha*,
Vehement men, and vengeful [are they;]
Five curved drinking horns, with five cloaks,
Five mantles let it be remembered.[169]
"Ten carved clasps to the king of *Raeilinn*,
And six royal steeds, I reckon,
Six mantles also to the champion,—
Six bondsmen to the same warrior.[170]
"Six steeds to the *Ui Criomhthannan* as ordered,
Six oxen in good condition,
Six drinking horns to hold in their hands,
Six mantles without mistake".[171]

XXIV. *Ui Feilmeadha*; king of *Raeilinn*; *Ui Criomhthannan*.

Next comes the tribute received by the king of Leinster from his tributary tribes, from which we select the following, as sung by the poet:—

Tributes to the king of Leinster from the: Galls;

"Seven hundred pigs in bacon, seven hundred hogs,
Seven hundred oxen, seven hundred good wethers,
Seven hundred cloaks, and seven hundred cows,
From the lands of the Galls all in one day.[172]
"Two hundred cloaks, no falsehood,
An hundred heavy hogs, heavy the herd,
And two hundred lively milch cows,
From the lands of the tribes of the *Forthuatha*.[173]
"From all the *Fotharta*
Are due two hundred prime cows,
And two hundred statute cloaks,
Two hundred wild oxen tamed.[174]
"Two hundred beeves, great the progeny,
Two hundred cloaks, and two hundred milch cows,
Two hundred wethers, great the relief
From the men of south Leinster".[175]

Forthuatha; *Fortharta*; men of south Leinster.

We come next to the king of *Emain Macha*, that is *Emania* in middle Ulster, and we have an enumeration of the gifts which the king of that important territory was entitled to from the monarch of Erinn, as well as his own liability to his tributary chiefs, and theirs to him in return. From the list of the gifts from the monarch to the petty king, as sung by our poet, we take the following stanza:—

Gifts from the monarch of Erinn to the king of *Emain Macha*.

"Twelve spears on which there is poison,
Twelve swords with razor edges,
Twelve suits of clothes of all colours,

(169) Ibid., p. 208. (170) Ibid., p. 200. (171) Ibid., p. 216.
(172) Ibid., p. 218. (173) Ibid., p. 220. (174) Ibid., p. 220.
(175) Ibid., p. 220.

XXIV.

For the use of the sons of high chiefs".[176]

Stipends of the king of *Emain Macha* to the kings of:

We find the king of *Emania's* gifts of clothes to his tributaries as limited as those made to himself by the monarch of Erinn. These gifts appear to have been limited to two chiefs only, the king of *Rath Mor Muighe*, i.e. of *Magh Line*, and the king of the *Conmaicne* in Connacht, who were of remote Ultonian origin. Thus sings the poet:—

Rathmor;

"Entitled is he [the king of *Rathmor*] shall any ask it?
Unless he be king over the men of Ulster,
To eight coloured cloaks and two ships,
With a bright shield on each shoulder.[177]

Ui Briuin;

"Entitled is the king of the noble *Ui Briuin*
To his truly noble French steed;

Conmaicne.

Entitled is the king of the fair *Conmaicne*
To a steed and a choice of raiment".[178]

Gifts bestowed on the king of Leinster by the monarch whenever he visited Tara.

We are told that whenever the king of Leinster paid a state visit to Tara, he received from the monarch—

"Seven chariots adorned with gold,
In which he goes forth to banquets,
Seven score suits of well coloured clothes,
For the wear of the sons of the high chiefs.[179]

"Upon which he goes back to his house,
The king of Leinster, with the champions,
Until he reaches the palace of Nas after a journey
Until he distributes his stipends".

Gift of king of Leinster to the king of the *Ui Fealain*.

Among these stipends, however, which the king of Leinster distributed after his return from Tara, we only find one of the chiefs entitled to a present of garments; as the poet sings:—

"Entitled is the king of fair *Ui Fealain*
To seven coloured cloaks, for cheerful banquets".[180]

Gift of the monarch of Erinn to king of *Caiseal* when at *Teamhair Luachra*.

We further find in this book, that the monarch of Erinn was bound by ancient usage to accept of a periodical invitation to a feast from the king of Cashel at *Teamhair Luachra* (an ancient palace situated in the neighbourhood of Abbeyfeale, on the borders of the counties of Limerick and Kerry). Here the monarch was bound to remain for a week, and in the meantime to hand over to the king of Cashel the gifts and stipends of dependance to which he was entitled from him. Among these were:—

"Eight score of cloaks in cloaks,
Eight bright shields over white hands,
Seven plough yokes in full range,
And seven score short horned cows".[181]

(176) Ibid., p. 242. (177) Ibid., p. 244. (178) Ibid., p. 246.
(179) Ibid., p. 251. (180) Ibid., p. 250. (181) Ibid., p. 254.

The king of Munster then distributed to his own subordinate chiefs and to their ladies his gifts and stipends in this manner, as sung by the poet:—

XXIV. Stipends given by the king of *Caiseal* at the visitation of the monarch of Erinn to the: *Deise*; *Ui Chonaill*.

"Eight good steeds of high degree
Are due to the king of the noble *Deise*,
And eight green cloaks besides,
With eight brooches of *Findruine* [or white bronze].[182]
"Entitled is the king of the fair *Ui Chonaill*
To an Easter dress from the king of *Caiseal*,
His beautiful sword of shining lustre
And his spear along with it".[183]

Again we find the provincial king of Connacht liable, among many other things, to the following items:—

Stipends paid by king of Connacht to the kings of: *Ui Maine*; *Luighne*.

"Entitled is the king of great *Ui Maine*
To four drinking horns for drinking occasions;
To twenty cows and twenty steeds,
To two hundred suits of clothes—no false award.[184]
"Entitled is the king of the valiant *Luighne*
To four shields for victories,
Four tunics with red gold,
Four ships, not a bad gift".[185]

I must, however, close here these extracts, having only desired to show at how early a period ornament was systematically applied to dress in ancient Erinn. I shall only add one more; because in leaving the subject of dresses of different colours, I cannot but lay before the reader a very curious example of a theory of colours in connection with the phenomena of winds, which I would wish to be able to investigate at much greater length than my narrow limits at present will allow.

Colours of winds according to *Seanchas Mór*.

Of the acquaintance of the ancient Irish with the nature and combinations of colours, an instance is preserved in the preface to the *Seanchas Mór*, that great law compilation, which is believed to have been compiled in St. Patrick's time. The writer of this preface, which is evidently not as old as the laws themselves, when speaking of the design and order of the creation, gives the following poetical description of the nature and character of winds.

"He (the Lord) then created the colours of the winds, so that the colour of each differs from the other; namely, the white and the crimson; the blue and the green; the yellow and the red; the black and the gray; the speckled and the dark; the dull black (*ciar*) and the grisly. From the east (he continues) comes the crimson wind; from the south, the white; from the

(182) Ibid., p. 256. (183) Ibid., p. 258. (184) Ibid., p. 264.
(185) Ibid., p. 264.

XXIV.

Colours of winds according to *Seanchas Mór.*

north, the black; from the west, the dun. The red and the yellow are produced between the white wind and the crimson; the green and the gray are produced between the grisly and the white; the gray and the dull black are produced between the grisly and the jet black; the dark and the mottled are produced between the black and the crimson; and those are all the sub-winds contained in each and all the cardinal winds".[186]

It would be a curious speculation to inquire into the meaning of this strange theory of coloured winds; but it contains at a glance evidence at least of the existence, when this most ancient preface was written, of a distinct theory of the relations and combinations of colours.[187]

(186) [original:—Ro delb dona daṫa na ngaeṫ, conid fain daṫ caċa gaeiṫe dib fri araile, .i. gel ocus corcra, glas ocus uaine, buiḋe ocus derg, dub ocus liaṫ, in alad ocus in timin, in ciar ocus in odur. Anair in gaeṫ corcra, anear in geal, a tuaiṫ an dub, aniar an odur. In derg ocus in buide itir ngaiṫ ngil ocus corcra bit; in uaine ocus in glas itir in uidir ocus in glegil bit; in liaṫ ocus in ċiar itir in uidir ocus in cirdub bit; in temin ocus in alad itir in dub ocus in corcra bit. Coni di fogaiṫ in caċ primgait insin.—Preface to *Seanchas Mór*, Harleian MSS. 432, Brit. Mus.]

(187) [This theory of coloured winds apparently refers to the more characteristic colours which the clouds assume about the rising and setting sun, and which to a certain extent seem to depend upon the wind which blows at the time.]

LECTURE XXV.

[Delivered July 12th, 1860.]

(VIII.) Dress and Ornaments (continued). Of *Conaire Mor* monarch of Erinn (circa B.C. 100 to B.C. 50) and the outlawed sons of *Dond Dess*, according to the ancient tale of the *Bruighean Daderga;* the sons of *Dond Dess* associate with the British outlaw *Ingcel* to plunder the coasts of Britain and Erinn; the monarch in returning from *Corca Bhaiscinn* in the Co. Clare, being unable to reach Tara, goes to the court of *Daderg; Ingcel* visits the court to ascertain the feasibility of plundering it; he gives descriptions on his return to his companions of those he saw there, and *Ferrogain* identifies them; *Ingcel's* description of the Ultonian warrior *Cormac Conloinges* and his companions; of the *Cruithentuath* or Picts; of the nine pipe players; of *Tuidle* the house steward; of *Oball, Oblini* and *Coirpre Findmor*, sons of *Conaire Mor;* of the champions *Mal Mac Telbaind, Muinremor* and *Birderg;* of the great Ultonian champion *Conall Cearnach;* of the monarch himself, *Conaire Mor;* of the six cup bearers; of *Tulchinne* the royal Druid and juggler; of the three swine-herds; of *Causcrach Mend;* of the Saxon princes and their companions; of the king's outriders; of the king's three judges; of the king's nine harpers; of the king's three jugglers; of the three chief cooks; of the king's three poets; of the king's two warders; of the king's nine guardsmen; of the king's two table attendants; of the champions *Sencha, Dubthach Dael Uladh* and *Goibniu;* of *Daderg* himself; of the king's three door keepers; of the British exiles at the court of the monarch; of the three jesters or clowns; of the three drink bearers. Summary of the classes of persons described. The exaggerations of such descriptions scarcely affect their value for the present purpose; very little exaggeration on the whole in the tales of the *Bruighean Daderga*, and *Táin Bo Chuailgne.* Antiquity and long continued use of the colour of certain garments shown by the tale of the *Amhra Chonrai*, by *Mac Liag's* elegy on *Tudgh* O'Kelly, and also by a poem of *Gillabrighde Mac Conmidhe.*

In the last two lectures I gave a short account of the military dress, chiefly in regard to colour and ornaments, of the ancient Irish, as preserved in the old historic tale of the *Táin Bo Chuailgne.* This was followed by a long account from the Brehon Laws and the life of St. *Ciaran* of Clonmacnois, of the mode of colouring and treating wool and flax, preparatory to their being manufactured into cloth, the instruments used in the various processes, and the laws which protected the workers, who, as far as we know, were always women, in the recovery of their wages, and any part of their property when pledged. I shall now proceed to give some account of the civil dress worn in courts, at state assemblies, public fairs, and great festivals, still treating the subject as far as can be in chronological order; and although we have not yet exhausted the rich descriptive stories of the *Táin*

XXV.

Bo Chuailgne, we shall now draw upon sources scarcely, if laid under contribution hitherto; and of these sources th of the *Bruighean Daderga*, will be the chief. As I have in a former lecture[188] an ample sketch of the tale of the *I hean Daderga*, I shall only have occasion to describe it h the briefest manner.

Of Conaire Mor and the outlawed sons of Dond Dess;

The reign of king *Conaire Mor*, or the Great, who ass the monarchy of Erinn a century before the Incarnation, prosperous one to his country, and extended to a period o: years. His rule of justice was so strict that several lawle discontented persons were forced to go into exile. Amon most desperate of these outlaws were the monarch's own f brothers, the four sons of *Dond Dess*, an important chieft Leinster. These refractory youths, with a large party o lowers, took to their ships and boats and scoured the coa Britain and Scotland as well as of their own country. H met on the sea with *Ingcel*, the son of the king of Britain for his misdeeds had been likewise banished by his own f both parties entered into a league, the first fruits of which the plunder and devastation of a great part of the British c after which they were to make a descent on that of E During this time the Irish monarch had occasion to go *Corca Bhaiscinn*, in the present county of Clare, to settle difference which had sprung up between two of the local c On his return, and when approaching his palace at Tara, a very small retinue, he found the whole country befor one sheet of fire; the plunderers having landed in his ab and carried fire and sword wherever they went. The accordingly turned away from Tara, taking the old *B Chualand* which was the great road that led from Tara, th Dublin, into Leinster; and having crossed the Liffey in s he repaired to the court of *Daderg*, which was situated o river *Dothra*, or Dodder (at the place now called fr *Bothar na Bruighne*, that is, "the road of the court") Tallaght in the present county of Dublin. This was one o six courts of universal hospitality, which at this time were lished in Erinn; and in this court the monarch was received the honour which his own dignity and munificence procur him everywhere within his dominions.

the latter associate with the British outlaw, Ingcel, to plunder the coasts;

the monarch unable to reach Tara goes to the court of Da-derg;

The plunderers having satisfied their vengeance, and l their vessels with spoils, put to sea again, and running the coast in the direction of the hill of Howth, they perc the monarch and his small but splendid company driving

[188] [See *Lectures on the MS. Materials of Ancient Irish History* xii, p. 258.]

the road towards Dublin. His own foster-brothers, who were among the leaders on board, immediately recognized him, and guessing the cause of his journeying in such a manner in such a direction, they took proper measures to keep him in view to the end of his journey. XXV.

The British outlaw chief, *Ingcel*, having received information of the monarch's resting place, ran his vessels on shore somewhere to the south of the mouth of the Liffey, and undertook when he came on shore to go with a small party to *Daderg*'s court, and ascertain with his own eyes the feasibility of plundering it and killing the monarch. On his return to his people, they formed a circle round him and the five sons of *Dond Dess*. *Ferrogain*, one of the five foster-brothers, was well acquainted with the monarch, and the functions and names of all the officers and official attendants who formed his ordinary company at Tara, and who attended him on all his excursions. *Ferrogain* therefore questioned the chief as to what he had seen in *Daderg*'s court. The chief described the different groups which he had seen there, and *Ferrogain* identified them; and it is this curious dialogue, which constitutes the chief part of the story, and, like the *Táin Bo Chuailgne*, contains those minute accounts of costume, etc., for the sake of which I proceed to make extracts at length.

Ingcel visit the court t ascertain the feasibility of plur dering it; gives descriptions on his return those he saw there and *Ferrogain* identifies them.

Ferrogain speaks first.

"I ask thee, O *Ingcel!* didst thou examine the house well?" said *Ferrogain*.

"My eye cast a rapid glance into it, and I will accept it as my share of the plunder, such as it is", said *Ingcel*.

"Well mightest thou do so if thou didst get it", said *Ferrogain*, "it is the foster-father of us all that is there, the high king of Erinn, *Conaire*, the son of *Eterscel*".

"I ask what thou sawest in the champion's seat of the house, before the king's face on the opposite side?" said *Ferrogain*.(189)

"I saw there", said he, "a large dark faced man with bright sparkling eyes, beautiful well set teeth, a face narrow below and broad above, and flaxen fair golden hair, upon him. He wore well-fitting clothes; a silver *Milech* or brooch in his cloak, and a gold-hilted sword in his hand. He had a shield with golden bosses; and a flesh-piercing spear in his hand. A manly, comely, crimson countenance has he, and he is beardless".

Ingcel's description of *Cormac Conloinges*

(189) [original:—Caċt inderċaċasu-ateċ commaiṫ a Ingcel? for Ferrogain. Rolá mo súilse luaṫċuaird and, acus gébait im ḟiaċu amail atá. Is deiṫbir dait a ingceil ciánó gabṫa ol Ferrogain, arnaiti uli fil and ardri hErenn Conaire mac Eterscceoil. Caċt cid atcondarcsu isind socluí feninnida in tige, fri eneċ ríg isin leiṫ anall?—*Leabhar na h-Uidhre*, f. 61. a. col. a.]

XXV.

"Pass that man by for the present", said *Ferrogain;* "and after him who didst thou see there?"(190)

d of his ne com- nions

"I saw there three men behind him, and three men before him, and three men close in front of the same man. Thou wouldst think that it was one mother and one father they had; and they are all of the same age, the same form, the same beauty, and same resemblance. They had long polls of hair; and green cloaks; they had *Tanaslaidhe*, or brooches, of gold in their cloaks; bent shields of red bronze upon them; ribbed spears above them; a bone-hilted sword in the hand of each man of them".(191)

Then *Ferrogain* identifies them as *Cormac Conloinges*, the son of *Conchobar*, king of Ulster, and his nine comrades.

the -uithen- ath or cts;

"I saw there another couch", said *Ingcel*, "and three men in it—three great brown men, with three round heads of hair, of equal length at poll and forehead. They wore three short, black cowls, reaching to their elbows, and long hoods to their cowls. They had three enormous black swords, and three black shields over them; and three black [handled] broad green spears over them [that is, standing by their sides and reaching above their heads"].

"It is not difficult for me to identify them", said *Ferrogain:* "I am not acquainted in Erinn with three such, unless they are those three [champions] from Pictland (*Cruithentuath*), who have passed into exile from their own country, and are now among king *Conaire*'s household. Their names are *Dubloinges*, the son of *Trebuait*, and *Trebuait*, the son of *Lonscae*, and *Curnach*, the son of *Ui Faich*. These are the three heroic victory-winning champions of *Cruitentuath* [Pictland].(192)

(190) [original:—Atċondarc and olse, fer gormaineċ már rosc nglan ngleórda lais, deit gen coir, aiged foċael forleṫan, lind-folt find fororda fair. Forti ċoir imbi; milec airgit inna brut, acus claideb oirduirn inalaim. Sciaṫ cocoicroṫ oir fair; sleg cóicrind inalaim. Cóinsa cóir ċáin ċorcorda lais, osé amulaċ. Ailm-mnaċ in fer sin, acus iar sin cia aca and.—*Leabhar na h-Uidhre*, f. 61. a. col. 2.]

(191) [original:—Atcondarc and triar fer fris aniar, acus triar fris anair, acus triar ar béla ind fir ċétnai. Atarlet is oenmathair acus oenathair dóib; ité comáesa, comċore, comalli, cosmaile uli. Cúlmongae foraib; bruit úainidi impu uli; tanaslaide óir inam-bruta; cuársceiṫ crend foraib; slega druimneċa úasaib; calg dét illáim caċ fir dib.—*Ibid.*, f. 61. a. col. 2.]

(192) [original:—Atcondarc and imdae, acus triar indi—tri dondfir móra, tri cruindberṫa foraib, ite comlebra forcúl acus etun. Tri gerr ċoċaill dubae impu, coulni, céinnidi fóta for na coċlaib. Tri claidib duba dimóra leo, acus teó ra dubboccóti úasaib; acus teóra dubslega leṫanglassa uassaib. . . Is andsa damsa a samail. Nis fe-tarsa in hErin intriarsin, manidhé in triar ucut di Cruiṫentúaiṫ, do deóċatár forlongais asa tír, conda fil hi teglaċ Chonaire. Ité anan-mand, Dubloinges mac Trebúait, acas Trebuait mac úi Lonscae, acus Curnaċ mac Ui Fáiċ. Tri láic ata-deċ gaibte gaisced la Cruiṫentuaiṫ intriarsin.—*Ibid*, f. 61. b. col. 1.]

"I saw there", said *Ingcel*, "a couch and nine persons upon it; they had fair yellow hair, and were like in beauty; they wore speckled, glossy cloaks, and had nine ornamented quadrangular caps (*Tennes*) over them. The emblazonment which is upon these quadrangular caps would be sufficient light for the royal house. These are nine pipe-players who came from the fairy hills of *Bregia* to *Conaire* to do him honour. Their names are *Bind, Robind, Riarbind, Sibe, Dibe, Deichrind, Umal, Cumal, Ciallglind*. They are the best pipe players in the whole world".[193] These nine names, I may observe, are symbolical of the nine perfections or highest performances of music, but, with the exception of the first and second names, they are now unintelligible. The first two names, *Bind* and *Robind*, that is, sweet and more sweet, or melodious and more melodious, are still living words.[194] XXV. of the nine Pipe players;

"I saw there", said *Ingcel*, "a couch with one man on it. He had coarse hair, so coarse that if a sack of wild apples were emptied upon his head, not an apple of them would fall to the ground, but each apple would stick upon his hair. He wore his great woollen cloak around him in the house. "Every discussion that arises in the house about seat or bed", said *Ingcel*, "is submitted to his decision. If a needle dropped in the house, its fall would be heard when he speaks. A huge black tree or mast stands over him; it is like the shaft of a mill with its cogs and wheel and axle. That man", said *Ferrogain*, "is *Tuidle* of Ulster, house-steward to [king] *Conaire*. He is a man", continues *Ferrogain*, "whose decisions are not to be impugned. He is the man that supplies seat, and bed, and food, to every one. It is his household staff (or wand) that stands above him".[195] of *Tuidle* the house steward;

"I saw another couch there", said *Ingcel*, "and three persons upon it. Three soft youths with three *Sirechdai* [or silken] cloaks upon them, and three brooches (*Bretnassa*) of gold in their cloaks. of *Oball, Oblini* and *Coirpri Find Mor*, sons of *Conaire Mor*;

(193) [original:—Atchondarc and imdai acus nonbur indi; mongae find buidi foraib, ite comalli uile; bruit brec ligda impu, acus noi tinne cetharchóire cumtachtai uasaib. Bá leór suillse isindorus tige a cumtach fil forsna tinnib cetharchóirib hisin. . . Nonbur cuslennach insin dorochtatar co Conaire ar a airscélaib asid Brég. Ité a n-anmand—Bind, Robind, Riarbind, Sibe, Dibe, Deichrind, Umal, Cumal, Ciallglind. Ite cuslennaig ata dec fil isin domon.—*Leabhar na h-Uidhre*, f. 61. b. col. 2.]

(194) [See *postea*, the lectures on music.]

(195) [original:—Atchondarc and imdai acas oénfer inti. Mael garb forsuidi, cia focerta miach fiadubull for a mául, ni tochriched ubull dib forlár, acht nogiuglad cach ubull for a finna. Abrat rolómar tarais isintig. Cach imresain bís isin tig imsuidiu no ligi isin areir tiagait uli. Do foethsad snathat isintig, rochechlastai a tothim intan labras béos. Dubcrand mór úasa; cosmail fri mol mulind conascialtaib acas a cendraig acus airmtiud. . . . Tuidle Ulad insin, rechtaire teglaig Chonaire. Is é cen aurchuasacht a breith inid fir sin. Fer connic suide, acus lige, acus biad do chách. Isi a lorg teglaig fuil úasa.—*Ibid.*, f. 61. b. col. 2.]

XXV.

They had three yellow golden heads of hair. When anger s upon them, their golden-yellow hair reaches to the points of shoulder blades. When they raise their eyes, the hair rises u that it descends no lower than the tips of their ears. It is curled than the forehead of a bleating ram (*retha copad*). golden shield and a candle of a royal house was over each of t Every one in the house admires their voice, their deeds, their words. Continue thy identifications, O *Ferrogain*". *rogain* now shed tears until his cloak in front was wet, an voice was heard from his head until a third part of the night past. "Alas!" said *Ferrogain*, "then, I have good caus what I do; these are *Oball*, and *Oblini*, and *Coirpri Finc* [that is, the fair and tall], the three sons of the king of Erinn

f the champions *Mal Mac Telbaind*, *Muinremor*, and *Birderg*;

"I saw there a couch", said *Ingcel*, "and three men i three large brown men, having three large brown beards. thick legs had they: thicker than the body of a man was e limb of theirs. They had three brown curled heads of majestically upon them. They wore red-spotted white Three black shields with devices of gold, and three flesh-pier spears, hang above them; and each of them has a bone-h sword". These were *Mal Mac Telbaind*, *Muinremor Mac G cind*, and *Birderg Mac Ruain*, three regal stems, three h of valour, three victory winning champions of Erinn.[187]

Then follows a strange description indeed.

f the great Ultonian champion *Conall Cearnach*

"I saw there on an ornamented couch", said *Ingcel*, " most beautiful man among the champions of Erinn. He a splendid crimson cloak upon him. One of his cheeks whiter than snow. Whiter and more red-tinged than the glove was the other cheek. One of his eyes was bluer tha violet; and the other blacker than the back of a cockchafer.

(186) [original:—Atconnarc ann imdae ocus triar indi, .i. tri móethóclaig ocus tri bruit sirecdai impu, teóra bretnassa órdai inna mbrattaib. Teóra monga órbuidi foraib. In tan folongat a bairbéiu taetmoing in mong órbuidi dóib cobraine a n-imdae. In tan conocbat arrosc cónócaib in folt connách isliu rind a n-uae. Cassithir rete copad. Coic roth óir ocus caindel rígthige úas cachae. Nach duni fil isin tig ar taceir guth, ocus gnim, ocus breithir. Samail lat a Firrogain. Roci Ferogain combofliuch a brat ros a bélaib, ocus ni hétas guth assáchind co trian na haidchi. A becu! or Ferrogain isdethbir dam; andogniu, Oball, ocus Oblini, ocus Co Findmór tri mic ríg hErenn in *Leabhar na h-Uidhre*, f. 62. a. c

(187) [original:—Atconnarc imdae ocus triar indi; triar móra, tri dond berrtha ro Duind colbthae remrae leó; ethir medon fir cach ball dib. dond foilt chassa forrib mórchind. Teóra lenna brec impu. Tri duibscéith cobuag óir, ocus teóra slega coicr úasaib; ocus claind dét cach fi . . . Mál mac Telbaind ocus M remor mac Gerrcind ocus Bir mac Ruain, tri rígdamnae, tri gaile, tri laich ocaide ísaicul, g in hErenn.—*Ibid*, f. 62, b. col.

large as a reaping basket is the bushy head of golden hair which is upon him. It touches the lower tips of his two shoulder blades. It is more curled than the forehead of a bleating ram".(198)

This was the celebrated *Conall Cearnach*, one of the great champions of the Royal Branch of Ulster.

of the monarch *Conaire Mor;*

"I saw there a couch", said *Ingcel*, "and its ornamentation was more splendid than all the other couches of the court. It is curtained around with silver cloth, and the couch itself is richly ornamented. I saw three persons on it. The outside two of them were fair both of hair and eyebrows, and [their skin was] whiter than snow. Upon the cheeks of each was a beautiful ruddiness. Between them in the middle [sat] a noble champion. He has the ardour and the action of a sovereign, and the wisdom of a historian. The cloak which I saw upon him can be likened only to the mist of a May morning. A different colour and complexion are seen upon it each moment; more splendid than the other is each hue. I saw in the cloak in front of him a wheel brooch of gold that reaches from his chin to his waist. Like unto the sheen of burnished gold is the colour of his hair. Of all the [human] forms of the world that I have seen, his is the most splendid. I saw his gold-hilted sword laid down near him. There was the breadth of a man's hand of the sword exposed out of the scabbard: From that hand's breadth the man who sits at the far end of the house could see even the smallest object by the light of that sword. More melodious is the melodious sound of that sword, than the melodious sounds of the golden pipes which play music in the royal house".(199)

And here follows a poem by *Ingcel* containing a minute description, so minute that I cannot do better than give it here at

(198) [original:—Atconndarc ann in imdae cumtachtae, fer ascáinem do láechaib herenn. Bratt caschorcra imbi. Gilithir snechtae indalagruaid do. Brec dergithir sion an gruaid naile. Is glasidir buga indala súil; is dubithir druim ndáil in tsúil aile. Meit cliab búana in dosbili find forordha fil fair. Benaid braini adaimdae. Is cassidir rethe corrad.—*Leabhar na h-Uidhre*, f. 62. b. col. 2.]

(199) [original:—Atconndarc ann imdae acas bacáimiu acomtach oldáta imdada in tigi olchena. Séolbrat nairgdidi impe, acas cumtaige isin dimdae. Atconndarc triar ninni. In dias imechtranach díb finna díb linaib conafoltaib acas a brataib, acas itgilithir snechtae. Rudiud róálaind forgruad cechtar nae. Móeth óclách etorro immedon. Bruth acas gnim ruirech lais, acas comairli senchad. Brat atconndarc imbi is cubes acas ceó cetamain. Is aindath acas ecosc cachahuairi tadbat fair; áildiu cach dath alailiu. Atconndarc roth nóir isin brut ar a bélaib adcomaic úasmech coaimlind. Is cosmail fritúidlig nóir forloscthi dath a fuilt. Dineoch atconndairc de delbaib betha is i delb as áldem díb. Atconndarc a claind nordduirn occo tís. Robói airthir láime din claind fri truaill anechtair: anairthir lámisin fer nobíd in airthiur in tigi tis cébad frigit fri foscad in claind. Isbinni bindfogrogod in claind, oldás bindfogra na cuslend nórdae fochanat céol isind rigthig. . .—*Ibid.*, f. 62. b. col. 2.]

XXV. of the monarch *Conaire Mor*;

full length. It mentions almost every article of dress or orna-ment in which a painter should pourtray an Irish king:—[200]

["I saw a tall illustrious chief
Starting forth upon the lovely earth,
Full-waxing in the springtide of dazzling beauty,
Of features gentle, yet of proportions bold.
"I saw a renowned placid king,
His legitimate place rightfully occupying,—
From the threshold even to the wall,—
For his couch.
"I saw his two blueish-white cheeks,
Dazzling white, and like unto the dawn
Upon the stainless colour of snow.
Two sparkling black pupils
In dark blue eyes glancing,
Under an arbour of chafer-black eyelashes.
"I saw his bright lordly diadem,
With its regal splendour,
Radiating its lofty refulgence
Upon his illustrious face.
"I saw the splendid *Ardroth*
Encircling his head,—enwreathing
With his hair its brightness,
The sheen of gold most brilliant,—
Above his curling yellow locks.
"I saw his many-hued red cloak of lustrous silk,
With its gorgeous ornamentation of precious gold be-
spangled upon its surface,
With its flowing capes dexterously embroidered.
"I saw in it a great large brooch,
The long pin was of pure gold;

(200) [original:—
Atchiu flaith nárd nairegdae
ara bith builled búredach brúchtas,
róimse robortae rechtbruth,
cáin cruth ciallachar.
Atchiu clothrig coscordach,
cotngaib innachert raind chóir,—
comchechbuid ó thraind cossaig,—
so a suidi.
Atchiu andángruaid ngormgela,
condossiriúamun find fuinechdae
sur dath sóerdath snechtaide.
didibriúilib sell glassaib glannu
a rosc ro búgad teninu achuins-
cliu,
caintocud itercleccor nduib
ndóelabrar.
Atchiu amind find flatha,
comdsfiressect suirech,
rat ordan suitan
a gnúis comdetae.
Atchiu ardroth ninnaisso
immachend,—co corre
cond sirsaltu sritchérur,
sordach nórda nollmaisse,—
sil uása berad buidechas.
Atchiu abrat nderg nildathach nátte
síric,
ar delbchor ndimaisse dindó
aurdéirc srethcisse sluind,
ail bend alathúaich noronaicdi.
Atchiu delg nand olladbol,
deór uili inclaisse;
lassaid ar lúth laneisci,
laine a cuaird corcorgemmach

XXV.

of the monarch *Conaire Mor*;

Bright shining like a full-moon
Was its ring, all around,—a crimson gemmed circlet
Of round sparkling pebbles,—
Filling the fine front of his noble breast
Atwixt his well proportioned fair shoulders.
"I saw his splendid linen kilt,
With its striped silken borders,—
A face-reflecting mirror of various hues,
The coveted of the eyes of many,—
Embracing his noble neck—enriching its beauty.
An embroidery of gold upon the lustrous silk—
[Extended] from his bosom to his noble knees.(301)
"I saw his long gold-hilted sword,
In its scabbard of bright silver,
Which through shields on champions cuts,
Until it reaches the illustrious blood.
"I saw his resplendent beautiful shield,
That towers above innumerable troops,
Inlaid with sparkling gold
On its polished rim of white metal,
Luminous like a glowing torch.
"A truncheon of gold, long as a king's arm,
Was near him on his right,
Which when grasped by the proud chief,
Summons forth, of hardy curly heroes,
Three hundred fighting champions
Around the victory-winning kingly chief,
And vultures from their eyries.
It is a court, a woful house I saw.]

"The noble warrior was asleep, with his legs upon the lap of one of the men, and his head in the lap of the other. He

caera cretir comraicte,
congaib aroreiċ ndenomaisse
eter adá gel gualaind ċoir.
Atċíu alenie ligdae linide,
cond srissebend sirechtaċ,—
scaṫderc scéo deilb ildaṫaig,
ingelt súla soċaide,—
cotgaib armeit muinenċor—
sóertar ar néim.
indenam ór sri siric srebċisse
o adbrund courglune.
Atċíu aċlaind nóradairn ninclaisse,
ma sindiuċ findargit,
airnéid ar ċeirr[n]? cóicroċ,
cond sricruaid naurdairc nair-
tir.

Atċíu ascíaṫ netroċt náilenda,
sail uásdorongaib dímes,
tréċur díor oibleċ
artor sceo bil ban bruṫ,
forosnai liṫ luaċet.
Turi díor inclaissi lam rig,
sris deiss,
dingabar sritrieċ tailc
taurgaib cond forcernu cruad-
ċassa,
tri cead corae comlána
ḃasindrurig raṫrúanaid,
sri boidb hi mbroin bertas.
is bruidin bróntig atċíu.
Atċíu flaiṫ nárd nairegdae.—
Leabhar na h-Uidhre, f. 63. a. col. 1.]

(301) [This passage clearly proves that the *Leinidh* was a *kilt* or petticoat reaching to the knees. See on this subject Lect. XXIII., *ante*, vol. ii. p. 106.]

XXV. awoke afterwards out of his sleep, stood up, and spake these words:

"I have dreamed of danger-crowding phantoms,
A host of creeping treacherous enemies,
A combat of men upon the [river] *Dothra;*
And early and alone
The king of *Teamair* was killed".[202]

"Identify for us, O *Ferrogain*, who it was that spoke that lay", said *Ingcel*.

"I do know his like", said *Ferrogain;* "it was not a sight without a king [thou sawest] indeed, it is the king most noble, most dignified, comely, and most powerful that has come of the whole world; the most polished, smooth, and precise that has ever appeared; namely, *Conairé Mór*, the son of *Eterscel;* it is he that was there, the high king of all Erinn".[203]

I believe it would be difficult to find in ancient poetry anything nobler or more beautiful than this vivid picture of a chivalrous king of the heroic ages in Erinn.

The tale continues:

of the six cupbearers;

"I saw there six men in front of the same couch, with fair-yellow hair. They wore green cloaks around them with brooches of red bronze fastening their cloaks; their faces were half red, half white, like *Conall Cearnach*'s. Each man of them is practised to throw his cloak around another quicker than a wheel in a cascade, and it is doubtful whether thy eye could follow them. These", said *Ferrogain*, "are the six cupbearers of the king of *Teamair*, namely, *Uan*, *Broen*, and *Banna* [that is, froth, drop, and stream], *Delt*, and *Drucht*, and *Dathen*.[204]

of *Tulchinne* the royal druid and juggler

"I saw there", continued *Ingcel*, "a large champion in front of the same couch, in the middle of the house. The blemish of baldness was upon him. Whiter than the cotton of the

(202) [original:—Robói iarum in móċtóclaċ inaċotlud, acas aċossa inuċt indalasir, acas a ċend inuċt araile. Doriusaig iarum assa ċotlud, acas atraraċt, acas roċaċain: . . .
Dommárfás imned immed siabrai,
slúag fáen fálgud námat,
comrac fer for Doċrai;
doċraite ríg Temraċ indoitid or-tac.—*Leabhar na h-Uidhre*, f. 63. a. col. 2.]

(203) [original:—Samail let a Fir-rogain ciaroċaċain in laidsin. Nin. Damsa a samail for Ferrogain; ní esce cenríg ón inm, isé rí asanoraiḋ [amra], acas as ordnidem, acas as cáinem, acas asċumaċtom ṫánic in domon uli; is hé rí arbláċem, acas as ṁinem, acas as becda do dánic, .i. Conaire mór mac Eterrsceoil; isé fil and ardri hErenn uli.—*Ibid.*, f. 63. a col. 2.]

(204) [original:—Atcondarc and seissiur ar bélaib na nimdad cétna, monga findbuidi foraib. Bruit úanidi impu, deilg créda in aurslocud ambrat; ite [let derga] let gabra amail Chonall Cernaċ. Fo-ccird caċ fer abrat imáraile, acas is luaċidir roċánṁbualed isingnaḋ indá arċét do súil . . . Nin. Damsá on. Sé dalemain ríg Temra[ch] insin, .i. Uan, acas Bróen, acas Banna, Delt acas Druċt acas Daċen.—*Ibid.*, f. 63. b. col. 2.]

mountains[305] is every hair that grows upon his head. He had ear-clasps of gold in his ears; and a speckled white cloak upon him. He had nine swords in his hand, and nine silvery shields, and nine balls of gold. He throws every one of them up [into the air], and none of them fall to the ground, and there is but one of them at the time upon his palm; and like the buzzing of bees on a beautiful day, was the motion of each passing the other". "Yes", said *Ferrogain*, "I know him; he is *Tulchinne*, the royal druid of the king of *Teamair;* he is *Conaire*'s juggler: a man of great powers is that man".[306] XXV.

"I saw three men in the east side of the house", said *Ingcel*, "with three black tufts of hair. They wore three green frocks upon them, and three black kilts [plaids or shawls?] wrapped around them. Three forked spears stood above them by the side of the wall. Who were these, *Ferrogain?* They are the king's three chief swine herds, *Dubh*, *Dond*, and *Dorcha*", answered *Ferrogain*.[307] of the three swine-herds;

Ingcel then describes the dress of the king's head charioteers. As this description is important in connection with the gold ornaments worn on the head, I shall reserve it for a future lecture.[308]

"I saw another couch", said *Ingcel*, "eight swordsmen on it, and a young champion between them. He had black hair, and stammers in his speech. All in the court listen to his counsel. The most beautiful of men is he. He wore a shirt, and a white and red cloak, and a silver brooch in his cloak. *Ferrogain* said this was *Causcrach Mend Macha*, [that is stammering *Causcrach* of *Emania*], the son of *Conchobar* [king of Ulster], who is in hostageship with the king [*Conaire*], and his guards are the eight swordsmen around him".[309] of *Causcrach Mend;*

(305) [*Canach sleibe*, the *Eriophorum polystachion* or common Cotton Grass. The name no doubt was applied also to *Eriophorum vaginatum*, or Haretail Cotton Grass, which in Ireland is a much rarer species than the *Eriophorum polystachion.*]

(306) [original:—Atcondarc and borróclaeċ ar bélaib naimdae cetnae, for lar in tige. Atis máile fair. Finnithir canaċ sléibe caċ finna ásas triana ċend. Unasca óir imáó; brat brecligda imbi. ix. claind ina láim, acas nói scéith airgdidi, acas .ix. nubla óir. Foċeird ceċ ai dib inardae, acas ní tuit ní dib forlár, acas ni bi aċt oen dib for abois; acas is cumma acas timṫireċt beċ illó ánli caċae seċ araile suas. . . . . Nin. Limsa asamail or Ferrogain Taulċinne rig druṫ ríg Temraċ, clessamnaċ Ċonaire insin: fer comaic móir inn fer sin.—*Leabhar na h-Uidhre*, f. 63. b. col. 2.]

(307) [original:—Atcondarc triar inairṫiur in tige, tri dubbertae foraib. Tri forti uánidi impu, tri dublenna tairsiu. Tri gabulgici úasaib hitóib sraigeo. . . . Ciasút a Firrogain. Nin. Ol Ferrogain, tri muccaidi inrig sin, Dub acas Dond acas Dorċa.—*Ibid.*, f. 64. a.]

(308) *Postea*, Lecture xxvii., vol. ii. p. 183.

(309) [original:—Atcondarc imdai naili, oċtur claidbeċ inti, acas máeṫoclaeċ etorro. Máeldub fair,

XXV.

We have next a description of the dress of apprentice chariot drivers, which I shall also reserve for a future lecture.[210]

of the Saxon princes and their companions;

"I saw", said *Ingcel*, "in the north side of the house nine men, with nine yellow heads of hair, wearing nine shirts upon them, and nine crimson kilts around them, and without brooches in the cloaks. Nine broad spears and nine curved red shields hung over them. "I know them, said he; "they are *Osalt* and his two companions; *Osbrit* the long-handed and his two companions; and *Lindas* and his two companions. These are three Saxon royal princes, who abide with the monarch".[211]

of the king's out riders;

"I saw three men more", said *Ingcel;* "the three have bald heads upon them; they wear shirts and cloaks wrapped around them; and a whip (or scourge) is in the hand of each. I know them", said he, "they are *Echdruim*, *Echruid*, *Echruathar*, the horse-back boys [or outriders of horse expeditions]. They are the king's three riders, that is, his three esquires (*Ritiri*)".[212]

of the king's three judges;

"I saw three others on the couch along with them", said *Ingcel*. "A comely man whose head was shorn was the first, and two young men along with him with long hair upon them. They wore three kilts of mixed colours, with a silver brooch in the cloak of each of them. Three swords hung over them at the wall. I know them", said he, "they are *Fergus Ferde*, and *Ferfordae*, and *Domaine Mossud*, the king's three judges".[213]

of the king's nine harpers;

"I saw nine others in front", said *Ingcel*, "with nine bushy curling heads of hair, nine light blue floating cloaks upon them, and nine brooches of gold in them. Nine crystal rings upon their hands; a thumbring of gold upon the thumb of each of them; ear clasps of gold upon the ears of each; a torque of silver around the neck of each. Nine shields with golden emblazonments over them on the wall. Nine wands of white silver were in their hands. I know them", said he, "they are the

acas belra formend leiss. Contuaset aes na bruidni uli acondelg. Ailđem di dainib hé. Caimsi imbi, acas brat gelderg, eo airgit inna brot. Ro fetursa sin ol Fergoban, .i. Cuscraid Mend Macha mac Conċobair sil hingialnai las in rig. Acometaidi inm in toċtar sil immi. —*Leabhar na h-Uidhre*, f. 64. a.]

(210) [*Postea*, Lecture xxvii., vol. ii., p. 183.]

(211) [original:—Atcondarc isind leiṫ atúaid din tig nonbur, noí monga for buidi foraib, noí caimsi forgarti impu, noílennae corcraidi tairsiu, cendelgae indib. Noí manaise, noí cromsceiṫ deirg úasaib. Russetamair ol se, .i. Osalt acas a dá ċomalta; Osbrit Lámfota acas a dá ċomalta; Lindas acas a dá ċomalta. Tri rigdomna do Saxanaib sin filead oconrig —*Ibid.*, f. 64.a]

(212) [original:—Atcondarc triar naili, teora máela foraib; tri lenti impu, acas tri broit hi forcepul; sraigell illam caċae. Russetarsa sin ol se, .i. Eċdruim, Eċruid, Eċruaċar, tri marcaig indrig sin, .i. a ṫri ritiri —*Ibid.*, f. 64. a.]

(213) [original:—Atcondarc triar naili isin dimdai ocaib. Fer cáin rogab a máelad hi cetad, dioclaig leis co mongaib foraib. Teora lenda cumascdai impu, eó argit imbrot caeċ naidib. Tri gascid

king's nine harpers, namely, *Side* and *Dide*, *Dulothe* and *Deichrinni Caumul*, and *Cellgen*, *Ol* and *Olene*, and *Olchoi*".[314]

of the king's three jugglers;

"I saw three more on the couch", said *Ingcel*, "wearing shirts of full length; carrying quadrangular shields in their hands, with bosses of gold upon them, and having with them balls of silver, and slender long darts. I know them", said he, "they are *Cless* and *Clessine* and *Clessamunn*, the king's three ordinary jugglers".[315]

of the three chief cooks;

"I saw three men cooking", continued *Ingcel*, "dressed in long aprons (*Berrbroca*); a fair gray-haired man, and two youths along with him". "I know them", said *Ferrogain*; "they are the king's three chief cooks, namely, the *Dagdae*, and his two apprentices, *Seig* and *Segdae*, the two sons of *Rofir* of the one spit".[316]

of the king's three poets;

Ingcel next describes the dress of the king's three poets, which to avoid repetition I shall omit here, but the reader will find it in a future lecture.[317]

of the king's two wardens;

"I saw there", said *Ingcel*, "two young warriors standing over the king, bearing two bent shields and having two great swords. They had red kilts, and brooches of bright silver in their cloaks. They", [said *Ferrogain*,] "are *Bun* and *Meccun*, the king's two wardens, the two sons of *Maffir Thuill*".[318]

of the king's nine guardsmen;

"I saw", said *Ingcel*, "nine men upon a couch there in front of the same king's couch. They had fair-yellow hair; they wore aprons (*Berrbroca*), and little speckled mantles, and carried protecting shields. Each of them had an ivory-hilted sword in his hand, and every man who attempts to enter the house, they

ceraib hi frais . . . Rufsetarsum olse, Fergus Ferde, Ferfordae, acas Domáine Mossud, tribriteman inorig sin.—*Leabhar na h-Uidhre*, f. 64. b.]

[314] [original:—Atchonnarc nonbur aile fris anair, nói monga craebacha casa forraib, .ix. mbroit glassa lúascaig impu, ix ndelce óir inambrataib. ix failge glana imdaláma; ordnasc óir imordain cachae; auchuimriuch nóir imóchach fir; dunnce airgit imbrágait cachae. ix. mbuilc conincaib ordaib uaraib [illegible]. ix. flesca findairgit ina lámaib. Rofetorsa sin olse. noi cruitire inoraig inosin, Side acas Dide, Dulothe acus Deichrinni, Caumul acas Cellgen, Ol acas Olene, acas Olchoi —*Ibid.*, f. 64. b.]

[315] [original:—Atcondarc triar aile isfindairiud, teora caimsi bruidib impu; sciatha cethrochairi ina lámaib, cotelaib óir foraib, acas ubla airgit, acas gai bic inclassi leu. Rosfetursa ol se Cless, acas Clessine, acas Clessamunn, tri clessamnaig inorigsin.—*Ibid.*, f. 64 b.]

[316] [original:—Atchondarc triar oc dénam fulachta imberrbrócaib inclaissib; fer findliath, acas di oclaig na farrad. Rusfetursa sin ol Ferrogan; tri primfulachtore inorig sin, .i. in Dagdae, acas ada daltae, .i. Séig, acas Segdae, da mac Rofir oenbero —*Ibid.*, f. 64. b.]

[317] *Postea*, Lecture xxvii., vol. ii., p. 183.]

[318] [original:—Atcondarc and dá óclaech innaseassom os cind inríg, dá cromsciath acas da bend claidiub mara occo. Lenna derca impu, delci findairgit is na bratraib. Bun acas Meccun sin olse de chometaib in ríg isin, dá mac Maffir Thuill —*Ibid.*, f. 65. a. col. 1.]

XXV. threaten to strike with the swords, and no person dares ap proach the couch without their leave. I know them", sai *Ferrogain*, "they are 'the three Early Mornings' of Meath the three symbols of victory of *Bregia;* the three pillars o Mount *Fuad*. These are the king's nine guardsmen", sai *Ferrogain*.[319]

of the king's two table attendants; "I saw another couch there", said *Ingcel*, "and two men o it, bold, gross and stout-firm. They wore aprons (*Berrbroca*) and their complexions were dark-brown. They had hair shor at their polls, and high upon their foreheads. As swift as waterwheel do they run past each other. The one to the [king's couch, the other to the fire. I know them", said *Ferrogain* "they are *Nia* and *Bruthni*, [king] *Conaire*'s two table atten dants".[320]

of the champions Sencha, Dubthach Dael Uladh, and Goibniu; "I saw", said *Ingcel*, "a couch, the nearest to [king] *Conair* and on it three prime champions. They wore black-blue kilts Every limb of theirs was thicker than the body of a man. They carried black, huge swords, each of them longer than the swor (or lath) of a weaver's beam; they would cut a hair upon water and the middle-man of them had a great spear in his hand These were three victory-winning, valiant champions of Erinn namely *Sencha* the beautiful son of *Ailill*, and *Dubthach Dae Uladh*, and *Goibniu* the son of *Lurgnech;* and the spear of *Celtchair Mac Uithidir*, which was in the battle of *Magh Tuireadh*, was in the hand of *Dubthach Dael Uladh*".[321] *Celt chair Mac Uithidir* was a famous Ulster champion whose residence was *Dun Cheltchair*, now Downpatrick, in the county of Down. His famous spear here alluded to was traced up t the battle of the second or northern *Magh Tuireadh*. Th

(319) [original:—Acconnarc nonbur in imdae and ar bélaib na imdai [himdae] cetnae. Mongae findbuidi foraib, berrbróca impu; acas coċléne brecca, acas scéiṫ béimneċa foraib. Claind dét illáim caċ fir dib, acas caċ fer do ċáec irateċ, fólóimeċár abéim cosna claind, nílomeċar neċ dul dond imdae cen airiasaċt dóib. . . Nin. Domsa ón tri moċ matnig Midi; tri búagelṫaig Breg; tri sortaig Slebe Fuáit. Nonbor cometaide indrig sin.—*Leabhar na h-Uidhre*, f. 65. a. col. 1.]

(320) [original:—Acconnarc imdae naile nand, acas dias indi icé dam dabċa balcremra. Berrbróca impu; ite gormdonna indib. Culmonga cumri foraib, ité aurarda for etun. Ic luaṫtoir roċ búale ceċtar de seċaraile. Indalahai dond im dai, alaile dontenid. . . Nin. Dams Nia acas Bruċni da soss mere Chon aire insin.—*Ibid.*, f. 65. a. col. 1.]

(321) [original:—Acconnarc imda ar nesam do Chonaire, tri primlái inti. Lenna dubglassa impu. Rem ċir medón fir caċball dib. Tr claind duba dimóra leo, ... claind ngarmnae caċae; nodole cáis finnae sorusciu; Lágén mór il láim indsin medónaig . . tri lá atadeċ gaibċe gaiscéd in hErenn, Senċa mac alaind Ailella, acas Dub ċaċ Dóel Ulaḋ, acas Goibnend ma Lurgnig; acas indlúin Chelṫċa mac Utidir forriċt hicaṫ Mag Tured, issi sil illáim Duibṫec Dá Ulaḋ.—*Ibid.*, f. 65. b. col. 2.]

XXV.

description of it in the tract relating to that battle is highly poetical.

Of Daderg himself;

"I saw another couch there", said *Ingcel*, "and one man on it with two *gilles* (or pages) in front of him; one fair, the other black-haired. The champion himself had red hair, and had a red cloak near him. He had crimson cheeks, and beautiful deep blue eyes, and had a green cloak upon him; he wore also a white shirt and collar, with beautiful interweaving [of gold thread] upon him; and a sword with an ivory hilt was in his hand; and he supplies every couch in the court with ale and food, and he is incessant in attending upon the whole company. Identify that man, *O Ferrogain*. I know that man", said he. "That, is *Daderg* himself. It was by him the court was built, and since he has taken [up his] residence in it, its doors have never closed, except the side to which the wind blows, it is to that side only that a door is put. Since he has taken to housekeeping, his boiler has never been taken off the fire, but continues ever to boil food for the men of Erinn. And the two who are in front of him, these are two boys, fostersons of his, namely the two sons of the king of Leinster, whose names are *Muredach* and *Corpri*.(222)

of the kin. three door keepers;

"I saw there three men on the floor of the house at the door", said *Ingcel*, "they had three clubs with chains in their hands. Each of them is swifter than a wild cat running around the other as they rush towards the door. They wore speckled aprons (*Berrbroca*) and pale cloaks. Identify those for us, O *Ferrogain*. These are the three door-keepers of the king of *Teamair* who are there, namely, *Echur* and *Tochyr* and *Techmang*, three sons renowned for valour and combat".(223)

(222) [original:—Atconnarc imdae naile and, acas oenfer inte, acas da gilla arabelaib; acas dimoing forraib, in dala hai is dub, alaile, is find. Folt derg forsindláeċ, acas a brait deirg lais. Dangruaid chorcorda lais, rosc roglas ro ċáin occa, acas brat uánídi immi; lene gel culpataċ condeg inclaid imbi; acas claind condmdurnd dét inalláim; acas arric airećtain caċa imdae isin tig dilind acas biúd, ossé cossalaċ oc timtirećt insloig uli. Samail l S. a. F. R. Nin. Rosetursa inna firusin, Daderga insain is lais do. Ronnad in bruiġean, acas ó gabais trebad ni ro dúnait a doirse, siam o do rigned act leṫ diambi ingáeṫ, is fris bis in ċomla. Acas o gabais trebad ni tuccad aċairi do ċenid, aċt no bíd oc bruiṫ bíd do feraib hErenn. Acas in días fil ar abélaib da dalta dosom, inda mac sin, .i. da mac ríġ Lagen, .i. Muredaċ acas Corpri —*Leabhar na h-Uidhre*, f. 65. b. col. 1.]

(223) [original:—Atconnarc and triar for lár in tige ocondorus, teóra lorga brebneca inna lámaib. Is lúaṫidir fiamain caċae dib timċull a raile doċum in dorais. Berr-bróca impu ite breca acas bruit laċtnae léo. Samail l S. a. F. R. Tri dorsaide ríg Temraċ insin, .i. Eċur acas Toċur acus Teċmang, tri-mic ersand acas comlad.—*Ibid.*, f. 65. b. col. 2.]

XXV.

of the British outlaws at the court of the monarch;

"I saw there", said *Ingcel*, "a couch, and three times nine men on it; they had fair-yellow hair, and were all of equal beauty. Each wore a small black mantle, and a white hood upon each mantle, and a red tuft upon every hood, and an iron brooch in the breast of each mantle; and each carried a huge black sword under his cloak, and they would sever a hair upon the surface of water; and they had shields with sharp etchings upon them. Identify those for us, O *Ferrogain*". "They", said *Ferrogain*, "are three times nine youthful outlaws of Britain".(224)

of the three jesters;

"I saw there", said *Ingcel*, "three jesters at the fire. They wore three dark gray cloaks; and if all the men of Erinn were in one place, and though the body of the mother or father of each man of them were lying dead before him, not one of them could refrain from laughing at them". "These were *Mael* (bald), and *Milithi* (pale), and *Admilithi* (more pale), the three jesters of the king of Erinn who are there", said *Ferrogain*.(225)

Lastly, and to end my long list of extracts, *Ingcel* says:—

of the three drink-bearers.

"I saw there a couch and three persons on it. They wore three gray, floating cloaks around them. A cup of water was before each man of them, and a tuft of watercress(226) upon each cup of them". Identify those for us, O *Ferrogain*. "They

(224) [original:—Atconnarc an imdae, acas tri nonbur inti; monga findbuidi foraib, icé comalli. Cochléne dub imcach nóenfer dib, acas cennuid find for cach cochull, acas cuirce derg for cach cennuid dib, acas delg niarind in aurslon cach chochaill; acas claind dub diamár fó brut cach fir dib, acas noidolsatais finna forusciu; acas scéith co faebar condualaforaib. Samail l. S. a. F. R. Nin. Diberg tri [nai] mic mbáitse di Bretnaib insin.—*Leabhar na h-Uidhre*, f. 65. b col. 2.]

(225) [original:—Atconnarc ann triár fuirchuitbidi hicind tened. Tri bruit odra impu; ond betis fir hErenn in oen magin, acas chénobed colaind amathar no athar ar bélaib cach fir dib, ni foelsad nech dib cen gáiri impu. . . . . Nin. Máel, acas Milich, acas Admilich, tri cuitbi ríg hErenn insin".—*Ibid.*, f. 65. b. col. 2.]

(226) [*Birur*, the *Nasturtium officinale* (R. Brown). The common Spanish name of this plant is *Bérro*. This name is thoroughly Spanish, as is proved by the popular expression *andar á la flor del bérro*, applied to strolling or straggling about, being borrowed from its mode of growth. The Basque name is *Berró-azarra*. Those words are evidently cognate with the Irish, and are, I think, Celtic and not Basque. The Spanish names of several other water-plants are connected with *Bérro*, thus the Great Water Parsnep (*Sium latifolium*) is called *Berrera* and *Berráza*. The common cabbage *Bérza* also appears to contain the same root. Was the latter name given to cabbage when first introduced as a substitute for Water cress? In Cormac's Glossary (Stokes' edition) the word *biror* is given: biror .i. bir tipra no sruth, hor .i. mong biror din mong chippat nossochat. "*Biror*, i.e., grass of a well or stream, *hor* (or *or*), i.e., the mane (that is, the growth). *Biror* consequently means the mane (or growth) of the well or stream". This derivation is at all events ingenious, for there cannot be a doubt that *Birur* contains the same root as *Birchi*, a water stream, and *Bir*, a well, a word which is still preserved in the Wallon tongue in the form of *Bure*, though now applied to a coal *pit*, that is, to the deep well or shaft by which the water is pumped up and the coal extracted.]

Dub (black), Dond (brown), and Dobur (dark), the three nkbearers of the king of *Teamhair*".[327] XXV.

In this very minute account we have not only a description the mode of arrangement of a regal household in the king's esence, but descriptions of the dress of several champions, and so of the characteristic costumes and insignia of such of the onarch's household attendants and officers as happened to accompany him in his ordinary excursions. We have the monarch mself, his sons, his nine wonderful pipers or wind instrument ayers, the king's cupbearers, that is the cupbearers of his whole ble or company; the king's chief druid-juggler, his three principal charioteers; their nine apprentice charioteers, his hostages, e Saxon princes and their companies, the monarch's equerries outriders, his three judges, his nine harpers, his three ordinary gglers, his three cooks, his three poets, his nine guardsmen, and s two private table attendants; then we have *Daderg* himlf, the lord of the mansion, the monarch's three doorkeepers, e British outlaws or exiles, and finally the king's private drinkarers, who were always prepared with three cups of water and ree bunches of watercresses in them. But it may be objected these descriptions, that the whole story with its gorgeous illustions is only poetry, and the romantic creation of a fertile imaination. There is, no doubt, a certain degree of exaggeration many of the descriptions, and there are some among those hich I have not quoted that are wholly improbable. But e existence of such poetical excrescences, or the introduction fairy mansions or *Tuatha Dé Danann* courts, no more inlidates the descriptions of what was undoubtedly real, though mewhat highly coloured, than the corresponding exaggerans and supernatural agencies do those in the Iliad of Homer. deed, it must be admitted that the descriptions in this tale, d in that of the *Táin Bo Chuailgne* also are on the whole very tle exaggerated, and bear the stamp of truth upon them. As gards the colours of the various cloaks described, we have many ancient references to them, that there can be no raonal doubt of their having existed in remote times. Then as gards the brooches, rings, bracelets, neck torques, diadems, rclets, and crescents of gold and silver, for the head, neck, and ms, the articles themselves still preserved in such great abunnce, afford the most complete evidence of the accuracy of e tale; while, with the exception of the extracts from the

Summary of the classes of persons described.

The exaggerations of such descriptions scarcely affect their value;

very little exaggeration on the whole in the tales of the *Bruighean Daderga* and *Táin Bo Chuailgne*.

[327] [original:—Accondaic ano ... acaf cpiap indi. Cpibpuic glar ... ṫeaċa impu. Cuaċ urce arbélaib ... ċ fin dib, acaf popp do biruf por caċ cúaċ. Samail. l. S. a. f. n. nin Dub, acaf Dono, acaf Dobup, cpi deogbairi píg Cempaċ inpin.—*Leabhar na h-Uidhre*, f. 66. a. col. 2.]

XXV. ancient tale of the *Táin Bo Chuailgne* already quoted, there no known existing authority for the manner of wearing th so decided or reasonable as this. It is to be regretted inde that it was not at Tara the scene of this most curious and i portant tale was laid, as then we should have doubtless had glowing description of the regal magnificence of the time its most ample dimensions; but it is no small evidence of t authenticity of the descriptions and incidents of the piece th it is a private house is made in the story to be the scene, an an unexpected incident the cause, of the death of the splendi *Conaire Mór*.

It would be tedious and unprofitable to attempt to trace th modifications of fashion from the eighth down to the twelfth an fifteenth centuries. These, indeed, are periods within which have scarcely entered at all in the course of these lectures; an although the references to costume during those times are abu dant and striking, still, as it is possible that the fashions m have been more or less influenced by the more intimate co tact and connection with other countries, they would not te to throw much light back on the more ancient and far more i teresting times which it is the special object of these lectur to illustrate.

antiquity and long-continued use of the colour of certain garments

Of the antiquity and the long continuance of the colour of ce tain garments in ancient Erinn, I may be allowed to refer conclusion to two very brief, but very valuable instances.

There is an ancient, but very little known tale or piec treasured in some of our old MSS., under the title of *Amh Chonrai*, that is, the death song or funeral oration of *Cur* This was the celebrated *Curoi Mac Daire*, whose history, a the account of whose residence at *Cathair Chonrai* in the coun of Kerry, I have already given at some length in a previo lecture.[328]

shown by the tale of *Amhra Chonrai*;

Curoi, as, on the occasion just alluded to, I showed had be treacherously killed by the Ulster champion *Cuchulaind*. Af his death, his household bard *Ferceirtne* wrote a panegyric him, in which, among others of his noble deeds, he enumera the gifts and presents made by him to himself in the course his professional connection with him. These gifts consisted drinking horns, forts, houses, sheep, hogs, bondmaids, gart (*Fernu*) of gold, head pieces or circlets of gold (*Eoburrud ói* white ancillae or anklets of silver, or of *Findruine*, white di or dishes of silver, neck rings or torques of gold, a scarlet clo scarlet horse-saddles or cloths, balls of gold for jugglery tric *Bollans* or small drinking vessels, *Tailliamna*, or slings, *Ructh*

(328) *Ante*, Lecture xxii., vol. ii. p. 75, *et seq.*

XXV.

which are explained as scarlet frocks, hats, white silver brooches, chessboards set with precious stones, bridles, and other gifts too numerous to name in this place. Of all these, however, the only articles we are immediately concerned with here are the scarlet cloaks (*Lor Lethna*), and the *Ruotha*, which our ancient writer glosses as either scarlet frocks (*Inar*) or scarlet pantaloons (*Triubhas*).

The colour of the garment in either case is one of rare occurrence, and it is on this account that I have deemed it worth while to quote another passage of a much more recent date, from which the scarlet *Inar*, or frock, would appear to have been a garment of rather general use, or else perhaps the badge of a particular tribe or clann. The passage to which I allude is from a poem by *Mac Liag*, preserved in the fragment of the great Book of *Ui Maine* in the British Museum, and which I have so fully described in a former lecture.[229] This poem is an elegy on the death of the bard's patron *Tadgh* O'Kelly, who was killed at the battle of Clontarf, in which he recounts all the exploits and triumphs of his life, and his munificence to all men, but more especially his gifts to himself. Among the many gifts which the sorrowing bard acknowledges to have received from his noble patron, after his various triumphs, he mentions the following, in the thirty-fourth and thirty-fifth stanzas of his poem:—

by *Mac Liag's* elegy on *Tadgh* O'Kelly;

Tadgh gave me on the day [of the battle] of *Loch Riach*
An hundred cows, an hundred swords, an hundred shields,
An hundred oxen for the ploughing season,
And an hundred halter horses.
He gave me on the night [of the battle] of *Glenngerg*
An hundred cloaks and an hundred scarlet frocks,
Thirty spears of bloodstained points,
Thirty tables and thirty chess boards.[230]

And the use, and therefore the manufacture, of similar dresses of the same bright colours, continued at least two hundred years later, as is proved by a quatrain from a spirited poem written by *Gillabrighde Mac Conmidhe* for *Donnchadh Cairbrech* O'Brien, upon the occasion of his inauguration at Limerick, after the death of his brave father *Domhnall Mór* O'Brien in the year 1194. I give this stanza from the poet's vivid description of the person and bearing of the young Dalcassian prince, merely to carry

and also by a poem of *Gillabrighd Mac Conmidhe.*

(229) [*Vide ante*, Lecture vi., vol. i., p. 124.]

(230) [original:—
tug dam Taḋg la Loca Riach
c bo c. claidim, ċ. sciath,
c. do damaib re huair nair,
acas c. each nadasdair.

tug tam aiḋċe Glindegerg
c. brat, is c inar nderg,
triḋa sleag báruaḋ reanda,
x. [xxx?] failbe x [xxx?] fichille.
—O'Curry's copy from the original.]

XXV. down the chain of evidence regarding colours from the mc ancient to the more recent, though still remote, times. Th speaks the poet:—

A dark brown red mantle, and a gauntlet,
A splendid shirt under his glossy hair,
A brown satin tunic lustrous and light,
A keen fine large eye of bright deep blue.(231)

(231) [original:—
Matal duḃ ḋunn dearg is laṁonn,
Léine caissíos fá 'ċeiḃ ttais,
ionnar donnsróil uir éadtruim
fán tsúil ċorrṁóir ngéag ḋui
nglais.
—O'Conor *Don's* MS., O'Curry's co
vol. ii., p. 641, No. $\frac{23}{D}$, R.I.A.]

LECTURE XXVI.

[Delivered July 17th, 1860.]

(VIII.) Dress and Ornaments (continued). Very early mention of ornaments of gold, etc., *e.g.* in the description of *Eladha* the Fomorian king, in the second battle of *Magh Tuireadh*. Champions sometimes wore a finger ring for each king killed. Allusion to bracelets in an ancient poetical name of the river Boyne. Ornaments mentioned in a description of a cavalcade given in an ancient preface to the *Táin Bo Chuailgne;* and in the description of another cavalcade in the same tract. Some of the richest descriptions of gold and silver ornaments are to be found in the romantic tale of the "Wanderings of *Maelduin*'s Canoe" (circa A.D. 700). Bronze *Budne* for the hair in Dr. Petrie's collection. Ornaments described in the tale of the *Tochmarc Bec Fola*. Story of *Aithirne Ailgisach*, king *Fergus Fairge*, and the gold brooch found at *Ard Brestine;* the finding of ornaments unconnected with human remains explained by this tale. Mention of a large sized brooch in the legendary history of Queen *Edain*. Ancient law respecting the mode of wearing large brooches. Large brooches mentioned in the tale of the "Wanderings of *Maelduin*'s Canoe". Thistle headed or Scottish brooches; reference to Scottish brooches in the story of *Cano* son of *Gartnan*. Carved brooches mentioned in the tale of the *Bruighean Daderga*. Reference to a carved brooch in the Book of Munster. Another reference to a carved brooch in a poem ascribed to *Oisin*. Brooches of bronze and *Findruine*. Chased gold pins used down to the beginning of the thirteenth century. Of the different kinds of rings. The *Fainne* used to confine the hair. Hair rings used in the seventeenth century. *Fails* were worn up the whole arm for the purpose of bestowing them upon poets, etc.; example of this from the Book of Lismore. Of the bracelet called a *Budne*.

I proceed now to another branch of the subject of dress; that, namely, of the ornaments made of the precious metals, used by the people of ancient Erinn.

All our ancient histories and romantic tales abound in references to splendid vesture and personal ornaments of gold, silver, precious stones, and fine bronze, from the first battle of *Magh Tuireadh* (said to have been fought more than seventeen hundred years B.C.), down to the fourteenth and fifteenth centuries. Thus, in the battle of the second, or northern *Magh Tuireadh*, fought between the *Tuatha Dé Danann* and the Fomorians, we are told that *Eladha*, king of the Fomorians, appeared suddenly before a *Tuatha Dé Danann* maiden in Connacht, dressed as follows:— Very early mention of ornaments of gold, etc., *e.g.*,

"He had golden hair down to his two shoulders. He wore a cloak braided with golden thread; a shirt interwoven with threads of gold; and a brooch of gold at his breast, emblazoned with brilliant precious stones. He carried two bright silver in the description of *Eladha*, the Fomorian king.

XXVI.

spears, with fine bronze handles, in his hand; a shield of gold over his shoulder; and a gold-hilted sword, with veins of silver and with paps of gold".[333]

We are further told, that at parting, the splendid Fomorian left the maiden his ring of gold, which he took off his middle finger.

Champions sometimes wore a finger ring for each king killed.

It would appear, too, that in ancient times (yet times more recent than that of the battle of *Magh Tuireadh*), some champions wore a gold ring on their fingers for every king they had killed in battle. As an instance of this fact, we are told in the Book of *Lecan*, that *Lughaidh Laga*, a prince and warrior of Munster, had slain seven kings in successive battles; of which great achievement the famous *Cormac Mac Airt*, monarch of Erinn (whose father, *Art*, was one of the seven), said: "His hand does not conceal from *Laga* what number of kings he has killed"; that is to say, "there were seven *Fails* [*Buinds*], or rings of gold, upon his hand [that is, upon his fingers"].[334]

Allusion to bracelets in an ancient poetical name of the river Boyne.

The river Boyne, from the clearness of its waters, was poetically called *Righ Mná Nuadhat;* that is, the wrist or forearm of *Nuadhat's* wife. This lady was one of the *Tuatha Dé Danann*; and the poetical allusion to her arm originated from her keeping it constantly covered with rings or bracelets of gold to bestow upon poets and musicians.

Ornaments mentioned in a description of a cavalcade in a preface to the *Táin Bo Chuailgne*;

The following gorgeous description of a cavalcade is preserved in one of the ancient prefaces to the *Táin Bo Chuailgne*, contained in an ancient vellum manuscript, sold in London in the year 1859, with the books and MSS. of Mr. William Monck Mason, but of which I have a copy. The story relates that *Bodhbh Dearg*, the great *Tuatha Dé Danann* chief of the hill or mountain now called *Sliabh na m-Ban* in the county of Tipperary, went one time on a friendly visit to his cousin *Ochall Oichne*, the great chief of the ancient hill of *Cruachan*, in the county of Roscommon, afterwards the royal residence of the kings of Connacht. The people of Connacht had a great meeting to receive *Bodhbh*, at *Loch Riach* (now *Loch Reagh*). Splendid indeed was the calvacade that attended *Bodhbh* on the occasion, says the story:—"Seven score chariots and seven score horsemen was their number. And of the same colour were all their steeds; they were speckled; they had silver bri-

[333] [original:—Mogg orbuide foir go dib guaillib. Brat go srethaib di orsnath imbe; alene gona dindlendaib de orsnath; delg noir ar ab-ruinde, go forranad de lic log-mara ann. Dia gelgae airgide, acar diremcradn srarai indib de credumae; coicroith oir uar amuin; cloidib ordduirn go fethaib air-geat, acar go cichib oir.—Egerton MSS., 5280, Brit. Mus., commencing f. 52.]

[334] [See original, note, Lect. xxvii., *postea*, Vol. ii., p. 177.]

dles. There was no person among them who was not the son of a king and a queen. They all wore green cloaks with four crimson *Heo*, or pendants, to each cloak; and silver cloak-brooches (*Broth-Gha*) in all their cloaks; and they wore kilts with red interweavings, and borders or fringes of gold thread upon them, and pendants of white bronze thread upon their leggings or greaves (*Ochrath*), and shoes with clasps (*Indeoil*) of red bronze in them. Their helmets were ornamented with crystal and white bronze; each of them had a collar (*Niamh-Land*) of radiant gold around his neck, with a gem worth a newly calved cow set in it. Each wore a twisted ring (*Bouinde do At*) of gold around him worth thirty ounces (*ungas*) [of gold]. All had white-faced shields, with ornamentations of gold and of silver. They carried flesh-seeking spears, with ribs of gold and silver and red bronze in their sides; and with collars (or rings) of silver upon the necks of the spears. They had gold-hilted swords with the forms of serpents of gold and carbuncles set in them. They astonished the whole assembly by this display".(334)

XXVI.

The same tract contains similar descriptions of other cavalcades of a like kind, such as the following short one:

and in the description of another cavalcade in the same tract.

When the great *Tuatha Dé Danann* chief of *Cruachan* saw the magnificence of his southern friends' retinue, he called a secret meeting of his people, and asked them if they were able to appear in the assembly in costumes of equal splendour with those of their visitors? They all answered that they were not; upon which *Ochal*, their chief, said that they were dishonoured for ever, and that they should acknowledge their own poverty. Whilst the noble chief was thus giving vent to his mortification, they saw coming towards them from the north of Connacht a troop of horsemen,—namely, "Three score bridle steeds and three score chariots. All the steeds were black: one would think that it was the sea that had cast them up; they had bridle-bits of gold. The men wore black-gray cloaks, with crimson loops; a wheel-brooch (*Roth*) of gold at the breast of each man of

(334) [original:—uii.xx. Carpat acas uii.xx. marcaċ ba he allion. Acas tondach for a nechuib uile, .i. bric uile; acas srein airgidi friu. Ni conbui ann aċt mac rig acas rigno. Brait huaniidi impuib uile, acas cetre heo corcra for gaċ brut; ubrothgha argat inambratuib huilib; acas lente connderg indlad, acas cocortarċaib orsnaiċ impuib. Inathi findruine as a nochruib; assai coni indeoil do credumo impuib dan. Cennbair conimdenum diglainne acas findruine for a cenduib; niamhlann oir imbragaid cech fiur, geim fiu laulgaid noig-echttar inda firsine. Bouinde do at im ceċ fer fiu xxx.ad huinge. Sceith thulgeulo foruib uile, conn-imcherduib oir ocas arccuid. [Acas sleagaib coicrinneċa conasnaib óir acas airgid] ocas credumui ina tae-buib; ocas go munchip argaid mam-braigoib na sleg. Claidum orduirn condelbuib naċraċ dior ocus char-mogul fuip. For uasnairiut indu-nud uile cossi ndeisium minimsin.]

them. Kilts of perfect whiteness, with crimson stripes dow their sides upon them. Black hair upon every man of them, an so sleek, that you would think it was a cow that licked them all. They carried shields with emblematic carvings, and shar scolloped rims of *Findruine*, at their shoulders. Ivory set sword at their sides, inlaid with figures of bronze. A pointless spea in the hand of each man of them, with rivets of silver. Fift coils (*Torrochta*) of burnished gold around each man. The had no sandals on their feet, nor head pieces (*Cennbair*) upo their heads, except a few of them. They did not come directl into the assembly, but set up a camp of their own; after whic they came to the assembly—three score in chariots, and th other three score on horseback".[(115)]

This party appears to have come in the same way as *Bodhb* to the great meeting of the men of Connacht at *Loch Riach*; they were under the command of a man named *Feryna*, chie of that territory in Ulster which afterwards received the nam of *Dal Riada*. At this time *Bodhbh Derg* had in his service professional champion whose name was *Rind*; and it happene also that *Ochall* the Connacht chief had in his service at th same time, and in the same capacity, this champion's brother whose name was *Falbhar*; but neither of the chiefs knew tha their champions were brothers. In the course of the meetin *Bodhbh* challenged his friend *Ochall* to find him a man t match his champion *Rind* in single combat. *Ochall* imme diately produced *Falbhar*, and thus the two brothers entere the circus, and unexpectedly met in deadly combat. The battl however, soon became general; the Connacht men had the wor of it; but the two brothers survived to act other prominent part in the wild mythological history of these remote times.

Some of the richest descriptions of gold and silver ornaments are to be found in the tale of the Wanderings of *Maelduin's* Canoe.

Among the romantic and highly-coloured descriptions int which personal ornaments of gold and silver enter, some of th richest will be found in the ancient tale of the Wanderings o *Maelduin*'s Canoe (*Imramh Curaigh Maeilduin*). The incident of this tale are assigned to a fixed date far within the period o

(115) [original :—.i. tri.xx eich fo a srianaib, acas tri .xx. carpat. Eich dubu fuchuib uile: in darlacc is muir fornaidriut; bellgid oir friu huili. Tri dubglasso collaib corcraib impu; roth oir for bruinnib gach fir dib. Leinti laingeala, connemaith corcraib iarmad taebuib impu. mbruc cirdub fur gac fer dib, indar latt, is bo ro lelaig cechae. Sceith co fechlaib condualae, acas commlib findruini foailtnigib for a muin Colga deta leo fo a cuimb, c fuighib humae foaib. Moel ga hillaim gach, fir dib, gu semannai airgit. Coeca torachc dior for loircci im gach nai. Ni bacar ialla iecraind impu, na cennbair in gcennuib, acht huathad dib. Indeir gaigi ned hirin darecht, dororbe catar indunad; chadeirinlocus t xx. dib a cairpetu, ocas hinneoch tri .xx. ii hindarecht.]

ur undoubted history—namely, about A.D. 700; and having n a former lecture[236] given a full account of the history and nature of the piece, I shall not now go into it again. I proceed at once to the description of the lady in the Twelfth Island reached by the voyagers, when she comes out to them, after their three days of enchanted sleep.

"Upon the fourth day", the story says, "the woman came forth to them, and splendidly did she come there. She wore a white robe and a twisted ring (*Budne*, or *Buinne*) of gold confining her hair. She had golden hair. She had two shoes of silver upon her crimson-white feet; a silver brooch, with chains of gold in her robe; and a striped smock of silk next her white skin".[237]

This story, it is true, is a wild legend of magic; but the description is certainly that of a rich dress, such as the writer was accustomed to regard as beautiful among those worn by the ladies of the very early period in which this tale was written.

It will be perceived that among the personal ornaments of this lady there are two articles that do not often appear in such descriptions, namely, a silver brooch with chains of gold attached; and a spiral ring of gold to confine her hair. This ring was, in fact, used only when the long hair of the head was plaited, or rolled into one roll at the poll; and it was on this roll that the spiral ring was put, to keep it from unrolling, and for an ornament. There are a few ancient specimens of this ornament in plain gold, and some in bronze, preserved in the Museum of the Royal Irish Academy. But Dr. Petrie's collection contains a beautiful, if not unique one, in gold bronze. This beautiful ring is formed of a hollow or half cylindrical thin fillet of elastic bronze; tapering from a breadth of about three-quarters of an inch at one end, to an obtuse point at the other. It has been coiled up spirally from the broad end, so that the whole fits, circle within circle, in the one great circle at the broad end; or, if the spirals are not pressed home, it will form a regular cone, with all the external appearance of a solid ropelike body. When the hair was rolled up, and the ring put upon it and expanded, from the thick butt of the hair down to its small top, the whole ring, from its convex spiral surface, appeared like a golden rope closely twisted around the hair.[238]

Bronze *Budne* for the hair in Dr. Petrie's collection.

(236) [The only reference to this tale in any previous lecture is to be found at p. 289 of the *Lectures on MS. Materials of Irish History*.]

(237) [original:—Isin cethramud lou iarum dolluid in banscal andochum, acas ba haluinn em tanaic ann. Brat geal impe, acas buinne oir imm a moing. Mong ordu fuiri. Da maelan airgit imma cossa gealcorcrai; bretnas arcaid conbreprib oir inabrut; acus lene srebnuide sitt fria gel cnes.—*Leabhar na h-Uidhre*, fol. 26. b. bot. *et seq.*, and Egerton MSS., 5280, Brit. Mus.]

(238) [See fig. 56.]

XXVI.

It would be impossible for me, with any degree of co tive arrangement, to press into one lecture all the referen those personal ornaments of gold, silver, bronze, and pr stones, which in the course of my readings I have broug gether; and I shall therefore, for the present, content n with a few only, and first translate the following extract a very curious story in an ancient MS. written in a very an style of diction.

Ornaments described in the tale of *Tochmarc Bec Fola.*

Diarmait and *Blathmac*, the two sons of *Aedh Slaine*, joint monarchs of Erinn for eight years, until they were carried off by the great mortality in the year of our Lord Our legend tells us:—"That *Diarmait*, the son of *Aedh S* was king of *Temair* [or Tara], and had in pupilage and hos ship from the province of Leinster, *Crimhthann*, the s *Aedh* [king of that country]—He [*Diarmait*] went one d *Ath Truim* [Trim], in the territory of *Laéghaire*, and his *Crimhthann* along with him, and attended by but one ser They saw a woman coming over the ford [on the Boyne] the western side, in a chariot. "She had on her [feet] pointless shoes of white-bronze (*Findruine*), ornamented two gems of precious stones; her kilt was interwoven thread of gold; she wore a crimson robe, and a brooch of fully chased and beset with many-coloured gems in that She had a necklace of burnished gold around her neck; diadem of gold upon her head. She drove two black steeds at her chariot with two golden bridles; and the yo the horses had trappings of silver".[330] After some p *Diarmait* took her with him to *Temair*. She, however, cast her attention on his [*Diarmait's*] pupil, that is, *Crimhthann*, the son of *Aedh*. The youth consented to her at *Cluain da Chaileach* (near the place now called B glass, in the county of Wicklow), at the third hour (or o'clock) on the Sunday following, in order to elope with l

The story goes on to say, that:—"The lady, *Bec Fola* her way in the wood of *Dubhthar* [near Baltinglass]; and seeing a fire, she went towards it, and there saw a young w cooking a pig. He had on a silk tunic of pure crimson, circlets of gold and of silver; he had a helmet of gold silver and crystal upon his head; he had meshes and ge gold upon every lock of his hair, down to the blades o

(330) [original:—Da maelassa fin-druine impe, dá gem do lic log-mair eistib; lene fodergindlaic óir impe; brat corcra, dealg óir lánecair co mbreactrad ngem il-dathach isin brut. Muinci dióp fors-loisce im a bragait.; mind no a cind. Da each dubglas carpat dá nall óir friu; cotuagmilaib airgdidib for H. 2. 16. f. 765; H. 3. 18. f. 75

shoulders; he wore two balls of gold upon the two forks or divisions of his hair (in front), each the size of a man's fist. He had a gold-hilted sword at his girdle; and he had two sharp flesh-seeking spears between the leathers of his shield, with rings of white bronze upon them. He wore a many-coloured cloak. His two arms were covered with bracelets of gold and silver up to his elbows".(240) XXVI.

Story of *Aithirne* and the brooch of *Ard Brestine*;

The next example is equally curious. There is a story told in the "Book of Leinster" of a satirical poet of the province of Ulster, in the reign of king *Conchobar Mac Nessa*, whose name was *Aithirne Ailgisach*, or *Aithirne* "the covetous".

Aithirne took it into his head to make a visitation of the other provinces of Erinn, for the purpose of raising contributions from the kings and chiefs, under the the terror of his satirical tongue. Having arrived in South Leinster, he met the king and people of that country assembled to meet him at the hill of *Ard Brestine*, a place which still preserves its ancient name, situated near Ahade (*Ath Fadat*), about three miles south of Tullow, in the county of Carlow.

The Leinster men were prepared with rich presents for the poet to purchase off his good words; but the satirist would accept nothing but the most valuable jewel on the hill, though no one knew what or where that jewel was. Whilst the king and his people were at a loss what to do in this difficulty, "there was a young man careering a steed on the hill, and in one of the turns that he made close to the royal seat, the horse threw up a clod of earth from his hinder legs, and which clod fell in the lap of the king, *Fergus Fairge*, who immediately perceived in it a brooch (*Dealg*) of red gold weighing eighty *ungas* or ounces. "What have I got in my lap, O *Aithirne*?" said the king to the poet. "Thou hast got a brooch (*dealg*) there", said *Aithirne*: and *Aithirne* then recited this verse:—

"A brooch that has been found in *Ard Brestine*,
From the hoofs of a steed it has been got;
Over it have been delivered many just judgments,
When in the cloak of *Maine*, son of *Durthacht*".

(240) [original:—Dorrala for merugad ann co trat daiochi contacartadar [condotarlatur, H. 3. 18. 756, bot.] coin altai coro marbrat an inilt acas luid ri hicrand for teched. Ambai isin crund confacai in tei for lar na cailli. Luid do chum in tened. Confacai in oclach imon teni ocurgnam na muici. Inar sirecdai ime conglanchorcair acas co circlaib óir acus arcait; cennbarr dior acas argut acas glainne im a chenn; mocoil acas fithisi oir im cach n-dual dia fult, conici clar a dá imdai; da uball oir for dei gabal amongi, med feardoirnn ceachtar nai. Achlaideb ordduirnn ara chris; acas a da fleg coicrinnd itir leathar a sceit, co cobruid findruine fora. Brut ildathach [leis, H. 3. 18. 757]. A da laim lana di failgib oir acas arcait co a diuillinn.—H. 2. 16. col. 766.; H. 3. 18. 757.]

XXVI.

"This brooch", said he, "is what I should prefer, because it was my mother's brother that put it into the earth, when defeated in a battle along with the Ultonians, namely, the battle of *Ard Brestine*". The brooch was there given to him.[341]

the finding of ornaments unconnected with human remains explained by this tale.

This curious, and probably true story, gives one satisfactory reason why ornaments of the precious metals, and of bronze, as well as arms and various other articles, have been, and still continue to be, turned up from the earth in places where no human remains are to be found. It would appear to have been the custom in ancient as well as in modern times, for retreating individuals or armies, to hide or destroy their most precious treasures, in order that they should not fall into the hands of their pursuers.

Mention of a large-sized brooch in the history of Queen Edain.

Another example of a very large sized brooch occurs at a very early period of history indeed. There is a fragment of a story preserved in *Leabhar na h-Uidhre* in the library of the Royal Irish Academy, relating to the birth and after history of a celebrated lady of ancient Erinn, whose name was *Edain*, and who became the wife of the monarch *Eochaidh Fedhleach*, one hundred years before the Incarnation. The lady *Edain* was the reputed daughter of an Ulster chieftain, whose name was *Etar;* and after her birth, the story says:—

"*Edain* was educated at *Inbiur Cichmuini* [in the east of Ulster], by her father *Etar*, and fifty maidens along with her, the daughters of neighbouring chiefs, and who were fed and clothed by *Etar* as the companions of his daughter. One day that all the maidens were bathing in the bay, they saw from the water a horseman riding towards them over the plain. He had under him a curveting, prancing, broad-rumped, curly maned, curly haired bay steed. He had on a long flowing green cloak, gathered around him, and a shirt interwoven with thread of red gold (under that). A brooch (*Eó*) of gold in his cloak [across] which reached his shoulders at either side. He had a shield of silver, with a rim of gold, at his back, and with trappings of silver and a boss of gold; and he had in his hand a sharp-pointed spear,

(341) [original:—Bui tra marcaċ ic air imrim a eiċ is tilaig doscuiched docum na hairecta nolinged uadib. Fecht and din ocsoud indeiċ dar colpta. Do cuirdar an teich fót mór da dibcroib [artarcoib] niro airig duine isindairiuċt conitarla inucht indrig, .i. Fergusa Fairge [mac Nuata Necht], conacca seḋ andelg inagid indfóid donleiṫ ontalmain, israbatar cetri fiċit unga didergóir. Cid fil imuchtsa a athairni? ol inri. Ata delc and, ol aitirni; isandasbert aitirni:

Dealc fil indard Brestini,
Do cruib eiċ dorinacht;
Tarir rucaḋ mór mbreṫ cert,
Imbrut Maini mac Durṫaċt.

Ise indelgsin ropál damsa, orathair, .i. braṫair maṫarsa fodracaib ocas do rat italam, iar maidm air ċata forullcu, .i. caṫ mBrestini, is andrin doratad dó indelg.—Harleian MSS., 5280, Brit. Mus.; and H. 2. 18. f. 74. a. a. top.]

covered with rings of gold from its socket to its heel. He wore fair yellow hair, coming over his forehead, and his forehead was bound with a fillet of gold to keep his hair from disorder".[242]

This richly-dressed man was *Midir*, the great *Tuatha Dé Danann* chief of *Bri Leith* in the county of Longford, whose history we shall not follow farther at present, since our concern now is with his dress only. And even as to this, the only circumstance connected with it which we shall now direct attention to is the great size of his brooch of gold, and the fact of his wearing it across his breast, reaching from shoulder to shoulder. No brooch of this description has been yet discovered in Ireland. Here, then, is another curious fact illustrative of the way in which these ancient massive brooches were worn. We find, indeed, in a passage from the Brehon Laws, that men were legally bound to wear, or perhaps rather to curtail, their brooches, whether they wore them at their breasts or at their shoulders, in such a way as that they should not be dangerous to the persons around them; a very good proof that they were the large, long-spiked pins, of which specimens are found in the museum of the Royal Irish Academy. The following is the passage alluded to:—"Men are guiltless of pins"—[that is, it is safe for the men to wear their brooches]—"upon their shoulders or upon their breasts; provided they don't project too far beyond it; and if they should, the case is to be adjudged by the criminal law".[243] Yet these large brooches, and other over large ornaments, continued to be worn. For, we are told in the story of the Navigation of *Maelduin*'s ship, already quoted, that the wanderers came to an island, landed, and entered a great house, where—

Ancient [laws] respectin[g] the mode [of] wearing large brooches

"They saw ranges (or ranks) upon the wall of the house all round from one door-post to the other: firstly, a range of brooches [*Bretnassa*] of gold and silver, stuck by their shanks into the wall; another range of great necklaces [*Muntorcs*], like the hoops of large tubs, made of gold and of silver;

large brooches mentione[d] in the tal[e] of the "W[an]derings o[f] *Maelduin*['s] Canoe".

(242) [original:—Alta iarom Etain ec Inbiur Cichmuini la Etar, ocus .i. ingen imre, di ingenaib tured, acus ba hessecom noda biatad ocus do necad ar comaitecht Etaini ainsin do gres. La nand doib an ingenaib silib isindinbiur oca fothrocud, conacatar in marcach isan magsech don duirciu. Ech dond tuagmar forletan casmongach cascair foasurdiu. A sidalbrat uaine illsed immi, ocus lene foderg fuad imbi. Acus eo oir ina brut, rosaiged agualaind for cach let. Sciath airgdidi, conimbiul oir imbi for a muin, sciathrach argit and, ocus tul noir fair; ocus sleg coicrind cosetan oir impi oirlond co cro inalaim. Folt find-buidi fair co hetun, snithe oir for a etun conna teilged a folt foagid.—*Leabhar na h-Uidhre*, folio 81, col, 1.]

(243) [The MS. containing this passage not being available to me, I cannot give the original.]

XXVI.

and a third range of great swords, with hilts of gold and silver".[344]

Now, it matters little to our present purpose, that this is an imaginative and exaggerated description. Our business is with the writer's evident acquaintance with the general existence and use of these precious ornaments in his own country; a fact sufficiently clear from the accuracy of his description.

Thistle-headed brooches.

Among the brooches in the collection of the Royal Irish Academy are some with round knobs, a little below the head, and deeply carved diagonally, so as to give the knob, with its flat-topped head, the exact appearance of a thistle head. I am not aware that our Scottish kindred have as yet put forth any claims to the exclusive right to this ancient type of their modern national emblem. Neither am I aware that they have as yet discovered any specimens of this brooch in their own country, or that there is any particular reference to it, or to any other type, in their ancient writings. The only reference I have met, with regard to Scottish brooches, is found in a very ancient story in my possession, which relates the adventures of *Cano*, the son of *Gartnan*, and grand-nephew to ***Aedh Mac Gartnan***, king of Scotland, a contemporary of St. *Colum Cillé*.

Reference to Scottish brooches in the story of *Cano* son of *Gartnan*.

This young prince, *Cano*, was compelled to fly from Scotland into Ireland, to avoid the jealousy of his grand-uncle, who had already slain his father, and killed or dispersed all his people. This was about the year 620. After the death of his father, the young prince took counsel with his people, as the story tells us, in these words:—" Well, now", said *Cano*, " it is better that we avoid this man, who has killed my father. We are not nearer to him than the man he has killed". " Where shall we go to?" said his people. " We will go into the land of Erinn", said he, " to a friend of ours". He caused canoes to be made. They went to the sea shore. This was the order in which they went down to the sea: fifty warriors; a crimson five-folding cloak upon each man, two flesh-seeking spears in his hand, a shield, with a rim of gold at his back, a gold-hilted sword at his girdle, his gold-yellow hair falling down at his back. This too was the order in which their fifty wives accompanied them: each wore a green cloak, with borders of silver, a smock interwoven with thread of red gold, brooches (*Deilgi*) of gold, with full carvings, bespangled with gems of many colours, necklaces (*Muinci*) of

(344) [original:—Conaccatár iarsin teóra sreta isindfraigid intuige immácuaird óndursaind dia rali: sret and cetamus di bretnasaib óir acas argit acas acosa isindfraigid; acas sret do muntorcaib óir agas argit, mar chircla dubcha cetéac; in tres sret diclaidbib mórаib conimdornaib óir agas airgit.—*Leabhar na h-Uidhre*, fol. 26, col. 1. See also Harleian MSS., Tract 1. 5280, Brit. Mus.]

highly burnished gold, a diadem (*Mind*) of gold upon the head of each. The fifty servants that attended them wore tunics of yellow silk. A chess board (*Fithchell*) upon the back of each servant, with men of gold and silver. A bronze *Timpan* (or harp) in the left hand of each servant; and two grayhounds, in a silver chain, in his right hand.[(245)]

Such then, is the very remarkable description of the noble Scottish exile and his retinue, on their visit to the monarch of Erinn, *Diarmait*, the son of *Aedh Slaine*, who received them hospitably, and rejected all the offers and solicitations of the King of Scotland, to betray them into his hands. I may remark further, in reference to these carved, or thistle-headed brooches, that not one of them has been yet discovered, with any kind of emblazonment or gems or composition; while several of the other types are found richly set with stones.

Carved brooches mentioned in the tale of the *Bruighean Da Derga*.

Again; in the ancient tale of the *Bruighean Dalerga*, or *Daderg's* court, we have the monarch *Conaire Mór's* own reasons for seeking the hospitality of *Daderg's* mansion, when forced to fly from Tara, to avoid the plunderers and rebels who made a sudden irruption into the district. This is the monarch's claim on *Daderg*, and in his own words:—"*Daderg* of Leinster", said *Conaire*, "came to solicit gifts from me; and he did not come to find a refusal. I bestowed upon him an hundred high class cows; an hundred fat hogs; an hundred crimson-mixed glossy cloaks; an hundred blue-coloured death-giving swords; ten carved brooches (*Deilci*) of gold; ten keeves, fine noble vessels; ten slaves; ten ewes; three times nine white hounds in their silver chains; with an hundred gifted steeds, as fleet as roebucks".[(246)]

We have another reference to the carved brooch, such as the

(245) [original:—Maith tra ar Cano, is ferr dun imgabail ind firse, ro marb ar nathair. Ni faicriu ar cairdeas do mac in fear ro marb. Cia leath regmais ar a muinter. Regmait sir nErinn co m-bratar dun. Do gniter curach lais. Lotar dochum traga. Is amlaid do dechadar dochum mara, .i. coeca laech; brat corcra coic diabalta im cach fear, da sleig coicrindi ina laim, sciath co m-buailig oir fair, claideb orduirn fora chris, a mong orbuide dara ais. As amlaid do deachadar in coeca ban: brat huaine co corcharaib argait, leine co n-derg indlead oir, deilgi oir lanecair co m-breachtrad n-gem n-ildathach, muinci dior forloisctha, mind oir fora chind cacha. In coeca n-gilla mara do sita buidi impu co n-argud. Fichell for muin cach gilla, co feraib oir acas airgid. Timpan creda in laim cli in gilla; da milchoin ar slabra airgid ina laim deis.—H. 2. 16. col. 789, mid.]

(246) [original:—Daderga di Laignib, ol Conaire, tanic chucumsa em ol Conaire do chuingid aisceda, acas ni chuidechid conera. Ranucsa imcet mbo bothana; rann im cet muc muccglassa; rann imcet mbrat cunagarsclach etach; rann imcet ngaisced ngorm data ngubae; rann imdeich ndeilci derca diorda; ran im deich ndabcha de olcha deich donnae; rann im .x. mogu; rann im .x. meile; rann im tri .ix. con nengel inna slabradaib airgdidib; rann im c. nech mbuada, hiseoganaib oss neg.—*Leabhar na h-Uidhre*, f. 59, col. 1 and 2.]

XXVI.

Reference of carved in Book of Munster.

Scottish ladies are represented above as having worn. This reference is found in the ancient Book of Munster, where we are told that after the unfair death of *Eoghan Mór*, king of Munster, at the hands of the friends of *Conn* of "the Hundred Battles", in the battle of *Magh Leana*, in the King's county, fought A.D. 180, we are told that after this occurrence, *Mac Niadh*, the son of *Eoghan*, the deceased king, threatened *Conn* with a new war unless he was paid the usual *eric*, or composition, for the death of his father. To this condition, we are told, king *Conn* was advised to assent; and therefore there were paid to *Mac Niadh* two hundred riding steeds, and two hundred chariots, and *Conn*'s own ring of gold, and his precious carved pin or brooch, and his sword and shield; with two hundred ships, two hundred spears, two hundred swords, two hundred hounds, two hundred slaves, and *Sadhbh Conn*'s daughter to wife.

Another reference to a carved brooch in a poem ascribed to *Oisin*.

I shall only give one more reference to this carved brooch, which, however, does not in this instance appear under the name *Dealg*, but under that of *Eó*. This reference occurs in an ancient poem; ascribed to *Oisin*, the celebrated son of *Find Mac Cumhaill*.

It appears that a dispute arose in the presence of *Find Mac Cumhaill* among some of his warriors as to their respective proficiency in chess-playing. The sons of *Cruimchenn* boasted that they would beat the celebrated *Diarmait O'Duibhne* and his comrade at this old game. *Find*, however, made peace between the disputants, and *Oisin* says:—(247)

"He, *Diarmait* of the brown hair, then challenged them,
The sons of *Cruimchenn* of the martial deeds,
Two *Fails* of gold from each of them
To stake upon the one game.

"It was not long after getting rid of our anger,
Till we saw coming towards us over the plain
A large, beautiful, admirable young champion,
Stern, manly, and truly brave.

"A silver sandal on his left foot,
With shining precious stones beset;
A golden sandal on his right foot:
Though strange, it was no ungraceful arrangement.

(247) [original:—

Ros ġreannaḋ iad Diarmad donn,
mac Cruimċinn conn iolar nglonn,
im dá ḟail óir ceċtarḋe
do ṫabairt anaon cluiċe
* * * * * * *

Gairid duinn iarsgur dar bfeirg,
go bfaicmid ċugain san leirg
óclaec mór, álainn, ampa,
fossaiġ, fearrḋa, fiorċalma.
Ass arcait ima cois cli,
go ligaib logmara li;
ass orrda ima ċois ndeis:

"A cloak over his breast the champion bore,
And a kilt of fine soft satin;
A brooch (*Eó*) well carved of brown gold,
In the splendid cloak of graceful points.
"A helmet of yellow gold upon his head,
With carved lions, at full spring;
A green shield at his back was seen,
With art of maiden hands displayed".

I have quoted more from this poem than was strictly necessary for my immediate object; but the whole passage is so curious, and at the same time illustrative of the subject of dress and ornament, that I could not well omit any of it. I shall return further on to the first stanza when discussing the subject of *Fails*.

Brooches of bronze and *Findruine*.

But the splendid pins of ancient times were not always of the precious metals. Besides the brooches of gold and silver to which we have so many ancient references, we have in the *Táin Bo Chuailgne*, instances of brooches of *Umha*, or ordinary bronze, and of *Findruine*, about which we are at a loss to know whether it was a distinct metallic alloy, a kind of white bronze, or gold, or silver, or some special style of carving and ornamentation of white metal.

Chased gold pins used down to the beginning of thirteenth century.

Before passing away from the subject of these old brooches, however, I think I may be justified in giving some reason to think that the use of chased gold pins came down to a comparatively late period. From a poem, written about the year 1190, by *Gillabrighdé Mac Conmidhé*, a distinguished poet of the province of Ulster, for Dermot O'Brien, chief of the Dalcassian race of Munster, and of which I possess, I believe, an unique copy, we discover that the manufacture of costly brooches and such articles had not then gone out of use. The poet complains of some hardships the lay literary orders of Ireland were labouring under at the time, and calls on the great Dalcassian chief to take the lead in redressing and correcting them. He dwells in glowing terms on the beauties and importance of general literature, but more particularly on poetry, which was his own profession. He compares the effect of his art on the words of a language, to the impress of the artist's hand on the raw material of gold; and in illustration of the latter idea, he writes the following stanza:

noċar ḃe an tindell aindeis.
brat os abruinne gon láeċ,
is léined domín sroill ṁáoṫ;
eó iar na eaccor d'or donn,
do ḃi isin mbrat mbláiṫ mbeann-
corr.
Caṫḃar orbuide ima ceann
go nealtaiḃ leoṁan laindeall;
sciáṫ uaine osa ḋruim gan aċt,
go ngres ingine macḋaċt.
—MSS. Royal Irish Academy, No. 23/L 22 (H. & S. collection), p. 441, bot., and 142, stanza 4.]

XXVI.

"The gold brooch (*Dealg*), though it gets the praise,
When the artist makes it lustrous by his art,
It is to the artist the praise is really due,
Who thus has beautified the brooch".[218]

Although I have not exhausted my list of pins under vari
names, I must through want of space pass for the present to
consideration of some other personal ornaments of the peopl
ancient Erinn. And as the ornaments nearest to the pins
order and frequency of allusion are perhaps rings, I shall p
ceed to describe them next.

the diffe- t kinds of gs.

Of rings there was a great variety, under the various nan *Fail*, *Fainne* or *Faidne*, *Fiam*, *Ornasc*, *Dornasc*, *Orduise*, *Bu* or *Buinne*, *Fornasc*, *Nasc*, *Idh*, etc. The *Fail*, I believe, w an open ring, or bracelet, for the wrist, arm, or ankle. *Fai* continues to be the ordinary name to this day for a closed fin ring. The *Fiam* was a chain which went round the neck. T *Ornasc* was also a finger-ring. The *Dornasc* was a bracelet the wrist. The *Orduise* were rings for the thumbs. The *Bu* was a twisted or corded ring, bracelet, or circle, formed out one twisted bar or several strands of gold or silver. The *N* was a fillet-ring, or garter, and when compounded with word *Niadh*, a champion, it signified something like a kni of the garter, exactly as these words are understood at this d because the *Nasc-Niadh* was in fact worn on the leg; but wearer was obliged to establish his title to it on the field battle, sword in hand. In those remote, and, if you will, r times, the fawning on prime ministers seems to have been a poor way of obtaining decorations and dignities.

Of the *Fornasc* I cannot well form an idea. The name occ in the enumeration of the trinkets of king *Ailill* and qu *Medbh* in the opening of the *Táin Bo Chuailgne*, along with *Fainne*, the *Fail*, and the *Orduise;* and as the word is co pounded of the intensitive or super-adjective prefix *for*, and noun *Nasc*, it very probably was the general name for th splendid gold bracelets, or armlets, which terminate at the ex mities in cups of various degrees of depth and regularity of sha

Fainne d to fine the r.

Of the *Fainne*, or ordinary finger-ring, we find a refere which shows that the article which bore that name was u for other personal purposes. Thus, in the Courtship of *Ma* the Connacht prince, and *Ferb*, the daughter of *Gerg*, preser in the "Book of Leinster", we are told of *Maine* and his att dants, that:—

(218) [original.—
an dealg óir cidh e mholtair,
mar as ceard crechu mhochdaibh,
ar don cheard ar mó ar molad
an dealg do dhachughadh.—
O'C. MSS., L. of Saints, vol. ii., p.

XXVI.

"They all had green shields; and if they owed a dish of gold, or silver, or bronze, one rivet from the spear of each man would pay it; and all with their hair confined by *Fainnes*, or rings of gold".(349)

Hair rings used in the seventeenth century.

I have already shown in a quotation from the Navigation of *Maelduin*'s Ship, and elsewhere, that the hair was sometimes confined by a spiral ring of gold or other metal. This custom came down to a very late period, as we find from a poem of *Eochaidh O'Beoghusa*, poet to Mac Guire of Fermanagh about the year 1630. The subject of this poem, which consists of forty-one stanzas, is a lament on the flagging energies of the Irish in opposing the English oppressor and wrong-doer. In comparing the then living generation with those which had gone before, he bursts into the following passionate strain in the tenth stanza:—

"No youth is now seen in the gage of combat,
Nor a warrior's armour close by his bed,
Nor a sword sucking the palm of the hand,
Nor does the frost bind the ring of the hair".(350)

Fails worn up the whole arm, for the purpose of bestowing them upon poets, etc.

Of the *Fail*, which appears to me to have been an open bracelet, I have already, from the Courtship of *Bec Fola*, given a most important instance of their being worn on the arms all up from the wrist to the shoulder; and the same is told of *Nuada*'s wife, a Leinster lady, that she had her arms covered with *Fails* of gold, for the purpose of bestowing them on the poets and other professors of arts who visited her court. That this species of munificence was not of a limited character, many instances could be adduced; but, as the case requires but little if any illustration, a little incident from the ancient tract of the "Dialogue of the Ancient Men", in the "Book of Lismore, will be sufficient as an example.

example of this from Book of Lismore.

"*Cailte*, the faithful lieutenant of *Find Mac Cumhaill*, being travelling through the country of Connacht on a certain day, met a certain chieftain's wife, attended by ten fair ladies. After some conversation as to whence *Cailte* had come and whither he was going, the lady, perceiving that he had a musician with him, asked:—'Who is this musician in thy company, O *Cailte*?' said the lady. '*Cas Corach*, the son of *Caincinde*, the best musician of all the *Tuatha Dé Danann*', said *Cailte*, 'and even the best musician in Erinn or *Alba*' [that is, Scotland]. 'His countenance is good', said the lady, 'if his performance is equally good'

(349) [I have not been able to find this passage.]

(350) [original:—

Ni faiċter gille ag geall treasa,
na treallaṁ laoiċ láiṁ re cuilt,
na colcc ag déol dearnann láiṁe,
ni ceanglann reodoiḋ fáinne fuilt.

—MSS. R.I.A. No. 23/F.16 (O'Gara MS.) p. 66, stanza 10.]

XXVI. 'On our word', said *Cailte*, 'though good his countenance, his music is better'. 'Take thy *Timpan*, O young man', said she. He did take it, and played, and freely performed for her. The lady then gave him the two *Fails* that were upon her arms".[231]

It would appear from the first stanza of the poem attributed to *Oisin*, which I quoted above,[232] that these *Fails* or armlets were sometimes pledged as stakes at the chess board.

Of the bracelet called a *Budne*.

From the bracelet called the *Fail*, let us now pass to the ring or bracelet, which was called *Budne*, or *Buinne*. The word literally means a wave of the sea, or, in domestic art, the wave or strong welt of rods which basket-makers weave like a rope in their work, to give it strength and firmness. In the metallic arts, this kind of work was produced by two different modes. The first was by twisting a round, square, or flat bar of metal, so as to give it a spiral or screw form. This is the ordinary mode still. The second mode was, by taking a solid square bar or prism of metal, and cutting out of it with a chisel along the lines of the longitudinal edges, at the four sides, all the solid metal, to within a thread or line of the centre, and leaving standing, along the edges, a thin leaf of the metal; so that when the whole is cleared out, what was a solid bar before, now consists of a mere skeleton, formed of four thin leaves standing out at right angles from a central axis, and proceeding, as it were, along its line, from the two solid ends, which were not at all hollowed out. Two specimens of *Budnes*, or ropes of gold, manufactured after the latter mode, have been found together at Tara, one smaller and more delicate than the other; the smaller one was perhaps intended for a woman. I shall have more to say on these two ornaments in the next lecture.

(231) original:—Cret in cairfideċ ut atfarra a Chailte? ar an ingen. Cas Corac mac Caincinde airfideċ T. D. D. uile ar Cailte, agas in cairfideċ is ferr a nEirinn agas a nAlbain. As maiṫ a dealb, ar an ingen, mara maith a airfited. Dar ar m-breiter ám, ar Cailte, gid maiṫ a dealb, is ferr a airfideċt. Gebh do timpan a oclaig, arsi. Agas ro-gab agas robói ica sennad, agas ica saeirseinm. Tuc iarum an ingen inna falad boi imma lamaib do.—*Book of Lismore* (O'Curry's copy, R.I.A.), f. 239. a. col. 1.]

(232) *Ante*, vol. ii. p. 166.

LECTURE XXVII.

[Delivered 19th July, 1860.]

(VIII.) **Dress and Ornaments** (continued). Anonymous notice of Irish Torques; description of two found at Tara; accounts of Torques found in England; no account of Torques in the works of older Irish antiquaries; those found at Tara bought in 1813 by Alderman West of Dublin; the author does not agree with the anonymous writer as to the mode of production of the Tara Torques. Uses of the Tara Torques; reference to such a ring of gold for the waist in an ancient preface to the *Táin Bo Chuailgne*; another reference to such a ring in an account of a dispute about the manner of death of *Fothadh Airgteach* between king *Mongan* and the poet *Dallan Forgaill* from the *Leabhar na h-Uidhre*; *Cailte*'s account of his mode of burial; a hoop or waist-torque among the ornaments placed on *Fothadh*'s stone coffin. Story of *Cormac Mac Airt* and *Lugaidh Laga* showing one of the uses of rings worn on the hands. Ornaments for the neck; the *Muinche*; first used in the time of *Muineamhon* (circa B.C. 1300); mentioned in a poem of *Ferceirtne* on *Curoi Mac Daire*; also in account of the Battle of *Magh Leana*. The *Niamh Land* or flat crescent of gold worn on the head, as well as on the neck. The Neck-Torque of *Cormac Mac Airt*. Descriptions of the dress and ornaments of *Bec Fola*. The *Muinche* mentioned in the tale of the "Wanderings of *Maelduin*'s Canoe", and in the story of *Cano*. *Muinche* and *Land* used also for the neck ornaments of animals and spears. Use of the term *Muintorcs*. Of the *Mael-Land* mentioned in the *Táin Bo Fraich*. The ferrule of a spear called a *Muinche* in the account of the Battle of *Magh Leana*; discovery of such a ring in Kerry; the term also used for the collars of grayhounds, chiefly in Fenian tales. Mention of the *Torc* in its simple form in the Book of Leinster. Of the *Land* or lunette; it formed part of the legal contents of a lady's workbag, and of the inheritance of daughters. The *Land* was worn on the head as well as on the neck, as shown by the descriptions of *Conaire Mór*'s head charioteer and apprentice charioteers; and also of his poets.

I SHOULD not have ventured to offer so unartistic, and indeed so very dry, a description of the very beautiful ornaments to which I alluded at the end of the last lecture, while I might have availed myself of a very learned and artistic description already published, but that I differ in opinion with the writer of that description, whoever he may be, as to the manner of manufacture and mode of wearing them. The description or account of these ornaments of which I have just spoken appeared anonymously in "Saunders's News-letter" of the 31st of December, 1830; and as it contains all that is known of the history of these articles, and the thoughts and observations of a scholar, I shall quote from it as much as appears pertinent to my present purpose. The article in question is headed "Antiquities: The Irish Torques". After which it proceeds:

Anonymous notice of Irish Torques;

XXVII.

description of two found at Tara;

"Two specimens of this ancient, and now extremely rare ornament, were discovered about eighteen years ago, in some reclaimed ground, at Tarah, in the county Meath. They are wreathed bars of pure gold, nearly five feet in length, bent into a circular form, flexible, but returning with elasticity into their natural curved shape; each bar consists of four flat bands, most accurately united along one of their edges, and then closely and spirally twisted throughout the whole length. The extremities end in smooth solid truncated cones, suddenly reflected backwards so as to form two hooks, which can be brought naturally to clasp in one another. Perpendicularly from the base of one of these cones proceeds a gold wire, a quarter of an inch thick and eight inches long, terminating also in a solid conical hook. This last appendage is deficient in every other torque that we have seen or read of, and adds considerable difficulty to what already existed in explaining the use of these expensive and singularly wrought ornaments. The weight of the larger is about twenty-five ounces; of the lesser, fifteen ounces.

"Three particulars contribute to render these ornaments objects of great interest to the antiquarian—their invariably wreathed or twisted form; the perfect purity of the gold they are composed of; and, lastly, there being no other ornament in the use of which so many nations have conspired. The Egyptians, Persians, Greeks, Romans, and almost every people of ancient Europe, have adorned themselves with them in the early periods of their history. . . . . Of English writers Lhuyd is the first who published an account of the torques. The one he describes was found A.D. 1692, at Harlech, Merioneth; its weight, eighty ounces; length, nearly four feet. Another is described by Woodward, in his 'Collection of Curiosities', published in 1728. In 1787, a torque weighing thirteen ounces was discovered by a labourer at Ware. Fearing that it might be claimed by the lord of the manor, he sold it to a Jew, who melted it; a drawing, however, had been previously taken, and appeared in the 'Gentleman's Magazine' for September, 1800.

accounts of Torques found in England;

no account of Torques in the works of older Irish antiquaries;

"It strikes us as not a little singular that this splendid proof of the ancient wealth and adornment of our island should hitherto have escaped the observation of every Irish antiquarian. No trace whatever can be discovered in the writings of Keating, Ware, Pocock, or Ledwich, which manifests the least acquaintance with it. It has even eluded the research of the patriotic Vallancey.

"The specimens which have given rise to this article", continues the writer, "were purchased in the year 1813 by the late Alderman West, and have since remained at his establishment in Skinner Row, open to the inspection of the curious. They are evidently the production of the most remote antiquity, and, with the exception of two others, much smaller in dimensions and inferior in design, are the only relics from the existence of which we can lay claim to an ornament so much prized by the civilized portion of the ancient world. On no other occasion have two torques been discovered together. The regal solidity of the one is contrasted with the feminine lightness of the other; and, if we are allowed to annex any importance to the site where they were found, we consider it rather surprising that monuments such as these should have so long remained unnoticed by the learned.

those found at Tara bought in 1813 by Alderman West.

"We are induced to offer the foregoing remarks in hopes that the attention of the curious will be directed to the acquisition of these invaluable ornaments, which will be offered for sale, this day, by the executors of the late Mr. West".

With the deepest respect and gratitude to the, to me unknown, writer of this learned and candid article, I feel that I must differ from his assumption and conclusions as to the mode of manufacturing these two particular ornaments, and their object and use. I do not believe—indeed they bear ample evidence to the contrary—that they were produced by twisting a wreathed bar of gold. Neither do I believe that these capacious circlets were ever intended to be worn as torques at the neck, although there is good reason to believe that ornaments of a similar form, but of much narrower compass, were so worn. In support of my first opinion I have only to direct an examination of the article itself, to convince any one, in my mind, that it was chiselled out of a solid bar of gold. In support of my second opinion, as to the object and use of ornaments of this size and type, I trust I shall be able in a few words to show, that they were not ornaments for the neck, as well as what they really were. I believe that they were girdles, or circlets, to go round the body; and it is singular that Gibbon, in his edition of Camden's 'Britannia', comes to the same conclusion, but with some modification; he thought they were belts from which the ancients suspended their quivers of arrows. There appears to me no better way of disposing of this curious and long standing question, than by bringing forward one or two examples from our ancient writings, in which various kinds of personal ornaments are enumerated, and by contrast and external knowledge, to define the use and place of each, and see if among them there

Author does not agree with anonymous writer as to the mode of production and use of the Tara Torques;

Uses of the Tara Torques;

shall not be found an appropriate description, name, and place, for these very articles.

reference to such a ring of gold for the waist in an ancient preface to Táin Bo Chuailgne.

It may be remembered that at the opening of the last lecture,[353] I translated from an ancient Gaedhelic MS., a gorgeous description of the cavalcade which attended upon *Bobhdh Dearg*, the great *Tuatha Dé Danann* chief of *Magh Femhen*, in Tipperary, when he went on a visit to his friend *Ochall Oichne*, at the hill of *Cruachan* in Connacht. Upon that occasion we are told that each man of the seven score charioteers and seven score horsemen of the retinue, wore, among other ornaments, a helmet, or cap (*Cend-Barr*), beset with crystal and *Findruine* upon his head; and a radiant blade (*Niamh-Land*) of gold around his neck, with a gem worth a new milch cow set in its centre (*Firsine*); and a wavy ring (*Bouinde do At* or *Bunne do At*) around each man, worth thirty ounces or *ungas* of gold.

Here we have the three most costly articles of personal ornamentation, set out with so much precision as to leave no difficulty whatever about their identification. There is, first, the *Cend-Barr*, or cap, or whatever its form may have been, upon the head, ornamented with crystal stones and *Findruine*. There is, in the second place, the *Niamh-Land*, or radiant crescent, of gold, with a gem worth a new milch cow, around the neck. This was a torque or gorget of the level fashion, and from its name, which is not an uncommon one, it could not possibly have been a spiral or twisted article. Next comes the *Bunne* or *Bouinde do At*, that is, the wavy or twisted ring, which we are told each man wore around him; and from its size, estimated by its value or weight of thirty ounces, it requires no argument to prove that it could only have been worn where we are told, around the body.

Another reference to such a ring from the Leabhar na h-Uidhre;

I shall only give one other reference to the wavy ring, or *Bunne do At*, where it is placed in such a contrast as, like the last case, to leave no room to doubt its use and destination. In an ancient story preserved in *Leabhar na h-Uidhre* in the library of the Royal Irish Academy, we are told, that at a certain time a dispute in historical questions arose between *Mongan*, king of Ulster, who died in the year 620, and *Dallan Forgaill*, so well known as the writer of the celebrated elegy on the death of Saint *Colum Cillé*. The king *Mongan* one day asked the poet, where and what was the manner of the death of *Fothadh Airgteach* [one of the three *Fothadh* brothers, who reigned conjointly over Erinn for one year, between the years of our Lord 284 and 285]; the poet answered that *Fothadh Airgteach* had been slain in the *Dubthir* of Leinster [now Duffern

dispute about the manner of death of Fothadh Airgteach between Dallan Forgaill and king Mongan;

[353] See Lect. xxvi., *ante*, vol. ii., p. 156.

in the county of Wexford]. The king *Mongan* said that this was not true, whereupon the poet said that he would satirize him for presuming to doubt his veracity, and not only that, but that he would satirize his father, and mother, and grandfather, who were a long time dead; that he would satirize the waters of the country, so that no fish could live or be caught in them; the trees, so that no fruit should be borne by them; and the plains, so that they should for ever remain barren of any produce. The king then agreed to pay to the poet whatever he should demand as far as three times seven cumhals, or sixty-three cows, if in three days' time he should not be able to prove that the poet's account of the death of *Fothadh Airgteach* was not true. This offer was accepted by the poet, out of respect to *Breothigirn*, the king's beautiful and bountiful wife. XXVII.

At the end of three days of great anxiety to the king and queen, a strange warrior appeared at their court with the headless handle of a spear in his hand. He made his way into the palace, took his seat near the king, and asked what they were concerned about. "A wager I have made", said Mongan, "with yonder poet about the place of death of *Fothadh Airgteach;* he said it happened in *Dubthir* of Leinster: I said it was false".[284] The warrior said it was false on the part of the poet. You will be sorry, said *Dallan Forgaill* [the poet], to have contradicted me. I shall not, said the warrior, I shall prove it. "We were along with *Find Mac Cumhaill*", said the warrior, "on our return from *Alba* [now Scotland], when we met with *Fothadh Airgteach* here at *Ollarbha* [near Larne in the county Antrim]. We fought a battle there. I threw a spear at him", said he, "which passed through him and entered the ground on the other side of him; and it left its iron blade in the ground there. This", said he, "is the handle which was in that spear. The bald rock from which I threw that cast will be found there; and the blade of the spear will be found in the ground; and the tomb of *Fothadh Airgteach* [will

Caille's account of Fothadh's death and burial;

[284] [original:—Imcomarcar Mongan a filid laa nand, cia haded Foṫaid Airgtig; asbert Forgoll góite in Dubṫair Laigen. Asbert Mongan ba gó; asbert in fili nod airfed aid aiṫgiud, acus no aerfad a aṫair, acus a maṫair, acus a senaṫair, acus do ceċnud forandusciu conna gebṫa iasc ina inberaib, do ceċnud for a fedaib cona tibritais torad, fora maige comtis ambriti ċaiḋċi caṫaṫlamde. Do fargaid Mongan aseir dó diretaib coticí secht cumala, no dásecht cumal, no tri secht cumal:— . . . . Traṫ mbátar and adfógarar fer dun raiṫ an des, abrut hi furcipul imi, acus dicoltur inna láim nadbúerbec. Toling fri sra crandsin tarna teóra ráṫa combói for lar lis; dirudiu combói for lár ind ríg ṫaige; dirudiu combói eter Mongan acus fraigid for sand-adart. In fili in iarṫar in taige fri ríg aniar. Segair incest isin tig, fead indoclaig dudánic. Cid daṫar sund olsudiu, ro gell som ol Mongan, acus in fili ucut im aidid

XXVII. be found] near it, a little on the east. There is a stone coffin around him there in the ground. His two *Fails* [or bracelets] of silver, and his *Bunne do At*, and his neck-torque [*Muintorc*] of silver, are laid upon his coffin; and there is a rock standing at his tomb; and there is an *Ogham* inscription in the end which is in the ground of the rock; and what is written in it is: '*Eochaidh* [or *Fothadh*] *Airgteach* is here, who was killed by *Cailte* in battle, on the side of *Find*'. Our warriors buried him as I have described", continues the young man, "and his funeral obsequies were performed [by us]".

It remains only to be told, that the warrior who had so timely come to the relief and rescue of king *Mongan* was no other than the spirit of the celebrated *Cailte*, the cousin and special favourite of *Find Mac Cumhaill*. This *Mongan* was the most learned and wise layman of his time: so remarkable were his knowledge and wisdom that people believed him to be *Find Mac Cumhaill* himself; and this belief or fact is asserted in the present legend. It is not, however, with *Mongan* personally that I am at present concerned, but with the important facts, for such I take them to be, connected with the tomb of the monarch *Fothadh Airgteach*. Of some of these facts I hope to make important use in my future lectures, if I be spared, and to the others I shall now refer with as much brevity as possible.

a hoop, or waist Torque, among the ornaments placed on *Fothadh's* stone coffin.

Indeed I have but to call attention back to the articles which are stated in this curious legend to have been deposited upon the stone coffin of king *Fothadh Airgteach*. These were his two *Fails*, or armlets of silver; his two *Bunnes do At*, or twisted hoops, but whether of silver or gold is not stated, and his *Muintorc*, or neck-torque of silver. Here, as in the former case—and in the absence of the diadem which is not mentioned—we find the three most important articles of ornament grouped in such a way as to leave no doubt in my mind of the use of each.

Ḟoṫaid airgtig; arrubart som isin Dubṫor Lagen: arrubartsa is gó. Asbert in tóclaċ ba gó dond filid. Bid aiṫ lig ol Forgoll cille da dummaiṫgeod. Ni baasom ol in tóclaċ, frosnriṫir. Bámárni latra lasin ol in tóclaċ; adaucc ol Mongan nimaiṫrin bámárni lafind tra olse dulodmur dialbae. Immarnacmár fri Foṫud nairgṫeċ hi sund accut forOllorbi. Fiċimmir scandul nund. Focartsid ercor fair co seċ tric collaid hi talmain friss anall; acus confacab a iarnd hi talam. Issin andi celtar foḃói isin gairin. Fugebṫar in mael cloċ dia polura arouder; acus fogebtar anair iarnn isin tallam; acus fogebṫar aulad Foṫaid airgtig fris anair bic. Ata comrar cloċe imbi and hi tallam. Atait a di fáil airgit, acus a di bunne do at, acus a muintorc airgit for a ċomrair; acus atá coirṫe ocaulaid; ocus ata ogom isin cind fil hi tallam din coirṫi; issin fil and: Eoċuid airgteaċ inso rambi Cailte immaeriuc fri Find.

Eche [.i. do gnítea] las inóclaiċ aniċt samlaid ule acus forerċa.—*Leabhar na h-Uidhre*, f. 83. b. a. col. 2.]

It is remarkable, however, that there are two *Budnes*, or hoops, mentioned here, but whether accurately or not, we have not now the means to ascertain. It is remarkable too, that while we are told the armlets and necklace were of silver, the metal of which the *Budne* or twisted ring was made is not specified: and might not this reserve imply that the article was invariably made of gold?

As I have already stated, *Budne* was a name descriptive of artistic fashion, and not of size or particular destination, and it is therefore that we have found it already confining a lady's hair, and in the following instance adorning a warrior's hands. *Lughaidh Laga*, as stated already, was a distinguished prince and warrior of Munster, brother to *Oilioll Oluim*, the celebrated king of Munster in the middle of the third century, and ancestor of all the great families of that province. When *Cormac Mac Airt* came to the sovereignty of Erinn in the year 227, he was immediately opposed by the three *Ferguses*, brothers, princes of Ulster, who drove him out of Tara, and forced him to fly to Munster for relief. His father's sister, *Sadhbh*, was the wife of *Oilioll Oluim*, the king of that province, and to her grandson, *Tadhg*, the son of *Cian*, son of *Oilioll Oluim*, he applied for relief and assistance to regain his inheritance. *Tadhg* consented, but advised the deposed monarch to procure the assistance of *Lughaidh Lagha*, his, *Tadhg*'s, grand-uncle, who was a superannuated warrior, and who had on a former occasion cut off *Cormac*'s father's head in the battle of *Magh Mucruimhe* in the county of Galway.

Story of *Cormac Mac Airt* and *Lughaidh Laga*, showing use of rings on the hands.

Cormac succeeded in this, and the Munstermen, under the command of *Tadhg* and *Lughaidh*, marched into Meath, and past Tara, to the place called *Crinna*, near the present ruined abbey of Mellifont. Here the hostile forces met; the Ulstermen were defeated, the three *Ferguses* killed by *Lugaidh*, who presented their three heads to *Cormac;* whereupon *Cormac* said: "His hand does not conceal from *Laga* that he has slain kings". And this is explained by the statement that he had "seven *Buinni* or twisted rings on his hand or on his fingers". This is found in the Book of *Lecan*, folio 124, a.; but in another reference to the same fact, at folio 137, b.a., of the same book, it is made seven *Failgi* or rings of gold upon his hands.(255) Whether the number of these *Budni*, or *Failgi*, worn by the warriors in general in the olden times, bore any relation to the number of

(255) [The original of the passage at f. 124. a. (marg. col. mid.) is:—is te asbert Cormac fris ni ceil a doid for Laga robi riga, .i. asreacht mbuindi oir ima doid no ma meor. The following is the original of the passage at f. 137. b. a. (top): ni ċeil a doid for Laga robiṫriga dorigai, .i. asreaċt failgi oir ima laim. See also Lect. xxvi., *ante*, vol. ii., p. 156.]

XXVII. kings or chiefs slain by them in battle, I cannot say, but in the remark of king *Cormac* upon *Lughaidh*'s hand, there is good reason to believe that he implied this curious fact.

Before passing away from this class of ornaments, I mean the ring, I shall have to speak more particularly, but still briefly, of the neck-torques, or gorgets, which have been so often incidentally introduced into those lectures.

Of ornaments for the neck. The necklace, or gorget, like the smaller rings, had several names, such as *Muinche*, *Muintorc*, *Land*, *Fiam*. Of these the *Muinche*, as the word literally signifies, was a generic name for any kind of ring or bracelet for the neck. The *Muintorc*, which is a name compounded of *Muin*, the neck, and *Torc*, a torque, means of course, a neck-torque. The *Land* was simply a blade or leaf of gold or silver, and *Fiam* was a real chain of either of these metals. The *Muinche* and the *Muintorc*, from what is known of them, were evidently blades or leaves of gold or silver, of a certain artistic fashion. While the *Land*, as its name implies, was a simple flat, or level blade of metal; and the *Fiam* was a chain of some fashion, or mode of linking, of which no specimen has as yet come within the range of my knowledge.[384]

The *Muinche*; There is mention of a *Muinche*, however, with a qualification, which leads me to think that it was not a blade or leaf of metal, but a wreath, a *Budne*, or twisted ring of metal, on a smaller scale than the *Budne*, which went around the body; this was the *Muinche do At*. It must be admitted too, that the name *Muinche* is often applied to any kind of ring or band for the human neck, or for the neck of a spear, a dog, or for any other purpose of that kind. The following recapitulation of the references to this article of personal ornament which have from time to time been introduced into these lectures may be useful. The

First used in the time of *Muineamhon* (circa B.C. 1300); first reference to the *Muinche* that I am acquainted with occurs in the "Annals of the Four Masters", so far back as the year of the world's age 3872, or about one thousand three hundred years before the Incarnation. Thus speak the Annals:—

"At the end of the fifth year of [the Milesian monarch] *Muineamhon*, he died of the plague in *Magh Aidhne*. It was this *Muineamhon* that first placed *Muinches* of gold upon the necks of kings and chiefs in Erinn".

And we are told by the old etymologists that this man's real name was *Maine Mór*, or *Maine* the great, but that after his institution of the order of the collar of gold he received and retained the name of *Muineamhon*, that is, of the rich neck, from *muin*, the neck, and *main*, richer.

The next instance of the *Muinche* that I remember occurs in

(384) [See fig. 57 (Fig. 3, pl. xvii., *Miscellanea Graphica*)].

the dirge already quoted, which was composed by the poet *Ferceirtne* for his master and patron *Curoi Mac Daire*, king of West Munster, in which he enumerates all the gifts and presents that he had received from the deceased chief, among which he reckons ten *Muinchi do At*, which, if I properly understand the words, were full rings, or bracelets, wreathed and hooked behind.

mentioned in a poem of *Ferceirtne* on *Curoi Mac Daire*,

Again: the battle of *Magh Leana* was fought in the year 137, between *Eoghan Mór*, the king of Munster, and *Conn* "of the Hundred Battles", monarch of Erinn. A copiously detailed account of this battle and the causes that led to it was published by the Celtic Society in the year 1855, and at page 113 of the volume we find the monarch, when arraying himself for the battle, putting his easy, thick, noble, light *Muinche* upon his neck, and his *Mind Aird Righ*, or chief king's diadem, upon his head.

also in account of Battle of *Magh Leana*.

I may next refer to the passage already quoted from the visit of *Bobhdh Derg*, the great *Tuatha Dé Danann* chief of Tipperary, to his friend *Ochall* of *Cruachan*, at *Loch Riach* (now Loch Reagh) in Connacht, where we are told that each of the seven score charioteers and seven score horsemen who composed his cavalcade wore a *Niamh Land*, or radiant leaf of gold, around his neck. This *Niamh Land*, or splendid flat crescent of gold, was worn not only around the neck, but was also worn upon or over the forehead. This may be seen from the following passage, which occurs in a volume of tales and adventures of *Find Mac Cumhaill*. The scene of this story is laid on the mountain called *Sliabh Crot*, a historical mountain in the south-west part of the county of Tipperary, and it is told by *Cailte*, one of *Find*'s most cherished and trusted officers, in the following words:—

The *Niamh Land*, or flat crescent of gold, worn on the head as well as on the neck.

"One day", said *Cailte*, "*Mac Cumhaill* was upon this mountain, and the Fenian warriors along with him; and we were not long here when we saw a lone woman coming towards us to the mountain. She wore a crimson deep-bordered cloak; a brooch (*Delg*) of enchased yellow gold in that cloak over her breast; and a *Niamh Land* (or radiant crescent) of gold upon her forehead".(257)

This lady was a resident of *Benn Edir*, now the hill of Howth in the county of Dublin, but as I shall have occasion to speak of her more at large on a future occasion, I shall not fol-

(257) [original:—Oen do laiṫib da raib mac Cumaill ar an telaig so ol Cailte, acas an ḟiann ina ḟarrad; acas noċar cian duinn ann go facamair an ain ingen cucainn go comdireċ gus an cnocsa. Brat corcra corcaraċ impi; delg ordaitbuide isin brat os a bruinne; niamlann oir ima hedan.—No. 2–36 of Hodges and Smith's collection of MSS. in the library of the Royal Irish Academy.]

XXVII. low her history any further here. This is but one of several references of the same kind that I could bring forward.

The neck Torque of *Cormac Mac Airt.*

We may, I think, next refer to the description of king *Cormac Mac Airt*'s personal appearance at the great feast of Tara, which has been printed in the first series of my lectures,[258] and from which I shall quote the following short passage as strictly pertinent to my present purpose:

"Splendid indeed was *Cormac*'s appearance at that assembly, sleek, curling, golden hair upon him. A red shield with engravings and animals of gold, and with trappings of silver upon him. A crimson, sleek, short-napped cloak upon him. A brooch of gold set with precious stones over his breast. A *Muintorc*, or 'neck-torque' of gold around his neck".

This, it must be admitted, is a decided reference to the *Muintorc* or Neck-*Torque* of gold, but still it does not convey any idea whatever of the particular shape or form of the article itself.

From the time of king *Cormac*, who lived in the middle of the third century, we may pass to that of the famous lady *Bec Fola*, the woman so romantically met, wooed, and won, by the monarch of Erinn, *Diarmaid*, the son of *Aedh Slaine*, about the year 640, and already described in a previous lecture.[259] I shall again quote here, in order to make my summary complete, the passage of the legend describing the lady *Bec Fola*'s costume:

Description of the dress and ornaments of *Bec Fola.*

"She had on her [feet] two pointless shoes of *Findruine*, ornamented with two gems of precious stones; her kilt was interwoven with thread of gold; she wore a crimson robe, and a *Dealg* or brooch of gold fully chased and beset with many-coloured gems in that robe. She had a *Muinche* or necklace of burnished gold around her neck".

The *Muinche* mentioned in tale of the "Wanderings of *Maelduin*'s Canoe";

I may also refer again too, to the story of *Maelduin*'s Navigation, or wanderings on the Atlantic Ocean, where they came to an island in which they saw a house, into which they entered, and saw upon the walls all around from door to door a range of brooches (*Bretnassa*) of silver and gold, sticking by their points; and another range of great *Muinchi* like the hoops of a great tub, all of gold and of silver. What has been said of the Scottish women who attended prince *Cano* into Erinn, about the year 600, may also be remembered. They wore brooches (*Delgi*) of gold with full carvings, and ornamented with gems of various colours, *Muinchi* of burnished gold (around their necks), and *Minds* or diadems of gold upon their heads.

and in story of *Cano.*

I could, were it necessary, multiply references to show the

[258] [See *Lectures on the Manuscript Materials of Ancient Irish History*, p. 45, and App. xxvi., p. 510.]

[259] [Lecture xxvi., *ante*, vol. ii. p. 160.]

niversal use of the *Muinche*, the *Land*, and the *Muintorc*, as rnaments for the neck in ancient and comparatively modern imes in this country. The names *Muinche* and *Land*, however, ppear to have been common not only to the necklaces of men nd women, but also to those of hounds, horses, and inanimate hings, such as spears, etc. The *Muintorc*, if wreathed as its ame implies, might be used in the same way, excepting as a ing or band, to grace the neck of a spear.

Muinche and *Land* used also for the neck ornaments of animals and spears. Use of the term *Muintorc*.

In the visit of *Fraech Mac Fidhaidh* to *Ailill* and *Medbh*, at he palace of *Cruachan* in Connacht, to demand the hand in narriage of their daughter *Findabair*, and of which I shall ave more to say by and bye, we are told that each of the ifty steeds which formed the cavalcade had upon its neck a *Mael-Land* of silver with little bells of gold. The word *Mael-Land* of silver used here would signify literally a pointless blade, r broad band, or crescent of silver, but as no recognizable specimen of this part of horse furniture has come under my notice, r probably exists at all, I cannot say more about it, than to give the simple analysis of the name.

Of the *Mael-Land* mentioned in the *Táin Bo Fraich*.

Again, in the passage already quoted in part from the Battle of *Magh Leana*, where the monarch *Conn* "of the Hundred Battles" is described as arraying and arming himself for the combat, we are told that "he placed his blue, sharp-edged, rich-hilted sword at his convenience; and his strong, triumphant, wonderful, firm, embossed shield, with beautiful devices, upon the convex slope of his back. He grasped his two thick-headed, wide socketed, battle-spears, with their *Muinchi* (or rings) of gold upon their necks, in his right hand". Here the word *Muinche* is applied to the ornamental ferrule, or ring of gold, placed upon the neck of a spear-handle, just where it enters the socket of the spear itself; and it is important enough that we have at least one specimen of what there is good reason to believe to be this particular *Muinche* or spear necklace. This ring, or hoop of pure gold was found many years ago on the estate of the late Daniel O'Connell, of ever glorious memory, in the county of Kerry. It was discovered in a small deposit of ancient bronze, namely—a bronze sword, some bronze hatchets, and a bronze *skian*, or oval-pointed dagger, to the decayed wooden shaft of which it appears to have belonged. These remains of certainly the most remote period of our history, were found under a large stone which stood in a river; and having passed into the hands of the great O'Connell, were subsequently presented by his son Maurice to the Royal Irish Academy, where they have for many years formed one of the most interesting and valuable groups of the collection of antiquities of

The ferrule of a spear called a *Muinche* in the account of the Battle of *Magh Leana*; discovery of such a ring in Kerry;

XXVII.

the term also used for the collars of grayhounds, chiefly in Fenian Tales.

that National Institution. The name *Muinche*, as I have already stated, is often found applied to the collars of noble grayhounds in the old books, and chiefly in the poems and tales which record the exploits and adventures of *Find Mac Cumhaill* and his *Fianna*. However, as it is not my intention to burthen these remarks with unnecessary illustrations or an idle display of research, I shall content myself for the present with what I have already said in proof of the existence, and the particular and general use of the *Muinche*, the *Muintorc*, and the *Land*, among the noble classes of Milesians in ancient Erinn.

Mention of the *Torc* in its simple form in the Book of Leinster.

I may, however, add that I have found the "torque" mentioned by itself, and not, as usual, compounded with *muin*, the neck, so as to make it a "neck-torque". In this form I have met the name but once; but in that instance it is very curious because its authority states that the articles there mentioned were of foreign manufacture. The passage is in a very curious poem in the "Book of Leinster", written in praise of the ancient palace of *Ailinn* in the county of Kildare. The poem consists of twenty-six stanzas, of which the following is the eleventh:—

"Its sweet music at all hours,
Its fair ships in the foaming waves,
Its showers of silver spangles magnificent,
Its 'torques' of gold from foreign lands".[260]

It would be idle to speculate on this curious passage, and I give it here merely for what it is worth.

Of the *Land* or lunette;

From the necklace in its various forms I shall now pass to the next ascending ornament of the person, referred to in our old writings, and this is the *Land*, or crescent, or lunette, as it is generally named at present. To this article as an ornament for the front of the head as well as for the neck, we have such references as shall leave no uncertainty of its very extensive use among those who were by rank entitled to wear it in ancient times. I have already quoted from the Brehon Laws a short article in reference to the work-bag or work-box of a chief's wife, and its legal contents, which consisted of four precious articles, namely, a veil of one colour, and a *Mind*, or diadem of gold for the head, and a blade or lunette of gold, evidently for the neck, and silver thread, or fine wire. If this lady's work-box or bag were stolen, and all these not in it, she was entitled but to the restitution of what had been stolen; whereas, if the legal complement of articles had been in it, she would be entitled to a fine of a breach of aristocratic inviolabi-

it formed part of the legal contents of a lady's work-bag;

(260) [original:—
Aceóil binni icach thrát,
aicin bárc fortondgur flannd,
afrairt airgit ordoi már,
atuirc óir a tirib gáll.—H. 2. 18. f. 27, a. b.]

lity, in addition. We find it laid down in our ancient laws that:— XXVII.

"As long as there are sons forthcoming, daughters do not receive any part of a deceased father's property, though he be their father as well as the father of the sons, nor anything but crescents of gold, and *Rand* or thread of silver, and *Bregda*, that is *Bricin*, or thread of various colours [for embroidery]".(361)

It formed part of the inheritance of daughters.

However clear it may appear from these and former passages that the *Land*, blade, or crescent of gold, was worn on the neck, the following few passages, out of many, will show with equal clearness that it was also worn on the front of the head, and probably sometimes across the head from ear to ear. The passages in question are from the tale of *Bruighean Da Derga*, and which I alluded to in a previous lecture,(362) and will, I think, be sufficient to prove this. These passages occur in the descriptions given by the pirate chief *Ingcel* to *Fer Rogain* of the interior of *Da Derga*'s court, and the disposition of the monarch *Conairé Mór* and his people within it.

The *Land* was worn on the head as well as on the neck, as shown by

"I saw there", said *Ingcel*, "three other men in front of these. [They wore] three *Lands* [blades or crescents] of gold upon the back of their heads. Three short aprons (*Berrbroca*) upon them of gray linen embroidered with gold. [They had] three short crimson capes (*Cochlini*) upon them, [and carried] goads of red bronze in their hands".

the description of *Conairé Mór*'s head charioteers,

These were the monarch's three head charioteers, *Cul*, *Frecul*, and *Forcul*.(363)

"I saw there", said *Ingcel* again, "nine [men] sitting upon [bare] wooden couches; they wore nine short capes upon them with crimson loops, and a *Land* (blade or crescent) of gold upon the head of each, [and carried] nine goads in their hands".

and of his apprentice charioteers;

"They", said *Fer Rogain*, "are nine apprentices who are learning chariot driving from the king's three chief chariot drivers".(364)

"I saw three others there", said *Ingcel*, "with three *Lands*

and also of his poets.

(361) [original:—Gein beit mic ann nocho berat, ingina ni do dibad in athar dogres, cid inann athair doib acas do na macaib, cin cob inann, acht mad lanna, acas ranna, acas bregda. Lann, .i. oir, acas rann, .i. in snaith airgit, acas breg da, .i. in bricin.—$\frac{23}{a.6}$ Acad. col.ect. R.I.A., f. 8. b.

(362) Lecture XXV., *ante*, vol. ii, p. 137, *et seq*.

(363) [original:—Atconnarc triar naili ar ambélaib Teora lanna oir for airchiur a cind; téora berrbróca impu delin glas imdentai dior; tri cochlini corcrai impu; tri broit credumi inaláim. Samailleat sin a Firrogain. Rosfetar olse, Cul, acas Frecul, acas Forcul, tri primaraid indrig.—*Leabhar na h-Uidhr*., f. 64. a.]

(364) [original:—Atchondarc nonbur forcranumad súil dóib; nói coclene impu colubun chorcrai, acas land oir sur cind cacháe, nói mbruit inalamaib . . . Nói naraid foglomma la tri primaradu indrig.—*Ibid*., f. 64. a.]

XXVII. (blades or crescents) of gold across their heads; [they wore] three speckled cloaks upon them; and three shirts with red interweavings [of gold]. They had three brooches of gold in their cloaks; three wooden spears [hung] over them at the wall".

"I know them", said *Fer Rogain;* "they are the king's three poets, namely, *Sui*, and *Ro Sui*, and *For Sui* [that is, sage, great sage, and greater sage], three of the same age, three brothers, and three sons of *Maphir Rochetuil*".(264)

(263) [original:—Atconnarc triar naile and; teóra landa óir tar a cend; trí broit bric impu; teóra camsi condergintlaid Teóra bretnassa óir ina mbrataib; teora bunsaca uasaib hi fraig, Ro fetarsa sin, or Ferrogin; tri filid in rig sin, .i. Sui, acas Ro-Sui, acas For-Sui, tri comais, tri bráthir, tri mic Maphir Roċetuil.—*Ibid.*, f. 64. b. bot.]

LECTURE XXVIII.

[Delivered July 23rd, 1860.]

(VIII.) Dress and Ornaments (continued). Of Ear-rings: the *Au-Nasc* mentioned in *Cormac*'s Glossary, and in the accounts of *Tulchinne* the druid and juggler, and the harpers in the tale of the *Bruighean Daderga*. Of the *Gibne*: it was a badge of office, especially of charioteers; it is mentioned in the description of *Rian Gabhra*, *Cuchulaind*'s charioteer; and also in a legend about him in *Leabhar na h-Uidhre*; the word *Gibne* is explained in an ancient glossary in a vellum MS.; the story of *Edain* and *Midir* shows that the *Gibne* was not worn exclusively by charioteers. The spiral ring for the hair mentioned in the "Wanderings of *Maelduin*'s Canoe". Men as well as women divided the hair. Hollow golden balls fastened to the tresses of the hair; mention of such ornaments in the tale of the *Bruighean Daderga*; curious poem from the tale of *Eochaidh Fedhleach* and *Edain* (foot note); golden balls for the hair also mentioned in the "Sick Bed of *Cuchulaind*"; two such balls mentioned in the tales of *Bec Fola* and *Bruighean Daderga*, and only one in that of the "Sick Bed". The *Mind óir* or crown not a *Land* or crescent; it is mentioned in the Brehon Laws, and in a tale in the *Leabhar na h-Uidhre*; the second name used in the tale in question proves that the *Mind* covered the head. The *Mind* of *Medb* at the *Táin Bo Chuailgne*. The *Mind* was also worn in Scotland, as is shown by the story of prince *Cano*. Men also wore a golden *Mind*, as appears from the *Táin Bo Chuailgne*; this ornament called in other parts of the tale an *Imscind*. The curious *Mind* worn by *Cormac Mac Airt* at the meeting of the States at *Uisnech*.

From these crescents or lunettes of gold, worn on the front, and sometimes farther back on the head, by men and women, we now pass to the next articles of ornament with which our remote ancestors adorned the head, namely ear-rings. To this class of ornament, however, I have met but few references, and in each case the wearers were men only. This ornament appears under two names, differing apparently in signification. The first name is *Au-Nasc*, or *U-Nasc*, which signifies literally an ear-ring. The second name is *Au-Chuimriuch*, which literally signifies ear-band, or ear-ligature.(366) For the precise value of the term *Au-Chuimriuch*, or ear-band, I have not been able to discover any authority further than the plain analysis of the name itself affords; but not so with the *Au-Nasc*, as we have the following clear definition of it in the ancient glossary, so well known as *Cormac*'s glossary:

Of Ear-rings;

"*Au-Nasc*, that is a ring for the ear, that is a ring of gold which is worn upon the fingers or in the ears of the sons of the free or noble families".

the *Au-Nasc* mentioned in *Cormac's* Glossary;

This explanation is clear enough; perfectly so, indeed, accord-

(366) [See Fig. 58.]

XXVIII.

ing to the composition of the word, and as far as rings for the ears are concerned; but I cannot help believing that the second meaning, that is, that they were rings for the fingers also, is wrong, and an interpolation of some thoughtless transcriber of more modern times.

and in the account of *Tulchinne*, the Druid and Juggler,

It may be remembered that in a former lecture of the present course,[267] when describing the various groups in the court of *Da Derg*, where the monarch *Conairé Mór* was killed, *Ingcel*, the captain of the piratical assailants, describes the monarch's chief juggler as follows:—

"I saw there a large champion in front of the same couch, in the middle of the house. The blemish of baldness was upon him. Whiter than the cotton of the mountains is every hair that grows upon his head. He had *U-Nasca* or ear-clasps of gold in his ears, and a speckled, glossy cloak upon him".

and also in that of the harpers in the tale of the *Brui-ghean Da-derga*.

The second reference to this ornament is found in the same important tale of the Court of *Da Derg*, where the harpers are described in the following words:—[268]

"I saw nine others in front, with nine bushy, curling heads of hair, nine light blue floating cloaks upon them, and nine brooches of gold in them. Nine crystal rings upon their hands; an *Ordnasc* or thumbring of gold upon the thumb of each of them; *Au-Chuimriuch* or ear-clasps of gold upon the ears of each; a *Muinche* or torque of silver around the neck of each".

The *Gibne*

There is another little ornament called a *Gibne*, connected with the head, which, I think, ought not to be overlooked here: it is the band or thread which was tied around the head to keep the hair down on the forehead and in its place otherwise. This ornament, however, appears to have been more particularly a badge of office, peculiar, but not exclusively so, to chariot-drivers, and the only instances of it that I remember, except one, are connected with *Laegh*, the son of *Rian Gabhra*, charioteer to the celebrated champion *Cuchulaind*. In the great combat fought by that champion against *Ferdiadh*, and which was so fully described in a former lecture,[269] we find the following passage in the description of the charioteer's dress:—

a badge of office, especially of charioteers;

mentioned in the description of the dress of *Rian Gabhra*, *Cuchulaind's* charioteer;

"The same charioteer put on his crested, gleaming, quadrangular helmet, with a variety of all colours and all devices, and falling over his two shoulders behind him. This was an addition of gracefulness to him, and not an incumbrance. He then with

(267) [See Lect. XXV., *ante*, vol. ii., p. 144.]

(268) [*Ubi supra*, p. 146.]

(269) [Lec., XIV. *ante*, vol. i. p. 302. See also Appendix for the whole episode of the *Táin Bo Chuailgne*, containing the fight of *Cuchulaind* with *Ferdiadh*.]

his hand placed to his forehead the red-yellow *Gibne*, like a crescent of red gold, of gold which had boiled over the edge of the purifying crucible: and this he put on in order to distinguish his office of charioteer from that of his master [who was the champion]". XXVIII.

Of the same champion and charioteer there is a very wild legend preserved in the ancient *Leabhar na h-Uidhre*, in which the *Gibne* appears again as part of the outfit of the latter. The story is shortly this.

and also in a legend about him in the *Leabhar na h-Uidhre*.

When Saint Patrick first appeared at Tara, and attempted the conversion from paganism of the very obstinate monarch, the *Laeghaire Mac Neill*, the latter refused to believe in the true God until the saint should raise to him from the dead *Cuchulaind*, the great champion of Ulster, who had been dead more than four hundred years at the time. The saint did not seem to assent to this condition, but, on the next morning, as the monarch was driving in his chariot northwards from Tara towards the river *Boind* (the present Boyne), the spirit of the famous champion appeared to him, splendidly dressed, with his chariot, horses, and charioteer, the same as when alive. After describing *Cuchulaind* himself, his chariot and horses, the king continues:—"There was a charioteer in front of him in the chariot. He was a lank, tall, stooped, freckle-faced man. He had curling, reddish hair upon his head. He had a *Gibne* of *Findruine* upon his forehead which kept his hair from his face; and *Cuache* (or little cups) of gold upon his poll behind, into which his hair coiled; a small winged *Cochall* or cape on him, with its buttoning at his two elbows. A goad of red gold in his hand by which he urged his horses".[(370)]

Let us examine what the ornaments of the charioteer were in this case. We have first a *Gibne* or thread of *Findruine* or white bronze upon his forehead, to keep his hair from falling over his face; and little cups at his poll behind, in which his hair was coiled up. Now this is a new piece of ornament, of which I have not found mention anywhere else; nor can I as yet recognize in the large collection in our national museum any article which could answer to this description. As regards the word *Gibne*, just mentioned, I find it explained in an ancient glossary in a vellum MS. in Trinity College, Dublin,

Meaning of *Gibne* explained in an ancient glossary;

(370) [original:—Ara ara bélaib isin carputsin araile forseng fánfota for brec, falt forcas for ruad for amulluċ. Gipne findruine for a étan nádleiced afolt fóagid Cuáċe deor for áoib cúlaid hi tairċellad afalt. Coiċline et teċ immi conaursloċud ar aoib nullennaib. Bruitne didergór ina láim diatarcellad a eoċu.—*Leabhar na h-Uidhre*, f. 74. a. b.]

XXVIII. as follows:—(271) "*Gibne*, that is a thread, as *Laegh* said when giving the description:—'I saw' said he, 'a man on the plain and a *Gibne* of *Findruine* upon his forehead'". The man who spoke the words was the *Laegh* just mentioned above, *Cuchulaind's* charioteer, but I have not been able to find the tract from which it is quoted.

the story of *Edain* and *Midir* shows that the *Gibne* was not worn exclusively by charioteers.

For the fact that the fillet, or thread of gold, or other metal which confined the hair on the forehead, and which must have gone round the head, was not exclusively worn by charioteers, I may refer back to the story of the lady *Edain* and *Midir*, the chieftain of *Bri Leith*, in the present county of Longford, given in a former lecture of the present course.(272) In this very ancient story it may be remembered that, whilst the lady and her fifty attendant maidens were bathing in the bay of *Inbiur Cichmuini* on the east coast of Ulster, they saw coming towards them over the plain the chieftain *Midir*, mounted on a splendid bay steed. Among the other rich ornaments already described which the horseman wore, was a thread of gold bound upon his forehead, to keep, as the story says, his hair from falling over his face.

There are a few more ornaments connected with the hair of the head, about which I shall now briefly speak. These are the ring, which confined the hair at the poll in one lock or bundle; and the hollow balls of gold in which the front side-locks, or divisions of the hair terminated. I need not refer back to a former lecture of the present course, where I described the beautiful, spiral, and elastic ring for the hair at the poll, in [the late] Dr. Petrie's fine cabinet of Irish antiquities;(273) but I may again call attention to the lady mentioned in the Navigation, or wanderings of *Maelduin's* Ship, where we are told that:—

The spiral ring for the hair mentioned in the "Navigation of *Maelduin's* Canoe".

"Upon the fourth day", the story says, "the woman came forth to them, and splendidly did she come there. She wore a white robe, and a *Budne* or twisted ring of gold confining her hair. She had golden hair. She had two *Maelann* or pointless shoes of silver upon her crimson-white feet; a *Bretnais* or silver brooch, with a chain of gold, in her robe; and a striped smock of silk next her white skin".(274)

I may here observe that the ring for the hair at the poll may be easily distinguished from all other rings, because it must of necessity have been of a spiral form, and gradually diminishing

(271) [original:—gibne, .i. snáithe, ut est, Laeg acctabairt na tuarasc-bála: Atconnarc ar sé fer isin mag acas gibne findruine for a édan.—H. 3. 18. 469. b. 650. a.]

(272) [*Ante*, Lecture xxvi., vol. ii., p. 162.]

(273) [*Ibid.*, p. 159.]

(274) [*Ibid.*, p. 159.]

from one end to the other, in order to fit the tapering character of the confined poll of hair, which diminished gradually in thickness from the root to the top. Such is the character of the beautiful hair *Budne* in Dr. Petrie's collection, and also of a smaller golden one in the Museum of the Royal Irish Academy.

Men as well as women divided the hair.

That men as well as women confined, either in one or several divisions, the hair of the poll, will be seen from the following instance. In the story of *Bec Fola* and king *Diarmait*, already several times referred to, we are told that the strange young man whom she met on the brink of a lake, when she lost her way after eloping from her husband's palace, had among other ornaments, "meshes, and a net of gold on every lock of his hair behind, reaching down to his shoulders; and two apples, or hollow balls of gold, the size of a man's fist, upon the two locks or forks, into which his hair was divided, but whether at the poll or the temples, we are not told, though it certainly must have been the latter. It would be very difficult to identify any of the hair-rings spoken of here, as they may have been of the ordinary circular form, and not spiral, since they were intended more for ornamenting separate small locks of the hair, than for confining the whole in one tapering bundle. Of the net of gold for the hair mentioned here, it is unnecessary to say anything further, as such nets are still used, not however by gentlemen, but by ladies, to whom in our matter-of-fact and democratic days, ornaments of gold for the hair are exclusively confined.

Hollow golden balls fastened to the tresses of the hair:

The next ornament we have to consider is the hollow ball of gold in which the tops of the two front, or rather side-locks, of the hair were generally received and fastened. The references to this ornament are not many, though from its character, simplicity, and luxury, there can be no doubt but that it was in extensive use with men and women in the olden times. Passing over the description of the two balls of gold just given from the story of king *Diarmait* and the lady *Bec Fola*, I have but two more references to this ornament, but one of these is so precise and characteristic as to explain clearly in what way these balls or hollow shells were attached to the hair. The very ancient and valuable tale of the *Bruighean Daderga*, so copiously drawn upon in the course of these lectures, opens with the following poetical passage:—

mentioned in the tale of the *Bruighean Daderga*;

"There was [of old] an admirable, illustrious king over Erinn, whose name was *Eochaidh Fedleach*. He on one occasion passed over the fair-green of *Bri Leith* [in the present county of Longford], where he saw a woman on the brink of a fountain, having a comb and a casket (*Cuirel*) of silver, ornamented with gold, washing her head in a silver basin with

XXVIII.

entioned in he tale of the ruighean aderga;

four birds of gold perched upon it, and little sparkling gems of crimson carbuncle (*Carrmogul*) upon the outer edges of the basin. A short, crimson cloak, with a beautiful gloss, lying near her; a *Dualldai* (or brooch) of silver, inlaid with sparkles of gold, in that cloak. A smock, long and warm, gathered and soft, of green silk, with a border of red gold, upon her. Wonderful clasps of gold and of silver at her breast, and at her shoulder-blades, and at her shoulders in that smock, on all sides. The sun shone upon it, while the men [that is the king, and his retinue] were all shaded in red, from the reflection of the gold against the sun, from the green silk. Two golden-yellow tresses upon her head, each of them plaited with four locks or strands, and a ball of gold upon the point of each tress [of the two]. The colour of that hair was like the flowers of the bog firs in the summer, or like red gold immediately after receiving its colouring. And there she was disentangling her hair, and her two arms out through the bosom of her smock".(275)

This is a curious description, and the old writer might fairly incur the charge of pure fiction, if we had not still extant, as far as combs, not of silver but of bone, gracefully carved, and little caskets of gold, clasps and fastenings of all sorts, and the balls of gold in which the two plaited tresses of the hair terminated, to prove the accuracy of his description of the ancient personal ornaments.

The name of the remarkable lady of whom we have just spoken was *Edain*, already mentioned; she was the daughter of *Etar*, a *Tuatha Dé Danann* chief, and grandmother of the monarch *Conairé Mór*, the hero of this tale of the *Bruighean Daderga*. When the monarch *Eochaidh Fedleach* had sufficiently observed and admired the beautiful *Edain* at her free toilette, he made proposals of marriage to her, which were at once accepted, and he returned to his palace at Tara in high spirits with his new queen. The lady, however, had not until

(275) [original:—Bui ri amra airegda for eiren Eochaidh Fedleach a ainm, do luidseacht; nann dar aenach mBreg Leith conaccai inmnai for ur in tobair, aċas cirr, ċuirrel argit conecor deor, acte oc folcud allaing argit, acas ceithri heoin oir for ri, acas gleoirgemai beccai dicharrmogul chorcrai hisorḟlescuib na luingi. Brat cas corcra foloicham aicte; dualldai airgoidi ecoirside deor oibinnu iribratt. Lene lebur culpatach iri ċotut le inor deistiu uainide foderginliud oirimpi. Tuagmila ingantai dior acas airget for a bruindi, acas a formnaib, acas a guallib isindlene dicaċleith. Taitned fria ingrian cobbasdearg dona feraib tuidleċ indoir frisin ngrein isin titiu uaindi. Da trilis norbuidi for a cind, ḟige ceitrinduail ceachtarnde acas mell for rind cach duail ba cosmail leo. Dath ind foilt sin fri barr nailestair hisamrad, no fri dergor iar ndenam a data. Is and bui oc taiṫbiuch a fuilt dia fulcad, acas a dalaim tria derc asedlaig immach.—H. 2. 16. col. 716. top.]

this time remained unobserved and unadmired by other men; and among those who ardently loved her was *Midir*, the *Tuatha Dé Danann* chief of *Bri Leith*, where she was first met by king *Eochaidh*. This was the gorgeously dressed and decorated *Midir*, who had previously surprised herself and her fifty attendant maidens when bathing in the bay of *Inbiur Cichmiuni* in Ulster, as I have already mentioned. XXVIII.

This *Midir*, like the rest of his race, was an accomplished magician; and in a short time after the marriage of *Edain*, he appeared in disguise at the palace of Tara. He was, in fact, the stranger who asked to play a game of chess with the monarch *Eochaidh Fedleach*, and won the queen *Edain* as the stake, the story of which I recounted in a former lecture,[276] and need

[276] [*Ante*, Lect. ix., vol. i., p. 192. It may be useful to give here a somewhat different version of this poem, together with the original:—

A befind in raga lim Itír ningnad hisil rind, Is barr sobarċe folt and, Is daṫ snecṫu ċorp coind?	O *Befind!* wilt thou come with me To a wonderful land that is mine, The hair is there like unto the blossom of the *Sobarche*, Of the colour of snow is the fair body?
Is and nad bi mui nutai; Gela det and dubui brai; Is li sula lin ar sluaig, Is dubrion [no is brecc] and ceċ gruad.	There will be nor grief or care; White are teeth there, black the brows; Pleasant to the eye is the number of our hosts, And on every cheek the hues of the fox-glove.
Is Corcair maige [no lossa] caċmuin, Is li sulu [no is dath] ugui luin; Cid cain deicsiu muigi Fail, Annum iargnais muige mair.	Crimson of the mead is each neck, As delightful to the eye as the blackbird's eggs; Though pleasant to behold be the plains of [*Innis*] *fail*, Rarely wouldst thou visit them after frequenting the great plain.
Cidmesc lib coirm Inse Fáil, Is mescu coirm tire máir; Amra tire tir asbiur, Ni ṫéit oac and resiun.	Though intoxicating to thee be the ale of *Innisfail*, More intoxicating are the ales of the great country; The only land is the land I speak of, There youth never grows into old age.
Sroṫa teit millsi tar tir; Rogu demid acus fin; Doim delgnaidi cenon; Combart cen peccad cen col.	Warm sweet streams traverse the land; The choicest of mead and of wine; Handsome people without blemish; Intercourse without sin, without prohibition.
Atċium caċ for caċ leṫ, Acus ni connacc neċ; temel imorbais Adaim Dodonarċeil ara raim?	We see every one on every side, And no one seeth us; The cloud of Adam's fault Has caused this concealment of which I speak.
A ben diaris mo ṫuaiṫ tind, Is barr oir bias fort ċind;	O Woman! if thou comest to my proud people,

XXVIII. not dwell further upon it here, especially as it is not further necessary for the purpose of my present subject. I may, however, remark that the poem addressed to *Edain* under the title of *Befind*, or Fair-haired Woman, and given in the lecture alluded to, is of undoubted primitive pastoral character, both in construction and in the allusions contained in it, and may in great part be safely referred to a very early period, if not to the age of *Eochaidh Fedhleach* himself.

and in the "Sick Bed of *Cuchulainn*"; The next and last reference to balls of gold for the hair, of which I shall at present avail myself, is found in the ancient Gaedhelic tale of the "Sick Bed of *Cuchulainn*",(277) of which I gave a very complete analysis in a former lecture.(278) It may be remembered that a woman with a green cloak, the wife of *Labraid* "the quick hand at sword", a fairy chieftain, was sent from the lady *Fand*, the wife of the great *Tuatha Dé Danann* navigator, *Manannan Mac Lir*, who had fallen in love with him, to invite him to visit her, and assist *Labraid* in a battle, and that his strength would be restored. *Cuchulaind*, before going himself, sent his charioteer *Laegh* to report on the country of *Magh Mell*, or "the Plains of Happiness". *Laegh* goes, and is well received by *Labraid;* and when he returns, he describes, in a poem of twenty-eight stanzas, his visit to *Labraid's* court. The following are the first two stanzas of this poem:—

"I arrived in my happy sportiveness
At an uncommon residence, though it was common,
At the court where were scores of troops,
Where I found *Labraid* of the long flowing hair.

"And I found him in the court,
Sitting among thousands of weapons,
Yellow hair upon him of a most splendid colour,
And an apple of gold closing it".(279)

two such balls mentioned in the Tales of *Bec Fola* and *Bruighean Daderga*, and only one in that of the "Sick Bed". In the previous instances there are two balls of gold mentioned, in which the two divisions into which the hair was divided in front terminated; here, however, there is but one ball of gold, which closed or terminated the whole of the hair. It is therefore quite clear that this ball could not have been in front or at the side of the head. It follows, then, that it must

Muc ur, laiċ lemnaċt lalind,
Rotbia lim. And a Befind!
—*Leabhar na h-Uidhre*, f. 82.]

It is a golden crown shall be upon thy head;
Fresh pork, banquets of new milk and ale,
Thou shalt have with me there, O *Befind!*]

(277) [Published in the *Atlantis*, vol. i., p. 362, and vol. ii., p. 96. Dublin, 1858–59.]

(278) [*Ante*, Lect. ix., vol. i., p. 195.]

(279) [See original in *Atlantis*, vol. ii., p. 103.]

XXVIII.

have been at the poll, and that the hair was either confined by a ring, or woven into one great plait behind, so that its arrangement was made firm and secure by its terminating point being received into, or passing through, this hollow ball of gold.

It does not appear, as far as I have been able to discover, that women in the olden times confined the hair in coils on the top or back part of the head with pins, brooches, or combs, although there is reason to believe that they did use pins and brooches for some purpose connected with its arrangement.

The *Mind óir*, or crown,

I shall now pass from the study of the minor ornaments of the head, which I have dwelt upon at such considerable length, to the chief of all, the *Mind óir*, or *Minn óir*, that is, the crown, or diadem of gold, of which we find frequent mention in our ancient writings. That the *Mind óir* was not an ordinary *Land*, that is, a frontlet or crescent of gold, must be at once acknowledged, when we find both mentioned together as different articles belonging to one and the same person, and when, besides this fact, it will be shown that, whilst the *Land* was worn either at the neck or on the forehead [and the back of the head. *vide* p. 183], the *Mind* invariably covered or surrounded the whole of the head. The first reference to the *Mind* or crown, to which I shall call attention, is an article in the Brehon Laws, and has been already mentioned in connection with the *Land*, or crescent of gold. In the article in question we are told that the workbag or workbox of a king's wife, when legally furnished, should contain "a veil of one colour, and a *Mind* (or crown) of gold; and a *Land* (or crescent) of gold; and thread (or fine wire) of silver". This instance alone would be sufficient to prove that the *Mind* and the *Land* of gold were different articles and worn in a different way.

not a *Land*, or crescent;

mentioned in the Brehon Laws;

and in a tale in *Leabhar na h-Uidhre*;

The following passage translated, from an ancient story in one of our oldest MSS., *Leabhar na h-Uidhre*, leaves, however, no doubt at all upon this matter.

"There was", says this story, "a great fair held at one time at *Taillte* [now absurdly called Teltown in the county Meath] by the Gaedhils [of Erinn]. The person who was king of Tara at this time was *Diarmait*, the son of *Fergus Cerbeoil* [who died in the year 588]. The men of Erinn took their places upon the stands and benches of the fair-place, each according to his dignity and possession and legal right, as had been at all previous times the custom. The women had a separate stand for themselves along with the king's two wives. The queens who were with [king] *Diarmait* at this time were, *Mairend Mael* [that is, *Mairend* the Bald]; and *Mugain*, the daughter of *Conraidh*, son of *Duach Dond*, of the men of Munster. *Mugain*

XXVIII. was deeply envious of *Mairend*", because she was herself barren, whilst *Mairend* was fruitful; "and she called unto her a satirical woman, and told her that she would pay her whatever she desired, if she went up and pulled the *Mind* of gold off the head of queen *Mairend*. The condition of queen *Mairend* was this, that she had no hair upon her head; wherefore she constantly wore a queen's *Mind* to conceal her blemish. The satirical woman went up then to where *Mairend* sat, and pertinaciously pressed her for a gift. The queen said that she had nothing to give her. Thou wilt have this then, said the women, pulling the golden *Cathbarr*, or diadem off her head. May God and St. *Ciaran* avenge this, said *Mairend*, at the same time clapping her two hands upon her bare head. No person in the assembly, however, had time to notice her disgrace before a mass of flowing golden hair started upon her head, falling down below her shoulder-blades; and all this through the miraculous interposition of St. *Ciaran*" [of Clonmacnois].(280)

With the peculiar morality of the royal court which this very interesting legend reveals, or the miraculous agency which it introduces, we are not concerned here; but the evidence which it affords of the meaning and use of the golden *Mind* is so conclusive as to require no further proof. If, however, further proof were required, the second name, that of *Cathbarr*, under which the diadem is mentioned, would amply supply it. The word *Cathbarr* is now, and has been at all times, well understood to signify a helmet, and in that sense it has come down as the proper name of a man, especially in the O'Donnell family of Donegal, to even so late a period as the year 1700. To call a queen's diadem a helmet would savour a little of robust poetry; but whatever be the idea which it was intended to convey, it is valuable to our inquiries so far as to bear out in full our conception of the character and use of the ancient golden *Mind*.

The second name, *Cathbarr*, used in this tale, proves that the *Mind* covered the head.

(280) [original:—Bai tra mór aénach mór, fecht and hi Talltin, la Diarmait mac Fergusa Cerbeóil. Ro hordaigit tra fir hErenn for foraidib ind oenaig, .i. cach ar miadaib, ocus dánaib, ocus dlestunus and, amail bágnath cossin. Bai dan forud ar leith oc na mnáib im dá setig ind rig. Ba hiat rígná batar hi fail Diarmata intansin, .i. Mairend Mael ocus Mugain ingen Chonchraid Mac Duach Duind do feraib Muman. Bái tnúth mór oc Mugain fri Mairind; ocus asbert Mugan frisin mbancainti do berad a breth féin di diamberad a mind oir do chind na rigna; ar as amlaid boi Mairend cenfolt, conid mind rigna no bid oc foloch alochta. Tanic tra in banchainti co airm imbái Mairend, ocus bói oc tothlugad neich forri. Asbert in rígán ná bái acci. Biaidh ocut ro orri octarraing in cathbairr orda dia cind. Dia ocus Ciaran riride im orro, or Mairend, oc tabairt a dálam mo cend. Nitarnic im orro doneoch issin tsluag descud fuirri, intan rosiachtat ada himdad in folt fand flescach forordda roasar furri tri nert Ciaran.—*Leabhar na h-Uidhre*, folio 42. b. col. 1.]

I have entered into this discussion because of a statement which has been made, and which has been frequently repeated and looked upon as final—namely, that the kings or queens of ancient Erinn did not wear any kind of head ornament which could be called a crown, because in none of our museums of antiquities can any such article be found. It is true the word *Mind* does not convey to the mind any precise or definite idea of the form or details of this diadem; but neither does the Latin word "corona", or the English word "crown", which is formed from it. If there be any advantage at all, it must be on the side of the Gaedhelic words *Mind* and *Cathbarr*, words which have been shown above to signify a helmet, or complete cap, or article of some such fashion, intended to cover and protect the whole head. XXVIII.

Our next reference to the *Mind* of gold is found in the *Táin Bo Chuailgne*, where we are told that when *Medb*, the queen of Connacht, was on her march with her army to ravage the country of Ulster, her progress was conducted in the following order,—She had nine chariots devoted to herself alone: two chariots of these before her, and two chariots after her, and two chariots at either side of her, and a chariot between them in the centre, in which she sat herself. And the reason [we are told] why queen *Medb* observed this order, was to prevent the clods from the hoofs of the horses, or the foam from their mouths, or the mire of a great army, or of great companies, from tarnishing the lustre of her queenly *Mind* of gold.(381)

The *Mind* of *Medb* at the *Táin Bo Chuailgne*.

And further of this same *Mind* of gold, we are told that when queen *Medb* and her forces entered the territory of *Cuailgne* (in the present county Louth), they encamped for the night on the brink of a river at a place ever since called *Redde Loiche*. The story proceeds to say that "*Medb* had ordered a comely handmaid of her household who had been in waiting upon her, to go to the river and fetch water for her to drink and wash in. *Loche* was the name of this maiden, and she, *Loche*, then went forth to the river accompanied by fifty women and carrying the queen's *Mind* of gold above her head. *Cuchulaind*, the opposing champion of Ulster, was concealed near the river, and perceiving the procession of women coming towards him preceded by a beautiful woman with a queenly *Mind* upon her head, whom he believed to be the queen herself, he let fly a stone

(381) [original:—Is amlaid no imthiged Medb ocus noi carpait fóthi a oenur: da charpat rempe dib, [ocus da charpat na diaid], ocus da charpat cechtar a da taeb, ocus carpat eturru ar medon cadessin. Is aire fo gnid Medb sin ar na ris tais fótbaige a cruib greg, no uanfad aglomraib srián, no dendgur mor sluaig, no mor buiden, ar na tisad diamrugud don mind óir na rigna.—H. 2. 18. f. 145. a.]

XXVIII.

from his sling at her head, which struck her, broke the *Mind* of gold in three places, and killed the maiden on the spot".[382]

The *Mind* was also worn in Scotland, as is shown by the story of Prince *Cano*.

The *Mind* or *Minn* of gold was also worn by the women of the Gaedhil of Scotland, as is shown by the story of prince *Cano*, which I told in a former lecture.[383] Each of the wives of the fifty warriors who accompanied the prince in his exile into Ireland, we are told, "wore a green cloak with borders of silver. A smock interwoven with thread of gold. Brooches (*Deilge Lacair*) of gold, with full carvings bespangled with gems of many colours. Necklaces (or 'torques') of highly burnished gold. A *Mind* (or diadem) of gold upon the head of each". As this story belongs to about the year 620, it affords proof of the knowledge and, no doubt, use of such ornaments in Ireland, and I think we may fairly assume in Scotland also, down to so comparatively late a period as the seventh century.

Men also wore a golden *Mind*, as appears from the *Táin Bo Chuailgne*;

That the *Mind* of gold, however, was not an ornament peculiar to females, will be seen from the following passage from the same old tale of the *Táin Bo Chuailgne*.

"It was at this time", says the story, "the youths of Ulster came southwards from *Emania* [to Louth]. Three times fifty boys, sons of the kings [and chiefs] of Ulster, was their number, under the leadership of *Folloman*, the son of *Conchobar*, king of Ulster. They fought three battles against queen *Medb* and her forces, in which they slew three times their own number, but the boys themselves were all killed except [their leader] *Folloman*, the son of *Conchobar*. *Folloman* vowed that he would never return to *Emania* until he should carry away with him [king] *Ailill*'s head and the *Mind* of gold which was over [or upon] it. This, however, [we are told] was not easy to accomplish, for the two sons of *Beithe*, son of *Ban*, [that is] the two sons of king *Ailill*'s nurse and fosterfather, came against the young prince and slew him".[384]

Farther on in the same story we find this same *Mind* of gold

(382) [original:—Radis Medb fria caem mailt comaitecta da muintir tecta ar cend urti, doil ocus innalta dochum na h-aba di. Loche comainm na h-ingene, ocus do chaet iarum Loche ocus coica ban impi, ocus mind n-óir na rigna os a cind. Ocus roceird Cuchulaind cloich assa chaball forri corróe bris in mind n-óir i tri, ocus coro marb in n-ingin inna reid.—H. 2. 18, f. 50. a. a. b.]

(383) See Lect. xxvi., *ante*, vol. ii., p. 164.

(384) [original.—Is hi sin aimser dollocar in maccradh a tuaid o h-Emain Macha; tri coicait mac do maccaib rig Ulad, im Folloman mac Conchobair; ocus dosbersat teora catha dona sluagaib co torcratar a tri comlin, ocus torcratar in maccrad dan acht Folloman mac Conchobair. Bagais Folloman na ragad ar culu co h-Emain cobrunni m-brátha ocus betha co m-beradh cend Ailella leis cos in mind óir boi uasa. Nir bo reid dosom a nisin, uair do rancatar dá mac Beithe mac Báin dá mac muimme ocus aite do Ailill, ocus ro gonat co torchair leo.—H. 2. 18. f. 154. a. b.]

designated by another name, that of *Imscim*, or *Imscing*, as may be seen from the following passage.

called in another part of this tale an *Imscim*.

"Then the men of Erinn desired *Taman* the buffoon to put on a suit of king *Ailill*'s clothes and his *Imscim* of gold, and go down to the ford of the river which was in their presence. He [the buffoon] did put on king *Ailill*'s clothes and his *Imscim* of gold, and went down to the ford. *Cuchulaind* perceived him, and taking him for king *Ailill* himself, he cast at him a stone from his *Cranntabaill* or sling, which struck and killed him on the spot".[285]

Curious *Mind* worn by *Cormac Mac Airt* at the meeting of the States at *Uisnech*.

In a former lecture,[286] an account of the occasion and manner in which the celebrated monarch *Cormac Mac Airt* was deprived of his eye in his palace at Tara by *Aengus Gai Buaifnech*, that is *Aengus* of "the poisoned spear", his own cousin, and chief of the *Deisé*, in the present barony of Deece in the county of Meath. When the king received this injury, he was obliged to abdicate the throne in favour of his son, *Cairbre Lifeachair*, because it was declared by the ancient laws and customs of the nation, that no man with any personal blemish or defect should ever be king of Tara. *Cormac* then retired to the palace of *Acaill*, now the hill of Screen near Tara, where he compiled the Book of *Acaill*, a volume of Laws. King *Cormac* did not submit tamely to the injury offered to his person, and the desecration of the sacred precincts of Tara and the violation of its ancient privileges. But he had been a constitutional monarch, and in place of calling out the national and regal power of the state against the offender, he called a national convention at the ancient place of meetings of the states, the hill of *Uisnech* in Westmeath; and before this assembly he summoned the offender to come forward and justify his regicidal act or receive the punishment due to so heinous a crime. The great meeting took place at the hill of *Uisnech*, where, we are told, "*Cormac* came with a king's *Mind* with him upon his head, with four-and-twenty small leaves of red gold, furnished with springs and rollers of white silver to maintain and suspend them, for the purpose of covering his injured eye and save his face from the disgrace".

(285) [original:—And sin ra raidsetar fir h-Erend ri Tamun drúth etgud Aililla ocas a imscimm nor-da do gabail immi, ocas tect sar in n-át bad fiadnaissi dóib. Roga-bastar som noetgud nAililla ocas a imscimm órda immi, ocas tanic bar in n-át . . . . Do connaic Cuchulaind e ocas indar leis in ecmais a fessa ocas a eolais ba sé Ailill bai and sadessin, ocas do srethi cloic ass a cranntabaill uad sair, conarc Tamun drúth can anmain bar sin náth issaibi.—H. 2. 18. f. 56. a. b. mid.]

(286) [See *Lectures on the MS. Materials of Ancient Irish History*, p. 48.]

XXVIII. I need not dwell further on this curious specimen of the kingly *Mind*, or the curious mechanism of the twenty-four leaves of red gold attached to it for the concealment of the king's blemish. These leaves must have been, I should think, small bits of gold leaf arranged and fastened together like the folds of plate armour, but I must confess my inability to comprehend the functions of the springs and rollers, or travellers, mentioned in connection with them.

LECTURE XXIX.

[Delivered July 26th, 1859.]

(VIII.) **Dress and Ornaments** (continued). Story of a *Mind* called the *Barr Bruinn* in the tale of the *Táin Bo Aingen*. Another legend about the same *Mind* from the Book of Lismore; another celebrated *Mind* mentioned in the latter legend; origin of the ancient name of the Lakes of Killarney from that of *Lén Linfhiaclach* the maker of this second *Mind*. The ancient goldsmiths appear to have worked at or near a gold mine. *Lén* the goldsmith appears to have flourished *circa* B.C. 300. The names of ancient artists are generally derived from those of their arts, but that of *Lén* is derived from a peculiarity of his teeth; this circumstance shows that he was not the legendary representative of his art, but a real artist. Gold ornaments found in a bog near Cullen in the county of Tipperary; circumstances under which they were found, and enumeration of the articles found—note. *Cerdraighe* or ancient territory of the goldsmiths near the present Cullen. Pedigree of the *Cerdraighe* of *Tulach Gossa;* this family of goldsmiths are brought down by this pedigree to *circa* A.D. 500; the eldest branch became extinct in St. *Mothemnioc, circa* A.D. 550; but other branches existed at a much later period. The mineral districts of Silvermines and Meanus are not far from Cullen. The *At* and *Cleitme*. The *Barr, Cennbarr, Eobarr,* and *Righbarr*. The goldsmith in ancient times was only an artizan; other artizans of the same class. *Creidne* the first *Cerd* or goldsmith; his death mentioned in a poem of *Flann* of Monasterboice; this poem shows that foreign gold was at one time imported into Ireland. The first recorded smelter of gold in Ireland was a native of Wicklow. References to the making of specific articles not likely to be found in our Chronicles; there is, however, abundant evidence of a belief that the metallic ornaments used in Ireland were of native manufacture.

Story of a *Mind* called the *Barr Bruinn* in the tale of the *Táin Bo Aingen*.

There is a very curious story about a *Mind*, or diadem of gold, preserved in the very ancient tale of the *Táin Bo Aingen* in the Book of Leinster. The story commences by telling us that *Ailill* and *Medb*, the king and queen of Connacht, so often mentioned in the course of these lectures, were one dark November eve enjoying themselves in their ancient palace of *Cruachan* (in the county of Roscommon, not far from Carrick-on-Shannon). Their majesties had had two culprits hung upon a tree the previous day; and king *Ailill*, in order to test the courage of his household, offered his own gold-hilted sword as a reward to whoever should go out to the gallows trees and tie a gad or twisted twig upon the leg of one of the still hanging culprits. This offer was accepted by a spirited young man whose name was *Nera*, who went forth in the darkness of the night and performed his work with becoming courage. However, upon *Nera*'s return towards the palace, he saw, as he thought, that building on fire, and he met a host of men on

XXIX

Story of a *Mind* called the *Barr Bruinn* in the tale of the *Táin Bo Aingen*.

the way who seemed to have plundered and set fire to th royal mansion. The men passed *Nera* without seeming to notice him, and he, anxious to know who they were, followed them as closely as he durst for that purpose. He had not far to go, however, as the party soon entered the well known cave of the hill of *Cruachan*, and *Nera*, still keeping at a respectabl distance behind them, entered the cave after them. The las man of the party discovered his entrance, and he was taken before the king of the royal residence of the *Tuatha Dé Danann*, which was supposed to exist, invisibly to external human eyes, within the cave. The king demanded and received an account from *Nera* how and why he had intruded into his secret palace. "Go", said the king, "to yonder house, where thou wilt find a lone woman, who will receive thee with kindness when thou tellest her that it is by me thou hast been sent; and thou shalt come every day to this mansion with a bundle of firewood for our kitchen".

Nera did as he was ordered. While thus occupied, *Ner* noticed every day a blind man leaving the door of the mansion carrying a lame man upon his back, until they reached the brink of a fountain which was at a short distance from the house, where they sat down; to this place he followed them unperceived. "I is not there", said the blind man. "It is indeed", said the lam man, "and let us go back now", said he. *Nera* inquired of th woman about this matter. "Why", said he, "do the blind an the lame men frequent the fountain?" "They frequent th *Barr* which is in the fountain", said the woman, "that is, *Mind* (or diadem) of gold which the king wears on his head and it is there it is kept". "Why is it that these two person frequent it?" said *Nera*. "Because", said the woman, "the are the persons that are most trusted by the king".(387)

Nera soon after, through the ingenuity of his wife, returne to his own people at *Cruachan*, and described to king *Aili*

(387) [original:—Erc don taig ud thall tra, ol in ri, ata bean aencuma ann, acas denad maith fris, abair fria is uaim ro faitcer cucu, acas tairri each dia co cuail condaig don taigsea. Do gnisum iaram an ni sin amail asbrech fris, fearaid iaram in bean failte fris, acas asbert. Rochen duid olsi; masa h-e in rig ro chind ille ise em, ol Nera. Ro thereadh Nera iaram co cuail condaig don dun cach dia, adchit as in dun amach, cach dia ara cind, dall, acas bacach for a muin, no teidis combidis for ur tibrad i n-dorus in duine. "Ni ann, ol in dall. Fil eicin, ol in ba cach, tiagam as din, ol in bacach Ro iarfacht Nera iaram in ni don mnai. Cid tachaigit, ol se, dall acus an bacach don tibrait Tacaigit in m-barr fil isin tibpa ol in ben, edon mindoir bis for cin in rig, is ann do coimetar. C ar imad in dias ucut nochachaige Ol Nera. Nin. Ol si, uair robo iad ro bo tairisi la in rig".—H. 16. col. 659 and 660.]

what he had seen in the cave. This was the time at which *Fergus Mac Roigh* and the other Ulster champions who exiled themselves after the treacherous death of the sons of *Uisneach*, arrived at *Cruachan*. King *Ailill*, availing himself of the presence of these valiant warriors, resolved with their aid to possess himself of the reported treasures of the cave of *Cruachan*, and accordingly on the November eve following, he, with a strong party, and through the contrivance of *Nera*'s wife, entered the subterranean mansion, and plundered it of all its treasures, including the diadem of gold which was called the *Barr Bruinn* or *Bruinn*'s diadem.

Another legend about the same *Mind* from the Book of Lismore;

It appears that this *Mind* or diadem was lost or rather carried back again by some unexplained agency to the same fountain in the cave from which it had been brought. This legendary statement is found in another ancient story preserved in that important part of the ancient "Book of Lismore", so singularly recovered some time since from the city of Cork. The story is shortly this. *Fingin Mac Luchta*, who was king of Munster about the year of our Lord 190, resided at his palace at *Druim Fingin*, or Fineen's Hill, in the county of Waterford. There was a certain prophetess from *Sliabh na m-Ban* in Tipperary, that visited him on every November eve, and related to him all the occurrences that took place in Erinn on that sacred night, and the results that should issue from them until that night twelvemonths. On one of those November eves that this lady visited the king, she related to him with peculiar emphasis one circumstance that happened on that night, and this was nothing else than the birth of the subsequently great monarch of Erinn, Conn of "the Hundred Battles". The birth of this great king and warrior was, according to our prophetess, ushered in with many strange and wonderful occurrences, all of which, however, were of a favourable character, and presaged the happy results to his country which were to result from the actions and reign of its future monarch. From the many singular and important events thus referred to in connection with that auspicious time, I have selected the following brief items, as quite pertinent to the subject of the present lecture, and bringing the older story of the golden diadem, called the *Barr Bruinn*, a few centuries later down than the *Táin Bo Aingen* just described.

The conversation between the king *Fingin* and the prophetess was carried on by way of question and answer.

"And what are the other wonders of this night?' said king *Fingin*. "These", said the woman.—"The three chief articles of manufacture in Erinn are this night found and revealed,

XXIX. namely, the *Barr* (or diadem) of *Bruinn*, the son of *Smetra*: it was the *Cerd* (or artificer) of *Aengus*, son of *Umór*, that made it. It is a *Cathbarr* (or helmet) of the pure crimson of eastern countries, with a ball of gold above it as large as a man's head, and a hundred strings around it of mixed [or variegated] carbuncle, and a hundred combed tufts of red burnished gold; and stitched with a hundred threads (or wires) of *Findruine* (or white bronze) in a variety of compartments. And it has been a great number of years in concealment in the fountain of the hill of *Cruachan* till this night, to save it from the *Mór Rigain*, [a celebrated *Tuatha Dé Danann* princess,] and so it has remained under cover of the earth until this night. And [another article, said she], the chess of *Crimthann Niad-Nair* [in the eighth year of whose reign the Saviour was born] which he brought away with him from *Aenuch Find* when he went with the lady *Nar* of *Bodhbh Derg*'s mansion [in Tipperary] on an adventure to the secret recesses of the sea, and which [chess] has been concealed in the *Rath* of *Uisnech* [in Westmeath] until this night. And [continued the prophetess] the *Mind* (or diadem) of *Laeghaire*, the son of *Luchta Laimfinn*, (or *Luchta* of the white hands), which was made by *Lén Linfhiaclach*, the son of *Banbulga*, and which has been found this night by the three daughters of *Faindle Mac Dubraith*, in *Sidh Findacha* [now *Sliabh g-Cuillenn* in Ulster] after having been concealed there since the time of the birth of *Conchobar Abrathruadh* [monarch of Erinn, who was slain in the year of our Saviour's birth], until this night".(288)

...ther cole-ted *Mind* ...ntioned his ...and;

It would seem that when these stories were written, it was a common occurrence, as it is now, to dig up from the earth ancient, elegant, and costly articles of the kind above mentioned, of the former existence and disappearance of which there still remained authentic written history, or a vivid and well-credited tradition.

(288) [original.—Ocus ciḋ .b. naili [?] for fingin. Nin, or an bean.—Teora primaicde Erenn innoċt fo frit ocus ro foillsigtea, .i. barr Bruinn meic Smeṫraċ: Cerd Aengusa meic Umoir do rigne, .i. caṫbarr do corcair glain thire nandind [?] ocus ubull oir uasa, ba meit fer cind, ocus cet ḟnathegna imme don carrṁocal cumuscda, ocus cet cailches circorcra do dergor forloiscti; ocus cead ronn findruinne aca uaimbreċtrad. Ita lina bhaḋna fo dichleit itiprait riḋe Cruaċain, ar in Mor Rigain cusanocht; ita iarum focceltar talman cusanoċt. Fidċeal Crimṫain Niad Nair tucca hAenuch Find dia luiḋ la Nair tuatċaeiċ issiḋ Buidb ro roċtra comboi fo diaṁaraib na fairrge, ata fo diċleit isin Raiṫh indUisnech cusanoċt. Minn Laeġaire, meic Luċta Laimfinn, do rigne Len Linḟiaclaċ, mac Banbulga, bainna foruaratur inocht teora hingina Faindle mac Dubraith, a Sid Findacha ar na beaḋ fo dicleit o ġein Concubair Abratruaiḋ, gus anoċt".—*Book of Lismore*, vel. copy by Joseph O'Longan, f. 188, p. 2, col. 1, top.]

XXIX. The name of the maker of the second *Mind*, *Lén Linfhiaclach*, the origin of the ancient name of the Lakes of Killarney.

To *Lén Linfhiaclach*, the maker of the second *Mind*, or diadem, mentioned above, namely that of *Laeghaire*, the son of *Liuchta* of the white hands, I have found another reference, which places his time, his character as an artist, and his identity with one or two Irish localities, in a light that cannot fail to give satisfaction to every genuine lover of Irish antiquarian researches.

In the very ancient Gaedhelic tract called the *Dinnseanchas*, or the etymological history of many of the most remarkable hills, mountains, rivers, lakes, etc., in Erinn, we find an article devoted to the origin of the name of *Loch Lein*, now the celebrated lake of Killarney. In this article we are told that *Lén Linfhiaclach* was *Cerd* (or goldsmith), to the chieftain *Bodhbh Dearg*'s noble mansion at *Sliabh na m-Ban* in Tipperary; that he went to this lake to make splendid vessels for *Fand*, the daughter of *Flidas;* and every night after his day's work was over, he would cast his anvil from him eastwards to the place called *Inneoin* (or anvil) near Clonmel, and he would throw three showers about him from his anvil, a shower of water, a shower of fire, and a shower of pure crimson gems; and the story adds that *Nemannach* (the artificer) used to do the same when shaping (gold) cups for king *Conchobar Mac Nessa* (king of Ulster) in the north. And *Lén* met his death at this lake, and hence the name *Loch Lein*, or *Lén*'s lake.

The prose account is followed by an ancient poem of thirteen stanzas, in which the history of *Loch Lein* is further discussed; but as my present concern is alone with the artificer, I shall only quote those stanzas which have special reference to him, namely the fourth, fifth, and sixth, which are as follows:

"I have heard of *Lén* with his many hammers,
Having been upon the margin of its yellow strand,
Where he fashioned without mishap, or flaw,
Splendid vessels for *Fand*, the daughter of *Flidas*.

"From *Bodhbh*'s court went forth reproachless
Lén Linfhiaclach, the son of *Bolcad*,
The firm son of *Bandad* of high renown,
The good son of *Blamad*, son of *Gomer*.

"Whether a chariot or a *Mind* of gold,
Whether a cup, or a musical instrument,
Was required from him by distinguished men,
It was quickly made before that night".[789]

[789] [original:—

Do chuala Len colin uird,	Niamlestar Faindi Flidais,
do bith forbuird a blath buird,	Ord Buidb fuchead canchair
diarchum cantiamge astaltais,	Lén Linfiaclach, mac Bolcaid,

XXIX.

The ancient goldsmith appears to have worked at or near the mine.

It would appear from this curious and valuable quotation, as well as from others that could be adduced, that the ancient custom in Ireland was, that the artist, or goldsmith, sometimes went to the gold or silver mine himself, and dug, or procured to be dug for him, the precious mineral, to smelt, or, as it is called in our ancient books, to boil the metal on the spot, in small quantities, whenever the locality suited, and then and there fabricate and fashion those splendid articles, the delicate mechanism of some of which is found to puzzle and astonish the most expert workmen of the present day, notwithstanding the great improvement in the processes and tools of the mechanical arts. This appears to me to be the explanation of that stanza of the poem which says that *Lén* went with many hammers or sledges to the borders of *Loch Lein*, where he actually made the splendid cups for the lady *Fand*, daughter of *Flidas*. But who was the lady *Fand* for whom these *Niamleastar*, or splendid vessels, were made? She was the daughter of *Flidas Foltchain*, that is, *Flidas* of "the beautiful hair", and sister by her mother to *Nia Seghamain*, of the Eberian race of Munster, who reigned as monarch of Erinn from the year of the world 4881 to 4887, when he was slain by *Enna Aighneach*, who succeeded him. So that, according to the chronology of the Annals of the Four Masters, the gifted artist *Lén*, and his royal patroness the princess *Fand*, flourished about three hundred years before the Incarnation of our Lord; and far within the sway of the Milesian dynasty.

Lén, the goldsmith, appears to have flourished circa B.C. 300.

I must confess that of all the references to native gold and famous native gold-workers which I have hitherto met, or may meet hereafter, this appears to me to be the most important. In the case of other artists of this class, the name of the artist is often derived from the art itself, or from the metal on which it is exercised. Thus, in the case of *Credne*, the celebrated *Cerd* or goldsmith of the *Tuatha Dé Danann*, and of whom we will have to speak hereafter, his name was derived from *credh*, the ore of the precious metals in which he worked, and, consequently, the fact of his real existence might be very fairly questioned, as savouring a little of the poetical and mythological. But in the case of *Lén Linfhiaclach* no such objection can be made, since the name is not descriptive of the art or the metal, but of the man proper, and signifying simply, *Lén* of "the many teeth", meaning evidently that he was remarkable for high, or a double row of teeth

The names of artists often derived from the art,

but that of *Lén* not.

blocach mac bandaid bladbil,
deg mac blamaid, mac goimair;
Cid carbad, cid cathbarr oir,
cid cuach, cid cairchi ciuil coir,
co lean farr deaghlaide,
ba gnim adbal ria naidche.
Book of Lecan, f. 239, a. a.]

XXIX.

The native manufacture of gold ornaments proved by the Brehon Laws.

But the following short article from the Brehon Laws settles completely the question of the native manufactures of these precious personal ornaments:—

"The law book tells us", says the commentator, "that the weight of the *Land óir* (or crescent of gold) was paid in silver to the *Cerd* or artist for making it".

We are told also in the same laws that the artists who made the articles of adornment and household splendour for a king, or a chief, were entitled to half the fine for injury to their property, or insult or injury to their persons, which would be paid to the king or chief himself for a like injury. This shows in what respect artists in the precious metals were held by the nobles, and the security afforded them by the laws of ancient Erinn.

In Guthrie's "General Gazetteer", published in Dublin in 1791, we find, as well as in other authorities, the following paragraph:

Gold ornaments found in a bog near Cullen, in the county of Tipperary.

"Cullen, a fair town in the county of Tipperary, province of Munster; fairs on 28th October. At the bog near this place was found a golden crown weighing six ounces; many other curiosities have been discovered in it, particularly some gorgets of gold, and gold-handled swords: for which reason it goes under the name of the golden bog".

This bog of Cullen is situated in the parish of Cullen, barony of Clanwilliam, and county of Tipperary, and on the immediate border of the county of Limerick. From time immemorial gold has been found in all conditions of preparation, from the primitive ore to the most beautiful of fashioned ornament, nay, even the very crucibles—small bronze saucepans, with the gold arrested in its progress of smelting or boiling—have been found in this bog and its neighbourhood. Within the last fourteen years, I have myself seen two bars of pure gold turned up out of this bog or its neighbourhood; the finders are not anxious to enlighten one much as to which. One of these bars was about five inches in length, an inch and a half in breadth, and more than half an inch in thickness. The other was somewhat smaller, but being plain bars without any artistic feature, they were not unfortunately secured by the Royal Irish Academy, and consequently they passed into the hands of a goldsmith, who of course has long since melted them down.[290]

[290] [In the year 1773 Governor T. Pownall exhibited to the Society of Antiquaries of London, two swords, and some other fragments, said to have been found in a bog at Cullen, in the county of Tipperary, on the lands of Lord Milton. On the 10th of February, 1774, he read a paper on the subject, which was afterwards published, illustrated by a plate, in vol. iii. (p. 555), of the *Archaeologia* for 1775. So far as we can judge from the drawings, the swords

XXIX.

Gold ornaments found in a bog near Cullen, in the county of Tipperary.

To return, however, to the golden bog of Cullen. It is not at all unreasonable to assume that this bog was anciently a

exhibited to the Society were not peculiar, being of one of the usual *forms* of bronze swords. The other object figured in the plate is a low conoidal disc of gold about four inches in diameter at the base. The apex of the conoid is chased so as to form a small stellated ornament; this is surrounded by the usual ridge, like chasings which are found on many Irish gold ornaments. These ridges form a series of complete concentric circles near the apex, but as they approach the base, the form being a conoid, and not a cone, they can only form segments of circles. Around the base, however, there is a border of complete circular ridges—the ridges being much larger than the centre ones. On the inner side of this border is a zigzag ornament which presents the appearance of rays pointing towards the centre or apex. This ornamentation does not go round the entire border, being wanting for about thirty degrees of the circle at the shortest slant-height of the conoid, that is, where it is nearest the stellated apex. Its conoidal shape would seem to show that it could not have been the boss of a shield, which it otherwise resembles. Governor Pownall thinks that it formed part of the gold plating of a wooden idol—this particular ornament being intended for the teat or nipple of the breast. The following is his account of the matter:

"The fragment, which was said to be part of an image found at the same time, is of a black wood, entirely covered and plated with thin gold, and seems to have been part of the breasts, the teat or nipple of which is radiated in hammered or chased work, in lines radiating from a centre, as is usual in the images of the sun; and round the periphery, or setting on of the breast, there are like radiations in a specific number, with other linear ornaments. There is another fragment of the same kind of wood which seems to be a fragment of an Ammonian horn; there are in it the golden studs or rivets by which it may be supposed to have been also plated with gold. The first account I had of this image was, that it was of an human form, with a *lion's face*; then, that it was indeed biform, but of what sort not specified. I have since been informed that the image, whatever it was, was of a size sufficient to make a gate post, to which use it was affixed".

It must be confessed that the evidence connecting the gold conoids with the image is not very satisfactory; for it appears by the report of the Rev. Mr. Armstrong, given by Governor Pownall, that the finding of the image occurred above sixty years before, and he found no one in the neighbourhood of Cullen who remembered anything about it. That some kind of carved wooden image was really found there, there appears to be no reasonable doubt; but whether it had golden nipples and was biformed, we have unfortunately no satisfactory evidence.

The report of the Rev. Mr. Armstong above alluded to, is a chronicle of the discoveries of gold ornaments, bronze weapons, etc., found in the same small bog near Cullen, between the years 1731 and 1753, made by a Mr. Nash, and between the years 1760 and 1773 by a Mr. Cleary. The golden articles found consisted of two chased cups, bosses, pieces of tube, plates, and ribbons, some of the former chased, gold wire, rings or ferrules, pommels of swords, the point of a scabbard, pieces with the links of a chain attached, a number of ingots, a quantity of small bits or clippings, amounting in all to above six pounds. The bronze articles consisted of a bronze cauldron and a quadrangular vessel, seven socketed spears five inches long with parts of the wooden shafts; thirteen socketed spears ten inches long with handles of quartered ash six feet long; two swords with pieces of gold attached to the rivets of the handle; a sword weighing 2lbs. 5oz., having a piece of white metal, called in the report pewter, inlaid in the bronze near the pommel; in this white metal was inlaid in copper, what are described as resembling four figures of 1; a piece of bronze tube; thirteen whole swords much hacked and notched; and forty-three parts of swords of the handle ends, and twenty-nine of the point ends; three ingots weighing

wooded valley, resorted to by a party, or parties, of gold smelters and smiths, on account, perhaps, of its contiguity to a gold mine, as well as the convenience of charcoal. But independently of these positive and assumed circumstances, there is extant a historical reference to this precise locality, which, I believe, identifies it with a family and a race of workers in the finer metals. There was anciently in this district a small chieftaincy called *Cerdraighe*, that is the territory of the goldsmiths; and this territory, as well as the tribe who owned and occupied it, had received the name from a man who bore it as his distinctive title in right of his profession of a *Cerd* or goldsmith. The tribe of the *Cerdraighe* were descended from *Oilioll Oluim*, the celebrated king of Munster, who died A.D. 234, and their pedigree is thus given in the "Book of Leinster":

Cerdraigh or the ter tory of th goldsmith near Cull

"The pedigree of the *Cerdraighe* of *Tulach Gossa*, that is, they were named *Cerdraighe* because every man of them was a *Cerd* (or goldsmith) for seven generations.

Pedigree the Cerdraighe of Tulach Gossa;

"*Oilioll Oluim* had a son whose name was *Tighernach*, who had a son *Cerdraighe* (or the king's goldsmith), who had a son *Cerd Beg* (or the little, or young goldsmith), who had a son *Cerdan*, the still more diminutive goldsmith, who had a son *Senach*, who had a son *Temnen*, who had a son *Lugaidh*, who had a son *Carban*, who had a son St. *Mothemnioc*, who, being a holy priest and not married, the family in this line became extinct in him; and the race of goldsmiths must have ceased in his father *Carban*, who was the sixth generation from *Cerdraighe*, the first of the artists, and grandson of king *Oilioll Oluim*".[391]

7lbs.; a piece of about 1lb. weight of what seemed to have been the residue left in the ladle after casting some article.

The number of articles noticed in this report must bear a very insignificant proportion to those actually found and silently disposed of by the peasantry during the last century. Indeed O'Halloran states (*History of Ireland*, vol. ii., p. 92; Dublin, 1819) that a gold crown was found in this bog in 1744, which he saw himself, and which, he says, was "like the close crowns of the eastern princes". From the number, as well as the variety of the articles, it seems certain, therefore, that gold and bronze working must have been anciently carried on in the district. It would appear that nothing had been found in cutting away the upper six feet of the peat, except the trunks of different kinds of trees, all of which, with the exception of those of the oak and fir, were rotten, and some horns, which from their size (they were said to be large enough to have a circle of about three feet in diameter described on each palm), may have been those of the red deer. It was in the second cutting below six feet that the first objects were discovered in 1731. The depth at which the articles were found, their number and character, and the interesting relation established in the text by Professor O'Curry between this locality and the tribe of the *Cerdraighe*, invest the bog of Cullen with special interest.]

(391) [original:—Genelaċ Cerddraige Tuilċe Gossa, .i. Cerddraige anmnid, ar ba cerda caċ fer dib co mor sessiur. Moṫemnioc (.i Temnen) mac Carban, mac Lugeda mac Themen, mac Themnen mac Senaig,

XXIX.

this family of gold-smiths is thus brought down to circa A.D. 500;

According to genealogical computations, the years of these seven generations would be 210, to which if we add the years of *Oilioll Oluim* himself and his immediate son *Tighernach*, the father of *Cerdraighe*, the last of the seven generations of artists would come down to the year 474, or say in round numbers to the year 500. And so we find that the trade and art of gold manufacture if not of gold smelting and mining, was carried on in this district, probably in this very spot, during the long period of 221 years. It is a singular fact that there still exists, some five miles to the west of Cullen, but in the county of Limerick, a well-known townland bearing the name of *Baile na g-Ceard*, or the town of the goldsmiths. I am, however, with great regret obliged to acknowledge that I have not as yet been able to discover the exact situation of *Tulach Gossa*, the ancient patrimonial residence of the family.

the eldest branch became extinct in St. Mothemnioc, circa A.D. 530;

But although this, the eldest, line of the family became extinct in the person of St. *Mothemnioc*, say about the year 530, it is quite certain that the whole race had not become so, as may be collected from an ancient Gaedhelic tract in my possession. This curious tract contains a more detailed account than the "Book of Rights", quoted in a former lecture, of the services rendered to the king of Cashel by several of the chieftaincies of the province of Munster, as well as of the particular territories which by ancient custom and privilege, supplied his court with certain officers. Thus, his doctors were furnished him by the *Dail Mughaidhe* in Tipperary; his harpers by the *Corcoiche* in the county of Limerick; his *Cerds*, or gold and silversmiths, and his *Umhaidhe*, or bronze-workers, from the *Cerdraighe;* the steward of his milch-cows and dairies from the *Boinraighe;* his poets and scholars from the *Muscraighe* of Ormond; and so on.

and other branches existed at a much later period.

The mineral districts of Silvermines and Meanus not far from Cullen.

It is worth mentioning here, that the mineral district of Silvermines, in the county of Tipperary, is only about twelve or fifteen miles to the north of Cullen, and that the ancient mineral land of *Mianus*, now Meanus in the county of Limerick, is only about the same distance to the west of that town.

I cannot conceal the satisfaction I feel in being able to connect the discovery of gold in all conditions of smelting and manufacture in this place, with a race of workers in the same metal, resident on the very spot, or in some contiguous locality, whose ancestry, term of existence, and period of time, I have, I trust, established on such satisfactory grounds as will be deemed sufficient for all the purposes of general history.

mac Cerddain, mac Cerdabicce —H. 2. 18. fol. 222. b., lower corner.]
mac Thighernaig mac Ailella Oloim.

Of the other names of a covering or ornament for the head, which have come under my notice in my readings among our ancient manuscripts, I shall give only a very brief notice, setting them down in alphabetical order. These names are:—*At; Barr; Cathbarr; Cenn Barr; Cleitme;* and *Eo-Barr*. XXIX.

The At and Cleitme.

The *At* had the same signification as the present English word "hat". The old British name was the same as the Gaedhelic, and had the same declensional forms, and, in my opinion, was borrowed from it. This word *At* signifies simply an ornamental case or covering; and the authority for the application of the name to an ornamental covering, or hat, for the head is found in the ancient elegy pronounced by the poet *Ferceirtne* on his prince and patron *Curoi Mac Dairé*, the king of West Munster. The poet, in enumerating the many gifts received by him from the bountiful deceased prince, counts ten *Cleitmes;* and an ancient glossarist explains the *Cleitme* to have been a *Righbharr* or *At*, that is, a king's radiating helmet, or a hat. The word *Cleitme* is also explained in a maxim of the Brehon Laws in this way:—

"Lattice precedes crest", that is, says the ancient commentator, "I prefer that the lattice walls of the house be built before the *Cleitme* (or crest)" (392)

The Barr, Cennbarr, Eobar, and Righbarr.

The *Barr*, which enters into the compound words *Cennbarr*, *Eobarr*, and *Righbarr*, signifies, like the *Cleitme*, a radius or crest compounded with *cenn*, the head; *eo*, the top, and *righ*, a king. When compounded with *cath*, a battle, as in the word and name *Cathbarr*, it signifies properly a battle cap or battle helmet, and not a mere ornamental crest, appendage, cap, or hat.

The goldsmith was only an artizan;

Having now completed what I had to say about the personal ornaments of the people of ancient Erinn, it only remains to say a few words on their artificers. The *Cerd* or goldsmith was not included among the professors of the free and liberal arts in ancient Erinn, although he was entitled to some high privileges. He belonged to the *Daer Nemhidh*, or base professors, that is, the higher class of artizans, of which we have a list in the Brehon Laws. Among these were the *Saer* or carpenter, the *Gobha* or blacksmith, the *Umhaidhe* the bronze worker, and the *Cerd* or smith, who worked in the precious metals. These several professions were considered to be base, because they performed the duties of their professions with their hands or fists In connection with these higher artizans may also be mentioned the *Rinnaidhe*, or engraver, and the *Ersco-*

other artizans of the same class.

(392) [original:—Do fet cliath cleithe, .i. as remtectai lium cliat iċtair in tiġi do denam ar dus, anas cleitme a mullaiġ.—*Felire beg*, 21. 23. a. a.]

LECTURE XXX.

[Delivered 10th June, 1862.]

(IX.) Of Music and Musical Instruments in ancient Erinn. Antiquity of the harp in Erinn. The first musical instrument mentioned in Gaedhelic writings is the *Cruit*, or harp, of the *Daghda*, a chief and druid of the *Tuatha Dé Danann*; his curious invocation to his harp; the three musical feats played upon it; examination of the names of this harp; the word *Coir*, forming part of the name of the *Daghda's* harp, came down to modern times, as is shown by a poem of Keating on *Tadgh* O'Coffey, his harper. The *Daghda's* invocation to his harp further examined; the three musical modes compared to the three seasons of the year in ancient Egypt; myth of the discovery of the lyre; Dr. Burney on the three musical modes of the Greeks; the three Greek modes represented by the Irish three feats; conjectural completion of the text of the *Daghda's* invocation; what were the bellies and pipes of the *Daghda's* harp; ancient painting of a lyre at Portici, with a pipe or flute for cross-bar, mentioned by Dr. Burney. Legend of the origin of the three feats, or modes of harp playing, from the *Táin Bo Fraich*; meaning of the name *Uaithne* in this legend. No mention of strings in the account of the *Daghda's* harp, but they are mentioned in the tale of the *Táin Bo Fraich*. Legend of *Find Mac Cumhaill; Scathach* and her magical harp; *Scathach's* harp had three strings; no mention of music having been played at either of the battles of the northern or southern *Magh Tuireadh*; this proves the antiquity of those accounts. The *Daghda's* harp was quadrangular; a Greek harp of the same form represented in the hand of a Grecian Apollo at Rome; example of Irish quadrangular harp on *theca* of an ancient missal. Dr. Ferguson on the antiquity and origin of music in Erinn; musical canon of the Welsh regulated by Irish harpers about A.D. 1100; his account of the *theca* above mentioned, and of figures of the harp from ancient Irish monumental crosses which resembled the old Egyptian one; he thinks this resemblance supports the Irish traditions; Irish MSS. little studied twenty years ago, but since then they have been; from this examination the author thinks the *Firbolgs* and *Tuatha Dé Danann* had nothing to do with Egypt, but that the Milesians had. Migration of the *Tuatha Dé Danann* from Greece; the author does not believe they went into Scandinavia; he believes their cities of *Falias, Gorias*, etc., were in Germany; they spoke German according to the Book of *Lecan*. The similarity of the harps on the monument of Orpheus at Petau in Styria and on the *theca* of the Stowe MS. may point to Murrhart as the *Murias* of the *Tuatha Dé Danann*.

Antiquity of the harp in Erinn.

The early cultivation of music and melody, and a special respect for the professors of the art, bespeak a peculiar civilization which implies no small degree of refinement of habit and of taste in a people. If there ever was a people gifted with a musical soul and sensibility in a higher degree than another, I would venture to assert that the Gaedhil of ancient Erinn were that people.

In no country in Europe, at least I believe so, is the antiquity and influence of the harp thrown so far back into the darker regions of history as in Erinn. Our traditions are more distinct than those of the Greeks; for, they give time and place, name and occasion. Ours is not the shadowy myth of Orpheus going to the realms of Pluto, and by his lyre softening the obdurate heart of the grim monarch of the infernal abodes. It possesses something much more of real life, and belongs more to definite history. It is, indeed, a remote tradition; but, it is identified with a people and with persons whose history, though obscure and exaggerated, is still embodied in our oldest chronicles, and has never departed from the memories of our living romances and popular traditions. And, from the very remotest period to which our oldest traditions with any degree of circumstantiality refer, we find music, musical instruments, musical performers, and the power and influence of music, spoken of.

The first musical instrument referred to in Gaedhelic writings

The first musical instrument to which we have any reference in our Gaedhelic writings, is the *Cruit*, or harp; and this reference is found in the history of that mysterious people called the *Tuatha Dé Danann*, of whom so much has been said in the course of these lectures. The reference to which I allude is found in the ancient detailed account of the battle of the second, or northern *Magh Tuireadh*, described in a former lecture; a battle which was gained by the *Tuatha Dé Danann* against those early piratical visitors of our shores, commonly called the Fomorians. This battle was fought, according to the "Annals of the Four Masters", in the year of the world 3330, or about eighteen hundred years before the Incarnation; and it was fought at *Magh Tuireadh*, a place still well known, situated in the parish of *Cill Mhic Trena*, barony of Tirerill (*Tir Oiliolla*), and county of Sligo.[395]

The Fomorians having been defeated with great slaughter, such of them as were still able, retreated from the field, under their surviving leader *Breas*, who had been captured, but obtained his liberty by a stratagem. The story proceeds in these words:—

is the *Cruit*, or harp, of the *Daghda*, a chief of the *Tuatha Dé Danann*;

"*Lugh* [the *Tuatha Dé Danann* king] and the *Daghda* [their great chief and druid] and *Ogma* [their bravest champion] followed the Fomorians, because they had carried off the *Daghda's* harper, *Uaithne* was his name. They [the pursuers] soon reached the banqueting house in which they [the Fomorian chiefs] *Breas*, the son of *Elathan*, and *Elathan*, the son of *Delbath*, were and where they found the harp hanging upon the wall. This was the harp in which the music was spell-bound, so that it would not answer when called forth, until the *Daghda* evoked it, when he said what follows here down:

(395) See about this battle, Lect. xii., *ante*, vol. i. p. 243.

XXX.

his invocation to his harp;

"'Come *Durdabla;* come *Cóircethairchuir;* come *Samh;* come *Gamh*' [that is, come summer, come winter] from the mouths of harps, and bellies and pipes. Two names now had the harp; namely, *Durdabla*, and *Cóircethairchuir.* The harp came forth from the wall then, and killed nine persons [in its passage]; and it came to the *Daghda;* and he played for them the three [musical] feats which give distinction to a harper, namely, the *Suantraighe* [which from its deep murmuring caused sleep]; the *Gentraighe* [which from its merriment caused laughter]; and the *Goltraighe* [which from its melting plaintiveness caused crying]. He played them the *Goltraighe* until their women cried tears. He played them the *Gentraighe* until their women and youths burst into laughter. He played them the *Suantraighe* until the entire host fell asleep. It was through that sleep they [the three champions] escaped from those [the Fomorians] who were desirous to kill them'".[299]

the three musical feats played upon it.

Examination of the names of the harp;

I must confess that these names applied to the harp of the great *Daghda*, and the musical sounds which he evoked from it —evidently descriptive names, as they are—are among the most unmanageable phrases I have ever met. The first name applied here to the harp, *Durdabla*, can, by taking its component parts at their ordinary value, be analysed in this way: *Durd*, or *dord*, a murmur, and *abla*, the possessive case of *aball*, a sweet apple tree. The second name, *Coircethaircuir*, can be analysed in the same way: *Coir*, signifies arrangement, adjustment, and *cethairchuir*, compounded of *cethair*, four, and *cor*, an angle, or rather a beak like the beak of an anvil, signifies quadrubeaked, or quadrangular; so that the second name would simply signify the quadrubeaked or quadrangular harmonious instrument.

the word Coir came down to modern times, as shown by a poem of Keating.

The word *Cóir*, as applied to the proper tuning or harmonizing of a harp, or any musical instrument, came down to my own early days; and we have a good instance of its ap-

(299) [original:—Loucur a ndiaid na Fomorach dno Lug acas an Dagdou agas Ogma ar cruitire [an Dagda ronucsad leo, Uaitniu a ainm.] Rosagad iarum a flecteċ amboi Bres mac Elaċan, acas Elaċan mac Delbaiṫ, isann boi in croc for in fraigid. Iss incruitsin ar a nenaisc na ceola connarofogradsetor tria gairm conuegart in Dagda in tan atbert annso sis. Tair Daurdablao, tair Coircetharċuirr, tair Sam, tair Gam (tair imbolc a) a beola croc acas bolg acus buinne. Dá nainm dno batar for an cruitsin, .i. Durdabla acas coircethairċuir. Dolluid an croc assan fraigid, acas marbad .ix. mar; acas tanuicc doċum an Dagda; acas seinnsé (?) a trédai for animichir cruitiri doib, .i. Súantraiġi acas genntraiġi, acas golltraiġi. Serainn golltraiġi doib congolsad amna dearáċa. Serainn genntraiġi doib contibsiot amna acas a macraith. Serainn Suantraiġi doib contuilsed an tsluaid. Is dered dierlatar ectriur slan uaidib cia ma dail a ngoin.—Battle of *Magh Tuireadh*, Harleian MSS. 5280, Brit. Mus. f. 59. a. last line.]

plication in the beautiful verses of the Rev. Doctor Geoffrey Keating, the historian, on his harper *Tadhg O'Cobthaigh*, or O'Coffey. In this poem he commences by asking, who is it that plays the enchanting music that dispels all the ills that man is heir to; and he goes on to enumerate several of the celebrated musicians of ancient Erinn, for any of whom he might be mistaken; he then answers himself in the fifth and sixth stanzas of the poem, which are as follow:—

"It is not any one that I have here named,
Of the necromantic *Tuatha Dé Danann;*
Nor of any race from these hither,
That has struck the *Cóir* of the harp.
"*Tadhg O'Cobthaigh* of beauteous form,—
The chief beguiler of women,
The intelligent concordance of all difficult tunes,
The thrill of music and of harmony".[297]

The term *Cóir*, for tune, or being in tune, and *Cornghadh*, for putting in tune or order, appears to apply more properly to a wind instrument, as may be seen from "O'Davoren's Ancient Irish Glossary", at the word—*Indell*,—to set or put in order, where he applies the word *Glés* to the tuning of the *Cruit* or harp; and the word *Corúighther*, to the tuning of the *Cuisleanna*, or pipes.[298]

But, to return to the account of the harp of the *Daghda*.

The *Daghda's* invocation to his harp further examined.

The two first names seem to symbolize the distinctive qualities, and the mechanical formation of his wonderful harp; but, in the remaining words of the address, he seems to invoke it in its varied musical character, when he says:—"Come summer, come winter [from] the mouths of harps and bags and pipes". It is difficult to understand these figurative invocations; but the difficulty of attempting an explanation of them is greatly increased by the circumstance that there seems to be a defect in this copy of the tract, the only one known to me; for something is left out between the word "winter", and the words—"mouths of harps and bags and pipes". It naturally occurs to ask—why it is, that the three seasons into which the year was formerly divided are not mentioned?—why it is the summer and the winter only, leaving out the spring? When first I saw

(297) [original:—
Ní haoin neach d'ar áirmheas ann,
Do Thuathaibh doilfe Dé Danann;
Na d'fóir o'n am sain ile it,
A d'aimsig cóir na cruite.
* * * * *
Tadhg ó Cobhthaigh cruth chorcra,—
Brannán bréagtha banntrochta,
Uaithne iúil fritir gach fuinn,
Critir an chiúil 'san choicedail.
—MSS. Egerton, 111, Brit. Mus., p. 282, col. 2.]

(298) [original:—Indell. .i. glés, ut est, indell crot, cuislennaig ced .i. gléasaigther na crota, acas coraigther na Cuislenna.]

XXX. this passage, it occurred to me that there were two seasons left out by some mistake, the spring and the autumn; but then, this number would not agree with the three musical feats, which, it is stated, gave the dignity of *Ollamh*, or doctor in music, to the professor of the harp. I found, however, that there was a very ancient authority for the three seasons of the year only being indicated or represented by three musical feats, corresponding to the Greek Modes. It is referred to in "Burney's General History of Music".

The three musical modes compared to three seasons of the year in ancient Egypt;

In speaking of a celebrated benefactor of the ancient Egyptians, Dr. Burney says that, "He was the first who out of the coarse and rude dialects of his time formed a regular language, and appellatives to the most useful things; he likewise invented the first characters or letters, and even regulated the harmony of words and phrases; he instituted several rites and ceremonies relative to the worship of the gods, and communicated to mankind the first principles of astronomy. He afterwards suggested to them, as amusements, wrestling and dancing, and invented the lyre, to which he gave three strings, in allusion to the seasons of the year: for these three strings, producing three different sounds—the grave, the mean, and the acute, the grave answered to winter, the mean to spring, and the acute to summer.

myth of the discovery of the lyre;

"Among the various opinions", continues Dr. Burney, "of the several ancient writers who have mentioned this circumstance, and confined the invention to the Egyptian Mercury, that of Apollodorus is the most intelligible and probable:—'The Nile', says this writer, 'after having overflowed the whole country of Egypt, when it returned within its natural bounds, left on the shore a great number of dead animals of various kinds, and among the rest a tortoise, the flesh of which being dried and wasted by the sun, nothing was left within the shell but nerves and cartilages, and these being braced and contracted by desiccation, were rendered sonorous. Mercury, in walking along the banks of the Nile, happening to strike his foot against the shell of this tortoise, was so pleased with the sound it produced, that it suggested to him the first idea of a lyre, which he afterwards constructed in the form of a tortoise, and strung it with dried sinews of dead animals'".[299]

Dr. Burney on the three musical modes of the Greeks;

Dr. Burney has the following observations also[300] upon what he calls the three musical modes, which may, I think, be regarded as explanatory of the three feats of music among the Gaedhil:—

(299) Burney's *General History of Music*, vol. i., p. 199.
(300) *Ibid.*, p. 194.

"Herodotus, in tracing the genealogy of the Dorians, one of the most ancient people of Greece, makes them natives of Egypt, and as the three musical modes of highest antiquity among the Greeks, are the Dorian, Phrygian, and Lydian, it is likely that the Egyptian colony which peopled the Dorian province, brought with them the music and instruments of their native country". XXX.

I have introduced these quotations here from Dr. Burney's work, with the view of showing the probability that our three ancient musical feats of sleeping, laughing, and crying, are represented, after the Egyptian or Greek manner, by the grave, the mean, and the acute; or winter, spring, and summer. And that, if so, there is one of them, the spring (*Errach* or *Imbolc*), left out in our copy of the *Daghda*'s invocation of his harp. It is very evident indeed, that there is a defect here, because the preposition *a*, from, is absent between *Gamh*, or winter; and the words *beóla Crot*, *acas Bolg*, *acas Buinne*—that is, mouths of harps and bags and pipes, which immediately follow, and the precise connection of which, on account of this defect, cannot be insisted upon. the three Greek modes represented by the Irish three feats;

If, then, this opinion be correct, the *Daghda*'s invocation would run in this way: come, *Durdabla;* come, *Cóircethairchuir;* come, *Samh* (that is, summer); come, *Gamh* (that is, winter); come, *Imbolc* (that is, spring), from the mouths of harps and bags and pipes: and another fact comes here in aid of this reading; for that the ancient Irish, at some remote period, did divide the year into the three seasons of *Samh*, summer, *Gamh*, winter, and *Imbolc*, spring (omitting the *Foghmhar*, or autumn), is quite evident from the fact, that *Cormac Mac Cuileannain* and the other old glossarists, explain *Samhain*, or November eve, by *Samh*, summer, and *fuin*, the end; that is, the end of *Samh*, or summer. That the year was also divided into four seasons at one time, and into but two at another time, will be seen from a chapter "On the Division of the Year among the ancient Irish", printed in the Introduction to the "Book of Rights" (p. xlviii.), published by the Celtic Society in 1847. conjectural completion of the text of *Daghda*'s invocation.

Another difficulty presents itself in this extraordinary address of the *Daghda* to his harp. What were the bellies or bags (for the word *bolg*, in the original means either), and the pipes from which he calls forth the mysterious music? It is clear from the context, that there was but the one instrument present, the *Daghda*'s own harp; and it must therefore follow that these were parts of it, each contributing its share to the production of the music. We can easily understand the belly to mean the sound-board or box; but then, what was the pipe? What were the bellies and pipes of the *Daghda*'s harp?

XXX. I must express my inability to answer this question. There is, however, a passage in Dr. Burney's work which is worth mentioning in connection with it, though it contains only a hint of what might possibly account for the mention of the pipe or tube alluded to by the *Daghda*.

Ancient painting of a lyre, with a flute for the bridge.

"In one of the ancient paintings at Portici", says Dr. Burney, "I saw a lyre with a pipe or flute for the cross-bar or bridge at the top; whether this tube was used as a wind instrument to accompany the lyre, or only a pitch-pipe, I know not; nor within the course of my inquiries has any example of such a junction occurred elsewhere".[304]

This is indeed a very loose account for our purpose; one that suggests nothing more than a vague hint: for we cannot learn from it anything of the precise form of the harp, or of the age and circumstances of the painting which Dr. Burney says he saw, nor to what period of antiquity his words "ancient paintings" might be referred. It would, however, be truly a remarkable fact in relation to our present inquiry, if there be still extant an ancient classic painting of a harp suggesting so curious an explanation (as far as we can understand it) of our most ancient account of the *Daghda's* harp, as regards the union of the tube with that instrument, whatever the particular use of that tube might have been. It seems to me evident indeed, as I have already said, from the *Daghda's* calling forth the music of summer, winter, and spring, from the mouths of *Cruit*, belly, and tube, that the latter did really contribute its own share to the sounds of the instrument: and hence, the very obscure words of our ancient text would receive some explanation, or at least some remarkable corroboration, if we are to depend upon the singular account of Dr. Burney.

Legend of the origin of the three feats or modes of harp-playing from the *Táin Bo Fraich*.

Let me, however, return to the subject of the three feats of harp-music, to which I have suggested an analogy in the three Greek modes. Concerning the origin of these three feats, there is extant a very ancient and singularly wild legend. The story forms one of the preludes to the *Táin Bo Chuailgne*, and is preserved under the name of *Táin Bo Fraich*, or the plunder of *Fraech's* cows. Of this *Fraech* I had occasion to speak in a former lecture, when describing some of the houses which formed part of the ancient palace of *Cruachan*, in Connacht,[305] but I shall have to introduce him here again.

Fraech was the son of *Fidhadh*, and a chieftain of West Connacht. His mother's name was *Bebinn*) a name which literally signifies the melodious woman), one of the *Tuatha Dé Danann*, and sister to that lady *Boand* from whom the river

(304) *Ubi supra*, vol. i., p. 493. (305) See Lect. xix., *ante*, vol. ii., p. 10.

Boyne (*Boind*) derives its name. This young chief, we are told, confident in the splendour of his retinue and in his own beauty of figure, proposed to himself to solicit the hand in marriage of no less celebrated a beauty than the princess *Findabar* (or "the fair-browed"), the daughter of *Ailill* and *Medb*, the king and queen of Connacht; and being sumptuously supplied with an outfit and attendance from the rich resources of *Tuath Dé Danann* wealth, by his aunt the lady *Boand*, he set out for the palace of *Cruachan* without any announcement of his intended visit. The description of his accoutrements is so rich that I am tempted to give it entire.

XXX. Legend of the origin of the three feats or modes of harp-playing from the *Táin Bo Fraich*.

The story proceeds to tell us that:—"He went southwards to his mother's sister, that is to *Boand*, in the plain of *Bregia;* and she gave him fifty black-blue cloaks, whose colour was like the backs of cockchafers, each cloak had four blue ears [or lappets]; and a brooch of red gold to each cloak She gave him besides fifty splendid white shirts with fastenings of gold; and fifty shields of silver with borders of gold. She gave him a great hard spear, flaming like the candle of a royal house, to place in the hand of each man of his party, and fifty rings of burnished gold upon each spear, all of them set off with carbuncles, and their handles studded with precious stones. They would light up the plain the same as the glittering light of the sun. And she gave him fifty gold-hilted swords, and fifty soft-gray steeds, on which his men sat; all with bridle-bits of gold, with a crescent of gold and bells of silver on the neck of each steed of them. And they had fifty crimson saddles, with pendants of silver thread, and with buckles of gold and silver, and with wonderful fastenings upon them (the steeds); and their riders had fifty horse-switches of *Findruine*, with a crook of gold upon the head of each horse-switch, in their hands; and they had besides, seven grayhounds in chains of silver, and a ball of gold upon (the chain) between each pair of them. They wore shoes of red bronze (*Cred-Uma*); and there was no colour which approached them that they did not reflect it. They had seven trumpeters among them, with trumpets of gold and silver, wearing many coloured raiments. Their hair was light golden; and they had splendid white shirts upon them. There were three buffoons preceding the party with silver-gilt coronets upon their heads, and each carried a shield with emblematic carvings upon it; and crested heads, and ribs of red bronze in the centres of these shields; and there were three harpers, each with the appearance of a king, both as to his dress, and his arms, and his steed".[303]

(303) [original:—Luid iarom fodes co siar a mathar edon (co Boind) co

XXX. Legend of the origin of the three feats or modes of harp-playing from the *Táin Bo Fraich.*

Having arrived at *Cruachan*, the party were hospitably received, and entertained for several days. One day after dinner, king *Ailill* spoke to *Fraech*, and requested that the harps should be played for them; and the story then tells us that:—

"This was the condition of these [harps]. There were harp-bags of the skins of otters about them, ornamented with coral, (*Partaing*) with an ornamentation of gold and of silver over that, lined inside with snow-white roebuck skins; and these again overlaid with black-gray strips [of skin]; and linen cloths, as white as the swan's coat, wrapped around the strings. Harps of gold, and silver, and *Findruine*, with figures of serpents, and birds, and grayhounds upon them. These figures were made of gold and of silver. Accordingly as the strings vibrated [these figures] ran around the men. They [the harpers] played for them then, until twelve men of *Ailill*'s and *Medb*'s household died of crying and emotion. Three comely men indeed were these [harpers], and sweet was the music which they played And they were the three sons of *Uaithne* [the harper] that were there. These were, indeed the three illustrious men so much spoken of, namely—*Goltraighe*, and *Suantraighe*, and *Gentraighe* [that is literally—crying music, sleeping music, and laughing music]. These three now were three brothers. *Boand* from the hills was the mother of the three. And it was this kind of music that *Uaithne* [their father] played upon the *Daghda*'s harp; and, it was from it the three [sons] were named. At the time that the woman [their mother] was in labour, it was then he [the husband] played the harp. When then the woman

imbai i Maig Breg; acas adbert dno, caeca brat n-dubgorm, acas ba cosmail a dath fri druimm n-daili, cethora dai dubglasa for cach brat; acas milech dergoir la cach m-brat. Caeca lena bangel co tuaidmilaib oir impu; acas caeca sciath airgdidi commlib oir impu. Oen gai cruadach mor i soillsithir rig caindell rigtaigi i laim cach fir dib; caeca coracht di or orlaiscthi im gach n-gai, eirmitiuda do charrmocol sodaib ainis uili, acas is do lecaib logmaraib indentai [anair iarn] a n-urdairn,—no lassair in faidbi amail ruithnib grene; acas caeca claideb n-ordurnd leo, acas caeca gabor m-bocglas fo suide; acas pellce [beilge] oir fri uili acas muillind [maellaind argait co cluicini oir] oir co cluicinu for bragaid cach ech dib, acas caeca srand [srian] corcra co snaithib argaid estib, acas co siblanaib oir acas argaid, acas co cendmilaib ingantaib foraib impu; acas caeca echlasc findruine co m-baccan orda for cind caca hechlaisci ina lamaib; acas secht milchoin i slabradaib airgid, acas ubull oir for cach [itir cech nae] slabrad dib. Brocca credumae umpu; acas ni raibi dath nad beith intib. Secht cornaire leo co cornaib ordaib acas airgdidib, co netaigib illdathacha umpu; co mongaib ordaib findbuidi foraib, co lentib etrochtaib umpu. Batar tri druith remib co mindaib [airgid] fordiór for a cendaib; sceith co sechlaib condualacha for cach nae; acas co cirbachlaib impu, acas co nesnadaib credumae iar na las [taebaib] ina sciach badar foraib. Triar cruitire co n-egosc rig im cach n-ai itir etaigib, acas armu, acas echu.—H. 2. 16. col. 649.]

XXX.
Legend of the origin of the three feats or modes of harp-playing from the *Táin Bo Fraich*.

was in her labour, it was crying and mourning with her in the intensity of her pains at the beginning. It was laughing and joy with her in the middle of them, at the pleasure of having brought forth two sons. It was repose and tranquillity with her on the birth of the last son after the weight of the labour; and it was on that account that each of them was named after a third part of the music. *Boand* then awoke from the repose. 'Accept thou thy three sons, O passionate *Uaithne*', said she, 'in return for thy generosity; namely, crying music (*Goltraighe*); and laughing music (*Geantraighe*); and sleeping music (*Suantraighe*); for men will [hereafter] die of hearing their ear-tuning if they go to play for *Medb* and *Ailill* [that is, when attuning their harps to their own ears]'".

"These sons", the story continues, "were afterwards nursed until they were men, and they it was whom *Fraech* took with him on his visit to court the princess *Findabar*, so that they played music at the desire of *Ailill*."[304]

This passage is, as I have said, from one of the most ancient of the historic tales; and I suppose I need hardly observe that it is by no means to be taken literally. It is, in fact, but an early form of one of our most ancient myths or legends, accounting for the lost history of the invention of music, or its introduction into the country; and, while on the one hand the words here used as proper names, are really words descriptive of the various kinds of music in which the most

(304) [original:—Is amlaid do badar side ono. Crotbuilcc do croicenn dobarcon umpu, cona n-imdenam do parṫaing, imdenam dior acas d'airged fairrside anuas, bian n-erb din impu ar-medon; sdialla dubglasa ima medonside; acas bruit lin giliter suan n-geissi imna teta. Crota di ór acas airged acas findruine, co n-delbaib n-athraċ, acas én acas milċon forraib. Di ór acas airged na delba sin; amail nogloisois na teda imrethidis im na firu imacuairt na dealba sin. Sendid daib iaram co n-ardatar da ḟer dec do muintir Aililla, acas Medba lacae acas toirsi. Ba cain tra in triarsa, acas ba bind an ceol do ronsad; acas ḃadar h-etri meic h-Uithni annsin. Iriad tra so in triar airdiric asberar, edon Goltraigi, acas Gentraigi, acas Suantraigi. Tri derbrathair tra in triar sai befind [Boind] a sidaib a maṫair atruar. Acas is din cheneolsa seḟaind Uaithni cruit in Dagdái; acas is de ainmnigther a triur. In tan robai an ben oc lamnad is and ro sendsem in ċruit. Ora bai iaram inbean oclomnad ba gol acas mairglee la guire na n-idan itosaċ. Ba gen acas gairi acas failte ar medon, edon ar imtholtain inda mac do breith. Ba suan acas ailgine ara breitċe in mac deidinach, edan ar truime na breithi; conad airi ro hainmniged triar [trian] in chiuil dib. Do dusaig iarum inboand as an suan. Arfuim firu olsi do tri meic a Uaithni arfoimsin olsi do ṫri maccu a Uaithni lan brota fo bith fele [file], edon Golltraigi, acas Geantraigi, acas Suantraigi, ar feraib sceo mnaib da tacdsad la Medb acas ailill adbelad fir la cluas ṅ-gléra doib. Ailter ina meic seo tra iarsuidiu, comdar mora, acas condait e tuc Fraech lais do tocmorc Findabrac. corabadar ocun senm la brethi n Aililla.—H. 2. 16. col. 650.]

XXX. ancient of musicians were practised, the very form of the myth itself proves how very ancient—how far before the farthest back commencement of the historic period, must have been the cultivation of an already regularly developed music in Erinn, at least among that superior race which preceded the Milesian colony.

Meaning of the name *Uaithne*.

The word *Uaithne*, the name given as that of the *Daghda's* harper, and father of the three musical sons, has three different significations in the ancient *Gaedhelic* language, namely, a post, or pillar, female parturition, and concord or harmony in poetry or music; so that, if the name be symbolical at all, it must be in the last sense.

It may be proper to pause here for a moment, and inquire what was the actual mechanical agency by which these three mechanical feats, or modes, or their wonderful effects, were produced.

No mention of strings in the *Daghda's* harp; but they are mentioned in the *Táin Bo Fraich*.

It may be remembered that in this allusion to the *Daghda's* own harp, the *Durd-abla*, there is no mention of any number of strings, or of strings at all, whilst in the description of the harps of the three sons of *Uaithne* in the palace of *Cruachan*, there is a clear reference to the strings, which not only produced the music, but also by their vibrations set the serpents, birds, and grayhounds, with which the harps were adorned, in motion. Here, however, there is no allusion to the number of the strings, and we are therefore still at a loss on that head.

The following curious story, taken from the old tract so often mentioned in the course of these lectures, called *Agallamh na Seanorach*, or the Dialogue of the Old Men, and which recounts a great many of the achievements and adventures of the celebrated champion, *Find Mac Cumhaill*, seems to show that the earliest harp was a three stringed instrument.

Legend of *Find Mac Cumhaill*, *Scathach* and her magical harp;

One day, we are told, that *Find* was hunting in that part of Erinn which is now known as the county of Donegal, attended by only eight chosen companions from among his warriors. Having sat down to take rest on the well-known mountain of *Bearnas Mór*, his party started a huge wild boar, and sent their dogs after him; but the boar killed them all except *Bran*, *Find's* own celebrated hound, which conquered and captured him. The boar, on being captured, screamed loudly and violently, whereupon a man of giant size came forth as it were from the hill, and requested of *Find* that his hog should be set at liberty. The eight men attacked him, but he soon vanquished, and bound them in tight bonds. He then invited *Find* to his *Sidh*, or enchanted mansion at *Glenndeirgdeis*, an

XXX.

Legend of *Find Mac Cumhaill*, *Scathach* and her magical harp;

invitation which *Find* and his friends gladly accepted. When they came to the door of the mansion, the giant struck the boar with his magical wand, and turned him into a young woman of great beauty. He then struck himself with the same wand, and restored himself to his natural size and beauty. The whole party then entered the mansion, where they were hospitably received, and sat down to a feast which had been specially prepared for them, presided over by the host's beautiful daughter, whose name was *Scathach*, or "the shadowy". *Find* fell in love with this fair damsel, and asked her from her father in marriage. Her father, of course, assented; and the champion and the fairy lady were forthwith united on the spot. Feasting and music continued until the hour of rest had arrived, when *Find* retired to the apartment assigned him, expecting to be soon followed by his bride.

So far the story. The following passage from the original poem, in which the whole is told, appears to me to support the idea of a three-stringed harp; and I translate it in full because in it such an instrument is described, possessing all the same wonderful gifts that distinguished the *Daghda*'s own harp:[(386)]

"The noble bed is prepared;
 Find is the first to approach it;
 Scathach asked before retiring,
 The loan of the musician's harp.
"The household harp was one of three strings,
 Methinks it was a pleasant jewel:
 A string of iron, a string of noble bronze,
 And a string of entire silver.
"The names of the not heavy strings
 Were *Suantorrglés; Geantorrglés* the great;
 Goltarrglés was the other string,
 Which sends all men to crying.
"If the pure *Goilteargl*és be played
 For the heavy hosts of the earth,
 The hosts of the world without delay
 Would all be sent to constant crying.
"If the merry *Gentorrglés* be played
 For the hosts of the earth, without heavy execution,

(386) [original:—

Orgaiċear an iomḋa ann,
 Toirċa Fionn ina coṁḋáil;
 Iar Sgaṫaċ ruil do luiġ,
 Iasaċt Cruite in airrfidiḋ.
Crut baoi isteiġ ar ṫri téad,
 Dar liom pa suléarr in séud:
 Téad iarainn, téad duṁa an,
 An teadna darccod iomlán.

Anmonn na ttéud nar ṫrom
 Suantoirrglés; geantoirrglés oll;
 Golltarrglés an téud oile,
 Chuirrear các ar ċiaṁoire.
Da sinntear an goilltearglés glan,
 Do ṡluaġaiḃ troma an talṁuin,
 Sloiġ an doṁuin gan dolba
 Do beiṫ uile acc bioṫ ḋogra.

XXX.

They would all be laughing from it,
From the hour of the one day to the same of the next.
"If the free *Suantorrglés* were played
To the hosts of the wide universe,
The men of the world,—great the wonder,—
Would fall into a long sleep.
"The gifted maiden plays
The slow sonorous *Suantorrglés*,
Until his heavy repose fell
Upon the son of *Muirin* [*Find*] the highly gifted.
"To deep sleep, above all others, she sent
Bran, and the eight warriors,—
Until the middle of the following day
They continued in their deep sleep.
"When the sun had arisen over the woods,
To them it was no mighty loss;
Where they found themselves was at *Bearnas*,
Which showed their diminished power".

The date of this curious poem cannot be fixed with any precision, but, in its present condition, it may be very fairly ascribed to the early part of the twelfth century, though I am satisfied that it is many centuries older. The question of age of the composition itself, however, is of very little moment to us, since it is with the very curious tradition preserved in it our concern lies; and the later the poem, the more curious would the existence of this clearly very remote tradition be. According to it, the fabled *Cruit* of the magical mansion of *Glenn-deirgdeis* had three strings; whilst the additional information that of these strings one was of iron, another of bronze, and the third of silver, shows that all these materials were used for different harp strings before the time of the writer; while, even if his reference to them be taken as the work of the poet's fancy, they may also be regarded as intended to represent the grave, the middle, and the acute musical modes already spoken of.

Scathach's harp had three strings.

Farther on in this, and in the lecture that shall next follow

Da seinntiċċe an ġeantorrġlés ġáḋ
  Do ṡlúaġ an talmuin ġan trom ár,
  Do beidis acc gáirfeḋe,
  On traċ raċṁor go roile.
Da seinntiċċe an ṡúantorrġlessáor
  Do ṡluaġuiḃ beaṫa na mbraon,
  Fir ḋomuin,—mór an moḋ,—
  Do beittis na ríor ċoḋlaḋ.
Seinnis an inġean faṫaċ
  An ṡuan tearġléas ríor ġnaṫaċ
  No gur ṫuit a toirrċimṡuam
  Ar mac Muirne go mór buaiḋ.
Cuirris na ccomṡúan tar ċáċ
  Bran,—isan toċtar óeclaċ,
  Go meaḋan laoi mor an moḋ
  Robádar na ccoḋlaḋ.
An uair do éirig grian orrioḋ,
  Dhoibriom níor baḋbal ancion;
  Ann robádor imbéarnuis,
  Ger luġa leo a ttiġernus.
—MS. No. $\frac{23}{\text{L. 22}}$ R.I.A., p. 420, bot.]

it, the existence of an ancient three-stringed harp, or *Timpan*, will receive much additional corroboration. XXX

No mention of music having been played at either of the battles of the two *Magh Tuireadhs*, and no allusion made to musicians in the account of them;

To return to the account of the *Daghda*'s harp in the story of the battle of the second, or northern *Magh Tuireadh;* that harp which its master called from the wall where it hung by the names *Durdabla*, and *Cóircethairchuir*, and in playing upon which he is described as evoking music from the mouths of harps, and bellies and pipes.

I have already endeavoured to show that the bellies and pipes, which he invokes, were component parts of the same harp; but, should I be mistaken, and that the tube alluded to was an independent instrument—in short a trumpet, then, indeed, it will appear very strange that with these references to the possession of music and martial musical instruments by the *Tuatha Dé Danann* at the time, there is nevertheless no mention whatever made of music of any kind having been played preparatory to, or in either of the battles of the two *Magh Tuireadhs;* and further, that *Lugh*, the great philosophical chief, who marshalled the *Tuatha Dé Danann* forces for the second battle, whilst he calls on the smith, the brazier, the carpenter, the hunters, the druids, the poets, etc., for their assistance in the coming battle (and, in doing so, is made to give an enumeration, apparently, of all classes about to be engaged in it), makes no mention whatever of any musician.

this proves their antiquity.

This is an important fact, and speaks much for the very great antiquity of the original accounts of these primitive battles of the Firbolgs, Fomorians, and *Tuatha Dé Danann;* for, certainly, if they had been historical romances of more modern times, full of the poetic embellishments of the *Táin Bo Chuailgne*, for example, and of other pieces even of this ancient class, there can be little doubt that in the enumeration of the professional parties mentioned by *Lugh*, the military performers on tubes and horns would have been included.[(306)]

As far, then, as we can ascertain with any degree of probability, the great *Daghda* invoked but the musical powers of his harp alone, excluding any idea of an independent musical tube, pipe, or trumpet; and, consequently, if there was a pipe at all, it formed part of that harp.

The *Daghda*'s harp was quadrangular;

I have already endeavoured to show from one of the names of the harp, that it was of a quadrubeaked or quadrangular

(306) I may also add here that I have not found any mention of music or of musical instruments among the Firbolgs in what has come down to us of their history; nor do I remember having met an instance of music having been played at any battle.

XXX. form; but it is curious, that, of the various forms of the harp and lyre taken from ancient Greek sculptures, and figured in the first volume of Dr. Burney's book, there is but one, No. 8, plate v., of precisely a quadrangular form; and this is a parallelogram with six strings, as represented in the hand of a Grecian Apollo, in the Capitoline Museum at Rome. This figure is an oblong square, with a sounding chamber, or belly, and somewhat resembles the high back of an old-fashioned chair. It is clumsy-looking in design, and apparently coarse in its mechanical details, considerably inferior to what we should be inclined to figure in our minds as consistent with the artistic skill of the *Tuatha Dé Danann*. These were themselves undoubtedly Greeks by education, if not by remote race, but they, or some others of our earliest colonists, have left in Erinn specimens of mechanical art in metals—the only material that could live to our times—which are not, I believe, excelled by anything of their kind that antiquarian researches have discovered in either Greece or Rome. It may be then that the *Tuatha Dé Danann* quadrangular harp, if not exactly the same, had been modelled, and, perhaps, improved upon the early Egypto-Grecian harp.

a Greek harp of same form on ancient sculptures

example of Irish quadrangular harp on *theca* of an ancient missal.

One curious example, at least, of the quadrangular harp of ancient Erinn is still extant in a carving on the shrine, or *theca*, of an ancient missal of the Irish Church, now unhappily, in the possession of Lord Ashburnham, in England. But, as the description of this figure, as well as other important points in the history of our ancient musical instruments, are so ably treated in a "Dissertation on the Antiquity of the Harp and Bagpipe in Ireland", written by my learned and accomplished friend, Samuel Ferguson, Esq., and published in Bunting's "Ancient Music of Ireland",[307] I shall quote the passage, in preference to anything I could myself say on the subject.

Mr. Ferguson on the antiquity and origin of music in Erinn;

Mr. Ferguson, after discussing the description of the music of Ireland written by Giraldus Cambrensis about the year 1180, continues his argument as follows:—

"Assuming, then, that the Irish, in the latter end of the twelfth century, possessed an instrument fit for the performance of such harp airs as were then known, with their appropriate basses, we come next to inquire how long had they possessed it. For, as Guido of Arezzo, the inventor, or at least revivor of counterpoint among the Italians, lived somewhat more than a century before that time, a suspicion reasonably arises, that they may have had their acquaintance with their improved style and method of playing from continental instruction. In answering the question proposed, and clearing away the preliminary objections, we

[307] Dublin, Hodges and Smith, 1840, p. 46.

draw our first assistance from the evidence of the Welsh. They, as is well known, had their musical canon regulated by Irish harpers about A.D. 1100. This they would hardly have submitted to had they not considered their instructors the greater proficients in the art; and yet the Welsh had before this time been noted for singing and performing in concert. But it may be objected by that numerous class, who would refer everything creditable among the ancient Irish to a Danish origin (confounding the Danes of the middle ages with the Tuath de Danans of tradition), that they were Danish-Irish to whom Griffith ap Conan referred for these instructions, namely, to Aulaf, king of Dublin, the son of Sitrick; and that, of the harpers sent by the Hiberno-Danish monarch, one only, Mathuloch Gwyddell, is mentioned as Irish, while the chief musician, Olar Gerdawwr, is manifestly one of the Ostmen. To this it may be answered, that there is no trace of northern phraseology in the Irish or Welsh musical nomenclature, but that, on the contrary, much, if not all, even of the Welsh vocabulary is pure Irish. Farther, that the harp, known from time immemorial to the Irish as *Cruit* and *Clairseach*, has never borne its Teutonic designation of *Hearpa* in any other of the languages of the united kingdom than the English; and finally, that these musical congresses, so far from being confined to the Danes of Dublin, were customary among the native Irish; for, not to dwell on similar assemblies at an earlier period, we find, that, at a meeting, identical in its character and objects, held before an Irish petty king, at Glendaloch, immediately after the one in question, the regulations of the Welsh synod were confirmed".[(308)]

XXX. musical canon of the Welsh regulated by Irish harpers about A.D. 1100;

"But, fortunately, the question rests on evidence of a more tangible nature than mere historical statement. Two monuments, one of the eleventh, and the other of a much earlier century, are now to be submitted, on which we have authentic contemporaneous delineations of the Irish harp executed by Irish artists.

Dr. Ferguson's account of the theca above mentioned;

"The first is the ornamental cover, or 'theca' of an Irish manuscript, containing, among other writings, a liturgy of the seventh century, now preserved at Stowe, in the library of the Duke of Buckingham, and elaborately described by Doctor Charles O'Conor in his catalogue of the MSS. of this magnificent collection.[(309)] The age of the ornamental cover is ascertained by the inscriptions remaining on it, from which it appears to have been made by Donnchadh *O'Tagan*, an artificer

(308) Welsh Archæology, vol. iii. p. 625.
(309) Vol. i., Appen. i.

XXX.

of the Irish monastery of Clonmacnoise, for *Donnchadh*, the son of Brian [*Boromha*], king of Ireland, and for Maccraith O'Donnchadh, king of Cashel, during the lifetimes and reign of the former, and, probably, during the lifetime of the latter also. But it is stated in the Annals of Tighearnach that Donnchadh was expelled from the sovereignty in the year 1064, and died the year after, and that *Maccraith*, king of Cashel, died in 1052. The 'theca' must therefore have been executed prior at least to the year 1064. Now, among the ornaments of this cover are five delineations of the harp of that period, containing, however, two pairs of duplicates, *fac similes* of which are given at the end of the second volume of O'Connor's '*Rerum Hibernicarum Scriptores Veteres*', whence the subjoined engravings have been accurately copied.

"The first, probably owing to the minuteness of the scale on which it is engraved on the silver plate of the *theca*, is unsatisfactory as to the shape of the instrument, which appears not of a triangular, but of a quadrangular form, and is represented with only two strings, the latter feature being, however, a manifest defect in the drawing. It is nevertheless valuable, as showing that the mode of holding and playing on the instrument had altered in nothing from the practice of the eleventh century, at the time when the MS. of Cambrensis, already alluded to, was illustrated.[310]

"The harps in the second ornament are represented on a large scale, but still not sufficiently so to enable the artist to show more than four or five strings on each. This piece of early Irish art, which combines embossing, enamelling, jeweling, and engraving, is thus described by Doctor O'Conor: 'Of the three central ornaments (*i.e.* of each marginal side) two are plates of silver; the third is the brazen image of a man dressed in a tunica, tightly fitted to his body, girdled round the waist, and reaching to the knees. The legs and feet are bare; the hands and arms are also bare, and are extended round two harps, which support the arms on either side. The heads of the harps resemble in shape a small *cornu ammonis* of blue enamelled glass, and in the breast of the figure a small square hole is filled with a garnet'.

ind of figures of harps rom ancient Irish monumental crosses resembling old Egyptian one;

"The instrument", Mr. Ferguson continues, "submitted to the reader from the other monument above referred to, is evidently of a much older date. The musical inquirer and general antiquary cannot fail to regard it with interest: *for it is the first specimen of a harp without a fore pillar that has hitherto been found out of Egypt;* and, but for the recent confirmation of

(310) The harp alluded to here is a triangular one. See "p 37 of the Introd."

Bruce's testimony with regard to its Egyptian prototype, might perhaps be received with equal incredulity; for, to the original difficulty of supposing such an instrument capable of supporting the tension of its strings, is now added the startling presumption that the Irish have had their harp originally out of Egypt. [The drawing follows here.] The drawing is taken from one of the ornamental compartments of a sculptured cross, at the old church of Ullard, in the county of Kilkenny. From the style of the workmanship, as well as from the worn condition of the cross, it seems older than the similar monument at Monasterboice, which is known to have been set up before the year 830. The sculpture is rude; the circular rim which binds the arms of the cross together is not pierced in the quadrants; and many of the figures originally represented in relievo are now wholly abraded. It is difficult to determine whether the number of strings represented is six or seven; but, as has been already remarked, accuracy in this respect cannot be expected either in sculptures or in many picturesque drawings. One hand only of the performer is shown, it probably being beyond the art of the sculptor to exhibit the other; and this, which is the right hand, is stretched, as in all the preceding examples, towards the longer strings of the instrument. The harp is also held on the knee as in the other instances; the only difference between the sculpture here and the first engraving on the *theca* of the Stowe MS., being, that the Ullard harp to all appearance has no front arm or pillar. In both cases the musician is naked; and yet both are associated with representations of churchmen and others in rich dresses; but it will be recollected that, in the hands of the figure in the ornamented tunic on the *theca*, there are represented harps of a perfect form; while that played by the naked musician in the adjoining compartment, is very rude in structure, and strongly resembles the Ullard instrument. Hence, we must by no means receive the latter as conclusive evidence that, at the time of its being sculptured, there was no other description of harp in use".

Mr. Ferguson continues further his learned discussion on the harp, and its progress to perfection, from its first fabulous invention by the Egyptian Mercury from the shell of a dead tortoise, as we have seen already, first the feeble bow or three-sided, to the four-sided, and from that to the triangular form. And from these circumstances the learned writer urges the probable truth of our ancient "bardic traditions" of the progress of the early colonists of Ireland from Egypt through Scythia; and he then continues as follows:— (he thinks this resemblance supports the Irish traditions.)

"There can be no question of the fact, that at a very early

XXX. period, a strong tide of civilization flowed into the east of Europe from the Nile, and thence spread northward and westward; and there are many grounds, extrinsic to this inquiry, on which it appears that a strong argument may be raised for intimate international relations between the original inhabitants of these islands and the ancient occupants of the east of Europe. If the various points of resemblance and even industry, on which such an argument might be rested, were advanced, it would probably appear something more than a coincidence, that in a monument erected at Petau, in Styria, during the lifetime of the emperor Aurelius, the Thracian Orpheus should be represented performing on an instrument in all respects resembling that on the *theca* of the Stowe MS.,[(311)] being in fact, what has just been surmised to be the Egyptian harp in a transition state, after it had received its forearm, and before it had acquired its perfect triangular form by the incorporation of the sounding chamber with the other upright" [here the figure is introduced].

It may be thought that I have quoted too copiously from Mr. Ferguson's essay; and that his arguments may have little to do with the bare accumulation of facts practically recorded, as they stand in our ancient chronicles, which was all that I ever proposed to myself here to make. But, although much of what he states in the able paper from which I quote has been known to us through other channels, yet I feel it due to him, as well as to my desire to strengthen my own opinions by the coincidence of his, to select his work especially for reference in this place.

Irish MSS. little studied twenty years ago, but since then they have been;

Even so recently as twenty years ago, when Dr. Petrie wrote his essay on the harp, improperly called *Brian Boromha's* harp, now in the museum of Trinity College, Dublin, the magnificent remains of ancient historical writings in our native tongue had been but little studied or examined. And those who did pretend to examine them never could find in them any thing that was of real value to true historical and antiquarian investigation. Within that time, however, these venerable records have undergone considerable examination; close readings have suggested and sustained new views and ideas, confirmed some old traditionary assertions, and are now opening up the true paths by which alone we can hope to become thoroughly acquainted with the origin, history, and vestiges of the people whose history our records profess to be.

I cannot, however, consistently with what I have read in these our ancient records, assent to the idea that the more pri-

(311) *Montfaucon*, vi. p. 252.

mitive colonists of Erinn, such as the Firbolgs and *Tuatha Dé Danann*, came indirectly from, or had any connection whatever with, the land of Egypt. The Milesians, I believe, had; but I am not at present concerned with that famous colony.

from this examination the author thinks the *Firbolgs* and *Tuatha Dé Danann* had nothing to do with Egypt, but that the Milesians had.

All our ancient traditions and writings are collected and chronologically set down in what is called the "Book of Conquests or Invasions"; and the account there preserved is just this: we are told that the lady *Ceasar* came to this island "from Palestine before the Flood" (whatever that may mean); that *Parthalon* came out of Migdonia in Greece, some three hundred years after the flood; that after the destruction of *Parthalon*'s people, *Nemidh* and his people came from the same country, or at least from that part of Scythia which our Gaedhelic writers say had been peopled by a Greek colony. That the Nemidians again, after a considerable time, were overpowered by the sea-robbers called Fomorians, and fled from the country in three parties; that one of these parties settled on the nearest coast of Britain, chiefly in the present island of Anglesea; that another of them went back to Greece, or at least to Thrace, which was then part of Greece, or subject to it; and that the third party settled in what are called the islands in the north of Greece. And we are told that this latter party were the people who afterwards took, or received, the name of *Tuatha Dé Danann*; a name said by some of our ancient etymologists to signify the people of the deities of science, because they venerated their professors of the social and occult sciences as deities.

Migration of the *Tuatha Dé Danann* from Greece;

These *Tuatha Dé Danann* are said to have inhabited that part of Greece in which the famous city of Athens was situated; and this territory having been invaded by a fleet from Syria, they are stated to have exercised their druidical powers in favour of their own friends successfully for some time; but their spells having become counteracted by a Syrian druid, they fled from Greece northwards and westwards (into Germany), and over the north of Europe (into Denmark, Sweden, and Norway), and on their way they are recorded to have established themselves and to have brought their arts into the four cities of *Falias*, *Gorias*, *Finias*, and *Murias*—those arts which they afterwards brought into Erinn.

the author does not believe they went into Scandinavia;

This is the common account of their travels, as may be seen reported in Keating and O'Flaherty, but not in older chronicles. I am inclined to dissent from this account of the *Tuatha Dé Danann*, as far as regards their having passed into Norway and Sweden. I think there is no good reason to believe that they ever inhabited these countries. As far as I am aware, no city is known to have existed in any one of these countries whose

XXX.

he believes their cities of Falias, Gorias, etc., were in Germany;

name resembles in any way any of the names of the four cities mentioned above. Not so, however, with Germany. I am certain that every one will at once perceive the close affinity, if not indeed complete identity, of *Falias*, and Westphalia; *Gorias* and Goritia, or Görtz; *Finias* and Vienna, or Pinneburg; *Murias* and Murrhart, all names of cities in Germany. And, without burthening this discussion with a collation of *Tuatha Dé Danann* and German personal names, I have still a very strong argument to adduce in favour of my opinion. It is this.

they spoke German, according to the Book of Lecan.

In a short article preserved in the Book of *Lecan* on the languages spoken by the different colonists who invaded ancient Erinn, we are told that German was the language of the *Tuatha Dé Danann*, and that they spoke Latin, Greek, and Gaedhelic too.[312] Now, it is quite certain that the old Gaedhelic writers would not confound the German with the Swedish or Norse languages; and, that therefore, whoever wrote this very old article had no idea that the *Tuatha Dé Danann* had ever been in these countries, or taught their arts and sciences in them.

I have gone into this, I fear, too long digression, for the purpose of endeavouring to show some remote reason for the quadrangular form of the *Tuatha Dé Danann* harp.

The similarity of the harps on the monument of Orpheus at Petau in Styria and on the theca may point to Murrhart as the Tuatha Dé Danann Murias.

You will remember that it has been already stated in the quotation from Mr. Ferguson's essay on the harp, that, in a monument erected at Petau in Styria, during the life of the emperor Aurelius, the Thracian Orpheus is represented performing on an instrument in all respects resembling the quadrangular harp on the *theca* of the Stowe MS. Now, Petau, where this monument stands, is an ancient town of Styria, on the river Drave, 35 miles north-east of Cilly, and 109 south of Vienna. And it is, indeed, a singular coincidence that the river Muer, upon which the town of Murrhart, already mentioned, is situated, and from which it takes its name, is only about sixteen miles east from the town of Petau. And if we could suppose that the present German town of Murrhart, or any other town on the river Muer, and taking its name from it, could be

(312) [Ebpa do Chearaip, acar Spe̱g do Pappthalan; Spec acar Laiden la Nemed cona muinteṗ; Spec acar Laiden acar Bpetnair ac Feapaib bolc, acar Belgaid acu i nÉpenn; acar Sepmain ac Tuathaib de Danand; Laiden acar Spe̱g acar Saidelg leo ror. Saidelg acar Laiden la macaib Mileað.—Book of *Lecan*, fol. 229, b. col. 1. bot.]

Hebrew [was the language] of *Cessar*, and Greek of *Parthalon*; Greek and Latin of *Nemed* and of his people; Greek and Latin and British of the Firbolgs, and who also had the Belgic in Ireland; and German of the *Tuatha Dé Danann*; who also had Latin, and Greek and Gaedhelic; Gaedhelic and Latin of the sons of Milesius.

A similar account is preserved in a poem in the Book of Lismore (O'Curry's copy, R. I. A., fol. 160, b. a. mid.]

XXX.

the ancient city of Murias, one of those into which the *Tuatha Dé Danann* brought their arts, then indeed, notwithstanding a wide distance in chronology, we might fairly enough imagine whence the quadrangular harp of the great *Daghda* came, and why the Thracian harp, which would appear to have been its prototype, appears on the Styrian monument.

The similarity of the harps on the monument of Orpheus at Petau in Styria and on the *theca* may point to Murrhart as the *Tuatha Dé Danann Murias.*

It must be admitted that the chronological difference between the arrival of the *Tuatha Dé Danann* in Ireland, and the erection of the Styrian monument, which took place in the third century of the Christian era, is very great, being more than fifteen hundred years, according to the chronology of the Annals of the Four Masters. But even so, we have no reason to think that ancient manners and customs did not, with little change, cover great spaces of time in various parts of the world, perhaps peculiarly situated and inhabited by people of peculiar dispositions. We know that at this day there is a traditional music preserved among the gypsies of Hungary, quite distinct in character from, and uninfluenced by, the more cultivated music of surrounding nations. We know that Thrace, where the quadrangular harp is believed to have been in early use, was part of that Greece in which the *Tuatha Dé Danann* cultivated and taught their arts and sciences; and if we compare the time which may have elapsed between the time of the invention of the quadrangular harp in Egypt, and of its being adopted in Greece by the *Tuatha Dé Danann*, with the time which elapsed in Ireland between the battle of *Magh Tuireadh*, where the harp is first mentioned, and the time of *Donogh*, the son of *Brian Boromha*, in whose reign, about the year 1060, the square harp was put on the *theca* or shrine of the Stowe MS., we will plainly see that notwithstanding the probable improvements and changes of time, old forms and old customs must have prevailed in Ireland at least for over two thousand years. To carry this discussion out to its legitimate conclusions, however, would require much more time, and I may say much greater abilities, than I can bring to it; and if I have by no inconsiderable expense of research and thought succeeded in presenting this interesting, and indeed most important, subject in a new point of view, I am quite content with having plucked a few green leaves from this new tree of knowledge, leaving to more competent and successful investigators to pluck the ripe fruit of success, which certainly awaits the hand of the honest and industrious inquirer in this difficult and devious path.

LECTURE XXXI.

(Delivered 12th June, 1862.)

(IX.) Of Music and Musical Instruments (continued). Legendary origin of the Harp according to the tale of *Imtheacht na Trom Dhaimhe*, or the "Adventures of the Great Bardic Company"; *Seanchan*'s visit to *Guaire*; interview of *Marbhan*, *Guaire*'s brother, with *Seanchan*; *Marbhan*'s legend of *Cuil* and *Canoclach Mhór* and the invention of the Harp; his legend of the invention of verse; his legend concerning the *Timpan*; the strand of *Camas* not identified. Signification of the word *Cruit*. The Irish *Timpan* was a stringed instrument. Another etymology for *Cruit*; Isidore not the authority for this explanation. Reference to the *Cruit* in the early history of the Milesians. *Eimher* and *Ereamhon* cast lots for a poet and harper. Skill in music one of the gifts of the *Eberian* or southern race of Erinn. Mention of the *Cruit* in the historical tale of *Orgain Dindrighe* or the "destruction of *Dindrigh*". First occurrence of the word *Ceis* in this tale; it occurs again in connection with the assembly of *Drom Ceat*, A.D. 573; *Aidbsi* or *Corus Cronain* mentioned in connection with poems in praise of St. *Colum Cille*, sung at this assembly; meaning of the word *Aidbsi*; the author heard the *Cronan* or throat accompaniment to dirges; origin of the word "crone"; the Irish *Aidbsi* known in Scotland as *Cepóg*; the word *Cepóg* known in Ireland also, as shown by a poem on the death of *Athairne*. The assembly of *Drom Ceat* continued; *Dallan Forgaill*'s elegy on St. *Colum Cille*; the word *Ceis* occurs in this poem also; *Ceis* here represents a part of the harp, as shown by a scholium in *Leabhar na h-Uidhre*; antiquity of the tale of the "Destruction of *Dindrigh*" proved by this scholium; the word *Ceis* glossed in all ancient copies of the elegy on St. *Colum Cille*; scholium on the same poem in the MS. H. 2. 16. T.C.D.; gloss on the poem in Liber Hymnorum; parts of the harp surmised to have been the *Ceis*,—the *Cobluighe* or "sisters", and the *Leithrind*; *Leithrind* or half harmony, and *Rind* or full harmony; difficulty of determining what *Ceis* was; it was not a part of the harp; summary of the views of the commentators as to the meaning of *Ceis*. Fourth reference to the word *Ceis* in an ancient tale in *Leabhar na h-Uidhre*. Fifth reference to *Ceis* in another ancient poem. *Coir*, another term for harmony, synonymous with *Ceis*; the author concludes that *Ceis* meant either harmony, or the mode of playing with a bass. The word *Glés* mentioned in the scholium in H. 2. 16. is still a living word; the *Crann Gleasta* mentioned in a poem of the eighteenth century; this poem contains the names of the principal parts of the harp; the names of the different classes of strings are only to be found in the scholium in the *Leabhar na h-Uidhre* to the elegy on St. *Colum Cille*.

So far, I have endeavoured to throw some light on the remote origin and the practical use of the Irish lyre; a light, if it be such, drawn, I must acknowledge, as much from inferences and probabilities, as from actual historical statements. But the ancient Gaedhelic literature is not entirely silent on the origin of the harp, any more than that of Greece; and the similarity of the two legends is so striking, that I must briefly narrate ours here.

Of the ancient tale called *Imtheacht na Trom Dhaimhe*, or the

XXXI.

Adventures of the Great Bardic Company, I gave a short, but rather free sketch in a former lecture.[313] At the risk of repeating something of what I said on that occasion, I must here again preface the portion of that tale which bears upon my present subject by a few observations sufficient to introduce the personages of the tale upon the scene.

Legendary origin of the harp according to the tale of the "Adventures of the Great Company";

On the death, in the year 592, of the poet *Dallan Forgaill*, the celebrated panegyrist of *St. Colum Cille*, and chief poet of Erinn, the vacant *Ollamh's* mantle and chair were by the unanimous voice of the profession, conferred on the young poet *Seanchan*.

It was the custom in those hospitable days, when a new chief-poet *Ollamh* of Erinn succeeded to the vacant place, that he selected, as a matter of high distinction, either the monarch of Erinn, at or near Tara, or some provincial king at his provincial court, to honour with his first visit. This pleasant custom *Seanchan* was resolved should not fail in his hands, and consulting his knowledge of the generous habits of the different kings in Erinn, he determined to bestow on *Guaire*, called the Hospitable, king of Connacht, the honour of the first visit of the new *Ard Ollamh*, or chief poet of Erinn. Thither, then, he went with his wife and children, and his accompanying retinue of *ollamhs*, tutors, and pupils, horses, dogs, and so forth. They were hospitably received and entertained by king *Guaire;* but soon some of them began to be pettish, and to ask for delicacies which were out of season and not procurable. The hospitable host was deeply pained when he found that he could not satisfy the desires of his unreasonable guests; but he had a brother named *Marbhan*, who some time previously had retired from court to the solitude of *Glenn Dallun*, where he led the life of a recluse, devoting his time to prayer, meditation, and philosophical reflections. To this gifted man the king repaired for counsel and assistance in his difficulty; nor was he disappointed, as the brother freed him from all his difficulties, and followed him shortly after to his court.

Seanchan's visit to *Guaire*;

Marbhan having arrived at *Guaire's* court, introduced himself at once to *Seanchan* and his learned, though cumbersome, company; and having expressed a desire to hear some of their musical performances, vocal and instrumental, his wish was freely complied with by various performers, with all of which, however, he seemed dissatisfied. The performance so far was, it seems, of the vocal character, and of the species called *Cronan* (a word which might be translated "purring"), a kind of monotonous chaunt, of which I shall have occasion to speak in a future

Interview of *Marbhan*, *Guaire's* brother, with *Seanchan*;

[313] Lecture iv., *ante*, vol. i., p. 86.

lecture. At this stage of the interview between the recluse and the poets, one of the latter came forward and offered to give him a specimen of his art, upon which the following dialogue took place between them:—

Marbhan's legend of Cuil and Canoclach Mhór and the invention of the harp;

" What art wilt thou display for me, and what is thy name?" said *Marbhan*. " I am a good *ollamh* of *Seanchan*'s in my art", said he, " and my name is *Casmael* the *Cruitire* (harper)". " I wish to ask thee, *Casmael* the harper", said *Marbhan*, " what was it that the *Cruit* was at first derived from; and who it was that composed the first song; and which of them was the first invented—the *Cruit*, or the *Timpan?*" " I do not know that, thou prophet of heaven and earth", said *Casmael*. " I know it", said *Marbhan*, " and I will tell it to thee:—There once lived a couple [a man and his wife], *Cuil* the son of *Midhuel* was the man, and *Canoclach Mhor* was his wife. And the wife conceived a hatred to him, and she was [always] flying from him through woods and wildernesses; and he continued to follow her constantly. And one day that the woman came to the sea shore of *Camas*, and was walking over the strand, she met a skeleton of a whale on the strand, and she heard the sounds of the wind passing through the sinews of the whale on the strand; and she fell asleep from the sounds. And her husband came after her [and found her asleep]; and he perceived that it was from the sounds the sleep fell upon her. And he then went forward into the wood, and made the form of the *Cruit;* and he put strings from the sinews of the whale into it; and that was the first *Cruit* that was ever made.

his legend of the invention of verse;

" And again", continues *Marbhan*, " *Lamec Bigamas* had two sons, *Jubal* and *Tubal Cain* were their names. One son of them was a smith, namely, *Jubal;* and he discovered from sounds of two sledges [on the anvil] in the forge one day, that it was verses (or notes) of equal length they spoke, and he composed a verse upon that cause, and that was the first verse that was ever composed". * * * * *

his legend concerning the tympan;

The tale goes on:—Another person in the house then said: " I will display an art for thee". " Who art thou", said *Marbhan*, " and what art dost thou profess?" " I am the *ollamh*-Timpanist of the great company", said he, " and *Cairche Ceolbhinn* (i.e. *Cairche* of the sweet music) " is my name". " I wish to ask, then, *Cairche*", said *Marbhan*, " why is the *Timpan* called *Timpan Naimh* [or saint's *Timpan*], and yet no saint ever took a *Timpan* into his hands?" " I do not know", said the timpanist. " Then I will tell it to thee", said *Marbhan*. " At the time that Noah, the son of Lamech, went into the ark, he took with him a number of instruments of music into it, together with a *Timpan*, which one of his sons had, who knew how to play it; and they remained in the ark during the time that the deluge was pouring down. Afterwards, when Noah and his children went forth from the ark, and his son was desirous to take the *Timpan* away with him". "Thou shalt not take it", said Noah, "until thou hast left its price [with me.]" The son asked him what the price was. He answered that he should require no greater price than to name the *Timpan* from himself. The son granted that price to his father; so that Noah's *Timpan* is its name from that time down; and that is not what ye, the ignorant timpanists, call it, but *Timpan* of the saints".[314] XXXI.

These are, indeed, two curious legends, well worthy, for more reasons than one, of careful consideration and comparison with the legends and traditions of other early nations. The legend of Tubal reminds us at once of Pythagoras, who is said to have been led to discover the musical effect of vibrations of a chord by observing the sound of various blows on an anvil; though the Irish legend (for the rest more vague) does not appear to bear on the tones so much as on the rhythm of music. The strand of *Camas*, on which the skeleton of the sea monster was found, cannot be identified, as there are a great many places of the name in Ireland. It was probably at the mouth of the lower Bann in the county of Antrim. The names of the husband and wife in the story are, of course, fictitious; and they are not in meaning symbolical of music in any way that I can discover. The word *Cruit*, which is our most ancient name for the harp, signifies literally, a sharp high breast, such as of a goose, a heron (miscalled a crane), or a curlew; indeed the Gaedhelic name of the curlew is *crottach*, or the sharp high breasted; it is what is commonly termed a chicken breast or chicken breasted. The word *Cruit*, at the present day, when signifying a personal deformity, is often applied to a hump on the back. This, however, is incorrect; and the more proper words *dronn*, *dronnog*, and *dronnaighe* are, in fact, also living words among the better informed speakers of the Irish language. As to the story of Noah's *Timpan* (*Timpan Naoi*), I must confess that I have never met with another reference to that name. Yet, the name, at least in its reputed corrupt form of *Timpan Naoimh*, or saint's *Timpan*, must have been well known in this country, otherwise the story would have never been written to correct it. And the story itself points to an early belief in the great anti-

The strand of *Camas* not identified.

Signification of the word *Cruit*.

[314] [See for original of these passages "*Imtheacht na Tromdhaimhe*", edited, with a translation, by Professor Connellan; Transactions of the Ossianic Society, vol. 5, p. 96. See also Book of Lismore, O'Longan's vel. copy, R. I. A., f. 191. a. b.]

XXXI. quity, and in the eastern origin of the instrument. But, a greater mystery than this attaches to the instrument itself, which the Gaedhil called a *Timpan*. We know that the English Tymbal and Latin Tympanum mean a drum of some sort; but it is beyond all doubt that the Irish *Timpan* spoken of in our ancient Irish MSS., was a stringed instrument, one of the kinds of harp, as I shall afterwards show.

The Irish *Timpan* was a stringed instrument.

Another etymology for *Cruit*;

The account just given is not, however, the only one of the origin of the *Cruit*. There is a very old and somewhat different etymology of the word given in an ancient Gaedhelic tract in my possession. This very ancient tract is a critical discussion on the origin and arrangement of the Book of Psalms, with the order for singing and playing them in the Jewish temple, made by king David himself. The following literal translation of the opening of this tract will give an idea of its character, as well as furnish the reference to the etymology of the *Cruit* just alluded to:—

"The title which is in the front of this book is 'Brightness to the minds of the Learned'. Its name in the Hebrew is *Hespertalim*, that is, a Volume of Hymns, in the same way that Liber Psalmorum (or Book of Psalms) is named, for the word psalm, or hymn of praise, is its interpretation. It is asked what is the name of this book in Hebrew, in Greek, in Latin? Answer. Nabla [is its name] in Hebrew; Psalterium in Greek; Laudatorium, or Organum, in the Latin. It is asked, why it was named by that name? Answer. From the *Cruit* through which David chaunted the psalms; for, Nabla was its name in Hebrew, Psalterium in Greek, Laudatorium, or Organum in Latin; in as much as Organum is a generic name for all musical instruments, because of its great nobleness. Nabla, however, is not a generic name for every musical instrument, but Cithera is the generic name for *Cruits*. Cithera, that is, Pectoralis; that is, the breast instrument; for as much, as that it is at the breast it is played. The Nabla is a ten-stringed *Cruit;* that is, which is furnished with ten strings, which are played with ten fingers; in which the ten commandments are concentrated. It is down upon it [that is at top] that its belly [or sounding chamber] is placed; and it is downwards it is played, or that music is performed on it. This name [of Nabla] is transferred, so that it is become the name of this Book, which is bound by the ten strings of the patriarchal law, upon which are played *de supremis mysteriis Spiritus Sanctis;* that is, 'the high noble mysteries of the Holy Spirit.'

"Psalterium. This is a Greek word; it is the derivative name of the book. These five words were invented in relation to each other, namely, Psalmus, Psalterium, Psalmista, Psalmodum, Psallo. It is asked: Whence came this nomenclature? Answer: What Isidore says is, that Psalmista is the name of the man who plays; Psalterium, what is played upon; Psalmodium, the name of the music which is played; Psallo, the words of the man who plays. . . . What David did in the latter times was: He selected four choice thousands of the sons of Israel to sing the psalms perpetually, without any interruption whatever. A third part of them at the choir; a third at *Croit;* and a third between choir and *Croit.* That which is entitled to the name of Psalmus is that which is arranged and practised upon the *Croit.* That which has a right to the name of Canticum, is that which is practised by the choir, and is chanted from the *Croit.* That which has a right to the name of Canticum Psalmus is what is carried from the *Croit* to the choir. That which has a right to be called Canticum Psalmi, is what is carried from the choir to the *Croit*".[318] XXXI.

Isidore not the authority for this explanation.

I am inclined to think that, although Isidore (a writer of the fifth century) is quoted in this tract in connection with the Psalms, it is not on his authority that the derivations of *Cithera* and *Cruit* are given, as may be seen from the following extract from his *Etymology:*—

[318] [original:—[Is] he titol fil indrech an leboirse "taitne do menmonaib na legnide". Is e a ainm isand ebre hesfertalim, .i. uolumen imnorum ainm asberar liber Psalmorum ar indi, is psalma is laus no imnus etercerter. Ceacht cia ainm anlibroirse a ebru, a Greg, illaitin? Nin. Nabla in ebra; Psaltium is an Greig; Laudatorium, no Organum is an laidin. Ceacht can ro ainmnigad do indainmsen? Nin. Din croit tresasocathoin Dabuid na salmo, .i. nabla a hainm isen ebru, Psaltorium in Greco, Laudatorium, no Organn in Laitin; ar indi is Organum is ainm cenelach ditech ciul ar ndairechus. Nabla immorro ni hainm cenelach do cech croit acht, is citera ainm cenelach cecha croite. Citera, .i. Pectoralis, in bruinde de, .i. issan ni sennor for bruindib. Nabla Cruit dechde, .i. cotarissetar o a x. tetaib, sennair o x. meruib, inacomaraitt na deich timna. Fuirme indair bid abolg di suidiu; acas isenduas sennoir, noc forniter icil inde. Tairmberar di inse conid ainm den libursa, contairissetar o x. tetaib an rach to fetorloic, doinfoir deisserenis mistepis srimtus sanctis; di nib drumir uaislib an srimta noib. Psaltorium for Gregda insen; issed ainm derbaroid forsenlibursa. Arethaiter na coic suin comainmnestae, .i. psalmus, psalterium, psalmista, psalmodium, psallo. Caecht, can do roic antainmnigadso? Nin. Issed isber Esidor, . . . psaltis ainm an fir notseinn; psalterium indi sennoir ann; psalmodium ainm an ciuil sennoir ann; psallo brethar ind fir notsennair. (MSS. Harleian, 5280, Br. Mus., f. 11. a. top.) . . . issed derigne Dabaid ridegenchoe: toi roecco cetri mile togaide di macoib Israel frietetol acas gnatogad na psalm dises, cenach toirmiusc etir. Trian dibh fri clais; trian fri croit; trian etir clais acas croit. Is dou as dir anni is Psalmus dendi airict, acas gnataiter hi croit. As do as dir anni is Canticum dini gnatoigead fria clais, acas canar o croit, is dou is dir anni is Canticum psalmus dini beror o croit a clais. As do is dir indi is Canticum Psalmi donindi do beror a clais hi croit. —*Ibid.*, f. 13. a. mid.]

XXXI.

"The form of the *Cithera* at first", says Isidore, "is said to have been like the human breast; because, as the voice [issues] from the breast, so from it [the Cithera] the sound is emitted; and it was named from that cause. For, in the Doric language the breast is called Cithara. . . . This is the difference between the Psalterium and the Cithara. The Psalterium has at the top [or upper side] that concave wood whence the sound is yielded, and the chords are struck downwards, and sound from above [or at the top]. The Cithara has the concavity of the wood underneath. There are ten chords used in the Hebrew Psalterium, from the number of the Decalogue".(316)

Passing on from this glimpse of an etymological connection between the *Cruit* and the harp of Greece, I proceed to the further consideration of the musical instruments of the ancient Gaedhil, such as we find them spoken of in our own ancient writings.

Reference to the *Cruit* in the early history of the Milesians.

The next reference to the *Cruit* is found in the history of the Milesians, who conquered and succeeded the *Tuatha Dé Danann* in Erinn. After the total overthrow of the *Tuatha Dé Danann* power by the Milesians in the battle of *Taillte*, in Meath, and the erection of their own power and government in its place, we are told (in the ancient "Book of Invasions") that the two leading brothers, *Eimher* (or *Eber*) and *Ereamhon* (or *Eremon*), divided the country between them, the first taking the southern half, and the second the northern half for his share. They next (as this record informs us) divided the surviving leaders, servants, and soldiers of the expedition, until nothing more remained for division but two professional men, a poet and a *Cruitire*, or harper, who had come on the expedition. The name of the poet was *Cir*, the son of *Cis*, and that of the *Cruitire* was *Cindfind*. Each of the brothers put forward a claim to both, but at last they agreed to decide their pretensions by lot. *Eimher*'s lot fell upon the *Cruitire*, and *Ereamhon*'s on the poet. The following quatrains commemorative of this curious event are quoted in the same ancient "Book of Invasions"; they are also quoted by Dr. Keating from the "Psaltair of Cashel":—

Eimher and *Ereamhon* cast lots for a poet and harper.

"The two sons of Milesius of bright renown,
Conquered *Eire* and *Alba*.
Along with them hither came
A comely poet and a *Cruitire* (or harper).
"*Cir*, the son of *Cis*, was the fair haired poet;
The name of the *Cruitire* was *Cindfind;*
For the sons of Milesius of bright renown,

(316) Isidore, *Etym*, lib. iii., cap. 22.

His *Cruit* was played by the *Cruitire*.
"These kings of many battles,
Who took the sovereignty of Erinn,
They made the clear sprightly contention,
Eimher and *Ereamhon*.
"They then nobly cast lots
Upon the great professional men,
Until to the southern leader fell
The tuneful, accomplished *Cruitire*.
"The sweetness of string-music, blandness, valour,
In the south, in the south of Erinn are found;
It so shall be to the end of time
With the illustrious race of *Eimher*.
"There fell to the share of the northern man
The professor of poetry with his noble gifts.
It is a matter of boast with the north that with them has remained
Excellence in poetry, and its chief abode".(317)

Skill in music one of the gifts of the Eberian or Southern race of Erinn.

It is a singular fact to find that so early and so late as the time of the holy *Cormac Mac Cuileannain* (A.D. 900), the author of the "Psaltair of Cashel", there should exist a tradition that preëminence in music, in blandness, and in personal strength, were of the most ancient times the peculiar natural gifts of the Eberian, or southern race of Ireland. This indeed is not the only place in which the same fact is alluded to, for in an ancient Gaedhelic tract in my possession, which purports to be an account of a meeting held at Tara in the time of king *Diarmait*, about the year A.D. 550, and at which the celebrated *Finntaan* was present, that ancient sage, in speaking of the characteristics of the west, east, north, and south of Erinn, uses these words:—"Her cataracts, her fairs (or assemblies), her kings, her warriors, her professors, her wheat, her melody, her harmony, her amuse-

(317) [original:—
Dá mhac Míle miadh nordain,
Gabsat Erinn is Albain.
Leo do ruachator alle,
File caomh is cruitire.
[illegible]r mac Cis, an file fiond;
Ainm don chruitire Cindfind;
La macaibh Míle miadh ngle,
Seaphnais cruit an cruitire.
[illegible]a flaithe coniolar nEreann,
Gabsat Righe na hEreann,
Gnisead cogle mer an glór,
Eimher acas Ereamhon.
Do chuirset crannchor co han
Iman aes ndana ndiomár,
Co ttarla don fior andeas
An cruitire coir comdheas.
Teidbinnes ciuil, caoine, drem,
Indes, indescert Erenn;
Is amladh bias co brath mbil
Ag siol airegdha Eimhir.
Do ralu don fior atuaidh
An tollamh gus an ollbuáidh.
As nos bága tuait dosnacht
Sos dana acas ollamnacht. Da.
—O'Clery's Book of Invasions, R.I.A., f. 81. A slightly different version of this poem has been already given in vol. i. p. 4. The editor did not wish, however, to omit it here, especially as it afforded him an opportunity of printing the original.]

XXXI. ments, her wisdom, her dignity, her order, her learning, teaching, her championship, her chess-playing, her rashness passion, her poetry, her advocacy (or lawyership), her h tality, her residences, her shipping, her fertility, all are her southern parts in the south".[318]

After what has been said in the last lecture of the Daghda and his Cruit, and of Uaithne and his three sons their Cruits, and the Milesian Cruitire just mentioned, the historical reference to the Cruit and its power, known to found in a historical tale described in a former lectur I allude to the ancient historic tale which gives an accou the early life and fortunes of Labraid Loingsiuch, monarc Erinn about four hundred years before the Incarnation.

Mention of the *Cruit* in the historical tale of the "Destruction of *Dindrigh*".

The father and grandfather of this prince were murdere his granduncle, *Cobhthach Cael*, while he was yet a child; he was committed to the care of two retainers of his fat house—namely, *Ferceirtne*, the poet, and *Craiftine*, the *Cru* or harper. When the young prince grew up, his presence uneasiness to his cruel granduncle, and his tutors fearing fo safety, fled with him into West Munster, where they were pitably received by *Scoriath*, the king of *Tir Morcha*. *Scoriath* had a beautiful daughter whose name was *Mor* and, as often happens under similar circumstances, an att ment was soon formed between this young lady and the Lei prince. The mother soon detected the mutual partiality o young people, and accordingly she contrived so to manage household arrangements, that they could never find an op tunity of being so long together alone as would allow the give expression to their thoughts. The young prince's fai tutors saw clearly enough the state of affairs, and *Craiftine Cruitire*, determined to lend them his aid. At this time *Sco* invited the nobles of his territory to a great feast. The y lovers immediately held council, through the means of the and the *Cruitire*, and they formed a plan of action. When time came, the company arrived; and in the course of the f the cup, the tale, and the song as usual went round. *Craif* the most famous of harpers, was requested in his turn to form, a request with which he readily complied; but gradu he led them on from a joyous to a more seductive strain;

(318) [original:—a hera, a hoenaigi, a donda, a diberga, a ruichi, a cruithnecht, a ceolchairecht, a binnis, a hairfitedad, a hecna, a hairmitniu, a feis, a foglaim, a foircetal, a fianna, a fichcellacht, a dene, a dirsere, a filidecht, a fechemnus, a fele, a sonus, a ta a torchaigi, ata deiscert ance H. 2. 16. col. 746, mid.; and *Lecan*, f. 277. b. a.]

(319) [See Lect. on the MS. rials, etc., p. 251.]

quences were those which always followed the *Suan-* r sleeping mode): the queen and all the company were nto a happy state of unconsciousness, and the young . time enough to open their minds in words, and pledge 's of love and fidelity to each other. The queen was the first to awaken from the trance into which had thrown his audience; and although she found her still innocently reclining at her side, still (says the guessed all that had happened, and quickly roused ill slumbering husband: "Arise, *Scoriath*", said she, ghter respires the breath of a plighted wife; hear her r the secret of her love has passed away from her". not who has got it", said the king, "but the druids oets shall lose their heads if they do not discover who this". The tale goes on. "It would be a disgrace to ng", said *Ferceirtne*, "to put thine own people to death". ad shall be struck off thee", said king *Scoriath*, "if not tell me". "Tell it", said [prince] *Labraid*, "it that I alone should suffer". It was then *Ferceirtne* conceal not that it was the musical *Ceis* of *Craiftine*'s t put upon the hosts a death sleep, so that friendship ged between *Main* [that is *Labraid*] and the youth- ith of *Morca; Labraid* is above all price. It was said he, "that embraced her after you were all sent by *Craiftine*'s *Cruit*". He (the poet) saved his people eans. "Good then", said [king] *Scoriath*, "we have ght of a husband for our daughter till this night, so re we loved her; but though we had been choosing could not select a better than he] whom God has sent a banquet be prepared in the house", said he, "and ife be given away to *Labraid;* and I shall not part until he is king of Leinster (*Laighin*)".(320)

XXXI.

Mention of the *Cruit* in the historical tale of the "Destruction of *Dindrigh*".

fe was then given to *Labraid*, we are told; and some wards, a muster of the men of Munster was made

:—Eirig a Scoriat, ol si. tlad a tai anal mna lat- te a hosnaid iar nodlam iadi. . . . Ni consear cia acind dona druidib acas aib osse mani fintar cia bid ainim duit, ar Fein- io muintir do marbad. ditsa fen, ar Scoriat, . abair, ar Labraid, is gugad ammoenur. Isand icheptni. Ni celt ceis ruit Chraiptine cocar- i sluagu suanbas, cons- ret coibneas iter sceo Main Mo- riat macdacht Morca; mo cech luag Labraid. Labraid, asse, condranic sse iar fortalgud do cruit Craip- tine. Romertsom a muinter a su- ide. Maith tra ar Scariath, ni contarglassamni cele diar ningin cosinnocht, ara seirc lind cia no bemis ica toga suide . . . do rad dia dun. Dentar ol isin tig, osse, acas tabar aben for laim Labrada; ocus ni scarsa sris osse cosossi Laigen.—H. 2. 16. col. 755, mid.; and H. 2. 18. f. 204. b. b.]

XXXI.

Mention of the *Cruit* in the historical tale of the "Destruction of *Dindrigh*".

and placed at his command, with whom he marched back into Leinster. He advanced to the walls of *Dindrigh* [near *Leithghlinn*, or Leighlin, in the county of Carlow], the palace of his father and grandfather; and here again the magical power of *Craiftine*'s musical skill was called into requisition. When they came to the ramparts of *Dindrigh*, they held a council of war, and the decision that they came to was, that *Craiftine* should mount the rampart, and play the sleeping strain (*Suantraighe*) for the parties inside, whilst his own friends were to lie down with their faces to the ground, and their fingers in their ears, so that they should not hear the music. This was done accordingly; and the result of course was that the guards within were slaughtered, and the palace taken.

Moriath, *Labraid*'s young wife, however (says the story), did not think it honourable to put her fingers into her ears against her own cherished music, and therefore she fell into a sleep which continued three days; for no one dared to move her. This circumstance is preserved in the following quatrain, quoted in this very ancient tract, from the poet *Fland Mac Lonain*, who died in the year 891; an extract which sufficiently marks the great antiquity of this celebrated tale:

"In the same way that noble *Moriath* slept,
Before the hosts of *Morca*, a long repose;
When they destroyed *Dindrigh*—an ungallant deed—
When the head-sleeping *Ceis* sent forth its music".[321]

I gave on a former occasion a full account of this ancient tale of the Destruction of *Dindrigh*;[322] and I introduce this reference to it again, only to call particular attention to two passages so remarkable as to the ancient Irish *Cruit*, and the three wonderful musical strains, or feats of performance which marked the *Cruitire* of eminence. Of themselves these references would give us but very little actual knowledge of the precise character of the *Cruit*, if the word *Ceis*, which occurs three times at periods remote from each other, in connection with the *Cruit*, did not occur also in another piece of composition of a period lying somewhere near midway between these periods.

First occurrence of the word *Ceis* in this tale;

When king *Scoriath* threatened *Ferceirtne* with the loss of his head, the poet's words were these: I conceal not that it was the musical *Ceis*, of *Craiftine*'s *Cruit*, that put upon the hosts a death sleep", etc.[323] This, the first occurrence of the word *Ceis*

[321] [original:—
Feib concatail Muiriach muad,
Fiad slúag Morca mochad seol;
Dianort Dindrig—rem cin cres—
Diaseraind ceis cendcoll ceol.
—*Ibid.* H. 2. 16. col. 755, bot.]

[322] [See Lectures on MS. Materials, etc., p. 252.]

[323] [See *ante*, vol. ii., p. 243.]

that I have met with, is referred to a sentence said to have been spoken by a poet who flourished about four hundred years before the Incarnation of our Lord, according to the chronology of the "Annals of the Four Masters". It occurs again under date of the year 592, in reference to the passage to which attention is now to be directed, though, I fear, in a discursive way.

occurs again in connection with the Assembly of *Drom Ceat*, A.D. 573;

In a former lecture, I gave an account of the National Assembly called by the monarch *Aedh Mac Ainmire* (A.D. 573) with a view to banish the surplus professors and students of the sciences out of the country, in consequence of the too great increase of their numbers as a privileged class, and the exorbitance of their demands upon the working people, and held at *Drom Ceat* (near the present town of Limavady [*Leim-a-Mhadaigh*], in the county of Derry).

St. *Colum Cille* having heard of this meeting and its objects, and being a great patron of literature, came over from his island home at *I*, or *Iona*, whither he had retired from the world to appease the king and the people, and quite unexpectedly appeared at the meeting. The poets at this time, with *Dallan Forgall* as their chief, were collected in all their numbers, in the vicinity of the hill of meeting, anxiously awaiting their fate; but their anxiety was soon relieved, as their able advocate had so much influence with the monarch and his people, as to procure a satisfactory termination to the misunderstanding between them and their poets.

The poets, on learning this happy turn in their favour, arose with their chiefs at their head, and went in a body to the meeting, each man of them who had a company (that is, who was a master) having a laudatory poem for the saint; and the chief of each band, we are told, sang his poem (all in chorus); and *Aidbsi*, that is *Corus Crondin*, (that is, scientific purring chorus) was the name of that music [i.e. the air to which they sang] and it was the most excellent of music, as *Colman Mac Lenene* said:

Aidbsi, or *Corus Crondin*, mentioned in connection with poems in praise of St. *Colum Cille* sung at this Assembly;

"As the blackbird to the swans,
As the ounce to the *Dirna*,
As the shapes of plebeian women to the shapes of queens,
As any other king to *Domnall*,
As a single murmur to an *Aidbsi*,
As a rushlight to a candle,
So is any other sword [compared] to my sword".[324]

[324] [original:—
.i. derolb na luin, farrad ne nela
Luin oc heolaib,
.i. dirna ainm tomais moir na ac dirnaib.
uingi o dirnaib,

XXXI.

That is to say, according to an interlined gloss on these lines: as the blackbirds are contemptible near the swans; as the ounce is contemptible near the *Dirna;* [the name for a large mass of metal]; as all kings are contemptible near king *Domnall;* as all music is contemptible near the *Aidbsi;* as one small candle is contemptible near a large royal candle; so was any other sword contemptible compared to his own sword. The sword would appear to have been a present from some great man to the poet. It will be seen that one of these seven lines (quoted from some ancient poem) cites an example of their author's low estimate of all kinds and combinations of music compared to the *Aidbsi*, which was that which was sung by the poets for St. *Colum Cille*.

meaning of the word *Aidbsi;*

The word *Aidbsi* in its simple, ordinary signification, means nothing more than great, or greatness; but, in its technical musical signification, it means the singing of a multitude in chorus. It would appear, however, that the *Aidbsi* was not the music to which the body of the poem in praise of St. *Colum Cille* was sung, because this was the performance of each person for himself, but it was the low murmuring accompaniment or chorus, in which the crowd took part at the end of each verse, and which, from its name of *Crónán*, must have been produced in the throat, like the purring of a cat. The word *Aidbsi* would appear to have been used also to denote the lamentation at great funerals, where one man or one woman sang the praises of the dead to a specially appropriate air, of which many varieties still live, and in which the whole concourse of the funeral took part, by taking up along with the singer, at the end of each verse, this curious, murmuring chorus; the sound of which, though produced in the throat, was not unmusical or monotonous, but one capable of various modifications of distinct, musical tones, ascending from the deepest bass to the highest treble.

the author heard the *Crónán*, or throat accompaniment to dirges;

I have, myself, often heard with pleasure this *Crónán*, or throat accompaniment, without words, performed to old Irish dirges; and I very well know how it was produced, and could even attempt an imitation of it. But, I have never heard the *Crónán* fully sung in concert; and I have known only two men

cróċa ban náeċeċ o crochaib rígna,
ríg ic Domnall,
.i. deroil caċ céol ifarrad aidbsi,
dord ic aidbsi,
.i. deróil oenċainnell bec hi farrad cainle more
adand oc caindill,
.i. claideb
colc oc mo choilcse. Acas innóenecht do gnitis in ceol sin.—*Leabhar na h-Uidhre*, f. 3. a. b. line 6.]

who were proficients in it; one of them was my own father; the other was John Molony, a younger and better performer. They were both large men. My father sang Irish songs better than any man I ever knew; but John Molony could not sing at all.

Many of our popular writers speak of an old woman "croning" in the corner; they mean by this that she is humming some sort of a tune. The word "croning", however, is a misapplied and shortened form of "cronaning", which is an Anglicised way of saying that she was singing a *Crónán*, which, as I have just said, was not humming, but a kind of purring. They have gone so far indeed as to form a generic noun from the corrupt word "croning"; and the word "crone", as an old woman, is now to be found in the English dictionaries, on the presumption, it may be observed, that every woman is old who hums in imitation of the old Irish *Crônán!*

origin of the word "crone";

There may be many persons still living in various parts of Ireland, who have heard this *Crónán* from their fathers; and there may be some who can produce it; but in my youthful days, and within the range of my acquaintance, though I have known many to attempt it, I never knew but the two persons already mentioned who succeeded in it.

The same practice of lauding the living and lamenting the dead, and in the same way, was anciently followed in Scotland; but what in Ireland was called *Aidbsi*, was there called *Cepóg*. This word *Cepóg* was well known in Ireland too; and it is singular to find that in neither country is either of these words now remembered. Both words, however, are entered in O'Reilly's "Irish-English Dictionary", but without sufficient explanation; and Stewart, in his "Gaelic Dictionary", has the word *Aidhbhsi* explained in the same way as O'Reilly, but he has not the *Cepóg*. That the word *Cepóg* for a song of praise or elegy, was well known in ancient Ireland as in Scotland, will be seen from a short story, preserved in the "Book of Ballymote" [which will be found in Lecture xxxvii., where the words *Aidbsi* and *Cepóg* are very fully discussed in their appropriate place].

the Irish *Aidbsi* known in Scotland as *Cepóg*;

the word *Cepóg* known in Ireland also.

But to return to St. *Colum Cille* and *Dallan Forgall*. The poets having chaunted their laudatory poems and performed their wonderful musical strain for their friend and patron, the chief poet of Erinn and head of all the others, whose name was *Dallan Forgall*, that is (*Forgall* the blind), came forward chaunting the commencement of an extempore poem in praise of St. *Colum Cille*. But when he had sung the first verse of it, the saint stopped him, saying that the strain was an elegiac one, and should not be composed until after his death. And he further

The Assembly of *Drom Ceat* continued:

XXXI.

Dallan Forgaill's elegy on St. Colum Cille;

said to the poet: "In whatever place you are, you shall hear of my death when it occurs".

After this the meeting of *Drom Ceat* broke up. St. *Colum Cille* returned to his home at *I*, or *Iona*, and the poets dispersed themselves throughout the country, in strict accordance with the arrangements made for them at the great meeting. Now, seven years after that event, the chief poet *Dallan Forgaill* was travelling with his retinue in the neighbourhood of *Loch Uair* (now Loch Owel, near the present town of Mullingar in Westmeath), and they were overtaken on the road by a strange horseman. Some of the poet's people asked the stranger if he had any news; and he answered that he had what was bad news for the *Ui Neill* (that is, for the people of Meath and Ulster), for that their great patron St. *Colum Cille* was dead. The moment the chief poet, *Dallan Forgall*, heard these words, he recollected what the saint had told him, and that he also charged him, that the very words in which his death should be announced to him, should be the words with which his poem on his death should commence; and immediately the poet commenced in the words of the stranger:

"It is not good news for the *Ui Neill*".(325)

And making straight for *Port Loman*, on the brink of the above lake, had finished his poem when he arrived there.

the word Ceis again occurs in this poem

It is in this very ancient and celebrated poem that the passage occurs to which I desire to direct notice: for in the nineteenth line the poet describes Ireland and Scotland after the loss of their great saint in these words:

"A *Cruit* without a *Ceis*, a church without an abbot".(326)

Ceis here represents part of the harp,

That the *Ceis* mentioned here, as well as in the former references to it, in the story of the princess *Moriath*, and *Craiftine's Cruit*, is represented as an essential part of the harp, and of remote antiquity, will be apparent from the following gloss, or rather commentary on the above line of *Dallan Forgall's* poem, as it is found in the *Leabhar na h-Uidhre*, of which the existing copy was made before the year 1106. And it is strange indeed that at this early time, and while the harp or *Cruit* was still the distinguishing instrument of the nation, that any doubt or difficulty could exist as to the precise signification and use of the *Ceis*.

as shown by a scholium in Leabhar na h-Uidhre;

Thus speaks the commentator just alluded to: "*Ceis*, that is, a means of fastening; or a path to the knowledge of the music; or *Ceis* is the name of a small *Cruit* which accompanies a large *Cruit* in co-playing; or, it is the name of the little pin (or key) which retains the string in the wood of the *Cruit;* or [it is the

(325) [original:—ni dirceóil d'ib néill.]

(326) [original:—ir crut cen ceir, ir cell cen abaid.]

name of] the *Cobhluigi* [the two strings called the sisters]; or it is the name of the heavy string [or bass]; or, the *Ceis* in the *Cruit* is what keeps the counterpart with its strings in it, as the poet said, that is, *Nos*, the son of *Find*, cecinit; or *Ferceirtne* the poet: XXXI.

"I conceal not [said he] that it was the *Ceis* of *Craiftine*'s *Cruit*
That threw the host into a death sleep,
Until *Labraid* and *Moriath* of *Morca* were united;—
Beyond all price did she prize *Labraid*,
Sweeter than all the music was the *Cruit*,
Which was played for *Labraid*, *Loingsiuch Lorc;*
Though the prince was before that dumb,
Craiftine's *Ceis* was not concealed".(327)

Even these stanzas have an interlined gloss, but it could not be made appreciable to the ear; and I must also indeed admit that it is difficult for a popular audience to catch the force and point of so necessarily stiff and close a translation as I have found myself bound to give of this important commentary.

antiquity of the tale of the "Destruction of *Dindrigh*" proved by this scholium;

It may be perceived that the commentator quotes two stanzas from *Ferceirtne*'s answer to king *Scoriath*, the father of the princess *Moriath;* but he appears to be uncertain whether the words

(327) [original:—

.i. ceis cai astuda, no coi dris in ciuil;
Is crut cen ceis, is cell cen abaid,
.i. céis ainm do ċruit bic bis i comaiteċt cruite móre hicomsinm;
no ainm don delgain bic fostas in teit himmude na crote;
no dona coblaigib; no ainm don trom ṫet; no isi in ceis isin cruit
an ní congbas in leṫrind cona tétaib inti, ut dixit poeta, Nos
mac Find cecinit; no Ferċertne file.

.i. Ni roċeil Nos mac Find no Ferċertne fili. .i. cruitire
Nicelt ceis ceol de cruit Craibtine
.i. do rat .i. bas codalta
cosrelastar for sluaga suanbas
.i. ꝑ
consert coibnius, eter sceo main Moriaet macdacht
.i. ꝑ gentis
Morca;
.i. Labrad do Loingsiuċ arba balb
bamo lé cech log Labreid,
ba binniu ceċ ceol in crot
.i. Labrad Longsiuc mac Ailiol mac Beg mac Ugaini Moir
airpete Laibraid Loingsec Lorc.
.i. ciar bo balb remi sin
ciarbodoċt for rune in ri
ni ro ċelt: ceis Craiptini.—*Leabhar na h-Uidhre*, f. 5. a. a. top.]

XXXI. were really to be ascribed to *Ferceirtne*, or to *Nos*, the son of *Find*, a poet to whom I have never met any other allusion. And this uncertainty places the antiquity and authenticity of the old tale of the Destruction of *Dindrigh* in a much higher and more important light; because, if its tradition or history had not been of remote antiquity, there could scarcely be any doubt about the identity of the poet at the early time at which this commentator must have lived. And we further collect from this commentary, that there must, in ancient times, have existed a much more extensive and detailed version of the destruction of *Dindrigh*, than the short condensed tract which is now extant; and that it contained a whole poem of the character of the additional ancient stanza quoted in this commentary, —that stanza which declares that "Sweeter than all music was the *Cruit*", which *Craiftine* played.

the word *Ceis* glossed in all ancient copies of the elegy on St. *Colum Cillé*.

It is strange indeed, as I have already observed, that at so early a date as about the year 1100, when our copy of the *Leabhar na h-Uidhre* was made, there should have been any difficulty as to the precise signification of the word *Ceis;* and not only then, but when the "Liber Hymnorum" was written, which was about the year 900; and not only at that time, but at a time much farther back—in fact at whatever time *Dallan Forgall's* elegy for St. *Colum Cille* first came to require an explanatory gloss. It is not only in the copy of this celebrated poem preserved in *Leabhar na h-Uidhre* that the gloss on the word *Ceis* is found, but in all the ancient copies of it that I am acquainted with, and which amount to four, namely, that already referred to in *Leabhar na h-Uidhre*, another in H. 2. 16, or the "Yellow Book of *Lecan*", in the library of Trinity College, Dublin; another in the "Liber Hymnorum" in the same library, and another in a vellum MS., lately purchased by the British Museum, at the sale of Mr. William Monck Mason's library.

The quotation and commentary that I have just quoted, are taken, as I mentioned, from the ancient *Leabhar na h-Uidhre;* but the following version of the same commentary is taken from the other ancient copy of the meeting at *Drom Ceat*, and the poem on St. *Colum Cille*, preserved in the "Yellow Book of Lecan", in the library of Trinity College, Dublin.

Scholium in MS. H. 2. 16. T.C.D.;

This version is as follows: "A *Cruit* without a *Ceis* (are Ireland and Scotland after him), that is, without a means of securing the strings [below], that is, without a knot [on the ends of the strings]. Or without *Cobhluighe* [that is, the strings called the sisters]; or they are a *Cruit* without a heavy string [a bass], or a *Cruit* without a string of knowledge such as *Cairbre* the harper had; that is the string of knowledge, which was in

Cairbre's harp; [and whenever he struck that string] there was not from the rising of the sun to its going down any secret of which he was ignorant. Ireland and Scotland, then, are a *Cruit* without a *Ceis* after him [St. *Colum Cille*], or, that it was for a small *Cruit*, *Ceis* was the name, and it was along with a large *Cruit* it used to be played; for the fine strings were in the small *Cruit*, and the heavy strings in the great *Cruit*, and it was together they were played; and Erinn and Scotland are [as] a *Cruit* without a *Ceis* after him, as the poet said, and it was *Dallan* himself that sang:— XXXI.

"The cure of a physician without a medicine-bag,
The parting of the marrow from the bone,
Singing with a *Cruit* without a *Ceis*,
Such are we after our noble protector".

"Or", continues the commentator, "it was a *Cruit* without any one of the three tunings (*Glésa*) which served to *Craiftine* the harper, namely *Suantraigh*, and *Goltraigh*, and *Gentraigh*, for the sleeping, the crying, and the laughing modes]".(328)

The copy in the British Museum adds nothing of value, except the words fastening below, introduced into the last version.

gloss in Liber Hymnorum;

The following is the short version in the "Liber Hymnorum": "*Ceis* is the name of a small *Cruit* which accompanied a large *Cruit* at playing upon; or the name of a nail on which the strings called *Lethrind* were fastened; or the name of the little pin; or the name of the [strings called the] *Cobhluighe* (or sisters); or the name of the heavy string".(329)

The word *Lethrind* we shall come to presently; it means here, probably, the treble strings.

parts of the harp surmised to have been the *Ceis*,—the *Cobhluighe*, or "sisters", and the *Leithrind*;

Among the other parts of the harp which the commentator surmises the *Ceis* to have been, were the *Cobhluighe* and the *Leithrind*. Now, the word *Cobhla*, which is the singular of

(328) [original:—As crot cen ċeis, .i. cen cae sais, .i. cen earrnaidm. No cen coblaigi; no as cruit cen trom theit, no ascruit cen teid sis amail ro boi ic Cairbri; .i. an téid sis ro bid a cruit Cairbri; acas an tan no gluaised an ted sin, nibid o turcbail co fuinead ni a nainfis do. Is cruit cen teid sis Eiri acas Alba dia essеam, no comad da ċruit bic bud ainm ces, acas maille re cruit moir; no sentea uair na goloca isin ċruit big, acas na trom ċeada sin ċruit moir, acas amail no senntea; agas as ċruit cen ċeol Eire acas Alba dia és, ut poeta dixit, acas comad e Dollan ses dixit.

As leiges lega cenles,
As deadail smeara sri smuas,
Is amran sri cruit cen ces,
Sinn deis ar nargari uais.

No as cruit cen gles do na tri glesaib do fognaidis do Ċhraiftine cruitiri, .i. suantraig, acas golltraig, acas gentraig, atiat sin an-anmann.—H. 2. 16. col. 689.]

(329) [original:—Ceis ainm do cruit bic bis hi comaitecht cruiti móiri h-ica seinm; no ainm do ṫarraing ar a mbi in leithrind; no ainm don delgain bic; no ainm dona coblaigib; no don trom theit.—E. 4. 2. Liber Hymnorum (in Amra Coluim), f. 32. b.]

XXXI. *Cobhluighe*, is explained in our ancient glossaries as *Camhlúth*, that is, simultaneous motion; and it is in this sense that *Comhladh* is the ancient name of a door; because, as stated in *Cormac's* Glossary, it moves simultaneously upon its hinges above and below.

It is remarkable that in the long apocryphal list of the names of the harp strings, printed by the late Edward Bunting in his "Ancient Music of Ireland", the word *Cobhluighe* occurs twice. In the first place, at page 21, concealed under the slightly corrupt orthography of *Caomhluighe*, and translated, "lying together"; and, in the second place, at page 32, where it is correctly enough written *comhluighe*, and translated, "stretched together". There can be no doubt, then, that Bunting's *Caomhluighe*, and our commentator's *Cobhluighe*, mean one and the same thing; and the following foot-note in Bunting's book, page 21, will very well maintain the etymology which I have ventured to give above, as well as the identity of the names of these strings:

"*Caomhluighe*, called by the harpers 'the sisters', were two strings in unison, which were the first tuned to the proper pitch; they answered to the tenor G, fourth string on the violin, and nearly divided the instrument into bass and treble".

That the practice of harmony—the use of the musical chord, existed in Ireland from a very remote period, is clearly shown in the commentary given above, where the writer at one time surmises that, perhaps, *Ceis* was the name of a small harp which accompanied a large harp; indicating that the large harp contained the heavy or bass strings, whilst the small harp contained the thin or treble strings, and that it was together they were played. Now, the harmonious unison of the two harps, when playing together—small string against large string, and large string against small string—exactly produces musical harmony.

Leithrind, or half harmony, and

It is evident that the word *Leithrind*, or half harmony, was not originally intended for either the large or the small harp, but for a constituent part of a single harp—namely, that part which held either the bass or the treble strings, divided by the *cobhluighe*, or "sisters".

Rind, or full harmony;

Along with this, in O'Davoren's "Irish Glossary", compiled in the latter half of the sixteenth century, I find the word *Rind*, i.e. music, with corresponding music against it".[339] In other words, *Rind* was music consisting of full harmony, while *Leithrind*, or half *Rind*, was one or either of the two corresponding parts which produced the harmonious whole, and these parts were the bass and treble notes, or the bass and treble strings—

(339) [original:—Rinn .i. ceol co cuibdius ina agaid.]

the *Trom Theada*, and the *Goloca*, or the heavy and the thin strings, either of which, the commentator on *Dallan Forgaill's* elegy on St. *Colum Cille* surmised to be the *Ceis* mentioned in that poem, and without which the harp had lost its life and harmony. XXXI.

So far I have endeavoured to give a description of the harp, and an idea of its musical powers, such as I could frame from the statements found in our most ancient historic tales and romantic writings. I am sorry to have to acknowledge, however, that I am not able to decide with certainty upon what the *Ceis* of the *Cruit* precisely was; but why should I take blame to myself for my shortcomings on this point, when we see how uncertain were the writers even of the eleventh and earlier centuries as to the exact meaning of this same word? All this difficulty of understanding this ancient term, however, goes to show the extreme antiquity of the harp, either as a complex whole, or as formed of two independent but imperfect parts—namely, the large and the small harps, the combination, or the co-playing of which was necessary to make a perfect harmonious whole. But, though I cannot speak with authority as to what exactly the *Ceis* was, yet there is good reason to think that it was no material part of the harp after all, but that the word signifies simply the harmonized tones or tune of the instrument. We have seen that on different occasions, the father, mother, and household of the princess *Moriath*, and herself afterwards, slept profoundly under the magical spell of the *Ceis* of *Craiftine's* harp. Surely it could not have been any material part of the harp, except the strings, that could have produced this extraordinary effect. Surely it could only have been the richness of the harmony of the instrument as so played. It is not easy to say whether the word *Ceis* refers to that harmony or that mode of playing, or to a necessary portion of the particular kind of harp played on.

difficulty of determining what *Ceis* was;

not a part of the harp;

We have seen from the words ascribed to the poet *Ferceirtne* in answer to *Scoriath*, the king of West Munster, that "I conceal not that it was the *Ceis* of *Craiftine's* harp" which sent the king with his household to sleep; and, strange to say, we find the scholiast on these lines in the eleventh and earlier centuries quite at a loss to understand what it was precisely that this word *Ceis* signified. The scholiast in *Leabhar na h-Uidhre*, copied before the year 1106, surmises, etymologically, that *Ceis* is a condensation of the two words *Cai Astuda*, that is, a means of fastening, or *Coi dfis in ciuil*, that is, a path to the knowledge of the music; or that *Ceis* was the name of a small harp which accompanied a large harp in co-playing; or that it

summary of the views of the commentators as to meaning of *Ceis*.

XXXI. was the name of the little pin which retains the string in the wood [that is, the harmonic curve] of the harp; or that it was the name of the strings which are called "the sisters", or of the bass string; or that the *Ceis* in the harp was what kept the counterpart strings of that part in their proper places in the harp. Again, in the scholium on the same line of *Dallan Forgall's* poem in the "Yellow Book of Lecan", compiled in the year 1391, we find that a harp without a *Ceis* was a harp without a means of tightening, that is, without a knot (on the ends of the string below), that is, without a fastening pin; or without a bass string; or without a string of knowledge such as *Cairbre* the harper (of whom I happen to know nothing more) had in his harp; or that *Ceis* was the name of a small harp which was played along with a large harp, for that the small strings were in the small harp, while the heavy strings were in the large harp; or that it was a harp without a *Glés* (that is a tuning) of the three *Glésa* which were known to *Craiftine* the harper, namely, the sleeping tune, the crying tune, and the laughing tune.

A fourth reference to the *Ceis* is found in the very ancient tale of *Toghail Bruidhne Da Choga*, or the Destruction of the mansion of the Two Equal Masters, who were two smiths by profession.

Fourth reference to the word *Ceis* in an ancient tale in *Leabhar na h-Uidhre.*

It may be remembered from former lectures, that *Fergus Mac Roigh*, the celebrated prince of Ulster, had exiled himself in Connacht after the tragical death of the sons of *Uisnech* while under his protection, by command of *Conchobar Mac Nessa*, the king of Ulster. *Fergus* was accompanied in his exile by *Cormac Conloinges*, son of king *Conchobar*. On the death of the latter, his son *Cormac* was invited back to Ulster, and having accepted the invitation, he set out from *Rath Cruachain* in Roscommon, crossed the Shannon at Athlone, and sought rest for the night at the mansion of the two smiths. [The ruined fort of this mansion is shown still on the hill of *Bruighean Mhor* or the Great Mansion, in the parish of Drumancy, barony of Kilkenny West, and county of Westmeath]. The house was beset in the night by the men of Leinster, and *Cormac* with the most of his people killed.

The tale of this slaughter relates that *Cormac* had been the former lover of a Connacht lady named *Sceanb*, who afterwards became the wife of a famous harper named *Craiftine;* and it is stated that on the night of the attack on *Cormac*, *Craiftine*, in a fit of jealousy, attended outside with his harp, and played for him a *Ceis Cendtoll*, that is, a head-sleeping, or a debilitating *Ceis*, or tune which left him an easy prey to his enemies.

A fifth reference to a *Cruit*, or harp without a *Ceis*, is found

XXXI.

Fifth reference to *Ceis* in an ancient poem.

in an ancient poem of general instructions to a new king, but evidently intended for a king of Munster, probably for *Cormac Mac Cuileannain* in the ninth century. The poem consists of thirty-seven quatrains, in the twenty-third of which the poet, dilating on the advantages of a good king to his people, says:

"This world is every man's world in his turn,
There is no prophet but the true God;
Like a company without a chief, like a harp without a *Ceis*,
Are the people after their king".[331]

Coir another term for harmony, synonymous with *Ceis*;

Another term for the harmony or proper tune of the harp was *Coir* (which literally signifies propriety), as has been already shown in speaking of the great *Tuath Dé Danann* harp, and in the quotation from Dr. Keating's poem on his harper. The following passage from the Brehon Laws will illustrate this fact:

"*Coir* is concealed from harps when one string is broken, that is *Coir* is completely concealed from the harp when one string is wanting to it, so that its harmony (or *Coicetal*) is destroyed, according to propriety. The *Coir* (or propriety) of harmony is dissolved, that is, the *Coir* (or propriety) of playing is concealed, when one string of the harp has been broken".[332]

Author concludes that *Ceis* meant either harmony or the mode of playing with a bass.

Now from all of the foregoing commentaries, and notwithstanding their uncertainty in many respects, it is, I think, a reasonable deduction on the whole, independently of the words of *Ferceirtne* and *Mac Lonain*, that the *Ceis* was the mere harmony of the harp, or that the word denoted only the mode of playing upon it in harmony, that is, with a bass. This point would seem to be in fact decided by the last paragraph of the scholium from the "Yellow Book of *Lecan*", which supposes the harp without a *Ceis* to be a harp without any one of the three *Glésa*, or tunings, by which *Craiftine*, as well as the other older harpers, produced such wonderful effect. Now it happens that the word *Glés*, which is here put for *Ceis*, has been a living word from the oldest times down to our own, and always understood to signify preparing, setting, or tuning; and not only this, but the name of the tuning-key itself is still on ancient record, and in such a position as to leave no doubt

The word *Glés* mentioned in scholium in H. 2. 16, a living word;

(331) [original:—
An bioṫ-so as bioṫ caiċ ar uair,
ni bfuil faiḋ aċt fiada fior;
cuire gan cenn, cruit gan ceis
samail na tuaiṫ d'eis an riġ.
O'Conor Don MSS., R.I.A., p. 917.]

(332) [original:—Diciallaiṫ coir a crotaiḃ conbongar aen téd, .i. abal diclithar a cóir ar in cruit o bus earbadaċ aon ted eiste, conid eipiltinach a coicetal uimpe do reir cóir. Taithmithe coir a coicetail, .i. diclither coir, in tseanma obrisdter aon ted isin cruit.—H. 3. 17. 438. Vide imṫeċt na Tromdaiṁe, Betham MSS., R.I.A., cxx. p. 39.]

XXXI. whatever of what it was, and its close relation to the word *Glés*. The name of this instrument was *Crann-Glésa*, or tuning-tree; and we find it mentioned in the Brehon Laws among the articles for which there was a special law for their prompt recovery, if borrowed and not duly returned. Here it is called *Comhobair gach ciuil, edhon Crann Glésa*, that is, "The instrument of all music, namely, the *Crann Glesa*, or tuning tree". [H. 3. 17. p. 403½.] With this instrument of course the strings were strictly tuned, so as to make it possible to play in full harmony of chords.

the Crann-Gléasta mentioned in a poem of the 18th century;

And again. In a single stanza, some hundreds of years old, preserved in a paper MS. of about the year 1740, in the library of Trinity College, Dublin, and prophetic of the decline of the harp in this country, the poet says:

"The *Crann-Gléasta* will be lost,
Strings will be thickly broken,
The *Corr* will drop out of the *Lamhchrann*,
And the *Com* will go down the stream".(333)

this poem contains the names of the principal parts of the harp;

This is an important stanza, for it gives us distinctly, what is exceedingly rare to be met with, the names of the chief members, or parts of the harp. The *Crann Gléasta* is clearly the tuning tree or key; the *Corr* is the cross tree, or harmonic curve; the *Lamhchrann* is the front pillar, and the *Com* is the belly or sound-board. The only loss is, that we have not in this, or in any other stanza, the distinctive names of the different classes of strings, such as *Trom-Théda* for the heavy string; *Cobhluighe*, for the strings called the sisters; and *Golóca*, for the light strings. These names indeed I have only met in the above scholium on *Dallan Forgall's* elegy on St. *Colum Cille*.

the names of the different classes of strings only found in this scholium to the elegy on St. Colum Cille.

(333) [original:—Caillfear an crann gléasta,
Brisfear téda go tiuġ,
Tuitfiḋ in corr as in Lámċrann,
Is raċaiḋ an com re sruṫ.—H. 4. 20. f. 92.]

LECTURE XXXII.

[Delivered June 17th, 1862.]

(IX.) OF MUSIC AND MUSICAL INSTRUMENTS (continued). Reference to the different parts of a harp in a poem of the seventeenth century. The number of strings not mentioned in references to harps, except in two instances; the first is in the tale of the *Iubar Mic Aingis* or the "Yew Tree of *Mac Aingis*"; the instrument mentioned in this tale was not a *Cruit*, but a three stringed *Timpan*; the second reference is to be found in the Book of *Lecan*, and the instrument is eight stringed. The instrument called "Brian Boru's Harp" has thirty strings. Reference to a many stringed harp in the seventeenth century. Attention paid to the harp in the twelfth and thirteenth centuries. References to the *Timpan* as late as the seventeenth century, proving it to have been a stringed instrument. The *Timpan* was distinguished from the *Cruit* or full harp. No very ancient harp preserved. The harp in Trinity College, Dublin; Dr. Petrie's account of it; summary of Dr. Petrie's conclusions. Dr. Petrie's serious charge against the Chevalier O'Gorman. Some curious references to harps belonging to O'Briens which the author has met with: *Mac Conmidhe*'s poem on *Donnchadh Cairbreach* O'Brien; *Mac Conmidhe*'s poem on the harp of the same O'Brien; the poem does not explain how the harp went to Scotland. What became of this harp? Was it the harp presented by Henry the Eighth to the Earl of Clanrickard? Perhaps it suggested the harp-coinage, which was in circulation in Henry the Eighth's time. The Chevalier O'Gorman only mistook one Donogh O'Brien for another. There can be no doubt that this harp did once belong to the Earl of Clanrickard. If the harp was an O'Neill harp, how could its story have been invented and published in the lifetime of those concerned? Arthur O'Neill may have played upon the harp, but it could not have been his; this harp is not an O'Neill, but an O'Brien one; Dr. Petrie's antiquarian difficulties: author's answer; as to the monogram I. H. S.; as to the arms on the escutcheon. The assertion of Dr. Petrie, that the sept of O'Neill is more illustrious than that of O'Brien, is incorrect.

AT the close of the last Lecture I quoted a stanza containing an old authority for the names of the three principal parts of the harp. But even in comparatively modern times also we may find authority for these names, and for the form of the instrument, which seems to have remained the same.

Reference to the different parts of a harp in a poem of the seventeenth century.

I have in my possession a curious poem of twenty-six quatrains, written by Pierce Ferriter, of Ferriter's Cove, on the coast of the county of Kerry, about the year 1640, on a harp which had been presented to him. Pierce Ferriter was a gentleman and a scholar, a poet and a musician; and he wrote this Gaedhelic poem in praise of a certain harp which was presented to him by Mr. Edmond *Mac an Daill*, the son of Mr. Donnell *Mac an Daill*, of *Magh Lorg*, in the county of Roscommon. In this poem he speaks of the harp under both the Gaedhelic names of *Cruit* and *Clairseach* (the former, of course, being by

XXXII.

Reference to the different parts of a harp in a poem of the seventeenth century.

far the more ancient name); and, as there are some interesting details introduced into his verses, I may quote a few stanzas of them here. At the tenth stanza, the poet, speaking of his harp, calls it—

"The key of music and its gate,
The wealth, the abode of poetry;
The skilful, neat Irishwoman,
The richly festive moaner.

"Children in dire sickness, men in deep wounds,
Sleep at the sounds of its crimson board;
The merry witch has chased all sorrow,
The festive home of music and delight.

"It found a *Cor* in a fruitful wood in [*Magh*] *Aoi;*
And a *Lamh-chrann* in the Fort of *Seantraoi,*—
The rich sonorous discourser of the musical notes;
And a comely *Com* from *Eas dá Ecconn.*

"It found *Mac Sithduill* to plan it,
It found *Cathal* to be its artificer,
And *Beannglan,*—great the honour,—
Got [to do] its fastenings of gold and its emblazoning.

"Excellent indeed was its other adorner in gold,
Parthalon More Mac Cathail,
The harp of the gold and of the gems,
The prince of decorators is *Parthalon*".[294]

This harp, the poet says, found its *Corr*, that is, its harmonic curve, or crosstree, was found in the fruitful woods of *Magh Aoi*, in the plains of Roscommon. It found its *Lamhchrann*, that is, its front pillar was found at the fort of *Seantraoi* (a place I am unable to identify); and it found its *Com*, that is, its sound-board was found at *Eas da Eccon*, now the falls of Ballyshannon, in the county of Donegal. In the same language he goes on to name the artificers. So it was *Mac Sithduill* that designed it, and *Cathal* that made it; and it was bound and emblazoned by *Bennglan*, and it was decorated with gold and gems by *Parthalon Mor Mac Cathail*. So that in this instance, so great was

(294) [original:—

Eoċair an ċeóil sa ċoṁla,
ionnṁus, teaġ na halaóna;
an éireannaċ ġasda ġlan,
ġeimeannaċ ḃlasda ḃiaḋmar.
Aos fírġalair, firġonta,
codlaid ris an cclar ccorcra;
an beó ḃaḋḃ donḃrón doḃris,
ceol aḋḃ an oil san aoiḃnis.
Fuair corr a cnuas ċoill i nAoi
agas Lamċrann a Lios Sentraoi,—
breasdaċ maoċlonn na ccles ccorr;—
is caoṁ ċom ó Eas [da] Ecconn.
Fuair Mac Siṫḋuill dá suiḋeaċt,
fuair Caṫal dá ceirduiġeċt,
is fuair Beannġlan, mór an moḋ,
a ceanglaḋ dór sa hionnloḋ.
Maiṫ a hoirċeard eile fuin,
Párṫalón Mór Mac Caṫuil,
clairseaċ an óir sna nallán,
dóiġ na ssairseaċ Párṫalán.

—Miscellaneous Poems, chiefly copied from the O'Connor Don's Book. O'Curry MSS., Cath. Univ., p. 294.]

the care bestowed on the manufacture of a harp, that it engaged the professional skill of four distinct artists,—the modeller, the wood-worker and carpenter, the binder and emblazoner, and the decorator; and the services of these artizans are referred to as if their occupations were in the usual course, each of them living by his own independent art. The shape and general design of the ancient harp, and the materials used in its framework, are then frequently alluded to; but there is, unfortunately, one great omission in all the references to the harp that I have met with—I mean the absence of any allusion to the number of strings which it properly contained. I have, indeed, met one or two references to harps of a certain limited number of strings; but it is evident from their being so particularized, that they were exceptions to the general rule. To these references I have next to direct your attention.

The number of strings not mentioned in references to harps except in two instances;

the first is in the tale of the "Yew Tree of *Mac Aingis*";

The first of them, and which is contained in the tale called *Iubhar Mic Aingis*, or the Yew Tree of *Mac Aingis* (which alludes to a harp of the kind called *Timpan*), is of undoubtedly great antiquity, though the tale is one of those belonging to the most fabulous class, as far as the incident connected with the harp is concerned. The tale is preserved in very old language in the "Book of Leinster", and may be shortly stated as follows:—

Oilioll Oluim (the ancestor of the great families of south and north Munster, and who was king of that province, died after a long reign, in the year of our Lord 234), was married to *Sadhbh* (or Sabia), the daughter of the monarch of Erinn *Conn* of the Hundred Battles, and widow of *Mac Niadh*, a distinguished Munster prince; and *Sadhbh* had a son by her first husband, named *Lugaidh*, more popularly called *Mac Con*, and several sons by *Oilioll*, her second husband, the eldest of whom was *Eoghan Mór*, or Eugene the Great. So much as to the personages mentioned in this story, which proceeds as follows:

"At a certain time [this] *Eoghan*, the son of *Oilioll* [*Oluim*], and *Lugaidh Mac Con*, his stepbrother, set out to pay a visit to *Art*, the son of *Conn* [monarch of Erinn], their mother's brother, who was then on a visit in Connacht, for the purpose of receiving some bridle-steeds from him. Now, as they were passing over the river *Maigh* or Maigue [at *Caher-ass*, in the county of Limerick], they heard music in a yew tree over the cataract, [and saw a little man playing there]. After that they returned back again to *Oilioll* with him, that is, with the [little] man whom they took out of the tree; because they were disputing about him [as to who should have him], so that *Oilioll* might give judgment between them. He was a little man, with three strings in his *Timpan*. 'What is your name?' [said

XXXII. the first is in the tale of the "Yew Tree of Mac Aingis";

Oilioll]. 'Fer-fi, the son of *Eogabhal*' [said he]. 'What has brought ye back?' said *Oilioll*. 'We are disputing about this man' [said they]. 'What sort of man is he?' [said *Oilioll*]. 'A good timpanist' [said they]. 'Let his music be played for us' [said *Oilioll*]. 'It shall be done', said he. So he played for them the crying tune (*Goltraighe*), and he put them to crying and lamenting and tear-shedding, and he was requested to desist from it. And then he played the laughing tune (*Gentraighe*), till they laughed with mouths so wide open, that all but their lungs were visible. He then played the sleeping tune (*Suantraighe*) for them, until they were cast into a sleep [so deep, that it lasted] from that hour till the same hour next day". "He then", continues the story, "went away from them to the place whence he was brought, leaving a bad feeling between them, such as he particularly wished should exist".[333]

The bad feeling which the little timpanist left between the stepbrothers arose not so much in regard to himself, as about the ownership of the wonderful yew tree in which he was found, and which appeared to have sprung up spontaneously by necromantic art for their misfortune.

The remainder of this wild story is too long for my present purpose, and it is therefore sufficient to say, that the little man was one of the *Tuatha Dé Danann* race from the neighbouring hill of Knockany (*Cnoc Ainé*). The famous *Tuatha Dé Danann* lady, *Aine*, from whom this hill takes its name, had been some short time previously abused, and herself and her brother *Eogabhal* slain in a fit of anger, by king *Oilioll Oluim*, and it was to have revenge for this deed that the little timpanist, *Fer-fi*, the son of *Eogabhal*, raised up the phantom yew tree at the falls of *Caher-ass*, in order to excite a dispute between the sons and the stepson of *Oilioll*. In this he succeeded to the full. *Oilioll* awarded the yew tree to his own son *Eoghan*, and *Mac Con* charged him with partiality, and challenged him, with all

(333) [original:—Luid dan fecht aile, Eogan mac Ailella acas Lugaid mac Con, .i. a comalta co Art mac Cuind diambái for cuairt Connacht, do ċabairt eċ srian úad, .i. brathair maċar do Eogan. Oc teċt doib seċ an Mag co cualatar in ceol issinduś ibair robúi ossindess. Berait leo co h-Ailill arisin, .i. infer tuctat asinduess; arbatar oc imresain imme, conrucad breith doib. Fer bec, tri chét ina thimpán. Ciatainm? Fer-fi mac Eogabail. Cid dobrintai? Or Ailill. Atáam oc imresain immo fessa. Cinnas firso? Timpanaċ maith. Sentar dún a ceol, or Ailill. Dogentar osse. Rosephaind dóib dan goltraide, conad cosartait ingol, acas i cói, acas derċóiniud. Rogess do anad de. Rosenid dan, gentraide, conadcosartar ingen ngaire, act nortar ecnai ascaim. Rosephaind dóib dán suantraige conadcorsattar isúan on trath coaraile. Atpullaiseom issuidiu allech dia tudċid acas forácaib droċimtel etarru ar bassran leis.—H. 2. 16. f. 206. b. b.]

his forces, to a battle, at a time to be fixed afterwards. When the appointed time came, both parties met at the hill of *Cenn-Abrat*, in the neighbourhood of Kilfinan, on the borders of the counties of Cork and Limerick, where a battle ensued, in which *Mac Con* was defeated, and forced to fly the country. He went into Scotland, but in some years returned with a large force of Scottish or Pictish and British adventurers, who sailed round by the south coast of Erinn, and entered the bay of Galway, and there, in the neighbourhood of Oranmore, at a place called *Magh Mucruimhé*, a battle was fought between them and the monarch *Art* and his forces, aided by his nephews, the seven sons of *Oilioll Oluim*, and the forces of Munster, under the leadership of *Eoghan Mór*, the eldest of them. This celebrated battle, which forms one of the cardinal points of the history of the period, proved fatal to the royal arms, the monarch himself having been slain in it, as well as *Eoghan Mór* and all the other six sons of *Oilioll Oluim*. So the little timpanist, *Fér-fi*, the son of *Eogabhail*, had ample revenge for the death of his father and his aunt.

There is a metrical version of the part of this story which relates to the little timpanist and the phantom yew tree preserved also in the "Book of Leinster". I believe *Cormac Mac Cuileannain* was the author of this piece, and that it was copied into the "Book of Leinster" from his "Psalter of Cashel". The authority, then, for this distinct allusion to the *Timpan* is old and high enough.

It must be observed that the three stringed instrument mentioned in this story, is not called a *Cruit*, or harp, but a *Timpan*. But even though it were not a *Cruit* of the ordinary kind, it certainly must have been some species of it; and it is important to know, on authority so undoubted, that the *Timpan* was a stringed instrument, and therefore some kind of harp, though perhaps of an inferior class.

the instrument mentioned in this tale was not a *Cruit*, but a three-stringed *Timpan*;

The next reference to an instrument with a definite number of strings, is found in the "Book of *Lecan*", in the library of the Royal Irish Academy; and this, as well as the last, was probably taken from the "Saltair of Cashel"; and the instrument referred to must also have been of a peculiar character both in shape and size.

the second reference is in the Book of *Lecan*;

I may premise that the *Feidlimid Mac Crimthain* mentioned in this story was king of Munster and monarch of Erinn, a distinguished scholar and a scribe or writer of books, and that he died at Cashel in the year 845. The *Ui Cormaic* mentioned in it were a tribe of the *Eoghanachts*, or Eugenians of *Ui Fidhgheinte*, who at an earlier period crossed the Shannon and the

XXXII. Fergus and settled beyond the latter in the northern part of *Corca-Bhaiscind*, their territory being nearly coextensive with the present barony of Islands in the county of Clare. In this story we are told that:

"On a certain day in the season of autumn, as *Feidhlimidh Mac Crimhthainn*, monarch of Erinn, was in Cashel of the kings, there came to him the abbot of a church of the *Ui Cormaic*, and he sat on the couch, and he took his little eight-stringed [instrument] (*Ocht-Tedach*) unto him from his girdle, and he played sweet music, and sang a poem to it, and he sang these words there.—

and the instrument is eight-stringed.

"Beware! beware! O chief and father!
Does the king of the *Eoghanacht* hear?
A tribe who are by the Shannon on the north:
Woe is it that they have ever gone into exile!

"The *Ui Cormaic*, O *Feidlimid!*
Do not love thy music-making;
The *Corca-Bhaiscind*, because of their strength,
Vouchsafe not justice to the *Eoghanachts*.

"My residence has been plundered;
And the men are not yet impeached;
The shrieks of its clerics and of its bells
Are not heard this day by *Feidlimid*.

"*Ui Cormaic* and *Tradraidhi*
Are much in want of relief;
They are from their friends far away,
And their great hardship is manifest.

"They are in want of relief,
The *Ui Cormaic* and *Tradraidhi;*
It is not now usual with [any one of] them
To be two days in his abbotship.[336]

[*i.e.*, such is the danger that no abbot, even, can be sure of his place for two days.]

[336] [original:—In aroile lo dain fogamair ro bi Feidlimid mac Crimthain rig Erind i Caisil na rig, dorachtoirchinneach cilli do hUib Cormac chuici ocus ro suid ar in colba, ocas tall a ochttedaich mbic chuici asa chris acas ro se-paind ceol mbind, acas rogob laid le, acas ro raid na briathra sa and.

Ababou abaid athair!
in cluineand rig Eoganacht?
tuath fil re Sinaind a tuaid:
mairg do chuaid andeoraidecht!
Hi Chormaic, a Feidlimid,
ni charaid do cheolaracht;
Corcobaiscind ara neirt,
nidamaid ceirt d'Eoganacht.
Rohaircedh mo bailsea
is fir gan aneiligid;
gair a cleireach isa cloc
ni cluin indocht Feidlimid.
Hi Cormaic is Tradraidi
regaid aleas foiridin;
siad ona tuathaib reraib,
isadmain amor deirir.
Recaid aleas foirithin,
i Cormaic is tradraidi;
ni tathair anois la cach
inda trach in abdaine. A.

—Book of *Lecan*, folio 183. a. a.]

XXXII.

What the effect of this singular appeal of the abbot from *Corca Bhaiscind* on the learned and just king *Feidlimid* was, we are not told; but we may presume that justice was rendered where it was due. It is, however, in reference to the musical instrument mentioned in it that the little article is of value to our present purpose. The date of king *Feidlimid's* death supplies us with two rather important historical facts; the first, that the tribe of the *Ui Cormaic* must have crossed the Shannon to the north some time before the year 845; and the second, that a portable eight-stringed harp was then an established instrument in the country; but whether as peculiar to the Church, or in common use, I am not at present able to say. There is no particular name given to this instrument, more than its being merely said that the abbot brought forth his little "eight-stringed" [harp] from his girdle; yet I think we need not hesitate to take it to have been a small eight-stringed harp; and we must look upon it as a small and light one indeed, when he could conveniently carry it at his girdle from Clare to Cashel. I confess myself unable to draw any conclusions from this little "eight-stringed" [instrument], as I cannot compare its compass with any musical standard of an earlier date: not having ever met with any reference to such standard, we must therefore come much farther down before we can speak with any certainty of the usual number of strings of the Irish harp, if it really had a standard number.

The instrument called "Brian Boru's harp" has thirty strings.

In the old harp preserved in the museum of Trinity College, Dublin, commonly called "Brian Boru's harp", and to which reference was made in my last lecture, the number of the strings is thirty; and we are told by Mr. Bunting, in the last volume of his "Ancient Music of Ireland", page 23, that this was the usual number of strings found on all the harps at the Belfast meeting in 1792. Yet, we find in the same writer's dissertation on the harp made for Sir John Fitzgerald of Cloyne, in the county of Cork, in the year 1621, that it contained forty-five strings.

Reference to a many-stringed harp in the seventeenth century.

An instance of authority for the use of a considerable number of strings in the harp, occurs in a fragment of a quaint English manuscript history of Kerry, written some time in the first half, I think, of the last century, and now preserved in the library of the Royal Irish Academy, in which we find at page 45, the following reference to a distinguished harper in that county: "As to the harp-playing, said county could well bragg, having the chiefest master of that instrument in the kingdom in his time, Mr. Nicholas Pierce of Clonmaurice, not only for his singular capacity of composing lamentations, funerals, additions

XXXII. and elevations, etc., but also by completing said instrument with more wires than ever before his time were used".

The writer of this tract does not speak of the precise time at which Mr. Pierce flourished; but we have his time from other sources, and in language which bears out the eulogium of our anonymous author on him. It appears that Mr. Pierce was blind, since we find him called, with reverence, "Blind Nicholas", in Pierce Ferriter's poem on his harp, already referred to. But, besides this reference, we have three distinct poems, by three different authors, written exclusively in his praise: one by *Ferflatha O'Gnimh*, a native of Ulster, who flourished about the year 1640, who calls him the *Craiftiné* of Cashel; another by *Maelmuiré Mac-an Bhaird*, of the county Donegal; the third is anonymous, and must, of course, have been written at the same time. The two latter of these curious poems are preserved in the O'Conor Don's volume of ancient poems, and will be found at pages 17 and 20 of my transcript from that volume.[337] *O'Gnimh's* poem is in my own possession.

Attention paid to the harp in the twelfth and thirteenth centuries.

Going back to a still earlier date we find the following curious entry in in the "Annals of *Loch Cé*" at the year 1225, showing that attention was paid long before to the improvement of the instrument.

"*Aedh* (or Hugh), the son of *Donnslebhe O'Sochlachann*, vicar of *Cunga*, a professor of singing and harp-tuning, as well as having invented a tuning (or arrangement) for himself that had not been done before him; and he was a proficient in all arts both of poetry and engraving and writing, and of all the arts that man executes. He died this year".[338]

What *O'Sochlachan's* arrangement of the harp was, however, whether an addition to, or diminution of the number of strings, or a new arrangement of the old number, whatever that might have been, our chronicler, unfortunately, does not say.

References to the *Timpan* as late as seventeenth century, proving it to have been a stringed instrument.

I have one reference more, though of a comparatively modern date, to the strings of the harp, or rather of the *Timpan*, and which I deem of sufficient value to add to these already brought forward. About the year 1680, a controversy sprang up among some of the bards of Ulster, as to what race, by ancient right, the armorial bearing of Ulster—the "Red Hand", belonged. Some person named *Cormac*, said or wrote something, which I have never seen, to the effect, that the Red Hand be-

(337) [Now in the library of the Royal Irish Academy.]

(338) [original:—Aeḋ mac Duinnsléibe i Soclaċain, aircinneaċ Cunga sai canntaireaċta ocus crotgléasa, maroen re gléas do deanam do féin naċ dearnaḋ reime, ocus ba sai in gaċ ceird, idir dán ocus gribdaċt, ocus scribend, ocus ar gach nealaḋuin do ni duine, do eg an bliadain sin.—Annals of *Loch Cé* (H. i. 19).]

longed by right to the *Clann Neill;* but he was called to account for saying so by *Diarmait*, the son of *Laoighseal Mac an Bhaird*, (called in English Louis Ward), who wrote a poem of seventeen quatrains, in which he adduces many historical reasons to prove that the Red Hand of Ulster belonged by right to the Ulidians of the Rudrician or Irian race, of whom *Mac Enis* (or Magenis) of the county Down was the chief. This poem begins: XXXII.

"O Cormac! remember what is right;
Take not from the Irian blood its honour.
Justice is the best argument:
The race is not now in bountiful affluence".[339]

To this poem an answer was given by *Eoghan O'Donnghaile*, or O'Donnelly, in a very clever poem of many stanzas, but of which I have never been able to procure more than the first thirty. O'Donnelly claims the "Red Hand" for the *Clann Neill*, and deals severely with his opponent's historical facts. The third stanza of this poem runs as follows:

"Three strings not of sweet melody,
I perceive in the middle of thy *Timpan;*
Small their power; bitter their sound;
They are no proof for the mighty great hand".[340]

It is true that the *Timpan* and its three strings are spoken of only figuratively here, as representing *Mac an Bhaird*'s historical assertion, and its three principal authorities; still the reference is curious, affording another proof of what I have said of the *Timpan*, by showing that even so late as the close of the seventeenth century, the *Timpan*, or Tympanum, was known in this country as a stringed instrument, and not by any means as a drum instrument of any kind. The humorous last will of Thomas Dease, Bishop of Meath, one of the Council of Kilkenny, 1643, speaks of the *Clairseach* or harp, and the *Timpan*.

There was, however, a distinction between the *Cruit*, or full harp, and the *Timpan*, as may be seen from the following passage from the Brehon laws in which the *Cruitirè*, or harper, is recognized as one of the distinguished artists, in a special clause in the following words: The *Timpan* was distinguished from the *Cruit* or full harp.

"A *Cruit;* that is, this is a *Cruit* in place of a *Timpan*, or a *Cruit* in its own proper state. This is the only species of music; that is, it is the only profession of music,—which is entitled to

(339) [original:—
A Chormaic cuiṁniġ an ċóir;
ná bean dfuil ir anonóir.
Irí a ċóir eagna ir ferr:
ni doiġ eḋála an fuirenn.
—H. and S. MSS., 208, R.I.A., cat. p. 616; 23. H. i. b. p. 49. top.]

(340) [original.—
Trí teada naċ binn dáin,
do ċím ar lár do ċiompain;
beag a mbriġ; searb a nglor;
ni dearbaḋ ar an laiṁ lán mór.
—*Ibid*, p. 50, top.]

XXXII.

be ennobled; that is, which is entitled to *Enechland;* [that is, to a fine in right of insult to the honour, as well as for personal injury to the performer], even though it does not attend on the illustrious, that is, although it is not retained by a nobleman, but it being noble in its own right".[341]

Here again we have the *Cruit*, or harp proper, and the *Timpan* as a species of harp, placed in such a relative position as to render it difficult to distinguish between them, although there is certainly a marked distinction.

No very ancient harp preserved.

It is very unfortunate that we cannot point to any examples in preservation, of any very ancient harp, an examination of which might at once solve the problems left unexplained in any of the many references I have given, to the power of this instrument as used by the great musicians of the golden age of ancient Irish civilization. There is, however, one valuable specimen of a purely Irish harp in existence, and one of the most beautiful workmanship too; though it is one of small size, and of an age not many centuries removed from our own time. I allude to the harp preserved in the museum of Trinity College, Dublin, with some observations upon which I may properly conclude this portion of my subject.

The harp in T.C.D.;

This harp has been the theme of much learned discussion already; and I confess I feel myself incompetent to offer any arguments concerning the theories broached upon the subject. It would, indeed, be a work of some effrontery, without a much greater share of historical, artistic, and antiquarian knowledge than I possess, to enter at all into a critical discussion of the evidences presented by this harp itself as to the period and style of instrument to which it belonged, after the cautious and accurate pen of such a writer as Dr. Petrie had recorded a decided opinion upon the matter.

Still in justice to Dr. Petrie himself, as well as to the cause of truthful investigation, of which he has long been a champion, though not with the view of offering opposition to any of his conclusions, I feel impelled to say a few words on the probable history of this harp; because I believe I am in position to place before him and the public some interesting facts hitherto unobserved, which may throw no little light on the subject.

In order, however, to introduce to you the few facts to which I allude, as bearing, I believe, on this subject, and for the better understanding of their point and value, I must premise by

(341) [original:—Cruit, .i. cruit ar timpan sin no cruit urri boden. Is he aen dan ciuil innsen, .i. ise oen dan oirfidead dligeas fairi, .i. dliges enicland cenimteid la hordan, .i. cen corab malle re huasal act abeadh aragaid a aenur.—H. 2. 16. p. 941.]

making another quotation from Dr. Petrie's "Memoir of an Ancient Harp preserved in Trinity College". XXXII. Dr. Petrie's account of it;

"The harp", says Dr. Petrie, "preserved in the museum of Trinity College, Dublin, and popularly known as the harp of Brian Boru, is not only the most ancient instrument of the kind known to exist in Ireland, but is, in all probability, the oldest harp now remaining in Europe. Still, however, it is very far from being of the remote age to which it is popularly supposed to belong; and the legendary story on which the supposition is grounded, and which has been fabricated to raise its antiquity and increase its historical interest, is but a clumsy forgery, which will not bear for a moment the test of critical antiquarian examination. We are told that Donogh, the son and successor of the celebrated Brian Boru, who was killed at the battle of Clontarf in 1014, having succeeded his brother Teigue in 1023, was deposed by his nephew, in consequence of which he retired to Rome, carrying with him the crown, harp, and *other* regalia of his father, which he presented to the Pope, in order to obtain absolution. 'Adrian the Fourth, surnamed Breakspear, alleged this circumstance as one of the principal titles he claimed to this kingdom, in his bull transferring it to Henry the Second. These regalia were kept in the Vatican till the Pope sent the harp to Henry the Eighth, with the title of Defender of the Faith, but kept the crown, which was of massive gold. Henry gave the harp to the first Earl of Clanricarde, in whose family it remained till the beginning of the last century, when it came by a lady of the De Burg family into that of Mac Mahon of Clenagh, in the county of Clare, after whose death it passed into the possession of Commissioner Macnamara of Limerick. In 1782 it was presented to the Right Honourable William [Burton] Conyngham, who deposited it in Trinity College, Dublin'. Such is the story, as framed by the Chevalier O'Gorman, by whom the harp was given to Colonel Burton Conyngham, and, as is usual, in the fabrication of most romantic legends, the fictitious allegations are so engrafted on real historical facts, the fable is so intermixed with truth, that few readers would think of doubting one more than the other, and even if they should doubt, would have the power of distinguishing between them".[342]

"It is scarcely necessary", continues Dr. Petrie, "to pursue the examination of this further, except, perhaps, to remark that the allegations in it respecting the gift of the harp from the Pope to king Henry the Eighth, and again from king Henry to the Earl of Clanricarde, have no better authority to rest on

(342) Bunting's *Ancient Music of Ireland*, p. 40.

XXXII.

Dr. Petrie's account of it.

than that of the chevalier himself. There is, however, one statement appended to the story, as an evidence of its truth, which should not be passed over in silence, as it exhibits in an equal degree the antiquarian ignorance and the daring mendacity of the writer. This statement is, that on the front arm of the harp 'are chased in silver the arms of the O'Brien family—the bloody hand supported by lions'. As already remarked by Mr. Moore, the circumstance of arms being on an instrument is fatal to its reputed antiquity, as the hereditary use of armorial ensigns was not introduced into Europe until the time of the crusades, and was not established in England until the reign of Henry the Third. The statement is altogether erroneous. The supporters are not lions, but dogs, probably wolf dogs, and the arms are not those of the O'Brien family, but of the more illustrious sept of O'Neil; and it is an interesting circumstance in the history of this harp, that the person who last awoke its long dormant harmonies, was a minstrel descended from the same royal race to whom it originally owed its existence, the celebrated Arthur O'Neill having played it through the streets of Limerick in the year 1760".[243]

"The legend so long connected with this interesting relic being now disposed of", continues Dr. Petrie, "it only remains to inquire—

"I. To what age the instrument belongs? and

"II. Whether it was originally intended for secular, or for ecclesiastical purposes?

"The first question might be determined by the skilful antiquary with sufficient accuracy from the style of workmanship of the armorial bearings already noticed, which evidently belongs to the close of the fourteenth, or, more probably, to the early part of the fifteenth century; and the general character of the interlaced ornaments on the harp, though derived from an earlier age, also points to the same period. But though hitherto unnoticed, there is one feature observable among those ornaments which decides this question with still greater certainty, namely, the letters I. H. S. carved in relievo in the Gothic or black-letter character, in general use at that period, and which is not found on monuments of an earlier age.

"That this harp did not belong to the class of bardic instruments, but rather to that smaller class used chiefly by the Irish ecclesiastics, as accompaniments to their voices in singing their hymns, would seem most probable from its very small size, which would unfit it for being used by the minstrel at the

(243) It is strange that Bunting, from whose volume I quote Dr. Petrie's Essay, should never have heard of this story.

festive board; and this conclusion seems to acquire support from the sacred monogram already noticed as being carved upon it". XXXII.

Summary of Dr. Petrie's conclusions.

So far Dr. Petrie, whose opinions on this curious old harp I have given in full in his own words, lest by any chance any account of them in mine should fail to convey their full force and meaning.

If I understand these observations aright, they amount to this:—

I. That the harp now in Trinity College, Dublin, and popularly known as *Brian Boru's* harp, is not, and could not have been, the harp of that illustrious monarch.

II. That there is no probability, much less certainty, that Donogh, the son of that *Brian* (who went on a pilgrimage to Rome about the year 1064), took with him this harp, along with the crown and other regalia of his great father, and made a present of it to the Pope.

III. That it is not true that another pope, in the early part of the sixteenth century, say in or about the year 1520, made a present of that same harp to Henry the Eighth, king of England; or that king Henry made a present of it to the first Earl of Clanrickard; or that from the Clanrickard family it passed, by the marriage of a lady of that house, into the family of Mac Mahon of Claenach in the county of Clare, ancestor of the present brave Duke of Magenta; or that it was next found in the possession of Commissioner Macnamara of Limerick; or that, in 1782, it was presented to Colonel Burton Conyngham, by the Chevalier Thomas O'Gorman; and that, finally, this whole story and history of the harp in question was false and unfounded, and a mere invention and fabrication by the same Chevalier Thomas O'Gorman.

Dr. Petrie's serious charge against the Chevalier O'Gorman.

This appears to me to be a very serious charge against any man, and one which ought not, I think, to have been made, unless grounded on his own precise words, and those words set out in the text; and it is a charge which I should be sorry to believe the Chevalier O'Gorman at all capable of deserving. There is in fact sufficient evidence that O'Gorman (or Mac Gorman, as he should have called himself) did really write or communicate verbally this, or some such account, either to Colonel Conyngham, to whom Mr. Ousely, and not O'Gorman, presented the harp, or to General Vallancey, who published it in his "Collectanea" (p. 32), as furnished by O'Gorman. It is very probable, indeed, that O'Gorman did write the story, as published by Vallancey, and by Walker in his "Irish Bards" (p. 61); but that he invented the whole story, and, for the first time gave to the instrument the name by which it has ever

XXXII. since been known, is surely more than questionable. For, though short the time since the year 1788, when Vallancey published this story, many an old tradition, originally founded in fact (however distorted afterwards), has disappeared since then; and the absence of evidence of such tradition is by no means to be taken as proof that it had no existence in the time of O'Gorman.

Some curious references to harps of the O'Briens;

I have been led into these observations by the circumstance of having met with one or two curious facts in connection with harps which at one time did belong to distinguished members of the great O'Brien family, one or either of which may have been the remote foundation of the story current concerning this harp, said to have belonged to *Brian Boromha*. But, whether they really were so or not, they are of themselves of sufficient interest to justify the propriety of introducing them into the discussion of a subject upon which so many learned dissertations, and so few genuine authorities or tangibly authentic references, have been produced.

There is in the possession of the O'Conor Don a manuscript volume of family and historical poems, in the Irish language, of various dates, say from the tenth to the seventeenth century. This volume, which is beautifully written, was compiled at Ostend in Belgium, in the year 1631, for a Captain Alexander Mac Donnell; but the compiler's name does not appear in it in its present somewhat damaged state. From this beautiful volume I copied, some years ago, one thousand quarto pages of my own writing, containing one hundred and fifty-eight rare family poems, of which, with a very few exceptions, no copies are known to me elsewhere in Ireland. Among these precious family records, I have fallen upon one which, as much for its gracefulness of composition as for its peculiar historic value as a very old authority bearing upon our present subject, I have always looked upon with great interest. The poem to which I allude was written by *Gilla-Brighde Mac Conmidhe*, otherwise called *Gilla-Brighde Albanach*, or of Scotland: he was so called because he was accustomed to spend so much of his time in that country; for, being a native of Ulster, the neighbouring land of Scotland came within his professional province as much as any part of Ireland.

Mac Conmidhe's poem on *Donnchadh Cairbreach* O'Brien;

Mac Conmidhe must have been born, I believe, about the year 1180, since we find him writing a poem descriptive of *Donnchadh Cairbreach* O'Brien, when he became chief of this name and of the Dalcassian tribes, which happened in the year 1204, that chieftain dying in the year 1242. In this poem the composer describes a vision in which he was carried on the deck of a ship to the city of Limerick, and how there he saw a young man sitting in the chieftain's chair or throne. He then describes this chief in glowing terms, giving an account not only of his personal appearance and costume, but also of his various accomplishments; and, among the latter, he makes special mention of music, to which he alludes in the following complimentary stanza, the third of the poem:

"Strings as sweet as his conversation,
On a willow harp no fingers have played;
Nor have the youth's white fingers touched
An instrument sweeter than his own mouth".(344)

This *Donnchadh Cairbreach* O'Brien was the first who took the distinctive chieftain name of "The O'Brien"; he was the son of *Domhnall Mór* O'Brien, the last king of Munster, who died in the year 1194.

It would appear that the warm feelings which inspired this poem, and the connection between the bard and the chieftain in whose praise it was written, did not terminate with the occasion of its composition. On the contrary, we can gather from *Mac Conmidhe*'s second poem—that which bears more directly on our subject—that, in many years afterwards, he had been sent by the same *Donnchadh Cairbreach* O'Brien on a special mission into Scotland to gain back—either freely, or by repurchase for an equivalent in Irish sheep—the small, sweet harp of the same O'Brien, which, by some means that I have not been able clearly to ascertain, had previously passed into that country.

It was on the occasion of this mission that *Mac Conmidhe* wrote this second poem; and as no words of mine could explain so well as the poem itself, either its historic value, or its beauty as a composition, and as the piece is not a long one, I may as well give it unbroken, in the following closely literal translation:—

Mac Conmidhe's poem on the harp of the same O'Brien;

"Bring unto me the harp (*Cruit*) of my king,
Until upon it I forget my grief—
A man's grief is soon banished
By the notes of that sweet-sounding tree.
"He to whom this music-tree belonged
Was a noble youth of sweetest performance.
Many an inspired song has he sweetly sung
To that elegant, sweet-voiced instrument.
"Many a splendid jewel has he bestowed

(344) [original:—
Téada buḋ coiṁbinn re a ċoṁráḋ,
ar clarṡoileaċ nír ṡeinn méar;
snír ṡeinn glanlaṁ an gilla
órgán buḋ binne ná a ḃéal.
—Miscellaneous Poems, chiefly copied from the O'Connor Don's Book, O'Curry MSS., Cath. Univ., p. 259.]

XXXII.

Mac Con-midhe's poem on the harp of the same O'Brien;

From behind this gem-set tree;
Often has he distributed the spoils of the race of *Conn*,
With its graceful curve placed to his shoulder.
"Beloved the hand that struck
The thin, slender-sided board:
A tall, brave youth was he who played upon it
With dexterous hand, with perfect facility.
"Whenever his hand touched
That home of music in perfection,
Its prolonged, soft, deep sigh
Took away from all of us our grief.
"When into the hall would come
The race of *Cas* of the waving hair,
A harp with pathetic strings within
Welcomed the comely men of Cashel.
"The maiden became known to all men,
Throughout the soft-bordered lands of *Banba:*
It is the harp of *Donnchadh!* cried every one—
The slender, thin, and fragrant tree.
"O'Brien's harp! sweet its melody
At the head of the banquet of fair *Gabhran;*
Oh! how the pillar of bright *Gabhran* called forth
The melting tones of the thrilling chords.
"No son of a bright Gaedhil shall get
The harp of O'Brien of the flowing hair;
No son of a foreigner shall obtain
The graceful, gem-set, fairy instrument!
"Woe! to have thought of sending to beg thee,
Thou harp of the chieftain of fair Limerick—
Woe! to have thought of sending to purchase thee
For a rich flock of Erinn's sheep.
"Sweet to me is thy melodious soft voice,
O maid! who wast once the arch-kings',
Thy sprightly voice to me is sweet,
Thou maiden from the island of Erinn.
"If to me were permitted in this eastern land
The life of the evergreen yew tree
The noble chief of Brendon's hill,
His hand-harp I would keep in repair.
"Beloved to me—it is natural for me—
Are the beautiful woods of Scotland.
Though strange, I love dearer still
This tree from the woods of Erinn".[348]

[348] [original:—
Tabraiḋ ċugam cruit mo ríoġ,
go ttréigim uirre m'imṡníoṁ,—
a brón da buing do ḋuine

XXXII.

Such is the address of *Mac Conmidhe;* but it is needless to y that it is impossible in a severe literal translation to do any ing like justice to the fervour and heartfelt pathos of this iching poem.

The poem does not explain how the harp went to Scotland.

The character of the poem, however, is such that it gives us clue to the circumstances under which O'Brien's hand-harp ssed into Scotland; but that it had gone there at the time, d that *Mac Conmidhe* was sent to recover it, either freely or an equivalent of Irish sheep. we have authority here that anot be questioned. It is equally certain that the mission of e diplomatic poet was a failure, and that the proverbial taste the Scotsman for our Irish mutton gave way to his higher ste for our ancient music, as evoked from this celebrated harp.

What became of the harp?

hat, then, became of this harp? Did it remain in the hands some chief, or king of Scotland till the conquest of that untry by Edward the Third, king of England, who died in e year 1307, but who had previously carried away from the cient palace of Scone, in Scotland, the ancient inaugural air and other regalia of the old Scottish monarchs, and deosited them in Westminster Abbey in London? May it be at the harp of *Donnchadh Cairbreach* O'Brien was by any ance among the spoils? and if that were possible, could it ave remained unnoticed and unappreciated at Westminster, ith the name of its original owner traditionally attached to it,

re glór an ċroinn cumruiḋe.
nte ga raiḃe an crann ciuil
giolla saor go rinn ttairḋiuir.
mor brátrann do ġab go grinn
rir an mblat-ċrann nglan ngut-
binn.
lor sead aluinn do ḟogail
ar cúl an ċroinn tslabraḋuiġ;
minic do ḃronn crod ó Ccoinn,
sa ċorr ġlan ré aġualoinn.
ṁuin an bas do ḃeanaḋ
an clar tana taoib-leabar:
gille seang narać ga seinm;
go ndeaġlaṁać go ndeiġḃearḃ.
i tan do ṫaiġleaḋ a láṁ
a naḋḃuiḋ ċiúil go cóṁlán,
a hosnaḋ leabar mín mór
do beanoḋ ḋinn ar ndoḃrón.
uair do ṫigeaḋ asttećt
rine Chair na ccul ndruimneać,
gruit go tteaduiḃ truaġa asttig
aggeagoiḃ cuanna Cairil.
gsad aiṫne ar an ingin,
tre son mḃanba mboigimlig
cruit Donnchaḋa! argać duine,—
an coṁṫana cúṁruiḋe.
uit iḃruan! binn a horgáin
re huċt bsleiġe brionngabráin;
ó ḃéanaḋ stuaiġ gabrain gloin,
argáin truaiġ as na téadaiḃ.
Ní bfuige mac Gaoiḋil gil
cruit iḃriain an barr druimniġ;
mac allmurḋaiġ ni ḟogaiḃ
an slabraḋaiġ sioḋaṁail!
Mairg do smuain cur read ċuingiḋ,
a ċruit ḟlaṫa fionnluimniġ,—
no do smuain cur réad ċeannać
ar ċraḋ uain Eirionnać.
Binn liom do guṫ milis mín,
a ḃean do ḃi gan airdriġ,
do ġuṫ mear is milis liom,
a ḃean a hinis Eirionn.
Da léiġṫi dam san tír ṫoir
saoġal na slaiti iuḃair
aoḋuire ban-ċnuic Ḃreanuinn
alam-ċruit do leiseaguinn.
Onṁoin leamsa,—dúṫċas daṁ,—
fioḋbuiḋe aille Alban
gioḋ iongnaḋ as annsa leam
ann crannsa dfioḋḃaiḋ Eireann.
Tabruiḋ.

—O'Connor Donn's MSS., O'Curry's copy, R.I.A., p. 228. b.]

XXXII. till the time of Henry the Eighth, who, it is said, presented a celebrated harp to the earl of Clanrickard, as the harp of a Donogh O'Brien?

Was it the harp presented by Henry VIII. to the Earl of Clanrickard?

It may indeed seem strange that, if Henry did present the harp to any one at this time, it was not Morrogh O'Brien that he should have selected for the gift, who deserted to the English and was created Earl of Thomond by him on the 1st of July, 1543, on the same day and at the same time that the Norman-Irish chief, Mac William Burke, exchanged his chieftain title for that of Earl of Clanrickard. This, however, is a question that cannot be cleared up now. But, assuming for a moment that this harp was preserved in Westminster when Henry the Eighth came to the throne in the year 1509, would it be too much to believe that it was the celebrity of this ancient instrument that suggested to that execrable monarch the first idea of placing the harp in the arms of Ireland, in the fashion of the heraldry of the time, and impressing it upon his coinage in this country? I cannot think the idea very fanciful.

Perhaps it suggested the idea of the harp coinage,

That the harp-coinage was in circulation in Ireland in Henry's time is well known; and the following brief extract from the Lord Deputy and council of Ireland to Henry the Eighth, dated at Dublin, the 15th of May, in the thirty-fifth year of that king's reign, and a few weeks before the creations of the earls of Thomond and Clanrickard, affords a curious illustration of this fact:

which was in circulation in Henry VIII.'s time.

"Fynally, for that ther ys no sterling money to be had within this your realme, thies gentlemen which now resorte to your highnes, wer utterly dysfurnished of money to bryng them thither, I, your magesties deputie, lent O'Brien an hundred pounds sterling in harp grotes, in default of other money, which I have delivered to your tresorer".

Supposing—believing, indeed, as I do—that the harp now in Trinity College, was given by Henry the Eighth to Clanrickard as the harp of a Donogh O'Brien, all then that the Chevalier O'Gorman, or some person before his time whose statements he followed, could have done was, to substitute a wrong name, that of Donogh the son of *Brian Boromha*, for *Donnchadh Cairbreach* O'Brien; for it is scarcely possible that O'Gorman or any one else could think of inventing the entire story; or that a tradition should be current that Henry the Eighth gave the earl of Clanrickard a harp at all, unless some such harp had been really presented or asserted to have been so presented, by the Clanrickard family. If O'Gorman had invented the story, how did it happen that he should not have selected the O'Brien himself, the newly created Earl of Thomond, as the recipient

The Chevalier O'Gorman only mistook one Donogh O'Brien for another.

of the royal gift? This, one would think, would make the invention much more appropriate and plausible, and should, in the absence of the question of the armorial bearings raised by Dr. Petrie, scarcely leave any room to deny the story by mere argument alone. It cannot, I think, be well denied, and indeed it has not been denied, that this particular harp did once belong to the Clanrickard family; that it passed from them with its traditional history (perhaps through the Mac Mahons of Claenach, in the county of Clare), certainly at last into the hands of Counsellor Macnamara of Limerick; and that from him it came into the possession of Ralph Ousely, who in 1782 presented it to Colonel Burton Conyngham.

There can b no doubt that this ha p did once belong to the Clanrickard.

Now, if this harp be a relic of the O'Neill family, and if as such it was played by the celebrated Arthur O'Neill in Limerick in the year 1760, how did it happen to have passed from him into the hands of Counsellor Macnamara? And how, too, could a story so glaringly false as this charged upon the Chevalier O'Gorman, be put so unblushingly before the world in conversation, in broad print in No. 13 of Vallancey's "Collectanea", 1788, while all those parties were still living? Arthur O'Neill himself lived down to the year 1818.

If the harp was an O'Neill harp how could it story have been invented and published in the life-time of those concerned?

Arthur O'Neill, according to Mr. Bunting (p. 80), made a professional tour of the four provinces when he was but nineteen years of age, and as he was born in the year 1734, the year in which Carolan died, this tour must have been made in 1753. It may be presumed that in this tour he must have passed through Limerick, and sojourned for some time in that hospitable city. Was this the harp he played at the time, as well as on the occasion of his alleged second visit in 1760? and if it was, how can it be believed for a moment that he could have quietly left it there, and parted for ever with so venerable a memorial of the noble sept from which he was so proud to claim descent? It could not be. It is entirely improbable. Is it not more probable, then, that this old harp was at the time in the possession of Counsellor Macnamara, whose hereditary hospitality, we may well suppose, the gifted young minstrel must have largely shared? And is it not very probable that during his visit with this gentleman, this venerable harp was brought under his notice; that he strung and tuned it anew; and that he did actually play it, not indeed as an itinerant through the streets of Limerick, for that was beneath him, but as a matter of courtesy to his host and his other patrons in the city? There can scarcely be a doubt but that the instrument was known as an O'Brien harp at this time, and that the Clanrickard tradition was well known, so that all that O'Gorman,

Arthur O'Neill may have played upon this harp, but it could not have been his;

XXXII. or whoever first framed the story, appears really to have done, was to endeavour to account for the way in which it came to Henry the Eighth. In doing this, he merely identified with it the name of the wrong Donogh, as being the most likely person of the name to fit the story, for of *Donnchadh Cairbreach*'s harp, I dare say, he had never heard.

this harp is not an O'Neill but an O'Brien one;

As far, then, as history, probability, and legitimate inference go, this is not an O'Neill, but an O'Brien harp. But then come Dr. Petrie's antiquarian difficulties; and I must confess that they are not easily if at all to be got over. Dr. Petrie's three objections are:—1. That the carving of the harp, though an imitation of an old style of carving, is not as old as the thirteenth century; 2. That the practice of carving the monogram I. H. S. in black letter, is not as old as that century; 3. That armorial bearings were not known in England till the reign of king Henry the Third, who began his reign in 1216, and died in 1272; that there are arms on the harp; and that they are not those of the O'Briens, but those of the more illustrious sept of the O'Neills.

Dr. Petrie's antiquarian difficulties;

author's answer; as to monogram I. H. S;

To the first objection I can say nothing more than that I believe it would be very difficult to find now any specimen of carving and design of the close of the fourteenth, or beginning of the fifteenth century, presenting the peculiar character of the tracery of the upright pillar of this harp, and that no such specimen has been shown to exist. Then as to the monogram I. H. S., I cannot doubt but that the letters so boldly, yet so rudely, carved in the curved bar of the harp, were intended to represent the sacred symbol. The H is rudely and inaccurately formed; and the S, the third letter of the monogram, is represented by a C; and this is more in accordance with the older Irish form of the sacred monogram, such as it is found in existing Irish MS. of the very early part of the fifteenth century, which may well carry us back still farther. There is an instance of this, for example, in the copy of *Cormac*'s Glossary now in the Library of the Royal Irish Academy, and which, there is reason to believe, formed at one time part of the great Book of *Dun Doighre*, now known as the *Leabhar Breac*, or Speckled Book, and which was compiled before the year 1412. In this copy of the Glossary, I say, we find the letter I in the Glossary commenced with the monogram ıħc, in hoc nomine est nomen nostri salutaris; and whether older copies of the Glossary had it written in the same way or not, I cannot say, as we have not an older copy now known. I may state, however, that in the other large portion of the great Book of *Dun Doighre* which remains, this symbol is not to be found, excepting at folio 100 b; but this is not in the original hand. Again, in part I. of the

XXXII.

book called the Liber Flavus, or Yellow Book, compiled in the year 1437, the monogram I. H. C. occurs in the top margin in two places.

It would indeed be easy to multiply instances of its occurrence in this form, and always in the top margin, in books of this and subsequent dates. It does not, however, appear in *Leabhar na h-Uidhre*, compiled before the year 1106; the Book of Leinster, compiled before the year 1150; the Book of Ballymote, compiled in 1391; or the Book of *Lecan*, compiled in 1413. In all these, and other books of their time, it is the word Emanuel, either written at length or in a contracted form, that appears in the place of the I. H. C. and always in the top margin, without any regard to the subject of the page underneath.

Upon an examination, then, of a regular succession of books from, say the year 1150 to the year 1500, it is not easy to determine with precision the time at which the old Emanuel was abandoned, and the monogram I. H. C. generally adopted.

As regards the monogram under discussion, however, I do not feel myself justified in disagreeing with such an authority as Dr. Petrie, that it cannot be older than the close of the fourteenth, or beginning of the fifteenth century. Indeed, I may even doubt that it is so old. But when I examine the workmanship of this harp, I may well doubt the conclusion he would draw from it; for I must say that I cannot believe that this monogram, so very rudely cut as it is, was ever executed by the same masterly hand that carved the other decorations of the instrument. It appears, indeed, that the place occupied now by this monogram was originally left vacant for some design, whether intended to be of a religious or a heraldic character. It is remarkable that whilst every other item of the carving is blunted and worn from age and friction, the outlines of the monogram now to be seen there are quite sharp and fresh. Is it unreasonable, then, to believe that the very old escutcheon now nailed to the hollow originally filled by a crystal, was designed to occupy the place now held by the monogram? The workmanship of the escutcheon appears to me to be much older than the monogram.

[A]s to the [ar]ms on the escutcheon;

Dr. Petrie asserts that the arms of this escutcheon, namely, an erect forearm and open hand with a shield, are not those of the O'Briens, but of the more illustrious sept of the O'Neills. Into the heraldic mystery of these arms I am quite incompetent to enter, but I may be allowed to say from their external features, that they appear to belong as much to the O'Briens as to the O'Neills. Even at the present day the chief emblems of both families are radically the same; though I am quite certain

XXXII.

that the use of the upright arm by the O'Briens is of an elder date than the Red Hand of the O'Neills. Indeed it was openly and publicly asserted in the seventeenth century by writers of the *Clann 'Neill* race themselves, that the Red Hand was the right of Magenis, but that the O'Neills wrested it to themselves, and have continued to usurp it to this day.[346]

The assertion of Dr. Petrie that the sept of O'Neill is more illustrious than that of O'Brien is incorrect.

I cannot but express my regret at the disparaging comparison which Dr. Petrie in his essay has thought well to draw, when he says that: "The arms on the harp are not those of the O'Brien's family, but of the more illustrious sept of O'Neill". It is true that, before the year 1002, the sept of O'Neill, in connection and concert, now with one now with another kindred sept of the same race, and either backed or unchecked by the two great provinces of Leinster and Connacht, did contrive to keep the regal power, such as it was, in its hands, to the wrong and prejudice of the single southern province, with its comparatively limited territory and military resources. But it would be utterly untrue to assert that the O'Neills were ever more brave, more munificent, more magnificent, or more true men than the O'Briens. Let the antiquarian and historian compare, even at this day, the ruined churches, abbeys, and castles of Clare, Limerick, and Tipperary, with those of O'Neill's country, and he will have little difficulty in settling with himself, from evidence the most enduring and conclusive, which sept has left behind the greater number and the noblest monuments of taste, of dignity, and of munificence. Let him take up our ancient manuscripts, our annals and our poetry, and he will find that the O'Brien name, in prose and verse, completely overshadows that of O'Neill. Let us then hear no more of this strange claim to superiority at the expense of a race to whose exploits we owe some of the most brilliant passages of our national history. Both races gave us great and noble princes: let our only feeling be, regret that they are of the past.

(346) [See ante, vol. ii., p. 264.]

LECTURE XXXIII.

(Delivered 26th June, 1862.)

(IX.) Of Music and Musical Instruments (continued). *Donnchadh Cairbreach* O'Brien sent some prized jewel to Scotland some time before *Mac Conmidhe*'s mission for *Donnchad*'s harp. The Four Masters' account of the pursuit of *Muireadhach* O'Daly by O'Donnell; O'Daly sues for peace in three poems, and is forgiven; no copies of these poems existing in Ireland; two of them are at Oxford. The Four Masters' account of O'Daly's banishment not accurate; his poems to Clanrickard and O'Brien give some particulars of his flight. Poem of O'Daly to Morogh O'Brien, giving some account of the poet after his flight to Scotland. The poet Brian O'Higgins and David Roche of Fermoy. O'Higgins writes a poem to him which is in the Book of Fermoy; this poem gives a somewhat different account of O'Daly's return from that of the Four Masters. O'Daly was perhaps not allowed to leave Scotland without ransom; what was the jewel paid as this ransom? The author believes that it was the harp of O'Brien. This harp did not come back to Ireland directly, and may have passed into the hands of Edward the First, and have been given by Henry the Eighth to Clanrickard. The armorial bearings and monogram not of the same age as the harp. Objects of the author in the previous discussion. Poem on another straying harp of an O'Brien, written in 1570; the O'Brien was Conor Earl of Thomond; the Four Masters' account of his submission to Queen Elizabeth; it was during his short absence that his harp passed into strange hands; the harp in T.C.D. not this harp. Mr. Lanigan's harp. Owners of rare antiquities should place them for a time in the museum of the R.I.A. Some notes on Irish harps by Dr. Petrie.—"He regrets the absence of any ancient harp"; "present indifference to Irish harps and music"; "some ecclesiastical relics preserved"; Dr. Petrie would have preferred the harp of St. Patrick or St. Kevin; "our bogs may yet give us an ancient harp"; Mr. Joy's account of such a harp found in the county Limerick; according to Dr. Petrie, this harp was at least 1000 years old. What has become of the harps of 1782 and 1792? A harp of 1509. "*Brian Boru's*" harp is the oldest of those now known; the Dalway harp is next in age; the inscriptions on this harp imperfectly translated in Mr. Joy's essay. Professor O'Curry's translation of them; Mr. Joy's description of this harp. The harp of the Marquis of Kildare. Harps of the eighteenth century: the one in the possession of Sir Hervey Bruce; the Castle Otway harp; a harp formerly belonging to Mr. Hehir of Limerick; a Magennis harp seen by Dr. Petrie in 1832; the harp in the possession of Sir G. Hodson; the harp in the museum of the R.I.A. purchased from Major Sirr; the so-called harp of Carolan in the museum of the R.I.A. The harps of the present century all made by Egan; one of them in Dr. Petrie's possession. Dr. Petrie's opinion of the exertions of the Harp Society of Belfast. "The Irish harp is dead for ever, but the music won't die". The harp in Scotland known as that of Mary Queen of Scots. Rev. Mr. Mac Lauchlan's "Book of the Dean of Lismore"; it contains three poems ascribed to O'Daly or *Muireadhach Albanach;* Mr. Mac Lauchlan's note on this poet; his description of one of the poems incorrect as regards O'Daly; Mr. Mac Lauchlan not aware that *Muireadhach Albanach* was an Irishman. The author has collected all that he believes authentic on the *Cruit.* The statements about ancient Irish music and musical instruments of Walker and Bunting

XXXIII. of no value; these writers did not know the Irish language; the author regrets to have to speak thus of the work of one who has rescued so much of our music.

In the last lecture I ventured to suggest some reasons for entertaining the opinion, that the instrument preserved in the Museum of Trinity College, Dublin, and popularly known as Brian Boru's harp, was really the harp of *Donnchadh Cairbreach* O'Brien, the sixth in descent from the great hero of Clontarf. I showed, with certainty, that some time, say about the year 1230, the poet *Mac Conmidhe* had been sent into Scotland to endeavour to bring back from that country the harp of *Donnchadh*, and which was certainly then in the possession of some potentate there. My next duty ought to be, to show, if possible, some probable cause for its having gone into that country at all. And it is singular enough that I have good authority to show that, some time before, this noble O'Brien did really send into Scotland some precious and much-prized jewel for a generous purpose and in a princely spirit. To make intelligible what occurs to me as connecting this act of the O'Brien with the subject of the present discussion, I shall first cite from the "Annals of the Four Masters", the following short entry in that invaluable record, which is set down under date 1213.—

Donnchadh Cairbreach O'Brien sent some jewel to Scotland.

Pursuit of the poet O'Daly by O'Donnell, according to "Four Masters".

"*Finn O'Brodlachain*, steward to the O'Donnell, that is Donnell Mór (prince of *Tir-Chonnail*), went into Connaught to collect O'Donnell's rent. The first place that he went to was *Cairpre* of Drumcliffe. He there went with his attendants to the house of the poet *Muireadhach* O'Daly, of Lissadill, where he fell to offering great abuse to the poet, for he was very exacting on behalf of a powerful man (not that it was his master that advised him to it). The poet was incensed by him, and he took up a keen-edged hatchet in his hand, and gave him a blow which left him dead without life. He went then himself to avoid O'Donnell, into Clanrickard's country. When O'Donnell came to know this, he collected a large force and went in pursuit of him, and he stopped not until he reached Derry O'Donnell in Clanrickard, which [place] received its name from his having been encamped there. He commenced spoiling and burning the country until Mac William at last submitted to him, and sent *Muireadhach* [O'Daly] into Thomond for protection. O'Donnell went after him, and fell to devastate and spoil that country too, until *Donnchadh Cairbreach* O'Brien sent *Muireadhach* away from him to the people of Limerick. O'Donnell followed him to the gate of Limerick, which he besieged from his camp at *Moin Ui Dhomhnaile* (which from him is named). The people of Limerick sent *Muireadhach* away from them by order of O'Donnell; so that he found no shelter, but to be conveyed from hand to hand until he reached Dublin.

O'Daly sues for peace in three poems, and is forgiven.

"O'Donnell returned home on that occasion, after having traversed and made a complete circuit of Connaught.

"He made another expedition again without delay and without rest, in that same year, to Dublin, until the people of Dublin were forced to send *Muireadhach* away from them into Scotland; and there he remained until he composed three laudatory poems, imploring peace, forgiveness, and protection from O'Donnell; and one of the three was:

'Oh! Donnell, good hand for [granting] peace', etc.

Peace was granted him for his laudations, and O'Donnell took him into his friendship afterwards, and gave him a holding and land, according to his wishes".

No copies of these poems in Ireland; two of them at Oxford.

Of the three poems addressed by O'Daly to O'Donnell, no copies are known to me to be extant in Ireland. There are, however, two of them preserved in the Bodleian Library in Oxford in the vellum MS. which contains O'Donnell's life of St. *Colum Cille*. One of these is that which is quoted above by the Four Masters; and it consists of thirty-eight stanzas. The other is addressed to O'Donnell's son, *Domhnall Oge*, written in the fifteenth year of the poet's exile, and descriptive of his sorrows and his wanderings on the Continent and up the Mediterranean Sea. This most curious poem consists of 29 stanzas, beginning:

"Long is it since I have drank the Lethean drink".

The account of O'Daly's banishment in "Four" Masters" not accurate; his poems to Clanrickard and O'Brien give some particulars of his flight.

There was a good deal more in the history of O'Daly's banishment than the Four Masters have recorded in this article; and there is some reason to think that part of what they have recorded partakes more of Donegal tradition than of historic fact. Of O'Daly's flying into the Clanrickard territory there is sufficient authority still extant in a remarkable poem addressed by the fugitive to Mac William Burke, the powerful chief of that territory, in which he avows his name and his crime, and implores protection. It is certain, too, that O'Daly passed into Thomond from Clanrickard, for, there is extant a poem addressed by him at the time to *Donnchadh Cairbreach* O'Brien, chief of that country, and of which the following is the first stanza:—

"Let me have my own bed, oh! *Donnchadh*,
I am entitled to honour from thy curled head;
I shall not be driven eastwards from Ireland [into Scotland]
In the reign of the noble fair-haired chief".[illegible]

[illegible] [original:—
mo leaba féin dam a donnchad
dligim cadaf ad cúl cas
ni leagair soir inn a heirinn
re linn an gloin ceibfinn cair.
—Betham MS., $\frac{23}{C.18}$, p. 73.]

XXXIII. This poem may, I think, be assigned to the year 1216, or thereabouts, a time that O'Brien, owing to family broils and English interference, was not in the best condition to shelter the fugitive from the vengeance of his pursuer; and O'Daly was compelled ultimately to fly to Scotland, where it appears he found shelter and protection from the Mac Donnells, Lords of the Isles, particulary the Clanranald. It will be seen, however, from Brian O'Higgins' poem, to which I shall come bye and bye, that it was against the advice and prohibition of the men of Thomond that he left that country.

O'Daly's history, from his flight to Scotland to his peace with O'Donnell and his return to his native country, would have been lost to us, were it not for the existence of his own poems, already mentioned, addressed to the O'Donnells, father and son; another addressed from Scotland to *Morogh* and *Donnchadh* O'Brien; and a fourth poem, addressed by Brian O'Higgin, a Connacht poet, to David Roche of Fermoy in the county of Cork, about the year 1450.

Poem of O'Daly to Morogh O'Brien, giving some account of the poet after his flight to Scotland.

O'Daly's poem is addressed to Morogh, the son of Brian O'Brien, who was the uncle of *Donnchadh Cairbreach*. It is a vigorous piece of composition, devoted chiefly to the praise and personal description of the young prince, who, from the poet, would appear to have been the heir apparent, or *tanaist* to his cousin *Donnchadh Cairbreach*. This poem, of which I possess a copy (made by myself from a vellum MS. in the British Museum), consists of twenty-six stanzas, of which the following is the first:—

"Guess who I am, O *Murchadh*,
Good is your inheritance of a well-directed cast;
Your father excelled all his acquaintance,
[He excelled] the arranged battalions".(348)

He continues then in the four stanzas which next follow, to address him thus:—"Guess what my profession is; guess what my name is; guess what country I come from". He then informs O'Brien that he has come from beyond the Mediterranean Sea; that he has been going about the world; that *Muireadhach Albanach*, or *Muireadhach* of Scotland, is his name; and that he is certain the *Clann Bloid* (that is the O'Briens, etc.) would take charge of him and protect him, even though he had committed theft itself. And so, after a good deal of strong praise and favourable prognostication of the

(348) [original:—
Tomais cia misi a Murċaiḋ,
maiṫ do ḋuṫċus deaġurċair;
do ċinn taċair ar aiṫni
ar na caṫaiḃ coraiġṫi.
—Additional MS. (vellum), 19,995. Brit. Mus., f. 4. a. top.]

future, the poet comes to the last stanza, in which he addresses *Donnchadh Cairbreach*, and which runs as follows:—

"Permit me to return to my country,
O *Donnchadh Cairbreach* of the smooth skin,
Out of Scotland of the feasts and of the grassy [fields],
Of steeds, of spears, [or, of suet], and of islands:
My run to Erinn on my return,
How soon shall I make! And guess".[(349)]

It is not to be understood that O'Daly was in Ireland at the time that he addressed this poem to *Murchadh*, the cousin of *Donnchadh* O'Brien, though intended for the more powerful chief himself. He not only asks *Murchadh* to guess who he is, but he admits distinctly that he has never seen his face or made his acquaintance.

After this poem we have no direct account of O'Daly but what the Four Masters state of the means by which he conciliated O'Donnell, and his having been received into favour by him on his return. This, however, is not the account of O'Daly's return contained in the poem of O'Higgin, above mentioned, a poem which is preserved in the old Book of Fermoy, a volume compiled in the year 1463. Brian O'Higgin, the author of this poem, was one of a learned family of bards and teachers of the province of Connacht. His name and fame appear to have reached the ears of David Roche, who at this time dispensed the hospitalities of a chieftain at his princely residence at Fermoy, in the county of Cork. The book called the Book of Fermoy was, in fact, compiled for this nobleman, in his own house, by the numerous poets and scholars who, by invitation, chance, or otherwise, repaired to him; and this is the reason that the book exhibits so many varieties of handwritings, each literary man writing his own poem or piece into it. Among the many scholars, then, who received an invitation to the court of Fermoy (and sufficient expenses for the journey, as he himself states) was Brian O'Higgin; and the present poem, in praise of the lord of that mansion, bears evidence to the fact that the author's reception was flattering and remunerative. It appears, however, that the bard was so well pleased with the hospitalities of the south that he felt inclined to abandon even the plains of Roscommon for the rich valleys of Munster. Nor does he hesitate to hint this desire rather broadly to David Roche; but as he appears anxious to save himself from a charge of singularity in

The poet Brian O'Higgins, and David Roche of Fermoy.

O'Higgins writes a poem to him which is in the "Book of Fermoy".

(349) [original:—
Ceadaiġ damsa dul am tír,
a Donnchaiḋ Cairbreaċ cnesmin,
a hAlbain fleḋaiġ féraiġ,
ngreġaiḋ, ngeraiġ, nolenaiġ:
ma ruaiġ i nErinn tar ṁais,
ni luaiṫ téġaim. Is tomais.
—Additional MS. (vellum), 19,995. Brit. Mus, f. 4. b. mid.]

XXXIII. preferring a strange country and people to his own, he, in the following stanzas, adduces the case of *Muireadhach* O'Daly in such a way as to lead us to think that the means through which he returned from Scotland were not exactly those recorded by the Four Masters. Thus speaks O'Higgin:—

This poem gives a somewhat different account of O'Daly's return from that of the "Four Masters".

" To abandon his native land,
On account of an insult to his profession,
Against the command of the southern land:
So did once a poet of my own peers.

" The jewel of *Donnchadh Cairbreach* having been sent
To release the chief poet of Scotland,
This it was that brought him over the sea,
Though it was a coming upon chance.

" His attention on the foreign Isles
He [*Donnchadh*] bestowed but a short time,
He brought *Muireadhach* over the sea,
Though he was an adopted son in Alba.

" When he [*Muireadhach*] was importuned,
At an after time, to go to his native place,
Seldom did he thither go
From the Dalcassians, as we have heard.

" My allusions to him have now come to an end,
To that *Donnchadh*, O David!
You and I are just like these
Two comrades in poetic science".[350]

And it was thus, by the example of O'Daly's preference of the O'Briens and Thomond to the O'Donnells and his native Connacht, that Brian O'Higgin justified his own preference of Roche and south Munster to his native province and its chiefs.

There can scarcely be any doubt of the correctness of the scrap of history contained in these few verses. The harsh course of O'Donnell, and the friendly interference of O'Brien in the case of O'Daly, must have been subjects of such interest to succeeding bards that we may be satisfied they were preserved with vivid accuracy.

(350) [original:—
Tréigean a tíre bunaid,
ar anonóir d'eladain,
dar aithne na tíre tes:
do rine maithghin deiges.
Seoid Donnchadh Cairbrig doċur
ar cenn ollaman Albun,
dobiat so a teċta tar tuinn,
ger techta sa tuaruim.
A agad ar innsib Gall
ni tabrad aċt do tamall,
tuc se Muireḋaċ tar muir,
gar fuineadaċ he anAlbain.
Da tugad aailgius air,
traṫ eigin dul na duchaid,
a ḋaul tarais gur annuth
o Dail Cais, do culamar.
Ar m' faiglib sis rainic criċ,
don Donnchad sin, a Daibiċ
meisi acas sib issamla
'soḋ feisi sir ealaḋna.
—Book of Fermoy, R. I. A., f. 117, bb.]

XXXIII.

It is, however, with the ransom sent into Scotland to release O'Daly that our chief concern lies now. We are to suppose that the Mac Donnells, or perhaps the king of Scotland,—for O'Daly was *Ollamh*, or chief poet, of all Scotland,—perhaps, I say, that either of these powerful parties would not allow him to pass out of it, without demanding some remarkable compensation for so great a loss,—something, in fact, which they hoped would not be given. What, then, was the jewel (*seoid*) which O'Brien sent over to purchase the liberty of his favourite bard, and enable him to return to his own country? It could not be money; and it could scarcely be cattle, the only other commodity that could have value in both countries at the time. We know, indeed, from *Mac Conmidhe's* poem, that whoever the person was in Scotland who had possession of O'Brien's harp, refused to part with it, either freely or for compensation in Irish sheep. And this clearly enough shows that property of this kind was deemed of less value in Scotland than the harp of an Irish chief; and it shows also, we may fairly argue, that so rich a treasure as the gifted poet could not be parted with in the same country for any amount of the ordinary commodities of Ireland.

O'Daly was perhaps not allowed to leave Scotland without ransom.

What was the jewel paid as this ransom?

What was it then that brought O'Brien's harp into Scotland at this particular time? I may state here that *Mac Conmidhe's* poem appears to be defective at the end. It does not, according to an invariable ancient usage, end with the same word with which it begins; and if it had been perfect, it is more than probable that we should have had some allusion to the circumstances under which the instrument had passed into Scotland. We have no direct authority on the subject; but from the allusions I have referred to, I may express my own belief that the harp was the jewel sent there to release *Muireadhach* O'Daly from the difficulties which stood in the way of his return to his own country.

The author believes that it was the harp of O'Brien.

The next question is, whether that harp ever came back direct to Ireland? and to this question I think we may answer with all the probability of truth, that it did not; for we have it on the authority of *Mac Conmidhe's* poem, that its restoration could not be obtained for love or money, at least in the owner's time. And now we may further ask, whether it is possible that the harp now preserved in the museum of Trinity College, Dublin, with its traditional history, such as it is, may be no other than this very harp of O'Brien? I answer that it possibly may be so; and that whether this harp passed from Scotland into England along with the regalia in the time of Edward the First; or whether it came there in any other way before

This harp did not come back to Ireland directly,

and may have passed into the hands of Edward I,

XXXIII.

and have been given by Henry VIII. to Clanrickard.

or after that time the tradition of its having been given by King Henry the Eighth to the Earl of Clanrickard, and of its having continued a long time in the Clanrickard family, under the name of Donogh O'Brien's harp, remains uncontradicted by any evidence or by any logical argument.

The armorial bearings and monogram not of same date as the harp.

Then, as regards the armorial bearings, by the character of which the age of this harp has been attempted to be determined, I venture to say that those armorial bearings, what family soever they may have belonged to, were no part of the original harp; and that there is not upon the entire instrument a spot left vacant in which they could fit, excepting that alone which is now occupied in the harmonic curve by the monogram I. H. C., so rude and inferior in artistic design and execution to the rest of the carving, into which it would appear to have been inserted, probably by some possessor of the instrument after it had passed from the hands of its original owner.

Objects of the author in this discussion.

In this tedious and perhaps shadowy discussion on the *Brian Boru* harp, I trust I shall be believed when I say, that I have had no object in view but the elucidation, as far as possible, of its true history; or if not that, the nearest possible guess at it; such a guess as might reasonably be given, from the few facts and circumstances that I have adduced, and which appear to me to supply coincidences bearing with remarkable point upon the subject. I don't want to offer any flat contradiction to high authority. I wish to place before these authorities such facts only as I have collected since Dr. Petrie's Essay was published, in the hope that if they do not lead to the certainty of the truth, they may be found useful landmarks in the further prosecution of this interesting antiquarian inquiry. And still further, to show that I am not trusting merely to speculations of my own in opposition to the opinions of well informed men, and that there is nothing at all improbable in what I have ventured to suggest as to the wanderings of the harp of *Donnchadh Cairbreach* O'Brien, I may here notice a reference to the straying harp of another distinguished, but much later nobleman of the great O'Brien family. This harp, indeed, might come within the range of Dr. Petrie's antiquarian tests, as to its age; but, if it is still extant, it is not accompanied by any known legend that would lead to its identification.

Poem on another straying harp of an O'Brien.

The reference to this harp that I have just mentioned, is found in an anonymous poem of considerable merit, which, like *Mac Conmidhe*'s poem on *Donnchadh Cairbreach*'s harp, was addressed to it, when heard played by a stranger, by the disconsolate bard of its exiled owner. This poem consist of ten quatrains, so appropriate to the present subject, and certainly so valuable a corroboration of an important historical event, that I shall give a literal translation of the whole of it. It is as follows:

Poem on another straying harp of an O'Brien.

"Musical thou art, O harp of my king!
The plaint of thy strings has brought me to grief;
It is little that my mind was not deranged
When I heard thy voice while being tuned.

"Seldom hast thou been seen upon a visitation,
O fount of music! who hath gained every prize!
Thou beautiful harp of the *Ollamhs* of [*Clann*] *Táil*.
Oftener was the visit of nobles to thee!

"Thou musical, fine-pointed, speckled harp!
Thou hast seen a time—did we of it wish to tell—
When to thee were sung the poems of sages,
For which *Ua Duach* [O'Brien] paid steeds and gold.

"Many a hand ran over thy ribs,
In that bright mansion, where pleasure reigned;
Thou of the noble breast, delightful and free,
Until thou didst allow him to sail over the waves.

"Thou musical harp of the race of Brian—
After them no one should in greatness trust,
Whilst I am like *Torna* after *Niall*,
And thou among strangers after my king!

"The foreigners have driven beyond the sea
The Earl of the *Clann Táil*—what greater wo!
From that time thither I have heard no harp
That has not a tone of wailing in its notes.

"Alas! that the fair, bountiful man did not consent,
The heir of the O'Briens, who gained all sway,
To suffer base deeds without anger
And guard himself against English treachery.

"Their oppressive demands were not borne
By the beloved of Cashel, of the foam white skin
His glowing billow of kingly blood [could not bear it],
Its consequence, alas! has come upon us.

"Erinn has ceased to live of the sorrows of the king,
Completely has her career gone down,
The nut produce of Inis Fail has ceased,
The happiness of all men has ceased, and their music.

"Sweet, O'Gilligan, are thy notes,
Sweet the voice of the strings in thy fingers;
Still 't was sweeter to me in the time of *Ua Luirc* [O'Brien],
Tho' this harp is always sweet for its music!"[351]

[351] [original:—

Ceolċar sin a cruit mo ríġ!
rom ċuir a snim sianra do téd;
suail naċar saobaḋ mo ċruṫ,
od cuala do ġuṫ dod ġlés

XXXIII.

written in 1570; This poem, whoever may have been the author of it, must have been written in the year 1570; for it was in that year, as we are told by the Annals of the Four Masters, that Conor O'Brien, Earl of Thomond, in consequence of the dissensions of his own people and the pressure of the English power, came to terms with the Earl of Ormond, Queen Elizabeth's representative, and promised to be counselled by him. The following is the account of this event, as chronicled by the Four Masters:—

the O'Brien was Conor, Earl of Thomond;

the "Four Masters" account of his submission to Q. Elizabeth; "He [the earl] gave up his towns, namely, Clonroad, Clarmor [now Clare Castle], and Bunratty, into the hands of the Earl of Ormond; and Donnell O'Brien and other chieftains of Thomond, whom the earl had as prisoners, were set at liberty, as were also the prisoners held by the president. The earl was afterwards seized with sorrow and regret for having given up his towns and prisoners, for he now retained only one of all his fortresses, namely, *Magh O'm-Bracain*, and in this he left ever-faithful warders; he resolved that he would never submit himself to the law or the mercy of the council of Ireland, choosing rather to be a wanderer and an outlaw, and even to abandon his estates and his fine patrimony, than to go among them. He afterwards concealed himself for some time in Clanmaurice [in Kerry], from whence he passed, about the festival of St. John, into France, where he stopped for some time. He afterwards went to England, and received favour, pardon, and honour from the queen of England, who sent letters to the council of Ireland, commanding them to honour the earl, and he returned to Ireland in the winter of the same year".

It must, then, have been in the precise year 1570 the above poem was written, for that was the year in which O'Brien was

Andaṁ leat craitcrin ar cuairt,
a ceolḟaoi do fuair gaċ geall!
a ċruit ċaem ollamna Táil,
sa mince cuaird ċaig ad ceann!
a ċruiṫ ċeolċar beannċorr breaċ!
tarairi seal,—gá ttám do—
do geabtái riot laeiċe ruaḋ,
ar a ttuc ua duaċ eiċ is ór.
Mor lam rolataḋ sad ċneas,
san mur ngeal, a bṡaiċċe muir-
inn;
a mórḋa bruinne ḟeargair saer,
gur leig tu a ċaeb re tuinn.
A ċruit ċeolċar clainne Bhriain,—
a ttrean na ndiaig nir ċoir brig,
is mise mar Tórna tar eis Neill,
is tusa ar eaċtra deis mo rig.
Do cuirsead allṁuraig tar sáil,
iarla ó Táil—cia craḋ as mó!
ó soin aleiċ ni ċuala cruit,
naċ biaiḋ soġar guil na glór.
as truaġ nar aentaig an rind sial,
ua na mBrian, re mbertċai barr,
sulang ċláin bert: cul re seirg,
beiċ ara ccoiṁne ar ċeilg nGall;
Nir ḟuilngeaḋ daeirse a mbreaċ
leannan Cairil, cneas mar ċuinn;
a ċonn mobraċ rola rig—
tarla a dearcaiḋ, sarior duinn.
Tairnig Eire diaċra an rig,
do ċuaiḋ uile sis a seol,
tairnig cnó ṁeas ċríċe Fáil,
tairnig aiḃnes ċaiċ sa cceol.
Binn, a Ui Gilligain do ġlór,
binn goċa na ttéd ad ṁeor;
binne lim i a bslaiċios Ui Luirc,
ge binn i an ċruit ara ceol.
Ceolċar.

—O'Curry MSS., C.U.I., Lives of Saints, vol. ii., p. 48.]

forced to fly over the sea from the English power. It is curious, however, to find that within the comparatively short time the earl was absent his harp had passed into a strange country, if not into strange hands; for, although the poet praises the performance of O'Gilligan, who appears to have been the possessor of this harp at the time, O'Gilligan is not a Munster name, and the bearer of that name could scarcely be expected to be raised to the distinction of chief *Ollamh* in music to the *Clann Tail*, or O'Briens, in preference to the musicians of their own country and race.

XXXIII. It was during his short absence that his harp passed into strange hands;

The harp now in Trinity College could not have been this harp of the Earl of Thomond, unless indeed that the latter harp might have come down some hundreds of years as an heirloom in the family; but this is not probable; and if this straying harp of Conor O'Brien, Earl of Thomond, of the year 1570, be in existence at all, it is not identified.

the harp in T. C. D. not this harp.

There is an old harp in the possession of John Lanigan, Esq., of Castle Fogarty, in the county of Tipperary; and I have heard Mr. Lanigan say that it exactly resembles in size and carving the harp in Trinity College, of which he saw a cast in the Royal Irish Academy. Mr. Lanigan's harp, however, has not been seen by any person who has given his attention to its comparative style and age, or who was qualified in any way to form and express an opinion on it. It is much to be regretted, and a great loss to inquiries of this kind, that the owners of rare relics of antiquity are not at all times willing to place for a time these curious remains in the Royal Irish Academy, where they could be properly examined and compared, duly understood, and appreciated by the general public as well as by the antiquary. There are generous exceptions to this rule, as in the case of Sir Richard O'Donnell, Bart., of Newport, county of Mayo, who has for many years allowed his precious relic, the *Cathach*, to add to the richness of the splendid museum of the Royal Irish Academy, and it would be greatly to be desired that his liberal example were more generally followed.

Mr. Lanigan's harp.

Owners of rare antiquities should place them for a time in the museum of the R.I.A.

In continuation of these observations of mine, and tracing still farther down the existence and abode of a few other surviving harps of the later times, the following communication from my own and Ireland's distinguished friend, Dr. Petrie, will, I am sure, be received with all the attention and respect due to his revered name. Thus writes Dr. Petrie.—

Some notes on Irish harps by Dr. Petrie.

"To the lovers of ancient Irish melody—a body, I regret to say, small in number amongst the educated classes in Ireland—it is a matter of deep regret that no very ancient specimen remains to us of the instrument which gave that melody a grace

"He regrets the absence of any ancient harp";

XXXIII.

"present indifference to Irish harps and music";

of form and depth of feeling which that of no other country has ever equalled, or will ever surpass. As a nation, indeed, we have been and are hopelessly indifferent in the matter. We suppose the Irish harp to have been a barbarous instrument, and believe the music to which it gave birth to be at best but rude and unsuited to civilized ears; and in truth it is not of a kind to touch the feelings or satisfy the conventional taste of society as at present constituted.

"Some ecclesiastical relics preserved";

"The religious sentiment, so strongly characteristic of the Gaedhelic mind, has, in despite of so many adverse circumstances, preserved to us a few relics of those saintly men who by their zeal in the propagation of Christianity, both at home and abroad, obtained for their country the title of *Insula Sanctorum;* and these relics are no less interesting as touching memorials of the good men of a remote age, than valuable as specimens exhibiting an intimacy with the elegant arts which without them would probably be more than doubted.

"Dr. Petrie would have preferred the harp of St. Patrick or St. Kevin";

"Highly, however, as I appreciate these remains, I confess that I would rather have possessed the harp of the apostle Patrick, or that of the gentle Keven of Glandalough, which we know to have been so long preserved, than their bells, shrines, or croziers, or any other of their relics; for such were only memorials of their professional existence, while their harps would present to our imagination the existence of that sensibility to 'the concordance of sweet sounds' which the Creator has bestowed upon man, as the most sensuous and pure of his leisure enjoyments. Unhappily, such touching memorials, however, we can never possess

"our bogs may yet give us an ancient harp";

"But we may still indulge the hope that our bogs, which have preserved for us so many interesting remains illustrative of the progress in civilization of our forefathers, may still conserve and present to us a specimen of our ancient harp; for at least one such they have already given us in our own time, but it seems to have been uncared for, and, consequently,—destroyed!

"Mr. Joy's account of such a harp found in the county of Limerick";

"The late Mr. Henry Joy, of Belfast, in his learned and admirable 'Historical Critical Dissertation on the Harp', printed in the late Mr. Edward Bunting's 'General Collection of the Ancient Music of Ireland' (vol. i.: London, 1811), has informed us that—

"'About ten or eleven years ago, a curious harp was found in the county of Limerick, on the estate of Sir Richard Harte, by whom it was given to the late Dr. O'Halloran. On the death of that gentleman it was thrown into a lumber room, and thence removed by a cook, who consigned it to the flames. Its exact figure we have not been able to obtain. Several gentlemen who saw it, declare that it totally differed in construction from the instrument now known in Ireland; that it was smaller in size, and still retained three metal strings, with pins for several others. It was raised by labourers at the depth of twelve spits or spadings under the earth in Coolness Moss, near Newcastle, between Limerick and Killarney. It seems extraordinary that any vestige of metal strings or pins should have remained, notwithstanding the qualities attributed to moss water'.

"From the great depth at which this harp was found", continues Dr. Petrie, "it could hardly have been less than one thousand years old. Nor is it improbable that amongst the harps belonging to the harpers of the last century and early part of the present, some of them may have been of a respectable though inferior antiquity to the Limerick harp. What, it may be asked, has become of the harps of the seven harpers who met at Granard in 1782, and the ten harpers at Belfast in 1792? Most of them, no doubt, have been used for firewood. Yet I have been informed by the late Mr. Christopher Dillon Bellew, and his lady, of Mount Bellew, in the county of Galway, that for many years a very aged harper, who was very probably one of those who attended the harp meetings, used, in making his annual rounds at the houses of the Connaught gentry, stop at their mansion for a fortnight, and that on those occasions they were always much struck with the antique character of his harp. 'It was', they said, 'small, and but simply ornamented', and on the front of the pillar, or forearm, there was a brass plate, on which was inscribed the name of the maker and the date—1509. The poor harper had often expressed his intention of bequeathing this harp to his kind entertainers; but a summer came without bringing him to his accustomed haunts, and the harp was never forwarded, nor its fate ascertained.

"According to Dr. Petrie this harp was at least 1000 years old".

"What has become of the harps of 1782 and 1792?"

"A harp of 1509";

"Of the harps now remaining to us, that preserved in the museum of Trinity College, and popularly called '*Brian Boru*'s', but which I would call 'O'Neill's', is, probably, the oldest. But, there can be no doubt of its being the work of a much later age than that of the Munster king: and it may be questioned if the ancient harps preserved in Scotland, and which are probably of Irish manufacture, are not of equal or even earlier antiquity. The next in age is the Fitzgerald, or, as it is now popularly called, the Dalway harp, having been in the possession of that old Antrim family for a considerable number of years. Of this harp, unhappily, only fragments remain, namely, the harmonic curve, or pin-board, and the fore-arm;

"'*Brian Boru*'s' harp is the oldest of those now known";

"the Dalway harp next in age";

XXXIII. the sound-board having been lost or destroyed. These fragments are, however, of great interest, not only on account of their elaborate and tasteful ornamentations, but, perhaps, still more from their being in great part covered with Latin and Irish inscriptions. From these inscriptions we learn that the harp was made for one of the Desmond Fitzgeralds, namely, John McEdmond Fitzgerald of *Cluain*, or Cloyne, whose arms are handsomely chased on the front of the fore-pillar, surmounted by the arms of England. It presents us also with the name of the maker, 'Donatus, Filius Thadei', and the date of its fabrication, 1621; and, in the Irish language and letters, the names of the servants of the household.

"the inscription on this harp imperfectly translated in Mr. Joy's essay".

"These inscriptions having been imperfectly translated in Mr. Joy's Essay, but recently read correctly by yourself, and printed for private distribution by the late Dr. Robert Ball, I think it desirable to give them a more secure record in your lectures as interesting memorials of domestic life in Ireland at that period".

"Professor O'Curry's translation of them";

The following is my translation of these Irish inscriptions:—

"These are they who were servitors to John Fitz Edmond [Fitz Gerald], at Cluain [Cloyne], at the time that I was made, viz.: the Steward there was James Fitz John; and Maurice Walsh was our Superintendent; and Dermod Fitz John, Wine Butler; and John Ruadhan was Beer Butler; and Philip Fitz Donnel was Cook there, Anno Domini 1621.

"Teige O'Ruarc was Chamberlain there, and James Russel was House Marshal; and Maurice Fitz Thomas and Maurice Fitz Edmond; these were all discreet attendants upon him. Philip Fitzteige Magrath was Tailor there; Donnchadh Fitz Teige was his Carpenter,—it was he that made me.

"Giollapatrick Mac Cridan was my Musician and Harmonist; and if I could have found a better, him should I have, and Dermot M'Cridan along with him, two highly accomplished men, whom I had to nurse me. And on every one of these, may God have mercy on them all".(346)

(346) [original:—triadso dob feidmanaig ag Seaan mac Emaind Gearalt, a gcluain, an tan doronadh misi, .i. dobo stiobard ann Semus mac Seaain; acas Muiris Breanach doba fadmanadach; acas Diarmuid mac Seaan buitileir fiona; acas Seaan Ruadhan buitileir na beorach; acas Pilip mac Domnaill ba cocaire ann, anno Domino 1621.

Tadg O Ruairc ba seomradoir ann, acas Semus Ruisel ba marasgal tige; acas Muiris mac Tomas acas Muiris mac Emainn; ba giollanaig dheisgcreideacha iad so uile. Pilip mac Taidg mhe Grath ba tailiuir ann; Donnc[a]dh mac Taidg na sa[e]r do ron.

Giollapadraig mac Cridain doba fear ceoil acas oirfidid dam; acas da fhaighin ni budh fear is se do bheag, acas Diarmaid mac Cridain maille ris, dias do tsaitheb glanna do bi agamsa dom alimaen. acas gach

"According to an old custom", Mr. Joy writes, "the instrument is supposed to be animated; and, among other matters, informs us of the names of two harpers who had produced the finest music on it; these were, it seems, Giolla Patrick M'Cridan and Diarmad M'Cridan". This harp, which was nearly twice the size of the last noticed, has been thus described by Mr. Joy:—"By the pins, which remain almost entire, it is found to have contained in the row forty-five strings, besides seven in the centre, probably for unisons to others, making in all fifty-two strings. In consequence of the sound-board being lost, different attempts to ascertain its scale have been unsuccessful. It contained twenty-four strings more than the noted harp called Brian Boiromhe's; and in point of workmanship, is beyond comparison superior to it, both for the elegance of its crowded ornaments, and for the general execution of those parts on which the general correctness of a musical instrument depends. The opposite side is equally beautiful with that of which the delineation is given; the fore-pillar appears to be sallow, the harmonic curve of yew. "Description of this harp".

"The instrument, in truth, deserves the epithet claimed by the inscription on itself—'*Ego sum Regina Cithararum*'".

"As following in age as well as in importance", continues Dr. Petrie, "the harp I have next to notice is, by a curious coincidence, also a Fitzgerald one—it is the harp of the great parent family of Kildare, and is happily in their keeping. The size and proportions of this harp are about the same as those of the Cloyne harp; and, like the latter, it is richly, but less elaborately ornamented In both harps, too, the style of the ornamentation is generally characteristic of an earlier age than that of their manufacture, as proved by the coats of arms and inscriptions upon them. In the Kildare harp, the inscription is, "The harp of the Marquis of Kildare".

ean diab go ndeapna Dia grasa orċa rom uile.

Beside the Irish inscription there is, in large Roman letters, near the figure of a queen, at the end of the harmonic curve,

I^oE & EB ME FIERI FECERUNT EGO SUM REGINA CITHARARUM.

Upon the bow the royal arms of England are carved; and it is to be remarked that the quartering for Ireland exhibits a harp which is a good representation of that known as the harp of Brian Boromha. Under the royal arms are those of Sir John FitzEdmond Fitzgerald, of Cloyne, impaled with those of his wife, the Hon. Ellen Barry, daughter of Viscount Buttevant; he was married in 1611, and died in 1640. The mottoes under the arms appear to be, "Virescit vulnere virtus, Boutez en avant". Upon the edge of the bow were Latin inscriptions (now partly lost); there remain, "Plecto vinco rego. . . . monstra viros. musica Dei donum. distractas solatur musica mentes. ut sonus . . . . transit sic gloria mundi. Vincit veritas". Upon the inside of the bow, in large letters, is inscribed, "Donatus filius Thadei me fecit, spes mea in Deo".]

XXXIII. indeed, a very simple one, namely, the letters R. F. G., and, in Arabic numerals, the date, 1672. Yet, brief as this inscription is, coupled with the escutcheon of arms above which it is carved, it is quite sufficient to identify the particular Fitzgerald for whom the harp was made. The escutcheon, which is carved in high relief upon the fore-pillar, exhibits the arms of the Kildare Fitzgeralds—pearl, a saltire, ruby; but they are charged with a crescent, to denote that they belong to the second son of the chief of the family; and thus informed, we are enabled by a reference to Lodge's Peerage, to determine, with certainty, that the R. F. G. of 1672, was Robert, the second son of George, the sixteenth earl of Kildare—who brought the name of Robert into that noble house—and who, during the minority of his nephew, John, the eighteenth earl, who was born in 1661, was appointed by the king to the government of the county. He was born in 1637, and he died in January 1697-8. On the death of George, the sixteenth earl, in 1707, the earldom passed to a second Robert, born in 1675, who was his first cousin, being the son of his uncle, for whom the harp was made, and from him, in a direct line, is descended the present estimable marquess, by whom, in the ancient castle of the family, at Kilkea, the harp is now most carefully conserved, and of his race may it never want conservators.

"Harps of the eighteenth century";

"I have now noticed all the harps of an age anterior to the eighteenth century known to me as existing in Ireland, and I have next to speak of those of a later age. The earliest harps of the eighteenth century which I have seen were made by Cormac Kelly, at Ballynascreen, in the county of Londonderry, 'a district', as Mr. Bunting informs us, 'long famous for the construction of such instruments'. Of these harps, the most remarkable is that preserved at Downhall, the seat of Sir Hervey Bruce, Bart., in the same county, and which had belonged till the time of his death to Denis Hampson, the well-known harper of Magilligan, who died in 1807, at the age of 112 years. Its sides and front are made of white sallow, and the back of bog fir, patched with copper and iron plates, and the following lines are sculptured on it:—

"the one in the possession of Sir Hervey Bruce";

'In the days of Noah I was grown,
After his flood I 've not been seen,
Until seventeen hundred and two:—I was found
By Cormac Kelly, under ground;
He raised me up to that degree,
Queen of music they call me'.

"the Castle Otway harp";

"A second, by the same maker, is preserved at Castle Otway, in the county of Tipperary, the seat of Captain Robert Jocelyn

Otway, R.N. and D.L., and bears the date 1707. This harp was the property of the harper and fiddler, Patrick Quin, a native of Portadown, in the county of Armagh, and who was the youngest of the harpers who attended at the assembly in July, 1792, Hampson being the eldest. Quin was brought to Dublin in 1809, as the only survivor of the old harpers, by the unfortunate John Bernard Trotter, who had made a visionary and fruitless attempt to organize a Harp Society, through whose patronage a school for the instruction of a new race of harpers might be established, of which Quin was to be the teacher; and many Dublin septuagenarians like myself may remember his performance at a Commemoration of Handel at the Rotundo in that year, and which was got up with the view to promote this object. XXXIII.

"A third harp of this period, which was, and, as I trust, is still preserved in the county of Limerick, is also, according to Mr. Bunting, the manufacture of this maker, and engravings of it are given in Walker's 'Irish Bards', and in Ledwich's 'Antiquities of Ireland'. But there can scarcely exist a doubt that my old friend was in error in this statement; for, in addition to the fact that this harp, in its form and style of ornamentation, differs essentially from those of Cormac, we have the statement of Mr. William Ousley, of Limerick, who drew the harp and supplied the information respecting it for Walker, that it bore the inscription 'Made by John Kelly, 1726'. It was also of greater size than any of the harps of Cormac Kelly, and which were never more than four feet in height; for we are informed that this harp was five feet high, and contained thirty-three strings. In 178[illegible] this harp was in the possession of Mr. John Hehir, of Limerick. What has since become of it I know not.

"a harp formerly belonging t[o] Mr. Hehir o[f] Limerick";

"Superior in many respects to any of the harps of this period I have now noticed, was one which, through the kindness of a friend, I had the pleasure of seeing in 1832, and of which, unhappily, I can now speak only from a faded recollection. It was at that time the property or in the keeping of a country solicitor, who had his Dublin office on Bachelor's Walk, and who was then out of town. This harp was of moderate size, about four feet in height, and, with the exception of a fracture which it was obvious it had recently received, was in the most perfect state of preservation. Its colour was that of a precious and well cared for Cremona violin, and no instrument of that class could exceed it in the beauty and perfection of its workmanship, while, from the antique character of its ornamentation, one would suppose it an instrument of much antiquity, but for the presence of an inscription which gives its history

"a Magenn[i] harp seen b[y] Dr. Petrie i[n] 1832";

XXXIII. and the year of its making. This inscription was not, as usual, engraved on the woodwork of the harp, but written in the Irish language and characters on parchment, which was under glass, on the sound-board, and, amongst other matters which I forget, it informed us that it was the property of a Captain Art Magennis, of some place in the county of Down, for whom it was made in the year 1725, or thereabout. Shortly after my seeing the instrument, the friend to whose kindness I was indebted for the privilege emigrated to America, where he died, and its owner having given up his lodgings, I could learn nothing from his successor as to his town and country residences. I can only, therefore, indulge the hope, I confess a feeble one, that this interesting memorial of a past state of feeling and condition of society in Ireland may have escaped the usual fate of such relics, and I have a pleasure in penning this imperfect notice of it, from the hope that, if it yet exists, such notice may lead to our acquiring a knowledge of its locality, and perhaps to a conserving appreciation of its interest and value.

"the harp in the possession of Sir G. Hodson";

"To this period I think we should also ascribe the harp preserved with an honoured place in the hall of Hollybrook House, county of Wicklow, the beautiful seat of Sir George F. J. Hodson, Bart. It is of small size, and without ornament or inscription. But it is not without a peculiar interest; for its presence carries our minds back to the joyous days in that district of the ancestor of Sir George, the 'Robin Adair' of many an old song. Which of us has not heard the 'You are welcome to Puckstown, Robin Adair', manufactured into 'You 're welcome to Paxton, Robin Adair' by the Scotch, and for a long time claimed as their own? or the still more popular ballad 'The Kilruddery Fox Hunt', in the opinion of Ritson, the best ballad-poem in the English language, in which we are told triumphantly that 'Robert Adair, too, was with us that day'? That line will preserve his name and memory for ever. And it also reminds us that in those days of simple living, social Irish merriment, and unconventional freedom of manners, the sound of the Irish harp, and the melodies of Ireland, whether gay or tender, were not forgotten; for the first of these songs was associated with the exquisitely beautiful and impassioned "Eileen aroon"; and the second with the tempered mirthfulness of 'Sighile ni Gara'. And, for my own part, I confess that I cannot banish from my mind the impression that there existed at this period, in the romantic district of the Bray river, a poet of the type of the ancient bards—one who combined with the powers of song the gift of composing exciting rhymes for the purpose of the hour. And he often presents himself to my imagination, seated in the old mansion of Hollybrooke, with Robert Adair and the bold hunters of Kilruddery—himself no doubt one of them—singing, with the accompaniment of this very harp, those simple songs which are yet remembered, and give pleasure in the remembrance, not only in the locality that gave them birth, but even in distant countries that have little knowledge or conception of its beauty.

"To this period may also be ascribed the harp preserved in the Museum of the Royal Irish Academy, though indeed there is, in my opinion, a possibility of its being of an earlier age. It is of medium size and of good workmanship, but its only ornamentation consists of a bird's head which adorns the fore pillar. This harp came into the possession of the Academy by the purchase of the second collection of Irish antiquities made by the late Major Sirr, his first and better collection having been disposed of to a Glasgow picture dealer, coupled with the singular condition that none of them should be offered for sale in Ireland; and I need hardly add, that, as a consequence, the whole collection passed into the hands of Scotch and English antiquaries.

"the harp in the R. I. A., purchased from Major Sirr";

"The Academy also possesses another harp, which, if it had any just claim to the name it bears—'Carolan's'—would be viewed by appreciators of musical genius with a deep interest. But, though it was sold to the Academy as such by a person who represented himself as the lineal descendant of the great minstrel, I have no doubt that he was a wretched impostor, whose statement was wholly unworthy of belief. We have trustworthy evidence that Carolan's harp was burned by the servants of Mac Dermot Roe at Alderford House, in which Carolan died. And even if such evidence were wanting, the character of the harp itself would belie the assertion; for it is of the rudest form and workmanship, and without any characteristic of Carolan's time. In short, I think it is a clumsy piece of work of the early part of the present century, and wholly unworthy a place in the great museum in which it is deposited.

"the so-called harp of Carolan in the R.I.A."

"I have now noticed all the old harps which have come under my own observation, and—with the exception of the Lanigan harp, in the county of Tipperary, which I have never seen, but I believe to be old—all those of whose present existence I have become cognizant. I have now, therefore, only to say a few words in reference to the harps manufactured in our own time.

"As far as I know, these harps are all the manufacture of Egan, the eminent Dublin harp-maker, and owe their origin to the necessity of providing instruments for a new race of harpers, the pupils of the school of the Belfast Harp Society. These

"Harps of the present century all made by Egan";

XXXIII. harps were of good form and size, about the height of pedal harps, rich in tone, and of excellent workmanship. But they were wholly without ornament, and had nothing about them to remind us of 'the loved harp of other days'. Where are these harps now? To what purpose have they been applied, now that their players have disappeared from amongst us? I cannot say. One, indeed, is in my own possession, and is an existing memorial of a great triumph of religious liberty—a triumph which I trust will yet obliterate the painful recollection of past divisions and sufferings, and unite Irishmen of all classes and creeds in the bonds of peace and brotherly affection. Many of us must, like myself, remember the triumphal procession of O'Connell through the leading streets of our city in 1829, after the passing of the Emancipation Act. The hero of the day was seated in a triumphal car, richly decorated with laurels; standing on his left hand, his henchman—one of my boy friends—the noble and lionhearted, and yet gentle, but not overwise Tom Steele; and seated before, but below them, a venerable minstrel, with abundant silvery locks and beard, arrayed in the supposed costume of the bardic race, and apparently drawing from his harp the joyous melodies of his country fitting for the occasion. It is true that he might as well have been a 'man who had no music in his soul', striking an instrument which could give forth no sound: for the never-ceasing Irish shout, which I believe is allowed to be far superior to all other shouts, of the assembled thousands who preceded, and surrounded, and followed the car, was a jealous shout, and would allow no other sound to be heard. The harp of that day was the one which is now mine; and the harper, whose appearance indicated a centogenarian age, and from whom, in a subsequent year, I bought it, was M'Loughlin, one of the *young* harpers of the Belfast school.

"one of them in Dr. Petrie's possession".

"Dr. Petrie's opinion of the exertions of the Harp Society of Belfast".

"The effort of the people of the north to perpetuate the existence of the harp in Ireland, by trying to give a harper's skill to a number of poor blind boys, was at once a benevolent and a patriotic one; but it was a delusion. The harp at the time was virtually dead; and such effort could give it for a while only a sort of galvanized vitality. The selection of blind boys, without any greater regard for their musical capacities than the possession of the organ of hearing, for a calling which doomed them to a wandering life, depending for existence mainly, if not wholly, on the sympathies of the poorer classes, and necessarily conducive to the formation of intemperate habits, was not a well-considered benevolence, and should never have had any fair hope of success. And besides, there were no competent teachers, imbued with a refined sense of the beauty of our finest melodies, to instruct them; none to select for them the most touching of those melodies, and unite them, anew, with a simple but correct harmony, such as has been preserved traditionally by the harpers of Wales, and give to their calling a continuance and a patronage not yet wholly extinguished. Thus imperfectly instructed—ignorant of counterpoint, and with a knowledge of only a few of our melodies, rarely of the first class, and scarcely ever perfectly preserved, how could it be expected that their performance could be tolerated by cultivated ears, accustomed to the 'tunes of the day', which are often of great beauty, and always correct and effective in their harmonies? But, even if it were otherwise—if those blind boys had been taught to play with skill and correctness the melodies of Ireland—the only melodies suited to their instrument—there was no longer in the country a generally diffused Celtic sentiment,—no national feeling, independent of class prejudices, like that of Scotland! A new phase of society, of which the struggle for wealth and the enjoyments of luxury are the characteristic features, has taken the place of that simpler one which gave a zest to the purer enjoyments, springing from man's sensibilities. Fashion will not now allow us to exhibit depth of feeling, or marked individuality of character. As a great poet has expressed this change.

"'The world is too much with us; late and soon,
Getting and spending, we lay waste our powers:
Little we see in nature that is ours;
We have given our hearts away, a sordid boon!'

"No. The Irish harp cannot be brought back to life: 't is dead for ever! And, even the music which it had created will never be felt again as it has been felt. But, IT won't die. A few minds, possessing the deeper sensibilities of our nature, and strong enough to spurn the deadening influences of fashion, will always be found, who, in the enjoyment of such music, will look for a solace amidst

"'The fretful stir and fever of the world'".

"the Irish harp is dead for ever, but the music won't die".

Passing from this valuable communication of Dr. Petrie, I shall now take up the thread of my own observations.

There is a harp in Scotland known as the harp of Mary Queen of Scots, described in "Gunn's Historical Enquiry", and said to resemble in a remarkable degree the Trinity College harp; but it has not, I believe, been yet examined by any person properly qualified to say how far this resemblance really exists. This may, for all we really know, be the harp of *Donnchadh Cairbreach* O'Brien.

The harp in Scotland known as that of Mary Queen of Scots.

XXXIII.

So far I have endeavoured to collect such references to the form, compass, and arrangement of the ancient harp,—our characteristic national instrument of music,—as well as to the history of the few existing examples of it known to us, as I have been able to gather in my readings of our ancient lore. But before I proceed to the next branch of my subject, and as I have said so much of *Muireadhach Albanach* O'Daly, I must be pardoned another short digression, in order to allow me to correct an error into which a learned Scottish writer, of whose acquaintance I feel proud to boast, has lately fallen respecting this celebrated Irish bard.

Rev. Mr. Mac Lauchlan's "Book of the Dean of Lismore";

The gentleman to whom I allude is the Reverend Thomas Mac Lauchlan of Edinburgh, who has within the present year published, with translation and notes, a volume of Gaedhelic poems selected from the Book of the Dean of Lismore in Scotland (a MS. of the year 1529). This book is a valuable contribution to the Gaedhelic literature of Ireland and Scotland. It is a work of great labour, most creditably executed, being enriched, besides the labours of the editor himself, by a long and deeply interesting introduction and additional notes from the learned pen of another valued friend of mine, William Forbes Skene, Esq., of Edinburgh. This is not, indeed, the place to enter into the merits of Mr. Mac Lauchlan's work, though I cannot resist the opportunity which the occurrence of *Muireadhach* O'Daly's name in it affords me of bearing my humble testimony to its merits. Among the curious selection of Ossianic and other poems in the volume, there are three short poems of a religious character ascribed to *Muireadhach Albanach* (O'Daly), of which I do not know of any copies existing in Ireland; and at page 109, in which is printed a poem ascribed to a John Mac Murrich, Mr. Mac Lauchlan appends the following note: "This John McMurrich, or McVurrich, was in all likelihood a member of the family who were so long bards to Clanranald, and who derived their name from their great ancestor in the thirteenth century, Muireach Albanach". And again, at page 157, where the first of O'Daly's poems occurs, the following note is appended:

It contains three poems ascribed to O'Daly or *Muireadhach Albanach*;

Mr. Mac Lauchlan's note on this poet;

"Murdoch of Scotland was the first of the great race of Mac Vurrichs, bards to Macdonald of Clanranald. From all that can be gathered regarding him, he was an ecclesiastic, and, according to the measure of light he possessed, a man of earnest and sincere religion. It was not known, until this volume of Dean McGregor's was searched, that any remains of his compositions existed; but here we find several, all very much of the same character. There is one long poem to the cross, which

XXXIII

appears to have been modelled on the early Latin hymns. Murdock of Scotland, or *Muireadhach Albanach*, would appear to have lived between A.D. 1180 and 1220. Mr. Standish H. O'Grady, late President of the Ossianic Society of Dublin, kindly sent to the writer some years ago a poem, still preserved in Ireland, containing a dialogue between *Muireadhach* and '*Cathal Croibhdhearg*', the red-handed Cathal O'Connor, king of Connaught, on the occasion of their embracing a religious life. Cathal's 'florish' is known to have been between A.D. 1184 and 1225".

his descri tion of or of the po incorrect regards O'Daly;

Mr. Mac Lauchlan prints the poem here, but the description of it is incorrect as far as O'Daly is concerned, for it contains no allusion whatever to his having embraced a religious life. On the contrary, he strongly urges the warrior king not to sheathe his sword, but rather to whet it for more battles, in place of whetting his knife for the purpose of tonsuring his head; and Cathal of the Red Hand did continue fighting his battles up to the year of his death in A.D. 1224, though he died in the habit of a Cistercian monk, in the abbey of *Cnoc Muaidh*, in the county of Galway, an abbey which he had himself founded in the year 1190.[348] Even in this poem O'Daly does not forget to pay a high and affectionate compliment to his friend *Donnchadh Cairbreach* O'Brien; but it is doubtful that he was in Ireland at all at the time of writing it. I possess a fine copy of this curious poem.

Mr. Mac Lauchlar not awar that *Mui eadhach Albanach* was an Irishman

It does not appear that Mr. Mac Lauchlan was aware that *Muireadhach Albanach* was an Irishman, but such he certainly was; and if the Mac Murdochs, or Mac Vuirrichs, of Scotland, are descended from him, they are the only posterity he is known to have left. For although his own pedigree is preserved by the O'Clerys and Mac Firbis, they do not seem to know that he had left any descendants. *Muireadhach Albanach* O'Daly, or, as he was called, *Muireadhach* of *Lios an-Doill*, was the third of six brothers, the second of whom was *Donnchadh Mor* O'Daly, abbot of Boyle, in the county of Roscommon, author of many religious Irish poems, some of them of great beauty, particularly those in praise of the Blessed Virgin Mary. The abbot died in the year 1244, and it is possible that some of the poems ascribed to his brother were his. This branch of the learned O'Daly family is set down by the O'Clerys and Mac Firbis as the O'Dalys of Breifney, and not of Meath, as some say. They were descended from Niall of the Nine Hostages, and of the same race as the O'Neills, or *Cinael Eoghain*.

From this digression I now return to my proper subject, and

(348) See the Annals of the Four Masters, A.D. 1224.

XXXIII. I shall accordingly proceed with our investigation into the records of the musical instruments used and the music performed in ancient Erinn.

The harp, of course, was the chief instrument employed in that music. And it is concerning the use of the harp that the greater part of the apocryphal statements current concerning ancient music have been made. I have here collected all that I believe to be really authentic on the subject of the perfect harp, or *Cruit;* the remainder of what I have to say upon this class of instrument will come in more properly when I have to speak of the *Telyn*, or Welsh harp, and to lay before the reader more full account of the *Timpán*. I have here but to add a few words by way of caution as to the speculations of some of the more popular writers on the subject.

The author has collected all that he believes authentic on the *Cruit*.

Much has been confidently written on the ancient Irish music and musical instruments, particularly by Mr. Joseph Cooper Walker and Mr. Edward Bunting; the former chiefly from imagination, and the latter from induction, aided by a high musical education; for Mr. Bunting's actual knowledge, or rather notions, of the ancient Irish harp, and the peculiarities of ancient Irish music, were derived by him only from the degenerate body of harpers who held their last synod in Belfast in the year 1792. That the information derived by him from those professors was apocryphal and corrupt will clearly be seen from the long list of musical terms published in his last volume (1840), all of which, with few exceptions (as I shall show by and bye), are, I may at once say, mere forgeries, or else the most commonplace and vulgar Hibernicisms of English terms supplied him by his informants, whoever they were. Mr. Bunting was not an Irish scholar. It may appear strange that in all that has been written on the subject of Irish music and musical instruments down to our own time, no example or instance of the performances in ancient times on the harp, or any other musical instrument, either singly or in concert, has been published on anything like authority by our musical writers. The reason of this, however, is obvious enough. These writers had no acquaintance with our ancient literature; they did not even understand our language; they had a reference to *Craiftine* and his wonderful harp from Keting, a few references to horns or trumpets in what are called the poems of Oisin, and to these their own imagination and effrontery made large additions.

The statements about ancient Irish music and musical instruments of Walker and Bunting of no value; these writers did not know the Irish language;

It is with the greatest reluctance that I venture to offer such strong remarks on the compilation published by Mr. Bunting, who has rescued so much of our precious music from loss and oblivion; but I must say, that it would have been more to his

XXXIII.

credit if he had left the whole discussion of the ancient Irish harp in such judicious hands as those of George Petrie and others of his stamp, whose deep learning and perfect conscientiousness would always keep them within the bounds of actual knowledge or fair rational induction. As for Mr. Cooper Walker, he appears to have been the sport of every pretender to antiquarian knowledge, but more especially the dupe of an unscrupulous person of the name of Beaufort,—not the learned author of the "Memoir of a Map of Ireland", but another clergyman of the name,—who unblushingly pawned his pretended knowledge of facts on the well-intentioned but credulous Walker.

the author regrets to have to speak thus of the work of one who has rescued so much of our music.

LECTURE XXXIV.

[Delivered July 1st, 1860.]

(IX.) Of Music and Musical Instruments (continued). Names of musical instruments found in our MSS.—The *Benn-Buabhaill;* the *Corn-Buabhaill* a drinking horn. The *Benn-Chroit.* The *Buinne.* The *Coir-Ceathairchuir.* The *Corn;* the *Cornaire* or horn-player mentioned in the *Táin Bo Fraich*, in the "Courtship of *Ferb*", and in a legendary version of the Book of Genesis; no reference to trumpets in the *Táin Bo Chuailgne*, but the playing of harps in the encampments is mentioned; instance of musicians in the trains of kings and chiefs on military expeditions:—the Battle of *Almhain* and the legend of *Dondbo.* Musical instruments mentioned in the Tale of the Battle of *Almhain*, and in the poem on the fair of *Carman.* The *Cornaire*, or horn-blower, also mentioned in the poem on the Banqueting-House of Tara. The *Craebh-Ciúil*, or Musical Branch, mentioned in the Tale of *Fledh Bricrind* or "*Bricriu's* Feast"; the musical branch a symbol of poets and used for commanding silence, as shown by the Tales of "*Bricriu's* Feast", and the "Courtship of *Emer*"; the Musical Branch mentioned in the Tale of the "Dialogue of the Two Sages"; and also in the Tale of the "Finding of *Cormac's* Branch"; and lastly in a poem of about the year A.D. 1500; the Musical Branch symbolical of repose and peace; it was analogous to the Turkish silver crescent and bells; some bronze bells in the museum of the R.I.A. belonged perhaps to such an instrument. The bells called "Crotals" described in the "Penny Journal"; Dr. Petrie's observations thereon; "Crotals" not used by Christian priests; explanation of the term; the Irish words *crothadh*, *crothla*, and *clothra;* they are the only words at all like *crotalum*, except *crotal*, the husks of fruit, i.e. castanets; bells put on the necks of cows, and on horses; the *Crotal* not known in Ireland,—everything written about it is pure invention. The *Crann-Ciúil*, or Musical Tree; it was a generic term for any kind of musical instrument, as is shown by a passage from the Book of Lismore, where it is a *Cruit; Cuisle*, a tube, explained in a vellum MS. as a Musical Tree; in another place in the Book of Lismore it is a *Timpan* that is so called. The *Cuiseach:* mentioned in the poem on the fair of *Carman*, and in the Tale of the Battle of *Almhain.* The *Cuisle Ciúil* another name for *Crann Ciúil; Cuisle* a living word meaning a vein, or a kind of cock; mentioned in the Book of Invasions; *Cuisle* explained, in H. 3. 18. T.C.D., as a Musical Tree.

It is not at all satisfactory, nor is it to be wondered at, that, although we find several musical instruments mentioned by name in our ancient writings, we have so few of them now existing among the specimens of ancient art preserved in the museum of the Royal Irish Academy. Those instruments have for ages ceased to be known in Ireland, and are now only occasionally found buried deep in the earth, from which they are from time to time recovered to bear their unimpeachable evidence to a remote era of civilization and art in the country. The best way, perhaps, in which we could enter upon the study of these objects would be to first give in alphabetical order a list of such musical instruments as I have found mentioned in old Gaedhelic writings, and then give in the same order a literal translation of these names as far as I can, together with the circumstances and ancient authorities in which they are found. After that I shall give (with such explanations as I can offer) the names for musical performers, and for the various species of music, and the occasions upon which they are mentioned, as far as I have been able to collect them.

The number of instruments, then, amounts to twenty, and the following are their names:

Names of musical instruments found in MSS.

Benn-buabhaill; Benn-Chroit; Buinde or *Buinne; Coir-Ceathairchuir; Corn; Craebh-Ciúil; Crann-Ciûil; Cruit; Cruiseach; Cuisle-Ciúil; Feadán; Fidil; Guth-Buinde; Ocht-Tedach; Oircin; Pip* or *Pipai; Stoc; Sturgan; Teillin; Timpan.*

The *Benn-Buabhaill*.

The first instrument, *Benn-buabhaill*, was certainly a compound name, formed from *benn*, a horn, and *buabhall*, a buffalo or wild ox. This real horn, as an instrument of music, is not mentioned, as far as I have found, in any composition older than those mediæval poems and writings known as the Finian tales and poems, so called because they pretend to record chiefly the life and achievements of *Find Mac Cumhaill*, and his warriors. In the modern copies of these pieces the name of this instrument is written *Barra-Buadh*, but this is manifestly a corruption from the old correct form of *Benn-Buabhaill*. The name will be found in several of the Finian poems, and in the Finian tale so well known as the *Bruighean Chaerthainn*, in all of which it is made the chief instrument by which the champion *Find* called his troops together for war or the chase.

The *Corn-Buabhaill* a drinking horn.

Mention of the use of the natural horn occurs, but under another name and for a different purpose, in other places where it is called a *Corn-Buabhaill*,—*corn* and *benn* both being names for a horn; but under this name it is always applied to a drinking cup or drinking horn, and not to a musical instrument;—as, for instance, in the Finian tract in the Book of Lismore:—"And the young warrior gave its full in a *Corn-Buabhaill* out of the cask of ale which he had, to *Cailte*".(349) Many other instances could be adduced of this use of the *Corn-Buabhaill*.

The *Benn-Chroit*.

The second instrument, *Benn-Chroit*, is explained in an ancient glossary thus: "The strings of a *Benn-Crot*, that is, the strings of a pinnacled (or triangular) *Cruit*, that is of a *Timpan*".(350) This is a curious interpretation, and if correct, it

(349) [original:—Ocus tuc an toclach a lán a mbeiand-buafball as in dabuig meada boi aige do Cailti.—Book of Lismore, fol. 339 [141] a. a.]

(350) [original:—Teta mbeanncrot, .i. na crot mbeannach, .i. na timpan.—H. 4. 22. 67 or 65].

XXXIV. would lead to the opinion that the real ancient *Cruit* was quadrangular, while the *Timpan* was triangular. The phrase, "As sweet as the strings of *Benn-Crot*", occurs very often in our ancient tales; and in deriving the name of *Geide Ollgothach*, or *Geide* of the great voice, one of our ante-Christian kings, we are told in the Book of Leinster and other equally ancient authorities, that he was so called because, from the peaceful, harmonious character of his reign, the people heard each other's words and voices with the same delight as if they had been the strings of the triangular [? melodious] harps, or *Benn-Chrotta*.

The Buinde. The third instrument is the *Buinde* or *Buinne;* and we have the best definition of its form that can be desired, from the old text quoted in Zeuss' "Grammatica Celtica", vol. I., p. 481, where we find: *Roboi buinne fochosmuilius nadarcae side*, that is "a cornet horn; which means that it was a trumpet in shape of a horn". The learned author of the "Grammatica Celtica" merely gives the passages for grammatical purposes from a codex at Milan in Italy, containing a commentary on the Psalms of David; but this passage contains an important authority for the meaning of the word *Buinne*, since the MS. is one of the ninth century. Again the same authority has, at page 77 of the same volume: *angaibther isind buinniu, no croit*, which is glossed thus: "quod canitur; i.e. tibia vel crotta"; that is, "what is chanted on the tibia, or the harp". Now Tibia is not exactly a horn, or an instrument of the horn form, but a flute, fife, or clarionet; but of such an instrument no ancient specimen that I know of has come down to our times. I have not met with the name *Buinne* itself as applying to any instrument of music in my readings of ancient Gaedhelic original writings; but the *Buinirê*, or performer on the *Buinne*, is mentioned in the ancient poem on the *Teach Midchuarta*, or Banqueting Hall of Tara; and he is placed at the same table with the *Cornair*, or horn-player, in the plan of that hall published by Dr. Petrie in his Essay on the Antiquities of Tara.

The Coir Ceathair chuir. The fourth instrument is the *Coir Ceathairchuir*,—the great harp of the *Tuatha Dé Danann*, so amply discussed in a former lecture; but, whether this was one of the special names for this particular harp, or the name of a particular fashion, or class of harps, it is at present quite beyond our reach to ascertain.

The Corn; The fifth instrument on my list is the *Corn;* a word which simply and literally signifies a horn, but which, certainly, was applied only to a metallic instrument of music of the trumpet kind. Of this fact, as well as of the use of the *Corn*, we have many examples, of which the following will be sufficient for our present purpose. In the very ancient tale of the *Táin Bo*

Fraich, already quoted in former lectures (where the three harpers, the sons of *Uaithne* and *Boand* who attended *Fraech* on his matrimonial visit to the palace of *Cruachan*, are described) we are told that the young prince was attended in his progress by seven *Cornaire*, or *Corn* players.

The Cornair or horn player mentioned in the *Tain Bo Fraich*;

"There were", says the tale, "seven *Cornaires* along with them, who had *Corns* of gold and of silver, and who wore clothes of various colours; their hair was fair-yellow, as if of gold, and they wore brilliant white shirts".[331]

We have a description of another group of *Cornaire* from a different source, and a different tale of equal antiquity, exactly similar; I mean that in the tale called *Tochmarc Feirbé*, or the Courship of *Ferb;* and which is one of the most celebrated of its class. *Ferb* was the beautiful daughter of *Gerg*, the chief of *Glenn-Geirg*, in Ulster, and she was beloved by *Máine*, one of the sons of *Ailill* and *Medb*, the celebrated king and queen of Connacht. We are told that this young prince having, with the consent of his father and mother, determined on paying a visit to the court of the lady *Ferb's* father, for the purpose of making a formal demand of her hand in marriage, he set out at the head of a splendid cavalcade to his father's palace of *Cruachan* to show himself to his royal parents and to receive their benediction and good wishes. Nothing can be more gorgeous than the description in this tale of prince *Máine*, and the cavalcade that attended his progress, as may be seen from the following short extract, which it will be observed includes the mention of the *Cornaire* or trumpeters, and of the *Cruitire* or harpers, as well as of the druids of the cavalcade.

in the "Courtship of Ferb";

"There were seven grayhounds attending his [prince *Maine's*] chariot, in chains of silver, with balls of gold upon each chain, so that the tingling of the balls against the chains would be music sufficient [for the march]. There was no known colour that was not to be seen upon these grayhounds. There were seven *Cornaire*, with *Corna* of gold and of silver, wearing clothes of many colours, and all having fair-yellow hair. Three druids also went in front of them, who wore *Minda* (or diadems) of silver upon their heads and speckled cloaks over their dresses, and who carried shields of bronze ornamented with red copper. Three *Cruitire* (or harpers) accompanied them; each of kingly aspect, and arrayed in a crimson cloak. It was so they arrived on the green of (the palace of) *Cruachan;* and they ran their three assembly-races upon the green of *Cruachan*".[332]

[331] [original already given; *ante*, Lect. xxx., vol. ii., p. 220.]

[332] [orginal:—Secht milcoin im-ma carpat ṡlabradaib airgit, agus

XXXIV.

After this the story tells us they went forth on their journey, which, however, happened to turn out an unfavourable one.

Of this fine old tale there remains a beautiful copy in the Book of Leinster, with the loss of, perhaps, a page at the beginning. I quote only that part of it in which the *Cornaire* are introduced.

and in a legendary version of the Book of Genesis;

The next reference to the *Corn* is from a very different source indeed, but it is one that sufficiently well defines the character and use of the instrument. It is to be found in a beautiful legendary version of the Book of Genesis, the creation of Adam and Eve, their temptation and fall, and expulsion from Eden.

"And it was then", says this legend, "that Adam heard the voice of Michael the Archangel, saying to Gabriel: 'Let a *Corn* and a *Stoc Focra* be sounded by thee, until they are heard throughout the seven heavens; and go all of ye to the presence of your Creator. And arise, all ye armies and host of angels of the seven heavens, until ye repair along with your Creator to paradise'".[383]

There can scarcely remain a doubt that the *Corn* spoken of here was the long curving trumpet of which we have such a magnificent specimen in the museum of the Royal Irish Academy, which is an instrument of the most powerful character;[384] and it appears to me equally certain that the *Stoc* was a clarion, a smaller, a more shrill and sharp-sounding instrument, of which, as far as we can surmise, no specimen has come down

ubull oir for cech slabrad, combaleor ceol sogur na nubull sris na slabradaib; noco rabi dach na rabi isna Conaib. Batar aice mor sessiur cornaire, co cornaib oir, acus argit leo, conetaigib illdathaib impu, co mongaib findbuide foraib. Ba tar tri drui rempu comindaib airgdidib uasa cennaib, combrattaib breccaib impu, acus cosciachaib umaidib acus conasnaidib credumai foraib. Tri cruittiri conecosc rigda for cechae machomair imbrattaib corcraib. Rancatar iarsin tachim sin co Cruachain, acus roselscat a tri graiphni aenaig for faichi na Cruachna.—H. 2. 18. fol 189. a. a. and a. b.

This passage is very similar to the corresponding one from the *Táin Bo Fraich*, given in lecture xxx. (*vide* vol. ii., p. 219). The buffoons, or as they ought perhaps more properly to be called jugglers, in the latter being here called Druids.]

(383) [original:—Conid ann sin rochualaid Adam guth Michil archaingil ocarad fri Gabriel aingel, seinnter olse corn ocus stoc focra lib co cluinn a sonn fona .uii. nimib; ocus ercid uile icomdail bar nduileman; ocus ercid uile a slogs ocus a airbriu aingel na .uii. nime comdechraid maraen ria bur nduileman dochum parduis.—*Leabhar Breac*, folio, 46. a. a. bot.]

(384) This grand instrument, fig. 61, when the two pieces are joined, measures eight feet five inches in length. The opening at the large end is three and a half inches wide, and five-eighths of an inch at the small end. There must have been another piece at least, as well as a mouth-piece. There is also in the Academy's museum the middle-piece of another great horn, fortunately preserving those circular bosses at the ends by which it was connected with the other two pieces.

to our time. Of this instrument, however, I shall have to speak again under its proper head.(355)

no reference to trumpets in the Táin Bo Chuailgne, but there is to the playing of harps in the encampments;

It is remarkable that there is no reference to instruments of the trumpet kind in the *Táin Bo Chuailgne*, nor in the *Bruighean Daderga*, two tales of a very warlike character, in which the mention of such instruments might naturally be expected. Indeed the only reference to music in the *Táin Bo Chuailgne* is where we are told that when the marching forces halted at night, they were regaled with the music of the harp and other instruments at and after dinner. Another instance of the attendance of musical performers upon kings and chiefs on their royal progresses and military expeditions, is found in the detailed account of the battle of *Almhain* (now the hill of Allen, in the county of Kildare) fought in the year 718; and this account contains so much that relates to our present subject, that although I have already used it in a former lecture,(356) I must go into it at some length here.

Instance of musicians in the train of kings and chiefs on military expeditions:

In the year 718, the monarch of Erinn, *Ferghal*, the son of *Maelduin*, of the northern *Ui Neill* race, and who at the time resided at *Aileach* (near Derry), proposed to re-impose, and levy from the people of Leinster, the old Borromean Tribute which had been remitted to them a few years previously by the then monarch, *Finnachta*, at the solicitation of St. *Moling*. He accordingly made great preparations for this dangerous expedition, as will be seen from the following extract:—

Legend of Donnbo.

"Long, indeed, was this muster being made; for what every man of the *Leith Chuinn* (or *Conn*'s half, i.e. the northern half of Erinn to whom the summons came) used to say, was: 'If *Donnbo* goes upon the expedition, I will'. Now *Donnbo* was the son of a widow belonging to the *Fera-Rois* (of the county of *Muineachan* or Monaghan); he had never gone away from his mother's house one day or one night; and there was not in all Erinn one more comely, or of better shape or face, or more graceful symmetry, than he; he was the best at singing amusing verses and telling of royal stories in the world; he was the best to equip horses, and to mount spears, and to plait hair; and his was the best mind in acuteness of intellect and in honour".(357)

(355) [See *postea*, Lect. XXXVI.]

(356) [See Lect. XVIII., *ante*, vol. i., p. 389.]

(357) [original:—Ba fada tra robás ag an tinolsain; uair assed ad beired gach fear do leith Chuinn gus a roichead fuacrad, .i. "dá d-ti Donnbó ar an sluagad ragadsa", Donnbó imurro mac baintreabthaige eiside d'Feraib Ross; agas ni deachaid lá na aidchi a taig a máthar imach riamh; acas ni raibe i n-Erinn uile bud coimhe, no bud ferr cruth no delb, no denam inás. Ni raba i n-Erinn uile bud griabdha, no bud segaine inás, acas as uad bud ferr rann ersa acas risgela for domhon; as e bud ferr do glesead,

XXXIV. Legend of *Dondbo* (continued).

Such was the description of *Donnbo*, the widow's son, who appeared so precious, we are told, in his mother's eyes, that when the king summoned him to his standard, she would not allow him to go until she had gotten the security of St. *Colum Cillé*, through his representative *Mael Mac Failbhe*, that he should return to his home from Leinster in safety. Not so, however, was the young man's fate, as the sequel will show.

King *Fergal* having completed his preparations, set out from *Aileach* upon his southern march, and in due time and after much toil, reached *Cluain Dobhail*, at *Almhain*, where he encamped and set up his own pavilion. It was then, the story says, that *Fergal* said to *Donnbo:* "Make amusement for us, *O Donnbo!* because thou art the best minstrel in Erinn, namely, at *Cuiseachs*, at pipes (or tubes), and at harps, and at poems, and at traditions, and at the royal stories of Erinn; and to-morrow morning we shall give battle to the Leinstermen". "Not so", said *Donnbo*, "I am not able to amuse thee this night; nor can I exhibit one single feat of all these to-night. But, wherever thou art to-morrow night, if I be alive, I shall make amusement for thee. Let then the royal buffoon, *Ua Maighlinne*, amuse thee to-night". So *Ua Maighlinne* was called to them then; and he commenced to narrate the battles and triumphs of *Leth-Chuinn* and Leinster from the destruction of *Tuaim Teanbath*, that is *Dind Righ*, in which *Cobhthach Cael-m Breagh* was killed, down to that time; and they slept not much that night, because of their great dread of the Leinstermen and the great tempest. For this was the eve of the festival of St. *Finnian* in the winter" (that is, the 11th of December).(336)

The story goes on to relate that the battle was fought on the next morning, and that the northerns were defeated with the loss of nine thousand men, including the monarch *Fergal* him-

acas do morma sleg, agas d-sighe folt, acus bud fer ri aicne [.i. ing-ne inntlechta] na einech.—Three Fragments of Irish Annals, pub. by I.A.S., p. 34; *vide* also H. 2. 16. 939; and Book of Fermoy, fol. 79. b.b.]

(336) [original:—As andsin asbert Fergal fria Donnbó: déna airfi-ded dúin, a Donnbó! fobith as tu as deach airfide fuil in-Erinn, .i. i cuisig, agas i cuislennoib, agas i cruitib, agas randaib, agas raid-sechoib, agas rigscelaib Erenn; agas is in maidin imbárach do bé-ram-ne cath do Laignib. Ach, as Donnbó, ni chumgaimsi airfide duit-si anocht, agas nimcha aon gniomh dib sin uile do taidbsin anocht. Agas cipsi airm i rabairsi a márach, agas imbeosa, do dénsa airfide duitsi. Dénadh imurro an rigdruth hua Mai-gléine airfide duit anocht. Tugadh hua Maigléni chuca iartain; ro gabhsaidhe og innisin cath, agas com-ramha Leithe Chuinn agus Laighen ó to-gail Tuama Tenbath, .i. Deanda Righ, in ra marbadh Cobthach Caolbregh, conigi an aimsir sin, agas ni ba mór codalta do rinnedlco in aid-chi sin, ra méd eagla leo Laighin, agas le méid na doininne, .i. uair aidhchi fele Fhinnain gaimhridhsin.—Three Fragments of Irish Annals, pub. by I. A. S., p. 38; *vide* also H. 2. 16. 939; and Book of Fermoy, fol. 79, b. b.]

self, and almost all the northern chiefs. It was *Aedh Menn*, a Leinster chief, that slew *Fergal*, but not before he had first slain the minstrel *Donnbo*, who appears to have lost his life in the special defence of the king. The buffoon, *Ua Maighlinne*, was taken prisoner; and we are told he was commanded to give his "buffoon's roar" (whatever that performance was), and that he did so. And the tale lays particular emphasis upon this performance, for we are told that loud and melodious was this roar; and that *Ua Maighlinne*'s roar remained with the buffoons of Erinn from that time to the time of the writer. This was not all, however, for we are further told that king *Fergal's* head was then cut off, and the buffoon's head was also cut off; and that the echo of the buffoon's roar continued to reverberate in the air for three days and three nights: a feat clearly showing to what class of the wonderful the tale I quote belongs. Then comes the passage in which the allusion to musical instruments occurs, in connection with which I shall quote this singular fiction.

XXXIV. Legend of Dondbo (continued).

"It was at *Condail* of the kings" (now Old Connall in the county of Kildare), continues the story, "that the Leinstermen encamped that night, drinking wine and mead pleasantly and in good spirits, after having fought the battle, and each of them relating his triumphs merrily and cheerfully. Then *Murchadh*, the son of *Bran* (king of Leinster), said: 'I would give a chariot worth four *cumhals* (that is, twelve cows) and a steed, and my dress, to any champion who would go to the field of slaughter, and who would bring us a token from it'. 'I will go', said *Baethghalach*, a champion of Munster. So he put on his battle-dress of battle and combat, and reached the spot where (king) *Fergal*'s body was; and he heard something near, above him, in the air, which said, for he heard it all: 'Here is a command to you from the king of the seven heavens. Make amusement for your master to-night, that is, for *Fergal*, the son of *Maelduin*, though you have all of you, the professional men, fallen here, both *Cuisleannchu* (that is, pipers), and *Cornaire* (that is, trumpeters), and *Cruitire* (that is, harpers); yet, let not terror nor debility prevent you this night from performing for *Fergal*'. And then the warrior heard the music both of singers, and trumpeters, and fifers, and harpers; and he heard the variety of music, and he never heard before nor after better music. And he heard in a cluster of rushes near him a *Dord-Fiansa* (or wild song), the sweetest of all the world's music The warrior went towards it. 'Do not come near me', said the head to him. 'I ask who thou art?' said the warrior. 'I am the head of *Donnbo*', said the head, 'and I was bound in a bond

XXXIV. Legend of Donnbo (continued).

last night to amuse the king this night; and do not you interrupt me!' 'Where is *Fergal's* body here?' said the warrior. 'It is it that shines beyond thee there', said the head. 'I ask', said the warrior, 'shall I take thee also away with me? It is thou that I prefer to take'. 'I prefer that nothing whatever should carry me away', said the head, 'unless Christ, the Son of God, should take me', continued the head; 'thou must give the guarantee of Christ that thou wilt bring me back to my body again'. 'I shall certainly bring thee (back)', said the warrior; and so the warrior returned with the head to *Condail* the same night, and he found the Leinstermen still drinking on his arrival.

"'Hast thou brought a token with thee?' said king *Murchadh*. 'I have', answered the warrior, 'the head of *Donnbo*'. 'Place it on yonder post', said (king) *Murchadh*. The whole host then knew it to be the head of *Donnbo;* and this was what they all said: 'Pity thy fate, O *Donnbo!* Comely was thy face! make amusement for us this night, the same as thou didst for thy lord yesterday'. So he turned his face to the wall of the house, in order that it should be the darker for him; and he raised his *Dord Fiansa* (or wild song) on high, and it was the sweetest of all music upon the surface of the earth! So that the host were all crying and lamenting from the plaintiveness and softness of the melody".[339]

[339] [Original:—I condail na ríog battur Laigin an aiḋċi, ag ol fina meda arccur an caṫa go subaċ soimenmaċ, agas caċ diob ag innsin a compania, is iad meḋraig meadarċaoin. As andsin ra ráiḋ Murchaḋ mac Briain: "do bearainn carpat ceṫre cumala, agas mo eaċ, agas m' erraḋ, don laoċ no ragaḋ isin árṁaċ, agas do ḃeraḋ comarṫa cugainn as". Raġad-sa ar Baotgalaċ, laoc dim[n] Muṁain. Gebiḋ a caṫerraḋ caṫa agas comlanna uime, go ráinig go hairm i mbaoi corp Fearġaile; go cuala ni i neagairgaire isin aeor ós a cinn, condeperc: ar closs uile, timarnaḋ duib ó ríg rećt nime. Dena airfide dá bur ttigerna anoċt, .i. d'Ferġal mac Maolduin, cia do roċrarair sinn uile in bar naoisdana etir cuisleanoċu, agas cornaire, acas, cruitire; na tairmescca erḟuaċ no héġ comnart sib d'airfideḋ anoċt di Fearġall. Go ccuala iaraṁ an toglaċ an cuisig. agas an ceol sireaċtaċ. Go ccuala dan 'san tum luaċra ba nesa ḋó an tórd-fiansa, ba binne (in ceol hisin oldac ceoil in domain.—B. of Fermoy, f. 80, a. b.]. Luiḋ an toglaċ na ḋóċum. Na tair ar m'amus, ar an cenn frir. Ceist, cia tu? ar an tóglaċ. Nin mise cenn Duinnbo, ar an cenn, agas naidm ro naidmeḋ frim a reir airfided an rig anoċt; agas ná ercóidiḋ ḋam! Caide corp Forġail sunn,? ar an t'oglaċ,? [Isé a ċorp in taiṫneamaċ sit anall, ar in ceand, ceist ar in toclaeċ cia no ber lium.—H. 2. 16. 989. et seq.] "as tu as deaċ lim", Nom béra, ar ann cenn; acht raċ crist dod ċinn da nom ruga, ga ttuga mé ar amus mo ċolla do ridisi. Do béir égin, ar an tóglaċ; agas imroi an tóglaċ agas an cennlais conige Condail, agas fuair Laigin ag ól ar a ċenn 'sin aiḋċi cétna. An ttugais comarṫa lat? ar Murċhaḋ. Tugas, ar an tóglaċ cend Duinnbó. Forairm ar an fuaiṫne ut ṫall, ar Murċaḋ. Tugsad an sluaġ uile aiṫne fair gur bé cenn Duinnbó; agas ased ro-

XXXIV.

However wild this strange story may be, the composition affords evidence sufficient to show, that in the middle ages, say in the seventh and eighth centuries, it was the custom in Erinn that music and song should attend on military expeditions, if not to cheer them on to the battle-field, at least to keep up their spirits and to dissipate the gloom which must naturally hang over an army on the night preceding the day of battle; and so also we gather from the context, that it was customary for the victors to celebrate their triumphs with wine, ale, music, and song. I may here observe that the musical instruments mentioned in this story were the *Cuiseach*, the *Cuisle*, the *Cruit*, and the *Corn*. Of the *Cruit* I have already said much; of the others I shall have more to say further on.

Musical instruments mentioned in the Tale of the "Battle of *Almhain*";

This represents one class of those occasions on which we find the music of the horn player referred to.

and the poem on the Fair of *Carman*.

Again, in the ancient poem preserved in the Book of Leinster, and described in a former lecture, which gives an account of the sports and entertainments practised at the fair of *Carman*[360] (now Wexford) in ancient times, we find several instruments of music mentioned as having been in requisition at these great national or provincial assemblies. This poem was written by *Fulartach*, a native of Leinster, about the year 1000; and, in speaking of and enumerating the various kinds of these entertainments, the poet tells us (at the fifty-fifth stanza), that among its favourite sources of enjoyment were the *Stuic*, the *Cruta*, the wide-mouthed *Corna*, the *Cuiseacha*, the *Timpain*, the *Pipai* (or pipes), the Fiddles, the *Fir-Cengail*, the *Cnamh-fhir*, and the *Cuislennachs*. I may observe that the last three names are those of performers, derived from the names of their instruments, of each of which I propose to speak under its particular head.

The *Cornair* or horn-blower also mentioned in the poem on the Banqueting House of Tara.

The *Cornair*, or horn-blower, is mentioned also in the ancient poem on the arrangement of the Banqueting House of Tara, the *Teach Midhchuarta;* and we find the particular place assigned to him in that great house marked on the plan of it published by Dr. Petrie in his "History of the Antiquities of Tara".

The *Craebh Ciúil* or Musical Branch;

The sixth instrument on our list is the *Craebh Ciúil*, or Musical Branch. This appears to have been a branch, or branchy

ráidhsed uile: dirsan duit a Dhuinn-bó! bá caomh do dealbh, dena airfide dúinn anocht, feb do rignis dot tigearna imbuarach. Impoigther a aighidh [fraighidh in tighi ar daig comad dorcha do.—H. 2. 16. 939. *et seq.*]; agas attracht a dord-fiansa attruagh ar aird, [combabindi cach céol ar tuind talman —H. 2. 16. 939. *et seq.*] go mbáttur uile ag caoi agas ag tuirsi [ria truaighi agas ri taitiusi in ciuil rochan. —H. 2. 16. 939. *et seq.*]—Three Fragments of Irish Annals, pub. by I.A.S., p. 46.

(360) [See Lect. II., *ante*, vol. ii. p. 38; and also Appendix, for the original of this important poem.]

XXXIV. pole, upon which a cluster of bells was suspended; something, perhaps, like the crescent with its bells, which, borrowed from the Turks within our memory, held a rather conspicuous place in the military bands of the British army. It is, perhaps, scarcely correct to call this a musical instrument, as we do not find it mentioned any where in connection with other instruments of music. The first reference to a musical branch that I have met is in the very ancient tale of *Fledh Bricrind* (*Bricriu's* feast), fully described in a former lecture.[361]

mentioned in the Tale of *Fledh Bricrind* or "*Bricriu's* Feast";

When at this feast the wives of the great champions of Ulster had got into a warm war of words in support of the merits of their respective husbands, the husbands themselves being present became excited, and ready to step beyond the limits of wordy argument to test the assertions of their spouses on the spot. As the passage is a very short one, I may as well give the following translation of it from the *Leabhar na h-Uidhre:*

"The house became a babel of words again with the women, in a contention about their husbands and themselves. And the husbands showed a disposition to quarrel again, namely, *Conall* [*Cearnach*], and *Laeghaire Buadhach*, and *Cuchulaind*. Then *Sencha* [the poet] son of *Ailill* arose, and he shook the *Craebh Shencha*, or *Sencha*'s Branch, whereupon all the Ultonians were silent to hear him".[362]

This *Sencha* was a distinguished scholar and poet, and held, besides, the post of chief judge to *Conchobar Mac Nessa*, king of Ulster at this time. In a former lecture[363] I have given a description of his person, arms, and dress, as told by *Mac Roth*, to *Ailill* and *Medbh*, the king and Queen of Connacht, at Sleimhain, in Westmeath, quoted from the *Tain Bo Chuailgne.*

the Musical Branch a symbol of poets, and used for commanding silence

That the Musical Branch was an appendage peculiar to the poets, and probably for the double purpose of distinction and of commanding silence, as in the present case, may be inferred from another passage in the same tale of *Bricriu*'s Feast, on the occasion of the first commotion of the women and their husbands referred to in the passage just quoted above. The contention in this case arose among the women when outside the house, as to who should be the first to get in, whereupon the tale says:

(361) [See *Lectures on the MS. Materials of Ancient Irish History*, p. 346; and also Lecture xix., *ante*, vol. ii. p. 17.]

(362) [original:—Do ṗala in teċ in-aráiṫreċaib briaṫar oc na mnáib, do ruiri oc imarbaig eter a feraib ocus fiat fesin. Co folmaisset inorin comergi debṫa doriṡi, .i. Conall ocus Loegaire ocus Cuċulainn. Atracht Senċa mac Ailella rocroiṫ in Craeib Senċa, ocus contoiset ula[ulcu] uli fris.—*Leabhar na h-Uidhre*, fol. 67 a. b. *et seq.*]

(363) [See Lecture xxiii., *ante*, vol. ii. p. 92.]

"Their husbands arose in the house; each man of them (anxious) to open the door for his wife, so that she should be the first woman to enter the house. 'It will be an evil night', said (king) *Conchobar;* and he struck the red bronze post of the couch with the spike of silver which he held in his hand, upon which the whole host sat down".[364]

XXXIV. as shown by "*Bricriu's* Feast",

That this was not an accidental circumstance as regards the king's means of commanding peace and silence, we have ample evidence from the following passage in the *Tóchmarc n-Eimire* (or, the Courtship of *Emer* and *Cuchulaind*), in which the same king *Conchobar Mac Nessa*, and his palace, the Royal Branch of *Emania*, are described:

"*Conchobhar's* couch was placed in the front of the house; it was ornamented with plates of silver, and it had posts of red bronze, with gilding of gold on their heads, inlaid with gems of carbuncle, so that day and night were of equal light in it. There was a plate of silver [i.e. a kind of gong] over the king, reaching to the roof of the royal house; and whenever *Conchobhar* struck with the royal wand this plate, the Ultonians all were silent".[365]

and the "Courtship of *Emer*";

The next reference to the *Craebh Ciuil*, or Musical Branch, is to be found in the ancient tale called *Agallamh an da Shuadh*, or the Dialogue of the two Sages or Professors, of which I gave a free analysis in a former lecture when treating of the pieces called ancient prophecies.[366] I shall give here a short analysis of the story by way of preface to the particular passage bearing upon my present subject.

the Musical Branch mentioned in the tale of the "Dialogue of the Two Sages";

Adhna, a learned man of the province of Connacht, was chief poet of Ulster, and attached to the court of the above *Conchobar Mac Nessa* at *Emania*, about the time of the Incarnation. This *Adhna* had a son, *Neithe*, who, after finishing his education at home, passed into Scotland, to add to his learning and knowledge of the world in the schools there. After spending some time there, at the school of a celebrated philosopher of the name of *Eochaidh Echbheoil*, he returned with a few companions to his father at Emania. When he reached that royal palace,

(364) [original:—[Conérget a fir isin tig; lasodan cach fer diib do oslogud ria na mnai combad aben cetna tísad issa tech artús. Bid olc indadaig, or Concobar; beraid acló nargit ro bói inaláim sisin nuáitni créduma in naimda. Condesitar in oslúaig innasudi.—*Leabhar na h-Uidhre*, folio 67. a. b. *et seq.*]

(365) [original:—Imdae Concobair indairenech in tige, co stioalooib airgid, co nuaitnib credumai, co-lígrud oir for a cendaib, co ngemoib corrmogul intib, comma comsolas laa ocus adaicc inte. Gona steill airgid uas an rig co ardlios an rigtigi; in nam no bualed Concobar co flesc rigdai an stell, contaitis ulaid uile ris.—MSS. Egerton 5280, Brit. Mus.]

(366) [See *Lectures on the MS. Materials of Ancient Irish History.*]

XXXIV.

the Musical Branch mentioned in the tale of the "Dialogue of the Two Sages";

however, he discovered that his father had died a few days previously; and having entered the court, he found the *Ollamh*'s or chief poet's chair which his father had filled, empty, with the chief poet's splendid cloak laid on the back of it, as no successor to the learned deceased had been yet appointed. The young man without hesitation put on the cloak and sat in the chair; but, shortly after the poet *Ferceirtne*, who was the presumptive successor to the vacant chair, walked in, and to his astonishment found it already occupied by a youthful stranger. *Ferceirtne* questioned him as to the chair and cloak of which he had possessed himself. The young man answered that his learning was his title to them, and he proposed to maintain it by a public discussion. The challenge was accepted, and the discussion was carried on in presence of king *Conchobar* and the nobles of Ulster; and this is the discussion, the report of which is what has ever since been called the *Agallamh an da Shuadh*, or the Dialogue of the two Sages or Professors. It is not, however, with the dialogue itself that we are at present concerned, but with a passage in the preface to it, which, in the following words, gives an account of the young poet's setting out from Scotland with his companions:

"*Neidhe* then set out from *Cenn Tiré* (now Kentire), and went from that to *Rinn Snog*. He after that set out from *Port Righ* (in Scotland) over the sea, and landed at *Rind Roiss* (in Ulster): from this he set out over *Seimhne*, and over *Lathairne* [now Larne], and over *Magh Line*, and over *Ollarbha*, and over *Tulach Ruse*, and over *Ard-Sleibhe*, and over *Craib Telca*, and over *Magh-Ercaithi*, and over the [river] *Banna* upper, and over *Glenn Righi*, and over the territories of *Ui Breasail* [in Armagh], and over *Ard Sailech*, that is *Ardmacha*, and over the hill of the palace of *Emhain* [or *Emania*]. And it is how he made his journey with a silver branch over him. This was what the *Anradhs* [that is the poets of the second order] carried over them; and it was a Branch of gold that the chief poets, that is the *Ollamhs*, carried over them; and it was a Branch of bronze that all other poets besides these carried over them".[367]

[367] [original: — Droictha dóib trać a cerca documlaisec do Chind Tire, ocus luid iar sin do Rind Snóc. Documlaisec iarum a Purt Rig dar fairgi, cor-ragabadar i Rind Roiss: assaide for Semniu for Latharnu, for Mag Line, for Ollorbai, for Tulaig Roisc, for Ard Slébe, for Craib Telca, for Mag nErcaite, for Banna iar nuachtar, for Glend Rige, for tuatha hi-mBresail, for Ard Sailech, frissaiter Ard .M. indiu, for sid bruig na hEmna. Is amlaid dan do cumlai in mac, ocus craeb airgdide uasa. Uair issed nobid uas na hanrothaib; craeb óir imorro uas na ollamain; craeb umai uas na filid ar chena.—H. 2. 18. folio 142. b. a. mid.]

This is a curious passage, as preserving to us an interesting feature in the professional equipment of the several degrees of the poets in the olden times, and one, too, hitherto unnoticed by all writers on Irish antiquities. XXXIV.

The third reference to a *Craebh Ciuil* or Musical Branch is found in an ancient tale, entitled, "The Finding of Cormac's Branch",—copies of which are preserved in the Books of Ballymote and Fermoy in the library of the Royal Irish Academy, and the Yellow Book of Lecan in the library of Trinity College. *Cormac Mac Airt*, the hero of this story, was monarch of Erinn in the middle of the third century; and the following is the opening passage of the tale, which gives an account of the way in which he obtained this Branch, as told in the Book of Fermoy.

and also in the Tale of "The Finding of *Cormac's* Branch";

"One time that *Cormac*, the grandson of *Conn* [of the hundred battles] was in *Liabh-Truim* [another name for Tara], he saw coming towards him on the green of the palace, a stately fair-gray-headed warrior. The warrior came up carrying in his hand a Branch of Peace, with three apples (or balls) of red gold upon it; and it is not known to what particular kind of wood it belonged. And when he [the warrior] shook it, sweeter than the world's music was the music which the apples produced; and all the wounded and sick men of the earth would go to sleep and repose with the music, and no sorrow or depression could rest upon the person who heard it".(368)

It is not necessary to our present purpose to enter farther into the details of this story, or show how king *Cormac* obtained, lost, and regained this wonderful Branch: it is proper to state, however, that, as long as *Cormac* had it, he used it in the same way that the poet *Sencha* used his Branch at *Bricriu's* feast, and king *Conchobur* his silver spike and wand, namely, to shake it, and produce peace and silence in his palace, whenever the high spirits of his courtiers approached the point of disturbance at the feast.

The next and last reference to a Musical Branch that I have met is of modern date, compared to those already given; but it is not the less valuable on that account, because, although the name is but figuratively applied to a harp, the figure is correctly carried out by ascribing to the particular harp referred to, the magically soothing properties of a Musical Branch.

and lastly in a poem of about the year A.D. 1500;

(368) [original:—Feċtus do bi Cormac huCuinn aLiatruim, cofaceaiḋ aenoclach furusta ḟinnliat agi ar faiġṫi in dúin. Is amla do ḃi an toclach ocus craeḃ siḋaṁail ana-laim, co tri hublaiḃ dergoir fuirre; ocus ni ḟes ca fiḋ hi; ocus an tan rocraiṫeaḋ hi ba binne anat ceoil an beata úile acandais na hubla; ocus roċoideldais fer[aib gonta agus aes galair] an beata lesin ceol sin, ocus nacabiṫ cúṁa na snim air na dáinib no eisteaḋ an ceol sin. —Book of Fermoy, folio 62 a. b.].

XXXIV. This reference is found in a sweet little Gaedhelic poem of eighteen stanzas, of which I possess a very good copy. The name and time of the author are unknown to me; but I should suppose that he flourished about the year 1500. The author appears to have been, or pretends to have been, abandoned or neglected by his friends and patrons; and in this state he addresses the poem to his historical manuscript book, calling on it to come to him, and not to abandon him like his other dear friends. He charges the book to come to him accompanied with his paper, his pens, his book of poems, and his handbook of arithmetic and astronomy, by means of which he was enabled to calculate chronology since the Deluge, and to count the stars of heaven. This brings him to the eighth stanza, which, with the ninth, tenth, and eleventh, he devotes to his harp, as will be seen from the following literal translation:—

"Do not forget the Musical Branch,
The red-boarded, dry, sweet-toned [instrument],
The soft-voiced, melodious moaner;
Which is a sleeping sedative to the mind.

"Do; bring me the musical lyre,
Speaking, brilliant, plaintive,
Polished, well-seasoned throughout,
Fine-stringed, and carved all round.

"Whenever I see the artistic harp,
The great brown-shaded, smooth-sided [instrument]
Under the bounding ardour of my swift-moving fingers
It excites my mind despite itself;

"Until I have played thrilling sweet tunes
From the very tips of my furiously rapid fingers,
Warm, thick-wove, and grave,
Filtered, hard-fingered, even".[369]

The Musical Branch symbolical of repose and peace; I scarcely need say any more to prove that the *Craebh Ciúil*, or Musical Branch, was an instrument indicative or symbolic of repose and peace, and used by those who were qualified by station or profession to command it. The particular form or parts of the Musical Branch we have now no means of discovering; but, from the qualities ascribed to the branches of the poet

(369) [original:—

Na dein dearmod don Chraoiḃ Chiuil,
Dearg ċláruiḋe, ċirim, ċaiġuir,
Uallanaċ bog, gotaċ binn;
Is suanan codalta dintinn.
Dáiliḋ daṁ an liric loinneaċ,
Eangaċ, eadtroċt, ioġlannaċ,
Niaṁ greanta, faḋairċe ar fod,
Teidleabair, coċailte tiomcol.
An tan adċiú an ċláirseaċ ċeardaċ,
Donnsgáileaċ ṁór, ṁínleargaċ,
Fa ġroidġeirg ríṁir mo ṁeoir
Do ḃrosduiġ mintinn daiṁḋeoin
Gur sinnioḋ linn criċre cor ṗort
Drisrinn mo meoir ḃrisċir grod,
go tirim, tiuġ ḋeantaċ, trom,
Sileaċ, cruitmearaċ, coċrom.
—O'Curry MSS., Cath. Univ., Historical Poems, vol. iv. p. 549, mid.]

Sencha and of king *Cormac*, we may assume that it resembled, in effect at least, if not in shape, the silver crescent of the Turks, with its gently-tingling bells, or that which, copied from it, some years ago had a place in British military bands. It happens that there are at present in the museum of the Royal Irish Academy two sets of little bells formed like hollow musket bullets, with stems, which may probably have formed parts of an instrument of this kind. One set of these bells consists at present of fifteen loose bells; they are formed of bronze of an ancient kind, having two small holes at both sides of the stem, and without any enclosure. The other set consists of thirteen; they are formed of a more modern kind of brass or bronze, and are a little smaller than the former, and not so regularly globular. They have each two similar perforations, and contain each of them a small loose ball or pea within, made, I suppose, of the same metal. They are at present—and were so when purchased by the Academy—slung loosely by their stems on a piece of wire bent into a series of regular bends, and the whole of them formed into a hoop or ring, like a cogged crown wheel, with a diameter of about four inches. Now, if this ring were fixed horizontally at the top of a thin pole or wand, and so shaken, the little bells being each slung upon its own bend of the wire, they could produce a small tingling noise, or music it may be, though certainly not of a very soothing quality. But I cannot refer to them as by any means an example of the effective instrument whose music is described in the ancient writings I have quoted.

It was analogous to the Turkish silver crescent and bells; bronze bells in the museum of the R.I.A. belonged perhaps to such an instrument.

There is another class of bells preserved in our national museum, of a different form from those just described, and of most undoubtedly remote antiquity. These bells were noticed in the "Dublin Penny Journal"[370] by a correspondent who signs himself with the letter B. The article is headed, "Ancient Irish Bells and Crotals", and goes on as follows:

The bells called "Crotals" described in the "Penny Journal";

"The annexed wood-cuts represent some ancient Irish bells, which, with a great variety of 'skeynes', 'celts', spears and arrow-heads, gongs, metallic pans, and other relics of antiquity, were found a few years ago in a bog near Birr in the King's county. Many specimens of the curiosities just enumerated, as well as of other rare remains of ancient times, including that antique work in metal called *Barnán Coolawn* [*Bearnán Culann*] (upwards of nine hundred years old), of which an account [a very silly account indeed] is given in the fourteenth volume of the 'Transactions of the Royal Irish Academy', are now in the collection of T. L. Cooke, Esq., of Birr. The bells are of

(370) No. 47, vol. i., p, 376, May 18th, 1833.

XXXIV. The bells called "Crotals" described in the "Penny Journal":

bell-metal, and appear as if gilt. No. 1 is five inches long by two and one and a-half in the greatest diameter; and No. 2 is three by two inches and a quarter.

"These bells were formerly called Crotals or bell-cymbals, and are supposed to have been used by the clergy. They consisted, as Dr. Ledwich writes, and as the specimens before us prove, of two hollow demispheres of bell-metal, joined together and enclosing a small piece of the same substance, to serve the use of a tongue or clapper, and produce the sound. The learned antiquary just referred to says, on the authority of John Sarisher, 'The Crotal seems not to have been a bardic instrument, but the bell-cymbal used by the clergy, and denominated a Crotalum by the Latins'. He adds, 'it was also used by the Roman pagan priests'.

"The name", continues this writer, "seems to be derived from the Irish *crotal*, a husk or pod, which was metaphorically used to express a cymbal. The venerable General Vallancey, in the twelfth number of his 'Collectanea', intimates that bells might have been employed by the Irish druids, and adduces instances of the ancient augurs having used them in pronouncing their oracles. Walker, in his 'History of the Irish Bards', vol. i., p. 127, tells us that these bells were formerly used by the priests to frighten ghosts".

Doctor Petrie, the learned editor of the "Penny Journal", offers the following observation on the communication from B, of which I have given the above extract.

"The ancient religious bells of the Irish, thus briefly noticed by our respectable correspondent B, is a subject of considerable interest, and which we shall return to in a future number at some length; we shall, therefore, only observe now that the bells represented by our correspondent, 1 and 2, as well as a third which we here add from the museum of the Dean of St. Patrick's, and which was found in the same bog, are evidently of that description called Crotal, or bell-cymbal—two of which were always connected together by means of a flexible rod. Beauford, in his essay on the ancient Irish musical instruments, published in Ledwich's 'Irish Antiquities', gives a plate of what he and Ledwich supposed to be the form of the Irish Crotals, but which are in reality only sheep-bells of the seventeenth century, and of which we subjoin a specimen from our own collection. The Crotals given above are the only true specimens of the kind which we have heard of as being found in Ireland; a great number of brazen trumpets, of the same metal, gilt in the same manner, and apparently the work of the same workman, were found along with them. These trumpets are in the possession of Lord Oxmantown [the late earl of Rosse], the Dean of St. Patrick's, and Mr. Cooke, of Parsonstown". XXXIV.

Of the collections of Irish antiquities alluded to in the preceding observations of Dr. Petrie, that of the Dean of St. Patrick's has since that time passed into the museum of the Royal Irish Academy, that of Mr. Cooke to the British Museum; but of Lord Rosse's collection I know nothing. If it were not humiliating to our national pride and degrading to our self-respect, it would be amusing to read these bold attempts of such ignorant, unscrupulous fabricators of facts, as Ledwich, Beauford, and Vallancey, to impose their audacious forgeries on our presumed ignorance of the written and existing records of our national history. A boldness to be the more wondered at from the well known fact, that not one of the three ever read, or ever could read, one chapter, one page, or one sentence of that history in the native tongue, although it encircled them all round in ponderous volumes, five, six, seven and more hundreds of years old. It is true that the Christian priests from St. Patrick down had the use of bells for the ordinary ecclesiastical purposes, but these were of the ordinary shape, round or square, open below, and with regular clappers of the ordinary kind. It is not true, however, as far as the most extensive reading leads, that *Crotals*, or *Crotalum*, were ever used by our Christian priests for any purpose whatsoever. In fact, the word "crotal" does not exist at all in the Gaedhelic language. It is a modern corruption of the Latin word, thus explained in "Ainsworth's Dictionary":

crotals not used by Christian priests;

"Crotali, or crotaliorum, jewels so worn that they jingle as they strike against one another. Crotalum, an instrument made of two brass plates or bones, which being struck together made a kind of music; a castanet".

explanation of the term;

Now I ask, whether there is the remotest resemblance between the "Crotals" or brass plates described here from Pliny and Cicero, and these curious bell-shaped instruments which are to be found in our national museum? I have, in former lectures, from time to time had occasion to describe poets, musicians, and druids in the actual exercise of their respective professions; but in no instance of these, nor anywhere else, have I found "Crotals", or bells of any kind forming any part of their professional paraphernalia, excepting in the instance of the poets and their Musical Branches, already described in this lecture. To follow these most impudent, because most ignorant, writers farther on the present subject, would be a positive waste of time and patience, and I shall therefore leave them for the present, and conclude this part of my subject with a few more words on the word Crotal, or Crotalum.

XXXIV.

the Irish words *crothadh*, *crothla*, and *clothra*;

It would, perhaps, be a question of some philological interest to collate the Latin word *Crotalum* with the Gaedhelic word *Crothadh*, to shake, and *Crothla*, and *Clothra*, anything which makes a noise by shaking. My meaning will be understood by giving the translation of the signification of these two words, as I find it in a Brehon Law Glossary, compiled by *Domhnall O'Dubhdabhoirenn*, or O'Davoren, an accomplished scholar and gentleman of Burren, in my native county of Clare, in the year 1569. The following are the glosses:—

"*Clothra*, that is, a thing which is heard being shaken, such as it is [in the Laws]: 'If it be a dog that is accustomed to spring upon people, there must be an alarm of a bell or a *Clothra* around its neck, that is, a little bell at its neck, or something else which is heard shaking [or ringing] when it is going to commit a trespass'.

"*Crothla*, such as the warning of a cross or a *Crothla*, that is, to pass over what is shaken there, that is, the forbidding *drolan* (or hasp), that is, the *Crothla* which is placed upon the garden door of the garden of an exile of God [that is, of a recluse or pilgrim]".(371)

From this curious explanation of the word *Crothla* we learn two interesting facts: the first, that in olden times in our country, the law allowed no person to enter into the hermitage of a religious recluse without due notice of his approach; and secondly, that the advance or garden door of this hermitage was furnished with a cross, hasp, or something else, which was struck against the door, like our knockers, or shaken, as the iron hasp of the door continues to be to this day, in the country parts of Ireland.

they are the only words at all like *Crotalum*

These two words, then, *Clothra* and *Crothla*, which actually mean the same thing, are the only words that I am acquainted with in the Gaedhelic language, which at all approach the Latin word *crotalum*; but we see clearly, from their assigned signification, that they are really as unlike bells of any kind as the crotalum or castanet itself.

except *crotal* the husks of fruit, i.e. castanets;

There is, to be sure, as the writer in the "Penny Journal" says, the word *crotal*, signifying the husks of fruit, or the scales of fish, and such like; but there is no great reason to imagine that the Gaedhils improvised the name of a bell from so remote and dissimilar an idea. We know

(371) [original:—Cloċra, .i. ni cluinteaṙ aga croċaḋ, amail ata [..] mad cú foilmeaċ bid urfogra cluicc, no cloċra fo a bragait, .i. cluigin ima bragait, no ni eile ic cluinfitheaḋ aga croċaḋ in tan ticfa do genaṁ fogla. O'Davoren, voce *Clothra*.

Croċla, ut, urfogra croiss no croċla, .i. dul tar an ni croċar ann, .i. in drolan urgurta, .i. croċla bis ar dorus airliss, airliss an deoraid dé. O'Davoren, voce *Crothla*.]

from the Brehon Laws that cows of the first class or quality in ancient times were, for distinction, furnished with bells (called *Cluig*) at their necks, and that cows so furnished were by law inviolate, so that they could not be taken in distraint even under a process of law, and if stolen or injured, the penalty was much higher than that which attached to the same offence when committed upon ordinary cows [v. *Senchus Mor*, vol. i. p. 143, pub. by Brehon Law Com.]. We know, too, that horses were furnished with little bells, sometimes of silver and gold, at their necks, long before the introduction of Christianity into this country. An instance of this fact is preserved in the very ancient tale of the *Táin Bo Fraich*, where we are told that *Fraech*, of whom so much has already been spoken in these lectures, when going to *Cruachan* to pay his addresses to the princess *Findabair*, went with a cortege of fifty horsemen in rich array, and each horse furnished, among other things, with a crescent of gold, and little golden *clogs*, or bells, at its neck. But again, I assert that there is no such instrument as a *Crotal* known in the Gaedhelic language, and that all that has been written about it for the last eighty years in books, and read in papers before the Royal Irish Academy, is pure fabrication, founded on the assumption of a fact that never had existence.

bells put on necks of cows;

and on horses;

the *Crotal* not known in Ireland—everything written about it pure invention.

Having, as I trust, disposed for ever of the "Crotal" as having been an ancient Irish instrument of music, I shall turn from this rather long digression, and again take up the alphabetical list, at the word next in order, namely, the *Crann Ciúil*, or Musical Tree; and, in the first place, I must observe that the word tree, in this as well as in various other instances, does not mean a tree in the ordinary sense of a growing plant. When I use the word here, I do so in translation of the Irish word *Crann*, and exactly in the sense in which we understand the word tree in some compound English words, as a spade-tree, an axle-tree, a boot-tree, a saddle-tree, and others of the same class. The *Crann Ciúil*, or Musical Tree, would imply by the very form of the words that the instrument was made of wood, but beyond this, even if so far, its natural signification does not extend. Indeed, I might say that the word *Crann-Ciúil* is a generic term for almost any kind of musical instrument; and as a discussion on the subject would be of little value, I shall content myself with two examples of this use of the term. In the old Book of Lismore, we find the following conversation recorded as having taken place between *Cailte* (the surviving historian of *Find Mac Cumhaill*), and St. Patrick:—

The *Crann Ciúil* or Musical Tree;

it was a generic term for any kind of musical instrument,

"It was then", says the story, "that St Patrick asked *Cailte* if they had musicians in the *Fenian* troops. 'We had, indeed'

XXXIV.

as is shown by a passage from the Book of Lismore,

said *Cailte*, 'the one best musician that could be found in Erinn or in Alba'. 'What was his name?' said St. Patrick. '*Cnu Deroil*', said *Cailte*. 'Where was he found?' said St. Patrick. 'Between *Crotta Cliach* and *Sidh Ban Find* (now *Sliabh na m-Ban*, in Tipperary) in the south', said *Cailte*. 'What was his description?' said St. Patrick. 'Four handsbreadths for *Find* was his height; and three handsbreadths for him was the height of the *Crann Ciúil* which he played', said *Cailte*. 'The other musicians of the *Tuatha Dé Danann* became jealous of him', said he, 'and turned him out of their court. *Find*', continues *Cailte*, 'happened to go on that day to *Sidh Ban Find* to a chase and hunt, and he sat there upon a raised mound. The Fenian chief having looked about him, perceived the little man tuning and playing his *Cruit* (or harp) upon the bank near him; and there he sat with his fair yellow hair floating down his back to his hips. And when he saw *Find* he came up to him, and put his hand into his hand [as a token of submission], for he [*Find*] was the first person he met after coming out of the [fairy] hill. And he continued to play his *Cruit* in *Find*'s presence until the rest of the Fenian warriors came up. And when they came up they heard the enchanting fairy music. Good, O beloved *Find*', said the *Fianna*, 'this is one of the three best gifts that you have ever received'. And he continued with him [*Find*] afterwards till his death".(372)

when it is a *Cruit*;

In this short article it will be seen that what was first described as a *Crann Ciúil*, or Musical Tree, of three hands in height, is twice afterwards described as a *Cruit*, or harp; and yet, in an ancient glossary preserved in a vellum MS. in the library of Trinity College, Dublin,(373) we find the word *Cuisle* (a tube) explained as a *Crann Ciúil*, or Musical Tree. We are told further in the same old Book of Lismore, that while *Cailte*

Cuisle, a tube, explained in a vellum MS. as a Musical Tree;

(372) [original:—Is andsin ro fiarfaig Patraic do Chailti in rabatar airfitig acuibsi isin feinn. Do bi immorro ar Cailti in taen airfitech is ferr do bi a nEirinn na a nAlbain. Ca hainm sin ar Patraic. Cnu Deroil ar Cailti, cait a fuiṫ e ar Patraig. Etoer Crota Cliaċ acus Sidh Bann bḟinn tis ar Cailti. Crec a tuarascbail ar Patraic. Ceiṫre duirnn Finn do bi ina airdi, acus tri duirnn do isin Crand Ciuil do ḟeined, ocus airfitig Tuaṫa De Dannain do rinde tuaċ fris. Luid Finn in la sin co Sidhban Finn fiar do feilg ocus dfiaġaċ, ocus suidis ar in bfirt fotbuig andsin. Sillis iarum in flaiṫ feine secha confaca in fer bec ac sesnad, ocus ac sairseinm a cruiti ar in fod ina focair, ocus is amlaid robui, acus folt fada finnbuidi co clar a da leas fair, ocus ar faicsin Finn tainic da ionnsaigid, ocus tuc alam na laim, or ase ced duine tapla do he iar tuidecht as in trid amach, ocus robui oc seinm a cruiti a fiadnuisi Finn no gu tancatar in fiann, ocus ar techt doib atcualatar in ceol sirechtach sidh. Maith a anum a Fhinn ar an fiann, ase suc in tres tiodlaicṫe as ferr fuarais riamh, ocus do bi ac Finn no go fuair bas. Book of Lismore, fol. 205 a.b.]

(373) [original:—H. 3. 18. f. 415.]

was on a visit to the king of Ulster, a young man came to the court dressed as a minstrel, and carrying his *Timpan* at his back. This young stranger turned out to be *Cas Corach*, son of *Bodhbh Derg*, the great *Tuatha Dé Danann* chief of *Magh Femen* in Tipperary, who had come to make acquaintance with *Cailte*, and add to his stock of story and song from the inexhaustible stores of the veteran Fenian warrior. *Cailte* received the young man with kindness and encouragement, and introduced him to St. Patrick, who was highly pleased with his wonderful performance on his *Timpan* or harp. The saint received his confession of faith, for which, and for his delightful performance, he promised him heaven, in the following words:

In another place in the Book of Lismore a *Timpan* is so called.

"Heaven is thine", said St. Patrick, "and may thy art be one of the three last arts by which a person shall realize his benefit in Erinn; and though the unwelcome which may be intended for a man of thy art, when he has played his music and [told] his stories, may be great, he shall not be any longer unwelcome; and the professors of thy art shall be at all times the couch fellows of kings, and they shall be prosperous provided they be not lazy". And then he (*Cas Corach*) put up his *Crann Ciúil* into its keep-place.[374]

From these few extracts, quite enough for my purpose, we see clearly that the term *Crann Ciúil* was applied indiscriminately to a *Cruit* or harp, a *Cuisle* or tube, and a *Timpan*, which was certainly a stringed instrument of the harp kind.

The next instrument in alphabetical order is the *Cruit*, of which I have already treated in the former lectures.

The *Cuiseach*:

Next in order is the instrument, the name of which is written *Cuiseach*, a word not obsolete, but which, from the position of gradation that it holds in relation to the other instruments mentioned along with it, I should take to signify a reed, or some such instrument of a very simple order. To this instrument I have never met more than two references, the first of which is in the ancient poem on the fair of *Carman* described in a former lecture,[375] and which I have also referred to in this lecture in connection with musical instruments. Among those I mentioned *Cuiseachs*. The word which actually occurs in the poem is *Cusigh*, which I take to be the plural of *Cuiseach* [? plur. *Cuiseacha*], and to signify reeds or small pipes. The

mentioned in the poem on the fair of *Carman*,

[374] [original:—Nem ḋuit ar Patraic, acus gurab i an trear ealaḋa ar a faguib nech a leasaġaḋ fria deread an Eirinn hi; acus ġiḋ mor in doichill bias re fear healadan aċt condearna airpited, acus conindisi scela gan doiċeall roime, ar Patraic; acus fear leapṫa rig tre biṫu ret healaḋuin, acus soirbeas doib act naċ dearnait leisce. Ocus ro cuirsium a Crann Ciuil ina coimead. Book of Lismore, f. 223 a.b.]

[375] [See Lecture ii., *ante*, vol. i. p. 38.]

XXXIV. and in the Tale of the battle of *Almhain.*

next, and only other reference that I have met to the *Cuiseach*, is found in the passage from the ancient account of the battle of *Almhain* which I have quoted above, where king *Fergal*, addressing *Donnbo*, says: "Make amusement for us, O *Donnbo*, because thou art the best minstrel in Erinn, namely, at *Cuiseachs*(376) at pipes (or tubes), and at harps, etc. In this combination of instruments we find the *Cuiseach* placed first, before the *Cuisle* (or tube) and the harp; leaving us room to infer that it was the minor or simplest instrument of the three. However, as I am not able to throw any further light upon the history or identification of this instrument, I shall pass from it for the present, leaving to future investigation the chance of carrying the inquiry farther.

The *Cuisle Ciúil* another name for *Crann Ciúil*;

The next instrument in alphabetical order is the *Cuisle Ciúil* (or musical tube). This is, simply, another name for the *Crann Ciúil*, or musical tree; and it is from this form of the name that the designation of the performers is derived, namely, that of *Cuislennach*, or tube performer, whilst there is no attempt at deriving a performer's name from the form "*Crann Ciúil*". The word *Cuisle* is a living one at this day, as well as in more ancient times, and is applied both to the veins of the living body through which the blood courses from the heart to the extremities, and also to a piece of reed, or hollowed wood, such as in country public houses is, or was in my youthful days, used with a stopper, in tapping a keg of whiskey or cask of ale, before the convenience of regular cocks for this purpose penetrated to the rural districts. In this sense it was also called *canaile*, or canal. And it is in these latter senses that it is mentioned in the ancient Book of Invasions of Ireland, in the story of the misbehaviour of *Dealgnad*, Parthalon's wife. This lady is stated, in this very old account, to have given her paramour a drink of ale from a special cask reserved for her husband, of which she was always entrusted with the *Cuisle* of gold through which the liquor was drawn. In the ancient poem which repeats the prose account of *Dealgnad's* misbehaviour, the *Cuisle* is glossed as *Corn Cael*, that is, a thin or slender horn or tube; and in an ancient glossary preserved in the vellum M.S. classed H. 3. 18. T.C.D., folio 415, *Cuisle* is explained as *Crann Ciúil*, or a musical tree. This old example of the word sufficiently indicates that a musical instrument of this name must have been of the pipe or tube class, and probably one of slight or thin bore.

cuisle a living word meaning a vein, or a kind of cock;

mentioned in the latter sense in the Book of Invasions;

Cuisle explained in H. 3. 18. T. C. D. as a Musical Tree.

(376) See *supra*, p. 310.

LECTURE XXXV.

[Delivered 4th July, 1862.]

(IX.) OF MUSIC AND MUSICAL INSTRUMENTS (continued). The *Fedán*; mentioned in the Book of Lismore; *Fedán* players mentioned in the Brehon Laws. The *Fidil* or Fiddle; mentioned in the poem on the fair of *Carman*; and in a poem written in 1680. The *Guth-Buinde;* mentioned in an Irish life of Alexander the Great; the *Ceólán* also mentioned in this tract; incorrect meaning given to this word in Macleod's and Dewar's Dictionary; *Ceólán* not a diminutive of *ceol*, but the name of a tinkling bell; the *Ceólán* mentioned in the Irish life of St. *Mac Creiche*. The *Guthbuinde* also mentioned in an Irish tract on the Siege of Troy. The *Oct Tedach*. The *Oircin;* mentioned in the Irish Triads; one of the bards of *Seanchan Torpeist's* "Great Bardic Company" called *Oircne;* no explanation of *Oircne* known, except that it was the name of the first lap-dog. Of the *Pip* or Pipe, and in the plural *Pipai* or Pipes; mentioned in the poem on the fair of *Carman;* the only ancient reference to the *Pipaireadha*, or *Piobaire*, or Piper, known to author is in a fragment of Brehon Law. Of the *Stoc;* mentioned in a paraphrase of the Book of Genesis in the *Leabhar Breac*, and in the version of the "Fall of Jericho" in the same book; and again in describing the coming of Antichrist; and in the plural form *Stuic* in the poem on the fair of *Carman*, and in the *Táin Bo Flidais*. Another instrument, the *Sturgan*, mentioned in this tract; and also in a poem on Randal lord of Arann. The *Sturganuidhe* or *Sturgan* player mentioned in Keating's "Three Shafts of Death". Specimens of the *Corn*, *Stoc*, and *Sturgan* are probably to be found in the museum of the R.I.A. The *Corn* was the Roman Cornua; specimens in the museum of the R.I.A. The *Stoc* represents the Roman Buccina. The *Sturgan* corresponds to the Roman Lituus. Mr. R. Ousley's description of the *Stuic* and the *Sturgana* in the museum of the R.I.A.; the specimens in the Academy's museum are parts of two instruments, and not of one; ancient Irish wind instruments of graduated scale and compass; the trumpets mentioned in Walker's "Irish Bards" first described and figured in Smith's History of Cork; Walker's observations on them; they are figured in Vetusta Monumenta; a similar trumpet found in England; the author agrees with Walker that there must have been another joint in the trumpets; discrepancy between the figures of Smith and the Vetusta Monumenta; Smith's opinion that they were Danish, erroneous; Smith's error that the Cork trumpets formed but one instrument, reproduced by Mr. R. MacAdam; Sir W. Wilde's novel idea of the use of the straight tubes; his idea that they were part of a "Commander's Staff", borrowed from Wagner; Sir William Wilde's illustration of the use of the straight part of a trumpet as a "Commander's Staff", unsatisfactory; his separation of the straight tube from the curved parts in the Museum of the R.I.A. a mistake which ought to be corrected. *Sturgana*, *Stuic*, and *Corna* in the museum of the Royal Irish Academy, and Trinity College, Dublin.

THE next musical instrument in alphabetical order from the list which I gave in my last lecture is the *Fedán*. The word *Fedán*, in the living language, signifies a thin, slender, musical pipe, or tube, and in the old medical manuscripts the term is applied to The *Fedán*

XXXV. a fistula. It was probably a whistle, since *fed* is the term, both ancient and modern, for a whistling with the mouth, and *Fedán* would therefore simply signify a whistling instrument. I don't remember having met with more than one written reference to this instrument, namely, in the Dialogue of the Ancient Men in the Book of Lismore. It is where *Cailte* is relating to St. Patrick how the palace of Tara was set on fire every November eve by *Ailean*, the son of *Midna*, a famous chief of the *Tuatha Dé Danann* race, who resided in the fairy mansion of *Sliabh Cuilluin* in Ulster. This chief, it appeared, was accustomed to approach Tara, playing one or more musical instruments in such soft and soothing strains, as to throw its guardians into a dead sleep till he had accomplished his purpose, for, as *Cailte* says, "even women in labour and wounded champions would be put to sleep by the plaintive fairy music, and the sweetly-tuned strain of song which the skilful performer raised who burned Tara every year".

This soothing musician, however, was killed at last by *Find Mac Cumhaill*, with a spear given to him by *Fiach Mac Conga*, a friend of his fathers; and, when giving him the spear, we are told that *Fiach* said to him: "When you hear the fairy music and the sweet-stringed *Timpan* and the melodious-sounding *Fedán*, uncover the blade of this spear, and apply its sharp edge to your forehead, or to some other member of your members, and it will keep you from falling asleep until *Ailean* comes within reach of you".[377] *Find* took this good advice, and when *Ailean* approached Tara, he found himself detected accordingly, and fled to his residence, followed closely by *Find*, who overtook and slew him as he was entering the door of his own mansion.

mentioned in the Book of Lismore;

Fedán players mentioned in the Brehon Laws.

In an ancient Brehon Law tract in the Book of Ballymote [f. 186. b. a. top], which gives a list of the rank and pay of the various professions, the *Fedánaigh*, or *Fedán* players, are set down among those who performed at the fairs and public sports.

The *Fidil* or fiddle;

The next musical instrument in alphabetical order is the *Fidil* or Fiddle, to which, however, I have met but two references in our old MSS., one considerably older than the other; but I cannot say that the old term *Fidil* was applied to the same kind of instrument as our present Fiddle. The first

(377) [original:—Uair do codeldais mna contonaib, ocus laeich ledairthe risin ceol sirechtach sidi, ocus risin ngadan nglestu nguithbinn do canad in fir foinemail sidi no loisced Temair gacha bliadain (.i. Aillen mac Midna) . . . isann do raid Fiacha, mar atcluinfe in ceol sidhe ocus an timpan teitbinn ocus an fedan fogurbinn, ben a cumdach do cenn na cruirigh agus tabuir red tedan, no ball eli dot ballaib, agus ni leicfe grain na sleagi neme codlad duit. Book of Lismore, f. 212. b.b.]

of these references is found in the version of the poem descriptive of the ancient fair of *Carman*, referred to in the last lecture, which is found in the Book of Leinster (a MS. of about the year 1150). Among the various instruments of music and musicians mentioned in this poem as having been present at this great assembly, are *Fidli*, or Fiddles;[378] the old word differing from the modern in having one *d* only, in accordance with the genius of the Gaedhelic language.

mentioned in the poem on the fair of *Carman*;

The second place in which I have met with the word "Fiddle" is in a poem written about the year 1680 by *Eoghan O'Donnghaile* (or Eugene O'Donnelly), a native of Ulster, for a harper, whose Christian name was *Feidhlimy*, who paid him a visit. The poet's praise is conveyed chiefly in a negative strain, not describing the artistic perfections of his visitor and his harp, but the defects and blemishes which they have not. This very clever poem consists of fifteen quatrains, of which the following, the third quatrain, will give a very good idea of the character of the whole:

and in a poem written in 1680.

"You are not Eugene of the bad tuning,
Who has the blubbering *Fidioll;*
It is not you who have the shifting posture,—
And there are no startings in your nerves".[379]

Here the fiddle is written *Fidioll;* and it is a curious fact that at the present day, in Munster at least, the instrument is called violin in speaking Irish, and fiddle in English; nor have the people any notion that the latter is the older name in their language. The word Fiddle is, I believe, an old word in the Saxon language too.

The next musical instrument in alphabetical order to which I have met with any historical reference, is the *Guth-buinde*, a word compounded of *guth*, the human voice, and *Buinde* or *Buinne*, a pipe or tube; probably some kind of speaking trumpet. I have never met this instrument named in any purely Gaedhelic composition, nor at all but in two instances, both of which are translations from the Latin. The first reference to the *Guth-buinde* is found in the life of Alexander the Great, translated from *Orus*, an unknown author, and preserved in the great book of *Dun Doighre*, or *Leabhar Breac*, in the library of the Royal Irish Academy,[380] into which it was copied from the ancient Book

The *Guth-Buinde*;

mentioned in an Irish life of Alexander the Great;

(378) [See lecture ii. *ante*, vol. i. p. 46; and see Appendix for the original of the whole poem.]

(379) [original:—
Ni tu Eogan is olc innioll,
ag a mbi an fidioll maosgain;
ni hionat bios an boċfaċ,—
sni ḃionn smotfaḋ ando smaosan.
—O'Curry MSS. Cath. Univ. Historical poems, vol. iv. p. 405.]

(380) [Fol. 105, a. b.]

XXXV.

The *Guth-buinde* mentioned in an Irish life of Alexander the Great;

of Saint *Berchan* of *Cluain Sosta*, now Cloonsost, in the King's county.[381]

The passage in which this reference occurs follows Alexander's epistle to his tutor Aristotle, in which he informs him of his victory over the great king Darius, and his subsequent overthrow of Por (Porus), king of India, whose chief city he captured and pillaged, and whom he then pursued into the country of the Bactrians, that is, as the story says, the country of the *Serrdha*, a people who manufactured for themselves clothes from the moss which grew upon the leaves of trees. The historian then goes on to say, that—

"Great was the army of Alexander at this time. Two hundred and fifty thousand foot soldiers, and thirty thousand horsemen, and one thousand elephants carrying gold and silver for them; and four hundred four-horse chariots; and two thousand [?] (ordinary [sicled, B. of Ballymote]) chariots; and two thousand mules; and fifty *Cassiandras*, that is a certain description of beasts of burden, and five hundred camels; and two score thousand [?] *Sumadas* (or nags) and *Mallas* (or mules) and oxen, and asses, and horses besides for carrying wheat. The herds were countless which were there to supply flesh meat to the army. It was straps of gold they had to whip the elephants and the camels, and the mules and the royal steeds with, when necessary. The arms and the helmets of the army were carved and ornamented by [order of] Alexander, with red gold and precious gems; in the same way were the *Guth-buinde* with their golden *Ceólána* adorned by him. Though it had been by night this army had marched they would have light sufficient from their clothes, and from their arms, adorned with gold and silver, and from their gems of precious stones, the same as if each man were a king".[382] All this

(381) [The copy of this tract in the *Leabhar Breac* is imperfect, but there is a complete but not so good a one in the Book of Ballymote. At *f.* 93. a. a. of the *Leabhar Breac* copy it is stated that the account is taken from Orus. Theophilus O'Flanagan has written at the beginning of the tract in the Book of Ballymote, in red ink, that the account is from the Latin of Justinus. The Orus alluded to is Paul Orosius, who drew the materials for his chapters relating to Alexander from Justinus. So that both statements are to a certain extent true. The tract appears to be to a certain extent an original work compiled from various sources, especially the two named. Professor O'Curry made a rough translation of this tract shortly before his death, which it is to be hoped will soon be published, along with several others relating to classical and mediæval history.]

(382) [Ba mor traċ slógad Alaxandair an inbuid sin .l. for. cc. m. do traiġṫeaċa, ocus .xxx. mile marcach, ocus .x. c. elefinnte oc immedain óir ocus argait doib; ocus .cccc. cethairriad; ocus .cc.x. cairrtech; ocus .xx.c. do mulaib; ocus .l. do cassiandaib, .i. araile anmannaib bertaid aire, ocus .u.c. camall; ocus .xx. [m.] do sumedaib, ocus malla, ocus dama, ocus asana, ocus echaib ar ċena sria hiomchar cruiṫnechta. Ba dirime na halma batar ann sriciméirecht feola

gold and silver, and these gems with which Alexander enriched his army, were taken from the treasury of *Por*, king of India, whose chief city he had taken and pillaged. Among the articles beautified and adorned from the precious stores of *Por's* unfortunate city, were the *Guth-buinde*, with their golden *Ceólána*. From the component parts of this word, namely, *Guth*, the voice, and *Buinde*, a tube, one would be inclined to infer that the instrument was a speaking trumpet; but it is rather a puzzle to understand how, if it were a speaking trumpet, it should have such appendages as *Ceólána*, that is, musical bells, attached to it!

XXXV.

the *Ceólán* also mentioned in this tract;

Of the name *Ceólán* itself, no authoritative signification has been hitherto published by any of our Irish lexicographers or historians. In Shaw's "Gaelic Dictionary", published in London in the year 1780, he gives *Ceólán*, as a little bell; and Edward O'Reilly, in his "Irish-English Dictionary", printed in Dublin in 1817, follows Shaw exactly. Not so, however, the Rev. Dr. Norman Macleod and the Rev. Dr. Daniel Dewar, in their Dictionary of the "Gaelic Language", printed in Glasgow in 1839, scorning to follow their own countryman Shaw, or the Irishman O'Reilly, they strike out a new path for themselves, and very learnedly tell us that *Ceólán* is a "diminutive of *Ceol*, faint music; a tender soft air". It is surprising to see two educated gentlemen, well versed, too, in the spoken dialect of the Gaedhelic of Scotland, fall into such a grammatical error as this. *Ceol*, in Irish, has no diminutive, any more than "music" in English; and if it had, it should be *Ceoilin*. *Ceólán*, then, is not a diminitive of *Ceol*, music; but it is a descriptive name for a sweet tingling, or chiming bell; and it cannot, as far as I am aware, be applied properly to any thing else. That it was a bell of some musical power, will be clearly enough understood from the passage in the Irish life of St. *Mac Creiche*, which I shall now quote.

Incorrect meaning given to this word in Macleod and Dewar's Dictionary.

Ceólán not a diminutive of *ceol*, but the name of a tinkling bell;

St. *Mac Creiche* was the contemporary and bosom friend of St. *Ailbhe* of *Imliuch Ibhair* (now Emly in the county of Tipperary), and must have been born before the death of St. Patrick. He was the founder of several churches in the present county of Clare, only one of which is named from him, namely,

the *Ceólán* mentioned in the Irish life of St. *Mac Creiche*.

dona slogaib. Ialla órda tra no-bítis fria groigib na nelefint ocus na camall, ocus na mul, ocus na nech rígda in tan ba himarcaide. Rorindad ocus ro ecrait airm ocus cathbairr na slog la halaxandar, do dergór ocus do gemmaib logmaraib; rocumdaiged lais tra son indus sin na guthbuinde conaceolanaib ordaib. Ciamad adaid no imthigitis in slogsin ba solas doib dia neiredaib, ocus dia narmcumdaigib dior, ocus diargat, dina gemmaib leag logmar amail bid ríg cech fer. *Leabhar Breac*, fol 95, a.b]

XXXV.

the Ceólan mentioned in the Irish life of St. Mac Creiche.

Cill Mic Creiche, near Innistimon in that county. In the early part of the sixth century, we are told, among other pestilential visitations which afflicted that country, was a dreadful amphibious monster called *Broic-Seach* (or the badger-monster), which suddenly appeared in *Loch Broicsighe*, or *Broicseach*'s lake, a lake not now known by this name,[383] but situated in the ancient territory of *Cineal Fermaic*, a district comprised in the present barony of Inchiquin, in the county of Clare, and some ten miles east by north of *Cill Mic Creiche*. The havoc which this monster caused among the people of the district and their cattle, induced them to call upon their clergy to exercise their sacred powers for its abatement. This call was readily responded to by the clergy, who, headed by saints *Maeldalna*, *Mac Aiblen*, and *Blathmac*, attended a great meeting of the people on a certain day. It happened at this time that the monster was chasing the cattle of the district up to the very precincts of the assembly. The ecclesiastics felt much alarmed, and what they did, says the legend, was to ring their bells (*Cluicc*) and their *Ceólána*, and make a great noise with their reliquaries and their croziers; and the [people of the] country shouted with them, both men, women, and children".[384] These proceedings, however, only gave additional vehemence and ferocity to the monster, so that the people were forced to disperse in all directions; and it was reserved for St. *Mac Creiche* to relieve them afterwards by chaining their enemy for ever at the bottom of its own lake. I have recounted this curious legend in detail, because this is the only precise and unmistakable reference I can recollect to have ever met to the name and use of the *Ceólán*.

The Guthbuinde also mentioned in an Irish tract on the Siege of Troy.

The second reference to the *Guthbuinde* that I have met is found in an ancient Irish translation of the Argonautic Expedition, and the Destruction of Troy, preserved in the Book of Ballymote, in the library of the Royal Irish Academy (a MS. book compiled in the year 1391), and of the same piece there is also a large fragment preserved in the Book of Leinster. The

(383) [The lake anciently called *Loch Broigseach*, that is, the "Badger's Lake", and now called *Loch-na-Ratha*, the "Lake of the Rath", is situated at the foot of the hill on which the old church of *Rath Blathmach* stands, in the parish of Rath, and barony of Inchiquin, and about two miles W. by S. from the town of Corofin. High up on the precipitous side of a hill, close to the lake, there is a hole or cavern, still called *Poll na Brocuidhe*, or the "Badger's Hole". The *Ceólána* alluded to in the legend are traditionally well remembered in the parish just named, and have, with other objects supposed to have belonged to Saint *Blathmac*, passed into the possession of the Royal Irish Academy.]

(384) [original:—gabais eccla, acus uaċbas mor na cleiriġ, acus ased do ronsat a ccluicc acas a cceolana do ḃuain acus tuargnaḋ mor da minnaib acas da mbaċlaib; acas do gairsiot an tir léo fearaib, macaib mnaib. Life of Saint *Mac Creha*, O'Curry's MSS., Cath. Univ. Lives of Saints, vol. I., p. 345, bot.]

passage in question occurs at folio 239, b. of the Book of Ballymote, where the second attack upon the city of Troy is described, beginning as follows:

"These were the kings and the chiefs who came to the battle from the Greeks: Agamemnon, the son of Ateri, son of Pilop, son of Tantal, son of Mercury, son of Jove, son of Saturn; and Menelaus his brother; and Achilles, and Patrocul, and the two Ajaxes, namely, Ajax the son of Olei, and Ajax the son of Talaman; and Ulysses, and Diomed, Nestor, and Polimnestor, and Palamides, and Mnestius, and many other leaders. All these high kings and chiefs of the Greeks came to the battle this day. It was a beautiful sight to look at them when they had arranged the battle. The sky blazed with the lustre and splendour of the various many coloured vestures, and the carbuncle gems of all colours, and the gold and silver *Guth-Buinde*, and the emblazoned battle shields, and the splendid various weapons which were over them".(385)

I have not been able to find any passages to agree, exactly, in phraseology with these in any version of the Life of Alexander, or of the Siege of Troy; and, consequently, no equivalent of the name *Guth-buinde*, in any other language, has as yet been found; so that I am unable, with any precision, to ascertain the nature of the instrument.

The Ocht Tedach.

The next musical instrument in alphabetical order on my list is the *Ocht-tedach*, literally the eight-stringed, which must from its very name, have been an instrument of the harp kind with eight strings. To this instrument I have met with but one reference. That reference, however, with its associations, is as good as many, and evidently typifies a class of instruments which must have been in extensive use, and probably with a particular profession, namely, the ecclesiastical. As, however, the legend of this instrument, and the curious metrical address of the abbot of *Ui Cormaic* to *Feidhlemidh Mac Crimhthainn*, king of Munster, have been amply dealt with in a previous lecture, it is not necessary to repeat the account I have already given of it.(386)

(385) [original:—Itesed rig ocus toisig tangadar isin cath o Grecaib. Agmemnon mac Ateri, mac Piloip, mac Tantail, mac Mercuir, mac Ioib, mac Saturn, agus Menelaus a brathair, ocus Aicil, ocus Patrocoil, ocus na da Aiax; .i. Aiax mac Olei, ocus Aiax mac Talamoin, ocus Uilixes, ocus Diomid, Nestor ocus Polimnestor ocus Palamides, ocus Mnestius, ocus toisig imda ele. Tancadar tra na huile airdrig ocus toisig Grec isin cath in lasin. Ba caem tra afaircsi icaregad iar corugud doib in cata. Rolasatar in taer do dellrad ocus do taitneam na tlacht nechsamail nildathach, na ngem carrmocal cach data, ocus na ngutbuinde ordae, ocus airgidi, ocus na cathsciath comochtai, ocus na narm nalainn nilarda badar uassaib. Book of Ballymote, f. 239, b.a]

(386) [See Lecture xxxii., *ante*, vol. ii. p. 261 *et seq*.]

XXXV.

The *Oircin*;

The next musical instrument, if indeed instrument it can be called, to which I have met reference, is the *Oircin*. To this *Oircin* I have met but one reference, and that not in connection with any other musical instrument, or with musical performance, but in comparison with other instruments. The name *Oircin* occurs in the ancient tract of which the ancient Irish triads form part. These tracts form a collection of short, pointed, wise sayings,—affirmative, negative, and comparative; and they are generally known as king *Cormac Mac Airt's* instructions to his son *Cairbre*. The section of these instructions in which the name *Oircin* occurs, is the comparative, and consists of twenty-four comparative affirmatives, beginning thus: "Every man is wise till he sells his inheritance". That is, any other act of folly is wisdom compared to the folly of selling one's inheritance. The next is: "Every one is a fool till he purchases land". That is to say, that all other exercises of prudence or acquisition of wealth was simple folly, compared to the purchase of land in perpetuity. These ancient sayings are curious evidences of the importance which at all times attached to the possession in fee of land in Ireland.

mentioned in the Irish Triads;

The nineteenth of these wise sayings runs thus: "All music is the music of cats, compared to the music of the *Cruit*". That is to say, all other music is but caterwauling, compared to the harp. And, in the twenty-third, we are told that "the sweetest of all music is the music of the *Oircin*".(387)

I have failed to find any further reference to this instrument, if instrument it was at all; and I have mentioned it merely for the purpose of pointing the attention of future archaeological readers to the fact of such a reference being extant. I should, however, note here, that among the great company of bards who attended *Seanchan Torpeist*, the chief poet of Erinn, in his visit to the court of *Guaire*, king of Connacht, as described in a former lecture,(388) there was one who was named *Oircne*, that is *Oircne*, the repeater, chief *Ollamh*, or professor of north Munster; but, unfortunately, the nature of his profession is not explained, any further than what his name implies. The name *Oircne*, however, must have been derived from *Oircin*, in the same way that *Cruitire*, a harper, is derived from *Cruit*, a harp. For the word *Oircne*, I have not found any explanation, but that it was the name of a specially gifted lap-dog or small

one of the bards of *Seanchan Torpeist's* "Great Bardic Company" called *Oircine*;

no explanation of *Oircne* known, except that it was the name of the first lap-dog.

(387) [original:—
1. Gaeṫ caċ coꞃanaꝺ ꞃeic a ꞅoꞃbbai.
2. Baeṫ caċ collaigiꞅ tiꞃe.
19. Caiꝺ caċ ceol co cꞃuit.
23. Milꞅem caċ ceol, ceol in-ꝺoiꞃcin.—H. 2. 18. f. 235. a. col. 4. mid.; H. 2. 17. f. 179, *et seq.*]

(388) [See Lecture XXXI., *ante*, vol. ii. p. 235.]

hound; but I do not know what relation existed between the dog and the musical performer, or professional *Oirene*. I may, however, remark that, according to the Brehon Laws, no one was allowed to have a lap-dog called *Oirene* but a *brugaidh*, or farmer, a queen, a doctor, and a harper. XXXV.

The next musical instrument in alphabetical order to which I have met any reference are the *Pipai* or pipes. To this instrument itself, under this, its proper name, I have met with but one ancient reference, and that in the poem in the Book of Leinster, already so often quoted in the course of these lectures: I allude to the poem describing the games and sports of the ancient fair of *Carman*, now the town of Wexford. In the list of musical instruments preserved in that poem, as having been in use at this great provincial fair, we find the *Pipai*, or pipes; and there is no reason to think these *Pipai* were not the bag-pipes of the times, whatever their simple or complex character may have been. *Pip*, or in the plural *Pipai*, that is pipe or pipes, continues to be the name of the bag-pipes to this day in Ireland. The following fugitive stanza, more than a century old, and taken down by me in 1855 from the lips of Mr. P. Mac Donogh, a native of Castlebar, in the county of Mayo, but now of the British Museum, preserves the Connacht popular name of the pipes. The first two lines of the stanza appear to have been addressed to an itinerant piper on his return from his wanderings to the residence of some hospitable patron; and the second two lines are significantly characteristic of the long established habits ascribed to this particular class of performers.

Of the *Pipai* or Pipes; mentioned in the poem on *Carman*;

"Play up the pipes, and thou shalt have payment,
Give us that melody which we have not for some time heard".
"The key is in the door, and draw us a horn of drink,
The pipes are thirsty; but they shall be so no more".[389]

Mr. Mac Donogh sings this stanza to a delicious simple air, of which he gave me an accurate score, to add to the ample and select collection of our great collector, Dr. Petrie.

Like the pipes themselves, I have not met in any ancient composition more than one reference to the *Pipaireadha*, or pipers. This reference is preserved in a fragment of our ancient laws consisting of but one single sheet of four pages, now bound up at the end of the ancient volume of laws so often referred to in the course of these lectures, and classed H. 3. 18. in the lib-

the only ancient reference to the *Pipaireadha* or Pipers known to the author is a fragment of Brehon Law.

[389] original:—

Seinn suas na pipai, is geaba tusa diolaigeaċt,
ta bair duin an binn úd, na cualamar go fóil.

Atá an eoċair annsa doras, agus tarraing corn dige duinn,
'tá tart ar na pipai, aċt ni biaidh nis mó.

XXXV. rary of Trinity College, Dublin. The article contains a list of the fines or recompense paid to professors of the mechanical arts for insults or bodily injury, and concludes in these words:

"These are base, that is, inferior professions, and are entitled to the same amount of fines as the *Pipaireadha*, or pipers; and the *Clesamhnaigh*, or jugglers; and the *Cornaireadha*, or trumpeters; and the *Cuislennaigh*, or pipe blowers".[390] This paragraph is valuable so far as to show that the *Cuislennach* or pipe-blower was a different person from the *Pipaire*, or piper.

Of the *Stoc*; The next of the musical instruments in alphabetical order to which I have reference is the *Stoc*. The only instance of the occurrence of this instrument, in its singular form, that I have met, is found in the passage from the paraphrase of the Book of *Genesis*, preserved in the Book of *Dun Doighre*, or *Leabhar Breac*, which I quoted in a previous lecture.[391]

mentioned in a paraphrase of the Book of Genesis in the *Leabhar Breac*.

In the passage referred to it will be seen that the *Corn*, that is a horn or trumpet, and the *Stoc Focra*, or alarm *Stoc*, are commanded to be sounded at the same time, and in such a way as to lead us to think that two distinct instruments are spoken of, namely, the *Corn* or horn, for congregating or calling attention, and the *Stoc Focra*, or alarm trumpet, to sound the marching blast. Could the ancient Irish writers have had any old romantic commentary on the following verses from the Old Testament (*Numbers*, chapter x.), which authorized them to make a distinction between the two silver trumpets which the Lord ordered Moses to make, one for mustering the tribes, and one to sound the march?

"1. And the Lord spoke to Moses, saying:

"2. Make thee two trumpets of beaten silver wherewith thou mayst call together the multitude when the camp is to be removed.

"3. And when thou shalt sound the trumpets, all the multitude shall gather unto thee to the door of the tabernacle of the covenant.

"4. If thou sound but once, the princes and the heads of the multitude of Israel shall come to thee.

"5. But if the sound of the trumpets be longer, and with interruptions, they that are on the east side shall first go forward.

"6. And at the second sounding and like noise of the trumpet, they who lie on the south side, shall take up their tents. And

[390] [original:—Daer nemid tra, .i. fodána na graidh tuas, ocus comh enechlann iad ocus na pipairedha, ocus na clesamnaig, ocus na cornairedha, ocus na cuislennaig.—H. 3. 18, loose sheet at the end of book.]

[391] [See Lecture XXXIV., *ante*, vol. ii. p. 308.]

fter this manner shall the rest do, when the trumpets shall sound or a march. XXXV.

"7. But when the people is to be gathered together, the sound f the trumpets shall be plain, and they shall not make a broken ound". mentioned in a paraphrase of the Book of Genesis in the *Leabhar Breac*,

Here it does not appear very clear whether the assembling umpets, and the alarm or marching trumpet, were one and the ame instrument, or whether the two were sounded at the same me and for the same purpose or not; but I believe they were ot.

We have in the same great authority another curious instance f the actual natural horn and the trumpet, from *Joshue*, chaper vi.

"1. Now Jericho was close shut up and fenced, for fear of the hildren of Israel, and no man durst go out or come in.

"2. And the Lord said to Joshue: Behold I have given ito thy hands Jericho, and the king thereof and all the aliant men.

"3. Go round about the city, all ye fighting men, once a day. o shall ye do for six days.

"4. And on the seventh day the priests shall take the seven umpets which are used in the jubilee, and shall go before the k of the covenant: and you shall go about the city seven times, id the priests shall sound the seven trumpets.

"5. And when the voice of the trumpet shall give a longer id broken time, and shall sound in your ears, all the people iall shout together with a very great shout, and the walls of ie city shall fall to the ground, and they shall enter in, every ie at the place against which they shall stand".

These five verses of the sixth chapter of *Joshue* are taken from ie Douay Bible, but other translations and commentators call iese trumpets which were sounded against the walls of Jericho, umpets of rams' horns. I need not follow these quotations irther; it is sufficient to say, that these trumpets continue to e spoken of down to the fall of the city of Jericho at the seveneenth verse of the chapter. The following passage from the istorical version of the fall of Jericho, from the Book of *Dun Doighre*, will show what the ancient Irish translator calls the umpets of rams' horns. and in the version of the "Fall of Jericho" in the same book;

"They [the Israelites] spread their flocks and their hosts over ie beautiful, wonderful plains of Jericho, that is, the chief city f Canaan. They collected their hosts and their scourers, and ieir battalions around about the city. There were seven strong npregnable walls around that city. There were sounded by ie sons of Israel seven powerful choice *Stuic* around the seven

XXXV.

walls of the city for a week, and a wall each day was what they knocked down".[392]

and again in describing the coming of Antichrist;

Again, in the same old book, where the coming of Antichrist, and his combat with, and overthrow of, Enoch and Elias are related, we find the passage of which the following is the translation:

"The day of judgment then will approach. Tuba canet Michael, et omnes resurgunt. Michael the archangel will sound his *Stoc*, and all [the dead] shall arise from their graves".[393]

And in the plural form *Stuic* in the poem on the fair of *Carman* and in the *Táin Bo Flidais*.

The *Stoc*, in its plural form of *Stuic*, is found in the enumeration of the musical instruments in the ancient poem on the fair of *Carman*, already referred to; and it occurs again in a more military sense in an ancient tale called *Táin Bo Flidais*, or the Cow Spoil of *Flidas*. This *Flidas* was a lady of great beauty and accomplishment, the wife of *Ailill Finn*, or *Ailell* the fair-haired, a valiant and powerful chief of *Irris* in Connacht, in the century preceding the Incarnation. This was the time at which *Ailill* and *Medb*, the celebrated king and queen of Connacht, were preparing to set out on that famous expedition into Ulster, so well known as the *Táin Bo Chuailgne*, to which frequent reference has been made in the course of these lectures. Preparatory to setting out on this expedition, these royal personages collected voluntary contributions from their provincial subjects, in the way of supplies for their army. One of the Connacht chiefs most celebrated for his flocks and herds was this *Ailill Finn*, or the fair-haired; and to him the king and queen sent a friendly request for a contribution to their commissariat. *Fergus*, the prince of Ulster, who was at this time in exile at the Connacht court, asked and obtained permission to go with this request to the court of *Ailill* the Fair-haired. But *Fergus* had motives of his own for preferring this request: he had seen and loved *Ailill's* wife, the beautiful *Flidas*, and he sought to make this an opportunity to see and converse with her in her own court. *Ailill* the Fair-haired, however, was not without his suspicions of the true motives of this visit, and when, therefore, *Fergus* arrived at his court, he received him coldly, refused him the supply, but offered him the hospitality

(392) [original:—Ro siset a creċa ocus a sloig sor muigib aille examla herico .i. primcathair na cannanca, timsaigit a sloig ocus a sirċe ocus a caṫa imon cathraig imacuairt. Seċt múir daingne dichoglaide imon cathraig sin. Rosennit oc maccu Israel .uii. stuic trena togharde im .uii. mura na cathrach co tend sectmaine .i. muir ceċ loei ised no legois remru.—*Leabhar Breac*, fol. 52. b. a.]

(393) [original:—Comfocsigid laithi braṫa iarsin. Tuba canet Michael et omnes resurgunt. Seinfid Michael a stocc condereċt in uli aranadnaċtib.—*Leabhar Breac*, fol. 52, b. a.]

of his house. *Fergus* refused this offer, whereupon a quarrel ensued, in which he was himself captured with two of his party, and twenty more of them killed, whilst the other eight fled to the royal palace of *Cruachan*, and apprised the king and queen of the dangerous state in which they left their chief. This news was not tamely received by king *Ailill* and queen *Medb*. They immediately set out with a large force, and having arrived at the fort of *Ailill* the Fair-haired, they laid siege to it, and after a long struggle, took and plundered it, killing himself and all its other brave defenders. It is in describing the attack on the fort of *Ailill* the Fair-haired the *Stoc* is mentioned. The passage is as follows:

"And then arose the men of the four great provinces of Erinn, and the dark exiles [of Ulster] along with them; and they were excited greatly by *Ailill* and *Fergus* and *Medb;* and they altogether faced the fortress; and they sounded their *Stuic*, and their *Sturgana* in proclamation of battle, and they raised tremendous terrific shouts".(394)

Another instrument the *Sturgan* mentioned in this tract;

This passage leaves no doubt of the ordinary use of the *Stoc*, whatever might have been its precise form. But we have here, along with the *Stoc*, another instrument, evidently of the trumpet kind, namely, the *Sturgán*. Of the *Sturgán* I have never met with any mention but the present, and two more, which, though coming down to comparatively recent times, do not throw any additional light on the kind or quality of the instrument.

And also a poem on Randall lord of Arran.

There is a poem in my possession, written for Randall, Lord of the island of Arann, in the Frith of Clyde in Scotland. This Randall was of Danish extraction, and the grandson of Godfrey Meranach, lord of the Danes of Dublin, who died in the year 1095. Randall, the subject of this poem, and who flourished about the year 1180, was of the Irish race by his mother's side; and in right of this descent, the poet exhorts him to come over to Ireland and establish his right to the throne of Tara. The poem consists of fifty stanzas. The stanza which contains the reference to the *Sturgán* is the last, and is as follows:

"O Randall, thou best of the world's kings,
Thou king to whom my warm affection clings;
After thee around O'Colman's Hill,
There will be a concert of *Stuic* and *Sturgána*".(395)

(394) [original:—Acus ro ergedar ceithre holl-cuigid erenn and sin, ocus in dubloingeas mar aen riu, ocus ro greis Ailill go mor, ocus Fergus, ocus Medb iat, ocus tucsat anaigthi a naenfecht ar in dunad, ocus ro fenoit a Stuic ocus a Sturgana leo i comfuagra catha, ocus ro thogbadar gairi aidbli uathmara.—H. 2. 16. col. 354.]

(395) [original:—
A Ragnaill a rig in domnan
a ri da tabraim talgrad
ad diaig um Cnoc ó Colmain
biaid organ, stoc, is sturgan.]

The O'Colman's hill spoken of here, was the Hill of Tara, so called in allusion to the O'Melachlainn family, the hereditary kings of Tara, but whose tribe name was *Clann Colmain*. In this stanza, as in the passage just quoted above, we have the *Stoc* and *Sturgan* in connection with military display.

The *Sturganuidhe* or *Sturgan* player mentioned in *Keating's* Three Shafts of Death.

In the Rev. Doctor Geoffry Keating's learned religious work, so well known under the name of the Three Shafts of Death, book 3, article 18, occurs the following paragraph:

"We read at *St. Matthew*, chapter ix., these words: 'Domine filia mea modo mortua, est, veni et impone manum tuam super eam, et vivet'. That is, 'Lord, my daughter is now dead: come and put thy hand upon her, and she shall be alive'. These words are found in *Matt.*, chap. ix., verses 18, 23, 24, 25, as follows:

"'18. While he spoke these things unto them, behold there came a certain ruler and worshipped him, saying, 'My daughter is even now dead: but come and lay thy hand upon her, and she shall live'.

"'23. And when Jesus came into the ruler's house, and saw the minstrels and the people making a noise,

"'24. He said unto them, 'Give place: for the maid is not dead, but sleepeth'. And they laughed him to scorn.

"'25. But when the people were put forth, he went in, and took her by the hand, and the maid arose'".

On this miracle Dr. Keating has the following short commentary:

"Understand that Christ did three things at the time of performing this miracle. Firstly, he put out of the house the crowd which were in it, both *Storganuidhe*, or *Sturgan* players; *Oirfidioch*, or musician, and *Piopaire*, or piper".[395]

Specimens of the *Corn*, *Stoc* and *Sturgan* are probably to be found in the museum of the R.I.A.

From all that I have read and seen of the *Corn*, the *Stoc*, and the *Sturgan*, the three chief military musical instruments of our remote ancestors, I have no doubt but we have ancient specimens of each of them still extant in the Museum of the Royal Irish Academy.

The *Corn* the Roman *Cornua*; specimens in the museum of the R.I.A.

I am satisfied that the *Corn* was the *Cornua* of the ancient Romans, which was bended almost round, and of which we have two, though still imperfect specimens in the museum of the Royal Irish Academy. Each of these instruments consists in its

(395) [original:—Léiġtear ag Mata san 9. ca. na briaṫra so "Domine filia mea modo mortua est, veni et impone manum tuam super eam et vivet". A ṫiġearna fuair m'inġen bás anois, tar agus cuir do láṁ féin uirre acas ba beó í.

. . . .

tuig go ndearnaid Críost trí neiṫe re linn na míorbaillsi do ḋeanam. Ar tus do ċuir as an tteaċ an tróċaire do bí ann, idir stoirganaiḋe, oirfidioċ acus píobaire. Mar an cceadna.—From a copy by Andrew Mac Curtin of Dunogain in the Co. of Clare, made in the year 1709; it will also be found at p. 351 MS. Egerton, 184, Brit. Museum.]

present state of two curved pieces, which were joined together for use by means of the boss which may be perceived on the small end of one of them, into which boss the end of each piece was received and made air-tight. It is evident that each instrument has lost one or more curved pieces, which had been attached in the same way, and continued until they formed the required circle of the instrument. They must have also had an ornamented mouthpiece, to correspond with the beautifully decorated disk which adorns the orifice of the one which has the boss just referred to. That these instruments consisted originally of three pieces at least, we have, I think, ample evidence in the fact of the middle piece of a third *Corn*, still retaining upon its ends the original bosses into which the ends of the other two pieces were received and attached. These unique *Corns* are composed of ancient bronze, not cast or welded, but joined by a riveted band of the same metal, which runs within the cylinder along the concave side, and upon which the edges of the moulded horn, which was originally a flat plate, are beautifully and, to modern artizans incomprehensibly, riveted down, the flat heads of the rivets being on the inside.

The *Stoc* represents the Roman *Buccina*.

The second of these instruments, the *Stoc*, represents, I am satisfied, the Buccina of the ancient Romans. The Buccina is described in Rees' Encyclopaedia as "an ancient military metallic instrument crooked like a horn used in war. The word", he continues, "comes from *bucca*, mouth, and *cano*, I sing". In no description, however, of the Roman Buccina that I am aware of, is there any definite reference to the way in which the instrument was blown; whether from the smaller end, in the ordinary way, or from an orifice in the side or in the concave surface. Indeed from the fact that the name Buccina is derived from *bucca*, the mouth, and *cano*, I sing, there appears good reason to think that the instrument was a speaking trumpet of a deep, loud, but not shrill compass.

It is remarkable that no specimen of a straight trumpet, pipe, or tube of any kind, of a musical character, has yet been discovered any where that I know of.

The *Sturgan* corresponds to the Roman Lituus.

The third of these instruments is that which I have ventured to identify as the *Sturgán;* and when we compare the following short description of the Roman Lituus from Rees' Encyclopaedia, and the figure of that instrument given in that work, with specimens in the Academy's museum, it requires no argument to prove that, however they may differ a little in the exact shape of the curve, they are identically the same in original conception and use.

"The Lituus", says the writer in Rees' Encyclopaedia, "which was almost straight, but crooked at the extremity, in the form of the augur's staff, whence its name, was a species of clarion or octave trumpet, made of metal, and extremely loud and shrill, used for horse, as the straight trumpet was for foot. The Lituus, among medallists, was the wand or staff, twisted at the top, used by the augurs, made in the form of a crozier, and the badge of the augurship. . . . . . . Aulus Gellius says it was bigger in the place where it was crooked than elsewhere".

The *Sturgán*, it will be seen, like the *Corn*, was composed of at least two parts, and perhaps of a third, with a bowl or mouth-piece; still, as far as we know of, no specimen of the instrument has yet been discovered consisting of more than two joints.

Mr. R. Ousley's description of the *Stuic* or *Sturgana* in the museum of the R.I.A.;

Of the *Stuic* and *Sturgana* in the museum of the Royal Irish Academy, the following brief account by Mr. Ralph Ousley, is preserved in the second volume of the Transactions of that learned body, for the year 1788, as follows:—

"An Account of three Metal Trumpets found in the county of Limerick, in the year 1787, by Ralph Ousley, Esq., M.R.I.A., communicated by Joseph Cooper Walker, Esq., Secretary to the Committee of Antiquities. [Read March 29, 1788.]

"As every attempt", says Mr. Ousley, "to elucidate the antiquities of this country has of late been favourably received, the following short description of three uncommon musical instruments is with great deference offered to the Royal Irish Academy.

"These trumpets were found by a peasant cutting turf in the bog of *Carrick O'Gunnell*, county of Limerick, in the month of May, 1787, and by him sold to a brazier in the city of Limerick, who reserved them for the present possessor. They are of a rich mixed metal, neither copper nor brass, but inclining rather to a copper colour. They resemble strongly those described in Walker's Historical Memoirs of the Irish Bards (page 109, Appendix), except in the middle, which differs from any I ever heard of, and is, I believe, an unique. This tube is $23\frac{6}{10}$ inches long, of one entire piece, and has a loop in the centre to run a cord through. At each end it has four holes, corresponding to four in each trumpet, through which two pins or pegs fastened the instrument. Both trumpets were fixed on the middle piece, like the points of a German flute, when first found, and very firm with rust and dirt, but the pins were lost. I should imagine this tube was only to hang them up by: Doctor Fisher (a celebrated performer on the violin, and doctor of music in the University of Oxford), who saw them with me in Limerick, conjectures fig. I. and II. are first and second. The mouth or large end of fig II. is four and a-half inches diameter, being one inch wider than the other. Fig. III. is the *Stoc* or *Stuic*, a sort of speaking trumpet described by Colonel Vallancey in the Collectanea, No. XIII., page 46, and Historical Memoirs of Irish Bards, page 83. The mouth-hole is oval, 1¾ inches long, by 1¼ wide, and was cut across by the turf spade; but the other two and middle piece are in fine preservation. They are all ornamented with little conical teats or projections at each end, as in the drawing, viz., four at the small end, and four near each extremity of the middle piece. Fig I. and fig III. have four holes at the wide ends, which seems as if some other tube was to be fastened occasionally within them, perhaps in the manner of Lord Drogheda's, described by Colonel Vallancey. It is natural to think there must have been mouthpieces for fig. I. and II., but none were found with them, nor with any others, I believe, in the kingdom, being made, probably, of perishable materials. The three trumpets and middle piece weigh 9 lbs. 11½ oz., viz.: middle piece, 1 lb. 11 oz.; fig. I., 2 lbs.; fig. II., 2 lbs. 9½ oz.; fig. III., 3 lbs. 7 oz. A very curious brass spur-rowel of 2 4/10 inches diameter, and eight prongs or rays, was dug up with the trumpets, and is now in my possession. XXXV.

"Ralph Ousley.

"Millsborough, near Castlerea, August 15, 1787".

The trumpets so accurately described in Mr. Ousley's communication are now in the museum of the Royal Irish Academy, and the drawings which accompany Mr. Ousley's paper are correct representations of them. It will, however, be apparent to any man of common sense that the three instruments could never have been the parts of only one instrument, as they might be supposed to have been, from the state in which they were found. To make sure that such was not the case, I have examined the originals, and the result of that examination enables me to assert positively, that they are parts of two, not of one instrument. For upon applying the straight tube to the smaller end of the larger trumpet, I found the opening of the latter much too wide for either of its ends, and that the rivet holes of neither end would match the holes of the opening. Again, upon applying the straight piece to the opening of the smaller trumpet, I found that one end fitted exactly, holes and all, showing by this simple method how easy it would have been for Mr. Ousley to satisfy himself that the two curved pieces were never intended to form with the one straight piece but one instrument. We may very well suppose, indeed, that the rivets which the finder of the trumpets said were lost by him, had not been present at all, and therefore that the two curved

the specimens in the Academy's museum are parts of two instruments, and not of one;

XXXV. pieces, if at all found as represented, were stuck only temporarily in some moment of hurry upon the one straight piece. The four holes at the wide ends of each of the curved pieces were for fastening a disk, such as may seem upon one of the *Corns* in the Academy's museum, and not, as Vallancey surmised, to fasten another tube to them.

Although this, or some such argument, would be sufficient of itself to prove that these were parts of two, not of one instrument, still we are not trusting to mere argument alone to put the assertion beyond dispute. It will be remembered that in Mr. Ousley's communication he says that these trumpets, then in his possession, resembled strongly those described in Walker's Historical Memoir of the Irish Bards, page 109 of the Appendix, excepting in the middle piece. It is singular that the instruments thus referred to should consist of three distinct specimens; and so like those of Mr. Ousley's are they, that, at first view, they could scarcely be distinguished from one another.

ancient Irish wind instruments of graduated scale and compass;

And this fact suggests good reason to think, that in ancient times in Ireland these wind instruments were grouped in instruments of graduated scale and compass; the great *Corn* forming the deep loud bass, and those others diminishing in compass and increasing in shrillness down to the smallest sizes of *Sturgan* which are in the museum of the Royal Irish Academy. There may have been still smaller, but as yet none such have been met with.

the trumpets mentioned in Walker's "Irish Bards" first described and figured in Smith's History of Cork;

The trumpets to which Mr. Ousley refers us in Walker's Memoir of the Irish Bards, published in 1786, were originally described and figured in Smith's History of Cork, vol. ii. p. 404, published in 1750.

"In a bog between *Cork* and *Mallow*", writes Charles Smith, "a few years ago, were discovered several brass trumpets, some of which are now in the possession of the Rev. Mr. Somerville of Castlehaven. One of them resembles that given us by Sir Thomas Molyneux in the Appendix to Boate's Natural History of Ireland. These of ours are drawn from the originals by a scale which shows their dimensions; the smaller end was entirely closed, the hole they sounded them by was at the side D, fig. 1, and not at the end as in our modern trumpets. It is not well known what kind of noise those who had skill in sounding this instrument could make before it had been injured by time; at present it gives but a very dull, heavy, uncouth noise, that cannot be heard at any great distance.[397] If the method of filling the German flute was lost, and a person was to find one, it

[397] Smith has a note here from Diodorus Siculus.

would be very difficult to guess what kind of sound it might afford; and the same may be said of our trumpets. XXXV.

"Fig. 2. is a kind of double trumpet, open at both ends, with no hole in the side as the former.

"From A to A are two brass pipes better than half an inch diameter; these pipes had been soldered at B, but at A A they exactly enter the small ends of the curved part of the instrument. The curved parts are both of a size; if joined when the pipe B was whole, it was impossible by blowing in the wider end to make any musical sound; but by blowing into either small end with one or both pipes fixed, it might have afforded no inharmonious noise. The wider, as well as the smaller ends of these instruments, are ornamented with a row of small pyramids, as in the figure. They are of cast brass, very smooth on the outside, but not quite so thin as a common brass trumpet. They undoubtedly belonged to the Danes, from their being found in one of their intrenchments, and there were thirteen or fourteen more discovered at the same time; but these were the most perfect and uncommon, particularly fig. 2".

That Smith, any more than Ousley, bestowed but little of close examination upon these trumpets which he figures, will be sufficiently evident from the following reference to them taken from the Appendix to Walker's Memoir of the Irish Bards, page 109:

"About thirty years since, the trumpets delivered above were found in a bog between Cork and Mallow. They were bought by a brazier in Cork, who was just going to melt them down, when they were rescued from his hands by the Rev Mr. Somerville of Castlehaven. Being afterwards exposed to sale, they were purchased by the Rev. Mr. Archdall for Dr. Pococke, bishop of Meath, to whom he was then chaplain. On the bishop's decease his valuable collection of curiosities was sold by auction in London. The trumpets fortunately getting into the possession of the Antiquarian Society of London, engravings of them appeared in the Vetusta Monumenta, a work which was conducted by that learned body. The engravings were illustrated by the following observations: Walker's observations on them; they are figured in Vetusta Monumenta;

"'Fig. I. II. III. Three brass trumpets found (with ten or a dozen more) in a bog between Cork and Mallow, in the kingdom of Ireland. They are imagined to be some of those instruments which the northern nations made use of in battle. 'They have amongst them', says Diodorus Siculus, speaking of the Gauls, 'trumpets, peculiar as well to themselves as to other nations: these, by inflation, emit an hoarse sound, well suited to the din of battle'. 'And', says Polybius, 'the parade and

XXXV. tumult of the army of the Celts terrified the Romans. For there was amongst them an infinite number of horns and trumpets which, with the shout of the whole army in concert, made a clamour so terrible and so loud, that every surrounding echo was awakened, and all the adjacent country seemed to join in the horrible din'.

"'Of these, fig. III. consists of one piece of fine brass, closed at the small end, near which it has a large oval hole for sounding, in the manner of the German flute at this day. The two rings were probably designed to receive a string, by which it was to be carried or supported. Fig. I. and II. are of a different construction; they consist of two pieces, viz., a curve pipe and a small straight tube, fitted exactly to enter into the small end of it. These were not sounded as the former, but from the end, in the manner of a common trumpet. The mouthpiece to both seems wanting.

"'More of this sort were found some years ago, near Carrickfergus, in the north of Ireland, two of which were brought to England, and are possibly the same which are now deposited in the British Museum'".[398]

Walker adds the following observations, which show what any man with ordinary discernment might see, that he did not believe these two curved and two straight tubes were ever intended to form but one instrument:

"Colonel Vallancey consulted Dr. Burney respecting these trumpets; the doctor and he concurred in opinion that fig. I. II. might have been a kind of musical trumpet. But the drawing does not show the instrument complete; there was certainly another joint. One Mr. Rawle, a gentleman of London, possesses a trumpet very much resembling the one in question, but with two joints and a perfect mouthpiece. This trumpet was found in England".

a similar instrument found in England;

So far Mr. Walker, and I have only to repeat that I agree with him fully in the opinion, indeed I may say certainty, that there must have been another joint to each of these trumpets, and that that joint, whether long or short, if not itself the mouthpiece, must have contained the mouthpiece.

author agrees with Walker that there must have been another joint in the trumpets;

I need not point attention to the discrepancy between the uniform figures of these two curved tubes, given by Smith, and the engravings of them, which must be more accurate, published in the Vetusta Monumenta, in which there is a marked difference to be seen between the suddenness of the curve in one from that of the other. A similar difference of curve will be seen in these two trumpets, figured as one by Mr. Ousley in the

discrepancy between the figs. of Smith and the Vet. Mon.;

(398) See Vestusta Monumenta, vol. ii., 1780, plate xx.

Transactions of the Royal Irish Academy. Smith's opinion, that these were Danish trumpets, because they were found in a Danish entrenchment, is as fallacious as his drawings evidently are. The Danes had no such trumpets at any time in this country, and the absurdity of their ever having an entrenchment in the bog in which these instruments were found does not require one word of refutation.

Smith's opinion that they were Danish erroneous;

I should not perhaps have dwelt so long on, I might say, the self-evident proof that the one group of these tubes, and consisting of three pieces, found in the county of Limerick, and the other, consisting of four pieces, found in the county of Cork, did not each form one but two instruments, if the contrary had not been put on record by such men as Smith and Ousley in their day, and reiterated, as regards the Cork tubes, in our own time. For, in the April number for 1860, of the Ulster Journal of Archaeology, edited by Mr. Robert Mac Adam of Belfast, and in a clever article written on Irish trumpets by that gentleman himself, we find Smith's engravings of the Cork trumpets, and his idea of their having formed but one instrument, reprinted, without any attempt on the part of the writer to show the utter absurdity of such an idea.

Smith's error that the Cork trumpets formed but one instrument reproduced by Mr. R. Mac Adam;

Dr. [now Sir William R.] Wilde, however, in his Catalogue of the Antiquities of the Museum of the Royal Irish Academy, page 624, takes a different, and to us in Ireland, a very novel view of the straight piece of tube found with these instruments. After shortly referring to Smith, Ousley, and Walker's account of them, Sir William Wilde says:

Sir W. Wilde's novel idea of the use of the straight tubes;

"One of these resembles No. 12 in our museum (see figs. 526 and 529), with a lateral aperture or mouth-hole; the other two were simple curved horns, like fig. 524; but with these were found pieces of straight tubing, like that represented by Ousley, and which were then believed to have formed parts of these trumpets. It does not, however, follow that they were portions of, or in any way attached to the horns with which they were discovered; and if (as we believe) they were portions of a commander's staff, as stated at page 492 (see fig. 360), it was not an unlikely place for such articles to be found, where the commander of a battalion had also his speaking-trumpet, as well as his trumpeters beside him, when he fell in battle. That a curved trumpet, attached to each end of a straight tube four feet long, could not be of any use known or conjectured in the present day, is manifest The subject, however, requires further illustration!" And so indeed the subject did require further illustration, and Sir William Wilde would have materially aided, if not altogether supplied that illustration, had he, as he ought to have done,

XXXV. given the engravings of these trumpets from Smith and the Vetusta Monumenta, neither of which he has done; for then he would have given to his readers the opportunity of using their own eyes, a very important aid in such an inquiry. It has, to some extent, been the custom with some Irish antiquaries to bow with great deference to the opinion of foreign writers, perhaps more from a desire to show their acquaintance with works in other languages, than from any real convictions of the soundness of such opinions. I should be sorry to assert that Sir William Wilde's opinion of the straight tube in question was a mere imitation; but why otherwise he should adopt it is to me a difficulty. His reason, however, will be found in the following extract and engravings from his catalogue, pages 490, 491, 492, where he is describing certain faulchion-shaped weapons, of which there are a good many in the museum:—"Heretofore these articles have been denominated 'war-scythes', and vague notions have existed as to the way in which they were used, as already stated at page 450. Their precise use may now, however, be learned from the following: In Holstein, Mecklenburg, and Saxony, bronze implements, with blades similar to some of those now under consideration, have been discovered, and to these the German antiquaries have given the name of Commandostab, a sort of military baton. Three of these have been figured in Wagner's Handbuch der Alterthümer, from fig. 1281 of which is copied the accompanying illustration, in which the blade corresponds, in many respects, with several of those in the Academy, and of which fig. 358 is the type. In the same work we find the curved variety, with a blade precisely similar to figs. 329 and 330, also represented. In the hill of Osterburg in Saxony, where the article here figured was discovered, there were found along with it one thousand urns, several stone war-axes (celts), and twelve oval metal disks, supposed by Wagner to have been attached occasionally to the commander's staff in signalizing.[1] The handles were hollow tubes, strengthened by wooden staves, which projected below a considerable distance, and thus also added to their length.

his idea that they were a part of a "Commander's Staff", borrowed from Wagner;

"Among the bronze articles heretofore unexplained in our collection is a hollow tube, $24\frac{1}{2}$ inches long and $1\frac{1}{4}$ in diameter, No. 296 in rail case O, with a moveable ring in the middle, and furnished with four circles of spikes (four in each row), two near the centre, and one at each end, where the collars and rivet holes show that it had been attached to other portions. Hitherto, this article has been regarded as a portion of a trumpet, and would appear to be [it really is] that figured as such in vol. ii. of the Transactions of the Academy, and de-

XXXV.

scribed by Ralph Ousley, Esq., one of our earliest collectors of antiquities; it was found in the county of Limerick in 1787. The trumpets found along with it are still in the Academy, and are described under the head of musical instruments. During the past year another and very beautiful form of bronze battle-axe blade has been procured from the bog of Rock Forest, near Roscrea, in the county of Tipperary; it is 7¼ inches long and 8⅝ measured along the base, where it has two perfect rivet-holes and two notches, as shown in the accompanying illustration, the lower portion of which represents the tube alluded to, the dotted line above marking its probable termination at top. It is possible, however, that the socket for holding the blade may have projected beyond the line of the shaft".

Sir W. Wilde's illustration of the use of the straight part of a trumpet as a Commander's Staff unsatisfactory;

The illustration which Sir William Wilde prints of the application of the Rock Forest war-scythe to the tube found with the Ousley trumpets, must appear rather unsatisfactory; for, if the too cumbersome tube were, as he says, "strengthened by wooden staves, which projected below to a considerable distance, and this also added to the length", then, indeed, not only would the collars or rings upon the tube be hidden by the overlapping laths, but the handle would then be too clumsy and too meaningless, either as a lever for so light a military weapon, or a graceful "commander's staff". It may be worth while to state that, in old Irish wars and battles, as far as they have come down to us, the "commanders" were always armed and equipped like the ordinary warrior, but in a more superb degree, trusting more to the example of their swords or spears, and the power of their arms, to raise and direct the courage of their followers, than the simple wave of so out-of-the-way a "*commandostab*" as that figured by either Wagner or Wilde.

his separation of the straight tube from the curved parts in the Mus. of the R.I.A., a mistake which ought to be corrected.

Sir William Wilde, in submission to the Wagner doctrine, has, in his arrangement of the Academy's museum, taken the straight tube in question away from the trumpets joined to which it was found, and placed it in company and connection with the war-scythes, swords, and spear-heads in the department assigned to them. This appears to me to be a grave mistake, and one which must be corrected, if not by Sir William Wilde himself, then, by the authority of the Academy, by restoring it to the place in its kindred group which it has filled for more than fifty years. I do not wish to enter here on any criticism of Sir Wm Wilde's catalogue, however I may dissent from many of his antiquarian dogmas. As a descriptive catalogue, it has its value; but the antiquarian speculations in which the writer indulges rather too freely, might, in my opinion, have been reserved for a more mature stage in the author's antiquarian studies.

XXXV.

Sturgana, Stuic and *Corna* in the museum of the R.I.A. and T.C.D.

Of these trumpets it only remains for me to say, that of the *Sturgana*, or Lituus, there are in the museum of the Royal Irish Academy the curved parts of four, differing more or less in size, and a straight piece which fits one of them. Of the *Stuic* or *Stocs* blown into from the side, there are four perfect ones and a broken one, of different sizes; and in the museum of Trinity College, Dublin, there are two very neat, small specimens of the same instrument. Of the *Corn*, or great horn, we have, as already stated, two fine specimens, consisting each of a curve and middle piece, and the middle piece of a third. Many more of these trumpets are known to exist, but I shall speak only of those I have myself seen, and those engraved in the Vetusta Monumenta.

LECTURE XXXVI.

[Delivered July 23rd, 1862.]

(IX.) OF MUSIC AND MUSICAL INSTRUMENTS (continued). The word *Teillin*, the name of a harp in Welsh, is not applied in Gaedhelic to a musical instrument; meaning of *Telyn* according to Owen's Welsh Dictionary; *Telyn* originally perhaps a derisive name; *Caradoc*'s account of the introduction of harp music from Ireland into Wales; author unable to find what Welsh word *Caradoc* used for harp; the *Telyn* and *Cruth* were the *Cruit* and *Timpan* of Ireland; Owen's definition of a Welsh *Cruit*. The Irish *Cruit* was a lyre, and not a cithara. The Welsh *Crud* or Crowd could not represent the Irish *Cruit*. The Welsh word *Telyn* apparently the same as the Irish *Teillin*, applied to the humming bee and humble bee; *Teillin* occurs in the *Dinnseanchas;* also in a poem about *Marbhan* and *Guaire;* and in one by O'Donnelly written about 1680. The word *Teillin* applied to the humming of bees; it has become obsolete in Ireland, but not in Scotland; occurs in the Highland Society's dictionary as *Seillean*. *Telyn* could not be a modification of the Greek chelys. Some think the fiddle represents the ancient *Cruit;* the poem on the fair of *Carman* proves this to be erroneous. Of the *Timpan: Cormac*'s derivation of this word gives us the materials of which the instrument was made; the *Timpan* mentioned in an ancient paraphrase of the Book of Exodus; also in the Tale of the Battle of *Magh Lena;* and in that of the Exile of the Sons of *Duil Dermait;* another reference in the Dialogue of the Ancient Men; the passage in the latter the only one which explains *Lethrind;* in this passage *Lethrind* signified the treble part; another description of the *Timpan* given in the Siege of *Dromdamhghaire*. The *Timpan* was a stringed instrument played with a bow; this is fully confirmed by a passage from a vellum MS.; which also shows that the harper and timpanist were not necessarily distinct professions; this MS. was compiled by Edmund *O'Deorain* near St. *Senan*'s lake; the passage was copied into it or first written in 1509; the same person may have played the harp and *Timpan*, but they were two distinct professions. The *Timpan* came down to the seventeenth century. Important passage from Brehon Law respecting the Timpanist; it would appear from this that, in addition to the bow, the deeper strings were struck with the nail. Harpers and Timpanists are separately mentioned in the *Tochmarc Eimere*. The harper alone always considered of the rank of the *Bo Aire;* the timpanist, only when chief Timpanist of a king. Relative power of harp and *Timpan* illustrated by a legend from the Book of Lismore. Professional names of musical performers: the *Buinnire;* the *Cnaimh-Fhear;* the *Cornair;* the *Cruitire;* the *Cuislennach;* the *Fedánach;* the *Fer Cengail;* the *Graice;* the *Pipaire;* the *Stocaire;* the *Sturganaidhe;* the *Timpanach*.

THE next musical instrument (if I may so use the term), and the nineteenth on my list, is the *Teillinn*. But, although I have, for an object which shall immediately be seen, taken this word, *Teillinn*, into my list of names of musical instruments, I have never met it so applied in the Irish language. The word *Teillinn*, however, is the name for a harp in the Welsh language; whilst the name for a fiddle, in the same language, is

The word *Teillin*, the name of a harp in Welsh, is not applied in Gaedhelic to a musical instrument;

XXXV. *Cruit*, or *Cruth*, as the Welsh write it; and I have heard respectable Irish antiquaries give it as their opinion that *Teillinn* was really the ancient Gaedhelic or Celtic name for the harp, as well as *Cruit* for the fiddle; and this on the mere assumption that the Welsh form must be correct, because they choose to regard it as a more primitive dialect of the ancient Celtic than the Gaedhelic. I do not mean to controvert these opinions by argument here; but I shall bring forward the few instances (very few, I am sorry to say) in which I have met the word *Teillinn* in my Gaedhelic readings, not, indeed (as already stated), as the name of an instrument of music, but so closely connected with music, as to throw some doubt on the correctness of the opinions just alluded to, as well as upon the antiquity and correct application of the name *Teillinn* to the *Cruit*, or harp, in the Welsh language.

meaning of *Telyn* according to Owen's Welsh Dictionary.

In William Owen's Welsh Dictionary, printed in London in 1803, we find the word *Telyn* thus explained:—"*Telyn:* what is stretched; what is compact or straight; what is in even row; a harp; also the ribs and whole side of a carcass, when divided into two". This, I think, is a very poor explanation of the word upon which to assume that it is to be taken to mean a harp. If *Telyn* signifies nothing more than "what is stretched, what is compact or straight, (or) what is even in a row", I don't see why the term should have been applied to the harp, any more than to the web in a weaver's loom, the lines on a ropemaker's spindles, the shrouds of a ship, or anything else in which any number of threads or lines are stretched straight, compact, and even. The name, so far, would be a merely arbitrary and conventional one, without the smallest reference to shape or form. It would appear, indeed, from the application of the word to the ribs and whole side of a carcass, that the Welsh might have had a tradition of our legend of the harp having been first taken from the playing of the wind upon the skeleton of a whale on the shore of the strand of Camas. If so, then, wherever this legend came from, it would have been common to the Gaedhelic and Britons, at some remote period; though, whilst the former retain it in its integrity, the latter remembered but a misty fragment of it, implying, in their sense, no relation whatever to the harp, to its actual form or characteristics. There was, however, a time, I am confident, when the name *Telyn* did apply properly to, and was well understood to describe, the then Welsh harp; or, rather the comparatively powerless instrument which stood the Welsh in place of that Irish harp, which, in after time, was introduced into their country. Indeed there is some reason to think that it was directly from Ireland that the

XXXVI.

Welsh got the word "*Telyn*", as a derisive name for a powerless buzzing instrument of music, perhaps of the guitar kind; and that with the decay of their language, they in some way, now inexplicable, retained the derisive name *Telyn* to denote the superior instrument, and transferred the real ancient Irish name of that instrument, the *Cruit*, to another altogether different and inferior.

Telyn originally perhaps a derisive name;

The old native historian of Wales, so well known as Caradoc of Lhancarvan, who died about the year 1156, when speaking of *Gruffyth ap Conan*, prince of North Wales, who died in the year 1136, writes as follows:—

Caradoc's account of the introduction of harp music from Ireland into Wales;

"There were several good and wholesome *Laws* and *Statutes* enacted in his time; and, among the rest, he reformed the great disorders of the Welsh minstrels, which were then grown to great abuse. Of these [minstrels] there were three sorts in Wales; the first were called *Beirdh* [or Bards], who composed several songs and odes of various measures, wherein the poet's skill was not only required, but also natural endowment or a vein, which the Latins term *Furos Poeticus*. These, likewise, kept the records of all gentlemen's arms and pedigrees, and were principally esteemed among all the degrees of the Welsh poets. The next were such as plaid upon musical instruments, chiefly the harp and crowd, which music *Gruffyth ap Conan* first brought over into Wales; who, having been born in Ireland, and descended by his mother's side of Irish parents, brought with him from thence several skilful musicians, who invented all the instruments as were plaid upon in Wales. The last sort [or class] were called *Athchanaidh*, whose business it was to sing to the instruments plaid upon by another".[398]

These are remarkable words from a native Welsh writer, who wrote in his native language, and flourished at the very time in which, as he informs us, the prince *Gruffyth ap Conan* introduced the Irish music, Irish musical instruments, and Irish instrument-makers, for the first time into his native country. Caradoc wrote in the Welsh language. I quote from an English translation, good enough for general purposes, but unfortunately not so for my present one, to ascertain the precise names by which Caradoc speaks of the harp and *Cruth*. After various applications to native Welsh scholars, I have failed to obtain any satisfactory information on this subject, and therefore feel myself compelled to believe that Humphry Lloyd, the first translator of Caradoc (about the year 1540?), has taken these terms as he found them in his original. Supposing that

author unable to find what Welsh words *Caradoc* used for harp;

(398) *Caradoc of Lhancarvan's The Hist. of Wales*, p. 158. W. Wynne's edition. Lond. 1697.

XXXVI

Caradoc, in his history, used the terms *Telyn* and *Cruth* to denote the chief instruments of music which *Gruffyth ap Conan* had a short time before introduced into Wales from Ireland, it will appear very strange that such a writer should designate these new instruments by names known in his own country only, and not by the names which they bore in the country whence they had been taken. It is quite clear, however, that the instruments mentioned here as the *Telyn* and *Cruth* were the *Cruit* and *Timpan* of Ireland; and I am only at a loss to understand how it has happened that the names have been confounded in Wales, so far as to give to our *Cruit* or harp the name of *Telyn*, and to our *Timpan* the name of *Cruit*, which was the ancient proper name for our harp.

the *Telyn* and *Cruth* were the *Cruit* and *Timpan* of Ireland;

I have already quoted from Owen's Welsh and English Dictionary, his definition of a *Telyn*. I shall now quote from the same author his definition of a Welsh *Cruit*: "*Cruth*", says Owen, is "any body swelling out or bulging; a paunch; a kind of box scooped out of a piece of wood, and rounded, except on the side where the excavation is made, which is flat and covered with a board ending in a tail, to hang it up by, when it appears much like a bottle, having a hole in the upper part of the rotundity through which it is filled. It is used mostly to hold salt; and hence a salt box of any form is called *Crowth Halen;* [that is a salt cruit]; also a musical instrument with six strings, the two lowest of which are touched by the thumb, whilst the others are touched with a bow. It is much on the same principle with the violin, of which it is the prototype; and the term [*Cruth*] is now indiscriminately used for both".

Owen's definition of a Welsh *Cruit*

So far, Mr Owen; and, without entering into any criticism on the application of the term *Cruit* to anything swelled out or to any kind of box, we can clearly understand that his *Cruth* is, in fact, the ancient *Testudo*, the body of which was formed like the shell of a tortoise, an object which would very well answer his description of the meaning of the word.

In a former lecture I showed that the harp which king David played, was called a *Cruit* in an Irish tract, as old, at least, as the year 800;—that it had ten strings, to represent the ten commandments; and that it was played with the ten fingers. It is surely clear that this *Cruit* must have been a lyre; that is, an instrument which, from the time of Pindar, was distinguished from the Cithera, by having the strings free at both sides, whilst the Cithera is described to have had the strings drawn partly across the sounding board, and consequently over a bridge; thus leaving them free, but at one side only. Our harp, then, represents the true ancient lyre; and, from the time of the battle

The Irish *Cruit* was a lyre, and not a Cithera.

of *Magh Tuireadh*, down to, I believe, the seventeenth century, I am certain it bore no other name than *Cruit*, excepting in those places where it seems to be alluded to under the name *Timpan*. I am equally certain that we have never borrowed the instrument, nor its name, from our neighbours and ancient Celtic cousins—the Britons; but that, if anything, they have borrowed it from us.

The Welsh *Cruth*, or *Crowd*, then, as described by Owen, with its six strings, and played with a bow, could not represent the ancient lyre, our *Cruit;* and the only ancient instrument which it really does represent in form appears to be the Testudo, or Chelys, so called from its likeness to a tortoise shell. If, however, the term *Telyn*, which the Welsh apply to their present harp, be an ancient form, and not a modification (as it is suggested by some Welsh authorities that it may be) of the word Chelys, a tortoise shell, and if it be intended to be a name descriptive of the power and quality of the instrument, then we have in the Gaedhelic language a word identical with it in sound and orthography, and indicative of a peculiar kind of music, if not derisively of a musical instrument. The word that I allude to is written *Teillin*, whilst the Welsh word pronounced in the same way, is written *Telyn*, which is apparently only a phonetic from our word. Of the occurrence of this ancient Irish word in composition, I have never met with more than three instances, in each of which it is used in reference to the buzzing or humming of bees, if not to that of the humble or larger wild buzzing bee in particular.

The Welsh *Cruth* or Crowd could not represent the Irish *Cruit*.

The Welsh word *Telyn* apparently the same as the Irish *Teillin*, applied to the humming bee and humble bee.

The first of these references to the word *Teillinn* is found in the ancient topographical tract called the *Dinnseanchas*, so often quoted in the course of these lectures, and in that article of it which gives the legendary origin of the hill of *Bri Leith*, in the present county of Longford. The story is shortly this:—

Teillin occurs in the *Dinnseanchus*;

Liath (or the gray man), the son of *Celtchair* of *Cualand* [in the county of Wicklow], was the comeliest son of a chief among the *Sidhe* [or fairy nobles] of Erinn; and he fell in love with *Bri*, called *Bri* of the freckled face, daughter of *Midir*, called *Midir* of the valiant deeds, son of *Indiu*, son of *Echtach*. *Bri* went with her attendant maidens to the Mound of the maidens, (*ferta na ninghen*) by the side of Tara, [to meet her lover, and] *Liath* came with his attendant youths to the Hill of Pursuit, (*Tulach na Hiarmaitrigh*) [to meet her and carry her off in elopement]. They failed, however, to approach each other nearer than this, by reason of the warders of the court of *Midir* [the lady's father], whose showers of darts were as thick as *Teillinn Bees* upon a summer's day. And they wounded *Cooh-*

XXXVI. *lan*, the servant of *Liath*, so that he died. The maiden returned to *Bri Leith* [her father's mansion,] where she died of a broken heart. And *Liath* said:—"Although I have not obtained the maiden, it is my name she shall bear". That is *Bri Leith*, that is *Bri*, who was owned by *Liath*; and hence the name of the hill at which she died; and which had previously been called *Sidh Midir*, or *Midir*'s fairy mansion.[400]

The value of this passage for our present purpose lies in the statement, that the showers of offensive missiles hurled by the battlement warders of *Midir*'s court were as thick as *Teilinn*, or humming wild bees, upon a fine summer's day.

also in a poem about Marbhan and Guaire; The next and second reference to the *Teillinn* is found in an ancient, and I believe well-authenticated poem, which is ascribed to a royal recluse of Connacht, who flourished about the year 640, and whose historic name was *Marbhan*, or the dead. This *Marbhan* was brother to *Guaire* the hospitable, king of Connacht, who died in the year 662. In the prime of life he abandoned his brother's court, and his share of his father's inheritance, and retired to the deep shades of a valley at a considerable distance, called *Glenn an Scail*, there, in seclusion and solitude, to devote his life to the service of God and the contemplation of heavenly things. After some time his brother, king *Guaire*, paid a visit to the recluse, and endeavoured to induce him to leave his solitude and return once more to the abode of man and the comforts of his own hospitable court. On this occasion the king addressed his brother in verse, and the brother answered in the same way. Of king *Guaire*'s poem I have found but two stanzas—the first and the last; but of *Marbhan*'s answer I have got thirty-one stanzas, which, I believe, formed the entire of it. Thus speaks king *Guaire*:—

"O *Marbhan!* thou recluse,
Why sleepest thou not upon a bed?
Thou sleepest oftener abroad,
With uneasy head in the middle of a fir-tree".[401]

(400) [original:—Bri Leith, canas ro hainmniged .i.n. Liath mac Celtchair Chualand, ise mac flatho caime boi hi sidaib Erenn. Cura carastar side Bri mBruach mBric ingen Midir mor glondaig mic Indui Echtaig. Do chodh dno Bri ocus a hingenraid co ferta na ningen i taeb Temrach. Luid Liath lin a macraid co mboi i taulach na hiarmaicris. Conseinnset comrac nibad nesam fria taibleoraib side Midir; ar ba lir bech teilleoin illo ainnle imsreagra a nuibraice co ra bris leo Cochlán, gilla Leith, co narad. Imsoi in ingen co Bri Léith cora bris a cride inte. Ocus atbert Liath: cen cotoasa in ingen, ise mo ainm-si bies fuirri, i. Bri Léith. .i. Bri, is la Liath.—H. 3. 3. folio 70. b. T.C.D.; *Book of Lecan*, f. 261. a. a.]

(401) [original:—
.i. Marban
A Marbain! a dithrubaig,
cid na cotla for colcaig?
Ba menci duit feis amuig,
cenn doroig for lar ochtgaig.]

To this friendly interrogation, the recluse answers, in thirty-one stanzas, beginning:— XXXVI.

"I shall not sleep upon a bed,
Even though offered safety there;
There are numbers abroad
Who would rise up to censure me!"[402]

Marbhan then goes on to say that of the friends of their youth and schoolfellows, a few only now remain; and he describes how, when he was abandoning the world, he distributed his little personal property among them. He then, in glowing terms, describes his little hermitage in the wood, and the natural beauties of water, shrub, tree, beast, and insect, that surround him and yield him food and consolation of body and mind. Among his musicians he enumerates the redbreast, the cuckoo, and the *Ciarann*, or beautiful large mottled wild bee, of which he says:—

"Dusky *Telinns*, round-bodied buzzers,
A gentle chorus;
The cackle of the wild-geese at approach of November,
The hoarse note of the merle-hen".[403]

The next and third reference to the term *Teillinn* that I have met with is much later. It is found in a poem written by Eugene *O'Donnghaile*, or *O'Donnelly*, who flourished so late as about the year 1680. This poem, as stated in a former lecture,[404] was written in praise of and bidding welcome to a harper whose Christian name was *Feidhlimy*. The poet's praises were bestowed negatively, by showing the imperfections which the subject of his praise has not; and after having disposed of the performance, he then turns to the instrument, with which he deals in the same way, as will be seen from the following, which is the ninth stanza:— and in one by O'Donnelly about 1680.

"It is not you that has the perverse harp,
Which makes the clattering noise upon the strings;
It is not it that has a confused tone
Like a *Teillinn* buzzing in the summer heat".[405]

Now, from these three instances of the word *Teillinn* we can plainly see that it is applied to the humming of bees, and,

(402) [original:—
Ni con cotluim for colcaig,
ge betheur com imslanud;
atait soċaiḋi amoig
atraig hoc imimradud.]

(403) [original:—
Tellinn ciarainn, certain cruinde,
cronan semh;
gigrainn caḋoin gair re samain,
seinm gairú ceir.]

(404) [See Lect. XXXV., *ante*, vol. ii., p. 329.]

(405) [original:—
Ni hagad ata an clairseċ crosda,
do gniḋ an brosgur ar teadaiḃ;
ni hinnte ata an guṫ boḋar
mar teilleann alaḃairt a neiḃ-
ioll.]

XXXVI.

The word *Teillin* applied to the humming of bees;

as in the last instance, to the humming bee itself, buzzing in the summer heat. It is strange that this word, which was known so late as 1680, has not found its way into any of our more ancient glossaries, or any of the several Irish lexicons of the last hundred and fifty years; neither is it, as far as I know, remembered in the spoken language in any part of the country. Not so, however, in the Highlands of Scotland. Here the word is still preserved in its original signification, and almost in its original orthography, the only modification being the substitution of the letter "S" for the initial letter T, and such details as must have arisen in consequence of the word having been taken from the spoken pronunciation, and not from any ancient written source. Shaw, the father of Scottish lexicographers, and who printed his work in 1780, gives the word as "*Seilloin*, a bee, humble bee". But this is the genitive form of the word, and, with the exception of the initial letter *S*, agrees exactly with the form in the *Dinnseanchas* of *Bri Leith*, where the words are written *Beich Teilleoin*, or humming bees. The Highland Society's Dictionary gives *Seillean dubh*, or black *Seillean*, as the equivalent for the bumble or humble bee; and this also, with the exception of the initial letter, agrees with the dusky *Teillinns* of *Marbhan* the hermit's poem.

it has become obsolete in Ireland, but not in Scotland;

occurs in the Highland Society's Dictionary as *Seillean*.

What, after all, if the Welsh term *Telyn* were at one time, then, but a name of contempt for a powerless harp or some other musical instrument? As for its being a transition form of the classic word Chelys, a tortoise shell, I have the authority of my learned friend [the late] Dr. Siegfried, to say that the transition of *ch* to *t* is unheard of between the Welsh and Greek or Latin languages.

Telyn could not be a modification of the Greek Chelys.

I shall not dwell farther on the words *Telyn* and *Cruth*, as applied by the Welsh to their musical instruments; but, as some friends of mine are inclined to think that it is the fiddle that really represents the ancient *Cruit* both of Ireland and Wales, I may direct attention only to the extracts from the old poem on the fair of *Carman*, in which *Cruits*, Timpans, and Fiddles, are enumerated:

Some think the fiddle represents the ancient *Cruit*;

the poem on the fair of *Carman* proves this to be erroneous.

"These are its peculiar privileges:
Trumpets, *Cruits*, open-mouthed horns,
Cuiseachs, timpanists without tiring,
Poets and poetasters,

. . . . .

"Pipes, fiddles, shackle men,
Bonemen and tube-players,

XXXVI.

A host of quill-men and of ornamental style-men,
Of roarers and of loud bellowers".[406]

Of the *Timpan*;

The twentieth and last instrument of music on my list is the *Timpan*, of which, although I have said much already, I have yet to say a little more here, so far as to quote some of the instances in which I have met it in the old books. The first reference to the *Timpan* that I shall produce is an attempt at the derivation, or rather analysis, of the name, taken from *Cormac's* Glossary, compiled about the year 900:—" *Timpan*, i. e. from *tim*, soft, i. e. the sally tree, and *bán*, i. e. bronze; of which (two) materials it is made, or, as it were, *Simpan*, from symphonia, sweetness".[407]

Cormac's derivation of this word

gives us the materials of which it was made;

With the speculations involved in this etymology we have little to do at present; but, the statement of the instrument being of sally-wood, and bronze or brass (as it may be supposed, the frame of wood, and the strings of brass), is of some value, as coming from an authority so old as *Cormac*.

the *Timpan* mentioned in an ancient paraphrase of Exodus;

The next place in which I meet the word *Timpan* is in the free translation of the Book of *Exodus* in the Great Book of *Dun Doighre*, where we are told, that after the Israelites had come up from the Red Sea, they assembled, " the men at the one side of Moses and Aaron, and the assembly of the women around Mirian; that is, Mirian the daughter of Amram and sister of Moses, and she playing a *Timpan*": " So Mary the prophetess, the sister of Aaron, took a timbrel in her hand, and all the women went forth after her with timbrels and with dances".[408] Now this passage agrees with *Exodus*, chap. xv., verse 20, where the instrument which Mirian played is called a timbrel, which at the present day would mean a tambourine or some such instrument, though it is certain that such was not the instrument which the Irish translator had in view.

also in the tale of the Battle of *Magh Lena*;

The word *Timpan* next occurs in the ancient historic tale of the Battle of *Magh Lena* (page 50), where *Eoghan Mór*, king

(406) [The greater part of this poem, according to the two versions of it found in the Books of Ballymote and Leinster, has been already given in Lect. ii., vol. i., p. 41 *et seq.* The two stanzas given here are from the version in the Book of Leinster, and differ somewhat from those given in Lect. ii. This poem is of such very great importance in connection with the manners and customs of the ancient Irish, that the Editor thinks it desirable to publish the whole of the original text, with a complete translation, in Appen. III.]

(407) [original:—Timpán, .i. tim, .i. bocc, .i. sail, acas ban, .i. uma bis-innti, vel quasi Simpan a symphonio, i.e. from the melodiousness.]

(408) [original:—Na fir don dara leth do Moyse ocus imm Aron, ocus oirecht namban imm Muire; .i. Muire ingen Amraim siuir do Moyse iside, ocus si oc sennaimm Timpain, ocus occantain ċiuil ar aen fri cach ic molad mac de.—*Leabhar Breacc*, fol. 49. b. b. line 41.]

XXXVI. of Munster in the second century, on his return from Spain to the Island of *Cregraidhe* in Berehaven, is received by the lady *Eadan*, whom he addresses in the following words:

"That is well, O high-minded *Eadan!*
Who ownest the battle-victorious bark;
O glory of women, dost thou still survive
In this island, where we were once before?"

To this address *Eadan* answers:

"Yes; the splendid chess-board still is here,
On which we played on the noble couch;
The pleasant sunny chamber also remains,
Where the sweet-stringed *Timpan* was heard".[409]

This stanza puts the character of the timpan beyond all question.

and in that of the Exile of the sons of Duil Dermaid;

So again, in another ancient tale, that of the *Loinges Mac Duil Dermaid*, or the exile of the sons of *Duil Dermaid*, which is referred to the period of the Incarnation, in which we are given an account of how the great Ulster champion *Cuchulaind* had been placed under the obligation to discover the retreat of these exiles. In this tale *Cuchulaind* sets out upon the sea, and sails to what appears to be the Western Islands of Scotland, and after describing his arrival at the first island, the tale says that "*Cuchulaind* landed upon the island, and came to a house with pillars of *Findruine*, or white bronze, in which he saw three times fifty couches, with a chessboard (*Fidchell*), a draught-board (*Brandub*), and a *Timpan* hung up over each of them".[410] But here the particular nature of the *Timpan* is not described.

another reference in the Dialogue of the Ancient Men;

Another curious reference to a splendid *Timpan* is found in the old romantic tract so often referred to in these lectures, the *Agallamh na Seanorach*, or Dialogue of the Ancient Men.

According to this piece, once that *Cailte* (one of the personages called ancient men) was sojourning with the king of Munster near Cashel in Tipperary, among many questions which the king asked the old man was, the reason why a certain ancient earthen fort which stood in their neighbourhood was called *Lis an Bhanntrachta*, or the Mansion of the Ladies. *Cailte* answered that this old mansion had been selected by his former friend and commander, *Find Mac Cumhaill*, as a place for the manufacture and embroidery of cloth for the special use of himself and his *Fianna* or warriors, and that the women there had a source of pleasure and delight beyond any other known com-

(409) [See Battle of *Magh Leana*, published by the Celtic Society, 1855, p. 50.]

(410) [original:—Gabais Cuċulainn isin insi, agas isin dun, connaccai a tech cona uaitnib findruinib and, cosaccai tri coecait imdae isin tig, fidchell, ocus brandub, ocus Timpan huas caċ imdai—H. 2. 16. col. 762, mid.]

pany of ladies, namely, a *Timpan*, which was played by the three daughters of the king of *Ui Ceinselaigh* (a district in the present county of Wexford), whose names were *Finnchas* (or the Crisp-Fair-Haired), and *Fionnbruinne* (or the Fair-Breasted) and *Finn-Inghean* (or the Fair-Daughter). "And this", continues *Cailte*, "was the description of that *Timpan*. It had its *Lethrind* (or treble-strings) of silver, and its pins (or keys) of gold, and its (bass) strings of *Findruine* (or white bronze); and wounded champions and warriors, however sore their sufferings, [and women in labour] would sleep under the influence of the plaintive fairy music which those princesses used to play for the maidens. And this", continues *Cailte*, "was the reason this old fort had been called *Lis-an-Bhanntrachta* (or the Mansion of the Ladies)".[411]

This is a curious passage, as being the only practical allusion I have ever met to the word *Lethrind*, which strictly signifies one half the musical strings; a term which clearly enough points to harmony, or the use of two different sets of strings one played with another. You will remember that this word *Lethrind* is one of the guessed explanations quoted in a former lecture as to the signification of the word *Ceis*. It is curious, too, that in Walshe's Latin-Irish Dictionary, compiled about 1690 (?) the author, at the word musical, puts the word *Rind* for melodia. Now, *Lethrind* would mean half this melodia; that is, I suppose, the treble of the bass played. In the instance of the *Timpan*, described by *Cailte*, it must have signified the treble part.

the passage in the latter the only one which explains *Lethrind*.

Lethrind in this passage signified the treble part;

Another short but curious description of a *Timpan*, is found in the ancient tale of the *Forbais*, or siege of *Dromdamhghaire*, now *Cnoc Luinge* or Knocklong, in the south-east corner of the county of Limerick. As I have already given the history of this tale, in connection with Druids and druidism,[412] I may at once proceed to that part of the tale connected with my present subject. At the opening of the tale, it is stated that *Cormac* was accustomed to shut himself up in a sacred chamber for the purpose of studying the laws and the wisest mode of administering them. He had, it seems, often heard his people

another description of the *Timpan* given in the "siege of *Dromdamhghaire*".

(411) [original:—Timpan, becc acu cona leiṫrind airgit, ocus cona deilgib oir buiḋi [ocus cona tedaib findruine (R.I.A. MSS., No 23. L. 22. p. 397) curaḋ acas caṫmileaḋ imreannoiḃ (*Ibid.*)] ocus mna re gur lamnad ro co codailfais fri sin ceol sireċtaċ siḋe do ṁeis in triur ingen sin don banntraċt.—Book of Lismore, f. 233. b. a

The following is the metrical version of this passage:—

Timpan bec ro boi ac na mnaib,
cona leichrind airgid bain,
con deilgib oir buiḋi,
cona tedaib findruine.

A small *Timpan* the women had,
With its *Lethriad* of bright silver,
With its pins of yellow gold,
With its strings of *Findruine*.

—*Ibid.* f. 233. b. b., and R.I.A. MSS., No. 23. L. 22. pp. 396, 397.]

(412) See Lec. X., *ante*, vol. i., p. 212.

XXXVI. speak of *Aengus Mac Inog*, the famous *Tuath Dé Danann* chief, and his palace of *Brugh-na-Boinne* (or palace of the Boyne, near Slane); and he had heard these stories with incredulity until one day that he happened to delay in his hall of judgment after all his attendants had gone away; looking around him, he perceived a comely youth at the far end of the hall, with whose person he was unacquainted, but whom he instinctively recognized at once as that of the very famous *Aengus*, of whose existence he had been so incredulous. To make sure, he asked the youth if he were really *Aengus*, and the youth answered that he was. So *Cormac* put some questions to him as to the destinies of his future, and after he had obtained a somewhat favourable answer, the youth disappeared. On *Cormac*'s return to his nobles, he described his interview with the seer in a poem of six quatrains; and it is from this poem that I have to quote the following, which are the first four verses of it:—

"There appeared to me, upon the brow of *Temair*
  A splendid youth of noble mien;
  More beautiful than all beauty was his form,
  And his dress ornamented with gold.
"He held a silver *Timpan* in his hand;
  Of red gold were the strings of that *Timpan;*
  Sweeter than all music under heaven
  Were the sounds of the strings of that *Timpan.*
"A wand with melody of music sweet an hundred fold;
  Over it [the *Timpan*] were two birds;
  And the birds, no silly mode,
  Used to be playing upon it.
"He sat beside me in pleasant fashion;
  He played for me his delicious sweet music;
  He prophesied most powerfully then,
  That which was intoxication to my mind".[413]

The Timpan was a stringed instrument played with a bow;

Now, although this account of king *Cormac*'s interview with the fairy chief of the *Tuatha-Dé-Danann* be the mere invention of the imagination, still the poem affords another proof that the *Timpan* was a stringed instrument; and, what is much more important to our purpose, it shows that it was an instrument

[413] [original:—

Tarfas dáṁ, ar bru Temraċ
  oclaċ aluinn ildealbaċ;
  caeime ina gaċ caem a cruth,
  cimċugaċ oir na edguċ.
Timpan airgit ana laiṁ;
  fa hor derg teta an timpain;
  binne ina gaċ ceol fo niṁ
  foghur tet a timpain sin.
Fleas gucairċe .c. ceol cain;
  uasa ċinn foda enaib;
  ocus na heoin, nir ṁod mer,
  bitis oca airfeited.
Do suiḋ acum etaim ngrinn;
  setrainn dom iceol caem binn;
  tarraiḋ co faithrenn iarsoin,
  ba hed medrad dom menmoin.—
Book of Lismore, O'Curry's copy, R.I.A., f. 169, a. b.]

played on with a wand and hair, words that plainly enough describe a fiddle-bow. So that at length we may consider that we have arrived at a clear determination of the hitherto undecided difference between the *Cruit*, or harp, and the *Timpan*, as well as of the latter being a stringed instrument, and not a drum, such as the name would imply. And this description will go far also to sustain our former view of the misnomers of the Welsh *Telyn* and *Cruth*, as there can now be little doubt that our *Cruit* is their *Telyn*, and our *Timpan* their *Cruth*. XXXVI.

One short reference more to the character of the *Timpan;* and the difference between that instrument and the *Cruit* or harp, and I have done with the subject. In a vellum MS. in the library of Trinity College, Dublin, chiefly occupied with Brehon Laws, there occurs the following curious note, standing by itself, and unconnected with any other subject: this is fully confirmed by a passage from a vellum MS;

"There are three qualities that give distinction to a *Cruit* (or harp), namely, the Crying Mode, the Laughing Mode, and the Sleeping Mode. The Timpanist has a wand, and hair, and doubling (or repetition). The harper has exclusive harping at this day against these. The Timpanist has exclusive timpaning (or *Timpan* playing) at this day against these".[414]

This curious, but to me somewhat obscure note, although not explicit enough to enable us to comprehend the meaning of the word doubling or repetition, is sufficiently clear on two points that are of importance to our discussion. First, it shows distinctly that the *Cruit* was of a very different and of a higher order than the *Timpan;* for that the three distinguishing and ennobling species of music, or melody, those which produced on the hearers the effect of crying, laughing, and sleeping, were peculiar to the *Cruit* only, and above the power of the *Timpan*. And secondly, it proves beyond all controversy that the *Timpan*, like that described by king *Cormac*, was played with a wand and hair, or, in other words, with a bow. It goes farther, indeed, than this, for we can plainly gather from it, this very curious fact, that, in the more ancient times the *Cruitire*, or harpist, and the *Timpanach*, or timpanist, did not of necessity form two distinct classes of performers, but that both the harp and the *Timpan* were common to the same performer. And this will at once account for the hitherto unexplained reason, that we so often find in the ancient Gaedhelic writings the same performer spoken of as a choice harpist and a choice timpanist. which also shows that the harper and timpanist were not necessarily distinct professions;

(414) [original:—Treiḋe nemtigther cruit, goltraiges, gentraiges, suantraiges. Ḟlescaċ acus emnad acus caircedh acon timpanaċ, imarcraig cruitireċt acon cruitire indiu na n-aguidsin. Imarcraig timpanaċta acon timpanuig indiu na nagaiḋ sin.—H. 3. 18. f. 87.]

XXXVI.

this MS. was compiled by Edmund O'Deórain near St. Senan's lake;

The MS. in which this note is found, was transcribed on the brink of *Loch Senain*, or St. *Senan*'s lake, in the year 1509, by Edmund *O'Deórain*. This lake had its name from the circumstance of St. *Senan*, the founder of the churches and round tower of Scattery Island (*Inis Cathargh*), near Kilrush, in the lower Shannon, having been born there about the year 540. This lake is well known to me. It lies about five miles to the east of the town of Kilrush in the county of Clare; and the ruins of an ancient church and oratory still mark the spot on which St. *Senan* was born; they are situated on the north side of the lake, near the east end. This book, then, having been compiled in the year 1509, the note on the harp and *Timpan* must have been copied from an older book, or written by the scribe himself, for the first time, that year. In either case it is plain that at this time, or possibly long before, the playing on the harp and on the *Timpan* had become distinct professions, notwithstanding that, as a matter of course, any person might play both instruments, though the professor but of one. From many sources we have authority to believe that the *Timpan* came down concurrently with the harp to the close of the seventeenth century; but what became of it then, or whether it merged into our present fiddle, I am quite at a loss to know. We find the harp, *Timpan*, and fiddle, mentioned in the ancient poem on the fair of Carman as already mentioned; and we have them again mentioned in Eugene O'Donnelly's poems, about the year 1680; but from that time down, I am not certain of having met with any reference whatsoever to the *Timpan*.

the passage was copied into it or first written in 1509; the same person may have played the harp and Timpan, but there were two distinct professions.

The Timpan came down to the 17th century.

Important passage from Brehon Law respecting the Timpanist;

To the above valuable passage taken from Edmund *O'Deórain*'s book of 1509, I may be permitted to add one short extract more from an article in the Brehon Laws, which provided as to wounds and injury to the person. The passage is as follows:

"If the top of his finger, from the root of the nail, or above the black, has been cut off a person, he is entitled to compensation for his [injured body], and a fine [for his outraged] honour, in proportion to the severity of the wound. If the blood has been drawn while cutting his nail off, he is entitled to the fine for blood-shedding for it. If it be from the black [circle] out that his nail has been taken off him, he is entitled to the same fine as for a white [or bloodless] blow; and if he be a Timpanist, then there is a quill [or feather] nail for him besides, by way of restitution".[418]

(418) [original:—Ma benad barr a meoir, ó bun na hingne, no ó thá a duban suas de, corpdire agas enechlann fo truma na cnedhi. No ma forcradh fuiliugad air ac buain a ingin de, is eiric fuiligthe do ann.

XXXVI.

This last reference to the *Timpan* so plainly implies its character, that nothing more need be said upon the subject. A question, however, for the first time arises out of the above extract from the Brehon Laws, and it is this: was the quill really used as a substitute for the bow, or, as we have it in this law, was it used as a substitute for the nail of the finger, or for the thumb, perhaps? It is not easy to determine this question with certainty: but it may easily be conceived as affording an explanation of how the two extra strings of the instrument now called *Cruit* by the Welsh were played. We may imagine the *Timpan* in fact to have been a kind of fiddle, played with a bow, but with two additional deeper strings, struck with the thumb or thumb-nail, so that if that nail were injured, it would be necessary to supply it with an artificial one.

It would appear from this that in addition to the bow the deeper strings were struck with the nail.

It is remarkable too, as just mentioned above, how constantly we find the *Cruit* and the *Timpan* accompanying each other, and that this is no modern confusion of the one with the other may be seen from a passage of the *Tochmarc Emire*, or courtship of the lady *Emer*, already referred to. The passage has reference to the splendour of the palace of the Royal Branch of the kings of Ulster at *Emania*, in the time of king *Conchobhar Mac Nessa*, and is as follows:

Harpers and timpanists are separately mentioned in the *Tochmarc Emire*.

"Great and numerous were the assemblies of that royal house; and of admirable performers, in gymnastics; and in singing; and in playing; for gymnasts contended; and poets sang; and Harpers and Timpanists played there".[416]

And again, in the Brehon Laws, we find that the *Cruit*, or harp, was the only instrument of music, the chief performer, or *Ollamh*, of which was recognized by the law as of the same grade as the best of the three classes of the gentry, or *Bó-Airech* class, so as to be entitled to four cows as his *Enechland*, or honour-price: that is, so as to be entitled, in case of personal injury or insult, to four cows for the insult to his wounded honour, in addition to whatever the fine and penalty for the actual injury may have been. It was only the chief or *Ollamh Cruitire*, or harpist, that was entitled to this distinction; and he was so entitled whether he was the state musician of a chief or king or not. The chief, or *Ollamh*-Timpanist, when he happened to be the chief musician of a chief or king, was indeed entitled to the

The harper alone always considered of the rank of *Bó Airech*;

the timpanist only when chief timpanist of a king.

mas ó duḃan suas ro benad de a ingu, eiric banḃéime ann; acus ingu ite don timpánaċ ar son aithgena nas de do benaḋ.—E. 3. 5. p. 41. col. 2.

(416) [original:—Ḃoi mar do immad ...euċ turcomraicc is an rigteċ; ocus ...e airfedaib adamraib arclis de; ocus arfendtee; ocus arcante ann; cdon arclistc errid; arcantis filid; arfendis cruitire ocus timpanoic.—O'C.'s copy from Egerton MS. 5280. f. 17. Brit. Mus., p. 43; H. 2. 18. f. 78.]

xxvi.

same *Enechland*, or honour-price, as the chief *Cruitire* or harper; but not otherwise.

tive r of and an rated legend the B. smore.

Of the relative power and compass of the *Timpan* and *Cruit* we have also a curious instance in the Book of Lismore, in that tract so often quoted in these lectures, the *Agallamh na-Seanorach*, or Dialogue of the Old Men. In this tract we are told that *Cailte*, the cousin and one of the chief captains under *Find Mac Cumhaill*, was sojourning at the fort of *Ilbhreac*, a *Tuath Dé Danann* at *Eas Ruaidh* (now the Falls of Ballyshannon, in the county Donegal). The time of *Cailte*'s visit was at the approach of November Eve; and when that night, so portentous in our fairy mythology, approached, the noble lord of the mansion, with his household and retainers, exhibited considerable uneasiness and alarm. On *Cailte* inquiring the cause of this, he was told that, on every November Eve, three large birds of a black colour came to the lawn of the mansion, and killed one or more of the youths amusing themselves there; and they were then expecting their visit. Accordingly, the night preceding the fatal eve was spent in council by the court of *Ilbhreas*, and in the morning they all went out upon the lawn to await the coming of the birds. Here they arranged themselves in groups, while the youths of the mansion commenced to play at the national game of hurling; and the story goes on:—"The *Tuatha Dé Danann* came to see the hurling; and there was brought to them a chess (*Fitceall*) for every six of them; and draughts (*Bronnaib*) for every five; and a *Timpan* for every ten; and a *Cruit* for every hundred; and a vigorous, accomplished tube-player (*Cuislennach*) for every nine".[117]

According to the scale of value or power suggested in this account, it will be seen that the *Cruit* was considered to have ten times that of the *Timpan*, or, in other words, that one *Cruit* was deemed equal to ten *Timpans*. There may be some exaggeration in the figures; but there can be no doubt of the very superior place which the *Cruit* held above the *Timpan* in the estimation of the original writer, as well as in that of all subsequent transcribers of the story.

So far I have, not without much labour, and I fear at tedious length, endeavoured to gather together, from all the sources available to me, such scattered and even minute references to all the ancient Irish instruments of music as would enable the reader to form some definite idea of their respective characters

[117] [original:—Ocus do eirgidor Tuatha Dé Danann arabnair na h-imana; ocus tugad fitceall gacha seisir doib; ocus brannaib gacha cuicir; ocus timpan gacha deichenbair; ocus cruit gacha .c.; ocus cuislenna feigi forbertaca gacha nonbair.—Book of Lismore, fol. 237. b. a.]

and identity. I shall now, in as few words as I can, proceed to give some account of the professional names of the performers on these instruments, and then (in the next lecture) a few of the ancient names of vocal and instrumental music, and, in the same way that I have taken the order of the instruments themselves, that is, alphabetically, so shall I proceed with the present list.

XXXVI. Professional names of musical performers

The first name on my list is *Buinnire*, or that of the musician who performed on the *Buinne*, which was some sort of tube, whether of the flute or fife or of the clarionet kind, as I have already mentioned. In the plan of the *Teach Midhchuarta*, or great Banqueting Hall of Tara, published in Dr. Petre's History and Antiquities of Tara, the *Buinnire* is assigned a place in the same compartment as the *Cornair*, or horn-blower.

the *Buinnire*;

The second name on my list is *Cnaimh-fhear*, a word which literally signifies a bone-man, though he is mentioned in the list of musical instruments and performers given in the ancient poem on the ancient fair of *Carman*,[418] already so frequently mentioned. What the instrument made of bone was upon which this performer played, I am not able to say; possibly some sort of castanets. We can only guess; for, unfortunately, our national museum at the Royal Irish Academy does not furnish us with any ancient specimen of such instruments.

the *Cnaimh-fhear*;

The third performer in alphabetical order is the *Cornair*, or great horn-blower. He is set down in the Brehon Laws among the meaner class of artists, and not entitled to price of honour, or any recognition of dignity above a mechanic. The *Cornaire*, as has just been shown above, has his place with the *Buinnire* in the great Banqueting Hall of Tara. The *Cornaire* is mentioned in the Progress of *Fraech*, the son of *Fidad*, in his visit to *Cruachan*, the royal palace of Connacht, to court the princess *Findabar*, as described at length in a former lecture;[419] and he is also mentioned in the Progress of *Mainé*, the brother of the same princess, in his visit to the residence of *Gerg* of *Glenngerg* in Ulster, to court the lady *Ferb*, that chieftain's daughter.[420]

the *Cornair*;

The fourth on my list is the *Cruitire* or harper. He is also mentioned in the two last-mentioned tales. He is assigned a special place in the Banqueting Hall of Tara, and accompanied by the *Timpanach*, or *Timpan* player. The *Cruitire* has a special place in the elaborate description of the state feast in the *Brui-*

the *Cruitire*;

(418) [Book of Leinster, fol. 152. And see Lect. ii., *ante*., vol i. p. 46.]
(419) [See Lect. xxx., *ante*, vol. ii. p. 219; also Lect. xxxiv., vol. ii. p. 307.]
(420) [See Lect. xxxiv., *ante*, vol. ii p. 307.]

XXXVI. *ghean Da-Derga*, where, as we have seen in a former lecture,[421] they formed a group of nine performers.

the *Cuislennach*; The fifth, is the *Cuislennach*, who played the *Cuislenna Ciuil*, or musical tubes, whatever they were. These performers have a distinct compartment assigned them in the accounts of the Banqueting Hall of Tara and the *Bruigheann Da Derga*. They are also grouped with the *Cruitire* and the *Timpanach*, in playing *Congal Claen*, the prince of Ulster, to sleep on the eve of the battle of *Magh Rath*.[422] Both the *Cuisleannach* and the *Cornair* are likewise mentioned in the lament of the lady *Deirdre* for the sons of *Uisnech*, printed in the edition of that very ancient tale contributed by me to the Atlantis.[423]

the *Feddnach*; The next, or sixth performer in alphabetical order is the *Feddnach* or performer on the *Fedan*, which was a shrill pipe or whistle. *Fead* is still the common name for a whistle with the mouth; and *Feadan* is still the name for any thin tube or pipe. I have met only one reference to this performer, and that among the lower class of musicians mentioned in the Brehon Laws, as attending great fairs and assemblies.

the *Fer-cengail*; The seventh performer is the *Fer-cengail*, a word which literally means a man of ties, bonds, or bindings: what this name is really intended to signify, as indicative of the man's profession, or whether he was strictly a musician of any kind at all, I am at a loss to know. I find the name mentioned (and in the plural number) only in the old poem on the fair of *Carman*, already referred to, among the performers at that assembly.

the *Graice*; The eighth class of performers are the *Graice* (literally croakers), who are otherwise called *Coirne*, or horn players, and who, as already described, produced from some description of horns, croaking sounds described as like those of ravens; probably of the same use in concerted music as those of the modern bassoon. They are mentioned in the Brehon Law as persons who were not entitled to any legal recognition of their profession.

the *Pipaire*; The ninth performer on my list is the *Pipaire*, or piper, who is mentioned in the Brehon Laws among the lower class of artists, ranking with the mechanics. The piper and fiddler are both referred to by implication in the old poem on the fair of *Carman*, where pipes and fiddles are enumerated among the musical instruments. *Ergolan* and *Scalfartach* are names for a piper preserved in some of our latter-day glossaries; but, as both words imply a loud noise, they must apply to that species of

(421) [See Lect. XXV., *ante*, vol. ii., p. 146.]

(422) See the ancient historic tale of the Battle of Magh Rath, published by Irish Archaeological Society, p. 168.

(423) No. VI., p. 410.

pipes which we know at present as the Highland Pipes of Scotland. XXXVII.

The tenth performer on my list is the *Stocaire*, that is, the performer on the *Stoc*, or short curved horn or speaking trumpet; the ancient Buccina, of which so much has already been said in a previous lecture. the *Stocaire*;

The eleventh performer on the list is the *Sturganaidhe*, that is, the performer on the *Sturgan*, or Lituus of the ancients; regarding which the reader is referred to the passage already quoted from the Rev. Dr. Keating's Three Shafts of Death. the *Sturganaidhe*;

The twelfth and last on my list is the *Timpanach*, or *Timpan*-player, of whose instrument so much has been said already. the *Timpanach*.

LECTURE XXXVII.

[Delivered 10th July, 1862.]

(IX.) Of Music and Musical Instruments (continued). The particular kinds of music mentioned in ancient manuscripts: the *Aidbsi*; the *Cepóc*; gloss on *Aidbsi* showing that *Cepóc* was only another name for it; the word *Cepóc* used in Ireland also, as shown by the Tale of "*Mac Datho*'s Pig", and in an elegy on *Aithirne* the poet. *Aidbsi* or *Cepóc* a kind of *Cronán* or guttural murmur. The *Certan*, referred to particularly in the *Cain Adamhnain*. The *Cronán*; mentioned in the account of the assembly of *Drom Ceat*; and also in the Adventures of the "Great Bardic Company". The *Crann-Dord*; it consisted of an accompaniment produced by the clashing of spear handles, as shown by a passage in the *Táin Bó Chuailgne*; and in a legend from the Book of Lismore in which the term occurs. Other musical terms used in this tale: the *Dordán*; the *Fodord*; the *Abran*; the *Fead*; the *Dord Fiansa*; the *Dord*; the *Fiansa*; the *Andord*; the latter word occurs in the Tale of the "Sons of *Uisnech*"; this passage shows that the pagan Gaedhil sang and played in chorus and in concert; though *Dord* and its derivatives imply music, the word *Dordán* was applied to the notes of thrushes. Character of the *Crann-Dord* shown by a passage from the "Dialogue of the Ancient Men"; and by another passage from the same Dialogue in a MS. in the Royal Irish Academy; the *Dord-Fiansa* was therefore a kind of wooden gong accompaniment. The *Duchand*, explained as *Luinneog* or music; *Luinneog* obsolete in Ireland, but used in Scotland for a ditty or chorus; *Duchand* was probably a dirge; *Duan*, a laudation; *Duchand* occurs in *Cormac*'s Glossary explaining *Esnad*; the latter a moaning air or tune in chorus. The *Esnad*. The Three Musical Modes. The *Géim Druadh* or "Druid's Shout", mentioned in the Tale of the Battle of *Almhain*. The *Golghaire Bansidhe*, or wail of the *Bansidhe*, mentioned in the *Táin Bó Fraich*; it probably came down to a late period. The *Gubha*. The *Logairecht* or funeral wail, occurs in *Cormac*'s Glossary at the word *Amrath*; meaning of the latter term. The *Luinneog*. The *Suanghuba*, or sea nymph's song as it is explained in an old glossary. The *Sian* or *Sianan*, applied in the Tale of the Battle of the second *Magh Tuireadh* to the whizzing of a spear; applied to a song in the Tale of the Sons of Uisnech; and also in the wanderings of the priests *Snedgus* and *Mac Riaghla*; it designates soft plaintive music. *Sirectach* applied to slow music; synonymous with *Adbond*; the latter word occurs in the Festology of *Aengus Ceilé Dé*; *Adbond Trirech*, or triple *Adbond*, explained in Michael O'Clery's glossary as the Three Musical Modes; *Trirech* occurs in Zeuss' Grammatica Celtica; *Trirech* was applied to a species of lyric poetry, as is shown by a passage in the Book of Leinster; the term *Trirech* not exclusively applied to the music or quantity of verse, but also to a particular kind of laudatory poem; the stanza in question sings to the air of: "For Ireland I would not tell who she is".

The particular kinds of music mentioned in ancient MS.:

From the names of the musical instruments and of the performers upon them, I shall now pass to such few names of particular kinds of music as I have met with in my readings,—setting them down also in alphabetical order. Before going into this list, I shall only premise, by observing that *Ceól* is the common name for music of all kinds; and *Ceolchairecht* is the verbal form, "a playing"; and that *Abhrann* (compounded of *Abh*, sweet, and *Rann*, a verse) is the name for a song of any measure, sung to a *Foun* or tune.

The *Aidbsi*;

The first species of music, in alphabetical order, is the *Aidbsi*, or great chorus, or vocal concert, such as that sung by the assembled poets of Erinn in honour of *St. Colum Cille*, at the meeting of *Drom Ceat*, in the year 590. This meeting and this music have been amply treated of in a former lecture.

the *Cepóc*;

The second word in order, denoting music, is *Cepóc;* but this was merely a name used by the people of *Alba* (or Scotland) to express the same performance, known amongst us as the *Aidbsi*, just mentioned. For this fact we have the authority of the gloss on a fragment of a beautiful copy of *Dallan Forgaill's* elegy on the death of *St. Colum Cille*, preserved in an ancient vellum MS., lately in the possession of Mr. William Monck Mason of London. This gloss or explanation is upon the word *Aidbsi* itself, and is as follows:—

gloss on *Aidbsi* showing that *Cepóc* was only another name for it;

"*Aidbsi* was the name of the music or *Cronán* which the greater part of the men of Erinn used to perform at this time; and *Cepóc* is its name with the men of Scotland, as the Scottish poet said:—

"It is better to praise the king of *Loch*
By performing our *Cepóc*".[424]

I am not able to say what part of Scotland this district called *Loch* was, for the king of which the poet proposed to raise the great chorus, which was perhaps a funeral song. It is a pity that our Scottish cousins of the Gadelian race have not preserved, as far as we yet know, any really ancient fragments of their early literature, for such a literature they certainly must have had. Even the single piece of which we have here but the two first lines, would be worth volumes of the spurious traditional poems of *Oisin*, to which the very best Gaelic scholars of that country attach such importance. As to the word *Cepóc*, it will be seen from the two following references that the use of it was not confined exclusively to Scotland, but that it was also common to Ireland. In the ancient tale of *Mac Datho's* Pig, described at considerable length in a former lecture,[425] we are told, that *Mac Datho* (whose real name was *Mesraeda*) was a prince of South Leinster, who flourished about the time of the Incar-

the word *Cepóc* used in Ireland also, as shown by the Tale of "*Mac Datho's* Pig";

(424) [original:—Aidbsi ainm in chiúil, no in cronáin do gnidis ur-mhor bfer nErenn in tan sin; ocus Cepóg a ainm ac feraib Alban amail atbert in file Albanach:—
Ferr molad ríg Lóicce
Do denum ar Chepoicce.
-*Amhra Choll. Chille*, Mason, p. 20. a.]

(425) [See Lect. on MS. Materials of Irish History, App. III., n. 49, p. 486.]

XXXVII.

the word *Cepóc* used in Ireland also as shown by the Tale of *Mac Datho's* Pig":

nation. It appears that he had reared a hound whose fame spread all over Erinn. So messengers came from *Ailill* and *Medb*, the king and queen of Connacht, begging from him a present of his hound; and at the same time, other messengers arrived on the same errand from the equally powerful prince *Conchobar Mac Nessa*, king of Ulster. *Mac Datho* saw in this coincidence a chance of being able to involve the two northern provinces in a conflict, or perhaps a war, which must tend to weaken the power of both, and thereby to strengthen that of his own province. Accordingly, he told the messengers of the two kings respectively, that he had already promised the hound to the master of the other, and that he saw no way of getting out of the difficulty but by both kings, with their nobles and choicest warriors, coming to his court at an appointed time to a feast which he would prepare for them, and where he might probably so arrange between them as to extricate himself from the difficulty. The emissaries of the two provincial kings accepted for them this invitation; and at the appointed time both potentates, each attended by a select band of nobles and warriors, arrived at *Mac Datho*'s court, which appears to have been situated in the southern extremity of the present county of Carlow. Their host prepared for them by ostentatiously killing for the occasion his famous pig,[426] and, as he anticipated, the rival parties quarrelled about the cutting up and distribution of this food for heroes. A conflict ensued; blood was spilled in abundance; and at last the men of Connacht retreated northward, whither they were followed by the Ultonians.

The story then tells us that when *Conchobar* arrived in the pursuit at the heath of *Fearbile* (in Westmeath), he came up with *Ferloga*, the charioteer of the king and queen of Connacht, who, it would appear, had deserted his post and concealed himself in the heath; and just as the king of Ulster was passing by, the charioteer started up and sprang into the chariot behind him, clasping his neck with both his hands. "Ransom thy head, O *Conchobar!*" said he. "Thou shalt have thy demand", said *Conchobar*". "It is not great, indeed", said *Ferloga*; "it is only that thou shalt take me along with you to *Emhain Macha* [the palace of *Emania*], and that the young women and girls of Ulster shall sing a *Cepóc* around me every evening, and each of them say: '*Ferloga* is my favourite' ".[427] To these rather fanciful

[426] Some account of this wonderful animal will be found in the edition of the *Battle of Magh Leana*, published by the Celtic Society, page 14, note a.

[427] [original:—Ic teċt iar sraeċ-rad inde siar, is and donarlaic Ferloga, .i. ara Aililla, ocus ro ling isin carpat ar cul Chonchobair co ro gab aċenn dar aiss. Beir buide n-anacuil, a Chonchobair! ar se. Toġmar, ar Conchabar. Ni ba mor, ar Ferloga, .i. mo breiṫ lat do

conditions king *Conchobar* was obliged to submit. The charioteer was brought to *Emania;* and in twelve months' time (the story tells us) he was conveyed over the river Shannon at Athlone, with a present to the king and queen of Connacht of king *Conchobar*'s two favourite steeds with their golden bridles; but we are told nothing more of his relations with the maidens of Ulster.

The third and final reference to the *Cepóc* is, like the last, from an Ulster tale of the same period as the last; and although I have had to give a sketch of the tale incidentally at some length in the second lecture of the present course, still, as this is the place in which it should appear in its proper order of illustration, I shall introduce it again in as few words as possible. and in an elegy on *Aithirne*, the poet.

After the tragical death of the sons of *Uisneach* on the green of *Emania*, through the malignant contrivance of the same king *Conchobar*, and the death for grief of them of the lady *Deirdri* in a year after, king *Conchobar*, we are told, fell into a state of grief and melancholy from which no effort of his courtiers could rouse him. At last it was proposed to search the province for the most beautiful maiden to be found in it, and to bring her to him to be his wife, in place of the unfortunate *Deirdri*. This was done; and a young lady, whose name was *Luain*, was selected and brought in triumph to *Emania*, where she was solemnly espoused by the king, after which happy event he soon forgot his grief and recovered his cheerfulness. It was at this time that *Aithirne* the poet flourished in Ulster: that vindictive poet and satirist who was known as *Aithirne Ailgesach*, or the importunate. He had two sons who were poets also, whose names were *Cuingedach* and *Abhartach;* and when they heard of the king's marriage with the lady *Luain*, they repaired to her to solicit the customary wedding presents. However, when they saw her, they both fell desperately in love with her, and each of them secretly sought her favour. These solicitations the young queen rejected with scorn, whereupon both the father and the sons satirized her so furiously that her face (according to the superstition of the time about the magical power of a poet's incantations) is said to have broken out in blotches, and she was forced to hide herself from public gaze in her father's house, where she soon died of shame and grief. Thereupon the king, furious, instigated the Ulstermen to take vengeance upon *Aithirne;* and they repaired straight way to his residence, where they killed, not only himself, but his two sons and his two daughters, and levelled the house with the ground.

emain Macha, ocur mná oentuma Ulad, ocur a n-ingena macdacht do gabail cepocce cech nona imum.—H. 2. 18. f. 73. b. a.]

XXXVII. The story proceeds to inform us that the other great poets of Ulster felt indignant at this profanation, as an indignity to their order, and that *Amergin* the poet pronounced an oration over the bodies of the slain (couched in the obscure language of the professional bards of the time), condemnatory of the act of the Ultonians, and lamenting the untimely death of *Aithirne*. This oration he afterwards put into the form of a poem of twenty-four lines, of which the following is the first:—

"*Aithirne's* grave, dig ye not here".

It is in this curious poem that the following quatrain occurs, which contains the word *Cepóc*, with which we are at present concerned:—

"I will make a *Cepóc* here,
And I will make his lamentation;
And here I will set up his tombstone;
And here I will make his graceful grave".[428]

From these three examples of the application of the term *Cepóc* we gather that the music for which, in common with *Aidbsi*, it was the name, was not, strictly speaking, reserved for any particular occasion, but that it might be used on occasions of joy, as in the cases of the meeting of *Dromceat* and the charioteer at *Emania;* and in grief, as (I think) in the case of the Scottish poet and the king of *Loch*, and certainly in that of the lament for *Aithirne*. Indeed the only distinction that appears to attach to the *Aidbsi* or *Cepóc* is, that it was a *Cronán* or purring, commenced in the chest or throat, on a low key, and rising gradually to the highest treble. It must, too, to have any effect, have been sung by a multitude; and there cannot be much doubt but the Irish funeral cry, as it is called, of our times is a remnant (though perhaps only a degenerate, uncultivated remnant) of the ancient *Aidbsi* or *Cepóc* of the Gaedhil. Even so late as the seventeenth century, Mr. Nicholas Pierce, the great harper of the county of Kerry, composed, or rather revived, some remarkable funeral lamentations, which came down to my own time, and I dare say are still chaunted in regular parts of bass and treble, by the voices of men and women, in concert, at funerals in the South of Ireland.

Aidbsi or *Cepóc* a kind of *Cronán* or guttural murmur.

The *Certan*; The second species of music in alphabetical order is the *Certan*, which is mentioned in the curious poem of the hermit *Marbhan* on his residence in the wilderness, already described; and it is there spoken of as if it were the sharp chirping of some

(428) [original:—
Do dena cepóc sunna,
Acas do dena aguba;
Acas saigsec sunna a lecc;
Acas do den a caemfert.
—H. 2. 17. p 468, and Book of Ballymote, fol. 142. a b.]

bird or insect. The *Certan* is mentioned also in a treatise on Irish grammar, in a MS. in the library of Trinity College, Dublin, where it is spoken of as a low and weak effusion of the lower class *Cronán*, or purring performances. The *Certan* is, however, somewhat more minutely referred to in the ancient *Cáin Adamhnain*, or law of Saint *Adamnan*. This law was made in the year 700, through the instrumentality or interposition of St. *Adamnan*. The object of this law was to prohibit women from being allowed to appear in fights and battles, and also to free female slaves from the degradation of abject bondage. The history of this curious and characteristic law may be told in a few words. It is said that St. *Adamnan* and his mother were once travelling through the country of *Bregia* in East Meath, near the present town of Drogheda, and that, when they came to the ford of the river (where, it would appear, there was then no bridge), St. *Adamnan* addressed his mother, and spoke in this way: "Get up on my back, my dearest mother", said he. "I shall not", answered she. "Why so? What dost thou mean?" said he. "I shall not, because thou art not a son that cares for his mother", said she. "Who", said he, "is more careful than I? Do I not constantly fasten thee to my back to carry thee everywhere, from one place to another, raising thee up safe from water and from wet? I do not know of any sort of service that a son of man pays to his mother that I do not pay to thee, except alone the *Certan*, which women perform with the long flesh-hooks of men-cooks. And since I do not indeed perform this *Certan*, I shall, at least, make a sweet harp (*Cruit*) to amuse thee, mother; and it shall have a yoke of *Findruine* (or white bronze) upon it";[429] and so on.

referred to particular in the *Cáin Adamhnain* or law of St. *Adamnan*.

Here we have a distinct and circumstantial, though still somewhat obscure, reference to the *Certan*. We cannot see why or how any thing like a flesh-hook should or could be turned into a musical instrument of any kind, and yet the words in the original are quite plain and intelligible. At all events, the instrument, whatever it was, appears to have been one exclusively used by women; though by what means they produced the sounds, and of what nature the sounds of the instrument were, we are entirely at a loss to know.

(429) [original:—Cid on? Cid taisiu? or sesium. Cia as goiriu innasa? Congbaim cris dar fochrus ocat immorchór as cech baili inaraile, ocdutursgabail fri fual acus ferat. Nifetar goire do gnet mac duine dia mathair na denuimsiu deitsiu, acht mad Certan do gniat mna leabar bael baclaich oca. Uair nadronaim in certan sin, do gentar crot binn linnsa deit, hic ut ersitiut; acus iris fionndruine esti.—*Cain Adamnain*, H. 3. 18. f. 291.]

XXXVII.

The Cronán;

The third species of music in alphabetical order is the *Cronán*, or purring, so freely discussed in a former lecture of this course. The word *Cronán* represents a sort of musical sound performed in the throat, for which the word purring is a very inadequate equivalent; though it may, to some extent, express the nature of the sound. The *Cronán* is mentioned in explanation of the term *Aidbsi*, in the account of the laudatory chaunt of the assembly of poets, raised in honour of St. *Colum Cille*, at the meeting of *Drom Ceat*, in the year 590.[430] The term occurs also in the account of the *Imtheacht-na-trom-Daimhe*, or Adventures of the Great Bardic Company, who, under their chief poet *Seanchan*, visited the court of *Guaire*, the hospitable king of Connacht, in the first half of the seventh century, an account amply described in a former lecture. The *Cronánaigh*, or *Cronán* performers are classed with the *Feadanaigh*, or whistle or pipe-players, in the Brehon Law tract on the different degrees of artists, preserved in the Book of Ballymote. The *Cronán* appears to have been a favourite performance with *Find Mac Cumhaill* and his warriors, as will be seen when we come to the term *Dordán*.

mentioned in the account of the Assembly of Drom Ceat; and also in the "Adventures of the Great Bardic Company".

The Crann-Dord;

The fourth species of music, in alphabetical order, is the *Crann-Dord*.

This term is compounded of the two words *Crann*, a tree, and *Dord*, a low humming noise or tune; and from this composition of the name and other circumstances to be mentioned, we may, I think, safely believe that originally the sounds designated by this name were produced by the measured clashing together of wooden poles or spear handles, although the term was sometimes extended to sounds somewhat dissimilar in volume and produced by a different agency. The following passage from the *Táin Bó Chuailgne*, descriptive of the *Dond Chuailgne*, or great brown bull of that territory, will sustain the latter assertion:

It consisted of an accompaniment produced by the clashing of spear handles, as shown by a passage in the Táin Bó Chuailgne;

"It was one of the gifts of the *Dond Chuailgne* that the *Crann-dord* which he performed every evening at coming home to his fastness and his cow-house and his cow-stand, was music and entertainment sufficient for the persons who were at the northern extremity, the southern extremity, and in the centre of the entire cantred of *Cuailgne*".[431]

There can be no doubt but that part of the word which refers to the *Crann* or tree in the compound name, would, in such

[430] See Lecture xxxi., *ante*, p. 245, vol. ii.

[431] [original:—ba do buadaib duindcualnge crandord do gnió cach nóna ic tiachtain ar ammus aliss ocas aléis ocas a machaid, ba leór céoil, ocas airfiti dondfir i tuaiscirt, ocas in-descirt, ocas in ecermedón tricháit chét Chualnge uili in crandord du gnió cach nóna.—*Táin Bó Cuailgne*, H. 2. 18. f. 50 a. a mid.]

a case as this at least, be misapplied in using the word in reference to the measured bellowing of the celebrated bull; and therefore, it may be contended the name must have been derived from the compounding of some other agent with a low murmuring sound. This will, I think, be found clearly established by the following references to the terms *Dord*, *Dordán*, and *Dord-Fiansa*, found chiefly in the ancient Book of Lismore.

legend from the Book of Lismore, in which this term occurs

The story describes how *Cailte*, the cousin, and one of the favourite captains of *Find Mac Cumhaill*, was travelling, when an old man, in the district comprised in the present county of Kerry, attended by a few of his superannuated companions in arms. They came one day to the ancient *Carn* or sepulchral heap of stones of *Letir Duibh*, and sat down for rest and refreshment at the foot of the *Carn*, on the brink of a stream. And whilst resting here, the herdsmen and shepherds of the neighbouring herds and flocks came and sat over *Cailte* on the *Carn*, and began to regale him with music and melody. And *Cailte* was charmed with the music, because, says the story, it was like the *Dord-Fiansa* [that is the murmuring music of *Find* and his warriors]. And he commanded his servant to be silent and to continue his fishing in the stream; and he then composed a poem of which the following quatrains will sufficiently show the character of the sort of music indicated by the terms *Dord*, *Dordán*, *Fodard*, *Fead*, and *Crann-Dord*:—

Other musical terms used in this tale;

"The shepherds of *Dubh*, from *Drom Leis*,
Imitate those who have gone before them;
Sweet music the equal of this
Was the *Dordán* of the three sons of *Dithreabhach*.

"The *Cronán* of *Faelchu* from *Fid Garb*;
The *Fodhord* of *Fland* from the slopes of *Latharn*;
The *Abran* of *Faelan*; the *Fead* of *Laind*;
The notes of the three sons of *Conchaind*.

"*Find* himself, and *Fland*, son of *Echaidh*,
Diarmait, *Raighne*, of the large eyes,
The *Dord-Fiansa* did sweetly sing;
It was sung, too, by *Cailte* of *Collamar*.

"At the fair of *Cruachan*, when of old
We chaunted the *Dord* when going to visit;
Sweet were the notes of the *Fiansa* on the march,
All men were glad to hear it".[432]

(432) [original:—

Aedaire Duiḃ a Druim Láis,
Anaiṫris fuabrait da néis;
Binn céol a macsaṁla sain
Dordan tri meic nDiṫreabaiġ.
Cronán Faolċon a Fid garḃ,
Foḋord Flaind do leirg Laṫarn,
Abrán Faolain; fead Laindi;
Fogur tri meic Conċainde.
. . . . .
Find fein, is Flann mac Eochaċ,
Diarmait, Raigne, rosclethan,

XXXVII.

Here we have a group of words to represent the different kinds of song supposed to have been used by *Find Mac Cumhaill* and his warriors; words intended to distinguish the various modifications of what appears to have been their ordinary, simple, vocal music. First, the *Dordán*, which, from the diminutive termination *an* of the name, seems to imply light murmuring sounds. Second, the *Fodord*, or, literally, under-murmur, implying the deepest and lowest murmuring sounds. Third, the *Abran*, which continues to this day to be the name for a song to any tune or measure. Fourth, the *Fead*, a term which continues to this day to be the name of a whistle with the mouth. Fifth, the *Dord-Fiansa*, a term which I should understand to signify a hunting whoop or wild song. Sixth, the *Dord* itself, which certainly means murmuring sounds in the ordinary measure. Seventh, the *Fiansa*, which, standing by itself, is a term quite new to me, and which I should take to be a species of military chorus or concert, peculiar to the *Fianna*, that is, to *Find Mac Cumhaill* and his warriors. There is another modification of the *Dord*, not introduced by *Cailte* into this curious poem: this is the *Andord*, or literally, Non-*dord* (for the particle *an* is deprivative in sense); that is, it is not exactly a *Dord* or murmur, but something next to it or higher than it. The word occurs in the following stanza from the lament of *Deirdre* in the tragical fate of the Sons of *Uisnech*:—

the Dordán; the Fodord; the Abran; the Fead; the Dord-Fiansa; the Dord; the Fiansa; the Andord; the latter word occurs in the Tale of the "Sons of Uisnech";

["The heavy wave-voice of *Nois*,
It was sweet music for ear to be ever hearing;
Ardan's Cobhlach was good;
And *Ainle's Andord* towards his wild hut".]

The whole of this ancient tale is published in the sixth number of the Atlantis, and the following note is appended to this quatrain at page 410:—"The heavy wave-voice of *Noisi*—that is, the loud bass voice of *Noisi;* the *Cobhlach*, or intermediate tones, or somewhat higher notes of *Dardan* [recté *Ardan*]; and the still higher notes of *Ainle* when returning to their huts in the evening. This is an important passage to show that the pagan or ancient Gaedhil sang and played in chorus and in concert. The words used are taken from the names applied to the different tones of the strings of the ancient harp. The tone of that part of the harp lower than the middle, but not quite so low as the longest and deepest strings, was called *Dord*, which may be translated 'bass'. Below that were the deepest of all

the passage shows that the pagan Gaedhil sang and played in chorus and in concert;

Canait in dord fiansa ar fuin;
Canaid Cailte Callamair.
. . . . . .
Anaonac Cruaċan, robae
Canmais dord ar nuul ar cae;
Ba bind fogur fiansa ar feaċt,
Ba maiċ le cáċ a eisteaċt.
—Book of Lismore, part ii. folio 60. b. b.]

XXXVII.

the strings, and to denote these the particle *fo* was prefixed to the word *Dord; Fo-Dord*, the 'deep bass'. On the other side, the tones of the next shorter strings to the *Dord* or bass strings, above the *Cobhlaighe*, or middle strings, were called *An-Dord*, adding the negative particle *an*, to signify literally '*not bass*'. Their tones answered, perhaps, to the modern tenor".

though *Dord* and its derivatives implies music, the word *Dordán* was applied to the notes of thrushes.

Still, notwithstanding that the word *Dord*, with its various modifications, as far as we are able to determine, invariably implies music or sounds of a deep tone; yet, in the lines already quoted in a former lecture from the poem on the hermitage of *Marbhan*, brother of *Guaire*, king of Connacht, we find that recluse enumerating among the various notes of the sylvan choir which regaled his ears, *Dordán* of the thrushes (*smólcha*), a term which, compared with the more shrill and less voluble notes of other birds, was appropriate enough. As to the real nature and character of the *Crann-Dord*, or tree music, already mentioned, the following two examples will be sufficient to show its character and the proper derivation of the name, although the word itself does not occur in these passages.

Character of the *Crann-Dord* shown by

a passage from the "Dialogue of the Ancient Men";

In the Dialogue of the Ancient Men, so often quoted in these lectures, and in that part of it in which the famous *Cailte*, whilst seated on the hill of Ardpatrick, in the county of Limerick, relates to St. Patrick the story of the courtship and espousals of *Coel O'Nemhain* and the princess *Credhi*, daughter of the king of Munster; and how it was from that hill that *Find* and his warriors went forth to accompany *Coel* on his love mission, as well as to fight the famous battle of *Finntraigh* (the white strand, now Ventry harbour in the bay of Dingle in Kerry), the following is the passage:—"And we determined on the battle on this hill (said *Cailte*), and we went forward over the sides of hills, and rocks, and highlands, until we reached *Loch Cuirrè* in the west of Erinn; and we came to the court [of the princess of Munster], and we performed the *Dord-Fiansa* with the trees (or handles) of our beautiful gold-socketed spears".[433] Now, there can be no doubt but that the music designated here by *Cailte* by the name of *Dord-Fiansa* was equally entitled to be called *Crann-Dord*, which it really was, as having been produced by the *Cranna*, or trees of their spears; and, if there could have been any reason to give it a different name, it must have arisen from the circumstance that the *Cran-Dord* of the

(433) [original:—Ocus do ailsedmar in cath don uladh sin, ocus tancamar romuinn tar taebhaib cnoc, ocus carraċ, ocus tulach, cu Loċ Cuirre amarċar Ereann; ocus tancamar cu dorus in Triḃa, ocus do censam in Dord Fiansa re crannaib ar sleg nurr nor ċrai.—Book of Lismore, f. 206.]

Fianna, or Fenian warriors, differed, perhaps, in its martial quality from that produced by the same agency by other performers and for other purposes.

and by another passage from the same Dialogue in a MS. in the R.I.A.;

Another reference to the *Dord-Fiansa*, as produced by the handles of spears, occurs in a fragment of the same Dialogue of the Ancient Men, preserved in another MS. in the Royal Irish Academy. In this case *Oisin*, the celebrated son of *Find Mac Cumhaill*, relates to St. Patrick how his (*Oisin's*) father, *Find*, fell in love with *Berach Breac*, or the Freckled, the beautiful daughter of *Cas Chuailgne*, king of Ulster. The old bard, in a poem of ninety-four quatrains, relates here how his father marched with his warriors, in full military pomp, to the gates of *Emania*, the palace of the king of Ulster, to demand from that prince the hand of his beautiful daughter, *Berach* the Freckled, in marriage. Having arrived at the palace gates, the bard says, in the sixth stanza of the poem:

"We chaunted with the trees of our spears
A *Dord-Fiansa*, with the voice of our men,
At the gate of green *Emania*,
For the assembly of the Red Branch".[434]

the *Dord-Fiansa* was therefore a kind of wooden gong accompaniment.

If we read this quatrain aright, the Fenian warriors mixed their voices (how high or low does not appear) with the sounds produced by the clashing of their spear-handles; so that, in fact, the *Dord-Fiansa* was a species of wooden gong music, produced by the striking together the handles of a number of brazen spears, so as to accompany or blend with the voices of a chorus of singers.

The *Duchand*; explained as *Luinneog* or music; *Luinneog* obsolete in Ireland, but used in Scotland for a ditty or chorus;

The fifth species of music in alphabetical order is the *Duchand*. This word is explained in O'Davoren's Glossary, as *Luinneog no Ceol*, that is, "*Luinneog*, or music". The word *Luinneog* is now obsolete in Ireland, but it still remains, or did until lately remain, in the Highlands of Scotland, and it is explained in the Highland Society's Dictionary, as a song, a ditty, a chorus; the last of which meanings I believe to be the most correct; but from finding the word *Duthchonna* often in conjunction with the word *Doghraing*, grieving or lamenting, I should be in-

Duchand was probably a dirge;

clined to think that the music of which it was the name, was of a melancholy or dirge-like character. In the description of a festive entertainment in the old tale of the Triumphs of *Conghal Claringneach*, we are told that poems (*Duana*) and *Duchonda* were sung for the company; from which we may perhaps infer

(434) [original:—
Canmaiḋ le crannaiḃ ar ſleġ
Dórd Fianſa, ḟoġar ar ḟear,
Andorar Emna uaine,
Do comṫinol na craeḃruaiḋe.
—MS. R.I.A., H. & Sm., No. $\frac{3}{86}$, p. 251.]

that the poems or *Duana* were laudations of the living heroes, whilst the *Duchonda* were the dirges of the meritorious dead. The word *Duchand* occurs in *Cormac*'s Glossary, in the explanation of the word *Esnad*, as follows: "*Esnad*, i.e. it is not a *Nath*, but a *Duchand;* for *Esnad* was the name of the music which the *Fianna* used to perform around the *fulacht fiansa*".[435] From this explanation it would appear that the word *Esnad* was compounded of *es*, a negative particle, equal to *non* in English, and *nath*, the name of any composition; so that the *Esnad* was a something not a poem or metrical composition, but only a *Duchand*, or mere musical moaning air or tune in chorus; and that this was what the *Fianna*, that is *Find Mac Cumhaill*'s warriors, chaunted around their *fulacht fiansa*, which were the rude cooking pits constructed by the warrior hunters after the day's chase, in which their well-earned meal was cooked, partly by baking between or upon red-hot stones, and partly on wooden roasting spits before their great fires. It was while assembled round these fires, before and during their long repasts, that they used to perform the music alluded to.

XXXVII. *Duan* a laudation; *Duchand* occurs in *Cormac's* Glossary explaining *Esnad;* the latter a moaning air or tune in chorus.

The sixth species of music in alphabetical order is the *Esnad* just described.

The *Esnad*.

The seventh of those enumerated in our ancient writings is the group of three modes so often mentioned already, namely, the *Gentraighe*, or laughing mode; the *Goltraighe*, or crying mode; and the *Suantraighe*, or sleeping mode. Unfortunately, I can add nothing specific upon these styles of musical composition.

The Three Musical Modes.

The next in order is a kind of musical performance called the *Géim Druadh*, or Druid's Shout, referred to in the ancient account of the battle of *Almhain* (now the Hill of Allen, in the county of Kildare), and which I have already given in full in a former Lecture, to which the reader is referred.[436]

The *Géim Druadh*, or "Druids' Shout"; mentioned in the Tale of the "Battle of *Almhain*".

Of this wonderful Druid's Shout, or whoop, or whatever it was, I have never met with any other notice but the one just referred to. But there seems no reason to doubt that the shout of *O'Maighlind*, *Fergal*'s Druid, continued to be popularly known and preserved by the musicians of Ireland down to the year 1391 when the vellum MS.[437] containing the historical tale of the battle of *Almhain* was compiled.

The ninth species of music in alphabetical order is the *Golghaire Bansidhe*, or the Wail of the *Bansidhes* (or fairy-women);

The *Golghaire Bansidhe*, or Wail of the *Bansidhe*;

(435) [original:—ערnaט, .ı. nı nach, acc ır ᴅuchanᴅ; aր ba neրnaᴅ ainm ın ċhıuıl ᴅı gnıċıր na ꝼıanae um an bꝼulachc ꝼıanրae.—Cormac's Gloss., *voc. Esnad.*]

(436) *Ante*, vol. ii. p. 809.

(437) Class H. 2. 16. Trinity College, Dublin.

XXXVII. and like the Druid's shout, to this cry, or wail, I have never met more than one reference, namely, in the story of *Fraech Mac Fidaid*. It will be remembered that this *Fraech* went to the palace of *Cruachan* in Connacht, to demand the hand in marriage of the beautiful princess *Findabar;* and that he was accompanied, among other officers of his train, by the three sons of *Uaithne*, the famous harpers, who gave names to the three musical modes just mentioned above. As I have already given the preliminary story of this tale,[438] I need not repeat it here, but pass at once to that part of the tale itself where the young prince, after being wounded by the river-monster, is taken by his attendants back to the palace to be treated for his wounds. The story tells us that his litter was preceded by his *Cornairidh* (or horn-players); and that so exquisite was their wailing performance that sixty youths of the household of king *Ailill* and queen *Medb* actually died of the melting plaintiveness of their music. They entered the court at last, and *Fraech* was placed in a medicated bath prepared for him by order of the king. He was then taken out and put to bed, upon which (continues the tale) there was heard around the palace of *Cruachan* a loud wailing or *Golghaire*. And immediately there were seen an hundred and fifty women dressed in crimson tunics, and green *Cennbarra*, or head-dresses, and wearing silver brooches on their breasts, in the vicinity of the palace. Some went out to them to learn their history, and to know whom it was that they bewailed. It is *Fraech* the son of *Fidad*, said one of them, that we bewail, the most heroic youth of all the fairy mansions of Erinn. *Fraech* then heard the *Golghaire* (or wail) of the women. Raise me up from this place immediately, said *Fraech* to his people. This is the wail of my mother, and of the women of the (river) *Boind*. He was then carried out, and they collected around him, and took him away from the palace of *Cruachan*. Great, says the story, was the bemoaning in the household of *Ailill* and *Medb* on that night; but they were delighted on the evening of the following day to see him coming back to them accompanied by fifty women, and he perfectly cured, without defacement or blemish. These women were all of the same age, the same features, the same loveliness, the same nobleness, the same splendour, the same symmetry of form, and the countenances of *Bansidhe* (or fairy women) on each of them, so that no one of them could be distinguished from another. Some of the people of the court were nearly suffocated in the pressure of the crowd to see them. They left him then at the door of the

mentioned in the Tale of the *Táin Bó Fraich;*

[438] See Lecture XXX., *ante*, vol. ii. p. 218.

court, and they renewed their wail at departing from him, so that several of the people of the court swooned at its overpowering effect; and it is from this event that the musicians of Erinn have retained the species of music called the *Golghaire*, or wail, of the *Bansidhe* to this day.[439]

This curious tale is preserved in the Book of Leinster, a MS. compiled about the year 1150; and I trust that the length of the extract will be found sufficiently compensated for by the scrap of *Bansidhe* mythology, and the clear evidence which it contains of the wonderful powers of our ancient musicians, as well as of the tender susceptibility of our remote ancestors to the influence of their performances. I am not aware that any trace of these old fairy strains is now to be found among our long neglected native musicians, at least with any name or traditional history; but I have no doubt but that the *Bensidhe*'s wail came down to a late period, though, perhaps, under a degenerate name and with some distortions, under the pretence of improvement, to meet the depraved taste of a mixed and declining race of people.

It probably came down to a late period.

The tenth species of music in alphabetical order was the *Gúbha*, a word which literally signifies sighing or moaning in grief. I cannot, however, say with certainty that the *Gúbha* came properly within the strict range of what can be termed vocal music, though I have authority to show that special funeral assemblies were held, which were called *Aenach Gúbha*, or moaning or mourning assemblies; but whether the lamentation was of a low moaning character or of the more ordinary passionate kind, I have not been able to ascertain.

The Gúbha.

(439) [original:—Acornaire iarum riamsom doċum duini Cruachan; sendaid suide riam iaram con arta tri fichid fer do macaemaib Aililla ocus Medba ara siraċt an t-senma. Do thegad iarum isin dun, acas teid Fraech isin fotracad, conerig ban curi in duine uile uime dia bliṫ, acas dia folcad a cind. Do beran as iaram acas do gniṫar dergad do. Co cuala ni, an golgaire for Cruachain, ai ina farrad conacca na tri chaecaid ban cona n-inaruib corcraib, cona cendbarraib uainidiḃ, cona mileċaib airgdidiḃ for a mbruinnib. Tiagar ċuċu dia fis a scel, dus cia ro chainset. Fraech mac Fidaid om, ol bean dib, ised chainmidni, mac dertell rig siḋe Erind uili. Lasodain ro chluin Fraech a ngolgairi na m-ban. Dom ócbaiḋ ass tra, ol Fraech fria muintir. Gol mo mathassa so, ol se, acas na m-ban m-Boinne. Tocabar imach lasodain; do ṫegaid uime, acas beraid as in Cruachain. Ba mor dno a ecaine i teglach Aililla acas Medba in aidchi sin; conaccadar iaram im traṫ nona ar na marach; do ṫaed chuco acas caeca ban uime, is he og slán, gan on, gan ainib, gan esbaid. Comaesa na mna uili, comdelba, comchaimne, comsaira, comailli, comcrota, con-ecosc ban siḋe umpu, cona bai aiċne nech dib sech araili. Bec nad muchad daine umpu. Tiagaid uad iarum in-dorus inlis atagad a ngol esoib, oc dul uad con cassadar na daine badar isin dunad ar cend; is de sin ata golgairi bansiḋe la haes ciuil Erend.—H. 2. 16. 646.]

XXXVII. The *Logairecht* or funeral wail;

The eleventh species of music (vocal) was the *Loçairecht*. This was simply the wild and scarcely regulated Irish funeral cry; that cry which is heard even to this day in the south and west of Ireland, raised and sustained chiefly by the women who follow a hearse or funeral to the grave. At the present day the cry is called *Logóireacht*, but in *Cormac*'s Glossary, a compilation of about the year 890, it is called *Logairecht*, and occurs in the explanation of the word *Amrath*. Now, the word *Amrath* is compounded of *am*, a negative particle, equal to the English non, and *rath*, which means the stock, bounty, or wages which a chief or landlord gave to a tenant or follower for rent and services that were to be returned to the chief or lord in accordance with stipulations mutually entered into. That was the affirmative *rath;* but the *Amrath* or non-*rath* was the bounty or payment given to the people who cried and lamented at the funeral of the chief, lord, or any body else, and for which bounty there was no further return ever to be made.

occurs in *Cormac's* Gloss. at the word *Amrath*; meaning of the latter term.

The *Luinneog*.

The twelfth species of music is the *Luinneog;* but all that could be said on the subject of this species has been said already under the word *Duchand*. The *Luinneog* is still the chorus or burden of a song in Scotland.

The *Sámhghúbha*, or sea nymph's song;

The thirteenth in alphabetical order is the *Sámhghúbha*, which is the old Irish name for the song of the *Murduchain*, that is, the sirens, mermaids, or sea-nymphs. The word *Sámhghúbha* appears to have been compounded of *sámh*, which signifies ease, tranquillity, or a sense of entrancing happiness, and *gúbha*, a plaintive, slow, melancholy moaning air or tune. The sirens or sea-nymphs who, in ancient classical mythology, are said to have practised this species of music, were able by the bewitching sweetness of their strains to draw mariners upon the rocks and then destroy them; and in the narrative of the wanderings and voyages of the Milesian or rather Gadelian tribes before their arrival in Spain, and ultimately in Ireland, we are told (in the Book of Invasions) that upon their passing through the Pontic Sea, between the Black Sea and the Mediterranean Sea, they were advised by their druids to stuff their ears with soft wax in order that they should not hear the music of the *Murduchans*, or mermaids, who were accustomed to sing to the mariners until they set them asleep, when they sprang on them and killed them. I have never met the word *Sámhghúbha* in any composition, but I find it in an old Irish Glossary in my possession, where it is said to be the name of the sirens [vide also O'Reilly, *in voc.*]; but this, unless figurative, is clearly a mistake or a mistranscript, as any Irish scholar will at once perceive.

It is mentioned in an old glossary.

The fourteenth species of music in alphabetical order is the

Sian, or *Sianan*. Whether this was any particular species of music, or only a popular name for a song or tune, I am not able to decide, as I have met only three references to it, two of which refer to the human voice, and one to the whizzing or whistling of a spear or dart, winging its way through the air. The oldest reference to the word *Sian*, in a musical sense, is found in the description of the Battle of the second or northern *Magh Tuireadh*, fought between the *Tuatha Dé Danann* and the Fomorians, where the clangour and clatter of the men and weapons are spoken of as follows: "The shout of the champions; the clashing of the shields; the flashing and clangour of the swords and of the *Colg dets;* the whistle and twang of the darts; the flying *Sian* of the spears and javelins; and the battle crash of the arms".(440) It is very difficult, indeed, to draw any distinction between the words whistle, twang, and *Sian* in this passage, and the writer seems only to give to the same, or nearly the same, sounds a variety of undistinguishable names.

XXXVII. The *Sian*, or *Sianan*; applied in the Tale of the Battle of the Second *Magh Tuireadh* to the whizzing of a spear;

The next place in which I have met with the word *Sian* is in the lament of *Deirdre* for the Sons of *Uisnech*, where she says:—

applied to a song in the tale of the "Sons of *Uisnech*;

"Sweet with *Conchobar* the king
Are the pipers and trumpeters;
Sweeter to me the *cloth nell*,
A *Sian* which the sons of *Uisle* sang".(441)

Here the word *Sian* refers to the song which the sons of *Uisle* sang.

The third place in which I have met the *Sian*, or *Sianan*, is in the wanderings of St. *Colum Cille*'s two priests, *Snedgus* and *Mac Riaghla*, who, on their return from Ireland to Iona on the coast of Scotland, were driven into the northern seas. Here they were driven for some time from one strange island to another, until at last, as they were approaching a new island, they heard the sweet voices of women singing on the shore, when immediately they recognized the music, and said: "This is the *Sianan* of the women of Erinn". These were Irish women belonging to a clann of people of the *Fera Rois*, or men of Ross, who had shortly before been forcibly sent out upon the sea at the mouth of the river Boyne, and driven by the winds to this island.(442)

and also in the wanderings of the priests *Snedgus* and *Mac Riaghla*;

From these two last instances of the word *Sian*, or *Sianan*, it would appear that it designated some kind of soft, plaintive

it designated soft plaintive music.

(440) [original:—Gair na Laechraidi, ocus presimb na sciath, loindrech ocus fedgairi na claidim, ocus na calc ndéd, cirċiu ocus grindegur na saigidbolc, ocus sian etigud na fogaid ocus na n-gabluch, ocus priscbemnech na narm.—Second Battle of *Magh Tuireadh*, MS. Egerton, 5280, Brit. Mus., O'C.'s copy, p. 28.]

(441) [See Atlantis, No. vi., p. 410.]

(442) [See *Lectures on the MS. Materials of Ancient Irish History*, p. 334.]

XXXVII. music, such as one would expect to hear from the Sons of *Uisnech* and from the *Fera Rois*, both of whom were in forcible exile from their native country.

Sirechtach applied to slow music; synonymous with *Adbond*; the latter word occurs in the Festology of *Aengus Ceilé Dé*.

Sirechtach was an adjectival term applied to music of a slow, plaintive, enchanting kind; and hence we often find in ancient tales the phrase *ceol sirechtach sidhe*, from *ceol*, music; *sirechtach*, slow or prolonged; and *sidhe*, fairy or enchanting. This term *Sirechtach* is explained in another place by the word *Adbond*, which in its turn is explained *bind*, that is, sweet or melodious. The word *Adbond* occurs again in such a way as to signify a song or a tune, as in a note in the Festology of *Aengus Ceilé Dé*, or the Culdee, on the festival day of St. *Mochae* of *Oendruim*, now Island Magee, on the coast of the county of Antrim. St. *Mochae* was a disciple of St. Patrick, and his festival is held on the 21st of June. This note tells us that one day he went out from his church upon the island, and that he turned into a little grove in its neighbourhood, where he sat down under a tree for prayer and contemplation. While sitting here he saw a bird of uncommon plumage perch upon a tree near him, and sing so sweetly that he could not take his eyes off it nor shut his ears against its notes for a full hour, when it ceased and flew away to the next tree. Here the bird resumed its melody, and again riveted the attention of the saint for another hour, when he flew away to another tree immediately near. Here again he renewed his enchanting notes, absorbing more than ever St. *Mochae's* whole mind and attention for another hour, after which he flew away and disappeared. St. *Mochae*, after reflecting some time on the strange appearance of this wonderful bird and his wonderful music, arose and returned to his church. The way back, however, appeared very strange to him. The grove in which he had sat had disappeared, and its place was occupied by a cultivated field. The path by which he reached it was no longer to be seen, the way having been crossed with hedges and ditches. At length he made his way to his church, but he found the edifice much altered since he had left it but three hours before. He saw there priests and monks, indeed; but he had never seen their faces before, and when he told them that he was *Mochae*, the original founder of their church, they smiled at him in pity, believing that he was some wandering pilgrim whose religious enthusiasm had got the better of his reason. They asked him why he believed himself to be St. *Mochae*, and he told them the story of the wonderful bird. "My good friend", said they, "you must be under some delusion, for our holy patron, the blessed *Mochae*, went to heaven one hundred and fifty years ago". On hearing this, *Mochae* besought the priest to hear his confession and prepare him for death. This was done, and immediately after his soul passed to heaven, and his body dropped into ashes and bare bones. On this beautiful legend an ancient poem, quoted in the Festology, says: XXXVII.

"For the gentle *Mochae* there sang,
The bird from the heavens,
Three *Adbonds*, from the top of the tree,
Each *Adbond* being fifty years."(443)

Father Michael O'Clery, in his glossary of ancient Irish words and phrases, gives the words *Adbond Trirech*, or triple *Adbond*, which he explains as a tune of music in which three parts are understood, namely, *Gentraighe*, *Goltraighe*, and *Suantraighe*. These, it will be recollected, are the three musical modes of the ancient Irish, of which we have already said so much. The word *Trirech* occurs in Zeuss' Grammatica Celtica, vol. ii. page 929, in an ancient stanza, which he quotes as an example of the rhyme or assonance of ancient Irish versification. The author of this quatrain would appear to have been a student, pursuing his studies in the solitude of a wood or grove, or else dreaming or imagining himself in such a place, when he says: *Adbond Trirech, or triple Adbond, explained in Michael O'Clery's gloss as the Three Musical modes; Trirech occurs in Zeuss' Gram. Celt.;*

Dom farcai fidbaidae fael,
Fomchain lóid luin luad nad cél
Huar mo lebrán indlintech.
Fomchain trírech inna nén.
Maraith sercc cein mardda
Aitne a máeletan.

[I was upon the wild wood's visitation,
The blackbirds sweetly sang notes which I conceal not.
Over my many-lined little book.
Melodious was the *Trirech* of the birds.
'T was my much-loved, long-coveted treasure
To understand their warbling.](444)

(443) [original:—
Ro ċachain do mochoe chain
in ténan dona nemdaib
Tri hadboind do barr inchroind
.L. bliadain cech adboind.
—*Felire*, 21st July.]

(444) [Zeuss gives the Irish thus:—
Dom | farcai | fidbaidae | fáel fomchain || lóid | luin | lúad nad cél huar mo lebrán | indlinech fomchain trírech inna ñén || maraith sercc céin | mardda aitne a | máeletán.

Mr. W. Stokes gives part of this stanza thus:—
Dom 'farcai fidbaide fél
fom' chain lóid luin lúath, nad cél
uar mo lebran indlinech
fom' chain trírech inna ñén.
The grove makes a festival for me;
A blackbird's swift lay sings to me—
I will not hide it—
Over my many lined booklet
A trilling (?) of the birds sings to me".
—"Irish Glosses", p. 70.]

XXXVII.

Trirech applied to a species of lyric poetry shown by a passage in the Book of Leinster;

That there was known to the ancient Irish a species of lyric poetry called *Trirech*, may be seen from the following specimens of versification, found among various other specimens preserved in the ancient Book of Leinster. This specimen stanza is quoted from holy *Cormac Mac Cuilennain*, king and bishop of Cashel, who died in the year of our Lord 903. It is headed:

Lorga fuach,
Cormac cc. isin trirug:

In tóceb mo ċurċan ciar,
for innocian nuchtleċan nán;
inraga rí richid réil,
ar mo thoil féin air in sal:
imba sessach, imba seng,
imba sressaċ corgib drong;
a Dhé, in cungene sum,
o thí oc techt for lind lond?—[H. 2. 18. fol. 19. a. b.]

Lorga Fuach,
Cormac cecinit in the Trirech.

Wilt thou steer my gloomy little bark,
Upon the broad-bosomed foamy ocean;
Wilt thou come, O bright King of Heaven,
While my own will inclines to go to sea:
With thee the great, with thee the small,
With thee the fall of hosts is but a shower;
O God, wilt thou assist me,
While coming over the boisterous seas?

It would be difficult to understand why this stanza should be called *Trirech*, or triple, in place of *Diablach*, or duplex, as it contained but two quatrains, or eight lines; and we should have been in perfect uncertainty whether it was to the music, the quantity of the stanza, or to the characteristics of the entire poem, that the term triple was intended by the writer, if we had not found the matter explained in a perfect copy of this tract on versification, which is preserved in the Book of Ballymote. In that copy of the tract we find that the term *Trirech*, or triple, was not exclusively applied either to the music or the quantity of a verse, but it was also applied to a species of laudatory poetic composition in which the writer mentioned the name, description, and residence of the person for whom it was written; and it was upon the circumstance of these three conditions being found in it, the poem was called triplex. If, therefore, we had the whole of *Cormac Mac Cuilennan's* poem, we should, according to this definition, have found in it

the term *Trirech* not exclusively applied to the music or quantity of verse, but also to a particular kind of laudatory poem;

the name, description, and residence of the person for whom he wrote. But, from the specimen verse here given, it is evident that it was for God, His attributes, and His kingdom, the poem was written.

The stanza under consideration, as I have already stated, consists of eight lines, and will sing in two parts to the ancient air popularly known in the south of Ireland as: "*Ar Eire ni inneosfainn cé hi*", or, "For Ireland I would not tell who she is". An air also known as set to the words of the song of "Nancy, the pride of the west", and in Scotland known as that of the song, "Tweed side".[445] This leads me, however, to the consideration of another subject, which I must postpone to my next lecture.

the stanza quoted sings to the air of "For Ireland I would not tell who she is".

[445] See an eloquent and elegant discussion on the parentage, Scotch or Irish, of this sweet melody, a discussion provoked by myself, in Dr. Petrie's Ancient Music of Ireland, vol. i. p. 97.

LECTURE XXXVIII.

[Delivered July 15th, 1862.]

(IX.) Of Music and Musical Instruments (concluded). The ancient lyric verse adapted to an ancient air referred to in last lecture; the existence of old lyric compositions having a peculiar structure of rhythm adapted to old airs still existing unknown in the musical history of any other country; many such known; there exists in the Book of Ballymote a special tract on versification containing specimen verses; the specimens are usually four lined verses; but they sing to certain simple solemn airs; these are chiefly the poems called Ossianic; the author has heard his father sing the Ossianic poems; and has heard of a very good singer of them named O'Brien; the author only heard one other poem sung to the air of the Ossianic poems; many other old poems would however sing to it. The tract on versification contains specimens which must read to music at first sight; three examples selected. The first called *Ocht-Foclach Corranach Beg*, or, "the little eight-line curved verse"; this class of poems written to a melody constructed like that known as the "Black Slender Boy"; description of this kind of verse. The second is the *Ocht Foclach Mór* or "great eight line verse"; this stanza was written to the musical metre of an air of which the first half of "John O'Dwyer of the Glen" is an example; description of this kind of verse. The third is the *Ocht Foclach Mór Corranach*, or "great curving eight line verse"; measure, accents, cadences, and rhyme are the same as in the second. Another specimen of verse from a long poem in the Book of *Lecan;* the kind called *Ocht Foclach h-Eimhin*, or the "eight line verse of *O' h-Eimhin*"; the *Ui* or *O* prefixed to the name of the author of the poem does not necessarily imply his having lived after the permanent assumption of surnames; description of this kind of poem; this poem written to a different air from the other stanzas quoted; will sing to any one of three well known airs. The author does not say that these verses were written for the airs mentioned, but only that they sing naturally to them. That these stanzas were not written by the writers on Irish prosody to support a theory, as shown by poems in the Tale of the *Táin Bó Chuailgne;* e.g. the poem containing the dialogue between *Medb* and *Ferdiad;* musical analysis of this poem; there are five poems of the same kind in this tale. The author does not want to establish a theory, but only to direct attention to the subject. Antiquity of the present version of the *Táin Bó Chuailgne:* the copy in the *Leabhar na h-Uidhre;* the copy in the Book of Leinster. At least one specimen of the same kind of ancient verse in the *Dinnseanchas*, e.g. in the legend of *Ath Fadad*, or Ahade: the *Dinnseanchas* was written about 590 by *Amergin* chief poet to *Diarmait*, son of *Fergus Ceirbheoil;* these various compositions are at least 900 years old, and prove that the most enchanting form of Irish music is indigenous. The author is conscious of his unfitness to deal with the subject of music technically; complaint on the neglect of Irish music; appeal to Irishmen in favour of it.

No clear allusion in very old Irish MSS. to dancing. The modern generic name for dancing is *Rinnceadh;* it is sometimes called *Damhsa;* meaning of those terms. *Fonn* and *Port* the modern names for singing and dancing music; Michael O'Clery applies the term *Port* to lyric music in general; *Cor*, in the plural *Cuir*, an old Irish word for music, perhaps connected with *Chŏrea;* the author suggests that *Port* was anciently, what it is now, a "jig", and *Cor*, a "reel"; "jig" borrowed from the French or Italian. *Rennceadh fada*, "long dance", not an ancient term; applied to a country dance. Conclusion. XXXVIII.

AT the conclusion of my last lecture I gave an instance of ancient Irish lyric verse perfectly adapting itself to one of those ancient Irish airs which have come down to us in a form, if not primitive, at least nearly that in which they must have been performed a thousand, probably even more than two thousand years ago. I allude to those verses of *Cormac Mac Cuilennain*, now almost a thousand years old, which sing to the air of "*Ar Eire ni inneosfainn ce hi*"; or, "For Ireland I would not tell who she is". I cannot, indeed, say that these particular verses were written to that particular air. I adduce it only as an interesting fact, that a fragment of a lyric poem, ascribed to a writer of the ninth century, and actually preserved in a MS. book so old as the year 1150, presents a peculiar structure of rhythm exactly corresponding with that of certain ancient Irish musical compositions still popular and well known, though traditionally as of the highest antiquity, one of which is the air I have named. I believe such a fact is unknown in the musical history of any other nation in Europe. And yet in ours, I believe, very many such instances could be adduced of ancient lyric music still in existence, in minutely exact agreement with forms of lyric poetry, used not only in, but peculiar to, the most ancient periods of our native literature. It would, however, be the work, not of a passing notice here, but rather of a course of lectures in itself, to investigate the numerous examples by means of which I think this connection of the existing remains of our ancient music with the earliest eras of our national civilization may be demonstrated. And the task itself is one which I should far rather see undertaken (with what assistance I could venture to offer him) by some master of Irish music as well as of Irish antiquities, such as our illustrious fellow-countryman, Dr. Petrie, than imperfectly accomplished in any such lectures as I, by myself, could lay before the public. We are by no means, then, confined to a solitary specimen of ancient Irish lyric composition, such as that which I quoted on the last evening; nor even to any vague deductions based on the chance analysis of such remains; for the Book of Ballymote, compiled from older books in the year 1391, contains a special tract on versification, in which specimen verses are given of all the poetic measures known to or practised by the ancient Irish.

The ancient lyric verse adapted to an ancient air referred to in last lecture;

the existence of old lyric compositions having a peculiar structure of rhythm adapted to old airs still existing unknown in the musical history of any other country;

many such known;

there exists a special tract on versification containing specimen verses;

Generally these specimens are verses of four lines only; so that, if intended for a musical accompaniment, the range of the

XXXVIII.

the specimens are usually four-lined verses; but they sing to certain simple solemn airs; these are chiefly the poems called Ossianic;

air was limited, and it must have been but little varied. Yet there are several ancient poems in this measure extant that will very well sing to particular airs, generally of a simple, solemn, or melancholy character. Of these I may mention the class of poems popularly called Ossianic, from their authorship being ascribed to *Oisin*, the famous son of *Finn Mac Cumhaill.* These so-called Ossianic verses are generally composed of seven syllables to the line, with alternate rhymes and a peculiarly delicate and exact rhythm, without return or burden of any kind.

the author has heard his father sing the Ossianic poems;

and has heard of a very good singer of them named O'Brien;

I have heard my father sing these Ossianic poems, and remember distinctly the air and the manner of their singing; and I have heard that there was, about the time that I was born, and of course beyond my recollection, a man named Anthony O'Brien, a schoolmaster, who spent much of his time in my father's house, and who was the best singer of Oisin's poems that his contemporaries had ever heard. He had a rich and powerful voice, and often, on a calm summer day, he used to go with a party into a boat on the Lower Shannon, at my native place, where the river is eight miles wide, and having rowed to the middle of the river, they used to lie on their oars there to uncork their whiskey jar and make themselves happy, on which occasions Anthony O'Brien was always prepared to sing his choicest pieces, among which were no greater favourites than *Oisin*'s poems. So powerful was the singer's voice that it often reached the shores at either side of the boat in Clare and Kerry, and often called the labouring men and women from the neighbouring fields at both sides down to the water's edge to enjoy the strains of such music (and such performance of it) as I fear is not often in these days to be heard even on the favoured banks of the soft flowing queen of Irish rivers.

the author only heard one other poem sung to the air of the Ossianic poems;

I do not remember having heard any other poem sung to the air of these Ossianic pieces but one, and that one is a beautiful ancient hymn to the Blessed Virgin, some seven hundred or more years old. My father sang this hymn, and well too, almost every night, so that the words and the air have been impressed on my memory from the earliest dawn of life. This sweet poem consists of twelve stanzas of four lines each, beginning:

"Direct me how to praise thee,—
Though I am not a master in poetry.—
O thou of the angelic countenance, without fault!
Thou who hast given the milk of thy breast to save me".[448]

[448] [original:—
Sciupaḋ me ḋoḋ ṁolaḋ
Cia nac ollaṁ me am eigir,—
A ġnúir ainglíḋe, gan loċ!
Tug rugaḋ t'uċta ḋom réiġteaċ.
—O'Longan's Irish MSS. R.I.A., No. $\frac{23}{C. 30}$ p. 69.]

XXXVIII.

The air of this hymn is not popular; I never heard it sung but by my own father. I know it myself very well, and I know several old poems that will sing to it, such as the above poems ascribed to *Oisin*, the son of *Find Mac Cumhaill*, and the great religious poem called "The Festology of *Aengus Ceilé Dé*", written in the year 798.

many other old poems would however sing to it;

Besides a great variety of specimens of the four-line verse, under various technical names, the tract in the Book of Ballymote contains a few specimens of a decidedly lyric character—verses which, from the measured positions of the accented vowels and cadences, must at first sight read to music. From these I have selected three of the longest kind of verse that occurs among them; but I may add that the names by which they are distinguished are names that do not occur in the prosody of any Irish grammar compiled or published within the last three hundred years.

the tract on versification contains specimens which must read to music at first sight; three examples selected—

The first of these specimens is a stanza of sixteen lines, called the *Ochtfoclach Corranach Beg*, that is literally, "The little eight-line curved verse". To make this name intelligible, it is necessary to state that the meaning of the word "*corranach*", or curved, in this name refers to the second part of eight lines which are added to the first eight lines, so as to make sixteen, in order to fill up the "curve", "turn", or second part of the tune. The example given here is certainly a Munster production, and appears to have been taken from a satirical poem written on some pretender to the divine art, who would indeed appear to have been a pupil to the author. It runs as follows:

The first called *Ochtfoclach Corranach Beg*, or "the little eight-line curved verse";

Oċt Foclaċ corranaċ beg.

A druith na nDéisi, acloicceand céisi,
Ni bia dar ndeisi, a muig og nabuaib;
A druim re seisi, noċo dumreirsi,
Noċo somċeilsi do ċuaḋ do chial;
Imthiġ adúini! ith im is uidi,
Roich uidi iar nuidi, adiu coróiṁ;
A Lorcan luigi, a bolcain buiḋi,
For tolclar tuiġi, ria nóin a niar.[447]

The Little Eight-line Curved Verse.

Thou fool of the *Deisi*, thou head of the small pig,
After us the cows shall not enjoy their plains;
Thou forsaker of science, not obedient to me,
'T is not under my counsel thy sense has vanished;

(447) [Book of Ballymote, folio 160. a. b.]

XXXVIII.

Go off, O man! eat butter and eggs,
Seek tutor after tutor, pursue [thy way] to Rome;
O Lorcan of the vows, O yellow *Bulcan*,
Upon the bare board, ere eve approaches from the west.

this class of poem written to a melody constructed like that known as "the Black Slender Boy";

Now, any one with an ordinary ear for Irish music, will at once see that the poem, of which this is a curious example, was written to a melody constructed precisely like that of the beautiful and well-known air, called in our times the *Buachaill Caeldubh*, or the "Black Slender Boy". This delightful air will be found in Dr. Petrie's Ancient Music of Ireland, vol. i., page 19, where three different versions of it are printed; none of them, I am sorry to say, agreeing exactly with my own impression of it, or with the song which accompanies them in that volume, and which was contributed by me. The air, as Dr. Petrie decides, is especially a Munster one; but those who supplied him with these settings of it were either unable to do it full justice, or must have taken it down in some other province.

description of this kind of verse.

I shall not undertake to scan our specimen verse, with reference to this exceedingly ancient air—indeed that is beyond my ability; but I will explain its peculiarity, and we shall then see how it differs from other metres, and by what peculiarities it may be distinguished. The first three lines of each of the four quatrains of which the stanza is composed, consist each of five syllables; the last word of each being a word of two syllables, with a strongly marked vowel assonance, indeed nearly a perfect rhyme. The fourth line of each quatrain consists but of four syllables, and the last word a monosyllable. The last words of the first and third quatrains do not make any rhyme or assonance with each other or with any other line in the stanza. The last words of the second and fourth quatrains make an assonance with each other, but not with any other word or line in the whole stanza. These peculiarities cannot, of course, be made apparent in a literal English translation; but an ordinary ear will detect them in the original:

The second is the *Ocht-foclach Mór*, or "great eight-line verse";

The second specimen is a stanza of eight lines; a stanza which is called the *Ocht foclach Mór*, or great eight line verse. From the context, these lines would appear to have been taken from a dialogue between the author and a student, who appears to be returning from his literary studies, at some place called *Cluain*, (very probably *Cluain Mac Nois*, now Clonmacnoise, in the King's county) and that it was at Kildare this interview with the author took place. The following is the stanza:—

XXXVIII.

Ochtfoclach mór.

Canas tic mac legind?
Ticim ó Chluain Celbind;
Iar legad molegind
Tegim sis co Sord.
Indis scela Cluana.
Indissed,—na cuala
Sinnaig Imahuadha
Etait bruana bolg.

Great eight-line verse.

Whence comest thou, O student?
I come from *Cluain Celbind* [of sweet music];
After reading my lesson,
I go down to *Sord* [Swords].
Tell [us] the news of *Cluain*.
I will tell it,—hast thou not heard
That the foxes of *Imahuadha*[448]
Have found [and] consumed the satchels.

These "satchels" were made of leather to hold books; and it may well be supposed that the offending "foxes" were only figurative of some objectionable persons, who found access to them.

this stanza was written to the musical metre of an air of which the first half of "John O'Dwyer of the Glenn" is an example;

Like the former stanza, any one with an ear for Irish music will, indeed must, at once perceive that this stanza was written to the musical metre of which the first half of that beautiful air, called now "*Seaghan O'Duibhir an Ghleanna*", or "John O'Dwyer of the Glenn", is an example. This specimen is called "the great eight-line verse", only because it has not that curve or turn, as it is called, which we understand to signify a full second part of eight lines, or two quatrains, like the first, which would be sung to the full double measure of the air, such as we know "John O'Dwyer of the Glenn" at the present day. This is a curious and important specimen of a verse and its music; and will, I may be allowed to hope, supply some valuable matter of discussion to Dr. Petrie, in that analysis of the Ancient Music of Ireland, so long expected from his learned pen.

description of this kind of verse.

The three first lines of each of the two quatrains of which this stanza is composed, consist of six syllables each, the last word of each consisting of two syllables and an assonance, or indeed, I might say, rhyme. The fourth line of each quatrain

(448) [Perhaps this may be Timahoe, in the Queen's County; the author's MS. has "about its graves".]

XXXVIII. consists but of five syllables, the last word of each being a monosyllable, and in assonance with each other.

The third is the *Ochtfoclach Mor Chorranach*, or "great curving eight line verse";

The third specimen is a stanza of sixteen lines, called the "*Ochtfoclach Mor Chorranach*", or great curving eight-line verse, and runs as follows:—

Ochtfoclach mor chorranach.

Domhnall ua Duibdala, in rainec Cill Dara
In brattuig no in tána, rucad uad co Sord;
Rainig Sliged nDala gemb mire mara:
Mo cride mo cara, ua Concorb na cerd,
Mac daingin Mail Caba, do brainn Inber Crara,
Cona milib ana, connadib na nord,—
Caelach feda ar faga, uair gerga acas gala,
Iarand lega ilaim laga, lorg draigin ar delg.[449]

Great curving eight-line verse.

Domhnall Ua Duibdala has pursued to Kildare
The plunder or the spoil, which was carried from him to Swords;
At *Slighed n-Dala* was heard the loud maddened bellowing [of the cows]:
The friend of my heart, the descendant of *Concorb* of the "poets",
The son of *Mael Caba*'s daughter, from the banks of *Inbher Crara*,
With his noble equipments, with the insignia of heroes of valour,—
A spear with slender wooden haft in time of strife and combat,
A surgeon's lancet in a surgeon's hand, a thorn upon a blackthorn staff.

This stanza, too, as well as the others, is of a satirical, humorous character, and appears to have some reference to the stanza immediately preceding; and to have arisen out of the dialogue between the author and the student returning from Clonmacnoise to Swords. This stanza, however, pretends to view the student in the light of a person who has been plundered of either captives or cattle, in search of which he is made to be on his way to Swords. The poet says that the maddened bellowing of the cows was heard upon *Slighed nDala*, which was the name of the ancient road that led from the passage across the Shannon (now called Shannon Bridge, near Clonmacnoise) to Tara. He speaks of the youth under the name of *Domhnall Ua Duibdala*, the friend of his heart, and descendant of *Con Corb* of the artists.

(449) [Book of Ballymote, fol. 160. a. b.]

He next styles him the son of *Maelcaba*'s daughter, from the brink of *Inbher Crara* (an *Inbher*, or river, with the situation of which I am unacquainted). And next the poet ridicules the hostile equipment of the young man for so daring an undertaking as the pursuit and recovery of his property. The slender handle of his spear; the blade of that spear like a lancet in the weak hand of a surgeon; the handle and blade together, being of no more formidable a character than a blackthorn staff mounted with a single thorn! XXXVIII.

It is a question whether any of these three specimens ever formed part of any lengthened piece; or whether, from their resemblance in lightness of character and sarcastic point, they were not fugitive stanzas written by way of "nonsense verses", as mere examples of rhyme and metre adapted to the rhythm of the known music of the day. Most of the prosodial illustrations of the fifteenth and sixteenth centuries are fugitive quatrains of a witty but fantastic character; and it is not at all improbable but that this was a custom derived from more remote times. This stanza was certainly written by the man who wrote the preceding stanza, or half-stanza of eight lines; it was evidently written at the same time, and on the same subject, but merely, as it were, an example for adaptation to the full or double measure of the tune. The measure, accents, cadences, and rhyme, are precisely the same as in the half-stanza, and will sing to the full length of the air of *Seaghan O'Duibhir an Ghleanna;* or, in other words, agree with the measure of the lyrical stanza called in ancient times the *Ocht-foclach Mor Chorranach*, or "great eight-line curving verse".

measure, accents, cadences, and rhyme, are the same as in the second.

I have one example more to give of this species of verse, but it is not a mere prosodial specimen, but part of a very ancient and very long poem of which a fine full copy is still extant. This poem is preserved in the Book of Lecan, in the Royal Irish Academy, and consists of seventy-nine stanzas of sixteen lines each, making 1264 lines in all. The poem is a religious one, devoted to the praise and supplication of God, the happiness of the good; and the doom of the wicked at the day of judgment. The poem is entitled, *In Ochtfoclach ui hi-Eimhin*, that is, "the eight-line verse of *O'h-Eimhin*", and, as at present written out, consists of eight lines to the stanza. But, although this is its present arrangement, it is evident from various reasons, into which I need not enter in detail, that the stanza originally consisted of sixteen lines, or two stanzas of the present arrangement, and consequently, that the piece should be classed under the name of the *Ocht-foclach Mor Chorranach*, or the "great eight-line return verse".

Another specimen of verse from a long poem in the B. of Lecan; this kind called *Ochtfoclach hi-Eimhin*, or the "great eight line verse of *O'h-Eimhin*".

XXXVIII.

The *Ui* or *O'* prefixed to the name of the author of this poem does not necessarily imply his having lived after the permanent assumption of surnames;

The *Ui* or *O'* prefixed to the name of the author of this poem does not of necessity imply that he must have lived after the establishment of permanently fixed family surnames, at the beginning of the eleventh century; it merely means that he was the grandson or descendant of a person named *Emin*. The prefixes *Mac* and *O'* (that is, son and grandson) had been in use in Ireland long before their establishment as distinctive prefixes to distinct and permanently fixed family names, though, until about the year 1000, they were never transmissible to posterity; so that the son of this *O' h-Eimhin* would not have been bound by any law or custom to call himself "*O' h-Eimhin*", unless he should prefer, for his time, to be named after his great-grandfather "*Emin*", rather than from his immediate father or grandfather, whatever their Christian names may have been. Whoever this *O' h-Eimhin* may have been, I have no doubt that this poem was written not later than the year 900.

description of this kind of poem;

This poem, like the preceding full lyrical stanza, consists of sixteen lines, or four distinct quatrains to the stanza. The three first lines consist each of six syllables; the last word of each containing three syllables, and forming an assonance or vowel rhyme, each with the other two. The fourth line of each quatrain, however, contains but four syllables, ending with a monosyllable, and not in assonance with the preceding three lines, but each does with the others throughout the four quatrains. The rhymes or final assonances of the lines in this poem are not, in any instance, as in the preceding stanzas, marked by long or full-sounding vowels; still the accents are decided and natural. These conditions, however, could not be detected in the mere literal translations of the former, any more than in that of the present, which runs as follows:

In ochtfoclach hi Eimin.

Dia mor dom imditen,
Dia mor dom imdedail,
Dia mor dom foirceadal,
Dia mor im fail,
Dia mor dom chaisearcad,
Dia mor dom imradad,
Dia mor dom imgnadad,
Dia mor dom romain.
In taṫair mor muinterach,
Mo choimdi cumaċtach,
Comsich mo chomairli,
Crist cathbarrcach;
M' oidi, ocus m' anmchara,—

Mac muiri ingine,
Rig in rigthig, rig nime,
Rigbili ós raith.[430]

The eight-line verse of O'h-Eimhin.

May the great God shelter me,
May the great God protect me,
May the great God instruct me,
May the great God be in my company,
May the great God bless me,
May the great God contemplate me,
May the great God be always with me,
May the great God save me.
The great merciful Father,
My powerful God-head,
The chief of my counsel,—
Christ the helmet of battle;
My teacher, and my soul's friend,—
The Son of Mary the virgin,
The King of the royal palace, King of Heaven,
The kingly tree of all grace.

This poem written to a different air from the stanzas quoted;

The trisyllabic termination of the leading lines of this remarkable poem would seem to indicate that the words were intended to be sung to an air different from those of the preceding stanzas; but whether this is or is not the reason, it is certain that it will not sing to music of the metre either of the air of the *Buachaill Cael Dubh*, or that of *Seaghan O'Duibhir an Ghleanna*, although it will sing quite smoothly to that of any one of three other well known airs, which differ as much from each other as they differ from the preceding airs. These three airs are: first, that which is so well known in connexion with the modern songs of Mary Lemore, the Exile of Erinn, and some others; second, the air now commonly known by the modern name of the *Rogaire Dubh*, or Black Rogue, sometimes called the Black Joke (but not the Black Joke, as published by Moore); third, a well known ancient air, popular in modern times only as a dance in Munster, and known to pipers under the name of the Humours of Glin. All these airs are, I believe very old, and the two last were not originally quick airs at all.

will sing to any one of three well known airs.

Author does not say that these verses were written for the airs

Now, I do not say—I cannot say, that any one of these specimen verses that I have given was actually written to any one

(430) [Book of *Lecan*, fol. 170. b. a.]

XXXVIII. mentioned, but only that they sing naturally to them.

of the airs which I have for the moment assigned to them. I only say that they will sing smoothly and naturally to these airs; and as my only object is to show that lyric music and melody were well known and practised in Ireland in ancient times, I feel that, even after my own unscientific way, I have sufficiently established that fact.

That these stanzas were not written by the writer on Irish Prosody to support a theory is shown by poems in the *Táin Bó Chuailgne*;

But that the specimens which I have just given from our ancient Irish prosody were not, all at least, mere stanzas compiled by the author of that tract for the illustration of a theory, there still exist means of a most conclusive character to prove. Such evidence we may find, for example, in the tale so often referred to of the *Táin Bó Chuailgne* which in the form in which it is preserved in *Leabhar na-h-Uidhri*, and in the Book of Leinster, is assigned to a period in or about the year 600. In this tale the verses I am about to refer to occur where *Medb*, the queen of Connacht, endeavours to rouse against the invincible *Cuchulaind* the scarcely less redoubtable warrior, *Ferdiad*, a famous champion from the western borders of Connacht, to whom she offers not only the freedom of his lands for ever, but also the hand of her beautiful daughter in marriage, as well as many other important gifts, if he would sustain her cause against *Cuchulaind*, his former friend and fellow-student in the military schools of Ireland and Scotland. The conversation between the queen and her champion, and the terms of their compact, are then given in a poem of ten stanzas, consisting each of eight lines, except the last, of which but four lines remain.

e. g. the poem containing the dialogue between *Medb* and *Ferdiad*;

The queen begins the dialogue as follows:—

M. Rat fia luaċ mór m-buinne,
raṫ ċuit maige is chaille,
ra saire do ċlainne
andiu co tí bráth,
a Fhirdiad mic Damáin,
eirggi guin is gabáil.
attecha ar ceċ anáil,
cid dait gan a gabáil
[a ni gabas cáċ?]

F. D. Ni gebsa gan áraċ;
daig nim láeċ gan lámaċ.
bud tromm ḟorm i m-báraċ,
bud forttrén in feidm.
cú dán comainm Culand;
is amnas in n-urrand;—
ní ḟursa a ḟulang;
bud tairpéch in teidm.

XXXVII

M. [I will give a great reward in rings,
With thy share of plain and forest,
And the freedom of thy children,
From this day to the end of time,—
O *Ferdiad*, son of *Daman*,
O champion of wounds and conquests.
Thou hast come out of every strife,
Why dost thou not receive that which others would accept?

F. I will not accept it without guarantee;
For a champion without security I will not be.
Heavily will it press on me to-morrow,
Terrible will be the battle.
Hound indeed is the name of *Culand;*
He is fierce in combat,—
'Tis not easy to withstand him;
Fearless will be the fight.]

And in this manner the dialogue is carried on to the end, until queen *Medb* grants all that *Ferdiad* requires, and until he accepts the post of her champion.(451)

The reader will have perceived, that as at present arranged in the old book, each stanza of this ancient poem consists of eight lines or two quatrains. The first three lines of each quatrain consist each of six syllables, ending with a word of two syllables, and are in well-marked assonance; whilst the fourth line of each quatrain consists but of five syllables, ending with a word of one syllable, not in assonance with the final words of the leading lines, but fully agreeing with the other. Now, according to the rule derived from the prosodial tract in the Book of Ballymote, this stanza belongs to the species of the *Ochtfoclach Mór*, or great eight-line verse, and will at once, like the former stanza of the same measure, sing to the first part of the air of "John O'Dwyer of the Glenn"; and if the response of the second speaker be taken into the measure of the music, it will flow smoothly and naturally into a second part, making the full measure of the whole air; in fact, the whole would be a musical recitative, carried on within the rigid limits of a well-defined and clearly ascertained piece of old lyric music; and then the full stanza would come under the name and class of the *Ochtfoclach Mór Choranach*, or great eight-line return or double verse.

musical analysis of this poem:

There are five poems in this style preserved in the *Táin Bó*

(451) [See Appendix I., p. 413, where the whole of the episode of the *Táin Bó Chuailgne*, relating to the combat of *Ferdiad* and *Cuchulaind* is given as an example of that great tale.]

XXXVIII

there are five poems of the same kind in this tale.

Chuailgne. The first (that already described) is the dialogue between queen *Medb* and the champion *Ferdiad*. The second is a poem of three stanzas of eight lines each, spoken or sung between *Ferdiad* and his own charioteer, in which the latter urges his master not to undertake the combat with *Cuchulaind*. The third is between the same charioteer and his master, in which the latter is informed of the approach of *Cuchulaind* to the ford of battle. This consists also of three stanzas of eight lines each, and would, indeed, appear to be a continuation of the preceding three stanzas, with as much of prose between them as was sufficient to explain the continuation of the dialogue. The fourth is a dialogue of three stanzas, between *Ferdiad* and his charioteer, in which he speaks confidently of his own success in the approaching combat. The fifth is a dialogue of nine stanzas, of eight lines each, between the champions themselves, that is, *Cuchulaind* and *Ferdiad*. In this dialogue *Cuchulaind* upbraids his opponent for coming against him in a mercenary spirit, while he is standing alone in defence of his patrimony and his province, against powerful and countless enemies. He reminds him, too, of the happy time they had spent together at the military college of the lady *Scathach* in Scotland, and the lesson of mutual friendship and fidelity, and the gifts of arms which that lady gave them.

It is curious that, although the last four of these poems are composed of odd numbers of stanzas of eight lines each, and make in all eighteen such stanzas, yet that if we compound these eighteen stanzas, or perhaps we ought to say half stanzas, they will exactly make nine full stanzas of sixteen lines each, and thus fill up the full measure of the air which we have provisionally assigned to them.

the author does not want to establish a theory, but only to direct attention to the subject.

In speaking thus of these various poems in connection with particular music, it must be understood that I want to establish no theory. I wish merely to place these curious ancient remains in such positions as might perhaps enable more competent persons to investigate further the structure at least of those classes of our national melodies to which I have referred. The task is rather for Dr. Petrie than for me to undertake as it ought to be undertaken.

Antiquity of the present version of the *Táin Bó Chuailgne*:

As to the antiquity of the present version of the tale of the *Táin Bó Chuailgne*, in which those latter five poems are found, I have already, in a former lecture,[438] pressed all the authorities that I could find into the discussion of that important subject, so that I may now state, in a few words only, the drift of the

(438) See Lectures on the MS. Materials of Ancient Irish History, Lect. II. p. 32.

evidences brought together upon that occasion. Saint *Ciaran*, the founder of the church at Clonmacnoise in ancient Westmeath and who died in the year 548, wrote this story with his own hand into a book which was called *Leabhar na h-Uidhri*, which book must of course have remained at Clonmacnoise for hundreds of years afterwards. There is a fragment of a large vellum book now in the library of the Royal Irish Academy, which was written at the same Clonmacnoise by a famous scribe named *Maelmuire*, the son of *Ceilechar*, who was killed there in the year 1106. This fragment of *Maelmuire's* book contains a large fragment of the *Táin Bó Chuailgne*, though, unfortunately, not the combat of *Cuchulaind* and *Ferdiad*, that part, with the remainder of the story, being lost. This book of *Maelmuire* has come down to us under the name of *Leabhar na h-Uidhri* also, from which we may very fairly infer that it originally contained a full transcript of St. *Ciaran's* original *Leabhar na h-Uidhri*, or at least as much of it as remained or was legible at the time, as well as other pieces collected or compiled from other ancient books, several of which are named by the writer. St. *Ciaran* died while in the prime of life, in 548; and if we suppose that he wrote his book, say in the year 540, and that *Maelmuire* copied it in the year 1100, that is six years before his death, we would find that the age of the book would then be but 560 years, an age by no means remarkable for a book which must have been preserved with religious care, and which, very probably, came down to the fourteenth or fifteenth century.

the copy in *Leabhar na h-Uidhri*;

The same tale is also preserved in the Book of Leinster, an almost contemporary manuscript, a large folio volume, of which a large portion of about 400 pages remains still in, with few exceptions, beautiful preservation. This book was written about the year 1150, by *Finn MacGorman*, who died as bishop of Kildare in the year 1160, so that at this day it is at least 712 years old. This book, then, which is nearly as old as *Leabhar na h-Uidhri*, contains a beautiful copy of the *Táin Bó Chuailgne;* and it is from this copy that I have taken the last five specimens of lyric verse to which I have called attention. So that, in fact, we have now in *Leabhar na h-Uidhri*, by the intervention of but a single hand, the *Táin Bó Chuailgne* (as much of it as remains there) in the same state probably that it came from the hand of St. *Ciaran* some time before the year 548. But although the copy in the Book of Leinster is not so old, it was not taken from *Maelmuire's*, but from some other ancient copy of the tale, and with some different readings; and *Maelmuire* himself observes, in some places, that other books contained readings of some passages different from his own.

the copy in the Book of Leinster.

XXXVIII.

At least one specimen of the same kind of ancient verse in the *Dinnseanchas*: e. g. in the legend of *Ath Fadad*, or Ahade;

We have not, however, to depend entirely on the specimen stanzas from the prosodial tract in the Book of Ballymote, and the five poems in the *Táin Bó Chuailgne*, for examples of ancient Irish lyric poetry, as it happens that there is to be found also in the very ancient topographical tract called the *Dinnseanchas*, at least one specimen of this kind of verse. The ancient legend in which this poem is found is preserved in the vellum MSS., the Books of Leinster, Ballymote, and *Lecan*. The place, of the name of which the story professes to give the etymology, is *Ath Fadad*, or the ford of *Fadad* (now Ahade on the river Slaney), about four miles below the town of Tullow, in the county of Carlow. The story is a short one, and the substance of it may be told in a few words. A battle was once fought among the men of Leinster themselves, that is, between *Etan Cend Derg* (of the Red-Head) with his household; and *Liath* of *Doire Leith* (at *Loch Lurcan*), with his children (namely, *Fadad* his son, and *Doe* and *Caichne*, his two daughters). for the right to the produce or fishing of the river Barrow; and *Liath* was killed in this battle. Some time after, *Fadad*, the son of *Liath*, with his two sisters, *Doe* and *Caichne*, mustered their friends, and another battle was fought at the same ford, in which *Fadad* was killed; and it was on that account that the ford obtained the name of *Ath Fadad*, or the ford of *Fadad*, a name which it retains to this day under the slightly anglicised form of Ahade. It would appear that before this last battle, *Etan* of the Red-Head endeavoured to deter *Fadad* from undertaking it; and the dialogue which passed between them on the occasion is preserved in a poem of five stanzas of eight lines each, which are precisely of the same measure and structure as those which have just been given from the *Táin Bó Chuailgne*, and like them, will sing to the same airs. *Etan* of the Read-Head begins the dialogue as follows:

Etan. Mo nuar ni fortachaid,
Ni ba deoch do blathaich;
Ni bera for machair
Mac orin amach.
Fadad o Loch Lorcan
Atber frib in tuddar
Do faeth do gaebulgach
Fri Laignib icath.

Fadad. Tiefa Doe ni doeneoch,
Co lind is co mileoch
Co narm ndairdrech ndoireoch
Do chur chorcuir cruaid;

Ticfai Caichne cobraid
Conarm nadmar narraid;
Roraid tarbar namsaib
Ar berear buaid. [B. of *Lecan*, f. 335, a. a.]

Etan. [Alas, they are not of the living,]
Nor will thy fame be better;
To a mother shall not be born
A son henceforth.
Fadad from *Loch Lorcan*,
The author says to you,
Was killed with sharp-piercing lances
By the Leinstermen in battle.

Fadad. [*Doe* will come not late,
With numbers and with heroes
With weapons sharp and straight
To make a hard battle;
Caichne the victorious will come
With fierce revengeful arms;
I say, over your mercenary forces
It is he who will take victory.]

the *Dinnseanchas* was written about 590 by *Amargin*, chief poet to *Diarmait*, son of *Fergus Ceirbheoil*;

We need not pause to examine the probability or improbability of this story, for the determination of the question is of no importance to our present inquiry. With regard to its antiquity, there are some circumstances preserved in another version of it, in the Books of Ballymote and *Lecan*, which would refer it to the latter part of the sixth century; say about the year 590. I may remind the reader that the original compilation of the exceedingly curious topographical tract, called the *Dinnseanchas*, is ascribed to *Amargin*, who was chief poet to *Diarmait*, the son of *Fergus Ceirbheoil*, monarch of Erinn, in whose time Tara was cursed and deserted, and who died in the year 558. But, without insisting on the correctness of the dates ascribed to the different compositions in which these specimens of versification are found, we may, without any fear of doubt or reasonable contradiction, throw them back a distance, at least, of nine hundred years from our own times; and this, with the aid of the strong testimony borne in detail by the libeller of the Irish Geraldus Cambrensis in the twelfth century, is assuredly quite sufficient to show that our music, in its most enchanting form, is purely native, independent of any Saxon, Danish, or Norman aid.

these various compositions are at least 900 years old;

and prove that the most enchanting form of Irish music is indigenous.

I am fully and painfully conscious of my utter unfitness to

XXXVIII.

Author conscious of his unfitness to deal with the subject of music technically; he wishes merely to record what little he knows himself.

deal intelligibly, much less, efficiently, with a subject so delicate, and requiring more or less of a technical musical education, as that upon which I have endeavoured in this lecture to set down some of the ideas which have occurred to me. Indeed, nothing on earth could induce me to touch upon it at all, but the desire, before I am called out of this world, to put on record, for the benefit of my dear country and for the assistance of future investigators, even the little rude acquaintance I have been able to make with a subject which has been the delight of my life from its earliest dawn to the present day. Oh! why do not Irishmen cultivate, encourage, cherish, and hoard up in their innermost souls, the priceless treasure of never-failing consolation and delight afforded by their matchless music, if but worthily understood and performed? Why have we banished to contempt, to poverty, and to the pauper's grave, the ever good-humoured and often talented, though, in their neglected state, but too ill-instructed, wandering professors of this, the proudest remnant of our ancient inheritance? and why, may not I also ask, has not Dr. Petrie been supported in the effort lately made to bring out his great collection of ancient airs? How is it that there could not be found in all Ireland as many subscribers of a pound a year, for two or three years, as would bring out a yearly volume of this splendid collection?—Oh! while it is not yet too late, let me even here entreat the coöperation of my countrymen in securing its completion, before that peculiarly gifted man, who has spent the greater part of a long life in collecting it, is snatched away from us for ever. It is little you know him; but I know him well, and I do not hesitate to say, that when you have once lost him, you shall never again look upon his like. How unlike the English! How immeasurably unlike the Scotch! There is scarcely in all Scotland, from the thrifty and well-taught labourer and mechanic up to the lordliest duke, a man in whose house volumes of the noble music of his native country, as well as of every scrap of national poetry or song, both in Gaelic and English, that from time to time issues from the active press of his country, may not be found.

Complaint on the neglect of Irish music; appeal to Irishmen in favour of it.

Having ventured so far to touch upon the subject of song and song-music, I have yet to say a few words, a very few words indeed, on dancing and dancing-music.

No clear allusion in very old Irish MSS. to dancing.

It is strange, and will, I am sure, appear to my readers almost incredible, that, as far as I have ever read, there is no reference that can be identified as containing a clear allusion to dancing in any of our really ancient MS. books. The present general, or generic, name for dancing, is *Rinnceadh*, but sometimes it is called

Damhsa. The word *Rinnceadh* is formed of *rinn*, an old name for a foot, and *ceadh*, a mere active termination like *ing* in English; so that from this plain analysis we might describe the word *Rinn-ceadh* to mean simply *Foot-ing;* and although we cannot find any ancient authority for its use, still we cannot but accept it as a correct native term, requiring little, if any, explanation to describe the action to which it has been given as the name. The term *Damhsa*, however, is not so easily analyzed or applied to that action; and I should, therefore, take it not to be an Irish term at all, but rather a Hibernicized form of the English word dance, for take, for example, this word *dance* in that form in which, among modern European languages, it most nearly approaches ours, the form *dansa*, and it will be seen that our term *damhsa* bears so direct a resemblance to it, that we can scarcely think of tracing it to any other source. The difference lies merely in that between *n* in the one and *m* in the other; a difference that can very easily be accounted for from the Irish preference to soft or aspirated and smooth consonants to those of a harder or harsher sound. The Gaedhils of Scotland have, in their older dictionaries, exactly our terms *Rinnceadh* and *Damsha;* but, singularly enough, Macleod and Dewar's Dictionary of the Gaelic Language (second edition, published at Glasgow in 1839), has the word *Damhsa*, but it refers us to *Dannsa* as the more correct form, though without giving any reason whatever for doing so.

XXXVIII. The modern generic name for dancing is *Rinnceadh*; it is sometimes called *Damhsa*; meaning of those terms.

The ordinary native name now known in Ireland for singing music is *Fonn*, and for dancing music, *Port*. The former is a very old word; but I have never met an instance of the latter in the older writings, though it occurs in medieval tales; but Father Michael O'Clery, in his Glossary, published in 1643, applies the term *Port* to lyric music in general in his explanation of the words *Adbond Trirech*. In some of the later middle-age tales, we sometimes meet with descriptions of social assemblies, in which it is said: "*Do sinneadh puirt agus cuir doibh*", that is, "*Ports* and *Cors* were played for them". Now, this word *Cor*, of which *Cuir* is the plural, is an old Irish word for music; and I may say that, wherever and whenever I met these two words *Ports* and *Cors*, I always understood them as signifying, if not dances, at least merry dancing tunes, such as we are now acquainted with. The *Cor*, however, has a precedent, if not its origin, in the Latin word chŏrea, which is explained, "a dance where many dance together; a ball". If I were to indulge in a little etymological speculation, I would venture to say that the *Port* was, as it really now is, the same as our Jig; while the *Cor*, which in Irish means a twist, a turn about, or out of a direct line, would very well describe the character of

Fonn and *Port*, the modern names for singing and dancing music; M. O'Clery applies the term *Port* to lyric music in general;

Cor, in the plural *Cuir*, an old Irish word for music—perhaps connected with *Chŏrea;* author suggests that *Port* was anciently what it is now, a "Jig", and *Cor* a "reel".

XXXVIII. the dance now called a Reel. Where the term Reel for a dance came from is not easily known, since it is not recognized by Webster in any such sense. Here is what Webster says: "*Reel*, from the Swedish *Ragla*, to stagger, to incline or move in walking, first to one side, and then to the other". It is curious to find that this Swedish word *Ragla*, from which Webster derives the word Reel, to stagger, would, by the interpolation of the aspirate *h* after *g*, form, as far as sound is concerned, a regular Irish genitive case of reel. For, if the word were written *Raghla*, it should be pronounced *Reela*, while its nominative form should be *Raghail*, and should be pronounced reel. The older Scotch dictionaries have the word reel as merely a *Rinnceadh*, or dance, without distinction from a Jig; but Macleod and Dewar make a Gaelic word for it, in accordance with the pronunciation, and print it *Righil*. My own present impression is, that the name may have come from Sweden or Norway into Scotland in modern times, and from that passed into Ireland.

etymology of "reel";

"Jig" borrowed from the French or Italian.

The modern term Jig for a certain kind of dance, is certainly taken from the French word gigue, or the Italian giga.

Rinnceadh Fada not an ancient term; applied to a "country dance".

The term *Rinnceadh Fada*, or long dance, which is so often introduced by modern writers, is not to be found in any manuscript Irish writing that I have ever seen. It appears to be a modern descriptive name for what is called a country dance, which is itself but a corruption of the French words "Contre Danse", a name merely descriptive of the simple arrangement of the dancers in two lines opposite to one another.

Conclusion.

With these few words as to dancing I here conclude this division of my general subject. I have, of necessity, abridged it; for it would have been impossible to go in detail into anything like a series of disquisitions upon what we may suppose to have been the exact forms, ornaments, and styles of our ancient musical instruments; and it would have been impossible as yet to give in detail any intelligible account of the employment of those instruments among our ancestors on all the various occasions on which our unequalled national music was in old times called into requisition. I have collected only some of the reliable authorities on the different parts of the subject, but still, as in the case of the other subjects which I have treated, by way of example only. Neither have I attempted to deal with subjects of music and dancing in themselves; because this would not be the place (even if I were the qualified person) to deal with them as they ought to be dealt with. I do not trespass on Dr. Petrie's province, but endeavour only to prepare the way for what, I hope, all will demand of him to complete for us, as I believe he only, of living men, can really explain what is yet untaught on the music of Erinn. It has been my province only to allude to the subject as one of those connectcd with the great subject of this entire course.—The Social Customs and Manners of Life among the People of Ancient Erinn.

APPENDIX.

I.

THE FIGHT OF FERDIAD AND CUCHULAIND.

AN EPISODE FROM THE ANCIENT TALE OF

THE TÁIN BÓ CHUAILGNE,

OR

THE CATTLE PREY OF COOLEY.

The original text from the vellum MS. in the Library of Trinity College, Dublin, known as the Book of Leinster (Class H. 2. 18), with a literal Translation.

The oldest copy of this tale known to exist is preserved in the vellum MS. known as the *Leabhar na h-Uidhre*, in the library of the Royal Irish Academy. This copy is, however, now imperfect at the end, and does not contain the "Fight of Ferdiad"—one of the finest episodes in the whole tale. It is to be regretted that the copy in this venerable manuscript is not complete, as it preserves the antique forms and the archaic purity of the language much better than any other existing one. There are, however, two ancient copies of the tale preserved in the Library of Trinity College, Dublin. The one in the vellum MS. H. 2. 16, which is, however, imperfect at the beginning, and differs somewhat from the older copies, to which it is inferior in form and in language. The second, which is the most complete copy known to us to exist, is contained in the vellum MS. Class H. 2. 18, better known as the Book of Leinster. This copy is perfect, and is nearly as old as that preserved in the *Leabhar na h-Uidhre.*

Although the grammatical endings are better preserved in the fragment in the *Leabhar na h-Uidhre*, the copy in the Book of Leinster is very nearly of the same antiquity; and the language, though a good deal modified in the antique forms and grammatical endings, is still very archaic and difficult.

The text of the MS. has been scrupulously followed, the only changes made being the lengthening out of the contractions, for which the Editor is indebted to the copy of the whole *Táin* made by Professor O'Curry from the Book of Leinster, and collated by him with all the ancient copies known to him, and now in the library of the Catholic University; and also the division of some words, and the punctuation of the whole. As the object the Editor has had in view in publishing this episode is to give an example of true Gaedhelic poetry, as distinguished from the inferior modernized legends and the confused jumble of traditions of various periods which Macpherson and others have fused together, and fabricated into the so-called poems of Ossian, to the prejudice of all that remains of genuine Ossianic poetry, he does not think it necessary to give various readings from other MSS., or to illustrate this tract as he would have wished to do if he did not expect soon to see the whole of the Tale of the *Táin Bó Chuailgne* published, and fully illustrated as it ought to be.

The marginal references to the Irish text indicate the folio and page of the original in the MS. H. 2. 18.

COMRAC FHIRDEAD INSO.

H. 2. 18. fol. 87. a. a.

Is andsin ra imraided oc feraib h-Erenn, cia bad ċóir do ċomlond ocas do ċomrac la Coinculaind ra h-uair na maitni muċi ar na bárach. Is sed ra raidsetar uile, combad é Ferdiad, mac Damain, mic Dáre, in milid mór ċalma dferaib Domnand. Daig ba cosmail ocas ba comadas a comlon acas a comrac. Ac oen muimme da ringsetar ceird gnimrada gaile ocas gaiscid da ra ḟoglaim: ac Scáthaig, ocas ac Uaṫaig, ocas ac Aife. Ocas ni bai immarcraid neich dib ac araile, aċt cless in gae bulga ac Coinculaind. Cid ed ón ba congancnessac Ferdiad ac comlund ocas ac comrac ra laeċ ar áṫ na agidside. Is andsin ra fáitea fessa ocas teċtaireda ar cend Fhirdiad. Ra erastar, ocas ra eittchestar, ocas ra rersetar Ferdiad na teċta sin, ocas ni tháinic leó, daig ra fitir a ní ma rabadar do,—do ċomlond ocas do comrac re ċaraid, re ċoclé, ocas re comalta, re Fern-diad mac n-Damain mic Dare, [re Conċulaind], ocas ni tháinic leó.

Is andsin fáitte Medb na druith ocas na glámma, ocas na cruadgressa ar cend Fhirdiad, ar co n-derntáis teóra aera fossaigte dó, ocas teóra glamma dicend, go tócbaitis teóra bolga bar a agid,—ail ocas anim, ocas athis; mur bud marb a ċetóir, bad marb re cind nomaide munu thised. Tanic Ferdiad leo dar cend a enig, daig ba h-ussu lessium a ṫuttim do gaib gaile, ocas gaiscid, ocas engnama, ná a ṫuttim de gaaib aire, ocas ecnaig, ocas imdergta. Ocas a da riaċt, ra fiadaiged ocus ra frithá-led é, ocas ra daled lind so óla so ċain so mesc fair, gor bo mesc medarċain é. Ocas ra gelta comada móra dó, ar in comlond, ocas ar in comrac do denam .i. carpat cethri secht cumal; ocas timthacht da ḟer deċ dechgud caċa daṫa; ocas co méit a ḟerainn de min Maige h-Ai, gan ċain, [gan chobach, ocas cen dunad cen sluaighed], cen ecendáil da ṁac, ocas da ua, ocus da iarmua, go bruinne m-bráṫa, ocas betha; ocas Findabair do én mnái, ocas in t-eó óir bae i m-brutt Medba fair anuas. Is amlaid ra bai Medb gá rada, ocas ra beir na briaṫra and, ocas ra reċair Ferdiad.

Rat ra luaċ mór m-buinne,
rat ċuit maige is chaille,

THE FIGHT OF FERDIAD.

And then it was discussed by the men of Eiriu, who should go to combat and do battle with Cuchulaind at the early hour of the morning of the morrow. What they all said was, that it was Ferdiad, son of Daman, son of Dáre, the great and valiant warrior of the men of Domnand. For their mode of combat and fight was equal and alike. They had learned the science of arms, bravery and valour with the same tutors: with Scáthach, and with Uathach, and with Aífe. And neither of them had an advantage over the other, except that Cuchulaind had the feat of the Gai Bulg. Nevertheless Ferdiad was clad in a skin-protecting armour to give combat and battle to a hero at the ford against him. Messages and messengers were then sent for Ferdiad. Ferdiad denied, and declined, and refused those messengers, and he came not with them, because he knew wherefore they wanted him—to fight and combat with his own friend, and companion, and fellow pupil, Cuchulaind, and he came not with them.

Ferdiad selected to fight Cuchulaind; He is invited by Medb;

It is then Medb sent the druids, and the satirists, and the violent exciters for Ferdiad, that they might compose three repressing satires, and three hilltop satires for him, that they might raise three blisters on his face,—shame, blemish, and disgrace; so that if he died not immediately, he would be dead before the end of nine days, if he came not with them. Ferdiad came with them for sake of his honour, for he preferred to fall rather by the shafts of valour, gallantry, and bravery, than by those of satire, abuse, and reproach. And when he arrived he was received with honour, and attendance, and he was served with pleasant, sweet, intoxicating liquor, so that he became intoxicated and gently merry. And great rewards were promised him for making the combat and the fight, namely: a chariot [worth] four times seven cumals; and the outfit of twelve men of clothes of every colour; and the extent of his own territory of the level plain of Magh Aié, free of tribute, without purchase and without courts or legions, without peril to his son, and to his grandson, and to their descendants, to the end of time and life; and Findabar as his wedded wife, and the golden brooch which was in Medb's cloak in addition to all these. And thus was Medb saying, and she spake these words there, and Ferdiad answered.—

Medb sends druids and satirists; to save his honour he comes; he is welcomed and promised rewards;

I will give a great reward in rings,
With thy share of plain and forest,

Dialogue between Medb and Ferdiad;

Fol. 87. a. a.

ra saire do ċlainne
aniu co tí brath,
a Ḟhirdiad mic Damáin,
eirggi guin is gabáil.
atteċha as ceċ anáil,
cid dait gan a gabáil
(—a ni gabar caċ?—)

F. d. Ni gebra gan áraċ;
daig nim láeċ gan lámaċ.
bud trom form i m-báraċ,
bud fortrén in feidm.
cú dán comainm Culand;
is amnas in n-urrand;
ní furursa a ḟulang;—
bud tairptech in teidm.

M. Ratfiat laich rat láma,
noċa raga ar dála:
srein ocas eiċ ána
da bertatar rit láim,
a Ḟhirdiad in n-ága.
dáig isat duni dána,
damsa bat fer gráda
seċ cách, gan naċ cáin.

F. d. Ni ragsa gan ráta
do ċluċi na h-áta.
meraid collá m-brátha
go m-bruċ is co m-brig.
noċo geb gé ersti,
ge ra bech dom rérci,
gan grein ocas ésci
la muir ocas tír.

M. Gachan: duit a ḟuireċ;
naiscsiu gorbat buideċ
for deiss rig is ruireċ,
do ragat rat láim.
sul sund naċat tuilfea—
ratsia caċ ni ċungfea,
daig ra fess co mairbfea
in fer ṫic it dáil.

F. d. Ni géb gan sé curu,—
ni ba ni bas lugu,—
sul do néor mo mudu
i m-bail i m-biat sluaig.
da nam ṫorrsed mardaric,
cinnset cun cur comnart,

Dialogue between Medb and Ferdiad;

And the freedom of thy children
From this day till the end of time,
O Ferdiad, son of Daman,
O champion of wounds and conquests,;
Thou hast come out of every strife:
Why dost thou not receive
(—that which others would accept?—)

F. I will not accept it without guarantee;
For a champion without security I will not be.
Heavily will it press upon me to-morrow,
Terrible will be the battle.
Hound indeed is the name of Culand;
He is fierce in combat;
'T is not easy to withstand him;
Fearless will be the fight.

M. I will give a champion's guarantee,
That thou shalt not be required at assemblies:
Bridles and noble steeds
Shall into thy hands be given,
O Ferdiad of valour.
Because thou art a brave man,
To me thou shalt be a bosom friend
Above all others, free of all tribute.

F. I will not go without securities
To the contest of the ford.
It will live [in fame] unto the judgment day
In full vigour and in force.
I will not accept though I die,
Though thou excitest me in language,
Without the sun and moon
Together with the sea and land.

M. Thou shalt have all: 't is to thyself to delay it;
Bind us until thou art satisfied
Upon the right hand of kings and princes,
Who will become thy security.
Here is one who will not refuse thee—
I will give thee whatever thou desirest,
For I well know that thou will kill
The man who comes against thee.

F. I will not accept without six securities,—
It shall not be any less,—
Before my destruction is wrought
There where hosts will be.
Even if my fame should be disparaged,
I will advance though the strength be equal,

Fol. 87. a. a. co n-dernur in comrac
ra Coinculaind cruaid.

M. Cid Domnal na cárpat,
na Niamán án airgne,
gid iat lucht na bairddne,
rotfiastu gid acht;
fonasc latt ar Morand;
madaill latt a chomal,
naisc Carpri Min Manand,
is naisc ar da macc.

F. D. A Medb, co mét m-buafaid,
nít cred caine nuachair;
is derb is tú is bracail
ar Cruachain na clad,
ard glór is ait gairgnert.
dom roiched sról santbrecc,
tuc dam t-ór is t-arget,
daig ro fairgged dam.

M. Nach tussu in caur codnach,
da tiber delgg n-drolmach?
o ndiu co ti domnach,
ni bá dál ba sia.
a láich blatnig bladmair,
cach sét caém ar talmain
da bérthar duit amlaid:
is uili rotfia. R.
Finnabair na fergga,
rígan iarthair Elgga,
ar n-dích con na cerdda,
a Fhirdiad, rodfia. R.

Is andsain ra siacht Medb maeth n-árais bar Ferdiad im comlond ocas im chomrac ra sessiur curad ar na bárach, na imchomlond ocas imchomrac ra Coinculaind, a oenur dambad assu leiss. Ra siacht Ferdiad maéth n-árais furriri no andar leis, im chur in t-seissir cetna im na comadaib ra gellad dó do chomallud riss madda toetsad Cuculaind leiss.

Andsain ra gabait a eich d'Fergus, ocas ra h-indled a charpat, ocas tánic reme co airm [a m-boi Cuculaind] co n-indised do sain. Firiss Cuculaind falti riss. "Mo chen do thichtu

Fol. 87. a. b. a mo popa Fherguis", bar Cuculaind. "Tairissi lim in m-falti a daltáin," bar Fergus. "Acht is do radechainsa da innisin duit inti ro thaet do chomlond ocas do chomrac rutt ra h-uair na maitne muche i m-bárach". "Clunemni latt din", bar Cuculaind. "Do chara fein ocas do chocle ocas

Dialogue between Medb and Ferdiad.

Till I make the battle
With Cuchulaind the brave.

M. Though it be Domnal in his chariot,
Or Niaman of the slaughter,
Though they are the patrons of the bards,
Even these, though difficult, I will give;
Bind it upon Morand;
If thou wishest for certain fulfilment,
Bind Carpri Min of Manand,
And our two sons, bind.

F. O Medb, abounding in venom,
Thou art not a sweet-tempered spouse to a consort;
It is true thou art the Brachail
Of Cruachan of the ramparts,
With lofty speech and despotic power.
Send me the beautiful speckled satin,
Give me thy gold and thy silver,
Since to me thou hast proffered them.

M. Art thou not the leading champion,
To whom I give a hooked pin?
From this day till Sunday,
The respite shall not be longer.
O thou famed and renowned hero,
All the splendid jewels of the earth
Shall to thee be also given;
And all in fulness I will give.

Findabar of the champions,
The princess of the west of Elgga,
On the slaying of the hound, of the feats,
O Ferdiad, [to thee] I will give.

Mutual binding of Medb and Ferdiad.

And then did Medb bind Ferdiad to combat and fight with six champions on the morrow, or to make combat and fight with Cuchulaind, whichever he thought easier. Ferdiad bound her, as he thought, on the sureties of the aforesaid six for the fulfilment of the promise of the rewards that was made to him should Cuchulaind fall by him.

Fergus visits Cuchulaind,

Then his horses were harnessed for Fergus, and his chariot was yoked, and he went forward to where Cuchulaind was, to tell him of it. Cuchulaind bade him welcome. "I am happy at thy coming, O my good friend, Fergus", said Cuchulaind. "I gladly accept that welcome, my pupil", said Fergus. "But what I have come for is to tell thee who the person is that comes to combat and fight with thee at the hour of early morning to-morrow". "We will listen to thee then", said Cuchulaind. "Thine own friend and companion and

and warns him of the approaching fight;

Fol. 47. a b. do ċomalta; ċ-fer comċliss, ocas comgascid, ocas comgnima, Ferdiad mac Damáin mic Dáre, in milid mór ċalma d'feraib Domnand". "Attear ar cobais", bar Cuculaind, "ni na[r] dáil duthracamar ar cara do ṫuideċt". "Is aire sein iarum", ale bar Fergus, "ar a n-airichlea ocas ara n-airelma, dáig ni mar caċ conarnecar comlund ocas comrac riut for táin bó Cualnge don ċursa Ferdiad mac Damáin mic Dáre". "Attúsa sund ám", bar Cuculaind, "ac fostud ocas ac imḟuireċ cethri n-ollċoiced nh-Erend oluan taite ṡamna co taite imbuilg, ocas ni rucas traig teċid re n-oenḟer riss in re sin, ocas is dóig lim ni mó bérat remisium". Acas issamlaid ra bai Fergus ga ráid ga báeglugad, ocas ra bert na briaṫra, ocas ra recair Cuculaind.

A Chuculaind comal n-gle,
atċiu is mitig duit eirge;
ata sund ċucut ra ferg
Ferdiad mac Damain dreċ derg.

Cc. A túsa sund, ni seól seng,
ac trén ḟasdud fer nh-Erend;
ni rucas for teċed traig
ar ara ċomlund oenḟir.

F. Amnas in fer da lae ferg
as luss a ċlaidib cró derg.
cnes congna im Fherrdiad na n-drong,
riss ni geib caṫ na comlond.

Cc. Bi tost—na taċair do scél,
a Fherguis nan-arm n-imthrén;
dar caċ ferand, dar caċ fond,
damsa, noċon, ecomlond.

F. Amnas in fer, fichtib gal
noċon ḟurusa a ṫroeċad;
nert cét na churp,—calma in mod,—
nin geib rind, nin tesc faebor.

Cc. Mad dia comairsem bar áṫ,
missi is Ferdiad gascid gnáṫ,
ni baé in scarad gan sceó:
bud ferggaċ ar faebar gleó.

F. Rapad ḟerr lem ann a luag,
a Cuculaind ċlaideb ruad,
combad tú ra berad sair
corcur Fhirdiad diummasaig.

Cc. A tiursa brethir co m-báig,
gon commaiṫse oc immarbáig,
is missi buadaigfes de

fellow pupil; thy co-feat, and co-deed, and co-valour-man, Ferdiad, son of Daman, son of Dáre, the great and valiant champion of the men of Domnand". "We give our word", said Cuchulaind, "it is not to fight ourselves we desire our friend to come". "It is now, therefore", said Fergus, "that thou requirest to be cautious and prepared, because, unlike any of those who have given thee combat and battle on the Táin Bó Chuailgne on this occasion is Ferdiad son of Daman, son of Dáre". "I am here", said Cuchulaind, "detaining and delaying the four great provinces of Eiriu since the first Monday of the beginning of Samhain [November] to the beginning of Imbulc [spring], and I have not yielded one foot in retreat before any one man during that time, and neither will I, I trust, yield before him". And so did Fergus continue to speak to put him on his guard, and he spake these words, and Cuchulaind answered.

Dialogue between Fergus and Cuchulaind.

F. O Cuchulaind brave in battle,
I see 't is time for thee to arise;
Here comes to thee with anger
Ferdiad, son of Daman of the ruddy face.

C. I am here, it is no light task,
Valiantly detaining the men of Eiriu;
I have not yielded a foot in retreat
To shun the combat of any man.

F. Fearless is the man in his excited rage
Because of his blood-red sword.
A skin-protecting armour wears Ferdiad of the troops,
Against it prevaileth not battle or combat.

C. Be silent—urge not thy story,
O Fergus of the arms brave;
On any land, on any ground,
I was not his inferior in battle.

F. Fierce is the man, in battles brave,
'T is not easy to vanquish him;
The strength of a hundred is in his body—gallant his bearing—
Spears pierce him not, swords cut him not.

C. Should we happen to meet at a ford,
I and Ferdiad of never-failing valour,
It shall not be a separation without history:
Fierce will be our sharp conflict.

F. I should prefer to a high reward,
O Cuchulaind of the blood-stained sword,
That it were thee that carried eastward
The purple of the haughty Ferdiad.

C. I pledge my word and my vow,
Though we may be much alike in the combat,
That it is I who shall gain the victory

Fol. 87, a.b.

bar mac n-Damáin mic Dáre.
F. Is me tarclaim na sluagu sair—
luag mo saraigṫe d'Ultaib.
Lim ṫancatar a tírub,—
a curaid a caṫ milid.
Cc. Munbud Conchobar na ċess
rarad ċruaid in comadcess;
ní tháinic Medb maige in Scáil
turus bad mo congáir.
F. Ra fail gním is mó bar do láim—
gleó ra Ferdiad mac n-Damáin;
arm cruaid catad cardda raind
bid acut, a Chuculaind. A.

Táinic Fergus reme doċum an-dunaid ocas longṗuirt. Luid Ferdiad doċum a ṗupla ocas a muintiri, ocas ra ċuaid dóib maeṫ n-áraig do tharraċtain do Medb sair imċomlond ocas imċomrac ra fessiur curad ar na bárach, na imċomlond ocas imċomrac ra Coinċulaind a oenur diambad assu leiss. Da ċuaid dóib no máeṫ n-áraig do tarraċtain dosum for Meidb im ċuir in t-seisir ċurad ċetna im na comadaib ra gellad dó do chomallad riss mad da taetsad Cuculaind leiss.

Nirdar subaig somaig sobbronac [luċt puirle Fhirdiad in aghaid sin]; aċt rarsat dubaig dobbronaig domenmnaig; doig ra fetatar airm condricfaitis na dá ċuraid ocas na dá ċliach bernaid ċét, co taetsad ceċtar dib and, nó co taetsaitis a n-dis; ocas dam neċtar dib; doig leosom gombad é a tigerna féin; daig ní ba réid comlond no comrac ra Coinculaind for táin bó Cualnge.

Ra chotail Ferdiad tossaċ na h-aidċi coro ṫromm, ocas a ṫáinic deired na h-aidchi, ra ċuaid a coċlud uad, ocas ra luid a mesci de, ocas da bái ceist in ċomlaind, ocas in chomraic sair. Ocas ra gab láim ar a araid ar a n-gabad a eoċo ocas ar a n-indled a ċarrat. Ra gab in t-ara ga im-thairmesc imme. Ra rad ḟerr duib [anad ina dul annsin], arse in gilla, [uair ní mó molas duibe na dimolas*].

Bi tost din, a gillai, ar Ferdiad, [uair ni gabam toirmesc oclaċ imo in siubal so], ocas iss amlaid ra boi ga rád, ocas ra bert na briaṫra and, ocas ra srecair in gilla.

F. Tiagaim issin dáil sea
do ċosnam ind ḟirsea,
gorrisem in n-aṫsa—
áth forr n-gera inbadb—

Of the son of Daman, son of Dáre.
F. It is I that gathered the forces eastward—
In revenge of my dishonour by the Ultonians.
With me they have come from their lands,—
Their champions and their battle warriors.

C. If Conchobar had not been in his debility
Hard would have been the strife;
Medb of Magh an Scail had not made
An expedition of louder shoutings.

F. A greater deed awaiteth thy hand—
To battle with Ferdiad son of Daman;
Hardened bloody weapons with obdurate points
Do thou have with thee, O Cuchulaind!

Fergus came back to the court and encampment. Ferdiad went to his tent and to his people, and told them that he was firmly bound by Medb to give combat and fight to six champions on the morrow, or to combat and fight with Cuchulaind alone if he thought it easier. He told how he had firmly bound Medb with the security of the same six champions for the fulfilment of the promise of rewards, should Cuchulaind fall by him. Ferdiad tells his people of his bond to Medb;

The inmates of Ferdiad's tent were not cheerful, happy, or in melancholy pleasure on that night; but they were cheerless, sorrowful, and dispirited; because they knew that wherever the two champions and the two hundred-slaying heroes met, that either of them should fall there, or that both of them would fall; and if it should be one of them, they were certain it would be their own master; because it was not possible to make combat or fight with Cuchulaind on the Táin Bó Chuailgne. their anxiety on his account.

Ferdiad slept the beginning of the night very heavily, and when the latter part of the night came, his sleep departed from him, and his intoxication had vanished, and the anxiety of the fight and the battle pressed upon him. And he commanded his charioteer to harness his horses and yoke his chariot. The charioteer began to dissuade him from it. It would be better for thee [to stay than to go there], said the servant, for to thee my approval of it is not more than my disapproval.* Ferdiad awakes and orders his chariot to be yoked; his charioteer dissuades him from the combat;

Be silent now, my servant, said Ferdiad [for we will not be persuaded by any youth from this journey], and so was he saying, and he spake these words then, and the servant answered him.—

Dialogue between Ferdiad and his charioteer;

F. Let us go to this challenge
To vanquish this man,
Till we reach this ford—
A ford over which the raven will croak—

* An idiomatic mode of saying he disapproved of it. The phrase is still current.

Fol. 87. a. b

i comdail Conculaind,
da guin tre chreitt cumaing
gorruca trít urraind,
coror de bur marb.

G. Ra pad ferr dúib anad.
ní ba mín far mbagar;
biaid neċ diamba galar;
bar scarad bud snéid,
techt i n-dáil ailt Ulad;
is dal dia m-bia ruḋar;
is fata bas ċuman;
mairg ragas in réim.

F. Ni coir ana rádi,
ní h-opair niad náre;
ní dlegar din ále;
ní anfam fad dáig.
bí tost, dín, a gillai;
bid calma ár sirt sinni;
ferr teinni na timmi;
[tiagam is in dáil.]* T.

Ra gabait a eich Firdiad ocas ra indled a ċarpat, ocas tánic reme co áċ in chomraic, ocas thánic lá cona lán-soilsi dó and itir.

"Maiṫ, a gillai", bar Ferdiad. "Scar dam fortcha ocas forgemen mo charpait fóm andso, co ro ṫobur mo thromthairthim suain ocas chotulta andso, daig ni ra chotlas deired na h-aidchi ra ceist in chomlaind ocas in chomraic".

Ra scoir in gilla na eiċ Ra discuir in carpat foe, toilis a ṫromṫairthim cotulta fair.

Imthusa Conculaind sunda innossa. Ni erracht side itir co tánic láa cona lán ḟoilse do, dáig na h-arraitis fir h-Erend, is ecla no is uamun do berad fair, madda n-eirged. Ocas ó ṫánic láa cona lán ḟoilsi, ra gab láim ar (a) araid ar a n-gabad a eoċo, ocas ar a n-indled a ċarpat. "Maith a gilla", bar Cuculaind, "geib ar n-eich dún, ocas innill ar carpat, daig is mocherseċ in laech ra dáil nar n-dáil, Ferdiad mac Damain mic Dáre".

Is gabṫa na eiċ, is innilti in carpat, cindsiu and, ocas ní tár dot gasciud. Is and sin cinnis in cur cetaċ, clessamnaċ, cath buadaċ, claideb derg Cuculaind mac Sualtaim ina charpat. Gura gairsetar imme boccánaig, ocas bananaig, ocas geniti glindi, ocas demna aeóir Daig da bertis Tuaṫa Dé Danann a n-gairiud immisium, combad móti a gráin, ocas a ecla, ocas a uruad, ocas a uruamain

To battle with Cuchulaind,
To wound him through his strong body
To crush his valour through him,
So that of it he shall die.

Dialogue between Ferdiad and his charioteer.

S. It were better for thee to stay.
Thy threats are not gentle;
One there will be to whom it will be disease;
Thy parting will be distressful,
To encounter the chief [hero] of Ulster;
It is a meeting of which grief will come;
Long will it be remembered;
Wo is he who goeth that journey.

F. What thou sayest is not right,
A brave champion should not refuse;
It is not our inheritance;
I therefore will not longer stay.
Be silent, then, my servant;
We will be brave in the field of battle;
Valour is better than timidity;
[Let us go to the challenge*].

Ferdiad's horses were harnessed and his chariot yoked, and he came forward to the ford of the battle, and the day with its full lights had now come upon him there. he goes to the ford;

"Good, my servant", said Ferdiad, "spread for me the cushions and skins of my chariot under me here, until I take my deep rest of repose and sleep here, because I slept not the end of the night through the anxiety of the combat and the battle". and sleeps in his chariot.

The servant unharnessed the horses. He arranged [the cushions and skins of] the chariot under him, and his heavy repose of sleep came upon him.

The history of Cuchulaind here now I will tell. He arose not at all until the day with all its light had come, in order that the men of Eiriu should not say that it was fear or dread that induced him, if he had arisen. And when day with all its lights came, he commanded his charioteer to harness his horses and yoke his chariot. "Good, my servant", said Cuchulaind, "harness our horses for us, and yoke our chariot, for he is an early rising champion who cometh to meet us to-day, Ferdiad, son of Daman, son of Dáre". Why Cuchulaind did not arise early that day; he orders his chariot;

The horses are harnessed, the chariot is yoked, step thou into it, and it will not disparage thy valour. And then the battle-fighting, dexterous, battle-winning, red-sworded hero, Cuchulaind, son of Sualtam, sprang into his chariot. And there shouted around him Bocanachs, and Bananachs, and Geniti Glindi, and demons of the air. For the Tuatha Dé Danann were used to set up their Bocannachs and other beings shout around him

* H. 2. 16. 614.

in caċ cath, ocas in caċ cathroi, incaċ comlund, ocas in caċ comruc i teiged.

Fol. 88. a. a. Nir bo ċian d'araid Fhirdiad co cuala in ni in fraim, ocas in foṫrom, ocas in fidren, in toirm, in torann, ocas in ses-tan, ocas in sesilbi, .i. scelugur na sciaṫ cliss, ocas slic-rech na sleg, ocas glondbéimneċ na claideb, ocas breisim-nech in chathbairr, ocas drongar na lurigi, ocas imchommilt na n-arm, dechraideċt na cles, teteinmneċ na tét, ocas nuallgrith na roṫ, ocas culgaire in ċarpat, ocas bass-chaire na n-ech, ocas trommċoblach in ċuraid ocas in chath-miled doċum in náṫa dá ṡaigid. Táinic in gilla ocas forromair a láim for a ṫigerna. "Maiṫ a Fhirdiad", bar in gilla, "comeirg, ocas aṫáṫar sund ċucut dochum in n-atha". Ocas ra bert in gilla na briaṫra and.—

Atchlunim cul carpait
ra cuing n-alaind n-argait
is fuath fir co forbairt.
as droiċ carpait ċruaid;
dar Breg Ros, dar Braine
fochengat in slige
seċ bun Báile in Bile—
is buadaċ a m-buaid
Is cú airgdeċ aiges,
is carpteċ glan geibes,
is seboc saer slaidess
a eocho fádess.
is cródatta in cua
is demin donrua.
ra fess ni ba tua
do beir dún in tress.
Mairg ḃias isin tulaig
ar cind in ċon cubaid.
bar rairngertsa anuraid
ticfad gired ċuin—
cú na h-Emna Maċa,
cu co n-deilb caċ daṫa,
cu ċriċi, cú caṫa,
do ċlunim, rar clum At.

"Maith, a gilla", bar Ferdiad, "ga faṫ mara molais in fer sain ó chánac ó tig? ocas is suail naċ faṫa conais dait a ro mét ros molais; ocas bar airngert Ailill ocas Medb damsa go taeṫsat in fer sain lemm. Ocas daig is dar cend luage loċerthair lemsa colluaṫ é. Ocas is mithig

shouts around him, so that the hatred, and the fear, and the abhorrence, and the great terror of him should be the greater in every battle, in every battle-field, in every combat, and in every fight into which he went.

And it was not long till Ferdiad's charioteer heard the noise [approaching, i.e.] the clamour, and the rattle, and the whistling, and the tramp, and the thunder, the clatter, and the buzz, namely, the shield-noise of the missive shields, and the hissing of the spears, and the loud clangour of the swords, and the tinkling of the helmet, and the ringing of the armour, and the friction of the arms; the dangling of the missive weapons, the straining of the ropes, and the loud clattering of the wheels, and the creaking of the chariot, and the tramping of the horses, and the triumphant advance of the champion and the warrior towards the ford approaching him. The servant came and placed his hand on his lord. "Good, O Ferdiad!" said the servant, "arise, here they come to thee to the ford". And the servant spake these words there.—

Ferdiad's charioteer hears the chariot approaching; and awakes his lord;

I hear the creaking of a chariot
With a beautiful silver yoke
And the form of a full grown man in it.
It is the roll of a warlike chariot;
Over Breg Ross, over Braine
They come over the highway
By the foot of Báile-in-Bile—
It is gifted with victories,

describes the chariot and its occupant;

He is a heroic hound who urges it,
He is a trusty charioteer who yokes it,
He is a noble hawk who speeds
His horses towards the south.
He is a martial hero,
He is [the presage of] bloody slaughter.
Surely 't is not with indexterity
He will give us the battle.

Woe to him who is on the hillock
Awaiting the hound of valour.
I foretold last year
That there would come a heroic hound—
The hound of Emain Macha,
A hound with complexion of all colours,
The hound of a territory, the hound of battle,
I hear, I have heard.

and foretels evil to his master;

"Good, my servant", said Ferdiad, "wherefore is it that thou hast been lauding that man ever since he came from his home? and it is likely that thou art not without wages for thy great praise of him; and Ailill and Medb have foretold that that man will fall by me. And certain it is that for sake of reward he shall be

Ferdiad upbraids him for praising Cuchulaind;

Fol. 58. a. a. in chobair". Ocus ra beirt na briathra ann, ocus ra recair in gilla.—

F. Is mithig in chabair;
bi tost din, na m-bladaig,
nar bu gnim ercodail.
daig ni bráth dar bruach
mac ċi ċurad Cualnge
co n-adabraid ualle?
daig is dar cend luage
locherthair colluath.

G. Mác chim curaid Cualnge
co n-adabraib ualle,
nir teiċed téit uainne,
aċt is cucaind tic,
rethid, is ni ro mall;
gid ro gaéṫ ni ro gand,
mar ḋusci d'ḟorall,
na marthoraind trice.

F. Suail naċ fotha [con ais]
a ro mét ras molais;
ga fáth ma ra thogais
ó ṫánac ó tig?
iss innossa thócbait,
atát aca ḟuacairt;
ni thecat da ḟuasairt,
aċt athigmith. M.

Nir bo ċian d'araid Firdiad dia m-boi ann co facca ni, in carpat cáin cúicrind cethir rind, gollúċ, golluas go lán gliccus, go pupaill uaníde, go creit chraesstana, ċraesstirim, ċlessaird, ċolgfata, ċurata; ar da n-eċaib luatha lémnecha, ó mair, bulid, ḃedgaig, bolgróin, uċt leṫna, beóċruidi, blenárda, basslethna, ċossċaela, fortrena, forránċa fua. Ec liath leslethan, lugléimneċ, lebormongach, fán dara ċuing don chárpait. Eċ dub dualaċ, dulbrass, dromleṫan fan ċuing anaill.

Ba samalta ra sebacc da ċlaiss illó ċruadgáiṫi; ná ra sidi sergaiṫi errraig illó márta, dar mani maċair; ná ra cet ag n-allaid ar na ċetgluasaċt do ċonaib do ċétrói, dá eċ Conculaind immon carpat, marbad ar licc áin tentidi; con criothsat ocus con bertsat in talmain, ra tricci na túrma.

Ocus da riaċt Cuculaind doċum in n-áṫa. Tarrasair Ferdiad bar fan leiṫ descertaċ ind áṫa. Dessid Cuculaind bár fán leiṫ tuascertac.

Ferais Ferdiad failte fri Conculaind. "Mo ċen do ticcu

quickly slain by me. And it is time for the relief". And he spake these words there, and the servant answered:

Dialogue between Ferdiad and his charioteer.

F. It is time for the relief;
Be silent then, don't extol,
That it be not a deferred deed of prophecy.
Surely 't is not a betrayal on the brink [of battle]
If thou seest the champion of Cuailgne
With his ostentatiousness of fame?
Surely, for the sake of reward,
He shall soon be slain.

S. If I see the champion of Cuailgne
With his ostentatiousness of fame,
It is not in retreat he goeth from us,
But it is towards us he cometh,
He runneth, and 't is not very slowly;
Though fleet as wind, not with difficulty,
But like water from a high cliff,
Or like the rapid thunder.

F. It seems thou art not without rewards
For thy great praises of him;
Why else hast thou chosen to do so
Since he has come from his home?
And now, when he appeareth,
Thou art proclaiming him;
Thou comest not to attack him,
But for glorifying him.

Description of Cuchulaind's chariot and horses;

Ferdiad's charioteer was not long there until he saw something, the beautiful, flesh-seeking, four-peaked chariot, with speed, with velocity, with full cunning, with a green pavilion, with a thin-bodied, dry-bodied, high-weaponed, long-speared, warlike Creit [body of the chariot]; upon two fleet-bounding, large eared, fierce, prancing, whale-bellied, broad-chested, lively-hearted, high-flanked, wide-hoofed, slender-legged, broad-rumped, resolute horses under it. A gray, broad-hipped, fleet, bounding, long maned steed under the one yoke of the chariot. A black tufty-maned, ready-going, broad backed steed under the other yoke.

and of the fleetness of their advance.

Like unto a hawk [swooping] from a cliff on a day of hard wind; or like a sweeping gust of the spring wind on a March day, over a smooth plain; or like the fleetness of a wild stag on his being first started by the hounds in his first field, were Cuchulaind's two horses with the chariot, as though they were on fiery flags; so that the earth shook and trembled with the velocity of their motion.

And Cuchulaind reached the ford. Ferdiad came on the south side of the ford. Cuchulaind drew up on the north side.

Ferdiad bade welcome to Cuchulaind. "I am happy at thy

Fol. 58. a. a. a Cuculaind", bar Ferdiad. "Tairissi lim ní ind ḟalti mad cos tráchtsa", bar Cuculaind; "ocas indiu ni dénaim tairissi de ċend. Acas a Ḟhirdiad", bar Cuculaind, "ra po ċorú damsa fálti d'ferthain fritsu, na daitsiu a ḟerthain rumsa. daig is tú dariaċt in crich ocas in coiced i túsa, ocas ni ra chóir .duitsiu tiċtain do ċomlund ocas do ċomrac rimsa, ocas ra pa ċorudamsa dol do ċomlond ocas do ċomrac rutsu. Dáig is romutsu atát mo mnása ocas mo meic, ocas mo maccaémi, m'eiċ ocas m'eċrada, m'albi ocas m'éiti ocas m'indili". "Maiṫ a Cuculaind", bar Ferdiad, "cid rot tucsu do ċomlund ocas do ċomrac rimsa itir? Dáig dá m-bammar ac Scáṫaig ocas ac Uaṫaig ocas ac Aifi, is tussu ba forbfer frithalma damsa .i. ra armad mo ḟlega ocas ra deirged mo lepaid.

"Is fír ám", ale bar Cuculaind, "ar oíce, ocas ar oítidċi do ninsea duitsiu, ocas ni hí sin tuarascbail ba túsa indiu itir: act ní ḟil bar sin bith laéch naċ dingebsa indiu". Ocas is andsin serais ceċtarnai dib athcossan n-aṫgér n-aṫcharatraid ra raile; ocas rabert Ferdiad na briaṫra and, ocas ra recair Cuculaind.

F. Cid ra tuc, a ċua,
do ṫroit ra niaḋ nua?
bud crodersg da chrua
as analaib ṫ-eċ;
mairg do thurus;
bud atód ra h-airer,
ricfa a less do legess,
mad da ris do ṫeċ.
Cc. Do dechad ré nóchaib,
im torc tretan tréṫaig,
re caṫaib, re céṫaib:—
dot ċursu san lind,
d'ḟeirg rut, is dot romad,
bar comrac cét conar,
corop dait bar ḟogal
do ċosnom do chind.
F. Fail sund neċ rat méla,
is missi rat gena.
dáig is dím facrith (.i. tic)
conugud a curad
i fiadnassi Ulad,
goroip ċian bar ċuman
gorop dóib bus dith.

[A line wanting—the stanza is not in H. 2. 16. or H. 1. 13.]

coming, O Cuchulaind", said Ferdiad. "The welcome would have been acceptable to me until this time", said Cuchulaind; "but this day I deem it not acceptable as friendship indeed. And Ferdiad", said Cuchulaind, "it were fitter that I bade thee welcome than that thou shouldst welcome me, because it is thou that hast come to me into the country and province in which I am, and it was not proper for thee to come to combat and fight with me, but it were more fit that I went to combat and fight with thee. Because it is out before thee my women and my children, and my youths, my horses and my steeds, my flocks, and my herds and my cattle are". "Good, O Cuchulaind", said Ferdiad, "what has brought thee to combat and to fight with me at all? Because when we were with Scáthach and with Uathach and with Aífe, thou wert my attendant man, namely to tie up my spears and to prepare my bed".

Ferdiad welcomes Cuchulaind; Cuchulaind upbraids him for coming to fight him; and Ferdiad retorts;

"It is true, indeed", said Cuchulaind, "but it was then as younger and junior to thee, I used to do so for thee; and this, however, is not the story that will be told hereafter of this day. For there is not in the world a champion that I would not fight this day". And it was then each of them uttered sharp, unfriendly invectives against the other; and Ferdiad spake these words there, and Cuchulaind answered.—

Dialogue between Ferdiad and Cuchulaind in which they upbraid each other.

F. What has brought thee, O hound,
To combat with a strong champion?
Crimson-red shall flow thy blood
Over the trappings of thy steeds;
Wo is thy journey;
Long shall it be told,
Thou shalt need to be healed,
Shouldst thou [alive] reach thy house.

C. I went to combat with warriors,
With lordly chiefs of hosts,
With battalions, with hundreds:—
To put thee under the water,
To do battle with thee, and to slay thee,
In our first path of battle,
So that 't is thou shalt suffer
In protecting thy head.

F. Here is one who will reproach thee,
'T is I that will do it.
Truly it is by me shall be accomplished
The overthrow of their champion
In presence of the Ultonians,
So that it shall long be remembered
That the loss was theirs.

[Line wanting.]

Fol. 58. a. a.

Cc. Car cinnas condricfam?
in ar collaib cneitfem?
gid leind rarrficfam
do ċomrac ar áṫ
in ar claidbib cruadaib,
ná 'nar rennaib ruadaib,
do t-ṡlaidi rit ṡluagaib,
má thánic a ṫrách?

F.D. Re funiud, re n-aidċi,
madit eicen airrċe,
comrac dait re bairche, (.i. sliab).
ni ba bán in gléo;
Ulaid acot gairmriu
ra n-gabastar aillriu.
bud olc dóib in taidbriu
raċthair thairriu is treó.

Cc. Dat rala i m-beirn ṁ-baegail,
tánic cend do ṡaegail;
imberċair fort fáebair
ni ba fóill in ráth;
bud mórglonnaċ biar.
condricfa caċ diár
ni ba toeseċ truas tú
andiú go ti bráċ.

F. Beirr ass din do robud,
is tú is brassi for domon,
nit ria luag na logud,
nidat doss ós duss,
is misi rat ḟitir.
a ċride ind eoin i ttig;
at gilla co n-gicgil,
gan gasced, gan gus.

Cc. Da m-bammar ac Scaċaig,
allos gaiscid gnaċaig,
is aroén imreidmís;
imthéigmís caċ ríċ.
tu mo ċocne cride;
tu m'aicme tu ṁ'ḟine.
ni fuar riam bad dile.
ba dursan do dith.

Fol. 58. a. b.

F. Ro mór facbai ċeineċ,
conna dernam deibeċ;
sul gairmes in cailech
biaid do ċend ar bir,
a Cuculaind Cualnge.

Dialogue between Ferdiad and Cuchulaind in which they upbraid each other.

C. How then shall we encounter?
Is it on our chariots we shall fight?
In what order shall we go to battle,
To fight upon the ford?
Is it with hard swords,
Or is it with bloody spears,
To hew thee down with thy hosts,
If the time has come?

F. Ere the setting [of the sun], ere the night,
If thou must be told,
Thou shalt fight against a mountain.
It shall not be a bloodless battle;
The Ultonians will extol thee
Thence thou wilt impetuous grow.
Sad to them will be the spectre
That over and through them will pass.

C. Thou hast fallen into the gap of danger,
The end of thy life hath come;
Sharp weapons shall be plied on thee,
It shall not be a deed of treachery;
Pompous thou wilt be
Until we both encounter.
Thou shalt not be a battle chief
From this day to the end of time.

F. Desist from thy vauntings,
Thou art the greatest vaunter in the world,
Nor pay nor reward hast thou received,
Thou art not the champion of champions,
It is I that well know it.
Thou heart of the bird in a cage;
Thou art a giggling fellow,
Without valour, without action.

C. When we were with Scathach,
In right of [our] respective bravery,
Together we used to practise;
Together we went to every battle.
Thou wert my heart-companion;
Thou wert my tribe, thou wert my family.
One dearer found I never.
Woful would be thy destruction.

F. Much of thy honour shalt thou lose,
It boots not that we hold contention;
Before the cock croweth
Thy head shall be on a stake,
O Cuchulaind of Cuailgne.

Fol. 58. a b.

roc gab baile is buadre,
rotria caċ olc uanne
daig is dait a ċin. C.

"Math, a Firdiad", bar Cuculaind, "nir ċóir duitsiu tiaċtain do ċomlund ocas do ċomrac rumsa tri indlaċ ocas etarcossait Aililla ocas Medba; ocas caċ oen tanic ni ruc buaid na bissech dóib: ocas da roċratar limmsa; ocas ni mó berar buaid na bissech duitsiu; ocas ra faéṫaisiu limm. Is amlaid ra bai ga rád, ocas rabert na briaṫra, ocas ra gab Ferdiad [i] clostecht fris.

Na tair ċucam, a láich láin!
a Fhirdiad mic Damáin!
is messu duit na m-bia de,
con tisse brón soċaide;
Na tair ċucam dar fir cert—
is limsa atá do tiglecht.
cid na brethand dait nammá
mo gleósa ra miledá?
Naċat n-diuchled ilarr cless,
gissat corcra, congancness,
in n-ingen as a taí oc báig
ní ba let, a mic Damáin.
Fineabair ingean Medba,
ge beiṫ d'febas a delba,
in ingen, gid caem a cruṫ,
noċos tibrea re cétluṫ.
Findabair ingen in ríg,
ind ráth atberar a fír,
soċaide mac tart bréic,
ocas do loitt do lethéit.
Na briss form lugi gan ḟess,
na briss ċig—na briss cairdes,
na briss brethir báig,
na tair ċucam, a láich láin.
Ra dáled do ċoicait láeċ
in ingen, ní dál dimbaeċ.
is limmsa ra said allecht,
ni rucsat uaim acht ċrandċert.
Gia ramaess menmnaċ Ferbáeṫ,
aca m-bái teglaċ daglaeċ,
gar uar gur ḟurmius a bruṫ—
ra marbas din oen urċur.
Srub Daire, serb seirge a gal,
ba run bale na cet m-ban.

Thou art seized with madness and grief,
All evil from us shalt thou have
Because thou it is that art in fault.

"Good, O Ferdiad", said Cuchulaind, "it was not proper for thee to have come to combat and fight with me through the instigation and intermeddling of Ailill and Medb; and to none of those who came before thee has it given victory or success: and they all fell by me; and neither shall it win victory or increase [of fame] for thee; by me shalt thou fall". Thus was he saying, and he spake these words, and Ferdiad listened to him.

Cuchulaind reproaches Ferdiad, and boasts that he shall not be victorious;

Poem of Cuchulaind in which he reproaches Ferdiad,

Come not unto me, O powerful champion!
O Ferdiad, son of Daman!
Worse to thee what shall come of it,
Though it will bring universal wo;

Come not to me in violation of rightful justice—
In my hands is thy last end.
Why hast thou not considered ere this time
My combat with champions?

Art thou not bought with diverse arms,
A purple girdle, a skin-protecting armour?
The maiden for whom thou makest battle
Shall not be thine, O son of Daman.

Findabar the daughter of Medb,
Though it be for the comeliness of her figure,
The maiden, though fair her form,
Will not be given thee to first enjoy.

Findabar the daughter of the king,
The reward which has been proffered thee,
To numbers before thee has been falsely promised,
And many like thee has [she] wounded.

and appeals to him not to break their bond of friendship;

Break not with me thy vow, not to combat,
Break not the bond—break not friendship,
Break not thy plighted word.
Come not to me, O champion bold.

and tells the fate of the other champions with whom he had fought;

Unto fifty champions has been proffered
The maiden, not slight the gift.
By me they have been sent to their graves,
From me they carried only a just fate.

Though vauntingly spirited was Ferbáeth,
Who had a household of brave men,
Short the time until his rage I lowered—
I killed him by the one cast.

Srub Daire, bitter the decline of his valour,
The repository of the secrets of hundreds of women.

Fol. 58. a b.

mór a blad alt ra bai thán,
ni ran, acht ór, na etgad.
Dambad dam ra naidmthea in bein
rirtib cend na coiced cain,
nocho dergfaindse do ċliab,
tess na tuaid, na tiar na tair.

"Maith, a Fhirdiad", bar Cuculaind, "is aire sin na ra ċoir duitsiu tiachtain do ċomlund ocas do ċomruc rimsa. Daig da m-bammar ac Scaṫaig, ocas ac Uathaig, ocas ac Aifi, is ar oén imthéigmis caċ caṫ ocas caċ caṫrói, caċ comlund ocas cac comrac, caċ fid ocas caċ fásaċ, caċ dorċa ocas caċ diamair. Ocas is aṁlaid ra bai ga ráda, ocas rabert na briaṫra and.

Ropḋar cocle cridi,
ropḋar caemṫe caille,
ropḋar fir chomdeirgide,
conculmis tromċotlud.
ar trom niṫaib
icrichaib, ilib echtrannaib,
ar oen imreidmis imtheigmis
caċ fid, forcetul fri Scaṫaig.

"A Chuculaind ċaem ċlessaċ", bar Ferdiad, "ra ċindsem ceird comdana, ra ċlóisét cuir caratraid, bocricha do ċetgune; na cumnig in comaltas, a ċua naċat ċobradar—a ċua naċat ċobraṫar".

"Ro fata atám amlaidseo ḃadesta", bar Ferdiad; "ocas ga gasced ar a ragam indiu, a Chuċulaind?" "Latsu do roga gascid ċaidchi indiu", bar Cuculaind; "daig is tu darraċt in n-áth ar tús".

"Indat meḃairsiu itir", bar Ferdiad, "is na airgtib gascid a nimmis ac Scathaig, ocas ac Uathaig, ocas ac Aife?" "Is amm meḃair ám écin", bar Cuculaind.

"Mara mebair tecam [forra", ar Ferdiad]. Do ċuatar bar a n-airgthib gascid. Ra gabsatar dá sciaṫ cliss ċomardaṫacha forro, ocas a n-oċt n-oċarċliss, ocas a n-oċt clettíni, ocas a n-oċt cuilg n-dét, ocas a n-oċt n-goṫnatta néit. Imréitis uatha ocas ċuccu mar beocho aille ainle. Ni thelgtis nad aimsitis. Ra gab cáċ dib ac diburgun araile dina clessaib sin ó dorblas na matne muċe go mide medoin lái, go ra ċloesetar a n-il ċlessarda ra tilib ocas ċobradaib ńa sciath cliss. Gia ra bai d'febas ind imdiburcṫi, ra boi d'febas na h-imdegla na ra fulig ocas na ra ḟordeirg cách dib bar araile sis in ré sin.

"Scuirem din gaiscedsa fodesta, a Cuculaind", bar Fer-

Great at one time was his high renown,
Not silver thread, but gold, was in his clothes.

Though it were to me the woman was betrothed
On whom the chiefs of the fair province smile,
I would not crimson thy body,
South or north, west or east.

"Good, O Ferdiad", said Cuchulaind, "therefore it is that thou shouldst not have come to combat and to fight with me. For when we were with Scathach, and with Uathach, and with Aife, it was together we used to go to every battle and every battle-field, to every fight and every combat, to every forest and every wilderness, through every darkness and every difficulty". And thus was he saying, and he spake these words there: Cuchulaind continues his reproaches;

We were heart companions, and alludes to their ancient friendship;
We were comrades in assemblies,
We were fellows of the same bed,
Where we used to sleep the deep sleep.
To hard battles,
In countries many and far distant,
Together we used to practise and go
Through each forest, learning with Scathach.

"O Cuchulaind of the beautiful feats", said Ferdiad, "though we have studied arts of equal science, and though I have heard our bonds of friendship, of me shall come thy first wounds; remember not the companionship, O Hound, it shall not avail thee—O Hound, it shall not avail thee". Ferdiad answers;

"Too long have we remained this way now", said Ferdiad; "and what arms shall we resort to to-day, Cuchulaind?" "Thine this day is the choice of arms till night", said Cuchulaind; "for it was thou that first reached the ford". proposes to select weapons.

"Dost thou remember at all", said Ferdiad, "the missive weapons we used to practise with Scathach, and with Uathach, and with Aife?" "I remember them indeed", said Cuchulaind. First day—weapons for first combat:

"If thou rememberest, let us resort [to them", said Ferdiad.] They resorted to their missive weapons. They took two emblematic missive shields upon them, and their eight turned handled spears, and their eight little quill spears, and their eight ivory-hilted swords, and their eight sharp ivory-hafted spears. They used to fly from them and to them like bees on the wing on a fine day. There was no cast that did not hit. Each continued to shoot at the other with those missiles from the twilight of the early morning to the mean midday, until all their missiles were blunted against the faces and bosses of the missive shields. And although the shooting was most excellent, so good was the defence that neither of them bled or reddened the other during that time. i.e. javelins;

"Let us drop these feats now, Cuchulaind", said Ferdiad, "for end of first combat;

Fol. 88. a. b. diad, dáig ní de seo tic ar n-etersgleód". "Scuirem ám écin ma thánic a thráth", bar Cuculaind.

Ra scoirsetar. Focheirdsetar a clessrada uaċaib illamaib a n-arad. "Ga gasced irragam i festa, a Cuċulaind?" bar Ferdiad. "Lettsu do roga gaiscid ċaidċe", bar Cuċulaind, "dáig is tú do riaċt in n-áċ ar tús". "Tiagam iarum", bar Ferdiad, "bar ar slegaib sneitti, snasta, slemunċruadi, go suanemnaib lín lán ċatut indib". "Tecam ám écin", bar Cuculaind. Is andsin ra gabsatar dá ċotut sciaċ ċomdaingni forro. Da ċuatar bar a slegaib snaitti, snasta, slemun chruadi, go suanemnaib lín lánċotut indi.

Ra gab cáċ dib ac dibursgun araile di na slegaib á mide medoin lái go tráth funid nóna. Gia rabui d'febas na h-imdegla, rabúi d'febas inddimdibairgċi, go ro fuilig, ocas go ro forderg, ocas go ra chrechtnaig cach dib bar araile ris in re sin.

"Scuirem de ḟodain badesta a Cuculaind", bar Ferdiad. "Scuirem ám écin ma ṫánic a ṫráċ", bar Cuculaind.

Ra scoirsetar. Bhaċeirdset a n-airm uathu illámaib a n-arad. Tánic cáċ dib d'indsaigid araile ass a aithle, ocas rabert cáċ dib lám dar brágit araile, ocas ra ṫairbir teóra póc. Ra bátar a n-eiċ in oen scur in n-aidċi sin, ocas a n-araid ic oen tenid; ocas bo gnísetar a n-araid cossair lepṫa úrluaċra doib, go fruthadartaib fer n-gona friu. Tancatar riallaċ icci ocas legis da n-icc ocas da leiges, ocas focheirdetar lubi ocas lossa icci ocas slánsen ra cnedaib ocas crecṫaib, rá n-áltaib ocas ra n-ilgonaib. Caċ lub ocas cac lossa icci ocas slánsen ra berthea ra cnedaib ocas crecṫaib, altaib ocas ilgonaib Conculaind, ra idnaicṫea comraind uad dib dar áċ siar d'Fhirdiad, na rabbraitis fir h-Erend, da tuited Ferdiad leissium, ba h-immarcraid legis da beraid sair.

Cach biad, ocas caċ lind, soóla, soċarċain so mesc da berthea ó ḟeraib h-Erend d'Fhirdiad, da idnaicṫea comraind uad dib dar áċ faċuaiċ do Coinċulaind; daig raptar lia biattaig Fhirdiad andá biattaig Conċulaind. Raptar biattaig fir-h-Ereno uli d'Firdiad ar Choinċulaind do dingbail dib. Raptar biattaig Brega daná, do Coinċulaind. Ticcis da acaldaim frí dé, .i. caċ n-aidċe.

Dessetar and in n-aidċi sin. Atrachtatar go moċ ar na bárac ocas tancatar rompu co áth in ċomraic. "Ga gasced ar a ragam indiu, a Fhirdead?" bar Cuċulaind. "Lettsu do roga n-gascid ċaidċi", bar Ferdiad, "daig is

it is not by such our battle will be decided". "Let us desist, indeed, if the time hath come", said Cuchulaind.

They ceased. They cast away their missiles into the hands of their charioteers. "What weapons shall we resort to now, O Cuchulaind?" said Ferdiad. "To thee belongs the choice of arms till night", said Cuchulaind, "because thou it was that first reached the ford". "Let us then", said Ferdiad, "resort to our straight, elegant, smooth, hardened spears, with their perfectly hardened flaxen strings in them". "Let us now, indeed", said Cuchulaind. And it was then they took two stout protecting shields upon them. They resorted to their straight, elegant, smooth, hardened spears, with their perfectly hardened flaxen strings in them.

they select weapons for second combat: i.e. spears with strings;

Each of them continued to shoot at the other with the spears from the middle of mid-day till even-tide. And though the defence was most excellent, still the shooting was so good, that each of them bled, and reddened, and wounded the other in that time.

"Let us desist from this now for the present, O Cuchulaind", said Ferdiad. "Let us, indeed, desist if the time hath come", said Cuchulaind.

end of first day's fighting;

They ceased. They threw away their arms from them into the hands of their charioteers. Each of them approached the other forthwith, and each put his hands around the other's neck, and gave him three kisses. Their horses were in the same paddock that night, and their charioteers at the same fire; and their charioteers spread beds of green rushes for them, with wounded men's pillows to them. The professors of healing and curing came to heal and cure them, and they applied herbs and plants of healing and curing to their stabs and their cuts and their gashes, and to all their wounds. Of every herb and of every healing and curing plant that was put to the stabs and cuts and gashes and to all the wounds of Cuchulaind, he would send an equal portion from him westward over the ford to Ferdiad, so that the men of Eiriu might not be able to say, should Ferdiad fall by him, that it was by better means of cure that he was enabled [to kill him].

knightly interchange of civilities after the fight.

Of each kind of food, and of palatable, pleasant, intoxicating drink that was sent by the men of Eiriu to Ferdiad, he would send a fair moiety over the ford northwards to Cuchulaind; because the purveyors of Ferdiad were more numerous than the purveyors of Cuchulaind. All the men of Eiriu were purveyors to Ferdiad for beating off Cuchulaind from them. The Bregians only were purveyors to Cuchulaind. They were used to come to converse with him at dusk, *i.e.*, every night.

They rested there that night. They arose early the next morning and came forward to the ford of battle. "What weapons shall we resort to to-day, O Ferdiad?" said Cuchulaind. "To thee belongs the choice of arms until night", said Ferdiad, "because it was I

Second day:

Fol. 53. a. a. missi bar roega mo roga n-gascid is ind lathi luid". "Tiagam iarum", bar Cuċulaind, "bar ar mánairib móra murniuċa indiu; dáig is foicsiu lind donág in t-imrubad indiu, anda dond imdiburgun inné".

"Gabṫar ar n-eiċ dún ocas indliṫer ar carpait, co n-dernam caṫugud dar neċaib ocas dar carptib indiu". "Tecam am ecin", bar Ferdiad.

Is and sin ra gabsatar dá leṫan sciath lán dangin forro in lá sin. Da chuatar bar a manáirib móra murnecha in lá sin.

Ra gab cách dib bar tollad, ocas bar tregdad, bar ruṫ, ocas bar regtad araile, á dorblas na matne muchi, go trách funid nóna. Dambad bés eóin ar luamain do ṫeċt tri ċorpaib doene, do ragtais tri na corpaib in lá sin, go m-bertáis na toċta fola ocas feóla tri na cnedaib ocas tri na creċtaib, in nélaib ocas in aeraib seċtair. Ocas á tháinic trách funid nóna, raptar sciṫa a n-eiċ, ocas raptar mertnig a n-araid, ocas raptar sciṫa som fadeisin,—na curaid ocas na laith gaile. "Scurem de ḟodain badesta a Fhirdead", bar Cuċulaind, "daig is at sciṫa ar n-eiċ ocas it mertnig ar n-araid; ocas in trách ata sciṫa iat, cid dúnni na bad scitha sind dan? Ocas is amlaid ra búi gá rád, ocas rabert na briaṫra and:

Ni dlegar din cuclaigi (bar ésium)
ra Fomorċaib feidm;
cuirṫer fóċu a n-urċomail,
a ro scaiċ an deilm.

"Scoirem ám écin, ma ṫánic a ṫráṫ", bar Ferdiad. Ra scorsetar.

Faċeirdset a n-airm uaṫu illámaib a n-arad. Tánic caċ dib d'innaigid a ċéile. Ra bert caċ lám dar brágit araile, ocas ra ṫairbir teóra póc. Ra bátar a n-eiċ in oén scur in aidċi sin, ocas a n-araid oc oen teind.

Do gnised a n-araid cossair lepṫa úrluaċra dóib go sruthadartaib fer n-gona friu. Tancatar siallaċ icci ocas leigis da fethium ocas dá fégad, ocas da forcomét in n-aidċi sin; dáig ni ni aile ra ċumgetar dóib, ra h-acbéile a cned, ocas a créċta, a n-álta ocas a n-ilgona, aċt iptha ocas éle ocas arṫana do ċur riu, do thairmesc a fola, ocas a fulliugu ocas a n-gae cró. Caċ iptha ocas gaċ ele ocas gaċ orṫana do berṫea ra cnedaib ocas ra creċtaib Conċulaind, ra idnaicṫea comraind uad dib dar áṫ siar d'Firdiad. Caċ biad, ocas caċ lind, soóla, soċarṫain somesc ra berthea o ḟeraib h-Erend do Fhirdiad, ra h-id-

that had my choice of weapons in the days that have passed". "Let us then", said Cuchulaind, "resort to our great broad spears this day; because we shall be nearer to our battle by the thrusting this day, than we were by the shooting yesterday". weapons for second day's fight,—heavy broad spears;

"Let our horses be harnessed for us and our chariots yoked, that we may do battle from our horses and from our chariots to-day". "Let us do so, indeed", said Ferdiad.

And it is then they took two broad full-firm shields upon them that day. They resorted to their great broad spears on that day.

Each of them continued to pierce, and to wound, to redden, and to lacerate the other, from the twilight of the early morning until evening's close. If it were the custom for birds in their flight to pass through the bodies of men, they could have passed through their bodies on that day, and they might carry pieces of flesh and blood through their stabs and cuts, into the clouds and sky all round. And when evening's close came, their horses were fatigued, and their charioteers were dispirited, and they were fatigued themselves, also—the champions and the heroes of valour. "Let us desist from this now, O Ferdiad", said Cuchulaind, "for our horses are fatigued and our charioteers are dispirited; and when they are fatigued, why should not we be fatigued too?" And so was he saying, and he spake these words there: fierceness of the combat;

We are not bound to persevere (said he)
With Fomorian obstinacy;
Let the cause be put in abeyance,
Now that the din of combat is over.

"Let us desist now, indeed, if the time has come", said Ferdiad. They ceased. end of combat;

They threw their arms from them into the hands of their charioteers. Each of them came towards the other. Each of them put his hands round the neck of the other, and bestowed three kisses on him. Their horses were in the same enclosure, and their charioteers at the same fire. repetition of knightly civilities;

Their charioteers made beds of green rushes for them with pillows for wounded men to them. The professors of healing and curing came to examine and take care of them that night; for they could do nothing more for them, because of the dangerous severity of their stabs, and their cuts, and their gashes, and their numerous wounds, than to apply witchcraft and incantations and charms to them, to staunch their blood, and their bleeding and gory mortal wounds. Every spell and incantation and charm that was applied to the stabs and cuts of Cuchulaind, he sent a full moiety of them over the ford westwards to Ferdiad. All sorts of food, and of palatable, pleasant, intoxicating drink that were sent by the men of Eiriu to Ferdiad, he would send a moiety of them over the the charioteers prepare beds for the wounded warriors; they interchange medicines and food.

ol. 83 a. a. naicctea comraind uad dib dar áth foċuaiṫ do Choinċulaind. Daig rartar lia biattaig Firdiad andá biattaig Conculaind. Daig rartar biattaig fir h-Erend uili d'Firdiad ar dingbail Choinċulaind dib. Raptar biattaig Brega no do Choinċulaind. Ticcis da iacallaim fri de, .i. caċ n-aidċe.

Desseter in n-aidċi sin and. Atráaċtatar co moċ ar na baraċ, ocas tancatar rempo co áṫ in chomraic. Ra ċondaic Cuċulaind midelb ocas miċemel mór in lá sin bar Ferdiad. "Is olc atairsiu indiu a Fhirdead", bar Cuċulaind. "Ra dorchaig t-folt indiu, ocas ra suanmig do rosc, ocas da ċuaid do ċruṫ ocas do delb ocas do denam dit". "Nir ṫeclasu na ar t-uamain formsa sain indiu ám", bar Ferdiad, "dáig ní ḟuil in h-Erind indiu láeċ nadingebsa". Ocas ra búi Cuċulaind ac écaini ocas ac airchisecht, ocas rabert na briaṫra, and ocas ra recair Ferdiad.

Cc. A Firdead, mása thú,
demin limm is at lom ṫrú,
tidaċt ar comairli mná
do ċomlund rit ċomalta.

F. d. A Chuċulaind, comall n-gaiṫ,
a ḟir ánraiṫ, a ḟir laiċ,
is éicen do neoċ a ṫeċt
co sin fót fois a m-bia ṫigleċt.

Cc. Findabair, ingean Medba,
gia beiṫ d'ḟebas a delba,
a tabairt dait ní ar do seirc,
aċt do romad do rigneirt.

F. Fromṫa mo nert a ċianaib
a ċu cos in caem riagail,
neċ bad ċalmu noco closs,
cos indiu nocon ḟuaross.

Cc. Tu fodera a fail de,
a mic Damáin mic Dáre
tiaċtain ar comairle mná
d'imċlaidbed rit chomalta.

F. Da scarainn gan troit is tú,
gidar comaltai, a ċaem ċú,
bud olc mo briathar is mo blad
ic Ailill is ac Meidb Chruċan.

Cc. Noco tard biad da belaib,
ocas noco mod ro genair,
do rig na rigain can ċess,
bar a n-dernaindse t-amles.

F. A Chuċulaind tolaib gal,

ıorthwards to Cuchulaind. Because the purveyors of Fer-
vere more numerous than those of Cuchulaind. For all the
of Eiriu were purveyors to Ferdiad for his warding off Cuchu-
from them. The Bregians only were purveyors to Cuchulaind.
used to come to talk to him at dusk, *i.e.*, at night.

ey rested there that night. They arose early the next morn- nd they came forward to the ford of battle. Cuchulaind per- l an ill visaged and a greatly lowering cloud on Fer- hat day. "Badly dost thou appear this day, O Ferdiad", 'uchulaind. "Thy hair has become dark this day, and thy is become drowsy, and thine own form and features and appear- ıave departed from thee". "It is not from fear or terror of hat I am so this day", said Ferdiad, "for there is not in Eiriu ay a champion that I could not subdue". And Cuchulaind omplaining and bemoaning, and he spake these words, and d answered.

Third day: the meeting;

dialogue between Cuchulaind and Ferdiad, in which the former reproaches the latter for having come to fight with his friend;

C. O Ferdiad, if it be thou,
Certain am I that thou art a degraded being,
To have come at the bidding of a woman
To fight with thy fellow-pupil.

F. O Cuchulaind, inflictor of wounds,
O valiant man, O true champion,
A man is constrained to come
Unto the sod where his final grave shall be.

C. Findabar, the daughter of Medb,
Though it be through her superior beauty,
Her bestowal upon thee was not for thy love,
But to test thy kingly might.

F. My might was tested long ago
O hound of the gentle rule,
Of none more valiant have I heard,
Nor to this day did I ever meet.

C. Thou art the cause of all that has happened,
O son of Daman, son of Dáre,
To have come by the counsel of a woman
To measure swords with thy fellow-pupil.

F. If I had returned without combat with thee,
Though we are fellow-pupils, O graceful hound,
Bad should be my word and my fame
With Ailill and with Medb of Cruachan.

C. Not one has yet put food unto his lips
Nor has there yet been born
Of king or queen without disgrace
One for whom I would do thee evil.

F. O Cuchulaind of battle-triumphs,

Fol. 83. a. a.

ni tú, act Medb, rarmarnestar,
bérasu buaid ocas blaid,
ni ḟort atát a cinaid.
Cc. Is caép cró mo ċride cain,
bec naċ rasclos ram anmain,
ni comnairt limm linib gal
compac rit, a Ḟhirdead. A.

"Meid a ċáirsiu ac cessaċt formsa indiu", bar Ferdiad. "Ga sasced for a ragam indiu?" "Lettsu do roga sascid ċaidċi, indiu", bar Cuċulaind, "dáig is missi bar roéga in laċe luid". "Tiagam iaram", bar Ferdiad, "bar ar claidbib tromma tortbulleċa indiu, dáig is factiu lind dondág in n-imṡlaidi indiu, andá dond imrubad indé". "Tecam ám écin", bar Cuculaind. Is andsain ra gabsatar dá lebor sciaċ lán móra forro in lá sain. Do chuatar bar a claidbib tromma tortbulleċa. Ra gab cách dib bar slaide, ocas bar sleċtad, bar airlech ocas bar essorgain, gomba meticir ri cend mic mis caċ thoṫoċt, ocas gaċ ċinmi do beired cáċ dib de guallib, ocas de ṡliastaib, ocas de ṡlinneoċaib araile.

Ra gab cáċ dib ac slaide araile, mán cóir sin, á dorblass na matni muċi co tráth funid nóna.

"Scuirem do ṡodain badesta, a Cuċulaind", bar Ferdiad. "Scoirem ám écin, ma ṫanic a ṫráṫ", bar Cuculaind. Ra scoirsetar.

Faċeirdsetar a n-airm uadaib illamaib a n-arad. Gir bo ċomraicthi dá ṡubaċ, sámaċ, sobbrónaċ, somenmnaċ, ra radascarṫain dá ndubaċ, n-dobbrónaċ, n-domenmnach, a scarṫain, in n-aidċi sin.

Ni rabatar a n-eiċ in oen scur in n-aidċi sin. Ni rabatar a n-araid ac oen tenid. Dessetar in n-aidċi sin and.

Is and sin atraact Ferdiad go moċ ar na báraċ ocas tanic reme a oenur co áth inchomraic. Dáig ra ḟitir ra pé sin lá etersgleoid in chomlaind ocas in chomraic; ocas ra ḟitir co táetsad neċtar de dib in lá sain and, noco taetsaitis a n-dis.

Is andsin ra gabastarsom a ċatherriud catha ocas comlaind ocas comraic immi, re tiaċtain do Choinċulaind da ṡaigid. Ocas ba don ċaṫ errud ċatha ocas comlaind ocas ċomraic: Ra gabastar a fuathbróic sirebnaide sróil, cona cimais d'órr bricc fria, fri gell chness. Ra gabastar fuaċbróic n-dond lethair, n-degḟuatai tairrsiside immaic a neċtair. Ra gabastar muadċloich móir méti cloċi mulind tairrsiside immuiċ a neċtair. Ra gabastar a fuaċbróic n-imdangin, n-imdomain, n-iarnaide, do iurn atlegṫa, dar in muadċloiċ móir méti cloċi mulind, ar ecla ocas ar uamun

It was not thee, but Medb, that betrayed me,
Take thou victory and fame,
Thine is not the fault.

C. My faithful heart is a clot of blood,
From me my soul hath nearly parted,
I have not strength for feats of valour
To fight with thee, O Ferdiad.

"Much as thou complainest of me this day", said Ferdiad. "To what arms shall we resort to-day?" "To thee belongs the choice of arms till night, this day", said Cuchulaind, "because it was I that took it the days that have passed". "Let us then", said Ferdiad, "resort to our heavy hard-smiting swords this day, for we are nearer the end of the battle by the hewing to-day, than by the thrusting yesterday". "Let us do so indeed", said Cuchulaind. And then they took two long very great shields upon them on that day. They resorted to their heavy hard-smiting swords. Each of them began to hew and cut down, to slaughter and destroy, until larger than the head of an infant of a month old, was every piece and every lump which each of them cut away from the shoulders, and from the thighs, and from the shoulder blades of the other. choice of weapons,—heavy swords;

Each of them continued to hew the other in that manner from the dawn of the early morning till the hour of evening's close.

"Let us desist now from this, O Cuchulaind", said Ferdiad. "Let us desist now, indeed, if the time hath come", said Cuchulaind. They ceased. End of third day's combat;

They cast their arms from them into the hands of their charioteers. Though it was the meeting—pleasant, happy, griefless, and spirited, of two [men], it was the separation—mournful, sorrowful, dispirited, of two [men], that night.

Their horses were not in the same enclosure that night. Their charioteers were not at the same fire. They rested that night there. no interchange of civilities on the third night.

Then Ferdiad arose early next morning and went forward alone to the ford of battle. For he knew that that day would decide the battle and the fight; and he knew that either of them should fall on that day there, or that they would both fall. Fourth day:

And it was then he put on his battle suit of battle and combat and fight, before the coming of Cuchulaind unto him. And that battle suit of battle and combat and fight was [as follows]: He put on his apron of striped silk, with its border of spangled gold upon it, next his white skin. He put on his apron of brown leather, well sewn over that outside on the lower part [of his body]. He put on a huge stone as big as a millstone over that outside on his lower part. He put on his firm, deep apron of iron, of purified iron, over the huge stone as large as a millstone, through fear and dread of the Gae Bulg on that day. He put his crested helmet of battle, Ferdiad puts on his armour;

Fol. 89. b. a. in gae bulga in lá sin. Ra gabastar a ċir ċaṫbarr catha, ocus comlaind, ocus comraic, imma chend, bar sa m-bátar ceṫracha gemm, carrmoccul, a caċ aén ċumtaċ; ar na ecur de chruan, ocus ċristaill, ocus carrmocaill, ocus de lubib soillsi airthir betad. Ra gabastar a ḟleig m-bairnig, m-bairend bailc ina deslaim. Ra gabastar a ċlaideb camṫuagaċ caṫa bar a ċliu, cona urdorn óir, ocus cona mul eltaib de derg óir. Ra gabastar a sciaṫ mór m-bua-balċain bar a tuagleirg a dromma, bar sa m-bátar coica cobrad, bar a taillfed torc taissealbṫa bar caċ comraid dib, cenmoṫa in comraid moir medonaig do derg óir.

Ba ċeird Ferdiad clessrada ána ilerda ingantaċa imda bar aird in lá sain, nad roeglaind ac neċ aile riam, ac mumme na ac aite, na ac Scaṫaig, na ac Uaṫaig, na ac Aife, aċt a n-denum uad féin in lá sain in agid Conċu-laind.

Da riaċt Cuċulaind doċum in n-áṫa nó, ocus ra ċonnaic na clessrada ána ilerda ingantaċa imda ba ċeird Ferdiad bar aird. "Atċiriu fút, a mo ṗopa Laig, na clessrada ána ilerda ingantaċa imda foceird Ferdiad bar aird, ocus bocotaidfer (.i. fogebsa) damsa ar n-uair innossa na cles-rada út, ocus is aire sin mad forumsa bus roén indiu, ar a n-dernaisiu mo grísad ocus mo glámad ocus olc do ráda rim, go ror móite éir ṁ-ḟir ocus ṁ-ḟergg ḟorromm. Mad romum bus roén, no ar a n-dernaisiu mo múnod, ocus mo molod ocus maiṫius do rád frim, go ror móti lim mo men-ma". "Da gentar ám écin, a Chucuc[laind]", bar Laeg.

Is and sin ra gabastar Cuculaind dno, a ċaṫerriud ċaṫa, ocus ċomluind, ocus comraic imbi. Ocus foċeird clessra-da ána ilerda ingantaċa imda bar aird in lá sain, nad roeglaind ac neoċ aile riam; ac Scathaig, na ac Uathaig na ac Aife. At ċondairc Ferdiad na clessrada sain, ocus ra fitir go fuigbiṫea dó ar nuair iat.

"Ga gaisced ara ragam a Fhirdead?" bar Cuċulaind. "Letssu do roga gaiscid chaidċi", bar Ferdiad. "Tiagam sar cluċi in n-áṫa iarum", bar Cuċulaind. "Tecam ám", bar Ferdiad. Giodbairt Ferdiad in ní sein, is air is doil-giu leis da ragad, daig ra fitir iss ass ra ḟorrged Cuċu-laind caċ caur ocus cac caṫmiled condriced friss bar cluchi in n-átha.

Ba mór in gnim ám da ringned bar sind áṫ in lá sain,— na da mad na dá anruiṫ; da eirrgi iarṫair Eorpa; da láim chidnaicṫi raṫa ocus ṫairberta ocus tuarastail iar-thair thuascirt in domain; da anċain dil gaiscid Gaedel; ocus da eoċair gaiscid Gaedel, a comraiccthi do chéin mair

and combat, and fight on his head, on which were forty [four, H. 2. 17. f. 116. a. a] gems, carbuncles, in each compartment; and it was studded with Cruan, and crystal, and carbuncles, and with brilliant rubies of the eastern world. He took his destructive, sharp-pointed, strong spear, into his right hand. He took his curved sword of battle upon his left side, with its golden hilt, with its pommels of red gold. He took his great, large-bossed, beautiful shield on the slope of his back, on which were fifty bosses, upon each of which bosses a full-grown hog would fit, not to mention the great central boss of red gold.

Ferdiad displayed many noble, varied, wonderful feats on high on that day, which he had never learned with any other person, neither with nurse or with tutor, or with Scathach, or with Uathach, or with Aife, but which were invented by himself that day against Cuchulaind. he performs many feats;

Cuchulaind came to the ford, and he saw the noble, varied, wonderful, numerous feats which Ferdiad displayed on high. "I perceive these, my friend, Laeg", [said Cuchulaind,] "the noble, varied, wonderful, numerous feats which Ferdiad displays on high, and all these feats will be tried on me in succession, and therefore it is that if it be I that shall begin to yield this day, thou art to excite, reproach, and speak evil to me, so that the ire of my rage and anger shall grow the more on me. If it be I that prevaileth, then shalt thou laud me, and praise me, and speak good words to me, that my courage may be the greater". "It shall so be done indeed, O Cuchulaind", said Laeg. Cuchulaind perceiving this instructs his charioteer;

And it was then Cuchulaind put his battle-suit of battle, and of combat and of fight on him. And he displayed noble, varied, wonderful, numerous feats on high on that day, that he never learned from anybody else; neither with Scathach, or with Uathach, or with Aife. Ferdiad saw those feats, and he knew they would be plied against him in succession. he arms for the fight;

"What weapons shall we resort to, O Ferdiad?" said Cuchulaind. "To thee belongs thy choice of weapons till night", said Ferdiad. "Let us try the Ford Feat then", said Cuchulaind. "Let us indeed", said Ferdiad. Although Ferdiad thus spoke his consent, it was a cause of grief to him to speak so, because he knew that Cuchulaind was used to destroy every hero and every champion who contended with him in the Feat of the Ford. weapons selected,—the "Ford Feat";

Great was the deed, now, that was performed on that day at the ford—the two heroes; the two warriors; the two champions of western Europe; the two gift and present and stipend-bestowing hands of the north-west of the world; the two beloved pillars of the valour of the Gaedhils; and the two keys of the bravery the fight;

Fol. 53. b. a. tri indlaċ ocus etarċossáit Aililla ocus Medba. Da gab caċ dib ac dibургun araile dona clessaidib sin á dorblass na matni muċi go midi medoin lái. Ocus ó thanic medón lai ra feoċraigseretar fergga na fer, ocus ra ċomfaicsigsetar cach dib da raile. Is and sin cindis Cuculaind feċtnoén and do ur in n-atha, go m-bai for cobraid scéiṫ Fhirdead mic Damáin do ṫetractain a ċind do bualad dar bil in scéith ar n-uaċtar. Is andsin ra bert Ferdiad béim da ullind clé sin sciath comdas rala Cuċulaind uad mar én bar ur in n-ácha. Cindis Cuculaind d'ur in n-áṫa aris co m-bai for cobraid sceiṫ Firdead mic Damáin, do ṫetarrachtain a ċind do bualad dar bil in sceiṫ ar n-uaċtar. Ra bert Ferdiad béim da glún ċlé sin sciaṫ gomdas rala Cuculaind uad mar mac ṁ-bec bar ur in n-áṫa.

Airgis Láeg in ní sein. "Amae", ale bar, Laeg, "rat ċur in caṫmilid ḟail it t-agid mar chúrsar ben báid a mac. Rot snigsetar mar ṡnegair cuir a lundu. Rat melastar mar milis mulend muadbraiċ. Rat regdastar mar thres-das fodb omnaid. Rat nascestar mar nascess-féith riou. Ras léic fort feib ras léic séig for mintu, conaċ fail do dluig, na do dual, na do díl ri gail na ra gaisced go brunni ṁ-bráṫa ocus betha badesta, a ṡiriti ṡiabarṫi bic, bar Loeg.

Is andsain atraaċt Cuculaind illuas na gaiṫi, ocus in aṫlaimi na fandli, ocus i n-dremni in drecain, ocus in nirt [in leogain i nellaib etarbuasaċa] in n-aeoir in tres feċt, go m-bai for ċomraid scéiṫ Firdead mic Damain, do thetar-raċtain a chind da bualad dar bil a scéiṫ ar n-uaċtar. Is andsin rabert in caṫmilid crioṫad bar sin sciaṫ, comdas rala Cuculaind uad bar lar in n-áṫa, mar bad é naċar lebad riam itir.

Is and sin ra ċét riastrad im Choinċulaind, go ros lín att ocus infiṫi, mar anáil illés, co n-derna thuaig n-uaṫ-mar, n-acbéil, n-ildaṫaig, n-ingantaig de; go m-ba metigir ra Fomóir, na re fer mara, in milid mór ċalma, ós chind Firdead i cert ardi.

Ba sé dlús n-imairic da ronsatar, go ra ċomraicsetar a cind ar n-uaċtar, ocus a cossa ar n íċtar, ocus allama ar n-irmedón dar bilib ocus cobradaib na sciaṫ. Ba sé dlús n-imairic da ronsadar, go ro dluigset ocus go ro dloingset a scéiṫ ó a m-bilib go a m brontib. Ba sé dlus n-immaric da ronsatar, go ro ḟillsetar, ocus go ro lupsatar, ocus go ro guasaigsetar a slega, ó a rennaib go a n-erlannaib. Ba sé dlús n-immaric da ronsatar, go ra gairsetar boccánaig,

of the Gaedhils, to be brought to fight from afar through the instigation and the intermeddling of Ailil and Medb. Each of them began to shoot at the other with those missive weapons from the dawn of early morning to the middle of midday. And when midday came the ire of the men became more furious, and each of them drew nearer to the other. And then it was that Cuchulaind, on one occasion, sprang from the brink of the ford, and came on the boss of the shield of Ferdiad, son of Daman, for the purpose of striking his head over the rim of his shield from above. And it was then that Ferdiad gave the shield a blow of his left elbow, and cast Cuchulaind from him like a bird on the brink of the ford. Cuchulaind sprang from the brink of the ford again till he came on the boss of the shield of Ferdiad, son of Daman, for the purpose of striking his head over the rim of his shield from above. Ferdiad gave the shield a stroke of his left knee, and cast Cuchulaind from him like a little child on the brink of the ford.

Laeg reproaches Cuchulaind

Laeg perceived that act. "Alas, indeed", said Laeg, "the warrior who is against thee casts thee away as a lewd woman would cast her child. He throws thee as foam is thrown by the river. He grinds thee as a mill would grind fresh malt. He pierces thee as the felling axe would pierce the oak. He binds thee as the woodbine binds the tree. He darts on thee as the hawk darts on small birds, so that henceforth thou hast not call, or right, or claim to valour or bravery to the end of time and life, thou little fairy phantom", said Laeg.

the latter renews the attack;

Then up sprang Cuchulaind with the rapidity of the wind, and with the readiness of the swallow, and with the fierceness of the dragon, and the strength [of the lion, into the troubled clouds of] the air the third time, until he alighted on the boss of the shield of Ferdiad, son of Daman, to endeavour to strike his head over the rim of his shield from above. And then it was the warrior gave the shield a shake, and cast Cuchulaind from him into the middle of the ford, the same as if he had never before been cast off at all.

his distortion;

And it was then that Cuchulaind's first distortion came on, and he was filled with swelling and great fulness, like breath in a bladder, until he became a terrible, fearful, many coloured, wonderful Tuaig (giant); and he became as big as a Fomor, or man of the sea, the great and valiant champion, in perfect height over Ferdiad.

description of their hand-to-hand combat;

So close was the fight they made now, that their heads met above, and their feet below, and their arms in the middle over the rims and bosses of their shields. So close was the fight they made, that they cleft and loosened their shields from their rims to their centres. So close was the fight which they made, that they turned, and bent, and shivered their spears, from their points to their hafts. Such was the closeness of the fight which they made, that the Bocanachs and Bananachs, and wild people of the glens, and demons of the air, screamed from the rims of their shields, and from the hilts of their

ocas bananaig, ocas gennitci glinni, ocus demnu aeóir, do bilib a sciaṫ, ocas d'imdornaib a claideb, ocas d'erlannaib a sleg. Ba sé dlús n-immaric da ronsatar, go ralasetar in n-abaind as a cuirp ocus assa cumaċta, gom ba imdaid indluigṫe indeirgiṫi do ríg nó rígain ar lar in n-áṫa, conná
Fol. 60. a. a. bái bánna d'usci and, acht muni siled ind sis in suaṫsadaig ocas ris in sloetradaig da ringsetar na da curad ocas na da caṫmilid bar lár in n-áṫa.

Ba sé dlús n-imaric da ronsatas, go ro memaid do graigib Gaedel sceċóin ocas sceinmnig, diallaib ocus dásaċt, go ro maidset a n-idi ocus a n-erċomaill, allómna ocas alleċrena; go ro memaid de mnaib, ocas maccaemaib, ocas mindoenib, midlaigib ocas meraigib fer nh-Erend tri sin dunud siar dess.

Batar sun ar faebar ċless claideb ris in ré sin. Is and sin ra siaċt Ferdiad uairbaeguil and feċt for Coinculaind, ocas ra bert béim din ċulg déṫ dó, go ra ḟolaig na ċliab, go torċar a ċrú na ċriss, cor b'forruamanda in t-áth do ċrú a cuirp in ċaṫmiled. Ni ferlangair Cuċulaind a ni féin, a ra gab Ferdiad bar a bráṫ balc bemmenaib, ocas fótalbemmennaib ocas muadalbemmennaib móra sair. Ocas conattaċt in n-gae bulga bar Laeg mac Riangabra. Is amlaid ra bairsde: ra sruṫ ra indiltea ocas illadair a ċoise ra teilgtea; álad oengae leis ac teċt i n-duni, ocas trichu farrindi ri taiṫmeċ, ocas ní gatta a cuirp duni go cosgairṫea immi. Ocas atċuala Ferdiad in n-gae m-bolga d'imrad, ra bert béim din sciath sis d'anacul ichtair a ċuirp. Do ruaraid Cuculaind in certgae delgṫi do láṁ a dernainni dar bil in sceith, ocas dar brollaċ in chongancnis, gor bo roén in leṫ n-alltarach de ar tregtad a chride na ċliab.

Rabert Ferdiad béim din sciaṫ suas d'anacul uaċtair a ċuirp. Giarbi "in ċobair iar n-assu". Da indill in gilla in gae ṁ-bolga ris in sruṫ, ocas ra ruċáil Cuculaind illadair a ċossi, ocas tarlaic rout n'urċoir de bar Ferndiad, co n-deċaid tri sin suaṫbróic n-imdangin n-imdomain, n-iarnaide, do iurn athlegṫa, gor róe bris in muadċloiċ máir méti cloċi mulind itrí, co n-deċaid dar timchirect a ċuirp an, gor bo lán caċ n-alt ocas caċ n-áge de da ḟorrindib. "Leor sain badesta", ale bar Ferdiad, "da rocarsa de ḟein. Aċt atá ni ċena is tén unnius ar do deiss. Acas nír bo ċoir dait ma ṫuittimsea doc laim". Is malaid ra bói ga rád, ocas rabert na briaṫra.

Achú na cless cain,
nír dess dait mo guin.

swords, and from the hafts of their spears. Such was the closeness of the fight which they made, that they cast the river out of its bed and out of its course, so that it might have been a reclining and reposing couch for a king or for a queen in the middle of the ford, so that there was not a drop of water in it, unless it dropped into it by the trampling and the hewing which the two champions and the two heroes made in the middle of the ford.

Such was the intensity of the fight which they made that, the stud of the Gaedhils darted away in fright and shyness, with fury and madness, breaking their chains and their yokes, their ropes and their traces; and that the women, and youths, and small people, and camp-followers, and non-combatants of the men of Eiriu, broke out of the camp south-westwards. terror inspired by the combat;

They were at the edge-feat of swords during the time. And it was then that Ferdiad found an unguarded moment upon Cuchulaind, and he gave him a stroke of the straight-edged sword, and buried it in his body, till his blood fell into his girdle, until the ford became reddened with the gore from the body of the battle-warrior. Cuchulaind could not endure this, for Ferdiad continued his unguarded stout strokes, and his quick strokes, and his tremendous great blows at him. And he asked Laeg, son of Riangabra, for the Gae Bulg. The manner of that was this: it used to be set down the stream and cast from between the toes; it made the wound of one spear in entering the body, but it had thirty barbs to open, and could not be drawn out of a person's body until it was cut open. And when Ferdiad heard the Gae-Bulg mentioned, he made a stroke of the shield down to protect his lower body. Cuchulaind thrust the unerring thorny spear off the centre of his palm over the rim of the shield, and through the breast of the skin-protecting armour, so that its farther half was visible after piercing his heart in his body. Cuchulaind is wounded; he asks for the Gae Bulg; Ferdiad is wounded;

Ferdiad gave a stroke of his shield up to protect the upper part of his body, though it was "the relief after the danger". The servant set the Gae-Bulg down the stream, and Cuchulaind caught it between the toes of his foot, and he threw an unerring cast of it at Ferdiad, and it passed through the firm deep iron apron of wrought iron, and broke the great stone, which was as large as a mill-stone, in three, and passed through the protections of his body into him, so that every crevice and every cavity of him was filled with its barbs. "That is enough now, indeed", said Ferdiad, "I fall of that. But I may say, indeed, that I am sickly now after thee. And it did not behove thee that I should fall by thy hand". So was he saying, and he spake these words.— Cuchulaind casts the Gae Bulg; Ferdiad is mortally wounded;

O Hound of the beautiful feats,
It was not befitting thee to kill me.

his dying words;

Fol. 60. a. a.

lett in loċt rom len.
is ḟort ra ḟer ṁ'ḟuil.
Ni lossat na troiċ
recait bernaid ṁ-braiṫ.
is galar mo guṫ.
uċ, do scarad scaith.
Mébait ṁ'asnae suidb.
mo ċridese is crú.
ni ma ra ḟeras báig.
da roċair a chú. A.

Rabert Cuculaind sidi da ḟaigid ass a aiṫle ocus ra iad a dá láim thairis, ocus tuargaib leiss cona arm ocus cona errud ocus cona etgud dar áth saṫuaid é, gombad ra áth atuaid ra beiṫ in coscur, ocus nabad ra áth aniar ac feraib h-Erend.

Da léic Cuċulaind ar lár Ferndiad; ocus do roċair nél, ocus tám, ocus tassi bar Coinculaind as ċind Fhirdiad and. At ċonnaic Láeg a ní sin, ocus atráigestar fir h-Erend uile do ṫiċtain dá ḟaigid. "Maith, a Chucuc[laind]", bar Láeg, "comerig badesta, ocus da roisset fir h-Erend dar saigid, ocus ní ba cumland óenḟir d'émait dúinn, ada roċair Ferdiad mac Damain mic Dáre latsu".

"Can damsa eirgi, a gillai", bar éssium, "ocus in ti da roċair limm?" Is amlaid ra bai in gilla ga rád, ocus rabert na briaṫra and, ocus ra recair Cuċulaind.

L. Eirg, a árċu Emna,
córu a ċaċ duit mór menma.
ra láis dit Fherndiad na n-drong.
debrad is cruaid do ċomlond.

Cc. Gaċana dam menma mór?
ram immart baeis ocus brón,
ithle in n-éċta do ringnius
iss in ċuirp ra ċruad ċlaidbius.

L. Ni ra ċóir dait a ċáiniud:
coru dait a ċommaidium.
rat rácaib in rúad rinneċ,
cainṫeċ, creċtaċ, crolindech.

Cc. Da m-benad mo lech ċoiss sláin,
dim is cor benad mo leṫ láim;
truag! naċ Ferdiad boi ar eċaib
tri biṫu na biṫ beṫaid.

L. Ferr leosom na n-dernad re—
ra ingenaib craebruaide.
sessium d'éc, tusu d'anad.
leó ní bec bar ṁ biṫ scarad.

Thine is the fault of my certain ruin.
On thee 't is best to have my blood.

The wretches escape not
Who go into the gap of destruction.
My voice is diseased.
Alas, I depart, my end hath come.

My lacerated ribs are bursting.
My heart is all gore.
Not well have I given battle.
Thou hast killed me, O Hound.

Cuchulaind ran towards him after that and clasped his two arms about him, and lifted him with his arms and his armour and his clothes across the ford northwards, in order that the slain should be by the ford on the north, and not by the ford on the west with the men of Eiriu. the victor carries off the body of the slain;

Cuchulaind laid Ferdiad down then; and a trance, and a faint, and a weakness fell on Cuchulaind over Ferdiad there. Laeg saw that, and the men of Eiriu all arose to come to him. "Good, O Cuchulaind", said Laeg, "arise now, for the men of Eiriu are coming to us, and it is not single combat they will give us, since Ferdiad, son of Daman, son of Dáre, has fallen by thee". the victor faints; Laeg urges him to arise;

"What availeth me to arise, O servant", said he, "after him that hath fallen by me?" And so was the servant saying, and he spake these words, and Cuchulaind answered.

Dialogue between Laeg and Cuchulaind;

L. Arise, O slaughter hound of Emania,
Exultation now beseemeth thee better.
Ferdiad of the hosts has fallen by thee.
Truly thy combat was hard.

C. What availeth me high spirit now?
To madness and grief I am driven,
After the deed I have done
And the body I have severely sworded.

L. It is not due of thee to lament him:
It were fitter for thee to exult in it.
At thee he flung the flying pointed spears,
Malicious, wounding, blood-streaming.

C. Even though he had cut my one leg off me,
And had he severed my one arm;
Alas! that Ferdiad mounts not his steeds
Through the endless time of perpetual life.

L. More pleasing to them is what thou hast done—
To the women of the Craebh Ruaidh.
He to die, thou to have remained.
To them seemeth not too small [the numbers] who have parted for ever.

Fol. 66. a. a.

An ló ṫanaċ a Cualnge
indiaid Medba mór gluaire,
is ár dáini le co m-blaid,
ra marbais da miledaib.
Ní ra ċotlais issáma
i n-degaid da mór ṫána.
giar b'uaṫed do dám malle,
mór maitne ba moċ ṫ-eirge. E.

Ra gab Cuculaind ac écaine ocas ac airċisecht Fhirdead and, ocas ra beirt na briaṫra.

"Maiṫ, a Fhirdead, bá dursan dait naċ nech dind ṙallaig ra ḟitir ma cheirt gnímradasa gaile ocas gaiscid ra acallais re comraċtain dúin comrac n-immairic. Ba dirsan dait naċ Laeg mac Riangabra, ruamnastar comairle ar co maltais. Ba dirsan dait náċ athere fír glan Fergusa fors emais. Ba dirsan duit naċ Conall caém, coscarac, commaidmeċ, caṫbuadaċ, cobrastar, comairle ar comaltais. Dáig ra fetatar in ḟir sin na gigne gein gabas gnimrada cutrumma commóra Connaċtaig rutsu go brunni ṁ-bráṫa ocas betha. Dáig mad iarrais ind ḟir sein de ḟessaib, na dúlib, na dálaib, na bruaṫraib brec ingill* ban cend ḟind Connaċt, etir imbeirt scell ocas sciaċ, etir imbeirt gae ocas ċlaideb, etir imbeirt m-brandub ocas ḟicheall, etir imbeirt eċ ocas ċarpat, ni ba lám laiċ letarar [latar] carna caurad, mar Fherndiad nel n-dáṫa, ni ba burind berna baidbi beldeirg do scoraib sciaṫṫa sceáṫ bricci, ni ba Cruaċain cossenas, gebas curu cutrumma rutsu go brunni ṁ-bráṫa ocas beṫa badesta, a mic drechdeirg Damáin", bar Cuculaind. Is and sin ra eirig Cuċulaind as ċind Fhirdead. "Maiṫ a Fhirdead", bar Cuċulaind, "is mór in brath ocas in trecun da bertatar fir h-Erend fort, do thabairt do comlund ocas do ċomruc rumsa. Dáig ni réid comlund na comrac rumsa bar Táin Bó Chuailnge. Is amlaid ra bai ga rád, ocas rabeirt na briaṫra.

Fol. 63. b. a.

A Fhirdead, ar dot ċloe brath.
dursan do dál dedenaċ,
tussu d'éc, missi d'anad.
sir dursan ar sír scarad.
Mad dammamar alla anall
ac Scáṫaig, buadaig Bhuanand
dar lind go bruṫe bross
noco biad ar n-aṫcharder.
Inmain lem do ruidiud rán,
inmain do chruṫ caem comlán,

* [Tingill, H. 1. 13. 281.]

From the day that thou camest out of Cuailgne
After Medb of great glory,
It is to her a grievous slaughter of [her] people,
All thou hast slain of her champions.

Thou hadst not slept in repose
After thy great plundered flocks.
Though few thy company along with thee
Many [were] the mornings of thy early arising.

Cuchulaind began to lament and moan for Ferdiad there, and he spake these words:

Lament of the victor over the slain;

"Well, O Ferdiad, it was unhappy for thee that it was not some one of the heroes who knew my real deeds of valour and prowess thou hadst consulted before thou hadst come to meet me in the too hard battle conflict. It was unhappy for thee that it was not Laeg, son of Riangabra, thou hadst consulted about our fellow-pupilship. It was unhappy for thee that thou didst not ask the truly sincere advice of Fergus. It was unhappy for thee that it was not the comely, ruddy, exultive, battle-victorious Conall thou hadst consulted for advice respecting our fellow-pupilship. For well do these men know that there will not be born a being of the Connacians who will perform deeds equal to thine till the end of time and life. For if thou hadst consulted these men respecting the places, the assemblies, the plightings, the false promises of the fair-haired women of Connaught, about playing at targets and shields, about playing at spears and swords, about playing backgammon and chess, about playing at horses and chariots, they would not have found the arm of a champion that would wound the flesh of a hero, like the cloud-coloured Ferdiad, nor one to raise the inviting croak of the red-mouthed vulture to the many coloured flocks, nor one that will contend for Cruachan, who shall equal thee to the end of time and life henceforth, O red-cheeked son of Daman", said Cuchulaind. And then Cuchulaind stood over Ferdiad. "Well, O Ferdiad", said Cuchulaind, "great was the treachery and abandonment played on thee by the men of Eiriu, to bring thee to combat and fight with me. For it was not easy to combat and fight with me on the Táin Bó Chuailgne". And so was he saying, and he spake these words:

O Ferdiad, treachery has defeated thee.
Unhappy was thy last fate,
Thou to die, I to remain.
Sorrowful for ever is our perpetual separation.

When we were far away, beyond
With Scathach, the gifted Buanand,
We then resolved that till the end of time
We should not be hostile to each other.

Dear to me was thy beautiful ruddiness,
Dear to me thy comely perfect form,

Fol. 80. b. a.

immain do rosc glass glanba,
inmain t-álaig is t-irlabra.
Nir ċing din tress tinbi ċness
nir gab feirg ra ferachas
ni ra ċongaib sciaṫ ar leirg láin,
ṫ-aiṫgintsiu a mic deirg Damáin
Ni tharla rumm sund cose,
áb a cear oenfer Aire,
da macsamla galaib gliad,—
ni ḟuaras sund, a Fhirdiad.
Findabair ingean Medba,
gé beiṫ d'ḟebas a delba
is gat im ganem, na im grian
a taidbriu duitsiu, a Fhirdiad. A.

Rá gab Cuċulaind ac fegad Firdiad and. "Maith a mo ṗopa Laig", bar Cuċulaind, "faubaig Fherndiad dadesta, ocas ben a errud ocas a étgud de, go faccursa in delg ar a n-derna in comlund ocas in comrac". Tanic Laeg, ocas ra ḟaubaig Fherndiad. Ra ben a errud ocas a étgud de, ocas ra ċonnaic in delg, ocas ra gab gá écaine ocas ga airchisecht, ocas rabert na briaṫra.

Dursan! a eó óir
a Fhirdiad na n-dám,
a balc bemnig buain,
ba buadaċ do láṁ,
Do barr bude brass,
ba cass, ba cain séd;
do ċriss duillech maeth
immut táeb gu t-éc.
Ar comaltas cain;
fadarc súla sáir;
do sciaṫ go m-bil óir;
th-fidċell ba fiu máin.
Do ṫuitim dom láim
tuci nar bé ċóir.
nir ba ċomlund ċáin
dursan! a eó óir! D.

"Maiṫ, a mo ṗopa Láig", bar Cuculaind, "coscair Ferndiad fadesta, ocas benin n-gae ṁ-bolga ass; dáig ni fétaimse beiṫ in écmais m'airm".

Tanic Laeg ocas ra ċosċair Fherndiad, ocas ra ben in n-gae ṁ-bolga ass, ocas ra ċonnaic rium a airm fuileċ for-derg ra taeb Fhirdiad, ocas rabert na briatra.

A Fhirdiad! is truag in dál!
t-acsin dam go ruad ro ban;

Dear to me thy gray clear-blue eye,
Dear to me thy wisdom and thy eloquence.
There hath not come to the body-cutting combat
There hath not been angered by manly exertion
There hath not held up shield on the field of spears,
Thine equal, O ruddy son of Daman.

Never until now have I met,
Since I slew Aife's only son,
Thy like in deeds of battle,
Never have I found, O Ferdiad.

Findabar the daughter of Medb,
Notwithstanding her excellent beauty
It is putting a gad on the sand or sunbeam
For thee to expect her, O Ferdiad.

Cuchulaind then continued to gaze on Ferdiad. "Well, my friend Laeg", said Cuchulaind, "strip Ferdiad now, and take his armour and his clothes off him, that I may see the brooch for the sake of which he undertook the combat and the fight". Laeg came, and he stripped Ferdiad. He took his armour and his clothes off him, and he saw the pin, and he began to lament and moan for him, and he spake these words.

the body of the slain is stripped in order that the victor may see Medb's brooch;

Alas! O golden brooch!
O Ferdiad of the poets,
O stout hero of slaughtering blows,
Valiant was thine arm,

lamentation of the victor on seeing the brooch;

Thy yellow flowing hair,
The curled, the beauteous jewel;
Thy soft foliated girdle
Upon thy side till thy death.

Delightful thy fellow-pupilship;
Beaming noble eyes;
Thy shield with its golden rim;
Thy chess which was worth riches,

Thy fall by my hand
I feel it was not right.
It was not a friendly consummation
Alas! O golden brooch! Alas!

"Good, O my friend Laeg", said Cuchulaind, "open Ferdiad now, and take the Gae-Bulg out of him; for I cannot afford to be without my weapon".

Laeg came and opened Ferdiad, and took the Gae-Bulg out of him, and he saw his weapon bloody and red-coloured by the side of Ferdiad, and he spake these words.

the body is opened and the Gae Bulg taken out of him;

O Ferdiad! sorrowful is the fate!
That I should see thee so gory and pale;

Fol. 60. b. a.

missi gan m'airm do nigi,
tussu it ċossair chroligi.
Mád dammamar alla anair
ac Scaṫaig, is ac Uaṫaig,
noċo betis beóil bána
etrainn, is airm i lága.
A dubairt Scáṫaċ go scenb
a athesc ruanaid ro derb;
ergid uli don ċaṫ ċass.
bar sicsa Germán garbglass.
A dubartsa ra Fherdiad,
ocas ra Lugaid, lán ḟial,
ocas ra mac ṁ-Baetain ṁ-báin,
teċt dún in agid Germain.
Lodmar go h-aille in ċomraic
ar leirg loċa Lind Fhormait.
tucsam chetri chét immaċ
a insib na n-Athisseċ.
Da m-basa is Ferdiad in n-áig
i n-dorus dune Germain,
ro marbusa Rind mac Niúil,
ro marbas Ruad mac Finniuil.
Ra marb Ferdiad ar in leirg
Bláth mac Calbai chlaideb deirg.
romarb Lugaid,—fer duairc dian,—
Mugairne mara Torrian.
Ra marbasa ar n-dula innond,
ceṫri ċoicait fern ferglond,
ro marb Ferdiad—duairc in drem—
dam n-dreimed is dam n-dilend.
Ra airgsem dún n-Germáin n-glicc,
ár fairgi leṫan lindbricc,
tucsam Germán i m-beṫaid
lind go Scaṫaig sciathleṫain.
Da nais ar mummi go m-blad
ar cró cotaig is oéntad,
conna betis ar ferga
etir fini find Elga.
Truag in maten, maten mairt,
rosbi mac Damáin diṫraiċt.
ucán, do ċara in cara
dara dalius dig n-derg fala!
Dambad and atċeindsea ṫ-éc,
etir miledaib mór Grec,

I having my weapon yet unwashed,
And thou a blood streaming mass.

the victor again laments the slain,

When we were away in the east
With Scathach, and with Uathach,
There would not have been angry words
Between us, and weapons of destruction.

Scathach eloquently spoke
In words of truly warlike import;
Go ye all to the furious battle
Which will be fought by German the terrible.

and recounts the story of a warlike expedition which they made together;

I said unto Ferdiad,
And to Lugaid, the ever generous,
And to the son of Baetan the fair,
Come [we] all of us against German.

We came all of us to the battle ground
On the shore of the lake of Lind Formait.
With us we brought four hundred out
Of the islands of the Athisech.

As I and Ferdiad the brave were
In the door of German's court,
I slew Rind, the son of Niul,
I killed Ruad, the son of Finniul.

Ferdiad slew upon the shore
Bláth, the son of Calba of the red swords.
Lugaid killed—a surly fierce man—
Mugarne of the Torrian sea.

I killed upon our going into the court
Four times fifty men of stern valour,
Ferdiad killed—surly was the party—
A clambering ox and a water ox.

We pillaged the court of the wily German.
Over the broad sea of spangled waters,
We brought German alive
With us to Scathach of the broad shield.

Our famous tutoress then bound
Our battle valour and amity,
So that our angers should not be [opposed]
Among the fair tribes of Elga.

after which they were bound in perpetual amity;

Sorrowful the morning, a Tuesday morning,
That the son of Daman was bereft of strength.
Alas, I loved the friend
To whom I have served a drink of red blood!

he continues to lament his fallen friend;

If it were there I saw thy death,
Among the great heroes of Greece,

Fol. 69. b. b.

ni beindsi i m-beṫaid dar ċéiss—
gombad aroén aṫbailméiss.
Is truag a ni narta de:
nar n-daltanaib Scáṫċe,
missi créċtaċ ḃa ċrú ruad,
tussu gan ċarptiu d'imluad.
Is truag a ni narta de:
nar n-daltanaib Scáṫaiċe,
missi créċtaċ bá ċrú garb,
ocas tussu úli marb.
Is truag a ni narta de:
nar n-daltanaib Scaṫaige,
tussu ḋ'éc—missi beó brass.
is gleó feirge in feraċas. A.

"Maith, a Chucuc[laind]", bar Laeg, "facbam in n-áthsa fadesta. Is ro ḟata atám and". "Faicfimmit ám écin, ámo ṗopa Láig", bar Cuċulaind, "acht is clúċi ocas is gaini lemsa caċ comlond ocas caċ comrac da rónas i farrad ċomlaind ocas ċomraic Ḟhirdiad".

Ocas is amlaid ra bai ga rád, ocas rabert na briaṫra.

Clúċi caċ, gáine caċ,
go roiċ Ferdiad iss in n-áċ;
inund foglaim friṫ dún,
innund rograim ráċ,
inund mummi máeṫ
rasslainni reċ cáċ.
Clúċi caċ, gáine caċ,
go roiċ Ferdiad iss in n-áth;
inund aisti ar uath dúinn,
inund gasced gnáṫ.
Scáṫaċ tuc da sciaṫ, damsa
is d'Ferdiad tráth.
Clúċi caċ, gaine caċ,
go roiċ Ferdiad iss in n-áċ;
inmain uatni óir
ra ḟuirmius ar áth,
a tairbga na tuath,
ba calma na cách!
Clúċi cáċ, gaine cáċ,
go roiċ Ferdiad iss in n-áċ;
in leoman lassamain lond,
in tond baéth ḃorr
immar bráth.
[MS. defective]
Clúċi caċ, gaine caċ,

I should not be alive after thee—
For it is together we should die.

Sad is the deed which has come of it:
We, the pupils of Scathach,
I all wounded and red with gore,
Thou thy chariot no longer driving.

Sad the deed which has come of it:
We the pupils of Scathach,
I wounded and rough with gore,
And thou entirely dead.

Sad the deed which has come of it:
We, the pupils of Scathach,
Thou to have died—I alive and strong.
The battle was an angry combat.

"Good, O Cuchulaind", said Laeg, "let us leave this ford now. Too long are we here". "We shall leave now, indeed, O my friend Laeg", said Cuchulaind; "but every other combat and fight that I have made was to me as a game and a sport compared with the combat and the fight of Ferdiad". *Laeg urges him to leave the ford; he prepares to go;*

And so he was saying, and he spake the words. *he magnifies his recent combat and eulogises his opponent.*

Each was a game, each was a sport,
Until Ferdiad came into the ford;
Alike was the tuition we received,
Alike were we called to rewards,
Alike was our tender tutoress
Who distinguished us above all others.

Each was a game, each was a sport,
Until Ferdiad came into the ford;
Alike were our individual habits,
Alike our ordinary achievements.
It was Scathach that gave two shields, to me
And to Ferdiad at the same time.

Each was a game, each was a sport.
Until Ferdiad came into the ford;
Dear to me the pillar of gold
Whom I vanquished on the ford;
Who assaulting the tribes,
Was more valiant than all!

Each was a game, each was a sport,
Until Ferdiad came into the ford,
The lion fiery and furious,
The swelling hideous wave
Threatening destruction.

[MS. defective.]

Each was a game, each was a sport,

go roiċ Ferdiad iss in n-áth.
indar limsa Fer dil diad;—
is am diad ra biad go bráċ.
indé ba meticir sliab;—
indiu ní fuil de aċt a scáth.

Tri dírime na tána
da roċratar dom láma,
formna bó, fer, ocus eċ,
ro das laidius ar caċ leċ.

Giribat linm- [illegible] a sluaig
tangatar [illegible] chruaċain ċruaid,
Mo triín r [illegible] u leti,
ro marbas [illegible] gaib ċluċi.

Noċo tarla [illegible] ċ cró,
ní ra alt [illegible] a da brú.
nír ra ċint [illegible] nuir na tír,
de maccail [illegible] buid forir clú. C.

Aideḋ Fhirdiad gonnicirin.

Until Ferdiad came into the ford.
Dear to me the beloved Ferdiad;—
It shall hang over me for ever.
Yesterday he was larger than a mountain;
To-day there remains of him but his shadow.

The three countless [legions] of the Táin
They all have fallen by my hands,
Their choicest cows, men, and horses,
I have slaughtered on either side.

The victor boasts of his feats.

Though more numerous were the hosts
That came out from destructive Cruachan,
Though my numbers were less by one half,
I killed them by my fierce contest.

There has not come to a gory battle,
Nor has Banba nursed upon her breast,
There has not come off sea or land
Of the sons of kings, one of better fame.

The victor extols the slain.

The Fate of Ferdiad so far.

II.

TWO OLD LAW TRACTS

ON

THE CLASSES OF SOCIETY AND THEIR PRIVILEGES

AMONG THE ANCIENT IRISH.

From the vellum MS. H. 3. 18., in the Library of Trinity College, Dublin.

WITH LITERAL TRANSLATIONS.

---

1. THE CRITH-GABLACH.

This, undoubtedly the most important document yet published on the social organization of the Gaedhil, or, indeed of the Celtic peoples of Europe, appears not to have been known in its complete form by Professor O'Curry, who has made the fragment of it known to him the subject of much valuable discussion in Lectures II., vol. i., and XX., vol. ii. The vellum MS. H. 3. 18. in the Library of Trinity College, Dublin, contains three unconnected fragments, from two of which the following copy of the whole tract has been made out. The first and larger fragment commences with part of a sentence (at the words bej bɩo cetħ-ɼaɼ, etc.), at page 1 of the MS. It is certain, however, that the Tract was originally complete in the first part of the MS., for what is now page 1 appears to have been formerly page 9: the first three leaves being so much defaced that they could not be read, and were not therefore taken into account in newly paging the MS., or by Dr. O'Donovan in his Descriptive Catalogue of the MSS. in the Library of Trinity College. The fourth leaf, which would have been pages 7 and 8 of this MS., has been torn away, and with it the first part of the Tract is thus lost from this part of it; as is clearly proved by a small portion of the lower end of the leaf which remains, and which contains some words and parts of words belonging to this Tract, the last being the connecting word between the lost part and the fragment now remaining. This word forms part of the sentence: Cıᴅ noᴅ m-beɼ ın ɼeɼɼa [a bó aıɼechuɼ? Aɼ] beɼ bıᴅ cetħaɼ no coıcıuɼ beıt hı comaɼbuɼ bó aıɼeċ, etc. "Why has this man not obtained [his Bó-aireship? Because] it is the custom to have four or five in the Comarbship of a Bó-Aire", etc. The words within the brackets are upon the remaining corner of the lost leaf, while the remainder of the sentence, beginning with the words ber bro, etc., is upon what is now p. 1 of the MS. There can then be no doubt that this copy of the Tract was originally complete. The page before the lost leaf is written in large characters, but so much defaced that it cannot now be read: it probably contained an introduction to the Tract.

The second fragment, and which contains the beginning of the tract, is found at p. 252 of the MS., and without title. The part common to both fragments led Mr. Bryan O'Looney to discover the connecting link between them, and thus we have been enabled to give this valuable tract in its complete form from the same MS. The translation of the first fragment was made by Mr. O'Looney. Professor O'Curry left a readable translation of the second part, which has served as the basis of the following one. The letters O'L. and O'C. on the margin, indicate the parts first translated by each respectively. The text of the copy in the beginning of the MS. being more correct than that of the second, which formed part of a different tract, has been accordingly adopted here, so far as it goes.

The third fragment is to be found on p. 419 of the MS. H. 3. 18., and consists of only a few paragraphs from the middle of the tract. With the exception of these three fragments, no other copy of the tract, or of any part of it, is known. The MS. H. 3. 18., like so many of our MS., is a mere scrap-book, into which the compiler copied everything he deemed worthy of preservation. It does not appear that the copyist recognized those three fragments, which were evidently copied from different MSS., as belonging to the same tract. Edward O'Reilly, in his *Irish Writers*, under the year 696, refers to the MS. H. 3. 18., and describes the tract, or at all events the chief fragment, as "a law tract on the privileges and punishments of persons in different ranks in society", and believed it to have been part of a great compilation of laws known as the ᴅa Leaban ᴅeag na ꜰuiċpime or ꜰuicpibċ, or The Twelve Books of the *Fuithrim*. At p. 78 a. of the MS. H. 4. 22. T. C. D., are to be found a few glosses under the heading "incipic maċcnaioce na cana ꜰuicpibċe", which show that at the period when those glosses were copied, the compilation in question existed. Judging from those glosses, from the internal evidence of the *Crith Gablach* itself, and many other considerations which cannot be entered into here, it is very probable that the *Crith Gablach* did really form part of the code of laws known as the *Cain Fuithrime*, compiled by *Amergin*, son of *Amalgad*, son of *Maelruan*, a distinguished poet, and a native of the *Decies*, in the time of *Finghin*, king of Munster, who died A.D. 694. Professor O'Curry has given an interesting account of this great Code of Laws from the MS. H. 3. 18., in vol. i., pp. 31 and 32, of the preceding lectures. But whether the *Crith Gablach* was once part of that code or not, there can be no doubt that it belongs to the middle or end of the seventh century.

AN CRITH GABLACH.

Cid ara nenper criṫ gablaċ? Nin. Ar indi crenas in fear tuaiṫe dia daġfoltaiḃ hi tuaiṫ co nairimther ina graḋ teċta imbi i tuaiṫ: no araili do gablaib i foolaither grad tuaiṫe.

H. 3. 18. p. 352. O'L.

Cair. Cislir foolai forsuidib? a .uii. Cid as a fordailti graid tuaiṫe? A urlann grad necalsa, ar nach graḋ bis a neclais is coir cia beṫ a urlann i tuaiṫ, deg fortaig,[453] no diṫiġ, no fiadnaise, no bretemnaċta, o cach do alailiu.

Cesc. Cadeat graid tuaiṫi? Fer midba, bó aire, aire desa, aire ard, aire tuise, aire forgill, ocus ri.

THE CRITH GABLACH.

What is it that is called Crith Gablach? Answer. The thing which the man of the tribe accumulates from his benefits in the territory till he is admitted to the rank of the legitimate possessors of the territory: or other increase [of property] by which distinction is given to the grades of the people.

Quære. Into how many grades are they [the people] divided? [Answer.] Into seven grades. In what manner are the grades of the people distinguished? In the same manner as the ecclesiastical grades, because it is proper that the grades which are in the church should be also in the people, for proof, or denial, or witness, or judgment, between man and man.

The privileged grades.

Quære. What are the grades of the people? A Fer-Midba, a Bó-Aire,[454] an Aire-Desa,[455] an Aire-Tuise,[456] an Aire-Forgaill,[457] and a Ri.

(453) *Fortig*, a law term which means proof for the negation, denial, or rebutting of a case at law.

(454) *Aire*. The ruling classes among the ancient Irish were called *Aires*. The corresponding term among the old Welsh was *Arglwydd*, which signifies a lord. These terms are, perhaps, to be connected with the parallel forms of the Sanskrit root *arh* and *argh*. From *arh* we have *arha*, honourable, *arhanâ*, honour. The Gothic *Airus*, man, ambassador, with its cognate forms: Old Saxon *eru*, Old Norse *âr*, *ári*, agent, ambassador, may also be connected with *Aire*. Another interesting cognate form is the Scythian *αἰώρ*, man. The Rugian man's name *Erarich* (Zeuss. Die Deutschen u. die Nachbarstämme, 486), is undoubtedly another relative, connected with a probable Gothic *áira*, and with the Old High German *êra*, *haera*, Frisian *êre*, Old Saxon *êra*, Ang. Saxon *âre*, *âr*, splendour, glory, honour. New High German *Ehre*, honour, and many other sister forms. With *argh* we may connect the Greek *ἀρκη*, sovereignty, power, in the plural *αἱ ἀρχαι*, authorities, magistrates; *ἄρχω* to govern, and *ἄρχων* a ruler; *ἀρχι* in arch-bishops, etc.; Gothic *airknis* [or *airkns?*] good, holy; and the Welsh *Arglwydd* above mentioned. The Sanskrit derivative *argha*, *arghya*, honour, offerings to gods, reward, and the Gothic *air*[illegible] suggest a possible, and if it coul[illegible]

The Crith Gablach. II. 3. 18. p. 232 'L.

Mad a dliged Fenechais, is menbud sunn fordailter na .uii. ngraidsi. Cia menbad bó aire cona ocht fodlaib, aire

The privileged grades.

In the same way that they are entitled to the Fenechas,[458] it is so they are divided into these seven grades. What are the ranks of the Bó-Aire with his eight (different) grades, Aire-Desa, Aire-Ech-

established, an interesting connection between the origin of the terms expressive of civil rule, and the priestly function.

In the Yaçna we meet with the word *airya*, which is the Zend representative of the Sanskrit *ârya*, from the root *r* (*ar*)=Zend *ërë*, to gain, to acquire. As an adjective, it means "venerable"; and as a noun it is the proper name from which has come the term "*Aryan*", now almost universally given to the Indo-European races and languages. Bopp compares the Old High German *êra*, above cited, and its cognate forms, with *arya*. It may be that this is so, and that the Irish *Aire* represented not only in blood but in name the primitive *Aryas*.

The modern German title "*Herr*", and its cognate forms in the German and Scandinavian dialects, is usually connected with the Gothic *hazjan*, to praise, O. H. G. *haer*, *heri*, venerable; the O. H. German comparative *heroro*, *haeroro*, etc., elder, major, etc., Anglo Saxon *Herra*, *Hearra*, Lord. Are these forms really connected with *hazjan*, or may they not be rather connected with the roots above, and therefore with our *Aire*?

There were two classes of *Aires*: 1. those who possessed "*Deis*", that is, who were owners of the soil; and 2. those whose wealth consisted of cattle and other personal property. The first class of *Aires* were distinguished as *Flaiths*, the "Wlad" of the Slavonians, and the "Hlaford" of the Anglo-Saxons. They constituted the "Haute Noblesse", and corresponded to the Eorls, Eorlcundmen, or Twelfhaendmen of the Anglo-Saxons. The second class were known as *Bó-Aires*, that is "Cow *Aires*", and corresponded to the Anglo-Saxon "Sixhaendmen", Sithcundmen, or Thanes.

(455) *Aire Desa*, the lowest grade of the *Flaiths*, or *Aires* who possessed *Deis* or real property. See vol. i. p. 37, and App. pp. 493, 494, and 516.

(456) *Aire Tuise*, i.e., the leading Aire; he took precedence in right of birth, and his rank, rights, and privileges were greater than those of most of the other Aires. He appears to have acted as a kind of president of the *Flaiths* on occasions of elections, etc. See vol. i. p. 37, App. pp. 499, and 516.

(457) *Aire Forgaill*, i.e. the testifying *Aire*. He was the *Flaith* next in rank after the *Righ* or king and his Tanist. One of his functions, from which he derived his name, was that of determining the qualifications, privileges, and rights of the suitors of the court and the various public functionaries. He corresponded to the *Canghellawr* of the Welsh; and was the prototype of the Cancellarius Regis in the mediæval states. Every *Righ* or king had his *Aire Forgaill*; and as there were three ranks of kings, there were also three ranks of *Aire Forgaills*; the *Aire Forgaill* of a *Righ Tuatha*; the *Aire Forgaill* of a *Righ Mor Tuatha*; and the *Aire Forgaill* of a *Righ Cuicidh* or provincial king. The *Ard Righ Erind* or high king had likewise an *Aire Forgaill*; we are not however in a position to determine whether, when the monarch was also provincial king, which was generally the case, he had two *Aire Forgaills*, one as monarch and one as *Righ Cuicidh*.

(458) See App., note 479, p. 472.

(459) *Aire Echta* was the *Flaith* who commanded the permanent military levy of the territory, consisting of five men equipped with arms. He was the king's Master of the Horse, and corresponded to the "Constable of the Host", the "Stallere" or "Constabularius Regis" of the Anglo-Saxon kings. See vol. i. p. 37, and App. p. 497.

desa, aire ecta, aire ard, aire tuire, aire forgaill, ta-naire ri, ocus ri? Cadeat fodlaib bo airech? Da fer midbota, ocus occ-aire, ocus aitech, ocus bo aire febra, — The Crith Gablach. H. 3 18. p. 252. O'L.

ta,[459] Aire-Ard,[460] Aire-Tuise, Aire-Forgaill, Tanaise-Ri,[461] and a Ri? What are the ranks of a Bó-Aire? Two Fer-Midbotha,[462] and an Oc-Aire,[463] and an Aithech,[464] and a Bó-Aire-Febsa,[465] — The privileged grades.

(460) *Aire Ard*, i.e., the High Aire. A *Flaith* who was higher in rank than the *Aire Desa*, and whose duties, rights, and privileges, were greater than those of the other grades of the nobility; he had precedence of the *Aire Desa*, and came next in rank, etc., to the *Aire Tuise*. See vol. i. p. 87, and Appendix, p. 497–8, and 515.

(461) *Tanaise Ri*, i.e., the Tanist of a king. He was next in rank to the king; and was elected as presumptive successor to the king by the people. His rank was much higher, and his rights and privileges much greater than those of the other nobles. See vol. i. p. 38, and App. p. 501.

(462) See App., note 481, p. 473.

(463) See App. note 511, p. 479.

(464) *Aithech*, *Athig*, *Athaig*, a word which has formed the subject of much discussion as to its true meaning. It corresponds to the Welsh *Taeog* in derivation and to a certain extent in meaning. It means literally "house-father", for there can be no doubt that it is a derivative of the old Irish *Aite*, nurturer, for *Aitte* (Zeuss, 1056, and Stokes' Irish Glosses, No 1078), corresponding to the Gothic *Atta*, father, of which many sister forms are to be found in the Old German dialects. A gloss in the Liber Hymnorum supports this primitive meaning of the word "*Athig .i. Fir muintir*", real family; the following gloss also supports it: "*Athaig .i. icaduighe* ut est *Athach tighe turc acus a setig*" —*Athaig*, i.e., payees, ut est, the *Athach* is the chief [i.e. the man of the house] and his wife" (MS. H. 3. 18. p. 5). As head of a house, the *Aithech* paid the tribute or rent levied by the *Flaith*, and hence his name became synonymous with "payee". The *Flaiths* who constituted the ruling classes, and no doubt many, if not most of the *Bó-Aires* also, belonged, as do the ruling classes in every other country, to the last intrusive race, and, like all conquerors, must have imposed as much of the burden of maintaining the state as the subject race could bear. Hence the better class of the latter in Eiriu, who were able to retain the position of independent householders, became mere tenants to the former. In time, such of the ruling class as were unable to maintain their position as *Flaiths*, sunk into the condition of *Aithechs*, when they did not descend to be mere retainers. In this way the *Aithech* became synonymous with "tenant", as distinguished from *Flaith*, or lord. The term *Flaith Athaig*, shows that an ancient proprietor might have even retained considerable possessions on payment of rent. Strictly speaking the *Bó Aires* were *Aithechs*, at least in all *Tuaths* where there were *Flaiths*. But the privileges which they acquired gradually transformed them into a gentry or intermediate aristocracy, so that the term *Aithech* gradually became restricted to those who did not possess sufficient wealth to be reckoned *Bó-Aires*. The *Aithech* in this more restricted sense, was a free man in the same sense that the Saxon *Ceorl*, or churl, and one class of the Welsh *Taeogs*, were free. See INTRODUCTION for a discussion of the whole subject of the occupation of land and the position of the occupiers amongst the ancient Irish.

(465) *Bó Aire Febsa*, i.e., the lowest grade of *Bó Aires*, a man who had merely the qualifications of the minor grade of the cow-owner nobility. He had twelve cows, and was entitled to fees or fines under the laws according to his dignity. See vol. i. p. 35; H. 3. 18. 257; see also Appendix, p. 484; and the different grades of *Bó Aire*.

The Crith Gabhlach. H. 3. 18. p. 252. O'L.

ocus mbruigfer, ocus fer fotlai, ocus aire cosraing. Caide imċach, ocus naidm, ocus raiṫ, ocus fiadnaise, ocus loᵹ

The privileged grades.

and a Brughfer,[466] and a Fer-Fothlai,[467] and an Aire-Cosraing.[468] What is the Imthach,[469] and the Naidm,[470] and the Raith,[471] and

(466) See App. note 531, p. 485.

(467) *Fer Fothlai*, i.e., a man of wealth. He was so called because he had more cattle than his own land could support; he let them out on hire to tenants, and paid his serving tenants in cattle. He was called the leader of *Bó Aires*, because of his wealth; and he was progressing to the rank of *Aire Desa* (i.e., a landlord). See vol. i. p. 36; and App. pp. 490–1.

(468) *Aire Cosraing*, i.e. the binding *Aire*, was a *Bó Aire* who represented the executive authority of the chief or king, in assemblies of the people and courts, which he appears to have had the authority to summon. He also was the provost of the chief or king over his *Ceiles*, *Bothachs*, *Sen-Cleithe* and *Fuidirs*, acting for them in all civil and criminal suits, contracts, etc., and determining the amount of dues and tolls in the shape of *Biatha*, *Bes Tigi*, etc., to which they were liable; and all of which as fiscal officer he settled. His title of *Cosraing* or *Nascaire*, as he was also called, was derived especially from his being the representative of the chief's *Ceiles*, etc., in all contracts and obligations. Though the executive officer of the chief or king he was elected by the people. As each chief or *Righ Tuatha*, *Righ Mor Tuatha*, and provincial king had an *Aire Cosraing*, there were at least three ranks of them, corresponding to the three ranks of *Aire Forgaills*. The *Aire Cosraing* was one of the Irish representatives of the Anglo-Saxon "Gerefa", of which there were, as is well known, several ranks also. Thus the *Aire Cosraing* of a *Tuath* corresponded to the "Gerefa" of the Hundred, and the *Aire Cosraing* of a *Mor Tuath*, to the Shire "Gerefa", who is now represented by the county Sheriffs or "Shire-reeves". The Welsh *Maer*, a title also known in Ireland and Scotland, was also the representative of the *Aire Cosraing*. See more on this subject in INTRODUCTION.

(469) *Imthach* (lit. progress, migration, departure, or adventure), but here it means rank, state, affluence, or position in society, in which sense the word is still used all over Munster.

(470) *Naidm*, literally a knot, that is a contract. All contracts, in order to be valid, should be made in the presence of a person privileged to execute them. This privileged person was called *Fer Nadma*, and corresponded to the *Gwr-Nod* or Nodman of the Welsh Laws. The editor of the Ancient Laws of Wales explains *Gwr-Nod* as a man of note or mark; the cognate Irish word shows that this explanation is incorrect. *Naidm* is the Latin *Nexum*, and the *Fer Nadma* or binder was like the Libripens who officiated in all transfers of res mancipi per aes et libram. The Irish functionary who bound the *Naidm* or *Nexum* appears to have had many responsibilities which there is no evidence to show that the Roman one undertook. He also acted in contracts and bargains which would not have been included in those considered by Roman Law necessary to be made per aes et libram. Thus, according to a passage in the MS. H. 3. 18, T.C.D. p. 29, the "knotter" was bound: to see that the *Naidm* or *Nexum* which he made was not in any way infringed upon, to give evidence on oath on the subject, and to honestly enforce the fulfilment of the contract. In the curt and elliptical language of the Brehon Laws, the *Naidm* or *Nexum* is put for the "knotter" or *Fer Nadma*. In the making of every contract, besides the latter functionary, two other persons should be present, a *Raith* or surety, and *Fiadnaise* or witness, "because it is a *Naidm* [recte a *Fernadma*] that binds, and it is a *Raith* that promises, and it is a *Fiadnaise* that proves the lawfulness of the suit" (MS. H. 3. 18. 21).

nenech, ocuꞅ bıaṫa, ocuꞅ oṫꞃauꞅ, ocuꞅ ꞅnaꝺa, ocuꞅ ꞇauꞃ- The Crith Gablach. H. 3 18. p. 252. O'L.

the Fiadnaise,[472] and the Loghenech,[473] and the Biatha,[474] and Their privileges.

Naidm, like *Nexum*, may be connected with the Sanskrit root *nah* = Zend *naz*, to bring together, to join, to enchain.

[471] *Raith* is usually, as in the foregoing note, explained as a bail or surety. According to the editor of the Welsh Laws, a *Rhaith* was a "verdict", of which there were different kinds according to the number of compurgators. Like *Naidm*, the *Raith* is put for the person who gives the decision. He was not strictly speaking a compurgator, but either a bail who bore testimony to the character and good faith of a party to a suit or contract, and promised that he should appear when called upon to fulfil a contract, or appear in court; or a person who was consulted respecting contracts, sales, etc.—an adviser in fact. His legal functions as bail appear to have been confined to the first hearing of a cause. *Raith*, in the sense of decision or counsel given, is perhaps to be connected with the Gothic *redan*, Old High German *râtan*, to consult, persuade, Anglo-Saxon *rædan* to give counsel, and many other Germanic and Scandinavian forms, including the New High German *Rath*, a councillor. We may also connect with it the Italian *rota*, Lithuanian *rotà*, a meeting of council. The cognate Irish words: *raidh*, which O'Reilly translates "arbiter", and which in many passages of Irish MSS. means a decision of a meeting or assembly, *râdh* to speak, *comhradh* conversation, the Lithuanian *rodas*, Lettish *râdu*, Polish *rada* counsel, are perhaps also to be connected with Gothic *redan* and not with *rodjan*.

[472] *Fiadnaise*, a witness. According to Dr. Ebel the latter English word is derived from *Fiadnaise*. See note 470, on *Naidm*, p. 470.

[473] There are four terms referring to the face used in the Laws: *Logh-Enech*, *Enechland*, *Enechruice*, *Enechgris*. *Loghenech* is always put for honour-price, or fine for any insult offered to a man's honour, which fine might be great or small in proportion to the rank of the offended person. *Enechland* was the fine due to a person for any insult, indignity, or injury done to any person or thing under his protection or sanctuary. That there was an essential difference between *Enechland* (an *Eiric* or fine) and *Loghenech* (honour price) is shown by the following curious gloss: "The *Aigne* (i.e. an arguer, i.e. a counsellor) was not entitled to *Loghenech*, because he was classed with the *Cainte* or satirist. He was only entitled to *Enechland* or *Eiric*, for the injury or insult which he had received; and the *Enechland* was as follows: for the counsellor who dispenses judgment, nine cows; for the pleading counsellor, six cows; for the highest rank of junior counsellor, four cows; for the next in order three cows (MS. H. 3. 18. p. 518). *Enechland* appears to have corresponded to the Welsh *Gwynebwarth*, which the editor of the Ancient Laws glosses "face-shame". Another word occurs in the Welsh Laws, *Gwynebwerth*, which is considered to be legally synonymous with the word just mentioned, but which is glossed in the same work as "face-worth". If these words are distinct they must have had different legal significations like the Irish words. *Gwynebwarth* may perhaps be compounded of two words equivalent to the Irish words, *enech*, face, and *gart*, interest or fine, i.e. the full fine or honour price, while *gwenebwert* may be formed from words corresponding to the Irish words, *enech*, face, and *bert* = *dliged*, a legal fine. *Enechruice* was a face-reddening reproach, i.e., "a blood-red face such as if your mother's son or your sister's son had taken an illegitimate companion". It was also applied to the insult offered to a tribe in which a murder was committed. (See in text under *Aire Echta*, p. 497.) (H. 3. 18. p. 120). *Enechgris*, a dishonour such as that of receiving stolen goods (*ibid.*). *Enech* is always translated "face", and this meaning has been adopted here; but if we may connect it with the Sanskrit *enas* = Zend *aênô*,

The Crith Gablach. H. 3. 18. p. 252 O'L.

creic, ocus bes tigi caċ ae? Nin. Amail ar in cain fenechas:

"Ara ferr grada fene
fri mes airechta adruimther".

Their privileges.

the Othraus,[475] and the Snadha,[476] and the Taurcreic,[477] and the Bes Tigi[478] of each of them? Answer. It is as laid down in the Cain Fenechas:[479]

"For whosoever is known to be of the Gradh Fine,[480]
To the rank of the Aireship he is reckoned".

offence, nuisance, the primitive meaning of the word must have been an insult or offence producing a blush on the face.

(474) *Biatha*. Part of the rent which the *Flaith* received from his *Ceiles* consisted of certain stated victuals, or *Biatha*. It was the *Daer Ceili* only who were bound to give refection, as in Wales, where the *Dawnbwyd* of the vassals represented the *Biatha* of the Irish base clients.

(475) See App. note 501, p 476.

(476) *Snadha*, means literally crossing or traversing. This word in the Laws means the protection and maintenance which one tribe or grade of society was bound to give to its co-grade, or any other grade, entitled to traverse its territory. *Snadha* is the equivalent of the term *Nawdd* used in the Welsh Laws for the legal protection which the king, his officers, and other persons of the higher classes had the privilege of according. See App. pp. 474-5, 481.

(477) *Taurcreic* was the term used for the stipends or gifts which a king or chieftain bestowed upon those who "commended" themselves and made homage to him as king or chief. The amount of *Taurcreic* depended both on the rank of the giver and of the receiver. The cattle and other property thus given received the name of *Sed Taurclaide*. The Book of Rights, edited for the Celtic Society by Dr. John O'Donovan, gives the nature and value of the *Taurcreic* of the king of Eiriu and of the provincial kings to the minor kings or sub reguli. The word *Rath* is sometimes used for *Taurcreic*, but there was an important distinction between them. *Rath*, i.e. wages, was the term applied to the cattle or other property given by a *Flaith* to his *Ceiles*. These cattle were only a loan, and reverted to the lord. If a *Ceile* gave more *Bes Tigi* to the lord than he was bound to give, the *Flaith* or lord gave him additional *Rath* in proportion to the *ardaig* or excess of his payment over his rent. But this additional *Rath* was looked upon as an absolute gift to the *Ceile*.

(478) *Bes Tigi*, i e. house tribute or rent. This was a stated rent or tribute in kind paid to a *Flaith* by every subject who had received his *Taurcreic* or stipend. The *Bes Tigi* was given by the free or *Saer Ceili*. This was also the case with the *Gwestea* of the Welsh (which is the same as the Irish *Bes Tigi*), which was fee farm rent, paid in kind by the free villes to the lord. The vassals gave refection, *Dawnbwyd*, the free villains *Gwestea*. H. 2. 15. f. 47.; and H. 3. 18. p. 2. See App. pp. 477-8, etc.

(479) *Cain Fenechas*. "The laws which are made by the Church, the people, and the *Flaith*, that is, what is called *Fenechas*" (H. 3. 18. p. 237 b. See O'C.'s Gloss.). *Cain* always implies a regular law, the *Cain Fenechas* forming what may be called the constitution of the whole nation; while the *Cain Urrudhas* were the customals or customary laws of the several *Tuatha*, or tribes, or of the provinces. The still more local By-Law was called a *Nos Tuatha*, and the inter-territorial treaty, or compact, a *Cairde*. The laws relating to the Occupancy of Land seem to have applied to every part of the country, and to have constituted so important a part of the *Fenechas* that *Cain Fenechas* is explained in M. S. H. 3. 18, p. 283, as "the Law of Occupancy in Land".

(480) *Gradh Fine*, the legal grades of the nobility and gentry.

Ꝺa fer miḋboṫa .i. ḟer miḋboṫ. — Imtuing smaċta, imtoing o snaṫait co dairt. Isseḋ Log a enech, dia air, dia diguin, dia esain, dia sarug,—isseḋ saidis a naidm, ocus a The Crith Gablach. H. 3. 18. p. 252. O L.

Two Fer Midbotha, i.e. a Fer Midboth.[481] He is an Imtuing Smachta, he is a Toing,[482] from a needle to a Dairt. It is his Log Enech[483] for his satire, for his Diguin,[484] for his Esain,[485] for his Sarugh,[486]—it is it that defines his Naidm and his Raith and his Fermidbo

(481) A *Fer Midbotha* appears to have been any one under a judgment of a court. There were accordingly several classes of persons included under this category. Thus a minor who was not of sufficient age to undertake the management of his property, or to fulfil the duties which his rank and property entailed upon him, appears to have been included in the category. Those whose paternal property was encumbered by debt; those who wasted their own property and ran into debt, and were under a *Nexum*; those who had committed homicide and were condemned to pay *Dire*, etc., constituted other classes of *Fer Midboth*.

(482) *Toing*, an oath, that is, of a compurgator. The *Fer Midboth* in the text is described as being *Imtoing*, "he is an oath", and *Imtuing Smachta*, "he is an oath of fine or penalty", which imply different functions in each case. As an oath simply, he could be a compurgator in all cases where the value in litigation did not exceed a heifer, or where he only counted to that extent. As a *Toing Smachta* I suppose him to have acted as compurgator, or in inquisitions, etc., in all petty cases of trespass, etc., in which *Smachts*, or fines, were summarily inflicted in the *Brugh's* court. As in the case of *Naidm*, *Raith*, etc., the oath is put for the person. The giver of the oath was properly a *Fer Tonga*. He was clearly the same as the "Ferdingus", or "Ferthingmen", of Anglo-Norman law. As the *Toing*, or oath of each grade differed in value, we can easily understand why the *Ferdingi*, mentioned in the twenty-ninth chapter of the laws of Henry the First, were ranked among the freemen of the lowest class, while in the statute of the gild at Berwick, A.D. 1284, the Ferthingmen are classed after the aldermen of the gild and before the decani. Thus the Irish laws fully explain a difficulty which has hitherto puzzled the legal antiquaries and historians of England. See "Ancient Laws and Institutes of England", p. 231.

(483) See App. note 473, p. 471.

(484) *Diguin* was the protection or sanctuary which legally belonged to the dwellings of the privileged classes, and for the forcible tresspass or wilful violation of which the owner was entitled to special *Enechland*. The extent of the ground about the house to which the right of sanctuary extended was called a *Maigin Digona* or "demesne of Sanctuary", and varied in extent according to the rank of the owner. See note 537, on *Cnairseach*, *post*, p. 488.

(485) *Esain* was the hindrance offered to a suitor by which he was prevented from appearing at courts or assemblies, etc., and which he could legally plead as an excuse for his non-appearance. A person so hindered could claim *Enechland*, that is damages, from those who were the cause of the hindrance. The Irish *Esain* represented the "Essoign" of the Norman law, and appears to have embraced the same categories, such as Malum viæ, seu de malo venendi, or the Norman "Commune Essonium", etc.

(486) *Sarughudh*, an insult or assault not amounting to the shedding of blood; female violation, the violation of a church or ecclesiastical dignity; the violation of any sanctuary. It is well explained in H. 3. 18, p. 159, etc. The Irish *Sarughudh* corresponded to the Welsh *Saraet* or *Sarhaet*, insult, which was also put for the fine or damages due for the offence.

The Crith Gablach, H. 3. 18. p. 202. O'L.

raiċ ocus a fiadnaise, ocus a aitire. A biatha aonar: Ass, ocus grus, no arbur; ni dlig imb. Snaidid a comgrad tar atuaiċ fadesin, ocus biadtar leis co ndeochaid tar crich.

Cid ara neper fer midboċ don fir so? Ara ni do nicet [ndicet] ammaici addligid altruma, ocus naid roig fertaig.

In forcmaithep aes fainsetech don fir midboċ ima tuing smachta? Forcmaithep aes ceitheora mbliadan ndeg. Is aire ni comruc innsgi na fiadnaise, ar ni h-in-

Fermidboth. Fiadnaise and his Aitire.(487) His Biatha to himself alone: Ass(488) and Grus(489) or Arba;(490) he is not entitled to butter. His compeers traverse his territory throughout, and he feeds them till they pass outside the bounds of his territory.

Why is this man called Fer-midboth? Because his tribe does not pay its lawful fosterage, and because it is not easy to sue it.

Is there a particular age at which the Fer Midba becomes eligible as a Tuing Smachta? He is eligible at the age of fourteen years. And it is the reason that he does not be a witness before

(487) *Aitire*, i.e., a security between two parties. He is described as a man between two *Feichems* or parties to a suit, or like that which binds or goes between the eye and the brow. There were three denominations of *Aitire*, viz.: the *Aitire Luige*, that is, the oath-bound *Aitire*; the *Aitire Fosme*, the *Aitire* of adoption, "resting" or "staying"; and the *Aitire Nadma*, the binding or knotting *Aitire*. If an *Aitire* became bail or surety for a person under a bond or *Naidm*, that is became an *Aitire Nadma*, or according to Roman Law a "Nexus", and that the obligation was not duly discharged at the stated time, and that the person for whom he was bail was not forthcoming, the *Aitire* became a *Cimbid*, or "victim", that is, his life was forfeit, but might be ransomed for seven Cumals, the price of a "victim". The condition of a *Cimbid* corresponded to that of a Roman "Nexus" when he became "addictus". The Irish law of "Nexum" was however more humane. The *Aitire Fosme* was the legal guardian of a minor, who was sometimes called *Mac Faesma* or the son of adoption, corresponding to our ward in Chancery. The *Aitire* who becomes bail after a judgment had been given, in order to stay execution, appears also to have been called an *Aitire Fosme*. If such a surety further entered into a bond before a *Fer Nadma* making himself fully responsible for the debt, he became an *Aitire Nadma* or "Nexus". *Aitire* seems to have been formed from *Aite* a nurturer, and *Aire*, that is he was a nurturing or fostering *Aire*. An *Ait-Urnaide* would be the nurturer or sponsor of a suit or pleading; and *Ath-urnaide* is perhaps the true origin of "attorney", and not that given by Diez, who connects it with "tornare".

(488) *Ass*, New milk.

(489) *Grus*, also *Gruth*, *Gruiten*, groats; Anglo-Saxon *grut*, Old High German *gruzi*, New High German *grütze*. There has been borrowing here on one side or the other; it is probable, however, that it took place from the Celtic, as we have a Welsh *grual* corresponding to the Old French *gruel*, whence the English *gruel*. The following gloss shows that in Irish *Grus* was applied to gruel or porridge also: grus, gruċ, gruiten, .i. grosso cibo, .i. ceaiblin, no braisech. H. 2. 16.

(490) *Arba*, *orba*, or *orbar*, the nom. singular of *Orbaind*, corn or grain of any kind. It is generally used in the sense of corn meal.

fiadnaise aċt fri caċ suaill re [roim] seċt mbliadna .x. Na ro gaib selḃ na comarbas, ria sin, manas comatheċ fer fene lais. Issed innsin imatoing, smaċta mbruiġreċta. The Crith Gablach. H. 3. 18. p. 252. O'L.

In midboṫ eile conoi innsgi is trebeiriu side; tecmaltar a innsci do in teora briaṫraiḃ. Co de treri? Co toi gin tor-mach gin diġbail imurtoing andiaiġ naċ aile, ar idfet a luga, ocus imtoing: colpdaig no a loġ issed loġ enech dia air, dia diġuin, dia esain, dia sarug; isseḋ saiḋis a naidm, a raiṫ, a fiadnaise, a aitire. A biaṫa aonar [.i. ar foluċ notrusa], ass ocus grus, no arbur; ni dliġ imb. Snaidid a comgraḋ tara tuaiṫa . . . . . co tabair diablad mbiḋ dó.

In toċra[s]: ni fil andiu, isin aimsirso aċt loġ a degfolta do caċ iar na miad, itir foċraic leġo, ocus lin, ocus

that [age], because none are fit to be witnesses before seventeen years, except such nobles who have not assumed proprietorship or Comarb-ship before that, unless a Fer Fene[(491)] is in co-partnership with him. It is then (he is entitled) for his Toing[(492)] to the Smacht[(493)] of Brugh-Law.[(494)] Second Fer Midboth.

The other Fer Midboth when he becomes eligible he is a Tre-baire;[(495)] his eligibility is confirmed to him on (in) three conditions. What are those three [conditions]? That he shall come [to give his evidence] without increase, or curtailment, for his oath after all others, for his price and his oath are defined: a Colpdach[(496)] or her price, is his honour price for his satire, for his Diguin, for his Esain, for his Sarugh; it is it that is also given for his Naidm, his Raith, his testimony, his Aitire. He is entitled to his feeding for himself alone (i.e. upon Folach nOtrusa)[(497)] of new milk and groats or corn-meal; he is not entitled to butter. His compeers traverse over his territory, ... and they give double food to him [?].

The diseased:[(498)]—he is now, in those times entitled only to the price of his deserts from them in their fulness, both the pay of the physician, and Lin,[(499)] and of food and the price of his insult

(491) *Fer Fine*, the family chief or tribe representative. See note 468, on *Aire Cosraing*, App p. 470.

(492) *Toing*, an oath. See note 482, on *Toing*, App. p. 473.

(493) *Smacht*, a fine. See note on *Toing*, App. p. 473, and note 574, on *Smacht*, etc., p. 511.

(494) See note 531, App., p. 485.

(495) *Trebaire*, i.e. a guardian, a security (a householder).

(496) See note 516, App., p. 480.

(497) See notes 501 and 528, App. pp. 476 and 483.

(498) There appears to be a gap of a few lines here so that we are abruptly introduced to the case of a *Fer Midboth* who has committed an aggravated assault, and wounded some one, and is obliged to take sanctuary with an *Aitire* until the wounded man is cured, giving bail in the mean time for all the expenses of the sick man, and fines and damages. The taking sanctuary was to prevent the reprisals of the wounded man's relatives in case the traverser appeared in public places.

(499) *Lin*. There appear to be two or three distinct words of this form. One is a name for ale or other malt drinks; another the name of flax, and thence extended to linen cloth, and to lint of that kind used for dressing wounds

The Crith Gablach II, 2. 18 p. 252. O'L.

biaḋa, ocus log nainme amairce eaboda; aċt bid coitcinn dligis caċ ngraḋ do graiḋib tuaiṫe i corus oṫrusa. Tongar fri corp ocus anmain, ocus do teit aitire ar fer ferus in fuil, icorus oṫrusa, im boin adnaig tar fot criuach. In ard nimed didite diein ardian tola sluaig ina urgell tareire, cen lepaid arcuile liaig; icargo lego co derosc in arslaine, ina iarslaine. Is slan lin lina (no lino) lepṫa arnadaḋ co forus tuaiṫe.

Second Fer Midboth.

together with his Eboda;[300] but every grade of the grades of the people is alike responsible for the amount of the sick maintenance. They make oath on the body and on the soul, and an Aitire is given for the man who sheds the blood, [according to] the Corus Othrusa[301] for the purpose of protection through every place of assembly. In high sanctuary he is to be kept, to be protected from the hard assaults of hosts, as a redeemed hostage, while he (i.e. the wounded man) lies upon the bed of a physician:—the physician certifies that the wound is curable, and becomes responsible for the after cure of it. The Slan[302] of the Lin is a responsibility that extends to the Forus Tuatha.[303]

in the text it means not only lint, but all things requisite for the cure, comfort, and nourishment of the *Othrus* or patient, as is shown by the following gloss.—"*Lin*, *Linn*, or *Len*, i.e. all remedial requisites, or all things necessary to the bedridden patient; ut est, let there be no want of medicinal remedies, that is, let there be no bad medicinal attendance, or bad cure-attendance, or a bad bed, or bad curative medicines; and he shall have security against neglect". MS. Egerton, Brit. Mus. 88, 88, a. 2, 3.

(300) *Eboda*, paid advocates, counsellors, attorneys. Vide fairbe:—

Fairbe .i. fior eibe, ut fear fairbe .i. fear fior eibe aoi .i. an fear bios ag fior ebe na cuiri maiġid neiċ ar loġ.

Fairbe, i.e. a true advocate, *ut Fear Fairbe*, i.e. a man who is a true advocate in a suit; i.e. the man who advocates a case faithfully against a person for fees (rewards).—Mac Firbis' Glossary.

(301) *Corus Othrusa*, i.e. the knowledge of the laws providing for the maintenance, care, and medical attendance of the sick and wounded. See note 528, App. *Folach nOthrusa*, p. 483.

(302) *Slan* was the entire liability incurred when an *Aitire* was given for the fulfilment of the stipulations of a bond. It represented an admission of the liability to the whole of the principal and costs, equivalent to the modern marking of a judgment.

(303) *Corus Tuatha*—that is the true knowledge of the *Aireacht*, or nobility, or that which is in perfect accordance with the *Aireacht* (or grades of the) nobility of the territory. *Corus Tuatha* is the knowledge of the grades of the territory, their respective rights, privileges, and responsibilities, in accordance to which any liability which fell upon the tribe, or was a general charge on the territory, could be levied on the several grades according to their ranks and property.

Forus, i.e., a house; the appointed or lawful place of payment (O'C.'s Gloss.) *Forus Tuatha* (i.e., the mansion of the territory or people), the house of the *Aire Forgaill*, which was the lawful place for the payment of all charges which extended to the *Corus Tuatha* (i.e., to the grades in proportion to rank). It was his function to pay all such charges, and he had the right to levy the amount on the nobles of the territory, and to distrain when any of the grades refused to pay their portion.

Cadeat a folai corai o cach fris, a curṫar aitire fri buiṫ? Reir lego:—og friteċt for rata, mana eta nech asreraḋ o fir cinaiḋ combi ar egin do bongar; is co rog dire,[504] ocus eneclánn fo miaḋ. Atgairter cid tre ednge rotoṫar, teit ocus aṁaṫair for folaċ. Uachtar ar leamlaċt dó hi trisi, a coicti, i nomad, a ndechmad, a ndomnaċ. The Crith Gablach. H 3. 18. p. 252 O'L.

In forcmaither o ċeṫeoraiḃ bliadnaib deg co ficṫiġ co cuairt ulċaid? Cia beiṫ ararogbad bo airechas riasin ro ba cuairdoid, ni ica a luga acht alluga fer midbota. Cia beiṫ gin gaḃail norbai dana, co crine, ni téit a luiġe o fir midboṫa beos. Biṫ a ṫurcreic coic setaib. Molt cona forais bes a tige. Asse bes oen cinneda innsin, fer na treabaiḋ selḃ na ferann do fadeisin. Forais in muilt: di bairgin deg, imbi, nem-beoil, imglaice, cainne co cennaib, H. 3. 18. p. 253.

What are his lawful benefits from them for the payment of which an Aitire is given? According to the physician,—the entire fulfilment of the bail, unless he can be exculpated from absolute guilt so that the liability is virtually dissolved; and the entire Dire,[504] and the full amount of the Enechland. Any three friends whom he appoints are called upon, they and his mother go with him upon Folach.[505] He is entitled to cream on new milk on third, on fifth, on ninth, on tenth, and on Sundays. Second Fer Midboth.

Is he made eligible from [the age of] fourteen years to twenty till he [his face] is encircled with beard? Any person whomsoever who has been elected to a Bó-aireship before he has been encircled [with beard] there is paid in his price but the price of a Fer Midba. Though he has not taken possession of patrimony [land] until he is bearded, his price does not exceed that of a Fer Midba still. His Taurcreic is five seds. His Bes Tigi is a wether with its accompaniments. He must be the last survivor of a family, a man who possesses neither property nor land of his own. The accompaniments of the wether: twelve loaves, butter, Nembeoil,[506] Im-

(504) *Dire* was the fine or penalty to which a man was entitled for injury to any of his property. The amount of the *Dire* was fixed by law according to the amount of the injury and to the rank of the owner of the injured property. *Dire* corresponded to the Welsh *Dirwy*, which, like the corresponding Irish word, appears to have originally varied in amount, but in the twelfth and thirteenth centuries was almost always twelve kine. The Anglo-Saxon *Were* or compensation paid for personal injuries or bloodshed is undoubtedly cognate with the Irish *Dire*. *Dire*, like *Sarughudh* and other words, originally meant the injury, and were afterwards put for the fine. It is apparently related to the Sanskrit *dru*, to wound, and must have consequently been the penalty or "damages" for bodily injury

Corpdire was the fine paid to a person for bodily injury to himself.—H. 4. 22, p. 54; and O'Curry's Gloss.

(505) See note 528 on *Folach*, *post*. p. 483.

(506) *Nemb-eoil* appears to have been some kind of beer or other drink. The second part of the word seems to represent the Ang. Sax. *Ealo* Old Norse *Öl*, English *Ale*. The liquor

The Crith Gablach, H. 3. 18. p. 252. O'C.

ian oil aiss, tri bassaib oċtar ocus lemlaċt; ocus draumce no blaṫach. Ni dligter focus [foċugad] a ṫige do neach cein mbis maici, co mbi tualaing saintrebṫa, ocus gabala sealba do fir midboṫa, cein bes noen ċinnid; acht ma frisnarar a flaiṫ, na fuilnge a bes tar molt cona forais; ma forberar folad a ṫigi co mbi folad mbó airech, no ni bes ardudu, torba [forbera], corus a tuircreicca dorom asuidiu: Tosormaig cadesin somaine combi bes a ṫige ann iar na ṁiad. Mana congla [.i. congelt] naċ flaiṫ aile fris, leṫ-

Second Fer Midboth.

glaice,[507] Cainne[508] with their tops, an Ian[509] for drinking new milk, three Bassaib[510] of cream and new milk; and skim milk or buttermilk. No person is entitled to the hospitality of his house while he is a youth, till he is fit to become an occupier, and to take possession of property from [being] a Fer Midbotha, while he is in his minority; but if he supplies his Flaith, his tribute is not allowed to exceed a wether with its accompaniments; if the wealth of his house increases till he has the wealth of a Bó-Aire or something more, the amount of his Taurcreic increases proportionately upon it: It increases according to his wealth till his Bes Tigi is in its fulness. Unless another Flaith co-grazes with him, he gives one half [the profits] of his fields in consideration of his advancement, after being duly proclaimed; one-third of his

anciently so designated is usually considered to have been fermented malt-infusion without hops or other bitter ingredient. But the O. N. *Öl*, and no doubt the Ang. Sax. *Ealo*, also seem to have been general names for intoxicating drinks. *Nemb-eoil* probably meant a kind of bitter ale. A drink called *Nenadmin*, made of the bitter juice of the wood berries or of the sour juice of wild apples (MS. Egerton, 88 Brit. Mus. p. 39. a. 3. b. and O'C.'s Gloss.), that is a kind of cider, was also used in Ireland.

(507) *Inglaice*, i.e. a handful. [Table accompaniments.; the "Opsonia" of the Romans.] Twice the full of a man's hand; the lawful allowance of garden vegetables, and a handful of green onions with their heads; four hands is the length of each stalk, and one handful of green vegetables, and the same length of a sausage, or two hands of a seasoned belly pudding of a pig with each loaf.

inglaice:—da inglaice do láim fir, coimri ceċta do lus lubgoirt ocus inglaici glas cainne cona cennaib, ceithri duirn fot cach buinde, ocus inglaice do bosslus fon fot cetna do tarsunn; no da dorn do mucruchc [.i. do ċaelan] saillṫe caċa bairgine . . . . . [the article is imperfect at the end].—H. 2. 15. 39. a. *Vide* O'Curry's Gloss.

(508) *Cainne*, or *Caininn*, onions, or some such thing; thus, in "Imram Bruin mic Febail", "The eyes shed tears under the influence of the Fir-Caininn (i.e. the true or strong onion). See also *Leabhar Breac*, fol. 109, b. a. bot. and No. 52, 4, p. 11, R.I.A.—*Vide* O'Curry's Glossary.

(509) *Ian*, a vessel which appears to have been generally used in the sense of a vat, though sometimes applied to a drinking vessel.

(510) *Bassib*, i.e., low drinking bowls or basins. The latter word is apparently derived from *Bas*, the palm of the hand, and *Ian*, a bowl or vat. The Irish word *Baisin* is still a living word for basin, bowl, skimming cup, or other vessel which is low and open-mouthed like the *bas* or palm of the hand.

drecht huad ingoirt dia treise iar focra; trian a ḋuinn ocus a mesca ocus a lesca, ocus a erca, do ḟlaiṫ. The Crith Gablach. H. 3. 18 p. 253. O'L.

Oc aire,—is ardu a airechasadi. Cid ara neper oc aire? Ar oitiu a airechais, ceḋh [giḋ] acht uaire is nue o ro gaḃ treaḃad. Caide a toṫacht? Folad seċta lais: .uii. mbae, cona tarḃ, .uii. muca co muic, forais, .uii. caire, capul itir ḟognum, ocus imrim. Tir tri .uii. cumal les, ise tir mbo la [fene] insin; foloing .uii. mbuu co cenn mbliadna, .i. adaigter .uii. mba inn, faccaib in seċtmad mboin dia bliadna a fochraiċ in tire. Cethraime arathair lais: Dam, soc, brot, cennose [cennforaiḋ], combi tualling coimse; cuit a náiṫ, immuilinn, isaḃall, scaball cócuis. Mét a ṫiġe, mou tiġ incis arit. .uii. traiġṫe .x. ameit side,

honour-price and of his fruits and his cattle sheds and his cows to the Flaith.

Oc-Aire,—his Aireship is higher. Why is he called Oc-Aire? Oc-Aire. From the youngness of his Aireship, howbeit, it is from a grandsire he has inherited property.[511] What is his stability (wealth)? He has properties sevenfold [viz.]: seven cows, and a bull, seven pigs, and a Muc Forais,[512] seven sheep, a horse for working, and [a horse] for riding. He has land sufficient to maintain three times seven Cumals[513] (twenty-one cows); then on the pasture land of the tribe, he supports seven cows for a whole year, i.e., he feeds seven cows upon it (the tribe land), he leaves the seventh cow at the end of the year to pay for the land (grass). He has the four essentials for ploughing [viz.] an ox, a sock, a yoke, a halter to enable him to control him [the ox]; he has a share in a kiln, in a mill, in a barn, and in a Scaball Cocuis.[514] The size of his house is greater than that of a Tigh Incis.[515] Seventeen feet is

(511) *Oc Aire.* It is very doubtful whether the interpretation given to *Oc* in the text be correct. We find in the laws a class of officials called *Sicc Oc*, in which *Oc* certainly does not mean young, but appears rather to be connected with Gothic: *ogjan* to terrify, O H. German *aki*, discipline. If this suggestion be correct, the *Oc Aire* was probably the crier of the court, who maintained order, and arraigned the prisoners, etc.

(512) *Muc Forais*, a household or house-fed pig. O'C.'s Gloss.

(513) *Cumal*, a mulct or fine generally of three cows, leviable for most offences. There appear to have been several kinds of *Cumals*, e.g.: "*Aire Ard* two *Cumals* (of *Cumal Cana*) is his *Enechland*". The *Cumal Cana* would appear to have been the *Cumal* of the National Law of the kingdom, and of a fixed quantity and value, while other *Cumals* were of arbitrary quantity and value according to the *Urrudhas*, or custumal, or customary laws (H. 3. 18.176. a.). The *Cumal* was the Welsh *Camlwrw*, which was also three cows, and was leviable for all offences except theft, violence, and fighting, for which *Dirwy* (Irish *Dire*) amounting to twelve kine, was leviable. Vide, note, 504, on *Dire*, App. p. 477.

(514) *Scaball Cocuis*, a cooking pot, H. 3. 18, 253 top. O'C.'s Gloss.; and Cormac *in voc. Caire.*

(515) A house of small dimensions, built for an old man who gives up his land to his friends or pupils on the condition that they shall maintain him. *Vide* Lect. xx., vol. ii. pp 30-31.

The Crith Gablach. H. 3. 18. p. 7a. O'L.

fiti co fordorus, diten itir cach dinti osuidiuga co cleite, dá dorus ann, comla ar alanai, cliath ar alaile, os he gin cliatha cen tulggu, udnocht coil imbi, clar ndara, inoir cach di caomdai. Is mo tech noc airech, noi traigi .x. amédruide. Tri troigi .x. a ircha. [No] ar a ro rand a aithir bes a tigi indi. Ocht mba a turcreic, ite .x. seoit insin. Ised diabal taurcreca in graid fil riam, ar is di thir giallaid in graidni: is di thir don a loga; .x. seoit dosom dia turcrec; bid dono athir sin for fola sris dó. Dartaid indi cona timtach bes a tige; tairr muca les as

Oc-Aire.

the size of it [the Tech Incis], woven to the lintel, a weather board between every two weavings from that up to the roof-ridge, two doorways upon it, a door to one of them, a hurdle to the other, and it without breaks or bulges, a roof of hazel upon it, and a board of oak between every two beds. The house of the Oc-Aire is larger, nineteen feet is its size (length). Thirteen feet is (the length of) his back-house. Or [he is a man] with whom his father has divided his Bes Tigi. Eight cows are his Taurcreic, that is ten Seds then. It is double the Taurcreic of the grade which is before (next under) him, because it is from land his rank is derived; it is from land his price is also derived; he is entitled to ten Seds[316] for his Taurcreic; his territory also contributes to his wealth. A Dartaid Inidi[316] with its supply of food is his Bes Tigi; he has a belly-

(316) *Sed*, a standard of value among the Gaedhil by which rents, fines, stipends, and prices were determined. Every kind of property was estimated by this standard, the unit being a milch cow, which was the prime *Sed*. From the king down to the *Dae* fines and stipends were paid in *Cumals*, equal to three cows; or in prime *Seds*; but from the *Dae* down they were paid in *Seds* of small cattle, and valuables of different kinds, in proportion to the rank, as laid down by the law. *Sed Bó Ceathra* was a *Sed* made up of small cattle; *Sed Bó Dile*, a *Sed* made up of any or different kinds of live stock; *Sed Marbh Dile*, a *Sed* of movable chattels, made up of inanimate objects; *Sed Bó-Slabra* was made up of every class of well bred cattle and thorough bred horses. *Coibche*, *Tochrai*, and *Tindscrai* constituted other kinds of *Seds*: *Coibchi* was a name for valuable cloths, personal ornaments, etc; *Tochrai* was a name for well bred sheep, and small pigs, etc.; *Tindscrai* was the name applied to gold, silver, and bronze articles of every country. The *Clithar Sed*, or king *Sed*, as the name indicates, was superior to all other *Seds*. It was the term applied to a prime cow when she was six years old, and when she had three calves: she was then at her highest value, and was worth twenty-four screpals. The last mentioned kind of *Sed* shows that while an average aged milch cow constituted the general unit of value of a *Sed*, the term *Sed* was also applied to cattle of different ages, and consequently of different values; thus *Sed Gabla* was the name for a yearling bull or yearling heifer, and was the smallest of all *Seds*. Yearling bulls and heifers of one year and up to two were also called by the name *Dairt*. Among the Continental Saxons the yearling ox was equivalent to the lesser "solidus", while an ox of sixteen months and upwards was equivalent to the greater "solidus". The heifer, if bulled at two years was called a *Dartaid*. A *Dairt* in the third year

…iccas la boin, no ṫine ordlaiġe inna chumbu coir, The Crith Gablach. H. 3. 18. p. 528. O'L.
s tri meich mbracha, ocus leiṫ meich tarai. Ar, amail
abul turchreaca in graid is isliu, turchreic in graid
rdu; is diabal somaine, dono, bés a tiġe. Snaidiġ a
grád, ar ni snaḋiġ naċ grád nech bes ardu. Biathad
n dó, di as ocus grus, no arbaim; ni dliġ imb; cuad
ordlaċ x. di draumcu ar lemlaċt ceċtar nai, ocus bair-
indruic, no di bairgin ban fuine. Adiis for foluċ; imb
iu a treissi, a coice, a nomad, a ndechmad, i ndomnaċ
seoit log a enech, aċt it seoit bo slabra. Dire naitire
Cid dia neirenaiter dósom in tseoit [.i. in boin] so?
Dia aoir, dia esain, dia diguin, dia tsaruġ, do loscaḋ

e of fat pork and a hog cured in bacon[517] with a cow, or a hog Oc-Aire.
flesh one inch high, in proper joints, and three bags of malt, half a bag of wheat. Because it is equal to double the rcreic of the grade which is lower that the Taurcreic of the er grade is; he is therefore entitled to double benefits for Bes Tigi. He traverses his compeers, but he traverses no e not as high as his own. He is entitled to the mainte-e of two of new milk, and groats, or corn-meal. He is not led to butter; a Cuad of twelve inches[518] of thick milk new milk every second day, a Bairgin Indriuc, or two gins of Banfuine.[519] Two upon Folach; butter at meals on l, on fifth, on ninth, on tenth, and on Sundays. His honour is three Seds, but they are Seds of Bó Slabra.[520] He is led to the Dire of an Aitire. For what is this Sed (i.e. the) awarded to him? Answer. For his satire, for his Esain, his Diguin, for his Sarugh, for the burning of his house,

rove-tide was called a *Dartaid-* A heifer in her third year until she was bulled was a *Sam-* before being bulled she was d at twelve screpalls, and after bulled at sixteen screpalls. A r of three years was a *Colpdach.* Gothic *Kalbo*, O.H G. *Kalba*, *pa*, and Ang. S. *Kalf* and *Cealf*, . *Calf.* A full-grown heifer about lve was called a *Laulghach*, and considered of equal value with the ghing ox. *Sed* is perhaps con-d with Gothic *Saths* or *Sads*, ient.—See MS. T.C.D. H. 3. 18. see also pp. 632, 651; H. 2. 17, 8, etc.

) *Tineiccas*, or smoke-cured ba-represents the Gallo-Roman word ACAE. "E queis [porcis] succi-Galli optimas et maximas facere ieverunt. Optimarum signum, quod etiamnunc quotannis e Gallia apportantur Romam pernae tomaci-nae et taniacae [*al.* tanacae], et peta-siones. De magnitudine Gallicarum succidiarum Cato scribit". Varro, *Re Rustica*, ii. c. 4.

(518) *Cuad*, a wooden bowl or cup. According to a marginal gloss in H. 3. 17. col. 658. a. T. C. D., a *Cuad* of twelve inches, was one which was six inches high, and six inches in dia-meter.

(519) The *Bairgin Indriuc* perfect, or household cake, appears to have been the same as the *Bairgin Ferfuine*, which was a cake or loaf sufficient for one man's meal, and to have been equal to two *Bairgins* of *Banfuine*, which was a loaf sufficient for one woman's meal.

(520) *Bó-slabra.* *Vide* note 516 on *Sed*, App., p. 480.

The Crith Gablach. H. 3. 18 p. 253. U.L.

a tigi, dia turorgain, do gait as a leċ [amuig], do gait inu; disforcuir amna, aingini,—aċt asbreċ la [fene]. Leċ dire gach grad ṫuaithe for amnai, ocus a ingin, ocus a maċ; aċt mad mac dormaine, no mac bes elodach ria ngairi, cethramha forruidiḋ log a eneċ, issed ima toing, ocus téd for a naidm, ocus a raith, ocus a aitire, ocus a fiadnaisi, os in da ṡet tesbanad aire [chus], huare nad noġ forrusa a ṫigi, ocus nad nimraith friu amail gaċ bo airi, ar loiged a folad.

Aithech ar aṫreba a deichride[332] a buaisride, .i. deich mbai lais, .x. muca, .x. cairig; cethraime arothair, .i. dam, ocus soc, ocus brod, ocus cennos rir; tech fichit traiged les, ċona irchai cetra traige ndeg; iii. seoit a dire dia air, dia esain, dia diguin, dia sarug. Imostoing, as naidm, is rath, is aitire, is fecham, is fiadnaisi friu; deich mba a turcreicc; forggu dine, ocus tine da mer, ina ċumbu coir,

Bo-Aire.

for his plunder, for a theft on the outside of it, for a theft from the interior of it; for the violation of his wife or of his daughter,—but it is a judgment which belongs to the tribe.[331] He is entitled to half the Dire of every grade of the people for his wife, and his daughter, and his son; but if he be the son of a meretricious woman, or a son who has strayed from his obedience to his guardians, his honour price then is one-fourth of them, and the same for his Toing, and they are also for his Naidm, and his Raith, and his Aitire, and for his witness, because it is in two Seds his Aire[ship] is manifested, and because the income of his house is not in its fulness, and that he is not capable of becoming a surety with them like every Bó-Aire, on account of the smallness of his wealth.

Aithech ar a Threba.

Aithech ar a Threba (i.e., a tribe tenant in his paternal home), his cattle are tenfold, viz., he has ten cows, and ten pigs, and ten sheep; and the four essentials for ploughing, viz., an ox, and a sock, and a yoke, and a halter; he has a house of twenty feet, with a back-house of fourteen feet. His fine for his satire, for his Esain, for his Diguin, for his Sarugh, is four Seds. He is a Toing, he is a Naidm, he is a Raith, he is an Aitire, he is a plaintiff, and a witness for them; ten cows are his Taurcreic; he has a Forggu Dine[333] and a salted hog with flesh two fingers [inches] high, is

(331) i.e., it is a case which is to be adjudged by the tribunals of, and according to the laws of the tribe.

(332) deich deichde, ten of tens, MS., p. 252.

(333) *Forggu dine*, the choicest or best cattle. *Forgab*, foods, i.e., a supply of food which is given to the *Flaith* by his tenants and vassals at certain festive seasons of the year; it was generally given between the Kalends and Shrovetide (H. 3. 17. p. 423). The following gloss on *Forcam*, which is synonymous with *Forgab*, will serve to give an idea of what this food consisted. "*Forcam* or *Forgab* (offal; mince meats?) It is supplied between two *Cairs* (festivals), i.e. food which is supplied between Shrove Sunday and [Ash-] Wednesday; or, that it was the feast of the festival between the Kalends and Shrove [-Tuesday]; or it is between two festivals it is supplied, i.e. between

ocus ceṫre (no ceṫir) meich braṫcha, ocus fidlan airmeide The Cilth Gablach.
di tara. Ise bés atiġe tincur, idir erna, ocus lestrai. H. 3. 18. p.
Ise aiteċ baitsiḋe inso dia mbe ina engai cin gait, cin braid, 253. O'L.
cin guin duine act lá a caṫa, no nech dosaid a cenn fair,
os hé cana lanamnas coir, ocús denmai in ainib ocus dom-
nachaib, ocus corgasaib. Cid nod mber in ferso a bo
airechas? Ar bes bid cethrar no coiciur beiṫ hi comar- H. 3. 18. pp. 1 and 253.
bus bo aireċ, conach assa bo aire do caċ ae. Biathad O'C.
deiri dó di ass ocus gruss no arbaimm, imb in ndom-
nachaib. Serccol tassain lasodain, dulesc, cainnenn,
salann. Dis dó for folach. Imim do ala tráṫ.

proper joints, and four bags of malt, and a Fidlan Armeide of wheat.[524] His Bes Tigi is furniture [of all kinds] both iron implements and vessels. Then he is an Aithech Baitsidhe [bachelor of Bó-Aireship],[525] if he be in his innocence without theft, without plunder, without wounding a man but on the day of battle, or a person who has given him defiant provocation, and that he has a lawful wife, and that he observes the Fridays, and the Sundays, and the Lents. Why has this man not obtained a Bó-aireship? Because it is the custom to have four or five in the Comarbship[526] of a Bó-Aire, so that it is not easy to call each of them a Bó-Aire. The feeding of two for him of new milk and groats or of corn-meal and butter on Sundays. He is entitled to seasoned fowl, Dulesc,[527] onions [or garlic], and salt. Two for him on Folach Othrusa.[528] Butter for him every second day. Aithech ar a Threba.

the Kalends and Shrove [-Tuesday], or between Easter and May; i.e. *Moroga* (or *Caelana*), (i.e. sausages) and *Cliathain* (neck, and breast pieces?), and *Dromana* (backs or chines). The *Furnaide* (lean meats), and the *Forcam* (offal), or the same [supply might be given in] round meats, i.e. joints (bacon, pork, or beef)".

(524) *Fidlan Airmeide*, a firkin or small cask, such as is still used for butter. It was formerly used as a dry measure. *Airmed* was applied to a measure of bulk, and *Airbid* to a measure of weight.

(525) *Aithech Baitsidhe* appears to have been a tenant entitled to the lowest degree of the Aireship, i.e., he was "tenant Bachelor of *Airechus*".

(526) *Comarbship* literally means "successorship"; here it means co-occupancy.

(527) Commonly called "Dillisk", the *Duilliosg* of the Highland, and the *Dulse* of the Lowland, Scotch. It is the *Rhodymenia Palmata* of botanists. As an example of the absurd etymologies current in books, wherein the authors, not being able to make a word Saxon, seek in every language, except the indigenous Celtic dialects for its origin, I may mention that of *Dulse* from the Latin dulcis!

(528) *Folach Othrusa*—the care and maintenance of a wounded person by him who wounded him (or by the next of kin in his territory whose rank was equal to that of the wounded man), in his own house and at his expense. If the person who inflicted the wound had no house, and was otherwise unable to support the wounded person, the *Aire Fine* was bound to provide for his maintenance, and he could then levy the amount on the branch of the tribe families to whom the offender belonged. Kings, bishops, chief poets, and others of the distinguished classes,

The Crith Gablach. H. 3. 18, pp. 1 and 258, O'C.

Bo Aire Febsa cid ara neipert? Ar is do buaib ata a airechass ocus a enecland. Tir da .uii. cumal leis. Tech .uii. traiged .xx. it, co nairchai coic traigid ndéac; cuit immuiliunn conair mil a muintir ocus a adáma; aith, saball, lias cairech, lias laég, mucfóil: it hé insin .uii. cleitiu ó ndirenar caċ boairi. Biid di bai .x leis; leṫ naraṫair; capul fognuma, ocus ech imrimme. Di bai .x. a ṫauracreice; colpdaiċ firend cona timchug bés a ṫiġi, in tsaimbiad ocus in gaimbiad. Coic seoit ina diriu doneoch iss sress do, dia enecland. Cid do bir na coic

H. 3. 18, p. 254.

seótu do enecland in bo airig? Nin. A grima.: Set a nadma; sét a raiṫi; set a fiadnairi; sét a aitiri; set a fosaiġṫi, ocus a briṫhemnais for mbruigreċt. Imtaing coic

Bó-Aire-Febsa.

Bó-Aire-Febsa, why so called? Because it is from cows his rank and honour price are derived. He holds the land of twice seven Cumals; a house of twenty-seven feet, with a back-house of fifteen feet; a share in a mill in which his family and his people may grind; a kiln, a barn, a sheep-pen, a calf-house, a pig-stye. These then are the seven prime possessions from which each Bó-Aire is qualified. He has twelve cows; half ploughing;[329] a working horse, and a riding steed. Twelve cows are his Taurcreic; a Colpdach Firend[330] with its accompaniments, is his Bes Tigi, in summer food and in winter food. Five Seds to him in his Dire for everything that is an insult to him, for his honour price. What is it that entitles the Bó-Aire to five Seds for his honour price? Answer: His deeds: A Sed for his Naidm; a Sed for his Raith; a Sed for his evidence; a Sed for his Aitire; a Sed for his arbitra-

and also women, did not go on *Foluch* to those who wounded them, but got its value and remained at their own homes.

The class of food and attendance to which each man was entitled was fixed by the law in proportion to his rank, in the same way as his *Corpdire* (*vide* note p. 477), his *Logeneck* (note 473, p. 471), and his *Enechland*. The family or tribe of the offender was obliged to entertain a certain number of the friends of the *Othrus* or wounded person, and provide the necessary attendance for the latter, e.g., physicians, nursetenders, nightwatchers; they were also bound to send a person to do the work of the *Othrus*, while under medical treatment, and, in a word, to defray all the expenses of his illness. If the patient died of injury, the family or tribe of the offender was accountable to that of the wounded man for the offender, and also for the price of the life of a man; and in case he recovered without a blemish, they had only to pay the fines; but if a blemish was occasioned by the wound, the price of it, which was fixed by law according to the nature of the blemish and the rank of the wounded person, should be paid in addition.

(329) half ploughing, i.e., half the necessary implements, etc., for ploughing.

(330) *Colpdach Firend*. The simple *Colpdach* was a three year old heifer. The *Colpdach Firend* literally means a male *Colpdach*, that is, a three year old bull. It may possibly also mean a prime three year old heifer. But the first interpretation is most likely to be the correct one.

seotu, tiagait for a naidm, ocus a raiṫ, ocus a aitiri, ocus a fiadnairi. A biathad triúr; triar do for folaċ. Imbim do i ndissi, i trissi, i cóicid, ind nomaid, i ndechmaid, i ndomnach. Fir cainnenn no saillti do tarsun. Ni terban di folcaib in bo airig terban dia diriu.

The Crith Gablach. H. 3. 18. pp. 1 and 254. O'C

Mbruigfer cid ara neiper? Di lin a mbruige. Tir tri .uii. cumal lasuide; isé bo aire reire breiṫe; bo aire gensa co cách in chruth a thiġe, inna átaib coraib: caire cona inbiurb cona lorggaib; dabaċ in roinnimdeltar bruṫ; caire fognuma folestrai, itir erna ocus loiste ocus choidiú coná héisedar;(532) ammbur indlait, ocus long foilcṫe;

tion and for his judgment in Brugh-Law. He is a Toing of five Seds, that is what he is entitled to for his Naidm, his Raith, his Aitire, and his evidence. He is entitled to the feeding of three together with himself; three for him upon Folach. Butter for him on second, third, fifth, ninth, tenth, and on Sundays. Strong onions for him, or salt meat with condiments. Anything that is deficient of the deserts of the Bó-Aire shall be wanting to his Dire.

Bó-Aire Febsa.

Mbruighfer,(531) why so called? From the extent of his lands. He hath the land of three times seven Cumals; he is the Bó-Aire for giving judgment; a Bó-Aire who instructs the people, by the arrangement of his household furniture in its proper places: a boiler with its spits and its skewers; a keeve in which broth is distributed; a serving pot with minor vessels, both irons and kneading troughs and wooden mugs with their ladles;(532) a washing

Mbruighfer.

(531) The *Brugh Fer* was one of the most important functionaries of the ancient Irish commonwealth. He was a *Bó-Aire* who enjoyed great immunities as regards exactions, mulcts, and amercements, and considerable appanages in order to afford hospitality and assistance to all public functionaries and persons entitled to maintenance at the public expense. The *Brugh*, in virtue of his office, appears to have enjoyed the privilege of having a *Dun* or wall and fosse about his house. It was at his residence the election of the chieftain or *Righ Tuatha* took place. The territory in which this residence was situated, consisting of twelve *Seisreachs* or plough-lands, constituted a *Brugh-Baile*, or as we might say, a "borough township". The *Brugh* corresponded to the *Breyr* or "moto-man" of South Wales, and appears to have acted as judge or magistrate, aided by other *Bó-Aires*, in all disputes between neighbours about pasturage, trespass of cattle, etc. The practice of this court was regulated by what was called *Brugh-recht* or *Brugh*-law, corresponding to the "Burlaw" or "Birlaw" of Scotland. The word may be safely connected with the Gothic *Baurgs*, a town, O. H. German *Purue*; M. H. German *Burc*; Anglo-Saxon, Old Saxon, etc., *Burg*; English *Burg*, *Burgh*, *Borough*; Greek, πύργος; Macedonian βύργος. As the chief function of the *Brugh* consisted in delivering judgment in disputes and arbitrations, it may perhaps be connected with the Sanskrit root *bru* = Zend *mru*, to speak, to say. See INTRODUCTION.

532 In H. 3. 18. p. 254, the word used is lieċrada, ladles, but it is almost obliterated. heisedar appears to represent the Welsh *Hestawr*, which is a modern form of *Lestar*. See *Lestar*, note 549, p. 495.

The Crith Gablach. H. 3. 18 pp 1 and 254 &c.

drochta; caindelbra; scena buana aine; lomna; tál; tarathar; tuiresc; dias fidhrann eirit; aicced fognama cacha raithe: Cach noeilm de cen iasacht; lia forcaid, fidba; biail; gai gona cethrai; teine bithbeó; caindel for caindelbrai cen mech; og narachair cona huile comopair.

Ite inso tra gnima bo airig reire breithe. Bit di iain inna ċig do gres, ian aiss ocus ian chorma. Fer tri sruba: sruib tuirc fochlaid scoltas ainechruicce cach aimsir; sruib tine for cruiċ; sruba arathair fo rinn [coltair], ar imtuolang gabala rig, no espuic, no suad, no brithemun do rout, fri tascra cecha dama. Fer tri miach inna tig do gres cech raiṫi: miach mbracha; miach muir luacha fri aithcumba naige dia ceithri; miach guaili fri erinna. Secht tige lais: aith, sabald, muilenn,—acuit isuidiu conid nairmil, tech .uii. traiged fichit, ircha .uii. traiged noec, mucfoil, lias loeg, liass cairech. Fichi bo, da tarbb, sé doim, fichi muc, fichi cairech; ceithri tuirce forais, di birit, each sliasta, srian cruain; sé méich dec i talmain.

Mbruighfer.

trough, and a bathing basin; tubs; candelabra;(333) knives for reaping rushes; a rope; an adze; an auger; a saw; a shears for clipping trees; implements for every quarter's work: Every item of these [shall he have] without borrowing; a grinding stone, a bill-hook, a hatchet, a spear for killing cattle, an ever-living fire, a candle upon a candelabrum without fail; a perfect plough, and all that appertains to it.

These, then, are the characteristics of the Bó-Aire who dispenses judgment. He has two vats in his house constantly, a vat of new milk and a vat of ale. He is a man who has three snouts: the snout of a rooting hog at all times, to shiver (or break) the blushes of his face; a snout of bacon upon the hooks; and the snout of a coulter under the earth, for the purpose of sustaining the visits of a king, or bishop, or a poet, or a judge from off the road, and for the entertainment of all companies. He is a man who has three sacks in his house each quarter perpetually: a sack of malt; a sack of bulrushes for dressing the wounds of his cattle; a sack of coals for [forging] the irons. He has seven houses: a kiln, a barn, a mill,—a share in it and in all that it grinds, a house of twenty-seven feet; a back-house of seventeen feet, a pig-stye, a calf-house, a sheep-house. Twenty cows, two bulls, six bullocks, twenty hogs, twenty sheep; four house-fed hogs, two sows, a riding steed, a bridle of Cruan.(334) Six-

(333) *Candelora*, i.e. a straight wand upon which the luminous fire is, and it must be in every man's house (or in the house of every Aire).

Caindelbra, .i. deil direach fo a mbi in breo taitnemach acus e codaire (.i. itec cac duinne). Mac Firb. Glos.

(334) *Cruan*, from many passages would appear to have been enamel, either set in like gems or covering the whole metal as a greenish glass. In other places it may mean some alloy—but I think the first meaning is the true one.

Taċai cairi humai i tallai toricc. Techtuig faithċi imbiṫ ḃiat cairig cen immirgi. Cethardḋa nuillata leis acas a ben. A ben ingen a chomgraid in na choir cetmuinteraiṡ. Os he maith alluga, a naidm, a raiṫ, a fiadnaise, a aitire, a ón, a airlicud; gen gait, cen brait, cen guin duine. Di chumal a thurcréicc. Bó cona timthuch, bés a thige itir gaim mbiaḋ ocus saim biaḋ. Triar a dam i tuaiṫ. Triur do for folach: Imb do cotarsund do grés. Snaḋid a chomgrad. Sall dó i triss, i coicti, i nomaid, i ndechmaid, i ndomnach. Imtoing se seotu; is naidm; is raiṫ; is aitiri; is feichem;[335] is fiadnaise friu;—isi a og eneclann. Aċt it .u. seotu i ndul tar a les dichmairec; diles a osolgud dimaich. Coic seoit in osolggud a thiġe dichmairc; bo i ndecsin ind; dartaid indlai de; dairt ina dó; colpdach i nairbir; samairch illeithbert; bo i mbert, ocus aiṫgin a tuiġe. Coic seoit i ndul tria tech, tria lias di brisiud a comlai; dartaid i fleisc ċis; dairt i fleisc ṫuas; samaisc i cleiṫ ċis; colpdach i cleit tuas. Dairt i

The Crith Gablach. H. 3. 18. pp. 2 and 254 O.C.

teen sacks [of seed] in the ground. He has a brass pot in which a hog fits. He has a suitable lawn in which sheep stay at all times without being driven off. He has four friends with him and his wife. His wife, the daughter of his own co-grade, in her proper bridal virginity. His oath is good, his Naidm, his Raith, his evidence, his Aitire, his loan, his lending on security and interest; [he must be] without theft, without robbery, without wounding [or killing] any person. Two Cumals are his Taurcreic. A cow with her accompaniments is his Bes Tigi both of winter and summer food. Three are his company in the territory. Three for him on Folach; he is entitled to butter with salt-meat at all times. He traverses his co-dignitaries. He is entitled to bacon on third, on fifth, on ninth, on tenth, on Sundays. He is a Toing of six Seds; he is a Naidm; he is a Raith; he is an Aitire; he is a suitor; he is a witness for them;—that is his full honour price. But he has five Seds for going within his yard unlawfully; it is lawful to open it for his good. Five Seds for unlawfully opening his house; a cow for looking into it; a Dartaid[336] for a lock [of thatch] from it; a Dairt[336] for taking two; a Colpdach[336] for an armful; a Samaisc[336] for half a truss; a cow for a truss, and restitution of the straw. Five Seds for going through his house or his cattle yard by breaking its door; a Dartaid for its [the door's] lower lath; a Dairt for the upper lath; a Samaisc for a lower wattle; a Colpdach for an upper wattle. A Dairt for the

Mbruighfer.

(335) *Feichem*, i.e., a party in a suit; he might be either the plaintiff or defendant.

(336) See note 516 on *Sed*, App. p. 480.

The Crith Gablach. H. 3. 18, pp. 1 and 254 O'C. naursain air-thir tige; dartaid i naursain iarthar tige.

Lech log enech caċ graid tuaithi i ngait nadlai ar a airlisi; un mad i ngait inte. Airchur sneid caċ lech is é corus a airlisi. Leċ dire forais forindra. Diles ocus indiles dobruud for lar tiġe. Diles caċ rochoém, indiles cach ndichaém. Diles ór ocus argat ocus umai. Indiles cach nombur caċ sreċ ascorus for lár.

H. 3. 18, pp. 2 and 251. Dairt i crand nairide ṫiar; dartaid i crann nairidi do thein, ocus dairt la haithgin cach nae, cid coém cid dichoém. Dairt caċ araire co sraiġ. Diles nindles nairidi dobruud. Diles ni bes islu ordd; indless ni bes ardd

Mbruighfer. front door-post of his house; a Dartaid for the back door-post of his house.

Half the honour price of every grade of society for stealing anything out of his yard; a seventh for stealing into it. The direct cast [of the Cnairseach[537]] in all directions [from the door of his house] is the proper extent of his yard. Half the Dire of the house for the enclosed ridge.[538] He may, or may not, have a water well in the floor of his house. All precious things are lawful, all things not precious are unlawful. Gold and silver and bronze are lawful. All troughs, and seats which are disarranged on the floor are unlawful.

A Dairt for the western lintel of the dairy; a Dartaid for cutting or breaking down the dairy-lintel, and a Dairt together with restitution of everything, be it small or non-small. A Dairt for every sheet of matting to the roof. He may or may not have a water well in his dairy. Lawful what is lower in order; unlawful what

(537) *Cnairseach*, a kind of crooked staff shod with iron, somewhat like a short "Alpenstock". The distance which the *Cnairseach* could be thrown by a *Bó Aireh* was the measure of his *Maigin Digona*, or "field of sanctuary", already described in note 484 on *Diguin*, p. 473. So that the *Airlis* of a *Bó-Aire* probably marked the extent of his field of sanctuary.

(538) *Indra*, a ridge. In the sense in which it is used in the text it means the enclosed garden which surrounded the house, and in which onions and other vegetables, and fruit, etc., were grown. This *Indra* or ridge was equal to nine ridges or beds in breadth (H. 3. 18. p. 571; and O'C.'s Gloss.), and it was surrounded by a special kind of fence, the crossing of which was called *dal tar Indra*, "i.e. going beyond the [fence of the] nine ridge garden", for which, and for any trespass done in the garden, there were certain stated penalties, such as that mentioned in the text. In the account of *Bricriu's* Feast, in Lect. xix. vol. ii. p. 19, the nine ridges mentioned therein evidently mean such an enclosed garden. In North Wales, the ancient mile, or more properly league, consisted of 1,000 "lands", *tyr*, which, according to the Ancient Laws of Wales, were called in modern Welsh (that is, the Welsh of the thirteenth or fourteenth century, which was modern to the compiler of the Venedotian Code), *Grwn*, a ridge equal to nine yards in length. The *Indra* or garden being nine ordinary *Indras* or ridges wide, and each such ridge being one yard wide, it corresponded to the Welsh *Grwn*.

orod. Foranu chuile a chumat direch nairidi. Noes nua dia esair

The Crith Gablach. H. 3. 18. pp. 2 and 254. O'C.

Direch nimda: diamolai do chind adairt, direnar dag chercaill; diamolai doneoch bis fo suidiu, direnar daggamun; diamoloi di ċossaib, direnár dag assaib; diamolui do fraig. ain nua dia essair; diam tochur tar cend, sét inn, ocus aithgin.

Diles ocus indless inimmid: Diles suide ocus freisligi inni, ocus cia brontar inni co comardda cinn issuidiu; innless inni bes ardou cinn; di loairgg direnaiter seot mad raitri chu a leṫ iarmoitá.

Mlech dicmairce immuiliunn mruġfir, coiċ seot, ocus dilse mine melar dicmairc, ocus log aenech dia toichne a da mám. Dia ma brondad, aineclann caich ara ai, ocus aithgin la tairgell mleche. Mada aith ro bronntar dichmairce, bo co ndairtt a dire, ocus aitgin. Diles ni ro bronntair inni, act adraimm tuarggar for lar, ocus assecha sét fadessnei. Dire a sabaill, coic seot, ocus aithgin conneoċ ro bronntair ann. Dire a mucḟolach, coic seoic mucaib, ocus aithgin. Dire a béla colpdaiċ; a leṫ dia fidba: Ría ré imbi, is colpdaċ i suidiú.

is higher in order. Breaking into his storehouse is the same fine as the dairy. He must get new rushes for its matting.

Mbrugh-fer.

The fine of a couch: If it be from the pillow that a lock is torn, a good pillow is paid for it; if the part for sitting on is stripped of a lock, a good cushion is paid; if the feet are stripped, good shoes [i.e. a covering] are paid; if it be a lock from the back roof, new rushes are paid for its matting; if it be an upsetting, a Sed for it, and restitution.

Of what is lawful and unlawful for a bed: It is lawful to sit and recline on it; even though it should be damaged to the height of the head; anything higher than the head is unlawful; for its tester a Sed is awarded, and it may progress to one-half after that [in proportion to the damage].

Grinding without leave in the mill of a Brugh Fer, five Seds, and the forfeiture of the meal that is unlawfully ground, and his honour price should he be deprived of two handsfull. Should it be damaged, it is the honour price of the party whose it is that is paid for it, and restitution, with a fine for the grinding. If it be a kiln that is unlawfully damaged, a cow with a heifer is its fine, and restitution also. Any damage done to it is lawful, except what is torn down of it, and its own proper coverings. The Dire of his barn is five Seds, and restitution for every damage done to it. The Dire of his pig-stye, is five Seds of pigs, and restitution. The Dire of his hatchet, is a Colpdach; half of that for his Fidba[(539)]. In the fencing season, a Colpdach is the fine for it.

(539) *Fidba*, some kind of bill-hook. Its exact character may be

The Crith Gablach. H. 3, 18 pp. 2 and 254. O'C. Fer fothlai cid ara neiper? Iré remibi bo Airechaib insin, ar in ni fótlen a bo aireċus do ṫaurcreicc ceili forcraid a cethrai, a bo, a mucc, a cáireg, nad fo chomlaing a thir fadeisin, ocus nad éta reicc ar thir, ni ric a less fadeisin, tabeir i thaurcreicc céile. Caiti somaine sét in H. 3, 18. pp. 2 and 255. nfir sin? Somaine grain diib. Lóg gérta cacha bó do grán arba biid. Ar ni dlig aithech mbraiċ corp flaith. Cesc cuin is flaiṫ an taithech din bo airechus, in dlis fruiċ faithce? In tan mbis diabol nairech desai lais, is ann is airi dissa.

Dia neper bo aire remibi bo airechaibh, beirid dib derrcugud dia taurcrua céileu. Nach aire dessa coniḋ roib de sir de, .i. diabol nairich deusa. Ocht seot illog a enech. Ni ar mrugfer, riam in tan din diablas feib mbo airech is and is airi desa; ar ni cumscaigi ainm ngraid dosum, cia do rormai a meclann, cosin anall. Imtoing ocht seotu; is naidm, is raiṫ, is aithiri, is fechem, is

Fer-Fothlai. A Fer-Fothlai, why so called? He takes precedence of the Bó-Aires, because his Bó-aireship extends to the payment of Ceiles by the excess of his cattle, i.e., his cows, his hogs, his sheep, which his own land cannot sustain, and which he cannot sell for land, and which he does not himself want, he gives as wages to his Ceiles. What are the profits of that man's cows? An equivalent of grain he gets from them. The value of the milk of each cow in corn grain he gets. For an Aithech is not entitled to malt until he is a Flaith. When does the Aithech become a Flaith out of the Bó-Aireship, entitled to go into a lawn?[340] When he has double as much as the Aire-Desa, it is then he is an Aire-Desa.

When a Bó-Aire is said to be a leader of Bó-Aires, he bears superiority from them by the payment of his Ceiles. He is not an Aire Desa until he has two with two, i.e., double what the Bó-Aire has. Eight Seds is his honour price. It is not among Brughfers he is counted, when he doubles the property of a Bó-Aire, it is then he is an Aire-Desa; for the title of the superior grade is not conferred upon him up to that, though his honour price is increased. He is a Toing of eight Seds; he is a Naidm, a Raith, an Aitire,

easily realized from the following description:—"A proper *Fidba* which gnaws not the timber, with its proper dimensions: its socket a fist; its crook three fingers; its edge a span; its snout or bill three fingers; its breadth at the back—its haft one inch, half an inch at the middle, and a third of an inch at the snout or bill".

[340] That is, entitled to go into, or live within a *Dun*, which has an enclosed lawn or pleasure-ground around it. No one below the rank of a *Flaith* was entitled to a residence of this class.

fiadnaise friu. Cetheora cumalai a thuracreic. Bo cona timthaċ cechla bliadnan bés a tigi: Colpdach firenn lee in mbliadain naili .uii. traigid ficit a thech; a .uii. ndec a airchai. Cethrar lin a dama: im co tarsun dó do gres. Cethrar dó for folach. Fursunduċ cethrair. Sall do hi treiss, i .u. ti, i nomad, i ndechmaith, i ndomnach. Is din grad so arcain Fenechus:

"Dligit firflaiṫe forcraid
for reir rimde.
Ro saigh ann-flaith leċ aithgin—
moine mogess inana deiċ seoit soerait
segait .u. seoit cundarṫa
combi oġ ninnrait naithgina,
ar itbaill leċ o ḟaill nessmacht.

Aire Coissring cid ara neper? Ar in ni consrenga tuath, ocus ri, ocus senod tar cenn a cheniuil. Na dlig a slan doib for cursu bel, acht atndaimet do thuisech, ocus airlabrai remid. Is hé aire fine innsin; tobeir gell tar ceann a ḟine do rig ocus senod, ocus aes cerdd, dia timorggain do reir. Cia meit in gill do ber? Gell coic seoit dineoċ rod mbi,—di arggat, no uma, no ibur. Cate slan a

The Crith Gablach. H. 3. 18. pp. 2, 255 and 418. O'C.

a suitor, and a witness for them. Four Cumals is his Taurcreic. His Bes Tigi is a cow with her accompaniments every second year, a Colpdach Firend[541] with her the other year. Twenty-seven feet his house; seventeen feet his back house. Four is the number of his retinue: they get butter with condiments at all times. Four for him on Folach. He is entitled to entertainment for four. Meat for him on third, on fifth, on ninth, on tenth, on Sundays. It is of this grade the Fenechas says:

Fer-Fothlai.

"The true Flaith is entitled to excess
In accordance with his counting.
The An-Flaith receives but half restitution—
If the price of the damage exceeds not ten Seds,
It is five lawful Seds he receives,
Which amounts to a perfect, faithful restitution",

The An-Flaith

—for one-half is forfeited in lieu of the despotic rule, or lordship.

An Aire-Coisring, why so called? Because he binds the people, the king, and the synod for his tribe. They are not bound to give him a fee for binding engagements; but they concede to him leadership, and to speak before (or for) them. He is the Aire-Fine (family-chief); he gives a pledge for his people to king and synod, and professional men, to restrain them in obedience [to the law]. How great is the pledge he gives? A pledge of five Seds of whatever kind it may be—of silver, of bronze, or of yew. What is the Slan

Aire-Coisring.

(541) See note 503, App. p. 484.

The Ceith Gabiach. H. 3. 18. pp. 2, 255, and 419. gill? Bo cacha aidchi ro fia tara cenn, tara tindnagar cenn co dechmaid; fuillem in gill ocus indeirce a gnimiu, ocus log a enech iar na miad iarsuidiu, mada gell coir do rata. Os mad do ratda forcraid ngill, is log a enech, ocus a gell slan cona fuillem do airicc amail sodain. Cesc cuin do tuitt a gell? Dia miss. Caitte a slan amail sodain? Bo cecha aidchi ro fia ro follaigter tar cenn neich cengell censuigell, de amel as indrubart mar. Coic seot dan co deċmaid Co fo thri an tucht sin: Ise slan a gill inso;* isse dan fuillem a set diandarera i cumtach. Noi seoit a enechlann.

Is naidm, is raith, is fiadnaise, is sechem, is aitiri friu. Coic cumala a ṫaurcreicc. Bo cona thimtag, ocus colpdaċ firend cona forrair i ngaimriud, co sambiud, bes a thige. H. 3. 18 pp. 2. 255, and 419. Tech trichat traiged, co nirċai noi troiged ndeacc. Coicciur a damam. Imb do, sercol tarrain. Sall do i triss, i coiccid, i nomaid, i ndecmaid, in ndomnach. Is óg log a inech cech graid dirunn, nin, mani aurcriat a folaid, .i. ar ná torchaires is naib sechtaib hi tuitet enech caich. Cateatside? Nin: A aer i torgábail cen gell dia inċaib;

Aire-Coisring of his pledge? A cow every night that passes, is what is given in security of them, as far as the tenth; the interest of the pledge and the fine of his deed, and his honour price in full besides, if it is a lawful pledge that has been given. But if an excess of pledge has been given, it is the price of his honour, and the full price of his pledge with its interest that is to be restored to him in that case. Question. When does his pledge fall [i.e. become forfeit]? After a month. What is the Slan in that case? A cow every night is given in full fine for every one for whom there is not pledge or security, as we have said. Five Seds as far as ten nights. Having thrice paid in this manner: This then is the Slan of his pledge; This then is the interest of his Seds if they have been richly ornamented. His honour price is nine Seds.

He is a Naidm, he is a Raith; he is a witness, he is a suitor, he is an Aitire for them. His Taurcreic is five Cumals. A cow with her accompaniments, and a Colpdach Firend with sufficient food in winter, till the time of summer food [i.e. pasturage], are his Bes Tigi. A house of thirty feet, with a back house of nineteen feet. Five are his company. Butter for him, and salt fowls. Bacon for him on third, on fifth, on ninth, on tenth, on Sundays. The honour price of every grade of these is perfect, unless their deeds diminish it, i.e., if they have not fallen into any of the seven things by which the honour of each is forfeit. What are they? Answer: To have been satirized for misdeeds

* Ise dno fuillim inso, "This is also its interest", H. 3. 18. p. 419.

gu fiadnaisi; gú test; ailsed naoma; elud rathaigis; The Crith Gablach. H. 3. 18. pp 3, 255, and 419. O'C.
dul tria aitiri im ni di chuat fuiri; cacc for a enech.
Cest cid di niġ di inċaib neich inna .uii. sa? Nin. Nach
sal as lenna ainech duine biit a tri oca diúnach, .i. sléic,
ocus usce, ocus anairt. Ised is sléic, cétamus fóisitiu in
midénmai fia doinib, acas in gell nád suisi friu aitherach,
in tusci imorro, icc nech atball tria mignimiu; anairt,
penait in midenmai ser lebor. Ité foðlai bo airech inso,
tesét cach ngrad ber sruthiu alaill.

Is iarsunn do innscanaitt gradða inna flaiṫe.

Fosus flatha, .i. flaith o déis co ríg. Cislir fuilleċta
for suidib? A secht. Cateat? Airi désa, airi eċtai,
aire ard, airi túsi, airi forggaill, tánairi ríg, ocus
ríg. Cid notai saesad? Andéis, a ndligid caċ ae, cid becc,
cid moor. Cais. Caitti deis flathai? Dég dligid [for-
taich, MS. p. 419] comditin dana. Dichussin cetheorai
déiri do flaitib: Sen chomditiu thuaiṫe; a dán i tuaiṫ,
im dán túisig, no tánairi thuisig i tuaiṫ, sechip dán

without having regard to his honour; false witness; false testimony; an intentional fraudulent knotting; to abscond from his guarantee; to break through his pledge in anything for which he became security; to befoul his face [or his honour]. Question. What is it that washes from a person's face [i.e. his honour] these seven blemishes? Answer. Every foulness that attaches to a person's face [i.e. honour], there are three things to wash it—viz., Sleic [soap], and water, and linen cloth. What Sleic is: firstly, a confession of the misdeeds in the presence of people, and a promise not to return to them again; the water now is the saving restitution given to the person who has suffered through the misdeeds; the cloth—the penance of the misdeeds according to books, These are the divisions [or distinctions] of the Bó-Aires, every higher grade takes precedence of the other. And after these the grades of the Flaiths [estated men] commence. *Aire-Coisring.*

The true knowledge of a Flaith—viz., a Flaith from a Deis to a king. How many grades of distinction are these divided into? Seven. Which are they? Aire-Désa, Aire-Echtai, Aire-Ard, Aire-Tuisi, Aire-Forgaill, Tanaisi Ri, and a Ri. What is [it] that ennobles them? Their Deis,[542] the rights of each, whether small or great. Question. What is the Deis of a Flaith? They are justly owed the protection of their rank. Four rights belong to a Flaith: The prescriptive protection of the Tuath; his rank in the Tuath, with his rank of leader, or Tanist leader in the Tuath, each rank of them; his bond Ceiles,[543] his free Ceiles, his Sen- *Grades of the Flaiths.*

(542) *Deis*, i.e. fee-simple land.—Mac Firbis and O'Curry's Glossaries.

(543) *Ceile*, a tenant, a dependent, a follower. There were two kinds of *Ceiles*, the *Saer Ceile* or free tenant, and the *Daer Ceile* or base *Ceile*. See

The Crith Gabhlach. H. 3. 18. pp. 8, 250, and 419. O'C.

dib; a ċeili gialnai, a soér cheili, a seincleṫhe; imsaebair cach giallnai, eislinniu glenomon; boċair ocus fuidirs fo a tir taberr, ar it moo a muine,—maithin ma beith fognum dib do flaithib co nómad naó; it bothaig it fuidri it senclete iarmoṫa.

Aire desa, cid ara neper? Ar indi is dia déis direnar. Nimṫa bo aire, is dia buaib direnar side. Caiti tochaṫt aireg désa? Deich céli leis—coic céli giallna, ocus coic saer céli. A coic celi giallna, dligid biathaḋ naircenn do cach ae: Bó cona timṫuċ, ocus colpdach firenn, ocus tri

cleithe;[344] the cutting of every bond, the punishment of culprits; Bothachs[345] and Fuidirs[346] he brings upon his land, in order that his wealth may be the greater,—they are set at large [i.e. naturalized][347] if there be service from them to the Flaiths, to the ninth generation; they are Bothachs, they are Fuidirs, they are Sencleithe notwithstanding.

Aire-Desa. Aire-Desa, why so called? Because of the fact that it is according to his property in land his Dire is regulated. Not so the Bo-Aire, it is according to his cows his Dire is regulated. What is the property of an Aire-Desa? He has ten Ceiles—five bond Ceiles, and five Saer Ceiles. His five bond Ceiles,—he is entitled to a fixed rent in provisions from each of them: A cow with her accompaniments, and a Colpdach Firend, and three Dartaids, every win-

INTRODUCTION for further information on the relations of the higher classes and the *Ceiles*.

(344) *Sen Cleithe*, hereditary followers, that is, families of followers who have adhered to the family of a *Flaith* for three successive generations. The *Flaith* and his descendants were bound to give aid and protection to his *Sen Cleiths* and their descendants. *Cleith*, *Cleithe*, i.e. the best or the head, or the head of the tribe, or the highest chief of the tribe. To the *Cleith* belongs the responsibility of the crime, i.e. to the chief of the tribe crime is carried when the criminal absconds—that is, he becomes responsible for the legal fines, etc. H. 2. 15, p. 121; see also *Cach Cleithe*, H. 3. 18. 15. Hence *Sen-Cleithe*, a follower of a chief. See INTRODUCTION.

(345) *Bothach*, a cottier tenant, of which there were two classes, corresponding to the two classes of *Ceiles*, the *Saer Bothach* or free cottier, and the *Daer Bothach* or base cottier. They were in a limited sense tenants-at-will on the land of a *Flaith*. See INTRODUCTION.

(346) *Fuidir*, a foreigner, that is one not recognized as a member of the tribe, but who has got the privilege of domicile. There were seven classes of *Fuidirs* under various denominations in a *Tuath;* but there were two principal classes of *Fuidirs*, the *Saer Fuidir*, who might at any time relinquish his land or domicile, and who appears to have generally, if not always, belonged to the privileged classes in his own native territory; and the *Daer Fuidir* or *Fuidir Fagnam* or serving or slave tenant, who either belonged to the base class in his own territory or had lost his privileges. The *Fuidirs* were in part the true tenants-at-will. See INTRODUCTION.

(347) *Maithin*. This appears to be the sense in which the word is to be understood here; because when a *Fuidir* family had served a *Flaith* family during nine generations, they became legally entitled to remain on the estate, but only as *Fuidirs*. From having no security of tenure they got perpetuity of tenure, and hence were, so far, improved

dartaidi cach gaimrid, cona saimmbiud dó ó .u. celi gialnai. Deich lanamna a ċosus for cui o calaind co hinitt. Os hé mac aireċ, ocus aue airech, thothocht a thigi, itir fossair, ocus fuirired, ocas enncai. Tech .uii. traiged .xx. it, co nairċai cóir; ocht nimmdai cona ṫinchur ann. Escrai cairi, cona lán lestrai[549] thigi aireċ, im dabaig. Imdich

The Crith Gablach. H. 3. 18. pp. 3 and 256 O'C.

H. 3. 18. pp. 3 and 256.

Aire-Desa.

ter, with their summer food, is paid him from each of his five bond Ceiles. His right on visitation[548] {Coshering] is ten couples from the Kalends to Shrovetide. As he is the son of an Aire, and the grandson of an Aire, he has the wealth of his house, both of accompaniments, provisions and hospitalities [broth or pottage]. A house of twenty-seven feet, with a back house to suit; eight beds with their furniture in it. Water vessels, pots, with the full supply of vessels[549] of an Aire's house, with keeves. He guards

(548) *For Cai*, i.e. upon coshering from the Kalends to Shrovetide, as the king and the *Ollamh* are wont to be, on one night's entertainment while making their visitation among their *Ceiles* (tenants). Mac Firbis' Gloss. The Irish *Cai*, or Coshering, corresponded to the Welsh *Kylch*, or progress. Somewhat analogous to the *Cai* was the *Fecht Fele*, one night's entertainment. "*For Fecht Fele*, i.e. the first night's entertainment we receive at each other's house. It is full refections we are entitled to on that night; but there is a difference between the treatment and the food which are given to the companies, and to the privileged grades, and to the nobles, and to their respective attendants, who accompany them. Howbeit any company that remains longer than that (i.e. the one night) they are only entitled to half refections, and they are not even entitled to that, unless it [the delay of departure] be occasioned by drink".

(549) *Lestar*, a small vessel, a milk pail, a drinking vessel, or basin. The *Lestar* varied in size and shape according to the use for which it was intended; and it might be made of any material whatever. As a milk pail or can, we find it mentioned in the Book of Leinster (H. 2. 18), and in the copy of *Copur na da mucada*, in the Mason collection of MSS., where *Medb Cruachna* is made to carry a *Findlestar Umaide*, that is a bright bronze vessel, in her hand going for milk, and where she is made to dip it into a certain stream, and to take its full of water, etc. As a drinking vessel it is frequently met with, sometimes made of gold, of silver, of bronze, or of wood. In the life of St. Brigid in the *Leabhar Breac*, and in the Book of Lismore, we find that the king of Taffia had a *Lestar Cumdactai*, that is, a richly ornamented drinking vessel, at a certain banquet in Taffia, that it was accidentally broken, and wonderfully renewed by the grace of St. Brigid. Again, the following gloss gives *Lestar* as a name for all kinds of drinking vessels, particularly of wood, as the name indicates. "*Fidlestar*, i.e. every kind of vessel (*Lestar*) which is used for drinking out of, both *Ardans* (piggins) and *Cuads* (mugs)—H. 2. 15. p. 34. There was another class of *Lestrai* called the *Lestar Lulaice*, or the *Lestar* of the new calved cow, which appears to have been so called from its having been made to contain the milk of one new calved cow. According to a gloss in the vellum MS. H. 3. 17. 645, under the word *Lestar Lulaice*: It contained twelve *Dirnas*, it was three hands broad at the mouth, one hand and a half at the bottom, and one-half hand deep; and the *Escra* was equal to one-third the size of the *Lestar Lulaice*". This description of the *Lestar Lulaice* very nearly corresponds with the milk pan (or biestings basin) of the present day. The Irish *Lestar* corresponded to the *Lester* or *Hestawr* of the Welsh Laws. A Welsh

The Crith Gablach. H. 3. 18. pp. 3 and 256. O'C.

dligiud a cheiliu cintaib coir cáin. Cairddi conneoch a tallen; lepaid daltu, comaltu, fiur, mnái, macc ingin. Ata suidiu for fobur [i. e. fobér] iar corus fine, ocus tuaithi, ocus flatha, ocus eclasa, ocus rechtgai, ocus chairddi. Sé cumala a taurcreicc o flaith. Di bai cona thimtachtai bés a thigi i ngaim, cona samthiud. Ech sliasta comadas, co srian airggait. Cethar ech lais co nglas srianaib; ocus clot delgg nungga. Cetmuinter dligtech comchenuil comadas fon óen timthach. .x. seoit a enechlann. Is mus toing, is naidm, is rath, is aitire, is feichem, is fiadnaise friú. Seisser a dam i tuaith. Imb dó do gres cotarsund

Aire Desa. the rights of his Ceiles, according to the statutes of appropriate law. Friendship to every one who comes; beds for foster children, foster brothers [or school-fellows], men, women, boys, girls. He is correct in the proprieties of his family according to the laws of the tribe, of his chief, and of the church, and of the national law, and of truces or local compacts. Six Cumals is his Taurcreic from his Flaith. Two cows with their accompaniments his Bes Tigi in winter, with their summer food. A riding steed becoming his rank, with a silver bridle. He has four steeds [besides] with green bridles; and a precious stone-brooch, worth an Unga.(550) A lawful wife of his own rank and equal, under the same attire.(551) Ten Seds for his honour price. He is a Toing, he is a Naidm, he is a Raith, he is an Aitire, he is a plaintiff, and a witness for them. Six his company in the territory; butter for him at all times, and seasoned salt meats. He is then a Flaith

"Hestor" is at present a measure containing two bushels.

The term *Dirna* mentioned above appears to have been used as the name of a measure of weight as well as of volume (see Lect. xxxi. vol. II. p. 245). As a measure of volume it appears to have varied in size. Probably the one referred to above was the *Dirna Umaide*, or bronze *Dirna*, a measure which was equal to a man's full drink, and the price of which was two and a-half pence (12th or 13th century?) MS. H. 3. 18. loose sheet at p. 445.

(550) *Unga*, i.e. a technical term for the sum of a legal penalty or reward, as *Unga Cana Domnaig*, thus: "Colpdach din no a llog is unga cana domnaig insin"—"A heifer now, or the price of her, is the amount of the *Unga* of the *Cain Domnaig* (Sunday Law)", *Leabhar Breac*, fol. 102, a. b. bot.

The amount or value of the *Unga* was not always the same; for example, it is made to be much less in another gloss in the same MS., fol. 73, a. a., and in O'Curry's copy of the Register of Clonmacnois, p. 5, we find the *Unga* as follows:—"The *Unga Mor* (or big *Unga*) was ten shillings, and the *Unga Beg* (or small *Unga*) was twenty pence".—*Vide* O'Curry's Glossary.

(551) That is, she should dress as the class in society to which he belonged did, or in other words she should be of equal rank with himself. From this it would appear that at the period when these laws were in force, the different classes were distinguished by different kinds of dress; and custom, if not law, operated against the intermarriage of the higher with the lower classes of the community.

saillti. Iss flaiċ mucleithe insin. Seissir dó for folach; forrugaḋ seissir; imb ocus sall dó i ndissi, i trissi, i coicid, i nomaid, i ndechmaid, i ndomnach. Cid do ber na .x. seotu do diriu innfir sin? Cóic seoit a ṫige fadeissin cétamus; ocus a cóic as in coictiġe. Adid ngiallna cen ni ascria no astha airechus, di ḟoltaib—beccaib ocus moraib, ar ná diá recht raltar. The Crith Gablach, H. 3. 18. pp. 3 and 256. O. C.

Aire eċtai, cid ara neper? Ar indi as naire [na aire] cóicir facabar frí dénum néchta i cairddiu, co cenn mis, di digail enechruccai tuaiṫi dia ndéntar dedenguin duine. Mani dernat co cenn mis do tiagat for cairddi. Nallenat a lepthai, chucai anall, cia rongonat doine din chairddiu—in ċoiciur chetnai—as comren airi eċta tara cenn. Na téit tír na humaċ airi ind, acht lestra loġa bo beirṫius dna dia nairitiuch sechtair co cenn cairdi, ar lín a chomairge, ocus a charat. A dam ocus a folach amail airig ndésai dligthir.

Aire ardd, cid ara neper? Ar indi as nardu oldas aire desa, ocus arse dotsét. Fiche ceili leis: .x. ceile

Mucleithe.[338] Six for him on Folach; entertainment for six; butter and bacon for him on second, on third, on fifth, on ninth, on tenth, and on Sunday. Why are there ten Seds in the fine of this man? Five Seds in right of his own house firstly; and five for the cook-house or refectory. He is supplied by his paying tenants without anything being wanting or deficient in his Aireship, of his perquisites—be they small or great, for it is not by law it is ruled.

Aire-Echtai, why so called? Because it is as the Aire [or chief] of five men he is assigned to perform his functions to enforce the observance of the "Peace", for a month, to avenge the insult offered to a tribe through the violent death of a person. If he does not [avenge] before the end of a month, he [i.e. the homicide] comes under the "Peace" laws. Whatever follows him into his bed [house], should they have killed a person under the "Peace"—the same five men—the Aire-Echtai pays for it for them. He does not receive the land or territory of an Aire for this, but only vessels of the value of a cow, which, now, are given for their maintenance outside during the "Peace", from the number of their clients and friends. He is entitled to his suite and his Folach, like those of the Aire-Desa. Aire-Echtai.

Aire-Ard [High Aire], why so called? Because of the fact that he is higher than the Aire Desa, and he precedes him. He has twenty Aire-Ard.

(338) This term is obscure, but perhaps means that he was then the *Flaith* or chief over the swine-herds in charge of the swine in the forests, and of the hunting of those forests.

The Crith Gablach, H. 3. 18, pp. 3. and 256, O'C.

giallna, ocus x saerceili. A deich ceili gialnai,—di bai cona timthug dó huaidib, ocus tri colpdachdai firinn, ocus coic dartaidi caich gaimriud, cona sammbiud. Arcuirether a céliu, cuir ocus chairdiu; cach ngrad as ic nislu bid dó i ceilsine. Cóic seot x. log a enech. Immus toing, is náidm, is rath, is aitiri, is sechem, is fiadnairi friú. Cid di beir coic seotu .x. do aineclann don firu? Coic seoit dó cétus ar tóchacht i tigi saderin; sét ceca céili dia ndlig biathad naircennai. Morseser a daim ind a tuaith. Coic fir fo leith. Imb cotarsunn doib do gress. Morseser for foluch. Forrusud morserir. Sall ocus imb do cotarsunn, i ndirri, i triri, i cóicid, i nomaid, i ndechmaid, i ndomnach. .uii. cumala a thaurcreic. Teoir [a] bai cona timthach bés a taigi. .xx. lanamain a cóirus for cui o calaind co init.

pp. 4 and 256.

Aire-Ard.

Ceiles: ten bond Ceiles and ten free Ceiles. His ten bond Ceiles—two cows with their accompaniments to him from them, and three Colpdachs Firind, and five Dartaids every winter, together with their summer food. He restrains his Ceiles, under the engagements and the "Peace"; every grade which is lower than himself is in obedience to him. His honour price is Fifteen Seds. He is a Toing, a Naidm, a Raith, an Aitire, a plaintiff, and a witness for them. What gives this man fifteen Seds for his honour price? Five Seds for him first for the stability of his own house; a Sed for every Ceile from whom he is entitled to fixed rent in provisions. Seven are his suite in his territory. Five men are his Foleithe.[353] They are always entitled to butter and condiments. Seven on Folach. The maintenance of seven. Bacon and butter, with condiments, are supplied them on second, on third, on fifth, on ninth, on tenth, and on Sundays. Seven Cumals are his Taurcreic. Three cows with their accompaniments are his Bes Tigi. Twenty couples are his right upon Coshering from the Kalends to Shrovetide.

[353] The *Foleithe* of a *Flaith* appears to have been a kind of retinue or body guard of retainers, which accompanied him when he held a judicial court or attended the popular assemblies. It is evidently related to the "Liti", "Lathen", "Litones" or "Lassi" of the German nations, a class below the nobility and above the serfs. In the new high German *Geleit*, we have almost the very word. The *Foleithe* included the persons who acted as *Naidms*, *Raiths*, *Fiadnaise*, etc. Several Hundreds were sometimes united in Kent under the name of "Lathes", and having the same jurisdiction as a Hundred. In other parts of England too the Hundred was sometimes called a "Leta", as for example, the "Leta de Brinkelow" in Warwickshire. The name of "Lething" given to the military levy in some parts of the north of England in Anglo-Saxon times, is undoubtedly connected with "Leta", on the one hand, and *Foleithe* on the other. "Leet", as in Court-Leet, "Leudes", "Lieges", etc., are also no doubt be connected. See INTRODUCTION,

Airi tuísi, ced ara nerer? Ar indi is toisech a cinul, ocus dosec airi ardd. .uii. ceili .xx. losuidi—cóic ceili .x. giallna, [ócus] da soerchéli .x. lais. A chéili giallna: cethcoir bai cona timthuch dó húadaib, acus .u. colpacha firinn, ocus sé dairtidi cach gaimrid, cona sambiud. Ocht cumala a thaurcreic ó rig. Cethcoir bai cona timtać bés a taigi. Ochtar a dám ina tuaith. Seisiur fo leithi. Imb cotarsunn dó do gres. Ochtar for foluch. Fossugud ochtair. Imb do cotarsunn ocus coirm no ass, ar it gella, i ndiss, i trissi, i coicaid, [i nomaid], i ndechmaid, i ndomnach. Fiči seot a eneclann. Immus toing, is naidm, is raith, is aitiri, is fechem, is fiadnaisi friú. Ac comren mat acra cen airech, cen airlicud. Tricha lanamna aice for cai o calaind co hinit, ar is a lin biadta bis a lin for cai. Noi traigead .xx. a tech, a noi .x. a airchai. Ocht nimdai isin tig, cona nos tincar tigi Airig túisi, im se brothracha cona corus tincair, itir corcailli ocus gaimniu suidi. Spe- The Crith Gablach, H. 3. 18. pp. 4 and 236. O'C.

Aire-Tuisi [Leading Aire], why so called? Because of the fact that his race is superior, and that he takes precedence of the Aire Ard. He has twenty-seven Ceiles—fifteen bond Ceiles, twelve free Ceiles. His bond Ceiles: four cows with their accompaniments to him from them, and five Colpdachs Firind and six Dartaids every winter, together with their summer food. Eight Cumals are his Taurcreic from his king. Four cows with their accompaniments are his Bes Tigi. Eight are his suite in his territory. Six his Foleithe. He is entitled to butter with condiments at all times. Eight upon Folach. The maintenance of eight. Butter with condiments is supplied them, and ale or new milk, because he is entitled to it on second, on third, on fifth, on ninth, on tenth, and on Sundays. Twenty Seds are his honour price. He is a Toing, he is a Naidm, he is a Raith, he is an Aitire, he is a plaintiff in a suit, and a witness for them. He pays if he is sued, without litigation, and without borrowing. He has thirty couples on Coshering from the Kalends to Shrovetide: for it is in proportion to the amount of his Biatha,[554] his number upon visitation [Coshering] is. Twenty-nine feet his house, nineteen [feet] his back-house. Eight beds in the house, with their perfect furniture equal to the house of an Aire-Tuisi, with six couches[555] properly furnished with pillows and sitting cushions. Suitable furniture Aire-Tuisi.

(554) See note 474, App. p. 472.

(555) *Brothach* always means a "blanket", though here translated "couch". As the permanent beds are already mentioned, it is probable that the meaning of the passage is that he should have six spare blankets, with a suitable number of pillows and sitting cushions, so that he could make up six additional beds when occasion required; the sitting cushions serving during the day as seats, and at night as beds. These cushions were made of skins stuffed with feathers.

The Crith Gablach, H. 3. 18, pp. 4 and 236.

cha corai isin tig, air odor [idar] cach meit, ocus iarn cach gnima ocus huma, lestrai im chairi i talla boin co tinne. Céili-coemeċtai lais, ise or [isaer] rathaib rig. Da echsrian .x. im rian [srian] noir, alaili airggait. Ni aisse do draetli milchu, laechraid, orcca. Lia a ben bithi acced cecha laubrai. La arathar cona óg corus dligteċ. Da ċapal do for sred. Cetmuinter co corus lán recta lanamna com ceniuil: Combi lan conggnam i tuaiṫ do aidbdenaib, do noilleċaib, do ġill, do giall, do cairdiu tar cenn ciniuil, tar crich, ocus i tech flaṫa. Ar neaṫ córus irráith a athar ocus a senathar. Docum baig a slan ara fornert. Fortoing forgraid arid nisliu,

End of tract beginning at p. 252 of MS.

ocus foserinnat a noillig.

Aire forggaill, cid ara nerer? Ar is he fortgella for na grada do ruirmisem nach airm inda tochrathar immesena, huaire asnuaiss a sebus indaċá a celi. Cethraċa céili la suide: fichi celi giallna, ocus fiċi soercéili. A fichi [ceili] gialnai, coic bai cona timtug do huadaib, ocus

Aire-Tuisi.

in the house with perfect workmanship,(556) and iron household tools for every work, and bronze vessels, together with a meat vessel(557) in which a cow and a hog will fit. He has an espoused wife, and he is in the free pay of the king. Twelve bridle-steeds, with a golden bridle, and another of silver. He is not liable for trespass by his grayhound, his calves, his young pigs. To his wife belongs the right to be consulted on every subject. He has a plough with its proper full set of implements. Two horses for him upon his journey. A virgin wife in the full propriety of matrimonial law, of equal tribe with himself: So that he shall have full assistance in the territory of prosecutors, of Noillechs,(558) of pledges, of hostages, to give, in order to secure the "Peace" for his tribe, outside of his territory, and into the house of the Flaith. He assumes the lawful fulfilment of the responsibilities of his father and grandfather. He redeems their guarantee of his own strength. He swears the grades that are lower than him, and he dissolves their enmities.(559)

Aire-Forgaill.

Aire-Forgaill, why so named? Because it is he that testifies as to character for the grades we have enumerated in every place they go to, to deny a charge, because his wealth is greater than that of his Ceiles. He has forty Ceiles; twenty bond Ceiles, and twenty free Ceiles. From his twenty bond he has five cows with

(556) Ornamental work in yew.

(557) Not a boiler or pot, but a vessel in which meat was salted, and which was usually kept behind the door of the house with meat preserved in it, to save the honour of the chief of the house. See O'Curry Gloss. at caire.

(558) *Noillechs*, a name given in the courts to the class of nobles who sat behind the judges, and acted as arbitrators.

(559) i.e., adjudges their disputes.

sé colpdaige firinn, ocus noi ndairtaide ceċ gaimrid, cona sammbiud. Coic seot déac a eneclann. Immus toing, is naidm, is raṫ, is aitiri, is fechem, is fiadnairi friu. Fer-ṫos cen airec, cen airlicud cia thaccrai. Noi cumala a thaurcreicc o mar flaiṫ. Cóicc bai cona thímṫug bes a thiġe. Nonbur a dam inna tuaṫ. Morseser folethe. Imm do cotarson, ocus saill, ocus cuirm no ass, ár it gellai i ndiss, i triss, i coicid, in nomad, i ndeċmaid, i ndomnach. Triċa traiged a teċ, .xx. traiged a irċai. A sreaṫai tiġe, a folud, a clete, a ech srein, a comopar caċ raithe, a cetmuinteras a cosuir dligid. The Crith Gablach, H. 3. 18. p. 4. O'C.

Tanassi rig, ced ara neper? Ar indi frisaicci tuath huili [do rigiu] cen cosnum friss. Coic sencleche forcraid laiss sech airig forggaill. Dechnebur a dam i tuaiṫ; oċtar foleiti; dechnenbur fo folach; co cetnu ċórus; co nínnrucus cleite; collín eochraide; co comopar ceċ raithe; co cetmuntesus dligid. Dech cumalai a thaurrcrecc. Sé bai bés a ṫige. Triċa sed a enechclann. Immus toing, is naidm, is raith, is aitiri, is fechem, is fiadnaise friu. Ferthos cen airec, cen airluccad cia ṫacrai.

their accompaniments, and six Colpdachs Firind, and nine Dartaids every winter, together with their summer-food. Fifteen Seds are his honour price. He is a Toing, a Naidm, a Raith, an Aitire, a plaintiff in a suit, and a witness for them. He pays without litigation, or without borrowing when sued. Nine Cumals are his Taurcreic from the great Flaith. Five cows with their accompaniments are his Bes Tigi. Nine are his company in his territory. Seven are his Foleithe. He gets butter with condiments and bacon, and ale or new milk, for he is entitled to them, on second, on third, on fifth, on ninth, on tenth, on Sundays. Thirty feet his house, twenty feet his back house. His household furniture; his wealth; his prime cattle; his bridle steeds; his working implements for the work of every quarter [of the year]; his espoused wife according to established law. Aire Forgaill.

Tanasi Righ [the tanist of a king], why so called? Because it is the whole territory [or people] that elects him without opposition to him. He has five Sencleithe more than the Aire-Forgaill. Ten are his company in the territory; eight his Foleithe; ten not Folach; with the same legal propriety; with the worthiness of a chief; with his full complement of horses; with implements for the work of each quarter of the year; with a lawful espoused wife. Ten Cumals are his Taurcreic. Six cows are his Bes Tigi. Thirty Seds his honour price. He is a Toing, a Naidm, a Raith, an Aitire, a party in a suit, and a witness for them. He pays without court litigation, or borrowing on a pledge, if he is sued. Tanasi Righ.

The Crith Gablach, H. 3. 18, p 4. O'C.

Ri, cid ara neper? Ar indi riges chumaċtui cuimriġ [ċuimniġ?] for a ṫuatai. Cair cislir foolai for rigaib? Teoir foola. Cateat? Rii ben, ri buden, ri bunaid caċ cinn. Rii benn cetamus, ced ar a neper? Is he ri tuaithi insin, las mbiat .uii. ngraid ḟene cona forodlaib i céilsine;

H. 3. 18, p. 5.

ar it he benna flaṫa do ruirmisium. Uii. cumalai a enechclann—cumal ceċ primgraid bis fo a ċumaċtu. Imus toing, is naidm, is raṫ, is aitiri, is fechem, is fiadnaise friu; ferċos cen aireċ, cen arliccud cia tacra. Da fer déc a dám na tuaith; nonbur foleithiu; dechenbur fos folach for a cosmus biata. Di cumal .x. a taurcreicc. Se ba bes a thige.

Rii buiden, cid ara nepersside? Ar indi as naurrai da buiden, no teora mbuiden;—secṫ .c. cacha buidne; isse ri teora tuaṫ, no cetheora tuaṫ insin. Oċt cumala a enechclann; huaire do foxla ilgiallu—a dáo, no a tri, no cethair, amail asḃeir [fenechus no Cormac Mac Airt]

The different ranks of kings.

Ri [a king], why so called? Because he possesses the power of binding over his people. It is asked how many are the ranks of kings. Three ranks. Which are they? A king with horns, a king of companies, a king the origin (or foundation) of all chiefs. The king of horns first, why so called? He is the king of tribes, who has the seven grades of the tribe with their tributaries in submission to him; for they are the horns of a Flaith which we have mentioned. Seven Cumals are his honour price—a Cumal for every prime grade that is subject to him. He is a Toing, he is a Naidm, he is a Raith, he is an Aitire, he is a plaintiff and a witness for them. He pays without court litigation or borrowing on a pledge when sued. Twelve men are his company in his territory; nine his Foleithe; ten on Folach according to his prescribed lawful maintenance. Twelve Cumals are his Taurcreic. Six cows are his Bes Tigi.

The Rii Ben.

The Rii Baiden.

The king of companies, why so called? Because he is the leader of two battalions, or three battalions;—seven hundred in each company;[560] he is the king of three territories, or of four territories then. Eight Cumals are his honour price; for he takes many hostages (or pledges)—two, or three, or four, as it is said [by either the Fenechas or Cormac Mac Airt].

[560] There were three grades of kings: 1, the *Righ Tuatha* or *Rii Ben*, who was chief of a *Tuath* or tribe, *Triucha Cead*, or 30 Hundreds, equivalent to a modern Barony; 2, the *Righ Mor Tuatha*, *Ri Buiden*, or *Righ Ruireach*, who had three, four, or more "Tribe Kings" or *Righ Tuathas* under him, equivalent to a modern county; and 3, the *Righ Cuicidh*, *Rii Bunad Cach Cin*, or "Provincial Kings", one of whom was generally *Ard Righ Eriund*, or High King of Eiriu.

"Rii Miċuarddu mescraid recht,
Na demogaid mesc maá,
Dligid cumal for a secht
Do a diriu dan".

The Crith Gablach, H. 3. 18. p. O'C.

Cethri fiċit fer a dám ina tuaiṫ; da fer deacc fo leithi. Coic cumala décc a thaurcreicc. Oct mbai bés a tiġi. Is difolaiġ rí buden: Oċt cumala ara gellat a ḟolaċ. Immus toing, is naidm, is rath, is aitiri, is fechem, is fiadnaisi friu; ferthos cen airec cen airlicud cia thacrad.

Rii bunaid cech cinn, dno, cid ara neper? Ar indí is fo cumaċtu a ċundriġ biid cech cenn nad timmairgg a coimdiu: huare fortét ceċ cenn bes tressai inní berétressa;— ise rii ruirech insin. Da .uii. cumala a enechclainni,— huaire mbite rí ocus tuaṫai fo cumaċtu ocus a chundriug. Immtoing, da .uii. cumalai, is naidm, is rath, is atire, is fechem, is fiadnaisi friú. Trica a dám inna tuaiṫ; secht cét folethe do cundriuġ la cach.

Difolaig rii ruirech, ocus rí écis, ocus brúgaid, i ngradaib tuaithi; leṫ folaċ ceċ gráid do a macc dligtheg, do

"The king of Michuaird of moderate inebriations,
Who obscures not his intellect with heavy intoxication,
He is entitled to a Cumal and seven,
To be paid him for the Dire of his state".

The Rii-Buiden.

Four-score men are his company in his territory; twelve men his Foleithe. Fifteen Cumals are his Taurcreic. Eight cows his Bes Tigi. A king of companies is non-Folach:[561] Eight Cumals are pledged to him for his Folach. He is a Toing, he is a Naidm, he is a Raith, he is an Aitire, he is a party in a suit, and a witness for them; and he pays without litigation or borrowing when sued.

The Ri Bunaid.

A king the origin of all chiefs, why so named? Because of the fact that it is under his control every chief is, who cannot be reduced to obedience by his own lord: For every chief who is the higher, constrains whosoever is lower;—he is then a king of kings. His honour price twice seven Cumals is,—for kings and peoples do be under his power and his direction. He is a Toing of twice seven Cumals, he is a Naidm, a Raith, an Aitire, a party to a suit, and a witness for them. Thirty are his company in his territory; seven hundred his Foleithe when governing the people.

The Folach of different ranks.

A king king, and a poet king, and a Brugaid, are non-Folach among the grades of the people; he is entitled to half the Folach of every grade for his lawful son, for his wife;—for it is

(561) Is nonsustainable that is, if he was wounded, he was not carried to the house of the man who inflicted the wound for his *Folach Othrusa*—it was paid him in his own house. See 5.35. R.I.A.

The Crith Gablach. H. 3. 18. p. 5 O'C.

a mnai;—ar is leth ceċ dligthig, cethramad caċ indligthig. Ban amus a folaċ a macaib maicc no céli. Rechtairi, techtairi folongthar leth folaċ a flatha. Gniitt cumala cainom a ngimo a folach fo a mbiathad lia flaiṫ. Cach dán do gni aicdi flatha, no ecalsa, folongar leṫ folach a miad caich asa aicdi do gni. Folach cech graid a eclais fo comgrad tuaiṫi. Caċ mathair lia mac for folaċ dia mathar.

Ité fodlai flaṫa do ruirmisem imaberat fullechtai flathemnais a somoinib féin. Cair ciade as sruthiu—in rí fa thuaṫ? Is sruthiu in rig. Cia do comsruithe? Ar is tuaṫ oirdnithes rig, ni rig oirdnithes tuaith. Caetet folaid rig do tuaith not noirdnither? Noaill tar a cenn fri rig oc [c]ur [oc cur, no oc cor] crichi. Istoing doib; fortoing huadaib .uii. cumala. Teit i combreith, i comfiadnaise fri rig tar cenn a thuaithi. Dligit conda bruthemain firian dóib. Dligit gell tar a cenn. Dligit foluch amail folongar. Dligit nad ngellai oenach forru nad timmell tuath uile aċd comaithe. Teora tomaltu ata corai do rig for a tuaitha: Oenach, ocus dál do cundrech, ocus

The Folach of different ranks.

half for every lawful, one-fourth for every unlawful. The wives of mercenaries have Folach in right of their sons or husbands. Stewards, and couriers, are sustained with half the Folach of their Flaith. They arrange that their share in Folach corresponds with their feeding by their Flaith. Every profession that performs the work of a Flaith, or of a church, is sustained with half Folach according to the grade whose work he performs. The Folach of every grade in the church is the same as that of its co-grade in the laity. Every mother goes with her son upon Folach, the same as his father.

Those ranks of Lords which we have enumerated, are those which receive the marks of Lord-ship from the amount of their property. It is asked which is the higher—the king or the people? The king is higher. What makes him higher? Because it is the people that ordain the king, not the king that ordains the people. What are the obligations of a king to the people that ordain him? He arbitrates for them with the king at the boundary of the territory. He is Toing for them; for his oath he gets seven Cumals from them. He goes into co-judgment, into co-evidence with the king for his people. They are entitled that he should keep righteous judges for them. They are entitled to pledges for the same. They are entitled to support as they support. They are entitled that he promises not a fair upon them at which the people at large shall not assemble with equal immunity. Three levies the king is justly entitled to from his people: A fair, and an assembly for rectifying the affairs of the

Obligations of a king.

tocomrac do crich. Is tuaithi cammae, comarggud oen-aiġ. Is riġ ni gellas ar oenoch, act rorcóir ni gellus. The Crith Gabhlach, H. 3. 18. p. 5. O'C.

Cair, cislir ata córai do riġ do giull for a tuaṫa? A tri. Cateat? Gell slaġad, gell rechtge, gell cairddi, ar it leisa tuaithi huli insin.

Cair, cislir slogad ata choorai do riġ do giull for a tuaitha? A tri. Cateat? Slogaḋ hi crich a medón fri indnaide slogid chairri; slogud co hor crichi fri forcsin fir ocus dligid, conic roib cath no cairdde; slogud tar crich fri tuaiṫ asatlui.

A taat dan, ceitheorai rechtgi gellus rig for a tuaitha Cateat? Rechtgai fenechais cétamus; it tuatha do deguisset; is riġ no dedluthai na teorai rechtgai eile, is ri do denimmairgg; rechtga iar cath comadmmaim furru, co ro dluthat a tuatha iarom ar namma conbba dóib; occus rechtga iar ndunebai; ocus rechtga rig, amail ron gab rechtga riġ Caisil, la Mumain Arataat teorai rechtgai ata córai do riġ do giull for a tuatha: Rechtgai do indarbbu echtarcimiul, .i. fri Saxanu; ocus rechtgai fri tuar torad; ocus recht cretme adannai, amail ron ngab rechta Adamnain.

people, and a convention of the government of the territory. It is the people that congregate, and contribute to the fair. And a king does not bind them to a fair, because it is only when it is appropriate he promises it. Obligations of a king.

It is asked, how many pledges is a king entitled to from his people? Three. Which are they? A pledge for hostings, a pledge for right, a pledge for peace, for all these things are for the good of the people. Rights of a king.

It is asked, how many hostings it is right for a king to bind upon his people? Three. Which are they? A hosting within the territory for the purpose of preparing a hosting beyond it; a hosting to the boundary of the territory to proclaim right and law, whether it be by battle or peace; a hosting over the boundary against an aggressive territory.

There are now four lawful rights which a king binds upon his people. What are they? The rights of Fenechas firstly; it is the people that enforce it; it is the king that exercises the other three rights, and it is the king that enforces them: a right after a battle has been broken upon them, to consolidate his people then, so that they be not disbanded; and a right after a mortality; and the right of a king; such as the right of the king of Cashel, in Munster. For there are three rights which it is proper for a king to exercise upon his people: a right to drive out foreign races, i.e. Saxons; and a right for the supply of fruits [or other produce]; and a right to kindle religion, such as the Law of Adamnan.

The Crith Gabhlach, H. 3. 18. p. 6. O'C.

Ité folaid fir flaitheman inso for a tuatha; ocus ni is forge goi na ecin, na forniurt. Rop slan etarggairech firion itir lobru ocus trenu.

Ataat dan a tri aili todacrat do ríg. Rop fer cach leiṫi lan dligid. Rop fer frecmairc fiss. Rop sorus ainmnet.

Ataat cethair toraic do berat dire naithig do ríg. Cateat? A thoraic for teora lorggaib athich: lorgg forgga, lorgg ṡamṫaiġi, lorgg rammai; ar cen mbis forraib is aiṫech. A ṫaraicc a aenur; ar ni corus do ríg imtheċt a aenur. Is ed laa insin fortoigg ben a aonur a macc for ríg; la na tabir neich a teist aċt nama. Ataa mi nad nimtéċ ri aċt cethrar. Cia ceṫrar? Ri, ocus brithemun, ocus dias i manchune. Cia mi in nimtéċ in tuċt sin? Mi silta. A guin inna diculaid dna oc teched, ar roi do ber diri naithaig dó. Aċt mad trió do cói, ar is amlaid sóon direnatar di cúlaid ríg ara inchaib.

Ata dna secht mónail i corus ríg: .i. domnach, do ól corma, ar ni flaith teċta nad ingella laiṫ ar cach ndomnich; luan, do breithemnas, do choccertad tuath; Máirt

Rights of a king.

These are the rights which a righteous king has over his people; and he exacts them not by falsehood, nor by force, nor by despotic might. His fostering care must be perfect to them all, both weak and strong.

Qualities of a king.

There are now three other qualities that pertain to the qualifications of a king. He must be a man fully qualified in every respect. He must be a man anxious to preserve knowledge. He must be the seat of equity.

Ways in which the dignity of a king is lowered.

There are four stoopings that bring the fine of an Aithech[563] or plebeian to a king. What are they? His stooping to the three shafts of an Aithech: The handle of a pitchfork, the handle of an axe, the handle of a spade; for as long as he is at them, he is an Aithech. His stooping to go alone; for it is not proper for a king to travel alone. That would be the day upon which a woman alone could swear her child upon a king; a day upon which no one else could give testimony but herself alone. There is a month in which the king travels but with four only. What four are they? A king, a judge, and two servants. In what month does he travel in that manner? The month of seed-sowing. To get wounded in the back, now, in retreating from a battle field gives him the Dire of an Aithech. But if it is through him it [the weapon] has passed, Dire is paid for the back of a king, the same as for his front.

Occupations of a king.

There are, now, seven occupations in the law of a king—viz. Sunday, at ale-drinking, for he is not a lawful Flaith who does not distribute ale every Sunday; Monday, at legislation, for the

(563) See *ante*, note 464, App. p. 469.

oic fidchill; Cétuin do deicsiu milchon oic toisonn; Taradain do lanamnas; Aindiden do rethaib ech; Saṫairn do brethaib.

The Crith Gablach, H. 3. 18, p. 6. O'C

Ataat tri toichnedai fris na ride corad (no tocrad) rig: Cia beth ri im choire iar ndul trit; toichniud iar néland aige dia folaid, acht ni ro fuiter dilcc dia guin; toichniuch iar netiuċ, ar is mo dosli oldáas aon, huare doslii loġ a enech.

Cair. Cia is cóir ocus is ceċtai do denum biḋ riġ? Fergnio tri forggaib. Cateat ridi? Fer fororggaib forggab for a comlonn, co trégda in fer tria sciath. Fer gaibes fer beogabail, ocus arit ngaib i roi. Fer benas dam oen bemmim nad fuidle. Fer forgaib cimbid cen aurlud. Fer forgaib eclann ar belaib sluaiġ, co tuit di aen forggub.

Ataat dno tri aurrach nad accladat rig: Errech ar tuaith asidlui oco nindriud; errech in tan mbis ri a nechtair leis ina thuaiṫ fadeisin, mani roa duini; errech diseiscc slabrai i ndithraib, iar tuidecht tar crich. Ad-

government of the tribe; Tuesday, at chess; Wednesday, seeing grayhounds coursing; Thursday, at the pleasures of love; Friday, at horse-racing; Saturday, at judgment.

Occupations of a king

There are three fastings which bring no disgrace to a king: [Fasting], when the king has a boiler which has leaked; fasting when a stranger has run away with his supplies, but no men have been sent to kill him [the absconder]; fasting after being refused [his supplies], for it is then his right to do so is greatest, because he is entitled to his honour price.

The fastings of a king.

Quere. Who is it that is fit and lawful to make the food of a king? A champion of three captures. Which are they? A man-captive whom he captures in his combat, after he has pierced the man through his shield. A man who has captured a man in living caption, and whom he has captured on the battle-field. A man who slays an ox with one stroke without default in the deed. A man who captures a Cimbid or "victim"[363] without a scuffle. A man who captures an assassin (or outlaw) in the front of an army, until he falls by one thrust.

Who should be the king's cook?

There are three extraordinary levies, which a king is not held responsible for; a levy upon a territory in revolt into which he goes to subjugate it; a levy when he has an extern king with him in his own territory, if his court is not sufficient to supply him; a levy of dry cattle in a waste,[364] after having gone

Levies for which a king is not responsible.

[363] A condemned person, whether for crime, or merely a "nexus" who had become "addictus". See note 470 on *Naidm*, *ante*, App. p. 470.

[364] That is land which had come into the hands of the chief through failure of heirs, confiscation, etc., and the management of which had not as yet been assumed by the proper authorities. It also included lands the ownership of which was disputed, etc. The *Brugh* of the district

Crith ...ach, ... 18. p. 8. genedar huad do cach bera cethrai, nad a neirrech ndede-nach, nad aithgenechar hi tuirech, acht mad inoruch nindligthech.

Cati chorus dono riġ bis hi forus do gress ar chinn a tuaiṫi? .uii. fichit traiged, di traigtib innraiccib, mett hi dune cach leith; .uii. traigid teiget a thalmatha, da traig .x. dna a domna. Is ann is rig an tan, dot nimcellat drechta gialna. Cati in drecht gialnai? Da traig .x. lethet a bél, ocus a domnai; ocus i fot fri dun; tricho traiġi a fot i nechtair. Cleirig do dénum itgi a thigi. Carr cóil, carr oine cech fir dia rogbai. Ind flaith bachoild ni dlig dénum a duni, act a chech namma. Uii. traigid trichot itech. Di immdai .x. hi rigṫiġ, co fernar tech riġ; amuis rig hi foitriu. Cair cis-né amuis ata corai la riġ? Fer soerus di triú, fer soerus di gabail,

over the boundary. He makes restitution for every class of cattle which belongs not to the last levy, for which he makes no restitution at first, but if it be an unlawful foray [he must make restitution].

...hts of a ...g as to house-...d. What are the lawful rights of the king who dwells perpetually at the head of his people? Seven score feet, of lawful feet, is the size of his Dun every way; seven feet is the depth into the ground; twelve feet now is its base. It is then only he is a king, when he is encircled by the Drecht Gialnai. What is the Drecht Gialnai [ditch of allegiance]? Twelve feet is the breadth of its mouth, and of its base; and its length encircles the Dun; thirty feet is the length it is out [i.e. from the Dun]. It is clerics that make the prayers of his house. A cart for firewood, and a cart for lending for every man who may require it. The Flaith Bachald[368] is not entitled to have his Dun built for him, but only his house. Seven feet and thirty is his house. Twelve beds in the royal mansion, with the array of a king's house; the body guard of the king in the south. It is asked who are the body-guard that a king ought to have? A man whom he has freed

appears to have had the usufruct of all such lands for a certain time, after which they passed into the possession of the *Righ Tuatha*, who held them as part of the *terra regis*, until they were regranted, or the dispute finally settled; hence the right of the king to levy his supplies there.

[368] The *Flaith Bachald* appears to have been the *Tanist* of a *Flaith*, a man fully qualified in every way by wealth, family, and rank, but not the ruling *Flaith*. *Bachald* is equivalent to *somaine flatha*, that is, having all the qualifications of a *Flaith*. *Flaith do arngair a bith bachald* was a *Flaith* who had ruined his estate, his rank, and his honour; he was one of the seven persons not entitled to *Enechland* or *Dire* (H. 3. 17. T.C.D., p. 372; and Egerton MS. 88. Brit. Mus.) The *Flaith Bachald* was perhaps equivalent to the *Athelings* of the Anglo-Saxons, that is, members of the ruling family, any one of whom was eligible to be elected Tanist or *Righ*.

fer soerus di cimmidecht; fer soerus di fognum di doer-bothus di doer fuidres. Ni bi occai fer soerus a roi; ar nach roimpe, no ar nach rubai, ar soethaib, ar ċonnalbi. Cia lin di amsaib as ċoir la riġ? Cethrar, .i. rigtiġ, ocus reirthith, ocus da taebtaid, ite a nanmann. Ite ata chorai do buith i foitriu taige riġ, ara choemtecht a taiġ immach, imaig i tech. Fer gill do gialnaib friu aniar. Cia miadrisi? Fer las mbi tir .uii. cumal, forbi a ḟetaib itir flaith ocus andoin, ocus chorus fein teċtai frisuidi iniar. Da ama iarsuidiu; eccis iarsuidib; cruitti iarsuidi; cuslennaiġ, cornairi, clesamnai a nairtiur foitri. Is innleċ eliu, fochlu fennid: fergnid fri forngairi ndorus; a charr ar belaib cechtirnaei do gres, fri cumascc churmtigi; soerceli na flaṫa friu aniar:—Oes insin bid coemtecht do flaiṫ; geil iarsuidiu; brithem iarsuidiu; i ben, no a brithem frisuidi inniar; ri iarsuidiu; gel dichma i nglasib i nairtiur fochlai.

The Crith Gablach, H. 3. 18. p. 6 (C.)

from death, a man whom he has freed from jail,[366] a man whom he has freed from the condition of a Cimmid or "victim", a man whom he frees from the servitude of bond Bothach-ship or from bond Fuidir-ship. He does not have a man whom he saves on the battle field; who has been forced to retreat, or who has been wounded, neither for castigation, nor for friendship. How many body-guards-men are proper for a king? Four, viz., a front-man, a rereman, and two sidemen, are their names. It is they that are proper to be in the southern part of a king's house, to guard him on the outside of his house, in a plain, in a house. A pledged man of the hostages by these behind. What is his rank? A man who has the land of seven Cumals, recognizable for his wealth both by his chief and his church, and his own lawful family faced forward seated by these behind. Two wardens behind these; poets behind these; harpers behind these; pipe players, horn players, and jugglers, in the back part of the south side. In the other side of the house in the champion's seat: warriors to guard the door; his spear in front of each of them at all times, to guard against the revel of the Ale House; the Flaith's privileged Ceiles behind them:—These are the parties who are the companions of the Flaith; hostages behind these; judges behind these; his wife, or his judge, faced forwards behind him; kings behind these; unredeemed hostages in locks in the east side of the champion's couch.

Rights of a king as to his household.

(366) *Gabail*, i.e., arrestation. A person under arrest being said to be in *Gabail*, that term no doubt gradually came to signify the place where the prisoner was secured. It is therefore probable that *Gabail* and the cognate words in other Celtic dialects appear to be the true origin of the English word *gaol*, *jail*, O. French, *gaole*, *jaiole*, modern French, *geôle*, Spanish, *gayola*, Portuguese, *gaiola*, Italian, *gabbia*, and not Latin, *cavea*, as is usually assumed.

The Crith Gablach, H. 3. 18, p. 7. O'C.

Rii tuaithe. Di feraib deacc do lessaib tuaithe folloing tuath fadessin fria taisteti. Dá fer deac dna dan espuic, di lesib ecelsi ocus tuaithi imteit cadesin. Ar ni racu tuath damrad rig ocus espuic, diam di gress for ngelat. Dam suad dna di ferib déac. Cia de is ruithiu, in rig fa espuc? Is ruithiu espuc, huaire ar nérig rig fobith creitme. Tuarguib espuc dno aglun ria rig

Dligthir brethim la rig rod bo brithim cadesin. Amal ar in can fenechas:

"Mad be rig
ro fessir recht flatha
fo thoth iar mbiad
meschaid a slóg,

The retinue of a king and a bishop.

Rii Tuaithe. Twelve men [are his retinue], when for the good of a Tuath, they are supported by the people on their excursions. Twelve men now are the retinue of a bishop, when he travels for the good of the church and the people. For the people could not sustain the retinues of a king and of a bishop, if they were constantly feeding on them. The company of the Suad(367) now is twelve men. Which is the higher, a king or bishop? The bishop is higher, because he binds the king in virtue of faith. A bishop, however, raises his knee to a king.

The retinue of a Sai.

It is lawful for a king to have a judge with him though he is himself a judge. As the Law of Fenechas says:—

Occupations of the Ale House.

"If he be a king
Who knoweth a king's lawful rights
With bounty, after meals
He regales his hosts.(368)

(367) *Suad*, or *Sai*, was the title of the class of literary men (poets, historiographs etc.) The highest rank of each profession was called an *Ollamh*—thus *Ollamh Brethemnas* was the highest rank of judge. The highest rank of *Sai* was accordingly styled an *Ollamh* also. He had the same rank as a *Righ Ruireach*; and was entitled to the same number in his retinue and to the same *Dire*. Cassiodorus (Variar. Libr. I. Epistola, xxiv.) speaks of a certain Nandius a Salo (*Gen.* Saionis), who acted as a kind of nuncio or ambassador to the Gothic king Theodoric. Other forms also occur, *Sajo*, *Sagio*, *Sago*, but always in Latin texts. Diefenbach suggests that the Gothic form may have been *Sagja*. In Anglo-Saxon we have *Secga*, *Secg*, an ambassador, and in Old Frisian in combinations *Sega* e.g. *ásega*, a judge, corresponding to Old Sax. *éosago*. O. H. German *êsago*. In the laws of the Salic Franks we also find mention of a class of persons called *Sagibarones*. It is worthy of remark that the Irish Historical Tales always give the function of ambassador to a *Sai*. The Anglo-Saxon *Secga*, suggests a relationship with the Irish *Sice Oc*, a name given to certain persons who formed part of the judicial courts, and performed the function apparently of announcing the decisions of the court. The Gothic *Saio* or *Sagio*, appears also to have signified a person who pronounced the sentence of the court. An old gloss mentioned by Diefenbach gives *Saio* poenator, which corresponds with the Spanish *Sayon*, an executioner. The term has thus descended from being the name of the highest legal functionary to that of the lowest.

(368) That is, his officials, *Fuidir* retainers, and mercenaries, etc.

sabaid cuirmmtigi,
cuirmesca,
mess tiri,
tomus forrag,
Forbesta diri,
Dithle messaid
Mor muin mrugrechtai,
mrogad coicrich,
cor cualne.
córus rinde,
rann itir comorbbo,
comaithig do gairmmaim.
Gaill comlaind caithigti
istoda, anagraitto rig,
raith commairgi
chorus co feisiur,
sédaib selb.
Slán cech comaithces,

The Crith Gablach, H 3. 18. p. 7. O'C.

The business[569] of the Ale House:
Verification of contracts,
Appraisement of land,
Measurement by pole,
Increase of Dire,
Taxing the assessment
Of chief tolls of Brugh-law,[570]
Extending boundaries,
Planting boundary stakes
According to law of allotment,
Dividing between Comarbs,[571]
Recognizing coöccupancies,
Adjudging foreign prisoners of war,
Adjusting the disputes of kings,
Giving security of sanctuary,
Promulgating the law,
Receiving Seds,[572]
The Slan[573] of each Commaithches,[574]

Occupations of the Ale House.

[569] *Sabaid*, plural of *Sab*, which ans literally a block or prop,—any- ng strong which supports. In the ws, as here, *Sabaid* signifies per- s powerful by their influence, ps of the state such as the chiefs, mpions, *Aires*, poets, etc., who with the king in the banquet l, while engaged in the business of state, in which the *Sabs* assisted a council. In the translation of text, the functions of the *Sabaid* are put for the council, and paraphrased as "business of the Banquet Hall".

[570] See note 531, App. p. 485.

[571] That is, determining the proportionate share of the capital, income, and responsibilities of each member of a copartnership or guild.

[572] See note 516, App. p. 480.

[573] See note 502, App. p. 476.

[574] See INTRODUCTION for an explanation of this term.

The Crith Gablach, H. 3. 18. p. 7. O'C.

curtar gellaib,
gelltar smachtuib miach;
molauga luag doirn.
Diri naurbai.
O dartaid co dairt.
dochum colpdaigi,
co cóic sétu cingit".

Occupations of the Ale House.

Pledges are given,
Sack[375] fines are promised,
Increasing the amount of Dires,—
The Dire of inheritance,
From a Dairt to a Dartaid.
Up to a Colpdach,
And to five Seds it progresses.

(375) *Smachtaib miach*, "sack-fines". *Smacht* appears everywhere in the Laws to mean tributes or rent in kind, or simple fines under the general law. *Miach*, in its original literal and general sense, means a sack, and is frequently used in the sense of bushel, peck, can, bucket, or other vessel of any shape or material; but in such cases it appears to have been so called from its being able to contain the same quantity as the *Miach* or sack; e.g. the *Miach Lestar*, a sack vessel, that is a vessel which contained the same quantity as the sack, and *Coidmiach*—from *Coid* or *Cuad*, a wooden vessel, and *Miach*, a sack; that is a wooden vessel or bucket, which contained a *Miach* or sack. In the *Táin Bó Flidais* it is expressly applied to a water vessel, but, as in the cases just mentioned, its name may have indicated its capacity. It is difficult to determine the capacity of the *Miach*, and therefore the value of the sack-fines, because it would appear to have been a variable measure, the capacity and quality of which depended upon the rank of the parties who received and paid the fines, and no doubt also upon the locality. The barrel or standard measure for grain which varied so much with the kind of grain and with the locality, is probably the modern representative of the ancient *Miach*. The following gloss will give some idea of the comparative capacity and value of the sack of different kinds of grain: *Miach Cruithnechta*, a sack of wheat. One-third of hulls hath the oats, i.e. it has one-third of husks upon it, i.e. upon the oats. It is in the proportion of two to three of food [shelled grain] that the oats is to the barley, and in the proportion of one to three in price; because a *Screpall* is the price of the sack of wheat, and two pence for the sack of barley, and one penny for the sack of oats. Eight score loaves in the sack of wheat, and six score loaves in the sack of barley, and four score loaves in the sack of oats. It is in the proportion of two to three of food [shelled grain] that the oats is to the barley here; and in the proportion of one to three the oats is to the wheat, and of one-third in price. It is in the proportion of three to four of *Arbo* [i.e. corn meal or good shelled grain] that the barley is to the wheat, and of two-thirds in price; and no other corn ranks in this proportion but oats and barley, nor is it in the same ratio that any one of them all yields loaves,— that is eight score loaves of *Banfhuine* are in the sack of wheat; and that is equal to four-score loaves of *Ferfhuine*; and four-score loaves of *Banfhuine* in the sack of barley; and that is equal to two-score loaves of *Ferfhuine*; and two score loaves of *Banfhuine* in the sack of oats; and that is equal to one-score loaves of *Ferfhuine*; but the wheat has a precedence, for it is the most noble, and the barley has an excess of *Tais* (dough) for malting, or for ale, and the oats, and that is the [reason of the] difference of price between them" (H. 3. 18. 279). O'Curry's Glossary, voce *Miach Cruithnechta*.

2. A LAW TRACT WITHOUT A TITLE, ON THE CLASSES OF SOCIETY.

This Tract will be found interesting in connection with the foregoing one, as it gives the titles of the different state officials by whom the government was administered, and a brief but distinct account of the rank, privileges, duties, and responsibilities of each, and of several other grades and officials of ancient Gaedhelic society not mentioned in the Crith Gablach. It forms in the vellum MS. H. 3. 18. T.C.D., one of a series of tracts on the classification and privileges, etc., of the various grades of learned men, and of the orders of the ancient Irish Church. The descriptions of these classes are brief, but it has not been thought necessary to give them here, especially as the subject of the classification of the learned classes will be treated of in the Introduction.

Cislir togarmand teċtaide miadleċta? Nin: a se .xx. it, .i. Triat, Ri Ri, Rig Tuaiṫi, Aire Forgill, Aire Ard, Aire Tuise, Aire Desa, Airi Fine, Idna, Ansruth, Dae, Ogflaiṫem, Leṫflaithem, Flaiṫem Oenescra, Bó Aire, Tanuise Bo Aire Tuisi, Huaitne, Seirchiud, Fas Faigḋe, Bogeltaċ Faiṫche, Aiṫeċ Baitse, Oinmit, Miḋlaċ, Reim, Riascaire, Sindach Brothlaige. H. 3. 18. p. 15. a.

Cislir a ndlige iar miadaiġeċt indeolaid is na miadleċtaib? Nin: A noi. Co festar cia meit i nastaither caċ dib, itir a lin, ocus a nuaite; itir a mbiathad, ocus a nesain; itir a nguin, ocus a ndiguin; itir a sar, ocus a sarugaḋ; itir a faesam, ocus a turrṫugaḋ; itir a nenec-lann ocus a nenechruice, ocus a neneċgris.

How many recognized titles of honour are there? Answer: Twenty-six, viz., a chief King, a King-king, a King of tribe (or territory), Aire Forgaill, Aire Ard, Aire Tuisi, Aire Desa, Aire Fine, Idna, Ansruth, Dae, Og-Flaithem, Leth-Flaithem, Flaithem Oenescra, Bó-Aire, Tanaise-Bó-Aire Tuisi, Huaithne, Seirthiud, Fas Faigdhe, Bogeltach Faithche, Aithech-Baitse, Oinmit, Midlach, Reim, Riascaire, Sindach Brothlaighe. Titles of Honour.

What is the extent of their lawful privileges as they progress in each rank of these distinctions? Answer: Their recognition, until it has been ascertained what are to be assigned to each of them, both as to their retinue and his own person; as to his Biathad, and their Esain; as to their wounding, and their Diguin; as to his insult and his Sarughudh; as to his Faesam[376] and his Turrthugadh; as to his Enechland, and his Enechruice, and his Enechgris. Their Privileges.

(376) An explanation of these terms will be found in the Introduction.

H. 3. 18. p. 14 Cislir do berad miaḋ ocus eneclann do caċ? Nin: A tri, airilliuḋ, ocus indrucus, ocus endce. A tri dno atlendai miaḋ contfe ar caċ, .i. anfolaḋ, ocus docerd, ocus anendge. Triaṫ .i. rig amail isber:

"Triach triom tremaetha Erind
tuaṫ o ṫuind co tuind
tairceLla tomus cond
iar na durn toimdither".

Dligiḋ a saerbiathaḋ fo lin, cin timdeibe, secib du timcella.

Dligiḋ .u. cumala dergóir,—scelig logmoir dia diguin, dia esain, no dia grisseḋ gruad; coic coicid Erenn tremaetha a mamu uile, amail roċet do Concobar:

"Ard mac rig, ro mac Nesa,
nenaisc iaċu fer fene".

Ri ri, .i. ri adgiallat .uii. rig tuaṫa; Cumal caċ rig do, dia air, dia esain, diatlu a dala, no a cuirmtiġe, no a oenuiḋ; dligiḋ a saerbiathad, fo lin cin timdeibe. Da .uii. cuṁal dia saruġuḋ, dia ésain, dia ainmed, amail isber Cormac:

"Bera do rig cloṫaċ Coirbre

What are they that give a man honour, and honour-price? Answer: Three things, viz., good works, righteousness, and innocence. There are three things moreover that injure the recognized rank of every one, viz., misdeeds, disgrace, and dishonour.

Triath. Triath, i.e., a king, as is said:

"The mighty powerful king of Eriu,
The territory from sea to sea
He secures with righteous judgments;—
Into his hand it is confided".

He is entitled to his free maintenance with his full retinue, without decrease, and to be encircled by a foss.

He is entitled to five Cumals of red gold,—sparkling precious for his Diguin, for his Esain, or for his cheek reddening; the five provinces of Eriu, he holds the allegiance of them all, as it was sung for Concobar.

"The high son of a king, the good son of Nessa,
Who governs the lands of the Fer Fene".

Ri Ri. Ri Ri, i.e., king king, i.e., a king to whom seven tribe kings are in submission; a Cumal from each king, for his satire, for his Esain, for his reproach at an assembly, or in an ale-house, or at a fair; he is entitled to his free maintenance, with his retinue, without decrease. Twice seven Cumals for his Sarughudh, for his Esain, for his disparagement, as Cormac said:

"Give unto the renowned king Cairbre

Loġ cimeda do cuṁalaib cáinib— H. 3. 18. p. 15.
co a .uii. saiġes aithirne [aiṫrine]
cend caċa cuindsen".

Comdilius dia diguin, no dia sarugud, no gruaide gris

"Rig tuaiṫi coimes co a .uii.:
dliġiḋ dia sarugaḋ sceo gruaide,
cumal inruic co a seċt,
saṁuither saerbreṫaib Cormaic".

Aire Ard, .i. Forgill, .i. tar cenn tuaiṫe; comsaera fris a cáin ocus a cairde, ocus ni he ar do nasc congiallna na dliged flaṫa; ocus acguidetrom na tuaṫa, ocus is rig ar do nasc. Dliġid a saerbiathaḋ corruice .xxx. oc learugud tuaiṫe. Dliġiḋ .uii. leṫ ċumal inraice dia diguin, dia sarugud, amail isbert Cormac:

"Aire Ard aird neme
cona tuaiṫe tesairg,
dliġiḋ dia sarugud,
sceo aiġṫe esain,
.uii. lana leṫ cumal,
ar caċ nurconn co ruice .uii.".

The price of a Cimid[577] of precious Cumals— Ri Ri.
To seven his fine progresses
In lieu of every violation of right".

He is entitled to equal retribution for his Diguin, and for his Sarughudh, and for his cheek reddening.

"Rig Tuatha, to seven his fine progresses: Rig Tuath
For his Sarughudh, for his cheek reddening he is entitled
To a full Cumal, to seven progressing;
Established by the just judgments of Cormac".

Aire Ard, i.e., who testifies, i.e., in behalf of the people; and he legalizes them under laws and treaties, and they cannot bind him in submission to the chieftaincy laws; and he vindicates the people, and it is a king that binds him. He is entitled to his free maintenance as far as thirty, while adjusting the territory. He is entitled to seven full half Cumals for his Diguin, for his Sarughudh, as Cormac said: Aire Ard Forgill.

"Aire Ard of high sanctuary
For the protection of his people.
He is entitled for his Sarughudh,
Also for his rank-Esain,
To seven full half Cumals;
From every chief as far as seven".

(577) See note 487, App. p. 474.

H. 3. 18. p. 15. Aire Tuisi: do ſet ſine comcenel do co ríg, ocus a ro slabra. Dligiḋ saerbiathaḋ xx., in tan bis ac lesugud tuaiṫe. Teora leṫ ċumala ina esain, ocus ina sarugud, ut dicitur Cormac:

"Cain bera do cach airig tuisi,
dia sarugud, dia esain,
teora leire letcumala,
la diabul fuirriud cin airbernad".

Aire desa, .i. fer conae deis nathar ocus a senathar, amail attota riam, ocus do tairchid. Dligiḋ saerbiathaḋ deiċnebuir do a tuaiṫ. Dligiḋ cumal caċ ain co morfe-siur dia sarugud, no dia esain:

"Aire desa dichli
dia diguin, dia sarugud,
dligiḋ slan cumal
caċ ain co morsesear,
la diablad fuirriud
do tortaibh".

Aire fine finnathar, .i. fer do et fine diambi arda feta co flaiṫ. Dligiḋ saerbiathaḋ .ui. ir a tuaiṫ; dligiḋ cumal caċa laime co cethrur dia sarugud no dia esain; ut dicitur Cormac:

Aire Tuisi. Aire Tuisi. He is known to be of a tribe equal in family and personal property to a king. He is entitled to the free maintenance of twenty, while adjusting the territory. He is entitled to three half Cumals for his Sarughudh and for his Esain, ut dicitur Cormac:

"The fine to be given to every Aire Tuisi
For his Sarughudh, for his Esain,
Is three full half Cumals,
With double supplies without diminution".

Aire Desa. Aire Desa, i.e., a man who has the property of his father and grandfather, as they always possessed, and as they accumulated. He is entitled to the free maintenance of ten in the territory. He is entitled to a Cumal from every one as far as seven for his Sarughudh, or for his Esain.

"Aire Desa as restitution,
For his Sarughudh, for his Esain,
He is entitled to a full Cumal
From every one as far as seven,
With double supplies
Of provisions".

Aire Fine. Aire Fine, be it known, i.e., a man who is of family of equal rank with a Flaith. He is entitled to the free maintenance of six from his tribe [territory]; he is entitled to a Cumal from every one as far as four for his Sarughudh, and for his Esain, ut dicitur Cormac:

"Aire fine findathar a techta, H. 3. 18. p. 15.
dia saruġuḋ dia tromġresaib,
sceo air indliġtiġ, sceo aiġte esain,
dliġiḋ cumal caċa laime co cethrur".

Idna, .i. fer oca mbi sochraiti do macuib berar do, ocus do braitrib, combi .xxx. uit gaisgedaċ. Dliġiḋ saerbiathaḋ .ui. ir oca fine; dliġiḋ leṫ ċumal co triar dia saruġuḋ, dia esain, ut dixit Cormac:

"Idna an diumsaċ,
sloind Coirpre Lifeċair
cia dligid dia saruġuḋ,
sceo ai esain an fir,—
dliġiḋ leir leṫ ċumal—
co tri firu seired,
la diablad fuirriud.
Connma imċartar Cormac".

Ansruth, .i. fer imdith a mennut ocus a criċ. Guin duine do in caċ treimsi do ceitrib raithuib na bliaḋna. Ni bes uaitiu .xx. fir crich a neċtair. Saerbiathad do caċa lete, no gaċa clete ina tuaith; dliġiḋ trian cumaile dia saruġuḋ, ocus dia esain; ocus dliġiḋ gaisceḋ inraic ina eneclann:

"Aire Fine let his lawful rights be known, Aire Fine.
For his Sarughudh, for his heavy insult,
For his unlawful satire, for his rank-Esain,
He is entitled to a Cumal from each to four".

Idna, i.e., a man who has a great number of sons born to him, Idna.
and of brothers, till they number thirty fighting men. He is entitled to free maintenance for six with his tribe; he is entitled to a half Cumal from each, to three for his Sarughudh, for his Esain, ut dixit Cormac:

"Idna the arrogant man,
Cairpri Lifechair defined
The fine for his Sarughudh,
For the rank-Esain of the man,—
He is entitled to a full half Cumal—
To three men it progresses,
With double rations.
As awarded him by Cormac".

Ansruth, i.e., a man who vindicates his people and his terri- Ansruth.
tory. He has the killing of a man in each division of the four quarters of the year. He does not have less than twenty men going into a neighbouring territory. He is entitled to free maintenance from every Leet,[578] or from every chief in his territory; he is entitled to one-third of a Cumal for his Sarughudh, and for his Esain; and he is entitled to a perfect sword for his honour price.

[578] See note 553, on *Foleithe*, p. 498.

H. 3. 18. p. 15. "Ansruth an imdich
a crich cethar aird,
conair gaile uad;
co ndligidh dia esain
ard cumal ceirt trian,
sceo gaisced inndraic
fri ruamna rus".

"Dae, .i. fer imerta fir ar a laime, connach tairted a comlonn; do fich a gressa cen adall fine aco. Dligidh a sarbiathad ocus a amus o cach leithe, ocus leth trian cumaile dia esain, no dia sarugudh, ocus gaisced no timthach, ut dicitur Cormac:

"Dae, ard ara srém laime,
luither, combi trelam, tenn—
dligidh cumal leth trian,
fria cuinnse cucht,
ara dinsem la dith clachta".

Otha sein tra ni cumalaib a ndire, acht a seotaib bó cethruib, no bó slabra—

Og flaithem, .i. fer tri seincleithe cona comorbaib techta. Dligidh saerbiathadh deichnebuir. Dligidh .x. seotu bee dile dia sarugudh no dia esain.

Ansruth. "Ansruth the protector
Of the territory on the four sides,
He guards off from it;
For his Esain he is entitled
To one full-third of a high Cumal,
With a perfect suit of valour arms
For battle conflict".

Dae. Dae, i.e., a man who vindicates justice by his strength, so that he cannot be overpowered in battle; he may be reproached without dishonour to his tribe. He is entitled to his free maintenance for himself and his mercenaries from each Leet, and one-third of a Cumal for his Esain, or for his Sarughudh, and a sword or a suit of clothes, ut dicitur Cormac:

"Dae noble, because of his powerful hand,
He must be fierce, equipped in arms, and brave—
He is entitled to a Cumal one-third,
For face reddening,
For his reproach and face insult.

From those [grades] now it is not in Cumals their Dire is paid, but in Seds of Bó Cethruib or B'Slabrad.

Og Flaithem. Og Flaithem, i.e., a man who has three Sen-cleithe with their lawful Comorbs. He is entitled to the free maintenance of ten men; he is entitled to ten Seds of chattels for his Sarughudh or for his Esain.

(579) See note 516, on *Sed*, App. p. 480.

Leth flaithem, .i. fer da cleithe cona comorbuib techtaib. Dligiḋ saerbiathaḋ ochtair, ocus .u. seotu dia sarugud ocus [dia] esain. H. 3. 18, p. 15.

Flaithem oen escra .i. fer aen cleithe, cona mur ocus a comarbaib techta. Dligiḋ saerbiathaḋ coicir, ocus .iiii. seotu beó slabra dia esain, ocus dia sarugud.

Bo Aire, .i. fer selba bunuid cona inud, no inniud do tir, .x. mba lais; ocus ni goin duine acht a ló catha. Ni toing luige acht fo aen a mbliadain; dligiḋ saerbiathaḋ .iiii. a tuaith, ocus tri seotu bó slabra dia sarugud, ocus dia esain.

Tanuise mbó Aire. Ocht mbai lais, a forus, cona inniud do tir. Dligiḋ saerbiathaḋ triir i tuaith, ocus da seoit bo slabra ina dire.

Huaitne fonluing ocus frisellaghar in fer, .i. frisellgeth troig ocus aideilgen. Fer folaing einech gresa cin imluad fine. Dligiḋ saerbiathaḋ deiri ocus boin leth gab[ala] .u. seotu diasa sarugaḋ, dia esain.

Leth Flaithem, i.e., a man who has two [Sen-]cleithe, with their lawful Comorbs. He is entitled to the free maintenance of eight men, and five Seds for his Sarughudh, and for his Esain. *Leth Flaithem.*

Flaithem oen escra, i.e., a man who has one [Sen-]cleithe, with his residence and his lawful Comorbs. He is entitled to the free maintenance of five men, and to four Seds of Beó-Slabrad for his Sarughudh, and for his Esain. *Flaithem oen escra.*

Bó Aire, i.e., a man who possesses a hereditary Selb with its habitation, or a habitation with its appropriate share of land, with ten cows; and who does not kill a man unless on the day of battle. He does not make oath but once a year; he is entitled to the free maintenance of four persons from his territory, and three Seds of Bó Slabrad for his Sarughudh and for his Esain. *Bó Aire*

Tanuise Bó Aire. He has eight cows, his residence, and sufficient land to maintain them. He is entitled to the free maintenance of three persons in his territory, and to two seds in Bó Slabrad for his Dire. *Tanuise Bó Aire.*

Huaithne fonluing ocus frisellaghar in Fer. "This man is a pillar of endurance and attendance", i.e., he attends the wants of the wretched and the wandering poor. He is a man who suffers the reddening of his face without insult to his tribe. He is entitled to the free maintenance of two persons, and a Boin Lethgabala.[380] He is entitled to five Seds for his Sarughudh and for his Esain. *Huaithne fonluing, etc.*

[380] Besides the regular stated rents and contributions under the name of *Biatha*, *Bes Tigi*, *Folach*, *Cai*, *Fossugud*, etc., there were occasionally special levies or rates in aid, to provide for certain wants of the chief, judges, and others, such as the *Errechs* or forced loans of a king, *Biatad Congbala*, supplies for a convocation for the promulgation of a law. Of this kind, too, was the *Boin Lethgabala*, or rate in aid of a cow levied to meet the requisition of the officer for the relief of the poor.

H. 3. 18. p. 15. Seirṫiud, .i. oclaċ do daġcenel, no fer forais, no mac túisiġ, .i. do nesa do feir túisiġ oc taideċt anndail, no a ndunad, no uair ro bo taiseċ a athair, no daġ a cinel, no ara ġais. Dliġiḋ saerbiathaḋ i tuaiṫ, ocus a ben, ocus sam- H. 3. 18. p. 16. seise focail; ocus colpdach inaeneclann, dia air, dia ainmed.

Na nai ngrada deidinach so, ni teċtait dliġiḋ dia mbret i nairecus, na damrad, na dire sainriuthach, mana narta sealb, no gaes, no sochraite. Ni caemchet dire di theċta, na di thir, na do chrait na hanfolta, uair natat indraice naḋma, na raithe, na haitire, na naill, na fiadnaise.

Fas faiġde, .i. fer ro creca a déis, ocus a ferann, ocus a selb ocus na techta fo tuaith co leir na cleiṫe; ocus co freisce cuile caich, ocus nitat diles, dod cois fri galar no

Seirthiud. Seirthiud, i.e., a young man of good family, or a Fer Forais,[illegible] or the son of a nobleman; he follows next after a chief in proceeding to an assembly or to a Dun, or because his father was a chief, or in right of his descent or of his profession. He is entitled to his free maintenance in the territory for himself and his wife, and to be politely addressed; and to a Colpdach for his honour price, and for his satire, and for his disparagement.

Those last nine grades, the law does not entitle them to the rank of the nobility, or to any special Dire unless they have either property, profession, or hosts. They do not get Dire by inheritance, or by land, or by wealth accumulated by oppression, because they are not eligible as Naidms, or Raiths, or Aitires, or Naillechs, or witnesses.

Fas Faigdhe. Fas Faigdhe, i.e., a man who has squandered his property and his land, and his own estate, and the legal privileges to which he is entitled in his territory, to the manifest knowledge of the chieftain; and though he attends the places of battle, yet it avails him not,

([illegible]) *Fer Forais.* *Forus* was a habitation or official residence of a dignitary of the *Tuath*, at which the fiscal business and a certain part of the legal business of the district was transacted. Thus, for instance, the yard or *Airlis* of a *Forus* was used as a "Pound"; pledges and goods and chattels distrained were kept there, legal fines and contributions levied by the *Flaith*, etc., were paid there (see note 503, App. p. 476). The proprietor of such a house was the *Fer Forais* or *Fer Airlisi*; he could receive payment of the principal sum and costs of a plaint or judgment, and deliver the pledges or articles distrained; when the distress was alleged to be illegal, he might return the articles distrained on the defendant giving sufficient security. The *Forus* was in fact the "office" of a court, and every one entitled to act as magistrate had a *Forus*. There were seven principal *Foruses* in a *Tuath*, viz.: the *Forus Ollomon*, or *Forus* of the *Ollamh*; *Forus Brethemon*, or *Forus* of the Brehon; *Forus Airech etir da Aire*; *Forus Airech Forgaill*; *Forus Aire Tuisi*; *Forus Airech Aird*; *Forus Airech Desa*. *Forus* appears to be related to *Foradh*=Latin *Forum*. Brit. Mus. MSS. Egerton 88, 59 b. a. *et seq.*

sreraid ocus is fas dno cia foighe, mana gata no mana creca H. 3. 18. p. 16.
a enech aire, amail [ar ċan Cormac]:

“Is fas do dno a faithce,
Fria galar ocus a reraid,
mana tabra neċ ni do ar Dia.
Is fas dno a saire ocus a dire
ocus a eneclann”.

Bo geltach faithce, .i. fer meite coimse, na teit tar criċ, naċ do airlisiġ riġ, aċt bid ina mendat fadeisin, ar imgaib comlonn aenḟir o robi cona gaisced fair cona dáim. Cáin cin ḟedain do ningarar. Bo geltach, .i. fer fogelta a bu a faithce ar cach nach déis etar coin allta ime, conadṡi máin insein. Ni dliġ dire na saire, ar is gnim meic no mna do gni.

Aitheċ baitse, .i. fer na saera dan na crebad; ni fuiled re daim in fer sin ina fuil gnimu láich lais. Ni téit a raith na i naitire fri flaiṫ na eclais, ar is gae greine do gairter.

Oinmit. [.i.] Fer miter im droch mnai co, no ona, [acas

being exhausted from an incurable disease, and he is consequently a wilderness although a Foighe,[582] unless he steals, or unless he befouls his Aire-honour as [Cormac said]: Fas Faighde.

“His fields to him are therefore a desert,
With a disease and [not] curable,
Unless one giveth him for sake of God.
His privileges, also his Dire
And honour price are lost”.

Bo-geltach Faithce, i.e., a man of great selfishness, who goes not outside of the territory, nor into the Airlis of the king, but who is always in his own cherished home, because he shuns the combat of one man when equipped in arms and with his company. He is not entitled to the fine of a worthy man. Bogeltach, i.e., a man who protects his cows in the field from everything that is dangerous and from marauding wolf-dogs, so that they are his whole treasure then. He is not entitled to Dire or privilege, because it is the deed of a boy or a woman he does. Bo-geltach Faithce.

Aithech Baitse, i.e., a man who is not ennobled by profession or property; this man who has not the qualificaiions of a man is not received among the grades of society. He does not become guarantee or security for chief or church, so that he is called “the sunbeam”. Aithech Baitse;

Oinmit, i.e., a man who is the husband of a bad wife, on ac- Oinmit.

(582) That is in the condition of such of the decent poor as are obliged to beg.

H. 3. 18. p. 18. ona], ndentar mear ocus fonachtaide, .i. forgenig. Ni dlig dire in fer sin.

Midlach, [.i. miliaig,] .i. midellach, .i. fer na ragaib fealb, na horba, na trebad, na trebtair do. No, midlach, .i. medon ellach insin, ar inni is mellach o delb ocus cinuil, cona damna cimeda insin tar cend tuaithe.

Reimm dno, .i. fuirseoir no druth; nach fer do beir remmad fo corp ocus a enech. Ni dlig dire, uair teit asa richt ar belaib sluag ocus sochaide.

Riascaire, .i. loingsech insin, ar imgaib a chenel ocus a fine, colith cáin ocus rechtge, ocus bidh o riasc do riasc, no o sleib [do sleib]. No riascaire, .i. rathmaige daer do flaith ocus eclais. Ni dlighinn dire.

Sindach brothlaige, .i. bruar cach bid, dó itir dilis ocus indlis, no cuma lais cidbedh bruides no do meala.

Seacht asa midithar duine: cruth, ocus cenel, tir ocus trebad, dán ocus indbus ocus inrucus.

count of whom he is made a fool of and laughed at, i.e., a Forgenigh, i.e., a laughing-stock. That man is not entitled to Dire.

Midlach. Midlach, i.e., a non-resident, i.e., a man without possessions, i.e., a man who has not occupied land or property, who does not work, or for whom there is no work done. Or, Midlach, i.e., he is the centre of deception, because he is deceitful in his appearance and in his nature, so that he is the material of a Cimid[388] then upon his Tuath.

Reimm. Reimm now, i.e., a juggler or a clown; every man who distorts his body or his face. He is not entitled to Dire, because he distorts himself out of his real state in presence of assemblies and crowds.

Riascaire. Riascaire, i.e., he is an outlaw, because he absconds from his family and from his tribe, to evade law and justice, and he goes from wilderness to wilderness, or from mountain to mountain. Or Riascaire, i.e., an ignoble rathbuilder for chiefs and ecclesiastics. He is not entitled to Dire.

Sindach Brothlaige. Sindach Brothlaige, i.e., the dregs of every kind of food for him, both lawful and unlawful, or he cares not what he eats or consumes.

Sechta as a midither duine. The seven things by which man is ennobled, viz., beauty and family, land and habitation, profession and wealth, and righteousness.

[The classification and account of the privileges of the various classes of churchmen, literary and professional men, follow here in MS. H. 3. 18. T.C.D.]

(388) *Cimid*, i.e. *Cimbid*, see note 487, App. p. 474.

III.

THE ANCIENT FAIR OF CARMAN.

From the Book of Ballymote in the Library of the Royal Irish Academy; and the MS. H. 2. 18. commonly known as the Book of Leinster, in the Library of Trinity College, Dublin.

WITH A LITERAL TRANSLATION.

The great fairs anciently held in Ireland were not, like their modern representatives, mere markets, but were assemblies of the people to celebrate funeral games, and other religious rites, during pagan times, to hold parliaments, promulgate laws, listen to the recitation of tales and poems, engage in, or witness, contests in feats of arms, horse racing, and other popular games. They were analogous in many ways to the Olympian, and other celebrated games of ancient Greece. The most—indeed, so far as the Editor knows, the only—satisfactory account we possess of any of those important meetings of the people, is that of the triennial fair held at Carman, now Wexford. This account consists of fragments of one or more poems preserved in the Book of Leinster, the Book of Ballymote, the MS. H. 2. 16. in the library of Trinity College, Dublin, and the MS. H. 3. 3. in the same library. The copies in the three last named manuscripts are substantially the same, and are principally occupied with an account of the origin of the name "Carman" and of the institution of the fair. The poem in the Book of Ballymote looks at first sight like a complete poem; but a closer examination shows that part of it at least is made up of more or less unconnected stanzas. Whether the transcriber of the MS. arranged the poem as it now stands from previous fragments, or merely copied the version of a previous transcriber, it is now perhaps impossible to determine. The copy in the Book of Leinster is apparently complete. Prof. O'Curry has given a translation of a fragment of it in his second lecture (see vol. i. p. 44 *et seq.*). This portion, which fortunately describes the fair itself, is manifestly the end of a long poem, of which the previous part is described in the lecture just referred to as illegible. It appears, however, that he laboured hard to decipher the illegible part, for among his papers has been found a copy of the poem containing twenty-five stanzas more than he had used in his lectures. This copy has all the appearance of having been made from a MS. difficult to be deciphered, and shows that he had expended much labour on the task. Among those unused stanzas are several that are identical with some of those found in the latter part of the copy in the Book of Ballymote, and others which, though agreeing in the subjects, and often in the words of whole lines, present some important deviations from those in the latter MS. This circumstance seems to show that all the fragments belonged originally to one continuous poem or to a series of connected poems; that the commencement of the poem is preserved in the Book of Ballymote, and apparently the whole in the Book of Leinster, the commencement being, however, almost illegible; and that the two copies overlap, and thus afford us a more or less complete copy of the whole. That this was also the opinion of Prof. O'Curry is proved by his efforts to construct a continuous text of the whole poem out of the two MSS.

The very great importance of this poem for the ancient history of Ireland, the fact that only a portion of it has been translated by Prof. O'Curry, and that portion given in his lectures without the original text, have induced the Editor to print the entire of the latter so far as it can be completed from the Books of Ballymote and Leinster, following in the case of the latter the transcript of Prof. O'Curry. From stanza 1 to 24 inclusive, the text is that of the Book of Ballymote, with the exception of stanza 14, which is inserted from Professor O'Curry's transcript, into what appears to be its proper position. From stanza 25 inclusive, the transcript of Prof. O'Curry is followed; the stanzas 25 to 48 inclusive being the part which he did not use in his lectures, and consequently did not translate, and which he probably had not deciphered when he wrote his second lecture.

The stanzas which are common to the Books of Ballymote and Leinster are those numbered 49, 50, 51, 52, 53, 70, 71, 72, 77 in the following pages. From this it will be seen that the copy in the former MS. is not a fragment complete as far as it goes, but an abridged version, either deliberately made, or, what is more probable, taken down from the dictation of some one who only remembered occasional stanzas. As has been above stated, some of the stanzas common to the two MSS. differ more or less. In such cases, the text follows the Book of Leinster, and the variations are printed from the Book of Ballymote as foot notes. The latter MS., contains a stanza which ought from its position to come between stanzas 69 and 70, but which is not found in the Book of Leinster copy. As the poem is now arranged it would be out of place there; the only place where it could have been introduced without interfering with the narrative of the poem is perhaps between stanzas 76 and 77. But as there is obviously something else wanting, it could not be introduced into the poem without injury to its continuity, and it has accordingly been put in a foot note.

In order to make the following edition of the poem as complete as possible, two prose introductions are also given; the one in the text from the Book of Ballymote; that given in the foot note, imperfect in the beginning and obscure in some passages, is from Prof. O'Curry's copy, and apparently belonging to the version of the Book of Leinster. The two stanzas with which the last introduction commences appear to have been the first two stanzas of a poem relating the history of the seven chief cemeteries of Eriu, namely *Tailtiu*, *Cruachan*, the *Brugh* of the Boyne, *Carman*, *Cuile*, *Tallacht*, and *Teamar* of *Dun Finntain*. The subject is of very great interest, and the poem may perhaps be still preserved in some Irish MSS. But if so, it is probably, like the following poem on Carman, only to be found in detached fragments in various MSS., and hitherto unknown in its complete form.

The old vellum MS. in the Library of the Royal Irish Academy, known as the *Leabhar na h-Uidhre*, contains two tracts on the ancient Cemetery of *Cruachan*, the first of which begins on fol. 41, b. b., and is headed senċas na relec inso, " the History of the Cemeteries here". It opens with a prose introduction which n printed with a translation by Dr. Petrie, at p. 96 of his Essays on the nd uses of the Round Towers', etc., and which he considers to have been re of the *Senchas na Relec*. It is, however, only the prose introduction es of pieces in prose and verse, on the Cemetery of *Cruachan*, which are und in the same MS., as parts of the two tracts above mentioned. Thus tely following the introduction printed by Dr. Petrie, is a poem of eighty-rses attributed to *Cuan O'Lotchain*, who died A.D. 1024, on the death ac *Mac Airt*, and his burial at *Ros na Righ* on the Boyne, and also on al of many of the distinguished nobles and chiefs of Eiriu. It begins: "An aig mic Indoc", on fol. 42, a. b., and ends on fol. 42. b. a. The second on the burial of King *Dathi*, commencing on fol. 35, b. a., with a short prose ction, which is followed by a poem of two stanzas addressed to the palace netery of *Cruachan*, by *Torna Eigeas*. Professor O'Curry has given a ranslation of this poem at p. 71, vol. i. of the present series of lectures, hout the original text, which begins: "A ta fotra ri rir find fail". followed by a short poem of *Dorban*, in which are preserved the names r of the nobles and chief poets buried at *Cruachan*, and which has been also d by Dr. Petrie in the work above mentioned. This poem ends on fol. 36, th the same words with which the first tract begins on fol. 41. b. b., namely, enċas na relec insin. "That is the History of the Cemeteries". Thus g with the well known custom of old writers, who invariably ended their nd other pieces with the same words with which they commenced, in indicate that the piece so far was complete. It would thence appear e two tracts just described, though now separated from each other in the d the end placed before the beginning, were originally parts of a large, doubt once complete history of the ancient pagan cemeteries of Eiriu. re now no means of ascertaining how much of this history has been lost, very probable that the two stanzas of the poem at the beginning of the introduction to the following poem, on the "Fair of Carman", formed the *Senchas na Relec*. It may be, too, that the poem on the "Fair of ", itself, as well as a poem on the "Fair of Tailltiu", which has not yet blished, also belonged to the same collection.

ssor O'Curry, in making out his copy of the text of the part of the poem ed in the Book of Leinster, made some emendations, no doubt the result re careful examination of the obscure text of the original. This will in part any variations in the translation of the whole poem, which the thought it desirable to add to the following edition of the text, from that y Professor O'Curry himself of the parts which he quoted in his second

s the Editor's intention at first to add copious notes explanatory of the whose names are mentioned in the following poem, and to endeavour to from it some chronological data—and from this point of view the poem is portant; but this he soon found would require a very long time. Not to delay the publication of the Lectures longer, he leaves to another to other hands this task.

AENACH CARMAIN.

B. of Ballymote, fol. 193, b. a.

Carmun canair ro hainmneḋ. Nin; triar fer tangadar a hAthain, agas oen ben leo, .i. tri mic Dibaid, mac Doirci, mac Aincheis iad .i Dian agas Dub, agus Doṫur a nanmann, agas Carmen ainm a mathar.

Tria briċtu, agas dicetla, agas cantana no luited in mathair caċ maigin; tria fogail agus esinnrucus imorro ro milloir na fir.

Doloḋar, dona, co hErenn ar ulc frì Tuata D. D. ducoll eta na hindsise forro. Olc iaram la Tuaiṫ D. D. innsin; do luid Ai, mac Olloman o filed; agas Creidenbel o caintib; agas Lug Laeban, .i. mac Caicair, o druidib; agus Becuille o na bantuathaib do cedal forrosom; agas ni ros carrsat friu cor cuirset in triar fer dar muir, agas facsat angiallu isus .i. Carmen a maṫair, ar na tisdais co hEre a frithisi; agus tucsat dia cind insecta nossognad, na ticfaidis airet beṫ muir im h-Ere.

Ba marb isus a mathair sin do cumaid ina giallaċt; agus rocuinnḋiġ for Tuatha D. D. airm maicfidea conagtais a haenuch and, agas combad é a h-ainm no beith an aenaċ sin; agas in maigin sinn; ocus unde Carman agus aenaċ Carman. Agas fognitsea T. D. D. hinnsin airet badar in hEre.

No ata, sean Garman tainic in degaid .uii. neṙc n-Echeċ tuc Lena, Mac Messroeda, agas Uca, ingen Oeca, ri Cerca a maṫair in mac sin; agas baben sen Messceagra mac Dato rig Laigen.

Iarom badar, dno, maraen la Lena, ic setaḋ in buair sin, hic Sen, mac Duirb; agas Locar Luaṫ, mac Smiraiġ; agas Gunnait, mac Succait; agas Altaċ, mac Duilb; agus Mucur, mac Largaiġ. For fuair sen Garman ic Rait Big, fri dun mic Daṫo anner. Marbṫair Uċa iarum, conabanntroċt, agas in miliḋ tucsat in mbuair, agas tucsat sen Garmun leis a buair comag Mersa, ingine Buidb, iar na breiṫ dosom a riḋ Finnchad isleḃ Monaid, i n-Albain; conabaṫ Mersa ar

THE FAIR OF CARMAN.

Carman, why so called? Answer. Three men who came from Athens, and one woman with them, i.e., the three sons of Dibad, son of Dorcha, son of Ainches, i.e., Dian, Dubh, and Dothur, were their names, and Carman was the name of their mother. Introduction.

By charms, and spells, and incantations the mother blighted every place, and it was through magical devastation and dishonesty that the men dealt out destruction.

They, however, came to Eriu to bring evil upon the Tuatha Dé Danann by blighting the fertility of this isle upon them. The Tuatha Dé Danann were incensed at this; and they sent against them Ai, the son of Ollamh, on the part of their Poets; and Credenbel on the part of their Satirists; and Lug Laeban, i.e., the son of Cacher, on the part of their Druids; and Becuille on the part of their Witches, to pronounce incantations against them; and they never parted from them until they forced the three men over the sea, and they left a pledge behind them, i.e., Carman, their mother, that they would never again return to Eriu; and they swore by the divinities they adored, that they would not return as long as the sea encircled Eriu.

Their mother, however, soon died of the grief of her hostageship; and she requested of the Tuatha Dé Danann that they would celebrate her fair in the place where she should be buried, and that the fair and the place should retain her name for ever; and hence Carman and the fair of Carman. And the Tuatha Dé Danann celebrated this fair as long as they occupied Eriu.

"Another version is that old Garman had followed the seven cows of Eochaidh, which cows had been carried off by Lena, the son of Mesroed; and Uca, the daughter of Occa, king of Cert, was his mother, and she was the wife of Mesceagra, son of Datho, king of Leinster.

There were also along with Lena, driving these cows away, Sen, the son of Durb; and Locar the swift, son of Smirach; and Gunnat, the son of Succat; and Altach, son of Dulbh; and Motur, the son of Largach. Old Garman discovered them at Rath Beg, on the south side of Datho's Dun. He killed Uca then, with her women, and the men who took away the cows, and old Garman drove away his cows to the plain of Mesc, the daughter of Bodb, whom he had carried away from Sidh Finnchaidh in Sliab Monad, in Alba; and Mesc died of shame in this place, and her grave was made

B. of Ballymote, fol. 193, b. a.

naire isin maighinsin, agas foclas a fert ann, .i. fert Mesca, ingini Buiḋḃ, agas rucsat .iiii. mic Daṫo, .i. Mes Seda, agas Mes Roeda, agas Mes Deda, acas Mes Delmon for sen Garmun[384] isin maigin sin, agas do ċear sean Garman ann; agas foclasa a fert ann, agas conait esin aeinuċ nguba do gnim ann; agas comḃeṫ a ainm inaenaċ sin agas in maigin sin do gres: agus unde Carmun agus sen Carmund ainmniugaḋ.

Agas fognitis Laigin in sin ar trebaib agas ar teallaigib, ca Caṫair mor. Ni sarlaig Caṫair, umorro, Carman, aċt dia maicnide agus otellaiġib fodeisin, agus remċus la sil Rosa Failgi, a forgabail; agas a ndeoraid, ilurg inaenaiġ; ut sunt Laigsi agas Foṫairt.

Seċt ngraifni ann, agas .uii. main sri agad breċa agus do cearta a cuicid sri tri bliadnaib.

Is ann fognitis Laigin dearggabair in laiṫi ndedenaċ de, is de adberar eċtres Osairgi. Forud a rig for deis ri Carmun, forud ri .h. Failgi for a cliu; agas is amlaḋ aman.

Hi Kailaind Augusd no teigdis ind, agas is seaċaid Augusd no tigdis as; agas gaċ tres bliadain fognidis; agas da bliaḋain fria ṫairec.

lxxx. agas u. bliadain oriognid an cetna aenaċ ann, cus in dara bliaḋain xl. flaṫas Octauam Augusti, irrogenair Crist.

Ich agas bliċt doib ar a denum, agas cen forran coigid in hEren forraib, agas sir riaglaig leo, agas suba la caċ saintreb, agas caċ mes martaidbsin, lina lanu o uscib. Agas meṫ agas mochleṫi rig oca doib, muna denut in sin. Eistig.

1. Estiḋ a Laigniu na lecht,
   a sluaig oraigni rad chert,
   co fagbaid uaim as ceċ aird,
   caem senċas carmuin cloċ aird.

2. Carman cete oenaig ḟeil,
   co faiċti roenaig ro reid;
   in tsluaig tictis dia taiċme,
   ar sigtis a glan graifni.

(384) This Garman may perhaps be the *German* of the *Táin Bó Chuailgne*. See the Fight of *Ferdiad*, *ante*, Appendix, p. 459.

e, namely, the grave of Mesc, the daughter of Bodb, and the sons of Mac Datho, namely, Mes Sed, and Mes Roed, and Ded, and Mes Delmon, overtook old Garman at this place, and Garman(584) fell by them there; and they made his grave there, so he begged of them to institute a fair of mourning for him e; and that the fair and the place should bear his name for : and hence Carman and old Carmund have their names".

nd the people of Leinster celebrated this fair by their tribes and heir families, down to the time of Cathair Mór. Cathair, how-, bequeathed Carman to his own sons and their families, and ave the precedence to the race of Ros Failgi, their dependent iches, and their exiles; to continue the fair; namely, the Laigsi the Fothairt.

here were seven races there, and a week for considering the laws the rights of the province for three years.

; was on the last day that the Leinstermen of Gabhra south l their fair, which was called the steed-contest of the Ossorians. Forud of their king was on the right of the king of Carman, Forud of the king of O Failge on his left; and their women were ed in the same manner.

t was on the Kalends of August they assembled there, and it on the sixth of August they used to leave it; and every d year they were wont to hold it; and two years for the parations.

t was five hundred and eighty years since the first fair was held e, to the forty-second year of the reign of Octavius Augustus, which Christ was born.

Corn and milk [were promised] to them for holding it, and that sway of no province in Eriu should be upon them, and brave gly heroes with them, and prosperity in every household, and ry fruit in great abundance, and plentiful supplies from their ers. And failure and early grayness of their young kings, if y did not hold it.(585) Listen.

1. Listen, O Lagenians of the monuments,
   Ye truth-upholding hosts,
   Until you get from me, from every source,
   The pleasant history of far-famed Carman.

2. Carman, the field of a splendid fair,
   With a widespread unobstructed green
   The hosts who came to celebrate it,
   On it they contested their noble races.

(585) The following somewhat different version of the prose introduction, igh imperfect, is very interesting, because it shows that the celebrated ient Fairs appear to have been always held around the ancient pagan eteries:—

3. Is reilec rig inruaim rán,
cid sainferc sluag co saergraid;
sailmor do dumaib dála,
da slog bunaid biṫġrada.

4. Do cainiud rigain is rig,
d'faidiud digal is mignim,
bat minci findsluaig fogmair,
dar slimgruaid saer sen Carmuin.

Sen Garman tanic indegaid .uii. nerc Echach, tuc Lena mac Mesroeda r.

Old Garman, who came in pursuit of the seven cows of Echad, which were carried off by Len the son of Mesroed, etc.

uii. primreilge h-Erenn ut dixit.

The seven principal cemeteries of Eriu, *ut dixit*:—

Ata sund .uii. relg dlaide:
relec Thalten ria ṫoga,
relec Cruaċna cimaire,
ocus relec in Broga,

These are the seven sepulchral cemeteries:
The cemetery of Tailtė to be chosen,
The cemetery of Cruachan of sai-ness,
And the cemetery of the Brugh.

Relec Carmain cuiredaig,
oenaċ Cuile cocimtaib,
martra muintire Partalain,
ocus Temair Dun Fintain.

The cemetery of Carman of heroes,
Oenach Culle with its appropriations,
The mortuary of the people of Parthalon,
And Tesmar of Dun Fintan.

Is amlaid do gnitis indoenaċsa, iar trebaib ocus cenelaib ocus tellaigib, co Caṫair Mar; ocus nis farlaic Cathair, imorro, acht da macnide fodein, ocus remthus le sil Rosa Failge, a forgabail ocus a ndeoraid, illurg indoenaig, ut .uii. Laigsi ocus Fothairt; ocus is leo sin a cor ocus a comairgi ic dul ind ocus ic tuideċt ass, ar caċ necraiti. Uii. n-graifni and in caċ ló, ocus .uii. laa fria denam, [aigid] ocus breṫa ocus coicerta a coicid fria tri bliadnaib. Is and no chindis Ossairge, imorro, in laṫe dedenaċ de, ocus tuairt ceċ laiṫe ria scur; is de asberar Eċtress Ossairge. Forud a rig for a dess rig Lagan, ocus forud rig hua Failge for a chliu; is amlaid a mnaa.

Thus it is they used to hold this fair, by their tribes and families and households, to the time of Cathair Mor; and Cathair, however, bequeathed not Carman unto any but to his own descendants, and the precedence is bequeathed to the race of Ros Failge, their followers and their exiles, to continue the fair *ut* the seven Laigsechs and the Fotharts; and to them belongs [the right] to celebrate it, and to secure it from every disaster [while] going thither and returning thence. There were seven races there every day, and seven days for celebrating it, and for considering the laws and rights of the province for three years. It was on the last day of it the Ossorians held their fair, and they coursed it every day before closing; and hence it was called the steed contest of the Ossorians. The Forud of their king was on the right hand of the king of Leinster, and the Forud of the king of Ua Failge was on his left hand; and in the same manner their women.

3. The renowned field is the cemetery of kings,
The dearly loved of noble grades;
There are many meeting mounds,
For their ever loved ancestral hosts.

4. To mourn for queens and for kings,
To denounce aggression and tyranny,
Often were the fair hosts in autumn
Upon the smooth brow of noble old Carman.

Kalaind August no tegtis ind,
us i sesid August tictis ass. Cech
es bliadain do gnithea; ocus da
iadain fria tairec. Lxxx ocus
ic cet bliadain ordgnaid in chet
nach i Carmain, cosin dara bliad-
.xl. [do flathus] Octavam Au-
sti ingenair Crist.

On the Kalends of August they assembled there, and on the sixth of August they left it. Every third year they were wont to hold it; and [it took] two years for the preparations. It was five hundred and eighty years from the holding of the first fair in Carman, to the forty-second year of [the reign of] Octavius Augustus, in which year Christ was born.

Tri marggaid ann .i. marggad
ocus etaig; marggad beochruid,
ocus ech, etc.; margga gall ocus
oraid itreice oir ocus argait,
. Lucht cech dana, eter primdan
is fodán, ocus michomic ic reice
is ic taisbenad a n-drécht ocus a
ligid do rig; ocus erned ar cech
an as dir ocus is dliged do reice
is daisein ocus do chlostecht.

Three markets there, viz., a market of food and clothes; a market of live stock, cows and horses, etc.; a market of foreigners and exiles selling gold and silver, etc. The professors of every art, both the noble arts and the base arts, and non-professionals were there selling and exhibiting their compositions and their professional works to kings; and rewards were given for every [work of] art that was just or lawful to be sold, or exhibited, or listened to.

ch ocus bliche doib ar a denam,
is cen forran coiced nechtrand
raib, acht co ro ainet, ocus co ro
issetet, feraib, mnaaib, maccaib
o ingenaib, deoraid, aurraid,
chaib ocus clercaib; mécha, ocus
a la cach saintreib, ocus cach
ss mára chaidbrin. ocus lina lán
ircib, ocus almuire co tir La-
.
Mech imorro ocus mechi ocus mo-
chi da feraib, ocus riglaic, ocus,
a; ocus tuitim a ferainn no a
g on ti ticfa taris, fir riglaich,
is mna; meach rig óca, etgud
uchach, ocus maili, meni dernta;
Fulartach, cc.

Corn and milk [were promised] to them for holding it, and that the sway of any invading province should not be over them, but that they should observe the Fridays, and that they should fast, men, women, boys, maidens, as well as exiles, chiefs, champions, and clerics. [They were also promised] prosperity and comfort in every household, and fruits of every kind in abundance, and abundant supplies from their waters, and fertility to the land of Leinster. And, moreover, that decay and failure and early grayness should come upon their men, kingly heroes, and women; and the forfeiture of his land or its price from him who evades it, men, kingly heroes, and women; [and that failure of] young kings, mean clothes, and baldness would come on them unless they celebrated it, Ut Fulartach cc.

34 B

5. In fir, no in fer co mét gal,
no in ben co nert anbal,
tuc ainm cen mes margnaid,
tuc ainm diles deg Carmain?

6. Ni fir, is ni fer fergaċ,
ach aenben dian, dibergaċ,
gluair a Carmun isa tairm,
o fuair Carman a cet ainm.

7. Carmun, ben mic Dibaid dein,
mic Doirce dirmaig dág féil,
mic Ancgeis, co met raṫa,
ba cend airdmeis ilċatha.

8. Nis tailced tairc tarba,
fri sainseirc na saerbanba,
daig ba smimaig ceċ amm tair,
cland mic Dibaid sa maċair.

9. Cengsat siar don dara cur,
Dian agus Dub agus Dothur,
ond Áṫain aidben anair,
agus Carmen a mathair.

10. Fognidis[366] im Tuathaib Dé,—
ind aes nuaċair[367] naimtide,—
torud caċ thalman co triaig:
bo fogal, adbal ecair.

11. Carmun as caċ briċt co m-blaid,
aidctgled caċ m-bliċt m-borrtoraid,
iar ngleicc as caċ dan nar dleċt,
na meic tria ág tria arreċt.

12. Ba luaṫ roratais Tuaṫ Dé,
rosbraṫaig uaṫ i samgné;
ar ceċ nomgnim gniset so,
sniset a comlin chucco.

13. Criṫenbel ba saibad sin,
Is Lug Laibaċ mac Caiċir;
Becuille ar caċ rae narag,
acas Ai mac Ollaman.

14. Ro raidsed riu iar roċtain,—
in ceṫrar cruaid comfortail,—
ben sund icend sarmaṫar,
triar fer don triur derbraṫar.

(366) no milcis in other copies.
(367) A d has been elided here; the word was originally n-duaċar, in mod

5. Was it men, or was it a man of great valour,
Or was it a woman of violent jealousy,
Gave the name without the merit of noble deeds,—
Bestowed the true name of beautiful Carman?

6. It was not men, and it was not a fierce man,
But a single woman fierce, rapacious,
Great her rustling and her tramp,
From whom Carman received its first name.

7. Carman, the wife of the fierce Mac Dibad,
Son of Dorcha, of legions and choice hospitality,
The son of Ancges, of rich rewards,
The renowned hero of many battles.

8. They sought not the profits of industry,
Through ardent love of noble Banba,
For they were at all times toilers in the east,—
The sons of Mac Dibad and their mother.

9. At length they westwards came,
Dian and Dubh and Dothur,
From delightful Athens westward,
And Carman their mother.

10. They used to destroy upon the Tuatha Dé,—
The wicked malignant race,—
The produce of every land unto the shore:
It was a great, an oppressive evil.

11. Carman by all powerful spells,
Destroyed every growing productive fruit,
After each unlawful art being tried [by]
The sons with violence, with injustice.

12. Soon as the Tuatha Dé perceived
What deprived them of their summer bloom,
For every evil deed which they wrought,
They hurled an equal deed upon them.

13. Critenbel, he was a Sab,[588]
And Lug Laibech, son of Cachir;
Becuille in every field entangled them,
And Ai the son of Ollam.[589]

14. They said to them when they arrived,—
The four warriors of equal valour,—
Here is a woman instead of your mother,
Three men for your three brothers.

Irish a cognate form of ᴅochaꞃ, evil,—the opposite of ꞅochaꞃ, good. The word as written in the text, would mean nuaċaꞃ, a companion, consort, husband, or wife.

[588] See note, 569, App. p. 511.

[589] These names also occur in the tale of the second battle of *Magh Tuired*.

15. Bas duib ni rogain roga,
ni soraid, ni saer toga;
facbaid go gle grind giall,
ercid a h-Erind oentriar.
16. Na srirsin do chuadar uain,—
sri a ruaca co roċruaid;
ciar bad ben leo facbait sund,
Carmun, beo na cru cumang.
17. Caċ fir dar na tecar slán,
muir, mil, nem, talam tondbán,
na tisat tess na tuir ċind,
cein no beiṫ muir im h-Erind.
18. Carman, ruc bas is báidi,
nosaidled a sencained,
fuair a haidid, mar ro dleċt,
etir dairib na n-dronfert.
19. Tancas sund, tria gaine gnó,
dia caine, dia cet gubo,
le Tuaiṫ De dar saersmag sain,
cetna oenaċ coir Carmain.
20. Fertan Carmain, cia roċlaid,
in fagbaid, no in fetabair,
iar mes ceċ deg atar dil,
Bres mac Eladan, eistid. E.

21. Ceṫri ficid coic cet cain,
fail uad, nibréc, do bliadnaib,
o Charmain fo ċirt caċt,
co salmgein isu iar n-doennaċt.
22. A da bliadain, trichat, ceiṫri cet,
o gein Crist,—ni saeb in séc—
co Crimthan os Carmuin cuċt,
co Patraic nadbal necruċt.
23. Coic ri trichat, cen trist tair,
do Laignib, ria Crist craitid,
a nuail os h-Erind rosaig,
dit ċuain celbind, a Charmain.
24. Coic rig coicait(590) saeċraċ se,
do Laeċraid na crisraide,
o Chrimthan, comdas na cned,
co Diarmait Dornmas Durgen.

(590) See note 502, App. p. 476.
(591) That is the four elements.

15. Death to ye we choose not nor desire,
It is neither [our] pleasure or free choice;
Assign with openness a proper pledge,
And depart out of Eriu each of you three.

16. Those men then from us departed,—
They were expelled with great difficulty;
Though a woman of theirs they left there,
Carman, alive in her narrow cell.

17. Every oath from which there is no release—[590]
Sea, fire, Heaven, and the fair-faced Earth,—[591]
That in power or weakness they ne'er would return,
As long as the sea encircled Eriu.

18. Carman, who gave death and battles,
Once so destructive with her spells,
Received her fate, as she well deserved,
Among the oaks of these firm mounds.

19. Hither came, to celebrate her [funeral] rites,
To lament her, to inaugurate her Guba,[592]
The Tuatha Dé, upon the noble beautiful plain:
This was the first regular fair of Carman.

20. The grave of Carman, by whom was it dug?
Will you learn, or do you know?
According to all our beloved forefathers,
It was Bres, son of Eladan. Listen.

21. Four score and five fair hundreds,
Is the number, not false, of years,
From Carman of demoniac spells,
To the manifested birth of Jesus after humanity.[593]

22. Two years, thirty, and four hundred,
From the birth of Christ—not small the span—
To Crimthan over Carman's plain,
To Patrick the great and glorious.

23. Five kings and thirty, without neglect of the tryst
Of Leinstermen, before the faith of Christ,
Their fame extended over Eriu,
From thy sweet-sounding harbour, O Carman.

24. Five and fifty vigilant kings,
Of the champions of Christianity,
From Crimthan, inflictor of wounds,
To Diarmad Dornmas Durgen.

(592) Wailings for the dead. See vol. ii. pp. 383, 384.
(593) That is, after he had assumed human nature.
(594) u. l. ıc ꞃıg, i.e. five times fifty kings.—H. 3 3.

25. Oċt mic Golaim lin a slog,
Donn h-Ir, Eber, is h-Eremon,
Amairgin, Colptha cenċriad,
h-Erech Febria, is Erennán.
26. Ropiad sain ratha ind oenaig,
ceċ trata re tren maidim,
oc toċt ind, oc tuideċt ass,
co tainic treitem n-amnas.
27. O Thuaiṫ Dé co Claind Miled,
ba din roban is rigfer;
o Claind Miled ba gnim n-gle
ba din co Patraic Machae.
28. Nem, talam, grian, esca, is muir,
toirthi, tnu, ocus turċuir,
beoil, cluasa, suili saobtha,
cosa, lama, sroin, is deta.
29. Eich, claidib, carpait caime,
gai, sceith, drecha doeine,
druchta, mess, daiten, la duli,
la is adaig, trais tromtuili.
30. do ratsat sain uile a nós,
buidni Banba cen biṫ brón,—
conna bech ro ċabair chéit,—
ceċ tresas bliadain tar tairmesc.
31. doringet genti gaedel,
i Carmain, re thrénmaidem;
oenaċ cen cáin, cen cinaid,
cen gnim aiġ, cen essidain.
32. Luċt baisti Crist na celid,
i Carmain, is daig, is deimin,
is mo dlegait crist ar teċt,
o Crist cosa cristaideċt.
33. Rigi ocus naem h-Erend,
im Patraic, is im Crimthann,
iat rathrenfastsat caċ cat,
ro bennaċsat in oenaċ.
34. A .ix. triċat oenaċ ard,
do bith os bruaċaib Carman;
coica na trenmedon trist,
ó hEremon co Patraic.
35. A coic ceṫri deiċ datta,
ar sreiṫ oenaig allatta;
o Bresal Broenaċ cen brat
cosin n-oenaċ n-dedenaċ.

25. The eight sons of Gollamh with their full host,
Dond, Ir, Eber, and Heremon,
Amergin, Colptha the griefless,
Ereach Febria, and Erennan.

26. These were the upholders of the fair,
To be ever highly boasted of,
Coming thither, going thence;
To the advent of the all-ruling faith.

27. Of the Tuatha Dé to the sons of Miledh,
Was a race of upright women and brave men;
Of the sons of Miledh of bright deeds
Was the race to Patrick of Macha.

28. Heaven, Earth, sun, moon, and sea,
Fruits, fire, and riches,
Mouths, ears, alluring eyes,
Feet, hands, noses, and teeth.

29. Steeds, swords, beautiful chariots,
Spears, shields, human faces,
Dew, fruits, blossoms, and foliage,
Day and night, a heavy flooded shore.

30. These in fulness all were there,
The tribes of Banba without lasting grief,—
To be under the protection of the fair,
Every third year without prohibition.

31. The gentiles of the Gaedhil did celebrate,
In Carman, to be highly boasted of,
A fair without [breach of] law, without crime,
Without a deed of violence, without dishonour.

32. The followers of Christ's baptism deny not,
That in Carman, right true,
More regular became the tryst
From Christ to the [introduction] of Christianity.

33. The kings and the saints of Eriu,
With Patrick, and with Crimthan,
Each clan they bravely controlled,
The fair they blessed.

34. Nine times thirty high fairs,
Were celebrated over the shores of Carman,
Fifty in its high central tryst,
From Heremon to Patrick.

35. Five four tens[595] is the date
Over which the noble fair extended,
From Breasal Broenach without guile
To the last holding of the fair.

(595) Five, and four tens, i.e. 540 years.

36. o Chrimthund in chroṫa cain
o Chathair . . . . .
a naoi raglana cen raind,
ra fil Labrada laechmaill.
37. Se rig dec ro derbaig dam,
ceċ fuil, ceċ fenċaid folam;
o Charmun na cuan craebaċ,
do rat sluag san slat oenaċ.
38. A h-ocht a Dothra doinich,—
sluag sochla ra srimaidim,—
gniset oenaċ coir Carmain
fo gloir, is fo glan armaib.
39. A do déc cen ruḋ imraind,
doenaigib urgna atmaim;
do ċuir gribda in gaisced,
on t-ḟil rigda ardo Marsiu.
40. A coiċ a fiogaible garg,
fichset os Carmain ċlotaird;
oenaċ saidbir, co sreṫaib,
co saidlib, co srian-eċaib.
41. Seisiur don raigni reimnig,
do ḟil Bresail Bric beimnig;
sluag find ra faglaib fuinid,
os ċruaid Carmain ċetguinig.
42. Patraic, Brigit immalle,
Caemgin is Colam Cille;
iat is airchech ar ceċ sluag,
na ro laimṫer amarcsluag.
43. Oenaċ na naeb nert dia chur,
ar tus is cert Dia ċorugud;
oenaċ ardrig flaiṫis glain,
issed bis ina degaid.
44. Cluchi ban Laigen iar ló,
on tṡluag ra gel—ni rad ngó:
bantraċt naċ bec mess immaċ,
issed a ceti in tress oenaċ.
45. Lairg Fothairt, fota a m-blad,
leo dareis coṫa na m-ban;
is leo Laigin lin a séd,
na dagḟir da h-imċomet.
46. Ra rigdamnaib sruthi sund,
in coiced cluċi i Carmund;

(569) See note 567, App. p. 510.

36. From Crimthan of the comely form,
From Cathair . . . .
Nine were celebrated without intermission
By the race of Labrad, the princely hero.

37. Sixteen kings to me have been recorded,
By every Sai,[396] and profound historian,
From Carman of the branchy harbours,
Who brought hosts unto the noble fair.

38. Eight from the populous Dodder,—
Renowned hosts ever to be boasted of,—
They celebrated the regular fair of Carman
With pomp and with bright arms.

39. Twelve, without an error in the counting,
Of festive fairs I acknowledge,
To the fierce champion, of valour,
Of the regal race of noble Maistiu.

40. Five from Fidgabhla the stern,
Celebrated over Carman of high renown,
A rich fair, with bridles,[397]
With saddles, with bridle-steeds.

41. Six by the royal triumphant heir,
Of the race of Breasal Breac of mighty blows—
A fair host with resplendent spears,
Over the cell of the battle-wounding Carman.

42. Patrick and Bridget together,
Caemgen and Colum Cille,
They are dominant over every host,
And they durst not be "cavalcaded".

43. The fair of the saints, with pomp is celebrated,
'T is meet at first to pay homage to God,
The fair of the high king of bright heaven,
It is after the [latter] it comes.

44. The fair of the women of Leinster in the afternoon,
A noble most delightful host—'t is no false assertion:
Women whose fame is not small abroad,
Their fair is the third fair.

45. The Laisechs of Fothairt, wide their fame:
To them is the stewardship of the coteries of the women:
Leinster with all her jewels to them belongs,
The chosen men for its protection.

46. To mirthful royal princes belongs
The fifth game at Carman;

(397) The *Sreith* was the double reined or parade bridle, as distinguished rom the *Srian* (= *sreith* + *ean*) i.e. the one-reined bridle.

sluaig enig h-Erend, mared,
doib ra ṫengell in ferred.
47. Ba deoid la Clannaib Condla,
cluċi Carmun dag comga,
seċ ceċ sluag, saer in soċar,—
os caċ roen, is rigthorud.
48. Seċt cluchi, mar damair dait,
issed forfacaib Patraic,
in caċ la ra seċtmain sain,
ar bar sercblaid sir eistid. E.

49. Do nitis Laigin in sain,
iar trebaib, iar tellaigib,
o Labraid Longseċ li sluag,[598]
co Cathair comseċ clethruaḋ.
50. Ni farlaic Cathair Carmain,
aċt dia maicni mor adbail;
na thossach co saidbri sain,
sil Rosa Failge segaid.
51. Forud rig Argat Rois ain,[599]
for deis rig Carmuin caemnair;
dia laim ċli cendaid, bri n-duail,
forud rig Gaible Gé-Cluain;
52. Is lorg ra sil Lugdaċ Loir
Laigsiċ, mac Conaill Cendmoir;
is Fothairt naċ taidli tair,
cen daibri dia marmoraċt.

(598) Li sluaġ, glittering hosts. In the Book of Ballymote version this is made lir suaḋ, i.e. of many poets, that is, he was patron of bards. Both terms are equally applicable to prince *Labrad*.

(599) The matter of stanzas 51, 52, and 53 is given in four stanzas in the Book of Ballymote, as follows:—

26. Forud riġ Argat rois ain,
for deis riġ Carmuin caem
nair;
dia cliu, sri gaċ luṫġair
luind,
forud riġ Cruaċain cleṫ
cuirr;

26. The *Forud* of the noble king of
Airget-Ros,
On the right of the king of beautiful Carman;
On his left, with all athletic
sports,
The *Forud* of the king of Cruachan—the lofty hero;*

27. Is lorg ra sil Lugdaċ Loir
Laigsiċ, mac Conaill Cendmoir;

27. And the progeny of the numerous
race of Lugad
Laigsech, son of Conall Cedmoir;

* The Cruachan here meant is Cruachan Claenta or Offaly.

The host of Eriu's bounteous men, with their jewels,
To them the sixth fair is assigned.

47. After this the Clan Cunla follow,
The fair of Carman duly celebrating,
Beyond each host, a noble race,—
On every field, a royal progeny.

48. Seven games, as to you we have told,
That is what Patrick ordained,
On every day of the sportive week,
Enjoining that to sweet devotions they should ever listen. Listen.

49. The Leinstermen continued to hold this fair,
By their tribes, by their families,
From Labrad Longsech of glittering hosts,
To the powerful red-speared Cathair.

50. Cathair bequeathed Carman,
Only to his own great and powerful race;
At their head with splendour bright,
The race of Ros Failge we behold.

51. The *Forud* [600] of the noble king of Airget Ros,
On the right of the king of beautiful Carman;
On his left hand stands, in right of inheritance,
The Forud of the king of Gaible Gé-Cluain;

52. And the progeny of the numerous race of Lugad
Laigsich, son of Conall Cendmor;
And the Fotharts who knew no thirst,
Without derogation to their ancestral inheritance.

is Fothairt co saidbir set,— cendaidbri don dichoimed.	And the Fotharts rich in jewels— Not degrading to the noble guardians.
28. Hi kalaind August cen ail, tiagdais ind gach tres bliadain, agtais .uii. ngraifne im gnim gle, secht laithe na sechtmaine.	28. On the Kalends of August without fail, They repaired thither every third year; They contested seven well-fought races, On the seven days of the week.
29. And luaigdis sin baga bil, certa acas cana in coig[ce],— cech recht riagla co rogan,— cech tres bliadain a corogad.	29. There they proclaimed in friendly words, The rights and laws of the province;— Every right of law they proclaimed,— Every third year they revised them.

[600] A *Forud* was the place in which each king sat surrounded by his *Sabaid* or counsellors, and his *Dam* or retinue. The seat of the king seems to have been on the top of a mound which was surrounded by an earthen wall or rampart. *Forud* is cognate with *Forus*, the residence of a magistrate, and with the Latin *Forum*.

53. I Kalaind August cen ail,
tiagait ind ceċ tres bliaḋain;
and luadit co dana ar daiġ,
cert ceċ cana ocus costaid.
54. Acra, tobaċ, frithir fiaċ,—
ecnaċ ecraite arriad,
ni lamar la graiffin ingaid,—
elad, aithni, athgabail.
55. Cen dul fer in airecṫ m-ban,
cen mna in aireaċt fer findglan;
mad aiṫed n ir [o] ċlunter,
cid aċḟer, cid aċmuinter.
56. Cipé ti dar reċt narriġ,—
Benen co beaċt ra buanscrib,—
na beṫ ar ár na fine,
aċt a bás na bithbine.
57. Is iat a ada olla:—
stuic, cruiti, cuirn ċraestolla,
cuisig, timpaig cen truamna,
filid ocus faen ċliara;
58. Fianruth Find,—fath cen dochta,—
togla, tana, toċmorca,
slisnige, is duile feda;
aera, rúne romera;
59. Arosc, roscada, rigail,
is tecusca Fira Fithail,
dubláidi, dindḟenċus dait,
tecusca Cairpri ocus Cormaic;
60. Na fessa, im feis truim Temra,
oenaige, im oenaċ Emna,
annallad and, is fir so,
caċ rand ro rannad Ered;
61 Scel tellaig Temra,—naċ timm,—
fis ceċ tuchait in h-Erind,
banḟenċas buidni baga,
bruidni, gessi, gabala;
62. Deiċ chimna Chathair Cetaig
dia claind, ra ceim rigmetaig;
foirb ceċ duni mar is dleċt,
combet uile co a eisteċt. E

[601] *Airecht*, a legal assembly or court. (See Introduction, p. cclxii.) T law for the protection of females appears to have prevailed among t Ancient Irish at all the national Assemblies and Fairs. See the poem

53. On the Kalends of August without fail,
They repaired thither every third year;
There aloud with boldness they proclaimed
The rights of every law, and the restraints.

54. To sue, to levy, to controvert debts,—
The abuse of steeds in their career,
Is not allowed to contending racers,—
Elopements, arrests, distraints.

55. That no man goes into the women's Airecht,[601]
That no women go into the Airecht of fair clean men;
That no abduction is heard of,
Nor repudiation of husbands or of wives.

56. Whoever transgresses the law of the assembly,—
Which Benen with accuracy indelibly wrote,—[602]
Cannot be spared upon family composition,
But he must die for his transgression.

57. These are its many great privileges:—
Trumpets, Cruits, wide-mouthed horns,
Cuisig, Timpanists without weariness,
Poets and petty rhymesters;

58. Fenian tales of Find,—an untiring entertainment,—
Destructions, Cattle-preys, Courtships,
Inscribed tablets, and books of trees,
Satires, and sharp edged runes;

59. Proverbs, maxims, royal precepts,
And the truthful instruction of Fithal,
Occult poetry, topographical etymologies,
The precepts of Cairpri and of Cormac;

60. The Feasts, with the great Feast of Teamar,
Fairs, with the fair of Emania,
Annals there are verified,
Every division into which Eriu was divided;

61. The history of the household of Teamar—not insignificant,
The knowledge of every territory in Eriu,
The history of the women of illustrious families,
Of Courts, Prohibitions, Conquests;

62. The noble Testament of Cathair the great
To his descendants, to direct the steps of royal rule
Each one sits in his lawful place,
So that all attend to them to listen. Listen.

he Fair of *Tailte* in the *Dindsenchas* of *Tailte*, and also in Keating's History
reign of *Tuathal Techtmar*, A.D. 79.
[602] See Note 14, vol. i., p. 45.

63. Pipai, fidli, fir cengail,
cnaṁḟir, ocus cuislennaig,
sluag etig engaċ egair,
béccaig ocus buiridaig.

64. Turcbait a fedma uile
do ríg Berba bruṫmaire;
co n-eirne in rí rán ramess,
ar caċ n-dan a miad diles.

65. Aitti, airggni, aidbsi ceoil,
coimgne cinti coemċeneoil;
a réim ríg raċ dar Bregmag,
aċaċ, saċruad engnam.

66. Is é sin scor ind oenaig,
on t-sluag beoda biṫḟaelid;—
co tabair doib on comdid
talaṁ cona caemthorṫib.

67. Gniset noem Lagen iarló,—
noem in cotaig—ni cloenró,—
ós raṫlind Carmain, co cáid,
Aifrinn, sleċtain, salmgabail.

68. Troscud i fogmur, foseċt,
i Carmun uile in oenḟeċt,—
ra Lagnib naċ samċerc sund,—
ra aireċt, ra écomlund,

69. Clerig, laeiċ Lagen ille,
mnaa na n-dagḟer co n-demne.
Dia, rositir mar rosolig,
ria n ictib ána eistid. E.

70. Oegidaċt .h. n-Dronade,
ocus eċtres Ossairge,
ocus nuall fri craunnu sleg,
on tsluag sunnu, isse a dered.

71. Cid firt Mersca atbermais de
ni h-essa, ni h-ecraite;
is sen Garman riar, a fer,
issand co cian ro claided.

72. Cid uadib sain no gairthe,
eter sluagaib samaigthe,
rosoleċt, cen daidbri, is rosolig;—
a Laigniu na leċt, estid. E.

63. Pipes, fiddles, chainmen,
Bone-men, and tube-players,
A crowd of babbling painted masks,
Roarers and loud bellowers.

64. They all exert their utmost powers
For the magnanimous king of the Barrow;
Until the noble king in proper measure bestows
Upon each art its rightful meed.

65. Elopements, slaughters, musical choruses,
The accurate synchronisms of noble races,
The succession of the sovereign kings of Bregia,
Their battles, and their stern valour.

66. Such is the arrangement of the fair,
By the lively ever happy host;—
May they receive from the Lord
A land with choicest fruits.

67. They, Leinster's saints, celebrate next day,—
The saints of the alliance—'t is no evil deed—
Over Carman's bounteous lake, with solemnity,
Masses, adorations, and psalm-singing.

68. They fast in the autumn, good the deed,
At Carman, all of them together,—
The Leinstermen without lack of humour,—
Against injustice, against oppression.

69. The clergy and the laity of Leinster all,
And the stainless women of the worthy men.
God, who knows how well they merit,
To their noble prayers will listen. Listen.

70. The hospitality of the Hy Drona,
And the steed contest of the men of Ossory,
And the clash of spear-handles,
From the entire host, that was the end.

71. Though we had called it Mesc's grave
It were not mockery, it were not enmity;
[For Mesc] and old crooked Garman, her husband.
Here in far ancient times were buried.

72. Even if from those the name had been derived
By hosts of etymological writers,
It wefe just, no doubt, and it were lawful,
O Leinstermen of the monuments, listen.

73. Rath ar fichit is buanblad,
i fail sluag fo ċaċ talman:
salmrailec corrablaid,
i fail sainserc saer Charmain.

74. Seċt n-dumai cen taidliud de,
do cáiniud marb co mence;
seċt maige, carmain cen teċ,
fo cluiċe Carmain chainteċ

75. Tri margaid sin tir treoraig:—
margad bid, margad beo crai,
margaid mor na n-gall n-Gregaċ,
i m-bid ór is ard étaċ.

76. Fán na n-eċ, fan na fuine,
fan na m-bandál fri druinne;
fer do sluag n-gaireċ
nis máided, nis imcáined.

77. Fil ara nemdenam de,—[603]
maili, meċi, moċ-leiṫe,
ri cen géin, cen grinni,
cen feile, cen firinne.[604]

78. Co se ba brigaċ bara,
sluag linmar lis Labrada;
caċ sluag, naċ saigtheċ bid secc,
laimther, ocus ni laimet. E.

79. Failte ic sluag nemda na noeb,
Dam ic dia delbda, degcaem;
ri corrath buidnib nosrig,
ri caċ n-aċċuingid estid. E

[603] The following stanza from the Book of Ballymote, indicating the advantages to be gained by holding the fair, seems to show that there is a gap of perhaps two stanzas here, and that this stanza is one of them: it is the thirtieth stanza in the Book of Ballymote (where it comes after the one numbered 29 in the foot note, page 535 *supra*), and is there obviously out of place. The only place where it could be introduced without disturbing the narrative of the poem would be after this stanza: it has however been thought better to give it as a foot note, than to introduce it into this part of the poem which is taken from the Book of Leinster.

30. Ith, blicht, siṫ, sama, sona,	Corn, milk, peace, ease, prosperity,
Lina lana lercola,	Waters full in great abundance.

Finit

73\. Twenty-one raths of enduring fame,
In which hosts are under earth confined:
A conspicuous cemetery of high renown,
By the side of delightful noble Carman.

74\. Seven mounds without touching each other,
Where the dead have often been lamented;
Seven plains, sacred without a house,
For the funeral games of Carman.

75\. Three markets in that auspicious country:—
A market of food, a market of live stock,
And the great market of the foreign Greeks,
Where gold and noble clothes were wont to be.

76\. The slope of the steeds, the slope of the cooking;
The slope of the embroidering women;
To no man of the friendly hosts
Will they give adulation, will they give reproach.

77\. There comes of not celebrating it,—[693]
Baldness, failure, and early grayness,
Kings without wisdom, without elegance,
Without hospitality, without truthfulness.[694]

78\. Hitherto warlike and brave have been
The numerous hosts of Labrad's house;
All assailing hosts, are compelled to be shy;
They are challenged, and they challenge not.

79\. A welcome with the saintly Host of Heaven,
May I receive, with the beautiful, all-perfect God;
The King of graceful hosts may I reach,
A king who to every prayer will listen! Listen.

ꞅıꞃ ꞃıᵹ-ꞁaıᵹ, cocombaıꝺ cınꝺ,	True kingly heroes, with loyalty to chiefs,
ꝺıꞃmaıᵹ ꞅoꞃꞃaın ꞅoꞃ Eꞃen.	With triumph of heroic hosts of Eriu.

[694] The following is the version of this stanza in the Book of Ballymote:—

72. ꞅaıl aꞃ a nemꝺenoım ꝺe—	There comes of its not being holden
maıle, ıꞅ meıch, ıꞅ moċleċe,	Baldness, decay, early grayness,
ꞃı ꝺana conamble hıl,	With many other evil fates,
ꝺo LLaıᵹnıb ana. Eꞅꞇıᵹ.	To the noble Leinstermen. Listen.

FINIS.

GLOSSARIAL INDEX

OF IRISH WORDS.

[In the case of important terms, such as *Aire*, etc., which are of frequent occurrence, only the references to places where their explanation is to be found are given here; the other references will be found in the General Index.]

Abairsech, a manufacturing woman, *iii.* 116.

Abh, sweet (see *Abhrann*), *iii.* 371.

Abh a cear, since I slew [the death of], *iii.* 456.

Abhrann, a song of any tune or measure, *iii.* 371, 377, 378.

Abrus, material, *iii.* 115, *n.* 87.

Aco, to him or with them, *iii.* 518.

Ach, a groan or sigh (see *Aileach*), *ii.* 152.

Achadh, a field, or division of land, *i.* clxxxii.

Acht-comaithe, with equal immunity *iii.* 504.

Acra, to sue, *iii.* 499.

Adabraid n-aille, ostentatiousness of fame, *iii.* 428.

Adairt, a pillow, *iii.* 489.

Adand, a small candle, *iii.* 246 (see *Caindill*).

Adannai, kindle, ignite, *iii.* 505.

Adbelad, will die, *iii.* 221.

Adbond, *bind*, sweet or melodious, a song or tune, *iii.* 386, 387.

Adbond Trirech, a triple *Adbond*, a tune in which three parts are understood, namely, *genntraighe*, *goltraighe*, and *suantraighe*, *iii.* 387.

Adbreth, a species of poetry peculiar to the order of poet called *Anradh*, *ii.* 171.

Adgensdar, *Aithgenethar*, to make restitution, *iii.* 508.

Adgiallat, they submit, or owe allegiance to, *iii.* 514.

Adhal, dishonour, blemish, or disgrace, *iii.* 518.

Adid, his two, *iii.* 497.

Admilithi, more pale: one of the jesters of Conaire Mór, monarch of Eriu, so called, *iii.* 150.

Aedh or *Udh*, "a spark of fire", from which is derived *Aedh*, the proper Christian name of a man, Anglicised Hugh, *ii.* 132.

Aenach, a fair, or general assembly, *i.* cclv.

Aenach Gubha, a moaning or mourning assembly, *iii.* 383.

Aes Sidhe, "dwellers in the hills", "the fairy people", *ii.* 198.

Agell do, [his pledge to him, *i.e.*, he is entitled to] his brooch and everything composed of gold and of silver—his pledged article, whatever it be, *iii.* 112.

Agid, *In Agid*, face to face, against the face of, *iii.* 458.

A h-Atham, "from Athens", *iii.* 526-7.

A h-Espain, "out of Spain", *iii.* 210.

Aicbeile, dangerous severity, etc., *iii.* 440.

Aiced-Fige, weaving implements, *iii.* 116.

Aicdi, work of art, *iii.* 504.

Aidbdenaib, prosecutors, *iii.* 500.

Aidbsi, great or greatness; its technical signification in music was the singing of a multitude in chorus, *iii.* 246, 247.

Aidbsi, *corus cronáin*, a kind of guttural or purring chorus; a great chorus or vocal concert (see *Cepóc*), *iii.* 245, 371, 374, 376.

Aideadh Uladh, the deaths of the Ultonians, *ii.* 94.

Ai Esain, same as *Aigthe Esain*, rank-*Esain*, *iii.* 517.

Aige, a stranger, *iii.* 507.

Aightha Esain, the proportional increase of a man's *Esain* due to his special rank or honour, *iii.* 515 (see *Esain*).

Aigne, an arguer, or pleading counsellor, *i.* ccxxiii, celii, cclxxiii.
Ail, a fence, a stake fence, *i.* clxxxi, cxxxii. cxci, ccl.
,, *comarbus*, a divisional fence between the lands of co-heirs, or shares of gavelled land, *i.* clxxxi.
Ail, a stone; *Ach*, a groan or sigh, hence *Aileach*, *ii.* 152.
Ail bend Alatuaith n-dronaicde, flowing capes dexterously embroidered, *iii.* 142.
Ailestar, *Ailastair*, the bog firs (*recte*, Iris pseudacorus, or common flag or Iris, now called *Feleastrom*), *i.* lxxiii; *iii.* 190.
Ailgine, tranquillity, etc., *iii.* 221.
Aili, other, *iii.* 506.
Ailsed-nadma, intentional fraudulent knotting, *iii.* 493.
Aimsir na c-curadh, the time of a champion's military education, *ii.* 367.
Ain, *Aine*, rushes, *iii.* 486, 489.
Aindiden, Friday, *iii.* 507.
Ainmed, disparagement, *iii.* 514, 520.
Airbernad, diminution, curtailment, *iii.* 516.
Airbid, a measure of weight, *iii.* 483, *n.* 524.
Airbi, a wooden fence, *i.* ccciv.
Airbir, an armful [*recte*, a shoulder bundle or load], *iii.* 487.
Aircend, a defined boundary or limit, *i.* ccl.
Airchinnech, a lay vicar, a land steward [of monastery or church land], *i.* celii; *ii.* 31, 169.
Airchisecht, bemoaning, *iii.* 442, 454.
Airech Feibhe, a chief of dignity, *iii.* 114, and 126–7.
Aire, a lord, a title of distinction, *iii.* 468.
Airech, litigation here, *iii.* 499.
Airecht, a court, *ii.* 20.
Airecht Fodeisin, his own court, *i.e.*
,, the court of the *Righ*, or court of king's bench, of a *Righ Tuatha*, *i.* ccxlix, cclxvi, cclxxii.
,, *Foleith*, a court leet, cclxii, cclxxii.
,, *Urnaide*, a court of pleas, *i.* cclxiii, cclxxii.
Aire Ard, the steward of a king, *i.* ccxliv; *iii.* 469, 515.
,, *Cosraing*, the Gerefa or Reeve of a *Fine*, *i.* cciii, ccxlvii, ccxlviii; *iii.* 470, 491.
Aire Desa, the lowest grade of *Flath*, *i.* ccxxxiv, ccxlvii; *iii.* 468, 494, 516
,, *Echtai*, a high constable of a *Crich* or territory, *i.* ccxlv, ccxlvii; *iii.* 468, 497.
,, *Fine*, the chief of kindred of a *Fine*, *i.* cci, ccxlvii; *iii.* 516.
,, *Forgaill*, an officer who corresponds to the Welsh *Canghellor* or chancellor, *i.* ccxliii; *iii.* 468, 500.
,, *Tuise*, commander of the levy of a *Tuath*, cf. *Dux* (Duc-s) and A. Sax. *Here-tog*, ccxliii; *iii.* 468, 469, 499, 516.
Airel, rooms, or compartments [in a house], *iii.* 7.
Aireman, *Airemh*, a ploughman, *i.* ci.
Airgetlach, a general name for a metallic ore, *i.* ccccix.
Airigis (perceives), he perceived, *iii.* 448.
Airigtib gaisced, missive weapons of valour, *ii.* 303.
Airilliud, good works, *iii.* 514.
Airinech, a frontage, *i.* ccccxlvi.
Airiliuth, maintenance, *iii.* 497.
Airlicud, *Airluccud*, borrowing or lending on a pledge, *iii.* 487, 49, 487.
Airlighe ar da cleth, chief or highest advisers; the members of the council of each *Fine*; the *Cuicer na Fine*, or the five chiefs of kindred of a *Fine*, *i.* cclxviii.
Airlis, a yard of a *Forus*, or enclosed paddock in which cattle were impounded, see note on *Fer Forais*, *i.* cclxxx, cccl, ccciv, *iii.* 520.
Airmed, a measure of bulk, *iii.* 483.
Airthind=*Airbind*, oats, *i.* ccclxiv.
Airthiur, the east, *Airthiur Foitsi*, the back part of the south side of the seat or couch, *iii.* 509.
Aisneis cleith, a private information against a nobleman, *i.* ccxlv.
,, *meirle*, a thief's information, *i.* cclxxxii.
Aite, a tutor, *iii.* 446.
Aitech Comaide, father or chief of a *Comaithches*, copartnership or gild, *i.* ccxvi.
Aiteog, a string which is put about the mouth of a bag, *iii.* 117.
Aith, a kiln, *iii.* 486.
Aithcumba n-aige, dressing of wounds, *iii.* 486.
Aithech, a tenant, a plebeian, *ii.* 36, *iii.* 469, 500.

Aithech ar a Treba, a tribe tenant on his ancestral home *iii.* 482, more correctly, the head of a copartnership or gild, *i.* cci.
Aithech Baitse, Aithech Baitsidhe, a man who aspired to belong to the privileged grades of society, a Bachelor of Bó-Aireship, a tenant bachelor of *Airechus*, probably connected with the Latin and Romance terms *Baccalaria* and *Bacele*, *i.* cci, ccli, *iii.* 438, 524.
Aitherach, a gain, *iii.* 493.
Aithgin, dat. pl. *Aithginnaib*, the equal of, restitution, *ii.* cxxiv, clxxxiii, cclxxx, cclxxxii, ccxci, ccxcii; *iii.* 112, 456, 487, 489.
Aitire, a security between two parties, a bail, cxcvii, cxcviii, cclxxv, cclxxxiv, cclxxxv, ccxcii; *iii.* 474.
Aitire Foesma, an *Aitire* of adoption, that is, a security for the liabilities incurred in affiliating a distant relative or a stranger to a *Fine*, *i.* ccxciii; *iii.* 474.
Aitire Laige, an oath-bound *Aitire*, *iii.* 474, *n.* 487.
Aitire Nadma, the binding or knotting *Aitire*; a security bound by a *Naidm* or bond, corresponding to the nexus of Roman law, *i.* ccxcii; *iii.* 474.
Aithirne, Aithrine, fixed lawful fines, rights, and privileges, *iii.* 514.
Aithlimi, readiness, swiftness, *iii.* 448.
Alad, a wound, *iii.* 450.
Alaile, Alaill, the other, *iii.* 480, 493.
Alaili, another=the other, *iii.* 500.
Alamu, her hands, see *Almhain*, *i.* ccciii.
Alanai, one of them, *iii.* 480.
Albanach, an Albanian or native of Alba, now Scotland, *i.* clxv.
All, the reins of a chariot; also the eyes or projections on the yoke through which the reins passed, *i.* cccclxxxi, cccclxxxii.
,, *Dualach*, a piece of harness almost identical with the *Cuirpi dualach*, or peaked straddle of the present time, *i.* cccclxxxi, cccclxxxii.
,, *oir*, golden bridles, *iii.* 160.
Alla, away (far off), *iii.* 456, 458.
Allaid, a wild stag, *iii.* 428.
Allugg, his oath, *iii.* 487.
Almsona, alms, *i.* ccxl.
Al-Tuath, another territory, and used for a man of another *Tuath* or territory, cf. A. Sax. elþeódig, strange; Welsh *Allmd*, a foreigner, *i.* cxxviii.
Alta, gashes, *iii.* 440.
Ama, wardens, *iii.* 509.
Amae, alas, indeed, *iii.* 448.
Amais, mercenaries [military retainers] *ii.* 389, 90, 91, 92.
Amh, indeed, *iii.* 430, 460.
Amh echin, now indeed, *iii.* 460.
Amhrath, *non-rath*, the bounty or payment given to the people who cried and lamented at the funeral of the chief, lord, or any body else, and for which bounty there was no further return ever to be made. It is compounded of the negative particle *Amh*, non, and *Rath*, wages, etc., *iii.* 384.
Amhus, or *Amhuis*, mercenaries corresponding to the Gaulish Ambacti, *i.* cxiii, ccxxxvi; *ii.* 389. See *Amais*.
Ammbur Indlait, a washing trough, *iii.* 486.
Amrus, suspicion, information based on suspicion, *i.* cclxxvii.
Amsaib, body-guards-men, *iii.* 509. See *Amais*.
Amuis righ, the body-guard of a king, *iii.* 508. See *Amais*.
Anad, a stay, *i.* cclxxxiii, cclxxxiv.
Anagraitto, disputes, quarrels, etc., *iii.* 511.
Andil, strife, *iii.* 416.
Anair, a species of negative laudatory poem, *ii.* 173.
Anamain, a species of poetry peculiar to the order of poet called *Ollamh*. The great *Anamain* was a species of poem which contained four different measures of composition, namely the *Nath*, the *Anair*, the *Laid*, and the *Eman*, and it was composed by an *Ollamh* only, *ii.* 171, 173.
Andoin, the church, *iii.* 509.
Andord, *Non-Dord* (for the particle *an* is deprivative in sense), that is, it is not exactly a *Dord* or murmur, but something higher than it, *iii.* 378, 379. See *Coblaighe*.
Anendge, dishonour (impurity, want of innocence), *iii.* 514.
Anflaith, *Anflath*, a rich tenant farmer, who has wealth, but is not a *Flath* or true lord; a middle man, *ii.* 36; *iii.* 491.
Anfoladh, misdeeds, *iii.* 514.

Anfolta=(*Anfolad*), misdeeds, oppression, *iii.* 520.

Anoi, their recognition, etc., *iii.* 513.

Anradh, a poet of the second order, *ii.* 171, 217; *iii.* 316.

Anruith, a warrior, *iii.* 446.

Ansruth, a man who vindicates the honour of his territory and people, a kind of territorial high constable, *i.* cexlvi; *iii.* 513, 517.

Antengtaid ar da Feth Airecht no Danaig, eloquent men having a recognized position derived from land or noble professions; they were the selected representatives of the *Fine*, corresponding to the Welsh *Taisbantyle*, i. cclxviii.

Aoir, satire, *iii.* 481.

Aos Ealadan, men of science, *i.* cccxxx.

Apa (same as *oba*), to shun (to refuse), *iii.* 420.

Apad, a legal notice, *i.* cclxxxiii, cclxxxv.

„ *nadma Aitire*, notice of bail bond, *i.* cclxxxv.

Apdatar, they died, *iii.* 220, 221.

Apdaines, persons whose rank was proclaimed or legally admitted, *i.* clxxxvii.

Ar, for *Atbert*, i.e., says or did say, *iii.* 510.

Arach, guarantee, *iii.* 416.

Aracol, a room or compartment, *i.* ccclx.

Araicecht, the grammar of the pupils *ii.* 172

Araid, charioteers, *iii.* 444, etc.

Arathar, a plough, *iii.* 500

Arba=*orba*=*arbar*, pl. *Orbain*, modern *arbhar*, corn, or corn-meal or shelled grain, *i.* ccclxii, ccclxv; *iii.* 474.

Arclisde, gymnasts, *iii.* 365.

Arcuirether, he restrains, *iii.* 498.

Ardaig, excess, *iii.* 472.

Ardan, a pigin, a drinking vessel, *i.* ccclv; *iii.* 495.

Ard Arcon imod Toisi, high nobles of great state. *Flaths* entitled to hold an *Airecht Foleith* or manorial court, *i.* cclxviii.

Ard neme, high sanctuary, *iii.* 515.

Ard Righ, high or paramount king, corresponding to the British *Gweledig*, and the Anglo-Saxon *Bretwalda*, *i.* ccxxxi

Ard Soius, hill of light, or hill upon which a signal light was burned, *i.* cccxviii.

Ardreth, a species of poetry peculiar to the order of poet called *Canu*, *ii.* 171.

Arfuin, *Arfoimsin*, accept thou [or I present to thee], *iii.* 221.

Arggat, or *Airgat*, silver, *i.* ccccxxii; *iii.* 491.

Arra, a charge, *i.* cclxxxi.

Arracur, filing a charge, *i.* cclxxix.

Arsanltee, singing? (*recte*, songsters), iii. 365.

Art Fine, the principal man of a *Fine*, *i.* cciv.

Arthana, charms, *iii.* 440.

Asathi, in revolt, aggressive, *iii.* 505.

Asana, asses, *iii.* 330.

Ascria, wanting, *iii.* 497.

Asne, it is he, *iii.* 497.

Ass, new milk, *i.* ccclxxi; *iii.* 474, 499.

Ass, pl. *Assai*, a sandal, a shoe. This term is frequently applied to women's shoes and bishops' sandals, both of which were sometimes made of *Findruine*, *i.* ccclxxxv, cccxcviii, dcxlii; *iii.* 104, 105, 157, 166.

Assu, danger [*recte*, to want, to require], *iii.* 450.

Astaither, assigned or confirmed to, *iii.* 513.

Astha, deficient, *iii.* 497.

At, a hat, an ornamental covering for the head (see *Righ Barr*), cf. Eng. *Hat*, Germ. *Hut*, Old Norse *Hött*, i. ccexvc; *iii* 209.

Atball, to suffer or fall, *iii.* 493.

Atchisiu, I perceive *iii.* 446.

Atcomren, he pays, *iii.* 499.

Atcota, they had, or they possessed, *iii.* 516.

Atguidhetsom, he vindicates, represents, *iii.* 515.

Athachs, tenants, but in this place used for such persons as performed the household service of a noble, or person of rank, *i.* dcxlii.

Athchanaidh (a reciter), a class of poet whose business it was to sing to the instruments played upon by another, *iii.* 353.

Athchardes, hostility, *iii.* 454.

Athgabail, a second or counter distress; the Withernam of the Anglo-Saxons, *i.* cclxxxv.

„ *Imbleogain*, a counter distress levied on a kinsman, *i.* ccxci.

Athigmith, glorifying, *iii.* 428.

Ath Solus, ford of light, or ford at which a signal light was burned, *i.* cccxviii.
Ath-urnaide, the nurturer or sponsor of a suit or pleading, probably the true origin of "Attorney", *iii.* 474.
Atlendai, to injure, to diminish, *iii.* 514.
Atlu, reproach, insult, *iii.* 514.
Atndamait, they concede, *iii.* 491.
Atod, long [space of time], *iii.* 430.
Atracht, arose [or did rise], *iii.* 444.
Atraigestar, they rose up, *iii.* 452.
Att, swelling, *iii.* 448.
Auchuimriach n-oir, ear-clasps of gold, *iii.* 146-7, 185, 186.
Aue, a grandson, *iii* 495, 548.
Aurcrait, to diminish.
Au-Nasc, *U-Nasc*, an ear-ring, "a ring for the ear, that is, a ring of gold which is worn upon the fingers or in the ears of the sons of the free or noble families", *Cor. Glossary*, *iii.* 185-6.
Aurrach, *Eirrech*, *Errech*, an extraordinary levy, *iii.* 507.
Aurscartadh, carving [or ornamentation], *iii.* 29, 30.
Aurslon, the breast of a mantle [*recte*, a fastening in the breast or opening of a mantle], *iii.* 150.
Baar, top or head, *i.* cccxcvii.
Bacanaig, hobgoblins, *ii.* 301.
Baccan, a crook, etc., *iii.* 219, 220.
Bachall, a bishop's crozier, *i* cclxxxix.
Badssta, now at once, forthwith, *iii.* 452, 456.
Badb, a raven, a vulture; *Fors n-gera in badb*, over which the raven will croak, *iii.* 422.
Badhba, conspicuous, *iii.* 58.
Baegul, unguarded: *uair baeguil*, an unguarded moment, *iii.* 450.
Bai, nom. plu. and gen. sing. of *Bó*, a cow, *iii.* 498, 501.
Bai Braisse, sudden death, *ii.* 372.
Baidhbhi, gen. of *Badbh*; *Baidbhi belderg*, of the red-mouthed vulture, *Badbh* is properly speaking a raven, or carrion crow, but here it must be a vulture, *iii.* 454.
Bhaiceirdset [same as *Focherdsat*], they threw, *iii.* 438.
Baile, the equivalent of the Latin Pagus, *i.* lxxxi.
Baile Biatach, the *Baile* of the victualler or steward, *i.* xci, xciii. cliii, cc.
Baile Maoir, steward's town, *i.* cliii.
„ *an gabhainn*, smith's town, *i.* ccvii.
„ *na cerd*, the town of the *Cerd* or worker in precious metals, *i.* ccvii.
Bairchi, .i. *Sliabh Bairche*, i.e. a mountain, *iii* 432.
Bairgin, or *Bairghin*, a cake or loaf of bread, *Bairgin Indruic*, a full household cake or loaf, *Bairgin Banfhuine*, a loaf or cake sufficient for one woman's meal, *Bairgin Ferfuine*, a cake or loaf sufficient for a man's meal, *i.* cxlii, ccclix, ccclxiv, ccclxvi, *iii.* 31, 481, 512.
Ballyboe, a division of land, *i.* lxxxix.
Ban amus, wives of mercenaries [mercenary women], *iii.* 504.
Bananaig, *Bananachs*, *iii.* 424, 425, 449, 450.
Ban-ghresa, woman's work, *ii.* 133.
Banna, a drop; it was also the name of one of the six cupbearers of Conaire Mór, monarch of Eriu, *iii.* 144.
Bansidhe, *Bansidhe*, fairy women, *ii.* 131, *iii.* 381, 382, 383.
Barc, a bond or hostage (?) *i.* dcxli.
Barficfa, will be fought, *iii.* 458.
Barr, a mind, diadem, or crest, *iii.* 202, 209, 200. *Cathbarr*, *Cenn Barr*, *Cleitme*, *Eo Barr*, all different names for a covering or ornament for the head, *iii.* 209, etc. *Barr Bruinn*, *Bruinn's* [golden] diadem, *iii.* 199 to 202,; a square cap like the old French Berret, and Spanish Barrete, *i.* cccxcvii.
Barra Buadh, the name of the instrument with which *Find Mac Cumhaill* called out his troops for war or for the chase; it is a corrupt form of the ancient word *Benn-Buabhaill*, or Buffalo-horn or trumpet, *iii.* 305.
Barréd, a warm covering for the head, worn chiefly by women, *i.* cccxcvi.
Bassaib, low drinking bowls or basins. The English word "basin", contains the same root, *iii.* 478.
Basschaire na n-ech, tramping of the horses, *iii.* 426.
Basslethna, wide-hoofed, *iii.* 428.
Beanna Flatha, horns of a *Flath* [of sovereignty], *iii.* 502.
Bean Comarba, a co-heiress, *i.* cxix.
Beanchara, a female friend, *i.* dcxliii.

Becc, small; abl. pl., *Beccaib* [with small things], *iii*. 497.
Bedgaig, prancing, *iii*. 428.
Beim co famus, [the subducing blow] cutting off his opponent's hair with his sword, *ii*. 372.
Beirn, a boat, *Beirn-Bróce*, boat-shaped shoes, *i*. cccxcviii.
Bellce ór, *Beilge oir*, bridle bits of gold, *iii*. 219, 220.
Bellgidh oir, bridle bits of gold, *iii*. 157-8.
Belra formend, stammering speech, *iii*. 145.
Bemmim, a stroke, a blow, *iii*. 507.
Ben baid, a lewd woman, Cf. Eng. *bawd*, *iii*. 448.
Benn, a horn, *iii*. 305.
Benn-crot, a pinnacled (or triangular) *cruit*; a *timpan*, *iii*. 305, 306.
Benn Buabhaill, a buffalo [or wild ox] horn, compounded of *Benn*, a horn, and *Buabhaill*, gen. of *Buaball*, a buffalo, a musical instrument so called, *iii*. 305.
Beo caindel, a living candle, *i.e.* positive evidence for the defence, *i*. cclxxix.
Beochride, lively-hearted, *iii*. 428.
Beolegud, living deposits, *i.e.* witnesses, *i*. cxcii.
Beoil, ale [lard, drawn butter, etc.,] *i*. dcxxxix; *iii*. 118.
Beolo Crot, mouths of harps, *iii*. 217.
Beor Lochlanach, "Norse beer", or popularly "Danish beer", *i*. ccclxxviii.
Berla Feine, technical law [language of the *Fenechas*], *ii*. 25.
Berra Airechta, decisions of a court, *i*. cclxviii.
Berrach, a junior barrister, *i*. cclxxiv.
Berrath, *i.e. mullach a cinn*; *Berrath*, that is the top of the head, *iii*. 107.
Berrbrocc, an apron, nearly corresponding to the modern petticoat called a kilt; the term appears to have been also applied to a part of a suit of skirted armour, the *Vorderschurz* of the Germans, and the large *Brayette* of the French. Cf. Gaulish *Braccae* or *Bracae*, *i*. ccclxxxiii, ccclxxiv, ccccl xxiv; *iii*. 147-8, 149, 183.
Bes Tigi, house tribute or rent in kind paid to a *Flath* by his free or *Saer Ceili*; the *Gwes-Tva* or rent of Welsh tenants; cf. also Welsh *Gwaesan*, *i*. cxiii, cxl, cxlii, ccxxvii; *iii*. 478.
Bhothais, the right of having *Bothachs* or cottier tenants, *iii*. 494. See *Both* and *Bothach*.
Biad Prointige, refectory commons, cf. Latin *Prandium*, *i*. ccclxviii.
Biadhadh naircennca; *Biathadh naircenn*, a fixed rent in provisions paid to a *Flath* by his bond or *Daer Ceili*, *iii*. 494, 498.
Bial, a bill-hook, billet-axe, or hatchet, *i*. cxci, ccclxi; *iii*. 486.
Bian n-erb, [snow-white] roebuck skins, *iii*. 220, 221.
Biata congbala, supplies of food for a convocation, etc., *iii*. 519.
Biatad, the food-supplies which formed part of the rent of *Daer Ceili*, *i*. cxii., cxliv, ccxl, dcxlii.
Biatha, a rent in kind paid to the *Flath* by his bond or *Daer Ceili*, *iii*. 471.
Biattaig, purveyors, *iii*. 438, 442.
Bil, a rim (as *bil na sceithe*, the rim of the shield), *iii*. 456.
Bille, bosses [small cups or dishes], *iii*. 104, 105.
Binidean, the same as *Binit*, and perhaps the same as the colour called *Bindean*, which was probably produced from the flowers of Galium verum *i*. cccci.
Binnit, *Binnet*, rennet, a name also apparently given to the Galium verum, or bed straw, *i*. ccclxviii, cccci.
Bir, (an iron) spit or spear, a lance, *i*. ccccxxxii; *ii*. 313; a lance [a spit, a skewer], 348; a stake, *iii*. 432.
Birit, a sow, *iii*. 486.
Birur, watercress, *i*. ccclxvi; *iii*. 151, 250.
Bith, constant (vide *bolc*, etc.), and *ii*. 133.
Blad, fame, *iii*. 442.
Bladmar, renowned, *iii*. 418.
Blai, a fence, a legal boundary, *i*. clxxxii.
Blatnig, famed, *iii*. 418.
Blath n-én n- óe gnaith, a bird plume of the usual feather, *i*. ccccl xxxi.
Blathach, buttermilk, *iii* 478.
Bleith, the costs of a distress, *i*. cxci.
Blenarda, high-flanked, *iii*. 428.
Blethach, the same as *Bocaire*, which see.
Blonoc, lard, *i*. dcxl.

for *do*; "*acas bo srethi*
is a "*Cranntabaill uadh*
l he cast at him a stone
Cranntabaill (sling), *iii.*

man who has a habitation
farm lands sufficient to
ten or more cows, etc.,

ısing [combing of wool]

see *Bacanaig*, *iii.* 424,

oatmeal cake, baked by
pported in an upright posi-
re the fire, *i.* ccclxiv.
, *Bó slabrad*, *Seds* of, see
Sed, *iii.* 480.
, *i.e. fogebsa*, *i.e.* will be
ied) against me, *iii.* 446.
tation or house, *i.* lxxxviii
faithce, a cow keeper,
who keeps or cares cows
grass land of his *Selb*)

tures, *iii.* 143.
abala, a rate in aid of a
d to meet the requisition
ficer for the relief of the
519.
Laighen, the cow-tribute
er, *i.* xxxiii; *iii.* 313.
ith Thellaigh, bellows, son
nt fireplace, *ii.* 133.
g or belly, *iii.* 217.
whale-bellied, *iii.* 428.
small drinking vessel, cf.
Bolli, a bowl, Ang. Sax.
German *Bolle*, English
ccclvi; *iii.* 152.
Borhuma, gen. of *Boireamh*,
cow tribute". See *Brian*

well bred cows, *iii.* 480,

in or shed, *i.* cxv.
cottier, corresponding to
darius, *Cottarius*, and *Co-*
of Domesday Book. See
xv, clxxxvi.
e modern name of a *Both*
, cf. the "Bothy" of Scot-
xv.
a cow-house, *i.* cxxv.
a fat ox, cf. German *Thier*,

raccae, a tartan-like trou-
cxci.
. *Braich*, or *Bracha*, malt;

cf. Welsh and Cornish *Brag*, whence Welsh *Bragaud*, old English *Bragot*, modern English *Bracket*, a kind of sweet ale, cf. also *Braga*, Russian white beer, *i.* cxli, cccxxxviii, ccclxxiii, dcxlii.

Brachail, a Bellona, *iii.* 418.

Braid, plunder, *i.* cclv.

Brandabh, *Brandub*, *Brannaib*, draughts, backgammon, or some similar game, *ii.* 359; *iii.* 365.

Brandub, a draughtboard, *iii.* 360.

Brat, a plaid or cloak, corresponding in some measure to the Roman *Sagum*, *i.* ccclxxxiii, ccclxxxviii.

„ *corcra cortharach*, a crimson deep-bordered cloak [a bordered purple cloak], *iii.* 179.

„ *posta*, a marriage cloak, veil, or cloth, *i.* clxxv.

Brath=*Brach*, which see.

Breacan mac Ban-ghresa, blanket, son of woman's work, *ii.* 133.

Breac-glas, green or gray-spotted cloth, *iii.* 113.

Brecan, *Breccan*, a blanket, properly any tartan like woollen cloth, *ii.* 133.

Brec dergithir sion, more red-tinged than the fox-glove, *iii.* 140, 141.

Brecadh, colouring, *iii.* 115.

Breeste gairid, short or knee breeches, *i.* ccclxxxv.

Bregda, *i.e.*, *an Bricin*, that is, thread of various colours [for embroidery], *iii.* 183.

Breid sida, a silk handkerchief, *iii.* 114.

Breisémnech, tinkling [of the helmet], *iii.* 426.

Breitheamnastair, "judicavit", *i.* cclxxv.

Brepnib oir, with chains of gold, *iii.* 159.

Bretha Fir Coire, "judgments of true calling", judgments obtained by *Crancur* or lot, as in the case of persons claiming to be members of a *Fine*, *i.* cliv, clxvi.

Bretha Chreidne, the judgments of *Creidne*, *iii.* 210.

Bretha Nemidh, laws of privileges, *ii.* 172. *Bretha Neimidh*, rules and precedents of the courts of *Neimids*, *i.* cclxiii.

Brethem, *no Dobeir*, judges or givers, —those who gave the *Berra Airechta* or decisions of th[e] court; they were the sam[e] called dispensers of justice, and were judges of inferior rank to the presiding judges, *i.* cclxviii, cclxxii, cclxxiv.

Bretheman, a Brehon or judge, *i.* cclxiv.

Bretnas, pl. *Bretnassa*, dat. pl. *Bretnassaib*, a brooch [a large headed pin], *iii.* 110, 139, 140, 159, 163, 164, 180, 188.

Briatharchath Ban Uladh, the battle speeches [wordy war] of the women of Ulster, *iii.* 21.

Bricin, see *Brigda*.

Brichtu, charms, *iii.* 526, 527.

Brisidh, to break, put for killed here, *ii.* 293.

Briseadh grisaig, breaking of cinders, a peculiar legal process of punishment, *i.* cclxxviii.

Bró, a quern or hand-mill, *i.* ccclx.

Brocc, a shoe [a living word], *Brocca cred-uma*, shoes of red bronze, *i.* ccexcvii; *iii.* 219, 220. *Brócc eile*, a thong-stitched shoe, sometimes made of horse-skin, *i.* ccexcviii.

Brodmuc feneda, a roast pig [from *Brod*, a spit, *muc* a pig, and *fuinedh*, to roast or cook], *i.* lxxxvi. See also Proc. R. I. A., Irish MS. Series I., p. 178.

Broen, a drop, *iii.* 144.

Broga croicne capuil, horse-skin shoes, *i.* dexl.

Broit, pl. of *Brod*, a goad, a spit. *Broit creduma*, goads of red bronze, *iii.* 183.

Brontar, is damaged [worn or broken], *iii.* 489.

Brosnacha, a species of poetry peculiar to the order of poet called *Sai*, *ii.* 171.

Brot, a yoke (a goad), *iii.* 479.

Brotha, small casks or barrels, *i.* ccclvi, ccclix, ccclxxi.

Brotha [gen. of *broth*, passion], *brotha*, passionate, *iii.* 221.

Brothachs [*recte*, *Brothrachs*], woollen blankets, etc., *i.* cccliii.

Brothgha, cloak-brooches, *iii.* 157.

Brothrach, pl. *Brothracha*, couches, [blankets, etc.,] *i.* cccxcix; *iii.* 28.

Brú, the breast [womb], *iii.* 462.

Bruar, dregs, *iii.* 522.

Brugad, *Bruguid*, *Brughaidh*. See *Brugh-Fer*, *i.* ccxliv; *ii.* 31, 368; *iii.* 503.

Brugh, the residence of a *Brughfer*, where elections were held, and around which grew the borough town, cf. Goth *Baurgs*, A Sax. *Burh*, O. Norse, *Burskap*, right of citizenship, *Bursprak*, a place of assembly, *i.* clx, clxi.

„ *Bhaile*, the township of a *Brugh*, corresponding probably to the districts called *Burhs*, *i.* ccxxviii.

„ *fer*, the man of the *Brugh*, a local magistrate having jurisdiction in all disputes concerning trespass of land, pasturage, tillage, forestry, and all other agricultural matters, cf. Welsh *Bregr*, *i.* ccxlix.

Brugh Recht, *Brugh*-law, or law of the court of the *Brughfer*, the "Birlaw" of Scotland, *i.* ccl, cclxxi.

Bruidhes, he eats, *iii.* 522.

Bruid-gine, the gnashing of the mouth *ii.* 372.

Bruindfine, the womb-sons and daughters of heiresses, or daughters of the *Gradh Fine*. From *Bruind*, the womb, *i.* clxiii.

Bruine, the neck and breast, corresponding to the Greek θώραξ, a hauberk or shirt of mail; cf. Irish *Brú* and *Bruund*, the womb, Old French *Broigne*, *Brunie* Provençal *Bronha*, Medieval Latin *Brunia*, Gothic *Brunjo*, O. High German *Brunne*, A. Sax. *Byrne*, Old Sax. *Brunjo*, O. Norse *Brynjd*, Old Slavonic, *Brynja*, *i.* cccclxxiii, cccclxxiv.

Bruitne, a goad:—*Bruitne di derg ór in a lam dia tarcellad a echu*, i.e., "a goad of red gold in his hand by which he urged his horses", *iii.* 151.

Bruth, broth, *i.* ccclxviii; *iii.* 485.

Buabhall, a buffalo or wild ox, *iii.* 805.

Buafad, venom, *iii.* 418.

Buagelltaigh, cowkeepers, etc., *iii.* 77.

Buaifneach, venomed, or poisonous, vide *gae buaifneach*, "the venomed spear", *ii.* 205, 324; *iii.* 197.

• *Buaile*, a cow keep or bawn, *ii.* 344.

Buanadh, permanent soldiers of the kings of Erin (the *Fianna Ereann*), *ii.* 379.

Bucanaig, see *Bacanaig*, *iii.* 424.

Budne, or *Buinne*, a twisted or corded ring, bracelet, or circle, formed out of one twisted bar or several strands of gold or silver; a helix or spiral coil used by ladies for confining the hair. Also twisted rings worn on the hands or fingers by ladies and warriors, see *Failgi*, *i.* ccccvii; *iii.* 168, 170, 172, 188.

Bugherane, bog-bean or buck-bean, Menyanthes trifoliata, *i.* ccccv.

Buiden, a battalion of seven hundred men, *iii.* 502.

Buidhechair, *i.e.* the *Buidhe Conaill*, or "yellow disease", which ravaged Eriu, etc., in the time of Diarmait and Blathmach, A.D. 664, *ii.* 91.

Buinde do at, or *Bunne do at*, a wavy or twisted ring worn around the waist, *iii.* 176, 177, 174, 157.

Buine, *Buinde*, or *Buinne*, a horn trumpet: *Roboi buinne fochosmilius n-adarcae side*, there was a cornet horn, it was in the shape of a horn:—(*Zeuss*, vol. i., p. 481); *a n-gabther isind buinniu, no croit, quod canitur tibia vel crotta*, what is chaunted on the *tibia* or the harp (*Zeuss*, vol. i., p. 77), a pipe or tube. Cf. Latin *Buccina*, Romance *Buisine*, *i.* dxxx; *iii.* 306, 329, 367.

Buinne (*m-buinne*), rings, *iii.* 414.

Buinne, pipes, *iii.* 217.

Buinire, *Buinnire*, *Bunaire*, the professional name of a musician who performed on the *Buine*, or *Buinne*, or tube, *i.* dxxi; *iii.* 367.

Buindi, rings, see *Fail*.

Burdoon, from the French *Bourdon*, not the *Burden* or refrain of a song, but a species of *Faux Bourdon*, in which three or more voices took part in the singing, *i.* dcvii.

Caco for a enech, to befoul his honour (or face), *iii.* 493.

Cachae, each or every one, *iii.* 494.

Cach nae, everything, *iii.* 488.

Cadhas, honour, *iii.* 281.

Cadesin, same as *Fodesin*, he himself, his own, *iii.* 510.

Cadhois, wild-geese, *iii.* 367.

Caelana, sausages, see *Forgaib*, *iii.* 104, 105, 482. *Caelana Tona*, bottom or belly-pudding, the same as *Mucriucht*, i. ccclxix.

Caer-clis, a sling-ball, a missive ball, see *Tathlum*, *ii.* 253, 252, 288, 289, 294.

Caer Comraic, "a ball of convergent ribs or lines", a mosaic *Caerclis* so called, *ii.* 253.

Cai, "coshering", *i.* cxl.

Cai Astuda, means of fastening, *iii.* 253.

Caich, gen. of *cach* or *cäch*, each, all, or every one, *iii.* 492.

Caichen do da Naill, testifiers of two oaths—the *Toings* or oathmen of the plaintiff, and the compurgators of the defendant, *i.* cclxvii.

Caile, chalk, *i.* cccclxx.

Cailches, tufts (or tassels), *iii.* 202.

Caille, a veil, cf. German *Hulla*, *i.* cccxciv; *iii.* 113, 114.

Caimsi, a loose blouse or smock-frock reaching to the knees, and sometimes to the middle of the calves of the legs. From the middle Latin *Camisia*, *i.* ccclxxxii.

Cain, statute law; also a tribute, or booty seized as a legal fine, cf. Anglo-Saxon *Cyne* in *Cyne-bot*, the king's share of legal fines, *i.* ccxxxiv, ccxlii, cclxxii, cclxxxii, ccccxx.

Cain Breathach, of mild judgments, *ii.* 21.

Cain Comithe acas comgaite, law of co-eating and co-stealing, *i.* cciv, cclxxvii.

Cain, *Cormaic*, "Cormac's law", a name given to "the twelve books of laws which Amergin compiled for the men of West Munster, the laws were called Cain Cormaic, or the laws of Cormac, at the instance of Cormac, the owner or chief, of the plain of *Fuithrim*, between the Lake of Killarney and the Mangerton Mountain in the county of Kerry, *i.* cclxxii; *ii.* 32, *iii.* 466.

Cain Domnaig, "Sunday law", *ii.* 32, 33. This law brought from Rome by St. Conall, son of Caelan, founder of the ancient church of Inis Cail (now Iniskeel), near the mouth of the Gweebarra bay, barony of Boylagh, county Donegal, was not promulgated for about a century after the death of St. Conall (circa 594?). Imperfect copies of this most curious tract are preserved in *Leab. Breac*, R.I.A., Yellow Book of Lecan, (class H. 2, 16, T.C.D.). A perfect copy in MS. Harleian, 5280, British Museum, and a copy from the latter in the O'Curry MSS., C.U.D.

Cain Fenechas, law of the *Fines*. The whole of the laws, both common and statute, by which ancient

Irish society was regulated, was called by this name, i. cclxxii; it also sometimes means the law of occupancy of land, see iii 472.

Cain Fuithrime, see *Cain Cormaic.*

Cain urrudhas, custumal or customary laws of the several tribes, or of the provinces, iii. 472.

Caindelbrai, *Caindelbra*, a candelabrum, iii. 486.

Cainne, *Cainnin*, *Cainnenn*, or *Cainnind*, onions (leeks) or some such, thing, iii. 478, 483; vide *Fircainnind*, iii. 104, 105.

Cainnill, a candle, iii. 246.

Cainthech, malicious, iii. 452.

Cair, a festival, see *Forgaib*.

Cair, quaere (or where), iii. 490.

Cairced, doubling [repetition or resonance], iii. 363.

Cairda [*recte Cairde*] interterritorial laws and contracts, etc., i cclxii.

Cairde, peace, friendship, amity, an interterritorial treaty or compact, [of peace and amity]; i. cclxii, iii. 472, 505.

Cairddi, friendship, iii. 496.

Caire, a cauldron or boiler, also a vessel for preserving meat, i. ccclxix, dcxiii; iii. 485, 495, 500.

„ *umae*, a bronze boiler in which cooked meats were always kept in readiness, i. ccclix.

„ *cuic dorn*, a five-fist cauldron, i. dcxxxix.

„ *colbthaige*, the meat-boiler of a *Brugh*, so called on account of its being large enough to contain or boil a *Colbthach* or heifer, i. cccxxxii.

„ *fognuma*, a serving pot (vessel), iii. 485.

Caireaman, a shoemaker, i. cii.

Cairi, see *Caire*.

Cairte Dearg, the "red stone",—the stone under which king Dathi was buried in *Relig-na-Righ*.

Caisel, *Caiseal*, an encircling stone wall, a stone building, a castle, i. ccciv; iii. 14, 15, 16, 34.

Caisleoir, a caiseal-builder, iii. 14, 73, 79.

Cathair, now *Cahir*, a chair or seat; a circular wall of dry masonry, a stone fort. The British "*Caer*", the Latin "*Castrum*", and the English "castle", iii. 4, 5, 68.

Cathair Atair, a bishop's seat, i. clvi.

Calad-Bolg (the hard bulging), the sword of *Leite*, ii. 320.

Calaind, Kalends, iii. 498.

Caluraigh, sites of ancient churches and burial grounds, iii. 71.

Cana, plural of *Cain*, which see.

Canach, a general term for moss and other mountain and marsh plants but specially applied to the Hypnum cupressiforme, used for dyeing. i. cccci.

Canach Sleibe, cotton of the mountain, the Eriophorum polystachion or common Cotton grass, iii. 144, 145.

Canaile, a canal, the *cuisle* or tale sometimes so called, iii. 326.

Cantana, incantations, iii. 526, 527.

Canticum, *Canticum Psalmi*, *Canticum Psalmus*, musical terms, iii. 239.

Caogdach, "fifty-man", the title of the lowest professor in a great public school, iii. 84.

Caomdai, beds, compartments, iii. 480.

Caomhluighe, or *Comhluighe*, a corrupt form of *cobluighe*, which see, iii. 252.

Cap, a bier or car, i. cccclxxv.

Capall, a horse, i. cccclxxv.

Capell-lands, or horse lands, i. xcii, cliii.

Carcair na n-giall, the prison of the hostages at Tara, ii. 16.

Cardda, obdurate, iii 422.

Carrmocaill, gen. of *Carmogal*, *Carmogul*, carbuncles, iii. 14, 414; *Carrmogul corcrai*, crimson carbuncles, iii. 190.

Carpat cethri secht cumal, a chariot worth four times seven *Cumals*, iii. 414.

Carr, a cart, or car, i. cccclxxvi; iii. 508.

Carr shlunain, a sliding car, cf. German *Schleife*, i. cccclxxvi.

Carn, a pile of stones made by each of a party going to a battle depositing a stone; each of the survivors afterwards taking away his stone; so that the number of stones that remained represented the number slain. The *Carn* was also piled over a grave, i. cccxxxv.

„ *cinn Cirb*, the carn of Cirb's head, i. cccxxxvii.

„ *an aen Fir*, the one man's Carn, i. cccxxxvii.

Carra (*i.e. carraic*), a rock, i. cxxi.

Cassán, a brooch, iii. 95, 100.

Casriandaib, a certain description of beasts of burden, iii. 330.

Cath, war, battle, *i.* cccxli, cccclviii; a battalion (3,000 men), *ii.* 381.
Cath Barr, a war hat or helmet, *i.* cccxcv.
Cath Carpat Serda, a scythed war chariot, *i.* ccccl xxxii.
Cathach (book) of battles, shrine of St. Colum Cille's copy of the gospels so called, see *ii.* 163.
Cathbar, a helmet, *iii.* 167, 194, 202, 209, 426. See *Barr*.
Catherriud, a battle-suit, *iii.* 444.
Cath-Mhiledh, a champion (or commander) over a battalion, *i.* cclxiv, *ii.* 138.
Cath cro, a gory battle, *iii.* 462.
Cathroi, a battle-field, *iii.* 436.
Catad, hardened, *iii.* 422.
Cateatside, what, or who, are they? *iii.* 492.
Caur [same as *Curad*], a hero, *iii.* 446.
Ceann-Barr, a covering or ornament for the head (a crest or diadem), *iii.* 209.
Ceann feadhna-cead, the captain of an hundred men, *ii.* 381.
Ceann-Corcra, crimson-headed [flowers], *i.* dcxliii.
Ceardcha, a forge, *i.* cccxxxv.
Ceasnaidhean, enchanted sleep, [childbirth, pains or debility], *ii.* 319.
Ceathramadh maoir, the *Maer's* or steward's quarter, *i.* cliii.
Cechtirnaei, each or every one of them, *iii.* 509.
Céd Coibche, the bridal gift at the first marriage of a woman, *i.* clxxiv.
Ceile, a client or vassal, a tenant, *i.* xcvii; *ii.* 34, 37; *iii.* 493, 494.
Ceile Coem[t]echtai, an espoused wife, *iii.* 500.
Ceilsine, submission, allegiance, tenancy, *i.* clxxxv, ccxxxviii, cclxviii; *ii.* 34; *iii.* 502.
Ceir, a merle-hen, *iii.* 357.
Ceirtle gela, balls of white bleached thread, *iii.* 116.
Ceis, a tune, vide *Ceis cendtoll*, *iii.* 243, 254; a condensation of the two words *Cai Astuda*, means of fastening, 253; or a path to the knowledge of the music; or *Ceis* is the name of a small *Cruit* which accompanies a large *Cruit* in co-playing; or it is the name of the little pin (or key) which retains the string in the wood of the *Cruit*; or [it is the name of] the *Coblaigi* [the two strings called the sisters]; or it is the name of the heavy string [or bass]; or the *Ceis* in the *Cruit* is what keeps the counterpart with its strings in it, etc. (*Leabhar na h-Uidhre*), *iii.* 248, 250, 253, etc.; or the name of the small *Cruit* which accompanied a large *Cruit* at playing upon; or the name of a nail on which the strings called *Lethrind* were fastened; or the name of the little pin; or the name of the strings called the *Cobluighe* (or sisters); or the name of the heavy string (*Liber. Hymnorum*), *iii.* 251, 253, etc.
Ceis cendtoll, a head sleeping, or debilitating *Ceis* or tune, *iii.* 254.
Ceiss, some kind of vessel, *i.* ccclxviii.
Cend-barr, or *Cenn barr*, a helmet or cap, *iii.* 174, 209.
Cenbert, a hat or helmet, *i.* cxv.
Cennbair, head pieces, *iii.* 158.
Cendfedhna Céd, a leader of one-hundred, *i* ccxliv.
Cengal (*Fer Cengal*), cognate with the Old French *Ginguer*, to move the feet. See *Fer Cengal*, *i.* dxli.
Cenud, *Ceniud*, a conical hood attached to a *Cochall*, *i.* cccxc, cccxci.
Cenniud find, a white hood for a mantle or cloak, *iii.* 150.
Cennas, (a head gier), a halter (same as *Cennose* and *Cennfhosaidh*, which see *iii.* 482.
Cennose, *Cennfhosaidh*, a head-gear, a halter to control the ox at the plough, etc., *iii.* 479.
Ceó cetamain, the mist of a May morning [the May mist], *iii.* 141.
Ceol, a generic name for music of all kinds, *iii.* 371.
Ceolán, pl. *Ceolana*, a tinkling bell or tintinnabulum; also elongated pear-shaped or globular closed bells, the mediæval *Crotal*, the French *Grelot*, *i.* dxxvi, dlxxxvii; *iii.* 330, 331, 332.
Ceolchairecht, a playing, *iii.* 371.
Cepóc, or *Cepóg*, a panegyric, a funeral chorus, see *Asdbsi*, *i.* cccxxiv; *iii.* 247, 371.
Cerd, a smith who worked in the precious metals, a goldsmith, an artificer, an armourer, *i.* ccclii; *ii.* 322-3, 362; *iii.* 43, 202, 204, 207, 208, 209, 210.

Cerdan, the smaller goldsmith, *iii.* 207.

Cerdbeg, the little (or young) goldsmith, *iii.* 207.

Cerdraighe, a tribe of hereditary goldsmiths, *iii.* 207.

Certan, a low and weak species of the lower class of *Cronán*, or purring performance, *iii* 375.

Cesc, quære, *iii.* 467, 490.

Cess, debility, *iii.* 412.

Cetamus, first, firstly, *iii.* 493.

Cetal Noith, "the illustrious narrative", an ancient grammatical term, the name of an ancient poetic rhythm and measure. It is that to which Fiace's metrical Life of St. Patrick is written, *ii.* 74–5.

Cetals, measured addresses or orations, *ii* 173.

Cethardiabail, four-folding, *iii.* 106.

Cethir-rind, four-peaked (four-speared), *iii.* 428.

Cethrai, quadrupeds,—cows, pigs, sheep, etc., *iii.* 490.

Cethraime Arathair, four essentials of ploughing, *iii.* 479.

Cetluth, to first enjoy (to first lie with), *iii.* 434.

Cetmunter, Cetmuintir, a wife, a virgin wife, *iii.* 496, 500.

Cetmuintir dligtech, a lawful wife, *iii.* 496.

Cetmuinterais coir, proper bridal virginity, *iii.* 487.

Cetmuinterus, espoused wife, [first espousal], *iii* 501.

Charr, (*a charr*), his spear, *iii.* 503.

Chercaill, (*dag chercaill*) a good pillow, *iii.* 489.

Choccertad, (*do choccertad*) for the government, *iii.* 506.

Ciar, a dull black colour, *iii.* 133, 134.

Ciarann, a beautiful, large, mottled, wild bee, *iii.* 403.

Ciar bo docht, Ciar bo balb remi sin, "though he was before that dumb", *iii.* 327.

Cig [*Cing*], a bond (a contract), *iii.* 434.

Cilorn, Cilurn, a pitcher with a handle at its side, it was usually made of yew wood, but a *Cilurn umaide*, or bronze cilurn, is mentioned (*i.* dcxlii), *i.* cclvi, ccclxviii; *iii.* 62.

Ciamhaire, crying, *iii.* 223.

Cimbid, a victim in the power of a plaintiff, *i.e.*, a nexus when he became addictus, *i.* cxx, cclxxxv, ccxcii, *iii.* 474.

Cimidecht, the condition of a victim, *iii.* 509.

Cindas, springs or did spring, *iii.* 448.

Cind Fine, the children of the senior chief in a family, *i.* clxiii.

Cinél, a race, cf. Welsh *Cenedl* and Greek Γένος, *i.* lxxviii, cxcviii.

Cing, to progress, to rise above, to come to (or to go), *i.* ccxxix, *iii.* 456.

Cing, a man who has excelled every *Mal* (prince or king); a man who has progressed above every *File*; it is the name for a man who is ennobled by having been placed above what is ennobled, cf. A.-Sax. *Cyning*, O. H. German *Chuning*, English, *King*, *i.* ccxxviii

Cinntech, a species of poetry peculiar to the order of poet called *Cli*, *ii.* 171.

Cintaib coir Cuin, statutes of appropriate law, *iii.* 496.

Cir cathbarr, a crested helmet, *iii.* 444.

Cir Bolg, a combing bag, *i.* ccclix.

Circlaib oir acas argait, with circlets of gold and of silver, *iii.* 160, 161.

Cis, rent, tribute, *i.* ccxxxix.

„ *Flatha*, tribute from *Flaiths*, *i.* ccxxxviii, ccxl.

„ *n-incis*, a special allowance made for the support of superannuated members of a *Fine*, *i.* clxv.

Ciste Cranachain, "a cake of the *Cranachan*", a cake which was baked with the *Cranachan* or three-pronged baking stick, *i.* ccclxiv.

Cislir, how many, *iii.* 513.

Cisne, who are they? *iii.* 508.

Cladh Cricha, a territorial boundary, *i* cccclxxix, dcxl.

Claide, earth and clay dug out of a grave, a trench, etc., *i.* cccxxi.

Claidheamh, a sword, cf. Welsh *Cledyf*, *i.* cccclxiv; *ii.* 225, 226. See *Claidem*.

Claidem, a sword, cf. Latin *Gladius*, a sword or glaive, *i.* ccccxxxvii, cccclix-vi. *Claidem Mór*, a large sword, the Scotch "claymore", Welsh, Llawmawr

Claidem corthair, a border or fringe sword or lath, upon which a border or fringe was woven, *iii.* 116.

Claidheamh a sword, generally fig-

leaf-shaped and pointed, and invariably double-edged", see *Claidem*, i. cccexliv; ii. 255, 295.
Claidbini, little swords, ii. 301.
Claidmib, na Slata Fige,—Claidmib, that is, the weaving rods, the heddles, iii. 116.
Claind det, an ivory-hilted sword, iii. 147-8.
Clairseach, a harp, iii. 227, 257, 265.
Claiss, a cliff, iii. 428.
Cland, a sword worn by distinguished warriors as a badge of championhood or knighthood, i. cccclix.
Cland or *Clann*, children, a family or house, representing the Latin *Gens*. In its territorial and general sense it comprised all the *Flaths* of a *Tuath* with their respective *Fines*, i. lxxviii, lxxix, clxvii.
Clanna, boundary planters, i. clxxxii.
Clais, Clauis, a choir, iii. 239.
Cleas-cait, the cat feat, ii. 372. *Cleas-cletenech*, the feathered dart feat, ii. 372-373. *Cleas for analaibh*, the feat of his breathings, ii. 372.
Cleasa, feats, ii. 371.
Cleith, a wattle, iii. 487.
Cleith, chief or head of a tribe, the highest or best person or thing, i. c; iii. 494.
Cleithe, the roof-ridge of a house, iii. 480.
Cleithiu, possessions (houses), iii. 484.
Cleitme, a *Righ-Barr*, or *At*, a king's radiating helmet or hat, a crest, i. ccexcv, ccexcvi; ii. 209.
Clera, a word synonymous with *crioll*. See *crioll*, iii. 117.
Clesamnai, jugglers, iii 509.
Clesamhnaighe, jugglers, iii. 336.
Clesrada ána, noble feats, iii. 446.
Clesraidib, missive weapons, iii. 448.
Cless, Clessamun, Clessine, a juggler, iii. 147.
Clethe, prime cattle, iii. 501.
Cletin, Cleitin, a short little quill spear, i. cccexxxvi, cccexlv, cccexlvi; ii. 301, 308; iii. 436. *Cletine*, Cuchulaind's spear, so called, ii. 298-299.
Cli, an order of poets, ii. 171, 217.
Cliabh Inar, a body *Inar*, a jerkin, i. ccexxxviii, ccclxxxvi.
Cliaraidhe, a *Criollaire*, a man who made bags, bottles, and all such things of leather, iii. 117.
Cliathain, neck and breast pieces, see *Forgaib*.
Clithar-sed, or king *sed*, see *Sed*, iii. 480.
Clocc, a bell, Latin clocca. See *Clog*, i. dxxxiv, dxxxv.
Cloch ind abaind, the river stone, or sounding flag, near the water's edge, i. ccexviii.
Cloch uachtair, the upper stone of the quern, i. ccclx.
Clochann, or *Clochan*, as here used means a beehive-shaped hut or house formed of dry masonry, having each stone overlapping the other, and terminating in a single stone, i. cccviii, *et seq.*; iii. 64–75.
Clog, gen. sing. and nom. pl. *Cluig*, or *Cluice*, a bell, iii. 323, 332.
Cloictech, gen. *Cloictigi*, the bell house known as a round tower, a belfry, i. dxxxvi; iii. 48, 50, 54.
Clois, a name for the body of a chariot, i. cccclxxviii.
Cloth delgg n-ungga, a gem-set brooch worth an *unga*, iii. 496.
Clothach, renowned, illustrious, iii. 514.
Clothra, a thing which is heard being shaken, iii. 322.
Cluas, the ear, but used here in the sense of the evidence of an ear-witness, i. clxxxvii, clxxxviii.
Cluas n-glesa, ear-tuning (of a harp, etc.), iii. 221.
Cluiche Caentech, the funeral rite; singing of dirges, and other rites and ceremonies of the dead, i. cccxxiii, cccxxv–vi.
Cluchi, a game, iii. 460.
Cluicine, Cluicini, little bells, i. dxxxv, dxxxvi.
Cluinim, I hear (see *Rar cluin*), iii. 426.
Cnaimh-fhear, pl. *Cnamhfir*, a bone man, a musical performer on the bones, iii. 313, 367, 544.
Cnairseach, probably a sledge or large hammer, i. clvi, ccxxx, iii. 488.
Cneitfem, we shall fight, iii. 432.
Cned, stabs [wounds inflicted by stabs], iii. 440.
Cnes congna, a skin protecting armour, made apparently of plates of horn, i. cccclxxv, iii. 420.
Cnes Lena, a skin shirt, i.e. a shirt worn next the skin, i. ccclxxxii.
Cnoc, in the sense of a tomb or monument of the dead was a round or conical hill or mound raised

over a grave, *i.* cccxxix, cccxxxv, dcxxviii.
Cobach, purchase, *iii.* 414.
Cobhla, pl. *Comhlath*, simultaneous motion, [more correctly, lying or stretching together], *iii.* 251, 252.
Coblaighe, or *Cobhluighe*, or *Coblaigi*, the middle strings [the music of] which was called *An-Dord*, adding the negative particle *an* to signify literally *not bass* (see *Andord*), the two strings (of the *Cruit*), called the sisters of the harp, *iii.* 379; *iii.* 248–9, (see *Ceis*), 250, 251, 252, 256.
Cobhlach, intermediate [notes] tones, etc., *iii.* 378.
Cobrad, *Comraid*, bosses [as of a shield], *iii.* 436, 446.
Cocart, [a servant or villanus, *B.* of *Rights*, p. 200, *n.*], tenants who gave service in dyeing, ect., and in dye-stuffs, *i.* ccccii; *iii.* 119.
Cochall, a short cloak or cape, the Gallo-Roman *Cucullus*, sometimes occurring in the combination *Bardo-Cucullus*, cf. English *Cowl*, *i.* ccccxc-ccccxcii; *iii.* 104, 105, 150, 187, 224.
Cochle, a companion, *iii.* 418.
Cochlin, diminutive of *Cochal* or *Cuchul*, pl. *cochlini*,—small hooded capes, which represented the Gallo-Roman *Cucullio*, *i.* ccccxci, cccccxxxiii; *iii.* 183. *Cochlini gobach*, bill-pointed little cochalls, *i.* dcxl. *Cochlene dub*, small black mantles, *iii.* 150. *Cochlene brecca*, little speckled mantles, *iii.* 147-8.
Cochne cride, a heart companion, *iii.* 432.
Coemtecht, companions, *iii.* 509.
Choemtecht, guard, protection, *iii.* 509.
Co Festar, till it has been ascertained, *iii.* 513.
Coi d-fis in ciuil, a path to the knowledge of the music, *iii.* 253.
Coi, passed or went, *iii.* 506.
Coibche, valuable or rich clothes, personal ornaments, etc., given as a marriage gift, *iii.* 27, 29, 480; a legal gift which the bridegroom gave to the bride after her marriage, the Welsh *Cowyll*, the German *Morgangaba*, the Norse *Hindradagsgaf*, *i.* clxxiii, clxxiv.
Coibsena, confessions, *i.* cccxl.
Coicedal, *Coicetal*, harmony, *iii.* 215, 255.
Coicrich, boundaries, *iii.* 511.
Coicriud, flesh-piercing, flesh-seeking; *Slegh coicriudi*, a flesh-seeking spear, *iii.* 137, 138, 161.
Coicti, fifth (fifth day), *iii.* 477.
Coictige, cook-house, *iii.* 497.
Coic-tighis, five houses, *iii.* 56 [*see* different meanings of, and mistake about, *iii.* 54-56].
Coicroth, the umbo of a shield, sometimes also a rim, *i.* cccxxxviii. *Coicroth oir*, a golden rim, or a golden umbo of a shield, *iii.* 137, 138.
Coidin, wooden mugs (drinking vessels), *iii.* 485.
Coidmiach, a bucket or peck which contained a *Miach* or sack, *iii.* 512.
Coinsund, consummation, *iii.* 456.
Coipe or *Coife*, a simple cap with a *Caille* or veil, *i.* ccccxciv.
Coir, propriety, *iii.* 255. *Coir Anmann*, appropriate etymology of names, *ii.* 11; a tract on the etymology of proper names so called, *ii.* 237.
Coir, tune, or being in tune, *iii.* 214, 215, 255. *Coir Ceathairchuir*, the name of the great harp of the Tuatha De Danann god, the *Dagda*, *iii.* 214, 306. [The true meaning of *Coir* when used in a musical sense is key or mode, which is that of its Welsh representative *Cywair*. *Coir Ceathairchuir*, the name of the mythical harp of the *Dagda*, meant, consequently, that the harp could be tuned in four keys, and not that it was quadrangular.]
Coire, a pot, *ii.* 133. *Coire mac Cruadhghobhann*, pot, son of hardy smith, *ii.* 133. *Coire sainte*, "pot of avarice", *ii.* 56. See *Caire*.
Coirm, ale, *iii.* 498. See *Cuirm*.
Coirte Flatha, the pillar stone of the *Flath*, *i.* clxxxvii.
Coisbert, covering for the feet, shoes, boots, etc., *i.* cxv.
Coisir Chonnachtach, the banqueting house of the Connaught people at Tara, *ii.* 15.
Coitcend Fiadnaise, a disinterested witness, *i.* cclxxix.
Colbtach, a heifer, *iii.* 112.
Colc, *Colg*, a sword, *i.* cccxxxviii–ix; *ii.* 243; *iii.* 246. *Colgdet*, a tooth-hilted or straight-edged sword, *ii.* 301. *Colg-dets*, ivory-hilted small swords, *i.* cccxxxviii, cccclvi; *ii.* 303.
Colith, to evade, to shun, *ii* 522.

Colpdach, Colpthach, a heifer three years old, *i.* clxxxiii; *iii.* 475. See *Sed. Colpdach Firen*, a three year old bull, etc., *iii.* 484.
Com, the belly or sound-board [of the harp, the waist], *iii.* 256, 358.
Comada, dat. pl. *Comadaibh*, rewards, *iii.* 414, 418.
Comadas, fit, becoming, appropriate, *iii.* 496.
Commae, to congregate, to contribute to, *iii.* 505.
Comairce, safe conduct or protection, which a man was entitled to after he left a house where he had remained on *cai* or *coshering*, *iii.* 513, 576.
Comairge, clients (followers), *iii.* 497.
Comairsem, we meet, *iii.* 420.
Comaitecht, companionship, *iii.* 162, 163.
Comaithi, neighbours, *i.* cciv. See *Comaithechs.*
Comaithechs, comaitheachs, cotenants or copartners, *i.* cxii, cxci.
Comaitches, Commaitches, a gild or copartnership, *i.* clix, clxxxi, cciv, ccxvi; *Comaitches Comaide*, cooccupancy of *Comaitches*, that is, of copartners, *i.* clxxxi, ccxvi.
Comalta, stepbrothers (fellow-pupils, etc.), *iii.* 260.
Comarbship, successorship, co-occupancy, *iii.* 483.
Comardathacha, emblematic [having devices carved or worked upon them], *iii.* 436.
Comdasrala, so that he cast, *iii.* 448
Comdiin, protection, *iii.* 493.
Comfhaicsigestar, they drew nearer to each other [the contest became closer], *iii.* 448.
Comgrad, co-grade, *iii.* 504.
Comhadhasa, the *Duthaig* or whole people of a territory, *i.* cxcvii, cxcviii.
Comhobair gach cinil, edon crann glesa, the instrument of all music, namely, the *Crann-glesa*, or tuning tree, *iii.* 256.
Comla, a door; a hole in the upper stone of the quern through which the corn was admitted from the hopper, or from the hand in the hand-quern, *i.* ccclx.
" *catha*, "gate of battle", the name of *Ceitchair Mac Uthaithir's* shield, *i.* cccclxxii; *ii.* 333.
Comobair na Fige, all the instruments used in weaving, *iii.* 116.
Comopair na bairse, the instrument of the manufacturing woman, namely, the winding bars, the tree upon which she prepares the yarn, the winding reel [bars], *iii.* 116.
Comopar cach raithe, working implements for the work of every quarter of the year, *iii.* 501.
Comorb, Comarb, a co-heir, *i.* clxxxi, clxxxiii, cclxxv.
Comracut, concentrated, *iii.* 238.
Comraid, see *Cobrad.*
Comthuagach, curved; *Claideb Comthuagach catha*, a curved sword of battle, *iii.* 446.
Conagtais, that they would celebrate, *iii.* 526-7.
Conairgaile uad, wards (beats) off from, *iii.* 518.
Conabath, died, or did die, *iii.* 526-7.
Conbba, disbanded (or broken up), *iii.* 505.
Conbongar, is broken, *iii.* 255.
Condriced, to contend (to meet or engage with), *iii.* 446.
Condricfim, we shall encounter, *iii.* 432.
Conecestar, a house of penitence? *iii.* 46.
Confe, recognized or confirmed, *iii.* 514.
Confled, a collective or common feast, *i.* cxcviii.
Congan, pl. *Congna*, a horn, *i.* cccclxxv.
Congancness, Congan cnessach, Conganchnis, a skin-protecting armour, a coat of mail probably made of plates of horn, *i.* cccclxxiv; *iii.* 434, 414, 450.
Congilda, a partnership for co-grazing, *i.* cciv, ccxvi, ccl, ccli. See *Comaitches.*
Congilt, co-grazing, *i.* ccxvi.
Congla, Congelt, co-grazing, *iii.* 478.
Co n-inrucus Cleithe, with the *Inrucus*, worthiness of a chief, *iii.* 501.
Conit roib, whether it be, *iii.* 505.
Conn Conda Secha, chiefs of kindred, who attended court to give testimony for the members of their *Fine*, to accept the verdict of the court, and give bail for any of them against whom a judgment was registered, *i.* cclxviii.
Connatacht, he asked, *iii.* 450.
Connalbi, friendship, *iii.* 509.

Consrenga, he binds, *iii.* 491.

Contarrisseter, is bound, *iii.* 238, 315.

Contoiseth, became silent, *iii.* 314.

Conugud, overthrow, *iii.* 430.

Cor, a kind of dance or dance tune, *iii.* 407, 408.

Corcailli, pillows, *iii.* 499.

Corco, oats, *i.* ccclxii.

Corcur, or *Corcar*, a purple colour obtained by the action of ammonia on lichens, chiefly the Lecanora tartarea and L. parella, *i.* cccc. The shade of colour is compared to that of the berries of the yew tree. *Corcur buicle* lustrous purple (?); *Corcair maige*, crimson of the plain, *i.* dcxliii.

Coriech n-Errid, the champion's salmon-sault or leap, *ii.* 372.

Corn, a horn, a metallic instrument of music of the trumpet kind, *iii.* 305, 306, 307, 308, 313, 336, 340, 350. *Corn cael*, a thin or slender horn or tube, a *crann ciuil*, *iii.* 324, 326.

Cornair, *Cornoir*, a horn-blower, a trumpeter, *iii.* 219, 306, 307, 308, 311, 312, 313, 367, 382, 509.

Cornair, a great horn-blower, a professional name for a musician, *iii.* 367.

Cornaireadha, trumpeters, *iii.* 336.

Corn-Buabhaill, a drinking cup or drinking horn, not a musical instrument, *iii.* 305.

Cornis, garlands, etc., *iii.* 104–5.

Corp, until, *iii.* 490. *Corp Dire*, a fine paid to a person for bodily injury done to himself, *i.* cxviii, cxxviii, clxxvii, ccxcii, *iii.* 477.

Corr, the cross tree, or harmonic curve [of the harp], *iii.* 256, 258.

Corthair a border or fringe, dat. plural *Corthoraib*, *iii.* 113, 116.

Corus, right, appropriate, *iii.* 498. *Corus a airlis*, the proper extent of his yard, *iii.* 488. *Corus biata*, prescribed lawful maintenance, *iii.* 502. *Corus Cronain*, a scientific purring chorus, *iii.* 245. *Corus dligid*, according to (established) law, *iii.* 501. *Corus othrusa*, the laws providing for the maintenance, care, and medical attendance of the sick and wounded, *iii.* 476. *Corus Tincur*, proper or lawful furniture, *iii.* 499. *Corus Tuatha*, the true knowledge of the rank, rights, privileges, and responsibilities of the various grades of a *Tuath*, or people of a territory, *iii.* 476.

Corughadh, putting in tune or order [the tuning of a harp or other musical instrument], *iii.* 214, 215.

Coselastar, i.e. *do rat*, that cast or threw [that set, or put, or that gave], *iii.* 249.

Cosnum, opposition, contention, *iii.* 501.

Cot, or *Cotha*, an enclosure; a place set apart at *Aenachs* for women called *Cota na m-Ban*. The French *Coterie* is obviously related to this word. The word is also cognate with the English *cot*, *cottage*, etc., and with the *cotarius* and *cotarelles* of Domesday Book, the *Cotsetlas* and the German *Kothsass*, *Erb*, and *Mark-Kotter*. The *Cot* was apparently the enclosed land upon which a *Both* was erected, so that *Bothach* was the same as *Cottier*, as is shown by the name *Coitinidhe chill inghine Baoith*, applied to the commons of Killinaboy in the county of Clare, from its villages of *Coitins* or cottagers, cabins. These cottagers were freeholders, possessing *Cots* on the commons of Killinaboy, who earned a livelihood as day-labourers until they were starved out by want of employment during the famine of 1847–8–9, and the misery and disease that followed. The Forty-shilling Freeholders, whose rights were unjustly swept away in 1829, like those of the higher classes of freeholders and copyholders at an earlier period, were *Saer Bothachs* or free *Cottini*, *i.* cxvi, cclvi, *iii.*

Cotarsunn, with condiments, *iii.* 498.

Craebh ciuil, a musical branch, *i.* dxxxvi–vii viii; *iii.* 313, 317, 318.

Craebhaigh, branchy, [a branch, or tree cutter], *ii.* 133.

Craebh-Dearg, red branch, *i.* cccxxxvii; *ii.* 332.

Craebh ruadh, red branch, one of the Royal Houses of Emania, *ii.* 9, 10, 332; *iii.* 453.

Crass, mouth, vide *Craeslinaidh*, *ii.* 133.

Craisech, a broad-blade spear, with an oval, not a pointed end (a Firbolg weapon), *i.* ccccxxxvii, ccccxxxviii, cccclvi; *ii.* 235, 241, 243, 255, 262, 295, 344, 345. *Craisecha cranmera-*

ra catha, thick-handled battle *Craisechs* (spears), *ii.* 241.

Crait, Chrait (*crait-cro*), wealth, property, *iii.* 520.

Cranachan, a three-legged stool, upon which the oatmeal-cake was supported before the fire, *i.* ccclxiv.

Crannur, Crannchur, casting lot, *i.* clxiv, cclxxix, cclxxxi.

Crandbolg lethair, a leathern tube-bag, *i.* ccclvii; *iii.* 117.

Crann ciuil, musical tree, a generic term for any kind of musical instrument, *i.* dxxxiii; *iii.* 323, 324, 325, 326.

Crann-Dord, "tree music", a species of music produced by the striking together of the handles of a number of spears so as to accompany or blend with the voices of a chorus of singers [this meaning is by mistake applied to *Dord-Fiansa* at *iii.* p. 380]; this word has also been applied to the measured bellowing of the celebrated brown bull of Cuailgne, in the tale of the *Táin Bó Chuailgne*, *i.* cclix; *iii.* 376-7, 379, 380, 432; see *Dord-Fiansa*.

Crann glesa, or *gleasta*, the tuning tree [of a harp] or cross bar in which the pegs are inserted, *iii.* 256.

Cranntabaill, a sling, or rather a kind of cross-bow for shooting stones or metal balls. The word has the same meaning as the French *Fustibale*, and the German *Stock-Schleuder*, *i.* cccclxi, cccclxii; *iii.* 195, 197, 291, 294.

Creachtach, wounding [woundful], *iii.* 452.

Crech Torretnach, free wages given in return for the *Biatad* of eight persons, *i.* cxi.

Crechta, cuts [wounds], *iii.* 440.

Cred, tin, *i.* ccccix, *n.* 748; *Cred-Ume*, or *Cred-Uma*, that is, *Cred*-copper or bronze; *Credne*, the first worker in bronze, his name derived from, *i.* ccci, cccxlvi, cccxlviii, cccclvi, dcxli; *iii.* 138, 219, 210, 220.

Cret or *Creit*, the *capsus* or body of a chariot. Cf. Latin *Crates*, English *Crate*. The *Cret* proper was the bottom and shell of the body of the chariot; the *Cret cuain* was the compartment in which the seat, or the reclining or resting couch was sheltered, and the *Cret cro* was the part where the champion stood when fighting, or when he wished to show himself, *i.* cccclxxviii, cccclxxxi; *iii.* 428.

Cretime, gen. of *Cretem*, religion, *iii.* 505.

Criathur, a sieve;—*cumang*, a narrow sieve;—*cairceach*, a hair sieve for preparing flour to dust over *Bairgins*, buns, etc., *i.* ccclx.

Crich, Criech, a territory, *i.* lxxxii, cliv, clxxxii, cxcviii, ccxlvi.

Crimall, the blood-spotted, the *Lain Celtchair*, so called, *ii.* 325.

Criol, a chest, *ii.* 133. *Criol mac Craeslinnidh*, "chest, son of fill-mouth", *ii.* 133.

Crioll, a bag formed of strips of leather stitched together with a thong, *i.* ccclviii; *iii.* 117.

Cris, a girdle, the *Zona* of the Romans, Welsh *Crys*, *i.* ccclxxx, ccclxxxii, ccclxxxvi, cccxcvi; *iii.* 104-5.

Crith gablach, a law tract on the classification and privileges, etc., of the grades of society, *ii.* 35; *iii.* 465, *et seq.*

Crithir ciuil, thrill of music, *iii.* 215.

Cruitire, a harper, *iii.* 236, 265, 266, 240, 241, 212, 307, 311, 367.

Crobh-Dearg, red hand, *iii.* 25.

Cro-derg, blood red, *i.* cccxxxvii.

Croi, now *Cró*, a shed, a hut, *i.* ccclxvi.

Crolindech, blood-streaming, *iii.* 452.

Crón, *i.* cccxxxvi. See *Cruan*.

Cronan [a sort of musical purring], a throat accompaniment without words; it was also called *Aidbsi* in Ireland, and *Cepóc* in Scotland, *iii.* 235, 246, 371, 375, 376, 377.

Crononaighe, a professional name for the musician who performed the *Cronán*, *iii.* 376.

Cronee cumdaigs, a preserving or cinerary urn, *i.* cccxxiii.

Crossach, a standard of weight for gold, silver, etc., *iii.* 102.

Crotal, the Parmelia Saxatilis and P. omphalodes, which give a yellowish brown dye, *i.* cccci.

Crottach, chicken-breasted, sharp, or high-breasted; it is also the Gaedhlic name for the curlew, *iii.* 237.

Crothla, such as the warning of a cross or a *Crothla*, that is to pass over what is shaken there, the forbidding *drolan* (or hasp), that is, the *Crothla* which is placed upon the garden door of the garden of an exile of God [of a recluse or pilgrim], *iii.* 322.

Cru, blood, death, *iii.* 450, 508.

Cruadh, hardy (hard), *ii.* 133. *Cruaidin Caidid-cheann*, the hard hard-headed, the name of the sword of Cuchulaind, which came down as an heir-loom through the family to Socht, son of Fithal, *ii.* 322.

Cruan, probably amber, but sometimes applied to enamelled metal, or ornaments in which amber was used with enamel; the plate or ornamented metal in which the ornaments were set seems also to have been sometimes included under the term, *i.* ccclv, ccccxxxvi, cccclxxxii.

Cruitnecht, wheat, *i.* ccclxii, dcxlii.

Crut, *Crot*, *Cruit*, a stringed musical instrument, supposed to have been the harp, cf. the British *Chrotta* in Venantius Fortunatus, the Old Welsh *Crud*, modern Welsh *Crwth*, English *Croude*, or *Crowd*, *i.* ccccxcvi, diii, div, dx, dxiii, dxix, dxxiii; *iii.* 213, 244, 261, 266.

Cruta, pl. of *Cruit*, *iii.* 313.

Cu, gen. *Conn*, *Con*, *Coin*, a hound; hence the British man's name *Cuneglasus*, the yellow or tawny hound, *i.* ccccxxxvi.

Cuachs di ór, little cups of gold [upon his poll behind, into which his hair coiled], *iii.* 187. *Cuagh mac Tormora*, "Wooden Mug, son of Turner".

Cuacleithe or *Cuach Cleithe*, a wicker cup roof, *i.* ccxcix, cccclxv.

Cuad, *cuagh*, a wooden bowl or cup, or more correctly a mug, *i.* ccclv, ccclvi; *ii.* 133; *iii* 481, 495.

Cuailne Gurt, stakes which marked the extent of a *Gort*, *i.* cxxxv.

Cuaille, a stake [of iron here] used as a pin in a cloak, *iii.* 95.

Cuairt ulcaid, encircled with beard. See it, *iii.* 477.

Cualne, boundary stakes, *iii.* 511.

Cuarans, skin shoes, *i.* cccxci, cccxcvii, cccxcviii, cccc; *iii.* 103, 105.

Cuaranaigh, a brogue-maker; he also made *criolls*, leather bags and *pails*, or leather bottles, *iii.* 117.

Cuarsceith cred, bent shields of God. *Cuar Sgiath*, a hollow, humpy shield, formed like a *Cuacleithe* or humpy cup-roof, *i.* cccclxv, *iii.* 188.

Cub, the cup in the cross-bar of the quern in which the *Milaire* or pivot worked. The word is also applied in a general way to the *Cub* and *Comla*, *i.e.* the cup and doorway of the quern itself, *i.* ccclx.

Cuglass, a "water hound", a term applied in the laws to a foreigner from beyond the sea who married an Irish woman, *i.* cxix.

Cui, *Cai*, coshering, visitation, etc., *iii.* 495, 498.

Cuic mera na Fine, the five fingers of the *Fine*, *i.* clxiv. See *Cuicer na Fine*.

Cuicer na Fine, the five of the *Fine*, that is, the five *Gialls* or pledges of the *Fine*, *i.e.* the family council of five, corresponding to the "Four men and the Reeve" of an Anglo-Saxon Township, *i.* clxiv, cclii, cclxviii, cclxxx.

Cuicidh, a province composed of five *Mór Tuatha*, *i.* lxxxiv.

Cuicil, *cuicil lin*, a distaff, the flax rock, *iii.* 116.

Cuicrind, flesh-seeking, *iii.* 425.

Cuig Rath Cedach, five pledges, or guarantors of one hundred of chattels, *i.* cxxiv, cxxv, clix, cciv, ccxl, cclxxv.

Cuilche, sack-cloth, some kind of coarse cloth, cf. *Culcais*, quilts, rugs, *i.* ccclxvi.

Cuilg n-deit, ivory hilted swords, *iii.* 436.

Cuilmen, the greatest book taught or known in the public schools of Eriu, *ii.* 84.

Cuil Tech, a store house, *i.* ccclxix.

Cuin, when, *iii.* 490.

Cuindsen—This word appears to be the accusative sing. of *cuinse*, the face; the old nom. form is *cuinch*, the face, which probably contains the root of *countenance*; but as used here it appears to convey the sense in which the word is used at present, namely, a covenant, a bond, any stated lawful right, *iii.* 515.

Cuing, a curved yoke, *i.* cccclxxx.

Cuirce derg, a red tuft [a tassel], *iii.* 150.

Cuirel, a casket? [a curling pin or comb, "*cirr, chuirrel argit conecor deor, acthe oc folcud alluing argit*, having a curling comb of silver ornamented with gold, washing her head in a silver basin"], *iii.* 189, 190.

Cuirm, gen. *Corma* or *Chorma*, ale, *i.* celii, ccxcix, ccclii, ccclix, ccclxiii, ccclxix, ccclxxi, ccclxxii, ccclxxvi, ccclxxvii; *iii.* 506.

Cuirmtech, gen. *Cuirmtigi*, *Cuirmtighe*, an ale house, *i.* ccclii, ccclix, ccclxxi; *iii.* 511, 514.

Cuirpi Dualach, a peaked straddle. The *Cuirpi* was the wooden straddle shaped to fit across the horse's back; the *Duals* were the two peaks or pegs which kept the reins from falling down. The *Dual* is represented by the *Stuirn* or pegs of the modern basket straddle on which the baskets are hung, *i.* cccclxxxi.

Cuiseach, pl. *Cuiseacha*, a reed or some such instrument, *iii.* 310, 313, 325. *Cuisigh*, reeds or small pipes, *iii.* 325, 326. [This word ought perhaps to have been written without the final *h*, *cuisig*, in which case it would refer to the performers on the *cuiseach*, and not to the instrument itself, as the context shows in the poem on the *Fair* of *Carman*.]

Cuisle, a tube, *iii.* 324, 326, a tube or cock for tapping an ale cask, *i.* ccclix. *Cuisle ciuil*, a musical tube, another name for the *crann ciuil*, or musical tree, *iii.* 326.

Cuisleanna, dat pl. *Cuisleandoib*, pipes or tubes [bag-pipes], *iii.* 215, 310.

Cuislennach, *cuislennaigh*, the name of the performer or performers on the *Cuislenna ciuil*, or musical tubes, not the pipers or *pipaireadh*, *iii.* 313, 326, 366, 368, 336, 509. *Cuisleannchu*, [recte, *cuisleandchu*], pipers, *iii.* 311. *Cuislenna ciuil*, musical tubes, *iii.* 368.

Cuitech Fuait, funeral games in honour of the dead, *i.* cccxxvi.

Cul, a name for the capsus or body of a chariot, *i.* cccclxxviii.

Cul Airecht, "rear court", the court of appeal, *i.* cclxii, cclxx, cclxxi, cclxxiii.

Culcais, a quilt, *i.* ccxcix.

Culgaire in carpait, creaking of the chariot, *iii.* 426.

Culg-det, a straight edged sword, *iii.* 450.

Culpat, *culpait* a hood for covering the head, *i* ccoxcv; the term is sometimes applied to a collar worn on the neck, but which probably had something attached for covering the head, vide *lene gel culpatach*, a shirt with a white collar, *iii.* 93.

Cumal, *cumhal*, three cows, *i.* lxxxix, clvi, clvii, clxv, clxxx, clxxxi, cxci, ccxliii, dcxliii; *ii.* 35, 60, *iii.* 29, 30, 101, 102, 139, 311, 479.

Cumalaibh cainibh, precious *cumals*, *iii.* 514.

Cumal Dé, God's *Cumal*, food supplied by a *Ceile* at the death of his *Flath* or lord, *i.* cxii.

Cumascc curmtigi, the revel of the ale house, *iii.* 509.

Cumbach Nadma, breaking or discharging of a bond, *i.* cclxxxv.

Cunnrigh, binding, *iii.* 502.

Cumscaigi, is conferred upon, *iii.* 490.

Cumthach, ornament, or ornamentation here, *iii.* 492.

Cundrech, governing, government, 504.

Chundring, direction, (control, or sway), *iii.* 503.

Cup [same as *gurab*, that it be], *iii.* 416.

Cur n-iach n-Erred, a champion's salmon-sault, *i.* ccxcix.

Curad, pl. *Curada*, a champion, *i.* cccxxix.

Curach, a canoe, *i.* dcxliii; *iii.* 53.

Curathmir, *Curadmir*, the champion's share, *i.* ccclvii, ccclxv.

Curn, a drinking horn made of an ox-horn, *i.* ccclvi.

Curthar, a border or fringe put to the facings of clothes, border of lace, *iii.* 107.

Curu-bel, binding engagements (or persons who had power to bind them), *iii.* 491.

Cusal, a long wooden bin (or box); also small wooden repositaries of prepared materials [of wool and flax] which the women kept in ancient times, *i.* ccclix; *iii.* 117.

Cusigh (*recte cuiscach*), a reed or musical pipe, *iii.* 325; *ii.* 45.

Dabach, *Dobach*, a keeve or tub;

Dabaig, keeves, *i.* ccclvi, ccclxvi, ccclxxii, ccclxxiii; *iii.* 485, 495.
Dabcha, tubs, *i.* ccclvii, ccclix.
Dae, the peace constable and commander of the armed levy of a *Fine*; he was the representative of the Welsh *Dialwr*, and the A. Sax. Ward Reeve, *i.* ccxlvi, ccxlvii, ccli, cclxxvii; *iii.* 518.
Daer, base, see the following words; this word is also used in the sense of sequestration, *i.* clxx.
,, *Accinti*, *Agenta*, base followers of a *Flath*, see *Daer Aicillne*, *i.* cxv, cxviii, cxxv.
,, *Aicillne*, base non-professional followers and tenants of a *Flath* or lord, *i.* cxv, ccxxxviii.
,, *Bothach*, base farm labourers of a *Flath* or lord, who occupied a *Both* or cabin on his demesne, *i.* cxv, cxvi. See *Saer Bothach* and *Cot*.
,, *Celes* or *Ceiles*, base tenants or villeins, corresponding to the Welsh *Taogs*, *i.* cxiv, cxxviii, cccii.
,, *Fuidir*, see *Fuider*.
Daer-Nemid, or *Nemhidh*, base professors, *i.* ccvii; *iii.* 209.
Dagdaine, good-men, nobles, *i.* cccxxix.
Daileman, *Dalemain*, cupbearers (or drink-bearers), *i.* cii; *iii.* 144.
Dairt, a generic name for yearling bulls, and heifers of one year and up to two years old, *i.* clxxvi, clxxxiii; *iii.* 29, 112, 480, 516. See *Dartaid*.
Dagh, good; *Dagh-shuaithe*, "good yarn" [texture], *ii.* 133.
Dal, *Dail*, an assembly where laws were enacted, *i.* ccliv.
Dalus, I have served, *iii.* 458.
Dám, retinue or company, the *Gefer-scipe* or *Folgoth* of the Anglo-Saxons, and the *Gefolge* of the Germans, *i* ccxxxv. *Damam*, company or retinue, *iii.* 491, 492, 496. *Damrad*, retinues, companies, *iii.* 510. See *Lin*.
Dam, pl. *Dama*, an ox, *i.* cccl, *iii.* 330, 479. *Dam n-Dreimned*, a clambering (or wild) ox,; *Dam n-Dilend*, a water ox, *iii.* 458. *Dam Dabach*, an ox-tub, or tub large enough to contain a whole ox; also a "Testudo" made with shields, *i.* cccclxix.
Damhliag, a stone-built, principal church, *iii.* 48, 49, 53.
Da n-All n-dualach dronudi [recte *dronbudi*], two rich yellow *All dualach*, *i.* cccclxxxi, see *All dualach*.
Damna, material, *Damna cinnada*, the material of a culprit, *iii.* 522. *Damna Righ*, the material of a king, *i.* ccxxxii, ccxxxiii.
Damsa, *Dambsa*, dancing, *iii* 407.
Dan, now, also, moreover, same as *dana*, *dna*, and *dno*, *iii.* 506.
Dáo, two, *iii.* 502.
Dartaid, a two year old heifer if bulled at that age. A yearling heifer entering on her second year was also commonly called a *Dartaid*, *i.* clxxxiii. *Dartaid Inide*, a heifer at shrove-tide (when passing into her third year), see *Sed*.
Dartaire, pl. *Dartairidhe*, square sods used for building sod fences and graves of the *Mur* kind where stones could not be obtained, *i.* cccxxxii.
Dechmad, tenth (tenth day); *Deich Deichde*, ten of tens; *Deichsaide*, tenfold, *iii.* 477, 482, 492.
Dechnebur, *Dechnenbur*, ten men, *iii.* 501.
Dedail, parting [separating] *iii.* 250.
Dedenguin duine, violent death of a person, *iii.* 497.
Dedluthai, exercised or enforced by, *iii.* 505.
Da fri de, two with two, double (or two to one), *iii.* 490.
Degfhuaitai, well sewn (or stitched), *iii.* 444.
Deguiset, they enforce, *iii.* 505.
Deibech, contention, *iii.* 432.
Deidinach, last, *iii.* 520.
Deilbh Caemh, the comely form, *i.* cccxxxiv.
Deil-clis, the common sling, *i.* cccclxi, *iii.* 292, 294.
Deirged, to prepare, *iii.* 430.
Delg, *Dealg*, a thorn, a plain breast pin or brooch, *i.* ccclxxxvii, dcxlii. *Delg duillech*, a foliated brooch, *iii.* 92. *Delg or dath buide*, a brooch of enchased yellow coloured gold, *iii.* 179. *Delg creda*, a brooch of *Cred* or tin, or of bronze coated with tin, *iii.* 144. *Delg niarind*, an iron brooch (pin), *iii.* 150. *Deilci derca diorda*, carved brooches of gold [recte, brooches of red gold], *iii.*

165. *Delci oir*, brooches of gold, *iii* 146, 147. *Deilge lacair* (*recte, lan ecair*), brooches fully carved [*recte* ornamented], *iii.* 196. *Deilgi oir*, brooches of gold, *iii.* 164, 165.

Delgaib, (dat. and abl. pl.) brooches, pins or keys [of a *Timpan*], *iii.* 361.

Demna Aeoir, demons of the air, *ii.* 301, *iii.* 424.

Demogaid, to obscure, to diminish, to tarnish, *iii.* 503.

Denemmairgg, that enforces, *iii.* 505.

Deoraidh, a wanderer, a stranger, *i.* cxxi, cxxv. *Deoraidh Dé*, a pilgrim, of God, clvi.

Derbforgail, the law term for a false charge of impropriety made by a husband against his wife, a defamation of character. The woman thus charged was sometimes called *Derbforgaill*, so that this legal term has been sometimes mistaken for a true proper name of a woman, and indeed appears to have been so used in later times. This mistake was made in the case of the wife of Fergal O'Rorc, who is maliciously said to have eloped with Diarmat Mac Morrough, king of Leinster, *i.* clxxvi.

Derbfine, relatives from the fifth to the ninth degree, *i.* clxiii, clxv, clxvi.

Derc, a grave, a hole or pit, *i.* cccxxix. *Derc talman*, a hole or pit in the ground, *i.* dcxxxix, dcxl.

Dergfine, or "red-[handed"] *Fine*, *i.* clxvi.

Dergud, a bed, *i.* cccxxix.

Deroil, contemptible, *iii.* 245, 246.

Des, *Deis*, gen. *Desai*, free land, an estate, ancestral lands, *i.* c, cxlii; *ii.* 37, *iii.* 28, 490, 493.

Dessetar, they rested, *iii.* 444.

Dessid, to draw up, to take a stand, to remain, *iii.* 428.

Dia, with, *iii.* 507.

Diabal Gae, a double spear, a military fork, *i.* ccccxlvii-viii.

Diabul corach, no do fille, literally a folder up, or doubler, of justice, *i.e.* persons who drew up or prepared cases for the pleader, like the attorneys of our courts. They seem to have been the equivalent of the Welsh *Kannlau* or guider, *i.* ccxxiii, cclxvii, cclxxii.

Diallait oenaig, an assembly cloak, *i.* ccclxxxvii, cccxxxviii.

Diam, if they were [*recte*, if it were], *iii.* 510.

Diamhraibh, deserts, *iii.* 41.

Dian, a species of poetry peculiar to the order of poet called *Fochlachan*, *ii.* 171.

Dias, a shears, *i.* ccclxi.

Diasa, for his [contracted from *dia-as-a*, to him-out-of-his, he is entitled to in lieu of his, etc.], *iii.* 519.

Diatlu a dala, for his reproach at an assembly (akin to *satlai*, revolt, which see), *iii.* 514.

Dibad, property of a deceased person; cf. Welsh *Difaith*, usually considered to mean unappropriated property, but properly meaning, like the Irish *Dibad*, the property before it was divided among the heirs, *i.* clxiii, ccxci.

Diberga, warriors, [free-booters, vikings], *iii.*. 241, 242.

Diburgun, throwing, casting, shooting, *iii.* 436, 448.

Dichetal do chennaibh, "the great extempore recital", a peculiar rite of Druidical divination, which did not come under the prohibition of St. Patrick, because there was no sacrifice to, or invocation of idols in it, *ii.* 135, 172, 209.

Dicetla, spells, *iii* 526, 527.

Diciallath, *Diclithar*, is covered or concealed, *iii.* 255.

Dichli, restitution here (lit. cover, concealment). *iii.* 516.

Diclither, is concealed, is dissolved, oetc., *iii.* 255.

Dichmairc, *Dichmaircc*, without leave, unlawfully, *iii.* 487, 489.

Did, two, see *Adid*.

Didhna, coverings, *i.* ccclix.

Didla, to cut, see *Didlastais*.

Didlastais, they would cut, *iii.* 150.

Difholaigh, *non-Folach*, *iii.* 503, see *Folach*.

Digail, revenges, *i.* cxii.

Digbaid, forfeitures, *i.* clxxxviii.

Diguin, strictly speaking, a wound, but usually used in the sense of a blood fine, equivalent to the *Galanas* of Welsh law, and the *Galnes* of Old Scotch law. Used in the genitive form in the term *Maigin Digona*, it meant the extent of sanctuary, within which no person could be wounded or arrested without legal process. The word may

be connected with Latin, *dign*-itas, *i.* ci, clvi, ccxcv; *iii.* 473.
Dib, from them, *iii.* 494.
Dillata, friends (favourites), *iii.* 487.
Dilsa, a legal assignment, *i.* clxxxviii
Dineoch rod mbi, of whatever kind it may be, *iii.* 491.
D'innaigid, towards each other, *iii.* 440.
Dinnseanchus, topography, *ii.* 172; an ancient topographical tract so called, *iii.* 41.
Diraind, waste or mountain lands, *i.* clx.
Dire, a fine or penalty as restitution for injury done to a man's property, and equivalent to the Welsh *Dirwy*, and Anglo-Saxon *Wer*, or *Wergild*. *Curp dire* was the fine paid to a person for bodily injury to himself, or any of his immediate family, *i.* cxvii, ccxxxiii, ccxcv; *iii.* 477.
Dire meba cana, fine of violation of *Cain;* the exact equivalent of the A. S. *Cynebot*, *i.* ccxxxiv.
Dirna, abl. pl. *Dirnaib*, a vessel used as a measure, and containing a man's full drink; a large measure (or weight), a large mass of metal; *iii.* 245, 246, 495, 496.
Dirim, innumerable, countless [legions], *iii.* 462.
Direnatar, *Dirinethar*, is paid [awarded], *iii.* 489, 506.
Diten, (a shelter), a weather board, *iii.* 480.
Dithig, denial, negation, etc., *iii.* 467.
Dithma, unredeemed [in O'D.'s supplement to O'Reilly's *Irish Dictionary*, this word is explained, "discharged or released", etc., in the passages there cited the word should have been more correctly translated "detention", and "period of detention". The passage in the text of the *Crith Gablach* shows that the word means unredeemed, forfeited, etc., e.g., *gel dithma i n-glasib i nairthiur fochlai*, unredeemed hostages *in locks* in the east side of the champion's couch], *iii.* 509.
Dithraib, a waste, *iii.* 507.
Dithraicht, bereft of strength, *iii.* 458.
Diubarcan, shooting, *i.* cccclili, cccclix. See *Diburgun*.
Diubarcu, a general name for darts of all kinds, and arrows shot with a bow, *i.* cccclili-iv.
Diuchled, bought (rewarded), *iii.* 484.
Diumsach, arrogant, *iii.* 517.
Dligidh, is entitled to, *iii.* 519, etc.
Dligi bes brathir, a mode of expurgation, according to which an accused person made oath on the gospels that he or she had no knowledge of the crime. This oath was made sometimes at the house of the accused, *i.* cclxxviii, cclxxi.
Dligi doith dithach, a solemn oath of denial made by an accused person at an altar, and corroborated by the oath of a "worthy" person, *i.* cclxxviii.
Dloingset, they cleft or loosened, *iii.* 448.
Dlui Fulla, or fluttering wisp, a wisp of straw, hay, or grass, on which a charm or incantation was pronounced for a person. It was called *Dlui Fulla* (*recte Fullon*,) from *Dlui*, a wisp, and *Fullon* or *Fulla*, the name of the druid who first practised the art of pronouncing charms or incantations on a wisp of straw or hay, etc., hence *Dlui Fullon* literally means *Fulla* or *Fullon's* wisp, *ii.* 203, 204.
Dluthat, to consolidate, *iii.* 505.
Dna, now, also, moreover, it is the same as *dan*, *dana*, *dno*, *iii.* 506.
Dno see *Dna*, *iii.* 507.
Dolar, water, dark, etc. One of the drink-bearers of *Conaire Mór*, monarch of Eriu, was so called, *i.* lxxiv; *iii.* 151, 227.
Dobachs, see *Dabachs*
Dobcha, see *Dabcha*.
Docerd, disgrace (malevolence, malpractices), *iii.* 514.
Documbaig, he redeems, dissolves, loosens, *iii.* 500.
Do et, is known, *iii.* 516. See *do fet*.
Do fet, is known, *iii.* 516. See *do et*.
Dofet, precedes, *iii.* 497.
Doghraing, grieving, or lamenting, etc., *iii.* 380.
Doich, suspicion, *i.* cclxxvii.
Doilfe, [occult] necromantic, *iii.* 215.
Doilgiu, cause of grief [saddening], *iii.* 446.
Domna, base of, *iii.* 508.
Dond, honour, *i.* cxxiii, cxxiv.
Dond, brown; one of the drink-bearers of *Conaire Mór*, monarch

of Eriu, was so called, *i* lxxiv, *iii.* 151.
Dorblas, twilight, *iii.* 436.
Dorcha, dark, *i.* lxxiv.
Dord, bass, murmuring sounds in the ordinary measure, *i.* dxxviii; *iii.* 377, 379, 378.
Dordan, light murmuring sounds, the notes or warbling of thrushes, *iii.* 377, 378.
Dord-Fiansa, the battle cry or war chorus; it appears to have been also applied to a hunting whoop, or to any wild song sung in chorus, *i.* dcxxxvi; *iii.* 311, 312, 377, 378, 380. In vol. iii., p. 380, this word is confounded with *Crann dord*, and hence incorrectly described as a species of wooden gong music, etc.
Dorman, gen. *Dormaine*, a meretricious woman, *iii.* 482.
Dornasc, a bracelet for the wrist, *iii.* 168. See *Ordnasc.*
Do rout, from off the road, *iii.* 486.
Dos Doss, a branch or pole; an order of poets, *ii.* 171, 217.
Dosaire, an officer who carried and planted the *Dos* or court pole, *i.* cclxiii.
Dos Airechta, a pole stuck in the ground as a symbol of authority to indicate the sitting and sanctuary of an *Airecht Foleith*, or Leet Court, *i.* cclxiii.
Dosli, *Doslii*, right, that which a man has a right to, or to which he is lawfully entitled, *iii.* 507.
Doss, a champion, *iii.* 432.
Dot mincellat, encircled by, *iii.* 508.
Draetli, trespass, *iii.* 500.
Draumce, *Draumchu*, thick milk (or skim milk), *iii.* 478, 481.
Drecht giallna, a trench made around the *Dun* of a king by his own tenants (or subjects), *iii.* 29; a ditch of allegiance, *iii.* 508. The true meaning of the term was, however, the wall and fosse which surrounded the king's *Dun* for the safety of the *Gialls* or pledges of allegiance, *i.* ccxxxviii, cccv.
Dreim fri foghuist, climbing against a rock, so as to stand straight at its top, *ii.* 372.
Dreimni, fierceness, *iii.* 448.
Drisechan Caorach, a kind of pudding made of sheep's blood, called in Cork a *Drisheen*, *i.* ccclxix.
Droch, the wheel of a chariot, cf. Greek τρόχος, N. H. G. *drehen*, *i.* cccclxxviii-ix.
Drochta, tubs, *iii.* 486.
Drolan, a hasp, *iii.* 322.
Dromana, backs or chines, see *Forgab.*
Dron argda, rich silvery; *Dron orda*, rich golden, *i.* cccclxxx.
Droncherd, a species of poetry peculiar to the order of poet called *Dos*, *ii.* 171.
Drongar na lurigi, the ringing of the armour, *iii.* 426.
Dronn, *Dronnog*, a hump, *Dronnaighe*, humpy-backed, *iii.* 237.
Druid, *Druadh*, "doctus", learned, *ii.* 48 (and *note*, 17.)
Druim Criaich, a proper name composed of *druim*, a hill, *cri*, the heart, and *ach*, a sigh or moan; a name given to this hill from the fact that upon it *Eochadh Feidhlech* received the heads of his three rebellious sons, and that his heart never after ceased to send forth sighs and moans, *ii.* 145, 146.
Druinech, or *Druinnech*, gen. *Druinige*, an embroideress, *iii.* 112.
Druith, buffoons, *iii.* 219, 220.
Drumchli, "the chief head", a literary professor who knew the whole course of learning, *ii.* 84.
Drumnech, curved, arched as applied to a yoke adapted to the shape of the horses' back, *i.* cccclxxx. The word *Druimnech* is used also in the sense of strong, rich, high coloured.
Du, a foss (as of a *Dun*), *iii.* 514.
Dual, a brush or lock of hair, *iii.* 210.
Dualaighe, a painter or brushman, from *dual*, a brush, *iii.* 210.
Dualdai, a brooch? [*dualdai* implies plurality, and the true meaning is perhaps hooks or clasps. *Dualdai airgdidi ecorside de ór oibiniu isi brat*, hooks or clasps of silver inlaid with burnished gold in the cloak], *iii.* 190.
Duan, pl. *Duana*, a poem or song of laudation of living heroes, *iii.* 381.
Duban, the black, from *dub* black, the name of the shield made for *Cuchulaind* by *Mac Enge*, *ii.* 329, 330.
Dubfine, *i.e.* the black, dark, or obscure *Fine*, a term applied to the

members of a family whose degree of consanguinity was doubtful, *i.* clxiv.

Dubhghilla, "the black page", the shield of *Aedh*, king of *Oirghiall*, *iii.* 111.

Duchand, pl. *Duchonda*, *i.e.* a *luinneog*, or music [of a melancholy or dirge like character], *iii.* 380, 381.

Ducoll, to blight, to destroy, *iii.* 526, 527.

Duile feda, *Duili fedha*, "Books of Trees", *i.e.* inscribed tablets, *i.* cccxliii; *ii.* 173; *iii.* 542.

Duillech, foliated, *iii.* 456.

Duilemain, the Creator, *iii.* 308.

Duillend Deale, a thorny or a speared brooch, *iii.* 102.

Duinn, honour price (benefits of lawful rank), *iii.* 479

Duir ime, a quick hedge, *i.* cxcl.

Duirtheach, an oratory, *iii.* 36, 37, 48, 49, 53.

Dul, *Dula*, legal property and other qualifications, cattle, etc., *i.* cxxiv, cxxv.

Dulbrass, ready, going, *iii.* 428.

Dulesc, literally water leaf, the "dillisk", or Rhodymenia palmata, *i.* ccclxvii; *iii.* 483.

Dum, *Duma*, pl. *Dumai*, a tumulus or burial mound containing a chamber (*Dum*, cf. Latin *domus*) for the ashes or bodies of the dead, *i.* cccxxviii, cccxxix, cccxxxv, dcxxxvii, dcxxxix. *Duma na n-Gall*, the mound or tomb of the foreigners at Tara, *i.* ccccxxvi. The term was also applied to the slopes or high ground on the margin of a flat plain, *i.* ccccxxxiv.

Dun, "two walls with water between them", the mounds and ditch which protected the residence of a *Righ* or king, cf. Welsh *Din*, Norse *Tun*, German *Zaun*, *i.* lxxxvii, cccv; *iii.* 3, 4. 7, 8, 29, 508.

Dunbai, a mortality, *iii.* 505.

Durd or *Dord*, a murmur, *iii.* 214. *Dord-Abla*, a name of the *Dagda's* harp, *iii.* 214.

Duthaig, natives or people legally belonging to the *Fines* of a *Tuath* or territory, *i.* clxiv, clxvi, cxcviii.

Duthaig Daine, the people at large; persons outside the seventeenth degree of kinship, who were not entitled to a share of the *Dibad* of deceased members of a *Fine*, *i.* clxiii, clxiv, clxv.

Each sliasta, a riding steed, *iii.* 486.

Eaboda, *Eboda*, paid advocates, counsellors, attorneys. See *Ebe*, and *Fairbe*, *iii.* 476.

Ebe, *Fir Ebe* or *Fairbe*, the fully qualified attorney entitled to practise in the higher courts, *i.* cclxxiii.

Ecaini, complaining [*recte*, lamenting], *iii.* 442.

Ecendál, peril [prejudice], *iii.* 414.

Echlasc, a horse switch or whip, *iii.* 219, 220.

Ech dond tuagmar, a curveting, prancing bay steed, *iii.* 162-3. *Ech imrime*, a riding steed. *Echsrein*, bridle-steeds, *iii.* 501.

Echrais Ulaidh, the Assembly House of Ulster at Tara, *ii.* 15.

Echtarcinail, foreign races, *i.e.* Saxons, *iii.* 505.

Ecin, force, compulsion, *iii.* 506.

Eclann, an assassin (or outlaw), *iii.* 507.

Eclais, a church, *i.* cxxviii. *Eclais glán*, pure or stainless church, *i.* clvi.

Ecna, wisdom; *Gradh Ecna*, grades or professors of knowledge or wisdom, *i.* clvi.

Ecsmacht, see *Necsmacht*, *iii.* 191.

Eibhioll, the summer heat, *iii.* 357.

Eigis, a sage, one of the grades of poets, *ii.* 171.

Eipiltinach, destroyed [dead[*iii.* 255,

Eirgg, a champion, *iii.* 416.

Eirnither, is paid, *iii.* 112.

Eirrgi, champions, *iii.* 446.

Eislinniu, punishment (or punishing), *iii.* 494.

Eitirgleo, the deciding or final combat. "*La etergleoid in chomlaind ocus in chomraic*, *i.e.*, the day which would decide the battle and the fight", *iii.* 444.

Eithne, the proper name of a woman, but which literally means the sweet kernel of a nut, *ii.* 290.

Eithrach, perjury, *i.* cciv.

Ele, incantations, *iii.* 440.

Emait, *d'emait duinn*, they will give or concede to us, *iii.* 452.

Emnad, hair, ii. 363.

Enan (recte *Eman?*), a species of metre, *ii.* 172-3.

Endce, innocence, *iii.* 514.

Enech, literally the face, but used

figuratively to express honour, *i.* cxiii.

Enechgris, a change of colour of the face caused by some act which brought dishonour on a family, such as that of receiving stolen goods, etc., *i.* ccxcv; see note on *Logh-Enech*, *iii.* 471.

Enecland, *Enechland*, *Enechlann*, honour price, a fine in right of insult to the honour, the amount of which depended on the rank of the person, *i.* ccxxxiii, ccxcv; *iii.* 266, 471.

Enechraice, gen. *Ennechruccai*, a face-reddening or blushing, caused by some act or scandal which brought shame on a family, *i.* ccxcv; see note on *Logheneck*, *iii.* 471.

Engai, innocence, *iii.* 483.

Engnam, bravery, *iii.* 414.

Enncai, soup, broth, or pottage, *iii.* 495.

Eó, a brooch, *iii.* 94, 96, 162. *Eó iarna caccor d'or donn*, a brooch well carved of brown gold, *iii.* 167.

Eó, the top; hence *Eó-Barr*, a hat, a head-dress or ornament worn on the head, *iii.* 207, 209. *Eoburrad óir*, head pieces or circlets of gold [more probably ear-rings of some peculiar form], *iii.* 152. *h Eo*, pendants: *h-Eo corcra for cach brut*, crimson pendants upon each cloak, *i.* cccxci; *iii.* 157. *Eó airgit*, a silver brooch, *iii.* 145. *Eó óir*, a brooch of gold, *iii.* 162, 163.

Eochraid, some kind of literary composition, *iii.* 173.

Eochraide, gen. plu. of *Each*, a steed, *iii.* 501.

Eó Feasa, "Salmon of knowledge", from *eó*, a salmon, and *feasa*, gen. of *fis*, knowledge, *ii.* 143, 144.

Eola, dat. pl. *h-Eolaib*, swans, *iii.* 245.

Eo Rosso, the yew tree of Ross, *ii.* 330, *iii.* 34.

Eorna, barley, *i.* ccclxii, ccclxiv.

Epistle, a necklace, *iii.* 104, 105.

Er, *Err*, *Erad*, a champion, a commander; *Er coga*, war chief; *Er catha*, battle chief; *Erad criche*, the commander of the levy of a *Crich*; *Er toga*, elected leader of the military force, corresponding to the Anglo-Saxon *Herstoga*, and the Scandinavian *Fylkir*, *i.* lxxxi, cv, ccxxxi.

Erca, cows, cattle, *iii.* 479.

Ercadh, pattern drawing and embroidery, *iii.* 123.

Ercomall, yokes (harness), *iii.* 450.

Eric, *Eiric*, a fine, composition for death, *ii.* 324; *iii.* 166.

Ercnat, an embroideress, *iii.* 123.

Erlannaib (dat. and abl. pl. of *Erlann*), hafts or handles, *iii.* 448.

Erlar chaich, a fore-hall, corresponding to the *Golf* of Norse houses, *i.* cccli.

Ereman, a ploughman, *i.* cii, where it is incorrectly printed *Erereman*.

Erna, irons for suspending the *Caire* or cauldron, etc., *i.* ccclix; *iii.* 483.

Erned, rewards, cf. O. Norse *arna*, to earn, etc.; A. Sax. *ge-earnian* to earn, to merit; English *to earn*, *iii.* 531.

Errach (or *Imbulc*), the spring (season), *iii.* 217.

Errach, a forced loan to which a king was entitled under certain circumstances, *iii.* 519, 507-8.

Erscoraidhe [recte, *Erscortaidhe*], a carver, that is, a wood engraver, or ornamental worker in wood, *iii.* 209-10.

Esain, hindrance offered to a suitor, by which he was prevented from appearing at courts or assemblies, etc.; the same as the *Essoign* or *Essoin* of the English law, the *Essoine* of French law, and the *Essoinzie* of Scotch law, *i.* ccxciii; *iii.* 473.

Escra, a vessel or a measure which contained one-third of the full of the *Lestar lulaice*, *iii.* 118, 495. A drinking cup, *i.* clxxiv, dcxlii, see *Tinnscra*. *Escrai*, water vessels, *i.* ccclix; *iii.* 495.

Esert, a defaulting tenant, or insolvent copartner in a *Comaitches*, cf. old English law term *Ossart*, appropriation, *i.* cxci.

Esinnraic, "unworthy" persons, that is, persons not legally qualified, or who had committed crimes, or who made base or unlawful use of their privileges, and were thereby rendered unworthy or disqualified from giving evidence, or doing other legal acts of a free man, *i.* cclxxvii.

Esnad, a word compounded of *Es*, a negative particle equal to *non* in

English, and *Nath*, the name of any [metrical] composition; so the *Es-Nath* was a something not a poem or a metrical composition, but a *Duchand*, *i.e.* a musical moaning air or tune in chorus, *iii.* 381.

Espuic, gen. of *Epscup*, *Espuc*, a bishop, *iii.* 510.

Eta, fertility, produce, *iii.* 526–7.

Eta, can or is able, *nad eta*, cannot or is not able, *iii.* 490.

Etarcossait, intermeddling, *iii.* 448.

Etarggairecht, fostering care, friendship, *iii.* 506.

Etarbuasach, troubled, confused, perhaps more correctly, hovering, *iii.* 448.

Fa, or; *Cia de is[s]riuthiu, in ri fa espuc?* which is the higher, a king, or a bishop, *iii.* 510.

Faccarsa, that I may see, *iii.* 458.

Facrith (.i. *tic*, it shall come), be accomplished, *iii.* 430.

Fadarc sula sair, long beaming noble eyes, *iii.* 456.

Fadeisin, Fadesin, his own, himself, *iii.* 490, 493.

Fadesta, the same as *Badesta*, the modern *Feasda*, forthwith, now, presently, *iii.* 460.

Faebhar-Chleas, the small sharp-edged shield feat, *ii.* 372, 373.

Faen-Chleas, the prostrate feat, *ii.* 372.

Faesam, the right possessed by freemen of entertaining strangers for a certain time, varying with the rank of the host, without being obliged to give bail or security for the guests, *i.* ccxciii; *iii.* 513.

Faethaisiu limm, thou shalt fall by me, *iii.* 434.

Faga Faegablaige, Faga Fagablach, Foga Fogablaigi, a small down-headed spear [a military fork], *i.* cccclxv, cccclxvii, cccclxviii; *iii.* 98.

Faga, Fagha, a short spear, a javelin, a dart, see *Faga Faegablaige*, *i.* cccxxxviii; *iii.* 317.

Fagnam, Fognam, serving; here it means the attendance and supplies of food which a *Flath* was entitled to get from his *Ceiles*, *i.* cxiii; *iii.* 509.

Fail, dat. and abl pl. *Failgib*, an open ring or bracelet for the wrist, arm, or ankle, *iii.* 156, 166 168–170, 176. *Fail-dearg-doid*, red rings on hands [red hand rings], *iii.* 211.

Failge glana, bright, polished, or crystal rings, *iii.* 146, 147, 161.

Faine Maighdena, a maiden's ring due to the king by every maiden at her marriage. It corresponded to the Welsh *Gobyr merch*, or king's share of the bride price, or *Amobyr*, *i.* ccxl.

Faine, Fainne, the ordinary finger-ring; also a ring for confining the hair, *iii.* 168, 169.

Fairbe, a paid advocate, a counsellor, a man who pleads, or advocates a case against another for fees, [not an advocate but an attorney, see *Ebe*], *i* cclxxiii; *iii.* 476.

Faisness, an information based on the positive knowledge of one or more eye-witnesses, *i.* cclxxvii, cclxxix.

Faitche, the enclosed ground or lawn about a homestead, *i.* cxxxv, clv, clvi, ccxxxiv, ccxci, ccciv, cccvii, cccxv, cccxviii. *Sechter Faithche*, outer farm, or pasture land beyond the *Faitche*, *i.* cxxxv.

Fal, a fence; the word is used also in the sense of the establishment of a prescriptive right, *i.* cxlv, clxxxvi, clxxxvii. [The reference at foot of note 226, p. cxlv, vol. *i.* to p. clxxvii, should be to p.p. clxxxvi-vii].

Fairgged, proffered, *iii.* 418.

Farrindi, barbs, *iii.* 450.

Fas Faigdhe, a squandering nobleman reduced to beggary by his own extravagance, *iii.* 520, 521.

Fasc, a summons, setting forth the nature of a plaint, *i.* cclxxxii, cclxxxiii.

Fastad, an attachment, the "attachiamenta bonorum" of Anglo-Norman law, *i.* cclxxxii.

Fastad nadma, fastening of a bond, *i.* cclxxxv.

Fathan, or *Fahan*, shelter, an enclosure, cf. *Faitche*, Goth. *bifahan*, *i.* cxlv, cccvii–viii.

Feadanaighe, the musician who played on the whistle or pipe (or *Feadan*, tube), *iii.* 376.

Fearan bó le fine, tribe cow land, the common grazing land of a *Fine* or tribe, *i.* clv.

Fearan commaitches, tribe land held in copartnership, *i.* clviii. See *Fearan congilta fine*.

Fearan comaide crithe, see *Fearan congilta fine*.

Fearan congilta fine, tribe land occupied by *Congilda*, or associations, *i.* clviii, ccxvi.
Fearan fine, tribe land, *i.* clv.
Fearan fuidri, *fuidir* land, or that part of the demesne land of a *Flath* or lord which he let to strangers and others as tenants-at-will, *i.* cliii, ccxxv.
Fearnog, the alder tree, Alnus glutinosa, *i.* cccevi.
Febus, goodness, wealth, rank, etc., *iii.* 500.
Fecht fele, one night's entertainment, *i.* cxl, ccxliii; *iii.* 495.
Fed, *Fead*, a whistle made with the mouth, *iii.* 328, 368, 377, 378.
Fedán, a thin, slender, musical or shrill pipe or thin tube; in medical MSS. a fistula, a whistling instrument, *iii.* 327, 228, 368.
Fedanach, *Fedanaigh*, *Feadanaighe*, he who played on the *Fedán*, *iii.* 328, 368, 376.
Fedhen, see *Fén*.
Fegi, vigorous, *iii.* 366.
Feib, real estate, property, riches, qualification, *i.* clxxii, *iii.* 490.
Feichem, a suitor, a party in a suit, defendant or plaintiff, *iii.* 487.
Feidm ochtair, eight-power, *i. e.* eight-pronged or having the power of eight spears, *i.* dcxl.
Feirtsib, abl. pl. with spindles, *iii.* 115. See *Fertais*.
Feis, a feast or meeting, a convention; "*Feis Droma Ceata*", the feast or convention of *Drom Ceat*, *ii.* 78. *Feis Teambrach*, the Feast of Tara, *i.* xxxiii, ccliii; *ii.* 12, 14–19.
Feis comarca, a species of poetry peculiar to the order of poet called *Filidh*, *ii.* 171.
Feith, woodbine, *iii.* 448.
Feith géir, the sleeking stick or bone which weavers still use to close and flatten linen cloth on the breast-beam of the loom while in process of being woven, *iii.* 116.
Felma, a wooden fence, the same as an *Ail*, *i* cxci.
Felmac, a pupil, *i.* ccccxxxiv.
Fén, *Fedhen*, *Feadhan*, a bier or hearse. Zeuss glosses it *Plaustrum*, cf. Old Norse, *vagn*, A.-Sax. *waegn*, English *wagon*, O. H. German, *wagan*, N. H. German, *wagen*, Latin *vehere*, *i.* cccclxxvi–cccclxxvii.
Fenechas, *Fenechus*, the general tribe and territorial law of the whole kingdom, or what might be called the national code, as it embraced all the laws regulating the occupation of land, and the social and territorial relations of all the *Fines* of the nation, *i.* clxxvi, clxxvii, clxxxix; *ii.* 31; *iii.* 468, 472.
Feneda, warriors, *i.* cccxxix.
Feneog, a window, from the Norse *vindauga*, literally "wind eye", whence English *window*, *i.* ccclii.
Fenester, a window, derived from the Latin *Fenestra*, *i.* ccclii.
Feochraigestar, became more furious or infuriated, *iii.* 448.
Feorling, a coin corresponding in value to the *Cingeog* or farthing, *i.* ccclxiv.
Ferachas, manly exertion, angry combat, *iii.* 456, 460.
Fer beogabail, a man in living caption, a man captured alive on the battle-field, *iii.* 507.
Ferbolgs, pawns for chess-playing, *i.* cccl.
Fer cengail, a "man of ties or bonds", more probably, however, one who danced the kind of dance known in the twelfth century as the *Espringale* or "springende tentz" of the Germans. A similar kind of springing dance, accompanied by a singing chorus of dance tunes, came down in Ireland to very recent times, *i.* dxl; *iii.* 313, 368.
Fer fene, *Fer fine*, family chief, or tribe representative, *iii.* 475.
Fer forais, or *foruis*, a Forus man, an *Aire*, whose house constituted a *Forus*, *i.* cclxxxiii, cclxxxv, cccxviii; *iii.* 520.
Fer fororggaib forggab, a man captive, whom he has captured in battle, *iii* 507.
Fer fothla, *Fer fothlai*, or *Anflath*, a wealthy middle-man, the wealthiest of the *Bo Aires*, so called from the abundance of his *Folad* or wealth, *ii* 36, *iii.* 470, 490, 491, 491.
Fergga, of champions, or, of the combats, *iii.* 418.
Fergill, a hostage man, *iii.* 509.
Fergnio, a warrior, a champion, *iii.* 507, 509.
Fer gigaoila, a giggle dancer, see *Cengal* and *Fer cengail*, *i.* dxli.

Fer legend, or *Ferlegenn*, a lector or law teacher, see *Fer leighinn*, *i.* celii.

Fer leighinn, head professor, or chief master in a literary school, *ii.* 84, 90, 168.

Fer luigi, an oathman, the same as *Fer tonga*, *i.* cclxxxvi.

Fermidba, see *Fermidbotha*, *i.* ccxlii; *iii.* 467.

Fer midbotha, any man under judgment of court, or not entitled by law as a free man in his own right, *i.* clxxxv, ccxli; *iii.* 467, 469, 473, 475–479.

Fer nadma, a knot-man, a magistrate who acted in making and proving the knot or bond of all legal contracts, *i.* cclxxv–vi; *iii.* 470, 474.

Fernu, garters [girdles], *iii.* 152.

Fersad, a club; *Fersad iarain*, an iron club, a *Ferbolg* weapon, *ii.* 256.

Fert, a mound, a grave, *i.* ccliii, cccvi, cccxxi, cccxxix, cccxli, dcxxxvii–dcxxxix. *Fert maigne no aonaig*, the mound of the assembly field or fair field, *i.* cccxxx; *Ferta na n-ingen*, the mound of the maidens at Tara, *i.* cccxxx.

Fertais, pl. *Fertsi*, a spindle, the spindles of the axle-tree of a chariot or wagon, *i.* ccccixxiv; *Fertais lin*, a flax spinning spindle, *iii.* 115.

Ferthos, he pays, *iii.* 501.

Fer tonga, *Fer toing*, a qualified oathman, who gave sworn testimony for a plaintiff or defendant, the "*Ferdingus*" or "*Ferthingman*" of English law, *i.* ccii, cclxxxvi, cclxxxix, ccxc; *iii.* 473.

Fessir, knoweth, *iii.* 510.

Fesius, [*recte Fesni*] themselves, *iii.* 314.

Fethal, a symbol, a mask or veil, *iii* 114.

Fethana, flat rings for spear rivets [*recte*, sinews; *Fethana agus cuislena and chuirp*, the sinews and veins of the body], *ii.* 241.

Fethlaib condualacha, *Fethlaib condualae*, emblematic carvings, *iii.* 158, 219, 220.

Fetorloic, patriarchal: *rachto fetorloic*, patriarchal law, *iii.* 239.

Fia, in presence of, *iii.* 493.

Fiachach, a defendant who became liable for the *Fiacha rechta*, or costs, etc., of a process, *i.* cclxxx.

Fiacha rechtge, *Fiacha rechta*, law costs, etc., *i.* cclxxx, ccxcii.

Fiadnaise, *Fiadnaisi*, pl. *Fiadnaisi*, a witness, one who proves the lawfulness of a suit, *i.* clxxv, clxxxviii, ccxxxix, cclxii, cclxxx; *iii.* 467, 470, 471.

Fialach icce acas leigis, professors of healing and curing, *iii.* 440.

Fialaig nom fialach, heroes (comrades), *iii.* 454.

Fiam, a chain, a peculiar kind of ornament of gold, silver, etc., worn round the neck, *iii.* 168, 178.

Fiaman, a wild cat [a hare], *iii.* 140.

Fianbhotha, hunting tents, *ii.* 380.

Fiann, mercenaries or militia retained by kings and chieftains to enforce the laws and to ward off enemies. *Fianna Eireann*, national militia or standing army of *Erin*, *ii.* 376, *et seq.* See *Amuis*.

Fianna fineadha, champions of families (or tribes), *ii.* 376, 377.

Fiansa, a species of military chorus or concert peculiar to the *Fians*, to *Find Mac Cumhaill* and his warriors, *iii.* 377, 378.

Fiarlann, pl. *Fiarlanna*, a curved blade, *i.* ccccxxxvii; *ii.* 239.

Fibtha do da crecha, *i.e.* axe-men of two cuttings, the apparitors who took charge of prisoners at the bar, and to whom traversers surrendered, *i.* cclxvii.

Fichtigh, twenty, *iii.* 477.

Fidba, *Fidbha*, a kind of bill-hook, *i.* cxci, ccclxi; *iii.* 486, 489. *Fidbha mac Fo Chrasbhaigh*, hatchet son of Tree Cutter; *ii.* 133.

Fidbac [*h*], a bow, *ii.* 287.

Fidbach, a wood gland, filberts, acorns, cf. Sanskrit *bhag*, Greek φάγω, *i.* ccclxiii.

Fidchell, *Fidchill*, *Fithcheall*, *Fithchell*, a chessboard, chess, *ii.* 359; *iii.* 165, 360, 366, 454, 507.

Fidil, *Fidioll*, pl. *Fidli*, *Fiodaill*, a fiddle, cf. A. S. *Fithele*, Old English, *Fidil*, O. H. German, *Fidula*, *i.* dxxiv–vii; *iii.* 313, 328, 329, 379.

Fidlan oirmeide, a firkin or small cask, formerly used as a dry measure, *iii.* 183.

Fidlestar, a name for every kind of drinking vessel made of wood, both *Ardans* and *Cuads*, *iii.* 483.

Fidren, whistling, *iii*. 426.
Fidu, a tree, *iii*. 448.
Figi, weaving, *iii*. 115.
File, a poet, *i*. cxxviii, etc.; *ii*. 48, 171. See *Fileadh*.
Fileadh, poets, philosophers, *ii*. 56, 208.
Filedheacht, poetry, philosophy, *ii*. 171–173.
Filidh, *i*. clvi; *ii*. 171. See *Fileadh*.
Filliud erred nair, the "whirl of a valiant champion", *iii*. 372.
Find Fine, "white *Fine*", the legitimate family, *i*. clxiv. See *Fine*.
Findathar, be it known, *iii*. 516, 517.
Findiuch, a scabbard, *iii*. 143.
Findlestar umaide, a bright bronze vessel, *iii*. 495.
Findruine, or *Findruini*, white bronze, *i.e.* a bronze containing a large proportion of tin, or bronze coated with tin, or perhaps some alloy of silver; sometimes used for ornamentation *i*. cccclxvi; *iii*. 101, 174.
Fine, or *Finead*, a family or house, cf. Latin *affinitas*, *affinis*, *i*. clxii.
„ *cis Flatha*, the lord's rent-paying *Fine*, or family of tenants, *i*. clxvi.
„ *duthaig*, the hereditary family entitled to share property according to the law of Gavelkind, corresponding to the original A.-Saxon *Maeght*, *i*. clxiv, clxvi.
„ *fingolach*, see *Dergfine*.
„ *Flatha*, the whole of the *Ceiles*, and other tenants and followers of a *Flath* or lord, *i*. cxvi.
„ *fognuma*, the serving *Fine* or family—the free and base *Ceiles* of a *Flath*, *i*. clxvii.
„ *uccomail*, members of a *Fine* who had been in exile, or who were out of their own country, and were received back into their *Fine* by *Fir Caire* or by lot-casting, *i*. clxvi.
„ *tacair*, *Fine*, or family by affiliation, *i*. clxv.
Finead, see *Fine*.
Finea, *i*. clxx, see *Fenechas*.
Fini, tribes, *iii*. 458.
Finnchas, the Crisp-Fair-Haired, a female name, *iii*. 361.
Fir Caire, true calling, *i*. clxiv.
Fir Dé, "truth of God", expurgation on the gospels, or at an altar, *i*. cciv, cclxxix, cclxxxvii.
Fir Ebe, a true, that is, a fully qualified attorney, *i*. cclxxiii.
Fircainnind, *Fir cainnenn*, true or strong onions or garlic, *iii*. 104, 105, 485.
Fireman, a witness, a compurgator, *i*. cii.
Fir, *Firian*, true, righteous, *iii*. 504–506.
Fir Flathaman, true right of a king, *iii*. 506
Fir Teist, true testification, compurgation, *i*. cclxxxi.
Firis, he or she bade: *Firis Failte*, he bade welcome, *iii*. 428.
Firsinne, the centre [radiation from], *iii*. 174.
Flaithem Oen escra, a small proprietor, not having property to qualify him as a *Flath*, *i*. clxxxiii; *iii*. 573.
Flath, *Flaith*, a lord, a nobleman, an estated gentleman, whose rank, etc., was derived from his having an estate in land for which he paid no rent himself, and which he let for rent to *Ceiles* (tenants). *Flath* is often used in the sense of landlord in the laws, etc. See *ii*. 34, 37, 38, *iii*. 493, *et seq*. *Flath bachald*, the *Flath* who invested an incoming *Flath* or *Rig* with the *Bachald* (=*Bachal*) or staff of office, and who acted as marshal, not the Tanist, as explained in *iii*. 508, *n*. 565. *Flaith mucleithe* has been explained in note 552, *iii*. 497, as the steward of swine herds. It may also be explained as formed from *cleith*, the best, the highest, a term applied to men as well as to cattle, and the prefix *mu*, the superlative degree of *mór*, great, that is, the highest *cleith* or chief. *Flath mucleithe* may therefore mean a man of the best family, and eligible for the highest offices, but not necessarily holding any.
Flath Geilfine, the chief of the *Gel Fine*, the chief proprietor in a *Fine*, *i*. clxxi, cciv.
Fled, pl. *Fleda*, a banquet, e.g. *Fled Bricrind*, "*Bricriu's* Feast", *i*. cccli; *Fleda Comadhasa*, common feasts, that is, banquets of the whole people, or supplies given by all the people of a territory to a king who attended a court, or made an expedition outside his territory, *i*. ccxiv.

Flesc, a wand, a lath, a blunt spear, or the bar of a door, etc., *i.* clvi, *iii.* 363, 487. *Flesc lin*, a flax scutching stick, *iii.* 116.

Flescach, a *Flesc* bearer, the retainer of a *Flath* who threw the *Flesc*, or *Cnairsech*, *i.* clvi.

Foach, marshes, rough, and waste lands, *i.* clx.

Fobiad fiach, a charge for debts or damages, *i.* cciv.

Fobiada, food rents, *i.* cxliv.

Fobith, because, in virtue of, *iii.* 510.

Fobrith, napping, [also pressing, or sleeking] of cloth, *iii.* 115.

Fochaireeh, one of the parts or books into which *Filedecht* or the philosophy and poetry of the Gaedhil was divided, and which formed the special study of the grade of *Filé* called the *Eiges*, *ii.* 171.

Focheir, *i.e.* its haft, *i.e.* the horn end of the *Cnairsech*, *i.* clvi, *n.* 267.

Fochlach, one of the orders or grades of *File*, *ii.* 217.

Fochlachan, "a learner of words", [properly a teacher] an order of poet, *ii.* 171, 172.

Fochla, an elevated seat or bench on which the master of the house sat; it corresponded to the *Oendvegi* of the Norse houses, *i.* cccxlix, cccl. *Fochla Fennid*, champion's seat, *i.* cccxlix; *iii.* 509.

Fochoire, native education, *iii.* 84.

Fochomlaing, to sustain, to feed or support, *iii.* 490.

Fo-Chraebhaigh, *i.e.* branch or tree-cutter, *ii.* 113.

Fochraic, *Fochraich*, pay, reward, *i.* ccxxxiv; *iii.* 479.

Focoisle ben ar a raille, anything which one woman takes or borrows from another, *iii.* 118.

Fodaer, a base bondsman, *i.* cxxv.

Fodb, a felling axe, *iii.* 448.

Fod-beim, *Fodhbeim*, the "sod-blow", with a sword, etc., *ii.* 372.

Fodessin, his own, himself, *iii.* 497.

Fodlai, divisions, ranks, etc., *iii.* 502.

Fodord, under murmur, that is the deepest and lowest murmuring sounds; deep bass, *iii.* 377, 378.

Foga, *Fogha*, *Fogad*, pl. *Fogaid*, a javelin, a short spear, *i.* cccxli; *ii.* 295; *Foga Fogaiblaige*, *Foga Fogablaigi*, a *Foga* with prongs, a military fork like the Sturmgabel of the Germans, *i.* cccxlvi, cccxlvii. See *Foga*, and *Gabal Gicca*.

Fogelt, the cost of grazing cattle under distraint; the pound-field fee of modern times, *i.* cxci, ccxvi.

Foghmhar, autumn, *iii.* 217.

Foglaim, education, *ii.* 372.

Foglantidh, "the teacher", the title of the professor of the *Fochaire* or native education in the public schools of *Eriu*, *ii.* 84.

Foglomantai, learners, apprentices, *i.* cccxxxiv.

Fognitset, they celebrated they made, *iii.* 526, 527.

Fogur, tingling, *iii.* 308.

Foil muc, a pig-stye, *i.* cxxv.

Foill, treachery, *iii.* 432.

Foircetlaidh, lecturer, the title of the professor of grammar, astronomy, and general science in the great public schools of Erinn, *ii.* 84.

Foisitin, confession, *iii.* 493.

Foitsiu, the south, *iii.* 508.

Folach, maintenance, attendance, etc., *i.* cclxxx; *iii.* 477.

Folach Othrusa, *Folach n-Othrusa*, the care and maintenance of a wounded person by him who wounded him or by his tribe, *i.* cclxxx; *iii.* 475, 483.

Folad, property, riches, etc., *iii.* 479.

Folai, benefits, rights, *iii.* 477. *Folaid*, rights, privileges, etc., *iii.* 506; obligations, *iii.* 504; prescribed supplies, *iii.* 507; deeds, *iii.* 492. *Folad*, wealth, *iii.* 501.

Foleith, the *Leet* or company of a *Flath*, *i.* ccxxxv; *iii.* 498. *Foleithis*, his *Foleith*, retinue or *Leet*, *iii.* 502. Cf. A. S. *Leode*, N. H. German *Geleute*.

Folestrai, small or minor vessels, *iii.* 485.

Folongar, are supported, *iii.* 504.

Folongthar, are sustained, *iii.* 504.

Foltchain, beautiful hair, *iii.* 204.

Foluch, [maintenance], a cooking pit, *i.* dcxxxix. See *Fulacht Fianna*.

Fonachtaide, a *fosgenigh*, an object of ridicule, a laughing-stock, *iii.* 522.

Fonaidm, the right of bail, or knot, which a chief of household possessed in favour of all those for whom he was legally responsible, *i.* ccxciv.

Fonaidhm niadh for rinnibh slegh the coiling or knotting of a champion around the blades [*recte* points], of upright spears, *ii.* 372.

Fodaing, the same as *Folaing*, to endure, to suffer, to bear or support, *iii.* 519.

Fonnad, the frame of a chariot, upon which was placed the *Cret* or capsus, *i.* cccclxxviii.

Fop, a ball or boss. *Fop a thona*, the ball of his rump, *i.* dcxl.

Foradh, a seat: a mound or bench as *Forad na Teamrach* at Tara, *i.* cccxxxiii; *iii.* 12. See *Forud* and *Forus*.

Foran, power, might, aggressive force; *Foranu chaile*, breaking into his storehouse by force or without permission, *iii.* 489.

Forbais, a siege, *iii.* 361.

Forbera, to increase (increases) *iii.* 478.

Forberta, diminution, remission, [*recte*, defining, perfecting], *iii.* 511.

Forcam, offal. See *Forgaib*.

Forcmaither, is qualified or made eligible, *iii.* 477.

Forcraid, excess, more than, *iii.* 490, 491, 492, 501.

Forcsin, to proclaim, to establish, *iii.* 505.

Forcuir, to violate; *Forcuir a mna, a ingine*, the violation of his wife, or of his daughter, *iii.* 482.

Fordorus, the door of the outer circumvallation of a *Dun*, *i.* cccv.

Forgab, *Forgaib*, contributions of certain kinds of provisions paid to the *Flath* at specified festivals, *i.* cxl; *iii.* 482.

Forge, to exact, *iii.* 506.

Forgemen, cushions, *iii.* 424.

Forggaib, captures, *iii.* 507.

Forggub, a thrust, *iii.* 507.

Forggu-dine, the choicest or best cattle, etc., *iii.* 482.

Forrancha, resolute, bold, *iii.* 428.

Forromair, to place upon, to press or strike, *iii.* 426.

Forrged, to destroy, to slay, *iii.* 446.

Forles, *Forless*, an outer *Less* or yard; the door of the principal house leading into the *Les* or enclosed ground of a *Dun*, *i.* ccclxx, dcxli.

Form-chleas the great prowess feat of *Cuchulaind's Roth chles* or wheel feat, *iii.* 78.

Formius, I vanquished, *iii.* 460.

Formna, choicest or best of, *iii.* 462.

Fornasc, a generic name for clasps, bracelets, rings, and probably for those gold ornaments which terminate at the extremities in cups of various degrees of depth and regularity of shape, *iii.* 168.

Forngairi, to guard, to ward off, *iii.* 503.

Forniart, despotic might, *iii.* 506.

Forrain, a portion of personal estate or property bequeathed by a *Flath*, *i.* clxxxviii.

Forrach, a measure of length, the Irish "Rope", equivalent to the modern chain, *i.* clxxx.

Fortaig, proof, etc., *iii.* 467.

Fortcha, the skins *i.e.* coverings of the chariot, *iii.* 424.

Fortche, curtains, hangings; *Fortche uanaide*, green hangings, *i.* cccclxxxi.

Fortgella, to testify, testifies, *iii.* 500.

Fortoigg, to prove upon, to swear upon, *iii.* App. 506.

Forttrena, brave rumped, *Forlethan*, broad rumped, *iii.* 428.

Forud, a seat, a mound, a bench; the place on which a king sat surrounded by his *Sabaid* when at an *Aenach*, etc., *i.* dcxxxviii; *iii.* 541. See *Foradh* and *Forus*.

Forun forlethan, aggressive, broad rumped, *iii.* 162, 163.

Forus, the house or residence of a magistrate, whose *Airlis* constituted a pound. Cf. *Forudh*, the the seat or bench of the place of assembly at Tara, *Forud*, the raised mound, or benches where a king and his retinue sat at a fair, Latin *Forum*, English *Fair*, French *Foire*, etc, *i.* ccxxiii, ccxlvi, ccxiix; *iii.* 476. *Forus ainmnet*, a seat (or centre) of equity, *iii.* 506. *Forus Flatha*, the true knowledge of a *Flath*, [used here for *Corus Flatha*] *iii.* 493. *Forus Tuatha*, the mansion of a territory, etc. See *Corus Tuatha*, *iii.* 476.

Fosernnat, he dissolves (settles or adjudges), *iii.* 500.

Fos-fuair, he found, *iii.* 526, 527.

Fosgenigh, a laughing-stock, an object of ridicule, the same as *Fonachtaide*, which see, *iii.* 522.

Fosngelait, they feed upon, *iii.* 510.

Fossair, accompaniments, sufficient supply of food, *iii.* 492.
Fossugadh, entertainment, maintenance, *iii.* 497, 498, 499.
Fostud, detaining, *iii.* 420.
Fotal-bemmennaib, abl. pl., with quick or vehement strokes, *iii.* 450.
Fótlen, adheres, extends to, *iii.* 490.
Fothrom, rattle, *iii.* 426.
Foun, a tune, the air of a song, *iii.* 371.
Foxla, to take or receive, *iii.* 502.
Fracc, a wife, cf. O. H. G. *Frouwa*, *Frâwd*, etc., a woman, the goddess *Frûd*, N. H. G. *Foran*, Swedish and New Lower German, *Fröken*, a young girl, etc., *i.* cccclxxvi.
Fraech-mheas, heath fruit, the modern *Fraochain*, *Fraochoga*, the Vaccinium myrtillus and V. uliginosum, commonly called "Frochans" or "whorts", *i.* cccclxxviii.
Fraig, the back or roof of a house; a limit, a wall, *iii.* 489.
Frecmaircc, to enquire for, to obtain, to preserve, *iii.* 506.
Frepa, to exculpate, to free from guilt or charge, to cure, *iii.* 477.
Frepaid, to cure, *no Frepaid*, incurable, *iii.* 521.
Friam, clamour, *iii.* 426.
Fri de, *i.e.*, *cech naidhche*, at dusk, *i.e.* every night, *iii.* 442.
Frisaicci, are consulted, they appoint, or elect, or respond? *iii.* 501.
Frisellagar, *Friseillget*, attendance, attends to or supplies, *iii.* 519.
Freissligi, to recline upon, 489.
Frisiudi uniar, faced forward behind him. *Suidi*, him, *sudiu*, these or those, *in* them, *e.g.*, *friu*, with them, *friu aniar*, behind them, *iii.* 509.
Frithadartaib, abl. pl., with pillows, etc., *iii.* 440.
Frithfaithce, with a *Faithche*, *i.e.* residing in a house or *Dun*, which has an enclosed lawn, or *Faithche* around it, *iii.* 490.
Frithisi (*a frithisi*), again, *iii.* 526–7.
Friu, for, with, or to them (always in the tract here referred to), *iii.* 492, 492.
Fhuaithne, a post, a pillar, *i.* cccxxxviii, ccclxxxvii; *iii.* 311, 312. See *Uaithne*, *Huaithne*.
Fuan, a tunic, *iii.* 92. *Fuan geise*, swan's coat (or down), *iii.* 220, 221.
Fuath, a pattern (or image), *iii.* 116.
Fuathbroic, an apron, *iii.* 444.
Fuba and *Ruba*, hewing and cutting, chasing, killing, and warding off, services rendered to a lord in clearing underwood, etc., and in chasing and keeping off wolves, foxes, wild dogs, plunderers, etc., *i.* cxii, cxci.
Fugell, security, *iii.* 492.
Fuib, lacerated (pierced), *iii.* 452.
Fuidhle, default (in a deed), 507.
Fuidir, a foreigner, a base tenant, not belonging to a tribe, and who held either at the will of the lord, or by special agreement, *i.* cxvii; *iii.* 449.
„ *auca set*, a tenant who was selected by a lord in preference to others, and to whom he gave land and cattle, *i.* cxxiii.
„ *crai findgal*, convicts guilty of capital crimes, *i.* cxx.
„ *dedla fri fine*, a man who separated himself from his *Fine* or family, *i.* cxxii.
„ *focsail a aithreab*, a man who abandoned his home and tribe, *i.* cxxii.
„ *grian*, a land Fuidir, a metayer, "a sky farmer", *i.* cxxii.
Fuidris, Fuidirship, or Fuidir-land *iii.* 494.
Fuilliechta, distinctions, orders, or ranks of society, *iii.* 493.
Fuiliem, *Fuillim*, interest upon a pledge or loan, *iii.* 112, 114, 492.
Fuirirud, rations, refections, etc. (same as *Suerbiathadh*, free maintenance, here), *i.* cxii; *iii.* 495, 516.
Fuirind, entertainment, *i.* cxii. See *Furirind*.
Fuirmid, one of the grades of *File*, *ii.* 171.
Fulacht-fiansa, the cooking pits of the *Fians* or warriors of Finn Mac Cumhaill, *iii.* 381.
Furbadh, the Caesarean operation (hence *MacFurbaidhe*), *iii.* 290.
Furis, the front part of a chariot, probably the charioteer's seat, *i.* cccclxxxii.
Furnaide, lean meats, see *Forgaib*.
Fursunduth, entertainment, *iii.* 491.
Gab laim, he enjoined, he commanded, *iii.* 422.
Gabail, a distress, also arrestation or committal to jail, a jail, a gallows, *i.* clxxxii, cclxxxv; *iii.* 508.
Gabail cotoral, a distress with as-

on or carrying away of the
s seized, *i.* cclxxxiv, cclxxxv.
en. *Gabla*), a fork, also ap-
the branches of trees, of a
etc., cf. German *Gabel*, *i.*
clxiii, ccccxlvi.
nd, gavelkind, A. Saxon
or *Gafol*, *i.* clxix.
ne, gavael or gabella, the
ing branches of a *Fine* or
. lxxxv, clxiii.
ici, a military fork, *i.*
ii.
blacksmith, *iii* 209.
steed, a horse, *iii.* 219, 220.
cca rothach feidhm ochtair,
led eight-pronged [of eight
] military fork, *i.* dcxl. See
logablaige.
gen. sing. and nom. pl. *gai*,
spears, javelins, *i.* ccccxli;
; a heavy spear, *ii* 316,
Gae-bolg, *Gae-bulga*, the
-dart", *i.* cccclxxiv; *ii.* 302,
10, 372, *iii.* 415. *Gae buaif-*
the venomed spear, one of
mes of the *Luin Chiltchair*,
xxxii; *ii.* 325–6–7. *Gae*
"a sunbeam", a name for a
or-nothing man, *iii.* 521.
velin, *ii.* 300.
lsehood, *iii.* 506.
"shame spear", *e g*, *Cor-*
aileng, *Cormac* Shamespear,
.
il (gen. form of *Gall bhial*),
ish, or perhaps simply a fo-
xe; a cooper's adze, *iii.* 29.
bhiadh, winter food, *iii.* 487.
, cushions, *iii.* 499.
l, *Gaimrid* (the same as
re), winter, *iii.* 492, 495.
ort, amusement, *iii.* 460.
hortness; *Gair-secle*, short
Gair-re, that is, *re-ghair*, [no
a short span of life], Cor-
. 217, 218.
, a sword, an equipment of
iii. 517, 518. *See* also *ii.*
c.
ift, *i.* cciv.
inter, *iii.* 214, 217.
a cushion, *iii* 489.
mhnach, the "cruel grave",
grave of the two daughters
e monarch *Tuathal Techt-*
Rath Inil, *iii.* 386.
, [weaving] beams, *iii.* 116.
rawn out of, *iii.* 450.

Geanntorrglés, one of the three strings of Scathach's magical harp, so called because it had the peculiar gift of causing all who heard it strung to burst into laughter and rejoicings; one of the ancient keys or musical modes of the Irish, *iii.* 220, 221, 223.

Gear Chonaill, the short spear of Congall, *ii.* 342.

Geim Druadh, a Druid's shout, or whoop, etc., *iii.* 381.

Geinti Glindi, wild people of the glen, mythological beings so called, *ii.* 301; *iii.* 424, 425, 450.

Geilfine, or *Gelfine*, the pledges of the *Fine*, or the family council; used also in the sense of relatives to the fifth degree, who constituted the pledges, *i.* clxiii, clxiv, clxv, clxix, cclxxx, cclxxxi, ccxci.

Gelt, or *Gilt*, to graze, *i.* ccxvi.

Gellas, he binds, *ii.* 505.

Gena (same as *Dena*), to do, *iii.* 430.

Gentraighe, *Geantraighe*, one of the three musical feats which gave distinction to a harper, and which characterised the harp and harper of the *Daghda*. The word is derived from *gen*, laughter or merriment, and *traighe*, time or mode, and was evidently the name of one of the ancient Irish musical keys, *i.* dcxxxiv, dcxxxvi; *iii.* 214, 220–21, 260, 381.

Gert, gen. *Gertha* milk, *iii.* 490.

Gialda, to be pledged or bound by giving security, *i.* ccxvi.

Gialdnaib, abl. pl. hostages, *iii.* 503.

Gibne, or *Gipne*, a band, fillet, or thread of gold, silver, or *Findruine*, worn around the head to keep the hair down on the forehead and in its proper place; also a crescent of red gold worn by charioteers to keep their hair in its proper place, and also as a distinguishing mark of their profession, *iii.* 186–188.

Gicgil, giggling, *iii.* 432.

Gigne, will be [was] born, *iii.* 454.

Gilech, the spike or spear of a shield; *Gilech cuach coicrindi*, a flesh mangling cup spear, *i.* cccclxix.

Gill, *Giall*, *Gial*, a pledge, a hostage, clxiv, ccxvi, ccxxxviii, cccv; *iii.* 491, 492; *Giall Cerda*, hostages given for the fulfilment of treaties and other interritorial contracts and laws, *i.* dcxli.

Gilla, a servant, a page, *ii*. 344; *iii*. 149.

Girsat, *Girrsat*, a sort of girdle or sash; *Girsat corcra*, a purple waist-scarf *i*. ccclxxx; *iii* 434.

Giall, *Gell*, to exercise [*recte*, to bind, to get pledges, hostages or security for the fulfilment of], a pledge, *iii*. 505.

Giuis, pine wood, now bog deal, *i*. cccxlviii, dcxli. Incorrectly written *Giis* in *iii* 11, 57, 58.

Glaissin, Isatis tinctoria, dyer's woad, and the blue dye-stuff prepared from it, the *Glastum* of the Gauls, i. cccciii; *iii*. 118, 120, 121.

Glam dichinn, "satire from the hill tops", *ii*. 216-218.

Glasba, clear blue, *iii*. 456.

Glas. There are probably two distinct words of this form: 1, *Glas*, signifying green when applied to fields, etc., but gray-blue or bluish gray when applied to other objects; 2, *Glas*, signifying yellow, *i*. cccexxxv-vi, ccccxiv; *iii*. 275. *Glas srianaib*, with yellow bridles, translated green in *iii*. 496.

Glasfine, kindred from beyond the sea, *i*. clxv.

Gled, a kind of cane sword, used by a class of bullies called *Gleidires*, cf. Welsh *Gleddyr*, *i*. cccexliv.

Gleidire, a gladiator, or fighting bully who fought with the *Gled*, *i*. cccexliv.

Glenomon, a culprit, *i*. cii; *iii*. 494.

Gles, to prepare, to tune a harp or *Crut*, *iii*. 215; *Glésa*, tuning, *iii*. 250, 254, 255.

Gletten, an obstinate, hard-fought battle, *i*. cccexliv.

Glond-beimneach, loud clangour, *iii*. 426.

Gluair, gen. *Gluaire*, glory, ostentation, *iii*. 454

Gnaim, corn, madder, and other cultivated crops, *i*. cxxii.

Gni, he does, iii. 521.

Gnimu, a deed or deeds, *iii*. 492.

Goba, gen. *Ghobhann*, a smith, *ii*. 133.

Goibniu, gen. *Goibnenn*, the mythycal smith of the *Tuatha Dé Danand*, *ii*. 247, 248.

Golghaire Bansidhe, the wail of the *Bansidhes* (or fairy women), *iii*. 381-383.

Goléa, the light or thin strings [of the harp], *iii*. 253, 256.

Goltarglés, one of the strings of *Scathach's* magical harp, which causing all who heard it strange to burst out in constant crying and lamentation; tuning a harp in one of the ancient keys, *iii*. 223.

Goltraighe, one of the three musical feats which give distinction to a harper, from *gol*, crying, and *traighe*, time or mode; one of the ancient keys of Irish music, *i*. dcxxxiv, dcxxxvi; 214, 220, [illegible], 250, 260, 381.

Gorm, blue; certain shades of blue, approaching the green called *Glasghorm*, *ii*. 275.

Gort, a garden, an enclosed field, cf. Gothic, *gardo*, Welsh, *garth*, *i*. xcviii-ix, cxxxv, cxxxvi, ccclxi.

Goth, *Gath*, a spear, *i*. ccccxli, cccexlviii; *Gothnada*, little darts, or perhaps rather arrows, *i*. ccccxxxviii, ccccxlviii-ix, cccclx; *ii*. 301; *Gothnatia neit*, ivory-hafted spears, or rather bone or walrus-ivory-pointed darts, *iii*. 436; *Gotha u-det*, ivory-shafted spears, more correctly bone walrus ivory, etc., pointed darts, *i*. ccccxxxviii, cccexlviii, cccexlix; *ii*. 301, 303; *Goth manais*, a broad war spear, *i*. ccccxxxvi, ccccxli.

Gradh Ecailsi, the different grades of ecclesiastics, i. clvi; *Gradh Fine*, the members of a *Fine* who belonged to the privileged classes, that is, were *Aires*, and had full political rights, derived from the possession of land, *i*. clxiii, clxxiii; *Gradh Flatha*, the different grades of *Flaths*, *i*. clxxiii.

Graice (croakers), a class of *Cornaire*, or horn players, who produced a croaking noise like ravens, *iii*. 368.

Greggaib, dat. pl. stud horses, *iii*. 436.

Gresa, designs? [recte *Gres*—*teora nuagres*, three new arts, finishing feats]. Here it means the *Gres Ceardchan*, the forge finishing of a weapon by the smith—tempering, polishing, and whetting, *iii*. 42.

Gres, gen. of *Gresa*, embroidery, figured weaving, ornamentation, etc., *iii*. 106.

Gresedh-gruadh, cheek-reddening, insult, *iii*. 514.

Gress, constant digress, constantly *iii*. 510.

Gressa, reproach, insult, *iii.* 518.
Grianan, a summer house, a chamber placed in a sunny aspect, *i.* cccii, cccclxxxi; *iii.* 13; *Grianan na n-Inghean*, the sunny house of the daughters at Tara, *ii.* 16.
Grisach, cinders, figuratively used for "shame"; *Grisach dearg inso*, "red cinders here", used in the sense of "burning shame", *i.* cclxxviii.
Grith in ceoil, the melody of the music, cf. sanskrit *gri*, to sing, *i.* dxxxi.
Gruaide gris, cheek reddening, or redness, *iii.* 515.
Grus, *Gruiten*, *Gruth*, groats, coarsely ground meal, cf. Anglo-Saxon *Grut*, *i.* ccclxv; *iii.* 474.
Gú, a lie, a falsehood; the same as *gó*, *iii.* 493; *Gu forgaile*, false testification, *i.* ccxxxix.
Gual, gen. *Guail*, *Guaili*, charcoal, *i.* ccclxii, ccclxxii; *iii.* 486.
Guasaigestar, they shivered or shook, *iii.* 448.
Guba, *Gubha*, sighing or moaning in grief; part of the ancient funeral rite, *i.* cccxxi, cccxxii, cccxxiv, cccxxv, cccxxvi dexli; *iii.* 383; *Gubai*, sorrowful, *Eithne in Gubai*, *Eithne* the sorrowful, *ii.* 196. See also *Sámhghúbha*, *iii.* 384.
Guin, death, a wound, *i.* cciv; *iii.* 450.
Guth, the human voice, *iii.* 329; *Guthbuine*, *Guthbuinde*, speaking or sounding trumpets, *i.* dxxx–i; *iii.* 329–331, 333.
Heisedar (or *Leisedar*), laddles for broth; probably a loan word from the Welsh, *i.* ccclix.
Herenech, the representative or steward in a *Fine*, of a church or monastic establishment having a share in the property of the *Fine*; a lay vicar, *i.* cclxxx.
Iadaig, *Tiag*, a bag, or wallet, *iii.* 113, 117.
Iaerna [sharp-pointed] irons, *i.* cccexxxiii; *ii.* 300.
Ialachrand, *Iallaiccraind*, sandals, shoes made probably of raw skin, worn by the *Tuatha Dé Danand*, *i.* cccxcviii; *iii.* 158.
Ian, a vat, a brewing vat; sometimes applied to a drinking vessel, *i.* ccclvi, ccclix, ccclxxi; *Ian ol aiss*, a bowl for drinking new milk, *iii.* 478; *Ian ais*, *ian chorma*, a vat of new milk, a vat of ale, *i.* ccclxxi; *iii.* 486.
Iarfine, relatives from the ninth to the thirteenth degree, *i.* clxiii–iv.
Iarmhua, descendants (great-grandchildren), *iii.* 414.
Iarmotha, notwithstanding, *iii.* 494.
Iarn cach gnima, iron household implements, tools, *iii.* 500.
Iarn-dota, gauntlets, *iii.* 97.
Iarsudhiu, behind them, *iii.* 509.
Iathu, lands, territories, etc., *iii.* 514.
Ibar, *Ibur*, yew, *iii.* 500; "*Ibar alainn fidhbhaidhe*, the yew the finest of timber; first name of the *Luin Cheltchair*, *iii.* 325, 491.
Icairddiu [*I Cairdiu*], within the provisions of the *Cairde* or interterritorial laws, *iii.* 497.
Id, pl. *Idi*, a chain, a collar, a wreath or collar made of a twig or rod of wood twisted round a pole or pillar stone, and upon which was inscribed an oghamic legend, *i.* cccxliv; *iii.* 450.
Idna, the father of a numerous family of fighting men, *iii.* 517.
Idnaicthea, would, or used to send, *iii.* 438.
Iern n-guala, *Iernguali*, probably means the "house of the coal" or brew-house, where the wort was boiled over a charcoal fire; cf. A. Sax. *aern*, a house, a room, *i.* ccclxxi.
Ilgiallu, many hostages, *iii.* 502.
Ilgona, many wounds, all the wounds, *iii.* 440.
Im, a preposition, to, for, with, on, about, *iii.* 500; *Im h-Ére*, around Eriu, *iii.* 526–7.
Imairic, fight, battle, *iii.* 448.
Imarchor n-delend, the proper carrying or using of the charioteer's switch, *ii.* 372.
Imb, butter, now written *Im*, but invariably written *Imb* in this tract, *iii.* 487, 492, 496, 498, etc.
Imbas forosnai, "illumination by the palms of the hands", a species of Druidical divination prohibited by St. Patrick, 208, 227; a species of poetical composition connected with the Druidical rite so called, *ii.* 135, 172.
Imbleogain, kinsmen, *i.* cclxxxvi.
Imbolc, *Imbuilg*, the spring season, *iii.* 217, 420.

Imchommilt na n-arm, the friction of the arms, *iii.* 426.

Imda, *Immda*, pl. *Imdai*, or *Immdai*, a bed, *i.* cccxlvii–viii, dcxxix; *iii.* 499.

Imdadh, compartments, couches, seats, etc., *iii.* 6.

Imdegail, gen. *Imdegla*, defence, protection, *iii.* 438.

Imdenam Druinechus, ornamentation, embroidery, etc., *iii.* 112, 113.

Imdith, *Imdich*, *Imdiuch*, to vindicate, to guard, to protect, a man who protects or guards others, *iii.* 495–6, 517, 518.

Ime, *Imi* a fence, *i.* clxxxii, cxci; *Ime indruic*, a perfect fence or legal boundary, *i.* clxxxiii.

Imfaebair, cutting, loosening of bonds, etc., *iii.* 494.

Imfuireach, delaying, *iii.* 420.

Imgabail, to avoid, to shun, *i.* lxxxv.

Imglaice, a handful, table accompaniments, the Opsonia of the Romans, *i.* ccclxvi; *iii.* 477, 478.

Imluad, the same as the modern *Amhluadh*, disturbance, insult, dishonour, *iii.* 519.

Imluada, see *Sluaighte*, *i.* ccxxii.

Immaich, outside of, *iii.* 444.

Immid a couch, a bed, *iii.* 489. See *Imda*.

Imirgi, driving out, *iii.* 487.

Imoatoing, *Immustoing*, he is a *Toing* (an oath), *i.e.* he was qualified to swear, *iii.* 482, 496, 498, 499, 501, 502, 503.

Imram, *Imramh*, rowing; a wandering on the sea; *Imramh curaigh Maelduin*, "wandering of *Maelduin's* boat", an ancient tale, so called, *iii.* 158; *Imram coraig Ua Corra*, wandering of the boat of the sons of *Ua Corra*, an ancient tale so called, *i.* dcxiii.

Imrubad, thrusting, fighting with the *Manais* or great spear, *iii.* 493.

Imsena, to deny a charge, *iii.* 500.

Imscim, *Imscing*, a name for the *Mind* or diadem worn by *Ailill*, king of Connaught, at the *Táin Bó Chuailgne*; *Imscim n-oir*, a diadem of gold, *iii.* 197.

Imslaidi, hewing (with a sword in battle), *iii.* 444.

Imtheacht, rank, state, affluence, or position in society, but literally progress, migration, going, departure, or adventure, *iii.* 470; *Imtheacht na Trom Dhaimhe*, "adventures or progress of the Great Company", a tale so called, *iii.* 234, 235.

Imtheigmis, we used to go, *iii.* 436.

Imtoltain, wish, desire, at the pleasure of, etc., *iii.* 221.

Inaicfidea [*In-adhnaicfidhea*], should or would be buried, *iii.* 526.

Inar, *Ionnar*, a tunic, a jacket, *i.* ccclxxxvi; *iii.* 104, 105, 153, 154; *Inar aodhar*, a bright coloured *Inar*, *i.* dcxl; *Inar n-derg*, a scarlet frock, *iii.* 153; *Inar sirecdai*, a silken tunic, *iii.* 161.

Inbir, dat. pl. *Inbiurb*, a spit, a skewer, *iii.* 485.

Incaib, in right of, *iii.* 504.

Incaib, *Inchaib*, dat. pl. of *Inech*=*Enech*, the face, the front, and figuratively honour; co *nincaib ordaib*, with golden emblazonments [with golden faces], *iii.* 147, 492, 504, 506.

Indar limsa, dear to me, *iii.* 460.

Indarbhu, banishing, driving out, *iii.* 505.

Indbas, wealth, wisdom, *iii.* 522.

Indéch, weft, *iii.* 115.

Indell, to arrange, to set or put in order, *iii.* 215.

Indeoil, clasps or buckles of shoes, 157.

Indergithi, fit to repose in, to strip and sleep in, *iii.* 450.

Inderiec, fine, payment, *iii.* 492.

Indeilb cloiche, a naked stone chamber over a grave, etc., *i.* cccxxx-i.

Indfine, relatives from the thirteenth to the seventeenth degree, *i.* clxiii.

In diss, on second, *iii.* 499.

Indlach, instigation, *iii.* 448.

Indled, to yoke. *Indled a carpat*, to yoke his chariot, *iii.* 422–424.

Indles, unlawful, *iii.* 488. See *Dilis*.

Indnaide, preparing, igniting, *iii.* 505.

Indra, a ridge, a certain measure of land; an enclosed garden annexed to a house, and in which onions and other vegetables and fruit, were grown, *iii.* 488.

Indrubart, have said; *amhail as indrubartmar*, as we have said, *iii.* 492.

Indruic, *Innraic*, *Iuraic*, whole, perfect. When applied to persons it means "worthy", that is, worthy man qualified to give evidence and perform other legal functions, *i.* ccxlv–vi, cclxxvii.

aind-dligthech, an unlawful
iii. 508.
righteousness, *iii.* 514.
alness, swelling, *iii.* 448.
to watch, seize, guard, re-
r take care of, *i.* lxxxv.
o distribute, *iii.* 506.
tt, Shrovetide, *iii.* 495, 498.
se, *iii.* 493.
, in it, *iii.* 489.
chcraft, spells, magic cures,

chai, (*i.e. iar-chai*), a back
iii. 480, 482.
ar-raith), that which re-
vith the heirs or successors
parent or ancestor, whether
ibilities or privileges, *iii.*

f Norway, *iii.* 101.
djusting, settling, etc., *iii.*

it, *iii.* 486.
lls or is forfeited, *iii.* 491.
they; these are they, *iii.*

entitled to, *iii.* 499.
vers, *iii.* 508.
aladh], after, *iii.* 452.
hat which is lower, *iii.*

yew tree; the wood of the
e, *i.* ccxcix; *iii.* 57.
t, vessels and furniture
f the wood of the yew tree,
working in yew wood, con-
in the making of the orna-
facings and carvings on the
and furniture, and also in
niture itself, and the wooden
], *iii.* 53, 57, 58.
modern *Ladhar*, a prong, a
ladair a chossi, between the
his foot, *iii.* 450.
heroes, *i.* cccxxix.
l, a form of the gen. plu. of
a calf, *iii.* 500.
lay, cf. German *Lied*, *i.*
ii; *ii.* 172; *Laidh Luascach*,
ne of a species of poetry;
which the poet *Ruaman*,
Colman, composed his poem
oratory of *Rathan ua Suan-*
i. 37.
aighin, a heavy spear; the
lance, *i.* xxi, cccxxxviii,
; *ii.* 256-259. *Laighen Lea-*
hlas, pl. *Laighne Leathna*
[not *ghlais*], "the broad
green thrusting-spear", the broad green (or, as it may here mean, yellow) blade of the Gauls, whence *Lagen*, Leinster, *ii.* 156-158, 262, 295.

Laith, *Lath*=*Cuirm*, ale, *i.* ccexxxii; *iii.* 506.

Lamhchrann, the fore pillar of a harp, *iii.* 256, 358.

Lamnad, parturition, child-birth, *iii.* 221.

Lamthoraid, hand produce, the work produced by hand-labour, etc., *iii.* 115.

Lamhonn, a gauntlet, *iii.* 154.

Lamthogha, choice hands, *ii.* 133.

Lanamnas, pleasures of love, *iii* 507.

Land, or *Lann*, a blade, or leaf, a crescent, lunette, or frontlet of gold or silver, *iii.* 113, 114, 182, 183, 178, 193, 204. It was applied to a necklace, whether for men or women, or to ornaments for spears and other inanimate objects when used after the manner of a necklace, *iii.* 181, 182. In the tale of the *Brudin Daderga*, charioteers are described as having *Lanna óir* on the back of the head, *iii.* 183.

Lassamain, fiery, flaming, furious, *e.g. Leoman lassaman*, a furious lion. *Laoch lassaman*, a fierce warrior, *iii.* 460.

Laulghach, a full grown heifer about to calve, the term is now applied to a milch cow, *iii.* 481.

Leac, see *Liace*.

Leacán laoich Milidh, a warrior champion's semi-flat stone, *ii.* 276, 277.

Leamlacht, new milk, *iii.* 477.

Lear, the plain of the sea, *iii* 38.

Leasugudh, adjusting, instructing, fostering, etc., *iii.* 505.

Lebhad, cast or thrown, *iii.* 448.

Lecad, an act or deed which binds a person indissolubly, *i.* clxxxvii.

Lecht, *Leacht*, a stone sepulchral monument, of unfashioned stones of various sizes piled over a grave or chamber, *i.* cccxxxi-ii; *Leacht an fhir mhairbh*, the dead man's *Lecht*, *i.* cccxxxix.

Lee, with her, *iii.* 491.

Lego, gen. of *Liagh*, a physician, *iii.* 475.

Leim dar neimh, *i.e.* a leap over a fence [a leap over the particular kind of thorn fence called the *Eim*, or *Ime*, which marked the *Nimedh* or sanctuary, the breaking of which was a violation of sanctuary according to the ancient laws] See H. 3, 15, 85, etc., *ii.* 372.

Leinidh, *Leined*, a kilt, or petticoat, *i.* ccclxxxii; *iii.* 103-107; *Leined do min shroil mhaoth*, a kilt of fine soft satin, *iii* 167; *Lenda cumascdai*, kilts of mixed colours, *iii.* 146.

Leine, *Lene*, *Lena*, a kind of inner garment which hung down to the knees, or below the knees, forming a kilt, *i.* ccclxxviii-ccclxxx, ccclxxxii; *Lene fo derg inliud ünbi*, a shirt [*recte*, a kilt] interwoven with thread of gold upon him, *iii.* 162, 163; *Lene fo derg indlait öir impe*, a *Lene*, or kilt with interweavings of red gold upon her, *iii.* 160; *Lene fri geal cnes*, a shirt to the white skin, *i.* ccclxxxii; *iii.* 104-107, 143; *Lena gel colptach co n-derg intlad öir*, a white collared *Lena* with red ornamentations of gold, *i.* ccclxxxiii.

Leirg, a bed, a plain, etc., *i.* ccclxi.

Leiter, a written deed or conveyance, *i.* clxxxviii.

Leithbért, a truss (an armful), *iii.* 487.

Leithe, a *Leet*, as in court-leet; *o cach leithe*, from every *Leet*, *iii.* 518.

Leithrind, the treble string of the *Cruit*? half harmony, *iii.* 251, 252.

Lelaig, licked, *Bó rolelaig*, it was a cow that licked, *iii.* 158.

Lente, kilts, *iii.* 157.

Leoman, a lion? *i.* cccclxxi; *ii.* 327.

Lepaid, beds, *iii.* 496.

Les, a physician's medicine-bag, or chest, *iii.* 250.

Lesan, a bag; *Lessan mac Daghshnaithe*, "Bag, son of good yarn", *ii.* 133.

Les lethan, broad hipped [*recte*, ribbed], *iii.* 428.

Lesca, gen. plu. of *Lias*, a cattle shed or yard, *iii.* 479.

Lestar, pl. *Lestra*, *Lestrai*, vessels; every kind of drinking vessels, *i.* ccclv, ccclvi; *iii.* 495. The *Lestar* varied in size and shape, and might be made of any material whatever, gold, silver, bronze, wood. *Lestar cumdachtai*, a richly ornamented or precious *Lestar*. *Lestar lulaice*, a *Lestar* which held the milk of a newly calved cow, *iii.* Cf. Welsh *Hestawr*, *Hestor*.

Leth Flaithem, "a half air", or poor gentleman; one whose property was not sufficient to entitle him to the privileges of a *Flath*, *i.* clxxxiii; *iii.* 519.

Leth narathair, half the necessary implements for ploughing, *iii.* 484.

Lethe=*clethe*, a chief or nobleman entitled to a *Foleithe*, that is, who had "sack and soke", and was entitled to hold a court-*Leet*, *iii.* 517.

Lethrena, their traces [leathers], *iii.* 450.

Lethrind, treble strings [of a *Timpan*], *iii.* 361.

Liach, plu. *Liachrada*, a ladle, *iii.* 485.

Lia, a stone, a flag, a headstone, *i.* clxxxvii, cccxli; *Lia forcaid*, a grinding stone, *i.* ccclxi; *iii.* 486; *Lia laimhe*, a hand stone, *ii.* 287; *Lia lamha laich* (also *laoich*), a champion's hand-stone, *i.* cccxxxviii, cccclvi; *ii.* 263, 264, 275, 295; *Lia mol*, the shaft-stone of a mill, *i.* ccclx; *Lia mbron*, a grinding stone, *i.* ccccxxxiv.

Liag, *Lüc*, a flag-stone, flat stone, *i.* cccxix, cccxxx; *Liag Find*, *Find's* champion flat-stone, *ii.* 283, 284; *Liag Mairgene*, *Mairgen's* sling-stone, *ii.* 289. *Lüc tailme*, a sling-stone, see *Tathlum*, *i.* ccccxxxviii, cccclxi; *ii.* 250, 288, 295; *Lüc curad*, a champion's flat-stone, *ii.* 283-286.

Liag, gen. *Liaigh*, *Leaga*, dat. and abl. *Lego*, *Legho*, a leech or doctor, *i.* cccxix; *iii.* 475-477; *Fingin fathliag*, *Fingin*, the prophetic leech, *iii.* 97.

Liás, *Liás Bó*, a cattle yard, *i.* ccclxvi; *iii.* 487; *Lias*, or *Liass cairech*, a sheep-house, or sheep-pen; *Lias laegh*, *Lias laogh*, a calf-house, *i.* cxxv; *iii.* 484, 486.

Lüc, see *Liag*, a flag-stone.

Lin, flax, linen cloth, lint for dressing wounds, etc., *iii.* 475.

Lin, number, amount of; *Lin a dama*, the number of his retinue, *iii.* 491, 499, 501; also applied to the retinue itself, *iii.* 513.

Lin, *Lind*, ale, etc. See *Linn*.

Lindamnus, dangerous waters, an angry sea, *iii.* 210.

Les, a cattle yard, *i.* clxxvi, viii; *iii.* 487. There seems to no clear distinction between and the following word; the amental idea in both is an en- ng mound or rampart.

s, a homestead surrounded by npart or earthen fence, cor- nding to the Welsh *Llys*, *i.* t, ccciv; *iii.* 4, 7, 8, 27.

ithe, *Caisc no notlaig*, a day lemnity, Easter or Christmas *iii.* 111, 112.

y, a tester, a cover, *iii.* 489.

"the wasting" or sale of ained chattels, *i.* cclxxxiv, xv.

weak, *recte*, wretched people, 06.

e price of a thing, wages, re- , *i.* ccxcv; *iii.* 115; *Log enech*, *enech*, honour-price, the fine or an insult offered to a man's ur, and the amount of which nded on his rank, *i.* cxix, viii, ccxcv; *ii.* 174; *iii.* 471; *lanamnais*, bride-price, cor- nding to the *Brautkauf* of lermans, and the *Munder* and *ygafe* of the Norsemen, *i.* v; *Log leaga*, leech-fee, the f a doctor, *i.* ccxxxiv.

cht, a funeral cry, *iii.* 384. See *rath* in Corm. Glos.

indich, weft, *iii.* 115.

a, a churnstaff [hand-work], 33. *Loimdha mac Lomthogha*. nstaff, son of choice hands d-work, son of choice hands], 3.

kneading troughs, *i.* ccclix; 85.

, strings, cords, or ropes, *iii.* 450.

n. *Luin*, a blackbird, *iii.* 245.

urious, *iii.* 460.

a ship, a boat shaped house, cxxxix; *Long Laghen*, the ster house at Tara, *ii.* 15; *Mumhan*, the Munster House ara, *ii.* 15; a boat-shaped ves- r bath, *e.g.*, *Long foilcthe*, a ng basin, *i.* ccclv; *iii.* 486.

Lurg, a handle, a shaft; *a brebneca*, clubs with chains, ained clubs, *iii.* 149; *Lorgaib* *ch*, the shafts of an *Aithech*— andle of a pitchfork, of an axe, f a spade; *Lorg fersad iarain*, a spiked iron club or mace, corresponding to the German "*Morgenstern*", *i.* ccccxxxviii, ccccIxii; *ii.* 224; *Lorg forgga*, the handle of a pitchfork; *Lorg rammai*, the handle of a spade; *Lorgg samthaigi*, the handle of an axe, *i.* ccclix; *iii.* 506; *Lorgga*, spits, skewers and other iron implements belonging to the cooking boiler, *iii.* 485.

Lor lethna? scarlet cloaks, *iii.* 153, [*Loa lethna* is probably older; *Loa* being a form of the nom. plu. of *Lua*, a red or scarlet cloak, and *lethna*, the plural form of the adjective *lethan*, broad; *Loa lethna* would consequently be "broad scarlet cloaks"].

Luaithrinde, ashes engraver, a name given by *Dubditha* to the prong of the fork by which the devices of *Cuchulaind's* shield were engraved, *ii.* 329, *et seq.*

Lucht Tighe, family, household troops, etc., *ii.* 392.

Lugarmain, the front beam of the loom upon which the warp was rolled, *iii.* 116.

Lugnasad, games and other funeral rites instituted by *Lug*, or *Lugad*, and celebrated at *Tailtiu*, *Cruachan*, etc., on *Lama's* or *Lamma's* day (first of August), *i.* cccxxvi; *ii.* 343.

Luin Cheltchir, *Celtchair's* spear, *ii.* 325.

Luinneog, music, a chorus, a song or ditty, *iii.* 380, 384. *Cf.* *Lon*, a blackbird.

Lumman, a name for a shield, etc., *i.* ccclxxi; *ii.* 327.

Lundu, a river, *iii.* 448.

Mad, great, heavy, excessive, *iii.* 503.

Mac Faesma, "a son of adoption", pl. *Mic Faesma*, "children of adoption", that is, persons adopted into a family or *Fine*; a minor was also called a *Mac Faesma*, *i.* clxv; *iii.* 474.

Mac Mecnachan, a species of poetry peculiar to the order of poet called *Fuirmid*, *ii.* 171.

Maclan airgit, shoes of silver, *iii.* 159, 188.

Mad, a hero, *iii.* 446.

Mad, when, *iii.* 454.

Mael Imme, "servant of butter", *iii.* 104, 105.

Mael Land airgit, a simple broad band or crescent of silver, *iii.* 181; *Mael Land*, an ornament of silver with little bells of gold [worn on the necks of riding steeds in royal processions], *iii.* 181.

Maelsaille, "servant of fat meat", *iii.* 104, 105.

Magh Rein, the plain of the sea, cf. Goth. *rinnan*, O. Norse, *renna*, Sanskr. *ri*, Greek, *ῥέω*, *i.* xxii.

Maidset, they broke, *iii.* 450.

Maigin, a place; *Maigin Digona*, "a demesne of sanctuary"; *Maigin Set*, *i.* clv–vi, cccxxxiv; *iii.* 473, 488, 526, 527.

Main, richer, [*recte*, riches], *iii.* 178.

Maithim, set at large, naturalized, improved, forgiven, *iii.* 494.

Malla, mules, *iii.* 330

Mám, a handful, *iii.* 489.

Manais, pl. *Manaisi*, dat. pl. *Manaisib*, a broad trowel-shaped thrusting spear, a heavy spear, *i.* ccclxxxvii, cccxli; *ii.* 238, 255, 262, 295, 298, 317; *iii.* 100, 146, 440. *Manais leathan-ghlas*, a broad green spear, *ii.* 316. *Manaisibh muirneacha*, with great heavy spears, *ii.* 304.

Manchaine, *Manchuine*, service. *I manchuine*, in attendance, *iii.* 506; the special services which an heir gave his lord, and in a more limited sense a heriot, *i.* cxi–cxii.

Man cor sin [*iman cor sin*], in that manner, *iii.* 444.

Mani, unless, *iii.* 492.

Mani dernat, if he have not done it, *iii.* 497.

Maothal, meal; food consisting of nut-meal and milk, oatmeal and milk, cheese, etc., *i.* ccclxv.

Mat, *Mad*, if, *iii.* 499.

Matal, a mantle, a cloak, the Norse *Möttul*, *i.* ccclxxxviii; *iii.* 154.

Mathluath, a *Dal* or assembly of the *Raths* and householders of a *Fine*; also an assembly of the chief men of a *Tuath*, cf. Goth. *Mathel*, A. Sax. *Methel*, O. H. German and O. Saxon, *Mahal*, a harangue, a place of assembly, Middle Latin *Mallum*, a convocation, *i.* clxxxix, ccliii, cclx.

M-Ba, *M-Bao*, *M-Bua*, gen. forms of *Bó*, a cow; dat. and abl. *M-Boin*, *iii.* 479.

Mbis, when he has, *iii.* 490.

M-Braith, of destruction, *iii.* 452.

Mbruighrechta, gen. of *Bruighrecht*, *iii.* 475.

Mbruth cirdub, black hair, *iii.* 158.

Meada, of ale [*recte*, of *Mead*, or *Mede*], *iii.* 305.

Mear, to befool, to mock, or deride, *iii.* 522.

Meath, to fail, to wither; to destroy. *i.* ccliii.

Mebait, are bursting, *iii.* 452.

Mecon, the parsnip, Pastinaca sativa, *i.* ccclxvi.

Medar, a yew vessel, smaller than the *Milan*, a mead-drinking mug, but also used for drinking beer. It was probably not a square vessel, as stated in vol. *iii.* p. 57, as it was reckoned among the hooped vessels by *Finntan*, *i.* ccclvi; *iii.* 57, 61, 62.

Mede, metheglin, cf. German *Metu*, A. Sax. *Medu* or *Meodu*, O. Norse *Mjöðr*, *i.* ccclxxvii.

Meill Bretha ("good judgments"). A book of laws drawn up by *Bodann*, the chief judge of Tara in the time of *Conn* of the Hundred Battles, for the future conduct of juvenile sports. The enactment of this law was due to *Fuaimnech*, the daughter of king *Conn*, *ii.* 30.

Meirge, a banner or handkerchief of silk, etc. [here it means a lady's silk veil], *iii.* 114.

Melastar, he grinds [*recte*, thou art ground], *iii.* 448.

Mell, a ball (of gold) worn by ladies on the points of the tresses of their hair when plaited, *iii.* 190.

Mellach, deceitful, *iii.* 522.

Memaid, frightened to flight, *iii.* 450.

Mendat fadeisin, his own cherished home, *iii.* 521.

Menedach, meal and milk, *i.* ccclx.

Meni oir, gold-ore, *iii.* 210.

Mennut, [*mían-oit*], his cherished native place and people, *iii.* 517.

Meragaib, non combatants (fugitives), *iii.* 450.

Mesc, dat. *Meisce*, intoxication, *i.* cxxiv; *iii.* 503; *mesc medarchain*, a gentle merry intoxication, *iii.* 414; *mescraid recht*, moderate inebriations, *iii.* 503.

Mesca, gen. pl. of *Mes*, fruits, *iii.* 479.

Mescbaid, he regales, *iii.* 510.

Metithir, larger than, *iii.* 460.

Miach, a sack, a measure, i. ccclxv, dcxliii; iii. 512; *Miach comaitches*, the sack-fine for multure, or as part of the rent of a copartnership, i. ccclxiv; *Miach lestar*, a vessel capable of holding a *miach*; *Miach cruithnechta*, a sack of wheat, iii. 512.

Miad, *Miadh*, honour, reward; cf. A. S. *mêd*, Engl. *meed*, iii. 514, 522.

Miadlechta, dat. pl. *Miadlechtaib*, titles of honour, iii. 513.

Mic cor n-bel, binding men, chiefs of kindred, i. cclxii.

Midelb, an ill visage, iii. 442.

Midenam, gen. of *Midenmai*, misdeeds, iii. 493.

Midhellach, a deceitful man; one who does not occupy land or possess property; who does not work, or for whom there is no work done, iii. 522. See *Midlach*.

Midi medon lai, middle of midday, iii. 448.

Midithar, is ennobled, iii. 522.

Midlach, *medhon ellach*, the centre of deception. *Midlach miliaig*, a homeless man, or a deceitful man, iii. 522. See *Midhellach*.

Midlaigib, camp followers, non-combatants, iii. 450.

Mignimu, misdeeds, iii. 493.

Milan, a vessel smaller than the *Cilorn*, made of the wood of the yew, i. ccclvi; iii. 61–62.

Milchu, gen. *Milchon*, a grayhound, iii. 500, 507.

Milech, a brooch, iii. 137, 138; *Milech iarnaige*, an iron pin, iii. 103.

Miliaig (a *Midlach*), a homeless or deceitful man, iii. 522.

Mind, *Minn*, pl. *Minda*, dat. pl. *Mindaib*, a diadem or coronet, i. lxxiv, cclxxxiv, cccxcv; iii. 180, 182, 193–203, 307. *Mind Aird Righ*, diadem of a high king, iii. 179; *Mind n-óir*, or *mind óir*, a diadem of gold, iii. 113, 114, 160, 165; *Mind riogda*, a kingly diadem (a curious one worn by King Cormac Mac Airt, at the meeting of the states at Tara), iii. 196, 197.

Mintu, small birds, iii. 448.

Miodhcuaird, mead-circling, i. ccclii.

Mí siltai, the month of seed sowing, iii. 506.

Mithemel, a lowering cloud; a countenance exhibiting dismay and dispiritedness, iii. 442.

Mithal, an assembly, a gathering of people, i. ccliii; *Mithal Tuatha*, an assembly of the freeholders of a *Tuath*, called together to make a *Dun*, house, *Fert* or grave, or for some general public purpose, i. ccliii; *Mithal Flatha*, a meeting of the tenants of a *Flath*, called together to give allegiance on his accession, to attend his wake and funeral, or for other purposes, i. ccliii; *Meath Míthli Flatha*, non-attendance at the lord's assembly, i. ccliii.

Mleth=*mbleth*, grinding, iii. 489.

Mocoil acas fithisi, meshes and gems [*recte*, clusters and weavings], iii. 161.

Mointech, bog moss, i. cccci.

Molt cona fosair, a wether with its accompaniments, iii. 477.

Mna caointe, mourning women, professional mourning women who performed the lamentation part of the *Cluiche caointe*, i. cccxxiv.

Monail, occupations, iii. 506.

Móo, greater, superl. of *Mór*, iii. 494.

Moraim, great (*recte*, greater things), iii. 497.

Morglonnach, pompous, iii. 432.

Moroga, sausages, puddings, i. ccclxix; iii. 482.

Mou, comparative form of *Mór*; great, iii. 479.

Mrogad, extending, enlarging, increasing, iii. 511.

Mrugrechtai, gen. of *Brughrecht*, Brugh Law, the initial *B* being displaced by a prosthetic *M*, iii. 511.

Muadalbemmennaib, abl. pl. tremendous great blows, iii. 450.

Mucfoil, gen. *Mucfholach*, a pig-stye, i. cxxv; iii. 484, 486, 489.

Muc-Forais, a house-fed pig, i. ccclxix; iii. 479.

Mucriucht, bottom or pig-belly pudding, i. ccclxix.

Mug Eimhe, "slave of the haft", the name of the first lap-dog brought into Eriu, i. xxxix; ii. 210–212.

Muilenn, a mill, iii. 486.

Muillind argait, the same as *Maelland argait*, iii. 219, 220.

Muin, the neck, iii. 178, 182.

Muinche, pl. *Muinci*, dat. pl. *Muincib*, or *Munchib*, a neck torque, or neck chain; a generic name for any kind of collar, ring, or necklace for the neck of men, women, dogs, horses, etc., and for the hafts of spears where the head was inserted. In the Fennian poems and tales it is especially used for the collars of noble grayhounds. It was either a blade, or leaf of gold or silver, twisted wire or a twisted wreath. The twisted kind was called a *Muintorc*, nom. pl. *Muintorca*, dat. pl. *Muintorcaib*. *Muincke do at*, a smaller variety of the *Budne do at*, which went round the body, and appears to have been the finest kind, *i.* lxxiv; *iii.* 146, 147, 157, 160, 163-165, 176, 178, 179, 180, 181, 182, 186, 211.

Muirchuirthe, the son of a foreigner by a free-born woman, *i.* cccxli.

Mur Luacha, [modern Irish *Muirluachra*=*Luachair*], bulrushes, *iii.* 486.

Mur Moena, see *Sruth Moena*, and *ii.* 186.

Mummi, a tutoress, *iii.* 458.

Mur, a wall, a sepulchral monument, a plague-grave; *Mur cloiche*, a stone rampart consisting of a block of dry masonry not less than two feet in height, which marked the graves of such as died of pestilential diseases; where stones could not be obtained, square sods called *Dartairidhe* were used; *Dartaire*, the singular form, has been inadvertently printed in the text, *i.* cccxxxiii, dcxxxviii-ix.

Murathaig, gen. of *Mur Fatha*, an enclosed *Gort* or garden, a kitchen garden, *i.* ccclxvi.

Murduchan, a siren, a mermaid or sea nymph. See *Sámhghúbha*, which was the old Irish name for the song of the Sirens, not of the Sirens themselves, as some writers have supposed, *iii.* 384.

Nacha ruba, shall not wound, *i.* cxi.

Nad acciadat, not responsible for, does not respond to, *iii.* 507.

Nadman, a functionary corresponding to the Welsh *Gwr Nod*, or *Nodman*, *i.* cclxxv-vi

Naib, the dative plural of the definite article *na*. *Is naib secktaib*, into the seven things (*iii.* 492), affords an interesting example of the inflexion of the article, and its agreement in number and case with the noun to which it belongs.

Naidm, a knot, a contract, or bond, cf. Latin *nexum*; it is used also for *Nadman*, that is, the magistrate who made the *Naidm*, *i.* cclx, cclxxv; *iii.* 470, 471. *Naidm Aitire*, the bond of an *Aitire* or bail, *i.* cclxxxv.

Nairide=*Airide*, (*Ind Airide*, *a* *i.* *Airidhe*) a dairy, a store-house, *iii.* 488.

Nama, only, alone, *iii.* 506.

Namma, so that they be not, *iii.* [illegible]

Namthorrsed, disparagement, *iii.* [illegible]

Narta de, has come of it, *iii.* 460.

Nasc, a ring, a band, a strap, a [illegible] ring, or garter, a bond or tie, *i.* clxxxviii, ccxlvii; *ii.* 331, 332; *iii.* 168.

Nascaire, a Nasc-man, that is, a binder, or knotting-man; a magistrate qualified to make a *Naidm* or bond; another name for *Fer Nadma* or *Nadman*, *i.* cclxvii-viii, cclxxv, cclxxvi.

Nath, the name of any [metrical] composition. The great and small *Nath* were certain kinds of poems, the learning of which formed the study of the sixth year in a course of *Filedecht*. *Esnath*, *Esnad*, that which is not a metrical composition, but only a *Duchand*, *ii.* 172, 173; *iii* 381.

Nathrach, gen. of *Nathair*, a serpent, *iii.* 157.

Na Tri Finn Emhna, "the three Fair Twins", or triplets, [the three *Finns* of Emania, *ii.* 261-264.

Naurrai [*Aurra*=*Urradh*], a leader or chief, *iii.* 502.

N-Dissi, on second, or second day, *iii.* 497.

Nechtair, *Nechtár*, *I nechtar*, outside, a distance out from, neighbouring, *iii.* 508, 517.

N-Ecsmacht, despotic rule, *iii.* 491.

Neime, a sacred object, a relic upon which an oath was sworn, *i.* cclxxxix, ccxci.

Neimid, a magistrate, a judge, a sacred person or thing, the highest class of privileged grades, *i.* cclxiii, cclxii.

Nel, a trance, *iii.* 452.

Nel Mac Laeich Lasamais, "Light, [*recte*, cloud], the son of Blazing Warrior", from *Nel*, "light", [*recte*, cloud], *Laech*, "a champion", and *Lasaman*, blazing, brilliant, *ii.* 122.

Nemh-thenga, poisoned [*recte*, poisonous] tongue, *iii.* 17.
Nembeoil, some kind of beer or cider [perhaps rather melted butter, or some savoury kind of sauce], *iii.* 477.
Nemed, a duly qualified "worthy man", *i.* clxxxiii.
Nena, a kind of literary composition forming part of the studies of the ninth and tenth years of the course of *Filedecht*, *ii.* 173
Nenadmin, a kind of cider made from the wild crab apple, and also from whorts, *i.* ccclxxviii.
Nenaisc, to bind, to govern, *iii.* 514.
Neper=eper, is said or called, *iii.* 491, 497.
Nesa, nearest or next to; *nesa do seir Tuisigh*, follows next after a chief, *iii.* 520.
Niadh, a champion, *iii.* 168,
Niamh Land, or *Lann* (*óir*), a flat crescent of gold, which was worn around the neck, and also upon or over the forehead; *e.g. Niamhlann óir in a hedan*, a radiant crescent of gold upon her forehead, *iii.* 157, 174, 179, 211.
Niamhleastar, a splendid vessel, *iii.* 204.
Nicelt, they did not conceal, *iii.* 249.
N-Immdai, beds, *iii.* 495.
Nin, "id est", that is, etc., *iii.* 492.
Noaill, to arbitrate (to go into co-judgment with), *iii.* 504.
Noes, rushes, *Noes nua*, new rushes, *iii.* 489.
Nog, *n-óg*, perfect, *Nog Cuir*, perfect bonds, *i.* clxxxviii; *Nog tincur*, perfect furniture, *iii.* 499.
Noill, to swear; used also in the sense of an oath and of the person who administered it, *i.e. Noillecha*, arbitrators or jurats who held sworn inquisitions, and who took part in planting, proclaiming, and ascertaining boundaries, *i.* clxiv, clxxxii, cclxxxix, cccxc; *iii.* 500.
Noillegh, enmities, disputes, *iii.* 500.
Noi-x, nineteen, *iii.* 499.
Nollenat, that which follows, *iii.* 497.
No-laited, blighted (or used to blight), *iii.* 526–7.
Nomad, ninth, ninth day, *iii.* 477.
Nomad nuá, the ninth generation, *iii.* 494.
Nomaide, nine days, *iii.* 414.
Nonbur, nine persons, *iii.* 501.
Nosad, funeral rites or games, *i.* cccxxvi, cccxxix.
Nos Tuatha, pl. *Nosa Tuatha*, a bylaw or territorial custumal, *i.* ccliv; *ii.* 31; *iii.* 472.
Nuaill, to proclaim or publish, *i.* clxxxii.
Nuaiss, *n-Uais* (comp. of *uas*, noble), greater, more noble, *iii.* 500.
Nuallgrith na roth, loud clattering of the wheels, *iii.* 426.
N-uath-ledb, a piece of leather upon which was made a pattern to be copied by a workwoman, *iii.* 116.
N-us, a grandsire, *iii.* 479.
Nurconn, *n-Urconn*, a chief man, *iii.* 515; cf. *Orc* a prince, *Ard Arcon*, high nobles, *Conn conda Secha*, chiefs of kindred.
O', from, *iii.* 495. *O bel acus O tengaig*, "from mouth and from tongue", record of court given". "Ore tenus", *i.* cclxviii.
O', dat. *U*, ears, *iii.* 145; *O' mair*, large-eared, *iii.* 107, 428.
Oc-Aire, a young *Aire* [an *Aire* who held by *socn* or sockage tenure], *i.* cxli-ii; *iii.* 479.
Ocbaidh, to raise up; *dom ocbaidh*, raise me up, *iii.* 383.
Ochar-chlis, "missive shields", [*recte* missive darts and not shields; *a nocht nochar-chlis*, their eight turned-handled missive darts], *ii.* 303; *iii.* 436.
Ochan Chonchobair, *i.e. Conchobar's* groaner, the name of *Concobar Mac Nessa's* great shield, *i.* ccclxxii; *ii.* 321.
Ochrath, pantaloons reaching to the *Ailt*, anckle, *iii.* 104–107; leggins or greaves, cf. Latin *Ocrea*, *i.* ccclxxxiv–v, cccxciv; *iii.* 157.
Ocht-Foclach mór, a kind of verse having eight lines in a stanza, of which the following varieties are mentioned: *Ocht foclach corranach beg*, or "little eight-lined curved verse"; *Ocht foclach mór chorronach*, or great eight-lined curved verse; *Ocht foclach h-i Eimin*, or eight-lined verse of *O' h-Eimhin*, *iii.* 393, 394, 395, 397–399.
Ocht-Tedach, an eight-stringed musical instrument of the harp or psalterium class, *i.* dxiii; *iii.* 262, 263, 333.
Octigernd, a petty or tributary king,

a lord having soke or jurisdiction, *i.* cccl.
Oé, to know, to recognize or acknowledge, see *a noi*, *iii.*513.
Oen-cinneda, the last survivor of a family, *iii.* 477.
Oenmit, the husband of a bad woman, a cuckold, *iii.* 521.
Oenudhe, gen. of *Oenuch*, a fair, an assembly, *iii.* 514.
Og-Aire, see *Oc-Aire*, *i.* cclxxx; *iii.* 26.
Og-Flaithem, a petty *Flath*, one of an inferior class of nobility holding part of a subdivided estate, corresponding perhaps to the German *Land-Adel*.
Oilec, *Oile*, men sent to arrest and pursue or execute a criminal; they probably formed the armed retinue of the *Dae*, *i.* ccxlvi; *iii.* 507.
Oircel, a small narrow house, shed, or cellar. In the *Lebhor Brec*, the shed in which Christ was born is called by this name; a mill sluice. *Oircil an fiona*, a wine cellar, *i.* ccclx.
Oircin, a musical instrument probably a loan-word from the Latin *Organum*; *Oircine*, a man's name, or rather title, *e.g.* the *Ollamh Oircne*, or chief professor of the *Oircin*. This name might also signify the "repeater", in allusion to the man's profession of *repeating* or singing, and derived from *oir* or *ór*, the mouth, and *cne*, a loan-word from the Latin *cano*, *i.* dxxx; *ii.* 210, 212; *iii.* 334–5.
Oircne, a lap-dog, *ii.* 210, 212; *iii.* 334–5.
Oirdniter, is ordained, that ordains, *iii.* 504.
Oirfidioch, musicians [fife-players], *iii.* 340.
Oitidchi, junior, *iii.* 430.
Oitiu, youth, newness, *iii.* 479.
Olla, wool, *iii.* 115.
Ollamh, the highest rank in any of the learned professions, *ii.* 78, 172; *iii.* 52, 53, 216, 235, 316, 365, 510; *Ollamh Aighne*, the highest rank of advocate or pleading barrister, *i.* cclxxiii; *Ollamh Brethamnuis*, chief justice of the *Airecht Fodeisin*, *i.* cclxxiii; *Ollamh Cruitire*, a chief harper; *Ollamh Ciuil*, an *Ollamh* or doctor of music; *Ollamh Tempanach*, a chief timpanist.
Omnaid, *Omnad*, an oak tree; a trunk of any tree, e.g. *omnad giuise*, a trunk of a pine tree; *omnad ibhair*, a trunk of a yew tree, *iii.* 448.
On, a loan (lending), *iii.* 487.
Or, *H-or*, a border, limit, extremity, or boundary of any place or thing; *H-or crichi*, the boundary of a territory, *iii.* 505.
Orb, an heir, as in *Comorb*, a co-heir, cf. German *Erbe*, *i.* clxxxii.
Orba, inherited estate, patrimony, *i.* clxxxii; *Orba cruib is sliasta*, "inheritance of hand and thigh", land settled on a daughter, and which passed away from the *Fine* to the husband and the children of the daughter and their descendants as long as they agreed with the *Fine*, and conformed to the *Fenechas*, or custumal law, *i.* clxx.
Orbainn, a generic name for corn, *i.* ccclxii.
Orcca, young pigs, *iii.* 500.
Ordain, renown, *iii.* 240, 241.
Ordain, the thumb, *iii.*146–7.
Ordd, order or rank, *iii* 488–9.
Ordnasc óir, a thumb-ring of gold, *iii.* 146–7, 186.
Orduise, thumb rings, *iii.* 168.
Orgain, slaughter, destruction, plunder, etc., *Orgain Chathrach Chonrai*, the slaughter of *Cathair Conrai*, *i.e.* the *Cathair* or residence of *Curoi*, *Mac Daire*, King of West Munster, *iii.* 81.
Ornai, the name of the sword of *Tethra*, *ii.* 254.
Ornasc, a gold ring, a finger ring, a clasp, *iii.* 168.
Or snath, gold thread, *i.* ccclxxxiii.
Os, a wild deer, hence *Ossairghe*, or Ossorians, *ii.* 208.
Osolgud, *Ossolggud*, opening, *iii.* 487.
Otha, from them, from that, or those, *iii.* 364.
Othar-chleas, the invalidating feat, *ii.* 352.
Othrans, a person sick or wounded, *iii.* 471, 472.
Pait, a leather bottle, cf. A. Sax. *Bytta* or *Butta*, English *Butt* or *Boat*, *i.* ccclviii; *iii.* 117; *Pait foilchthi*, a leather bottle with cosmetic and scented oil—literally a bathing or washing bottle, *i.* ccclvii; *iii.* 117.
Partaing, coral, *iii.* 110, 220, 221.

tuina dearg, the berry of the
ntain ash.
e, a maker of leather bottles,
clvii; *iii.* 117.
horse, *i.* ccclxxv.
it, penance, penalty, *i.* clvi.
olg, a foot bag in which sorted
l is kept by carding women, *i.*
viii; *iii.* 115.
a wooden drinking vessel with
pright handle, larger than the
n, or mug, *i.* ccclv–vi
a, a penny, *i.* cclxxx, cclxxxi,
civ; *iii.* 37.
bag-pipes, Welsh *Pybeu*, *i.*
lxxxiv, dxxxii; *iii.* 313, 335.
e, *piopaire*, pl. *Pipaireadha*, a
r, *iii.* 335, 336, 340, 368, 369.
can, etc., *iii.* 31.
e, a satchel, a book wallet, *i.*
viii.
a friend, a tutor, master, or
er, *iii.* 446, 456; sometimes
as "my dear", as in *iii.* 418.
, a tent, an awning or cover-
of a chariot, from the Latin
lio, *i* cccclxxx.
kind of dance-music, *iii.* 407.
lach, legal limit of pursuit, *i.*
xxvii.
each, decorators, *iii.* 258.
aid, prime grade, *iii.* 502.
, supper, a meal, from the
n *Prandium*, *i.* ccclxvi.
, he spake, he said, iii. 450.
a special levy, etc., *i.* ccxl.
to sustain, etc. *Ni racu*, could
sustain, *iii.* 510.
saying, *iii.* 414.
haidsa, I have come, *iii.* 418.
choib, poems and traditions,
sodies, *iii.* 310.
Raith, pl. *Ratha*, a bail or
ty, a spokesman for another,
tii, clxxxviii, cclxii; *iii.* 416,
Rath Trebaire, a chief of
sehold, *i.* clxxvi; *Raith com-*
gi, security of sanctuary, *iii.*

, is ruled, *iii.* 497.
, a spade, *i.* cxi.
oble, *iii.* 454.
Rand, thread; *Rand-airgid*, sil-
thread, *iii.* 113, 114, 183.
a verse (see *Abhram*), *iii.* 371.
in, I have heard, *iii.* 426.
rnastar, that betrayed me, *iii.*

ertso, I foretold, *iii.* 426.

Ratregdastar, art pierced, *iii.* 448.

Rath, wages; the cattle, etc., given by a lord to his *Ceiles*, for which the latter were to pay service, rent, etc., according to mutual agreement, *i.* cx–cxiii; *iii.* 384, 472.

Rath, a residence surrounded by an earthen rampart; the residence of an *Aire* entitled to act as a *Raith*, *i.* cccv, cccxxx; *iii.* 14. See *Lis* and *Dun*.

Rathaigis, he guarantees, *iii.* 493.

Rathbhuidhe, a *Rath*-builder who constructed the *Rath*, *Lis*, and *Dun*, *iii.* 14, 15.

Rathmaighe, a rath builder, *iii.* 522.

Ratfia, I will give, *iii.* 400, 414.

Realta na Bh-Filiodh, "the star of the poets", *i.e.*, the house of the poets at Tara, *ii.* 16.

Recht, law, *i.* cclxxi; *iii.* 497; *Recht Adhamnain*, the law of *Adamnan*, *iii.* 505; *Rechta lanamna*, gen. of marriage law, *iii.* 500.

Rechtaire, pl. *Rechtairi*, a house steward, corresponding to the *Pincerna* or butler of the Anglo-Saxons, *i.* ccxxxix, cccli, ccclii; *iii.* 504.

Rechtgi, *Rechtge* (pl. of *Recht*), lawful rights, *iii.* 505.

Redithma, the time of detention of hostages, pledges, etc.; and in case of cattle in pound, it meant the time between the expiration of the *Anad* or stay, and the *Re Fiascla* or time of release, when notice of *Lobad* or wasting, that is, of forfeiture and sale, was given, *i.* ccxxxiv. See *Dithma*.

Refedaib, "rollers, bodkins, or pins" [*recte* twisted cords or thongs], *ii.* 300. See *Lebor na h-Uidhri*, p. 63, col. 1, line 18.

Ré Imbi, the fencing season, *iii.* 489.

Reimm, a juggler, a clown, *iii.* 522.

Remmad, distortion of the body and face, *iii.* 522.

Rend, *Renn*, dat. and abl. pl. *Rennaib*, a point, *ii.* 300, *iii.* 448.

Repaid, to cure=*Frepaid*, which see.

Repsetar, they refused, *iii.* 414.

Retha copad, a bleating ram, *iii.* 140.

Rethaib ech, horse-racing, *iii.* 507.

Ri, a king, *iii.* 469, 502.

Riascaire, an outlaw, a wanderer or exile, a man who absconds from his family, tribe, and territory to evade justice; an ignoble *Rath* builder who builds for chiefs and ecclesiastics. Cf. English *rascal*, *iii.* 522.

Riastartha, the gigantic distorted, cf. German *Riese*, Old Norse *Risi*, a giant, i. cccxxxviii.

Riastrad, distortion, *iii.* 448.

Ric a less, to want or require, *iii.* 490.

Ricce, Rige, a kingdom, i. lxxxiv.

Richt, form, appearance, state of being, *iii.* 522.

Rig, Righ, Rii, Ri, forms of the generic name of a king. Cf. Gaulish *Rig-s* or *Rix*, Latin *Reg-s*, or *Rex* (see also *Cing*), *i.* ccxxviii, ccxxxi; *iii.* 469, 502, etc.; *Ard Ri Erind*, the high or paramount king of Ireland, *i.* ccxxxi; *Righ* or *Rii Ben*, king of horns, see *Righ Tuatha*, ccxxix; *iii.* 502; *Rii Buiden*, a king of companies, see *Righ Mór Tuatha*, *i.* ccxxix; *iii.* 502; *Rii bunaid cech cinn*, the *Rii Rurech*, or king of kings, see *Righ Cuicidh*, ccxxix; *iii.* 502, 503; *Righ Cuicidh*, one of the provincial kings of the Irish Pentarchy; he was the same as the *Righ Bunid* or *Righ Rurech*, *i.* ccxxix; *Ri eicis* or *Righ eigeas*, a king sage, or poet-king, *ii.* 57; *iii.* 503; *Ri Ri*, a king-king, who holds the allegiance of seven tribe kings, *iii.* 574; see *Righ Mór Tuatha*; *Rigflath*, a king-*Flath*, or royal chief, *i.* cxxviii; *Rii Rurech*, the same as the *Righ Cuicidh*; *Rig Treaba*, the king of a tribe, *i.* ccxxx; *Righ Tuatha*, the king or chief of a *Tuath* or *Triucha Céd*; he was the same as the *Righ Ben* or *Righ Benn*, *i.* ccxxix; *Righ Mór Tuatha*, a king of a great *Tuath*, he was the *Dux* or leader of the armed forces of the union of small *Tuaths* comprised in the *Mór Tuath*, and corresponded to the Ealdorman of a Trithing, while the *Rig Tuatha* corresponded to the Ealdorman of a Hundred. The *Righ Mór Tuatha* was also called a *Righ Buiden*, or king of companies, from his office of military leader, *i.* ccxxix, ccxxxi, cclxviii.

Rigán, a queen, *i.* cccl-cccli.

Righ-Barr, a royal *Barr* or diadem; any ornament or covering worn by a king on his head, *i.* ccoxlv; *iii.* 209.

Righdamna, Rigdomna, "the material of a king", a prince, a royal heir, *i.* cccl, cccli; *iii.* 146.

Righ Tech, Rig Tech, gen. *Rigthigh*, "a king house", a kingly or royal residence, *iii.* 508.

Rigthigh, a frontman. A king was entitled to have four mercenary attendants or body-guardsmen in his retinue, viz.: a *Righthigh* or frontman, a *Sairthith* or rear-man, and two *Taobtaid*, or sidemen, *iii.* 500.

Rinceadh, dance, *iii.* 406-408.

Rind, "music with corresponding music against it"; melody, *iii.* 232, 361.

Rinde, a round wooden bucket, *iii.* 117.

Rinnaidhe, an engraver or carver, *iii.* 209.

Ritiri, a horseman, an esquire, cf. German *Reiter*, *iii.* 146.

Robhud, vauntings, warnings, etc., *iii.* 432.

Rochair, has fallen, died, *iii.* 452.

Rochet, was sung, *iii.* 514.

Rochraphair, you have fallen or died, *iii.* 311, 312.

Rochratar, they fell or died, *iii.* 434.

Rochul, a shroud or grave cloth, *i.* cccxli, ccclxxxvii, cccxciv.

Rocuindigh, did request, *iii.* 526-7.

Rod, though: *Rod be*, though he be (is), *iii.* 510.

Rodh, see *Rud*, *Rudh*.

Rodoslaidius, I have slaughtered, *iii.* 462.

Roeglaind, learned, *iii.* 446.

Roen, visible, *iii.* 450.

Rofia, that passes, *iii.* 491.

Rofuiter, have been sent, *iii.* 507

Rogbai, to require or desire for, *iii.* 508.

Roi, a battle; a battle field, *iii.* 506.

Roidh, see *Rudh*, *iii.* 119, 120.

Roilbe, common mountain pasture, a morass, waste land in general, *i.* clx.

Roinimdeltar, is distributed, *iii.* 485.

Romad=Fromad and *Fromad*, to test, to prove, to rouse, *iii.* 442.

Roure, retreat, defeat, *iii.* 509.

Rop, is, it is, *iii.* 506.

Ropcoir, is appropriate, *iii.* 505.

Ropp, a tuft; *Ropp do birur*, a tuft of water cress, *iii.* 150, 151.

Rormai, is increased, *iii.* 490.

Rosca catha, battle songs, war odes, and harangues, *i.* cccxxvii.

Roslaic, he darts, bounds, or lets go, *iii.* 448.

Roth, a wheel, cf. Latin *Roto*, *i.* ccccIxxviii-ix; *Roth-chleas*, the wheel feat, some such game as throwing the sledge or the quoit, *ii.* 372; *Roth croi*, *Roth righ*, a royal wheel shaped brooch, *ii.* 56-7; *Roth n-ór* a gold wheel brooch, *iii.* 141, 157-8.

Rout, a road, *iii.* 486.

Rui, a wood, *i.* clx.

Ruadan, probably rye, and cognate with Lettish *Rudzi*, *i.* ccclxii.

Ruaim, *Rime*, the Alnus glutinosa, alder tree, the branches of which are used for dying wool, *i.* ccccv; *iii.* 119.

Ruamadh, "riming", the first process of wool dyeing, effected by boiling the wool with the twigs of the alder tree, *iii.* 119. This process is still called *Ruamughadh*, *i.e.*, alder-colouring.

Ruamna rus, battle conflict, triumph; cf. O. H. G., O. Sax. *hruom*, *hrôm*, clamor, jactantia, gloria, N. H. German *Ruhm*, fame, *iii.* 518.

Ruanaid, warlike, *iii.* 458.

Ruaraid, he thrust, *iii.* 450.

Ruba, wounding, cutting, killing, driving off trespassing cattle, or animals of prey, etc., *i.* cxii. See *Fuba*.

Rubai, wounded, *iii.* 509.

Rucht, pl. *Ruchta*, a scarlet frock or coat, *iii.* 152, 153. See *Inar*.

Rud, *Rudh*, *Roidh*, *Rú*, *Run*, Galium verum, the yellow bedstraw, also a cultivated plant, probably madder, used for dyeing wool of a red colour, *i.* cccci, dcxliii; *iii.* 119, 120. A *Rig Tuatha*, was entitled to get from his subjects every year a quantity of *Corcur* and of *Rud* of the value of one *Scrapal*.

Rudrad, prescription, *i.* clxxxvii, clxxxix, cxc; *Rudrad cascait*, a prescription of fifty [years], *i.* clxxxvii; *Rudrad trichat*, a prescription of thirty [years], *i.* clxxxvii.

Ruide, reddening, disgrace, literally blushing, *iii.* 507.

Ruidiud, ruddiness, *iii.* 454.

Ruirmisem, *Ruirmisium*, we have enumerated or mentioned, *iii.* 500, 501.

Rungcin, a channel or moulding plane, *iii.* 29, 30.

Ruriud, a first crossing or trespassing over a defined boundary, *i.* ccl.

Rutsu, with you, to you, *iii.* 454.

Sab, pl. *Sabaid*, a prop of state, a councillor of state; *Sabaid* is frequently used in the sense of a council, *i.* cxxxi, clxxxvi, ccxlii, ccclxxi; *iii.* 511; *Sabaid Cuirmtigi*, the Council of the Ale House, *i.* ccxlii, cclii; *Sabh Ildanach*, the polytechnical block, or trunk of all the arts, a name given to *Lughaidh Mac Eithlinn*, *iii.* 40, 42.

Sabald, *Saball*, a barn, *iii.* 479, 486.

Saer, a carpenter, a mason, a builder, *iii.* 40-42, 209, 210.

Saer, free; *Saer Biathad*, free maintenance, *iii.* 514; *Saer Bothach*, free-service cottiers living in a *Both* or cabin on common or tribe lands, *i.* cxv, clxxxvi. See *Cot*. *Saer Ceile*, a free client or vassal, *i.* cxxix. *Saer Fuidir*, a free *Fuidir*, *i.* cxvii; *Saer rath*, the gifts or wages given by a lord to a free *Ceile* or vassal, *i.* cx.

Sai, a literary title given to historiographs and other learned men, *i.* ci; *iii.* 510. See *Suad*. *Sai canoine*, a professor of canon law, etc., *ii.* 84; *Sai Treab*, a *Righ Treaba* or tribe king, *i.* ccxx x.

Saiget, an arrow, a dart, *ii.* 287, 301; *Saiget Bolc*, *Saget Bolc*, *Saighead Bolg*, a belly spear; ore probably an ordinary bow, cf. *sagitta*, an arrow, *i.* ccccliii; *ii.* 295, 301.

Saigid, unto; *da saigid*, unto him, unto us, *iii.* 444, 452.

Saig-uar, nomen fontis, whence *Saigir Ciaran* in Ossory, *i.* cccvi.

Sailti, salted meat, *i.* ccclxix; *Sailti do tarsun*, salt meat with condiments, *iii.* 485.

Saim biad, *Saimmbiad*, summer food, *iii.* 487, 495.

Saintrebtha, householding, household troops, *iii.* 478.

Sál, foulness, dirt, dishonour, *iii.* 493.

Saland, salt, *iii.* 483.

Saill, *Sall*, a generic name for flesh meats of all kinds; bacon, *i.* ccclxix; *iii.* 487, 492; *Saill t-salnd*, salted meat, the *Sialfacti* of the Norse, *i.* ccclix, ccclxvii.

Samh, summer, *iii.* 214. See *Samhain*, *Sámghubha*, *Sambiad*, etc.

Samach, happy, *iii.* 444.
Samaisc, a heifer in her third year, not bulled, *i.* cxi, cxii; *iii.* 49, 114, 481. See *Sed.*
Sambiad, *Sambiud*, summer food, *iii.* 492, 500.
Samain, *Samhain*, gen. *Samna*, November eve, from *samh*, summer, and *fuin*, end, *ii.* 13; *iii.* 124, 217, 420.
Sāmhghūbha, the song of the *Murduchans*, mermaids or sea nymphs, from *samh*, which signifies here tranquillity, entrancing happiness, and *gubha*, a slow plaintive air, *iii.* 384.
Samhuither, arranged, established, confirmed, etc., *iii.* 515.
Samseisc focail, polite address, gentle conversation, *iii.* 520.
Santbrecc, beautifully speckled, *iii.* 418.
Sar, an insult, an assault in which blood was not shed, female violation, violation of sanctuary, i. ccxcv; *iii.* 473, 482.
Sarugud, *Saragh*, a fine or compensation paid for a *sar*; it was the same as the Welsh *Saraad*, *i.* cxxviii, clxxvi, ccxcv.
Satlui, revolt, aggression, *iii.* 505.
Scabal, a pot; *Scabal cocais*, a cooking pot, *i.* ccclx; *iii.* 479; *Scabal tigi*, a house or family pot, *i.* dcxl.
Scadere, *Scaiderc*, a mirror, *i.* ccclvii; *iii.* 117.
Scalfartach, a loud, sharp, shrill sound or noise; the chirping of birds; *e.g.*, *scalfartach lon*, chirping of blackbirds; this word is incorrectly explained in some latter day glossaries as a piper, *iii.* 368.
Scāthān, a mirror. See *Scaiderc*, *iii.* 117.
Sceinmnig, shyness, wild flight, *iii.* 450.
Sceith beimnecha, protecting shields, *iii.* 147-8.
Scell, a target, *iii.* 454.
Sceo gruaidhe, *gruadhgrissa*, cheek-reddening, *iii.* 515.
Scian, pl. *Scena*, a knife, *i.* ccclxi; *Scian gailia* (recte, *gaili*, gen. of *gail*, slaughter warfare, rage of battle, etc.; there is also a form *gal*, heat, battle, valour, etc.), a curved war knife called by the Scotch a "gully-knife", *i.* cccclxiv.
Sciath, a shield, a scuttle, *ii.* 330, 331; *Sciath clis*, pl. *Sciatha clis*, missive shields, *ii.* 301; *iii.* 436; light shields used in fighting with javelins and other missive weapons, *i.* cccclxv, cccclxvii.
Sciathrach, the straps and trappings of a shield, *ii.* 331; *iii.* 162, 163.
Scilde, see *Skilda*.
Scolb, a "scollop", a thin rod or twig, pointed at both ends, and used for fastening thatch, *iii.* 32.
Screcin, fright, *iii.* 450.
Screpall, a standard of value which varied in many cases, but here it is = three pence, *i.* cclxxx-i; *iii.* 112.
Scuaird Lena, a *Lena* made like the Norse *Skyrta*, *i.* ccclxxxiii.
Scur, an enclosure, a grazing field, a paddock, *iii.* 444.
Sdan (=*stan*), tin, from the Latin *Stannum*, *i.* ccccix.
Sdarga, a shield, *i.* cccclxv; *ii.* 344.
Sebān, a small wooden mug, *i.* ccclvi.
Seagdair, *Seaghdair*, one of the grades of *Fili*, or poet, *ii.* 171.
Seanchaid, *Senchaid*, persons qualified to make "record of court", *i.* cxci; *Seanchaid n-imaic*, fully qualified *Senchaids*, *i.* clxxxii.
Seanoir, a senior, *i.* clvi.
Sechip, each of them, *iii.* 493.
Sechtar Faitche, an outer farm or lawn annexed to the *Faitche*, farm or lawn proper, *i.* cxxxv.
Sechtaib, seven things, septinary grades, see *Naib*, *iii.* 492.
Secib, together with, outside of, *iii.* 514.
Secul, rye, a loan word from the Latin *Secale*, *i.* ccclxii.
Sed, pl. *Seoit*, *Seoid*, *Seota*, a standard of value by which rents, fines, stipends, and prices were determined. There were many kinds of the *Sed*, but a milch cow represented the prime *Sed*. *Sed-bó-Ceathra*, a *Sed* of small cattle; *Sed-bó-dile*, a *Sed* made up of any or of different kinds of live stock; *Sed-bó-siabra*, a *Sed* made up of every class of well bred cattle and thorough bred horses. *Sed gabla*, a yearling bull, or a yearling heifer, the smallest of all *Seds*. *Sed-marbh-aile*, a *Sed* of moveable chattels made up of inanimate objects; *Seoid turclaide*, *Seds* of

revertible chattels, *i.* cxii, clxxxiii; *iii.* 27, 29, 30, 480, 481.

Seig, a hawk, *iii.* 448.

Seir, the rear, the back part, see *Nesa do seir tuisig*, *iii.* 520.

Seired, progresses, follows, *iii.* 517.

Seirglige, a sick bed, [or bed of decline]; *Seirglige Coinchulaind*, "the sick bed of *Cuchulaind*", *ii.* 367; *iii.* 192, etc.

Seirtiud, a young man of noble race, *iii.* 520.

Seisec slabrai, dry cattle, *iii.* 507.

Seisreach, a ploughland, *i.* xcii, xcv; some kind of measure of bulk; "a *Seisrech* of new milk" was probably a quantity sufficient for six persons, *i.* cxxxix.

Selb, a homestead, equivalent to the Danish *Toft*, *i.* cxix, cxxxv, clv.

Semannaib, abl. pl. with rivets, *iii.* 158.

Sen cleithe, hereditary followers of chiefs, a class of tenants having legal rights acquired by living on the estate for three generations, *i.* cxvi, cxxi; *ii.* 37, 38; *iii.* 493, 494.

Sendata, a species of poetry peculiar to the order of poet called *Seaghdair*, *ii.* 171.

Sennat, some kind of literary composition forming part of the studies of the ninth and tenth years of a course of *Filedecht*, or philosophy, *ii.* 173.

Seoid, pl. of *Sed*, frequently used in the sense of jewels, precious objects, *iii.* 285.

Seol siraichte, a silken motion, applied to an easy death, *i.* cccclxxvi.

Sercol, fowl meat; *Serc/heoil na g-coilech feadha*, fowl meat of the woodcocks; *Sercol tarsain*, seasoned or salt fowl, *iii.* 483, 492.

Serda, set with scythes, cf. A. Sax. *sceran*, to shear, to cut, O. English *sheres*, Modern English *shears*, *i.* cccclxxxiii.

Seruan, some kind of corn or seed, cf. Latin *saurion*, Sansk. *sūrū*, Sinapis nigra, black mustard, *i.* ccclxiii.

Sesca Ced, *i.e.* sixty hundred, six thousand, *ii.* 391.

Sessigh, a subdivision of a Ballyboe, *i.* xcv.

Sesilbi, buzzing, *iii.* 426.

Sestan, clatter, *iii.* 426.

Setadh, driving away, *iii.* 526-7.

Sgiorta, a skirt or shirt, from the Norse *Skyrta*, a shirt, *i.* ccclxxxiii.

Sian, or *Sianan*, soft plaintive music, *iii.* 385, 386; *Sian curadh*, the champion's war-whoop, *ii.* 372.

Sicc Occ, *Sic Oc*, a name given to *Aires* having *Sac* and *Soke*, that is, to those entitled to hold the *Airecht Foleithe* or Court Leet, *i.* ccxxxv, cclxii, cclxviii, cclxx; *iii.* 510.

Sidhal Brat, a loose flowing cloak, *iii.* 162, 163.

Sidhe, a fairy mansion; sometimes used for fairy, or fairies, *e.g.*, *sluagh sidhe*, a fairy host, *i.* cccclxvi; *ii.* 198.

Sidlui=Satlui, revolt, *iii.* 507.

Sillas, he looked, *iii.* 324.

Sindach Brothlaige, a term of contempt; literally, a cooking-pit fox, a pot watch-dog, a pot-watcher, applied here to a man of the lowest class of society, who watched and attended the cooking pits and houses of the wealthy, and lived on the offal, whether acquired legally or illegally, *iii.* 522.

Sion, the foxglove, Digitalis purpurea, *brec dergitir sion*, more red-spotted than the foxglove, *iii.* 140, 141.

Sirechdái, silken; *bruit sirechdái*, silken cloaks, or garments, *iii.* 139, 140.

Sirechtach, silken, slow, plaintive, *iii.* 316.

Siriac, silk, *iii.* 90.

Sirith siabarthi, a fairy phantom, *iii.* 448.

Sith ails, boundary, or peace arbitration, *i.* cxcii.

Sith ballrad=casa fata, long-limbed, having long legs, *iii.* 96.

Sithbe, the pole of a chariot, etc. *i.* cccclxxx.

Skiida Oir, a golden shield, a loan word from one of the Teutonic languages, *i.* cccclxiv. *Scilde óir*, a plate or flattened piece of gold sometimes given like the *Fail óir*, by way of reward or gift: "he put his hand into his *bassan* (hand-bag, or purse), and took three *Scildes* of gold out of it, and gave them to him" (Second Battle of *Magh Tuired*). The *Scilde*, which represented a kind of coin, was no doubt named from its resembling the *Skilda* (shield) in shape.

Slaghad, hosting, *iii.* 505.

Slán represents in the legal sense an admission of the liability for the whole of principal sum and costs, equivalent to the modern marking judgment; also the rehabilitation of a person by the payment of all charges and fines imposed upon him, *i.* cclxxxii; *iii.* 476.

Sleaghaibh coicrinnecha, with flesh-seeking spears, *iii.* 157.

Sleg, *Slegh*, pl. *Slegha*, a long light spear which was hurled or cast with an amentum, *i.* cccexxxvii; *ii.* 98, 255, 295, 300, 304, 314, 317, 344, 345, 348, 382. *Sleg coicrind co fethan óir impi*, a sharp pointed spear with rings of gold upon it; a flesh-mangling spear with veins of gold upon it, *iii.* 163; *Sleig coicrinni*, a flesh-seeking spear [*recte* a five-pronged *Sleg* or military fork?], *iii.* 99.

Sleich, soap, *iii.* 493.

Slegin, *Sligin*, pl. *Sleigini*, *Sligini*, small light javelins, darts, *i.* cccexxviii, cccexlviii; *ii.* 301.

Slicrich, hissing of spears, *iii.* 426.

Slimred, no do nuiben, cleaners or burnishers, a class of pleaders whose business it was to make the cases of their clients as bright as possible, *i.* cclxviii, cclxxiii.

Sliocht, a race, a family, cf. *Schlacht*, a race, a family in Ditmarsch, German *Geschlecht*, *i.* ccxviii.

Slogh comfleda, the collective feasting of a levy accompanying a *Flath* beyond his own territory, and who, while on the expedition, were entitled to be maintained at the joint expense of the whole territory, *i.* cxcviii.

Sluagh, a host, a tribe, *i.* ccliv. See *Sliocht*, *Sluaighte*.

Sluaighte=*Luaite*, related to *Laeti*, *Leudes*, etc., cf. *Tochomlad*, etc. Ang-Sax. *Léode*, O. H. G. *Leudi*, N. H. German *Leute*, people, *i.* ccxxii.

Sluaite (incorrectly printed *Shluaite*, *i.* ccxxii.), see *Sluaighte*.

Sluican, recte *Sleabhacan*, sloke or slouk, made by boiling the Porphyra vulgaris and Porphyra laciniata, *i.* ccclxvii.

Smacht, pl. *Smachta*, fines, penalties, *i.* cxci, ccxxxviii, ccxxxix; abl. pl., *Smachtaib miach*, sack fines, *iii.* 512.

Smiramair, a marrow bath, *iii.* 101.

Smolcha, thrushes, *iii.* 379.

Smuas, a bone, *iii.* 250.

Snadad, *Snadha*, to traverse, *i.e.* the right of *Aires* to cross the lands of others, and to receive protection, hospitality, etc., in accordance to their rank. It represented the Welsh *Nawd*, the initial *s* having been lost in the latter, *i.* ccxliv; *iii.* 472; *Snadigh*, he traverses; a traverser, *iii.* 481.

Snath, thread; *Snathe liga*, ornamental or coloured thread, *iii.* 107; *Snath oir*, gold thread.

Snathait, a needle, from *snath*, thread, and *sét*, a passage, *iii.* 117.

Snegair, is thrown, *iii.* 448.

Snigestar, thou art thrown, *iii.* 448.

Snimaire, a spindle; *Snimaire olla*, a wool-spindle, *iii.* 115.

Snithe oir for a etum, etc., a fillet or thread of gold upon his forehead, *iii.* 163.

Sobairche, *Sabairche*, Hypericum quadrangulum, *Lin.*, the St. John's Wort, also called the "Herba Sancti Petri", *i.* lxxiii; *ii.* 60, 191.

Sobronach, griefless, *iii.* 444.

Sobus, *Sobes*, good morals, *iii.* 496.

Soc, the sock of a plough, a crowbar, *i.* cxci; *iii.* 479.

Soethaib, for castigations, punishments, *iii.* 509.

Somaine, profits, benefits, amount of, the value of, *iii.* 490.

Somenmnach, spirited, magnanimous, *iii.* 444.

Sonn, a sound, from the Latin *sonus*, *iii.* 308.

Sonnach umaide, a paling or wall of bronze, *i.* dcxiii.

Spara, a spear, cf. O. Norse, *Spior*, English, *spear*, *i.* ccccli.

Sraigell, a whip or scourge, *iii.* 146.

Srethai, gen. furniture, etc.; *Sreathai tighe*, furniture of a house, *iii.* 500, 501.

Srebnaid, striped; gen., *Srebnaide sroil*, of striped satin, *ii.* 301; *iii.* 159.

Srian, a bridle; *Srian argait*, a silver bridle, *iii.* 496; *Srian cruan*, a bridle of *Cruan*, iii. 186.

Sról, gen. *Sróil*, satin; *srebnaide sroil*, of striped satin, *ii.* 301; *iii.* 113; *Sról rig*, kingly satin, iii. 96.

Srub tine, a snout of bacon, *iii.* 486.

Sruith, high, comp. *Sruithiu*, higher, *iii.* 493, 504, 510; superl. *Sruithem*, a term applied to an *Aire Forgaill*, or highest *Aire*, *i.* cclxxvii. See *Ansruth*.

Sruth, some kind of literary composition forming part of the course of *Filedecht* during the ninth and tenth years, *ii.* 173.

Stadeir, *Staideir*, a homestead or family seat, cf. Ang. Sax. *stede*, as in homestead, German *Stadt*, *i.* cxlvi.

Staraidhe, a historian; the title of the professor of history in the public schools, *ii.* 84.

Steill, a canopy, *i.* cccxlvii.

Stoc, pl. *Stuic*, a trumpet, a short, curved horn, *iii.* 313, 336-342, 350; *Stoc focra*, *Stoc fogri*, *Stuc fogri*, a warning trumpet for sounding to arms, etc., *i.* dxxxi; *iii.* 308, 336, 339, 341, 350, 369.

Stocaire, a performer on the *Stoc*, *iii.* 369.

Stocuidhe ruiliera, "roll" stockings, thick woollen stockings made from yarn spun from the roll, *i.* ccclxxxv.

Stuc fogri, see *Stoc*.

Sturgan, pl. *Sturgana*, a species of trumpet, *i.* dxxxi; *iii.* 329-342, 350, 369.

Sturganaidhe, pl. *Sturganaidhe*, a sturgan player, *iii.* 340, 369.

Suad, *Suadh*=*Sai*, a literary professor of the highest order, entitled to sit in the "Council of the Ale House", *i.* ci; iii. 510.

Suafatach, gen. *Suafadaig*, trampling, puddle-mixing, *iii.* 450.

Suaineamain loga, hard twisted strings, *ii.* 317.

Suanbas, a death sleep, cf. English *swoon*, *iii.* 249.

Suantorglés, one of the three strings of *Scathach's* magical harp, which caused all who heard it to fall into a heavy, balmy sleep; one of the ancient musical keys of the Irish, *iii.* 223, 250.

Suantraighe, the sleeping mode, one of the three musical feats that gave distinction to a harper; those who listened to a harp played in this mode are fabled to have fallen into a deep sleep for the time. The word is formed from *suan*, sleep, and *traigh*, time, *i.* dcxxxiv, dcxxxvi; *iii.* 214, 220, 221, 243, 244, 250, 260.

Subach, pleasant, *iii.* 444.

Suidha, followers, the suit of a *Rig* or *Flath*, his *Sobaid*, *i.* cxcviii.

Suidiu, a seat, a place to sit upon, *iii.* 489; *Suidhe faire*, "the watching seat", see *Cathair Conrai*, *iii.* 79.

Suifi, to return or fall back into vice, *iii.* 493.

Súist, a flail, *i.* ccccxlii; *Súist iarainn*, an iron flail, "the Holy Water Sprinkler", or armed whip of medieval warriors, *i.* cccxxxviii, ccccxlii.

Súith, the suite of a prince, *i.* clvi. See *Suidha*, *Suad*, *Sai*.

Suitengaid, *no do fethaigther*, the *Suith* or suite of tongues entitled to be heard in court, that is, the *Sabaid* who made record of court, that is, who bore witness to the judgments given and acts done in their presence, *i.* cclxviii.

Sumadas, dat. and abl. pl. *Saimedaib*, nags, pack-horses, cf. French, *somme*, *som*, a burden, *iii.* 330.

Sutaire, a follower, a suitor; *Sutaire a mathar*, his mother's pet; *Sutaire an tiagherna*, the pet or follower of the landlord, *i.* ci.

Taball, gen. *Tabaill*, a sling, *ii.* 252, 288, 289. See *Crann tabaill*.

Taccrai, sued, *Cia taccrai*, if sued, *iii.* 501.

Tachim, manner, state of being, order, array, *iii.* 307.

Taeb Airecht, a side court, a high court for the trial of causes arising between different territories, such as the *Tuaths* forming a *Mór Tuath*, and all questions of *Cairde* or international treaties and laws, *i.* cclviii-cclxxi.

Taebtaid, sidemen, *iii.* 509.

Taetsad, would fall, *iii.* 422.

Taetsaitis, they would fall, *iii.* 444.

Taidbsiu, *i.e.* expecting, shadowing, an idiomatic expression still in use in Munster, as in the current phrase: *na bidh da taidhbsiu duit féin*, do not be shadowing her (or it) for yourself, that is expecting or hoping for her (or it) for yourself]. Cf. *Taidbsi*, a shadow, *iii.* 456.

Tailliamna, slings, *iii.* 152.

Tailm, a kind of sling. *Cormac* derives it from *tell* and *fuaim*, which he explains as "the clashing of the thongs and their clangour", *i.* cccclxi; *ii.* 292, 294.

Tairberta, pl. gifts, presents, *iii.* 446.

Tairchid, they accumulated, *iii.* 516.

Taircella, secures, governs, *iii.* 514.

Tairgell, a fine, *iii.* 489.

Tairids, [*recte*, *Tairside*] upon him (H. 2, 18, f. 65, a. a.), *iii.* 92.

Tairptheck, fearless, intrepid, *iii.* 416.

Tairriside, over that, *iii.* 444.

Tairsce, a crossing over, *e. g. Tairsce n-imbe*, crossing over a fence, *i.* ccl.

Taiscedi, excursions, *iii.* 510.

Taite, the beginning of; *Luan taite samna*, the first Monday of the beginning of November, *iii.* 420.

Taithbeim, a peculiar blow given with the flat of a sword, *ii.* 195, 372.

Taithmeach, to open, *iii.* 450.

Taithne, brightness, *iii.* 238.

Tal, an adze, *i.* cclxi.

Talla, to contain, to fit in, *iii.* 500.

Tam, *Tamh*, a faint, a sudden or unnatural death, *iii.* 452; *Tamleacht*, a pestilence *Leacht*, or sepulchral monument, *e. g.*, *Tamhlaachta muintire Phartolain*, the graves of the people of *Partolan*, now Tallaght, near Dublin, *i.* cccxxxii; *iii.* 2, 3.

Tanaise Righ, *Tanassi Righ*, the Tanist of a king, a man elected during the life time of a *Rig* to be his successor, and who, during the lifetime of the king, was next in rank to him; an heir apparent, *ii.* 88; *iii.* 501.

Tanaiste, see *Tanaise*, *i.* clxi.; *iii.* 282.

Tanaslaidhe, brooches, *iii.* 138.

Tanuise Bó Airé, the Tanist of a *Bo Airé*, *i.* clxxxiii.; *Tanuise Bó Airé Tuisi*, the Tanist of a *Bó Airé Tuisi*, *iii.* 513.

Taoisech, a commander or captain, but sometimes used in the sense of a prince, like the corresponding Welsh word *Tywysawg*, the title by which the chief princes of Wales are called in the Welsh chronicles. The Irish *Righ Thaoiseach*, royal or king captain, and the *Taoisech Tuatha*, territorial or cantred captain, who was eligible to be king, corresponded exactly with the Welsh title. The *Aire Tuisi* of the *Crith Gabhlach*, was the same as *Taoiseach*, both words being cognate with the Latin *Duc-s* or *Dux*, and the *tog* in Augl.-Sax., *Here-tog*, Germ., *Herzog*, *i.* ccxliii, ccxliv; *Taoiseach com-óil*, master of banquets, *i.* ccxliv; *Taoiseach caogaid*, the captain of fifty men, *ii.* 381; *Taoiseach Eallaig*, master of chattels, etc., *i. e.* a treasurer, *i.* ccxliv; *Taoiseach nonbair*, the commander of nine men, *ii.* 381; *Taoisech Scuir*, master of the horse, or commander of the cavalry, *i.* ccxliv; *Taoiseach tri nonbair*, leader of three times nine men, *ii.* 381.

Tár, disparagement, *iii.* 424.

Tara, gen. *Tarai*, wheat, *i.* ccclxii; *iii.* 481.

Taradain, Thursday, *iii.* 507.

Tarathar, an augur, *i.* ccclxi.

Tarbh, a bull, *iii.* 486.

Tarbga, assaulting, beating off, *iii.* 460.

Targlaim, to gather, *iii.* 429.

Targu, a target, *i.* cccclxv.

Tarmberar, is transferred, *iii.* 238.

Tarrasair, he came, *iii.* 428.

Tarsnu, *Tarsund*, sausages, seasoned mince-meats, condiments, etc., *i.* ccclxix, ccclxx; *iii.* 487, 491, 496, 499.

Tathlum, a sling stone, a concrete ball, *i.* cccxxxvii, ccccl xi; *ii.* 252, 253, 288, 289, 291, 295, 311, 395.

Taurclaide, see *Scoid Taurclaide*, *i.* cxv.

Taurcrech, *Taurcreic*, a gift or stipend which a *Flath* gave to such as became his *Ceiles*, that is, acknowledged him as their lord, and paid *Biathad* to him. It was also called *Rath*, wages (which see), *i.* cx, cxii, ccxl, cccixxxvi; *iii.* 472, 477, 490.

Teallach, gen. *Teallaig*, a fire place, *ii.* 132.

Tech, *Teach*, gen. *Tigh*, a house; *Teach caoel cumang*, a long narrow house, *i.* ccclx; *Tech darach*, an oak house, *i.* ccxcix, ccclviii; *Tech incis*, gen. *Tigh inichis*, a small house provided for a superannuated member of a *Fine*, who gave up his land on condition of receiving maintenance and attendance, *i.* ccxcviii; *iii.* 479, 480;

Tech merage, the house of a fool, or of a needy wanderer, i. ccclxv; *Tech Midchuorda*, mead-circling house, the banqueting hall at Tara, i. ccexlvi–vii., dxxxi; *Tech óil*, a drinking house, gen. *Tigh óil*=*Cuirm tech*, an ale house, i. cclii; *Tech n-imacalmo*, a conversation house, i. dcxlii.

Techta, inheritance, iii. 520.

Techta, lawful, *Techta dlighthecha*, legal rights, iii. 107.

Techtairi, curriers, iii. 504.

Techtait, entitled to, iii. 520

Ted-chleas, *Ted chlis*, a rope feat, or feats, ii. 371, 372.

Tedud, the bass strings of a *Cruit* or *Timpan*, iii. 361.

Tegin, or *Tuigin*, an *Ollamh's* cloak, cf. Norse *tign*, i. ci.

Teglech, a household, i. cccl.

Teilleoin, humming. See *Beich teilleoin*, humming bees=mod. Gaelic, *Seilloin*; *Teillinn*, humming wild bees, *recte* buzzing or humming bees, iii. 355, 356, 357, 358.

Teist, testimony; also used for the person who gives it, i. cciv, cclxxxix.

Teinm, laeghda, "the illumination of rhymes", a rite of Druidic divination prohibited by St. Patrick; a rhyme charm, ii. 135, 208, 209, 212.

Tene, *Teine*, a fire; *Teine bithbeo*, an ever-living fire, iii. 486; *Teine* or *Tene geallain*, a blazing or wild fire, i. cccxviii; *Tene n-aen beime*, fire of one stroke, iii. 132.

Tesairg, to protect, etc., iii. 515.

Teta bena crot, the strings of a pinnacled or triangular *Cruit*, or of a *Timpan*; [more probably=*binn* or *bind*, sweet, *i.e.* a string of a sweet or melodious *Cruit*], iii. 305.

Teti, *Tete*, a house, or rather homestead, *e.g. Teti Brice*, *Teiti Brec*, "the Speckled House of Emania", corresponding to the Welsh *Tydden* or *Tyden*, i. lxxxix, xcvi, clxxix, ccciii; ii. 332. *Toiden* occurs several times in the M.S. H. 2. 18. in the sense of a house or homestead, and is evidently the exact equivalent of the Welsh word. Thus, "one time *Moling* was in [his] *Toiden*, he saw *Mael Daborchon*, son of *Cellach*, coming towards him, to ask him for his horse" (f. 204 a.); "another time, as *Moling* was in [his] *Toiden*, he saw nine of the *Dibergs* approaching him" (fol. 205, a.). "Another day, as *Moling* was in front of his *Toiden*", etc.

Tetrachtain, endeavouring to strike, iii. 448.

Thein, to cut or break down, etc., iii. 468.

Thidnaicthe ratha, stipend-bestowing, iii. 446.

Tiag, a bag, a leather wallet, i. ccclvii–viii; iii. 113, 117.

Tidnagar, security or pledge, a binding, iii. 499.

Tighearna, a lord, cf. Welsh, *Teyrn*, Breton, *Mac Tiern*, O. Norse, *tign* =Latin *dign-us*, O. N. *Tignarmathr*, a nobleman, i. ci.

Tii, cloaks; *Tii dubglasso*, black gray cloaks, iii. 157, 158.

Tilib, on the faces, literally bosses (of shields), the modern form *Tóll*, abl. pl., *Tollaib*, ii. 303; iii. 436. See *Tul*.

Timdeibe, decrease, deficiency, iii. 514.

Timorgain, to restrain or govern, iii. 491.

Timpan, a stringed musical instrument one kind of which was played with a bow, i. ccccxcviii, dxvii, dxviii; iii. 238, 261, 265, 266, 305, 306, 359.

Timpanach, a *Timpan* player, iii. 367, 369.

Timthach, *Timthacht*, outfit, attire, clothes, i. cxi; iii. 414, 496.

Timtherecht bech, the buzzing of bees, iii. 145.

Timthuch, accompaniments, iii. 487, 492, 494.

Tincur, *Tinchur*, a marriage portion, i. clxxiii; furniture, iii. 483, 495.

Tindscra, *Tinnscra*, *Tindscrai*, bride-price, a bridal gift, which from the composition of the word, was made up, at least at one period, and for some particular rank, of *Tinde* or *Tinne*, a neck chain, value three *Ungas*, and *Escra*, a drinking vessel, value six *Ungas*, i. clxxiv; gold, silver, or bronze articles of every country, iii. 480.

Tinne, a bacon pig, i. cccl; iii. 500.

Tinneicas, smoke-cured bacon, the Gallo-Roman *Taniacae*, or *Tanacae*, i. ccclxix; iii. 481.

Tinne, a kind of quadrangular cap, *iii.* 139.

Tir, a country, a portion of land; *Tir Cumail*, the extent of the landed estate of an *Aire* which could be taken in distraint for the fines and other liabilities of his *Fine*; this, in one case at least, was a piece of land twelve *Forrachs* (ropes or chains) long and six wide, *i.* clxxxi, ccxci.

Tobar, a well, a pond; *Tobar tuinne*, or *tuinde*, a mill pond, *i.* ccclix.

Tocbhait, *Thocbhait*, appeareth, or has come, *iii.* 428.

Tochair, a causeway, *iii.* 34.

Tochomlad, pl. *Tochomlada*, the emigration of a military band, *i.* ccxxii. See *Sluaighte*.

Tochra, *Tochrai*, well-bred sheep and small pigs, *i.* clxxv; *iii.* 480.

Tocomrac, *Tocomrach*, a convocation or assembly; *Tocomracc Tuaithe*, a convocation of a *Tuath* for lay or ecclesiastical business, *i.* ccliv; *iii.* 111, 112; *Tocomrac do crich*, a convocation or convention of a *Crich* or territory, *iii.* 505.

Tochratar, they went, *iii.* 500.

Tochur tar cend, an upsetting (topsy-turvy), *iii.* 489.

Tod, a residence and land attached, *i.* cxxii.

Todacrat, to pertain to, proper or appropriate to, *iii.* 506.

Tofet, takes precedence of, *iii.* 493.

Togarmand, a title of distinction or honour; *Togarmund techtaide miadlechta*, recognized or lawful titles of honour, *iii* 513.

Togmall, a squirrel, *ii.* 293.

Toiteog, a base tenant or *Daer Ceile*, the equivalent of the Welsh *Taeg*, *i.* cxiv.

Tomadmmaim, to break up the ranks of an army, and scatter them in disorder; a rout, defeat, an irruption, etc., *iii.* 505.

Tomalta, pl., levies or wastings, *iii.* 504.

Toichne, to fast, to take away; *Toichnedai*, fastings, *iii.* 489, 507.

Toifonn, coursing with dogs, *iii.* 507.

Toimdither, is confided, *iii.* 514.

Toimes, progresses, *iii.* 515.

Toing, an oath; used also for the person who gave it, *e.g.* *Fer tonga*, an oathman, a compurgator, *iii.* 473; *Toing laighe*, to make oath, *iii.* 519.

Toirm, a tramp, noise, *iii.* 426.

Toraic, any act which lowered the dignity of a person, *iii.* 506; a private information made in the presence of *Inaraics* or competent magistrates, etc., *i.* ccxiv, ccxlvi, cclxxvii.

Torann, thunder, *iii.* 426. *Toranchleas*, the "thunder feat", *ii.* 372; *Torann* or *Toraud na beim tar sgiath*, thunder or shield rattle, *i.* ccccxviii.

Torc, a torque, *i.* ccclvi; *iii.* 182.

Torc, a hog, a wild boar; *Torc fochluide*, a rooting hog, *iii.* 486.

Tornoir, gen. *Tornoira*, a turner, *ii.* 133.

Torracht, a coil; *Torrachta di ór forloisctí*, coils of burnished gold, such as those worn round the waist, *iii.* 158.

Torthaib, dat. and abl. pl., food supplies, fruit, vegetables, etc., *iii.* 516.

Torthaiset, they fall, they have fallen, *iii.* 492.

Toth, *Thoth*, bounty, *iii.* 510.

Tothacht, property, position, rank, wealth, stability, independence, *iii.* 494, 495, 498.

Traigtib innraiccib, dat. and abl. pl., in lawful feet, that is, in lawful measure, *iii.* 508.

Treb, *Trebh*, a homestead; used also in the sense of a household; a tribe, *i.* lxxix, clii, ccciv.

Trebad, a house; the five *Trebads* were a residence, a cow-house, a calf shed, a sheep house, and a pig-stye, *i.* cxxiv–v.

Trebaire, a householder, one entitled to act as a guardian, a security, etc.; the buildings, etc., the possession of which constituted a man a householder, *i.* clxv, clxxxviii, cxci, cci, ccl, ccxciii; *iii.* 475.

Tregda, *Tregtad*, pierced, to pass through, *iii.* 450, 507.

Tremaetha, he binds, controls, holds in allegiance, the same as *nenaisc*, to bind, to govern here, *iii.* 514.

Treó, through, *iii.* 506.

Trena, *Trennai*, the three days devoted to the *Guba* or funeral rites of deceased persons of distinction, *i.* cccxxxi, dxli.

Tressai, higher, more powerful, *iii.* 503.

Trian tinsoil, the one-third share of property which the daughter of one of the *Floth*-grade got as her marriage portion, when married to one of the *Gradh Fine* or estated members of a *Fine*. This portion was equal to half the wealth of the bridegroom, hence her share was equal to one-third of the joint wealth, *i.* clxxiii.

Triath, a chief king, *iii.* 514.

Trilis, the modern *Trillsi*, tresses of hair, etc., *iii.* 190.

Tricci, velocity, suddenness, *iii.* 428.

Triucha cél, Tricha céd, thirty hundred, a *Tuath* cantred or hundred, the principality of a *Rig Tuatha*. It is represented by the modern barony, *i.* xcii, ccxxix; *ii.* 392; *iii.* 502.

Tri Cuilceda na Feinne, the three beddings of the *Fianna*, *ii.* 380.

Trirech, triplex; the name of a species of Irish lyric poetry. This name was not exclusively applied either to the music or the quantity of the verse, but was also applied to a kind of laudatory poem which gave the name and described the person of the subject of the poem, and mentioned where he lived, and hence it was called Triplex, when it fulfilled these three conditions, *iii.* 388.

Trisi, the third day, *iii.* 477.

Triubas, Triubhas, misprinted sometimes in the text *Truibhas*, a pantaloons or trousers, *i.* ccclxxxiv-ccclxxxvi, cccxciv; *iii.* 153.

Triunu, strong powerful men, *iii.* 506.

Troich, wretches, lepers, *iii.* 452.

Tromchoblach, triumphant advance, *iii.* 426.

Tromgresaib (dat. and abl.), heavy insult, *iii.* 517.

Trom Theta, the heavy strings of the harp, *iii.* 253, 256.

Trosca, fasting, *i.* ccxxiii, *recte*, cclxxxiii).

Trosdan, a staff or support used by all classes of pilgrims, clerical students, and religious men and women, cf. Goth, *trausti*, O. N. *traust*, O. M. and N. High German, *trôst*, Engl., *trust*, *i.* ccxli.

T-Saland, salted; a term applied to salt meat and butter, *i.* ccclxvii.

Tuagleirg=*Stuagleirg*, a broad slope, *iii.* 446.

Tuagmar, curveting, prancing, see *Ech dond*.

Tuagmila, dat. and abl. pl. *Tuagmilaib*, crooks, clasps or buckles, trappings, *iii.* 160, 190.

Tuairgnidhe catha, the leader of an army in battle, *ii.* 388.

Tualaing, mighty, competent, *i.* cccxl; *Tualaing coimse*, competent to control, *iii.* 479.

Tuarascbail, description, account, relation, *iii.* 324.

Tuarastal, positive evidence, proof; it is explained in an old gloss as "a door, that is, a means of admitting light to the blind". It appears to have been also used as the name of the gifts given by the higher kings to the inferior kings, the acceptance of which was *positive proof* of fealty, *i.* cciv, cclxxix; *Tuarastal fastaide fiach*, evidence which fastened the liability of a debt and costs, when the accused failed to clear himself by expurgation, *i.* cclxxxi.

Tuarggar, is torn down or broken, *iii.* 489.

Tuarguib, raises up, *iii.* 510.

Tuar torad, supply of fruits, *frumentarius*, *iii.* 505.

Tuath, originally the people or tribe that occupied a given district, but afterwards the territorial division called also a *Triucha Ced*, a cantred; cf. Goth. *Thiuda*, O. Norse *Thjoth*, O. H. German *Diut*, *i.* lxxx, lxxxi, xcii, clvi, ccxxix.

Tuidhen (recte, *Tuighean*) *filidh*, a poet's gown, *ii.* 20.

Tuidlig noir forlosti, the sheen of burnished gold, *iii.* 141.

Tuinell, to assemble, *iii.* 501.

Tuirc oir a tirib gall, torques of gold from foreign lands, or from the country of the Gauls, *iii.* 182.

Tuirc forais, gen. and nom. pl. of *Torc forais*, a house-fed hog, *iii* 486.

Tuireadh, a tower, a stout post or column; *iii.* 32.

Tuiresc, a saw, *i.* ccclxi; *iii.* 486.

Tuirm, gen. *Turma*, motion, tramp; enumeration, *iii.* 428.

Tuirnn, Tuirnd, wheat, *i.* ccclxii.

Tul, the boss of a shield, *iii.* 162, 163. See *Tilib*.

Tulach, a hillock, a certain form of grave or sepulchral mound, *i.* dcxxxvii.
Tulogu, breaks, bulges, holes, *iii.* 480.
Tum luachra, a cluster of rushes, *iii.* 311, 312.
Turcairthe, gifts, *iii.* 324.
Turrthugadh, protection, exemption from arrest; the right which a chief of household had of his premises not being liable to be searched without notice and due process of law, *i.* ccxciv; *iii.* 513.
U, *Uo*, the ear, *iii.* 107.
Ua, a grandson, *iii.* 414.
Uadaib, from them, *iii.* 500.
Uaithiu, less than, *iii.* 517.
Uair, *Huaire*, because, *iii.* 510.
Uaithne, a post, a pillar; parturition; concord in music or poetry, *iii.* 221, 222; *Huaithne fonluing ocus frisellaghar*, "a pillar of endurance and attendance"; a term applied to a man appointed to attend to and supply the wants of the wretched and homeless poor; the relieving officer of the ancient Irish, *iii.* 519; *Uaithne iuil frithir gach fuinn*, the intelligent concordance of all (difficult sounds), *iii.* 215; *Uaithni óir*, a pillar of gold, *iii.* 460.
Uan, froth, *iii.* 114.
Uatha, alone, by himself; *a n-uatha*, their individual right, *iii.* 513.
Ubhall, an apple, a ball; *Ubhall chleas*, the ball feat, *ii.* 372, 373.
Uchan, alas! *iii.* 458.
Udnacht, *Udnocht*, a wattle roof, a covering, a railing or palisade, *iii.* 46; *Udnacht coil*, a roof or a palisade of hazel, *iii.* 480.
Uma, *Umha*, gen. *Umae*, copper, ordinary bronze, *iii.* 167, 491; *Cred uma*, red bronze, *iii.* 219; an alloy of a certain shade of red (*Cred* = a mixed colour); tin-copper (*Cred* = tin), *i.* cccclx, *n* 748.
Umhaidhe, a bronze worker, *iii.* 208, 209, 210.
Umai lestrai, *Humai lestrai*, bronze vessels, *iii.* 500.
Ummairrith, bronze stream, *i.* cccxxxvi.
U-Nasca oir, ear-clasps of gold, *iii.* 145, 186.
Unga, *Uinga*, an ounce; a technical term for the amount of a legal penalty, reward, or price; there were different kinds of *Ungas*, and the value varied according to the kind and name, *i.* clxxiv, ccxl; *ii.* 87; *iii.* 102, 113, 116, 145, 157, 161, 162, 174, 245; *Unga beg*, the small *Unga*, of the value of twenty pence; *Unga cana domnaig*, the *Unga* or fine of the Sunday law, the value of which was a heifer, or the price of her; *Unga mór*, the big *Unga*, the value of which was ten shillings, *iii.* 496.
Ur, the border, *e.g.* *Ur*, or *Or Tuatha*, the border of a territory, *i.* cxcviii.
Urchomail, abeyance, *iii.* 440.
Urgell tareise, a redeemed hostage, *iii.* 476.
Urgnam, cooking, *iii.* 161.
Urnaim, a fast bond, *i.* clxxxviii.
Urrad, a counsellor, a bail or surety, *i.* cxx, cxxv, cciv, cclxxi.
Urramain, counsellors; *Urramain na criche*, chiefs or chief counsellors of a *Crich* or territory, *i.* cclxxi.
Urrand, *Urraind*, valour, power, supremacy, *iii.* 424; mistranslated combat, *iii.* 416.
Urrudas, *Urrudhas*, common or traditional law, cf. Angl. Sax., *or*, N. H. German, *ur*, ancient, and A. S. *raed*, counsel, *quasi orraed*, ancient counsel, *i.* ccxivi, cclxviii, cclxxi. It is misprinted *Urrhudas* in cclxxxii. See *Urrad*.
Ussa, shoes, see *Ass*, *iii.* 107.

INDEX NOMINUM.

Abban, St., *iii.* 41, 45.
Abbo, St., *i.* dcxliv.
Abdalrahman I. and II., *i.* dxxi.
Abdul Kadir, *i.* dcxxxvi.
Aben Esra, *i.* dxiv.
Abhartach, son of Aithirne the poet, *iii.* 373.
Abhcan, son of Beccelmas, *iii.* 42.
Abruin, wife of Mac Liag, *ii.* 123, n. 90.
Abul Abbas al Hakem II., *i.* dxxi, dxxii.
Acaill, daughter of Cairpri Nia Fer, *iii.* 96.
Achenbach, *i.* cli.
Acrisius, king of Argos, *i.* xciii.
Adam de la Hale, *i.* dxxxii, dlvii, dlviii.
,, of Bremen, *i.* ccxii, ccxcvii.
Adamnan, St., *ii.* 77, 79, 80, 85; *iii.* 375, 505.
Adenès, *i.* dxxvi.
Adhar, son of Umor, *ii.* 122.
Adhna, chief poet of Ulster, *ii.* 53; *iii.* 315.
Admilithi, the jester, *ii.* 150.
Adolfi Johan, see Neocorus.
Aedan, son of Gabran, king of Scotland, *ii.* 52, 77, 78.
Aedh, or Hugh, derivation of, *ii.* 132.
,, Abrat, the daughter of, *ii.* 196, 197.
,, Allech, *ii.* 95.
,, Caemh, of the Clanna Morna, *ii.* 387.
,, from the banks of the Boyne, *ii.* 386.
,, Guaire, king of Ui Maine, *ii.* 336, 337.
,, keeper of St. Patrick's tooth, *ii.* 160.
,, king of Oirghiall, *i.* dcxliii, *iii.* 110, 111.
,, Lurgnech, *i.* dcxxxix.
,, Mac Ainmire, Ard Righ, *ii.* 52, 55, 56, 57, 77, 78, 337, 338, 340, 341; *iii.* 245.
,, Mac Gabrain, see Aedan.
Aedh, Mac Gartnan, king of Scotland, *iii.* 164.
,, Menn of Leinster, *iii.* 311.
,, of Rath Aedh, in Meath, *ii.* 158, 159.
,, Slainge or Slaine, Ard Righ, *i.* ccciii, dcxli; *ii.* 91, 106, 158, 159; *iii.* 160.
,, Oirdnidhe, Ard Righ, *ii.* 95, 176, 177.
,, son of Bran, king of South Leinster, *ii.* 390, 391.
,, son of the Dagda, *i.* cccxxvii; *ii.* 152, 155; *iii.* 8.
,, son of Duach Dubh, *iii.* 330.
,, son of Eochadh, king of Connaught, *ii.* 18.
,, son of Eoghan O'Connor, *iii.* 25.
,, son of Finnliath, Ard Righ, *ii.* 95, 155.
,, the poet, Fer Leighin, of Meath, *ii.* 78.
Æneas, *i.* ccclxxx, ccclxxxi, cccclxxii.
Aengabha, of Iruaidh, *ii.* 39.
Aengus, *ii.* 322.
,, Ceilé De, St *ii.* 76, 85, 95, 175; *iii.* 123, 386, 387, 393.
,, Crundmael, *i.* dcxxxix.
,, Gae-buaifnech, *ii.* 205, 326, 327; *iii.* 197.
,, Gae-fuiltech, king of Bregia, *ii.* 18.
,, grandson of Corc, king of Munster, *ii.* 64, 67, 68.
,, Mac Inog, *iii.* 122, 362.
,, Mac Umor, chief of the Clan Umoir, *ii.* 122; *iii.* 122, 202.
,, na Diadhachta of the divinity, *i.e.*, Aengus Finn O'Daly, *iii.* 144; *ii.* 148.
,, Olmucadha, *i.* xx, xxi.
,, of the Boyne, *iii.* 122.
,, of Monasterboice, *ii.* 162.
,, son of Aedh Abrat, *ii.* 196, 197.
,, son of Art Corb, see Aengus Gae-buaifnech.
,, son of Carrach of Meath, *ii.* 121.

Aengus, son of the Dagda, *ii.* 18.
„ son of Natfrach, *ii.* 66, 151, 206; *iii.* 15.
Aete, daughter of Ochond, and second wife of Enna Nos, *ii.* 288-9.
Agnes the beautiful, *i.* dxxvii.
Agricola, *i.* xxi, xl, dxxvi.
„ Alexander, musician, *i.* dlix.
Agruan of Magh Ene, a Fennian chief, *ii.* 386.
Ai, son of Ollam, poet, *ii.* 39, 42; *iii.* 533; son of Olloman, *iii.* 527.
Aichleach, son of Duibhdrenn, *ii.* 387.
Aicil [Achilles], *i.* cccxxv.
Aidleo, son of Allai, a Tuatha De Danand champion; *i.* dcxxxviii; *ii.* 238, 241.
Aife, daughter of Lugad Delbaeth, *ii.* 220, 226.
„ daughter of Scathach, *ii.* 302, 307, 311, 312, 371, 415, 431, 437, 447, 457.
Ailbe, or Ailbhe, St., *ii.* 76; *iii.* 331.
Ailech, daughter of Fubtaire, king of Scotland, *ii.* 153; *iii.* 10.
Ailian, Solomon's caisel builder, *iii.* 15.
„ son of Midna, a Tuatha Dé Danand chief, *iii.* 328.
Ailill, king of Connaught, *i.* iii, xx, xxiv, xxv, lxxii, cxix, cclxii, cccxix, cccii, cccxliii, cccxlviii, cccliii, ccclvii, ccclx, ccclxi, ccclxxi, ccclxxv, ccclxxxi, cccxxxii, ccccxxxvi, dxi, dxli; *ii.* 122, 199, 259, 260, 291, 293, 296, 306, 312, 314, 318, 319, 320, 357, 361, 362, 363; *iii.* 74, 89, 90, 97, 98, 99, 101, 106, 181, 196, 197, 199, 219, 200, 201, 220, 221, 222, 307, 314, 338, 339, 372, 382, 443, 449.
„ Ceasdach, *ii.* 322.
„ diabalgai, *i.* ccccxlvii.
„ Finn, chief of Irris, *iii.* 338, 339.
„ Flann Beg, king of Munster, *ii.* 211.
„ Molt, *ii.* 339.
„ son of Dunlaing, *ii.* 339.
„ son of Eochad Muighmeadhan, *i.* cccxxi; *ii.* 102, 147.
Ainceas, Ainches, *ii.* 39, 41.
Aindelbadh, son of Lugadh Delbaeth, *ii.* 220.
Aine, a Tuatha De Danann lady, *i.* xxiv, xxv; *iii.* 260.
Aininn, son of Nemid, *ii.* 184.
Ainle, *iii.* 378.
Ainmire, grandson of Conall, Ard Righ, *ii.* 342.
Aireran, St., "the wise", *ii.* 85
Airnelach, *ii.* 342.
Aisidhe, son of Sida an Eich bhuidhe, *ii.* 101.
Aithirne Ailgisach, chief poet, *ii.* 20, 21; *iii.* 161, 373, 374.
Alain of Lille, *i.* dxxv.
Alaric, *i.* xlv, xlvi.
Alcuin, *i.* dvii, dxxxiv.
Aldhelm, St., *i.* dvii, dcxliv.
Alen, caisel-builder, *iii.* 15.
Alexander Severus, *i.* ccviii.
Alfarabi, *i.* dcxxxvi.
Alfred, king, *i.* cccxxviii.
Alian, see Ailian.
Allou, M., *i.* cccexix.
Almu, *i.* ccciii.
Altach, son of Dubh, *ii.* 40; *iii.* 527.
Amalgad, *i.* xlvi, cccxxii.
Amalgadh, son of Maelruan, *ii.* 31.
Ambrose, *i.* ccccxxxiv, ccccxxxv.
Ambros, A. W., *i.* ccccIxxxvi, ccccIxxxviii, dxi, dxxxviii, dlx, dlxi, dlxii.
Amergin, son of Milesius, poet, judge, and druid, *ii.* 3, 20, 51, 54, 188, 189, 190, 226.
„ a poet, *iii.* 374.
„ father of Conall Cernach, *ii.* 263, 333.
„ pupil of Dithirne, *ii.* 171.
„ son of Amalgad, son of Maelruan, compiler of the twelve books of West Munster laws, called the Cain Cormaic, and Cain Fuithrinne, *i.* cclxxii; *ii.* 31, 32; *iii.* 466.
„ son of Dubh, *i.* cccxxii.
„ son of Ecalsalach, the smith of Ulster, *i.* ccclxxxi, ccclxxxiii; *ii.* 51; *iii.* 94, 95.
Amenhotep IV., *i.* ccccIxxxv.
Amhalgaidh, see Amalgad.
Amlaff, son of the king of Lochland, *ii.* 346.
Amlaibh (Amlaff), a king of Dublin, *ii.* 125.
Ammianus Marcellinus, *i.* xxxi, cexxix, cexxxv, ccccIxxxii, ccccIxxxix.
Amosis, king of Egypt, *i.* ccccIxxxiv.
Amphictyon, *i.* xciv.
Anand the goddess, *i.* xxxii, lxxvi.
Anderson, Adam, *i.* ccclxxvi.
Aneurin, poet, *i.* xiii.
Anier Mac Conglinde, *iii.* 103. See Mac Conglinde.

)ueen, *i.* cxciv.
son of Uisnech, *ii.* 358.
i. cxciv.
usne or Busnois, *i.* dlviii.
t, *i.* dlx.
son of Uisnech, *ii.* 358, 378.
rb, *ii.* 326, 327.
of Conn, Ard Righ, *i.* ccxxxiv; *ii.* 22, 139, 140, 327, 8, 331; *iii.* 259, 260, 261.
solitary, *ii.* 58.
e, *i.* ccccixxxvi.
enos, *i.* cccclxxxv.
ong, *i* dii.
Dr., *i.* dcxxiv.
Dr. Th., *i.* ii.
Bruck, *i.* dlix.
king, *i.* xl.
musician, *i.* dlxv.
l, Earl of, Justiciary of N.
s, *i.* cxlii.
, *i.* iii.
e, poet and satirist, *ii.* 57.
ane, *i.* cci, ccii, cclxxxviii.
, the goddess, *i.* iii.
us, *i.* ccclxxi, cccclxxxvi, cxxvii, dx, dxi.
xlvi, xlvii, xlviii, lxxii, :viii. See l athi.
M. l' abbé, *i.* lxiii, lxiv.
ine, St., *i.* dix, dx, dxxix, dlxx.
ine (see Austin), *i.* dcxxxi.
us (Caesar), *i.* ccviii, ccix, cxii.
Danish king of Dublin, *iii.*
is, *i.* lxxx.
St., *i.* dcxxxi.
, a Tuatha De Danann dru- *ii.* 187.
, son of Ninne, *iii.* 342.
of Lugad Delbaeth, *ii.* 220.
the Fair, *iii.* 459.
ialach, a Munster champion, 1, 312.
, son of Esse Enchinn, *ii.* 371.
. xxiv, xxvi.
, *iii.* 15, 16.
, or Bailche, son of Dobhur,
. 311.
of Buarainech, *iii.* 15.
the evil eye, Fomorian chief, 251, 252, 288, 324; *iii.* 43.
on of Buanlamhach, *iii.* 15.
or Banbha, *ii.* 71, 128; *iii.* 463.
:a, *iii.* 202.
Bandad, *iii.* 203.
Banim, J., *i.* dcxiii.
Baoithin, St., *iii.* 32, 33.
Barnal, *iii.* 15.
Barnib, *iii.* 15.
Barra or Finnbarr, St., *i.* cccxxii.
Barrington, Mr. Daines, *i.* ccccxcvi, ccccxcvii, ccccxcviii.
Barthelemon, musician, *i.* dcxxix, dcxxxii.
Baudelot, M., *i.* lxiii.
Baxter, William, *i.* xxi.
Bearchan, St., of Clonfert, iii. 66.
Beathach, grandson of Buiredach, *ii.* 51.
Beauford, *i.* dxxxvi; *iii.* 303, 320, 321.
Bebhinn, daughter of Eignechan, *ii.* 102.
Bebinn, mother of Fraech, son of Fidad, *iii.* 10, 218.
Bebuadha, daughter of Eignechan, son of Dalach, *ii.* 102.
Becain, *i.* ccciii.
Bec Fola, *iii.* 160, 169, 180 189.
Becker, Prof. J., *i.* lxii, *n.* 48; lxiv, lxxx, *n.* 90.
Beckmann, *i.* ccclxxvi.
Bec Mac De, a poet and prophet of Munster, *ii.* 173.
Becuille, a witch, one of the chief druidesses of the Tuatha Dè Danann, *ii.* 39, 42, 187; *iii.* 527.
Becuma, *i.* cccxxii, cccxxxiii, cccxxxiv.
Bede, the Venerable, *i.* xxxv, xciv, ccxxx; *ii.* 82.
Befind, Befinn, Queen Edain, *i.* ccclxix; *ii.* 191, 192, 193, 194, 226; *iii.* 191. See Edain.
Beg, a poet, see Beg Mac Dè.
Beli, *i.* xxxvii.
Belloguet, Roget de, *i.* lviii, lxiv.
Benen, St., *ii.* 25, 45, 66; *iii.* 543.
Bennglann, a harp enblazoner, *iii.* 258.
Beort, *i.* xxxvi.
Beothach, son of Jarbonel the prophet, *ii.* 185.
Beowulf, *i.* ccxxxvii.
Bera, *i.* xx.
Berach Breac, daughter of Cas Cuailgne, king of Ulster, *iii.* 380.
Berchan of Cluain Sosta, *iii.* 330.
Betha, son of Ban, *iii.* 196.
Bethuinde, the Nymph of the Waves, *ii* 283, 284.
Bibra, E. von, *i.* ccccxii, ccccxvi, ccccxvii, ccccxxix.

Bicrenn, or Tuirend Bicriu, *ii.* 325.
Bignon, *i.* cix.
Binchois, Egidius, *i.* dlv.
Bind, *iii.* 189.
Birc, son of Esse Enchinn, *ii.* 371.
Birderg, son of Ruan, *iii*, 140.
Birger, Earl, *i.* clxx.
Bith, i.e. life, fourth son of Noah, *iii.* 59, 61.
Blackstone, *i.* lxxxi, *n.* 95.
Blaithnaid, see Blanat.
Blamad, *iii.* 203.
Blanat, Blathnat, wife of Curoi Mac Daire, *i.* ccclvii; *ii.* 76, 79, 80, 81, 97.
Blance, son of Dalran, *iii.* 15.
Blanchini, *i.* dx.
Blar, *iii.* 15.
Bláth, son of Colba, *iii.* 459.
Blathach, *ii.* 340, 341.
Blathmac, son of Aedh Slaine, *i.* xxxviii; *ii.* 91; *iii.* 160.
Blathmac, St., *iii* 332.
Blocc, son of Blar, *iii.* 15.
Blom, Prof., *i.* cxlviii.
Boand, from the Hills, *iii.* 218, 219, 220, 221, 307.
Bodann, or Modann, *ii.* 30.
Bodb, chieftain of Finnchadh, etc., in Scotland, *ii.* 40.
Bodhbh Derg, *iii.* 156, 157, 158, 174, 179, 202, 325.
Bœckh, *i.* cccclxxxvi, dxlvii.
Boethius, *i.* dcxxxiv, dcxxxv.
Boieldieu, *i.* dcxiii.
Boind, *i.* dcxxxix.
Bolc (or Bloc), son of Blar, *iii.* 15.
,, Mac Bith Thellaigh, Bellows, son of Constant fireplace, *ii.* 433.
Bolcad, *iii.* 203.
Bolg Mac Buain, *ii.* 311.
Bolur of Rath Breisi, *iii.* 15.
Bonifacius, St., ccexlix, dxxxiv.
Bopp, Prof., *i.* liii.
Bose, *i.* dcxxxvi.
Boudard, M., *i.* lxv.
Boudicca, Queen, *i.* lxxiii, lxxiv.
Bourignon de Saintes, M., *i.* lxiii.
Bracton, *i.* cclxxxviii.
Braen, son of Conga, *ii.* 385.
Brainne, *iii.* 427.
Bran, son of Eochad Abrad Ruaidh, *ii.* 283, 284, 390.
„ Bairne, of Burren, *iii.* 61.
,, Dubh, king of Leinster, *ii.* 338, 339, 340, 341.
Brard, C. P., *i.* cccexix.
Brath, son of Detha, *ii.* 191.
Breaghmaine, *ii.* 91.
Breas, Tuatha De Danann chief and Fomorian leader, *i.* xxiii; *ii.* 190, 235, 236, 237, 239, 244, 245, 246; *iii.* 5, 6, 15.
,, son of Ealathan, *ii.* 43.
„ „ „ Eochad Feidhlech, *ii.* 202, 145, 146.
Breasal, grandson of Baiscne, *ii.* 386.
„ Belach, king of Leinster, *ii.* 208, 383–386.
,, Mac Firb, *i.* xxv.
Brecan, St., iii. 66.
Brecan Mac Ban-Ghresa, Blanket, son of Woman's Work, *ii.* 133.
Brendan, St., of Birr, *ii.* 333; *iii.* 66.
Brendan, St., of Clonfert, *ii.* 78, 89.
Brennus, *i.* cccexlii.
Breothigirn, wife of king Mongan, *iii.* 175.
Bresal, the farmer, *ii.* 52.
Brethán, *i.* lxxxix.
Bri, daughter of Midir, *iii.* 355, 356.
Brian, *ii.* 127, 177, 178, 349; *iii.* 287. See Brian Boromha.
Brian Banba, see Brian Boromha.
„ Boromha, *i.* cccclxvii; *ii.* 98, 99, 115, 116, 117, 118, 120, 121, 12 , 127, 128, 151, 175, 177, 178, 346, 347, 348, 350, 351; *iii.* 228, 230, 233, 274.
„ Borumha, *iii.* 24. See Brian Boromha.
„ Boru, *ii.* 263, 267, 269, 270, 280, 286, 291, 293 See Brian Boromha.
„ brother of Nial of the Nine Hostages, *ii.* 62.
„ one of the chief druids of the T.D.D., *ii.* 187.
„ son of Eochadh Muighmeadhan, *i.* cccxx; *ii.* 102, 147, 344.
,, son of Tuirend, *i.* ccccxxxii.
Bricin, St., *ii.* 77, 92.
Bricrind, genitive of Bricriu, which see.
Bricriu, *i.* cccli, ccclii, ccclxv, ccclxviii, ccclxxii, cccclxxxvi; *ii.* 51, 372; *iii.* 17, 18, 19, 20, 21, 22, 23, 75, 314, 315, 316.
Bridget, St., *i.* xxiii, ccclxi, ccclxx; *ii.* 71, 338; *iii.* 495.
Brig Ambui, Brigh, or Brighit, daughter of Senchad, *i.* clxxi; *ii.* 21.
„ daughter of the Dagda, *ii.* 250.
Brig ban brughad, *i.* clxxi.
„ brethach, *i.* clxxi

fe of Tadg O'Kelly, chief
ine, ii. 122.
iii. 539; see Bridget, St.
n's wife, ii. 87.
l, son of Fergus, i. xxxviii;
85.
of Bethar, ii. 252.
of the king of Lochland,
51.
144, n. 204.
r Valentine, i. cccvi.
. 144, n. 204.
uinn, son of Smetar, i.
; iii. 199, 200, 202.
i. 148.
the learned wife, ii. 190.
, i. dcxxxix.
xii, dcxxxvii.
hter of Samer, i.
ii.
anann, Buanand, i. xxxii;
iii. 345.
ch, iii. 15.
, iii. 15.
i. 15.
m, Duke of, ii. 124.
lvii, dcxliv.
ii. 51.
son of Bronach, ii. 77,
113, 149, 168, 169.
. 394.
9, 147.
i. dci, dcii, dciii, dcvi,
xiv, dcxv, dcxvii, dcxliv;
252, 263, 275, 290, 294,
, 303.
r., i. dcxiii, dcxviii, dcxxv,
, dcxxix, dcxxxi, dcxxxii;
217, 218, 226, 346.
cWilliam, iii. 274, 281.
our, iii. 14.
dlxiv.
yr, i. ccccxciii.
Brethach, i. cccxxiii; ii. 20.
2, 13.
. dcxxxvii.
i. 386.
Caemghin, Caemhghin
St., ii. 70, 85; iii. 539.
xxxiv, lxxxiii, lxxxviii,
xxi, cxxxiii, cxxxvi, cli,
ccxxxvi, cclviii, cccxx,
ccclxxi, ccclxxxi, cccciv,
ccccixii, ccccixxvii.
on of Eidirsgul, ii. 39, 219.
, Cachir, druid, ii. 188;
27, 533.
aughter of Liath, iii. 404,

Caier, king of Connaught, ii. 217, 219.
Caillin, St., ii. 89.
Cailte, i. ccciii, ccccxxxiv; ii. 59; iii. 169, 170, 175, 176, 179, 323, 324, 325, 328, 360. 361, 366, 377, 379.
Caimin, St., ii. 76.
Caincind, iii. 169.
Caindi, i. xxiv.
Cainech, St. (St. Canice), ii. 81.
Cairbre, ii. 45, 51, 52, 209, 210; iii. 543.
„ Ard Righ, ii. 387.
„ brother of Conall Gulban, and son of Niall, ii. 161, 164.
„ Lifeachair, ii. 52, 282, 382, 383, 384, 386, 387; iii. 197, 205.
„ Musc, ii. 210, 211, 212.
„ Niadh-fear, see C. Nia Fear.
„ Nia Fear, ii. 122, 199; iii. 96.
„ son of Cormac Mac Airt, iii. 334.
„ son of Dian, i. dcxxxvii.
„ the harper, iii. 250, 251, 254.
„ the stooped, ii. 52.
Cairce Ceoil-bhinn, Ollamh timpanist, iii. 236.
Cairen, mother of Niall, i. lxxiii; ii. 66.
Cairnech, St., ii. 25, 66.
Cairpre of Dromcliffe, iii. 280.
„ Lifechair, i. dcxxxix. See Cairbre.
„ Min of Manand, iii. 419.
„ son of Niall, see Cairbre.
„ the poet, son of Etain, i. cccxxvii; ii. 50, 51.
Cairpri Cindcait, i. xxiv, xxv, xxvi, xxxi, xxxii, xxxiii.
„ Nia-Fear i. xcix. See Cairbre.
„ ua Cuind, i. cccxli, cccxlii.
Calad, son of Concinn, ii. 283.
Callaghan of Cashel, i. ccccliii.
Camden, iii. 173.
Canannan, ii. 98.
Canari, Giovanni Maria, i. dxvi.
Cano, son of Gartnan, i. cclxxiv, cclxxv, cclxxvi, iii. 164, 180, 196.
Canoclach Mhór, wife of Cuil, iii. 236.
Canute, i. ccxiii, cclxxxviii.
Caplait, a druid, ii. 72.
Capponi, G., cxxiii.
Caradoc of Lhancarvan, i. ccccxci, ccccxcii, ccccxciii, ccccxciv; iii. 353.
„ king, i dcxxvi.
Caratniad, chief judge of Conn, ii. 22.
Carausius, i. xlii, xliv.
Carban, son of Lugad, iii. 207.
Caredig, Ceredig, i. xlviii.
Carlus, son of the king of France, ii. 347.

Carman, *ii.* 39, 42, 49; *iii.* 527, 533, 535.
Carmen, see Carman.
Carolan, *i.* dxciv, dcix; *iii.* 275, 297.
Caron, Firmin, *i.* dlviii.
Carpri, see Cairpre and Cairbre.
Carter, Mr., *i.* dcxxii.
Carthach, St., *iii.* 4. See Mochuda, St.
Carthair, Inghen Druinighe, i.e. Fringe, daughter of Embroideress, *ii.* 133.
Cas, Corach, son of Bodhbh Derg, *iii.* 325.
„ „ son of Concind, *iii.* 169.
„ of the wavy hair, ancestor of the Dalcassians, *ii.* 117, 220; *iii.* 272.
„ son of Glas Gamhna, *ii.* 288.
„ son of Ros Ruadh, *ii.* 314.
Casaubon, *i.* cccclxxi.
Casmael, the cruitire or harper, *iii.* 236.
Casruba of stone-hewing hatchets, *iii.* 15.
Cassiodorus, *i.* cxciv, dcxxxiv, dcxxxv.
Castren, *i.* viii.
Caswallawn, *i.* xxxvii.
Cathair, *ii.* 43.
„ Mór, Ard Rig, *ii.* 12, 40, 43, 44, 46, 376; *iii.* 529, 530, 539, 541, 543.
Cathais, Danish pirate, *ii.* 102, 103.
Cathal, harp maker, *iii.* 258.
„ Mac Finguin, king of Munster, *ii.* 32, 76, 81, 82.
„ son of Ragallach, *ii.* 83, 84, 343.
Cathbadh, druid, *ii.* 51, 200, 226, 319, 363, 364.
Cathbarr, destined king of Ulster, *ii.* 163.
„ destined Ard Righ, *ii.* 163.
„ son of Domhnall Mór O'Donnell, *ii.* 163.
Cathelan, son of Maelfabhaill, *ii.* 103.
Caumul, harper, *iii.* 147.
Causcrach Mend, son of Concobar, *iii.* 145; see Causcrad.
Causcrad, *i.* ccclxxxii; *ii.* 333; *iii.* 93.
Caylus, *i.* ccclvi, ccclxxxi.
Ceadarn [or Ceasarn], king of the Fomorians, *ii.* 356 [? Cæsar, king of the Romans].
Ceallach, the diviner, *ii.* 205, 326, 327.
„ of Cearna, son of Flannagan, *ii.* 96.
Ceallachan Chaisil, *ii.* 275.
Ceanfaeladh, son of Ailill, *iii.* 61.
„ successor of St. Patrick, *iii.* 61.
„ the learned, *ii.* 52, 92, 93, 94, 95.
Ceannmor, Ceannmhair, a Munster druid, pupil of Mogh Ruith, *ii.* 214, 277.
Cearbhall, son of Muiregan, king of Leinster, *iii.* 25, 105.
Ceasair, wife of Eogan Mor, *ii.* 113, 109, 110; *iii.* 59, 231, 232.
Ceat Mac Magach, *ii.* 107, 122, 290, 325.
„ son of Scathach, *ii.* 370, 371.
Cecht, a druid, *ii.* 215.
Cecrops, *i.* xciv.
Ceinneidigh (Kennedy), father of Brian Boromha, *ii.* 117.
Ceirtle Inghen Snimhaire, i.e. Ball or Bottom, daughter of Distaff, *ii.* 133.
Cellach, *i.* dcxxxix.
„ son of Ragallach, *ii.* 343, 344.
Cellgen, a harper, *iii.* 147.
Celtcar or Celtchair Mac Uithir, (Uthichair, Mac Uthair, Mac Uithidir), *i.* clxxi, cccoxxxii, ccoclxxii; *ii.* 325,333, 357; *iii.* 95, 148.
Cenethryth, wife of Offa, *i.* cccxxxiv.
Cennedigh or Kennedy, *ii.* 349.
Cennfaeladh, *i.* xxxvii, xxxviii.
„ son of Conga, *ii.* 385.
Centwine, *i.* dvii.
Cerdan, son of Cerd beg, *iii.* 207.
Cerd beg, *iii.* 207.
Cerdraighe, son of Tighearnach, *iii.* 207, 208.
Cermat, or Cermait, son of the Dagda, *i.* cccxxvii; *iii.* 43.
Cermn, *ii.* 111, 118.
Cesarn, poet, *ii.* 57.
„ chief druid to Eochad Mac Erc, *ii.* 188, 189, 226, 263.
Cet, son of Magach, see Ceat Mac Magach, *ii.* 263.
„ Cuimnig, king of Munster, *ii.* 7.
Cethern, Mac Finntain, *i.* cccoxxxii; *ii.* 59, 97, 98, 209, 313, 314, 318.
Charlemagne, *i.* ccxiii, ccxiv, ccxviii, cccliv.
Charles the Bald, *i.* dxii.
„ I., dcxxviii; *iii.* 85.
„ II., *iii.* 85.
Chaucer, *i.* dxxv.
Chevallet, M. A. de, *i.* lix.
Chlodowig, or Clovis, *i.* dcxxxiv.
Chlotilde, *i.* dcxxxiv.
Chrestien de Troyes, *i.* xxxix.
Chrodomar, *i.* ccxxxv.
Chunrat, *i.* cccliii.

Cialiglind, a pipe player, *ii.* 139.
Cian, *i.* ccccxxxii; *ii.* 325.
„ son of Oilioll Oluim, *ii.* 139, 149.
Ciaran, St., *i.* ccclviii, ccccv, cccev; *ii.* 76, 81; *iii.* 403.
„ of Clonmacnoise, *ii.* 85, 89, 221, 335; *iii.* 120, 121, 135, 194.
„ of Saighir, *i.* ccclxvi; *ii.* 85.
Cicero, *i.* lx, cccxcvii, ccccixxvii.
Cimbaeth, Ard Righ, and husband of Queen Macha Mong Ruadh, *ii.* 112, 356.
„ king of Emania, *ii.* 374.
Cime, son of Umor, *ii.* 122.
Cinead, *i.* dcxxxix.
Cined or Cineadh O'Hartagan, *i.* ccxxxvii; *ii.* 105, 377.
„ of Cnodhbha, *ii.* 96.
Cind Find, harper, *ii.* 240, 241.
Cing, son of Umor, *ii.* 122.
Cingdorn, *iii.* 79, 15.
Cinneadh O'Hartagain, see Cined or Cineadh O'Hartagan.
Ciothe, druid, *ii.* 215.
Ciothruadh, chief druid, *ii.* 213, 214, 215.
Cir, *iii.* 15.
„ Inghen Scribaire, i.e. Comb, daughter of Scrubber *ii.* 133.
„ son of Cis, poet, *ii.* 4; *iii.* 240, 241.
Cirb, *i.* cccxxxvii.
Cire, son of Esse Enchinn, *ii.* 371.
Cirr, *i.* dcxxxix.
Cirril, *i.* dcxxxix.
Clarac, M. de, *i.* cexcviii.
Claudian, *i.* xliv, cccexlii.
Claudius, *i.* ccviii.
Clement of Alexandria, *i.* dxi.
Cleothar, *iii.* 15.
Clothra, *ii.* 71.
Cnucha, *ii.* 288.
Cnu Deroil, musician to the Fianns, *iii.* 324.
Cobhthach Cael, *ii.* 72, 256; *iii.* 242, 310.
Coc, embroiderers, *iii.* 122, 123.
Cochet, M. l'abbé, *i.* ccxcviii, cccclix.
Cochlan, *iii.* 355, 356.
Codrus, *i.* xciv.
Coinchenn, *ii.* 311.
Coire Mac Cruadh Ghobhan, i.e. Pot, son of hardy Smith, *ii.* 133.
Coke, Sir Edward, *i.* xciv.
Colgan, Rev. J., *i.* xcii.; *ii.* 64; *iii.* 66.
Colla, the three brothers, *ii.* 17, 12; *iii.* 84.
„ Uais king of Leinster, *ii.* 18.
Collins, Catherine, *iii.* 119.
Colman, *i.* dcxxxviii.
„ Ela, St., *iii.* 32, 33, 34.
„ four [*recte* two]—s, *ii.* 284.
„ Mac Lenin, St., *ii.* 76.
„ O'Cluasaighe, *ii.* 76, 90, 91.
„ St., *i.* dcxliv; *ii.* 82; *iii.* 33.
„ son of Comgellann, *ii.* 52.
Colptha, a chief druid, *ii.* 278, 279, 280; *iii.* 537.
Columbanus, St., *i.* xvi, dlxix, dcxliv.
Colum Cille, St., *ii.* 33, 52, 77, 78, 81, 85, 89, 91, 155, 163, 202; *iii.* 32, 122, 123, 164, 174, 235, 245, 247, 248, 253, 256, 281, 310, 371, 376, 385, 539.
Colum Cuaellemeach, a smith, *iii.* 42.
Comgall, St., of Benchuir, *i.* dcxliv; *ii.* 76, 81, 85.
Comgan, son of Maelochtar and Nuad Fullan, *ii.* 204, 205, 226.
Con, Conn, *i.* dcxxxviii; *ii.* 10, 18.
„ or Conn of the Hundred Battles, *i.* xxi, xxv, xxvi, cccxxii, cccxxxiii, cccxxxiv, cccxl, dcxxxix; *ii.* 11, 21, 30, 57, 149, 205, 209, 212, 324, 327, 374, 375, 376, 384; *iii.* 166, 179, 201, 272, 317.
„ son of Dalach, *ii.* 163.
Conaing, nephew of Brian Boromha, *ii.* 124.
„ Beg-eaglach, Ard Righ, *ii.* 330.
„ Fomorian chief, *ii.* 109, 184, 185.
„ son of Donncuan, *ii.* 349.
Conaire Mór, *i.* xx, lxxiv, cccl, ccclxx, ccclxxix, ccclxxxii, ccexc, cccxcvii, ccccxxxiii, ccccIxii; *ii.* 18, 97, 199, 212, 226; *iii.* 136, 137, 138, 139, 144, 145, 148, 152 165, 183, 186, 190, 382.
„ son of Mogh Lamha, *i.* cclxiv.
Conaladh, *iii.* 61.
Conall, *i.* dcxxxviii.
„ Cael, an Umorian chief, *ii.* 48, 122, 165, 284, 434, 455.
„ Cearnach, *i.* xxii, ccclvii, ccclxii, ccccixvi, ccccIxx, ccccIxxxi; *ii.* 55, 107, 108, 122, 196, 263, 291, 331, 333, 357, 358, 366, 367, 373, 374; *iii.* 19, 21, 75, 77, 144.
„ Cendmor, *iii.* 540, 541.
„ Cremthainné, *ii.* 151, 161.
„ Cruachna, king of Scotland, *ii.* 374.
„ Dearg Ua Corra Finn, *i.* dcxlii.
Eachluaith, king of Munster, *ii.* 64, 65, 220, 375.

Conall, Gulban, *ii.* 161, 162, 163, 164, 165, 375.
„ St., *ii.* 33; *iii.* 66.
„ son of Baedan, *ii.* 342. 443.
„ son of Niall, *ii.* 60, 163, 164.
„ son of Umor, *ii.* 122.
Concend, *i.* cccclxii, cccclxiii.
Conchaind, *iii.* 377.
Conchobar, king of Meath, *ii.* 151.
„ Abrath Ruadh, *iii.* 202.
„ Mac Nessa, see Concobar Mac Nessa.
Conchobhar Mac Nessa, see Concobar Mac Nessa.
Concobar Abradh-Ruadh, *ii.* 53.
„ Mac Nessa, *i.* xx, xcix, clxxi, ccxxxvii, cccxxviii, cccxlviii, ccliii, ccclxxi, ccclxxii, ccclxxix, ccclxxx, ccclxxxii, ccclxxxiii. cccclxx, cccclxxii; *ii.* 8, 20, 51, 55, 106, 107, 112, 197, 199, 200, 290, 291, 292, 300, 319, 320, 321, 325, 329, 330, 332, 333, 357, 358, 359, 361, 362, 363, 364, 368; *iii.* 17, 18, 19, 20. 91, 92, 95, 96, 97, 109, 138, 151, 161, 196, 203, 254, 315, 365, 372, 373, 376, 385, 423, 514.
„ son of Cathbadh, *ii.* 18.
„ son of Fachtna Fathach, *ii.* 321.
Concorb of the Artists, *iii.* 396.
Concraidh, son of Duach, king of S. Munster, *ii.* 158, 159, 193, 194.
Condere, *ii.* 383.
Conga, *ii.* 385.
Congal Clairingnech, Ard Righ, *ii.* 274, 276, 277; *iii.* 380.
„ Clean, *ii.* 341; *iii.* 368.
Congallach of Colt, *ii.* 96.
Conglas, *i.* cccexxxvi.
Conla, Cain Breathach, *ii.* 21.
„ son of Cormac Cas, *ii.* 387.
„ *ii.* 143, 144.
„ son of Tadg, son of Cian, *ii.* 212, 375.
„ son of Tadhg, *ii.* 140.
Conlaech, son of Cuchulaind, *ii.* 310, 312, 331.
Connal, see Conal.
Connington, Prof., *i.* ccclxxx.
Connlaid, St. Brigid's artificer, *ii.* 338.
Connor Mac Nessa, see Concobar Mac Nessa.
Connu, worker in precious metals, *ii.* 322, 323.
Connud Mac Morna, *i.* ccclxxvii, ccclxxx, *iii.* 94.
Conor, *iii.* 14.
Conra, *i.* xxv.
Conroi Mac Daire, see Curoi Mac Daire.
Constantine, *i.* xlv.
„ king of the Britons, *iii.* 38.
„ the Great, *i.* xlii; *ii.* 160.
Constantius, *i.* xliii, xlvi.
„ Chlorus, *i.* xlii.
Conyngham, Col. Burton, *iii.* 267, 269, 275.
Cooke, Mr. T. L., *iii.* 321.
Coplait, a druid, *ii.* 72, 201.
Corb of the Artists, *iii.* 396.
„ Mac Ciarain, *ii.* 327, 328.
„ Olum, *i.* xxv.
„ poet, *ii.* 57.
Corc, king of Cashel, *ii.* 25, 62, 68, 69, 72, 375.
Corcran Cleirech, *ii.* 137.
Corelli, *i.* dcix.
Cormac, *ii.* 32; *iii.* 514 543.
„ *iii.* 264, 265.
„ an Eigeas, poet, *ii.* 105.
„ Cas, king of Munster, *ii.* 18, 65, 387.
„ Conloingeas, *i.* cccclix; *ii.* 361, 362; *iii.* 91, 109, 137, 138, 254.
„ File, poet, *ii.* 105; *iii.* 6.
„ Gaileng, *ii.* 139, 140.
„ Kelly, *iii.* 295.
„ Mac Airt, *i.* xxii, xcvii, ccclxx, cccexxxii, cccexxxiv; *ii.* 18, 19, 22, 23, 27, 45, 51, 52, 58, 89, 165, 139, 140, 205, 206, 211, 212, 213, 215, 277, 278, 280, 321, 323, 324, 326, 327, 333, 334, 354, 375, 382, 525; *iii.* 5, 6, 7, 11, 12, 24, 156, 177, 178, 180, 197, 317, 319, 334, 361, 362, 363, 388.
„ Mac Cullinan, *i.* dvii; *ii.* 11, 48, 52, 54, 64, 89, 101, 144, 166, 173, 209, 210, 217, 218, 227, 380; *iii.* 25, 252, 261, 276, 338, 381, 384.
„ son of Colamarig, *iii.* 100.
„ son of Maelefogha, *iii.* 100.
Coroticus, *i.* xlviii.
Corpri, son of a king of Leinster, *iii.* 149.
Corrgenn, *ii.* 151, 152; *iii.* 8.
Cothbadh, see Cathbadh.
Cotton, John, *i.* dxxxii, dlii.
Coulson, Capt., *i.* lxiii.
Coussemaker, M. de, *i.* cccexci, cccexcv, cccexcvii, cccexcviii.

cccc xcix, d, di, dii, dvi, dxii, dxiii, dxiv, dxv, dxviii, dxix, dxxv, dxxvi, dxxix, dxxxix, dxlvii, dl, dli, dlii, dliii, dliv, dlv, dlvi, dlvii.
Craifné, son of Aife, *ii.* 371.
Craiftine, *ii.* 51; *iii.* 242, 243, 244, 248, 249, 250, 253, 254, 255, 264, 302.
Cran, son of Oilioll Oluim, *ii.* 375.
Crede, *iii.* 12, 13, 14.
Credenbel, *iii.* 527.
Credne, *iii.* 204, 210, 211. See Creidne.
Creide, daughter of the king of Munster, *iii.* 379.
Creidne, the first worker in precious metals, *iii.* 43, 211, 246, 248, 249.
Crichel, son of Dubhraith, *iii.* 15, 16.
Cridenbel, Critenbel, satirist, *ii.* 89; *iii.* 533, see Credenbel.
Crimthan, Crimhthann, *i.* dcxxxix, *ii.* 386.
„ Ard Righ, son of Daire Cerb, *ii.* 64, 67.
„ Mór Mac Fiodhaidh, Ard Righ, *ii.* 211, 220, 375.
„ Nia Nair (also Niad-nair), *i.* xxii, xxiv, xxvi, xxix; *ii.* 55, 200, 202.
„ son of Aedh, king of Leinster, *iii.* 160.
„ (son of Enna) king of Leinster, *ii.* 43, 206, 337, 338, 339, 340; *iii.* 535, 539.
„ son of Fidad, *i.* cccxx.
„ son of Finntan, *ii* 314.
Criol Mac Craeslinaidh, i.e. Chest, son of Fill Mouth, *ii.* 133.
Criomthan, see Crimthan.
Critine, poet, *ii.* 51.
Crofinn, a Tuatha De Danann lady, *ii.* 189.
Cromdereoil, *i.* ccxcix.
Crompton, *i.* xciv.
Cron, mother of the Tuatha De Danann Fianlugh, *ii.* 250.
Cronan, St., *ii.* 76.
Crotch, Dr., *i.* dcxxvii.
Cruife, *i.* xxiv, xxv.
Cruimchenn, *iii.* 166.
Cruimthoris of Cenngoba, embroideress to St. Patrick, *iii.* 122.
Cruithne, *i.* xxxii.
Crundmael, *i.* dcxxxix.
Csaplovics, *i.* cl.
Cu, the comely, i.e. Cuchulaind, *ii.* 306.
Cuag Mac Tornora, i.e. Wooden Mug, son of Turner, *ii.* 133.
Cualad, *iii.* 61.
Cuan O'Lothchain, or O'Lochain, *ii.* 22, 131, 378.
„ the victorious, *ii.* 386.
Cuar, killed by Cuchulaind, *ii.* 293.
„ son of Scathach, *ii.* 370, 371.
„ *iii.* 15.
Cuara, or Cuaradh, *ii.* 154, 155.
Cubretan, son of Aengus, *ii.* 390.
Cuchulaind, *i.* xx, xxii, xxxii, xxxviii, lxxii, lxxvi, xc, clxi, ccvii, ccxcix, ccc, ccciv, cccxxxii, cccxxxviii, cccxl, cccxliii, cccliv, ccclvii, ccclx, ccclxi, ccclxv, ccclxxi, ccclxxii, ccclxxix, ccclxxxiii, ccclxxxvi, ccclxxxviii, ccccxc, ccccix, ccccxxxiii, ccccxxxiv, ccccxxxvi, ccccxlv, ccccxlvi, cccclii, ccccliv, cccclxii, cccclxiii, cccclxix, cccclxx, cccclxxiv, cccclxxviii, cccclxxix, cccclxxx, cccclxxxii, cccclxxxiii; *ii.* 10, 94, 97, 122, 181, 194, 195, 196, 197, 198, 199, 200, 226, 291, 292, 293, 294, 296, 297, 298, 299, 300, 301, 302, 303 to 312, 313, 314, 315, 317, 318, 319, 321, 322, 323, 324, 329, 331, 333, 357, 358, 359, 361, 362, 363, 364, 365, 366, 367, 368, 369, 370, 371, 372, 373, 374; *iii.* 11, 20, 21, 75, 77, 78, 79, 80, 81, 82, 97 to 102, 110, 122, 152, 186, 187, 188, 192, 195, 196, 199, 315, 360, 400, 401, 402, 413, 414, 415, 419, 421, 423, 425, 429, 431, 435, 437, 439, 440, 441, 443, 445, 447, 449, 451, 453, 457, 459, 461.
Cuchulainn, see Cuchulaind.
Cuchuland, see Cuchulaind.
Cudiuligh, son of Kennedy, *ii.* 349.
Cuil, son of Midhuil, *iii.* 236.
Cuingedach, son of Aithirne, *iii.* 373.
Cul, a charioteer, *iii*, 183.
Culand, Culann, the smith, *i.* ccvii; *ii.* 362 363; *iii.* 401, 417.
Cumall, Cumhall, son of Trenmor, *i.* cccxxii; *ii.* 283, 375, 385.
Cumascach, son of Aedh Mac Ainmire, *ii.* 338, 340.
Cumin, or Cumain Fada, *ii.* 90, 202; *iii.* 33.
Cummen, *i.* lxxxix.
Cumscraigh Menn, *ii*, 325.
Cunedda, *i.* xxxvii, xxxviii, xl, xlviii.
Cuneglasus, *i.* ccccxxxvi.
Cunnla, *ii.* 144.
Curnach, son of Ui Faich, *iii.* 138.
Curoi Mac Daire, *i.* xxii, xxxviii,

cccxxxvi, cccxiii, ccclvii; *ii.* 9, 10, 97, 199, 358; *iii.* 15, 75, 76, 78, 79, 80, 81, 82, 152, 179, 209.
Curruid, *ii.* 311.
Cuscrach, *i.* xx. See Causcrach.
Cutra, son of Umor.
Daderg, *i.* ccclxxix, cccсxxxiii, ccccxxxv, ccccIxii; *ii.* 199; *iii.* 136, 137, 149, 151, 165, 163, 186, 189, 368.
Dae, son of Umar, *ii.* 122.
Dagda, the Tuatha Dé Danann god, *i.* xxxii, cccxxviii, dcxxxiv, dcxxxv, dcxxxvi, dcxxxix, dcxl; *ii.* 50, 51, 110, 132, 151, 152, 187, 215, 217, 220, 221, 222, 223, 225, 272; *iii.* 8, 43, 73, 147, 213, 214, 233, 242.
Dagdai Mór. See Dagda.
Daghda, see Dagda.
Dahana, *i.* iii.
Dahlmann, *i.* cxlv, cli.
Daire, king of Ulster, *ii.* 25, 67, 122.
" Cearb, Cerb, *ii.* 67.
" Domthig, *iii.* 88.
" grandfather of Ferdiad, *ii.* 306.
" Mac Feachna, *iii.* 90.
Daithe, *iii.* 43.
Dalach, druid, *ii.* ii.
" Prince of Tirconnell, *ii.* 102, 104, see Eignechan.
" son of Muircertach, *ii.* 162, 163; *iii.* 90.
Dalbh, Dulbh, *ii.* 40; *iii.* 527.
Dallan, druid of king Eochad, *ii.* 193, 194.
" Forgaill, *ii.* 33, 52, 78, 85, 86; *iii.* 110, 111, 174, 175, 235, 245, 247, 248, 250, 253, 254, 256, 371.
" Mac More, a Leinster poet, *ii.* 105.
Dalran, *iii.* 15.
Daman, son of Dare, *ii.* 306; *iii.* 419, 421, 423, 435, 443, 449, 455, 457.
Danann, a chief druidess, *ii.* 187.
Danjou, M., *i.* dliv.
Daolach [recte Dael], son of Umor, *ii.* 122; *iii.* 74, 75.
Daphne, *i.* iii.
Dathen, *iii.* 144.
Dathghel, *ii.* 133.
Dathi (see Athi), *ii.* 70, 71, 72, 150, 226; *iii.* 525.
Datho, king of Leinster, *ii.* 40; *iii.* 527.
Dauney, Mr., *i.* ccccxc.
David, king, *i.* cccxcvii, dlvi, dlviii; *iii.* 7, 238, 239, 354.
Dé, *i.* lxxvi.
Dealgnad, wife of Partholon, *iii.* 326.
Dearbhail, son of, *ii.* 96.
Dease, Thomas, Bishop of Meath, *iii.* 265.
Deaus, or Deuce, *i.* iii.
De Burg, family of, *iii.* 267.
Dectere, mother of Cuchulaind, *ii.* 360.
Deichrind, Deichrinni, a harper, *iii.* 139, 147.
Deilbh Caemh. See Bécuma.
Deirbrin, *ii.* 71.
Deirdre, *ii.* 369; *iii.* 368, 373, 378, 385.
Delbaeth, or Delbath, *ii.* 51; *iii.* 213.
Delt, *iii.* 43, 144.
Demmin, *i.* ccccxliii, ccccxliv, ccccxlvi.
De Muris, *i.* d.
Denewulf of Winchester, *i.* cxlii.
Derg Damhsa, *i.* cccxl.
Dermeil, *ii.* 311.
Dermot Mac Ferguss Ceirbheoil, see Diarmait, son of Fergus Ceirbheoil.
Detha, *ii.* 191.
Deucalion, *i.* xciii.
Dewar, Rev. Daniel, *iii.* 331.
Dian, *ii.* 39, 42; *iii.* 527 533.
Diancecht, the great physician, *ii.* 284; *iii.* 40, 43.
Diarmaid the poet, *ii.* 55, see also Diarmait.
Diarmait, son of Aedh Slaine, *ii.* 91; *iii.* 160, 165, 173, 180, 189.
" Dornmas Duirgen, *ii.* 43; *iii.* 533.
" father of Aedh Slaine, *ii.* 158; *iii.* 241.
" king of Corcabascen, *ii.* 349.
" O'Duibhne, *iii.* 166; 377.
" son of Fergus Ceirbheoil, or Cerrbheoil, or Cerbhall, *i.* cccxl, cccxli; *ii.* 16, 18, 115, 159, 233, 336, 337; *iii.* 24, 193, 194, 465.
Dibad, son of Dorcha, *ii.* 39, 41, 42; *iii.* 527, 533.
Dibdin, Charles, *i.* dcxxxiv.
Dibe, *iii.* 139.
Dicholl of Drum Da Chonor, *ii.* 356.
Dicuil, *i.* xvi.
Dide, a harper, *iii.* 147.
Didron, M., *i.* dxv.
Diefenbach, Lorenz, *i.* lvii, cexxxvi cclxiv, ccccіv, ccccxliii, ccccxliv, ccccIxxvii, ccccxcix.
Diez, *i.* ccxxi, cclxxiv, cccxciii, ccccliv.

Dill, a druid, *ii.* 204, 208, 226, 375.
Diocassius, *i.* ccclxx.
Diocletian, *i.* xlii.
Diodorus Siculus, *i.* cccclxxxix.
Diogenes, the tragic poet, *i.* cccclxxxvii.
Dionysius, *i.* lxxvii.
Dioscorides, *i.* lx.
Dithorba, *ii.* 357.
Dithrabach, *ii.* 386; *iii.* 377.
Dithrinne, poet, *ii.* 171.
Dobrowsky, *i* cccclxxiii.
Dobur, drink bearer, *iii.* 151.
Doche Mac Magach, *ii.* 315.
Doe, daughter of Liath, *iii.* 404, 405.
Domaine Mossud, *iii.* 146, 213.
Domhnall (Donnell), *ii.* 132, 156, 368-9.
„ Mac Eimhin, Mòr Maer, or high steward of Scotland, *ii.* 349.
„ Mór O'Brien, *iii.* 153, 271.
„ son of Aedh, *ii.* 341, 342.
„ son of Donchadh, *ii.* 146; *iii.* 15, 16.
„ the brown haired, *ii.* 127.
„ Ua Duibdala, *iii.* 396.
Domnall, *iii.* 245, 246, see also Domhnall.
„ king of Ulster, *ii.* 335.
„ son of Diarmait, k. of Corcobaiscenn, *ii.* 349.
Donagh, son of Brian Boromha, *iii.* 267, 269.
Donatus, *ii.* 54; *iii.* 292.
Donbo, *iii.* 309-312.
Donchadh, son of Fland, *i.* cccxxvii.
Dond, *i.* lxxiv; *iii.* 145, 150.
„ Dess, *iii.* 136, 137.
Doni, *i.* dxx.
Donn, Dond, son of Milesius, *ii.* 189; *iii.* 537.
„ Mac Doghar, *ii.* 386.
„ -Og, *iii.* 25.
Donnbo, Dondbo, see Donbo.
Donnchadh or Donagh, son of Flann Sinna, *ii.* 148, 149.
„ Cairbreach, *ii.* 272, 276, 284.
„ Mac Gilla Padraicc, king of Ossory, *ii.* 351, 352.
„ O'Brien, *iii.* 351-352.
„ son of Brian Boromha, *ii.* 121, 151, 351, 352; *iii.* 228.
Donncuan, *ii.* 349.
Donnsleibhe, king of Ulidia, *ii.* 156.
Donogh, son of Brian Boromha, *iii.* 233, 274, see Donnchadh.
Dorban, a poet, *ii.* 72; *iii.* 525.
Dorcha, *i.* lxxiv; *iii.* 145.
Dôrcha, son of Ainches, *ii.* 39, 41; *iii.* 527, 533.
Dornmar the Musical, *iii.* 77.
Dornröschen, romance of, *i.* ccci.
Dothur, *ii* 39, 42; *iii.* 527, 533.
Drac, *iii.* 35.
Drucht, *iii.* 43, 144.
Duach, son of Conall, *ii.* 343.
„ Dubh, king of Oirghiall, *ii.* 330.
„ king of South Munster, *ii.* 159.
„ Teimin, *i.* cccxxvi.
Dual Mac Firbis, *ii.* 169.
Dub, *i.* lxxiv; *iii.* 151.
Duban, son of Degha, *iii.* 61.
„ from Druim Daoile, *ii.* 386.
Dubchluithe, *iii.* 15.
Dubdachonn, *ii.* 15.
Dubditha, *ii.* 329.
Dubh, *ii.* 252, 253, 288, 289; *iii.* 145, 527.
„ from Drom Leis, *iii.* 377.
„ son of Dibad, *ii.* 39, 42; *iii.*
„ the Fomorian Smith, *ii.* 249.
Dubhaltach Mac Firbisigh, *iii.* 15.
Dubhchruit, *iii.* 15.
Dubhreann, son of Uirgreann, *ii.* 322.
Dubhthach, Dael Tenga, *ii.* 373.
„ Dael Uladh, *i.* cccxxxviii, ccccxxxi, ccccxxxii; *ii.* 333, 357; *iii.* 148.
„ of Dublin, *ii.* 339.
Dubloinges, *iii.* 138.
Dubthach, chief poet, *i.* ccclxi; *ii.* 25, 52, 66, 67, 72, 74, 284, 339, 340.
Ducange, *i.* cii, cv, cccl.
Dufay, Guillaume, *i.* dlv, dlvi, dlviii.
Duibhdreann, *ii.* 387.
Duibhlinn, daughter of Eignechan, *ii.* 102-3.
Duildermait, *iii.* 106, 360.
Duinechadh, *iii.* 34.
Duirb, *i.* cccclviii.
Dunadach, *ii.* 349.
Dunchadh, king of Leinster, *ii.* 38
Dungalach, *ii.* 70, 71.
Dunlang, or Dunlaing, son of Enda, or Enna, *i.* ccclxi; *ii.* 18, 339.
Dunne, Dr. Charles, *i.* xcvi.
„ See O'Doyne, *i.* cliv.
Du Noyer, G. V., *i.* cccvii, cccix, cccxii, cccliv, ccccxxxviii; *ii.* 242; *iii.* 67-72, 74.
Dunraven, Earl of, *i.* cccvii.
Durand, M. Germer, *i.* lxiii.
Durb, *ii.* 40; *iii.* 527.
Dussaussoy, M., *i.* ccccxvii.
Dyaus Pater, *i.* iii.
Eadan, *iii.* 360.

Ebel, Dr. Hermann, *i.* lii, liii, liv, lviii, lxv, lxxvi, cclxxxviii, cccccxxii.
Eber, *ii.* 4, 20, 75, 88, 190; *iii.* 537.
Ebn Hayan, *i.* dxxii.
Ebric, son of the king of France, *ii.* 347.
„ son of the king of Lochlann, *ii.* 350.
Ecalsalach, the smith, *i.* ccclxxxi. See Ecsolach.
Echad, *iii.* 530.
Echdruim, *iii.* 146.
Echruathar, *iii.* 146.
Echruid, *iii.* 146.
Echtach, *iii.* 355.
Echtigbern, *ii.* 169.
Echur, *iii.* 149.
Ecsolach, *ii.* 51.
Edain, or Etain, wife of Eochad Fedhleach, *ii.* 192, 194, 226; *iii.* 162, 163, 188, 190, 191, 192, 360.
„ the poetess, *i.* lxxiii; *ii.* 133.
Edchu [Eochu] Rond, king of Ui Maine, *iii.* 106.
Edgar, king, *i.* cccxc.
Edward, king, *i.* cclxxxviii.
„ the Elder, *i.* cxcix.
Egan, Mr., harp maker, *iii.* 297.
Egbert, *ii.* 82.
„ St., *i.* ccccxlix.
Egfrid, *i.* xxxv.
Egidius de Murino, *i.* dliv.
Egilsson, *i.* lxxxvii.
Eichhorn, *i.* cviii, cix, cxciv, cclix.
Eidersgeal, Eidersgul, *ii.* 18, 218, 219.
Eignechan, son of Dalach, *ii.* 98, 102, 103, 104, 163.
Eimher [recte Eber], *iii.* 240, 241.
Einar Skalaglum, *i.* ccccclxxi.
Einglan, king of birds, *i.* ccclxx.
Eirrge Echbel, *iii.* 95, 96.
Eithear, a chief druid, *ii.* 188.
Eithne, *i.* cxxiv.
„ daughter of Emangaeth, *ii.* 52.
„ in Gubai, *ii.* 194, 195, 196.
„ queen of Cashel.
„ "the fair", daughter of king Laeghaire, *ii.* 201.
„ Uathach, daughter of Dill the Druid, *ii.* 204, 208.
„ wife of Concobar Mac Nessa, *ii.* 290.
„ wife of Conn, *i.* ccccxxxiv.
Ekkehard, *i.* dxii, dlxvii, dlxix.
Eladha, king of the Fomorians, *iii.* 155, 156.
Elathan, Eladan, son of Delbaeth, *ii.* 51; *iii.* 213, 535.
Elim, *i.* xxv, xxxi.
Elizabeth, Queen, *i.* dcxxxiii; *iii.* 85, 288.
Emangaeth, *ii.* 52.
Emer, wife of Cuchulaind, *i.* ccclxxi, ccclxxxvii; *ii.* 195, 197, 198, 226, 365, 368, 369, 371, 372; *iii.* 11, 20, 122, 315.
En, son of Ethoman, *iii.* 342.
Enda, king of Leinster, *i.* ccclxi. See Enna Cinnselach.
„ son of Niall, see Enna.
Endach, son of Umor, *iii.* 74.
Engel, Carl, *i.* cccxciv, dix, dx, dxi, dxvii, dc, dcxix, dcxx, dcxxi.
Enna, Aighneach (Aigneach), *ii.* 6, 328, 204.
„ Airgtheach, see Enna Aigneach.
„ brother of Conall Gulban, *ii.* 161, 342.
„ Cinnselach, Ceinselach, or Ceinnselach, king of Leinster, *ii.* 59, 69, 70, 285, 337, 339, 340.
„ son of Niall, *ii.* 60, 163, 164.
„ son of Nos, *ii.* 238.
Eocaid, *i.* ccccxxi.
Eochach Muidhmeadhan. See Eochad.
Eochad, or Eochadh, *i.* ccccxxxvii.
„ Abrad Ruaidh, *ii.* 283.
„ Airem, or Airemh, *i.* ccci, cccclxxx; *ii.* 71, 72, 105, 192, 194, 226, 283.
„ Beg, *ii.* 357.
„ Belbuidhe, *ii.* 39, 40; *iii.*
„ [Dagda], *iii.* 9.
„ Domlen, *ii.* 386.
„ Echbeoil, *iii.* 315.
„ Edgudach, *ii.* 6; *iii.* 88.
„ Eolach O'Ceirin, *ii.* 113.
„ Erann, son of Flann Mainistrech, *ii.* 169.
„ Fedleach, *i.* lxxiii; *ii.* 13, 71, 72 98, 145, 146, 150, 199, 261, 274, 290, 295; *iii.* 190, 191, 192.
„ Finn, *ii.* 374.
„ [Fothadh] Airgteach, *iii.* 175, 176.
„ Garbh, *i.* cccxxvi, cccxxxiii, cccxxxvi, cccxxxix, dcxxxviii.
„ Gunnat, king of Ulster, *ii.* 18, 70, 147, 338; *iii.* 527.
„ Iuil, *ii.* 197.
„ king of Munster, *ii.* 65.
„ Mac Erc, *i.* dcxxxvii; 237, 239.

241; *ii.* 148, 188, 226, 235, See Eochad Garbh.
Eochad Muidhmeodhan, *i.* lxxiij, cccxx; *ii.* 60, 147.
„ Mac Luchta, *ii.* 21.
„ O'Ceirin, the learned, *ii.* 55, 153, 154, 155. See Eochadh Eolach.
„ O'Cleircein, *ii.* 167.
„ O'Flanagan, *ii.* 113.
„ O'Flinn, O'Floinn, 103 et seq.
„ Righ Eigas, *ii.* 57, 76, 85, 86, see Dallan Forgaill.
„ son of Cairbre Liffeachair, *ii.* 336.
„ son of Dunadach, *ii.* 349.
„ son of Enna Ceinsellach, *i.* xlv; *ii.* 59, 69, 70, 285, 286, 287, 295, 339.
„ the druid, *ii.* 330.
Eocho Mumho, *ii.* 9.
Eogabhail, *iii.* 260.
Eogan, *i.* cccxl; *ii.* 212.
„ Mac Durthachta, *ii.* 20, 357; *iii.* 19, 93.
Eoghan, or Eogan, Bel, *ii.* 335.
„ Mac Duirtheacht, Eoghan Mac Durthacht, or Mac Durthach, see Eogan Mac Durthachta.
„ brother of Conall Gulban, *ii.* 161.
„ Inbhir, *ii.* 197.
„ or Eogan Mór, king of Munster, *i.* ccxxvi; *ii.* 50, 51, 57, 65, 112, 155, 218, 357, 374, 375; *iii.* 5. 166, 179, 259, 261, 359, 360.
„ son of Echtighern, *ii.* 169, 329.
„ son of Niall, *ii.* 60, 142, 154, 155, 156, 161, 164, 344.
Eolus, a druid, *ii.* 184.
Erc Culbuidhe, *i.* lxxii.
„ daughter of king Daire, *iii.* 122.
„ daughter of Loarn Mór, king of Alba, *ii.* 156.
„ son of Cairbre Niadh-fear, *ii.* 199; *iii* 96.
Ercc, *iii.* 96, see Erc.
Ercnat, the virgin nun, *iii.* 123.
Ereach Febria, *iii.* 537.
Ereamhon, see Eremon.
Eremon, *ii.* 7, 75, 106, 164, 189, 190; *iii.* 12, 240, 241.
Erennan, *iii.* 537.
Erich, St., *i.* clxx.
Erinys, *i.* iii.
Eros, *i.* iii.
Err, *i.* cccxlv.
Errard Mac Coise, *ii.* 128.
Errg, *ii.* 333.
Ergge Echbel, *iii.* 96.
Erumas, *ii.* 251.
Esclan the Dagda's judge, *i.* dcxxxix.
Essa, daughter of Eochad Airemh, *ii.* 105.
Esse Enchinn, *ii.* 371.
Etain, queen, *i.* ccci, cccxxvii, ccclxxxi, ccclxxix. See Edain.
„ the poetess, *ii.* 50, 51.
Etan Cend Derg, *iii.* 404, 405.
Etar, *iii.* 162, 190.
Etercomol, *i.* cccxli.
Ethan, *ii.* 57.
Ethelhun, *ii.* 82.
Ethelwin, *ii.* 82.
Ethor, *ii.* 281, 282.
Etuscel, *iii.* 187.
Euphorion, *i.* ccccxxxvi, cccclxxxvii.
Ewers, *i.* cl.
Fabius, *i.* xciii.
Fabritio Caroso da Sermoneta, *i.* dlxii.
Fachtna Fathach, *ii.* 321.
„ St., *ii.* 76.
„ the wise son of Sencha, *ii.* 20, 322.
Fadad, son of Liath, *iii.* 404.
Fadg, *ii.* 375.
Faelan, *iii.* 375.
Faelchu, *iii.* 377.
Fail-dearg-doid, *ii.* 7; *iii.* 241.
Faindle Mac Dubraith, *iii.* 202.
Falbhar, *iii.* 158.
Fallaman, son of Concobar Mac Nessa, *ii.* 360.
Fand, daughter of Flidais, *iii.* 204.
„ daughter of Aedh Abrat, *ii.* 196, 197, 198; *iii.* 192.
Fathach, a Firbolg druid, *ii.* 187.
„ poet, *i.* dcxxxvii.
Fauriel, M., *i.* cviii
Feargna, *ii.* 169.
Fechen, St., *ii.* 85, 119, 120; *iii.* 67.
Fedelm, *iii.* 109, 110.
„ Noi Chridhe, "the ever blooming", *iii.* 19.
Fedelmid Rechtmer, *i.* dcxxxix See Feidhlimid.
Fedelm Nucruthach, daughter of Concobar Mac Nessa, *i* cccxliii; *iii.* 96.
„ "the Rosy", one of king Laeghaire's daughters, *ii.* 201.
Feidhlim, son of Flann of the Monastery, *ii.* 169.
„ son of Laeghaire, *ii.* 166.
Feidhlimid Mac Crimthain, Ard Righ, *ii.* 376; *iii* 261, 262.
Feidhlimid, Feidlimidh, Rechtmhar, *i.* xxvi; *ii.* 21, 22.
Feidhlimy, the harper, *iii.* 329, 357.

Feidlimid, *i.* dxiii.
Fellenberg, von, *i.* ccccxvi.
Fenius Farsaidh, *ii.* 20, 53, 54, 113, 174.
Feradach, son of Rocuirp, *i.* ccccxl.
Feradhach Finn or Find Feachtnach, Ard Righ, *i* xxiv, xxv, xxvi, xxix, xxxi, xxxiii; *ii.* 21; *iii.* 95.
„ son of Assal, *ii.* 18.
Ferb, the daughter of Gerg, *i.* ccclxxv, *iii.* 168, 169, 307.
Ferbaeth, *i.* cccclii; *iii.* 435.
Ferberna, poet and warrior, *i.* cccclxxi; *ii.* 328.
Ferceirtne, also Fercertne, *ii.* 8, 9, 12, 51, 53, 54, 57, 97, 133, 257; *iii.* 152, 153, 179, 209, 242, 243, 244, 249, 250, 253, 255, 316.
Fercertne, Concobar Mac Nessa's poet, *ii.* 51.
Fercu, *i.* ccccxxxii.
Ferdiad, *i.* xx, xxxii, lxxii, clv, clxxxv, ccxxxvi, ccclxxx, ccclxxxiii, cccclxvi, cccclxix, cccclxxiv, *ii.* 302, 303, 304, 305, 306, 307, 308, 309, 310, 312, 313, 317, 318, 319, 358, 369; *iii.* 101, 102, 186, 215, 302, 400, 401, 402, 409, 413, 414, 417, 419, 421, 423, 425, 427, 429, 431, 435, 436, 439, 441, 443, 445, 447, 449, 451, 453, 455, 457, 459, 461, 463, 584.
Fer-fi, son of Eogabhal, *i.* dxxiii; *iii.* 259, 261.
Ferfirb Mac Muireadhaig, *ii.* 78.
Ferfordae, *iii.* 146.
Fergal Mac Maoileduin, Ard Righ, *ii.* 389, 390, 391; *iii.* 309, 310, 311, 312, 326, 381.
Fergna, son of Findconna, *iii.* 96.
„ *iii.* 158.
Fergus, son of Aithirne, *ii.* 21, 25, 57, 66, 67, 72, 74.
„ Cirrbheoil or Cerrbheoil, *i.* ccxl; *ii.* 335; *iii.* 193, 194.
„ Dubh deadach, i.e. of the black tooth, *ii.* 18, 139.
„ Fairge, *iii.* 161, 162.
„ Ferde, *iii.* 146.
„ Fiannaite, *ii.* 21.
„ Fogha, *ii.* 112; *iii.* 25.
„ Mac Leite, *ii.* 320, 357.
„ Mac Roigh, *i.* cccxli, cccxliii, cccxliv, cccxlviii; *ii.* 89, 195, 196, 256, 257, 297, 298, 315 to 318, 320, 321, 323, 335, 357, 358, 360, 367, 374; *iii.* 18, 91 to 97, 201, 254, 338, 339, 367, 373, 374, 419, 421, 453.
Fergus, son of Eochad, *ii.* 147.
„ son of Finn Mac Cumhaill, *ii.* 59.
„ son of king Ragallach, *ii.* 343.
„ son of Rossa, *ii.* 85.
„ the half red son of Nemid, *ii.* 184, 185.
„ the novelist, *ii.* 55.
Ferguses, the three brothers, so called, *iii.* 177.
Ferguson, Dr. Samuel, *i.* cclxxxv, dvi, dvii, dxix, dcxliv; *iii.* 226-230, 232.
Ferloga, charioteer, *iii.* 372, 373.
Ferriter, Pierce, *iii.* 257, 258, 264.
Ferrogan, *i.* ccccxxxii, ccccxxxiii, cccclxiii; *iii.* 137, 138, 139, 144, 145, 147, 148, 149, 150, 151, 183, 184.
Festus Pompeius, *i.* ccxxxvi, ccclxxix.
Fetis, M., *i.* cccclxxxvi, dix, dxiv, dlix, dlxii, dcv.
Fiacc, bishop of Sleibhte, *i.* xlvii; *ii.* 74.
Fiach, son of Dubhthach's sister, *ii.* 339.
„ Araidhe, king of Ulster, *ii.* 17.
„ brother of Niall, *ii.* 388.
„ Finnailghes, *ii* 7.
„ Mac Conga, *iii.* 328.
„ Mac Fir Aba, *ii.* 363, 364.
„ Muillethan, *ii.* 18, 57, 65, 213, 278, 375
„ son of Eochad Muighmheadhoin, *ii.* 102.
„ son of Niall, *ii.* 60, 220.
„ Sraibtine, Sraipthine, *i.* dcxxxix; *ii.* 152, 153, 386; *iii.* 386.
„ Suidhe, *ii.* 205.
„ tutor of Conal Gulban, *ii.* 161.
Fiacha Finnfolaidh, *i.* xxv.
„ Finscothach, *ii.* 11.
Fiachaig, *iii.* 95.
Fiachna, *iii.* 95.
„ king of West Munster, *ii.* 90.
„ son of Baetan, king of Ulster, *ii.* 55, 155.
„ "The Festive", Ard Righ, *ii.* 79, 80, 106, 107.
Fiachnadh Finnolaidh, *i.* xxv, xxvi, xxix, xxx.
Fiachra, son of Eochad, Muidhmedhan, *i.* cccxxi, cccxxiii; *ii.* 102, 147.
„ son of Nadruig, *iii.* 61.
„ son of Niall, *ii.* 161.
„ tutor of Conal Gulban, *ii.* 375.
Fing, *ii.* 9.
Fiamain Mac Forai, *ii.* 369.
Fianlugh, *ii.* 250.

Fidad, *i.* cccxx.
Fidba Mac Fo-Chraebhaig, i.e. Hatched, son of Tree Cutter, *ii.* 133.
Fidfech, *i.* xxv.
Fidgabhla, *iii.* 539.
Fidgarb, *iii.* 377.
Figulus, *i.* dcxxxv.
Finan, Bishop, *ii.* 82.
Findabar, Findabair, daughter of Medb, *i.* cccii, cccliii, cccclxxxi; *ii.* 293, 302, 306; *iii.* 10, 101, 181, 221. 323, 367, 382, 415, 419, 435, 443, 457.
Find Mac Cumhaill, *i.* ccxliv, cccxlii, ccccxxxiv; *ii.* 12, 45, 166, 169, 175, 176, 179, 182, 222, 223, 283, 305, 323, 324, 328, 388; *iii.* 52, 59, 82, 99, 209, 210, 227, 283, 284, 295, 354, 360, 361, 366, 376, 377, 378, 379, 380, 381, 382, 383, 385, 386, 387, 392, 393.
Find Mac Rossa, king of Leinster. *ii.* 199.
Fingal, Earl of, *i.* cclxxix.
Finghin, *i.* cclxxii.
„ Mac Luchta, king of Munster, *ii.* 31; *iii.* 201, 202, 466.
Fingin Fathliag, physician, *iii.* 97, note 59; *ii.* 318.
„ Mac Rudhraidhe, *ii.* 374.
„ poet, *ii.* 83, 85, 343.
Fink, Dr. H., *i.* dlix, dcxix.
Finn, king of Leinster, *ii.* 53.
„ see Find Mac Cumhaill.
„ Mac Cumhaill, see Find Mac Cumhaill.
„ Ua Baiscne, see Find Mac Cumhaill.
Finn-Abhair, see Findabair.
Finnachta, Ard Righ, *iii.* 309.
„ "the Festive", see Fiachna.
Finnargam, *i.* cccclviii.
Finnbar, *ii.* 76. 90.
Finnbruinne, *iii.* 361.
Finnchadh, *iii.* 61.
Finnchaomh, poet.
Finnchas, *iii.* 361.
Finne, son of Cormac Cas.
Finnen, St., *ii.* 71, 76, 80.
„ of Magh Bile, *ii.* 52, 159.
Finnia of Magh Bile, St., *ii.* 52. See Finnen
Finnian, St., *iii.* 310.
Finn-Inghean, *iii.* 361.
Finntan, son of Bochra, *i.* xcvi, cccclviii; *ii.* 52, 183; *iii.* 59, 60, 61, 241, 242.
„ father of Cethern, *ii.* 59, 314.
Fisher, Dr., *iii.* 342.
Fithal, Judge, *i.* ccccxxxiv.
„ the Wise, *ii.* 22, 45, 51, 52, 133, 322, 323.
Fitzgeralds of Kildare, *iii.* 294.
Flaithbertach, *ii.* 98.
„ O'Neill, *ii.* 156.
Flaithchins, "the valiant", *ii.* 386.
Flaithri, son of Fithal, *ii.* 22.
Fland, son of Eochad Abrad-Ruaidh, *ii.* 283, 284: *iii.* 377.
„ from the Slopes of Latharn, *iii.* 377.
„ Mac Lonain, *iii.* 244.
Flangus, *ii.* 70, 71.
Flann Abra, Lord of Gabra, *ii.* 97.
„ Mac Lonain, *ii.* 98, 99, 100.
„ Mainistrech *ii.* 89, 113, 140, 149 to 169: *iii.* 9, 210.
„ of Buite. See Flann Mainistrech.
„ Sinna, or Sionna, *i.* cccxxvii; *ii.* 97, 98, 104, 146, 148.
Flannagan, son of Ceallach, *ii.* 95, 96, 97.
Flannan, St., *ii.* 76.
Flidas Foltchain, *ii.* 333: *iii.* 203, 204.
Flore and Blanscheflur, *i.* ccci
Florus, *i.* cccclxxvii.
Flos, a druid, *ii.* 184.
Flotow, *i.* dcxiii.
Fochlachan, *ii.* 171.
Fochlainn, *i.* cccxlv.
Fochmorc, *ii.* 184.
Fodhla, one of the names of Ireland personified, *ii.* 8, 71.
Fogartach, *ii.* 96.
Foich, *i.* cccxlv.
Foill, eldest son of Nechtan Scene, *ii.* 292.
Foirsem, *i.* cccclviii.
Folloman, son of Concobar Mac Nessa, *iii.* 196.
Fonnam, *i.* cccclviii
Fontenay, M. de, *i.* lxiv.
Forann, *i.* dcxxxix.
Forcul, charioteer to Conaire Mór, *iii.* 183.
Ford, William, musician, *i.* dciii.
Forgal Manach, *ii.* 195, 368: *ii.* 20, 122
Forkel, *i.* dxxxviii.
For Sai, one of Conaire's poets, *iii.* 184.
Fothadh, Fothaid, *i.* ccccxxxiv; *iii.* 174.
„ Airgteach, Airgdech *iii.* 174, 175, 176.
„ na Canoine, *ii.* 61, 95, 175, 176.
Fortchern, St, *ii.* 166.

Fraech Mac Fidaid, *i.* xxii, dcxli, dcxlii; *iii.* 10, 11, 23, 57, 58, 181, 219, 220, 221, 222, 367, 382.
Fraechan, son of Sanasan, *ii.* 343.
Franciscus Bossinensis, *i.* dlxi.
Francon of Cologne, *i.* dliv, dlv, dlvi.
Franks, Mr., *i.* ccccl xiv.
Frecul, charioteer, *iii.* 183.
Frigrind, *ii.* 153; *iii.* 10.
Frigrinn. See Frigrind.
Frisch, *i.* ccccl xxiii.
Frithiof, *i.* cclv.
Fuaimnech, daughter of Conn, *ii.* 30.
Fuaman, *i.* cccclxxix.
Fuatach, poet, *ii.* 51.
Fubtaire, king of Scotland, *ii.* 153.
Fuentes, Mariano Soriano, *i.* dxxiv.
Fulartach, poet, *iii.* 313, 581.
Fullon, druid, *ii.* 204.
Furbaide, or Furbaid Ferrbeann, son of Concobar Mac Nessa, *i.* cccxxxvi, ccclxi; *ii.* 290, 291, 333; *iii.* 19.
Fursa, St., *iii.* 66.
Gabhlan, *iii.* 15.
Gabran, *i.* cccclviii.
Gabrieli, Giovanni, *i.* dlxi, dlxiii.
Gaiar, *i.* cccxxxiv.
Gaibniu the Smith, *ii.* 246. See Goibniu.
Gall, St., *i.* xvi, lvi.
Gallilei Vincenzio, *i.* dxix.
Ganfael, *i.* xxxvii, xxxviii.
Gann, *i.* dcxxxvii.
Gar, *i.* dcxxxviii.
Garad, *ii.* 386.
Garb, *i.* cccclviii.
Garban, or Garbhan, *iii.* 9, 15, 73.
Garcia, king of Navarre, *i.* dxxii.
Garman, *ii.* 40, 44, 46; *iii.* 527, 528.
Garnett, Rev. R., *i.* li, liv.
Gartnan, *i.* ccclxxiv.
Geide Ollgothach, *iii.* 9, 306.
Geijer, Prof., *i.* clxx.
Geine, *ii.* 386.
Geminiani, *i.* dxciv, dcix.
Genand, *i.* dcxxxviii.
Gentraighe, *iii.* 220, 221.
George III., *i.* clxxxiv.
Gerard, *i.* ccclxxxii.
Gerbert, *i.* cccexc, d, diii, dv, dviii, dxx, dxxi, dxxxvii, dxliv, dxlix.
Gereind, *iii.* 94.
Gerg, *i.* ccclxxii, ccclxxiii; *iii.* 307.
Gerhard, E., *i.* cccclxxxix.
Germaine, or Germanus, St., *i.* xlvii, dcxliv.
German, *iii.* 459.
Gersdorf, *i.* cxlvii.
Gerson, *i.* cccexci.
Gildas, *i.* cccexxxvi.
Gilla Brighde Albanach, or Mac Connidhe, *iii.* 270.
Giolla Caeimhghin, *ii.* 222.
Giraldus Cambrensis, *i.* cccc..., ccccxcviii, dxxxi, dcviii, dcxxiv; *ii.* 226, 228.
Glacedh, *i.* cccclviii.
Glan, cup-bearer, *iii.* 43.
Glangein, son of Seich, *ii.* 322.
Glareanus, *i.* dxx, dlxxix, dlxxx, ...
Glas Mac Cais, *ii.* 211.
Glass Donn, *ii.* 377.
Glas Gamhna, *ii.* 288.
Glei, cup-bearer, *iii.* 43.
Gleisi, cup-bearer, *iii.* 43.
Gluck, *i.* lviii.
Glück, *i.* dlx.
Glum, *i.* cccxciii.
Gnathach, a druid, *ii.* 187.
Gno Beg, son of Lugad Delbaeth, *ii.* 220.
„ Mor, do., *ii.* 220, 221.
Gobban Saer, *iii.* 34 to 36, 39 to ..., 44, 45.
Göbel, Prof., *i.* ccccxviii, ccccxix.
Götelinde, *i.* dxxvii.
Goibniu, the smith, *ii.* 248; *iii.* 40.
„ son of Lurgnech, *i.* ccccxxxii.
Goll, *iii.* 15.
„ Mac Morna, *ii.* 377.
Gollamh or Milesius, *ii.* 94.
Golltraighe, *iii.* 220, 221.
Gombert, *i.* dlx.
Gomer, *iii.* 203.
Gomm, *i.* dliii.
Gormlaith, *ii.* 104.
Gortigern, a British king, *i.* cccxxxiii, cccxxxiv, cccxxxv; *ii.* 222.
Gortniat, *i.* xxiv.
Gottfried of Strasburg, *i.* xxxi..., ccclliii, dlii.
Goudimel, Claude, musician, *i.* dl..., dlx, dlxiii.
Graham, M. G. Farquahar, *i.* dxvii.
Graves, Dr., Bishop of Limerick, *i.* lxvi.
Greene, Dr., musician, *i.* dcxxiv.
Gregory, St., the Great, Pope, *i.* dxlvii, dxlviii, dlxvii, dcxxx..., dcxxxii.
„ XIII., Pope, *i.* cxlix.
Grellan, or Greallan, St., *iii.* 84.
Gressach, a smith, *ii.* 338.
Grewingk, C., *i.* ccccxxix.
Griffith, Sir Richard, *ii.* 267, 2..., 269, 271.

Grimm, Jacob, *i.* ix, lix, lx, lxxvi, ciii, civ, cv, cxlvi, cxlviii, clvii, ccxv, ccxxxvi, cccclxiv, cccclxxiii, ccccxcix.
„ the Brothers, *i.* ccoclviii.
Grivaud de la Vincelle, *i.* coclxxxi, cccxci.
Gruasalt, *i.* cccclviii.
Gruffydd ab Cynan; also Gruffyth ap Conan, Griffith ap Conon, *i.* ccxliv, ccccxci, ccccxciii, dcxxiv, dcxxv, dcxxvii, dcxxviii; *iii.* 227, 353, 354.
Gruibo, *i.* xxiv, xxv.
Guairé, "the hospitable", king of Connaught, *ii.* 87, 88, 150; *iii.* 235, 334, 356, 376, 379.
„ Gull (i.e. Oisin, son of Find), *ii.* 283, 284.
Guden, *i.* cxlvii.
Guerard, *i* cxlvii.
Guhl, E. and Koner, W., *i.* ccoclxxxix.
Guido d'Arezzo, *i.* dlii, dcxxx; *iii.* 226.
Guillaume de St. Pair, *i.* dxxvii, dliii.
„ Le Breton, *i.* ccccxliv.
Guizot, M., *i.* cv, cxxxii, clxvii, clxviii.
Gunhild, mother of Harold Grafeld, *i.* ccxcvi.
Gunnat, son of Succat, *ii.* 40; *iii.* 527.
Guornemet, *i.* cclxiv.
Guthar, Guthor, *ii.* 218.
Hagny, *i.* lxxv.
Hakon Jarl, *i.* cccclxxi.
Halthaus, *i.* ccxxix.
Hampson, Mr. R. T., *i.* ccli, cclxx, cclxxxviii.
„ Denis, harper, *iii.* 294, 295.
Hanssen, *i.* cli.
Hardiman, James, *ii.* 118, 125; *iii.* 65.
Hardinge, Mr. W. H, *i.* xcviii, xcix.
Hawkins, Sir John, *i.* ccccxcvii, dcxxxi.
Haxthausen, von, *i.* cxlix, cli.
Haydn, musician, *i.* dcxii.
Hearne, *i.* ccccxcvi.
Heinrich von Veldeck, *i.* cccliii.
„ Isaak, musician, *i.* dlix.
Helen, *i.* iii.
Helenus, *i.* cccclxxii.
Helmholtz, Prof., *i.* dlxiii, dlxvi, dlxxix, dcxix.
Hendrik van Ghizeghem, *i.* dlviii.
Hengist, *i.* vi, xxxiv.
Hennessy, Mr. W. M., *i.* dcxliii.
Henry I., *i.* ccii.
Henry II., *iii.* 267.
„ III., *iii.* 268, 276.
„ VI., *i.* cclxxxvii.
„ VIII., *i.* clxxxiv; *iii.* 267, 269, 274, 276, 286.
Hercules, *i.* ii.
Heremon, *iii.* 537. See Eremon.
Herraud, *i.* dcxxxvi.
Hickes, *i.* cclxxiv.
Hieronymus de Moravia, *i.* dxxv, dxxix.
Hilary, St., *i.* dx.
Hincmar, *i.* ccxi, ccxii.
Hior Halfson, *i.* lxxv.
Hitchcock, Mr. R., *i.* cccvii.
Hobrecht, Jacob, musician, *i.* dlix.
Hodson, Sir George T. J. *iii.* 296.
Holtzmann, Prof., *i.* lxxv.
Homer, *i.* ccccx.
Honorius, *i.* xliv, xlv.
Horsa, *i.* xxxiv.
Horsley, *i.* xxi.
Houard, M., *i.* ccii.
Houghton, *i.* ccclxxvi.
Howel Dha, *i.* cclxvi.
Hrafn, *i.* lxxiv.
Hrolf Sturlungsson, *i.* lxxiv.
Hrothgar, king, *i.* ccxxxvii.
Hucbald, *i.* dli, dlii.
Hugdietrich, romance of, *i.* ccci.
Hugues de Méry, *i* dxxviii
Hŷmir, *i.* ccclxxii.
Iarbonel, son of Nemid, *ii.* 184.
Iargas, son of Umor, *ii.* 122.
Iarlaithe or Jarlath, St., *ii.* 77.
Ibar, bishop, *iii.* 45.
„ charioteer, *ii.* 292, 364, 365.
Idland, *ii.* 386.
Ilbreac, *iii.* 366.
Ilbreachtach, a harper, *ii.* 99, 100.
Iliach, son of Cas, *ii.* 314.
Ilian, *iii.* 14.
Illand, Illan, son of Fergus, *i.* ccccxlvi; *iii.* 98.
Ilsuanach, *ii.* 371.
Imchell, *iii.* 9, 73.
Indai, *iii.* 9.
Indiu, son of Echtach, *iii.* 355.
Ine, *i.* ccxiii.
Inell, *i.* cccxlv.
Ingcel, *i.* xx; *iii.* 136, 137, 138, 139, 140, 141, 142, 143, 144, 145, 146, 147, 148, 149, 150, 151, 183, 184, 186.
Ingeborg, *i.* cclv.
Ingnathach, a druid, *ii.* 187.
Iobath, *ii.* 187.
Iphigenia, *i.* cccxxxiii.
Ir, *ii.* 190; *iii.* 537.
Irgalach, *i.* dcxxxix.

Isaac Jarchi, called Rashi, *i.* dxiv.
Iseult, *i.* xxxix, xlviii.
Isidore, St., *i* ccclxxix, ccclxxxviii, cccexlv, d, div, dxii, dxxxv, dxlvii, dxlix, dli.
Ismail Sahib, *i.* dcxxxvi.
Ite, St., *ii.* 85.
Ith, *iii.* 88.
Iubal, *iii.* 236.
Iuchadan, *ii.* 5; *iii.* 88, 211.
Iuchar, a chief druid, *ii.* 187.
,, son of Tuirend, *i.* cccexxxii.
Iucharba, *i.* cccexxxii; *ii.* 187.
Jacini, *i.* clix.
James I., *i.* cccciii.
,, ,, of Scotland, *i.* dcxxii, dcxxiii.
Japhet, *ii.* 184.
Jason, *i.* ccoclxxxviii.
Jean du Roy, or Regis, musician, *i.* dlviii.
Jerome, St., *i.* xxxi, xxxiii, cccexc, dcxliv.
Jocelyn, *ii.* 165, 166.
John, St., *iii.* 288.
John, *i.* dlxvii, dcxxxi.
,, XXII., Pope, *i.* dlxvi.
,, of Salisbury, *i.* dxxxvi.
,, Scotus Erigena, *i.* dl, dli.
Jones, Rev. W. B., *i.* xxxvii, xl, xlviii.
,, Edward, *i.* cccexciii.
,, Sir William, *i.* xlviii, l.
Jornandes, *i.* lxxxviii.
Joseph, son of Jacob, *i.* ccoclxxxiv.
,, St., *ii.* 92.
Josephus, *i.* dviii, dxi.
Josquin de Près, *i.* dlviii, dlix, dlx, dlxii.
Joy, Mr. Henry, *iii.* 290.
Joyce, Dr. P. W., *i.* dxcvi.
Judenkunig, Hans, *i.* dcxxx, dcxxxii.
Julius Caesar, *i.* ccviii. See Cæsar.
,, Capitolinus, *i.* cccxcii.
Jumilhac, Dom, *i.* dxlvii.
Jupiter, *i.* iii.
Juvenal, *i.* ccclxxx, cccxc, cccxci.
Karamsin, *i.* cl.
Keating, Rev Dr. G. *i.* xxvi, xxx, xlvii, ccxliv, cccxxv, cccxxx, cccxxxi, cccxxxii, cccxl, cccexlv; *ii.* 12, 14, 15, 19, 25, 38, 64, 65, 71, 78, 113, 114, 257, 354, 377, 378, 379, 380, 382; *iii.* 89, 172, 215, 231, 240, 255, 340, 369.
Kelly, Cormac, *iii.* 294.
,, John, *iii.* 295.
Kemble, J. Mitchell, *i.* lxxix, cxxxvii, cxl, cxlii, cxlvii, clxxix, ccii, ccxvii, ccxviii; *ii.* 247, 270, 271.
Kiaran, St., *i.* xvii. See Ciaran.
Kircher, Father, *i.* dxvi.
Kluber, *i.* ciii, civ.
Kopp, *i.* ccclxxxv.
Krug, *i.* cl.
Kruse, Prof., *i.* cccexxix.
Labbe, *i.* cccciv.
Labhraidh, see Labrad.
Labrad, *i.* cccxxii, cccxxxiv; *iii.* 243.
,, Loingsech, *i.* iii, xxi, cccexliv; *ii.* 9, 43, 44, 47, 51, 71, 196, 197, 256, 259, 261, 295; *iii.* 192, 242, 243, 244, 249, 541, 547.
Labraid, see Labrad.
Lachtna, *iii.* 24.
Lacomblet, *i.* cxlvii.
Lacroix, *i.* dxv.
Ladcend, son of Barced, *ii.* 69, 70, 173, 286, 287.
Ladcuin Mac Barceda, see Ladcend.
Ladra, *iii.* 59.
Laech Liathmhuim, *ii.* 183.
Laeg, *i.* cccxc, cccexxxvi, cccexlvi, ccoclxxxiii; *ii.* 197, 297, 298, 299, 308, 309, 310, 358, 373; *iii.* 97, 186, 187, 188, 192, 447, 449, 451, 453, 455, 457, 461.
Laegh, see Laeg.
Laeghaire Buadach, *i.* ccclxii, cccexxxvi, ccoclxvi, ccoclxix, ccoclxx, ccoclxxi; *ii.* 75, 76, 77, 315, 358, 373; *iii.* 19, 21, 93, 314.
,, Lorc, *i.* xxi.
,, Mac Neill, *ii.* 14, 25, 29, 30, 52, 60, 66, 67, 72, 75, 150, 166, 201, 202, 333, 338; *iii.* 24, 37, 160, 187, 202, 203.
,, of the mantles, *ii.* 339.
,, son of Luchta Laimhfinn, *iii.* 202.
Laidcend. See Ladcend.
Laidcenn, son of Baircead. See Ladcend.
Laidech, *ii.* 183.
Laigsech of the large head, son of Conall, *ii.* 43, 44; *iii.* 374.
,, son of Conall Cendmor, *iii.* 541.
Laind, *iii.* 377.
Laing, Capt., *i.* cccexcv.
Laitheog, poetess, *ii.* 98.
Lamec Bigamus, *iii.* 236.
Lampadius, Prof., *i.* cccexv.
Lampridius, *i.* ccviii.
Langethal, *i.* cli.
Lanigan, Rev. Dr., *ii.* 68, 75.
Lappenberg, *i.* cccexcii.
Larcom, Sir T. A., *i.* xcvi, cxix.
Lear, *ii.* 142.

Le Grand d'Aussy, *i.* cccxlix, ccclxxvii.
Ledwich, Dr., *i.* dxxxvi.
Leete [*recte* Leeves], Rev. Mr., *i.* dcxxii.
Leibnitz, *i.* lxiii.
Leine Inghen Lin Ghuirt, i.e. Shirt, daughter of Flax-field, *ii.* 133.
Lein Linfhiaclach, *iii.* 202, 203. See Len.
Leite, *ii.* 320.
Lemaire, *i.* cccexciv.
Len, Lena, son of Mesred, or Mesroed, *ii.* 40, 311; *iii.* 527, 530.
Len Inghen Lamhthoraidh, i.e. Linen, daughter of Handwork, *ii.* 133.
Len Linfhiaclach, *iii.* 203, 204. See Leîn.
Lendabar, Lendabair, wife of Conall Cearnach, *i.* cccliii; *iii.* 19.
Lenihan, M. Maurice, *i.* cccclxvii.
Lenormant and De Witte, *i.* cccclxxxvii.
Leo, St., *iii.* 67.
Le Play, *i.* ccccxiv.
Lepsius, Prof., *i.* cccclxxxv.
Lesan Mac Dagh-Shuaithe, i.e Bag, son of Good Yarn, *ii.* 133.
Lesbothemis, *i.* cccclxxxvii.
Leschner, *i.* ccccxv.
Lescurel Jehannot, *i.* dlix.
Lettenhoven, M. Kervyn de, *i.* ccxii.
Levey, R. M., Mr., *i.* dcii, dcxv.
Lhoyd, or Lloyd, Humphry, *i.* ccccxcii, ccccxciii; *iii.* 353.
Lhwyd, R., *i.* ccccxcii.
Liath of Doire Leith, *iii.* 404.
,, son of Celtchair, *iii.* 355, 356.
Liathan, *i.* xxxviii, xxxix.
Liban, wife of Labrad, *ii.* 196, 197.
Lindas, *i.* ccclxxxii; *iii.* 146.
Lindenschmidt, *i.* ccccxxxviii, ccccxxxix.
Lir, or Lear, *ii.* 325.
Liruti, *i.* ciii, cvi.
Livy, *i.* ccclxxxviii.
Llewelyn, Prince of Wales, *i.* clxxvii.
Llwyd, or Lhuyd, Edward, *i.* xxxvii, xlviii; *iii.* 172.
Loarn, king of Alba or Scotland, *ii.* 156, 287.
Lobel, *i.* cviii.
Lobineau, Dom Alexis, *i.* lxiii.
Locar, Lochar the Swift, *ii.* 40; *iii.* 527.
Loccenius, *i.* ccxxvii.
Loch, *i.* cccclxxiv; *iii.* 195, 196.
Loch Mor Mac Morfebis [Mofemis, or Emonis], *ii.* 369.
Lodan, son of Lir, or Lear, *ii.* 142.
Lodtmann, *i.* cxlvi
Loeghaire Buadach, *i.* ccclvii. See Laeghaire.
Loimdha Mac Lomthogha, [*recte*, Lamhdha Mac Lamhthoga] i.e. Handwork, son of Choice Hands, *ii.* 133.
Loingsech, Ard Righ, *ii.* 25.
Loki, Logi, son of Nâl, *i.* ccccxlvii.
Loman, *ii.* 166.
Lommon, *i.* ccxl, ccxli.
Lomna, *ii.* 209, 210.
Long, *i.* dcxxxviii.
Longuemar, M. de, *i.* lxvi.
Long Mac Emonis, *iii.* 101.
Lorcan, king of Munster, *ii.* 98.
Lorcan, of the vows, *iii.* 394.
Lorga, a druid, *ii.* 279, 280, 281, 282.
Lorgach, Largach, *ii.* 40; *iii.* 527.
Lort, *i* dcxxxviii.
Lothar, or Lothor, son of Eochad Feidhlech, *ii.* 145, 146, 262, 263, 276, 277.
Lottner, Prof., *i.* lxv, lvi.
Louis le Debonnaire, *i.* ccxi, ccxiv.
Loyset Compère, *i.* dlviii, dlix, dlxii.
Luan, *iii.* 373.
Luath Mac Derera, *i.* xxiv.
Lucan, *i.* cccclxxviii.
Luchta, son of Luchad, *ii.* 199; *iii.* 42.
Luchtaine, *ii.* 246, 249.
Lucretius, *i.* ccccxc.
Lug, *i.* cccxxvii.
„ Laeban, or Laibach, son of Cacher, *ii.* 39, 42; *iii.* 527, 533.
„ or Lugad Mac Eithlenn, or Ethlend, *i.* ccccxxxii, ccccxlvi, ccccxlvii, cccclxvi; *ii.* 110, 225, 248, 251, 252, 288, 324, 325; *iii.* 40, 41, 42, 43, 213.
,, son of Cian, *ii.* 131, 132, 148.
Lugad Delbaeth, *ii.* 219, 220, 221, 226.
,, Laga, *ii.* 140; *iii.* 156, 177.
,, Lamfhind, *ii.* 355.
„ Lamh-fada, *ii.* 356; *iii.* 41, 42.
„ Laigsech, *ii.* 43, 44; *iii.* 459.
„ Luaighne, or Laighne, *ii.* 7, 274.
,, Mac Con, son of Mac Nia, *iii.* 259.
„ Mal, *i.* cccxxxvi.
,, "Master of all the arts", *ii.* 131.
„ Reo Derg, *ii.* 196, 198, 199, 200.
„ Riabh-Derg, *ii.* 367, 374.
,, son of Ith, *iii.* 88.

Lugad, son of Laeghaire, *iii.* 67.
,, son of Nuadad, *i.* dcxxxvii
,, son of Seal Balb, *i.* ccexxvii.
,, son of Temnen, *iii.* 207.
Lugar, son of Lugad, king of Munster, *ii.* 356.
Lugard, *ii.* 986.
Lughaidh. See Lugad.
Lughna Firtri, *ii.* 375.
Luigech, a poet, *ii.* 51.
Luitprand, *i.* clx.
Lupat or Lupait, *iii.* 122.
Lupus, *i.* dlx, dcxliv.
Lurc, *i.* dcxxxviii.
Lurgnech, *i.* ccccxxxii.
Luscinius, Ottomarus, *i.* dcxxxi.
Lynch, Dr. John, "Gratianus Lucius", *i.* xxiii, xxvi; *ii.* 32.
Mabillon, *i.* dxxiii, dcxliv.
Mac Adam, Mr. R., *iii.* 347.
,, Aibhlin, St., *iii.* 332.
,, Aingis, *i.* dxxiii; *iii.* 259, 260.
,, an Bhaird, Diarmat, *iii.* 265.
,, an Daill, *iii.* 257.
,, Brics, *ii.* 284.
,, Buain, *ii.* 311.
,, Carthy, *i.* clxvii.
,, Cecht, *i.* ccccxxxiii; *ii.* 71, 189.
,, Coise, Errard, or Erad, 11, 76, 77, 116, 118, 127 to 135, 139.
,, Con, *i.* xxi, xlii, ccccxxxiv; *ii.* 22, 57, 139, 211, 331,; *iii.* 259, 260, 261.
,, Conglinde, *i.* ccclxxxiv, ccclxxxv, cccxcviii; *iii.* 102 to 106. See Anier Mac Conglinde.
,, Conmidhe, Brian Ruadh, *ii.* 98.
,, ,, Gilla Brighde, *ii.* 162, 163, 164, 165, 166; *iii.* 58, 153, 154, 167, 168, 270, 271, 273, 280, 285, 286.
,, Conrai, *ii.* 221.
,, Cormac, *ii.* 140; *iii.* 44.
,, Creiche, St., *i.* cclxxxix; *iii.* 331, 332.
,, Cridan, Diarmad, *iii.* 292, 293.
,, ,, Giolla Patrick, *iii.* 292, 293.
,, Crimthainn, Feidhlemidh, king of Munster, *iii.* 333.
,, Cuill, *ii.* 71, 188; *iii.* 43.
,, Cuillennain, Cormac, *ii.* 94, 104, 250; *iii.* 217, 241, 255, 388, 389.
,, Cumhaill, Find, see Find Mac Cumhaill.
,, Curtin, Andrew, *i.* ccccxxxiv.
,, Datho, *iii.* 372, 529.
,, Dermot, *iii.* 129; *iii.* 297.
,, Donagh, *ii.* 129.
,, Donald, *i.* dcxxi
Mac Donald, Lord of Clanranald, *iii.* 300.
,, Donnell, Capt. Alex., *iii.* 270.
,, Donnells, Lords of the Isles, *ii.* 282, 285.
,, Donogh, Mr. P., *iii.* 335.
,, Enge *i.* ccccixx; *iii.* 265.
,, Enis. See Magennis.
,, Eochagan, *ii.* 161, 220.
,, Eoghan Ruadh, *ii.* 166.
,, Erachtaigh, Donn óg, *iii.* 25.
,, Erc, *i.* dcxli. See Eochad Mac Erc.
,, Firbis Dudley, *iii.* 15. See Mac Firbisigh, Dubhaltach.
,, Firbisigh or Mac Firbis, Gilla Isa Mór, *ii.* 383.
,, ,, Dubhaltach, or Dud, *i.* 79, 117, 239; *iii.* 15, 16, 201
,, Geoghegan, Abbé, *ii.* 138.
,, Gillapatrick, Donagh, *ii.* 38
,, Gorman, Finn, Bishop of Kildare, *iii.* 169, 408.
,, Greine, *ii.* 71, 189.
,, Guire, *iii.* 169.
,, ,, Hugh, Lord of Fermanagh, *ii.* 392.
,, -in-Egis, *ii.* 339.
,, Iubar, *ii.* 311.
,, Lauchlan, Rev. Thomas, *iii.* 301.
,, Lenene, Colman, *iii.* 245.
,, Liag, *ii.* 93, 116, 117, 118, 119, 120, 121, 122, 124, 126, 140; *iii.* 153.
,, Lonain, *ii.* 96, 98 to 104, 134, 154, 163; *iii.* 253.
,, Loughlin, harper, *iii.* 295.
,, Maelnuire, *iii.* 264.
,, Mahon of Claenach, *iii.* 267, 269, 275.
,, ,, of Monaghan, *ii.* 392.
,, Murdochs of Scotland, *iii.* 301. See Mac Vurrich.
,, Murrich, John, *iii.* 300. See Mac Vurrich.
,, Murrough, Dermot, king of Leinster, *ii.* 107.
,, na g-Cuach, *ii.* 102.
,, Namaras of Clare, *ii.* 10[illegible].
,, Namara, Mr. Commissioner, *iii.* 267, 269, 275.
,, Nessa, see Concobar Mac Nessa.
,, Nia, *iii.* 166, 259.
,, Occ, *i.* ccccixxix.
,, Pherson, *iii.* 413.
,, Ranall, or Reynolds, *ii.* 33.
,, Riagbla, *iii.* 385.
,, Roth, *i.* ccclx; *ii.* 297, 315 to 318; *iii.* 91-97, 98, 314.
,, Sithduill, *iii.* 258.

Mac Solly, John, *ii.* 116, 146, 311.
,, Vurrich, *iii.* 300, 301. See Mac Murdoch.
,, William of Clanrickard.
Maccraith O'Donnchadh, king of Cashel, *iii.* 228.
Macha, daughter of Erumas, *ii.* 187, 251.
,, Mong Ruadh, *ii.* 112, 357; *iii.* 11, 102.
Machaut, Guillaume de, *i.* d, dxx, dxxxii.
Machta, St., *ii.* 77.
Maculloch, *i.* cxlviii
Maedhog, St., of Cluain Mór, or Clonmore, *ii.* 338, 339.
Mael, a druid, *ii.* 72, 201, 202.
Maelbrighde, son of Mothlachan, *ii.* 83, 342.
Mael Coba, Maelchoba, *i.* dcxxxix; *ii.* 55; *iii.* 396, 297.
Maelcrund, *ii.* 386. See Crundmael.
Maeldalua, St., *iii.* 332.
Maeldoran, or O'Muldory, *ii.* 98.
Maelduin, *i.* xxviii, ccciii, ccclvi, ccclvii, ccclviii, ccclxviii; *iii.* 158, 163, 169, 180, 188.
Maelgwyn, *i.* xlviii.
Mael Mac Failbhe, *iii.* 310.
Maelmilscothach, *ii.* 131, 135.
Mael Mór, *ii.* 71.
Maelmordha, *ii.* 335, 336, 347.
Maelmuire, *iii.* 403.
Mael Mura of Fahan, *ii.* 97, 98.
Maelochtair, *ii.* 204, 205, 226.
Maelruan, St., *ii.* 76.
,, St., of Tallaght, *ii.* 85, 175.
Maelruanagh, *ii.* 121.
Maelruanaidh, *ii.* 129.
Maelseachlain, Maelsechlann, *i.* cccxxvii; *ii.* 119, 121, 126, 128, 137, 146, 150, 159, 346.
,, O'Donnell, *ii.* 162.
Maelsuthain, O'Carroll, *ii.* 175, 177
Maelugra, *ii.* 386.
Maen, *ii.* 51.
Maen Mac Etnae, *ii.* 212, 227.
Maffir Thuill, *iii.* 147.
Magach, *ii.* 260; *iii.* 90, 91, 109.
Magennis, *i.* xxv; *iii.* 265, 278.
Maghmor, *i.* cccxxvi; *ii.* 148.
Magnus Berfaeta, *i.* ccclxxxix.
,, Ericson.
Mahon, *ii.* 115, 177, 178.
Maidulph, *i.* dvii.
Maighnean, St., *i.* ccxl, ccli.
Main, *iii.* 243.
Maine, *i.* ccclxxv; *ii.* 342; *iii.* 90.
,, Aithremail, do. *iii.* 100, 101.
Maine Andoe, son of Ailill and Medb, *ii.* 318.
,, Mathremail, do. *iii.* 100, 101.
,, Mor or Muineamhon, *iii.* 84, 178.
,, son of Ailill and Medb, *iii.* 168, 169, 307, 367.
,, son of Durthacht, *iii.* 161.
,, son of Niall, *ii.* 161.
Mainmairic, *ii.* 7.
Mairend Mael, *i.* cccxcv; *iii.* 193, 194.
Mairgen, *ii.* 252, 288, 289.
Maistiu, *iii.* 122.
Mal, *ii.* 51.
Manach, father of Emer, *i.* clxi.
,, Mac Teibaind, *iii.* 140.
,, the jester, *iii.* 150.
Mananand, or Manannan Mac Lir, *i.* xxxviii, cccxxii, cccxxxiv; *ii.* 140, 197, 198 301; *iii.* 40, 192.
Mangan, James Clarence, *ii* 118.
Manogan, *i.* xxxvii.
Maolmuire, son of Celtchair, *iii.* 403.
Maothagan, *i.* cccxxxi.
Marban or Marbhan, *ii.* 88; *iii.* 235, 238, 307, 356, 357, 358, 374, 379.
Marcellus, *i.* xvi, dlxvii. See Moengal.
,, Burdigallensis, *i.* lviii, lix, lx.
Marco Polo, *i.* cccxxii.
Marculfus, *i.* cviii, clxx.
Marcus, *i.* xlv, dlxviii.
Marini, *i.* ccxiv.
Mark, St., *i* dcxliv.
Martial, *i.* ccclxxxviii.
Martin, M. Henri, *i.* cxxxviii.
Mathuloch Gwyddell, *iii.* 227.
Matthew, St., *iii.* 340.
,, of Paris, cccxcii.
Maurer, *i.* cxlv, cxlvi, cxlvii.
Maximian, *i.* xliii.
Maximus, *i.* xliii, xliv.
Meadhbh, see Medb.
Meconn, *iii.* 99.
Mecun, *iii.* 147.
Medb, *i.* xx, xxxii, lxxiii, lxxiv, cccii, cccv, cccxxxvi, cccxxxviii, ccclviii ccclvii, ccclx, ccclxi, ccclxxv, ccclxxx, cccxxii, ccclii, cccliv, cccclxix, cccclxxiv, cccclxxix, cccclxxxi, dcxli; *ii.* 71, 145, 199, 259, 260, 261, 290, 291, 293, 296, 297, 298, 302, 303, 306, 310, 314, 315, 318, 319, 357; *iii.* 10, 11, 74, 89, 90, 91, 98, 101, 102, 106, 109, 110, 195, 196, 220, 221, 307, 314, 338, 372, 400, 401, 402, 415, 417, 419, 423, 427, 435, 443, 445, 449, 455, 458, 495.

Meibomius, *i.* cclxvi.
Mellitus, *i.* dcxxxi, dlxvii.
Memmi, Simone, *i.* dxvi.
Mend or Menn, son of Salcholgan, *ii.* 96, 333.
Mesbuachala, *i.* ccclxx.
Mesc, daughter of Bodbh, *ii.* 40, 44, 46; *iii.* 527, 529.
Mesceagra, son of Datho *iii.* 527.
Mesded, *ii.* 40; *iii.* 529.
Mesdelmon, son of Datho, *ii.* 40; *iii.* 529.
Mesgedhra, king of Leinster, *ii.* 107, 290.
Mesroed, Mesred Misroed, *ii.* 40; *iii.* 371, 529, 530.
Messed, *ii.* 40; *iii.* 529.
Midas, *i.* iii.
Midhe, son of Brath, *ii.* 191, 226.
Midhuil, *iii.* 236.
Midir, *i.* lxxiii, ccci, ccclxix, cccclxxix; *ii.* 71; *iii.* 79, 80, 163, 188, 190, 191, 192, 355, 356.
Milesius, *i.* cccxxxiii; *ii.* 189, 191; *iii.* 232, 240, 241.
Milin, *i.* ccclxxxi.
Milithi, *iii.* 150.
Mobi, St., *ii.* 76, 91.
Mochae, St., of Oendruim, *iii.* 386, 387.
Mochuda, St., of Rathan, *ii.* 204; *iii.* 4, 38.
Modan, see Bodan.
Moengal, or Marcellus, . dlxvii. dlxviii.
Mofemis, *ii.* 9.
Mogcorb, *ii.* 65, 387.
Moghad Neid, *i.* ccccxl.
Mogh Lamha, *i.* cclxiv.
Mogh Ruith, *ii.* 213, 214, 215, 227, 278, 279, 280, 281, 282, 295, 375.
Moke, Prof., *i.* lxxv, ccxii.
Molaise, St. of Damhinis, *ii.* 85.
" " of Leithglinn, *iii.* 34, etc.
Moling, St., *i.* ccclxv; *ii.* 85; *iii.* 34, 36, 39, 45, 309.
Molling, the swift, *ii.* 385.
Mommsen, Prof., *i.* ii. lxv, lxvi.
Monafinn, *ii.* 147.
Mone, *i.* lviii, lix.
Mongan, *i.* cccxlix, cccl; *ii.* 283; *iii* 174, 175, 176.
Monin, M., *i.* lviii, lix, lx, lxii, lxvi.
Monteverde, Claudio, *i.* dlxiv, dlxv.
Montfaucon, *i.* lxiii, ccclxxxi.
Moore, Thomas, *i.* dxci, dxcii, dcxiii, dcxv, dcxvii.
Mophir Rochetuil, *iii.* 184.
Morán, *ii.* 133.
Morand, Moen, see Morann Moen.
" son of Cairbre the stooped, *ii.* 52.
Morann Moen, *i.* xxv, xxvi, xxxii, xxxiii; *ii.* 21, 51, 324; *iii.* 419.
Morc, son of Dela, *ii.* 185.
Morewood, *i.* ccclxxvii.
Morgan, *i.* cccxxxiv.
" John, *i.* ccccxcvii.
Morhault, *i.* xxxix.
Moriath, *iii.* 242, 243, 244, 248, 249, 252.
Mor Mumhan, *ii.* 133.
Morogh, son of Flann Moelseachlainn, *ii.* 151.
Mór Rigán, *ii.* 50, 51, 187, 202.
Mór Rigu, *i.* dcxxxix. See Mór Rigan.
Moser, *i.* cxciv.
Moses, *i.* dlxx, *ii.* 20.
Mothemnioc, St., *i.* ccvii; *iii.* 207, 208.
Mothlachan, *ii.* 342.
Motur, Mothur, son of Largach, *ii.* 40; *iii.* 527.
Mugain, see Mugan.
Mugairne, *iii.* 459.
Mugan, *i.* clxxi; *ii.* 158, 159; *iii.* 193.
Mughain, see Mugan.
Muineamon, Ard Righ, *ii.* 7; *iii.* 178, 211.
Muinremor Mac Gerrcend, *iii.* 93, 94, 140.
Muirceartach Mac Erca, *ii.* 156.
" *ii.* 162.
" king of Meath, *ii.* 159.
" son of Muiredhach, *ii.* 156.
" son of Niall, *ii.* 105, 134, 135; *iii.* 25.
Muired, *i.* dcxxxix.
Muiredach Albanach O'Daly, of Lis an Doill, or Lissadill, *iii.* 280, 281, 282, 284, 285, 300, 301.
" Meann, *ii.* 375.
" son of Eoghan, *ii.* 130.
Muirenn, *ii.* 343.
Muirenn Mael, *ii.* 343.
Muiresg, *ii.* 71.
Muirin, *iii.* 224.
Muirn Molbthach, *ii.* 276.
Muirni Muncaem [Nom. Muirin], *i.* ccccxxii.
Müller, Johann von, *i.* ciii.
" Prof. Max, *i.* ix.
Munch, Prof., *i.* lxxxi, lxxxii, cccxl, cccxix.
Munnu, *ii.* 51.
Munremur, see Muinremor.
Muratori, *i.* cii, cv, ccccxciv.

Murchadh, *ii.* 347.
,, son of Brian Boromha, *ii.* 117, 121, 124, 349, 350, 351.
Murchadh, son of Bran Muite, k. of Leinster, *ii.* 389, 390, 391; *iii.* 311, 312.
Muredach, son of the king of Leinster, *iii.* 149.
Nachtigall, Othmar. See Luscinius.
Nandâ (O. H. G.), goddess, *i.* cccxxxix.
Nanna, wife of Baldr, *i.* cccxxxix.
Nanþo (Goth.), *i.* cccxxxix.
Naoise, see Nois.
Nar, son of Eochad Feidhlech, *ii.* 262.
,, the lady of Badb Derg's mansion. [This was Nar, daughter of the king of Cruitentuath or Pictland, and wife of Crimthan Nia Nair, and should not be confounded with Nar the swine herd to Badb Derg], *iii.* 202.
Natfraech, k. of Munster, *ii.* 66; *iii.* 15.
Nathchrantail, *i.* cccclii.
Nechtan Scene, *ii.* 292, 366.
Necker de Saussure, L. A., *i.* dcxviii.
Neid, chief poet of Ulster, *ii.* 53.
,, son of Adhna, *ii.* 20, 21, 217, 218, 219; *iii.* 315, 316.
,, son of Indai, a Tuatha De Danann god, *ii.* 152; *iii.* 9.
Neidhe, see Neid
Neithe, see Neid.
Nemannach, *iii.* 203.
Nemetona, a goddess, *i.* cclxiv.
Nemid, Neimid, *i.* xxxviii, xxxix, cclxiv, cccxxxix, dcxxxvii; *ii.* 110, 184, 186, 187, 233; *iii.* 3, 231, 232.
Nennius, *i.* xxxviii, cccxxxiii; *ii.* 222.
Neocorus, *i.* ccxviii, ccxix.
Nera or Nere, of Cruachan, *iii.* 199, 200, 201.
,, poet, *ii.* 133.
,, son of Fincholl, *ii.* 52.
,, son of Morann, *ii.* 21, 51, 324.
Nertchu, *ii.* 238, 241.
Ness, *iii.* 514, see Concobar Mac Nessa
Nessa, see Ness.
Nessan, *ii.* 76.
Nia, *iii.* 148.
,, Mór, *ii.* 18.
,, Seghamain, *ii.* 204.
Nial Glundubh, *ii.* 105, 154.
,, O'Ciunn, *ii.* 349.
Niall or Nell, *ii.* 132.
,, of the nine hostages, *i.* xliv. xlv, xlvi, xlvii, xlviii, lxxiii; *ii.* 50, 59, 60, 61, 62, 64, 67, 69, 72, 210, 108, 147, 151, 161, 163, 164, 173, 285, 287, 338, 339, 375, 388; *iii.* 37, 60, 287, 301.
Niaman, goddess of war, *iii.* 419.
Niebuhr, *i.* ii. lxxvii, xciii.
Nigra, Cav. C., *i.* dcxliii.
Ninde, *ii.* 343, see Ninne.
Ninne, *ii.* 342, 344.
Niul, *ii.* 113, 160.
Noenenach, a goddess, *i.* cccxxxiv, cccxxxviii.
Nois, son of Uisnech, *ii.* 333, 358, 369; *iii.* 378
Nonnius Marcellus, *i.* xciii.
Nor, son of Eochad Feidhlech, *ii.* 145, 146.
Nos, *ii.* 288.
,, son of Find, *iii.* 249, 250.
,, son of Sighi, [nom. Sig], *ii.* 221
Noðe (Ang. Sax.), *i.* cccxxxix.
Notker, *i.* ccxxix.
,, Balbulus, *i.* dl, dlxviii.
,, Labeo, *i.* diii, div, dx.
Nowel, Laurence, Dean of Lichfield, *i.* xcix.
Nuada Dearg, *ii.* 375.
,, Fullon, king of Leinster, *ii.* 2[illegible]4, 226.
,, Necht, Ard Righ, *ii.* 53.
,, Tuatha, De Danann King, *i.* ccccliii; *ii.* 236, 237, 239, 242, 246, 251, 333; *iii.* 156, 169.
Nuadat, a druid, *i.* ccciii.
Nuadha. See Nuada.
Numa, *i.* ccviii.
Oc, son of Olloman, *i.* cccxxvii.
Ochall Oichne, *iii.* 156, 157, 158, 174, 179.
Ochand, son of Cnucha, *ii.* 288, 299.
Ochinn, *ii.* 253.
Odin, *i.* cclxv.
Oeca, *iii.* 527. See Osca.
Oedan Mac Gabhrain, *i.* ccclxxiv.
Oengus, *i.* clxxiv. See Aengus.
,, Céle Dé, *i.* ccclxvi. See Aengus.
Oengus, son of the Dagda, *i.* cccxxvii. See Aengus.
Offa, king of Mercia, *i.* cccxxxiv, dcxxvi.
Ogma, son of Eithlinn, *i.* cccxxvii; *iii.* 42, 213; *ii.* 51, 254.
Oilen, *iii.* 15.
Oilioll Flann Beg, *ii.* 65, 67.
,, Flann Mor, *ii.* 65.
,, Olum, *i.* xxv, cclxiv; *ii.* 57, 58, 65, 106, 139, 149, 206, 213, 261, 375; *iii.* 5, 43, 44, 177, 207, 208, 259, 260.
Oisin, son of Find, *i.* cccxxv; *ii.* 57,

283, 387; *iii.* 166, 303, 371, 380, 392, 393.
Okeghem, Johannes, *i.* dlviiii.
Ol, *iii.* 147. Oll, *iii.* 98, 99.
Olaf the peaceful, *i.* cexcvi.
Olar Gerdawwr, harper, *iii.* 227.
Olavius, *i.* ccc.
Olchoi, a harper, *iii.* 147.
Olene, a harper, *iii.* 147.
Olivier de la Marche, *i.* cccexliii.
Ollaig, *iii.* 88.
Ollam, Ollamh, *ii.* 42; *iii.* 527, 533.
Ollamh Fodhla, or Fotla, a name applied to a king called Eochad, *i.* ccxliv, cccxxvii; *ii.* 8, 10, 12, 18, 53.
Olloman, *i.* cccxxvii. See Ollam.
Oluim. See Oilioll Olum.
Olussen, *i.* cli.
Ona, harper, *ii.* 4.
Orcagna, Andrea, *i.* dxv, dxvi.
Orosius, Paulus, *i.* xxxviii, cccxcvii, ccccxlii; *iii.* 329, 330.
Orrdan, *i.* dcxxxvii.
Orpheus, *iii.* 213, 230.
Orus. See Orosius.
Osalt, *i.* ccclxxxi; *iii.* 146.
Osbrit, *i.* ccclxxxi; *iii.* 146.
Osca, king of Certa, *ii.* 10
Oscar, Oscur, son of Oisin, *i.* cccxli, cccxlii; *ii.* 387.
Osirtasen I., *i.* cccclxxxiv.
Othan, *i.* cccxxx.
Othme, *iii.* 99.
Ottfried, *i.* ccxxix.
Ottokar, *i.* dxxvii.
Otway, Captain Robert Jocelyn, *iii.* 294, 295.
Ouranos, *i.* iii.
Ousley, Ralph, *iii.* 269, 275, 342, 343, 344, 345, 346, 347, 349.
,, William, *iii.* 295.
Overbeck, *i.* ccccIxxxix.
Ovid, *i.* ccccIxi, ccccIxxx, cccexc, dxii.
Owen, Aneurin, *i.* cccexciv.
Owens, William, *iii.* 352, 354, 355.
O'Beoghusa [*recte* O'Heogusa], poet to Maguire, *iii.* 169.
O'Briene, his art of poetry, *ii.* 173.
O'Brien, *i.* clxvii.
,, Anthony, *iii.* 392.
,, arms of, *iii.* 268, 277, 283.
,, Brian, uncle of Donnchadh Cairbrech, *iii.* 283.
,, Conor, Earl of Thomond, *iii.* 288, 289.
,, Dermot, *ii.* 167, 168.
,, Domhnall Connachtach, *iii.* 375.
,, Domhnal Mór, king of Munster, *i.* ccclxxxix; *iii.* 153, 271.
O'Brien, Donnchadh Cairbrech, *i.* ccclxxxix; *ii.* 162, 163, 375; *iii.* 153, 154, 270, 271, 272, 273, 274, 280, 281, 282, 283, 284, 286, 299, 301.
,, Donnell, *iii.* 288.
,, Donogh, *iii.* 274, 286.
,, family, harps of, *iii.* 270, 274, 275, 276, 285, 286.
,, Morogh, *iii.* 274, 282.
,, Murchadh, or Morogh, son of Brian O'Brien, *iii.* 282, 283.
,, Torlogh, king of Munster, *ii.* 107.
O'Brothlachain, Finn, steward to O'Donnell, killed by the poet O'Daly, *iii.* 280.
O'Cadhla (or Keely), Bishop Malachius, *iii.* 66.
O'Carroll, *i.* cliv.
,, Maelsuthain, tutor to Brian Borumha, *ii.* 175, 177, 178.
O'Ceirinn Eochadh Eolach, author of the poem on Loch Garman, *ii.* 12, 13, 113, 114.
O'Cethernaighs of Teaffi (called the Foxes), *ii.* 161.
O'Clerigh Diarmait, his school, *ii.* 98.
,, Michael, *ii.* 25, 167; *iii.* 201, 387, 407.
,, or O'Clery, Tadg Cam, his school, *ii.* 98.
O'Clery's Book of Invasions, *iii.* 240, 241.
O'Cluasaigh Colman, *ii.* 90, 92.
O'Cobhthaigh, Tadhg, (or O'Coffey), Dr. Keating's poem on, *iii.* 215.
,, teachers, *ii.* 77.
O'Connells, ancestor of, *ii.* 212.
,, Daniel, *iii.* 181, 293.
,, Maurice, *iii.* 181.
O'Connor, family of, *ii.* 129.
,, Brian Luighnech, *ii.* 375, 376.
,, Cathal Crobh Dearg, *iii.* 23, 301.
,, Charles of Balanagare, *ii.* 138.
,, Clare, *ii.* 85.
,, Connaught, *ii.* 375.
,, Don, *iii.* 264, 270.
,, Dr. Charles, *i.* xxiii, ccccxc; *iii.* 27, 228.
,, Hugh, son of Cathal, *iii.* 23.
,, Kerry, *ii.* 85.
,, Roderick, Ard Righ, *i.* cccxxvii.
,, Torlogh, *ii.* 107.
O'Cronin, *ii.* 215, 216.
O'Cuinn, Niall, *ii.* 349.
O'Curry, Prof., *i.* xx, xxii, xxiii, lxvii, lxx, lxxiii, lxxxviii, xc, xcvi, cclix, cccvi, cccvii, cccviii, cccix, cccxix, ccclxxviii, ccclxxxiii,

cccclxxxiv, ccclxxxv, ccccxli, cccliv, ccclvii, ccccxcv, cccccvii, ccocviii, ccccxxx, ccccxxxvii, ccccxxxviii, ccccxxxix, ccccxlv, ccccxlvi, ccccxlviii, ccccl, cccclii, ccccliv, cccclvi, ccccclxii, ccccclxvii, ccccxci, ccccxcii, ccccciv, dvii, dxiii, dxxviii, dxxx, dxxxvi, dxl, dxli, dcxxxiv; *ii.* 127, 240, 367; *iii.* 101, 207, 240, 292, 330, 418, 465, 466, 512, 523, 524, 525.

O'Daly, Aengus Finn, *ii.* 143, 144.
„ Donchadh Mór, *iii.* 301.
„ Muireadhach, *iii.* 280, 281, 282, 284, 285, 300, 301. See Muiredach Albanach.

O'Davoren, *iii.* 215, 252, 322, 380.
O'Dempseys, *i.* cliv.
O'Deorain, Edmund, *iii.* 364.
O'Donnell, *i.* clxvii; *ii.* 161, 164, 166; *iii.* 194.
„ Conn, *ii* 162.
„ Domhnal Oge, *iii.* 281, 282.
„ Donnell Mór, *iii.* 280, 281, 282, 283, 284.
„ Neachtan, *ii.* 98.
„ Red Hugh, *ii.* 166.
„ Sir Richard, *iii.* 289.

O'Donnghaile, or O'Donnelly, *iii.* 265, 329, 357, 364.
O'Donovan, Dr. John, *i.* xxiii, xxvi, xxviii, xcii, xcvi, xcviii, cclxxiv, ccclxxxviii, ccceiii; *ii.* 77, 127, 137, 138; *iii.* 465.
O'Doyne, *i* cliv.
„ Teige, chief of O'Regan, *i.* xcvi.
O'Duban, *ii* 146.
O'Dubhagain, or O'Duvegan, Seann Mór, *ii.* 59, 65, 124, 354.
O'Dubhdabhoirenn, or O'Davoren, Domhnall, *iii.* 322.
O'Dugan, *i.* xxviii; *ii.* 215, 216.
O'Falveys, *ii* 212.
O'Ferrall, *ii.* 85.
O'Flaherty, Roderick, *i.* ccccxxxix; *ii.* 63, 64, 65, 66, 68, 256–259, 354; *iii* 65, 231.
O'Flanagan, Theophilus, *iii.* 330.
O Flinn, Eochadh, *ii.* 110, 111, 113.
O'Gara, *ii.* 140.
O'Gilligan, *iii.* 287, 289.
O'Glinn, Ferflatha, *iii.* 264.
O'Gorman, the Chevalier Thomas, *iii.* 267, 269, 270, 274, 275.
O'Grady, Mr. Standish H., *iii.* 301.
O'Griobtha (or Griffin), *ii.* 86.
O'Halloran, Dr., *iii.* 207, 290.
O'Hara of Sligo, *ii.* 140.
„ „ Leyney, *ii.* 376.

O'Hartagan, Cinneadh, *ii.* 107, 108, 325, 377, 378; *iii.* 6.
O'h-Eimhin, *iii.* 397, 398, 399.
O'h'-Eogusa, Eochadh, *iii.* 25.
O'Higgin, teachers, *ii.* 77.
„ Brian, *iii.* 282, 283.
O'Kelly, *ii.* 336; *iii.* 84.
„ Denis H., *ii.* 15.
„ Donnchadh Muimhnech, and Donnchadh Cennieelach, *ii.* 376.
„ Tadg, *ii.* 115, 122, 126, 127, 143, 153, 392.
O'Lochain, *ii.* 139. See O'Lothchain.
O'Lomthuile, Nuadha, poet, *ii.* 391.
O'Looney, Mr. Brian, *i.* cclxxxix, ccexviii, ccexxix, ccccxxxiv, dxxiv; *iii.* 466.
O'Lothchains of Meath, *ii.* 140.
O'Lothchain, Cuan, poet, *ii.* 137, 139, 140, 141, 142, 144, 145, 147, 148, 149, 378; *iii.* 6, 12, 525.
O'Loughlin of Clare, *ii.* 85.
O'Maelchonaire, Tornaidhe, *ii.* 237, 241.
O'Maelseachlainn, *ii.* 161; *iii.* 24.
„ Flann, *ii.* 151.
O'Maighlind, *iii.* 381.
O'Meachair of Tipperary, *ii.* 140.
O'Melachlainn, *iii.* 340.
O'Moradh, or O'Moore of Leix, *ii.* 374.
O'Mulchonry, teachers, *ii.* 77.
„ Tornaidhe, poet, *ii.* 237.
O'Mulloy, *ii.* 161, 220.
O'Neill, sept of, or Cinel Eoghain, *iii.* 268, 277, 278, 301.
„ *i.* clxvii; *ii.* 25.
„ Aedh, king of Ulster, *ii.* 126.
„ Arthur, harper, *iii.* 268.
„ Domhnall, Ard Righ, *ii.* 130, 131, 132, 133, 134, 135, 154.
O'Nemhain, Coel, *iii.* 379.
O'Reardons of Tipperary, *ii.* 140.
O'Reilly, Edward, *ii.* 32, 86, 98, 99, 104, 105, 108, 113, 115, 128, 137, 138, 145, 150, 158, 159, 162, 163, 164, 165, 166, 167; *iii.* 247, 331, 384, 466.
O'Ruairc of Breifney, *ii.* 129.
„ Fergal, *ii.* 129, 130, 392.
„ Teige, *iii.* 292.
O'Shea, *ii.* 212.
O'Sochlachain, Aedh, son of Donslebhe, *iii.* 264.
O'Sullivan, *i.* clxvii.
Palacky, *i.* cxlix, cl.
Palestrina, *i.* dlvi, dlviii' dlx, dlxiii, dlxxxvi.
Palgrave, Sir Francis, *i.* xxxiv, cxxxiv, cxcviii, cxcix, cc, ccii, ccv,

cccxl, cccxli, cccxliv, cccxlix, cccxc.
Pani, *i.* iii.
Paris, *i.* iii.
Parry, Mr. John, *i.* dcxxvi, dcxxix.
Parthalon, or Partholon, *ii.* 50, 108, 109, 110, 232, 233; *iii.* 2, 3, 231, 232, 258, 326.
Patrick, St., *i.* vii, xiii, xvi, xvii, xix, xlvii, xlviii, cccxxxiv, ccclxx, dcxliv; *ii.* 23, 24, 25, 26, 29, 43, 52, 57, 63, 64, 66, 67, 69, 75, 84, 85, 92, 154, 155, 159, 160, 165, 166, 167, 170, 178, 201, 202, 206, 211, 216, 227, 290, 324, 334, 339, 346; *iii.* 24, 57, 61, 122, 133, 187, 320, 321, 323, 324, 325, 328, 331, 379, 380, 386.
Paul of Nola, St., *i.* dxxxv.
„ Herr O., *i.* dli, dlv.
Pauli, Prof., *i.* cccexcii.
Paullus the Notary, *i.* xliii.
Penllyn, William, *i.* dcxxviii, dcxxxii.
Pennant, *i.* dxiii.
Pepin, *i.* dxxx.
Peri, Jacopo, *i.* dlxiv.
Perseus, *i.* iii.
Persius, *i.* ccclxx.
Peter the Great, *i.* cxlix.
Petrie, Dr., *i.* cccli, dxciv, dxcvi, dxcviii, dxcix, dcxiii, dcxv, dcxvii, dcxviii; *ii.* 68, 141, 153, 200, 377; *iii.* 6, 8, 24, 36, 40, 41, 50, 51, 52, 54, 55, 159, 188, 189, 230, 266, 267, 268, 269, 275, 276, 277, 278, 286, 289, 291, 293, 298, 299, 303, 306, 320, 335, 367, 389, 391, 394, 395, 402, 405, 408, 409, 525.
Petrocul [Patrocles], *i.* cccxxv.
Philemon, *i.* dxi.
Phillips, Ambrose Lyle, *i.* dcxxxv.
Pictet, M. Adolphe, *i.* lii, liii, lx, lxiv, lxv, lxvi, ccclxii, cccix, cccclxxvi, dxxxi.
Pierce, Mr. Nich. *iii.* 263, 264, 374.
Pierre de la Rue, *i.* dlviii, dlx.
Pietro Perugino, *i.* dlx.
Pigot, John E., *i.* cccexxxvii.
Pilop, son of Tantal, *iii.* 3 3.
Pinkerton, Mr., *i.* xlix.
Pirris, *ii.* 325.
Pithou, *i.* cix.
Plait, son of the king of Lochland, *ii.* 347, 349.
Pliny, *i.* lx, ccclxii, ccclxvi, ccccix, cccclxvi, cccclxxvii, dxxxix.
Plutarch, *i.* ccviii, cccclxx, cccclxxii, dxlviii.
Polybius, *i.* cccexliii.
Pomponius Mela, *i.* clxxi, ccccv, cccclxxvii, cccclxxviii.
Por, king of India, *iii.* 330.
Porsenna, *i.* dxxxix.
Posidonios, *i.* ccclxxi.
Possevin, Father Antoine, *i.* cxlix.
Powel, Dr., *i.* cccexcii, cccexciii, dcxxvii.
Praetorius, *i.* d.
Prichard, Dr., *i.* l, lii.
Priscian, *i.* cccxciv.
Propertius, *i.* cccexliii, cccclxxvii, cccclxxviii.
Psyche, *i.* iii.
Ptolemaeus, *i.* cccclxxxviii.
Pylagoras, *i.* xciv.
Pythagoras, *i.* dxliv.
Quin, Patrick, harper, *iii.* 295.
Ragallach, *i.* cccxxxvii, ccclxv; *ii.* 83, 342 to 345, 389; *ii.* 25.
Ragnar Lodbrok, *i.* dcvi, dcxxiii.
Raigne "Rosgadach", or the Glossarist, *ii.* 51.
„ or Raighne of the large eyes, *iii.* 377.
Ranieri, St., *i.* dxvi.
Raphael, *i.* dlx.
Rath, G. vom, *i.* cccexiv.
Ratpert, *i.* dlxviii.
Raumer, F. von, *i.* cxxiii, ccclxxvii.
Raynouard, *i.* dii.
Redg, *i.* cccxxxvi, cccexlv; *ii.* 298, 299.
Reeves, Rev. Dr. W., *i.* xvii, lxxxv, lxxxix, xc, xcii, xciv, xcvi, xcviii, cxix.
Reilbeo, *ii.* 184, 185.
Reochad, son of Fathaman, *iii.* 94.
Rhabanus Maurus, *i.* dvii.
Rhys, Dr. John David, *i.* cccexciii.
Riangabra, *i.* cccexxxvi.
Riarbind, *iii.* 139.
Richard II., *i.* ccxiii.
Righairled, king of Munster, *ii.* 7.
Rigrin, or Frigrinn, *iii.* 15. See Ailech and Oilech.
Rigru, see Rigrin.
Rind, *iii.* 158.
„ son of Niul, *iii.* 459.
Ringin, or Rigrin. See Rigrin and Frigrinn.
Rinnall, *ii.* 237, 241.
Ritson, *i.* xxxvii; *iii.* 296.
Rizzio, David, *i.* dcxxii.
Robert, C., *i.* cxlix.
Robert ab Huw, *i.* dcxxviii.
Robind, *iii.* 139.
Roche, David, of Fermoy, *i.* 282, 283, 284.

Rocuirp, *i.* cccxl

Rodubh, son of Cas, *ii.* 253, 288, 289.

Rofir Aenbero, *iii.* 147.

Roitheachtaigh, *ii.* 7.

Ronan, *i.* cccxxv.

Roquefort. See Le Grand d'Aussy.

Ros Mac Trichim, a poet, *ii.* 25, 66, 67, 72, 74.

Ros Failge, *ii.* 40, 43, 44; *iii.* 529, 530, 541.

Ros, or Ross Mac Deaghaidh, *ii.* 122.

„ Ruadh, *ii.* 314, 321.

Roscher, *i.* cxcv.

Rossellini, *i.* ccccIxxxv.

Rossini, *i.* dcxii, dcxvii.

Ro Sui, a poet, *iii.* 186.

Rotharit, king, *i.* ciii.

Rowland, *ii.* 182, 183.

Ruad, son of Finniul, *iii.* 459.

Ruadan, St., *ii.* 336, 337; *iii.* 18, 76, 115.

„ son of Breas, *ii.* 250.

Ruadh Rofheasa, *ii.* 132.

Ruadhan, John, *iii.* 292.

Ruadsech Derg, *iii.* 35, 36.

Ruaman, see Ruman, *ii.* 95; *iii.* 37, 38.

Rudhradh, Ard Righ, *ii.* 85, 274.

„ king of Ulster, *ii.* 321, 314,

„ son of Torloch O'Connor, Ard Righ, *iii.* 24.

Rudhraighe, see Rudhradh.

Rughraidhe, see Rudhradh.

Ruiz, Juan, *i.* dxxiii.

Ruman, a poet, *ii.* 95; *iii.* 37, 38.

Russell, James, *iii.* 292.

Sabhairce, Ard Righ, *ii.* 111.

Sadb, wife of Oilioll Olum, *ii.* 139, 140, 206; *iii.* 166, 177, 259.

Sadhbh, see Sadb.

Saemund, *i.* ccxx.

Safa, Ressai Akhuan el, *i.* dcxxxvi.

Saighead, daughter of Carrtunn Cor, *ii.* 276.

Salcbolga, *ii.* 314.

Samer, *i.* xxxii.

Samhair, daughter of Find Mac Cumhaill, *ii.* 387.

Samtan, son of Lugad Delbaeth *iii.* 220.

Sarama, *i.* iii.

Saranyu, *i.* iii.

Sanasan, *ii.* 343.

Saul, *i.* dviii.

Savigny, von, *i.* ciii, civ, cv, cvi, cvii, cviii, cix.

Scal Balb, *i.* cccxxvii.

Scathach, *ii.* 302, 303, 307, 311, 329, 368, 369, 370, 371; *iii.* 223, 402, 415, 431, 333, 437, 447, 455, 459, 461.

Sceanb, wife of the harper Craiftine, *iii.* 254.

Scene, *i.* ccccIxii, ccccIxiii.

Schafarik, *i.* cxlix.

Schlegel, Fred. von, *i.* l, ccxx.

Schmeller, *i.* cccl, ccccIxxxi.

Schmid, *i.* ccccxcii.

Schubiger, Father Anselm, *i.* diii, dlxix.

Scoriath, *iii.* 242, 243, 244, 249, 253.

Scotus Erigena, John, *i.* xvi, dl.

Scuap Inghen Gaironta, i.e. Broom, daughter of Clean Tidiness, *ii.* 133.

Sealbach, *ii.* 166.

Sean Mac Ardhne, a Brehon, *ii.* 21.

Seanach, son of Eochadh Abrad-Ruadh, *ii.* 283.

„ son of Durb, *ii.* 40; *iii.* 527.

Seanan, see Senan, *ii.* 283, 284.

Seancha, a Brehon, *i.* ccccIxx; *ii.* 21.

Seanchadh, *ii.* 322.

Seanchan Torpeist, see Senchan Torpeist.

Segdae, *iii.* 147.

Seich, *ii.* 322.

Seig, *iii.* 147.

Seigeng, or Sideng the Fair, *ii.* 283.

Selden, *i.* cclxxxviii.

Semeon, *ii.* 241.

Senach, son of Cerdan, *iii.* 207.

„ bishop, *ii.* 337.

„ son of Eochadh Abrad Ruadh, *ii.* 283, 284.

„ successor of St. Patrick, *ii.* 92, 93.

„ the distorted, *ii.* 197.

Senan, St, of Iniscathaig, *i.* cccxxix. *iii.* 364.

Sen Bec, *ii.* 50, 51.

Sencha, son of Ailill, poet, *ii.* 21, 51, 333; *iii.* 19, 20, 148, 310, 314, 317.

„ the beautiful, son of Ailill, *i.* ccclxxix, ccccxxxii.

Senchan, or Sencha, the orator, *i.* ccclxxix; *iii.* 92, 93.

„ judge and poet, *i.* clxxi.

„ Mac Cuairfertaigh, *ii.* 78.

„ son of Cairbre, *ii.* 52.

„ Torpeist, *ii.* 85, 86, 87, 88, 89, 91, 150; *iii.* 235, 236, 334, 376.

Septimus Severus, *i.* ccclxii, ccccIxxii.

Serret. See Lacroix.

Servius, *i.* xciii.

Setanta, *i.* ccvii. See Cuchulaind.

„ son of Soaltann, i.e. Cuchulaind.

Shearman, Rev. John, *i.* lxvii.
Shield, musician, *i.* dcxxxiv.
Siadhail, *i.* xxix.
Siauve, M. E. M., *i.* lxiii.
Sibe, *iii.* 139.
Sida-an-Eich-Bhuidhe, i.e. Sida, or Sheedy of the bay steed, *ii.* 109.
Side, *iii.* 147.
Sideng, daughter of Mongan, *ii.* 283.
Sidney, Sir Henry, *i.* cccexcii.
Sidonius Apollinaris, *i.* cccxcii cccxcvii, cccxcix.
Siegfried, Dr., *i.* lxv, lxvi, lxxx.
Sighl, son of Lugad Delbaeth, *ii.* 221, 222.
Sigrad Mac Lotar, *iii.* 347. See Sitric.
Sigurd, *i.* iii.
Silius Italicus, *i.* ccclxxxviii.
Simeon, or Semeon Breac, son of Starn, *ii.* 185, 187.
Simon, see Simeon.
„ Magus, *ii.* 213, 282, 300.
„ son of Cerb, *ii.* 387.
Simrock, Karl, *i.* lxxxviii.
Sinann, daughter of Lodan, *ii.* 142, 144.
Siorna Saeghlach, Ard Righ, *ii.* 356.
Sismondi, *i.* cli, cxxiii, cxxxiii, cxxxiv.
Sithach, *i.* dcxxxviii.
Sitric, *ii.* 350; *iii.* 227.
Sixtus IV., Pope, *i.* dlix.
Skene, John, *i.* ccii, ccl.
„ Wm. Forbes, *iii.* 300.
Skinner, *i.* clxxix, ccxxxiii.
Slainge, *i.* dcxxxvii; *ii.* 239, 242; *iii.* 6.
Slanoll, *ii.* 9.
Smaragdus, *i.* ccccclxxvi.
Smetra, *i.* cccxcvii.
Smirach, *ii.* 40; *iii.* 527.
Smith, Dr. Charles, *iii.* 8, 75, 76, 344, 345, 347.
„ Dr. William, *i.* ccclxxx.
Snathad Inghen Inumai, i.e. Needle, daughter of Stitcher, *iii.* 133.
Snedgus, *iii.* 385.
Soalta, Soaltann, or Soaltainn. See Sualtan.
Socht, son of Fithal, *i.* cccexxxiv; *ii.* 322, 323, 324.
Somerville, Rev. Mr., *iii.* 344, 345.
Somner, *i.* clxix.
Sopater, *i.* dx.
Sophocles, *i.* ccccclxxxvii.
Spangenberg, *i.* cccxcviii.
Spelman, *i.* clxix, cclxxxviii, cccxcii, dcxliv.
Spenser, Edmund, *i.* cxxvi.
Sreng, son of Sengann, *i.* cccexxxii; *ii.* 235, 236, 237, 239, 242, 244; *iii.* 5, 6.
Sroibheinn, or Sruibhghean, *i.* cclxiv.
Srub Daire, *i.* cccexxxi, cccclxii, cccclxiii; *iii.* 435.
Starn, son of Nemid, *ii.* 184.
Steele, Tom, *iii.* 298.
Stephen, St. *ii.* 99.
Stetten, Paul von, *i.* cccxcvi.
Stevenson, Sir John, *i.* dxci, dxciii, dcxiv, dcxvii.
Stilicho, *i.* xliv.
Stokes, Miss M., *i.* lxvi, cccevii.
„ Dr. Whitley, *i.* lviii, lxv, lxvii, lxxxv, lxxxix, clxxxv, cccexli; *iii.* 387.
Strabo, *i.* clxxi, ccclxxix, cccxcvii, cccclxxii.
Struben, *i.* cxcv.
Sualtainn, see Soalta, etc.
Sualtan, father of Cuchulaind, *i.* ccexliii; *ii.* 196, 309, 319, 360. See Saolta, etc.
Succut, Succat, *ii.* 40; *iii.* 527.
Suetonius, Caius Tranq., *i.* xxi, cccexc.
„ Paullinus, *i.* xxxviii.
Sui, son of Mophir Rochetuil, poet, *iii.* 184.
Suibhne, *ii.* 284.
„ Menn, Ard Righ, *ii.* 341.
Surenne. J. T., *i.* dxvii.
Sust Inghen Tren Tuairenigh, i.e. Flail, daughter of Powerful Thresher, *iii.* 133.
Sylvester, Pope, St., *i.* dxlvi.
Tacitus, *i.* xxi, xl, xli, xlii, lxxvii, lxxix, lxxxiii, cxxxi, cli, clxxi, ccxxxi, ccxxxii, ccxxxv, ccxxxviii, cclix, ccxcvi, ccxcvii, ccclxxxviii, cccexxxv, cccclxxii.
Tadg, son of Brian, *ii.* 121
„ Mac Brody, *ii.* 61.
„ of the tower, king of Connaught, *ii.* 129.
„ O'Kelly, *ii.* 121, 125.
„ son of Cian, *ii.* 139, 149; *iii.* 177.
Taei, cup-bearer, *iii.* 43.
Tailte, see Tailtiu.
Tailtiu, *i.* cccxxvi, cccexxxiii, dcxxxviii; *ii.* 148, 149.
Taliesin, *i.* xiii.
Talom, *iii.* 43.
Taman, *iii.* 197.
Taran, *i.* cccclvii.
Tassach, bishop, *ii.* 75.
Taylor, Silas, *i.* clxix.

Tea, wife of Eremon, *i.* cccxxxiii; *ii.* 108, 189.
Teascach, *i.* cccclvii.
Techmang, *iii.* 149.
Tegner, *i.* dxix.
Teidm, *i.* cccclviii.
Teige, see Tadg.
Temnen, son of Senach, *iii.* 207.
Teora Soillsi, *iii.* 99.
Terpander, *i.* dxliv.
Tethra, Fomorian king, *ii.* 254.
Theoderich, king, *i.* dcxxxiv, dcxxxv.
Theodore, *i.* dlxvii, dcxxxi.
Theodosius, *i.* xliii, xliv, xlviii, ccix; *ii.* 160.
Theseus, *i.* lii, xciv.
Theudlind, *i.* cccxciv, cccxcv.
Thierry, M. Amadée, *i.* cxxxii.
Thomas the Trouvère, *i.* dlii.
,, Mr. John, *i.* dcxxx, dcxxxi, dcxxxii, dcxxxiii.
Thomson, George, *i.* dcxviii.
Thor, *i.* ccclxxii, ccclxxxi, cccclvii.
Thorleif Kimbri, *i.* cccclxxi.
Thorngyr, Iarl of Jutland, *i.* lxxv.
Thorpe, Mr. Benjamin, *i.* cccxxxi.
Thrael and Thye, *i.* ccxxxvii.
Tibraidhe, or Tipralt Tirech, *i.* xxiv, xxv; *ii.* 324.
Tighernach Tetbannach, *ii.* 199.
,, son of Oilioll Olum, *iii.* 207, 208.
,, the annalist, *i.* cccxxii, ccclxxv; *ii.* 128, 129, 130, 137; *iii.* 37, 228.
Tighernmas, Ard Righ, *i.* xxi; *ii.* 5, 6, 247; *iii.* 88, 210, 211.
Tius, *i.* iii.
Tlirenmor, see Trenmor.
Tochur, *iii.* 149.
Todd, Rev. Dr., *i.* xlvii; *ii.* 92, 205, 222, 271.
Tolc, *i* cccclviii.
Tomoltach, *ii.* 70, 71.
Torloch Mór O'Connor, Ard Righ, *iii.* 24.
Torlogh, son of Murchadh, *ii.* 349.
Torna Eigas, *i.* lxxiii; *ii.* 59, 60, 61, 62, 63, 64, 65, 66, 69, 70, 71, 72, 147, 148, 375; *iii.* 287, 525.
Totilo, *i.* lxxx. See Tuotilo.
Tradd, son of Tassach, *ii.* 220.
Traiglethan, *iii.* 15, 16.
Trajan, *i* cccclxxii.
Trebellius, Pollio, *i.* ccclxxxviii.
Trebuait, son of Lonscae, *iii.* 138.
Trenfer, *i.* cccclviii.
Trenmiled, *i.* cccclviii.
Trenmor, *ii.* 283.
Trese, *i.* dcxxxix.
Tristan, *i.* xxxix, xlviii.
Trivet, Nicholas, *i.* cccxcii.
Trog, *iii.* 43.
Trogaidhe, *ii.* 356.
Troighlethan, see Traiglethan.
Tromboncino, Bartolomeo, *i.* dlxi.
Trotter, John Bernard, *iii.* 295.
Tuan Mac Carrill, *iii.* 61, 62.
Tuathal, *i* lxxx; *ii.* 70, 71.
,, Maelgarbh, Ard Righ, *ii.* 335.
,, Teachtmar, Ard Righ, *i.* xxv, xxvi, xxix, xxx, xxxiii, xcix; *ii.* 14, 261, 383, 386; *iii.* 84.
Tubal Cain, *iii.* 236, 237.
Tuidle, *iii.* 139.
Tuile, *iii.* 13.
Tuirbi Tragmar, or Tuirbhi Traghmhar, *iii.* 41, 42, 43.
Tuireand Brierend, *i.* iii. cccxxxii.
Tulchinne, *iii.* 145.
Tuotilo, *i.* dxii, dlxviii, dlxix.
Turgeis, *ii.* 102, 103.
Ua Corra, *i.* dcxlii, dcxliii.
Ua Crotta, *ii.* 173.
Ua Duach (O'Brien), *iii.* 287.
Ualad, *i.* cccxxxii.
Ua Luirc [O'Brien], *iii.* 287.
Ua Maighlinne, *iii.* 310, 311.
Ua Maine, *ii.* 115, *iii.* 126
Uaithne, *ii.* 213, 214, 220, 221, 222; *iii.* 125, 242, 307, 382.
Uan, *iii.* 144.
Uar, druid, *ii.* 184.
Uathach, daughter of Scathach, *ii.* 370, 308; *iii.* 415, 431, 437, 447, 459.
,, father of Ragallach, king of Connaught, *ii.* 389.
Ua Torpa, *ii.* 287.
Ubtaire [*recte*, Fubtaire, which see] *iii.* 10.
Uca, daughter of Osca, *ii.* 40; *iii.* 527.
Ugaine Mór, *i.* xxii.
U-gairbh, *iii.* 15.
Uisle, *iii.* 385.
Uisnech, *ii.* 320, 321, 325, 358, *iii.* 201, 254, 368, 373, 378, 385.
Ulphilas, *i.* lviii, ccxxix, ccxxxvii.
Ulysses, *iii.* 333.
Umal, *iii.* 139.
Umor, *ii.* 122.
Urmael, *ii.* 78.
Usher, *i.* dcxliv.
Uthidir, *i.* cccxxxii.
Vallancey, General, *i.* dxxxvi; *iii.* 172, 269, 270, 275, 320, 321, 343, 344, 346.

Valentinus, *i.* xliii.
Varro, *i.* lx. xciii, ccxxxiii, ccclxix, dxxxix.
Varunas, *i.* iii.
Veleda, *i.* clxxi.
Venantius Fortunatus, *i.* cccxliii, cccxlii, cccexc, ccccxcv, ccccxcix.
Veneziano, Antonio, *i.* dxvi.
Viadana, Ludovico, *i.* dlxiv.
Villemarque, M. de, *i.* lxviii, dxxii.
Villoteau, *i.* dxi, dxiv.
Vincent, M., *i.* dxlvii.
Virdung, Sebastian, *i.* dcxii.
Virgil, *i.* xvi, ccclxxx, ccclxxxi, cccexlii, ccceclxxii, ccceclxxviii.
Virgil the grammarian, *i.* lviii, lix.
Vitalian, Pope, *i.* dlxvii, dcxxxi.
Vivaldi, *i.* dcix.
Vopiscus, *i.* cccxcvii.
Wagner, *iii.* 348, 349.
Waitz, *i.* cxl, cxlvi.
Walafrid Strabo, *i.* dxxxv.
Walker, Mr. Joseph Cooper, *iii.* 269, 295, 302, 308, 320, 342, 344, 345, 346, 347.
Walsh, Maurice, *iii.* 322.
Walshe, *iii.* 361.
Walters, Ferdinand, *i*, cviii, ccccxcii.
Wandilochus, St., *i.* dcxliv.
Ward, Father, *ii.* 166.
Ware, *iii.* 172.
Weber, *i.* dcxii.
Weinhold, Karl, *i.* clxxiii, ccxcvi, ccc, cccxxxvii, ccclxxiv, ccclxxvi, ccclxxvii, ccclxxiv, ccclxxviii, cccliv, ccclxxxii, ccclxxxv, ccclxxxvi, cccxcviii, cccxciii, cccxciv, ccccli, cccclxxii, cccclxxiii, cccclxxxi.
Wenzel II., *i.* dxxvii.
West, Alderman, *iii.* 173.
Westwood, Mr., *i.* lxvii.
Wiarda, *i.* cli.
Wibel, Dr. F., *i.* ccccxvii.
Wilda, *i.* ccxiii, ccxiv, ccxviii, ccxx.
Wilde, Sir William, *i.* ccccxxxvii, ccccxxxviii; *ii.* 240, 271; *iii.* 347, 348, 349.
Wilkinson, Sir G., *i.* cccclxxxv.
Williams, Miss Jane, *i.* dcxxviii.
Winterfeld, *i.* dlxi, dlxii, dlxvi.
Woden, *i.* ccxxxii.
Woodward, *iii.* 172.
Worsaae, Prof. J. J. A., *ii.* 266, 267.
Wulfgar, *i.* ccxxxvii.
Wynne, W., *i.* cccclxcii.
Yates, Mr. James, *i.* ccclxxx.
Zeus, *i.* iii.
,, Hetaireios, *i.* cccclxxxviii.
Zeuss, J. K., *i.* lvi, lvii, lix, lx, ccccxliii, cccclxxvi, dxxxi; *ii.* 248; *iii.* 306, 386.
Zio, *i.* iii.
Zoroaster, *ii.* 183.

INDEX LOCORUM.

Aachen, *i.* ccclxxxvi.
Abbeville, *i.* ccccxxv.
Abbeyfeale, *iii.* 132.
Aberdeen, *i.* xc.
Acaill, *i.* xxv; *ii.* 22, 327; *iii.* 96, 197.
Achadh Abhall, *ii.* 160.
„ Bo, *ii.* 81.
„ Dorbchon, *i.* cccxxii.
„ Leith Dearg, *ii.* 112.
Ache, the river, *i.* ccccxvi.
Achonry, diocese of, *i.* xxix.
Aenach Ailbi, *i.* cccxxvii.
„ an Bruga, *i.* cccxxviii.
„ Cuile, *i.* cccxxvii.
„ Colman, *i.* cccxxvii.
„ Cruachan, *i.* cccxxvii. See Cruachan.
„ Tuaighe, *i.* ccccliii.
Aenach Find, *iii.* 202.
Ahade, ford of, *iii.* 161, 404.
Ai. See Magh Aie.
Aicill, Aichill. See Acaill.
Aidhne, *ii.* 122.
Aileach, *i.* cccvii; *ii.* 105, 130, 151, 152, 153, 154, 155, 156, 160, 161, 340, 341, 389; *iii.* 8, 9, 10, 12, 15, 24, 25, 73, 83, 126, 127, 152, 153.
Ailinn in W. Munster, *ii.* 107.
„ (Knockaulin, Hill of Allen, Co. of Kildare), *ii.* 356; *iii.* 15, 16, 182.
Aillinn. See Ailinn.
Aine, *i.* xxviii.
Airget Ros (Ossory), *ii.* 43, 328; *iii.*
Airghioll. See Oirghiall.
Alba, *i.* xxii, xxiv, xxv, xxxii, xlvi, cccxxxvi, cccxxxviii, ccccxxxiv; *ii.* 156, 211, 359, 367, 368, 370, 371, 372, 373; *iii.* 169, 175, 240, 241, 284, 324, 371, 527.
Albain, gen. of Alba. See Alba.
Albion, *ii.* 210. See Alba.
Alcluaide, *iii.* 38.
Allen, hill of. See Almhain.
Alexandria, *i.* ccix.
Alexandropol, *i.* ccccxxii.
Alinn. See Ailinn.
Almeidan, the, *i.* dxxix.
Almhain, *i.* xxvii, ccciii; *ii.* 389, 390, 391; *iii.* 309, 310, 326, 381.
Almu. See Almhain.
Almuim[n], *i.* xxvii.
Alps, the, *i.* xxii, xlvi, xlvii, ccccxliii.
„ the German, *i.* ccclxxviii.
Altenberg, *i.* ccccxix.
Altmark, *i.* cli.
America, *i.* cccxciii.
Amiens, *i.* d, dxv, dxxvi.
Angers, *i.* ccccxci, dxii.
Anglesey, *i.* xxxix, ccccxcvii, dcxxviii; *iii.* 185, 186.
Anglia, East, *i.* xcii.
Anhalt, *i.* ccccxxv.
Annagais, the river, *i.* xxx.
Antrim, *i.* xxviii, xxxviii, ccclxxv; *ii.* 283, 315; *iii.* 8, 128, 175, 237, 291, 386.
Appleby, *i.* lxxxviii.
Ara, *iii.* 124, 125.
Araidh, *iii.* 128.
Arainn. See Arann Islands.
Arann Island, in the Clyde, *iii.* 339.
„ Islands, coast of Clare, *i.* xxviii; *ii.* 122; *iii.* 5, 65, 66, 74, 122.
Ardagh, Co. of Limerick, *i.* ccclxxiv.
„ Co. Longford, *ii.* 193.
Ard Brestiné, *iii.* 161, 162.
„ Gul, *i.* xxx.
„ Oilean, *ii.* 66, 67.
„ Neimhidh, *i.* xxxix.
„ Patrick, Co. of Limerick, *iii.* 379.
„ Sailech, *iii.* 316.
„ Sleibhe, *iii.* 316.
„ Solus, *i.* cccxviii.
Ardee, *i.* ccclxxv; *ii.* 297, 310; *iii.* 25, 102.
Ardmacha (Armagh), *ii.* 76.
Argat Ros, *ii.* 43; *iii.*
Argyleshire, *i.* xc, cxlviii.
Arles, *i.* xlv, dxxvii.
Armagh, *i.* xxix, lxxxix, xcv; *ii.* 67,

75, 76, 92, 156, 178, 233; *iii.* 3, 57, 58, 61, 97, 103, 117, 295, 316.
Armorean Sea, *ii.* 252.
Asia, *i.* cccexi.
„ Minor, *i.* ccccIxxxviii.
„ Central, *i.* cccex, ccccxii, ccccxxviii.
„ Southern, *i.* cccxi.
„ Western, *i.* ccccIxxxvi.
Asia, *ii.* 167, 228, 232.
Askeaton, *ii.* 386.
Asturias, *i.* ccccxix.
„ Western, ccccxxviii.
Assyria, *i.* ccccxxiii, ccccIxxxviii.
Ath an Righ (Athenry), *i.* xxi; *ii.* 139, 331.
Athenry, *i.* xxi. See Ath an Righ.
Athens, *i.* dxxxiii.
Athiseachs, Islands of, *iii.* 459.
Ath Blair, *iii.* 16.
„ Bres, *ii.* 387.
„ Cliath, *iii.* 37.
„ Comair, *ii.* 262, 271, 276, 277, 295.
„ Fadat. See Ahade
„ Ferdiadh. See Ardee.
„ Liag Find, *ii.* 283, 284.
„ Liag Mairgene, *ii.* 289.
„ Mogho, *i.* xxix.
„ an Roide, *i.* xxviii.
Athlone, *i.* xxix; *ii.* 145, 259, 283, 284, 291, 315; *iii.* 25, 85, 254, 373.
Ath-na Foraire, *ii.* 365.
„ n-Gabla, *i.* cccxlv.
„ Sennaigh (Ballyshannon), *ii.* 343.
„ Solus, *i.* cccxviii.
„ Tolam Sed, *ii.* 299.
„ Truim (now Trim), *ii.* 166, 160.
Athy, *ii.* 351.
Atlantic Ocean, *i.* ccccxi; *iii.* 180.
Attica, *i.* xciii, xciv.
Åtvidaberg, *i.* ccccxv, ccccxvi.
Augsburg, *i.* ccexciii.
Αὐγουστονέμετον in Gaul, *i.* cclxiv.
Austria, *i.* ccccxxv.
Autun, *i.* lxiv.
Auxerre, *i.* xlvii.
Avignon, the Musée Calvet at, *i.* lxiii.
„ *i.* dlxxxvi.
Ayr, *i.* xc.
Babylon, *i.* dviii.
Baile Atha Aoi (Athy), *ii.* 351–352.
„ an Scáil, *ii.* 57.
„ in Bile, *iii.* 427.
„ na Ceard, or na g Ceard, *i.* ccvii; *iii.* 208.
Baile, an Gabhain, *i.* ccvii.
"Baily" Light House at Howth, *ii.* 200.
Balasadare, *ii.* 344.
Balbriggan, *i.* xc.
Baldoyle, *i.* xc.
Baldungan, *i.* xc.
Balglais, *i.* xc.
Ballinrobe, *i.* xxix
Ballinvogher, *iii.* 68.
Ballyadams, barony of, *iii.* 45.
Ballybrack, near Dingle, *i.* cccxv.
Ballybrit, barony of, *i.* xxviii, cclxxiv.
Ballydeely. See Davil and Daelach.
Ballyheabought, *i.* cccxv, cccxvii.
Ballyleague. See Ath Liag Find.
Ballymagauran, *i.* xxx.
Ballynascreen, *iii.* 294.
Bally O'Dowda, *iii.* 16.
Ballyshannon, *ii.* 162, 232, 262, 343; *iii.* 258, 366.
Balrothery, *i.* xc.
Balscaddan, *i.* xc.
Baltic Provinces, *i.* cccxl, ccccxxiv, ccccxxix.
„ coast, *i.* ccccxxxv.
„ region, *i.* ccccxxxv.
Baltinglass, *ii.* 338, 341.
Bangor, *i.* dcxliv.
Bann, river, *i.* xxix; *ii.* 275; *iii.* 144, 237, 314, 316.
Barehaven, Bearehaven, *iii.* 360. See Beara.
Barrow, river, *i.* ccclxxiv; *ii.* 46, 144, 351, 383, 384, 385; *iii.* 16, 35, 45, 404.
Barry's Cross, Co. of Carlow, *iii.* 45.
Barrymore, barony of, *i.* xxvii.
Bavaria, *i.* ccccxxv, ccccxli, ccccIv.
Bavon, St., at Ghent, *i.* ccxii.
Bealach Conglais. See Baltinglass.
„ Mugna, *ii.* 104, 105.
Beannchoir (Bangor), *ii.* 76, 81, 85.
Beara (Barehaven), *ii.* 360, 377.
Bearba. See Barrow, the river.
Beare and Bantry, bar. of, *i.* xxvii.
Bearnan Eile, the Devil's Bit, *ii.* 62.
Bearnas Mór, Co. of Donegal, *i.* xxix; *ii.* 164; *iii.* 222, 223, 224.
Bedg, a river, *iii.* 97.
Beinn Edair (the Hill of Howth), *ii.* 106, 200; *iii.* 179.
„ Gulban, *ii.* 375.
Belfast, *i.* dxcii, dcxiv.
Belfast, *iii.* 203, 291, 297, 298, 303.
Belgatan mountain, *ii.* 236.
Belgia, *i.* ccclvi.
Belgium, *i.* xxxv, clix, dli, dlvi, dlviii, dcxxxiii.

Bellech Caelli, *i.* cccxlv.
Ben Lomond, *i.* dcxvii.
Bennchuir. See Beannchoir.
Benn Edair. See Beinn Edair.
Bergen, *i.* ccxcvi.
Bernas of Tir Oililla. *i.* xxix.
" of Tir Hugh. See Bearnas Mór.
Berwick, *i.* cciii.
Besançon, *i.* ccclxxxi.
Biel, Lake of, *i.* cccxxxix.
Bir, river, *iii.* 97.
Birr, King's County, *ii.* 76, 337; *iii.* 319.
Biscay, Bay of, *i.* lxxvi.
Bishop's Island, *iii.* 67.
Bithlain river, *iii.* 97.
Bithynia, *i.* xciv.
Black Sea, *i.* cccxii; *ii.* 228; *iii.* 384.
Blackwater, the river, *i.* xxviii.
Blarney, *i.* dcxiii.
Bobbio, *i.* dcxliv.
Bocherville, *i.* dxiv.
Bodwigen, *i.* dcxxviii.
Bohemia, *i.* cccxxiv, cccxxviii, ccclxiii, dxxvii.
Boind, the river Boyne, *ii.* 111, 195; *iii.* 96, 187, 218, 219, 382, 383. See also Boyne, the river.
Boinn. See Boind.
Boirinn, or Burren, *iii.* 124, 125.
Boromha, poetical name for Ceann Coradh, *ii.* 120, 121.
Borsbaanya, *i.* cccxv.
Borysthenes, *i.* cccxxiv.
Bothar na Bruighne, *iii.* 136.
" Chualand, *iii.* 136.
Boulogne-sûr-mer, *i.* xlv, cccxi, cccxliii, dv, dxv, dxxxix, dxli.
Bourdeaux, *i.* lviii.
Boylagh, barony of, *ii.* 83.
Boyle, *iii* 301.
Boyne, the river, *i.* ccclxxv; *ii.* 141, 144, 156, 195, 292, 314, 366, 386; *iii.* 44, 122, 156, 160, 187, 362.
" the estuary of the, *i.* xxx.
Braquemont, near Dieppe, *i.* ccxcvii.
Bray, *i.* ccclxxiv, ccclxxvi.
Breagha, *i.* xxx. See Bregia, 443.
Brefny, *i.* ccclxxv.
Brega, *i.* ccciv.
Bregia, *i.* ccclxxv; *ii.* 30, 46, 91, 141, 155, 292, 326; *iii.* 41, 43, 77, 139, 148, 219, 375.
Breg Ross, *iii.* 427.
Breguin, *i.* xxviii.
Breifne, or Breifney, *i.* xxx; *ii.* 129, 392; *iii.* 301.
Brendon's Hill, *iii.* 272.
Brenide, the river, *iii.* 97.
Brentir, or Breintre, *i.* xciii.
Bri Leith, *i.* ccclxxviii, cccliv; *ii.* 141, 192, 194; *iii.* 163, 188, 189, 190, 191, 355, 356.
Briole, *i.* xxix.
Britain, *i.* v, xvi, xvii, xix, xx, xxii, xxiii, xxiv, xxxiv, xxxvi, xxxvii, xxxviii, xxxix, xl, xlii, xliii, xliv, xlv, xlvi, xlviii, l, liii, ccxcvi, cccx, cccxi, cccxxi, cccxxviii, cccxxix, ccclv, cccxciii, dii, dlxvii, dcxxxi; *ii.* 82, 183, 186, 190, 210, 222, 223, 225, 231, 233, 266, 273, 338, 341; *iii.* 136.
Britanny, *i.* xxii, xliv, dxxii, dxxiii.
British Islands, *i.* xliii, cccxcix, dxviii, dxx.
Bristol, *i.* ccv.
Brislech Mór, *i.* cccv, cccxlvi.
Brogail, Bruigheol, *i.* xxix.
Brosnach, the river, *ii.* 141.
Bruck in the Pinzgau, *i.* cccxvi.
Brugh na Boinne, or Brugh Mic an oig, *i.* dcxxxix; *ii.* 105, 106; *iii.* 122, 305, 362, 524.
Brugh of the Boyne, *iii.* 524. See Brugh na Boinne.
Brughean Mhór, *iii.* 254.
Bruree, Co. of Limerick, *i.* clxi.
Brussels, *i.* dii; *ii.* 79, 167, 353.
Burdigala. See Bourdeaux.
Burgundy, *i.* ccxcvii.
Buaigh (Bann), *i.* xxix.
Buain, the river, *iii.* 97.
Buais, the river, *iii.* 95.
Bunratty Castle, *iii.* 288.
Burach, *iii.* 96.
Burren, *iii* 5, 61, 74.
Burrishole, barony of, *i.* xxix.
Cáenraigh, now Kenry, *ii.* 388.
Caer Edris, Anglesey, *ii.* 182.
Caher, Co. of Tipperary, *iii.* 5.
" Ass, *iii.* 250, 260.
" Conlish, *iii.* 5.
" Fada an dorais, *iii.* 72.
" na Mac Tirech, *iii.* 72.
Caill Gartan Coille, *i.* ccclxxiv.
Caille, *iii* 99.
Cailledh, *ii.* 106.
Cairbre ua Ciardha, now Carbry, Co. of Kildare, *iii.* 123.
Cairpre, or Cairpri of Drom Cliabh, *i.* xxix.
" Gabhra, *i.* xxx.
Caiseal, now Cashel, *iii.* 15, 133.
Caladh, *i.* cclxv.
Calatum, *i.* xxi.
Callamar, *iii.* 377.

Calland, *iii.* 94.
Calt, *ii.* 96.
Camas, *iii.* 236, 237, 352.
Cambridgeshire, *i.* lxxiii.
Campania, *i.* dxxxiv, dxxxv.
Camros, *iii.* 44, 45.
Canterbury, *i.* ccxiii.
Cappadocia, *i.* xciv.
Carbery, *ii.* 375.
„
Carbry, Co. of Kildare, *iii.* 123.
„ bar. of, East and West, *i.* xxvii, xxviii.
Carcassonne, *i.* cccxci.
Carlow, *i.* xvi, xxvii, cclv, cclvii, cccxliii, cccexeviii, dxxi, dxxxi, dxxxiii, dxl; *ii.* 330; *iii.* 34, 45, 161, 244, 372, 404.
Carlsruhe, *i.* lvi.
Carinthia, *i.* ccclxxviii.
Carman, *ii.* 38, 39, 40, 41 to 44, 46, 47; *iii.* 313, 325, 329, 335, 338, 358, 364, 368, 523, 524, 525, 526, 527.
Carn Achaidh Leth Derg, *ii.* 17.
„ An aen Fir, *i.* cccxxxvii.
„ Chonaill, *ii.* 121, 122, 123.
„ Ciun Firb, *i.* cccxxxviii.
„ Eochach, *i.* cccxxxix.
„ Feradaig, *i.* cccxl.
„ Fiachach, *ii.* 220, 221.
„ Furbaide acus Eithne, *i.* cccxxxvi.
„ Leca, *i* cccxxxvi.
„ Lugdach, *i.* cccxxxvi.
„ Mail, *i.* cccxxxvi.
Carnoel, *i.* ccccxxxix.
Carnteel, *i.* xxix.
Carn Tsiadhail, *i.* xxix.
Carpentoracte, *i.* ccccixxvii.
Carra, bar. of, *i.* xxix.
Carraic Bracraighe, *ii.* 102.
Carrickfergus, *iii.* 346.
„ O'Gunnell, *iii.* 342.
„ On Shannon, *ii.* 70, 259; *iii.* 199.
Carthage, *i.* ccccxxiii.
Cashel, *i.* xxvii; *ii.* 61, 62, 101, 226, 250; *iii.* 15, 25, 124, 125, 132, 208, 228, 240, 241, 261, 262, 263, 264, 272, 287, 360, 388, 505.
Caspian Sea, *i.* ccccxii.
Castlebellingham, *i.* ccclxxv.
Castle Connor, *iii.* 16.
„ Dermot, *ii.* 144. See Disert Diarmada.
„ Fogarty, *iii.* 289.
„ Island, *i.* xxviii.
Castlemaine, barony of, *iii.* 85.
Castle Otway, *iii.* 294.
Castlerea, *i.* ccclxxiv
Castlereagh, *i.* xxix.
Castletown, bar. of, *i.* xxviii.
Castletown Delvin, *ii.* 221.
Cathair Chinn Lis, *iii.* 5.
„ Chonroi, or Conrai, *i.* cccxiii; *ii.* 9, 97; *iii.* 15, 75 to 80, 81, 82, 152.
„ Crofinn, *ii.* 189; *iii.* 73.
„ Dun Iascaigh, *iii.* 5. See Caher.
„ Maothal, *i.* ccclxvi.
„ na Claen Ratha, *iii.* 83. See Cathair Chonrai.
„ na Mac Tirech, or "Fort of the Wolves", *i.* cccx-cccxi. See Caher na Mac Tirech.
Cathermoyle, *i.* ccclxvi. See Cathair Maothal.
Cat, Island of, *ii.* 347.
Caucasus, *i.* ccccxii.
Cavan, Co. of, *i.* xxv, xxx, xcv.
Cean Abrat, Cenn Abrat, or Feabrat, *ii.* 57; *iii.* 261.
Ceannanus, now Kells, *iii.* 123.
Ceann Coradh, *ii.* 98, 99, 115, 117, 118, 119, 120, 121, 126, 156; *iii.* 24.
Ceann Crochan, *ii.* 99.
Ceannfeabhrat, *i.* cclxiv. See Cean Abrat.
Ceanntire, or Cenntire, now Kentire, *ii.* 39; *iii.* 316.
Cearna, *ii.* 96.
Ceara, *i.* xxix.
Cell Belaigh, *iii.* 38.
Cenngoba, *iii.* 123.
Cerna, *i* ccclxxiv.
Cert, *ii.* 40; *iii.* 527.
Cerrig Brudyn, *ii.* 182.
Cetgueli, now Kidwelly, *i.* xxxviii.
Champagne, *i.* ccxcvii.
China, *i.* dxliii.
Cianacht, *ii.* 140, 356. See Mons Trogaidh.
Ciaraidhe Luachra, now Kerry, *i.* xxviii; *iii.* 82.
Ciarraige, Ciarraidhe Aei, *i.* ccclxxiv.
„ Locha na n-Airneadh, *i.* ccclxxiv.
Cill Abbain, *iii.* 44, 45.
„ Coirne, *ii.* 220.
Cilie Choca, *iii.* 123.
Cill Da Lua, now Killaloe, *ii.* 98.
„ Dara, now Kildare, *iii.* 396.
„ Eoin, *ii.* 220.
„ Finan, *ii.* 57.
„ Gobban, *iii.* 40.
„ Ita, *ii.* 85.

Cill Malluighre, *ii.* 220.
„ Mic Creiche, *iii.* 332.
„ Mic Nenain, *ii.* 161, 163.
„ Mic Trena, *iii.* 213.
„ Na n-Daighre, *ii.* 155.
„ Ogh-na-Suloch.
„ Osnadh, *ii.* 68, 151.
„ Rannarach, *ii.* 340.
Cinge, or Cine, *i.* xlvi.
Cingil, *i.* cccxxxii.
Cinncha, *ii.* 376.
Cité de Limes, *i.* ccxcvii.
Claenach, *iii.* 267, 269, 275.
Claen Raith, *iii.* 130.
Claire (Munster), *ii.* 214, 279.
Clanbrassil, *i.* xcv.
Clanca, *i.* xcv.
Cland Flathuisa, *i.* ccxxix.
Clara, *ii.* 315. See Clartha.
Clare, *i.* xv, xxix, xciii, cl, cccvii, cccxviii, ccclxi, ccccvi, dcv; *ii.* 101, 122, 268; *iii.* 5, 24, 61, 65, 67, 74, 85, 119, 186, 262, 263, 267, 275, 278, 288, 331, 332, 340, 364, 392.
„ barony of, *i.* xxviii.
Clartha, *iii.* 130, 135, 315, 320, 321. See Clara.
Cleitech, *ii.* 27, 156.
Clenagh. See Claenach.
Cliach, *ii.* 357, 383.
Clibech, *ii.* 201, 202.
Clithar Bó Ulad, *i.* cccvi.
Clochan Leo, *iii.* 67.
Clochar, *iii.* 15. See Manister.
Clonard, *i.* xxx; *ii.* 76, 79, 81, 83, 84, 85, 343.
Clondalkin, *ii.* 389.
Clonderlaw [Clonderalaw], *i.* xxviii.
Clonfert, *ii.* 90; *iii.* 33.
Clonlisk, barony of, *i.* xxviii, ccclxxiv.
Clonmacnoise, *i.* xxix; *ii.* 76, 81, 134, 221, 335; *iii.* 120, 121, 133, 194, 228, 394, 396.
Clonmel, *iii.* 203.
Clonmore, *ii.* 339.
Clonroad, *iii.* 288.
Cloonsost, *iii.* 330.
Clontarf, *i.* cccexxxiii, ccccIxx; *ii.* 116, 345 to 352, 358, 392; *iii.* 153, 267.
Cloyne, *iii.* 263, 292, 293. See Cluain.
Cluain, *iii.* 292, 394, 395.
„ Celbind, *iii.* 395.
„ Crema, *i.* dxxx.
„ Da Chaileach, *iii.* 360.
„ Dobhail, *iii.* 310.
„ Dolcain, *ii.* 389, 390. See Clondalkin.
Cluain Fraich, *iii.* 25.
„ Fuiche, *i.* xxix.
„ Lochain, *ii.* 220.
„ Mor Maedhog, *ii.* 338.
„ Muc Nois, *ii.* 85, 221; *iii.* 394.
„ Sosta, now Cloonsost, *iii.* 330.
Cluain Uamha (Cloyne), *ii.* 76.
Cluny, Hotel, at Paris, *i.* lxiii, lxv.
Clwyd, the river, *i.* xxxviii.
Clyde, the river, *iii.* 339.
Cnamhros, battle of, *ii.* 386.
Cnoc Aine (now Knockany), *ii.* 357; *iii.* 260.
„ Luinge, now Knocklong, *ii.* 213.
„ Muadh, *iii.* 301.
„ O'Colmain, *iii.* 339, 340.
„ Raffan,
Cnodba, or Cnodhbha, *ii.* 96.
Cnogba, *i.* ccexlv.
Cnuca, *i.* ccciii, cccxxii.
Cobhas, *iii.* 128.
Coirte, *i.* xlvi.
Colom, *i.* xlvi.
Comor, *ii.* 141, 146.
Comung, the river, *iii.* 97.
Condail, now Old Connall, Co. of Kildare, *iii.* 311, 312.
Condons and Clangibbon, barony of, *i.* xxviii.
Cong, *ii.* 119, 187, 236.
Connells, bar. of, *i.* xxviii.
Congign, on the borders of Thibet, *i.* cccxxiii.
Congnaig, the river, *i.* xxix.
Congo, *i.* ccccxcv.
Conmaicne, *i.* xxix; *iii.* 126, 132.
Connacht, *i.* xxix, lxxiii; *ii.* 10, 11, 296.
Connaught, *i.* xx, xxiv, xxv, ccxxx, ccxxxvii, cccvii, dcxlii; *ii.* 13, 53, 78, 85, 87, 105, 121, 129, 164, 187, 199, 201, 217, 218, 236, 259, 260, 262, 290, 291, 302, 314, 315, 324, 335, 343, 347, 357, 358, 374, 375, 377, 389; *iii.* 10, 15, 25, 44, 60, 74, 83, 85, 91, 102, 106, 109, 125, 126, 132, 133, 155, 156, 157, 158, 168, 169, 179, 199, 218, 219, 234, 254, 259, 278, 282, 283, 291, 301, 307, 314, 334, 335, 338, 342, 345, 356, 372, 373, 376, 379, 382, 400.
Constantinople, *i.* dxxix.
Conway, *i.* ccccxcii.
Cooley, *iii.* 413. See Cuailgne, and also Táin Bó Chuailgne.
Coolness Moss, *iii.* 291.
Coranroe, *i.* xxviii.
Corbey, Abbey of, *i.* ccclxvi.

Corca Bhaiscind, Corca Bhaiscinn, Corca Baiscen, *i.* xxviii; *ii.* 349; *iii.* 136, 262, 263.
Corca Muichi, *i.* xxviii.
Corcaguiny, bar. of, *i.* xxviii.
Corcmodhruadh. See Corcomruadh.
Corco Duibhne, *i.* xxviii.
Corcolaige, *i.* xxviii.
Corco Luigde, *i.* cccix.
Corcomruadh, lxxviii; *iii.* 125.
Corcortri, *i.* ccxxix.
Cordova, *i.* dxxii.
Cork, County of, *i.* xxvii, xxviii, xxxix, cccvii, ccclxxviii, dcv; *ii.* 375; *iii.* 85, 261, 263, 282, 283, 344, 345, 347.
„ City, *i.* clvii, ccclxix, ccccl x, cccclxi, dciii, dcxiii; *ii.* 76; *iii.* 103, 104, 345.
Cork Harbour, *i.* xxvii.
Cornwall, *i.* xxii, xxxix, xlviii, ccccxi, ccccxix, ccccxxviii; *ii.* 211, 347.
Corofin, *iii.* 332.
Corpar, *i.* xlvi.
Corsica, *i.* cccxcii.
Corra an Ruaid, *i.* xxviii.
Corran, Corann, *i.* xxix; *ii.* 344.
„ barony of, *i.* xxix.
Corrsliabh, the Curlew Mountains, *ii.* 341.
Cosles, bar. of, *i.* xxviii.
Costello, barony of, *i.* ccclxxiv.
Coumeenole, *iii.* 68.
Craeb Derg, or Red Branch at Emania, *i.* cccxxxvii.
Craebh, *iii.* 127.
„ Tulchadh, *ii.* 167.
Craib Telca, *iii.* 316.
Craemhchaill, *ii.* 386.
Craig Liath, *ii.* 115; *iii.* 24.
Cregraidhe, Island of, *iii.* 360.
Cremthann, *i.* xxx.
Cremorne, bar. of, *i.* xxx.
Crich Liathain, *i.* xxxix.
Crimea, *i.* ccccxxiii.
Crinna, *ii.* 140; *iii.* 177.
Croatia, *i.* cxlix.
Croghan, Hill of, *i.* xxvii.
Croisic, *i.* ccccxix.
Cromarty, *i.* xc.
Croom, *ii.* 215.
Crotta Cliach, *iii.* 324.
Cruachan Ai, *i.* cclvii, cccv, cccxxvii, ccclii, cccclv, cccclxvi, cccclxxxii, ccclxxxi, dcxli; *ii.* 70, 71, 72, 83, 84, 107, 129, 201, 202, 259, 260, 262, 291, 343, 345, 357, 389; *iii.* 10, 11, 15, 23, 25, 57, 59, 61, 89, 91, 106, 109, 110, 126, 156, 157, 179, 181, 199, 200, 218, 219, 220, 222, 254, 307, 323, 339, 367, 377, 382, 383, 412, 413, 443, 455, 463, 524, 525.
„ Claenta, in Offaly, *ii.* 43; *iii.*
Cuailgne, *ii.* 200, 236, 315; *iii.* 90, 128, 195, 376, 414, 429, 433, 455. See also Cooley and Táin Bó Chuailgne.
Cualand, or Cualann, *i.* ccclxxiv; *iii.* 130, 136, 211, 255.
Cuarna, *ii.* 328.
Cuil Cuilleann, *ii.* 383.
Cuile, *iii.* 524.
Cuillen, *ii.* 141.
Cuil Silinné, *ii.* 259, 260.
Cuil Tola, *i.* ccclxxiv.
Cuirene, *i.* xxix; *iii.* 129.
Culend, the river, *iii.* 97.
Cullen, *iii.* 205, 206, 207, 208.
Cumar na Tri n-Uisce, *i.* ccclxxiv; *ii.* 383.
Curlew Mountains, *ii.* 344.
Cyprus, *i.* cccclxxxviii, dviii.
Daolach, the river Davil or Deely, and the townland of Ballydeely, County of Clare, *ii.* 122.
Damh, Inis, Daimhinis, *i.* ccclxxii; *ii.* 85.
Dal Araidhe, *i.* xxix, ccclxxv; *ii.* 17, 232, 337.
„ Cais, *i.* xxviii.
Dalriad, *i.* ccclxxv.
Davil, the river, *iii.* 74. See Daolach.
Dealbna, Dealbhna, now Delvin. See Delbhna.
Decies, *ii.* 31; *iii.* 346.
„ of Munster, *i.* xxvii, xxviii.
Deece, barony of, Co. of Meath, *iii.* 197.
Delbhna, *ii.* 220; *iii.* 126.
„ Beg and Dealbna Mór, *i.* xxx.
Delvin, *i.* xxx; *ii.* 124, 145, 221, 262. See Delbhna.
Demi Fore, bar. of, *i.* xxx.
Denbighshire, *i.* xxxviii.
Denmark, *i.* clxx, ccxiii, ccxix, ccxx, ccccx, ccccxxiv, cccclxvii; *ii.* 231, 266, 267, 273; *iii.* 231.
Derry, *ii.* 151, 153, 340, 389; *iii.* 8, 24, 245.
„ O'Donnell, *iii.* 230.
Diamraibh, now Diamor, *iii.* 41.
Dicaem, the river, *iii.* 97.
Dieppe, *i.* ccxcvii.
Dijon, *i.* lxiv.
Dind-Righ, or Dinn-Righ, *i.* cccv; *ii.* 256; *iii.* 242, 244, 250, 310.

Dingle, i. cccxv, ccclіv; iii. 70, 71, 75, 379.
„ Bay of, i. cccxii.
„ Promontory of, i. cccvii, cccix.
Disert Diarmada, now Castle Dermot, ii. 104, 144.
Ditmarsh, i. xciii, ccxviii, ccxix.
Dniepr, river, i. cccсxxii, ccccxxiv.
Dodder, river. See Dothra.
Dodona, i. dxl.
Dogmael, St., in Cardiganshire, i. lxvii.
Domnand, iii. 415, 421.
Don, river, i. ccccxxiv.
Donegal, i. xxviii, xxix; ii. 62, 184, 185; iii. 194, 222, 258, 264, 281, 366.
Donnegore, i. xxxviii.
Doon, Hill of, cccclxvii.
Dordogne, i. ccccxxv.
Dorind, i. ccclxxiv.
Dorsetshire, i. lxix, lxxii.
Dothra, river, iii. 136, 144. See Dodder.
Down, Co. of, i. xxix, ccclxxv, dcxliv; ii. 325; iii. 5, 17, 128, 148, 296.
Downhall, iii. 194.
Downpatrick, ii. 325; iii. 5, 95, 148.
Dover, i. xxxiv, xxxv.
Drogheda, ii. 292, 296, 366; iii. 375.
Drom Ceat, ii. 77, 78; iii. 245 247, 250, 371, 374, 376.
„ Ceata, *recte* Drom Ceat.
„ Cruachain, ii. 165.
„ Damhghaire, ii. 212 to 215, 227, 278; iii. 361.
Dromiskin, ii. 140.
Drom Cliabh, i. xxix.
„ Leis, iii. 377.
„ Lighin, ii. 220.
„ Sneachta, ii. 51.
Drong, river, iii. 97.
Drowes, river, i. xxix.
Druim Airthir, ii. 145, 146.
„ Asail, ii. 215.
„ Cain, ii. 189.
„ Criadh, ii. 262.
„ Criaich, now Drum Cree, ii. 145, 146, 147.
„ Cro, ii. 145. See Druim Criach.
„ Da Chonair, ii. 386.
„ Dairbreach, ii. 146.
„ Daoile, ii. 386.
„ Decsain, ii. 189.
„ Fingen, ii. 201.
„ Gale, i. xv.
Druim Inniscіaimh, ii. 95.
„ Leith (or Liath), iii. 126.
„ Lethan, i. ccclxxiv.
„ na n-Druadh, ii. 71.
Drumany, iii. 254.
Drumcliffe, i. xxix; iii. 280.
Drumcree, ii. 145, 262. See Druim Criaich.
Drumlane, i. ccclxxv.
Drung, iii. 125.
Dubh Chathair, iii. 5, 74.
„ Chomar, ii. 152, 10.
Dubglas, the river, iii. 97.
Dubhlinn, ii. 288, 289, 252.
Dubhthair, iii. 160.
Dublin, i. xxiv, dcix, dcxiii; ii. 288, 289, 346, 347, 353, 383; iii. 2, 5, 37, 41, 122, 136, 137, 179, 205, 227, 274, 281, 295, 297, 298, 301, 319, 331, 339.
Dublin, County of, i. xc, ccclxxiv.
Duffern, iii. 174.
Duibthir, iii. 174, 175.
Duma Eire, ii. 106.
Dun Aenghuis, or Dun Aengus, ii. 1 2; iii. 5, 74, 122.
Dunbarton, i. xc.
„ -beg, i. cccxiii-cccxv; iii. 68, 72.
„ -bolg, ii. 340, 341.
„ Bric, ii. 96.
„ Celtchair, iii. 325.
„ Cermna, or Cearmna, ii. 111, 218, 219.
„ Cheltchair, or Chealtchair, iii. 5, 148. See Dun Celtchair.
„ Chonchraidhe. See Dun Concraid.
„ Concraid, iii. 66, 74.
„ Da Bheann, ii. 314.
„ Da Leath Glass, ii. 75; iii. 5, 95. See Dun Celtchair.
Dundalk, i. ccclxxv, xxx; ii. 197, 310; iii. 5. See Dundelca.
Dundelca, ii. 197; iii. 5. See Dundalk.
„ drum, ii. 341; iii. 17, 40.
„ Duibh Linne, iii. 5. See Dublin.
„ Eoghanacht, ii. 5.
Dungannon, barony of, i xxix.
„ Geirg (Dun Geirg Faebhur Geal), ccclxxii; i. ccclxxv.
„ Map Lethan, ii. 211.
„ Mór, iii. 71, 72.
„ More. See Dunmór.
„ na n-Gedh, ii. 342.
Dungarvan, na Sciath, iii. 24.
„ na h-Uidhre, iii. 127.
„ nechtain, ii. 366.

Dungarvan Ochaill, *iii.* 5, 74.
„ Ogain, *iii.* 340.
„ Quin, *iii.* 68.
„ Rudhraidhe, *iii.* 17.
„ Severick, *ii.* 315. See Dun Sobhairce.
„ Shaughlin, *i.* xxvii.
„ Sobhairce, *ii.* 111, 315.
„ Tradin, or Tredin, *ii.* 211.
„ Tulcha, or Tulchadh, *iii.* 59, 61.
Durlas Muaidhe, or Durlas Guaire, *ii.* 87, 88, 150, 151.
Eas da Eccon, *iii.* 258. See Eas-ruadh.
„ darra, or Balasadare, *ii.* 344.
„ ruadh, or Easroe, *i.* xxix; *ii.* 85, 145, 162; *iii.* 366.
Edinburgh, *i.* dcxxiv, *ii.* 353.
Edmuind, *i.* ccciv.
Egypt, *i.* lxxviii, cccxxiii, ccccxxviii, ccccIxxxiv, ccccIxxxvi, ccccIxxxviii, dxiv; *ii.* 20, 113, 188; *iii.* 216, 217, 226, 228, 229, 230, 231, 233.
Eithne, river, now the Inny, *ii.* 2[illegible]0.
El Amara, *i.* ccccIxxxv.
Elbe, *i.* xxxiv.
Ele, *i.* ccclxxiv.
Elga, Ealga, *iii.* 129, 419, 459.
Elgin, *i.* xc.
Elies, the, *i.* xxviii.
Eliogarty, *i.* xxviii, ccclxxiv.
Ely, *ii.* 62.
Ely O'Carroll, *i.* xxviii, ccclxxiv.
Emain Macha, *i.* cccxiii, cccxxxvii, ccclxxii; *ii.* 199; *iii.* 17, 18, 131, 199, 372, 427. See Emania.
Emania, *i.* lxxxix, ccclvii, ccccIxxxii; *ii.* 9, 45, 53, 54, 97, 107, 112, 145, 196, 198, 199, 200, 297, 319, 332, 333, 357, 358, 359 to 367, 368, 372, 373; *iii.* 11, 15, 17, 23, 25, 57, 59, 80, 102, 122, 132, 145, 196, 315, 365, 372, 373, 374, 380, 453.
Emhain, *iii.* 316. See Emania.
Emiligh, now Emly, *ii.* 76; *iii* 331.
England, *i.* xxxix, xlv, lxviii, lxxii, lxxxvii, xciv, clxix, clxxvii, ccv, ccvi, ccxiii, ccxiv, cclx, cclxxxiii, cclxxxv, cclxxxvii, ccxcvii, cccvi, cccliii, ccclxxvi, ccclxxviii, ccccxi, ccccxxvi, ccccIviii, ccccxcvi, ccccxcviii, dvii, dxviii, dxix, dlxvi, dlxvii, dcxiii, dcxiv, dcxxiii, dcxxv, dcxxvi, dcxxxiii, dcxxxiv; *iii.* 392.
English Channel, *i.* xlv.
Eoganacht of Cashel, *i.* xxvii.
„ Inassa, *i.* xxviii.
„ n-Inais = n-Inussa, *i.* xxviii.
Eoganacht of Loch Lein, *i.* xxv[illegible]
„ of Ross Argait, *i.* xxviii.
Erne, river, *i.* xxix.
Erris, *i.* xxix; *ii.* 302.
Erzebirge, *i.* ccccxviii, cc[illegible] ccccxxviii.
Etruria, *i*, xciv, dxxxix.
Exeter, *i.* ccxiii.
Eybenstock, *i.* ccccxix.
Fahan, County of Kerry, *i.* [illegible] cccvii, cccxiii; *ii.* 68-71, 97, [illegible]
Fahlun, *i.* ccccxvi.
Faile, *i.* xlvi.
Falias, *iii.* 281, 282.
Farney, *iii.* 93.
Fathan Mura, *ii.* 176 See Fah[illegible]
Feaa, *ii.* 383.
Feara Arda, *i.* xxx; *iii.* 130.
„ Cuile, *i.* ccclxxv.
„ Feara, *i.* xxx.
„ Lurg, *i.* xxx.
„ Manach, *iii.* 128.
„ Muighe, *i.* xxvii, xcvii.
Fearbile, *iii.* 372.
Fearnmaige, *ii.* 21; *iii.* 93.
Fearta na n-inghen, *iii.* 353.
Fechi, *i.* cccxxvii.
Feenach, *ii.* 88.
Fehmarn, in Ditmarsch, *i.* ccxix.
Femin, *i.* xxviii.
Fera, or Feara, Rois, *i.* xxx; *iii.* 385.
Fer Dryid (Anglesey), *ii.* 182.
Fer Falga, Fer Folga, *i.* ccc[illegible] ccclxiii.
Fergus, river, *ii.* 22[illegible].
Fermanagh, *i.* xxix, lxxxix; *ii.* [illegible] *iii.* 169.
Fermir, *i.* xlvi.
Fermoy, *i.* xcvii; *ii.* 215; *iii.* 283, 317. See Feara Muighe.
„ barony of, *i.* xxviii.
Ferns, *ii.* 339.
Ferrard, barony of, *i.* xxx.
Ferriters Cove, *iii.* 257.
Fer Ruide, *i.* xxviii.
Ferta Fingin, *iii.* 97.
Fifeshire, *i.* xc.
Findbo in Sweden, *i.* ccccxix.
Finisterre, Dept. of, *i.* ccccxxxix
Finland, *i.* ccccxciv.
Finnglas, river, *iii.* 80-81.
Finntraigh, *iii.* 82, 379. See [illegible]tracht.
Fintracht, now Ventry, *i.* ccclx.
Fiodhnach, *ii.* 220.
Firfalgia, (*recte*, Fir Falga) *iii.* 7[illegible]
Flanders, *i.* cxciv, ccxi, ccxix, [illegible] dlvii, dcv.

Florence, *i.* dlxiv, dcxxxi.
Fobar, now Fore, *ii.* 85.
Forchartan, *ii.* 288, 289.
Forfarshire, *i.* xc.
Forlochra Ardda, *i.* ccclxxiv.
Forth, *ii.* 387.
Forthuats, *i.* xxvii.
Forud, *i.* ccccxx.
Fothairt, *ii.* 40, 43, 44; *iii.* 130.
Fotharta Airbrech, *i.* xxvii.
France, *i.* v, xvii, xxxiii, xlv, cxciv, cxcv, ccix, ccx, cclxv, ccxc, ccxcvii, cccxlix, cccliv, ccclxxvii, ccclxxxi, ccccxxv, ccccxxviii, cccclvi, dxvi, dliii, dlvii, dlviii, dlix, dlxiii, dlxvii, dcv, dcviii, dcxxxii; *ii.* 231, 256, 287, 347; *iii.* 288.
„ northern, *i.* dxxiv.
„ south of, *i.* dxxix.
Freiberg, *i.* ccccxv.
Friesland, *i.* clix, ccccxcviii.
Fuibthirbe, (*recte*, Fuithirbe) coast of, *i.* ccccxxxv.
Fuithrim, Fuithribthe, *ii.* 32; *iii.* 466.
Gabar, Gabor, *i.* xxvii.
Gabhar, *ii.* 40.
Gabhra Aicle, *ii.* 382, 383, 386, 387. See Skreen.
„ South, *iii.* 529.
Gabhran, *iii.* 272.
Gaible Gó-Cluain, Gaibhle, *ii.* 44; *iii.* 541.
Gaela, *ii.* 124.
Gailenga, Galenga, great and little, *i.* xxix; *ii.* 130, 139, 140.
Gainemain, river, *i.* xxix; *iii.* 97.
Galicia, *i.* lxxvi, ccccxix, ccccxxviii.
Gallia Braccata, *i.* ccclxxxi.
„ Comata, *i.* ccclvi.
Galmoy, bar. of, *i.* xxviii.
Galway, *i.* xxiv, xxviii, ccxlv, cccvii; *ii.* 122, 268, 331; *iii.* 5, 65, 67, 74, 84, 85, 106, 121, 261, 291, 301.
„ Bay of, *i.* xxviii.
Garbhthamhnach, *ii.* 386. See Rath Inil.
Garristown, *ii.* 328.
Gaul, *i.* v, vi, xvii, xli, xlv, xlviii, liii, lvii, clxii, ccxi, ccxxiv, ccxxxv, ccxxxviii, cclviii, ccxcvi, ccxcviii, ccc, cccxc, cccxci, ccccxxix, cccclxxiv, cccclxv, d, dvii, dxxxiv, dl, dli, dlxvii, dcxliv; *ii.* 225, 256.
„ Transalpine, *i.* ccclxix.
Gergin, *i.* ccclxxv.
Germany, *i.* v, vi, xli, lvii, lxxvi, clxxxv, cxciv, cxcv, ccxi, ccxxiv, ccxxx, ccxxxv, cclviii, ccxcvi, cccliii, cccliv, ccclv, ccclxxvi, ccclxxvii, ccccxcii, ccccx, ccccxxii, ccccxxix, ccccxli, ccccxliv, cccclv, cccclviii, cccclxv, dvii, dxviii, dxxvii, dlvi, dlvii, dlxiii, dlxvii, dcxxxii, dcxxxiii.
„ Central, *i.* ccccxxv.
„ Eastern, *i.* ccccxxiv.
„ Northern, *i.* ccccxxv; *ii.* 231.
Gesoriacum, *i.* ccccxliii.
Geyer, *i.* ccccxix.
Giants' Causeway, *ii.* 315.
Gibraltar, Straits of, *i.* ccccxi.
Giehren, *i.* ccccxix.
Gizeh, Giseh, *i.* cccclxxxiv, cccclxxxv, dxi.
Glais Bearramain, river, now the Inny, *ii.* 290.
„ Nera, the river, *ii.* 140.
Glamorganshire, *i.* xxxviii.
Glandalough. See Glendaloch.
Glanworth, *i.* xxviii.
Glas Naoidhen, now Glasnevin, *ii.* 9, 76, 81.
Glastimberi (Glastonbury), *ii.* 211.
Glastonbury, *i.* xxxix, dvii, dviii, dcxliv.
Gleanamain, river, *iii.* 97.
Glendaloch, *ii.* 77, 85; *iii.* 50, 227 290.
Glendalough. See Glendaloch.
Glennamhnach, *i.* xxviii.
Glenn an Scail, *ii.* 88; *iii.* 346, 347. See Glenn Dallun.
„ Dallun, *iii.* 235. See Glenn an Scail.
„ Fahan, *i.* cxlv, cccvii; *iii.* 70 71, 72, 73.
„ Geirg, in Ulster, *iii.* 307, 367.
„ Gerg, *iii.* 153.
„ Righi, Righe, *i.* xxix; *iii.* 316.
„ Treithim, *ii.* 246.
Gleoir, river, *iii.* 97.
Göttingen, *i.* cxcv.
Gorias, *iii.* 231, 232.
Gort Insi Guire, now Gort, *i.* xxx; *ii.* 87.
Gothland, *i.* ccc.
„ East, *i.* clxxv.
Gower. See Guir.
Granairud, *i.* ccccxliii. See Granard.
Granard, *iii.* 291. See Granairud.
Great Britain, *i.* cccclxvii, dcxvii.
Great Island, Cork Harbour, *i.* xxxix.
Greece, *i.* iii, ccccxxiii, ccccxxviii, cccclxxxviii, dviii; *ii.* 188, 232; *iii.* 226, 231, 233, 234, 459, 523.
Grellach, *i.* ccccxliii.
„ Dullaigh, *ii.* 166.

Grellach Eilti, *ii.* 335.
Grenius, *i.* xlvi.
Grianan-Lachtna, *ii.* 115 ; *iii.* 24.
Guined, *ii.* 222.
Guir, now Gower, *i.* xxxviii.
Gweebarra Bay, *ii.* 33.
Gwent (South Wales), *i.* cxli.
Gwynedd (North Wales), *i.* xxxvii, cxlii.
Hagenow, *i.* ccccxvi.
Hallstadt, *i.* ccccxxii, ccccxxv.
Hamath, *i.* dviii.
Hanover, *i.* ccccxxv, ccccxli.
Hastings, *i.* cccclix.
Hebrides, *ii.* 122, 328.
Heidelberg, *i.* ccclxxxi.
Heror, *ii.* 222.
Highlands of Scotland, *i.* cccc.
Hildesheim, *i.* cxcv.
Hita, *i.* dxxiii.
Holland, *i.* clix.
Horse Leap Castle, *i.* xxviii.
Howth, Hill of, *i.* xxiv, cccxxxiv ; *iii.* 136, 179.
Huntingdonshire, *i.* lxxiii.
Hy Censella, *ii.* 376.
„ Drona, *ii.* 44 ; *iii.* 544.
„ Maine, *ii.* 376 ; *iii.* 84. See Hymany.
„ Nelland, *ii.* 233.
Hymany, *i.* ccxlv, ccliv. See Ui Maine.
Ibricken, bar. of, *i.* xxviii.
Iceland, *i.* dcxxiii.
Ictian Sea, *i.* xxxv.
Ierne, *i.* xliv.
Iffa and Offa East, bar. of, *i.* xxvii, xxviii.
Ikerrin, bar. of, *i.* xxviii.
Imahuadha, now Timahoe, *iii.* 395.
Imliuch Iobhair, or Ibhair, now Emly, *ii.* 82 ; *iii.* 331.
Immail, *iii.* 93.
Imokilly, bar. of, *i.* xxvii.
Inber Colpa, *i.* xxx ; *ii.* 111.
„ Crara, *iii.* 396.
„ Ferna, *i.* ccclxxiv.
„ in Rig, *i.* ccclxxv.
„ Mór, *ii.* 54.
Inbher Colptha. See Inber Colpa.
Inbiur Cichmaine, *iii.* 188.
Inchiquin, *iii.* 332, 349.
„ barony of, *i.* xciii.
India, *i.* lxxvii.
Inis Bo Finne, *iii.* 67.
„ Cail, now Iniskeel, *ii.* 33.
Iniscaltra, *iii.* 51.
Inis Carthaigh, (*recte*, Cathaigh) *i.* cccxxix.
Inis Catharg (*recte*, Cathaigh), *ii.* 364.
„ Celtra, *ii.* 76.
„ Clothrann, *ii.* 291.
„ da Dhrom, *ii.* 220.
„ Derglocha, *ii.* 383.
„ Eoghain, now Inishowen, *ii.* 163
„ Erca, *iii.* 67.
„ Fail, a poetic name of Ireland, *ii.* 71, 191, 192 ; *iii.* 287.
„ Faithlenn, now Inisfallen, *ii.* 177.
„ (Innse) Gall, the Hebrides, *ii.* 120.
„ Gluaire, *iii.* 66.
„ Salmer, *ii.* 232.
Inneoin, *ii.* 207, 208 ; *iii.* 203.
Innisfallen, *ii.* 137. See Inis Faithlenn.
Innistymon, *iii.* 332.
Innse an Ghaill Duibh, *ii.* 120.
Inny, the river, *i.* xxx ; *ii.* 290.
Inverness, *i.* xc.
Iona or I, *ii.* 80, 85 ; *iii.* 245, 385.
Irard Cuilland, *i.* ccxliii.
Ireland, *i.* ccccxxvi, ccccxxix, ccccxxx, ccccxc, ccccxci, ccccxcviii—*passim*.
Irrus Domnain, *ii.* 302.
Irruadh (Norway), *iii.* 100, 102.
Island Magee, *iii.* 3, 386.
Isle of Man, *ii.* 88.
Italy, *i.* cxciv, ccxi, ccclxii, ccclxix, cccxciv, ccccvi, ccccixxxviii, dxiv, dxvi, dxx, dxxxii, dxxxiv, dl, dli, dlviii, dlix, dlxvii, dcxvii.
Iveagh, Barony of Upper and Lower, *i.* xxix.
Iveragh, Mountains, *i.* cccxii.
Joachimsthal, *i.* ccccxix.
Jutland (the Jutic Moor), *i.* cli.
Kalenberg, *i.* cxcv.
Καρβαντόριγον, *i.* ccccixxvii.
Keelogue Ford, *ii.* 267-271.
Kells, *i.* xxvii, cccxcvi ; *ii.* 123, 148, 149.
„ Barony of, *i.* ccclxxv.
Kenmare, Bay of, *iii.* 59.
Kent, *i.* xcvii, clxix, clxxxiv.
Kentire, *ii.* 39 ; *iii.* 316.
Kerry, *i.* xxviii, cccvi, cccvii, cccviii, cccix, et seq., ccclív, ccclxxiv, ccccvi, dcv ; *ii.* 278, 375, 383 ; *iii.* 5, 12, 15, 45, 59, 61, 65, 70, 71, 75, 80, 85, 125, 132, 152, 181, 257, 264, 288, 374, 377, 379, 392.
Kidwelly, see Cetgueli.
Kilbarron Castle, *ii.* 93.
Kilcock, *iii.* 123.

Kilconnell, Barony of, *i.* cexlv.
Kilcumny, *ii.* 145, 262.
Kildare, *i.* xxvii; *ii.* 73, 77, 148, 328, 351, 390, 391; *iii.* 45, 122, 182, 309, 311, 381, 394, 395, 396.
„ and Leighlin, diocese of, *i.* xxvii.
Kilfinane, *iii.* 261.
Kilgobbin, *iii.* 40.
Kilkea, *iii.* 294.
Kilkee, *iii.* 67.
Kilkenny, County of, *i.* xxviii, cliv; *ii.* 328; *iii.* 45, 229.
„ barony of, *i.* xxx; *iii.* 254.
„ church of, *ii.* 81.
Killabban, *iii.* 45.
Killaloe, *ii.* 115; *iii.* 24.
Killarney, Lakes of, *i.* xxxviii; *ii.* 32, 177; *iii.* 203, 291.
Killeen Cormac, *i.* lxvii.
Kilmacduach, diocese of, *i.* xxviii.
Kilmacrennan, bar. of, *i.* xxix.
Kilmactranny, bar. of, *i.* xxix.
Kilmaine, bar. of, *i.* xxix.
Kilmainham, *ii.* 346.
Kilrush, *iii.* 364.
Kincardine, *i.* xc.
Kinelmeaky, bar. of, *i.* xxviii.
King's County, *i.* xxvii, xxviii, cliv; *ii.* 268; *iii.* 4, 45, 166, 319, 394.
Kinsale, *ii.* 166.
„ Old Head of, *ii.* 218.
Kirch Jessar, *i.* ccccxvi, ccccxviii.
Kirkcudbright, *i.* xc.
Kition, *i.* dviii.
Knockany, *i.* xxviii; *iii.* 260. See Cnoc Aine.
Knockaulin, *ii.* 358.
Knocklong, *ii.* 27; *iii.* 361.
Kotterbach, *i.* ccccxiv.
Kujundschik, *i.* dix.
Kurnah, *i.* cccclxxxv.
Laaland, *i.* cccx.
La Cave, at Volnay, *i.* lxiv.
Laeghaire, *i.* xxix.
Lagney, barony of, *i.* xxx.
Laigen, Laighen, *i.* cccxlv; *ii.* 9, 10; *iii.* 243. See Leinster.
Laighdi, *i.* xxviii.
Laighis, or Leix, *ii.* 374.
Laigne, *i.* cexxix.
Lambeth, library of, *i.* xcvi.
Lancashire, *i.* cccvi.
Lanesborough, *ii.* 283.
Langres, *i.* ccclvi.
Larne, *iii.* 175, 316. See Latharn.
Latharn, *iii.* 316, 377.
Lattringen, *i.* ccccxxxix.
Leac na n-Giall, *ii.* 310.
Leath Chuinn, *ii.* 384. See Leith Chuinn.
Lecale, *i.* ccclxxv.
Leim a Mhadaigh, *iii.* 245.
Leim an Eich, Castle of, *i.* xxviii.
Leimne, *ii.* 233.
Leinster, *i.* xxi, xxvii, xxxiii, ccxxx, cccvii, ccexlii, ccclxi, ccccii, ccccxlv; *ii.* 5, 13, 40, 46, 74, 105, 121, 155, 199, 256, 257, 295, 296, 325, 338, 346, 347, 348, 357, 376, 377, 383, 386, 389, 390, 391; *iii.* 15, 25, 44, 61, 85, 118, 119, 124, 130, 131, 132, 136, 149, 160, 210, 211, 242, 244, 255, 278, 309, 310, 311, 313, 371, 527.
„ South, *i.* xxvii.
Leipzig, *i.* dcxix.
Leiter Duibh, *iii.* 377.
Leith, *ii.* 386.
Leith Chuinn, *iii.* 309. See Leath Chuinn.
Leithglinn, now Leighlin, *ii.* 68, 330; *iii.* 34, 244.
Leitrim, County of, *i.* xxx.
Leix, *i.* xcv; *ii.* 374.
Lena, *i.* viii.
Leon, *i.* dxxii.
Lercaib, *i.* cccvi.
Lethard, *ii.* 214.
Letterkenny, *ii.* 164.
Levant, the, *i.* ccccvi.
Leyney, *ii.* 376.
Lewis, Island of, *ii.* 347.
Liabh Truim (recte Liathruim, or Liath Druim), *ii.* 189; *iii.* 317.
Liag Tuill, *i.* xxviii.
Life, river, *ii.* 246, 247. See Liffey.
Liffey, river, *i.* xxvii; *ii.* 140, 233, 246, 247, 252, 253, 288, 289; *iii.* 5, 44, 88, 136, 137.
„ the plain of, *ii.* 233.
Lifford, *ii.* 164.
Limavady, *iii.* 245.
Limerick, County of, *i.* xxviii, cccvii, ccclxvi, ccclxxiv, cccclxvii; *ii.* 357, 383; *iii.* 5, 15, 82, 85, 132, 205, 208, 259, 261, 278, 290, 291, 342, 347, 361, 379.
„ City of, *ii.* 76, 276; *iii.* 120, 153, 154, 267, 268, 269, 271, 272, 275, 280, 295.
Limoges, *i.* ccccxix.
Lindesse or Lincoln, *i.* xcvii.
Lind Formait, *iii.* 459.
Lios an Doill, *iii.* 301. See Lissadill
Lismaothal, *i.* ccclxvi.

Lis Mór, *iii.* 4, 5. See Lismore.
Lismore, Co. of Waterford, *ii.* 85, 204; *iii.* 4, 5.
„ in Scotland, *iii.* 300.
Lis na Banntrachta, *iii.* 360, 361.
Lissadill, *iii.* 280.
Listowel, *iii.* 5.
Lis Tuathail. See Listowel.
Lobbes, the ancient Liptinae, or Liptinas, *i.* cclxiv.
Loch in Scotland, *iii.* 371, 374.
„ Aininn, now Loch Ennel, *iii.* 24.
„ Bricrend, see Lough Bricland, *iii.* 17.
„ Broicsighe, or Broigseach, *iii.* 332.
„ Carman, *ii.* 113, 114.
„ Cé, *i.* xxix; *iii.* 25, 264.
„ Cime, *i.* xxix.
„ Cuain, *i.* ccclxxv.
„ Cuire, *iii.* 379.
„ Cutra, now Loch Cooter, *ii.* 122.
„ Dairbrech, *ii.* 262.
„ Dearg, *ii.* 144.
„ Echtrann, *ii.* 366.
„ En, *ii.* 89; *iii.* 24, 25.
„ Ennel, *iii.* 24.
„ Erne, *ii.* 85.
„ Feabhail (Loch Foyle), *ii.* 152.
„ Gair, *i.* cccclxvii. See Lough Gurr.
„ Garman, *ii.* 13. See Loch Carman.
„ Gile, *ii.* 335.
„ n-Guala, *i.* ccclxxii.
„ Lein, *i.* xciii; *ii.* 177; *iii.* 203, 204.
„ Lugh-Phorta, *ii.* 221.
„ Lurcan, *iii.* 404, 405
„ Mór, *ii.* 369.
„ Na Ratha, *iii.* 332.
„ Owel, *iii.* 248. See Loch Uair.
„ Reagh, *iii.* 156, 179. See Loch Riach.
„ Ree, *ii.* 291.
„ Riach, *ii.* 99; *iii.* 153, 156, 158, 179. See Loch Reagh.
„ Senain, *iii.* 364.
„ Silen, *i.* xxx.
„ Techad, *i.* xxix.
„ Uair, *i.* ccxl; *iii.* 248. See Lough Owel.
Lochland, *ii.* 346, 347, 350.
Logore. See Lough Gower.
Loire, river, in France, *i.* xxii, xlv, lxxvi; *ii.* 59, 166, 287.
Lolland, *i.* cli.
Lombardy, *i.* xxii, clix.
London, *i.* cci, ccii, ccxii, ccxii, ccciii, dxv.
Londonderry, County of, *iii.* 294.
Longerie, *i.* cccxxv.
Longford, County of, *i.* xxx, ccclxxv; *ii.* 161; *iii.* 85, 163, 188, 189, 190, 355.
Lothar, now Lorra, *ii.* 62, 76, 115, 337.
Lothra, *recte* Lothar, which see.
„ Bricland, *iii.* 17.
Lough Foyle, *i.* xxix.
„ Gabhon. See Lough Gower.
„ Gower, *i.* xxvii.
„ Gurr, *i.* cccclxvii.
„ Erne, *i.* xxix.
„ Gara, *i.* xxix.
„ Hackett, *i* xxix.
„ Neagh, *i.* xxix.
„ Ree, *i.* xxix.
„ Shealin, *i.* xxx.
Louth, *i.* xxix, xxx, ccclxxv; *ii.* 5, 101, 195; *iii.* 77, 149, 293, 310.
Louvaine, *i.* dcxliv.
Low Countries, *i.* dcviii.
Lowicz, *i.* cl.
Luachair Deagaid, *i.* xxviii.
Luachar, *ii.* 107.
Luaighne, *iii.* 126.
Lüneberg, *i.* cxcv.
Luibnech, *ii.* 141.
Luighne, *i.* xxix; *ii.* 140, 209, 216; *iii.* 130.
Luininn, *ii.* 208.
Lumman, *ii.* 328.
Lundun, *i.* xlvii.
Lupfen, *i.* cccxcviii.
Lurg, barony of, *i.* xxx.
Lusc, now Lusk, *ii.* 195, 368; *iii.* 122.
Mac Dermot's Rock, Castle of, *iii.* 25.
Macedonia, *i.* lxxx.
Maela Mide, na tri, the three bald hills of Meath, *ii.* 321.
Mag, Adhair, *ii.* 122, 156, 336.
„ Ai, Aie, or Aoi, *i.* xxix, clv, clxxxv; *ii.* 11, 201; *iii.* 102, 258, 415.
„ Aidhne, *iii.* 178.
„ Ailbhe, *ii.* 105.
„ an Scail, *iii.* 423.
„ Bile, *ii.* 52, 159.
„ Bolg, now Moybolgue, *i.* xxv.
„ Breguin, *i.* xxvii.
„ Cetne, *i.* xxix.
„ Cobha, *i.* xxix.
„ Constantine, *iii.* 58.
„ Cro, *i.* xxiv.

Mag Eithrighe, *ii.* 232.
„ Ene, *ii.* 386.
„ Ercaithe, *iii.* 316.
„ Femen, *iii.* 325.
„ Inis, *i.* ccclxxv.
„ Ita, *ii.* 232.
„ Locha, *iii.* 129.
„ Lathairne, *ii.* 232.
„ Lena, or Leana, *i.* ccxxvi; *ii.* 65; *iii.* 8, 166, 179, 181, 359.
„ Line, *iii.* 152, 316. See Rath Mór Muighe Line.
„ Lir, *ii.* 232.
„ Lurg, *i.* xxix; *ii.* 129, 232; *iii.* 257.
„ Meine, *ii.* 215.
„ Mell, *ii.* 197; *iii.* 192.
„ Mia, *ii.* 236.
„ Mis, *ii.* 383
„ Misca, *ii.* 40.
„ Mucceda, *i.* cccxliii.
„ Mucruimhe, Macroimhe, *i.* xxi, xlii, ccccxxxiv, cccclii; *ii.* 57, 139, 140, 331; *iii.* 177, 261.
„ O'm-Bricain, *iii.* 288.
„ Raighne, *ii.* 215.
„ Rath, *ii.* 305, 341, 342; *iii.* 78, 368.
„ Rein, *i.* xxii; *ii.* 88.
„ Slecht, *i.* xxx; *ii.* 6, 227; *iii.* 88.
„ Techt, *i.* xxii.
„ Tuired, or Tuireadh, *i.* cccxxix, cccxxxvi, ccccxxxix, ccclii, ccccxxxi, ccccxxxii, cccclvii, cccclxiv, cccclxxiv, dcxxxvii, dcxxxix; *ii.* 59, 110, 111, 122, 132, 148, 181, 188, 222, 225, et seq. 231, 234, 235, 240, 242, 244, 245, 250, 252, 253, 254, 272, 288, 289, 295, 296, 311, 325, 328; *iii.* 5, 8, 42, 43, 74, 148, 155, 156, 210, 213, 214, 225, 233, 354, 355, 385.
„ „ na bh-Fomorach, *i.* xxix, cccxcvii, cccliii, cccclxxiv, dcxxxix-xl; *ii.* 45, et seq., 248, et seq., 253-254, 288; *iii.* 42-43, 155-156, 213-214, 385.
„ Tulaing, *i.* cccxl.
„ Uladh, *i.* cccxxxvi.
Maige, river, or Mague, *iii.* 82, 259.
Maigin, *ii.* 141.
Mainister Buite, now Monasterboice, *ii.* 107.
Maintz, *i.* cccclv.
Mallow, *iii.* 344, 345.
Malmesbury, *i.* dvii.
Man, Isle of, *i.* xxii, xxxviii, cccclxiii; *ii.* 142, 143, 198, 347; *iii.* 80. See Manand.
Manand or Manann, *i.* xx; *ii.* 141, 198; *iii.* 419.
Mangerton, *ii.* 32.
Manister, Co. of Limerick, *iii.* 15, n. 11. See Clochar.
Mansfeldt, *i.* ccccxv, ccccxvi.
Mantua, *i.* dlxiv.
Map Liathan, *ii.* 211.
Martra, Cataract of Balasadare, *ii.* 344. See Eas-darra.
Mattock, the river, *ii.* 292, 366.
Maurice's Mills, *i.* ccclxvi.
Mayo, County of, *i.* xxix, ccclxxv; *iii.* 85, 835.
Meanus or Mianus, *iii.* 208.
Meath, East, Co. of, *i.* xxx.
„ *i.* xxvii, xxviii, xxx, ccclxxv; *ii* 78, 116, 121, 122, 126, 127, 148, 151, 161, 172, 259, 292, 293, 311, 326, 335, 346, 347, 358, 366; *iii.* 41, 43, 60, 123, 148, 177, 193, 197, 265, 301.
„ Sub-Kingdom of, *i.* xxxiii, xcvii, xcix, c, cccxx.
Mecklenburg, *i.* ccccxvi, ccccxviii, ccccxxii, ccccxxv, cccclv.
Medionemeton in Britain, *i.* cclxiv.
Mediterranean Sea, *i.* xxii, cccxcii, ccccxl, ccccxii, ccccxix, ccccxxviii, cccclxxii, cccclxxxvii; *iii.* 281, 282, 384.
Meithe an Eoin, *ii.* 293.
„ Togh, *ii.* 293.
Melifont, *ii.* 140; *iii.* 177.
Melrose Abbey, *i* ccccxcvi.
Menai Street, *ii.* 186.
Menpiscus, *i.* ccxix.
Mercia, *i.* cccxxxiv, dcxxvi.
Methin Port, *ii.* 293.
Midhe, *ii.* 13, 190, 19. See Meath.
Migdonia, *iii.* 231, 232.
Milan, *i.* lvi, dxxxi.
Military Frontier, *i.* cl.
Miliuc, river, *iii.* 97.
Miscal, *i.* xlvi.
Mitylene, *i.* cccclxxxvii.
Modicia or Monza, *i.* cccxciv.
Modurn, *iii.* 94.
Mœn Chonaing, sometimes incorrectly Moin Chonaing, *ii.* 185, 186.
Mohar ui Ruaidhin, *i.* xxviii.
Moile, *i.* xlvi.

Moin Mór, *ii.* 107.
„ Trogaidhe, *ii.* 356.
„ Ui Domhnaill, *iii.* 280.
Moira, see Magh Rath.
Mona, Island of Anglesey, *i.* xxix, xxx, xxxviii; *ii.* 182, 183, 185, 186.
Monaghan, *i.* lxxxix, xcv; *ii.* 392; *iii.* 309. See Muineachan.
Monasterboice, *ii.* 77, 107, 113, 114, 140, 149, 168, 169; *iii.* 210, 229.
Mont Afrique, near Dijon, *i.* lxiv.
„ Brigitte at Besançon, *i.* cccxci.
Monte Rey, *i.* cccexix.
Mont St. Michel, *i.* dxxvii.
Morbihan, *i.* cccexix.
Morca, *iii.* 243, 244, 249.
Morgallion, *i.* xxx; *ii.* 39.
Mount Eagle, *i.* cccvii; *iii.* 68.
„ Fuad (Sleibe Fuad or Fuat), *iii.* 148.
Moy, river, *iii.* 16. See Muaidhe.
„ the plain of, *i.* xxix.
Moyarta, barony of, *i.* xxviii.
Moycarne, barony of, *iii.* 85.
Moyfenrath, *i.* xxx.
Moyhill, *i.* ccclxvi.
Moylena. See Mag Lena.
Moylinny, *i.* xxxviii.
Muach, river, *iii.* 97.
Muaidhe, *ii.* 87.
Mughdorn, Muighdhorn, *i.* xxx; *iii.* 128.
Muigh Meadba (*recte* Magh Medba), *ii.* 129.
Muilchearn, river, *i.* ccclxxiv.
Muineachan. See Monaghan.
Muir (*recte* Mur) Meena, *ii.* 186.
Muir Nicht (Muir n-Icht), *i.* xxii.
„ Toirrian, *i.* xxii.
Muirtheimne, *i.* cccv, ccclxxv; *ii.* 195, 196, 311, 359; *iii.* 97, 128.
Mullach Maisten, *ii.* 246; *iii.* 122.
Mullaghmast. See Mullach Maisten.
Mullingar, *ii.* 315; *iii.* 24, 91, 248.
Mumha, *i.* cccxl. See Munster.
Mumhan, *ii.* 9, 10. See Munster.
Mungaret, or Mungret, *ii.* 76.
Munich, *i.* ccccl xxxvii, ccccl xxxix.
Munster, *i* xxv, xci, ccxxx, cccxxi, cccxlii; *ii.* 13, 31, 51, 61, 64, 65, 66, 78, 101, 105, 147, 151, 155, 177, 199, 205, 212, 213, 216, 250, 259, 281, 296, 331, 346, 347, 356, 357, 358, 375, 376, 377, 387, 388; *iii.* 5, 25, 44, 45, 61, 83, 85, 103, 106, 121, 133, 156, 166, 167, 168, 177, 193, 201, 204, 205, 207, 208, 209, 242, 243, 244, 255, 259, 260, 261, 271, 273, 283, 289, 291, 31[illegible] 329, 330, 334, 360, 379, 393, 39[illegible] 399, 466, 505.
Munster, West, *i.* xxviii, ccxx[illegible] cccvii, cccix, cccxiii.
Munster, North, *i.* ccccl xx.
Murias, *iii.* 231, 232, 233.
Mur Ollamhan, *ii.* 8.
„ Tea, *iii.* 12.
Murresk, barony of, *i.* xxix.
Murvey Strand, *iii.* 66.
Muscraidhe Breoghain, *i.* xxviii.
„ Luachra, *i.* xxviii.
Muscraighe, *i* cccxxii.
„ Mitaine, *i.* xxviii.
Muskerry, West, *i.* cccxxiv.
Myfyrion, *ii.* 182.
Nantes, *i.* xvii, ccxii, cccexix.
Nás, now Naas, *ii.* 105, 141, 145; *iii.* 25, 132.
Navan, barony of U. and L., *i.* xx[illegible]
Navarre, *i.* dxxii.
Νεμετόβριγα, in Spain, *i.* cclxiv.
Nemetocenna, of the Atrebati, *i* cclxiv.
Nevers, *i.* lxiii, lxiv.
Newburgh, *i.* ccccxcvii.
Newcastle, *iii.* 291.
New Grange, *ii.* 386.
Newry, the vale of, *i.* xxix.
Newtown Limavady, *ii.* 77.
Nikopol, *i.* cccexxii.
Nile, the, *i.* dxliii.
Niniveh, *i.* cccexxiii.
Nismes, or Nemausus, *i.* lxii, lxiii, lxv, lxxx.
Nola, *i.* dxxxiv, dxxxv.
Nore, river, *i.* ccclxxiv; *ii.* 144.
Norfolk, *i.* lxxiii, lxxxix, xcvii.
Normandy, *i.* lxviii.
North Sea Region, *i.* cccexxv.
Northumbria, *i.* xxxv, ccv, ccvi; *ii.* 82.
Norway, *i.* cxxxvii, cxlviii, clxx[illegible] ccxxviii, cclxv, ccclxxiv, ccclxx[illegible]; *ii.* 231; *iii.* 100, 101, 231, 408.
Norwich, *i.* ccxiii.
Nowo-Tscherkask, *i.* cccexxiv.
Ocha, *ii.* 339, 340.
Ochter n-Achad, *i.* lxxxix.
Ochun, *ii.* 108.
O'Colman's Hill (Tara), *iii.* 339, 34[illegible]
O'Dorney, *i.* ccclxxiv; *ii.* 59.
Oendruim, now Island Magee, *ii.* 386, 387.
O'Failge (Offaly), *ii.* 40; *iii.* 529, 53[illegible]
Offaly, barony of, E. and W., *i.* xxvii.
Offerlane, *iii.* 44, 45

Oilen Dairbre, ii. 278.
Oirghiall, i. dcxliii; ii. 17, 110, 111, 127.
Olbha, ii. 96.
Olbia, i. ccccxxiv.
Oldenburg, i. ccccxxv.
Ollarbha, iii. 175, 316.
Olnegmacht (Connaught), ii. 10, 71.
O'Neilland, barony of, iii. 8.
Orange, i. cccclxiv.
Oranmore, iii. 261.
Orbraidhe, iii. 125.
Orcades, i. xliii.
O'Regan, i. xcvi.
Oriel. See Oirghiall, i. xxix; iii. 127, 128.
Orior, i. xcv.
Orkney, i. dxix.
Ormond, i. xxviii; ii. 62, 143, 337; iii. 208, 288.
„ barony of Lower, i. xxviii.
Ossory, i. clxxiv; ii. 40, 43, 77, 226, 351, 352.
„ diocese of, i. xxvii.
Ostend, iii. 270.
Osterburg, iii. 348.
O'Torna, ii. 375.
Owney, barony of, i. xxviii.
Oxford, i. lvi; ii. 353; iii. 37, 281, 342.
Paris, i. ccccxxxix, ccccxcviii, d, dii, dvi; ii. 170.
Pavia, i. dlxii.
Pays de Grimberghe, i. clxxix.
„ de Liège, i. cclxiv.
Persia, i. ccccxxxii; ii. 18?, 325.
Perth, i. xc.
Petau, i. dvi; iii. 230, 232.
Pfalz, the, i. cccliii.
Phrygia, i. xciv, cccclxxxviii.
Pisa, i. dxv, dxvi.
Poitiers, Vieux, i. lxiii, lxiv.
Polentia, i. xlv.
Poll Begg (Poolbeg Street), ii. 288.
Poll na Brocuidhe, iii. 332.
Pomerania, i. ccccxxv.
Pompeii, i. dv, dvi.
Pontic Sea, iii. 381.
Portadown, iii. 295.
Portland, Isle of, i. clxix.
Portloman, iii. 248.
Portnahinch, bar. of, i. xxvii.
Portrigh, iii. 316.
Portugal, ii. 301.
Portumna, ii. 144.
Portus Iccius, i. xlv.
Provençe, i. dxxii.
Provincia, i. ccclxxxi, ccclxxxiv. See Provençe.
Prussia, i. ccccxxxv.
Puy-les-Vignes, i. ccccxix.
Pyriac, i. ccccxix.
Queen's County, i. xxvii, xcv, cliv, ccclxxiv; iii. 44, 45, 85.
Quin Abbey, Co. of Clare, i. cccxviii.
Raeilinn, iii. 131.
Rahen, iii. 37, 38.
Raighne, Flags of, ii. 215.
Raithlinn, i. xxviii.
Rath Aedh, ii. 159.
„ Becce, ii. 69.
„ Beg, iii. 527.
„ Beggan, ii. 69, 70. See Rath Becce.
„ Betha, ii. 7.
„ Bhiligh, ii. 339.
„ Blathmach, iii. 332.
„ Boith (Raphoe), ii 25, 80, 85.
„ Breisi, iii. 15.
„ Ceannaid, ii. 78.
„ Cimbaoith, ii. 233; iii. 3.
„ Cinn-Eich, ii. 283; iii. 3.
„ Cruachan, ii. 145; iii. 80. See Cruachan.
„ Essa, ii. 105, 106.
„ Gaela (now Rathkeale), iii. 5.
„ Inil, ii. 384, 386.
Rathain ua Suanaigh, iii. 37. See Rahen.
Rathin, iii. 4,
Rathkeale, see Rathgeala.
Rathlenn, Rathlend, i. cccxxii; iii. 125.
Rath Mailcatha, iii. 16.
Rathmore, i. xxxviii.
Rath-Mór Maighe Line. See Rathmore.
„ Mor Muighe, iii. 132.
„ na Righ, iii. 5, 6, 7, 12.
„ Naoi (now Rathnew), iii. 5
„ Rudhraidhe, iii. 23.
Ravenna, i. dcxxxv.
Red Sea, i. ccccxii, dlxx; ii. 252, 311; iii. 359.
Rede Loiche, iii. 195, 196.
Reichelsdorf, i. ccccxvi.
Reichenau, i. dxii.
Relig na Righ, i. cccxxviii; ii. 70.
Rhenish Hesse, i. ccccxxxviii.
Rhine, the, i. xxxv, cccclv.
„ Land, i. ccccxxv.
Rhodez, see Segodunum.
Rhone, river, i. ccccxliii
Rhuddlan, i. clxxviii.
Rigdond, iii. 94.
Righ, river, ii. 17.
Righ Mna Nuadhat, the river Boyne, iii. 156.
Rind, river, iii. 97.

Rind Roiss, *iii.* 316.
Rinn Cinn Beara, *ii.* 97.
Rinn Dubhain, *ii.* 384.
„ Snog, *iii.* 316.
Roadford, *i.* xxviii.
Robe, river, *i.* xxix.
Rock Forest, Co. of Tipperary, *iii.* 349.
Rodb, river, *i.* xxix.
Rome, *i.* iii, ccvii, ccviii, cclx, ccclxix, ccclxxix, cccexxii, cccexxiv, ccccIxxviii, dxvi, dxxxiii, dlxviii.
Ros, *iii.* 128.
„ Broc (now St. Mullins), *ii.* 385.
Roscommon, *i.* xxix, cliv, ccclxxiv; *ii.* 259, 291; *iii.* 24, 84, 85, 102, 103, 105, 106, 156, 199, 254, 257, 258, 283, 301.
Roscrea, *iii.* 349.
Ros na Rīgh, *ii.* 55, 295; *iii.* 525.
Ross, *i.* xc; *iii.* 385, 386.
„ *ii.* 330; *iii.* 34.
„ Ailithir, *i.* ccclx; *ii.* 76, 77.
„ diocese of, *i.* xxviii.
„ Guill, or Gull, *i.* xxix.
Rouen, *i.* ccccxxxviii, dxii; *ii.* 242, 243.
Roxburgh, *i.* cxlviii.
Ruddlan Marsh, *i.* dcxxvi. See Rhuddlan.
Russia, *i.* cxlix, ccccxi, ccccxxiv.
Saighir, *i.* ccclx, ccclxvi.
Sainte Reine d'Alise, *i.* lxiii, lxiv.
Salop, *i.* ccv.
Savoy, *i.* ccccxxv.
"Saxon Shore", *i.* xxxiv.
Saxony, *i.* xxii, cxlvii, ccccxxiv, ccccxxviii; *iii.* 348.
Scandinavia, *i.* lxxvi, clxxii, ccxiii, ccxcvi, ccccxix, ccccxxiv; *ii.* 276; *iii.* 231.
Schaffhausen, *i.* ccccxvi.
Schlaggenwald, *i.* ccccxix.
Schleswig-Holstein, *i.* ccccxxv.
Scilly Islands, *i.* ccccxi.
Scotia, exclusively applied to Ireland in ancient times, *ii.* 210.
Scotland, *i.* xxxv, xlviii, lxviii, xc, xci, clix, clxvii, ccxiv, ccl, ccclxxiv, ccccxxvi, ccccxxxiv, cccclxxi, ccccxc, ccccxci, dxix, dlxvi, dcxiii, dcxviii, dcxx, dcxxii, dcxxiii; *ii.* 88, 266, 287, 302, 341, 349, 368, 369, 380, 381; *iii.* 10, 38, 91, 136, 164, 165, 169, 180, 196, 247, 248, 250, 251, 261, 270, 271, 272, 273, 280, 281, 282, 283, 284, 285, 291, 296, 299, 300, 301, 315, 331, 339, 358, 360, 369, 371, 380, 384, 38[illegible], 400, 402, 406, 407, 408.
Scotland, Highlands of, *i.* cxlviii.
Screen, or Skreene, Hill of, *ii.* 10[illegible], 387; *iii.* 96, 197.
Scythia, *i.* lxxvi, ccccxxiii; *ii.* 18, 233; *iii.* 229, 231.
Segodunum, *i.* lxxxviii.
Seimhne, *iii.* 3, 316. See Semhne
Seine Inferieure, *i.* ccxcvii.
Seiscenn Uairbeoil, *iii.* 77.
Semhne, *iii.* 129.
Semira, near Kuranko, *i.* ccccxcv.
Sentraoia, Fort of, *iii.* 258.
Sequania, *i.* ccclxxxi.
Serrdha, country of, *iii.* 330.
Servia, *i.* cxlix.
Seven Churches of St. Brecan, *iii.* 6[illegible]
Shannon, river, *i.* xxix; *ii.* 14[illegible] to 144, 145, 201, 259, 26[illegible], 2[illegible]-271, 291, 335, 337; *iii.* 8[illegible], 254 262, 263, 364, 373, 392, 396. See Sinann.
Shenar, *ii.* 53.
Shruthru, *i.* ccexliii.
Siberia, *i.* ccccxvi.
Sicily, *i.* ccccxxiii.
Sidhan, *i.* xxix.
Sidhe an Caradh, *ii.* 221.
Sidh Ban Find, now Sliabh na m-Ban, *iii.* 324.
„ Femen, *ii.* 52, 383. See Sidh Ban Find.
„ Finnchaidh, *iii.* 527.
„ Findacha, now Sliabh g-Cullen, *iii.* 202.
„ Midir, *iii.* 355, 356.
Siegen, *i.* cl.
Sigtun, Odin's, *i.* lxxxviii, cclxv.
Silesia, *i.* ccccxix, ccccxxiv.
Silvermines, *iii.* 208.
Sinann, river (now the Shannon) *ii.* 142, 143, 144.
Siöberg, *i.* ccxx.
Sith Seapsa, *ii.* 343.
Skreen, Hill of, *i.* xxv.
Skye, Island of, *ii.* 347.
Slain, see Slane,
Slane, *i.* xxx; *ii.* 292, 358; *iii.* 122, [illegible]
Slaney, the river, *ii.* 144
Slebe Fuaid [recte Sliabh Fuaid], *iii.* 97.
Sleibhte, *ii.* 74.
Slemain, *iii.* 91, 92, 93, 94, 96, 97.
Slemish Mountain, *i.* xxix.
Sleswig, *i.* ccxv. See Schleswig-Holstein.
Sliabh an Chairn, *i.* xxix.
„ Bregh, *i.* xxx.

Sliabh Crot, *ii.* 386; *iii.* 179.
„ Cua, *ii.* 155, 156.
„ Cuilluin, or Sliabh g-Cuillen, *iii.* 202, 328.
„ Dallain, *ii.* 193.
„ Echtge, *ii.* 93.
„ Eibhline, *i.* xxviii.
„ Fuaid or Fuait, *i.* ccciv; *ii.* 359, 365.
„ Gamh, *ii.* 343.
„ Loughra, *i.* xxviii.
„ Mis, *i.* cccxiii; *ii.* 188, 383; *iii.* 75, 80, 81.
„ Monad in Alba, *iii.* 527.
„ Na m-ban, *i.* xxviii; *ii.* 383; *iii.* 156, 201, 203, 324.
„ Ughmoir (the Caucasus), *ii.* 232.
„ Uillin, *i.* cccxxxvi.
Slieve, see Sliabh.
Sligech (Sligo), *ii.* 344.
Slighed n-Dala, *iii.* 396.
Sligo, *i.* xxix; *ii.* 145, 335, 344; *iii.* 213.
Small County, bar. of, *i.* xxviii.
Smarmore, *iii.* 101. See Smiramair.
Smerwick, *iii.* 73.
Smiramair, *iii.* 101.
Sonderherred, *i.* ccxx.
Sorcha (Portugal), *ii.* 301.
Sord (now Swords), *iii.* 395.
Spain, *i.* xvii, lxxvi, lxxvii, xcv, cccxxvi, ccccxii, ccccxxviii dxxi, dxxxiv, dli; *ii.* 188; *iii.* 210, 360, 384.
Sruth Moena (the Menai Strait), *ii.* 186.
Stackallen, *ii.* 116.
Staigue Fort, *i.* cccvi.
St. Amand, *i.* dli.
St. Bavon at Ghent, *i.* ccxii.
St. Blaise or Blasien, *i.* cccexc, cccexcv, d, dviii, dxviii, dxix, dxxxvii.
St. Emeran, *i.* d, dxviii, dxxxviii.
St. Gall, *i.* cccclxvii, diii, div, dxii, dl, dlxvii, dlxviii, dlxix.
St. Germain des Pres, *i.* cxlvii.
St. Mullins, *ii.* 85; *iii.* 34, etc.
St. Omer, *i.* dxv.
St. Pierre, Abbey of, at Ghent, *i.* ccxii.
Stirling, *i.* xc.
Stour, river, *i.* lxxiii.
Straffan, *ii.* 328. See Tech Straffain.
Strangford Lough, *i.* ccclxxv.
Stratfleur, *i.* cccexcii.
Strokestown, *iii.* 25.
Styria, *iii.* 232.
Suck, river, *i.* xxix.
Sudermannland, *i.* ccc.
Suffolk, *i.* lxxiii, lxxxix.
Suilidh, river, now the Swilly.
Suir, river, *i.* ccclxxiv.
Suir, river, *ii.* 144, 206.
Sussex, *i.* xcvii.
Swansea, *i.* xxxviii, ccccxiv.
Sweden, *i.* clxx, ccxxviii, ccxxxi, cclxv, cclxvi, ccc, ccclxxiv, cccci, ccccxv, ccccxix.
Sweden, *iii.* 231, 403.
Switzerland, *i.* ccxcvi, ccccxxii, ccccxxv.
Swords, *ii.* 77; *iii.* 395, 396. See Sord.
Sylt, Island of, *i.* cli.
Syria, *iii.* 231.
Taffia, Northern, *i.* cccxliii.
Taillte. See Tailte.
Tailltin. See Tailte.
Tailte, *i.* xxxiii, cclvii, cccxxvi, cccxxvii, cccxxxiii, dcxxxviii, dcxl, dcxli; *ii.* 148, 381; *iii.* 193, 194, 524, 525.
Tailtiu. See Tailte.
Tallaght, Tallacht, *i.* cccxxxii; *ii.* 76, 85, 233; *iii.* 2, 136, 521.
Taman, peninsula of, *i.* ccccxxiii.
Tamhlacht. See Tallaght.
Tamlacht O'Crilly, *i.* cccxxxii.
Tanais, Old, *i.* ccccxxiv.
Tara, *i.* xxv, xxxiii, ccxxxi, ccliii, ccciii, cccxxvi, cccxxx, cccxxxiii, cccxxxiv, cccli, ccclxxvii, dxxxi; *ii.* 8, 12, 14, 15, 17, 30, 31, 38, 61, 64, 66, 68, 69, 72, 94, 106, 107, 141, 147, 152, 187, 189, 190, 201, 235, 236, 237, 262, 290, 327, 337, 377, 381, 383, 387, 389; *iii.* 2, 5, 6, 7, 8, 12, 14, 15, 24, 41, 42, 43, 59, 60, 61, 96, 105, 129, 130, 132, 136, 145, 152, 170, 172, 177, 180, 187, 193, 194, 197, 241, 306, 313, 317, 328, 339, 340, 355, 356, 367, 368, 377, 378, 396. See Teamair and Teamar.
Tasinemetum in Noricum, *i.* cclxiv.
Tattybrack, *i.* lxxxix.
Teabtha, *i.* xxx.
Teach Eandach, *iii.* 74.
„ Midchuarta, *ii.* 16, 49, 94, 105; *iii.* 6, 7, 17, 24, 74, 313, 367.
„ Moling, *ii.* 384; *iii.* 34, 45.
„ Mór Milib Amus, *iii.* 6, 24.
Teamair. See Teamar.
Temar, *i.* ccciii.

Teamar, Temar, *i.* xxx; *ii.* 12, 13, 14, 15, 16, 18, 19, 25, 45, 51, 106, 141, 148, 149, 150, 189, 192, 199, 285, 286, 287; *iii.* 7, 8, 15, 130, 144, 160, 362. See Tara.
„ of Dun Finntain, *iii.* 524.
Teamhair Luachra, *iii.* 182
Teampall Muire, cccxxix.
Tech Straffain, *ii.* 328.
Tees, river, *i.* lxix, lxxii.
Teffia, *i.* cccxxi; *ii.* 124, 137, 161.
Telameit, river, *iii.* 97.
Teltown, *ii.* 193. See Tailte.
Temair. See Teamar and Tara.
Temair Erind, *i.* cccxxvii.
Tempall Benen, *iii.* 66.
„ an Cheathrair Aluinn, *iii.* 66.
Templemore, Parish of, *iii.* 8.
Temur, or Teamur, see Teamar and Tara.
Teti Brice, *i.* lxxxix. See Teti Breac.
Teti Breac, Teitĕ Brec, *ii.* 196, 332.
Thames, river, *i.* cccclxiv.
Thebes, *i.* cccclxxxiv.
Thomond, *i.* xxviii; *ii.* 62, 162, 219, 375, 387; *iii.* 274, 280, 281, 282, 288.
Thrace, *ii.* 187, 233; *iii.* 231, 233.
Thule, *i.* xliii.
Thuringia, *i.* cli.
Tigh Moling, see Tech Moling.
Tigh Temrach, *iii.* 6, 7. See Tara.
Tinnahinch, bar. of, *i.* xxvii.
Tipperary, *i.* xxvii, xxviii, xcv, cliv, ccclxxiv; *ii.* 268, 383; *iii.* 5, 85, 158, 179, 202, 205, 208, 278, 324, 325, 331, 349.
Tir Aeda, *i.* xxviii.
„ Awley, bar. of, *i.* xxix.
„ Chonaill, *ii.* 102, 121, 160, 161, 162, 342, 343; *iii.* 280.
„ Connail, see Tir Chonaill.
„ Connell, see Tir Chonaill.
„ Erill, bar. of, *i.* xxix; *iii.* 213.
„ Enna, *ii.* 164.
„ Eoghain, or Tyrone, *i.* xxix; *ii.* 121, 134, 154, 345; *iii.* 126, 127.
„ Fhiachrach, *iii.* 16.
„ Hugh, bar. of, *i.* xxviii.
„ Morcha, *iii.* 242.
„ Olliolla, *i.* xxix; *iii.* 213.
„ Oiulla, *i.* xxix.
„ Tairngire, *i.* cccxxxiii.
Titchbourn, *i.* cxlii.
Tlachtga, *i.* xxxiii; *ii.* 141.
Todi in N. Italy, *i.* lxv.
Toledo, *i.* dxiv.
Tolka, river, *ii.* 81.
Tor Chonaing, Tory Island, *ii.* 186. See Tor Inis.
„ Inis, Tory Island, *ii.* 186. See Tor Chonaing.
Torrian Sea, *iii.* 459.
Tory Hill, Co. of Limerick, *ii.* 215.
Tory Island, *i.* cccccxxxv; *ii.* 184, 185, 186. See Tor Chonaing.
Toulouse, *i.* cccxcvii.
Tracht Ebe, *i.* dcxl.
Tradraidhe, *ii.* 220.
Traig Rudhraidhe, Port of, *ii.* 341.
„ Tuirbhe, Strand of Turvey, *iii.* 41.
Tralee, Bay of, *iii.* 15, 75, 80, 82.
Trent, river, *i.* ccvi.
Treoit, now Trevit, in Meath, *ii.* 52.
Treves, *i.* xliii, cl.
Trim, *i.* xxx; *ii.* 166; *iii.* 160. See Ath Truim.
Troyes, *i.* dxiv.
Tuaheran, *i.* xxviii.
Tuaim Drecain, now Toomregan, Co. of Cavan, *ii.* 77, 92, 93.
„ Finnlocha, *ii.* 220.
„ Teanbath, *iii.* 310.
Tuam, *ii.* 77.
Tuath Ranna, *i.* xxviii.
Tuirbhi (Turvey), *iii.* 41. See Turvey and Turbi.
Tulach Dathi, *ii.* 342.
„ Felmedha (now Tullow, in the Co. of Carlow), *ii.* 286.
„ Na Iliarmaitrigh, *iii.* 355, etc.
„ Og, *iii.* 127.
„ Ruse, *iii.* 316.
„ Gassa, *i.* ccvii; *iii.* 207, 208.
„ Thind, *i.* cccix.
Tuladh an Bhiail, *iii.* 41.
Tulchlaen, river. See Tolka, *ii.* 81.
Tullamore, *ii.* 81; *iii.* 4, 37.
Tullow, *iii.* 161, 404.
Turbi, *iii.* 41. See Tuirbhi and Turvey.
Turvey, strand of, *iii.* 41. See Turbi and Tuirbhi.
Tuscan Sea. See Tyrrhian Sea.
Tyndale in Northumberland, *i.* cclxxxviii.
Tyrone, *i.* xxix, lxxxix, xcv.
Tyrrhian Sea, *i.* xxii.
Uaithni, *i.* xxviii.
Uamh Leo, Leo's Cave, *iii.* 67.
Ui Amalgad, *i.* xxix.
„ Becon, *iii.* 130.
„ Breasail, *iii.* 127, 316.
„ Briuin, *i.* xxix.
„ Briuin of Breifne, *i.* xxx.

Ui Briuin Archoill, *iii*. 128, 132.
" Cairpre, *i*. xxviii.
" Ceinnselaigh, *i*. xxvii; *ii*. 74; *iii*. 361.
" Cella, *i*. cccxxxvi.
" Chonaill, *i*. xxviii.
" " Gabhra, *i*. xxviii.
" Cormaic, *iii* 261, 262, 263, 333.
" Criomhthannan, *iii*. 131.
" Deaghaidh, *iii* 45.
" Dortain, *iii*. 128.
" Doona, *ii*. 46; *iii*.
" Echach, *iii*. 128.
" " of Munster, *i*. xxviii.
" Failge, *i*. xxvii; *iii*. 529, 530.
" Fealain, *iii*. 130, 132.
" Feilmeadha, *iii*. 131.
" Fiachra, *ii*. 121.
" Fiachrach, *i*. xxix.
" " Aidni, *i*. xxviii.
" Fidhgheinte, *iii*. 261.
" Liathan, *i*. xxvii.
" Mac Cailli, *i*. xxvii.
" Mac Uais, *i*. xxx, cccxx.
" Maine, *i*. xxviii, xxix; *ii*. 58, 121, 122, 123, 124, 125, 126, 336, 337, 392; *iii*. 106, 126, 133.
" Meith, *iii*. 128.
" Mic Caerthainn, *iii*. 121, 127.
" Neill, *i*. xxix.
" Niallain, barony of, *ii*. 233; *iii*. 3.
" Torna, *ii*. 59.
" Tuirtre, *iii*. 127, 128.
Uib Saghain, *i*. xxx.
Uisnech, or Uisneach, *i*. xxxiii; *ii*. 13, 190, 191, 381; *iii*. 197, 202.
Ulad, Uladh, or Ulidia, *i*. xxix, cccxliii, ccclxxii; *ii*. 9, 10, 17, 55; *iii*. 128, 129. See Ulster.
Ullard, *i*. dxix; *iii*. 129.
Ulster, *i*. xxv, ccxxx, cccvii, cccxlii, cccliі, ccccііі; *ii*. 13, 66, 78, 121, 126, 164, 199, 290, 296, 313, 314, 315, 320, 357, 361, 366; *iii*. 17, 23, 25, 75, 85, 91-97, 109, 122, 131, 132, 141, 145, 161, 167, 168, 174, 175, 177, 187, 196, 202, 203, 248, 254, 261, 264, 265, 270, 307, 314, 315, 316, 325, 328, 329, 338, 339, 360, 365, 367, 368, 372, 373, 374, 380, 425.
Umall, *i*. xxix; *iii*. 125, 126.
Uman Sruth [Uma Shruth], *i.e.* bronze stream, *ii*. 299.
Ummairrith, *i*. cccсxxxvi
Upland, *i*. ccc.
Upper Wood, barony of, *iii*. 44.
Upsala, *i*. ccxxx.
Ural Mountains, *i*. cxlix, ccccxi.
Urchenfeld, Herefordshire, *i*. clxix.
Vaison, *i*. lxiii, lxiv, lxxx, cclxiv.
Valencia, Island of, *ii*. 278.
Valentia Bay, *i*. cccxii.
Vaulry, *i*. ccccxix, ccccxxviii.
Vauxhall Gardens, *i*. dcxxiv.
Venice, *i*. dlxii.
Ventry, *iii*. 65, 68, 70, 71, 82, 379.
Vesontio, *i*. ccclxxxi.
Vieil-Evreux, *i*. ccccxliii.
Vienna, *i*. dcxxxii; *iii*. 232.
Vigna Ammendola, *i*. ccсclxiv.
Villedar, *i*. ccccxix.
Volnay, *i*. lxiv.
Volterra, *i*. ccсclxxxviii.
Wales, *i*. xxxvii, xxxviii, xl, xcii, cxxxix, cxlii, cxliii, clvii, clix, clxiv, clxxii, clxxviii, clxxix, ccxxxviii, ccxli, ccxliv, cccxcii, ccccxv, ccccxc, ccccxci, ccccxcii, ccccxciii, ccccxciv, ccccxcvi, ccccxcvii, dxix, dlxvi, dxxiii, dcxxvi; *ii*. 337; *iii*. 299, 353, 358.
Wales, North, *i*. ccccclxiv.
Wash, the, *i*. lxix.
Waterford, *i*. xxvii, xxviii, xxx, cccxxiv; *ii*. 383; *iii*. 4, 5, 85, 201.
Weissing, *i*. ccccxvi.
Wessex, *i*. xxiv, xl, dvii.
Westmannland, *i*. ccc.
Westmeath, *ii*. 91, 145, 161, 262, 291; *iii*. 24, 248, 254, 372, 403.
Westminster, *iii*. 274.
West Munster, *i*. xxii; *ii*. 97; *iii*. 179, 253. See Munster.
Westphalia, *iii*. 232.
Wexford, *ii*. 38, 286, 383; *iii*. 174, 313, 335, 361.
Wicklow, *i*. xxvii, xcv, cliv, ccclxxiv; *ii*. 247, 338; *iii*. 5, 160, 211, 296.
Wigton, *i*. xc.
Winchelsea, *i*. cclxxxvii.
Witham, river, *i*. ccccіxiv.
Wittenberg, *i*. dlxii.
Wladimir, *i*. ccccxxiv.
Wolfenbüttel, *i*. cxcv, ccclxxxi.
Wood Quay, Dublin, *ii*. 289.
Worcester, *i*. ccv.
Worms, *i*. ccclxxvi.
Wurzburg, *i*. lvi.
York, *i*. dcxxv.
Yorkshire, *i*. xcvii.
Zinnwald, *i*. ccccxix.

GENERAL INDEX.

Acchillea millefolium, *i.* ccclxxiii.
Accompaniment, instrumental, *i.* dlxi, dlxii.
Acorns, *i.* ccclxv.
Adrian IV., bull of Pope, *iii.* 267.
Adscriptio glebae, *i.* cxiv.
Adze, *i.* ccclxi.
Aenech, the, or fair, *i.* cclii; functions of the —, originated in funeral games, *i.* cclv; was an organized assembly; the enclosure for women at—, *i.* cclvi; the great —s were chronological units, *i.* cclvii' cclxi.
Ager publicus, *i.* cexxiii.
Ages, the three, of human culture, *i.* cccoviii.
Agilofings, the Bavarian, *i.* ccxxxii.
Agweddi, or Gwaddol of the Welsh, *i.* clxxii, clxxiv, clxxviii.
Aillt, pl. Eilltion, *i.* cxxvii, clii, cliv.
Aire, *i.* xcvi, c, ci, cii; represented the Lombard Ariman, *i.* cv, cviii; political rights of, cix, cliv, clv, clvi, clvii, clviii, clxxii, clxxiv, clxxxiv, cciii, cciv, ccv, ccxxiii, ccxl, ccxlii, ccxliv, ccxlii, ccliv, cclviii, cclxx, cclxxv, cclxxvi, cclxxvii, cclxxxii, ccxciv, ccc, cccl, cccli, cccliii, ccclv, ccclxi, ccclxx; *iii.* 467. See Bó-Aire.
„ Ard, the, *i.* cxliii, cliii, ccxlii, ccxliii, ccxliv, ccxlv, ccxlvi, ccxlvii, cclxvi, cclxx, cclxxxii, ccxci, ccclxvii, ccclxxxviii, cccc; *ii.* 34–37, 38; *iii.* 26, 28, 469, 493, 497, 498, 513, 515.
„ Cosraing, *i.* clviii, clxi, clxxiv, cci, ccii, ccv, ccxliii; his functions, ccxlvii - ccxlviii; he represented the A. Sax. Gerefa; he did not hold a court, ccxlviii, ccxlix, cclxii, cclxvi; *ii.* 36; *iii.* 470, 491, 492, 493.
Aire Desa, *i.* cxiii, cxliii, cliii, clvi, cciv, ccxxiv, ccxlvi; his functions, ccxlvii, cclxv, cclxviii, cclxxx, cclxxxii, ccxci, cccliv, ccclv, ccclxvii; *ii.* 37; *iii.* 28, 29, 467, 468, 490, 493, 494-497, 513.
„ Echtai, *i.* cliv, cciv, ccxlv; was master of the horse, or commander of the permanent military force of a Tuath, ccxlvi, ccxlvii; *ii.* 37; his function, 326; *iii.* 468, 493, 497.
„ Febsa, *ii.* 469; *iii.* 469.
„ Feibe, *i.* clxxii, clxxiii; *iii.* 114.
„ Fine, *i.* clxi, clxxiii, clxxxiv, cxci, cci, cciii, cciv, ccv, ccxliii, ccxlvii, ccxlviii, ccli, ccliii, ccliv, cclv, cclvii, cclxi, cclxii, cclxviii, cclxxx; *ii.* 36; *iii.* 491, 513, 516, 517.
„ Forgaill, three ranks of, *i.* ccxlii; corresponded to the Welsh Canghellor or Chancellor, ccxliii; cclii, cclxvi, cclxvii, cclxx, cclxxx, ccxc, ccxci; *ii.* 38; *iii.* 28, 467, 468, 493, 500, 501, 513.
„ Tuisi, *i.* cciv, ccxlii; name cognate, with Dux and Heretog; was the Taoiseech of later times, ccxliii; the latter corresponded to the Welsh Twysawg, ccxliv, cclxx, ccxci; house of ——, cccli, ccclii, ccclv; *ii.* 37; *iii.* 28, 467, 468, 493, 499, 513.
Airecht, *i.* clxxxviii, cclxii.
„ Fodeisin, *i.* ccxlix, cclxii, cclxvi, cclxvii, cclxxii, cclxxiii.
„ Foleith, *i.* cclviii, cclxii, cclxiii, cclxxii.
„ Urnaide, *i.* cclxii, cclxiii, cclxxii.
Airoman, *i.* cii.
Airlis, *i.* clxxx, cclxxxiii, ccci, ccciv, cccxviii.

Airs to which ancient lyric verses sing, *iii.* 389, 391; air of Seaghan O'Duibhir an Ghleanna, 395, 397, 399.
„ Irish, *i.* dxc, dxcii, dxciii, dxciv, dxcvi, dxcviii, dxcix, dc, dci, dcii, dciv, dcvii, dcxiii; caprice of collectors in dealing with —, dcxiv; distinction between the object of the archaeologist and of the artist in dealing with —; duties of the musical archaeologist, dcxvi; rights and duties of the musical artist, dcxvii.
„ Scottish, in the key of *C*, dcxix; in the keys of *D*, *E*, *G*, and *A*, dcxxii.
„ the Welsh and English dispute concerning the paternity of certain, *i.* dcxxvi.
„ Welsh, traces of true Welsh music to be still found in old *i.* dcxxvii.
Aitbech, Aitheach, *i.* cxxx; explanation of, *iii.* 469, 484, 490, 506.
„ ar a Threba, *i.* cci, ccii, cciv, ccxvi, ccl, ccli; *i.* cclviii, cclxxv, ccclxvii; *ii.* 26; *iii.* 26, 482-489.
„ Baitsi, *iii.* 482, 483, 513. See A. Baitsidhe.
„ Baitsidhe, the latter word connected with bachelor, *i.* ccl; and with Baccalaria and Bacele, *i.* ccli.
„ Comaide, *i.* ccxvi.
„ Tuatha or Atticotti, *i.* xxiii; first revolution of the, xxiv; second do., xxv; accounts of those revolutions confused, xxvi; Keating's view of those revolutions, xxvi, xxvii; they show the Scotic power to have been recent, xxviii; Morand, Cairpri, and Feradhach, gods of the —, xxxii; distribution of the conquered tribes throughout the country, xxvii, xxx-xxxi, xxxiv, xlvi, lxxvii, clii; *iii.* 83, 84. See Atticotti.
Albanians (Scotchmen), *i.* xxi; *iii.* 7.
Alder, *i.* ccccv.
Ale, *i.* ccclxix, ccclxxii, ccclxxiii, ccclxxiv, ccclxxv, dcxlii. See Cuirm, Beer.
Ale Bank, see Brugge.
„ House, *i.* ccclxxi. See Cuirmtech.
Allelujah Victory, the end of Scotic Invasions of Britain, *i.* xlvii.
Allemannen, *i.* civ.
Allodial land of Ethelings, *i.* cxxxviii; — in Wales, cxxxix.
Almoghen, *i.* cclxv.
Alnus glutinosa, *i.* ccccv.
Alod and cognate words, *i.* cxxxiv, clxxxv.
Altud, *i.* cxxvii, cxxviii, cxxix.
Alum, *i.* ccccii, ccccv, ccccvi.
Amalgad or Awley, son of Athi or Dathi, battles fought by in returning from the Loire, *i.* xlvi.
Ambacti, ccxxxvi. See Amhus.
Amber, *i.* cccciv, ccccxxxv, ccccxxxvi.
Amentum, the, used with the Sleg and the Laigen, *i.* ccccxlv.
Amhuis, see Amhus.
Amhus, or Ambus, *i.* cxiii; *ii.* 389, 391.
Amobyr, *i.* ccxl.
Amphictyonic league, *i.* xciii.
Amus, Amuis, Ambus, *i.* ccxxxvi. See Amhus.
Andbahts, Andbahtos, *i.* ccxxxvi, ccxxxvii.
Anelace, or Verona dagger, *i.* cccclvi.
Anglo-Normans, *i.* xxiv.
„ Saxons, *i.* v; English people not all —, lxix, lxxxi, cxxviii, cxxix, cxxxix, cxl, cxliii, cxlvii, clxix, clxxix, cxcix, cci, ccv, ccxxxiii, cclviii, cclv, cclxxxviii, ccxcvi, cccliii, ccclx, ccclxxvii, cccclxxiii.
Annals of the Four Masters, *i.* xxi, xxii, xxiii, xxiv, xxv, xxvi, xxvii, xxix, xxx, xxxi, xxxii, xxxvii, xxxviii, xlvi, lxxxvi, xcii, ccxliv, ccl, cclviii, cclxiv, cccxxvii; *ii.* 3, 5-7, 19, 50, 90, 95, 129, 130, 137, 146, 156, 159, 167, 169, 234, 235, 294; *iii.* 2, 178, 280, 283, 284. 288.
Au-Nasc, See Ear-rings and Glos.
Ansruth, see Dae.
Antiphonary of Bangor, *i.* dcxliv.
Antiphony, *i.* dxlviii.
Antiquities, owners of rare, should place them in the Museum of the R.I.A., *iii.* 289.
Antrustio, *i.* cviii.

Aombetsman, *i.* ccxxxvii.
Apple-trees, *i.* ccclxxviii.
Arabic rule in Spain, *i.* dxxi.
Arbalète a Galet, *i.* cccclxi.
Archaeology, prehistoric, *i.* i; crude views of writers on, ccccviii.
„ Irish, importance of, in comparative history of Aryan race, *i.* iv; and in the history of the laws, etc. of England, France, etc., v.
Archil, *i.* cccci.
Ard Righ Erind, *i.* ccxxxi, ccxxxviii, ccclxxi.
Argonautic Expedition, Irish version of the, *iii.* 332.
Argyvreu, *i.* clxxviii.
Arimann, the, of the Lombards, *i.* cii; different opinions regarding, cii, et seq.; etymology of, ciii, civ; the quality of —, did not exclude that of Antrustio, Leude, or Vassal, civ; —s mentioned as freemen, cvi.
Arimannen, relation of, to the Comes or Graf, the same as that of Aires to the Rig Tuatha, *i.* cvi; — only could have slaves; — as Scabini, and as burghers of towns, cvii.
Arimannia, used for the Arimanni of a district; — mentioned by Marculfus, *i.* cviii; — used for household property; — used for rents, etc., cix.
Arimenni, *i.* ciii. See Arimann.
Armed Whip, *i.* cccclxii. See Suist.
Armour, defensive, *i.* cccclxxii, et seq.; — of the Irish, cccclxxiv; — at the Battle of Magh Tuired, *ii.* 253.
Arms, warriors buried with their, *i.* cccexxxix; different types of, referred by O'Curry to different races, ccccxxxvii; — of Sreng, *ii.* 235; construction of —, alluded to in the tale of the Battle of Magh Tuired, *ii.* 238; — of the Firbolgs, 240; — of the Tuatha Dé Danand; descriptions of — in the tale of the second Battle of Magh Tuired, 245; manufacture and repair of — by the T. Dé Danand, 248, 250; — of the time of Eochad Feidlech, 261; — used in the Battle of Ath Comair, 262; — found at Keelogue Ford in the Shannon, 271; — used at the battle of Aenech Tuaighe, 275; — of Illiach, [illegible] Descriptions of — in the Táin [illegible] Chuailgne, 315, 318; description [illegible] — at the Battle of Clontarf, [illegible] 347, 348.
Army, the standing, of the [illegible] Righ Cairbre, the Clann Morna, *ii.* 387; instances of a regular —, after the Battle of Gabhra, [illegible]
Array of Battle of the Firbolgs, [illegible] 238.
Arrow Heads, flint, *ii.* 271; barbed —, *ii.* 273.
Arrow, *i.* cccclii, cccclv; *ii.* 272, [illegible]; Niall of the Nine Hostages killed by an —, 287.
Artificers, the three great, of the T. De D., *ii.* 246.
Artistic Music of the Continent known in Ireland, *i.* dlxvi; Irishmen living abroad acquainted with —, dlxvii.
Artizans, *iii.* 209.
Aryan, *i.* iii, iv, v, lxii, lxviii, lxix, lxx.
„ language, an, not a proof that a race is Aryan, *i.* lxix.
Aryans, *i.* lxxvii, lxxxiv, lxxxvii, ccxiv, ccxxiv, ccxcvi, ccccxxxiii.
Ashburnham, Lord, the Book of O'Duvegan, or of Ui Maine, in the possession of, and access to it refused to Irish scholars, *ii.* [illegible], 124-125, 354.
Asor, the, *i.* dx. See Nebel Nassa.
Assemblies of the people, names of the, *i.* celii.
Assembly, manner of convening each kind of, *i.* cclviii; persons entitled to vote at each kind of popular —, celviii.
Assyrian Kings, names of, given in Flann's poem, *ii.* 160, 244.
Atlantis, the, *i.* cccxiv, ccccxxxii; *ii.* 195, 196, 325, 367; *iii.* 1[illegible], [illegible] 378, 385.
Ataman of the Cossacks, *i.* ciii.
Athelings, *i.* c, cxxxviii, ccxxxii.
Atrebati, *i.* cclxiv.
Attachiamenta bonorum, *i.* cclxxiii.
Attachment, *i.* ccxxxiii; — Court of Verderers, cclxxxiii.
Atticotti, *i.* xxiii, xxvi, xxx, xxxi, xxxii, xlvi; *iii.* 84. See Aithech Tuatha.
Attorney, etymology of the name, *i.* cclxxiii.
Augadòra (Goth.), Augatora (O.H.G.). See Window.
Auger, *i.* ccclxi.

Auguries, from birds; from the croaking of ravens; chirping of birds; chirping of the wren; stars and clouds by night, *ii.* 224.
Aurlaind, *i.* cccv.
Authentic Tones, see Tones.
Avenger of a Kindred, see Dialwr.
Axe, *i.* cccclvii, cccclviii; — not mentioned in the Táin Bó Chuailgne, *ii.* 318; the Lochlan, —, *ii.* 348; — of the Danes and Dalcassians, *ii.* 348-350.
Axle-spindle, *i.* cccclxxix.
Axle-tree, *i.* cccclxxix.
Baccalaria, *i.* ccli.
Bacele, *i.* ccli.
Bacon, *i.* ccclxix; *iii*, 481, 483.
Bagpipe, the, *i.* ccccxc, ccccxcviii, dxxxi; not used in war by the Irish; Celtic, Romance, and Teutonic names of the —, *i.* dxxxii; Irish name borrowed from the Romance; medieval Irish —, the same as the modern Scotch —, *i.* dxxxiii; dcxx, dcxxi.
Bail, or Aitire, *i.* ccxcii; the Aitire Nadma or Roman Nexus; the Cimbid or Nexus become "addictus", *i.* ccxcii; the Aitire Foesma, *i.* ccxciii. See Aîtire in Glos.
Baile, or Bally, *i.* lxxxiv, lxxxv, lxxxvi, lxxxvii, lxxxviii, xc, xci, xciii, cxxxv, clxxvi, ccxliv, ccclxii.
„ Biathach, *i.* lxxxvii, lxxxviii, cliii.
„ Maoir, or stewards' Baile, *i.* cliii.
"**Bairn Breac**", *i.* ccclxiv. See Bairgin in Glos.
Bal. See Bol.
Ballestre, *i.* cccclxi.
Ballium, the Middle Latin, *i.* lxxxiv.
Balls, hollow golden, for the hair, *iii.* 189, 190, 192.
Bally, conclusions deducible from the geographical distribution of Bal and — in topographical names, *i.* xci. See Baile and Bol.
Ballybiatach, *i.* xcii, xciii, xcv, xcvi, xcviii, xcix, c. See Baile Biathach.
Ballyboe, *i.* lxxxvii, lxxxviii, lxxxix, xc, xci, xcv, xcvi, xcviii, cxv.
Banqueting Hall of Tara, *i.* cccxlvi, cccxlvii, cccli, ccclxxi.
Barc, a kind of grave, *i.* dcxxxix.
Bardo Cucullus. See Cucullus.
Bards, *ii.* 172.
Baretta, *i.* cccxcvi.
Barley, *i.* ccclxii, ccclxiii, ccclxiv, ccclxvi, ccclxxiii.
„ meal, *i.* ccclxxiv.
"**Barnan Coolann**". See Bearnan Cualann.
Baronies represent ancient Tuaths, *i* xcviii.
Barr, the, *i.* cccxcv, cccxcvii; *iii.* 199, 200, 201, 202, 209.
Barrack, great, of Tara, described by Cineadh O'Hartagan, *ii.* 377; mentioned in Cuan O'Lothchain's poem on Tara, *ii.* 378; description of the —, *iii.* 6-7.
Barréd, the, *i.* cccxcvi, cccxcvii.
Barrels, *i.* ccclvi.
Barrenness a cause of reproach among the ancient Irish, *ii.* 158.
Barrete, Barrette, *i.* cccxcvi, cccxcvii.
Barrister, four grades of, among the ancient Irish, *i.* cclxxiii; origin of the word, cclxxiv; a — not entitled to Log Enech, cclxxv.
Bass, invention of figured or fundamental, *i.* dlxiv.
Bassoon, the, *i.* dxxx.
Battle of Achadh Leith Dearg, *ii.* 112. (See Carn Achaidh Leith Dearg).
„ Aenach Tuaighe, *i.* ccccliii.
„ Almhain, *ii.* 391.
„ Ath Comair, *ii.* 146, 276, 277, 295.
„ „ Ferdiad, *iii.* 25.
„ Beallach Mughna, *ii.* 104, 105.
„ Caenraighe, *ii.* 388.
„ Carn Achaidh Leith Dearg, *ii.* 17.
„ Cenn Abrat, *ii.* 57; *iii.* 261.
„ Cill na n-Daighre, *ii.* 155.
„ Cill Osnadh, *ii.* 68, 151.
„ Cinncha, *ii.* 371.
„ Cliach, *ii.* 383.
„ Clontarf, *i.* cccсxxxiii, cccclxx; *ii.* 116, 345 to 352, 353, 392; *iii.* 153, 267.
„ Cnamhros, *ii.* 383-386.
„ Cnuca, *i.* ccciii, cccxxii.
„ Craebh Tulchadh, *ii.* 167.
„ Crinna, *ii.* 140.
„ Cuarna, the Hill of, *ii.* 328.
„ Cuil Cuillean, *ii.* 383.
„ Cumar na Tri n-Uisce, *ii.* 383.
„ Dinn Righ, *ii.* 256.
„ Druim Criaich (second), *ii* 146.
„ Dubh Chomar, *ii.* 152; *iii.* 10
„ Dunbolg, *ii.* 340, 341.

Battle of Fea, *ii.* 383.
„ Finntragh, or Ventry, *iii.* 83.
„ Gabhra, *ii.* 382, 383, 386, 387.
„ Glengerg, *iii.* 153.
„ Inis Derglocha, *ii.* 383.
„ Kinsale, *ii.* 166.
„ Knockaulin, *ii.* 358.
„ Loch Riach, *iii.* 153.
„ Magh Adair, *ii.* 156.
„ Magh Ailbhe, *ii.* 105.
„ „ Ita, *ii.* 232.
„ „ Leana, or Lena, *ii.* 265; *iii.* 179, 180.
„ „ Mis, *ii.* 383.
„ „ Mucruimhe, *i.* ccccxxxiv; *ii.* 57.
„ „ Rath, *ii.* 341, 342.
„ „ Tuired, *i.* ccclvii, ccccxxxi, ccccxxxii, cccclii, cccclii, cccclviii, cccclxxiv; *iii.* 225.
„ Moin Mór, *ii.* 107.
„ „ Trogaidh, *ii.* 356.
„ Ocha, *ii.* 339, 340.
„ Rath Inil, *ii.* 384, 386.
„ Ros na Righ, *ii.* 55.
„ Sidh Femen, *ii.* 383.
„ Sliabh Mis, *ii.* 383.
Battle-axe, *i.* ccccxliii, ccccxlix, cccclі.
Battles won by the Fianna of Find Mac Cumhaill, *ii.* 383.
Bauer, the German, *i.* lxxxiv.
"Beauty and the Beast", *i.* iii.
"Bearnan Cualann", *iii.* 319.
Beds, *i.* ccclxi.
„ Feather —, *i.* ccclііі.
Bedstraw, the yellow, *i.* ccclxxiv, ccccl, ccccv.
Beef, *i.* ccclxviii, ccclxix.
Beer, *i.* ccclxiii; — the chief drink of the Irish, ccclxxi; plants infused in —, to make it bitter, ccclxxiii; ccclxxiv, ccclxxv, ccclxxvi, ccclxxvii.
"Beestings milk", *i.* ccclxviii.
Beiträge, Kuhn u. Schleicher's, *i.* lxvii.
Bells, antiquity of; uses made of — by the Greeks and Romans, *i.* dxxxiii; probably known in W. Europe before the Christian era; open and closed —; Clocc, the Irish name of the open —, borrowed from the L. Latin Clocca; origin of the latter word obscure; it was used in the eighth and ninth centuries for hand-bells, etc., afterwards applied to large — in belfries; Campana and Nola, other names for —, dxxxiv; origin of these names; the Irish Cluisine; early use of — in Irish churches; — were measures of church rights, dxxxv; use of small closed —; the pear-shaped closed — called Ceolans; the — bells called Crotals, *iii.* 319-323; *i.* dxxxvi; the Crotals described in the *Penny Journal;* the bronze Ceolans in the Museum of the R. I. A. formed part of a musical branch, *iii.* 319; Crotals not used by Christian priests; explanation of the term, *iii.* 321; they were put on the necks of cows and horses, *iii.* 323; O'Curry's objection to the use of the term Crotal; Ledwich's and O'Curry's mistake concerning the Crotal, *i.* dxxxvi.
Belt, *i.* ccclxxxvi.
Beltis, *i.* ccclxxxvi.
Benefice, original meaning of, *i.* ccxxiii; modified by the German conquest, ccxxiv.
Benna, the, *i.* cccclxxvi, cccclxxviii.
Benn Buabhaill, *iii.* 305.
Benn Chroit, *iii.* 305
Beowulf, *i.* ccxv, ccxxxii, ccxxxvii, ccliii.
Bequest, *i.* clxxxvii. See Manach in Glos.
Berngal, a king of the race of Ollamh Fodhla, *ii.* 9.
Berrbrocc, *i.* ccсxxxviii, ccclxxxiii, ccclxxxiv, cccclxxiv.
Bes Tigi, *i.* lxxxvii, cxiii, cxl, cxli, cxlii, cxliii, cliv, clxxxvi, ccxxvii.
Beste Houbet, *i.* cxii.
Biatach, *i.* cxiv.
Biatad, *i.* cxi, cxii, cxiii, cxxiii, cxxiv, cxxv, cxl, cxliv, cexl, dcxlii.
Bifahen, the Gothic, *i.* cxlv.
Bifänge, *i.* ccviii.
Bill-hook or Fidba, *i.* ccclxi.
Bin, *i.* ccclix.
Bindean, *iii.* 119.
Binidean, *i.* ccccii.
Binnit, or Binnet, *i.* ccclxviii, ccccii.
Bir, *i.* ccccxxxii, ccccxxxiii, ccccxliv, ccccxlvi.
Birds, *i.* ccclxx.
Birlaw, *i.* clx, cclxxi. See Brughrecht.
„ Courts, *i.* ccl.
Birret, Birrets, *i.* cccxcvi, cccxcvii.

Birur, *i.* ccclxvi, *iii.* 150. See Water Cress.
Birrhus, *i.* ccexci.
Birrus, *i.* cccxcvii.
Bishop, retinue of a, *iii.* 510.
Blanket. See Brothrach.
Blackthorn, the, used for capping fences, *i.* clxxxii; use of, in druidical rites, *ii.* 216, 227.
Blood-wite, *i.* ccxlviii.
Bó Airech, *ii.* 35; a harper always considered to be of the rank of a, *iii.* 365. See Bó Aire.
Bó Aire, *i.* lxxxix, ci, cx, cxi, cxiii, cxiv, cxxix, cxxx, cxliii, cliv, clv, clvi, clxv, clxxii, clxxiii, clxxxii, clxxxiii, cxcviii, cciv, ccxxxii, ccxxxiv, ccxxxv, ccxli, ccxlii, ccxlvii, cclviii, cclxv, cclxxx, ccxci, ccсliii, ccclxvii, ccc; *ii.* 25; *iii.* 26, 29, 365, 465, 466, 467, 469, 478, 482, 483, 486, 493, 513, 519.
„ „ Febsa, *i.* cxl, ccc; *ii.* 35; *iii.* 26, 484, 485.
„ „ Gensa, *iii.* 27.
„ „ Remibi, *iii.* 490. See Fer Fotlai.
Boar, the wild, *i.* ccclxx.
Bôc Land, *i.* cxxix, cxxxvii, cxxxviii, cxxxix, clxix, cciii.
Bœ, meaning of, *i.* lxxxviii, lxxxix.
Bœli, the Norse. See Bol.
Bœndr or Buendr, *i.* lxxxiv.
Bog, corpse exhumed from a in Friesland, *i.* cccxcviii; shoes found in a Danish turf ——, cccxcviii.
Bog-bean, *i.* cccccv.
"Bog-Butter", *i* ccclxvii.
Boiler, *i.* ccclix, ccclxxiii.
Bol, the Norse, *i.* lxxxiv, lxxxvii, lxxxviii, lxxxix, xc, xci, cxlix.
Bolla (A. Sax.), *i.* ccclvi.
Bollan, *i.* ccclvi; *iii.* 152.
Bolli, the Norse, *i.* ccclvi.
Bombalum, the, a kind of Musical Branch, *i.* dxxxviii; description of — in the Epistle to Dardanus, *i.* dxxxix.
Bonde, the A. Sax., *i.* lxxxiv.
Bondes, *i.* cclxv.
Bondwomen, *i.* ccclxi, ccclx.
Book of the Dean of Lismore, *iii.* 300.
Book of Kells, illuminations of the, prove knowledge of colours, 123.
Book of Navan, *ii.* 13, 321, 377. See Manuscripts.
„ Ui Maine, compiled by Sean Mór O'Dubhagan, *ii.* 58, 59, 124, 125, 126, 354.
Bordarii of Domesday Book, *i.* cxv, cxvi.
Borgh, free, *i.* cci.
Borh, a, *i.* cci.
Borough, representation of a; the Bruighfer, the mayor of a —, *i.* clxi; — represented the Saxon Burgh, clxii.
Borough-English, *i.* clxxix.
Borromean Tribute, *iii.* 313. See Boireamh Laighen.
Boŏ, *i.* cclvii.
Both, Bothan, *i.* cxv.
Bothach, *i.* xcvi, cxv, cxxviii, cxxix, cxl, cxliii, cli, clii, clx, clxxxvi, cxcvii. ccxl, ccli, cclxxvi; *iii.* 494.
"Bothy", the, of Scotland, *i.* cxv.
Bottles, Leather, *i.* ccclvii,
Boulagh, *i.* ccclxviii.
Bourdon, the, of Hieronymus de Moravia, *i.* dxxix.
Bow, *i.* cccclii-ccccliv; *ii.* 272-273. See Arrows.
„ (of musical instruments), the use of, learned from the Spanish Arabs by the Joglars, *i.* dxxii.
Bowed musical instruments did not come into Europe at the crusades, *i.* dxx; — were in use in Ireland in the beginning of the twelfth century; — are of Arabic origin; — were not in use before the eighth century, dxxi; — mentioned in Irish MSS., dxxvii.
Bovata, the Latin, *i.* lxxxix.
Bowls, *i.* ccclvi.
Box and chest, *i.* ccclix.
Bracae, *i.* ccclxxxiv, cccxci.
Brace, the Gaulish, *i.* cxli
Bracelets, *iii.* 156, 170.
Brach, malt, *i.* ccclxxiii.
Bracket, Bragot, *i.* ccclxxvi, ccclxxii, ccclxxiii.
Braga Cup, the, *i.* ccxiv.
Bragaud, Bragaut, *i.* cxli, ccclxxiii, ccclxxvi.
Braket or Bragget. See Bragaut.
Bramble, the, or Blackberry, *i.* ccccv.
Bran, the hound of Find Mac Cumhaill, *iii.* 222.
Brat, *i.* ccclxxxii, ccclxxxiii, cccxxxvii, ccclxxxviii, cccc, dcxlii.

Blemishes — and kingship, iii. 197.

Brayette, the large, *i.* ccclxxxiv, cccclxxiv.
Bread, *i.* ccclxiii, ccclxiv, ccclxv.
Breaking of cinders, *i.* cclxxviii.
Breeches, *i.* ccclxxxiv.
Breeste gairid, *i.* ccclxxxiv.
Brehon Laws, *i.* cxxxviii; *ii.* 326, 355, 375; *iii.* 135, 205, 255, 256, 323, 328, 334, 335, 363, 364, 368.
Brein Gwynn, one of the druidic courts of Anglesea, *ii.* 182.
Breithmn, *i.* cclxxiv.
Brennin, the Welsh, *i.* ccxliv.
Bretheman or Brehon, *i.* cclxiii.
Brethyn, *i.* ccclxxxvii.
Bretwalda, the Saxon, *i.* lxx, ccxxxi.
Brewing, privilege of, *i.* ccclxxvi, dcxlii.
„ Vat, the, called the Daradach, *i.* ccclxxii.
Breyr or Breyer, *i.* cxvii.
Bricriu's Feast, *i.* cccclxx; *ii.* 372; *iii.* 17-21, 314, 315. See Tales.
Bridal Gift. See Coibche in Glos.
Bride Price, *i.* clxxiv, clxxv.
Bridles, *i.* ccclv.
Brigantes, *i.* xx, xxi.
British tribes in Ireland, *i.* xx.
„ Museum, *i.* cccclxiv; Mr. Cook's Collection of Antiquities in the —, *iii.* 321; trumpets found in Ireland, now in the —, 346.
Britons, *i.* v, xxi, xxxv, xxxvii, xl, xli, xlv, xlvii, xlviii, lxx, lxxv, cclxxxviii, cccxxxiii, ccclxiii, ccclxx, ccclxxi, cccxc, cccciv, cccclxxvii; *ii.* 185; *iii.* 38, 355.
Bró or Quern, *i.* ccclx.
Broce, the, *i.* cccxcvii, cccxcviii, cccc.
Broigne, derivation of the word, *i.* cccclxxiii, cccclxxiv.
Bronze, no evidence that it was known before iron, *i.* ccccviii; Irish name of, ccccix; manufacture of, ccccx; supposed Phenician origin of, ccccxi; use of analyses of; early analyses of — defective; newer analyses more perfect; new ones wanted, ccccxii; no analyses of Spanish —s, ccccxiii; — may contain lead as an accidental ingredient, ccccxv; Wibel's theory of the making of —, ccccxvii; — was probably made from crude copper and tin stone; the impurities in —s serve to indicate the nature of the ores; Göbel's classification of the alloys of; tin — the oldest alloy, ccccxviii; composition of ancient —s definite, ccccxix; classification of ancient —s, ccccxx; lead —s; zinc —s, ccccxxii; constitution of the —s of different countries; Assyria, ccccxxiii; Austria, ccccxxv; Bavaria, ccccxxv; Bohemia, ccccxxiv; Carthage, ccccxxiii; Denmark, ccccxxiv; Egypt, ccccxxiii; England, ccccxxvi; France, ccccxxv; Germany (Eastern), ccccxxiv; Germany (Northern and Central), ccccxxv; Greece, ccccxxiii; Ireland, ccccxxvi; Rhine Land, ccccxxv; Rome, ccccxxiv; Russia, ccccxxiv; Savoy, ccccxxv; Scandinavia, ccccxxiv; Scotland, ccccxxvi; Scythia, ccccxxiii; Switzerland, ccccxxv; general conclusions as to the comparative constituents of the Bronzes of different countries, ccccxxvii; evidence of the use of — in historic times, ccccxxxvi.
Bronze Age, true use of the term, *i.* ccccx; *ii.* 266.
„ Implements found in Holstein, *iii.* 348.
„ Sling Balls, *ii.* 291.
„ Swords easily made, *i.* ccccix.
„ Weapons, *i.* ccccvii, ccccx; number and classification of analyses of, *i.* ccccxx; percentage of tin in each type of, ccccxxi; iron and — frequently mentioned in Irish MSS., ccccxxxi; *ii.* 340.
Brooch, *i.* ccclxxxvii; gold — of Medb, *iii.* 102; Aitherne and the gold — of Ard Brestine, 161, 162; large-size — mentioned in the story of Queen Edain, 162; law regarding the wearing of —es, 162; large —es mentioned in the tale of the wandering of Maelduin's Curach; Thistle-headed —es, 164; Scottish —es mentioned in the story of Cano, 164, 165; carved —es, 165, 166; —es of bronze and Findruine, 167.

Broth, *i.* ccclix, ccclxvi, ccclxviii.
Brown Type, or pre-Aryan race in Europe; more numerous in England than in Ireland, *i.* lxxvii.
Brudin Da Derga, tale of the, referred to, *i.* xx, lxxii, lxxiv, cccxlvi, cccl, ccclv, ccclxxxii, ccclxxxiii, ccccxc, ccccxxxi, ccccxxxiii, ccccxlvii, ccccIxii; *iii.* 107, 136, 152, 189, 190. See Tales.
Brugge of the Norse, the, *i.* cccli, ccclxxi, ccclxxiii.
Brugh, *i.* clx; development of a — into a city, *i.* clxii, ccxlix, cclvii, ccclxii.
„ *i.* cclii, ccclxxxix. See Brughfer.
„ Town, the, a prototype of a borough, *i.* clx.
„ Court, *i.* clxii, ccl, cclxii, cclxxxiii.
Brughfer, *i.* ccc, cccxviii, ccclv, ccclxi; *iii.* 370, 485-490. See Bruighfer.
Brughrecht, *i.* clx, ccl, cclxxi.
Bruighean Da Derga, *ii.* 325. See Brudin Da Derga.
Bruighfer, *i* cliv, clx, clxi, cxcviii, ccxxxiii, ccxxxv, ccxxxix, ccxli, ccxlvii; his functions, his duties, and privileges; his court, ccxlix; it corresponded to the Birlaw Court of Scotland, and was of great antiquity, ccl, cclvii, cccxlvi, cccxlix, ccclvii, ccclxii, ccclxxvi; *ii.* 35. See Brughfer.
Bruine, the, *i.* ccccIxxiv.
Brunjo, the Gothic, *i.* ccccIxxiii-iv.
Bruoch, *i.* ccclxxxiv-v.
Bruth, *i.* ccclxvi. See Broth.
Buachaill cael Dubh, "black slender boy", the tune of, *iii.* 394, 3 9.
Buaile, *ii.* 344.
Buccina, the Roman, *i.* dxxx.
Buckbean, *i.* ccclxxiv.
Buckles, *i.* ccclxxx.
Budne of bronze for the hair, *iii.* 159. See Buidne.
Buff jerkin, *i.* ccclxxxvi.
Bugherane, *i.* ccccv.
Buildings, Mac Firbis on stone, in Erinn, *iii.* 16; stone —, *iii.* 64; ancient stone — of Kerry, *iii* 67-71; stone buildings not all pre-Milesian, *iii.* 83.
Buinde, the, *iii.* 306. See Buine.
Buine, the, *i.* dxxx, dxxxi.
Buinire, Buinnire, the, *i.* dxxxi; *iii.* 367.
Buisine, the, *i.* dxxx.
Bull, the Papal, *Docta Sanctorum*, *i.* dlxvi.
Buonaccordo, *i.* dxvi.
Burden of a song. See Refrain.
Burdoon, the kind of singing called, *i.* dcv; not a refrain, but a species of Faux Bourdon, *i.* dcvii; nature of the Irish —, *i.* dcvii.
Burgh, *i.* clxii.
Burgundians, *i.* ccii.
Burhs, *i.* ccxxviii.
Burial of the dead, reasons for writing on, *i.* cccxix.
„ of Eoghan Bel with his r d spears, *ii.* 325.
Burlaw, *i.* ccl. See Birlaw.
Butter, *i.* ccclxvii-viii; *iii.* 474, 475, 477, 481, 483, 485, 487, 491, 492, 496, 498, 499, 501.
Buttermilk, *iii.* 478. See Milk.
Buttons, gold, *i.* ccclxxxiii.
By, meaning of, *i.* lxxxviii-ix.
Byme, the Anglo-Saxon. *i.* dxxxi.
Byrlaw. See Burlaw and Birlaw.
Caeth, *i* xxxi
Caethion, *i.* cxxvii viii.
Cahir. See Cathair.
Cai, *i.* cxl.
Caille, *i.* cccxciv-v. See Veil.
Caimsi, the, *i.* ccclxxxii.
Cain, pl Cana, *i.* cxxiii, cxxiv, clvi, cciv, ccxxxiv, ccxxxviii, ccxlii, ccxliii, ccxlv, ccxlvi, ccliv, cclxxi-ii, cclxxxii, cccxxx.
„ Adamnain, *i.* cclxxii.
„ Cormaic, *i.* cclxxii.
„ Domnaigh, *ii* 32-33.
„ Fenechas, *i.* cclxxii.
„ Fuithrime, *i.* xviii, cclxxii; *ii.* 31-32.
„ Righ Erind, *i*, cclxxi.
Cainte, *i.* cclxxii.
Caire, *i.* ccclix, ccclxix, dcxxxix, dcxl, dcxlii.
Cairde, *i.* cxxiii-iv, ccxliii, cclxxi.
Cairte, Cairti, *i.* cccxxxi, cccxxxii, dcxxxvii, dcxxxviii.
Caisel, the, *i.* ccxcvii, ccciv-v, cccix, dcxxxix; *iii.* 4, 14, 15.
„ Builders, *iii.* 14, 15, 16.
Cake, unleavened barley and oat, *i.* ccclxiii; the Bocaire or oatmeal —; different sizes of, *i.* ccclxiv. See Bairgin in Glos.
Caledonians at Tara, *iii.* 7.
Caluraigh, or ancient burial grounds, *iii.* 71.

Camisia, the, *i.* ccclxxxii.
Campana, *i.* dxxxiv, dxxxv.
Camps of Caesar, *i.* cccvi.
Camsilis, the, *i.* ccclxxxii.
Cana, an order of poets *ii.* 171, 217.
Canach, *i.* cccci.
Candelabrum, *i.* ccexlvi.
Candlestick, *i.* ccclііі.
Canghellor, the Welsh, *i.* cci, ccxliii, ccxliv.
Canon, a musical instrument, *i.* dxv-dxvii.
„ a musical term, *i.* dlv, dlvii-viii, dlxii.
Canonical Repetition, *i.* dlvii, dlxii.
Canteredus, or Cantred. See Triucha Ced.
Canto-Fermo. See Cantus Firmus.
Cantref of Wales, *i.* xcii.
Cantus Firmus, *i.* dxlix, dliii-iv, dlxiv, dlxxvi-viii, dlxxxvii.
Cape, *i.* ccexci, cccxciii.
Capel or Horse-land, *i.* xcv, cliii-iv.
Capp, the, *i.* cccclxxv.
Carcar, a prison, Carcair Leith Macha, *i.* dcxxxix; Carcair na n-giall, *ii.* 16.
Carew Papers, *i.* xcv, xcvi.
Carlovingians, *i.* cclx, cclxi.
Carn, the, mode of making, *i.* cccxxxv; use of the —, to ascertain the number slain in a battle; instance of a — being placed over a corpse, cccxxxvi; and over the heads of those slain; custom of cutting off the heads of the slain, and of protecting them by a —, cccxxxvii; stones subsequently added to —s, cccxxxix; dcxxxvii-viii-ix.
Carol, *i.* dxl.
Carpat, the, *i.* cccclxxv; the name a loan word, cccclxxvii; the vehicle itself of Roman origin, cccclxxviii; names of the different parts of the —, cccclxxviii-cccclxxxii.
„ Serda or Scythed Chariot, *i.* cccclxxxii-iii.
Carpentum, the, *i.* cccclxxvii.
Carr, the, *i.* cccclxxv.
„ sliunain or sliding car, *i.* cccexliii, cccclxxvi, cccclxxxii.
Carriages. See wheeled carriages.
Carrow, the, *i.* xcviii. See Ceathramhadh.
Carrucate, *i.* lxxxiv.
Carrus, the, *i.* cccclxxvi.
Carving in yew-wood, *iii.* 57, 59.
Casati, *i.* cxvi.
Casks, *i.* ccclix.
Casque, or War-hat, *i.* cccxcv.
Castes, classes of Irish society as, *i.* cxxix, cxxx.
Cathach, or "Book" of Battles, *ii.* 163; *iii.* 289.
Cathair, the, *i.* cccvii, cccviii, cccix; the — or "Fort of the wolves" at Fahan, *i.* cccx-cccxii, ccclxvi; *iii.* 4, 64, 65, 66–75; townland names derived from, 85; — Chonrai, *ii.* 81–82; guardroom or warder's seat, *i.* cccxi-xii; *iii.* 79.
Cathbarr. See Barr.
Cattle, *i.* cclxxi
„ shed, *i.* ccclxvi.
„ yard, *i.* ccclxvi.
Cauchi, the, *i.* ccclxxiii.
Ceathramhadh, the, *i.* lxxxiv, xci, xcv.
„ Bhaile, *i.* xci.
„ Maoir or Maer quarter, *i.* cliii. See Baile Maer.
Ceile, *i.* xcvii; Saer and Daer, or free and base—, *i.* cx, cxiv; duties of a —, on the death of his Flath, cxi; relation of the heirs of a — to the Flath, cxii, cxiii; persons included under the term, cxiv; rights of —s, cxv, cxxvi, cxxvii, cxxix; —s only had political rights, cxxix; they were not necessarily related by blood to the Flath, cxxix, cxl, cxli; amount of rent of base —s, cxliii, cli, clii; extent of holdings of —s, cli, clv, clviii, clxii-clxiii, clxxxii, clxxxvi-ix, cxciii-vi, cxcvii, ccvi, ccxxv, ccxlii-iii, cccviii, ccclxxii; *ii.* 34; *iii.* 493-496, 498-500, 502.
Ceileship, nature of, *i.* cx. See Ceilsine.
Ceilsine, *i.* cviii, cxii, cxxvii, cxlix, clxxxv, ccxxxviii, cclxix.
Ceis, *i.* dxli; *ii.* 344; *iii.* 243-256.
„ Corann, *ii.* 343.
Ceiss, a vessel, *i.* ccclxviii.
Celtic Languages, connection of the, with the Sanskrit; difficulties in the way of their scientific study, *i.* xlviii-ix; not included in Indo-Germanic family; Prichard's early opinion on the relationships of the —, l; his work on the —, li; Ad. Pictet's and Bopp's works on the —, lii.

Celtic Grammar, causes of its difficulty, *i.* liv; Mr. Garnett's way of accounting for case-endings in Irish, *i.* liv.

"Celts", weapons so called, *i.* cccexli, cccexliv, cccexlix; *ii.* 264-265.

Celts, *i.* lxix, lxxv, cxxxviii, ccxcvi.

Cemeteries, poem on the chief ancient royal, *i.* cccxxvii.

Cenedl, of the Welsh, *i.* lxxviii. See Cinel.

Cennbarr. See Barr.

Centena, the German, *i.* lxxxii-iii, xcii, ccxxx.

Centivillaria regis, *i.* xcii.

Cenuid, the, *i.* cccxcv.

Ceolan, the, *i.* cclxxxix, dxxxvi-vii; *iii.* 331, 332.

Ceorl, the Saxon, *i.* cclviii.

Cepóc, Cepóg, the, *i.* cccxxiv; *iii.* 247, 371-375.

Cerbyd, the Welsh, *i.* cccclxxviii.

Cerd, the, *i.* ccclii; *iii.* 209, 210.

Cerdraighe, tribe of the, or goldsmiths, *iii.* 207, 208.

Cetal, Ceatal, the, *ii.* 173.

Certan, the, *iii.* 374.

Chains of gold, *ii.* 7.

Champion's "flat stone". See *Liic Curad.*

„ "Handstone", *i.* cccclvi; *ii.* 263, 264, 275, 295. See *Lia Lamha Laich.*

„ Share, the, *i.* ccclxviii; *iii.* 75-79.

Chanting, the, of the liturgy, like the Greek recitative, *i.* dxlvii, practised in the west of England in the seventh century, *i.* dlxvii.

Charcoal, *i.* ccclxii.

Chariot, the, *i.* ccclxi; description of Cuchulaind's —, cccclxxviii-ix; description of Conall Cernach's —, cccclxxxi; description of Laeghaire Buadach's —, cccclxxxi; the Scythed —, cccclxxxii; *ii.* 299-302. See Carpat.

Charmed weapons, *ii.* 254.

Chaste tree, *i.* ccclxxiii.

Cheese, *i.* ccclxv, ccclxvii-viii.

Chess, *i.* ccci; *ii.* 190; *iii.* 191; chessboard, *i.* ccci, dcxlii; *ii.* 192; *iii.* 165.

Chest, *i.* ccclix.

Chevalier d'Ost, *i.* ccli.

Chief of Kindred. See Aire Fine.

Chifonie, the, *i.* d, dxxiv. See Ciphonie and Symphonie.

Chimneys, *i.* cccliv, ccclv.

Chord of the seventh, first use of, *i.* dlxv.

Chorus, the, cccexc, cccexci.

Choruses, Greek system of, ill adapted for Christian congregations, *i.* dxlviii.

Chronicon Scotorum, *ii.* 130.

Chronology in Ireland not older than Christianity, *i.* lxxi.

Chrotta, the British, of the fifth century, *i.* cccexcv; supposed — of a MS of the eleventh century, cccexcviii, di; opinions of J. Grimm, de Coussemaker, and Diefenbach regarding the —, cccexcix.

Chunine, the O. H. G., *i.* ccxxviii-ix.

Chunrats, or Ruolandes Liet, *i.* cccliv.

Church, civil organization of ancient Irish, *i.* cccviii.

„ chants, early practice of, in Ireland, *i.* dcxliv.

„ music, influence of Celtic and German poetry on, *i.* dxlviii; early —, constructed on the quinquegrade scale, the natural scale now used in —, dlxxxvi; Irish music is to be compared with old —, dlxxxvii.

Church tones, *i.* dlxiv, dlxv, dlxxi, dlxxiii-dlxxvi, dlxxviii-ix, dxcvi, dxcvii, dxcviii.

Cider, *i.* ccclxxviii; *iii.* 478.

Cilorn, Cilurn, *i.* ccclvi, ccclxviii; Cilurn umaide, *i.* dcxlii.

Cimbal, the, *i.* dxvii.

Cimbid, *i.* cxx, cclxxxv, ccxcii, ccxciii; *iii.* 507.

Cimbri, the, *i.* ccxcvii, cccvi, ccclxxiii.

Cimbrian Horsemen, *i.* cccclxx, cccclxxiv.

Cindfine, *i.* clxiii.

Cinel, Cineal, *i.* lxxviii, lxxxvii, cxcviii, ccxviii.

„ Boghaine, *iii.* 127.

„ Chonaill, *ii* 160, 161.

„ Enna, *iii.* 127.

„ Eoghain, or Eogain, *ii.* 155, 156.

„ Fermaic, *iii.* 332.

„ Fiachrach, *i* ccccv; *iii.* 121.

Cinerary Urn, *i.* cccxxiii.

Cing, *i.* ccxxviii-ix.

Cir Bolg, *i.* ccclix.

Circulus tintinnabulis instructus, *i.* dxxxvii.

Cis, *i.* clxv, ccxxxiv; Cis Flatha, *i.* ccxxxviii, ccxl; Cis n-incis, *i.* clxv.

Cithera, *i.* cccccxc, dviii; *iii.* 354; difference between the lyre and the —, *i.* dix; difference between the psalterium and the —, dx; Cithara Anglica, dxviii; Cithara Teutonica, d, di, dxviii.
Civilization, definite system in Eriu, *ii.* 2.
Clad, Claid, Cladh, *i.* ccciv, cccxxx; Cladh coicriche, *i.* dcxl
Claideamh, *i.* cccccxliv, cccclv.
Claidem, *i.* cccccxxxviii, cccccxliii, cccclv-vi.
Claidhem Mór, *i.* cccclv.
Clan, Clann, nobles only were of the; constitution of the —, *i.* cxxix; clan names were eponyms; M. Guizot's different view of the —, clxvii; his comparison of the —, with the feudal family; they were not, however, very different, clxviii; the responsibility of the —, partly territorial; the clan system better preserved among the Irish than among the Anglo-Saxons, cxcix.
" Baoiscne, *ii.* 387.
" Bloid, *iii.* 282.
" Colla, peculiar privileges of the, *ii.* 16, 169.
" Colmain, *ii.* 159; *iii.* 24, 340.
" Cuilein, *ii.* 101.
" Deaghaidh, *ii.* 358, 377.
" Feara Rois, *iii.* 309, 385.
" Luigdech, *ii.* 349, 350.
" Maurice, *iii.* 288.
" Neill, *ii.* 154, 155, 343, 344; *iii.* 278.
" Raṅald, *iii.* 282, 300.
" Rickarde, or Ricard, *iii.* 267, 269, 274, 275, 280, 281, 286.
" Tail, *iii.* 287, 289.
" Umoir, *iii.* 15, 205.
" William, *iii.* 205.
Clanna, *i.* clxxxii.
" Deagadh, Clanna Deaghaidh, *i.* cclxxvii; *ii.* 358.
" Morna, *ii.* 377, 387.
Clasps, carved, *i.* ccclxxxi, ccclxxxiii.
Classes of society in Eriu, *ii.* 33. See Crith Gablach.
Clavacin, *i.* dxv.
Clavicembalo, Clavicimbalo, *i.* dxv, dxvi.
Clavicordo, *i.* dxvi.
"Claymore", *i.* cccccxliv.
Cledyf, the Welsh, *i.* cccccxliv.
Cleith, Cleithe, *i.* c.
Cleitme, the, *i.* ccexcv-vi; *iii.* 209.
Cleitones. See Athelingo.
Cless, *iii.* 147.
Clessamun, *iii.* 147.
Clessine, *iii.* 147.
Cletin, Cletine, the, *i.* cccccxxxvi, cccccxxxviii, cccccxl, cccccxlv-vi; *ii.* 298, 299.
Cli, an order of poets, *ii.* 171, 217.
Cliabh Inar, *i.* ccexxxviii, ccclxxxvi.
Clientes of the Romans, *i.* cexxiv; Clients Leuds, and Ceiles, essentially the same, *i* cexxiv.
Clitones of the Anglo-Saxons, *i.* c. See Cleitones.
Cloak. See Brat, Fuan, Matal.
Clocc, *i.* dxxxiv-v,
Clocca, *i.* diii, dxxxiv.
Clochan, *i.* cccviii, cccxi, cccxii, cccxiv-vii; *iii.* 64, 65, 66-75.
Clochur, the, or stone bed, *i.* dcxxxviii.
Cloictech, *i.* dxxvi.
Cloin, the, of a chariot, *i.* ccccclxxviii.
Clos Blancs, *i.* ccxcvii.
Clothra. See Crotal, *iii.* 322
Clouds. See Stars.
Cluiche Caentech, not a pyre, though sometimes used in that sense *i.* cccxxiii, cccxxv-vi.
Cluicini, *i.* dxxxvi.
Cnairsech, the, *i.* clvi, ccxxxiv.
Cnamh-fher, a castenet or bone player, *iii.* 367, 544.
Cnoc, *i.* ccexxix, ccexxxv, dcxxxviii.
Cobhluige, the harp strings so called, *iii.* 251.
Cocarts, tenants who paid tribute in dye-stuffs, *i.* cccclii; *iii.* 119.
Cochal, Cocul, *i.* ccexci-iii, ccexcv, dcxl; *iii.* 105. See Cucullus.
Cochlin, Cochline, the small hooded cloak called the, *i.* ccexc; it corresponded to the Gallo-Roman Cucullio, ccexci; *Cochlini Gobach*, dcxl.
Cocolla, the, *i.* ccexcii. See Cochall.
Cocull. See Cochal.
Cogadh Gall, re Gaoidhealth, "the Wars of the Danes with the Gaedhil", quoted, *ii* 346.
Colbche, *i.* clxxiii-clxxvii, clxxxviii.
Coic Tighis, explanation of, *iii.* 56.
Coif, the, *i.* ccexciv.
Coipe, or Coife, *i.* ccexciv.
Coir, *iii.* 214, 215, 255.
Colaisti, *i.* xx, xxi.

Colg, the, *i.* ccccxxxviii-ix; *ii.* 243; Colg-det, the, *i.* ccccIvi.
Collective Frankpledge. See Frankpledge.
Collegia, or Colleges, rise of in towns, *i.* ccvii; their privileges abused; they were suppressed and re-established several times; the name was applied to two kinds of corporations, the collegium proper, and the sodalitas, ccviii; the trade colleges survived the Roman Empire, ccix.
Colonization, early, *ii.* 232, 233, 234.
Coloured thread. See Thread.
„ garments, antiquity of, *iii.* 152, 153.
Colours used to distinguish different classes of society, *iii.* 89, 124; knowledge of —, 123; colours of vestments, clothes of different colours part of the tribute of Flaths and Ceiles, 124; colours of winds, 183, 184.
Column of Antoninus, *i.* ccxcviii-ix, ccçii, ccclxxxvi.
Comarb, *i.* cxi, cxiii, clvi, clix, clxiii, ccli.
Combat, description of the, between Cuchulaind and Ferdiad, *ii.* 303-312; *iii.* 414, *et seq.*
Comites of the Germans, *i.* ccxxxv.
Comma, signification of in music, *i.* dxlv.
Commons land, settlers on, had at first only the usufruct, *i.* cxxxvi; their position in Scandinavia, *i.* cxxxvi. See Folcland.
„ representation of the, *i.* cxcvi.
Commôt, or half cantref of Wales, *i.* clii, cliv, cclxvi-vii.
Communism, M. H. Martin on the alleged, of the early Celts, *i.* cxxxviii; system of — in Russia and other Sclavonic countries, cxlix.
Comorb, see Comarb.
Comorbship, *i.* clxxxi, cxcii, ccxvi.
Compass, *i.* ccclvi; *ii.* 329, 330.
Compensation to tenants for improvements, *i.* cxc.
Compurgators, *i.* cclvii, cclxxxvi; relation of — to juries, *i.* cclxxxvi.
Comtincur, or marriage portion, *i.* clxxvii.
Concilium, the, of Tacitus, *i.* cclix.
Concords used by the Romans in the second century; those mentioned by St. Isidore, *i.* dxlviii.
Conduits, *i.* dlxi, dlxvi.
Confréries, or Confraternities, *i.* ccix, ccx, ccxiii.
Congilda, *i.* cciv, ccvi, ccl, ccli, cclxxv.
Congildones, *i* ccxvi.
Conjurati sodales, *i.* ccxii.
Constable of the Host, *i.* ccxlvi; constable of a Hundred, ccxlvii.
Constabularius regis, *i.* ccxlvi.
Conseil des Prud'hommes, *i.* ccl.
Co-partners, see Comarbs.
Cope, or pluviale, *i.* cccxc.
Copper ores, *i.* ccccxiii; foreign minerals mixed with —, ccccIv.
„ crude, composition of, *i.* ccccxiv.
Copperas, *i.* ccccvi.
Coppers, ancient, *i.* ccccxv, ccccxvi; origin of small quantities of tin in —, ccccxvii.
Corn, different kinds of, grown in Ireland, *i.* ccclxii; the kind of — chiefly grown, ccclxiii.
Corna, in Museums of R. I. Academy and Trinity College, Dublin, *iii.* 350.
Corporations in towns, rise of, *i.* ccvii.
Corporations des Arts at Metiers, *i.* ccix, ccxi, ccxiii.
Costume of Amargin, *iii.* 94-95.
„ „ Bec Fola, or Folad, *i.* dxxxv; *iii.* 180.
„ „ British vikings, *iii.* 150.
„ „ Britons (Mic Baitsi of the), *i.* ccccxxxiii.
„ „ Broen and Brudni, *iii.* 99.
„ „ Causcrach or Causcraigh Mend, *iii.* 92, 145
„ „ Cavalcades described in preface to Táin Bó Chuailgne, *iii.* 156, 157, 158.
„ „ Celtchair Mac Uthair and his clan, *iii.* 95.
„ „ Charioteers of Conaire Mór, *iii.* 183.
„ „ Clans at the Táin Bó Chuailgne, *iii.* 91.
„ „ Conaire Mòr, Ard Righ, *iii.* 142-143.
„ „ Conall Cernach, *iii.* 140-141.
„ „ Concobar Mac Nessa, *iii.* 91.
„ „ Conud, son of Morna, *iii.* 94.

Costume of Cooks of Conaire Mór, *iii.* 147.
„ „ Cormac Conloinges and his companions, *iii.* 137-138.
„ „ Cruithentuath, or Picts, *iii.* 138.
„ „ Cuchulaind, *i.* ccclxxxvii; —— 's clan, *iii.* 96-97.
„ „ Cupbearers of Conaire Mór, *iii.* 144.
„ „ Da Derg, *iii.* 149.
„ „ Domhnall Mór O'Brien, king of Munster, *iii.* 153-154.
„ „ Door-keepers of Conaire Mór, 149; curious —— of a door-keeper described by Mac Conglinde, 104-105.
„ „ Drink bearers of Conaire Mór, *iii.* 150-151.
„ „ Edchu or Eochadh Rond, *iii.* 106.
„ „ Eirrge Echbel, *iii.* 95, 96.
„ „ Eladha, the Fomorian king, *iii.* 155.
„ „ Eogan Mac Durthachta, *iii.* 98.
„ „ Errc, son of Carpri, and of his clan, *iii.* 96.
„ „ Etain, *i.* ccclxxxi.
„ „ Fedelm the Prophetess, *iii.* 109.
„ „ Feradach Finn Fechtnach, *iii.* 95.
„ „ Fergna, son of Findconna, *iii.* 96.
„ „ Fergus Mach Roigh or Roich, *i.* cccexlvi; *ii.* 298.
„ „ Fiachaig and Fiachna, *iii.* 95.
„ „ figures on the cross of Clonnacnoise, *i.* cccxcv, cccxcvi; — figures on the market cross of Kells, cccxcvi.
„ „ a son of a German king, *i.* cccxcix.
„ „ old German, compared with the Irish, *i.* cccxcix.
„ „ freemen of western Goths, cccxcix.
„ „ guardsmen of Conaire Mór, *iii.* 147-148.
„ „ Harpers, *iii.* 146, 147, 186.
Costume of Jesters of Conaire Mór, *iii.* 150.
„ „ Judges of „ „ *iii.* 146.
„ „ Jugglers of „ „ *iii.* 147.
„ „ Laegh, son of Rian Gabhra, *iii.* 186, 187; battle — of, *ii.* 299, 300.
„ „ Loeghaire Buadach, *iii.* 93.
„ „ Lug, son of Erblend, *i.* cccexlvi.
„ „ Muinreamhar, *iii.* 93, 94.
„ „ Mac Conglinde, *iii.* 102-105
„ „ Mac Roth, the herald, *ii.* 297.
„ „ Mal Mac Telbaind, Muinremor and Birderg, *iii.* 140.
„ „ Mind, son of Salcholgan, *iii.* 96.
„ „ Oball, Oblini and Cairpri Find Mór, *iii.* 139.
„ „ outriders of Conaire Mór, *iii.* 146.
„ „ Pipe-players of Conaire Mór, *iii.* 139.
„ „ Poets of Conaire Mór, *iii.* 147, 183-184.
„ „ Reochad son of Fatheman, *iii.* 94.
„ „ Saxon princes, and their companions, *iii.* 145.
„ „ Sencha, *iii.* 92, 93.
„ „ Sencha, Dubthach Dael Uladh and Goibniu, *iii.* 148.
„ „ Srubdaire, Concend Cind Maige and Sceme, *i.* cccexxxi, ccccxiii.
„ „ swine-herds of Conaire Mór, *iii.* 145.
„ „ table attendants of Conaire Mór, *iii.* 148.
„ „ Theudlind, the Lombard queen, *i.* cccxcv.
„ „ Tuidle, Conaire's house steward, *iii.* 139.
„ „ Tulchinne, the royal druid and juggler, *iii.* 144, 145, 186.
„ „ wardens of Conaire Mór, *iii.* 147.
Cotarellus, *i.* cxvi, clxxxvi.
Cotarius, etymology of, *i.* cxvi; clxxxvi.

Coterie, *i.* cclvi.
Cotsetlas, *i.* cxv.
Cottarii of Domesday Book, *i.* cxv, cxvi.
Couches (Immdai), position and number of, etc., *i.* ccexlviii; decorations of —, cccxlix; places of the — of the officers of the house hold, etc., cccli–ccclii; beds, pillows, etc., for —, cccliii.
Council of Elders of a Cantrev, *i.* ccxli.
Counterpoint, *i.* dlv, dlvi; equal —, dlv; figured or unequal —, dlv; mixed or flowered —, dlv; double —, dlviii.
Counties, formation of, *i.* xcvii.
Court, Irish term for a; five distinct courts in Ireland, cclxii; the court leet or court of the Foleith, ccxlviii, cclxii, cclxx, cclxxii, cclxxiii; the — of pleas or Airecht Urnaidi, cclxiii, cclxxii; the Neimid; connection of this word with ethnical, topographical, and personal names, cclxiii; and with the Scandinavian Nemda, cclxiv, cclxv; Court of King's Bench, or Airecht Fodeisin, ccxlix, cclxvi; names of the different classes of persons forming this court, very difficult to analyse, cclxvii; the twelve classes, cclxvii-viii, cclxxii; the interterritorial court, Taeb Airecht, or side court, cclxviii; meaning of the term Sic Oc, cclxix; its connection with "Sak" and "Sok", cclxx; the High Court of Appeal, or Cul Airecht, cclxx; the Brugh —, ccxlix; it corresponded to the Birlaw-court of Scotland, ccl.
„ of the Ealdorman, *i.* ccxlix.
„ attachment, of the Verderors, *i.* cclxxxiii.
Covinus, Covinnus, *i.* cccclxxvii.
Cowl, see Cochal and Cucullus.
Cowyl; the Welsh, *i.* clxxiii, clxxiv, clxxviii.
Craft Gilds, *i.* ccx.
Cremation of the dead practised in Ireland, *i.* cccxx; the Gaulish custom of burning slaves, etc., common to all Aryan nations, cccxx; the mere occurrence of burnt bones, not sufficient evidence of —, because some criminals were burnt alive, cccxxi-cccxxiii.
Criol, *i.* ccclviii.
Crith Gablach, *i.* xvi, xxxiii, xxxvi, lxxxi, xcvi, c, cv, cxiii, cxxi, cxxx, cxl, cxlii, cxliii, cliii, cliv, clvi, clxxxi, clxxxiv, cxciv, cci, ccii, ccxxix, ccxxxiv, ccxxxv, ccxxxvi, ccxxxvii, ccxxxviii, ccxxxix, ccxli, ccxlii, ccxliii, ccxlvi, ccxlvii, ccxlix, ccl, cclii, ccliii, cclxix, cclxxiii, cclxxv, cclxxvi, cclxxxii, ccxciii, ccxciv, ccxcv, ccxcviii, cccxlvi, cccxlvii, cccxlix, cccl, cccli, ccclii, cccliii, cccliv, ccclv, ccclvii, ccclix, ccclxi, ccclxv, ccclxvi, ccclxvii, ccclxxi, ccclxxvi; *ii.* 35; *iii.* 465 to 512.
Croit, *i.* dlvii. See Crut and Cruit.
Crom Cruach, an idol of the Milesians, worshipped at Magh Slecht, *ii.* 6, 227; *iii.* 88.
Cromlech, *i.* cccxxxii.
Crone, origin of the word, *iii.* 247. See Cronan and Aidbsi.
Cross, the market, of Kells, *i.* cccxcvi; the — of Clonmacnoise, cccxcvi.
Crotal, *i.* cccci, dxxxvi-vii; *iii.* 319-323. See Bell.
Crowd, the, *i.* ccccxcvi, ccccxcix. See Crwth.
Crud, the Welsh, *i.* ccccxcvi-viii, d, div, dxxix. See Crwth.
Cruit, *i.* dlvi; signification of the word, *iii.* 237-240; the — referred to in the early history of the Milesians, 240; mentioned in the story of the destruction of Dindrigh, 242-244; the Irish — was a lyre, not a cithara, 354; the —, mentioned in the poem on the Fair of Carman, 358, 543; distinction betweeen the — and the Timpan, 363; relative power of the — and the Timpan, 366. See Crut and Harp.
Cruitentuath, *i.* xxiv, xxxii; *iii.* 138. See Picts.
Cruithneans or Picts at Tara, *iii.* 7.
Crut, the, *i.* cccclxxxiv, ccccxcvi, diii, div, dx. dxiii, dxix, dxxiii.
Crwth, description of the Welsh, *i.* ccccxcvi-vii, di, dxxiii, dxxix, dcxxxi, dcxxxiii; the Welsh —

was the same as the Irish Timpan, *iii.* 354; definition of the word —, 354; it could not be the same as the Irish Cruit. 354.

Cucullus, the Cochall was the Gallo-Roman —, *i.* cccxc; Gaulish figures with the —, cccxci; its use confined to monks in later times; names by which it was known in different countries, cccxcii; hooded cloaks of the Norse, cccxciii.

Cugulla, the, *i.* cccxcii.

Cuirass, the, of the Romans; the — used also by the Gauls; not used at first by the Germans; horn — of the Quadi, cccclxxii, cccclxxv; the Anglo-Saxon —; it was made originally of leather, whence the name, cccclxxiii.

Culinary Vessels, *i.* ccclix.
„ Vegetables, *i.* ccclxvi.

Cumal-land, see Tir-Cumaill.

Cumôt (a sepulchral mound), *i.* dcxxxix.

Cups, introduction into Ireland of ornamental drinking —, *ii.* 5.

Curds, *i.* ccclxv, ccclxvii-viii.

Curtains, *i.* cccclxxxi.

Curtis, *i.* cxlv, ccci. See Hof.

Cwyn, *i.* ccxxxiv.

Cymbalum, *i.* dxxxvii.

Cynebôt, Cynbote, *i.* ccxxxiv; cclxxii.

Cyning, *i.* ccxxviii.

Cyvar, a tenant copartnery in Wales, *i.* clix.

Dacians, *i.* ccxcviii.

Daer Bothach, *i.* cxv, cxvi, cxxi, clxxxvi.
„ Ceiles, *i.* cxiv, cxxviii, cxxix, cxxxix, clii, cliii, clxvi, clxxxvi, cxcvii, ccxxii, ccxl.
„ Fuidir, *i.* cxiv, cxvii-cxxi, cxxiii, cxxvii, cxl.

Daggers, *i.* cccxxxviii.

Dal, the, *i.* clvi, clxxxix, ccliii, ccliv, cclvii, cclviii, cclix, cclxi, cclxxvi, cclxxvii, cclxxxix; *iii.* 111, 112.

Dalcassians, *i.* cccclxx; *ii.* 99, 100, 107, 127; battle axes of the —, 348-350; straight-backed swords of the —, 350, 351, 352, 379, 387; *iii.* 167, 270, 284.

Dalcassian clans, *ii.* 177, 178.
„ race, Lugad Delbaeth, the druid of the —, *ii.* 219
„ prince, description of the, *iii.* 153-154.

Dalriada of Scotland, the, *ii.* 52, 77.

Dam, *i.* cxliv, ccxxxv, ccxxxvii, ccxxxix, cccl.

Damascening, process of, known in Ireland, *i.* cccxxxiii.

Damnonians, the Connaught, *i.* xx.

Danauns, the, *ii.* 42, 187.

Dance music of Ireland, the, *i.* dcxv.

Dances, the, *i.* xvii, xxxvi, cclir, ccclxxviii; *ii.* 119, 155, 177, 334; *iii.* 25, 38, 44, 227, 339, 345; account of the weapons of, *ii.* 345, 346; steel loricas of —, 347; axes of the —, 348-351, 391.

Damnonii, *i.* xx.

Danish beer, *i.* ccclxxviii.
„ pirates, *ii.* 102, 103.
„ veterans, *ii.* 348.
„ wars, *i.* xcvii.

Dawnbwyd, *i.* cxiv.

Decachordon, *i.* dlv.

Dechant. See Discant.

Decies, territories of the, *ii.* 206, 207. See Deise.

Decimatio. See Tithing.

Deele, the Danish, *i.* cxlviii.

Deer, the red, *i.* ccclxx.

Degen, *i.* cl.

Deise, *ii.* 205-208; *iii.* 4, 125, 128, 197. See Decies.

Deme, *i.* xciii.

Demi Canon, *i.* dxvii.

Descriptions of dress, etc., from the Táin Bó Chuailgne, *ii.* 296-312, 315-318; *iii.* 91-101.

Dialwr, the Welsh, *i.* ccxlvi-vii.

Diaphony, *i.* dli, dliv.

Diatonic scale, *i.* dlxxii, dlxxx; existence of two —— scales; these scales lead to different systems of music, dlxxxii; exemplified by the tuning of two violins, dlxxxiii-v;—church scale, dcxxv. See Scale.

Dibad, *i.* cxviii, clxiii, clxiv, clxvi, clxix, clxx, ccliii, ccxci.

"Dieu des Jardins", cccxci.

Diguin, *i.* cl, clvi, clxxxi, ccxciv, ccxcv.

Din. See Dun.

Dinnsenchas See Tracts, Irish.

Dire, *i.* cxvii, cxviii, cxxiv, cxxv, cxxviii, cxxix, clviii, clxxxii, ccxxxiii, ccxxxix, ccxl, ccxlvii, ccliv, cclxxi, cclxxvi, cclxxx, ccxci, ccxcv.

Dirwy of Welsh law, *i.* ccxcv.

Discant, rise of the kind of polyphony called, *i.* dliii; original mode of making a —; different names given to it; supposed origin of —; it was a measured harmony; the rules of — given by Francon of Cologne, refer only to simple counterpoint, dliv; but figured and flowered counterpoint were known in his time; voices not connected in early —; the connection effected by Canon and Imitation; coloured —; — with words gave rise to masses, dlv; — with words and partly without words; this kind probably practised in Ireland, dlvi, dcv; — first used in ecclesiastical chant, dlvii; action of secular music on —, dlviii.

Discantus. See Discant.

Distaff, *i.* ccclxx.

Distress. See Gabhail and Athgabhail.

Divination, instances of, *ii.* 208; peculiar rights of — prohibited by St. Patrick, 208-209; — by interpretation of dreams and omens, 223-224.

Dogs, hunting, *i.* ccclxx.
,, wolf —, *i.* ccclxx.

Dominants of church modes, *i.* dlxxvi.

Domnans, a party of king Labrad's Gaulish troops called, *ii.* 259-261.

Dond, or Donn Chuailgne, the brown bull of Cuailgne, *ii.* 296; *iii.* 90, 376.

Doors, *i.* cccxlv, cccxlvi.

Dream, Mac Conglinde's, a Rabelaistic story, *iii.* 104; divination by interpretation of dreams, *ii.* 223, 224.

Dress of an ancient Gaulish figure, *i.* cclxxxi. See Costume.

"Drisheen", *i.* ccclxix.

Drink of oblivion, *ii.* 226.

Drinking vessels, *i.* ccclv; evidence of the use of the lathe and compass in making —, ccclvi; the larger vessels made of staves bound by hoops, ccclvi.

Druidesses of the Tuatha Dé Danand, *ii* 187.

Druidical Academy of Cerrig Brudyn, Anglesey, *ii.* 182.
,, charms, — the Dlui fulla, "Fluttering Wisp", *ii.* 203, 204, 205.
,, creed, according to Pliny, *ii.* 182.

Druidical Drinks of oblivion, *ii.* 226.
,, Fire, *ii.* 191; story of the siege of Damhghaire, 212-215, 219-221, 226.
,, Glam Dichinn, or satire from the Hill Tops, *ii.* 216-219.
,, Incantations on Cuchulaind, *ii.* 226.
,, Oracles, *ii.* 226.
,, Orations pronounced against Cuchulaind, *ii.* 198.
,, Rites, *ii.* 216.

Druidic Academy at Caer Edris in Anglesey, *ii.* 182.
,, Rites, the roan-tree used in, *ii.* 213, 214; the blackthorn used in — rites, 216.
,, spells, fountains gifted by, *ii.* 225.
,, Wand, *ii.* 205.
,, Wisp, *ii.* 205-207.

Druidism, instances of the use of — at a very early age, *ii.* 187-188; — among the Tuatha Dé Danand, 187; — among the Firbolgs, 188; — among the Milesians, 188, 189; — not introduced into Ireland from Britain or Anglesey, 191; references to — in ancient Irish writers, 191; peculiar characteristics of Irish —, 194; ancient medley of — and fairyism, 198; — in king Conchobar Mac Nessa's time, 200; and in king Laeghaire's time, 201, 202; it did not cease with the introduction of Christianity, 201, 202; characteristic examples of — from Irish MSS., 203-225; recapitulation of instances of — in Irish MSS. 225-227; ancient poetical satire as a branch of —, 216.

Druids, spoken of by Herodotus; Cæsar on —, *ii.* 180; three kinds of — distinguished by Strabo; the several classes of — mentioned by writers, 181; no specific account of — in Gaul or Britain, 181, 225; voluminous essays written on British —, 222; the orders and doctrines of — not sufficiently defined, 225; little known of the religion and organization of —, 227; no foundation for the modern theories concerning druids and druidism, 228; the chief settlement of the — of Britain, 181; Rowland's account of the — of Anglesey, 182; nothing definite known of the — of Britain, 183; origin of — in Ireland, 184; the — of Parthalon, of the Nemedians, of the Fomorians, 184; the — of Anglesey a colony from Ireland, 186; origin of the name, 48; position and rank in Ireland, 49; the wand of divination of Irish —; use of Ogam by the —, 194; the — as teachers in Eriu, 201, 202. Tulchinne, the royal druid of Conaire Mór, *iii.* 144, 145; Cathbadh the druid of Conchobar Mac Nessa and his school, *ii.* 200; the — of king Laeghaire Mac Neill, 201. The Teinm Laeghdha, or "illumination of rhymes", of the —, 172, 208-212; the Imbas Forosnai illumination by the palms of the hands, 172, 227; the Dichetal do Chennaibh, 172, 209; the druid's fire, 212-215, 219-221; the Glam Dichen, 216-217; the Geim Druadh, or Druids' shout, 381; contests of spells between —, *ii.* 225; pillar stones of — at the battle of Magh Tuired, *i.* cccclviii.

Drum, the, *i.* dcxi.

Drunaimetos, *i.* cclxiv.

Dulcimer, the, *i.* dxv, dxvii.

Dun, the, *i.* lxxxiv, lxxxvii, lxxxviii, clii, ccxxxiv, ccxxxviii, ccliii, cclxix, ccxcvii, cccii, ccciii, cccv, cccvii, cccviii, cccx, cccxv, cccxvii, ccclvii, dcxlii; *iii.* 3, 4, 5, 7, 8, 11, 12, 14, 15, 70, 75, etc.

"Dung". See Tune.

Duodenary system in topographical divisions, *i.* xcii-xciv.

Dux, the, *i.* ccxxxi, ccxliii.

Dyeing, art of, among the ancient Irish, *i.* cccc; lichens used as dye-stuffs, cccci, dcxliii; use of moss for dyeing wool, cccci, red and yellow dye-stuffs, — Gallium verum, yellow bed-straw, and madder, ccccii; *iii.* 119-120. Saffron not used in early times, *i.* cccciii; the blue dye-stuff Glaissin or woad, ccccii; *iii.* 120; it was the Glastum of the Gauls, *i.* cccciv; *iii.* 120; legend about St. Ciaran and the Glaissin, *i.* cccciv; *iii.* 120; ancient custom of dyeing animals, *i.* ccccv; green dyes, black and brown dyes, ccccv; *iii.* 119; mordants used by the ancient Irish, *i.* ccccvi.

Dye-stuffs, the, used in Ireland of native growth, *iii.* 119.

Dýna, *i.* ccexlix.

Dyngja, *i.* ccci.

Eaguare, *i.* ccciI.

Ealdorman, the Angl. Sax., *i.* ccxx, cclxv.

Ealga, Elga, one of the poetic names of Ireland, *iii.* 129, 419, 459.

Ear-rings, *iii.* 185, 186.

Ebediw, *i.* cxii.

Eberian Race, *iii.* 204, 241.

Ecclesiastics, distinguished as literary men, *ii.* 85.

Echevins, *i.* cvii.

Edda, the, *i.* ccxv, ccxxxvii, ccclxxvi

Education in Eriu in early times, *ii.* 48, 169; lay — in Eriu, 81; literary education of Finn Mac Cumhaill, 59; revision of the system of national — at Drum Ceat, 78; system of academic — in early times, 171; value of — appreciated by the ancient Irish, 174, 175; — of boys and girls in Eriu, 355.

Egyptians, torques worn by the, *iii.* 172.

"Eibhlin a rúin", the air, *i.* dcx, dcxii, dcxiii.

Eiric, *i.* clvi, cclxxiii, ccxcii, ccxciii, ccxcv.

Embroidery, *iii.* 122; — of gold, *i.* ccclxxix.

Embroidress, legal rights of the pledged needle of an, *iii.* 112-116; Coca, the — of Colum Cille, 122.

Emphyteusis, *i.* cxciv.

Enech of Scotch law, *i.* ccxcv.

Enecland, *i.* cxii, cxviii, cxix, cxxv, cxxviii, clvi, clxxvii, ccxxxii, ccxxxix, ccxlii, ccxliii, ccxlvii, ccxci-ccxcv, cccix, dcxliii; *iii.* 356, 471.

Eneit of Heinrich von Veldeck, *i.* cccliii.

English music was completely transformed in the sixteenth and seventeenth centuries; rise of harmonic music, *i.* dcxxxiii; opinion that the English have no national music erroneous, dcxxxiv.

Eoganachts, or Eugenians, *iii.* 3, 261, 262; Eoganacht of Loch Lein, *ii.* 177, 178.

Eorleundmen, *i.* ci.

Eorls, *i.* ci.

Eraic, *i.* cxviii, cxxiv, clxxvi. See Eiric.

Erbpacht, *i.* cxciv.
Eric, *i.* clxxxvii. See Eiric and Eraic.
Erws, *i.* clvii, clix.
Esain, *i.* ccxlviii, ccxciii; *iii.* 473, 514, 515, 516, 517, 518, 519.
Escreune, or Ecraigne, *i.* ccxcvii.
Esnas, *i.* cxxvii.
Espringal, *i.* dxl.
Esquimaux, *i.* cccliv.
Essedum, *i.* cccclxxvii, cccclxxviii.
Essoign, *i.* ccxciii. See Esain.
Estate, life, lapsed into — in fee, *i.* cliv.
Estavelle, or Ystavell, *i.* ccc.
Esthetic effects of ancient Greek modes, *i.* dcxxxiv; and of the church modes, *i.* dcxxxv.
"Exile of Erin", the air, *iii.* 399.
Faesam, *i.* cxl, clxv, ccxlii, ccxliii, ccxciii, dcxliii.
Fails, *iii.* 169-170.
Faine, *iii.* 168; Faine Maighdena, *i.* ccxl.
Fair, the, was always held in a cemetery, *i.* cccxxvi; — of Ailech, *ii.* 152; — of Carman, *i.* cxvi; *ii.* 38-47; *iii.* 528, et seq.; — of Tailte, *i.* cccxxvi, cccxxvii, dcxl, dcxli; *ii.* 148.
Fair-haired races of Europe, identity of the, *i.* lxxv.
Fairies, or Aes Sidhe, true ancient doctrine concerning the, *ii.* 198.
Falso bordone, *i.* dxlix.
Fanega, *i.* xcv.
Fanegada, *i.* xcv.
Faux bourdon, *i.* dxlix, dlxxxvi, dcvii.
Feats of championship, *ii.* 370-373.
Fees of oathmen, witnesses, etc., *i.* ccxc.
Feis, or Feast of Tara, Dr Keating's account of, *ii.* 14-16; Cormac Mac Airt at the —, 18-19.
Feldgemeinschaft in Germany, *i.* clx.
Fenestra, *i.* cccii.
Fennian officers, list of, in Yellow Book of Lecan, *ii.* 383.
Ferdingus, *i.* ccii, cclxxxvi; *iii.* 473.
Ferthingman. See Ferdingus.
Festingafê, *i.* clxxiv.
Feud, hypotheses of the etymology of; Palgrave's objection to them, *i.* ccxxi; not more fortunate in his own attempt, ccxxii; essential principle of a —, ccxxii-ccxxiii; origin of the words feodum and —, ccxxvi.
Feudal system, Irish freedom older than the bondage of the —, *i.* cxiv.
Feudalism, neglect of the Celtic languages, etc., injurious to the study of, *i.* ccxx.
Ferrules of spears, *ii.* 241.
Fiadnaise, *i.* clxxxv, clxxxviii, ccxxxix, cclxii, cclxxv, cclxxvi, cclxxvii, cclxxxii, cclxxxviii, cclxxxix, ccxc, ccxcii; *iii.* 467, 470, 471, 474, 475, 482, 485, 487, 491, 492, 496, 498, 499, 501, 502, 503.
Fiddle, the, *i.* dxxi, dxxiv, dxxvii; *iii.* 328, 329; mentioned in the poem on the Fair of Carman, 358, 364; the opinion that it represents the ancient Crwth of the Welsh shown to be erroneous, 358.
Fidula, *i.* dxxiv.
Filberts, *i.* ccclxv.
File, *i.* cxxviii, cxl, clvi, ccxli, cclii; *ii.* 48, 56, 136, 171.
Findruine, *i.* cccxxxviii, cccxcviii, cccclxvi, cccclxxviii, cccclxxix, dcxlii; *iii.* 92, 101, 106, 109, 138, 152, 158, 160, 167, 174, 180, 187, 188, 219, 220.
Fine or House, *i.* lxxix, lxxxvi, cxviii, cxxv, cxxvi, cxxix, cxliv, clviii; meaning of, *i* clxii; branches of a, *i.* clxiii; the council of a —; remotely related kindred of a —; mode of establishing claim to the rights of a —, clxiv; adoption by a —; rights of legally adopted members of a —; fees paid for adoption, clxv; kindred of exiles and emigrants; kindred of murderers, clxvi; the rent paying — of a Flath, clxvi; clxvii, clxix, clxx, clxxii, clxxxiii, clxxxiv, clxxxvii, clxxxviii, clxxxix, cxci, cxcii, cxciii; the — and the Gild, the sources of the representation of the Commons, cxcvi, cxcvii, cciii, cciv, ccxvii, ccxviii, ccxliii, ccxlvi, ccxlviii, ccli, ccliii, ccliv, cclv, cclviii, cclxi, cclxii, cclxviii, cclxxii, cclxxxvi, cclxxxvii, ccxci, ccxcii, ccxciii, ccxciv, ccxcv, ccxcviii, cccl, ccclxi.
Finncharn, the white, a sepulchral mound near the Boyne, *ii.* 386.
Firbolgs, *i.* xxiii, xxvi, xxxix, lxxi, lxxvi cclxiv, cccxxvii, cccxxxvi, cccxxxvii, cccxxxix, ccccxxxii,

cccexxxvii, cccexxxviii, cccel, ccecliii, ccecIxii; *ii.* 2, 5, 50, 111, 122, 148, 153, 185, 187, 231, 233, 234, 235, 236, 237, 238, 239, 240, 241, 242, 243, 244, 255, 256, 272, 295, 302, 328, 334, 346, 358, 374; *iii.* 5, 6, 59, 73, 74, 83, 84, 85, 106, 122, 210.

Fire, position of in houses, *i.* cccxlvi.

Fish, *i.* ccclxvii, ccclxx.

Fithele, *i.* dxxiv.

Flail, the war. See Suist.

Flaith, see Flath.

Flat Seventh, use of the; originated with the Bagpipe, according to Engel, *i.* dcxx; this opinion not correct; the true origin; Macdonald's rule about "flats and sharps" in pipe music correct, dcxxi.

Flath, *i.* ci, cvii, cix, cxiii-cxxxi, cxxxix, cxl, cxliii, cxliv, clii-clvi, clviii-clxii, clxv, clxvii, clxx, clxxi, clxxii, clxxiii, clxxxv-clxxxvii, clxxxix, cxcvii, cxcviii, cciv, ccxxv, ccxxxii, ccxxxiii-ccxxxv, ccxxxviii, ccxl, ccxli, ccxlii, ccxlv, ccli, ccliii, cclviii, cclxi, cclxii, cclxviii, cclxxv, ccxc, ccxcviii, ccciv, cccviii, cccxlvi, cccxlvii, cccli, ccclii, cccliv, ccclxxiv, ccclxxvi, ccclxxvii, ccclxxxix, dcxlii; *ii.* 34, 37; *iii.* 26, 490, 493, 508.

Flemish Schools of Music, rise of the; influence of the — on music in Italy, *i.* dlix; Palestrina's relation to —, dlix.

„ Composers, character of the masses of the, *i.* dlix.

Flint Arrow Heads, *i.* cccliv; — found in Ireland, *ii.* 271.

Flitches, *i.* ccclxix.

Florentine, early, School of Music, *i.* dlix.

Flute, the German, *iii.* 342, 346.

Folach, *i.* ccxxxiv, cclxxx, ccclxvii-viii; *iii.* 477.

Folc-gemôt, *i.* cxxxvii, cclix-cclxi.

Folc land, *i.* ci, civ, cxxxvii, cxxxviii, cxli, clxix, clxxxvi.

„ man, *i.* ciii.

Folcith, *i.* cviii, ccxxxv, ccxxxvi, ccxlv, cclxii, cclxiii, cclxx, cclxxiii, ccclxviii; *iii.* 498, 499, 501, 502, 503.

Folghers, *i.* cxiii.

Folgoth, *i.* ccxxxv.

Folk, *i.* lxxx.

Folkmoot, *i.* cciii, cclxxxviii.

Fomorians, *i.* xxiv, xxxviii, lxx, cccxxxix, cccliii, ccccIxxii, dcxxxix, dcxl; *ii.* 108, 109, 110, 184, 185, 225, 232, 245, 248, 250, 251, 253, 255, 256, 295, 300, 358; *iii.* 3, 8, 43, 155, 213, 214, 231, 232, 384.

Foreigners, frequent mention of, in Irish wars, *i.* xxi; position of — in Ireland, cxvii; seven streets of — at Cill Belaigh, *iii.* 38.

Fore-oath, *i.* cclxxxvi.

Forest laws of England, *i.* cclxxxiii.

Forge, the, *i.* ccclxii; description of an armourer's —, ccccxxxiv; — of Goibniu, situation of, *ii.* 246, 247.

Fork, flesh, *i.* ccclix.

„ the military, *i.* ccccxlvi-viii. See Foga.

Forts, the, of Nemid, *iii.* 3; — of Dunbeg, 72, 73.

Forud, *i.* dcxxxviii; *iii.* 530, 541. See Forus.

Forum, *i.* ccxxxiii. See Forus and Forud.

Forus, the, of a Brughfer, the place of election of a Rig, *i.* clxi, ccxxxiii, cclxxxiii, ccxlix, cccv; the lawn light and signals of a —, cccxviii; *iii.* 476.

Fosses aux prêcheux, *i.* ccxcvii.

Fossils of human time, *i.* ccxcvii.

Fosterage, ancient system of, explained, *ii.* 355; instance of — under Eochadh Beg, 357; Irish law of —, adopted by the Anglo-Normans, 375.

Fōtpallr, *i.* cccxlix.

Fountains, healing, *ii.* 225.

Fowd, or deputy governor of Zetland, *i.* cclxx.

Fowl, *i.* ccclxx.

Foxes, the O'Cethernaighs of Teffia or, *ii.* 161.

Frankpledge, view of, *i.* cc, cci.

„ collective, nature of, *i.* cc; representatives of —, cc; the Aire Fine, or chief of family or kindred, and the Aithech ar a Threba, or elected Aire Fine, cci, ccii; the Hindena of London; the Ferthingmen or Ferdings, ccii; was — a political right? the "four men and the reeve" of an Anglo-Saxon township;

the Aire Cosraing or chief Aire Fine, the chief of kindred or family, the Cuicer na Fine or "family council of five", *i.* cciii; the chief of kindred or of family always acted for minors, ccv; the Anglo-Saxons had originally a family council, which became "the four men and the reeve", ccv; Palgrave's opinion that — was not universal harmonizes with the Editor's views of its origin, ccv-vi; rise of —, ccvi.

Franks became known to the Irish in the time of Carausins, *i.* xxi, xlii, lxx; ciii, civ, cvi, cxiv; Salic and Ripuarian —, cxxxi, cccxcvi, cccxcviii; *iii.* 7.

Free Borgh. See Frankpledge.

Freehold, the Ballyboe or Teti, a type of a, *i.* xcvi.

Freeholders, number of, in Erin, *i.* xcvi, cliii.

Freemen, position of, in town and country, *i.* cx; extent of land in usufruct of — not being Aires, clvii. See Aires.

Freepledge. See Frankpledge.

French school of music, *i.* dlix.

Freomen, *i.* civ.

Freyfeld Gericht, *i.* cclxvi.

Friborgi, *i.* civ.

Frilingi, *i.* civ.

Fringe of gold and of silver thread, *i.* ccclxxix, ccclxxxvii; mention of the weaving of a border or —; the — sword, *iii.* 111, 112.

Frisian, old, language, *i.* ix.

Frisians, *i.* cccxvi, ccci; *iii.* 7.

Frith Gild, *i.* cxcvii, ccii, ccv, cexii.

Frithiof Saga, *i.* dxix.

Frithskiöldr, *i.* ccccIxx.

Frock, the, *i.* ccclxxxv.

Frohner, *i.* cclxvi.

Frommen Bruderschaften, *i.* ccx.

Frottole, *i.* dlxi.

Fugue, *i.* dliii, dlxii.

Fuidirs, *i.* xcvi; the position of, cxvii, cxviii; their Log Enech determined by that of their lords; exceptions, cxx; persons included in the category of —; St. Patrick a Daer —; voluntary Daer —, cxx; Irish law of promotion, cxxi; different categories of free —; the — focsail a aithrib, — dedla fri Fine, — Grian, cxxii, cxxiii; a certain class of — treated like base Ceiles, cxxiii; — auca set, cxxiii; different categories of Daer —; — golbhle, — Cinnad O'Muir, etc., cxx; cxix, cxxvi, cxxviii, cxxix, cxxxi, cxxxix, cxliii, clii-cliv, clviii-clx, clxii, cxciii-cxcv, cxcvii, cciv, ccxxiii, ccxxv, ccxxvi, ccxl, ccli, cclxxv, ccc; *iii.* 494.

Fuidir land, should be the property of a Flath, *i.* cxxviii, cliii.

„ partnerships, *i.* cxxiv, clviii.

Fuidirship under a strange lord a tenancy from year to year; error of Spenser on this subject, *i.* cxxv-cxxvi.

Funeral cry, *iii.* 374.

„ dirges or guba, *i.* cccxxiii; the cepóc or panegyric; example of a modern cepóc; manner of chanting the dirges; the Mná Caointe or professional mourning women, cccxxiv; the panegyric of Rigs and Flaths made by the historian or bard of the family; prostration and plucking of hair and beard accompanied the Guba, cccxxv.

„ games, or Cuitech Fuait, *i.* cccxxv.

Furniture, fines for damaging the — of a Bruighfer, *i.* ccclix; *iii.* 477, 478; articles of — made of yew wood, 62.

Fustibale, *i.* cccclx, cccclxi.

Fustibalus, *i.* cccclxi.

Fylk, the, *i.* lxxx-lxxxii, cv, cclxv.

Fylkir, *i.* ccxxxi.

Ga, Gae, etc., cccxxxxvii, ccexxxviii, cccclxi, cccclvii; *ii.* 300, 316, 317

Gabal Gialda, *i.* cxiv.

Gabellae, Gavellae. See Gavael.

Gabella libera; — nativa, *i.* lxxxvi.

Gaedhelic language, ecclesiastics were educated in the, *ii.* 170.

Gaedhil, the, do not acknowledge to have received the druidic system from any neighbouring country, *ii.* 184.

Gaesum, the, *i.* cccxliii.

Gafol, *i.* clxix.

Gaisas, the, *i.* ccccxli.

Gaisatias, the, *i.* ccccxli.

Gaisatoi, the, *i.* ccccxliii.

Galanas of Welsh law, *i.* cxxviii, cxxix, ccxlv.

Galium verum, *i.* ccclxxiv, cccci, ccccii.
Gallians, *ii.* 259, 260.
Gallo-Roman altar in Musée des Thermes, Paris, *i.* lxiii.
Galls, *ii.* 347, 348, 368; *iii.* 7, 37, 38.
Galnes of old Scotch law, *i.* ccxcv.
Gamanrians, *i.* ccxxxvii; *ii.* 358
Game, *i.* ccclxx.
Gamut, knowledge of, in Ireland in thirteenth century, *i.* dlxx.
Gapped scale, *i.* dlxxx, dlxxxix, dxci, dxcv, dxcvii; history of the recognition of the — in Irish music, *ii.* dciii.
Garda, the Gothic, *i.* cxxxv.
Garde reins, *i.* ccclxxxiv.
Garth, *i.* cxxxvi.
Gasindu. See Gisindo.
Gau, or Gavi, the Gothic, *i.* lxxx, lxxxi, lxxxiii.
Gauding, the German, *i.* cclix.
Gaulish inscriptions, Grimm on the absence of; many now known, *i.* lxi; enumeration of the more important ones, *i.* lxii-lxvi.
Gauls, *i.* v, xxiv, xli, lxx, lxxv, xcii, cxxxvi, clxviii, clxxi, ccxxxvi, cccxx, ccclxxvi, cccxcvii, cccxcix, cccclvi, cccclxi, cccclxv, cccclxvi, cccclxxii; *ii.* 258, 345.
Gavael, *i.* lxxxvi.
Gavelkind, *i.* lxxxvi; the ancient custom, explanation of the term; position of women under this custom, clxix; Irish custom of —, clxx; position of women under it, clxxi-clxxii; division of property among heirs; custom in Wales, clxxix; the Irish custom, clxxx-clxxxii; law of tanistry, clxxxii; estates of Flaths sub-divided; the estate of a Bó Aire might also be subjected to the law of tanistry, clxxxiii; Irish customs not recognized in English courts in Ireland; revival of gavelkind in Ireland in the reign of queen Anne as a penal enactment against Catholics; comparison of the gavelkind custom in Kent and in Ireland, clxxxiv
Geferscipe, *i.* ccxxxv.
Gefolge, *i.* ccxxxv.
Gegilda, *i.* ccxii.
Gegildan, *i.* ccxii, ccxvi, ccxvii.
Gegylden, *i.* ccxvii.
Geige, *i.* dxxvi.
Geldonia. See Gildonia.
Gelef, the Welsh, *i.* ccccxliv.
Geleute, the, of the Germans, *i.* cclxiii.
Gell, *i.* cxii, cclxxxiv, cclxxxv.
Gems, *i.* ccclxxxvii.
Genealogies, Irish, tacked on to biblical ones, *i.* lxxi.
Genos, the Greek, *i.* lxxviii.
Gens, the Latin, *i.* lxxix.
Geology, rise and growth of, *i.* i.
Gerefa or Reeve, the, *i.* lxxxi, clxi, cciii, ccxxxi, ccxlviii.
German, the, language spoken by the Tuatha Dé Danand, *iii.* 232.
Germanen, *i.* civ.
Germans, *i.* iv, v, xxxiv, xli, lxx, lxxiv, lxxv, lxxix, xcii, xciii, cvi, cxxxviii, cxl, clxviii, clxxi, clxxv, ccxx, cclviii, cclx, cclii, cclv, ccxcvi, ccc, ccci, ccciii, cccxliii, ccclii, ccclxxvi, ccclxxvii, ccclxxxvi, ccclxxxviii, cccxcii, ccccxlvi, cccclvi, cccclxi, cccclxx, cccclxxii, cccclxxiv, cccclxv.
Gesa, the medieval, *i.* ccccxliii, ccccxliv.
Gesatorii, *i.* ccccxliii.
Gèse, the old French, *i.* ccccxliii.
Gesith, the Saxon, *i.* ci, cii.
Gesum, the Gallo-Roman, *i.* ccccxlii; the Gauls carried two Gaesa, the Irish two Gae, *i.* ccccxlii-iii.
Gifts to the king of Tara, *iii.* 129; — from the king of Tara to the king of Emain Macha, 131; — of the Ard Righ to the king of Leinster when the latter visited Tara, 132; — of the king of Leinster to the king of the Ui Fealge, 182; — of the Ard Righ to the king of Cashel when at Temair Luachra, 132; — given by Ailill to Medb, 98; — promised by Medb to Long Mac Emonis, 101; — promised by Medb to Ferdiad, 102.
Giga. See Gigue.
Gigue, the, *i.* d, dxxv; origin of the word, dxxvi, dxxviii.
Giguéours d'Allemagne, *i.* dxxvi, dxxvii.
Gild, the medieval, *i.* ccxii; — and the Fine the sources of representation of the Commons, ccvi, ccix; the — of kalenders, gild merchants, craft gilds, confraternities, ccx; the gilds of kalenders and the confraternities, cl

Christian origin; protective or true gilds; the Frankish Gildonia sworn Societies in Flanders, etc., ccxi; Flemish gilds of great interest; Frisian Conjurati Sodales; Anglo-Saxon Gegildan; Frith Gilds, ccxii; the term Gild extended to different associations; supposed pagan origin of Gilds; — supposed to have originated in England, ccxiv; no ground for this opinion; alleged connection between — and banquets, ccxiv; etymology of the word —, *i.* ccxvi; Kemble's suggestion that Gegildan embraced the whole population, not correct, ccxvii; ancient organization of Friesland, *i.* ccxviii; relation between it and that of Ireland; later civic character of —, compatible with a rural origin, *i.* ccxix.

Gilda, *i.* ccxv.

Gildscipe, *i.* ccxv.

Girdle, see Cris.

Gisacus, a God-appellative, *i.* ccccxliii.

Gisarma, see Guisarma.

Gisindo, *i.* ci.

Gladius, *i.* ccccxxxviii, ccccxliv.

Glaesum or Glessum, *i.* ccccir, ccccxxxv, ccccxxxvi.

Glaisin, *i.* ccccili-ccccv, ccccxxxvi; *iii.* 118, 120, 121.

Glaive, the, *i.* ccccxxxviii, ccccxliii, ccccxliv, ccccliv.

„ Guisarme, *i.* ccccxxxix, ccccxliii, ccccxliv.

Glandes, *i.* ccccixi.

Glastum, *i.* ccccir, ccccxxxv, ccccxxxvi.

Gled, *i.* ccccxliv.

Gleddyr, Cleddyr, *i.* ccccxliv.

Gleefe, the German, *i.* ccccxliv.

Gneeve, *i.* xcv, xcviii.

Goat, *i.* dcxxxix.

Goat's flesh, *i.* ccclxviii.

Gobyr Merch, see Amobyr.

„ -Estyn, *i.* cxii.

Gold embroidery, *i.* ccclxxix; concealment of golden ornaments, etc., in springs, etc., ccxcvii; chains of —, *ii.* 7; Juchadan the first worker in —, 5; first smelting of —, *iii.* 88, 211; early use of ornaments of —, 155; native manufacture of ornaments of —, 205; ornaments of —, found in a bog near Cullen, 205; Mr. Clery's account of, 206; Mr. Nashe's chronicle of finds of — in Cullen bog, 206; importation of —, 210.

Gold mines, *ii.* 5; goldsmiths worked at or near —, *iii.* 204.

Goldsmith, a, named Lin Linfhiaclach, *iii.* 203; territory of the goldsmiths, 207; pedigree of a family of —s, 207, 208. See Cerd.

Golf, the Norse, *i.* cccli.

Goose, the, *i.* ccclxx.

Goths, *i.* xlv, civ; the western —, ccccxcix.

Grammar, an ancient Gaedhelic, *ii.* 53, 54.

Grammatica Celtica, the, of J. C. Zeuss, *i.* lvi, lvii, lviii, lix, lxii, dxxxi; *iii.* 306.

Graphio or Graff, *i.* cclxvi.

Grave, making a dishonoured, *i.* cccxxiii.

Grave-cloth, the Rochull or, *i.* cccxli.

Greaves, *i.* ccclxxxiv.

Greek recitative, *i.* dxlvii; — system of choruses, dxlviii.

Greeks, *i.* xvii, cccxxxiii; the — used harmony only in the form of antiphony, *i.* dxlviii.

Gregorian chant, *i.* dlix.

Grelots, *i.* dxxxvi, dxxxix.

Griddles, *i.* ccclix, ccclxiv.

Grinding stone, *i.* ccclxi.

Grith-breeh, *i.* cexlviii.

Groats, *i.* ccclxv.

Gudrun, poem of, *i.* xl.

Gugel, Kogel, Kugel, *i.* ccexcii.

Guider, the Welsh, *i.* cclxxviii.

Guisards, *i.* ccccxliii.

Guisarma, *i.* ccccxliii.

"Gully", the, *i.* ccccxliv.

Guma, *i.* cccxciii.

Gurda, the Welsh, *i.* cclxvi.

Gwaddol, see Agweddi.

Gwaesav, *i.* ccxxvi, ccxxvii.

Gwaesavwr, *i.* ccxxvi.

Gweledig, *i.* ccxxxi.

Gwelly, or Wele, the, of Wales, *i.* lxxxv, lxxxvii.

Gwelygordd, *i.* lxxxvii.

Gwes, *i.* ccxxvii.

Gwes-tva, the equivalent of the Irish Bes Tigi, *i.* lxxxvii, cxiii, ccxxvii; the — of a tref, cxli; commutation of — into "tunc rent", which proves that the Sacr Ceile had a freehold, cxlii; such freeholds recognized in Wales, but not in Ireland, cxlii-iii.

Gwr Nod, *i.* cclxxvi.

Gwynebwerth, *i.* clxxviii.
Gyle, or porter-wort, *i.* ccclxxiii.
Hackbrett, the, *i.* dxv, dxvii
Hätta, the Danish, *i.* cccxciii.
Haesthûs, *i.* ccci.
Hair, Coil or Buidne, for the, *i.* ccccvii; men and women divided the —, *iii.* 189; hollow golden balls fastened to tresses of the —, 189, 190, 192; — the colour of the blossom of the sobarche, 191.
Halsberg, the, cccclxxiv.
Hammer, the War, *i.* cccclvii-ix.
Hams, *i.* ccclxix.
Handicrafts in ancient times hereditary, *i.* ccvii; each lord had his own base craftsmen, ccvii.
Hare, the, ccclxx.
Hariman. See Arimann.
Harjis, the Gothic, *i.* cv.
Harmony, St. Isidore's definition of, *i.* dxlviii; M. de Coussemaker's conclusions as to — in the twelfth, thirteenth, and fourteenth centuries, dlvii-viii.
Harp, the Egyptian, *i.* cccclxxxiv; *iii.* 229; the Assyrian —, *i.* cccclxxxv; — in the hands of one of the muses, cccclxxxvi; antiquity of the — in Ireland, *iii.* 213; mention of the — in the Táin Bó Chuailgne, 309; legendary origin of the Irish —; Marbham's legend of the invention of the —; the Irish legend similar to the Greek one, 234, 235; the Cruit of the Dagda was a —, 213; the Dagda's invocation to his —, 214, 215, 217; names of the Dagda's —, 214; his three musical feats, 214; they represented different keys; existence of similar keys among the Greeks; esthetic effects of the ancient Greek modes and of the ancient church tones; Arabic and Norse legends similar to that of the Dagda, *i.* dcxxxiv-vi; bellies and pipes of the Dagda's —, *iii.* 217; no mention made of strings in the Dagda's —, 222; Scathach's had three strings, 222-224; the Dagda's — was quadrangular, 225; a quadrangular — on the theca of an Irish missal, *i.* dvi; *iii.* 226; a Greek — of the same form, from an ancient sculpture, 226; figure of a — from the monumental cross of Ullard, 228; this the first specimen of — a without a fore-pillar found out of Egypt, 228, 229; the quadrangular — invented in Egypt, 233; similarity of the — sculptured on the monument of Petun to that on the Irish Theca, 232, 233. Welsh name of the —, *i.* ccccxci-cccxcii; *iii.* 351, 352; Caradoc's statement about the introduction of — music into Wales from Ireland, 353; the Welsh hair-strung —, *i.* cccxciv; the Irish and Welsh —s were called in Latin, Cithara, ccccxcv; the quadrangular instruments figured on the Theca, the cross of Ullard, etc., represented the Psalterium, dvi; replacement of the Psalterium by the —, after the twelfth century, dvi; the Manx —, dxiii; the oldest figure of the true — known, dxviii; the modern harp originated in the British Islands, and was a modification of the Trigonon, dxviii; the Cruit was a true —, dxix; improvement in the —s in Ireland in the twelfth and thirteenth centuries, *iii.* 264; improvement of French —s, and introduction of the — into Italy due to visits of Irish harpers about the same period, *i.* dxix; introduction of the — into the arms of Ireland by Henry VIII., and issue of the — coinage, *iii.* 274. Ceis of a Cruit, 248, et seq.; parts of the — surmised to have been the Ceis, 251; principal parts of a —, 256, 257; reference to the different parts of a — in a poem of the seventeenth century, 258; names of the different classes of strings, 256; number of strings in early —s, *i.* dxx; instances where the number of strings is mentioned, *iii.* 259-263; relative powers of the Irish — and Timpan, 265. The — in Trinity College, Dublin, commonly known as Brian Boru's —, 263, 266, 291; Dr. Petrie's account of it, 267-269; it was probably the — of Donchad Cairbrech O'Brien, 280; Mac Connidhe's poem on the — of Donchadh Cairbrech, 271-273; this — was probably sent to Scotland, 285; what became of this harp? 273; it was probably the

harp given by Henry VIII. to the Earl of Clanrickarde, and perhaps suggested the harp-coinage, 274; the — in Trinity College did belong to the Clanrickarde family; it was not an O'Neill harp, though Arthur O'Neill may have played upon it, 275; Dr. Petrie's antiquarian difficulties on this subject, 276; O'Curry's answer, 276, 277; the — known in Scotland as that of Mary Queen of Scots, may be the — of Donchad Cairbrech, 299; poem on another straying harp of the O'Briens, 286, 287; the owner of this — was Conor O'Brien, Earl of Thomond, 288; this is not the — in Trinity College, 289; the — in the possession of John Lanigan, Esq., of Castlefogarty, 289, 297. Dr. Petrie's notes on Irish —s, 289 et seq.; the ancient— found on the estate of Sir Richard Harte in the County of Limerick, and given by him to Dr. O'Halloran, 290; the —s of the harpers who met at Granard in 1782, and at Belfast in 1792, 291; "Brian Boru's harp", in Trinity College, Dr. Petrie's opinion that it should be called O'Neill's —, 276, 291; the — of Sir John Fitzgerald of Cloyne, now known as the Dalway —, 263, 291-293; the — belonging to the Marquis of Kildare, 293, 294; —s of the eighteenth century, 294; — in the possession of Sir Harvey Bruce at Downhall, 294; the Castle Otway —, 294; a — formerly belonging to Mr. Hehir of Limerick, 295; a Magennis — seen by Dr. Petrie in 1832, 295; the — in the possession of Sir George Hodson of Hollybrook House, 296; the — in the Royal Irish Academy, purchased from Major Sirr, 297; the so-called Carolan — in the Royal Irish Academy, 297; —s made by Egan of Dublin, 297, 298; Dr. Petrie's opinion of the Harp Society of Belfast, 298.

Harpa, the, of the Teutonic nations, *i.* cccclxxxix, dxviii.

Harper, Emher and Ereamhon cast lots for a poet and a, *iii.* 210; the — and timpanist not necessarily distinct persons, 263; the — considered to be of the rank of a Bò Airech, 365.

Harpicordo, *i.* dxvi.

Harpsichord, *i.* dxvi.

Hat, the, *i.* ccexcv.

Hatchet, *i.* cccxli.

Haube, *i.* cccxcv.

Hauberk. See Broigne.

Haugr, *i.* cclv.

Head, coverings for, *i.* cccxcv.

Heads of the slain, custom of cutting off the, *i.* cccxxxvii-cccxxxviii.

Heath fruit, *i.* ccclviii.

Heather beer of the Danes, a myth, *i.* ccclxxviii.

Heerman, *i.* ciii.

Heimgiöff of the Norse, *i.* clxxii.

Helice, the Greek, *i.* cccclxxvi.

Hendinos, *i.* ccii, ccxxix.

Heorth fastmen, *i.* cxiii.

Herads, *i.* ccxxxi.

Herath, the, *i.* lxxxi, lxxxii, cv, cclxv.

Heraths-Hofding, *i.* cclxv.

Herathțhing, *i.* cclvi, cclix, cclxiv.

Here, the Anglo-Saxon, *i.* cv.

Herereita, *i.* lxxxii, cv.

Heretog, the Anglo.-Sax., *i.* ccxliii.

Heretoga, *i.* ccxxxi,

Heriot, *i.* cxii. See Manchaine.

Herizogo, Herizoho, *i.* ccxxxi.

Hertugi, Hertogi, *i.* ccxxxi.

Hetta, the Norwegian, *i.* cccxciii.

Hezlagh, *i.* ccxv.

Hhasor, the, *i.* dix.

Highland Society's Dictionary, *iii.* 358, 380.

Highlanders, *i.* ccclxiii, ccclxxxv, ccclxxxvi.

Hindena, *i.* ccii.

Hindradagsgaf, *i.* clxxiii.

Historians of the Tuatha De Danands, *ii.* 50; — of the Milesians, 51, 52.

History, inductive method, applied to, *i.* ii; scope and object of, iii; importance of Irish — in comparative history of Aryan race, and history of the laws of England, France, etc., iv, v; sources of ancient Irish —, vi; — anciently taught in verse, *ii.* 167; — and annals of the wars and battles of Eriu, by Mac Liag, 116.

Hlaford of the Anglo-Saxons, *i.* ci.

Hökulbroekr or Oekulbroekr, *i.* ccclxxxv.

Höttr, *i.* cccxcv.

Hof or Curtis, *i.* ccci.

Hofding, *i.* ccxxxi.

Hoffmen, *i.* cclxv.

Hog. See Pig.

"Holy-water sprinkler". See Suist.

Homestead, purchase of a, in early Irish Christian times, *i.* lxxxix; — early, in severalty, cxxxv; —s, did not form villages, cxxxvi.

Homophonous music, always combined with poetry, *i.* dxlii; every tone of a scale used as a tonic in —, dxlv; Greek tragedies and epic poems musically recited; the rhythm of this music different from metre; the chanting of the liturgy like the Greek recitative; Christian hymns were rhythmed, dxlvii.

Honey, *i.* ccclxiv-ccclxvii, ccclxxvi, dcxliii.

Hood, *i.* ccccxc, ccccxcv.

Hooks, *i.* ccclxix.

Hoops, *i.* ccclvi.

Hops, *i.* ccclxxiii, ccclxxvi, cccciii; field —, ccclxxiii-iv.

Horn, — cuirasses, *i.* cccclxxv; no implements of, found in Ireland, *ii.* 271.

Horns, drinking, *i.* ccclvi.

Horseback, instance of a combat on, *ii.* 340, 341.

Horseskin shoes, *i.* dcxl.

Hosaneu, *i.* ccclxxxv.

Hose, the, or stocking, *i.* ccclxxxv.

Hosewaus, *i.* ccclxxxv.

Hospites, the barbarian, were Fuidirs, *i.* ccxxv.

Hostages, their position in a royal house, *i.* cccli, ccclv.

Hotr, *i.* ccccxciii.

Houbittuoch, *i.* ccccxciv.

House: the houses of the Celts, Germans, and Slaves were built of wood, *i.* ccxcvi; shape of ancient Irish houses, ccxcvii; *iii.* 30, 31; the round wicker —, construction of the round wicker —; *i.* ccxcviii; *iii.* 31, et seq; account of the building of a round wicker —, 32, 33; weather boards on wicker —, *i.* ccxcviii; circular wicker houses of the Gauls as represented on the column of Antoninus in the Louvre, ccxcviii-ix; the cup roofs of Irish wicker houses like those of the Gaulish ones, ccxcix; the residence of an Aire consisted of several houses; the custom of having each room an isolated —, existed in Gaul, Wales, Norway, and Sweden, ccc; the German farm-buildings generally under one roof; divisions or rooms in Irish, Anglo-Saxon, etc., farmsteadings; the women's — a separate building; it was cut off from the other houses; Norse and German names of women's houses, ccci; the Irish Grianan; it seems to have been sometimes erected on the wall of the Dun, cccii; windows and shutters mentioned in Irish tales, cccii; fences and trees about Irish homesteads, ccciv; a spring of water in the dairy of a Bruighfer, and a stream of running water in the Lios or Airless of a Fer Forais, and of a leech or physician, cccxviii; *iii.* 148. The principal — had but one room, *i.* cccxlv; number and position of doors, cccxlvi; number of doors in a Leech's —, cccxix; doors of German houses, cccxlvi; position of Immdai or couches, cccxlvi; number of Immdai or couches, cccxlvii-viii; decorations of the Immdai; the Fochlu or seat of the chief of Household, cccxlix; the position of the occupants of Immdai as regarded the Fochlu determined by their rank, cccl; position of the seats of the members of the household of a Righ Tuatha, cccli; the Erlarchaich or Fore-hall, cccli; seats of the Rigán or queen, and of the other women, ccclii; feather beds and pillows in the Immdai; blankets and coverlets; covering of the walls at the back of the Immdai; the whole family slept in one room, as was also the case with the Anglo-Saxons, Germans, and other northern regions, cccliii; early marriage customs connected with this custom, auccliv; in the Duns of Righs, etc., there were distinct houses for the different members of the same family, *iii.* 70; the early houses had no chimneys, *i.* cccliv; they were only one-storied buildings; introduction of lofts; the common living room contained all the furniture, tools, etc.; the arms of the men, the bridles of horses, drinking vessels, etc., were arranged on the walls, ccclv; dimensions of the houses, and general character of the furniture of the different classes of society, *ii.* 33, et seq.; *iii.* 25-32, and *Crith Gablach*, 477, et seq.; the — of an Oc Aire, 26, 479-480; the Tech incis, or house of a superannuated man, 30, 31, 479, 480; the — of an Aithech ar a Threba, 26, 482; the — of a Bó Aire Febsa, 26, 27, 484; the — of the Aire Reire Breithé, 27; the — of a Bruighfer, 486; the — of a Fer Fothlai, 491; the — of the Aire Cosraing, 492; the — of an Aire Desa, 28, 495; the — of an Aire Tuise, 28, 499; the — of an Aire Forgaill, 28, 501; the — of a Rig Tuatha, 508; the — of Bricriu, *i.* cccxlvii; *iii.* 17-21; the — of Crede, 12-14; the royal — of Cruachan, *i.* cccxlviii, dcxli; the royal — of Emania, cccxlvii; the — of the Royal Branch, *iii.* 11; houses of the Norse, *i.* cccl ccclii; the ale —, ccclii, ccclxxi; *iii.* 509, 511; the Tech darach, or oak —, *i.* cccxlviii; fines for injury to the —s and furniture of the several classes of Aires, *iii.* 27, 29, 30.

Household of a King, Cormac's order regulating the, *ii.* 23.

Hufe, *i.* cxlv, cxlvii, cccxcv.

Hulls, *i.* cccxciv-v.

Human Sacrifice, reference to, in poem on the Fair of Tailté, *i.* dcxl; *ii.* 222.

Hundafaths, *i.* ccxxix.

Hundari, the Swedish, *i.* lxxxii.

Hundred, the, *i.* lxxxi, lxxxii, lxxxiv, xcii, ccii, ccxvii, ccxxx, cccxxxi, cclvi, cclviii.

„ the Constable of the, *i.* ccxlvii.

„ Gemôt, *i.* cclix.

Hundredes Ealdor, *i.* ccxxix.

Hunones or Hunnones, *i.* ccxxix.

Huns, *i* cccxxxvii.

Hurling-match between the Tuatha Dé Danand and the Firbolgs, *ii.* 237.

Hûs Karlar, *i.* cxvi

Hut, *i.* cccxcv.

Hyde or Hide of land, *i.* xciv, ci, cxlvii.

Hymanfylgja, *i.* clxxii.

Hymns, Christian, were rhythmed, *i.* dxlvii.

Hynaviaid Cantrev, the Welsh, *i.* ccxlii.

Hynden, *i.* ccii.

Hy Niall, the Southern, *ii.* 161.

Hypnum cupressiforme, *i.* cccci.

Iberians, *i.* lxxvii.

Icelanders, *i.* ccxcvii, ccclxxviii.

Iceni, the, *i.* lxxiii, lxxiv.

Idols invoked in the Teinm Laegdha; — taken into the druid's bed to influence his vision; the — called the Crom Cruach, *ii.* 6, 227; *iii.* 88; — worshipped by the Druids, *ii.* 227.

Imitation (musical), early use of, *i.* dlv, dlviii.

Inar, the, or jacket; it corresponded to the Norse Kyrtil; materials and colours of, *i.* ccclxxxvi; cccxci, cccxcvi, cccciii, dcxl, dcxlii; *iii.* 105.

Incantation of Amergin, *ii.* 190; druidical —, 226.

Indigo, *i.* ccccili, ccccⅳ.

Indigofera tinctoria, *i.* ccccili.

Inductive method applied to history, *i.* ii.

Information, criminal, of three kinds, *i.* cclxxvii.

Inheritance of daughters, *iii.* 183.

Inille, chattels, *i* cxxv.

Inscribed swords, *ii.* 254.

Inscriptions, Celtic, in North Etruscan alphabet, *i.* lxvi.

Intervals of typical scales, *i.* dlxxx.

Invista hûs, *i.* ccci.

Irishmen, distinguished, living abroad in the middle ages, very little known concerning, *i.* dlxviii.

Irish inscriptions, *i.* lxvi, lxvii.

„ language, Aryan character of, established by Dr. Ebel, *i.* lviii.

„ music, peculiarities of, *i.* dlxx; — constructed on a gapped quinquegrade scale, or in the diatonic quinquegrade scale of the old Church tones, dlxxi; historical position of, dciii; influence of ecclesiastical music on, dciv; — was homophonous, and not affected by harmony, dciv; a rude harmony, the organum of the Church practised in medieval times, dciv, dcv; the successive developments of harmony known to the Irish; discant probably known, dcv; the conditions necessary for the growth of polyphonous music did not exist in Ireland; effect of the introduction of Protestantism on —; social and political state of Ireland in the eighteenth century, dcviii; state of — in the eighteenth century; influence of foreign music as in the compositions of Carolan, dcix; transformation of homophonous —; rise of a school of — impossible; artistic development of — entirely arrested, dcx; inevitable death of homophonous —, dcxi; causes which hasten this event, dcxi; disappearance of old — inevitable, dcxii; Irish musicians do nothing for —, dcxvii; duty of Irish Academy of Music, dcxviii.

Irish power, strong for offence, but weak for defence, *i.* xii; this explains the conquest of Gaul by the Romans, xii; state of — in the time of Carausius, xliii.

„ writers, Edward O'Reilly's, *ii.* 32, 86, 94, 98, 104, 105, 108, 113, 115, 128, 129, 137, 145, 150, 166.

Irminseule, *i.* cclxvi.

Iron known to all European Aryans, *i.* ccccix; evidence of the early use of — in Ireland, cccexxxi; — age, *ii.* 266; — defensive armour, 347; — Loricas on the horses of Cuchulaind's chariot, 300; — sling balls, 291; — spears, *i.* cccexlv; — spear of Cethern, *ii.* 313; — weapons, *i.* ccccvii; *ii.* 340; use of — of considerable antiquity; — frequently mentioned in Irish MSS., *i.* cccexxxi.

Irrian race, chief of, *iii.* 265.

Japhetian race, *ii.* 184, 188, 233.

Jarl, *i.* ccxx.

Jarðhus, *i.* ccxcvii, cccii, cccxii.

Javelin, *i.* cccexxxiii, cccexxxvii; the Cletin or feathered —, cccexlv.

Jig, *iii.* 408.

Judges, the, of the various courts, *i.* cclxxii; remarkable — of Eriu, *ii.* 21; profession of poet — deprived of its privileges, 21.

Judicial system. See legislature, etc.

Jurats, or Noillechs, *i.* ccxc; a jury of Noillechs formed apparently of twelve, ccxc.

Kaino-Anthropic epoch, *i.* ccccvii.

Kalendars, gilds of, *i.* ccx.

Kannlau, or Guider, the, *i.* cclxvii.

Kâpa, Kapi, *i.* cccxciii, cccxcv.

Καπάνη the Thessalian, *i.* ccccIxxvi.

Kappa, *i.* cccxciii.

Keeve, *i.* ccclxv.

Keile, *i.* cccexliv.

Kemangeh a guz, the Arabic, *i.* cccexcv.

Kemenate, *i.* cccl.

Key of *C*, *i.* dlxxxix; Irish airs composed in the — of *C*, dxc; Scotch airs in the — of *C*, dcxix; — of *D*, dxci; Irish airs in the — of *D*, dxcii-dxciv; Scotch airs in the — of *D*, dcxx; — of *E*, dxcv; Irish airs in the — of *E*, dxcvi; Scotch airs in the — of *E*, dcxx; — of *G*, dxcvii; Irish airs in the — of *G*, dxcviii, dxcix; Scotch airs in the — of *G*, dcxx; the — of *A*, dci; Irish airs in the — of *A*, dcii; Scotch airs in the — of *A*, dcxxi.

Keys of gapped quinquegrade scale, *i.* dlxxi; ancient — of diatonic scale, dlxxii; the five ancient Irish —, dlxxxix; the old — of Irish music the same as those of the Plain Chant, dlxxii.

Kiafal, *i.* cccxciii, cccxciv.

Kilt, the, *i.* ccclxxviii, ccclxxxiv, ccclxxxvi, ccclxxxix; *iii.* 105.

"Kilruddery Fox Hunt", the ballad called the, *iii.* 296, 297.

Kindins, *i.* ccxxix.

Kindred. See Fine.

Kindred, chief of. See Aire Fine

King, of a Territory, *ii.* 28; different ranks of —, *iii.* 502, 503; rank, rights, and obligations of a —, 503-512; occupation of a —, 507; occupation of a — in his Ale House, 510-512; retinue of a —, 510; body-guard of a —, 508, 509; lawful cooks of a —, 507; three levies of a —, 507; three ways in which the dignity of a — is lowered, 506, 507; three fastings of a —, 507. See Righ.

Kingdoms, threefold subdivision of ancient, *i.* lxxxiii; sub- — of Ireland, xcix.

Kinnor, the, an important instrument of the Phenicians; it was the origin of the Trigonon; the —, and the Assyrian harp, dviii; the — incorrectly called a Cithara, dix, dx.

Kinyrva. See Kinnor.

Kitchen, the, *i.* ccclxix.

Kitchen garden, *i.* ccclxvi.
Kluffte, *i.* ccxviii, ccxix.
Kneading troughs, *i.* ccclix.
Knife, *i.* ccclxi.
Knighthood, *ii.* 200, 226.
Knives, law as to seizure for debt of, *ii.* 332.
Konungr, *i.* ccxxix.
Κόρμα, κοῦρμι, *i.* ccclxxi.
Kote Setlan or Cotsetlers, *i.* clvii.
Kothsass, *i.* cxv.
Kotter, *i.* cxv, cxvi; Erb —, Mark —, cxvi.
Kufl, *i.* cccxciii.
Kvennahûs, *i.* cccii.
Kymri, the, *i.* cxxix.
Kyrtil, *i.* ccclxxxvi, ccclxxxix.
Lacerna, *i.* cccxci.
Lād, *i.* cci.
Ladle, *i.* ccclix, dcxl.
Laeti, *i.* ccxxii.
Laetic grants, *i.* ccxxv.
Lagenians, *i.* ccclxxiv.
Laghaehus, *i.* ccc.
Laghman, *i.* cclxv, cclxxiv.
Lagrett, *i.* cclvi, cclxxiv.
Laigen, *i.* xxi, cccxxxi, ccccxxxviii; the — was probably made of bronze, ccccxlv; *ii.* 256-261.
Lamb, *i.* ccclxviii.
Lambahûs, *i.* ccci.
Lance, *i.* ccccxxxiii, ccccxlv.
Land, measured by quality, *i.* xcv; curious measures of — in Cavan, xcv; effect on occupiers of — substitution of measurement by area for that by quality, cxv.
Land. See in Glos., *Land*, *Niamh Land*, *Mael Land*
Land laws, four classes of society, the result of, *i.* cxliv-cl.
Landlord class, *ii.* 37, 38.
"Land of Promise" of the Gaedhil, *iii.* 11.
Land system in the time of Cæsar and Tacitus, *i* cli.
Language, decay and growth of, *i.* vii, ix; a — does not change uniformly, vii; dynamic action of nature on —; action of contact with other languages on a —, viii; a literary — becomes a dead language, ix; case of the Irish —; the — of Irish poems and tales constantly adapted to the spoken language, x; genealogical classification of —s, liv, lv; difficulty of the — of Ferceirtne's poems, *ii.* 9, 10; cultivation of the Gaedhelic — in the early ages of the Church, 73, 170, 171.
Lapdog. See Muʒ Eimhe.
Lappets *i.* ccccxci.
Lard, *i.* dcxxxix, dcxl.
Lassi, *i.* ccxxii.
Lathe, the, *i.* ccclvi.
Laths or Letas of Kent, *i.* lxxxi, lxxxiv.
Latin verse, influence of Celtic and German poetry on, *i.* dxlviii.
Law, date of Irish, fragments, *i.* xiii; age of Irish — MSS., xiv; general term for — in Irish, cclxxi; common —, Cairde, or interterritorial —, and Cain or statute —, cclxxi; portions of Irish —s unintelligible in the year 1509; —s of nations do not change rapidly, xv; Irish —s incompatible with the state of things in the Dano-Irish and Anglo-Norman times, but compatible with that from the fifth to the eighth century, xvi; the Irish —s belong to the latter period; Irish —s originally written in verse, xviii; Lombard —s, cvi; Salic —, "De corporibus expoliatis', cclv; Welsh —s, how drawn up, cclxvi; —s of Edward and Athelstane, cclxxxviii; accounts of the passing of particular —s, *ii.* 29; codification of Irish —s; revision of the laws in the time of St. Patrick, *ii.* 25; the twelve books of laws for West Munster, 31; local —s, mode of making, 31; —s or ordinances not passed in an assembly, 32; old Irish —s continued in force in the Co. of Clare down to the year 1600, 25; —s relating to co-stealing and co-eating, or to *Accessories*, *i.* cclxxvii; — of *Adamnan*, *ii.* 26; — regulating provision for the *Aged*, 30; — respecting the mode of wearing large *Brooches*, 163; *Brugh* —, or Birlaw, *i.* ccl; — regulating the price of *Buildings*, *iii.* 49, 50; — regulating the *Colour* of dress, *ii* 6; *iii.* 88; — of *Contracts*, *ii.* 26; was like that of the Jews, 29; *Criminal* —, 26; —s regulating *Distress*, etc., of objects connected with *Dyeing*, weaving, and embroidery, *iii.* 115-117; — of *Eric* introduced by St. Patrick, *ii.* 29; —s against damage of *Houses* and furniture, *iii.* 29; — concerning the *House* of a leech or doctor, *i.* cccxix; — as to the division of property of a *Husband* and wife when legally separated, *iii.*

118; —s as to *Land*, ii. 27, see also Crith Gablach; — as to the wearing of the *Leinidh* or kilt, and the Ochrath or greaves, iii. 107; *Meill Bretha*, or —s regulating juvenile sports, ii. 30; *Military* —s, 27; — of *Moses*, see Moses; — concerning the *Oirens*, iii. 334-335; — regulating the stipend of an *Ollamh*, 52; — against overholding *Pledged* articles of gold or silver, 122; — regulating the *Ranks* and classes of society, and houses and lands, see Crith Gablach, ii. 27; —s in *Seanchas Mór*, 26-29; various *Special* —s, 27; — concerning the profession of *Teaching*, 78; — as to the relation between *Teacher* and pupil, 174; — regulating the separation of a *Wife* from her husband, i. clxxvi; — for the protection of articles belonging to *Women*, iii. 114-115; — as to the pledging of ornaments and articles belonging to *Women*, 111-115; — of distress for the *wages* or for articles belonging to *Women*, 115-120.

Lawn lights and signals of a Forus, i. cccxviii.

Leabhar na h-ua Chongbhala, ii. 13, 321, 377.

Lead, the use of, indicates a knowledge of silver, i. cccexxii; — in bronzes, cccexv; difficulty of determining whether it be accidentally or intentionally present, cccexxi; localities of the — bronzes which have been analysed, cccexxii.

"Leading Note", i. dlxv.

Learning, men of, in the time of Concobar Mac Nessa, ii. 55, 57; state of — under Niall Naoi Ghiallach, 59; profession of — established by law, 136.

Leather, i. ccclxxxiii; — bags, — bottles, and book wallets, ccclviii.

Lecanora tartarea and L. parella, i. cccc.

"Leech fee", i. ccxxxiv.

Leeks, i. ccclxvi.

Leet, or Leta, i. xciii, ccxxxv; — court, cci; the roll of the, cciii; — jury, ccxlviii.

Legend of Aithirne and the Brooch of Ard Brestine, iii. 161, 162.

„ Ambrose and Gortigern's Dun, i. cccxxxiv.

„ Amergin the smith, and the mother of St. Finnbar, i. cccxxii.

Legend of Becuma and Conn Ced Cathach, i. cccxxxiii.

„ Blanat, or Blathnad, and Cuchulaind, iii. 80-82.

„ Blanat and Ferceirtne the poet, ii. 97.

„ the Broicseach and the Ceolans, iii. 332.

„ the Cathair of Curoi Mac Daire, iii. 75-79.

„ Prince Comgan, ii. 204, 205.

„ Connla's Well, the Eo Feasa and the Seven Streams of Knowledge, ii. 142-144.

„ Corrgenn, ii. 152.

„ Cuchulaind and Eithne, ii. 195-198.

„ Dagda's Harp, iii. 213-214.

„ Dondbo, iii. 308-312.

„ Edain and Eochad Airemh, ii. 192-194.

„ Einglan, king of birds, and Mesbuachala, i. ccclxx.

„ Eithne Uathach, the Deisi, and the druid Dill, ii. 205-208.

„ Fer-fi and the yew tree of Mac Aingis, iii. 260.

„ Find Mac Cumhaill, Scathach and her magical harp, iii. 222-224.

„ Fingin Mac Luchta, king of Munster, iii. 201, 202.

„ Finntann, son of Bochra, iii. 59-62.

„ the three modes of harp playing, iii. 218-221.

„ Labrad Loingsech and Moriath, or the magic Cruit of Craiftine, iii. 243, 244.

„ Lomna and Find, Mac Cumhaill, ii. 209-210.

„ Lugad Delbaeth, the fire producer, ii. 220, 221.

„ Lugadh Reo Derg, ii. 198-203.

„ Lug Mac Eithlenn, iii. 42, 43.

„ Mac Lonain, the poet and the clown, ii. 100.

„ Mairend Mael and Mugain, iii. 193-194.

„ Marbhan's legend of the invention of the harp, of verse, and of the Timpan, iii. 235-237.

„ Mog Eimhe, or Mug Eimhé, the first lap dog brought into Ireland, ii. 210-212.

Legend of Mogh Ruith and his druidical fire, *ii.* 212-215.
„ Mongan and Dallan Forgaill, *iii.* 174-176.
„ Muirni Muncaem, *i.* cccxxii.
„ Neidhe and Caier, *ii.* 218-219.
„ Nera and the Barr Briunn, *iii.* 200.
„ St. Ciaran and the dye-stuff Glaisin, *i.* cccciv; *iii.* 120.
„ St. Mochae, *iii.* 386, 387.
„ St. Moling and Gobban Saer, *iii.* 34-36.
„ St. Patrick and Eithne and Fedelim, daughters of King Laeghaire, *ii.* 201.
„ Seanchan Torpeist's rhyming rats to death, *ii.* 87.
„ Tuirbhi, father of Gobban Saer, *iii.* 41.
Legislation, local, *ii.* 30.
Legislative and judicial, system of the Irish, information fragmentary regarding the, *i.* cclii.
„ functions separated in Ireland at an early period, *i.* cclxii.
Leidgreve, or Gerefa of a Leet, *i.* ccxlviii.
Leirwite, *i.* ccxlviii.
Lena, or Lene, its form, *i.* ccclxxviii; its material and colour; the Roman Lena, ccclxxix; it was perhaps different from the Irish one; the Irish — was like the Greek Chiton and the Roman Tunica; ornamented Lenas, ccclxxx; the — worn by women, ccclxxxi; ccclxxxii, ccclxxxvi, ccclxxxvii, ccclxxxix, cccxciv, cccxcvi, cccciii, dcxliii.
Leode of the Anglo-Saxons, *i.* cclxiii.
Less, Les, *i.* clii, clxxvi, ccciv, cccxii. See Lis.
Lethrind, Leithrind, *iii.* 251, 252, 361.
Lia Lamha Laich, *i.* ccccxxxviii, ccccl vi; *ii.* 263, 264, 273, 274, 277, 278-282, 283, 284, 285.
Liath Macha, Cuchulaind's gray steed, *ii.* 319.
Libellarii, *i.* cxciv.
Liber Hymnorum Notkeri, *i.* dlxix.
Libripens, the Roman, *i.* cclxxvi.
Lichens, *i* cccc, cccci.
Ligurians, *i.* lxxvii.
Lime, use of for whitewashing, known at an early period, *i.* ccciii.
Lin. See Liun.
Linde, the, *i.* cccclxv.
Lindi, the, *i.* ccclxxxvi.
Linen, *i.* ccclxxix, ccclxxxii; — sheets, ccdiii.
Linté, *i.* clxxiv.
Lis, the, *i.* clxxx, ccciv, cccvi, cccxiv, cccxlviii, ccclxvi, ccclxxv, dcxlii *iii.* 4, 12, 70.
Literary offices connected with the monarch's court, *ii.* 55.
„ men, ecclesiastics distinguished as, *ii.* 85.
Literature and education in Eriu in the earlier ages, *ii.* 48.
Lith, *i.* cclxxxi.
Liti, *i.* ccxxii.
Liun, ale, etc., *i.* ccclviii, ccclxxiii, ccclxxvi, dcxlii.
Lives of Saints. See Saints.
Llawmawr, the, *i.* ccccxliv.
Llys, *i.* ccciv.
Loaf. See Bairgin.
Lochlann, or foreign battle-axes, *ii.* 348, 349.
Lodentappert, *i.* cccxciii.
Loen-lands, the lands of Ceiles were, *i.* ccxxiv.
Lofts, *i.* ccclv.
Log Enech, *i.* cxix, cxxvii, clxxxviii, cclxxii, ccxcv.
Logwood, *i.* cccevi.
Loin-guard. See Garde Reins.
Lombards, *i.* cvi, cccxcviii. See Longbards
Longbards, *iii.* 7.
Longobardai, *i.* xxi.
Lopt. See Loft.
Loricas of the Fomorians, *ii.* 253; — on the horses of Cuchulaind's chariots, 300; steel — of the Danes, 347. See Cuirass.
Lute, the first instrument used in accompaniment, *i.* dlxi.
Lyre, the, of the Britons, *i.* cccclxxxix; discovery and construction of the —, *iii.* 216; ancient painting of a — with a flute for a bridge, 218, 354.
Lyric verse, ancient, *iii.* 391.
Mac Fiurmedh, an order of poets, *ii.* 217.
Madder, *i.* ccclxxiv, ccccii-iii, dcxliii.
Madra, *i.* ccclxxiv, ccccii.
Madrigals, *i.* dlvii, dlxii.
Maegh-Burh, *i.* lxxix.
Maegth, the Anglo-Saxon, *i.* lxxix, lxxxvi, clxiii, cxcix, ccv, ccvi, ccxvii, ccxlvii, cclix, cclxxxvi.
Maegscaft, the, *i.* lxxix.

Maer, or Steward, the, *i.* cliii, clxi; — governed the towns of lords, clxii, cci; the — Mór of Scotland, ccxlv.
Maer Tref, *i.* clii.
Magi, Asiatic, *ii.* 228.
Magic wisp, *ii.* 226. See Druidical Fire.
Magical fire. See Druidical Fire.
Magl, or Magyl, *i.* clix.
Mahal, Old Saxon, *i.* cclx.
Malgin Digona, *i.* xcix, clv, clvi, clxxix, ccxxxiv, ccxciv.
Mail, the coat or shirt of, *i.* cccclxxii.
Maire of the palace of the Merovingian kings; the French —, *i.* ccxlv.
Malberg Glosses, *i.* lviii. lix.
Mallum, the, of Charlemagne, *i.* cclix; the word is cognate with Mathluagh; character and functions of —; those of the Mathluagh were analogous, *i.* cclx.
Malt, *i.* ccclxxiii, dcxlii.
Malting, privilege of, *i.* dcxlii.
Mandoline, *i.* dxxi.
Mansus, the *Frankish*, *i.* lxxxix, cxlvii.
Mantle. See Matal and Möttull.
Manuscripts, Irish, *i.* vii; — little more than scrap books, xviii; causes that led to this fragmentary character, xix; — little studied twenty years ago, *iii.* 230.
Manuscripts quoted:
Bibliotheque Royale, Brussels:
Vol. containing Nos. 2324–2340, *i.* cclxxxix; *iii.* 32–33, 35, 44, 331–332.
Vol. containing Nos. 2569, 2572, (*Cogadh Gaedhel re Gallaib*) *ii.* 347–352.
Vol. containing Nos. 4190–4200, *iii.* 4, 34–36, 45.
"Duald Mac Firbis'" Annals, No. 5301 (in vol. containing 5301 to 5320), *ii.* 79, 390–391; *iii.* 310, 311, 312, 313.
No. 9025, *i.* dii.
Bibliotheque Nationale, Paris:
Fonds Latin, No. 1118, *i.* cccccxcviii, dvi.
„ Lavalliere, No. 14, *i.* dii.
„ Sorbonne, No. 1817, *i.* dxxv.
Bodleian Library, Oxford, Rawlinson, 487, *i.* cxxvii, cxxxv–vi, clxxii–iii, clxxvi–viii, clxxxi–ii, clxxxix, cxc–cxci, ccl, ccclxiv.
„ „ „ Laud. 610, *iii.* 46.
Manuscripts quoted:
British Museum, Library:
Additional MSS. No. 11,108, *i.* ccxxxvii.
„ „ „ 19,995, *iii.* 282, 283.
Egerton, No. 88, *i.* lxxxv, lxxxvi, clvi, cciv, ccxxix, ccxxx, ccxlv–vi, cclxxvii, cclxxix, cclxxxix, cccxc, ccccviii, dcxliii; *ii.* 8–9.
Egerton, No. 90, *ii.* 124, 125, 153.
„ No. 91, *i.* cccxl–ccxli; *iii.* 4, 44.
„ No. 93 (Tripartite Life of St. Patrick), *i.* lxxxv; *ii.* 67, 74 201.
„ No. 111, *i.* 215.
„ No. 184, *iii.* 34.
„ Plut. cl. xvi. Miscellanea Hibernica, *ii.* 123, 143.
„ No. 1783, *ii.* 343–345.
Harleian, Titus D. II., *i.* cccccxciv.
„ No. 432, *iii.* 115, 116, 117, 118, 134.
„ No. 5280, *i.* ccccxxix, ccccxlvii, div, dcxxxix–xl; *ii.* 33, 135, 253, 254, 369–370, 371, 372–373; *iii.* 42, 43, 156, 159, 162, 164, 214, 239, 315, 365, 385.
Catholic University Library—O'Curry MSS.:
Forbais Droma Dambgaire, and other tracts, *iii.* 356–357.
Lives of Saints, vol. ii., *iii.* 58, 168 (from Book of Fearan Connail).
Historical Poems, vol. iv., *iii.* 318, 329, 339.
Keating's History of Ireland, *ii.* 257, 379–382.
Lives of Saints, (copies from MSS. in Burgundian Library, Brussels), vol. i., *i.* cclxxxix; *iii.* 32–33, 34–5, 37–38, 332.
Historical Poems from the Book of Delvin, bound up in vol. *ii.* of Lives of Saints, *iii.* 168, 287–288.
Miscellaneous Poems, *iii.* 253, 271.
O'Davoren's Glossary, *iii.* 215, 252, 322, 380.
Einsiedeln,—Codex, No. 121, *i.* dlxix.
Lambeth Library, No. 614 (Carew Papers), *i.* xcv.

Manuscripts quoted:
Liber Flavus (the property of, James Marinus Kennedy, Esq.), *ii.* 205-208, 357; *iii.* 277, 385.
Marsh's Library, Dublin, v. 3 tab. ii. No. 20, *i.* xcvi.
Monk Mason's MSS. (now dispersed), exclusive of the Book of Fermoy, *ii.* 79-80, 252; *iii.* 156, 157, 371.
Monastery of St. Paul, Carinthia, Codex, No. 2 (extracts made from by Herr Mone), *iii.* 46, 47.
O'Conor Don's Book, *ii.* 98, 104, 165, 154; *iii.* 25, 255, 272, 273.
O'Duvegan's Book, (part of this book, now in the possession of Lord Ashburnham, which is in the British Museum) *iii.* 58, 65.
O'Looney's, Mr. Brian, MSS.:
Battle of Magh Lena, *i.* cccxl
„ of Magh Mucreimbe (Andrew M'Curtin's copy from the Book of Munster), *i.* cccexxxiv-v.
Keating's Tri Bir Gaithe an Bhais, *i.* cccxl, cccxxv, cccxxx; *iii.* 340.
Vita Senani, *i.* cccxxix. (Andrew M'Curtin's copy).
Royal Irish Academy Library:
Book of Ballymote, *i.* xxiv, xxvi, xxx, lxvi, ccxxix, cccxxi, cccxxv-vi, dxxviii, dcxxxix, dcxl-dcxli; *ii.* 18, 39, 44-47, 65, 106, 109, 110, 111, 117, 121, 123, 142, 145, 147, 149, 151, 153, 154, 155, 171-173, 216 217, 237, 257, 287, 322-324, 377, 378, 388; *iii.* 11-12, 41, 52-54, 83, 124, 277, 317, 328, 330, 333, 374, 376, 388, 391, 393, 395, 396, 401, 405, 526-535.
Book of Fermoy, *i.* cccxxxiii, dcxlii, dcxlii; *ii.* 390-391; *iii.* 204, 309-310, 317.
Book of Lecan, *i.* xx, xlvi, cccxxvi, cccxxx, cccxxxi, cccxxxiii, cccxxxvi, ccclxxii-iii, cccexlvii, dcxxxviii, dcxl-xli; *ii.* 12, 86, 94, 105, 106, 108, 109, 110, 111, 112, 113, 117, 123, 147, 149, 150, 154, 155, 156, 159, 160, 166, 237, 252, 253, 284-285, 325, 385; *iii.* 8, 41, 83, 122, 177, 203-204, 232, 262, 277, 356, 398-399, 405.

Manuscripts quoted:
Book of Lismore (copies of), *i.* cccxxii, cccxxiii, ccclviii, ccc xlviii, dxiii; *ii.* 276, 279-281; *iii.* 12, 14, 121, 170, 202, 232, 237, 305, 324, 325, 328, 361, 362, 366, 377-378, 379.
Lebor Brec, *i.* cccix, cccxli, ccclviii, ccclx, ccclxi, ccclxii, ccclxvi, ccclxviii, ccccxlv; *ii.* 11, 33, 56, 81-82, 85, 175, 202; *iii.* 103, 105, 308, 329, 330, 331, 338, 359, 381, 387.
Lebor na h-Uidhri, *i.* xxxii, xlvi, xc, clxxi, clxxiv, clxxv, ccxcix-ccc, ccci, cccii, ccciii, ccciv, cccv, cccxxi, cccxxii, cccxxvii-viii, cccxxxii, cccxxxvi, cccxxxvii, cccxli, cccxliii, cccxliv-v, cccxlvii, cccxlviii, cccli, ccclii, cccliii, ccclv, ccclvi, ccclvii, ccclviii, ccclx, ccclxi, ccclxiv, ccclxv, ccclxviii, ccclxix, ccclxx, ccclxxi, ccclxxii, ccclxxxvi, ccclxxxvii, cccxc, cccxcv, ccccxxxi-ii, ccccxxxiii, ccccxxxiv, ccccxxxvi, ccccxlvi, cccclii, ccccliv, cccclxiii, cccclxvi, cccclxix, cccclxx, cccclxxiv, cccclxxv, cccclxxvi, cccclxxviii, cccclxxix, cccclxxx, cccclxxxi, cccclxxxiii, ccccxcvi; *ii.* 25, 71, 106, 113-114, 192-193, 299-301; *iii.* 17-21, 57, 76-79, 137, 138, 139, 140, 141, 142, 143, 144, 145, 146, 147, 148, 149, 150, 151, 159, 163, 164, 165, 175, 176, 183, 184, 186, 187, 191, 192, 194, 245, 246, 248, 249, 253, 314, 315.

23 A. 6 Brehon Law, MS. *iii.* 183.

23 C. 18 Betham MSS. *iii.* 281.

CXX, „ „ *iii.* 255.

23 C. 20 O'Longan MSS. *iii.* 392.

23 D. 5 *ii.* 10, 65.

Manuscripts quoted:
23 D. O'Conor Don's Book of Historical Poems, *ii.* 144; *iii.* 154.
23 E. 22 *iii.* 222, 223, 224.
23 F. 16 O'Gara MS. *ii.* 118; *iii.* 169.
23 G. 8. *ii.* 121.
23 H. 1-b (H. and S. MS. 208), *iii* 265.
23 K. 26 O'Clery's Book of Invasions, *i.* xxxii; *ii.* 4, 20, 109, 110, 112; *iii.* 240, 241.
23 K. 37 *ii.* 311.
23 L. 22 H. and S. *iii.* 166, 167, 361.
23 L. 24 *ii.* 129.
23 M. 24 *ii.* 61.
23 P. 1 Mac Firbis' Book of Genealogies, *i.* xxx; *ii* 65-66, *iii.* 15, 16, 83.
23 P. 3 Felire Beg, *iii.* 203.
23 P. 8 *ii.* 160, 162, 163, 164, 165.
23 P. 13 *ii.* 120.
23 Q. 1 *ii.* 160.
2, 25, *ii.* 129.
2, 36, H. and S. *iii.* 179, 380.
13, 5, *ii.* 116.
22, 5, *ii.* 118.
32, 5, *ii.* 121.
35, 5, *i.* cclxxx–cclxxxi, ccxcii.
205, H. and S. *ii.* 275, 277.
No. 208, H. and S. *iii.* 265.
Trinity College Library, Dublin:
Book of Armagh, *i.* xlvii, lxxxv, lxxxix, cxxxv.
Class E. 3, 5, *i.* clxxxi, clxxxvi–viii, clxxxix–cxc; *iii.* 365.

Manuscripts quoted:
Class E. 4, 2 (Liber Hymnorum), *ii.* 74–75, 91–92; *iii.* 251.
Class H. 1, 15, *i.* cccii; *iii.* 7, 107.
Class H. 1, 19 (Annals of Loch Cé), *iii.* 204.
Class H. 2, 15, *i.* cxi, cxii, cxiii, cxvi, cxvii, cxviii, cxix, cxx, cxxi, cxxii, cxxiii–iv, cxxv, cxxviii, cxliii–iv, clxx, clxxi, clxxxvii, clxxxviii, clxxxix, ccxxix, ccxxxviii–ix, cclxxiv–v; *ii.* 119, 127, 128; *iii.* 11–12, 111, 112, 113, 114, 118.
Class H. 2, 16 (Yellow Book of Lecan), *i.* lxxiii, cccli, ccclxx, ccclxxiv–v, ccclxxxi; *ii.* 33, 60, 96–97, 99, 102, 287, 333, 383, 390–391; *iii.* 52, 54, 102, 106, 160, 161, 190, 200, 219–220, 221, 242, 243, 244, 251, 266, 312, 313, 339, 360, 381, 383.
Class H. 2, 17, *i.* cccxxxvii, cccxxxix, cccclvii–viii, dcxxxviii; *iii.* 334, 371.
Class H. 2, 18 (Book of Leinster), *i.* cccxxvii, cccxxxii, cccxli, cccxliii, cccxlviii, cccli, cccxcviii, ccccxxxvi, ccccli, ccccIvi, ccccIxix, cccclxxxii, dxxxiii, dcxii–dcxiii; *ii.* 8, 39–44, 86, 99, 106, 107, 108, 110, 111, 112, 123, 138, 147, 148, 149, 150, 151, 154, 155, 156, 158–159, 165, 176, 237, 260, 292, 293, 294, 297, 298, 302–310, 316–318, 319, 320, 333, 338–339, 340, 356, 357, 359–366; *iii.* 6, 10–11, 14, 34–36, 37 38, 59–62, 81, 88, 90, 92, 93, 94, 95, 96, 97, 98, 99, 100, 101, 109, 110, 162, 168–169, 182, 195, 196, 197, 199, 207–208, 210, 243, 266, 277, 306, 308, 313, 316, 329, 334, 358, 365, 367, 372–373, 376, 383, 388, 400, 404–405, 536–547.
Class H. 3, 3, *ii.* 284–285, 356, 377.
Class H. 3, 17, *i.* ccclxv; *ii.* 14, 216, 329; *iii.* 48–50, 255, 256.
Class H. 3, 18, *i.* xv, xviii, lxxxv–vi, cx, cxvii, cxxxvi, cxliii, cxliv, clvi, clx, clxxiv

Manuscripts quoted:
clxxx, clxxxii, clxxxiii, clxxxvii, cxc–cxci, cxci–cxcii, cxcviii, ccvii, ccxxviii, ccxxx, ccxxxviii, cclii, cclxii–iii, cclxvii, cclxxix, cclxx, cclxxi, cclxxiv, cclxxv, ccxci, cccxxiii, cccxxx, ccclxxii, cccxciv, ccccix, cccclxiii, cccclxvii, ccclxxviii, ccclxxxii, dlxx, dcxliii; ii. 8–9, 31, 93, 186, 376, iii. 3, 26–30, 56, 152, 153, 160, 161, 188, 254, 326, 336, 368, 375.
Class H. 4, 4, i. ccclxv.
Class H. 4, 20, iii. 256.
Class H. 4, 22, i. cliii, ccxlii, ccxliii, ccxliv, cclxxi; ii. 61; iii. 305.
Marcellian Formulae, the, i. lviii-ix.
Mardelles, Margelles, i. ccxcvii.
Markgenossenschaft, the German, i. cxlvi.
Markvogt of the Germans, i. clx.
Marraba, the Arabic, i. cccexcv.
Marriage of the Irish with the Picts, Britons, etc., i. xx.
Marriage customs of the Irish; the Tincur or — portion, i. clxxii; the Coibche or bridal gift, clxxiii; the Tindscra, Log Lanamnais, or "Bride Price", clxxiv; rights of married women, clxxv-vi; separation and divorce in Wales, clxxvii; separation and divorce in Ireland, clxxviii; position of women in Wales as to inheritance, clxxviii.
Mart lands, i. xcv, cliv.
Matting, i. cccliii.
Maynaul, the, of North Wales, i. xcii.
Mayor or Mayer, i. ccxlv.
Meal, i. ccclx, dcxxxix.
Meal and milk, i. ccclix, ccclx.
Meat, different kinds of flesh, i. ccclxviii; persons entitled to —, ccclxvii; salt —, ccclxix.
Melodies, uses of national, i. dcxii.
Menyanthes trifoliata, i. ccclxxiv, ccccv.
Mercenaries, Gaulish, in the pay of Ailill and Medb, i. xx.
Meso-Anthropic epoch, i. ccccvii.
Metals, M. Ad. Pictet's researches on the — of the Aryans, i. ccccix.
Metayer, the, i. cxxiii.
Metempsychosis, no trace of the doctrine of, among the Gaedhil, iii. 60.
Metheglin, not the only or chief intoxicating drink of the Irish, i. ccclxxvii.
Metre, i. dxlvii.
Meyer, the German, i. ccxlv.
Mezzajuolo, the, i. cxxiii.
Mi-Canon, i. dxvii.
Milesian colony and colonists, ii. 50, 51, 183, 222, 226; — Gaedhils, 231; — or Gadelian tribes, iii. 384; — dynasty, 204; — sovereignty, foundation of, ii. 3.
Milesians, i. xxiii, xxiv, lxxi, lxxvi, lxxvii, cccviii, ccccxxxviii, cccclxvii; historians and poets of the —, ii. 51, 52; 153, 169, 170, 188, 189, 234, 256; iii. 2, 43, 73, 82; inferiority of the —, a modern hypothesis, 83, 85; 89, 182, 231, 240, 241.
Military education in Eriu, a system of fosterage, ii. 375.
" Fork, i. ccccxlvi, ccccxlvii, ccccxlviii; a wheeled eight-pronged —, dcxl. See Foga.
" organization, ii. 12.
" School, ii 354.
" Teacher, first historical allusion to a, ii. 356.
" Tutors of celebrated champions, ii. 374-5.
Milk, i. ccclxi, ccclxiv, ccclxv, ccclxvii, ccclxix, ccclxxi, dcxxxix.
Mill, i. ccclix, ccclx; — pond, ccclix; — shaft, ccclx; — stone, ccclx.
Millet, i. ccclxiii.
Mince meats, i. ccclxix.
Mine, gold, ii. 5; iii. 204; mineral district of Silver Mines and Meanus, 208.
Minor key, supposed predominance of the, in the national music of all nations, i. dc.
Minor scale, modern, of *E*, i. dxcvi; modern — of *A*, dciii.
Minor seventh, change of the, into the major seventh, i. dlxv.
Mirrors, i. ccclvii.
Missus, the, of the Emperor, i. cclx.
Mitgift, i. clxxii.
Mjöðkarm, i. ccclvi.
Mlat, the Bohemian, i. cccclvii, cccclix.
Modes, the three ancient musical, iii. 381.
Möttul, the; the Tiglar —, i cclxxxix.
Möttulköp or Mantlepurchase, i. clxxv.
Μολυβδίδες, i. cccclxi.

Momonians, *i.* ccccxxi, ccclxxiv.
Monodon monoceros, *i.* cccclxix.
Moraches, *i.* dxvii.
Mordants, *i.* cccciii, ccccvi.
Morgangaba, *i.* clxxiii.
Morgenstern, the, *i.* cccclxii.
"Morning Star", the, *i.* cccclxii.
Mortar not used in the earliest stone buildings, *i.* ccciii.
Mor Tuath, *i.* xcvii, xcviii, ccliii, ccliv, cclviii, cclxviii, cclxix, cclxx, ccclxxix.
Motet, *i.* dliv, dlxii.
Mouldings of red yew, *i.* dcxli.
Muudbora, *i.* cxvii.
Munder, *i.* clxxiv.
Mundiburdus, *i.* cxvii.
Muse, the, *i.* dxxxii.
Music, object of the discussion of Irish, *i.* dxli; three epochs of development of —, dxlii; introduction of — into the service of the church, dxlvi; *genus* of church — different from that of modern —; developement of — according to caprice, dlxxvii; causes which led to the emancipation of —, from the dominating influence of plain chant, dlxxviii; principal defect in modern —, due to this cause, dlxxix; professors of —, *ii.* 4; — not played at the battle of Magh Tuired, *iii.* 225; Dr. Ferguson on the antiquity of — in Ireland, 226; skill in — a characteristic of the Eberian race, 231; — traditionally preserved by gipsies of Spain, 233; present indifference to Irish —, 290; testimony of Giraldus Cambrensis to excellency of Irish —, 405; particular kinds of — mentioned in ancient MSS., 370.
Musical branch, the; was used in other countries also; the Circulus tintinnabulis instructus; the cymbalum; the Irish — was a lay instrument; similar instruments may have been elsewhere used in churches, *i.* dxxxvii; the Bombalum, dxxxviii; — of Porsenna, king of Etruria, dxxxix; *iii.* 313; — was a symbol of poets, and used for commanding silence, 314; 315, 316; the finding of the — of king Cormac Mac Airt, 317; — was symbolical of peace and repose; a poem on —, 318; — was analogous to the Turkish crescent and bells, 319.
Musical Canon of the Welsh, *iii.* 227.
„ Feats, the, of the Dagda, *i.* dcxxxiv; *iii.* 214; they represented different keys; existence of similar keys amongst the early Greeks, *i.* dcxxxiv; *iii.* 216, 217; similar legends to be found in other countries, *i.* dcxxxv; — of the Norse harper Bose, dcxxxv; — compared to different seasons of the year in Egypt, *iii.* 216; legend of the origin of the three —, 218-222.
„ Instruments of the Irish, *i.* cccclxxxiv; — of Ireland, Scotland, and Wales, according to Giraldus Cambrensis, ccccxc; — mentioned under the name of Cruit in Irish MSS., probably of the Psalterium or Nablum class, dxiii; — of the east in use in Spain, dxxii; existing — adapted to the bow when the latter was first introduced; the same — was played with a plectrum, a bow, or with the fingers, dxxiii; statements of Walker and Bunting regarding Irish — of no value, *iii.* 302; names of Irish — found in Irish MSS., 306; — mentioned in the tale of the Battle of Almhain, and in the poem on the Fair of Carman, 313.
„ Modes, *iii.* 214, 216, 217, 218-222, 381. See Musical Feats.
„ Performers, professional names of, *iii.* 367; — mentioned in the Brehon laws, *iii.* 368.
Musicians, instance of, in the train of a king on a military expedition, *iii.* 309-312.
Mustard, *i.* ccclxiii.
Mutton, *i.* ccclxviii.
Myrica gale, *i.* ccclxxiii.
Mythology, comparative, of Aryan nations, *i.* iii.
Myvirian Archaiology, the, *i.* dcxxviii-dcxxx.
Nabla, or Nablum, the, *i.* diii, dvi, dx; — was considered a superior instrument by the Greeks, dxi; —

was an instrument of the elegant Roman world, dxii; — may have been used by Tuotilo, dxii, dxiii.
Naidm, *i.* cxcvii, cxcviii, cclxii, cclxvii, cclxxv, cclxxvi, cclxxxiv, ccxc, ccxcii; *iii.* 470, 471.
Nâlgund, *i.* ccccxlvii.
Nam, *i.* cclxxxii, cclxxxv.
Narwhale, *i.* ccccxlix.
National music, sources of error in noting down, *i.* dcxiv, dcxv.
Natural diatonic scale now used in Plain Chant, *i.* dlxxxvi, dlxxxix, dxci.
Nawd, the Welsh, *i.* ccxciv.
Nebel, the, *i.* dix, dx, dxi; — Nassor, dx.
Needle, the pledging of a, *iii.* 112; legal fines for overholding a pledged —, 112, 113.
Nemds, the court or jury called a, *i.* cxxxvi, cxciii, cclxiv, cclxv, cclxvi.
Nemedians, *i.* xxxviii, xxxix, lxxi, lxxvi; *ii.* 50, 109, 184, 185, 225, 233, 234; *iii.* 2, 231.
Nemet, *i.* cclxiv, cclxxxix.
Νεμῆται, Nemetes, the tribe name, *i.* cclxiv.
Nemeton, *i.* cclxiv.
Neuad, of the Welsh, *i.* ccc.
Neumes, *i.* dlxix.
Nexum, *i.* cclxxv. See Nexus.
Nexus, *i.* ccxcii, ccxciii.
Niebelungen Lay, *i.* cclxxvii, ccccxlix, dxxvii.
Nimidas, *i.* cclxiv.
Nodman, *i.* cclxxvi; *iii.* 470.
Nofre, *i.* dxi.
Nola, *i.* dxxxiv, dxxxv.
Nomenclature, confusion of musical, *i.* dlxxix.
Normans, *i.* xlii, lxviii, lxix, cxxxix, cxcvii.
Norse, or Norsemen, *i.* xxxvi, lxxiv, xc, xcii, cclv, ccxlix, ccclx, ccclxix, ccclxxviii, ccclxxxix, ccccxlix, ccccli.
"Norse-beer", *i.* ccclxxviii.
Norse Saga, *i.* ccccxliv, cccclxx.
Northmen. See Norsemen.
Norwegians, *i.* xxiv, ccc, ccclxxvii, ccccxcii.
Notation, no example of musical, in Irish MSS., *i.* dlxix; supposed musical — of the Britons; the Welsh musical MS.; Dr. Burney's opinion of it, dcxxviii; he deciphered a little of it; the greater part was deciphered by Barthelemon; Mr. Parry's pretended *fac-simile* of the Welsh MS.; Dr. Burney's *fac-simile*; the transcript in the *Myvirian Archaiology* not a fac-simile at all, dcxxix; the five Welsh keys of Mr. Thomas; they are modern keys; the keys in the Welsh MS. as given by Mr. Thomas are unintelligible, dcxxx; Mr. Thomas thinks the music of the Welsh MS. was for the *Crwth*; he has deciphered some of it; he thinks the — was that of St. Gregory, dcxxxi; it is the tablature of a stringed instrument, and is not older than the sixteenth century; this instrument may have been the Crwth, dcxxxii.
Numbers, preference of the ancient Irish, for certain, *i.* ccxli; this has no political importance, ccxlii.
Numismatics, Celtic, *i.* lxvii.
Nut of Knowledge, *ii.* 144.
Nutmeal, *i.* ccclxv.
Oak bark, *i.* ccclxxiii.
Oathmen, *i.* cclxvii.
Oaths of different kinds, *i.* cclxxxix.
Oatmeal, *i.* ccclxiii-vi.
Oats, *i.* ccclxii, ccclxiii, ccclxxiii.
Obai, the Spartan, *i.* lxxxi; — subdivisions of the —, xciii.
Oblivion, drink of, given to Cuchulaind and Emer, *ii.* 226.
Oc Aire, *i.* cxxx, cxli, cxlii, clv, clvii, clxv, ccxli, cclxix, ccxcviii, cccliv, ccclix, ccclxvi, ccclxvii; *iii.* 469, 479, 480, 481, 482.
Ocrath, Ochrath, *i.* ccclxxiv, ccclxxxv; *iii.* 105.
Oendvegi, *i.* cccl.
Offices, literary, of the Irish monarchs, *ii.* 35.
Og Aire, *i.* cclxxx; *iii.* 26. See Oc Aire.
Ogam, Ogham, tract on, in Book of Ballymote, *i.* lxvi, cccvii; writing the name of a deceased person in —, part of the burial rite, ccc xx, cccxli; — inscriptions usually cut in wood in pagan times; the old Germans cut their runes on tablets of ash, cccxlii; the Irish *Duile feda* were probably tablets of this kind, cccxliii; instances from Irish MSS. of — being cut on sticks, cccxliii-cccxiv; *ii.* 210; instances of an —

cut on stone, ccoxli; — inscriptions cut on stone probably not older than the Roman occupation of Britain, cccxlii; some — inscriptions may be cryptic, but all are not, cccxliii; why — inscriptions may show traces of Latin influence, cccxliv; — not borrowed from the Norse runes, cccxliv, cccxlv; first — inscriptions, *ii.* 7, 172; — cut or written by Dallan, 192-194; — used by the druids, 194; — stones and monuments, 194; Lomna communicates with Find in — characters, 209, 210; — letters, 226; — inscriptions on swords, 254; — stone of Dunmore, *iii.* 71; Mr. Richard Hitchcock's manuscript book of notes on —, 71.

Odal land, *i.* clxxxv.

Ollamh, *i.* clvi, cclii, cclxx, cclxxii, cclxxx; *ii.* 39, 42, 217; *iii.* 43; meaning of —, *ii.* 136; *iii.* 52, etc.; Book of —s, *ii.* 171-173; the stipend of an — builder, *iii.* 53-55; artistic work of an —, 57; great stories an — was bound to tell before a king, 81.

„ Aighne, *i.* cclxxiii.

„ Brethemnais, *i.* cclxvi.

„ Cruitire, and — timpanist, *iii.* 365.

Ol na Guala, *i.* ccclxxi-ccclxxiii.

Omens, of a day, *ii.* 226.

Onions, *i.* ccclxvi.

Opera, influence of the, on the change of polyphonous into harmonic music, *i.* dlxiv.

Opsonia, *i.* ccclxvi.

Oracles, druidical, *ii.* 226.

Ordeal by fire, use of the roan tree in, *ii.* 216.

Ordnance Memoir of Derry, *ii.* 153; *iii.* 8.

Organ, the pneumatic, *i.* dxxix; — may have been known in Ireland, dxxx.

Organistrum, *i.* dxxiv.

Organum, *i.* dxxx; use of the term —; was probably known in the time of St. Isidore, but not generally practised, as shown by the choir of St. Gall in the ninth century, dxlix; rules for the — existed however in the ninth century, dl; first kind of —; second kind of —, or diaphony; Herr O. Paul's view as to the nature of —, dli; the first kind of —, disused before the eleventh century; the — had no independent meaning; — not used in secular music, according to some writers; proof that — was sometimes used in secular music, dliii.

Ornaments, description of gold and silver, in the tale of the Wandering of Maeldun's Boat, *iii.* 158 et seq; — described in the Tochmarc Bec Fola, 150; explanation of the finding of — unconnected with human remains, 162; — mentioned in the description of a cavelcade, 156-158; — for the neck, 178; — for the necks of animals, 180; — of native manufactures, 211.

Orobus niger and Or. tuberosum, *i.* ccclxiii.

Ossart, *i.* cxci.

Ossianic poems, *iii.* 300, 392; — Society, *i.* xii.

Ossorians, *ii.* 46, 206, 207.

Ownership of land, sources of information regarding, *i.* cxxxi; medieval sources; modern French writers on the —, cxxxii; M. Guizot's opinion, cxxxii, cxxxiii; M. Sismondi's opinion; the state conjectured by the latter that of nomadic tribes, cxxxiii; assumed absence of ownership in severalty among the Germans; individual property in lands known to the Germans, cxxxiv.

Oxen, *i.* ccclxviii.

Oxgang, the Anglo-Saxon, *i.* lxxxix, cxlviii.

Paalstab, *i.* cccel

Pagus, the Latin, *i.* lxxxii, lxxxiii, lxxxiv, lxxxviii, xci, ccxxx.

Palaeo-anthropic Epoch, *i.* cccvii.

Paling of bronze, *i.* dcxlii.

Palli, the Sanskrit, *i.* lxxxiv.

Pallium, *i.* ccclxxx.

Pál-stair, *i.* cccel.

"Palstave", *i.* cccexliv, cccexlix, cccel, cccell.

Papal choir in the Sistine Chapel, *i.* dlxxxviii.

Parmelia saxatilis, P. omphalodes, *i.* cccci.

Parsnips, *i.* ccclxvi.

Partnership Tenure, nature of, *i.* cxlviii; form of entering into copartnery, cxci; protection one object of —, cxcvi.

Partnerships, their advantages, *i.* clviii; Fuidir —, cxxiv, clviii; co-

tillage — in Wales, Scotland, Friesland, etc.; rundale, or runrig, the relics of partnership, *i.* clix; insolvent members of —, cxc-cxci; absent members of —, cxcii. See Gilds.
Pastinaca sativa, *i.* ccclxvi.
Pavana, *i.* dlxii.
Pavaniglia, *i.* dlxii.
Pencedl, *i.* cci.
Pennpits, *i.* ccxcvii.
Persians, *ii.* 160; *iii.* 72.
Pertuisane, *i.* cccexliii.
Philology, Irish, works on, *i.* lvii.
Phœnician origin of the Irish, *i.* lxviii; — trade with Cornwall a mere assumption, cccexi.
Phratry, *i.* lxxviii, xciii.
Phrygian musical mode, *i.* dcxxv; *iii.* 217.
Phyle, the Greek, *i.* lxxx; sub divisions of the —, lxxxi, xciii.
Pianoforte, *i.* dxvi.
Picts, *i.* xx, xxiv, xxxiv, xxxv, xliii, xliv, xc, ccxxxix; *iii.* 7, 34; Irish —, *i.* ccclxxv. See Cruithentuath.
Pig, *i.* ccclxv, ccclxviii, ccclxix, dcxxxix.
Pin, *i.* ccclxxxvii; chased gold —s, *iii.* 167.
Pillows, *i.* cccliii.
Pilum, the, *i.* cccexxxiii.
Pipa. See Bagpipe.
Pipe. See Bagpipe.
Pirete, *i.* cccxcvi.
Pi-santir, the, *i.* dxiv.
Pitch of *A* adopted in France, *i.* dlxxxii.
Pitcher, *i.* dcxlii.
Placitum, the general; it corresponded to the Aenech, *i.* cclx-cclxi.
Plagal Church Tones, relation of, to Irish music, *i.* dxcix-dc. See Tones.
„ Modes, *i.* dlxxv, dxcix.
Plain Chant, *i.* dxlviii, dlxxvii, dlxxviii, dlxxix, dlxxxvi, dxcix, dc.
Planxties, *i.* dcix.
Plaustrum, the, *i.* cccclxxvi; — majus, *i.* ccclvi.
Plebs, *i.* cclviii.
Ploughlands. See Seisreach.
Plume, the bird, *i.* cccclxxxi.
Plunder of the Castle of Maelmilscothach, a Rabelaistic tale, *ii.* 130-135.
Poems quoted:
Aedh Abrat's poetical invitation to Cuchulaind, *ii.* 196.
Anonymous, to a harp of Conor O'Brien, Earl of Thomond, *iii.* 287.
„ to a MSS. book, and to the harp of the author, *iii.* 318.
On the origin of the name *Ath Liag Find*, *ii.* 283-284.
Stanza from Zeuss on the singing of *blackbirds*, *iii.* 387.
Breasal Belach's appeal to Find Mac Cumhaill, *ii.* 384, 385.
On the modes of *Burial*, *i.* cccxxx, cccxxxi.
Cailte's description of the vocal music of Find and his warriors, *iii.* 377.
Of *Cano* on the celebrated ales of Ireland, *i.* ccclxxiv-v.
Ceannmhair's invocation to his handstone, *ii.* 281, 282.
On the chief *cemeteries*, *i.* cccxxvii.
Cinnaeth O'Hartagan's, on the Tech Midchuarda, *ii.* 378.
Fragment of a, on the *Clann* Colla, *ii.* 16.
Colman Mac Lenene's, on his sword, *iii.* 245.
On *Cormac's* interview with Aengus Mac Inog, *iii.* 362.
Cormac Mac Cuilennain, fragment of a religious, of, *iii.* 388.
On *Craiftine's* harp, by Nos, son of Find, or by Ferceirtne, *iii.* 249.
On the Courtship of *Credé* and Cael, *iii.* 13, 14.
Of *Cuan* O'Lothchain, on the privileges, etc., of the Ard Righ, and provincial kings, *ii.* 142.
Of *Crubretan*, son of Aengus, on violence done to a leper, *ii.* 390.
On *Dubh* Gilla, the shield of Aedh, king of Oirghiall, *i.* dcxliii.
Of *Dubthach Dael Uladh* on Cuchulaind, *i.* cccxxxviii.
Of *Dubthach Ua Lugair*, *ii.* 340.
Story of *Duiblinn*, *ii.* 289.
On the lot casting of *Eber* and Ereamhon, *ii.* 4; *iii.* 240-241.
Of *Eochaidh Eolach O'Ceirin* on the history of Ailech, *iii.* 8, 9.
Of *Eochaidh Eolach O'Ceirin* on the origin of the name and ancient history of Loch Garman, and on the Feis of Tara, *ii.* 12-13.

Poems quoted:
Eogan Mór's address to Eadan and her answer, *iii.* 360.
Of *Fercertne* on Ollamh Fodhla, *ii.* 8, 9, 257.
On the Fight of *Ferdiad* and Cuchulaind, *i.* dcvi; *ii.* 303, 305, 306; *iii.* 400-401, 415-463.
Of *Fergus* on an Ogham inscription on an Id, *i.* cccxliv-v.
Pierce *Ferriter's* panegyric on a harp, *iii.* 258.
Fionntan's elegy on the death of king Raghallach, *ii.* 81-82, 343-345.
Of *Flanagan*, son of Ceallach, on the death of Aedh Finnliath, *ii.* 96.
Of *Flanagan* on the death of his son Ceallach, *ii.* 96.
Of *Flanagan* on the historical tales which an Ollamh should know, and on the deaths of eminent persons, *ii.* 96-97.
Of *Flann Mac Lonain* on the death of the sons of Flanagan, *ii.* 96.
Flann Mainistrech's pedigree of the saints of Ireland, *ii.* 166, 167.
Fothadh na Canoine, stanzas on the death of king Aedh Finnliath, *ii.* 95.
Fulartach on the Fair of Carman or Garman, *ii.* 38 to 47; *iii.* 358-359, 526 to 547.
Discovery of the *Gae Bulga*, *ii.* 311, 312.
Giolla Brighde Mac Conmidhe on the Church of Armagh, *iii.* 58.
Geoffrey Keating on his harper Tadgh O'Coffey, *iii.* 215.
Laegh's description of his visit to the court of Labrad, *iii.* 192.
Loch Lein and *Len* the goldsmith, *iii.* 203.
Mac Conmidhe on the harp of Donnchadh Cairbrech O'Brien, *iii.* 271-272.
Mac Liag's elegy on the death of Tadgh O'Kelly, *ii.* 125.
,, topographical poem, *ii.* 100.
,, and Mac Coise, dialogue of, *ii.* 127-128.
Midir's address to Edain as Befinn, *ii.* 192-193; *iii.* 191.
On the death of *Mogh Neid*, *i.* cccxl.
Mogh Ruith's address to his Lia Laimhé, or hand-stone, *ii.* 279, 280.

Poems quoted:
On the Battle of *Móin Trogaidhé*, *ii.* 356, 389.
Nuadha O'Lomthuilé on the Battle of Almhain, *ii.* 391.
O'h-Eimhin, a prayer, *iii.* 399.
Brian *O'Higgins'* address to David Roche of Fermoy, *iii.* 284.
Oisin, on the chess playing of Diarmait O'Duibhne, and other Fenian chiefs, *iii.* 166-167.
,, from the fragment of the battle of Gabhra, *i.* cccxli-ii.
,, lament of, for his son Oscar, *i.* cccxxv.
Satire of a master on his pupil, *iii.* 393-394.
,, on a student, *iii.* 396.
Satirical dialogue with a student, *iii.* 395.
Rath and Caiseal builders, metrical list of, *iii.* 15, 16.
Rumain Mac Colmain, quatrain of, enumerating the number of boards for an oratory, *iii.* 37.
Saint Baoithin's lesson from the building of a round house, *iii.* 33.
,, Maedhog of Cluan Mór, address of, to Bran, King of Leinster, *ii.* 338, 339.
,, Moling, panegyric on King Aedh, *iii.* 46, 47.
,, ,, appeal of, to the Ui Deagha, *iii.* 36.
Scathach, the magic harp playing of, *iii.* 223-224.
Seanchan Torpeist, elegy on the death of Dallan Forgaill, *ii.* 85, 86.
,, fragments of the Satire on rats of, *ii.* 87.
,, farewell to Guairé, *ii.* 88.
Suibne, the mad, on a building made by Gobban Saer, *iii.* 46.
On the Fair of *Tailté*, *i.* dcxl-dcxli.
Tanaidhe O'Maelchonaire, on the Firbolg kings, *ii.* 237.
On *Tara*, *iii.* 7.
Tathlum, on the making of a, *ii.* 252.
Torna Eiges, on the death of Niall, *i.* lxxiii; *ii.* 60.
,, on Niall and Corc, King of Cashel, *ii.* 63.
,, on Religh na Righ, *ii.* 71-72.
Tuirbhi, father of Gobban Saer, legend of, *iii.* 41.
Ui Cormaic, appeal of the Abbot

of, to Feidhlimidh Mac Crimhthainn, Ard Righ, *iii.* 262.
Poems referred to:
Aengus na Diadachta, or Aengus Finn O'Daly, *ii.* 143, 144,
Amergin, lament for Aithirne, *iii.* 374.
Anonymous, in praise of the palace of Ailinn, *iii.* 182.
„ instructions to a new king, *iii.* 255,
„ on the Fair of Tailté, *i.* ccxxxvi, cccxxxiii.
„ Address to Randall, Lord of Arann, *iii.* 339.
Art "the Solitary" son of Conn, prophecy of, *ii.* 58.
Blessed Virgin, ancient hymn to, *iii.* 392.
Brian Ruadh Mac Conmidhe, panegyric of Neachtan O'Donnell, *ii.* 98.
Cenfaeladh, on the migrations of Golamh or Milesius, *ii.* 94.
„ Aidedhaibh Uladh, on the death of the Ultonians, *ii.* 94.
Cimbaeth, on, *ii.* 357.
Cinaedh or Cinnaeth O'Hartagan, on the death of the sons of Aedh Slane, *ii.* 106.
„ on Brugh Mic an Oig, *ii.* 106.
„ on Dumha Eirc, and the Hill of Acaill, *ii.* 106.
„ on the Champions of Eriu, *ii.* 106, 107.
„ on the death of Niall, *ii.* 108.
„ on Rath Essa, *ii.* 105, 106.
„ on the manner of the deaths of the chief heroes of the Red Branch, *ii.* 325.
„ on the pillar of St. Buite, *ii.* 107.
„ on the origin of Tara, *ii.* 106.
„ on the Tech Midchuarta, *ii.* 105.
Colman O'Clusaigh, elegy on St. Cumain Fadda, *ii.* 90.
„ hymn against the Yellow Plague, *ii.* 91.
Cormac an Eigeas, circuit of Muirchertach "of the leather cloaks", *ii.* 105.
Cormac Filé, poem on Tara, *iii.* 6.
Cuan O'Lothchain, panegyric of Cormac Mac Airt, *ii.* 140, 141.
„ on the origin of the name and ancient history of Druim Criaich, *ii.* 145, 146, 147.
„ on the privileges, prerogatives, etc., of the Ard Righ and Provincial Kings, *ii.* 141, 142.
Poems referred to:
„ on the origin of the name of the river Shannon, *ii.* 142.
„ on the history of Tailté, *ii.* 148, 149.
„ Panegyric on Tara, and on Noall of the Nine Hostages, *ii.* 147, 148, 378.
Cuaradh on Aileach, *ii.* 155.
Dallan Forgaill, Amra or elegy on St. Colum Cille, *i.* cccclxxv-vi, cccclxxix, ccccxcvi; *ii.* 52, 78, 85; *iii.* 245-246. 247-249, 250-251, 253, 371, 376.
Deirdre, lament of, *iii.* 378, 385.
Diarmait, son of Laoighseal Mac an Bhaird, on the right of the Ulidians to the "Red Hand", *iii.* 265.
Dorban on interments in Cruachan, *ii.* 72.
Dubhthach, panegyric of Crimhthann, son of Enna Cinselach, *ii.* 340.
Eochaid Eolach O'Cerin on the origin of the name of Loch Carman, *ii.* 12, 18, 113, 114.
„ on the history of Aileach, *ii.* 153; *iii.* 8, 9.
„ O'Beoghusa, lament on the decay of the warlike energies of the Irish, *iii.* 169.
„ O'Cleircin. See Flann, Pedigree of the saints of Ireland, *ii.* 167.
„ O'Flinn, on the invasion of Ireland by Partholan, *ii.* 108-109.
„ „ on the colonization of Ireland by Caesar and Partholan, *ii.* 109.
„ „ on the division of Eriu between the sons of Partholan, *ii.* 109.
„ „ on the names of the druids, etc., of Partholan, *ii.* 109.
„ „ on the destruction of Conaing's tower, *ii.* 109.
„ „ the colonization of Ireland, *ii.* 109.
„ „ the invasion of Ireland by the Tuatha Dé Danand, *ii.* 110-111.
„ „ on the chiefs of the Milesian expedition, *ii.* 111.
„ „ on the accession of Sobharcé and Cermna, *ii.* 111.
„ „ on the coming of the Gadelians, *ii.* 111.

Poems referred to:
- Eochaid O'Flinn, on the building of Emania, *ii.* 112.
  - „ „ on the kings of Ulster from Cimbaeth to Concobar Mac Nessa, *ii.* 112.
  - „ „ on the reign of the monarch Eogan Mór, *ii.* 112.
  - „ „ on the creation of the world, *ii.* 113.
- Eoghan O'Donnghaile, on a harper named Feidhlimy, *ii.* 329, 357.
  - „ „ on the right of the O'Neills to the "Red Hand", *iii.* 265.
  - „ Ruadh Mac an Bhaird on the baptism of Conal Gulban, *ii.* 165.
- Errard Mac Coisé, panegyric of Maelseachlain or Malachy and the chief princes of Eriu, *ii.* 127.
  - „ Dialogue between, and Mac Liag, *ii.* 127, 128.
  - „ Panegyric of Maelbrunnaidh, son of Tadgh of the Tower, *i.* 128, 129.
  - „ on the death of Fergal O'Ruairc, *ii.* 129.
  - „ Address to the plunderers of his Castle, *ii.* 135.
- Fercertne, Amra Chonrai, *i.* ccclvi; *iii.* 152-153, 179, 209.
- Fiacc, Bishop, metrical life of St. Patrick, *ii.* 74-75.
- Find Mac Cumhaill, poems attributed to, *ii.* 59.
- Flann Mac Lonain, elegy on the death of Eignechan, *ii.* 102-105.
  - „ on the sons of Eochaidh Muighmheadoin, *ii.* 102.
  - „ Address to Forester, Son of Entangled Forest, *ii.* 102.
  - „ on the qualifications of an Ollamh, *ii.* 96-97.
- Flann Mainistrech, on the death and place of sepulture of the Tuatha Dé Danand, *ii.* 150; *iii.* 210.
  - „ on the length of the reign and manner of death of each of the Pagan monarchs of Eriu from Eochaidh Feidhlech to Dathi, *ii.* 150.
  - „ on the manner of death of the Christian monarchs of Eriu, *ii.* 150.
  - „ a satirical poem on the names of the Tróm Daimh, *ii.* 89, 150, 151.
- Flann Mainistrech, on the names length of reign, and manner of death of the Christian Kings of Munster, *ii.* 151.
  - „ on the monarchs of Eriu and kings of Meath descended from Niall, *ii.* 151.
  - „ on the origin and history of Aileach, *ii.* 151-153.
  - „ on Aileach (a second), *ii.* 154.
  - „ on the battles and deeds of valour of the descendants of Eoghan, son of Niall, *ii.* 155.
  - „ on the battles and deeds of valour of the Cinel Eoghain, *ii* 156.
  - „ on the life of Muirchertach Mac Erca, *ii.* 156.
  - „ on the birth and history of Aedh Slainé, *ii.* 158, 159.
  - „ on the monarchs of Eriu and kings of Meath of the race of Aedh Slainé, *ii.* 159.
- Flann Mainistrech, on the household of St. Patrick, *ii.* 159, 160.
  - „ a metrical abstract of ancient history, *ii.* 160.
  - „ on the taxes and tributes paid to the King of Tir Chonaill, *ii.* 160.
  - „ on the rights and privileges of the kings of Aileach, and the kings of Tir Chonaill, *ii.* 160.
  - „ Panegyric of Conall Gulban, *ii.* 161.
  - „ Pedigree of the Saints of Ireland, *ii.* 166.
- Fothadh na Canoiné, metrical precepts on the duties of a king, *ii.* 176.
- Fulartach, Fair of Carman, *i.* cxvi, ccxxxii, ccliv, cclvii, cclix, cccxxvi, cccxiii, cccxliii, dxxi, dxxxii; *iii.* 313, 325, 335, 338, 364, 367, 368.
- Giolla Brighde Mac Conmidhe on Dalach, son of Muirchertach, *ii.* 162.
  - „ on Maelseachlain O'Donnell, Lord of Tir Connell, *ii.* 162.
  - „ on the territories of Conall Gulban and his brothers, *ii.* 163, 164.
  - „ on the territory and race of Enna, *ii.* 164.
  - „ on the division of territory between Conall Gulban and Eoghan, *ii.* 164, 165.

Poems referred to:
Giolla Brighde Mac Conmidhe on the hardships of the literary orders, *iii.* 167.
" Panegyric on Donnchadh Cairbreach O'Brien, *iii.* 271.
Laitheog's address to her son Flann Mac Lonain, *ii.* 98.
Mac Liag, topographcal poem, *ii.* 99.
" on the sons of Cas, *ii.* 117.
" on the sons of Ceineidigh, *ii.* 117.
" on the fall of Brian Borumha, *ii.* 117-118.
" Address of Errard Mac Coisé on the death of Brian, *ii.* 118-119.
" Lament for his absence from Ceann Coradh, *ii.* 120.
" on giving the name Borumha to Ceann Coradh, *ii.* 120, 121.
" on Carn Chonaill, *ii.* 121, 122.
" Panegyric on Tadgh O'Kelly, *ii.* 123, 143.
" Panegyric on Tadgh O'Kelly and other chieftains, *ii.* 124.
Maelmura of Fahan, in praise of Flann Sionna, *ii.* 98.
Marbhan, dialogue between, and his brother Guaire, *iii.* 356, 357.
Muireadhach Albanach O'Daly—three laudatory poems addressed to O'Donnell, *iii.* 281.
" appeal to Donchadh Cairbrech O'Brian, *iii.* 281.
" appeal to Morrogh, son of Brian O'Brien, *iii.* 282-283.
O'Duibhagan, Sean Mór, panegyric on Tara, *ii.* 58-59, 65, 66.
Olioll Oluim, poems of, in Book of Leinster, *ii.* 57.
Oisin, account of the wooing of Berach Breac by his father Find, *iii.* 380.
Ruman Mac Colman, poem written for the Galls or foreigners of Dublin, *iii.* 37.
Saint Mochae, poems relating to the legend of, *iii* 387.
Seanchan Torpeist, on the battles of the monarch Ruadhraidhe, *iii.* 86.
Torna Eigas, poems attributed to, *ii.* 60, et seq.
Poet, a, governed Ireland conjointly with a priest, *ii.* 138, 139.
Poet-judges, profession of, deprived of their privileges in the time of Concobar Mac Nessa, *ii.* 20.
Poets of the Milesians, *ii.* 51, 52; — at the court of Laeghaire, 72; the different orders of —, and the kind of poetry peculiar to each, 171.
Poetry, professors of, *ii.* 4; the twelve books of —, *ii.* 381.
Pole, the, of a chariot, *i.* ccccIxxx.
Pole hammer, the, *i.* cccclix.
Polis, the Greek, *i.* lxxxiv.
Polychord instruments known to the Greeks, who looked upon them as foreign, *i.* ccccIxxxvi; the absence of — from sculptures, etc., not a proof that they were not in extensive use, *i.* ccccIxxxvii.
Polyphonous music, *i.* dxlvi.
Poor, relieving officer of the, *i.* ccli.
"Poor scholars", *ii.* 279.
Population, distribution of, in Ireland; demesne of the Flath; comparison with Wales; Fuidirland; number of freeholders, *i.* cliii; extent of the holdings of Ceiles; public land; was gradually converted into allodium, cliv; life estates lapsed into estates in fee; tribe land; rights of freemen on it; establishment of a Selb, clv; the Maigin Digona, clv, clvi; extent of, land in usufruct of freemen not Aires, clvii; partnerships or gilds, their advantages, clviii; Fuidir-partnerships; co-tillage partnerships in Wales, in Scotland, in Friesland, etc.; rundale or runrig, the relics of partnership, clix; Brughrecht, or Birlaw; the Brughfer, the Brughtown, it was the prototype of a borough, clx; different ranks of Brughfers; the Forus of a Brughfer the place of election of a king; representation of a borough, the Brughfer, the mayor, clxi; the Brugh town represented the Saxon Burgh; development of a Brugh town into a city; the towns of lords were governed by their Maers or stewards, clxii.
Pork, *i.* ccclxix.
Porphyra vulgaris, and P. laciniata, *i.* ccclxvii.
Porridge, *i.* ccclix, ccclxiii, ccclxvi.
Port Gerefa, *i.* cclxxxviii.
Posaune, the, *i.* dxxx.
Possessores among the Salic Franks, *i.* cxiv.
Pot, cooking, *i.* ccclix.
Precarium, nature of, *i.* ccxxiii; the land held by a Fuidir, was a —, *i.* ccxxiii.

Prerogatives of the Ard Righ and provincial kings, *ii*. 140, 141; a knowledge of the — necessary for the chief poet and historian, *ii*. 142.
Prescription of different kinds, *i*. clxxxvii, clxxxviii, clxxxix.
Prescriptive rights, evasion of, in Ireland, *i*. ccxxv.
Prestariae or Praestitae, *i*. ccxxiii.
Priapus, *i*. cccxc.
Priest, provisional government of Ireland by a, and a poet, *ii*. 138, 139.
Probi-homines, *i*. ccxc.
Procedure, legal, in criminal trials, *i*. cclxxvii; worthy and unworthy witnesses, cclxxvii; different kinds of criminal information, cclxxvii; confirmation of a criminal charge; simple expurgation, cclxxviii; the Tuarastal or proof; the Fir Dé, or truth of God; the Crannchur or lot-casting; complainant might proceed either by criminal indictment or civil process, cclxxix; costs and damages; the leech fee, cclxxx; compurgation, cclxxxi; information of an accomplice or accessory, cclxxx; private information of an accomplice or accessory should be made to three magistrates or to a "worthy" priest, cclxxxii.
„ in civil actions; the Fasc or summons; the Gabhail or distress, *i*. cclxxxii; the Trosca or fasting; the Anad or stay; the pound or Airlis of a Forus, cclxxxiii; Replevin; immediate distress; the Re Dithma or detention in pound; the Lobad or sale of the distress, cclxxxiv; trial in Replevin; forfeiture of a Gell or pledge; the Athgabhaill or Withernam, cclxxxv.
Profession of learning established by law, *ii*. 136; — of teaching not confined to the clergy, *ii*. 176-177.
Professors of music and poetry, *ii*. 4; — in a public school, 84; — as rulers and Ministers of State, 137.
Prohibitions of the Ard Righ and provincial kings, *ii*. 140, 141; a knowledge of — necessary to the chief poet and historian, *ii*. 142.
"Promotion", English law of, *i*. cxxx.
Property, the descent of, among the Gauls and Germans was according to the custom of Gavelkind, *i*. clxviii-clxix.
Prostates, *i*. cxvii.
Protestant Hymnology in relation to the history of music, *i*. dlxiii.
Proverbs, poetical, *ii*. 173.
Provisional Government of Eriu by a poet and a priest, *ii*. 137-139.
Prud'hommes, *i*. ccxc.
Psalterium, the, *i*. diii; two forms of it in use before the eleventh century; the rectangular —, div; the — in modum clypei, dv; — must have been known to the Irish, dvii; the triangular — represented the Kinnor, dviii; dx, dxiii, dxxx, dlvi.
Psaltery. See Saltaire.
Public land gradually converted into allodium, *i*. cliv.
Puddings, ccclxix.
Pulk, the Sclavonic, *i*. lxxx.
Purple, *i*. ccclxxx, ccclxxxvii, cccc, dcxliii.
Pybeu. See Bagpipe.
Quadi, the, *i*. cccxxii, ccccxxv.
Quadrilateral musical instruments of the harp kind in common use down to the twelfth century, *i*. dv; these were ecclesiastical instruments, *i*. dvi.
Quadruplum, *i*. dliv.
Quanon, the, *i*. dxv; number of strings in a —; transformation of the — into the pianoforte, dxvi; Mr. F. Graham's statement that the — came into Europe as the tympanum, dxvii.
Queen, see Rigán.
Quern, the; it was worked by women who were slaves among the rich, *i*. ccclx.
Quinnabenkr, *i*. ccclii, dcxlii.
Quinquegrade scale, early Church music constructed on the, *i*. dlxxxvi, dcxxv.
„ diatonic scale, *i*. dlxxx, dlxxxix, dxci dxcvi, dxcviii, dciii. See Scale.
Rabe, the, *i*. dxxiii.
Races, constant struggles of, in Ireland, *i*. xxiii; effect of mixture of — on language, lxviii-lxix; Ireland peopled by different —, lxx; Irish traditions about — not fully

worked up, lxxi; existence of two types in Ireland, lxxii; early —, fair-haired, lxxiii; governing classes fair-haired, menial classes dark-haired, lxxv; prejudice of Norsemen against black hair, lxxiv; identity of all fair-haired — in Europe, lxxv; this explains why words that are Celtic to some are German to others, lxxv; difference of rights among tribes due to difference of race, lxxvii.

Rachimburgen, *i.* civ.

Rade Knights of Bracton, *i.* cclxxxviii.

Radechenistres, *i.* cclxxxviii.

Radman, *i.* cclxxxvii.

Raith (a householder), *i.* clxxxviii, cxcvii, cxcviii, cci, cclxii, cclxxv, cclxxvi, ccxxxvi, cclxxxvii, cclxxxii, cclxxxviii, ccxc, ccxcii.

Raithmann, *i.* cclxxvi.

Randir of the Gwentian and Dimetian codes, *i.* xcii.

Rapes of Sussex, *i.* lxxxi, lxxxiv.

Rath, the (a fort or mound), *i.* ccxcvii, cccii, ccv, cccvii, cccxxx, cccl, ccclxxiv, dcxxxvii, dcxxxviii; *iii.* 3, 4, 5, 7, 8, 12, 14, 15, 70, 75, etc.; — chambers, *i.* ccxcvii; — na Righ at Tara, *iii.* 5, 12; — of Ailech, 8, 9, 10, 12; — Cruachain, description of, 11, 12; — builders, 14, 15, 16.

Rath (wages), *i.* cx, cxi, cxii, cxiii, cxxiii, cxxiv, cxliv. See Taurcrech.

Rath, or Raith (a householder, etc.), *i.* clxxvi, cclii, cclviii, cclxxxii. See Raith.

Rebab. See Rebec.

Rebebe. See Rebec.

Rebec, the, used in Britanny, *i.* dxxii; — in Ireland and in Wales, dxxiii; dxxv, dxxvii.

Recitative, invention of, *i.* dlxiv.

Red Branch House, *iii.* 380.

„ Hand, the, the armorial bearings of Ulster, *iii.* 264; — the arms of the O'Neills belonged of right to Magenis, 278.

Reel, *i.* dcxx; origin of the word, *iii.* 408.

Reel (for winding yarn), *i.* ccclix.

Rees' Encyclopædia, article on druids in, *ii.* 179, 182; *iii.* 341.

Reeve, *i.* cciii, ccxxxi. See Gerefa.

Refrain, nature of; called in Norse Stef; the Vidkvædi, a particular kind of it; a similar kind of — in Irish, *i.* dcvi; the Irish *Burdoon* not a —, dcvii.

Reiterhammer, the, *i.* ccccclix.

Rennet, *i.* ccclxviii.

Replevin, *i.* cclxxxiii.

Residences of the Ard Righ after the desertion of Tara, *iii.* 24.

Revolution in music foreshadowed in works of Palestrina, *i.* dlxii; cause of that revolution, dlxiii; effect of similar causes on music of Palestrina, dlxiii.

Rhaith Llys, *i.* ccliv.

„ Gwlad, *i.* ccliv.

Rhingyl, the Welsh, *i.* ccxliii.

Rhodymenia palmata, *i.* ccclxvii.

Rhythm, musical, *i.* dxlvii; — and tonality of popular music, dlvii.

Ri, *iii.* 469, 493, 502, 513, 514; — Ard Erind, *i.* clvi. See Rig.

Rice, the Anglo-Saxon, *i.* lxxxiv.

Rig, the, or Righ, *i.* lxxxiv, clii, cliii, cliv, clv, clviii, clx, clxi, clxv, clxxxv, cxcviii; other names for —; corresponding titles among the Norsemen, ccxxxviii; different ranks of, ccxxix; the — Tuatha represented the Ealdorman of the Hundred, ccxxx; the Dux, and the Ealdorman of a Trithing corresponded to the — Mór Tuatha; the — Ard Erind, ccxxxi; the office of — elective, but confined to certain families, hence the value of genealogies; the — was elected by the Aires; the Tanaiste, ccxxxii; the election of officers took place at a Brugh; the power of a — limited, ccxxxiii; extent of the sanctuary of a —; the Folach or leech fee of a — Tuatha, and of a — Mór Tuatha, ccxxxiv; a — not permitted to do servile work; the Dam of a —; its composition, ccxxxv; the Foleith of a — Tuatha, of a — Mór Tuatha, and of a — Rurech; the Amus or Ambus of a —, ccxxxvi; the residence or Dun of a —, ccxxxviii; the household of the — Ard Erind, ccxxxix; the revenue of a —, ccxl-ccxli; ccxlii, ccxlviii, cclii, ccliii, cclvii, cclxii, cclxvi, cclxxxiii, cccv, cccviii, cccxvii, ccclxxvi; *ii.* 38.

„ Ben, *i.* ccxxix; *iii.* 111, 502.

„ Buiden, *i.* ccxxix, ccxxxi, ccxxxiv; *iii.* 502, 503.

Rig Bunad, *i.* cexxix; *iii.* 503.
„ Culcid, or Cuicidh, *i.* cexxix, cccix.
„ Damna, *i.* cccl, cccli.
„ Flath, *i.* cxxviii.
„ Mór Tuatha, *i.* cviii, clxxxv, cexxix, ccxxx, ccxxxi, ccxxxvi, cclxix, cccl.
„ Rurech, or Ruirech, *i.* clvi, ccxxix, ccxxxiv, ccxxxv, ccxxxvi, ccxxxviii.
„ Treaba, *i.* ccxxx.
„ Tuatha, Rii Tuaithe, *i.* cvii, cviii, cx, clvi, clxxxv, cxcviii, ccvi, ccxxix, ccxxxi, ccxxxiv, ccxxxv, ccxxxvi, ccxxxviii, ccxl, ccxliii, ccexlv, ccxlix, cclxxiii, ccevili, ccclxxi, dexliii; *iii.* 510, 513, 515.
Right of Sanctuary, tradition of the, among the Irish peasantry, the true cause of their harbouring criminals, *i.* clvii.
Rigsmál, the, *i.* cxxxiv, ccxx, ccxxxvii, ccclvi.
Rii. See Rig.
Riki, the Norse, *i.* lxxxiv.
Rikir, *i.* ccxxix.
Rings, different kinds of, *iii.* 168; finger — used to indicate the number of warriors slain by a champion, 156; hair — used in the seventeenth century, 169, 174, 175; spiral — for the hair mentioned in the Wanderings of Maeldun's Boat, 188. See Ear-rings and An-Nasc.
Roan tree, quickbean or mountain ash, use of in druidical rites, *ii.* 213, 214, 227; use of the — in the ordeal by fire, 216, 227.
"Robin Adair", the air called, *iii.* 296, 297.
Rock, the German. See Frock.
"Rogaire Dubh", the air called, *iii.* 399.
Romans, *i.* xxi, xxxiv, xl, xliv, lxix, lxxiii, xciii, cvi, ccclxxvii, ccclxxix, ccclxxx, ccclxxxii, cccclxxii, cccclxxvii, cccclxxx; *ii.* 160, 300, 381; — at Tara, *iii.* 7; 172, 340, 341, 346.
Roman singers sent to England in the seventh century, *i.* dlxvii.
Rondeau, *i.* dxl.
Ross-schinder, *i.* cccexliv.
Rote, two different instruments called, in use in the middle ages, *i.* dl; difference between them; one of them was played with the fingers, dii, diii; the triangular Psalterium called a —, dxiv; dxvii, dxxiii, dxxv, dxxvii, dxxviii, dxxix.
Rotta, Rota, supposed derivation of the word, from Chrotta, *i.* cccexcix; the — not the ancient or modern Viéle, or the harp, d, di; the German — in the ninth and tenth centuries described as a Psalterium, *i.* diii. See Rote.
Round Towers, price of erection of a —, *iii.* 50; origin and use of —, *i.* dxxxvi; evidence of the Christian character of —, *iii.* 46; Dr Petrie's view regarding — unassailable, 52.
Royal Branch, house of the, at Emania, *ii.* 261; heroes of —, 325, 356, 357, 367; *iii.* 11, 12.
Royal Irish Academy, library of the, MSS. in the, *i.* lvi; *ii.* 353; *iii.* 162, 163, 174, 261, 263, 276, 317, 329, 332, 380, 397, 403, 413, 523, 525; Mr. Hitchcock's MS. book of Notes on Ogams —, 71.
„ Museum of the, *i.* cccclir, ccccl xii; *iii.* 181, 182, 189, 205, 289, 297, 303, 308, 319, 321, 340, 342, 344, 350, 357.
„ Transactions of the, *iii.* 347, 348, 549.
„ Papers read before the, *i.* lxviii; *iii.* 71.
Rubebe. See Rebec.
Rubia tinctorum, *i.* cccciI.
Rubus fruticosus, *i.* ccccv.
Rudrician race, chief of, *iii.* 265.
Rudzi, *i.* ccclxii.
Rumex acetosa, *i.* ccccvi.
Runes, *i.* ccexliii, ccexliv.
Rye, *i.* cccclxii.
Sab, pl. Sabaid, *i.* xcvi, cxxxi, clxxxvi, ccxlii, cclii, ccliii, cclvi, cclxviii, ccciii, ccclxxi; *iii.* 41, 42, 511.
Sachsenspiegel, *i.* ccclxxxv.
Sackcloth, *i.* ccclxvi.
Sacrifice (human); one instance of the sacrifice of hostages recorded in Irish MSS., *i.* cccxx; legend of Gortigern, cccxxiii; similar legend of Conn and Becuma, cccxxiii-iv; — referred to in a poem on the Fair of Tailté, dxxl.
„ of animals; instance of the slaying of the animals of a

deceased person, *i.* cccxxi; reference to the slaying of animals in a poem on the Fair of Tailté, *i.* dcxl.
Saer Bothach, *i.* cxv, cxvi, clxxxvi.
„ Ceile, *i* cxiii. cxxix, cxxxix, cxli, cxliii, clii, clxvi, clxxxvi, ccxl, cccl.
„ Fuidir, *i.* cxvii, cxxi, cxxvii, cxxix.
Saffron, *i.* ccccii.
Sagum, the, *i.* ccclxxxviii.
Sai, *i.* ci, clxxx, ccxx, cclxxx; *ii.* 171; *iii.* 510.
Saints, manuscript lives of, quoted:
Beatha Abbain (St. Abban), *iii.* 44.
„ Brighte (St. Brigit), *i.* ccclxi.
„ Cholmain Ela (St. Colman Ela), *iii.* 32-33.
„ Cholum Cille (St. Colum Cille), *ii.* 81, 202.
„ Ciarain (St. Ciaran), *i.* cccciv; *iii.* 120-121.
„ Coemghin (St. Kevin), *i.* ccclxv.
„ Cumine Fata (St. Cumin Fada), *iii.* 35.
„ Finnbairr (St. Finnbar), *i.* cccxxii.
„ Greallain (St. Grelan), *iii.* 34.
„ Maic Creiche (St. Mac Creiche, or Croha), *i.* cclxxxix; *iii.* 331-332.
„ Maighnein (St. Maighnen), *i.* ccxl-ccxli.
„ Mochuda (St. Mochuda, or Carthach), *iii.* 4.
„ Moedog (St. Moedog of Cluan Mór), *ii.* 338-339.
„ Moling (St. Moling), *iii.* 34-36, 45.
„ Patraicc (Tripartite life of St. Patrick), *i.* lxxxv; *ii.* 67, 166, 201-202.
„ Ruadain (St. Ruadan), *ii.* 336-337.
„ Senain (St. Senan), *i.* cccxxix.
"Sak and Soke", *i.* cclxx.
Salad, *i.* ccclxvii
Salmon, *i.* ccclxx; — of knowledge. See Eo Feasa.
Salt, *i.* ccclxvii, dcxlii.
Salteire, the, of the Trouverès a different instrument from the Psalterium, *i.* dxiv; method of playing the —; figures of the —, dxiv-xv; transformation of the — into the pianoforte; the — in use in the seventeenth century, dxvi.
Salterio tedesco, *i.* dxvii.
Sambucus, *i.* dxx.
Sanskrit grammar, Wilkins', *i.* li.
Santir, the, *i.* dxvii.
Saraad, *i.* cxxviii, cxxix, clxxviii. See Sarhaet.
Sarcilis, the, *i.* ccclxxxii.
Sarhaet, *i.* ccxcv. See Saraad.
Sarugh, Sarughudh, Sarugud, *i* cxxviii; clxxviii, ccxl, ccxlviii, ccli, ccxciv, ccxcv; *iii.* 473, 481, 482, 514, 515, 516, 517, 518, 519.
Satin, striped, *i.* ccclxxxiii, ccclxxxvi.
Satire, power and nature of, *ii.* 217, 218, 219; poetical effects of —, 227.
Satrap, *i.* ccxxx.
Saudahûs, *i.* ccci.
Saurion, *i.* ccclxiii.
Sausage, *i.* ccclxix.
Sautrie, see Salteire.
Saw, *i.* ccclxi.
Saxon, music *i.* dcxxii; — nation, students of the, in the schools of Eriu *ii.* 82; treachery of the — invaders of Britain, 222; the descendants of Brutus and Britan Mael driven out by the — settlers, 185.
"Saxon ale of bitterness", *i.* ccclxxv-vi.
Saxons, *i.* xx, xxi, xxiv, xxxiv; early acquaintance of the — and the Irish; their hostility the result of political relations in the north, xxxv; the — first mentioned as enemies of the Irish in the seventh century; importance of this fact, xxxvi, xl, xlii, xliii, xliv, lxxv, cxxxix, cxcvii, ccxxxix, ccclxxxii; *ii.* 185; *iii.* 7, 146; the old —, *i.* ccxxxi.
Scabini, *i.* cvi, cviii.
Scale; existence of many musical —s; origin of the notes of a —, *i.* dxlii; mode in which the quinquegrade — was obtained, dxliii; relation of the notes of the quinquegrade — to each other, dxliv; no natural tonic among them; way in which the diatonic — was completed, dxliv; — thus obtained not identical with the modern one; every tone of a — used as a tonic in homophonous music, dxlv; comparison of mu-

sical — s, dlxxxi; modern — of *G*, dxcviii.

Scandinavians, *i.* xxxiv, lxxv, clxxv, cclv, cclvi, cclxv, cccxxxvii, cccxliii, cclliii, ccclxxiii, ccclxxxiii, cccli, ccclvii, ccclxiv, ccclxx.

Scena, *i.* ccclxi.

Schellen, *i.* dxxxvii.

Schlachten, *i.* ccxix.

Schöffen, *i.* cvii. See Schöppen.

School, Moengal, teacher of the inner, of St. Gall, *i.* dlxviii; his scholar Tuotilo probably an Irishman, dlxviii-ix; — of Fileadh, *ii.* 49; — of St. Ailbhi at Imliuch, 76; — of Beannchoir under St. Comgall, 76; — of Birr, under St. Cronan, 76; — of Cluain Uamha, now Cloyne, 76; — of Clonard, 76, 79, 81, 83, 84, 34?; — of Clonmacnoise, 76; — of St. Finnbar at Cork; lay — of Colman Ua Cluasaigh at Cork; — of Mungaret, near Limerick; of Lothar, 76; — of Ross Ailither, 76, 77; — of Swords, 77; — or college under St. Bricin at Tuaim Drecain, 77, 93, 94; — of Kildare, 77; foreign students at — of Armagh, 82; qualifications of a Fer Leighinn, or master of a public —, 84; professors or teachers in a public —, 84; — of Cathbadh the Druid, 200.

Schools, the ecclesiastical, of the early Christian period, *ii.* 76; lay national — at the same period, 77; revision of the system of teaching in — made at Drom Ceat, 78; sizars and poor scholars in those schools, 79; hut encampments of students at Irish —, 81; Bede's allusion to Saxon and British students at Irish —, 82.

„ of music, Flemish, *i.* dlviii, dlix, dlx; French —, dlix; early Florentine —, dlix.

Schöppen, *i.* cclxvi. See Schöffen.

Sciath, the, *i.* ccccIxiii; *ii.* 330, 331; — clis, *i.* ccccIxv, ccccIxvii. See Shield.

„ Arglan, the shield of the poet Senchad, *i.* 333.

Scire Gerefa, *i.* ccxlviii; — Gemôt, cclviii.

Sclavonians, *i.* cccxxxvii.

"Scorpion" the. See Suist.

Scotch, the, *i.* ccccxliv.

Scoti, Scots, *i.* xxiii, xxxi, xxxiv, xxxv, xliii, xliv, xlv, xlvi, xlvii, lxxvi, xci; *iii.* 2.

Scotic power was recent at the period of the Atticotic revolution, *i.* xxviii; — conquests on the coast of Britain, xxxiii.

Scottish music, two kinds of; Highland —, nearly the same as the Irish, *i.* dcxviii; recognition of the gapped scale in —, dcxviii-ix; Lowland — has the scale and keys of Irish music, dcxix; the conventional style of —; difference between Highland and Lowland —; hypotheses to explain this difference, dcxxii; Highland — not affected by polyphonous music; influence of foreign music on Lowland —, dcxxiii; preservation of —; growth of a conventional style in —, dcxxiv.

Screpal, Screpall, Scrapal, *i.* clxxxi, ccxl, ccl, cclxxx, cclxxxi, dcxliii.

Screuna of the Franks, *i.* ccxcvi.

Secular national schools in early Christian times in Ireland, *ii.* 77.

Secular Song, difference between, and ecclesiastical chant recognised by early composers, *i.* dlxii.

Seilloin, see Teillin.

Senchas Mór, *iii.* 20; account of the more remarkable judges of Erin from the —, 21; 23, 25, 26-29, 31; — said to have been drawn up by a committee of nine, 52; presence of Corc, king of Munster, at Tara during the revision of the —, 63-68; colours of winds according to —, *iii.* 133.

Sencleithe, *i.* xcvi, cxv, cxvi; rights of —; tradition of those rights still preserved, *i.* cxxi; cxxix, cxxx, clii, clxxxxiii; *iii.* 494.

Sepulchral monuments, names of; the Dere, *i.* cccxxix; the Fert, cccxxx; the Indeilb cloiche, cccxxx; the Fyhrt of Anglo-Saxon law; the Leacht, cccxxxi; the Leac or Liace; Cairte or pillar stones; the Tamleacht; the Mur, cccxxxii; the Cnoc, cccxxxv; the Carn; use of a Carn to ascertain the number slain in battle; instance of a Carn placed over the corpse of a warrior, cccxxxvi; and over the heads of those slain; custom of cutting off the heads of

the slain; the Cairn used to protect the heads of the slain from being carried away as trophies, *i.* cccxxxvii-viii; stones afterwards added to the Leacht; the Carn invariably connected with the Firbolgs, cccxxxix; — referred to as existing on the plain of Magh Tuired, dcxxxvii; — mentioned in the Dindsenchas of the Fair of Tailte, dcxxxviii; — mentioned in the Dindsenchas of Brugh na Boine, dcxxxix.
Sequences, *i.* dl, dlxix.
Shears, *i.* ccclxi.
Sheep, *i.* dcxxxix.
Sheriff, *i.* ccxlviii, ccxlix; —'s Tourn, cclxii.
Shield, the, form and material of —s, *i.* cccclxiii-iv; names of —, cccclxiv; *ii.* 333; wooden —s; rims of —s, *i.* cccclxv; bosses and umbo of —s; rivets of —s; sharp and wave-edged —s, cccclxvi; small —s or Sciatha Clis, cccclxvii; Bronze — in the Museum of the R. I. Academy, cccclxvii-viii; large —s used by the Irish, cccclxix; German and Danish —s, cccclxix; colours of shields; —s ornamented with devices, cccclxx; —s ornamented with precious metals, etc.; —s presented to poets; —s were heirlooms, cccclxxi; personification of —s, cccclxxii; silver —s, when and where first made, *ii.* 6, 328; —s with sharp rims, 319; missive —s, 318-319; Ochain the — of Concobar Mac Nessa, 321; —s used in ancient Eriu, 327; — of Corb Mac Ciarain, 327; early references to the —, 328-329; metal —s used by the Gaedhil at a very early period, 328; Cuchulaind's — Duban, 329; — of Aedh, son of Duach Dubh king of Oirghiall, made of the Eo Rossa, 330; — of Mac Conn, 331-332; the — strap, 331-332; names of celebrated shields, 332-333.
Shirt. See Caimsi and Skyrta.
Shoes, different kinds of, *i.* cccxcvii, dcxl; bronze —, cccxcviii.
Shutters, *i.* dcxli.
Sialfaeti of the Norse, *i.* ccclxix.
Sic Oc, *i.* ccxxxv, cclxii, cclxix, cclxx, cclxxi.
Sieve, *i.* ccclx.
"Sighile ni Gara", the air, *iii.* 296.
Silk, *i.* ccclxxix, ccclxxxii, ccclxxxvi.
Silures, *i.* lxxvii.
Silver, knowledge of, indicated by the use of lead, *i.* ccccxxii; — ornaments mentioned in MSS. along with gold and bronze, ccccxxii; shields of —, *ii.* 6.
Sinapis nigra, *i.* ccclxiii.
Sith, *i.* ci.
Sithar, *i.* ci.
Sithcundman, *i.* cxxx, cxl.
Sixhaendmen, *i.* ci.
Sizarships, *ii.* 279.
Skalks, *i.* ccxxxvii.
Skemma, *i.* ccci, cccii, cccxviii.
Skewers, *i.* ccclix.
Skickjá, the, *i.* ccclxxxix.
"Sky-farmer", *i.* cxxiii.
Skyrta, or Serker, the Scandinavian, *i.* ccclxxxiii.
Slaves, *i.* ccxcvi, ccclxi.
Sleeping room, *i.* cccliii.
Slegh, the, *i.* lxxiv.
Sling, *i.* cccxxxviii, cccclx, cccclxi; *ii.* 195, 287, 288, 292, 294, 318.
„ Balls, *ii.* 288, 289, 290, 291.
Sling Stones of iron and bronze, *ii* 251, 252, 291.
Sloke, *i.* ccclxvii.
Sluice, mill, *i.* ccclx.
Smith, *i.* ccclxii.
Smithy, *i.* ccclxii.
Smock-frock, *i.* ccclxxxii.
Social state of Ireland, the, was advanced in the period from the fifth to the eighth century, *i.* xvii.
Society, political organization of, in England before the Norman Conquest, *i.* cxcvi-vii; organization of Irish — very similar, *i.* cxcvii.
Sock (a stocking), *i.* ccclxxxv.
Soc-men of a Tuath, the, *i.* ccxlii.
Socn, *i.* cclxx.
Sodales, *i.* ccviii, ccix, ccxii.
Sodalitas, Sodalitates, the religious associations so-called, *i.* ccviii-ix.
Soke. See Socn.
Soldurii, *i.* ccxxxvii.
Solo-airs, invention of harmonized, *i.* dlxiv.
Sonata, *i.* dliii.
Soothsaying, *ii.* 219-222.
Sorrel, *i.* ccccvi.
"Sortes", the barbarian, *i.* ccxxiv; Palgrave's idea that the — were allodial, ccxxiv.

Spara, the, *i.* ccccl.
Spardha, the, *i.* cccclii.
Sparða, the, *i.* ccccl.
Spear, *i.* cccexxxi - cccexxxvii; pointed —s known to the Firbolgs, *ii.* 237; double-bladed —s, 314; the — of Assal, King of Persia, 325; the — of Celtchar, called the Luin Cheiltchair, 325; the iron — of Cethern, 313; the — of Conall, son of Baedan, 342; the — of Congall, called Gearr, 342; the venomed — of Cormac. See Gae Buaifnech; the — of Cuchulaind, called a Cletiné, 298, 299; the Gaulish or "broad green" — introduced by Labrad Loingsech. See Laigen; the — of the Tuatha Dé Danand, 245-246; a — of honour one of the emblems of royalty, 336.
„ points, mounting of, among the Firbolgs, *ii.* 241.
„ rivets. See Fethana.
Spelt Wheat, *i.* cxli, ccclxiii.
Spinetta, *i.* dxvi.
Spinning Wheel, *i.* ccclix.
Spits, *i.* ccclix.
Spjöt, the Norse, *i.* ccccxlvi.
Squirrel, the, of Medb, *ii.* 293.
"Staff of Jesus", or Crozier of St. Patrick, *ii.* 165.
Staiga, *i.* cccvi.
Staimbart, *i.* cccclviii.
Stars and clouds, observation of the, *ii.* 226.
Staves, *i.* ccclvi.
Stee. See Steigh.
Steigh, *i.* cccvi. See Stee and Stig.
Steva, *i.* ccc.
Stig, the Angl.-Sax., *i.* cccvi.
Stipends paid by kings to their Subreguli, *iii.* 125-133.
Stirabout, *i.* ccclxv, dcxxxix, dcxl.
Stocking. See Hose.
Stockschleuder, *i.* ccclx, cccclxi.
Stone, age, *ii.* 266.
„ axes, *i.* cccclviii.
„ buildings; use of stone as a building material borrowed from the Romans; earliest churches built of stone belong to the sixth century, *i.* ccxcvi; mortar not used in the most ancient buildings, ccciii; the Caisel and Cathair built of stone, *iii.* 4; stone-built Duns, Cathairs, etc., chiefly found in the S.W. and W. of Ireland; ancient — of Kerry, *i.* ccevii; these are very old, but were probably ecclesiastical, cccvii; they are constructed like the Duns, etc., described in Irish tales; three types of buildings—the Caiseal, the fort, and the Dun, cccix; ancient — at Ailech, *iii.* 8, 9, 10; ancient — on Aran Islands, 5.
Stone house, *i.* ccclxix.
„ missiles, *ii.* 271, 278.
„ weapons, *i.* ccccvii, ccccxxxvii, cccclvi.
Stones used in battle, *i.* cccclvii, cccclviii; *ii.* 275.
Story telling, the three sorrows of, *ii.* 325.
Stowe Library, ornamented cover or theca of a MS. in the, *iii.* 227, 228, 229, 230, 233.
Straddle, the peaked, *i.* cccclxxxii.
Strainers, *i.* dcxlii.
Strangers, naturalization of, *i.* cxxii.
Strathclyde Britons, *i.* cxxviii.
Strathspeys, *i.* dcxx.
Streitkeils, Streite-kewl, *i.* ccccxli, ccccxliv.
Students, hut-encampments of, *ii.* 81; foreign — at Armagh, 82; Bede's allusion to Saxon and British — at Irish Schools, 82.
Sturmgabel, *i.* ccccxlvi.
Subdivision of land, early, *i.* cxlvii.
Sucking Pigs, *i.* ccclxix.
Suitors, Aires only could be; various capacities in which — acted, *i.* cclxxv.
Supper, *i.* ccclxvi.
Sûri, *i.* ccclxiii.
Svefnskemma, *i.* cccii.
Svinasteuer, *i.* ccci.
Sweet Gale, *i.* ccclxxiii.
Sword, *i.* ccccxxxiii, ccccxxxiv, ccccxxxviii, cccclix, cccclv; different shapes of — blades, *ii.* 243; a two-handed —; Calad Bolg the — of Leite, 320; the inscribed — of Cuchulaind, 322; the — of Crimthann, 337-9, 350; —s, etc., found in Cullen Bog, *iii.* 205.
Symphonia, *i.* dxxiv.

Symphonie, the. See Chifonie.
Synchronisms of Flann, *ii.* 167.
Tales, Irish, internal evidence of the antiquity of many, *i.* xi; localization of personages and events—a characteristic of —, xii; absence of this characteristic from Welsh and Old German poems and Tales, xiii; the — of the Heroic Period the most valuable, and those principally used by O'Curry, xxi.
Tales, Irish, quoted and referred to:
Agallamh na Seanorach (Dialogue of the Seniors), *iii.* 169-170, 179, 222-224, 315-316, 323-324, 325, 328, 360-361, 366, 376, 377, 379, 380.
Aided Aithirne Ailgisech (the Death of Aithirne), *iii.* 373-374.
„ n-Athi acas a adnacol (the Death of Athi and his burial), *i.* cccxxvii-viii.
„ Blathnaite ingen Paill Mic Fidaid le Conculainn (the Death of Blathnat, daughter of Pall, son of Fidad), *ii.* 97.
„ Chloinne Tuirend (Death of the Sons of Turend), *i.* ccccxxxii; *ii.* 325.
„ Conrui, *i.* cccxxxvi; *iii.* 81, 82. See Argain Cathrach Chonrai.
„ Firdiaid (Death of Ferdiad), "Fight of Ferdiad", *i.* ccccxlvi, ccccliv, cccclxvi, cccclxxii, cccclxxv; *ii.* 302 to 310; *iii.* 413 to 463. See Táin Bó Chuailgne.
„ Meidbe (Death of Medb), *ii.* 290-291.
Aisling Maic Conglinne (the Vision of Mac Conglinde), *i.* cccxxxiv-v, cccxcviii; *ii.* 81, 82; *iii.* 102-104.
Aithirne and the brooch of Ard Brestiné, *iii.* 161-162.
Ani dia fil Aidid Fothaid Airgdech (Death of Fothad Airgdech), *i.* ccccxxxiv.
Argain Cairpri Cinn Cait for Soer Clannaibh Erenn, *i.* xxiii, xxxiv; *iii.* 84.
„ Orgain Cathrach Conrai (the Plunder of the Cathair of Curoi Mac Dare), *i.* xxii; *iii.* 81, 82.
„ Cathrach Maoil Milscothach
Tales, Irish, quoted and referred to:
(the Plunder of the Cathair of Mael Milscothach), *ii.* 130-135.
Argain Dindrigh (the Destruction of Dindrigh), *iii.* 242-244, 249-250.
Cath Aenach Tuaighe (Battle of Aenach Tuaighe), *ii.* 275, 276.
„ Almhaine (Battle of Almhain), *ii.* 389-391; *iii.* 309-313, 326, 381.
„ Atha Comair (Battle of the Ford of Comar), *ii* 261-263.
„ Caenraighe (Battle of Caenraigh), *ii.* 388.
„ Cnamhros (Battle of Cnamhros), *ii.* 383-386.
„ Dunbolg (Battle of Dunbolg), *ii.* 338-339, 340-341.
„ Finntragha (Battle of Ventry Harbour), *iii.* 82.
„ Gabhra (Battle of Gabhra), *i.* cccxli-ii; *ii.* 387.
„ Maige Lena (Battle of Moylena), *i.* ccxxvi, cccxl; *iii.* 179, 181, 359.
„ Maige Rath (Battle of Moyrath), *ii.* 341, 342; *iii.* 368.
„ Moin Trogaidhe (Battle of Moin Trogaidhe), *ii.* 356.
„ Muige Mucroima (Battle of Magh Muchruimhe), *i.* ccccxxxiv.
„ Muige Tuired Conga (Battle of Moytura of Cong), *i.* cccxxix, cccxxxix, cccclvii, dcxxxvii; *ii.* 188, 225, et seq.; *iii.* 5.
„ Muige Tuired na bh-Fomorach (Battle of Moytura of the Fomorians), *i.* cccxcvii, ccccliii, cccclxxiv, dcxxxix-xl; *ii.* 45 et seq., 248 et seq., 253-254, 288; *iii.* 42-43, 155-156, 213-214, 385.
Cathreim Cheallachain Chaisil (Warfare of Callaghan of Cashel), *ii.* 276.
„ Chonghail Clairingnigh (Warfare of Congal Clairingnigh), *ii.* 274, 276; *iii.* 380-381.
Cogadh Gaedhel re Gallaibh (Wars of the Gaedhil with the Danes), *ii.* 346-352.
Compert Conculaind (Conception of Cuchulaind), *i.* ccciv.

Tales, Irish quoted and referred to:
Cormac Mac Airt's Adventures in the Land of Promise, *iii.* 11.
Dinnsenchas, *i.* cccxxvii, cccxxxvi; *ii.* 106, 172, 191, 252, 283-284, 288-289, 329; *iii.* 41, 80, 82, 122, 203, 355-356, 404-405.
Exile of Cano, son of Gartnan, *i.* ccclxxiv-v; *iii.* 164-165, 180, 196.
Feis Temra (Feast of Tara), *iii.* 180, 197.
Finding of Cormac's Branch, *iii.* 317.
Fled Bricrind (Bricriu's Feast), *i.* ccxxxix, cccii, cccxlvii, ccclii, ccclxv, ccclxxii, ccclxxvii, cccc x x x v i, ccccl xvi, ccccl xx; *ii.* 198-200; *iii.* 17, 22, 31, 315.
„ (Curathmir Emna Macha, dispute about the Champion's Bit), *iii.* 75-79.
„ (Tochim Ulad do Chruachnaib Ai. Progress of the Ultonians to Cruachan Ai), *i.* ccii, cccv, cccxlviii, ccclvii, ccclxiii, ccccliv, ccccl xvi, ccccl xxx, ccccl xxxii.
„ Dun na n-Gedh, *ii.* 342.
Forbais Droma Damhgaire, *ii.* 212, 215, 278-282; *ii.* 361-362.
„ Fer Falga, *i.* ccccl xii.
Fotha Catha Cnucha (cause of the Battle of Cnuca), *i.* ccciii.
Genemain Aéda Sláne (Birth of Aedh Slane), *ii.* 335-336; *iii.* 193, 194.
Immram Curaig Mailduin (Wandering of Maeldun's Boat), *i.* ccciii, ccliii, ccclvi, ccclvii, ccclxviii; *iii.* 158-159, 163-164, 180, 188.
„ Snedgus ocus Maic Righail (or Voyage of Snedgus and Mac Riaghla), *iii.* 385.
„ h-Ua Corra (Wandering of Ua Corra), *i.* dcxlii-dcxliii.
Imtheacht na Trom Daimhe (Progress of the Great Company), *ii.* 89; *iii* 234-237, 317, 334, 376.
Iomarbhadh na bh-Filidhe (Contention of the Bards), *ii.* 62.
Iubhar Mic Aingis (The Yew tree of Mac Aingis), *iii.* 259-261.
Longes Labrada Loingsech (Exile of Labrad Loingsech), *ii.* 256, et seq.

Tales, Irish, quoted and referred to:
Longes Mac n-Duildermata (Exile of the Sons of Duildermat), *iii.* 106, 360.
„ Mac n-Uisleand (Exile of the Sons of Uisnech), *iii.* 368, 378, 385.
„ Ulaid (Exile of the Ultonians), *ii.* 320
Mesca Ulad (Intoxication of the Ultonians), *i.* cexcix-ccc.
Scel Muicce Mic Datho (Story of Mac Datho's Pig), *iii.* 371-373.
Seirgligi Conculaind (Sick Bed of Cuchulaind), *i.* cccxlv; *ii.* 195-198, 367; *iii.* 192.
Senchas na Relec (History of Cemeteries), *ii.* 114; *iii.* 524-525.
Siabur Charpat Conculaind (Phantom Chariot of Cuchulaind), *i.* ccclxxxvii, ccexc, ccccl xxix; *iii.* 187.
Sluagad Neill Mic Echach co Muir Nicht (Expedition of Nial, son of Eochad, to the Ictian Sea), *ii.* 287.
Succession of the kings of Tara, *iii.* 177.
Story of Finntan, son of Bochra, *iii.* 59-62, 241-242.
„ of Lugad Delbaeth, *ii.* 221.
Táin Bó Aingen (Prey of the Cows of Aingen), *iii.* 199-201, 202.
„ Chuailgne (Cattle Prey of Cooley), *i.* xi, xviii, xx, xxxii, lxxii, lxxiii, lxxiv, ccvii, cccv, cccxxxviii, cccxli, cccxliii, cccxliv-v, ccclx, ccclxxix, ccclxxxiii, ccclxxxvi, ccclxxxvii, ccclxxxix, ccc x c v i i i, ccccxxxv, cccc x x x v i, ccccxlv, ccccxlvi, ccccxlvii, ccccliv, ccccl vi, ccccl xvi, ccccl xix, ccccl xx, ccccl xxii, ccccl xxiv, cccc l x x v, ccccl xxx, ccccl xxxiii; *ii.* 89, 200, 259-260, 292-293, 296-310, 313-321, 358-366; *iii.* 89-102, 109-110, 186-187, 195, 196, 197, 376, 400-401, 414-463.
„ (Preface to —), *iii.* 156-158.
„ Bó Dartada (Prey of the Cows of Dartad), *ii.* 357.
„ Flidais (Prey of the Cows of Flidas), *iii.* 338-339, 512.

Táin Fraich (Prey of the Cows of Fraech), *i.* ccexlviii, dxxxv, dxxxvi; *iii.* 10-11, 181, 218-221, 307, 323, 382-383.

Tochmorc Bec Fola (Courtship of Bec Fola), *i.* ccxl, dxxxv, *iii.* 160-161, 180

" Creide (Courtship of Crede), *iii.* 12-14.

" Delbh Chaime ingine Morgain (Courtship of Delbh Caem, and visit of Conn Ced Cathach to Tir Tairngire, and his courtship with Becuma Cnesgel), *i.* cccxxxiii.

" Emere ocas Foglaim Conculaind (Courtship of Emer and education of Cuchulaind), *i.* lxxii, cccxlvii, ccclxxi, ccclxxxvii, ccccix, ccccIxxviii; *ii.* 322-324, 368-373; *iii.* 11, 122, 365.

" Etaine, (courtship of Etain or Edain), *i* lxxiii, ccci, cccii, ccclxix, ccclxxx; *iii.* 162-163, 190-192, 193-194.

" Feirbe (courtship of Ferb), *iii.* 307-308, 367.

" Treblainne (courtship of Treblain), *i.* xxii.

Tochomlad Loingsi Fergusa a h-Ultaib (Emigration of Fergus and his companions from the Ultonians), *ii.* 320.

" na n-Deisi o Themraig, or as it is elsewhere called Tucait Innarba na n-Dessi Immumain acas Aided Cormaic (Emigration of the Deisi from Tara to Munster), *ii.* 205-208, 326.

Togail Bruighean Chaertain (Destruction of the Bruighean of Chaertain), *iii.* 305.

Bruidne Da Choga (Destruction of the Brudin Da Choga), *i.* ccccix, ccccIxxviii; *iii.* 254.

" Dá Derga (Destruction of the Brudin of Da Derg), *i.* xx, lxxii, lxxiv, ccxxxix, cccxxxv, cccxlvii, cccl, ccclv, ccclxx, ccclxxix, ccclxxxiii, ccclxxxvii, cccxc, ccccxxxi, ccccxxxiii, ccccxlvii, ccccIviii, ccccIxii-ccccIxiii; *iii.* 136-150, 165, 183-184, 186, 189-190, 367-368.

Bruidne Tuir Chonaing (Destruction of the Tower of Conaing), *ii.* 109.

Tamarix Germanica, *i.* ccclxxiii.

Tamboura, *i.* dxi.

Tanacetum vulgare, *i.* ccclxix.

Tanaise Righ or Ri, *ii.* 39; *iii.* 469, 493, 501, 502.

Tanaiste, *i.* clxi, clxxxiii, ccxxxii, ccxxxiii, ccxxxv, ccxxxvi, ccxlii, cclxvi.

Taniaccae, Tanacae, *i.* ccclxix.

Tanist of a king, *ii.* 39. See Tanaise Righ and Tanaiste.

Tanistry, custom of, *i.* cxxxix, clxxxii; estates of Bó Aires might be subjected to the —, *i.* clxxxiii.

Tansey, *i.* ccclxix.

Taran, Jupiter Taranis, *i.* ccclxxxi.

Tassels, *i.* ccclxxxvii, cccxc.

Tassets, the, *i.* ccclxxxiv.

Tate, Tath, or Tatty, *i.* lxxxix, xcv, xcviii.

Tatooing, *i.* cccciv.

Teacher, legal relation between, and pupil, *ii.* 174; office of —, a layman's function in Christian times, 176, 177.

Teachers in a public school, *ii.* 84; — employed as ministers of state by their former pupils, 175.

Tectosagi, *i.* xciv, cccxcvii.

Teillin, not the name of a musical instrument in Irish, *iii.* 351; occurrence of — in MSS., 355-357; applied to humming bees, 358; has become obsolete in Ireland, but exists in Scotland in the form *Seilloin*, 358. See Telyn.

Teisbantyle, *i.* cci, cclxviii.

Telyn, the, *i.* cccexc, ccccxci-ccccxciii; — the Welsh name of the harp, and the Chronicle of Caradoc, ccccxci - ccccxciii; O'Curry's etymology of —, ccccxcv; ccccxcvii; — the Welsh name of the harp, *iii.* 351; meaning of —, 352; was perhaps originally a derisive name, 353; the — was the Cruit of Ireland, 354; the word — the equivalent of the Irish Teillin, descriptive of the humming bee, 355; — could not be derived from the Greek Chelys, 358.

"Tempered" Scale, the, *i.* dlxxxvii-dlxxxviii.

Tenancy, hereditary, in the middle ages, *i.* cxciv.

Tenant, the Irish law protected the —, *i.* cxxvi; preference given by —s to Irish laws discreditable to English rule, cxxvii; damages of large —, how estimated, cxxvii; the — class, *ii.* 35, 36.
Tenor, origin of the term, *i.* dlv.
Tenure en bordelage, *i.* cl.
Tenures of Ceiles, *i.* cxxiv; nature of the estate of a Flath, clxxxv; — of a Saer Ceile; — of a Daer Ceile; — of Bothachs; privileged villenage, or villein-socage, burgage —, a kind of socage tenure, free Socage —, copyholders, clxxxvi; the Daer Ceile represented a copyholder, clxxxvi-vii; Taurcrech and Rath paid to Ceiles, clxxxviii; relation of lord and Ceile; land let to freemen of a Tuath, clxxxix; compensation to tenants for improvements, cxc; insolvent members of partnerships, cxc-cxci; absent members of partnerships, cxcii; insolvent owners, cxcii-cxciii; — of Fuidirs, cxciii; Irish — throw light on those of Europe, cxciv-v; contrast between the Irish and Continental land systems, cxcvi.
Teog, *i.* cxiv, cxxviii, clii.
Teothing. See Tithing.
Terra dominica, demesne land of a lord, *i.* clii
Testudo, the, *i.* cccclxix.
Textile arts, *iii.* 118, 121.
Theca, or case of a missal at Stowe, *iii.* 226, 227, 232, 233.
Thegn, *i.* ci, cii, cxxxi, cxxxviii, cciii, cclviii, cclxxxvii; — land, ci.
"The Last Rose of Summer", *i.* dcxiii.
Theows, *i.* cxxvii-viii; Wite —, cxxviii.
Thing, *i.* cclvii.
Thjoth, the Scandinavian, *i.* lxxx, lxxxiv.
"Thorough Bass", *i.* dlxiv.
Thread, gold, *i.* ccclxxix, ccclxxxiii; coloured — paid as rent, *iii.* 118.
Thiuda, the Gothic, *i.* lxxx, lxxxiii.
Θώραξ, the, *i.* cccclxxiv.
Thverpaller, *i.* ccclii.
Tign, *i.* ci.
Tignar Konur; — Mathr, *i.* ci.
Tilgiöf, *i.* clxxv.
Time, three epochs of human, *i.* cccevii.
Timpan, the, *i.* ccclxxxiv, cccexc, cccexcviii, dxxi, dxxiii; two kinds of —, dxxviii; one played with a bow, some strings being touched with the finger nail; no evidence as to whether the — was a Rote or a Viele; the — and Welsh Crwth were borrowed from the Continent, dxxix; legend concerning the —, *iii.* 236; mystery attached by the Gaedhil to the —, 238; the — was a stringed instrument, 234, 264; reference to strings of the —, 264; the — distinguished from the Cruit, 265; the — mentioned in the poem on the Fair of Carman, 358, 364; derivation of the word —, 359; reference to the — in MSS., 359, 360, 361; — played by Miriam, sister of Moses, 359; — mentioned in dialogue of Ancient Men, 360, 361; description of the — in the tale of the Forbais or Siege of Dromdamhghaire, 361-362; the — was a stringed instrument played with a bow, 362, 363; the Irish — was the same as the Welsh Crwth; difference between the — and the Irish Cruit, 363; the — continued in use down to the seventeenth century, 364; the deeper strings of the — were struck with the nail, 365; relative powers of the Cruit or harp and the —, 366.
Timpanist, the chief, of a king had the rank of a Bó Airech, *iii.* 365.
Tin, Irish names of, *i.* ccccix; the Phoenicians obtained their — from Asia, ccccxi; — abundant in the Caucasus, ccccxii; European localities of tin-ore, ccccxix.
Tintinabulum, *i.* diii, dxxxxiv, dxxxvii, dxl.
Tir-Connellians, their standard, *ii.* 165.
Tir Gwelyawg, *i.* lxxxvii, cxliii.
Tithing, the English, *i.* lxxxii, lxxxiv, cc, ccxvii.
Tocomrach, the, *i.* cclii, ccliv, cclvi, cclvii, cclviii, cclix, cclxi.
Toft, the Danish, *i.* cxxxv, clv; the English — and Croft, cxxxv.
Toilet, articles for the —, *i.* ccclvii.
Toing, Tuing, *i.* cclxxv, cclxxxix, ccxc, ccxci; *iii.* 473, 474, 475, 482, 485, 487, 490, 496, 498, 499, 501, 502, 503.
Tolisto Bogii, *i.* xciv.

Tompt, the Swedish, *i.* cxxxv.
Tonality, development of modern, *i.* dlxvi; the sentiment of — of modern growth; all the notes of the Irish scale served as tonics, dlxxi.
Tones, fusion of the old Church, into the major and minor modes, *i.* dlxv; five melodic families of —; authentic — of St. Ambrose, dlxiii; extent and tonality of pieces in old Church —; extension below and curtailment above the tonic; peculiarity of the — thus developed, dlxxiv; ordinal designation of Church —; plagal —; origin of the term plagal; the eight Church —. dlxxv; no Church — having *C* or *A* for tonic, dlxxvi; the twelve — of Glareanus, dlxxix.
Tonic, no natural — among the notes of the quinquegrade scale, *i.* dxliv; every tone of a scale used in homophonous music as a —, dxlv. See Keys.
Tools which a Brughfer should have, *i.* ccclxi.
Tooutious. the Gaulish, *i.* lxxv.
Topographical divisions, occurrence of the numbers twelve and thirty in, *i.* cxiii.
Torques, worn by the ancient Egyptians, and by every people of ancient Europe; account of — first published by Lhuyd; no account of — in works of older antiquaries; — found at Harlech in Merioneth; drawing of a — in the *Gentleman's Magazine*, *iii.* 172; anonymous notice of Irish —, 171; description of two — found at Tara, and bought by Alderman West, 172, 173; Gibbon's conclusions as to the uses of —, 173; use of the Tara —, 173-174; waist — of Fothadh Airgtech, 174, 175; neck — of Cormac Mac Airt, 180. See Torc.
Tothland, *i.* lxxxix.
Tourn. Turn of the Sheriff, *i.* ccxlix, cclxii.
Town, *i.* cccv.
Townland, the modern, the representative of several different denominations of land, *i.* xcviii.
Tracts, Irish Miscellaneous, quoted and referred to:
Amra Choluim Cille (Elegy on the death of St. Colum Cille, *i.* cccclxxv-vi, cccclxxix, ccccxcvi; *ii.* 52, 78, 85; *iii.* 245-246, 247, 248, 249. 250-251, 253, 371, 376.
Annals, Duald Mac Firbiss' manuscript, *ii.* 79.
Bible, old Irish version of the, Exodus, *iii.* 359; Genesis, 308, 336-338; I. Kings, *i.* ccclviii.
Cain Adamnain (Law of Adamnan), *ii.* 26; *iii.* 375.
„ Domhnaigh (Law of Sunday), *ii.* 32-33.
Chronicon Scotorum, *ii.* 391.
Coir Anmann (Etymology of Names), *ii.* 204, 287.
Felere Oenghuis (Festology of Aengus Cele Dé), *i.* cccix, ccclxvi; *iii.* 123, 386-387.
Fis Adamnain (Vision of Adamnan), *i.* cccxcv.
Grammar, on ancient Gaedhelic, *ii.* 53-54, 93-94.
Leabhar Gabhala (Book of Invasions or Conquests), *ii.* 3, 4, 20, 109, 110, 111, 112; *iii.* 3, 240, 241, 326, 384.
„ na g-Ceart (Book of Rights), *i.* ccxl, cccii, ccciii, cccxxxviii, ccclxvii, ccclxxxix, ccccii, ccccciii; *ii.* 45; *iii.* 124-133.
„ Olloman (Book of Ollamhs), *ii.* 171-173.
Liber Hymnorum, *ii.* 90; *iii.* 251.
Life of Alexander the Great, *iii.* 239-330.
On Omens, Dreams, and Visions, *ii.* 223-224.
Origin and arrangement of the Book of Psalms, *iii.* 238-239.
Sanas Cormaic (Cormac's Glossary), *ii.* 11, 48, 89, 208, 209, 210-212, 217-219, 250, 324, 335, 342, 356, 383; *iii.* 185, 276, 384, 388.
Sean Raite Fitbail (Precepts of Fithal), *ii.* 22.
Siege and Destruction of Troy, *i.* cccxxv-vi; *ii.* 89; *iii.* 332-333.
Travels of Marco Polo, *i.* cccxxiii.
Traha, Trahea, Traga, *i.* cccclxxvi.
Tref, the Welsh, *i.* xcii, cxiii; the Gwestva paid in Gwent for a —, *i.* cxli, clii.
Trehingreve or Gerefa of a Trithing or Riding, *i.* ccxlviii.
Triads, the Welsh, *i.* xxxvii.
Tribe, of Boinraighe, *iii.* 208; — of

Ceardraighe, 207, 208; — of Ciaraidhe, 126; — of Coircoiche, 208; — of Crothraidhe, 129; — of Dal Mughaide, 208; — Forthuatha, 131; — of Greaghraidhe, 126; — of Muscraighe, 208; — of Ossairghe, 208; — of Tradraidhe, *ii.* 220; *iii.* 262.

Tribes (Free —), Benntraighe, Bibraighe, Bladraighe, Boecraighe, Bondraighe, Brughraide, Callraighe, Carraighe, Cathraighe, Condraighe, Corco Ainge, Corco Bili, Corco Bruidi, Corco Dega, Corcoige, Corco Maige, Corco Muich, Corco Soilchend, Crothraigh, Curaigh, Dal n-Didail, Dal Maigni, Dal Mathrach, Dal Mecon, Dal Mendato, Dal Mochoirp, Dal Mochon, Dal Muide, Dal Muigid, Dal Tidilli, Dal h-Uiscide, Gabhraigh, Glosraighe, Granraighe, Lathraige, Ludraige, Luffraighe, Mendraighe, Nudhraige, Rathraighe, Saithrighe, Scothraighe, Sedraighe, Semrighe, Teocraighe, h-Uraighe, *i.* xxvii.

Tribes (Rent:)— Tuath Airbri, — Aithechtha, — Benntraighe, — Bibraighe, — Biobraighe, — Brecraighe, — Buain, — Cairige, — Cathbarr, — Cathraige, — Chonchobairni, — Connraighe, — Cregraighe, — Cruithnech, — Cruitnech of the North, — Currat, — Domnann, — n-Eibluirg, — Emenrighe, — Farduis, — Fer-Buidi, — Fer More, — Fer Ninais, — Fidhga, — Firbh, — Fochmond, — Gaileoin, — Gebtine, — Glasraighi, — Guaire, — Ligmuine, — Luaigne, — Mac Derbchon, — Mac Umoir, — Mac Umor, — Maistini, — Masraighe, — Ochuinne, — Resent Umoir, — Selli, — Semonn, — Sen-Chenéoil, — Sen Erann, — Sen Mogad, — Tregae, — Treithirni, *i.* xxvii-xxx.

Tribes, made up of Fines or Houses, *i.* lxxviii.

Tribe land, rights of persons on; establishment of a Selb, *i.* clv.

Tribus, the Latin, *i.* lxxxi.

Tributes due to kings from their sub-reguli, *iii.* 124, 125, 126, 129, 130, 131.

Trichaeus rosmarus, *i.* ccccxlviii.

Triding, *i.* lxxxi. See Trithing.

Tri Finn Eambna, "the three fair twins", *recte* "the three fair [youths] of Emania", *ii.* 145, 146.

Trigonon, the, *i.* cccclxxxvii; has relief of a — on a sarcophagus of Volterra, cccclxxxviii; figure of a — on an Apuleian vase; this — has a fore pillar, and is the prototype of the harp, cccclxxxix; the Kinnor was probably the origin of the —, dviii; Doni's opinion that the harp is a modified —, *i.* dxx.

Trinity College, Dublin, MSS. in Library of, *i.* lvi; *ii.* 327, 330, 353; *iii.* 7, 117, 187, 250, 256, 317, 324, 326, 336, 363, 375, 413, 414, 466, 523; harp in museum of —, *iii.* 230, 263, 266, 267, 268, 269, 274, 280, 285, 289, 291, 299; Stuic, Sturgana, etc., in museum of —, 350.

Triplum, a, *i.* dliv.

Tristan and Iseult, romance of, *i.* xxxix.

" of Gottfried von Strasburg, *i.* ccciii.

Trithing, *i.* lxxxi, ccxxxi. See Triding.

Triticum sativum, *i.* ccclxii; — spelta, ccclxiii. See Wheat.

Tritonus, *i.* dlxxvi, dlxxviii.

Triucha ced, *i.* xcii, xciii, xcvi, xcviii, xcix, c; *ii.* 392; *iii.* 502.

Troemi, *i.* xciv.

Tropes, *i.* dlxix, dlxxviii.

Trousers, the, *i.* ccclxxxiv.

Trumpets, possessed by Lord Oxmantown, *iii.* 320, 321; Mr. Ralph Ousley's account of the trumpets in the museum of R.I.A. found in the County of Limerick, 342-343; — of Lord Drogheda, 343; — described in Walker's *Irish Bards*, 342, 345, 346; these were first described and figured in Smith's *History of Cork*, 344; — figured in *Vetusta Monumenta*, 345, 346; Smith's errors regarding these —, 346, 347; Smith's error that the Cork — formed but one instrument, reproduced by Mr. R. Mac Adam, 347; Sir William Wilde's novel idea as to the use of the straight tube of the Cork —, 348-349.

Tuath, the, *i.* xxxiii; —, a territorial political unit, lxxix, cxcviii; cognate forms of the word —, lxxx;

the Mór — was made up of several Tuaths, lxxx, lxxxii, lxxxiv, xci; number of Ballybiatachs in a —, xcii, xciii, xcvi, xcvii, xcviii, xcix, cxxv, cxxix, cxxxi, cxxxix, cliii, cliv, clvi, clx, clxvii, clxxxiii, clxxxv, clxxxix, cxcii, cci, cciii, ccxxviii, ccxxix, ccxli, ccxlii, ccxliii, ccxlvi, ccxlvii, ccxlviii, ccxlix, ccliii, ccliv, cclvii, cclxii, cclxx, cclxxvii, cclxxxiii, cclxxxv, cccviii, ccclxii, ccclxxix.

Tuatha Dé Danann, or Danand, *i.* xxiii, xxiv, xxxii, xxxix, lxxi, lxxiii, lxxvi, ccxxviii, ccxxix, cclviii, cclxiv, cccxxvii, ccccxxxii, ccccxxxvii, ccccxxxix, ccccxl, ccccxlvi, ccccl, cccclii, ccccIvii, ccccIviii; *ii.* 3, 39, 42, 50, 51, 52, 71, 106, 110, 122, 128, 131, 142, 148, 150, 151, 152, 153, 185, 187, 188, 189, 198, 226, 231, 232, 233, 234, 235, 236, 237, 238, 241, 243, 245, 246, 248, 249, 250, 251, 252, 255, 258, 272, 288, 295, 301, 324, 328; *iii.* 2, 5, 8, 10, 12, 15, 40, 42, 43, 59, 60, 73, 83, 97, 122, 151, 155, 156, 157, 163, 169, 174, 179, 190, 191, 192, 200, 202, 204, 210, 211, 213, 215, 218, 219, 225, 226, 227, 231, 232, 233, 240, 255, 260, 306, 324, 325, 328, 362, 366, 384, 425, 527.

Tuathas of Fort, *iii.* 127; — of rent-paying tribes, *i.* xxvii-xxx.

Tubs, *i.* ccclvi, ccclvii, ccclix, ccclxvi.

Tuceta, *i.* ccclxx.

Tuguria, *i.* ccxcvii.

Tuirnd, Tuirnn, *i.* ccclxii. See Tarai and Wheat.

Tûn, the old Norse, *i.* lxxxvii, cccv; the Anglo-Saxon —, or town, lxxxviii.

Tunc, the, or "Dungs" of the old Germans, *i.* ccxcvi.

Tunes of savage nations, extent of, *i.* dxliii.

Tunginus, the, of a Salic village, *i.* clxi.

Turks, *i.* viii; *iii.* 314, 319.

Twelfhaendmen, *i.* ci, cxcvi.

Twysawg, the Welsh, *i.* ccxliv.

Tydden, the Welsh, *i.* lxxxix, clxxix, clxxx.

Tyggi, Tiggi, *i.* ci.

Tympanon, *i.* dxvii,

Tympanum, *i.* ccccxc, dxvii.

Tyr Cyfrif of the Welsh, *i.* cxxxix.

Uchelwyr, *i.* cxvii, cxxviii.

Ui Neill, *iii.* 24, 25, 248, 309.

Ulidians, *ii.* 156; *iii.* 265.

Ulster Journal of Archaeology, *iii.* 347.

Ulstermen, *ii.* 335.

Ultonians, *i.* ccclxi, ccclxxi, cccclxvi, cccclxx; *ii.* 319, 329; *iii.* 314, 372 423, 431, 433.

Umorians, *i.* xxiv, lxxi; *ii.* 122.

University, ancient academic or — course; order of the studies of the twelve-years course of study, *ii.* 171-173.

Uthûs, *i.* ccci.

Vaccinium myrtillus; — uliginosum, *i.* ccclxxviii.

Vaisla. See Veisla.

Valhumal Voldhumle, *i.* ccclxxiii, ccclxxiv.

Vassal, etymology of, *i.* ccxxvi; tribute of food given by the vassal to the lord, and not by the lord to the —, ccxxvii.

Vassalage, military service not the essential characteristic of —, *i.* ccxxviii.

Vasseur, etymology of, *i.* ccxxvi.

Vat, Ale, *i.* ccclxxiii; brewing —, *i.* ccclix.

Vavassor, *i.* ccxxvi.

Veal, *i.* ccclxviii.

Veil, *i.* ccclvii, ccccxciv.

Veisla, *i.* ccxxvii.

Veislu-maðr, *i.* ccxxvii.

Veitsla, Veizla. *i.* ccxv. See Veisla.

Verkmenn, *i.* cxvi.

Verse, history anciently taught in, *ii.* 167; legend of the invention of —, *iii.* 236.

Verses, four-lined, which sing to certain airs, *iii.* 392, 393.

Versification, tract on Irish, in the Book of Ballymote, *iii.* 388, 391.

Vessels. See Culinary Vessels and Drinking Vessels.

Vetch, the black bitter, and the tuberous bitter —, *i.* ccclxiii.

Vièle, the, *i.* ccccxcix, d; Teutonic names for —; form of —, up to the eleventh century, dxxiv; the Rote, Rebec, Gigue, and —, like each other; change of form of these instruments after the eleventh century, dxxv, dxxvi; — a favourite instrument; it was played by women as well as by men, dxxvii, dxxviii, dxxix, dcxxiv.

Vielle. See Vièle.
Videla, *i.* dxxiv.
Vigele, *i.* dxxiv.
Vihuela, *i.* dxxiii-iv; — de arco, dxxiii-iv; — de peñola, dxxiii-iv.
Villa, *i.* cc.
Villae liberae, *i.* cxiii; — nativae, cxiv.
Villeins, *i.* clxxxvi; free — in Wales, cxiii.
Villenage, *i.* clxxxvi.
Vindauga, *i.* cccii.
Viol, the modern, *i.* dxxiv.
Viola, the. See Viula.
Viole, the. See Vièle.
Violin, the, *i.* d.
Virginal, the, *i.* dxvi.
Vitex agnus castus, *i.* ccclxxiii.
Viðarmundr, or counterpurchase, *i.* clxxv.
Vitrum, *i.* ccccív, cccexxxv.
Viula, *i.* dxxiv.
Volcae-Tectosages, *i.* lxxx.
Volk, *i.* cv.
Vorderschurz, *i.* cccclxxiv.
Vryccan, or Welsh Plaid, *i.* ccclxxxvii.
Wagon, the. See Fedhen.
Wainscotting, *i.* ccciiii.
Waislumen, *i.* cexxvii.
Waist-piece, the, *i.* cccclxxv. See Brayette.
Walhalla, the doors of, *i.* cccxlvi.
Walrus, the, *i.* ccccxlviii, ccccxlix.
Wapentake, the, *i.* lxxxiv, cexxxi.
Warda or Ward, the, *i.* cc.
"Warder's Seat", the, of Irish tales, *i.* cccxiii.
Ward-Reeve, the Anglo-Saxon, *i* ccxlvii.
Warp, *i* ccclix.
Water, a spring of, in the house of a Bruighfer; a running stream of — in the Lios or Airless of a Fer Forais, and in the house of a Leech, *i.* cccxviii.
„ Cress, *i.* ccclxvi-vii.
"Wayland Smith", Cualand the Irish, *i.* ccvii.
Weapons, the words *dubh*, *gorm*, and *glas*, as applied to, *i.* ccccxxxv; — mentioned in Irish MSS., *i.* ccccxxxvii; scope of lectures on — of warfare, *ii.* 230; earliest descriptions of — in Irish MSS., 231; — of the Milesians; distinction between the — of the Tuatha Dé Danand and of the Firbolgs, 256; recapitulation of — anciently in use, 295; law as to seizure for debt of —, 332; continued use of the same — down to the ninth century, 335, 345; no account of the — of the Danes before the Battle of Clontarf; — used at the Battle of Clontarf, 345.
Weft, *i.* ccclix.
Wele. See Gwelly.
Welsh music, not derived from the Irish; old — merely restored by Gruffyd ab Cynan; story of Giraldus Cambrensis concerning the existence of part-singing among the Welsh, *i.* dcxxiv; — was constructed on a gapped scale, but was more affected by Church music than was the Irish music, dcxxv; and by polyphonous music also, dcxxvi; the old — was extinguished by Protestant hymnology; modern — does not differ essentially from English music; the Welsh not cognizant of the great change which has taken place in their music, dcxxvi; evidence of this change to be found in the works of the Welsh bards; traces of the true — to be found still in old airs, dcxxvii.
Wends, *i.* ccclxxxv.
Wer, *i.* cci, ccxcv.
Wergild, *i.* cxvii, cxxviii, clviii, clxix, ccxlviii.
Wheat, *i.* ccclxii, ccclxiii, ccclxiv, dcxlii.
Wheeled carriages used by the Irish in peace and war; Irish names of, cccclxxv.
Wheels of a chariot, *i.* cccclxxvii.
Whorts, *i.* ccclxxviii.
Wind instruments, *i.* dxxix; ancient Irish — of graduated scale and compass, *iii.* 344.
Windows and shutters mentioned in Irish tales, *i.* cccii; dcxli.
Wine, *i.* ccclxxvii.
Wine cellar, *i.* ccclx.
Withernam of the Anglo-Saxons, *i.* cclxxxv.
Witness, *i.* cclxxxviii; the Irish — affirmed, cclxxxix, ccxc; penalties for false witness, ccxci.
Wlad, the, of the Sclavonians, *i.* ci.
Woad, *i.* ccciii, ccccv; — cultivated in Limerick, *iii.* 120.
Women, custom as to inheritance by, in Ireland, among the Ger-

mans, Franks, Burgundians, in Denmark and in Sweden, *i.* clxx; "inheritance of Hand and Thigh", clxx-clxxii; female judges, Σαμνιτῶν γυναῖκες, the Barrigenae or Senae, Matres familiae, Matrae, Mairae, etc., Dames Souveraines des pensées, etc., clxxi; dress of Irish —, cccxciv; character of — tested by ordeal by fire, *ii.* 227.
Wool paid as rent or tribute, *iii.* 118.
Woollen cloth, *i.* ccclxxix.
Workbag, pledging a queen's; its lawful contents, *iii.* 113; — of the wife of an Airech Feibhe, 114; the contents of a — only a small part of a lady's personal ornaments, 114; the Land formed part of the contents of a —, 182.
Wort-boiler, the, of Gerg, *i.* ccclxxii.
Writers, Gaedhelic —, in early Christian times, *ii* 74.
Wurfpfeil, the, *i.* cccclxvi.
Wylisc gafol gilda, *i.* cxiv.
Wynebwerth. See Gwynebwerth.
Venison, *i.* ccclxvii.
Yarrow, the, *i.* ccclxxiii.
Year, divisions of the, *iii.* 217.
Yeast, *i.* ccclxiii.
Yennissei Oztyaks, *i.* viii.
Yew, Druids' wand of divination made of —, *ii.* 194; the —, a sacred tree of Irish druids, 226; articles of furniture made of —, *iii.* 62.
Yoke, the, *i.* cccclxxx.
Ystavell, or Estavelle of the Welsh, *i.* ccc.
Zaun, the German, *i.* lxxxvii, cccv.
Zinc bronzes of Roman origin, *i.* ccccxxii.
Zünfte, *i.* ccx, ccxi, ccxiii.
Zukkarah, the, *i.* dxi.
Zûn, *i.* cccv.

THE END.

John F. Fowler, Printer, 3 Crow Street, Dame Street, Dublin.

nted in the United States
85LV00002B/226/A

9 781432 682149